Special Collections in College and University Libraries

Special Collections in College and University Libraries

Compiled by
MODOC PRESS, INC.

With an Introduction
by
Leona Rostenberg and Madeleine B. Stern

MACMILLAN PUBLISHING COMPANY
NEW YORK

Collier Macmillan Publishers
LONDON

Macmillan Publishing Company
866 Third Avenue
New York, NY 10022

Collier Macmillan Canada, Inc.

Library of Congress Catalog Card Number: 88-36849

Printed in the United States of America

printing number

1 2 3 4 5 6 7 8 9 10

Library of Congress Cataloging-in-Publication Data

Special collections in college and university libraries / compiled by
Modoc Press, Inc. ; with an introduction by Leona Rostenberg and
Madeleine B. Stern.
p. cm.
Includes index.
ISBN 0-02-921651-6
1. Libraries—United States—Special collections—Directories.
2. Library resources—United States—Directories. 3. Libraries,
University and college—United States—Directories. 4. Rare books–
–Library resources—United States—Directories. 5. Manuscripts–
–Library resources—United States—Directories. I. Modoc Press.
Z731.S73 1989
027.7'025'73—dc19 88-36849
CIP

CONTENTS

Introduction	vii
About This Book	xiii
Main Entries	1
General Index	547
Institution Index	623

INTRODUCTION

Leona Rostenberg and Madeleine B. Stern

It is sometimes called The Treasure Room, and that is an apt description. It is also known in some libraries as The Locked Room, and that, unfortunately, is also an apt description. In many institutions the division is classified as The Rare Books and Manuscripts Department, an umbrella nomenclature that often shields a great variety of holdings. Generally, however, it is characterized as *Special Collections,* a term that also includes "Specialized Collections" found within general library stacks. Special Collections may sometimes be equated with a Treasure Room, and more frequently though not invariably with a Rare Books and Manuscripts Division. It is devoutly to be hoped that it will not merit the forbidding name of The Locked Room. Whatever it is called, the Special Collection is special indeed.

The scope of Special Collections in college and university libraries is staggering. Whether large or small in number of volumes, and although often highly specialized in coverage, the *range* of subject matter in Special Collections is so vast that it could provide the seeds of new scholarship for generations to come. Indeed it would be difficult to name a discipline not covered by some Special Collection.

There are Special Collections devoted to almost all of ancient, medieval, and modern learning. Voyages, travel, and exploration, and the geographical areas they opened up are represented, from America and Alaska to the Baltic and the Pacific Islands, Iran and Afghanistan. Western America and the Deep South, Appalachia and the Ozarks may be studied. Special Collections chronology stretches from the earliest recorded history to the Space Age, illuminating the wars and persecutions of the past, from Inquisition to Holocaust. The social problems and movements of the more immediate past may be researched: populism, prohibition, depression.

Religion in all its aspects finds a significant place: Jewish and Hebrew studies, Catholica, the Reformation, Bible collections, the Jesuits in America, Sufi mysteries, Pietistic literature, and Puritan literature. In addition, the diverse sects that have raised fervor in their time have found their place: from Anabaptism to Methodism, from Anglicanism to the Millerite Movement, from the Mennonites to Creationism.

The trades, professions, and aspirations of men and women are here: education; the law and its philosophy; military and naval history; pure and applied sciences; literature and the stage; political thought, diplomacy and diplomatica; mining the earth and scanning the sky.

To the disciplines of medieval quadrivium and trivium have been added the concerns and achievements of modernity, from riverboats, steamboats and railroads to aviation and the problems of the nuclear community. Special topical collections include all facets of society and all pursuits of the genus humanum. Not only our world and our work, but our pleasures and pastimes are represented; from angling to weaving, from ice skating to track and field, from embroidery to jewelry, from gastronomy to costume, from gaming to mountaineering. And of course, highlighted in many Special Collections are the history and continuing struggles of earth's minorities, notably blacks and women.

Close on the heels of topical collections are Special Collections whose nucleus is a single individual, very often an author. Such collections are often, but not always, appropriate to the institutions where the materials are deposited. Thus it is fitting for portfolios of specific artists' works (for example, an Ansel Adams Portfolio) to be found in a College of Design, and a scholar would certainly expect a John Greenleaf Whittier Collection to be located in an institution named after the poet. The papers of Julia Morgan, American architect known for her work on Hearst's estate at San Simeon as well as for the Goethe Sacramento Residence, seem to belong in California libraries. Because of their relationship to specific geographical areas during periods of their lives, the relicts of certain individuals have been appropriately housed: those of Helen Hunt Jackson in Colorado Springs, of Upton Sinclair in California. The raison d'être for the placement of some author collections is less obvious, although a raison d'être usually exists. It is supremely fitting for the papers of the New England author Louisa May Alcott and of her family to be deposited at Harvard University's Houghton Library in Cambridge, Massachusetts. The fact that a sizable collection of her books and letters is also located in the University of Virginia becomes understandable only when the source of the collection is traced to the interests of a resident donor. Appropriately placed or not, even at times misplaced, Special Collections focusing upon individuals are of incalculable value to scholars researching their lives, their works, and their times. From Newton to Einstein, from Lafayette to Lincoln, from William Jennings Bryan to Eugene V. Debs, from Theodore Roosevelt to Franklin Roosevelt, from Beethoven to Elvis Presley, from Goethe to Rilke, from Vergil to Chaucer and Shakespeare, from Tennyson to Emerson and Henry James, from Hawthorne, Whitman and Mark Twain to John Steinbeck, Flannery O'Connor and James Jones, from Bret Harte and Stephen Crane to Stephen King—even to the author of "The Night before Christmas" and "the last poet laureate to Kansas," Special Collections exist in institutions across the country, receiving or awaiting the close attention of scholars.

Although topical and individual collections account for the vast majority of Special Collections, there are other focuses as well. Numerous Special Collections have centered upon regionalism, the history of the area in question, the ledgers and records, papers and scrapbooks of its counties, the books and documents that elucidate a geographical development. Then, too, many Special Collections are formed on the basis of genre: children's books, fables, poetry, ballads, diaries, mystery, detective and science fiction, historical novels, drama, genealogies, dictionaries and textbooks, the Little Blue Books of Haldeman-Julius.

One of the most interesting bases for Special Collections is the art and science of the book. Books about books make fascinating libraries for bibliophiles, elucidating as they do the history of printing and publishing. The University of California at Los Angeles offers an extraordinary Special Collection of early printed books that emerged from the first movable presses of the Italian States. The Harold B. Lee Library of Brigham Young University is the center of a fine collection of fifteenth- and sixteenth-century works published by the House of Aldus Manutius in Venice and by the Estienne family in Paris and Geneva. The University of Delaware has a collection of extremely rare works printed by the sixteenth-century freethinker Etienne Dolet. From the beginnings of the printed word to the productions of fine modern presses, from incunables to the imprints of Ward Ritchie, the products of the Ars Typographica have been gathered in Special Collections throughout the country.

The tremendous range of subject matter covered by Special Collections includes finally those collections that may be characterized as "curious," unlikely, unusual, uncommon. One thinks, for example, of the manuscript collections devoted to the Crédit Foncier; a Utopian community in Topolobampo, Sinaloa, Mexico; the library concerned with the Mutiny on the Bounty, the adventures of Captain Bligh, and Pitcairn Island; the collection of publications of the American Welding Society; and books on plumbing fixtures. One thinks of Special Collections pertaining to scientific recreations such as the magic lantern, or to Arabian horses and their breeding. From cabbages to kings, it is all here in Special Collections, whose infinite variety must attract scholars in multifaceted fields.

The forms taken by materials in Special Collections are as diversified as their subjects. By no means do all these sources of information appear in book form. Special Collections find space for manuscripts and letters, diaries and ledgers, periodicals and newspapers, for ephemeral pamphlets and broadsides, papyri and scrolls, photographs and maps. And since these are, or should be, continuing collections, evidences of modernity creep in, in the shape of oral history tapes or audio and video cassettes. Tightly knit though it may be in its topicality, the Special Collection is often protean in its shape.

The Arabian Horse Collection at California State Polytechnic University, Pomona, was inspired by a donation from the king of cereals, W.K. Kellogg, who in 1925 purchased hundreds of acres in Pomona, California, for what became his own Arabian Horse Ranch. The origin of Special Collections is often fascinating, and their shaping and expansion throw light not only upon their past but upon their future.

The personnel involved in the creation of a Special Collection includes donor, Special Collections librarian, and antiquarian bookseller. Of prime importance in most cases is the donor who often actually originates the collection. The donor may be a member of the faculty who delighted in collecting American bestsellers and later presented the collection to his or her university library. The donor may be an alumna or an alumnus. It was a Wartburg alumna, Kathryn Koob, who, having survived 444 days of captivity as an Iranian hostage, presented to her college library a collection related to peace. The donor may be a librarian, such as Dr. Lawrence Clark Powell, whose continuing contributions have enriched the holdings of so many institutions. Then again, the donor may be an antiquarian bookseller. Friends of Libraries often become donors, and sometimes individuals in quest of income tax deductions join the all-important category of benefactors who provide a nucleus for the formation of Special Collections. Unfortunately, and all too often, the original deed of gift does not carry with it the potential for expansion, the necessary funds to augment a collection and so keep it alive.

Such funds are vital for the second important method of library acquisition, the purchase of books and related materials. An ongoing collection needs to be continued by purchase which is often made direct from an individual collector. In that way the collection of books about Abraham Lincoln and the Civil War, rich in pamphlet material and memorabilia, was acquired by Occidental College from a Los Angeles lawyer; in that way numerous significant Special Collections have been obtained by librarians throughout the country. In such purchases, Friends of the Library often play a role by raising necessary funds, and the interests of Special Collections librarians themselves may be instrumental in initiating acquisitions. Indeed, some remarkably alert Special Collections librarians have been known to follow obituary notices very closely in order to pounce upon collections before they are placed on the market.

Through donation and purchase a Special Collection is started and sometimes enhanced. A strong faculty member with a devoted student following can do much to stimulate a strong collecting program. But the persistence and aggressive determination of the Special Collections librarian are of prime importance in originating and shaping a Special Collection. It is he or she who has the imagination to perceive what is suitable for acquisition. In the words of one librarian, "The decision to acquire collections is determined by . . . how well [the material] complements other collection strengths, and, to some extent, the existence of a strong academic program." A Special Collections librarian with knowledge and imagination can help mold the collection so that it too plays a role, stimulating augmentation by its very nature. Donation coupled with endowment, and leadership invested in faculty members and Special Collections librarian, must make for an ongoing library productive of scholarship.

At times, unfortunately, such a salutary combination of forces does not exist. A librarian may discontinue purchases in a specific field of interest when the faculty member who inspired such purchases departs the campus. A professor of romance languages deeply involved in seventeenth-century French novels, for example, may convince the Special Collections librarian that such a genre collection would be highly desirable and much used. The library buys and the search proceeds. Items are purchased either individually or en bloc, at auction or from dealers' catalogues and dealers' shops. The dealers themselves, alerted to the library's desiderata, climb toppling ladders across the European continent in quest of plums to offer. Meanwhile, the professor of romance languages with the taste for seventeenth-century French novels has left the university, and just now the most ardent searcher after rare books on the faculty is a professor of Byzantine history. The library is left—alas—with the meagre beginnings of a Special Collection that has now been discontinued. It is, as one Special Collections librarian puts it, "not being added to unless we have an occasional gift." Such a collection is static and of dubious research value.

Along with faculty member and librarian, the antiquarian dealer may play a vital role in the formation and development of a Special Collection. It was the California dealer, the late David Magee, who remarked to the Special Collections librarian of Brigham Young University during a conversation about incunables: "Why have them just on the East and West coasts?" The remark initiated a prestigious incunable collection in Utah. Although the part played by antiquarian dealer may be, and usually is, overlooked and unacknowledged, it exists at almost every stage of a history that begins with the assemblage of a collection and continues after the transfer of that collection to a college or university library. The dealer was almost certainly involved in the original acquisition, and will as certainly be involved when the collection, on deposit in a library, is expanded.

Here we speak from the experience of over forty years in the business of rare books. Those years have been punctuated by our building collections for Special Collections libraries, and the details of such building may provide insight not only into the role of the dealer, but into the nature of the Special Collection. Not without a degree of pride, we look back over those years and note that we have amassed and transferred libraries that fall into most of the categories featured in Special Collections: topical collections and individual collections, genre collections and collections related to the history, art and science of the book.

The first topical collection we formed and designed for an en bloc sale was an outgrowth of our passion for France and its history, especially the dramatic events of the sixteenth and seventeenth centuries. An assemblage of ephemera—broadsides, pamphlets, "plaquettes" issued between the mid-sixteenth and mid-seventeenth centuries—would, we considered, be an on-the-spot reflection of those events: the violent struggle among Guise, Valois and Bourbon claimants to the throne; the assassination of Henry IV, the regency of Marie de Medici; the rise of Richelieu; the advent of Mazarin; the Fronde. Moreover, we felt that if a scholarly catalogue accompanied the collection it would provide a sourcebook of sorts for the century covered. And so we assembled 755 ephemera, the harvest of numerous visits to the shops of French dealers, of inquiries galore, and close examination of stocks, ladder climbing, perusal of catalogues, attendance at auctions. Once in our hands, each tract was studied and catalogued, and the whole finally made its bow under the title *One Hundred Years of France (1547–1652): A Documentary History*. Our uncertainty as to a successful en bloc sale is reflected in the preface: "As a unique group of documentary material—unlikely to be amassed again in many years—the collection is offered preferably en bloc. It forms a precious nucleus for the study of the political, religious, social, and economic history of the period. As such it is of invaluable significance. Its purchase as a unit is advised. Inquiries will be welcomed. VIVE LA FRANCE!"

Despite the ambivalence demonstrated, we had three inquiries in fairly prompt succession. The first of course was made by the successful purchaser, a northeastern library alerted to the collection by an enthusiastic professor of French history. The second inquiry came from Michigan State University, and the third from Yale. In the case of *One Hundred Years of France,* the collection unfortunately went to the wrong institution. The eager professor of French history who had instigated its purchase moved on to areas unknown, and our carefully culled library of documentary French history hibernated, having joined the all too numerous ranks of static holdings never enhanced by further acquisition.

Nonetheless, the important words in the catalogue preface defining the collection as "a precious nucleus for . . . study" remain significant. Rarely if ever is a collection complete, but it is, or should be, a nucleus subject to the goal of completeness. Collections to be useful must not only be planted but must grow. Placing the right collection in the right place becomes almost as vital a matter as assembling the collection in the first place. It must be placed where it will be augmented, and where it will be used.

And so it has been with many other topical collections whose seeds we have planted through the years in institutional Special Collections: collections based upon the violent history of the Huguenots, the sensational but productive history of the Medici, the far-reaching influence of the Holy Roman Empire, the blood-stained annals of the French Revolution.

From time to time we have formed genre collections for libraries: French novels or Italian plays, Utopias or German political pamphlets; usually gearing them to selected Special Collections where they will best be used.

One of our major author collections is based upon the strong interest we have in America's best-loved author of juveniles, Louisa May Alcott. In the course of our researches, our writings, and our collecting of Alcott, we have been able to expand her bibliography and to strengthen her standing in the history of American literature. Our studies have yielded the fact that Ms. Alcott was not only an internationally popular and influential writer for children but a literary experimenter who succeeded in a variety of genres. One of the major sections of her *oeuvre,* it turns out, consists of sensational stories written in secret and published either anonymously or pseudonymously. In those narratives the advocate of apples and ginger cookies concerned herself with incest and madness, violence and revenge, feminist passion and power, hashish experimentation, and opium addiction. Her skills when she delved into darkness are as notable as when she wove a domestic drama from a fabric of sweetness and light. She is not only more interesting than had been supposed, but more important, and far more collectible. Our Alcott holdings are now the holdings of Brigham Young University's Special Collections, where they form a well used and continuing library.

As booksellers we have been fascinated by the history of the book, and in this category we have built up several major collections. The bookseller is in a sense the natural descendant of the early printer-publisher-stationer who made the first printed texts available to a small reading world. Of them all, Aldus Pius Romanus, founder of the House of Aldus which flourished in Venice from about 1495 to 1595, was pre-eminent. We determined to build a collection of books published by this great scholar-printer and his family during the high Renaissance in Italy. Among the treasures of our collection were our 1502 Dante in pocket format, the first edition of the complete works of Plato, the 1513 Caesar with captions penned in Aldus' own hand, a magnificent copy of Castiglione's *Courtier*. The Aldine Anchor, which was the device of the Press, is symbolic of firmness and deliberation, and it took a great deal of both for us to assemble more than 250 Aldines in our collection. We expanded our Aldine library by including books issued by the related Giunta Press of Venice and Florence as well as by Aldine imitators, and, as in the case of our French documentary history collection, we issued a catalogue that described our holdings. Our foreword ended with a flourish: "These . . . titles bear witness to the unrivalled position of the Aldine family as the greatest publishing dynasty of all time, whose Press made the past serve the present and enrich the future." The collection itself found its en bloc way to a university's Special Collections library. In time we were able to assemble another fine Aldine collection, as well as smaller collections of works printed by the Estiennes of Paris and by Etienne Dolet of Lyons—all reflections of printed legacies to the mind of man, and all placed in libraries that strive to expand the nucleus they obtained from us.

For us as dealers, and for Special Collections librarians as well, one collection may often lead to another. Thus a library devoted to Louisa May Alcott may eventually be enlarged to become a library devoted to the New England Transcendentalists; a library devoted to Martin Luther may evolve into one devoted to other great Reformers; a library concerned with Etienne Dolet may be enriched with the writings of Lyonese philosophers and scholars who, like Dolet, helped shape the French Renaissance. Such imaginative conceptions in the building of Special Collections must result in the broader usefulness of the library to students and researchers. In order to attain maximum usefulness, such collections—needless to say—must be catalogued.

What would a university be without its department of Special Collections? It would assuredly have no strong graduate program and no interchange among graduate students, no resources for faculty research or professorial development. The community too is served by a wholesome, vital, and expanding division of Special Collections. Exhibitions, newsletters, and lectures sponsored by the division engage public attention and educate society. Moreover, such devices indirectly help enrich the library. As one scholar commented recently: ''Every librarian worth his or her salt knows that the way to build up a collection on a chosen subject is to have an exhibition.'' The exhibition may strengthen the collection by attracting donations as well as other collections.

It is in the department of Special Collections that major literary discoveries have been made. Our own personal experience in this connection took place many years ago in Houghton Library's Special Collections at Harvard University, where, in a group of letters from a Boston publisher to Louisa May Alcott, Leona Rostenberg discovered Miss Louisa M. Alcott's pseudonym and the titles of her sensational stories. Original source material such as those letters are often the basis of new scholarly insights. And where, if not in the department of Special Collections, are such original sources to be found? It is there that we can see the dime novel—not on microfilm but in its original gaudy wrappers, as we would see in a museum the painting and not a slide of the painting. It is in Special Collections that we find the sources of our history assembled for our study, our interpretation, our enlightenment. Here the past enriches the present and here future scholarship takes shape.

ABOUT THIS BOOK

This directory of special collections in college and university libraries has been developed not just for reference librarians and researchers, but also for those interested in BOOKS—collectors, booksellers, designers, typographers, and all others for whom BOOKS represent a resource for their trade, profession, or personal interest.

Included herein are those four-year institutions of higher education as well as two-year community, technical, and junior colleges that have special collections. These institutions were sent questionnaires designed specifically to elicit detailed information from which to create interesting, readable narrative as well as a detailed and extensive index. Institutions were given the option of sending descriptive brochures or other printed matter containing the information requested. Many chose the latter method of response.

The term ''special collections'' can be considered a twofold concept. For that reason, libraries were asked to differentiate between ''specialized'' collections that exist within the general stacks of the library and the ''rare books and manuscripts'' collections. The specialized collections are envisioned as being curriculum materials, native son/daughter collections, maps, photographs, or other material that represents a definite ''specialty'' unique to the general holdings of the library. The rare books and manuscripts collections are to be considered those that are often isolated in a separate location within the library and administratively may be identified as a ''division of special collections.'' Department libraries are not included as they are indeed ''special libraries'' dealing with a curricular subject, e.g., business, engineering, geology, law, music. Nonetheless, any specialized collections within a departmental library were deemed appropriate for inclusion—a collection of annual corporate reports, architectural drawings of Frank Lloyd Wright, maps of the Permian Basin, international law, or nineteenth-century sheet music, for example.

This volume differs from others that sail similar waters. It is not a directory of special libraries nor is it a listing by subject of a library's holdings. Rather, it is a compilation of detailed, descriptive information concerning special collections, rare books, and manuscripts to be found in the libraries of colleges and universities throughout the United States. These collections may represent: local interests (e.g., county histories, genealogical records, native American Indian tribes); literary interests (e.g., first editions of a local author); specific periods (e.g., Reformation Period, Italian Renaissance, British Restoration Period); faculty interests (e.g., Baltic studies, French Revolutionary pamphlets, religious tracts); institutional interests (e.g., oral history archives, college/university archives); or national interests (e.g., diplomatic history, military history, U.S. Presidents). It is emphasized that respondents to questionnaires listed those collections of importance to the library and did not list all titles in those collections.

The various special collections are described under the name of the collection, be it named for the donor or the subject covered.

The importance of donors in building special collections cannot be overemphasized. Donations are of several forms—bequests of collections with funds to catalogue and perpetuate their existence; or donation of funds to purchase new acquisitions and thereby assist in building a collection or adding to an existing one; or outright gifts of either money or books to be used at the discretion of the special collections librarian. Although many library budgets include funds for building special collections, the role of donors in a library's acquisition policy is of great assistance in preventing the devastation of an extremely tight budget. The high cost of rare items in today's marketplace is astounding and prevents many libraries from obtaining that one missing unit so greatly desired. In a recent auction of items from the Doheny Collection of St. John's College of Camarillo, California, held in New York at Christie's, the original 1813 edition of the novel *Pride and Prejudice* fetched $49,500. Prices of this magnitude are far beyond the budgets of most colleges and universities. However, there are individuals who do purchase such rare books and donate them to their alma maters.

Donors are responsible not only for building collections, but often for the structures in which they are housed. Most of the libraries listed in this volume have official names and generally these are the names of individuals who contributed to the library's growth. Many libraries also have memorial rooms dedicated to preserving the memorabilia and books donated by a past president, faculty member, or graduate.

Not all college and university libraries have special or rare book collections as defined above. The general collections of the various libraries reflect the mission and goals of the institution in terms of degree programs offered. The lack of special collections with a staff to care for them is not to be considered a diminished interest in preserving our heritage, but rather an emphasis on the curriculum of the institution as opposed to an expansion of subject areas not germane to the various departmental needs. Therefore, the omission of an institution from this volume indicates only that no special or rare book collections were reported or that further research yielded no information to support an entry.

There may be collections housed in a library that are not available to the public and thus will not be listed in this volume. For example, Princeton University houses more than a thousand letters that T.S. Eliot wrote between 1927 and 1947 to Emily Hale, an American school-teacher whom Eliot had met in Boston as a young man. Although many of Eliot's letters have been edited by his widow, Valerie Eliot, and published (*The Letters of T.S. Eliot, Volume I, 1898–1922*, Harcourt Brace Jovanovich, 1988), the letters to Emily Hale will remain secluded at Princeton and unavailable for examination or publication until the year 2019.

Main Entry Section

The major arrangement of the entries is alphabetical by institution within state. Main entries are numbered consecutively throughout the volume and appear directly above the name of the institution. Running heads at the top of each page also carry the entry number to assist the user.

Introductory information about the institution includes address, telephone number, a brief statement regarding institutional affiliation and enrollment, library administrators, and general holdings. Special collections are then described with their names appearing in boldface. Rare book collections are listed under that heading if they have been identified as being a separate element of special collections.

General Index

The General Index to this volume follows the main entry section. It includes personal names, subjects, geographic place names, and titles of books and magazines. Following each item are the entry numbers referring the user to the institutions in the main entry section. The General Index also gives the names of the institutions included in this volume. These appear in boldface.

Institution Index

A separate Institution Index follows the General Index. This index is an alphabetical listing of all institutions whose special collections are included in the book.

Reference Sources

In addition to college catalogs, the following sources were relied upon as authority lists for proper name spelling, enrollment statistics, dates, affiliations, and other peripheral information.

1987–88 Accredited Institutions of Postsecondary Education. Sherry S. Harris, Editor. Published for the Council on Postsecondary Education. American Council on Education/ Macmillan Publishing Company, New York, 1988.

American Community, Technical, and Junior Colleges. 9th Edition. Dale Parnell and Jack W. Peltason, Editors. American Council of Education/Macmillan Publishing Company, New York, 1984.

Benet's Reader's Encyclopedia. 3rd Edition. Harper & Row, New York, 1987.

The College Blue Book. 20th Edition. Macmillan Publishing Company, New York, 1987.

Dictionary of American Biography. 20 volumes with 8 supplements. Published under the auspices of the American Council of Learned Societies. Charles Scribner's Sons, New York, 1928–1937, 1944–1988.

The New Century Cyclopedia of Names. Clarence L. Barnhart, Editor. Appleton-Century-Crofts, New York. 1954.

Acknowledgments

It is hoped that those with items to donate, books to sell, research materials to be found, books to design, or words to put into type will find herein the sources and resources that will assist them in their goals of scholarship and professional development.

The compilers express their sincere appreciation to all of the institutions listed herein for their cooperation in answering our numerous questions and supplying the information in various forms. Of particular note are several to be singled out—the Rare Book and Manuscript Library of Columbia University, Lilly Library of Indiana University, Joseph Mark Lauinger Memorial Library of Georgetown University, Hargrett Rare Book and Manuscript Library of the University of Georgia, University of Illinois Library at Urbana-Champaign, the Kenneth Spencer Research Library of the University of Kansas, Hillman Library of the University of Pittsburgh, Beinecke Rare Book and Manuscript Library of the Yale University Library, and Houghton Library of Harvard University. Gratitude is also due to the archivists, special collections librarians, rare book specialists, antiquarian booksellers, and book collectors who offered advice and suggestions.

There are others too numerous to mention, but the result of their assistance is found on the pages that follow.

Alabama

1
Alabama Agricultural and Mechanical University
J. F. Drake Memorial Learning Resources Center
P.O. Box 285
Normal, Alabama 35762

Telephone. (205) 859-7468

Institutional Description. The publicly supported university was founded in 1875 as the Huntsville Normal School. A land-grant institution, it became a university in 1969. Enrollment: 3,457.

Library Administration. Birdie O. Weir, Director, Learning Resources Center.

Library General Holdings. 300,000 volumes; 1,100 periodical subscriptions.

Special Collections

Archival and Historical Collections. These collections are comprised of documents, records, letters, manuscripts, videotapes, audiotapes, photographs, publications, and memorabilia of University origin.

Black Collection. Contains books and a limited number of journals and microfilms by and about Black Americans. These materials cover the Black experiences from slavery to the present.

International Studies Collection. This collection is a diverse gathering of books, videotapes, and other resources which support the International Studies Program of the School of Agriculture. The collection provides scientific information on solving food, nutrition, and agricultural development programs of developing countries.

2
Alabama State University
University Library and Learning Resources
P.O. Box 271
915 South Jackson Street
Montgomery, Alabama 36195

Telephone. (205) 262-3581

Institutional Description. The publicly supported university was founded in 1887, and for years was devoted to the training of public school teachers. Enrollment: 3,438.

Library Administration. John L. Buskey, Director, University Library and Learning Resources; Bertha P. Williams, Special Collections Librarian.

Library General Holdings. 195,000 volumes; 1,016 current periodical subscriptions.

Special Collections

Ollie L. Brown Afro-American Heritage Collection. A compilation of multimedia materials representing the Black man's contribution to society. The collection consists of more than 6,000 books, exhibits, artifacts, and audiovisual materials depicting Black "Alabamana" and the life and history of Blacks in the nation and the world, as well as a collection of rare books.

Educational Media Center. Houses the audiovisual collection, including audiotapes, cassettes, filmstrips, motion pictures, filmloops, phonorecords, slides, and transparencies.

E.D. Nixon Collection. Includes the papers, trophies, plaques, portraits, and photographs of the noted civil rights leader.

University Archives. Consists of administrative records and other materials of importance to the University.

3
Alexander City State Junior College
Thomas D. Russell Library
Highway 63 South
Alexander City, Alabama 35010

Telephone. (205) 234-6346

Institutional Description. The publicly supported junior college held its first classes in 1965 and moved to its permanent location in 1966. Enrollment: 925.

Library Administration. Ella Frances W. Tapley, Acting Head Librarian.

Library General Holdings. 36,000 books; 447 current periodical titles; 19 newspaper subscriptions.

Special Collections

The **Alabama Room** of the library contains artifacts, documents, and memorabilia, with special emphasis on Tallapoosa County.

4
Athens State College
College Library
301 Beaty Street
Athens, Alabama 35611

Telephone. (205) 232-2802

Institutional Description. Athens State College was established as Athens Female Academy in 1822 and became coeducational in 1931. Enrollment: 1,133.

Library Administration. James D. Ballew, Director.

Library General Holdings. 64,000 volumes; 400 periodicals.

Special Collections

Special collections include books and records of the Methodist Church Annual Convention in Alabama from 1842 to the present; a collection of diaries from the Civil War era; and a collection of rare nineteenth-century periodicals.

5
Auburn University
Ralph Brown Draughon Library
Auburn, Alabama 36849

Telephone. (205) 826-4500

Institutional Description. The publicly supported university was chartered in 1856 by the Methodist Church and became part of the State University System in 1872. Enrollment: 17,985.

Library Administration. William C. Highfill, University Librarian; Gene Geiger, Special Collections Librarian.

Library General Holdings. 1,451,974 volumes; 18,797 periodical subscriptions; 1,674,500 microforms; 25,967 audiovisual materials; 112,856 maps.

Special Collections

The Draughon Library has specialized collections dealing with aerospace engineering, architecture, fisheries, railroads, genealogy, and mathematics; the Veterinary Medical Library's collection encompasses all aspects of veterinary medicine, including material in foreign languages, videocassette, slides; the Architecture Library maintains a large collection of slides. The Archives contains extensive collections dealing with Alabama agriculture and rural life, twentieth century Alabama politics, Alabama military history, and the institutional records of Auburn University.

Rare Book Collections

Rare Books Collections. The Library maintains material relating to Alabama, Auburn University, the South in general, rare editions, some Confederate imprints, maps, photographs, university archives, and Alabama state publications. Included in the holdings are historic Bibles (1613 King James Version, 1566 Great Bible, the Geneva Bible) selected first editions, contemporary fashions, and a collection of eighteenth century imprints; the papers of James H. Lane, Holland M. Smith, Jeremiah Denton, George Andrews, Joseph L. Stewart, William F. Nichols, and Fob James. The manuscript collection includes Eugene Current-Garcia, Walton Patrick, Clyde Cantrell, Madison Jones, Jelks Barksdale, James S. Edson, Anne Rivers Siddons, and Paul Hemphill.

6
Auburn University at Montgomery
Library and Resource Center
Montgomery, Alabama 36193

Telephone. (205) 279-3000

Institutional Description. Auburn University at Montgomery was established in 1967. Enrollment: 4,191.

Library Administration. Lawrence J. McCrank, Dean.

Library General Holdings. 1,499,000 bibliographic units, including 1,836 periodical subscriptions and a book collection of 174,660 titles; 850,000 government publications.

Special Collections

The Library and Resource Center's collection of government publications includes many documents that date back to the mid-nineteenth century.

7
Birmingham-Southern College
Charles Andrew Rush Learning Center/N.E. Miles Library
Arkadelphia Road
Birmingham, Alabama 35254

Telephone. (205) 226-4742

Institutional Description. Birmingham-Southern College is a privately supported liberal arts college operated under the auspices of the Alabama-West Florida and North Alabama Conferences of the United Methodist Church. Enrollment: 1,656.

Library Administration. Billy Pennington, Director.

Library General Holdings. 147,613 bound volumes (131,223 books and 15,444 bound periodicals); 758 periodicals; 10 daily and weekly newspapers; 19,104 microforms; 33,093 government documents; music scores, 5,000 recordings, and audiovisual materials.

Special Collections

Branscomb Collection. A current collection of books by and about women that is funded by Dr. Louise Branscomb.

Shugerman Collection. Musical recordings (popular and classical) donated by Mr. Albert Shugerman; 1,500 recordings cataloged to date; another 10,000 are to be organized and cataloged over the next five years.

Rare Book Collections

Archives Collection. Publications of the College and publications by and about faculty and alumni of the College.

Methodist Archives Collection. Documents of and about Methodism in Alabama, including publications of the Alabama Conference of the United Methodist Church.

Townes Collection. Materials on Alabama history.

Whitmire Collection. Materials by Alabama and other Southern writers; a number of late nineteenth century music scores.

8
Enterprise State Junior College
Learning Resources Center
U.S. 84 East
P.O. Box 1300
Enterprise, Alabama 36331

Telephone. (205) 347-2623

Institutional Description. The publicaly supported junior college was crated during a Special Education Session called in 1963 by Governor George C. Wallace. The new campus was occupied in 1966. Enrollment: 1,989.

Library Administration. Susan S. Sumblin, Director.

Library General Holdings. 30,000 accessioned volumes; 81,350 unaccessioned government publications; 420 periodical titles.

Special Collections

The library maintains a special collection of genealogical books and magazines.

9
Faulkner University
Gus Nichols Library and Learning Center
5345 Atlanta Highway
Montgomery, Alabama 36193

Telephone. (205) 272-5820

Institutional Description. The privately supported liberal arts institution, formerly named Alabama Christian College, is supported by the Churches of Christ. Enrollment: 1,448.

Library Administration. Bernice Weaver, Chief Librarian.

Library General Holdings. 47,459 volumes; 305 current periodical subscriptions.

Special Collections

The Gus Nichols Library and Learning Center contains a collection of books, serials, and audiovisuals to support the curriculum of the University which places emphasis on a cultural Christian education. The **Restoration Collection** includes historical material relating to Churches of Christ.

10
Gadsden State Junior College
Meadows Learning Resouces Center
100 Wallace Drive
Gadsden, Alabama 35999

Telephone. (205) 546-0484

Institutional Description. Gadsden State Junior College was founded in 1965 as the Gadsden Technical Junior College. The name was changed to Robert E. Lee in 1966 and a few months later the current name was adopted. Classes began in new buildings at the present location in 1966. Enrollment: 2,625.

Library Administration. John B. White, Librarian.

Library General Holdings. 80,000 volumes; 700 periodical titles.

Special Collections

The **Alabama Collection** and a special collection of juvenile and young adult books are maintained by the library.

11
George C. Wallace State Community College - Dothan
Library/Media Department
Dothan, Alabama 36303

Telephone. (205) 983-3521

Institutional Description. The two-year college offers general education programs, university-parallel transfer programs, technical programs, and health-related studies. Enrollment: 2,643.

Library Administration. Martha Louise Moon, Department Chairperson.

Library General Holdings. 41,500 books; 395 periodical and 25 newspaper subscriptions.

Special Collections

The library maintains a collection of books and microfilm resources on genealogy.

12
George Corley Wallace State Community College
Library
Range Line Road
P.O. Box 1049
Selma, Alabama 36702

Telephone. (205) 875-2634

Institutional Description. The college enrolled its first students in 1965 and offers two-year programs. Enrollment: 1,241.

Library Administration. Patricia Ann Mobbs, Librarian.

Library General Holdings. 30,000 volumes; 220 periodical subscriptions.

Special Collections

The library has a **Rare Book Collection** of 52 items.

13
Huntingdon College
Houghton Memorial Library
1500 East Fairview Avenue
Montgomery, Alabama 36194

Telephone. (205) 265-0511

Institutional Description. Huntingdon College is a privately supported United Methodist liberal arts college. Enrollment: 688.

Library Administration. Eric A. Kidwell, Director; Mary Ann Pickard, Archivist.

Library General Holdings. 90,582 bound volumes; 369 periodical subscriptions; 8 newspaper subscriptions; 3,799 micorforms; 942 audiovisual materials.

Special Collections

Huntingdon Collection. 1854-present. Diplomas and genealogical data on graduates; school publications; some artifacts; records of different departments; Board of Trustees records; many pictures (unarranged); some manuscripts.

Spang Collection. 80 original drawings of the cartoonist for the *Montgomery Advertiser;* supplements another collection of cartoons in the Montgomery Museum.

Methodist Collection. 1808-present. The Alabama-West Florida Conference of the United Methodist Church was given space in 1977 for the Franklin S. Moseley Depository. These records have been arranged according to the following record groups: Officers, Districts, Annual Conference Sessions, Program Agencies, Administrative Agencies, Auxiliary Agencies, Connectional Agencies, Local Church Records, Personal Papers, Pictorial Collection, Artifact Collection, Methodist Historical Library (which now has over 1,000 rare and recent books and publications), Miscellaneous and Historical Sketches.

Autograph Collection. Special collection being compiled; included are *Personal Memoirs of Ulysses S. Grant* and a three-volume set entitled *Windsor Castle: An Architectural History* (inscribed by Queen Mary).

Alabama Collection. An extensive collection on the State of Alabama and its people; includes fictional works by authors from Alabama as well as biographical works on Alabamians.

Rare Book Collections

Nineteenth-Century and Rare Book Collection. A 130-volume set of *War of the Rebellion: Official Records of the Union and Confederate Armies,* published by the War Department from 1880-1901; other books on a variety of subjects and persons.

14
Jefferson Davis State Junior College
Leigh Library
P.O. Box 958
Brewton, Alabama 36427

Telephone. (205) 867-4832

Institutional Description. The college began classes in the fall of 1965 in the Methodist Church in Brewton and moved to its present location in the spring of 1966. Enrollment: 762.

Library Administration. Janel Redditt, Librarian.

Library General Holdings. 27,649 volumes.

Special Collections

The library has an **Alabama Collection** and maintains the archives of the Escambia County Historical Society.

15
Judson College
Brown Newell Learning Center
P.O. Box 120
Marion, Alabama 36756

Telephone. (215) 683-6161

Institutional Description. Privately supported Judson College is a distinctly Christian liberal arts college for women and is affiliated with the Alabama Baptist State Convention. Enrollment: 356.

Library Administration. Mildred Griffin Yelverton, Director of Library Services.

Library General Holdings. 54,000 volumes; 410 current periodical subscriptions.

Special Collections

Special collections include the **Gwen Bristow Collection** and the **Judson Collection.**

16
Lawson State Community College
Library/Learning Resources Center
3060 Wilson Road
Birmingham, Alabama 35221

Telephone. (205) 925-1666

Institutional Description. Lawson State Community College offers associate degree and career preparation programs. Enrollment: 1,552.

Library Administration. Gertrude Bloom, Librarian.

Library General Holdings. 16,000 volumes; 1,200 periodical titles; 3,500 microforms.

Special Collections

The Ebony Room of the library houses the **Dr. Martin Luther King, Jr. Memorial Black Collection.** It provides a vast collection of the world's accumulated knowledge for students about their Black heritage.

17
Livingston University
Julia Tutwiler Library
Livingston, Alabama 35470

Telephone. (205) 652-9661

Institutional Description. The publicly supported state liberal arts university was founded in 1835 as a female academy. It is now coeducational and composed of four colleges. Enrollment: 1,353.

Library Administration. Monroe C. Snider, Director.

Library General Holdings. 120,000 volumes; 698 periodical subscriptions; 16 newspaper subscriptions.

Special Collections

Alabama Room. Houses a collection of historical materials relating to the state of Alabama. Includes the **Ruby Pickens Tartt Collection** of regional Black folklore (folk songs and ring games of Sumter County, Alabama).

18
Lurleen B. Wallace State Junior College Library
P.O. Box 1418
Andalusia, Alabama 36420

Telephone. (205) 222-6591

Institutional Description. The two-year community college opened in 1969 in temporary quarters and moved to its present campus in 1970. Enrollment: 740.

Library Administration. Sandra A. King, Library Services Director.

Library General Holdings. 24,000 volumes; 150 periodical subscriptions; 5,000 audiovisual materials.

Special Collections

A special collection is maintained in the area of marriage and family relations. There is also an **Alabama Collection.**

19
Miles College
Learning Resources Center
P.O. Box 3800
Birmingham, Alabama 35208

Telephone. (205) 923-2771

Institutional Description. The privately supported liberal arts college was established in 1907. It is affiliated with the Christian Methodist Episcopal Church. Enrollment: 573.

Library Administration. Hazel R. Patterson, Director of Learning Resources.

Library General Holdings. 81,000 volumes.

Special Collections

Although the curriculum, faculty, and student body are nondenominational, the College emphasizes the development of strong Christian values and the preparation of students for lives of Christian service. The Learning Resources collections support the academic programs of the College.

20
Mobile College
College Library
P.O. Box 13220
Mobile, Alabama 36613

Telephone. (205) 675-5990

Institutional Description. The privately supported liberal arts college was founded in 1961 and is affiliated with the Alabama Baptist State Convention. Enrollment: 696.

Library Administration. Brantley H. Parsley, Director.

Library General Holdings. 100,000 volumes; 450 periodicals.

Special Collections

The library maintains a collection of 2,000 volumes in its children's collection as well as a special collection of rare, historic books.

21
Northwest Alabama State Junior College
James A. Glasgow Library
Route 3, Box 48
Phil Campbell, Alabama 35581

Telephone. (205) 993-5331

Institutional Description. Northwest Alabama State Junior College offers transfer courses in the first two years of most baccalaureate programs. Northwest has a strong Registered Nursing program. Enrollment: 1,179.

Library Administration. Debbie Chaffin, Head Librarian.

Library General Holdings. 42,000 volumes.

Special Collections

The library has special collections on Alabama and women's studies.

22
Oakwood College
Eva B. Dykes Library
Oakwood Road, N.W.
Huntsville, Alabama 35896

Telephone. (205) 837-1630

Institutional Description. The privately supported liberal arts college was founded in 1896 as an industrial and manual training school. It is owned by the General Conference of Seventh-day Adventists. Enrollment: 1,147.

Library Administration. Jannith Lewis, Chief Librarian.

Library General Holdings. 85,000 volumes.

Special Collections

The library maintains a special collection related to Seventh-day Adventist Black history, Oakwood College history, and artifacts donated by Mr. P.W. Ridgeway from his many travels around the world. There is also a collection of 5,000 volumes on Black studies and a collection of children's books.

23
Patrick Henry State Junior College
John Dennis Forte Library
Frisco City Highway
P.O. Box 2000
Monroeville, Alabama 36460

Telephone. (205) 575-3156

Institutional Description. The two-year junior college was founded in 1963. Enrollment: 629.

Library Administration. Dale Welch, Head Librarian.

Library General Holdings. 30,000 volumes; 71 current periodical subscriptions.

Special Collections

Special collections are maintained on Alabama, forestry, law enforcement, and career planning.

24
S. D. Bishop State Junior College
College Library
351 North Broad Street
Mobile, Alabama 36690

Telephone. (205) 690-6416

Institutional Description. Founded in the summer of 1927, the college was originally a branch of the Alabama State University. In 1936, the college was established as a two-year college. Enrollment: 1,351.

Library Administration. Robert Parker, Director, Library Services.

Library General Holdings. 34,707 volumes.

Special Collections

The library maintains the **Black Authors Collection** and a collection of materials for staff development of junior college instructors.

25
Samford University
Harwell Goddwin Davis Library
800 Lakeshore Drive
Birmingham, Alabama 35229

Telephone. (205) 870-2846

Institutional Description. The privately supported university is owned and operated by the Alabama Baptist State Convention. Enrollment: 3,669.

Library Administration. William N. Nelson, Librarian; Elizabeth C. Wells, Special Collections Librarian.

Library General Holdings. 167,000 volumes; 141,000 microforms; 1,000 serial subscriptions; 138,232 government documents; 38,281 Learning Resource Center materials.

Special Collections

The Special Collection Department houses Alabama history, literature, and imprints, particularly antebellum and Reconstruction Periods. Early Southeast materials include whose concerning Indians, travel, and law.

Also housed are the books and manuscripts of William H. Brantley, Jr. (eighteenth-, nineteenth-, and twentieth-century books, manuscripts, and maps); **Albert E. Casey Collection** (books, manuscripts, periodicals, maps of Ireland, especially Cork and Kerry Counties); the **John Ruskin Collection;** the **John Masefield Collection;** the **Alfred Tennyson Collection;** and the **Lafcadio Hearn Collection.**

The Special Collection department serves as the depository for the Alabama Baptist State Convention housing Baptist church records, association and state convention annuals and reports (nineteenth- and twentieth-century) as well as other church records of other denominations in the state.

The Department also serves as the archives for Howard College, now Samford University, 1841 to the present (publications, manuscripts, and departmental and administrative records).

26
Southeastern Bible College
Rowe Memorial Library
2901 Pawnee Avenue
Birmingham, Alabama 35256

Telephone. (205) 251-2311
Institutional Description. The privately supported Bible college is interdenominational. Enrollment: 127.
Library Administration. Edith S. Taff, Librarian.
Library General Holdings. 30,000 volumes; 132 periodical subscriptions.

Special Collections

The library maintains special collections in theology, education, and Biblical literature.

27
Spring Hill College
Thomas Byrne Memorial Library
4000 Dauphin Street
Mobile, Alabama 36608

Telephone. (205) 460-2121
Institutional Description. The privately supported Roman Catholic liberal arts college was founded in 1830. It is owned and operated by the Jesuits. Enrollment: 1,052.
Library Administration. Mary K. Sellen, Director.
Library General Holdings. 150,000 volumes; 635 current periodical subscriptions; 14,000 microforms; 33,000 government documents.

Special Collections

The library maintains a special collection of Mobiliana, the college Archives, and a rare book collection.

28
Stillman College
William H. Sheppard Learning Resources Center
P.O. Drawer 1430
Tuscaloosa, Alabama 35403

Telephone. (205) 349-4240
Institutional Description. The privately supported liberal arts college was founded in 1876 with the purpose of training ministers. It now concentrates on Christian education rather than training for the ministry. It is affiliated with the Presbyterian Church. Enrollment: 730.
Library Administration. Robert Heath, Director.
Library General Holdings. 84,000 volumes; 359 periodical subscriptions.

Special Collections

Special collections in the library include the **Martha L. O'Rourke Afro-American Collection.** The College's Media Center, Curriculum Laboratory, Educational Development Laboratory, and the **College Archives** are also housed.

29
Talladega College
Savery Library
627 West Battle Street
Talladega, Alabama 35160

Telephone. (205) 362-0206
Institutional Description. The privately supported liberal arts college was founded in 1867 as a primary school. In 1895, it graduated its first class of baccalaureate degrees. It is affiliated with the United Church of Christ and the American Missionary Association. Enrollment: 482.
Library Administration. Juliette Summerville Smith, College Librarian.
Library General Holdings. 86,000 volumes; 1,500 bound periodicals; 400 current periodical subscriptions.

Special Collections

The library maintains the **College Archives** and a **Black Studies Collection.**

30
Troy State University
Lurleen B. Wallace Library
Troy, Alabama 36082

Telephone. (205) 566-3000
Institutional Description. The publicly supported state university began in 1887 as a normal school. Enrollment: 4,741.
Library Administration. Thomas A. Souter, Dean of Library Services; Ethel Sanders, Special Collections/Rare Book Librarian.
Library General Holdings. 205,357 volumes; 1,793 current periodicals; 148,771 microforms; 30,457 audiovisual materials; 14,480 other library materials.

Special Collections

Marching Band Collection. A collection of 2,000 volumes including scores and dissertations.
Creek Indian Collection. Includes 200 titles including the Smithsonian Bureau of American Ethnology microfiche collection.
Origins and Development of the U.S. Constitution. Includes 702 items.

Special Education/Interpersonal Communications and Early Childhood. Consists of 3,500 items.

Curriculum Materials. Special collection of 16,000 volumes including children's literature, textbooks, educational tests and measurements.

31
Tuskegee University
Dr. Hollis Burke Frissell Library
Tuskegee, Alabama 36088

Telephone. (205) 727-8011

Institutional Description. The privately supported university was founded in 1881 by Booker T. Washington as a normal school. It now consists of 6 colleges and schools. Enrollment: 3,210.

Library Administration. Annie G. King, Librarian.

Library General Holdings. 250,000 volumes; 1,000 periodicals; 20 foreign and domestic newspapers; 25,000 government documents.

Special Collections

The Washington Collection and Archives. A collection of manuscripts, books, rare books, photographs, and other artifacts by and about Africa and Afro-Americans, containing more than 100,000 items.

32
University of Alabama
W.S. Hoole Special Collections Library
P.O. Box S
Tuscaloosa, Alabama 35487

Telephone. (205) 348-5512

Institutional Description. The publicly supported university was founded in 1831 by the State Legislature. Enrollment: 14,005.

Library Administration. Joyce Lamont, Assistant Dean for Special Collections and Preservation; Joan Sibley, Reference Archivist.

Library General Holdings. 1,654,865 volumes; 1,193,-565 microforms; 28,280 audiovisual materials; 15,760 periodical subscriptions; 1,049,704 government documents.

Special Collections

William Stanley Hoole Special Collections Library. Contains materials primarily related to Alabama and the Deep South. The Special Collections Library had its genesis in the T.P. Thompson Collection (10,000 books, pamphlets, maps, sheet music) and is therefore rich in materials dealing with Louisiana, especially New Orleans. Over the years this has been augmented with the addition of several discrete collections, such as the first editions of Sir Walter Scott, Lafcadio Hearn, and Robinson Jeffers, a large collection of Confederate imprints, a nearly complete set of Editions for the Armed Services, as well as substantial book collections contributed by Rucker Agee, Hudson Strode, and the Wyman-Jack Family.

The Alabama Collection is a rapidly expanding comprehensive collection of books, periodicals, pamphlets, and ephemera relating to Alabama and Alabamians, inlcuding Alabama State documents and University of Alabama publications.

Among the notable manuscript collections are the papers of Basil Manly, the Gorgas Family, Robert Jemison, Henry DeLamar Clayton, James Bowron, Oliver Day Street, John Sparkman, Carl Elliott, Lister Hill, Albert Rains, Armistead Selden, and the Alabama section of the Charles Lanman Congressional Papers.

Also housed in the Special Collections Library is the Archive of American Minority Cultures which focuses on the special subject areas of ethnic, folk, minority, and women's history and culture consisting primarily of nonprint formats such as oral histories on audio and video tape.

Three other collections emphasize information in various formats: the **Photograph Collection** includes pictorial matter depicting the people, places, and events of Alabama, especially the University of Alabama; the **Newspaper Collection** consisting mainly of nineteenth-century Alabama newspapers, but also includes nineteenth-century Southern newspapers, particularly those of the Civil War era; the **Map Collection** includes maps dating from 1511 to the present, primarily of Alabama and the southeastern region of the United States.

33
University of Alabama at Birmingham
Mervyn H. Sterne Library
University Station
Birmingham, Alabama 35294

Telephone. (205) 934-4011

Institutional Description. The publicly supported state university was founded in 1831 by the state legislature. It lay dormant after the Civil War until 1871. Now encompassing a 900-acre campus, it offers a wide variety of programs. Enrollment: 11,332.

Library Administration. Jerry W. Stephens, Director.

Library General Holdings. 650,000 items; 2,500 current periodical subscriptions.

Special Collections

Important special collections of the Sterne Library include the **Reynolds Historical Library,** a collection of over 10,000 items including rare books; incunabula; medical mannequins; the **Pittman Collection on Endocrinology,,** the **Daniel Drake Collection,** and letters of William Osler, Louis Pasteur, Florence Nightingale, Oliver Wendell Holmes, Sr., Pierre Curie, George and Martha Washington. The personal papers of George C. Wallace are also maintained.

34
University of Alabama in Huntsville
UAH Library
4701 University Drive, N.W.
Huntsville, Alabama 35899

Telephone. (205) 895-6120

Institutional Description. The publicly supported branch campus of the University of Alabama grants associate, baccalaureate, master's, and doctoral degrees. Enrollment: 4,884.

Library Administration. Delmus E. Williams, Director.

Library General Holdings. 100,000 volumes; 2,415 current periodical subscriptions.

Special Collections

The library maintains a space and rocket collection, including the **Willy Ley Memorial Collection.** It also holds the papers of Congressman Robert Jones.

35
University of Montevallo
University Library
Station 6050
Montevallo, Alabama 35115

Telephone. (205) 665-6000

Institutional Description. The publicly supported liberal arts university was founded in 1896 as a girl's school. It became coeducational in 1955. Enrollment: 2,279.

Library Administration. Robert B. Somers, Director.

Library General Holdings. 177,000 books; 1,300 periodical titles; 340,000 microforms.

Special Collections

The University's library supports a curriculum that is broad-based in the liberal arts and sciences and designed for the student's intellectual and personal growth. The University is comprised of a College of Arts and Sciences, College of Business, College of Education, and a College of Fine Arts.

36
University of North Alabama
Collier Library
Wesleyan Avenue
Florence, Alabama 35632

Telephone. (205) 766-4100

Institutional Description. The publicly supported liberal arts and teachers university was founded in 1872. Enrollment: 4,478.

Library Administration. Fred M. Heath, Dean of Library Services.

Library General Holdings. 212,00 volumes; 1,400 journal subscriptions; 341,000 microforms.

Special Collections

The library's special collections include strength in a carefully maintained **Alabama Collection** which includes valuable materials for historical research; the **Flippo Collection;** the **Rudolfo Halffter Collection;** and the **Wesleyan Collection.** Additional collections of books and audiovisual materials are maintained in other campus resource units including the Media Center, the Kilby School Library, the Music Department, and the Learning Resources Center.

37
University of South Alabama
University Libraries
308 University Boulevard
Mobile, Alabama 36688

Telephone. (205) 460-6101

Institutional Description. The publicly supported (state) liberal arts university was founded in 1963. It features business, teacher education, and health sciences, among other programs. Enrollment: 7,418.

Library Administration. Robert M. Donnell, Director.

Library General Holdings. 296,000 volumes; 4,631 current periodical subscriptions; 321,000 microforms; 538,000 government documents.

Special Collections

The collections of the library provide information and access to materials needed to fulfill the teaching, scholarship, and service goals of the University. Among the collections is the **University of South Alabama Photographic Archives.** The Biomedical Library, part of the University's library system houses material which supports the programs of the Medical Center on the campus.

Alaska

38
Alaska Pacific University
Library/Information Service
312 University Hall
4101 University Drive
Anchorage, Alaska 99508

Telephone. (907) 564-8284

Institutional Description. Alaska Pacific University is a private institution affiliated with the United Methodist Church. Enrollment: 942.

Library Administration. Elizabeth Morrissett, University Librarian; Lylia Peck, Special Collections Librarian.

Library General Holdings. The Library is a participant in the Anchorage University Consortium Library at the neighboring campus of the University of Alaska.

Special Collections

Alaska Arctic Exploration Collection. A research collection of 3,000 volumes including material in Russian and Native Alaskan languages.

39
Islands Community College
Stratton Library
1101 Sawmill Creek Boulevard
Sitka, Alaska 99835

Telephone. (907) 747-6653

Institutional Description. Islands Community College, formerly known as Sitka Community College, is a unit in the University of Alaska's statewide system. Enrollment: 755.

Library General Holdings. Stratton Library, operated jointly with Sheldon Jackson College, is located on the SJC campus. *See* **Sheldon Jackson College.**

40
Ketchikan Community College
College Library
7th and Madison
Ketchikan, Alaska 99901

Telephone. (907) 225-6177

Institutional Description. Located on Alaska's Inside passage, Ketchikan is the first port of call for ships heading north. The two-year college was foundced in 1954 and occupied its present location in 1969. Enrollment: 632.

Library Administration. Robert D. Warner, Librarian.

Library General Holdings. 41,000 volumes; 150 current periodical subscriptions.

Special Collections

The library maintains the **History of the Sea Collection** and materials on the American West.

41
Kuskokwim Community College
Kuskokwim Consortium Library
P.O. Box 368
Bethel, Alaska 99559

Telephone. (907) 543-2621

Institutional Description. The two-year community college serves 50 villages spread over an area of 60,000 square miles. Enrollment: 484.

Library Administration. Theodora Wintersteen, Librarian.

Library General Holdings. 20,000 volumes; 210 periodical titles.

Special Collections

The **Northern Collection** consists of 1,750 volumes on Alaska and other northern areas.

42
Northwest Community College
Emily Ivanoff Brown Learning Resource Center
Pouch 400
Nome, Alaska 99762

Telephone. (907) 443-2201

Institutional Description. Located in Nome, a town of 300 people on the Bering Sea, the Northwest Community

College is the continent's westernmost college. It gives strong emphasis in multicultural education, office occupations, human services, and arctic technology. Enrollment: 485.

Library Administration. Kathleen Hansen, Acting Librarian.

Library General Holdings. 12,000 volumes; 130 periodical subscriptions.

Special Collections

The library has a 1,500-volume special collection of Alaskana.

43
Sheldon Jackson College
Stratton Library
801 Lincoln Street
Sitka, Alaska 99835

Telephone. (907) 747-5234

Institutional Description. Sheldon Jackson College is affiliated with the Presbyterian Church. Enrollment: 298.

Library Administration. Evelyn K. Bonner, College Librarian.

Library General Holdings. 67,000 books; 500 periodical and 30 newspaper subscriptions; over 3,000 recordings and tapes; rapidly growing collection of microfiche and microfilm.

Special Collections

Andrews Collection. Comprises the major portion of the library of Clarence L. Andrews (1862-1948), author of numerous articles and books on Alaska; includes rare and first edition books and periodicals about Alaska and the Northwest Coast.

Elbridge Warren Merrill Photographic Collection. Over 900 glass plate negatives taken by E. W. Merrill (1899-1929), an early Sitka photographer; a large portion of the collection is genre type studies depicting Tlingit life and represents a photographic record of the Tlingit people for three decades.

44
University of Alaska - Anchorage
University Library
3211 Portage Drive
Anchorage, Alaska 99508

Telephone. (907) 786-1800

Institutional Description. The University of Alaska - Anchorage was established in 1970. Enrollment: 4,755.

Library Administration. Jack W. O'Bar, Director; Dennis F. Walle, Archivist and Manuscripts Curator.

Library General Holdings. 445,000 volumes.

Special Collections

Special collections include materials on Alaska and the polar region; 62,000 pieces of choral music; 50,650 pieces of symphonic music; and collections of unpublished archives and manuscripts.

45
University of Alaska - Fairbanks
Elmer E. Rasmuson Library
Fairbanks, Alaska 99775

Telephone. (907) 474-7224

Institutional Description. The publicly supported university was founded in 1917, and in 1935 became the University of Alaska. Enrollment: 5,299.

Library Administration. Paul H. McCarthy, Acting Director; C. Eugene West, Arctic Bibliographer; Marvin Falk, Rare Books Librarian.

Library General Holdings. 1,493,082 volumes; 640,181 U.S. government documents; 4,391 media units; 35,171 serial/periodical titles.

Special Collections

Alaska and Polar Regions Collection. Contains materials related to the subjects indicated in the title of the collection. An attempt is made to acquire everything published about Alaska regardless of format or language. These include: monographs, maps, government documents, film products, and pamphlets. Acquisition of monographs related to the following geographic regions is also strongly emphasized: Canada north of 60 degrees latitude; Greenland; Antarctica; northern portions of Norway, Sweden, Finland, and the Soviet Union, especially Siberia. The collection currently numbers more than 70,000 monographs, 1,000 newspapers and serials, and 25,000 maps.

Archives. These are almost wholly related to Alaska and document its political and social history, business and economic development, and personal and religious experience. Strengths include papers of Alaska territorial delegates to Congress, and U.S. Senators and Representatives. State records include the Alaska Constitutional Convention and Governor's personal papers. Archives has a collection of more than 200,000 historical photographs and is especially strong in images of the Alaska Gold Rush Era. Archives has an estimated 25,000 manuscript maps related to Alaska.

Rare Book Collections

Rare Book and Maps Collection. Contains materials related to Alaska and associated northern polar regions. Strengths include the history of Russian America and Alaska together with north polar exploration in all languages. These include the Lada-Morcarski Collection, extremely rare books on Russian America, unique items relating to the Collins Overland Telegraph Expedition, and the George Davidson collection of maps and charts. The Shur Collection contains film reproductions of Russian manuscript material and drawings which are the only reproductions outside the Soviet Union. The collection currently contains 3,210 monographs and 1,200 maps.

46
University of Alaska - Juneau
Library and Media Services
11120 Glacier Highway
Juneau, Alaska 99801

Telephone. (907) 789-4458

Institutional Description. The University of Alaska - Juneau offered its first instruction at the postsecondary level in 1956. Enrollment: 2,234.

Library Administration. Michael Herbison, Director.

Library General Holdings. 70,000 volumes; 1,400 serial titles; 275,000 microforms; 2,000 phonorecords and audiocassettes.

Special Collections

The resources available in the library are supplemented by cooperative arrangements with the Juneau Memorial Library and the Alaska State Library. A common catalog, the Capital Cities Catalog, is used by all three libraries. As a designated Alaska State Documents depository, the library houses 6,000 state publications. The library is also a selective federal depository library.

Arizona

47
American Graduate School of International Management
Barton Kyle Yount Memorial Library
Thunderbird Campus
59th Avenue and Greenway Road
Glendale, Arizona 85306

Telephone. (602) 978-7200

Institutional Description. The privately supported institution is the only graduate school in the United States devoted entirely to training for international business, languages, and interdisciplinary studies. Enrollment: 1,018.

Library Administration. Lora Jeanne Wheeler, Chief Librarian.

Library General Holdings. 90,000 volumes; 1,016 domestic and international periodicals.

Special Collections

The resources of the library are specifically chosen to support the unique Thunderbird curriculum with concentration on the various phases of international management, international relations, and the history and background of various areas of the world. Language study is reinforced by collections in Arabic, Chinese, French, German, Japanese, Portuguese, and Spanish. An extensive vertical file is maintained, containing current material covering countries, industries, commodities, business firms, and all other subjects pertaining to the curriculum.

48
Arizona State University
Charles Trumbull Hayden Library
Tempe, Arizona 85287

Telephone. (602) 965-9011

Institutional Description. The publicly supported state university was founded in 1885. It is now composed of 11 colleges, an extension program, and summer sessions. Enrollment: 31,283.

Library Administration. Donald E. Riggs, University Librarian; Marilyn J. Wurzburger, Head, Special Collections; Shelley Grebles, Assistant Librarian, Arizona Collection.

Library General Holdings. 2,160,000 volumes; 28,900 periodical and serial subscriptions; 2,340,000 microforms; 75,000 audiovisual materials.

Special Collections

The Charles Trumbull Hayden Library is the main library and houses the largest multidisciplinary collection. The **Arizona Collection** includes the papers of several major Arizona political figures. Other important collections are the **William Burroughs Archives** and the **Alberto Pradeau Archives.**

Architecture Library. In additions to books and periodicals, this library houses the Paolo Soleri archives.

Music Library. Maintains a large collection of music scores, recordings, and music reference materials. Special collections include the **Wayne King Collection,** the **Pablo Casals International Cello Library,** and the **International Percussion Reference Library.**

Daniel E. Noble Science and Engineering Library. Special collections include the **Solar Energy Collection** and the **Map Collection.**

49
Central Arizona College
Learning Resource Center
Woodruff at Overfield Road
Coolidge, Arizona 85228

Telephone. (602) 723-4141

Institutional Description. Central Arizona College is a multi-campus institution offering two-year programs at locations throughout the central part of Arizona. Enrollment: 1,755.

Library Administration. Patrick W. Parker, Director.

Library General Holdings. 75,000 volumes; 1,500 current periodical subscriptions.

Special Collections

The library has a small collection of rare books and maintains the **Early Arizona Collection.**

50
Cochise College
College Libraries
Bisbee Douglas Highway
Douglas, Arizona 85607

Telephone. (602) 364-7943

Institutional Description. The two-year community college was opened in 1964 and serves both commuter and resident students. Enrollment: 2,531.

Library Administration. Catherin Lincer, Director.

Library General Holdings. 57,000 volumes; 232 periodical subscriptions.

Special Collections

The library has special collections on anthropology, nursing, Oriental and Southwestern art.

51
Eastern Arizona College
Learning Resources Center
6100 Church Street
Thatcher, Arizona 85552

Telephone. (602) 428-1133

Institutional Description. Eastern Arizona College is a community college offering university-parallel programs and vocational-technical courses. Enrollment: 1,781.

Library Administration. Crystal Melton, Librarian.

Library General Holdings. 36,000 books; 250 magazine, newspapers, and microfiche serial titles.

Special Collections

The Learning Resources Center maintains the **Faculty Collection,** the **Arizona Collection,** and the **Native Americans Collection.**

52
Grand Canyon College
Fleming Library
3300 West Camelback Road
Phoenix, Arizona 85017

Telephone. (602) 249-3300

Institutional Description. The privately supported Christian liberal arts and teachers college is affiliated with the Arizona Southern Baptist Convention. Enrollment: 1,565.

Library Administration. Cathy Poplin, Director, Resource Learning Center.

Library General Holdings. 100,000 volumes; 350 current periodical subscriptions.

Special Collections

Vera Butler Collection. Contains 120 children's books dating from the 1800s.

Library of Recordings. There are over 3,000 sound recordings in Fleming Library. Many were donated by Chet Brantner, an Arizona cowboy and Bud Glaze, a Phoenix businessman.

53
Mohave Community College
Resource Center
1971 Jagerson Avenue
Kingman, Arizona 86401

Telephone. (602) 757-4331

Institutional Description. The two-year community college offers university-parallel and career-oriented programs leading to the associate degree, certificate, and diploma. Enrollment: 1,241.

Library Administration. Kathleen M. Stanley, Reference Librarian.

Library General Holdings. 29,500 volumes; 371 periodical subscriptions.

Special Collections

The library maintains a special collection of materials on Mohave County.

54
Navajo Community College
Learning Resource Center
Tsaila Rural Post Office
Tsaila, Arizona 86556

Telephone. (602) 724-3311

Institutional Description. Navajo Community College is a junior college and is the nation's first Indian-owned and Indian-operated institution of higher learning. Enrollment: 819.

Library Administration. Raghbir Jassal, Director of Library Services.

Library General Holdings. 35,000 volumes; 490 periodical titles; 11,457 microforms; 2,100 audiovisual materials.

Special Collections

In keeping with the philosophy of the College, the Learning Resource Center (Naaltsoos Ba Hoogan or "House of Papers") established the **Moses-Donner Collection of Indian Materials.** This reference section on American Indians and the Southwest includes books, periodicals, newspapers, phonorecords, maps, and films.

55
Northern Arizona University
Special Collections Library
NAU Box 6022
Flagstaff, Arizona 86011

Telephone. (602) 523-5551

Institutional Description. The publicly supported university began in 1899 as a two-year college. Enrollment: 10,973.

Library Administration. Jean D. Collins, University Librarian; William H. Mullane, Special Collections Librarian.

Library General Holdings. 1,500,000 volumes.

Special Collections

Arizona Research Collection. This collection reflects all aspects of Arizona and the Southwest—its history, art, people, culture, civilization, and literature through a variety of formats, including books, periodicals, manuscripts, photographs, pamphlets, and ephemera. One interesting adjunct to this collection is an assortment of books on lost mines and treasure hunting in the Southwest.

Norman Allderdice Memorial Collection. This collection of materials is named after its collector who methodically acquired and preserved an abundance of information on social and political issues spanning the years from the 1930s to the 1970s. The books, pamphlets, and periodicals, many of them rare, collected by Mr. Allderdice through his lifetime reflect his concerns. They are basic documents in the fields of political and economic philosophy, communism, socialism, Russian history, anti-communism, and Soviet-American relations.

Elbert Hubbard/Roycroft Press Collection. This collection consists of approximately 650 items printed by the Roycroft Press. Most of the items have been printed on a handmade press on handmade paper. They are also illuminated by hand and bound in handmade leather bindings.

Photograph Collection. The library has extensive collections of photographs, including the Emery Kolb Collection (Grand Canyon); repository of Jo Mora (Hopi photographer, painter, sculptor) photograph collection; repository for photographs and manuscripts of Pioneer Museum of the Arizona Historical Society (Flagstaff).

Zane Grey Collection. One of the most significant Zane Grey collection of books and manuscripts ever collected privately and donated to an institution.

Local and State Collections of Businesses. Includes the archives of the First Interstate Bank of Arizona, Arizona AFL-CIO, Arizona Woolgrowers, Arizona Lumber and Timber Co., United Verde Mine (Jerome).

George F. Wales Checker Collection. The collection contains everything for people interested in checkers, from beginning to championship levels. It deals with introductory information, history, strategy, tournament games, and solutions to hypothetical situations.

Manuscript Collections. The majority of the collections contain materials pertaining to the history and development of Flagstaff and northern Arizona.

Rare Book Collections

The library does not emphasize the collection of rare books and manuscripts, only as they may pertain—and are "rare" to—the history of Arizona and the Colorado Plateau. However, numerous rare items will be found, e.g., *A Universal Etymological Dictionary,* N. Bailey, 1726; *Gerardiionnis Vossii de Historicus Latinus, 1651; The Tales of the Heike* (Kamakura Period, 1185-1334).

George, Babbitt, Jr. and Madeline Babbitt Rare Book Collection. One of the finest private collections of historical lore devoted almost exclusively to Arizona and the Southwest, the collection represents a broad and complete approach to all published materials available relating to Arizona. The collection includes rare and first edition books, maps, manuscripts, records, photographs and pamphlets—3,000 items collected by George Babbitt, Jr. (1899-1980).

56
Scottsdale Community College Library
9000 East Chaparral Road
Scottsdale, Arizona 85256

Telephone. (602) 423-6650

Institutional Description. Scottsdale Community College is part of the Maricopa County Community College system. Enrollment: 3,903.

Library Administration. Sharon Howard, Library Director; Karen Biglin, Technical Services Librarian.

Library General Holdings. 36,487 volumes; 475 periodical and 20 newspaper subscriptions; 19,303 microforms; 748 recordings; 54 realia; 1,740 pamphlets; 595 paperbacks; 613 leisure reading volumes.

Special Collections

Arizona Collection. 1,009 books and periodicals pertaining to Arizona.

College and Career Collection. 684 books, pamphlets, audio recordings, and microfiche on all aspects of careers and career planning; materials on colleges.

Foreign Language Collection. 376 books written primarily in Spanish, French, and German.

Indian Collection. 1,389 volumes, periodicals, and audio recordings on Indians of the Southwest.

57
University of Arizona
University Libraries
Tucson, Arizona 85721

Telephone. (602) 621-2211

Institutional Description. The publicly supported university was founded in 1885. It is now composed of 13 colleges. Enrollment: 25,799.

Library Administration. W. David Laird, Librarian, University Library.

Library General Holdings. 5,000,000 items, including books, periodicals, microforms, maps, government publications, manuscripts, and non-book media.

Special Collections

Basic holdings of the University Libraries cover all fields of instruction and there are especially strong collections in anthropology, geology, Spanish and Latin American languages and literature, American agriculture, Southwestern Americana, Arizoniana, twentieth-century photography, history of science, science fiction, and eighteenth- and nineteenth-century British and American literature.

Center for Creative Photography. Contains the library's archive of over 100 famous twentieth-century photographers.

Library Science Library. Houses the library's collection of professional library literature in support of the Graduate School of Library Science.

Map Collection. A depository for USGS maps; houses a fully cataloged collection of 130,000 maps on every subject.

Music Collection. Houses the library's collection of 50,000 scores, 26,000 sheet music items, and 25,000 recordings.

Oriental Studies Collection. Contains over 182,000 items including books, periodicals, and newspapers in the Chinese, Japanese, Arabic, Persian, Hindi, Urdu, Turkish, and other Oriental languages.

Southwest Folkore Center. Consists of the library's collection of musical tapes and manuscript archives of Southwest music and folklore.

Special Collections. Houses the library's collections of Arizoniana and Southwestern Americana, science fiction, rare books, fine printing, manuscripts, and the University of Arizona archives. The Lecomte du Nouy Memorial Room preserves the manuscripts and first editions of the works of Pierre Lecomte du Nouy and of other important figures in the history of scientific development.

Arkansas

58
Arkansas College
Mabee Learning Resources Center
P.O. Box 2317
Batesville, Arkansas 72501

Telephone. (501) 793-9813

Institutional Description. The privately supported liberal arts college was founded in 1872. It is affiliated with the Presbyterian Church, U.S.A. Enrollment: 692.

Library Administration. Ellen I. Watson, Director.

Library General Holdings. The **Dorothy P. Sydenstricker Room** houses the College Archives and rare books collection and a collection of reproductions of William Hogarth given to the College by Mr. and Mrs. W. Edwards. The library also maintains a region collection on Arkansas and the Ozarks which includes the **J. Quincy Wolf Collection.**

59
Arkansas State University
Dean B. Ellis Library
State University, Arkansas 72467

Telephone. (501) 972-3030

Institutional Description. The publicly supported state university was founded in 1909 as a two-year agricultural school. Enrollment: 6,739.

Library Administration. James W. Hansard, Director.

Library General Holdings. 415,731 books and bound periodical volumes; 2,300 current periodical subscriptions; 257,989 physical units of microtext; 298,605 federal and state documents.

Special Collections

Children's Literature. Includes an outstanding collection of Lois Lenski books for children and related materials, as well as collections of notable Arkansas authors of children's books: Charlie May Simon, Lois Snelling, and Faith Yingling Knoop.

Creation Science Papers. A collection donated by Arkansas Attorney General Steve Clark includes the state's side of the landmark creation science case.

John Gould Fletcher Collection. A collection of the works of the Arkansas writer.

Honorable E.C. Gathings Collection. Made up principally of correspondence of Arkansas' long-time congressional representative.

Cass S. Hough Aeronautical Collection. Consists of 14,000 books and memorabilia which an expert in the field has described as the single most valuable collection of aviation materials in private hands.

Juvenile Literature. There is a special collection of literature for juveniles and adolescents which is maintained as a teaching resource.

Tom Love Collection. Forms the nucleus of an extensive Arkansas collection comprised of manuscripts, documents, and other historic materials relating to the state of Arkansas.

Rare Book Collections

Robert E. Lee Wilson III Collection. Includes 250 rare books from the library of Robert Dale Owen, the nineteenth-century legislator, diplomat, and author.

60
Arkansas Tech University
Tomlinson Library
Russellville, Arkansas 72801

Telephone. (501) 968-0237

Institutional Description. The publicly supported (state) university was founded in 1909 as an Agricultural school, offering the first two years of college. It became a four-year institution in 1950. Enrollment: 2,881.

Library Administration. William A. Vaughn, Librarian.

Library General Holdings. 125,000 volumes; 1,160 current periodicals; 59,000 government documents; 475,000 microforms.

Special Collections

The library maintains a special **Americana Collection** as well as holdings in music and recreation and park administration.

61
Central Baptist College
Cobb Memorial Library
CBC Station
Conway, Arkansas 72032

Telephone. (501) 329-6872

Institutional Description. The privately supported liberal arts college was founded in 1952 as a junior college. Baccalaureate and master's programs have been added. The college is affiliated with the Baptist Missionary Association of Arkansas. Enrollment: 253.

Library Administration. Ellen R. Hornaday, Librarian.

Library General Holdings. 30,000 books; 200 current periodical subscriptions.

Special Collections

Special holdings of the library include the local association minutes of the Baptist Missionary Society of Arkansas and microfilm copies of the **Baptist Missionary Society Archives.**

62
Harding University
Beaumont Memorial Library
Searcy, Arkansas 72143

Telephone. (501) 268-6161

Institutional Description. The privately supported liberal arts university is affiliated with the Churches of Christ. It grants baccalaureate and master's degrees. Enrollment: 2,666.

Library Administration. Winnie Elizabeth Bell, Librarian.

Library General Holdings. 286,186 volumes; 1,337 current periodicals; 12 daily and weekly newspapers.

Special Collections

Special collections include the personal library of the late G.C. Brewer, an influential writer and minister in the Churches of Christ; and the **Juvenile Collection** for use by students in elementary education. The **Harding Room** houses materials related to the history of the school and tapes in the Oral History Collection. A collection of 1,200 science books, some unusually old and rare, were presented to the library by Dr. Wyndham Davies Miles.

63
Henderson State University
Huie Library
Arkadelphia, Arkansas 71923

Telephone. (501) 246-5511

Institutional Description. The publicly supported state university was established in 1929. Enrollment: 2,-569.

Library Administration. Donald J. Pennington, Director of Information.

Library General Holdings. 230,000 volumes; 1,500 periodical subscriptions; 250,000 microforms; 23,000 audiovisual materials.

Special Collections

Major collections such as the **Library of English Literature** and **Library of American Civilization** are available on microfiche. Also maintained are the **Arkansas History Collection** and the **Howard A. Dawson Memorial Collection.**

64
Hendrix College
Olin C. Bailey Library
Conway, Arkansas 72032

Telephone. (501) 329-6811

Institutional Description. The privately supported liberal arts college offers academic cooperative programs with Columbia University, Vanderbilt University, Washington University, and American University. It is affiliated with the United Methodist Church.Enrollment: 998.

Library Administration. Henry L. Alsmeyer, Jr., Director.

Library General Holdings. 174,000 volumes; 600 current periodicals; 69,000 microforms.

Special Collections

The library maintains the **Hendrix Archives** and has a collection of Arkansas Methodist materials. The rare book room is named for Ethel K. Millar, alumna and former librarian.

65
Ouachita Baptist University
Library
410 Ouachita Street
Arkadelphia, Arkansas 71923

Telephone. (501) 246-4531

Institutional Description. The privately supported university was founded in 1885 by the Arkansas Baptist State Convention. It is affiliated with the Southern Baptist Church. Enrollment: 1,158.

Library Administration. Samuel Ray Granade, Director.

Library General Holdings. 123,000 volumes; 300,000 non-book titles; 650 serial titles.

Special Collections

Special collections include **American Baptist History Collection;** the **Clark County Historical Archives;** and the papers of Senator John L. McClellan.

66
Philander Smith College
M.L. Harris Library
812 West 13th Street
Little Rock, Arkansas 72202

Telephone. (501) 375-5257

Institutional Description. The privately supported liberal arts college was founded in 1877. It is affiliated with the United Methodist Church. Enrollment: 490.

Library Administration. Mary N. Russell, Acting Librarian.

Library General Holdings. 66,000 volumes; 300 current periodical subscriptions.

Special Collections

The library supports the curriculum of the College and maintains a special collection of juvenile literature.

67
Phillips County Community College
Library
Helena, Arkansas 72342

Telephone. (501) 338-6474

Institutional Description. The college was the first community college in Arkansas and offered its first courses in 1966. Enrollment: 1,009.

Library Administration. Joseph Forte, Head Librarian.

Library General Holdings. 31,000 volumes; 390 periodical titles; 24,000 audiovisual materials.

Special Collections

Special collections are maintained in auto mechanics and practical electronics.

68
Southern Arkansas University
John F. and Joanna G. Magale Library
Magnolia, Arkansas 71753

Telephone. (501) 235-4001

Institutional Description. The publicly supported (state) liberal arts and teachers university has two branch campuses, in El Dorado and East Camden. Enrollment: 1,839.

Library Administration. Robert Wallace Reid, Head Librarian.

Library General Holdings. 150,000 volumes; 1,000 periodical titles.

Special Collections

The library maintains the **Arkansas Collection.**

69
University of Arkansas at Fayetteville
David W. Mullins Library
Fayetteville, Arkansas 72701

Telephone. (501) 575-2000

Institutional Description. The publicly supported university was founded in 1871 as a land grant institution. It offers a wide variety of programs. Enrollment: 12,415; Medical Center (at Little Rock) 1,787.

Library Administration. John A. Harrison, Director.

Library General Holdings. 1,181,000 volumes; 12,000 journal and serial subscriptions; 1,196,000 microforms; 536,000 government documents.

Special Collections

The Special Collections Department in Mullins Library acquires and preserves material for research in the history, literature, and culture of Arkansas and surrounding regions. Among the more than 3,300 linear feet of fully processed manuscript collections available are the papers of J. William Fullbright, Joe T. Robinson, Edward Durrell Stone, Orval Faubus, Brooks Hays, John Gould Fletcher, and Vance Randolph. In addition, the department maintains a special collection of books written by Arkansas authors as well as a collection of the articles and books published by faculty members of the University. The department also houses the library's Rare Book Collection and other material.

70
University of Arkansas at Little Rock
Ottenheimer Library
2801 South University Avenue
Little Rock, Arkansas 72204

Telephone. (501) 569-3120

Institutional Description. The publicly supported university was founded in 1927 as a junior college. Enrollment: 6,910.

Library Administration. Bobby L. Roberts, Special Collections/Rare Book Librarian.

Library General Holdings. 242,516 volumes; 2,700 serial subscription titles; 179,127 microfiche titles; 9,300 microfilm reels; 2,600 maps.

Special Collections

The University of Alabama at Little Rock Archives and Special Collections contains approximately 200 manuscript collections (plus 500 small manuscript collections); 11,000 books; 4,000 pamphlets; 600 maps; 800 newspapers; 15,000 photographs relating primarily to Arkansas. Its book collection relates not only to Arkansas but also the antebellum lower Mississippi Valley. There is a book collection of Pultizer Prize poet John Gould Fletcher and children's writer Charlie May Simon. The U.M. Rose Collection of European Imprints includes imprints collected between 1870 and 1900.

Manuscript collections include: the **J.N. Heiskell Historical Collection;** the **Winthrop Rockefeller Collection;** the **Dale Bumpers Papers;** the editorial cartoon collections of Bill Graham *(Arkansas Gazette)* and Jon Kennedy *(Arkansas Democrat);* legal and judicial materials relating to Arkansas prisons, labor issues, and creation science; FBI Reports and other papers relating to the Little Rock School Crisis; the **Lum and Abner Archives** of tapes, films, and scripts; the **Fletcher-Terry Papers;** the State Land Commission records and maps; newspapers of the Japanese-American relocation camps in Arkansas; and materials on labor organizations in Arkansas.

Native American Press Archives. A Collection of materials relating to the Native American Press including 800 titles comprising 25,000 issues; microfilm, including documents and newspapers; a vertical file; pamphlet file; and biographical files on Indian writers.

71
University of Arkansas at Monticello
University Library
P.O. Box 3596
Monticello, Arkansas 71655

Telephone. (501) 367-6811

Institutional Description. The publicly supported liberal arts and technological campus of the University of Arkansas was founded as the Arkansas Agricultural and Mechanical College. It became part of the state system in 1971. Enrollment: 1,667.

Library Administration. William F. Droessler, Librarian.

Library General Holdings. 114,000 volumes; 870 current periodical subscriptions; 113,000 government documents; 7,200 microforms.

Special Collections

The library supports special collections in the areas of forestry, government documents, and Arkansas history.

72
University of Arkansas at Pine Bluff
Watson Memorial Library
Pine Bluff, Arkansas 71601

Telephone. (501) 541-6500

Institutional Description. The publicly supported liberal arts and professional campus of the University of Arkansas was founded in 1873 as a land grant institution. Enrollment: 2,479.

Library Administration. Edward Fontenette, Library Director.

Library General Holdings. 126,000 volumes; 1,050 current periodical subscriptions; 147,000 microforms.

Special Collections

The Watson Memorial Library maintains the **John M. Ross Collection;** the **Knox Nelson Collection,** and the **J.B. Watson Collection** (President of the University 1929-1942).

73
University of Arkansas for Medical Sciences
Medical Sciences Library
4301 West Markham, Slot 586
Little Rock, Arkansas 72205

Telephone. (501) 661-5980

Institutional Description. The University of Arkansas for Medical Sciences Library is a health sciences collection serving the Colleges of Health Related Professions, Medicine, Nursing, Pharmacy, and the Graduate School.

Library Administration. Rose Hogan, Director; Edwina Walls, Special Collections/Rare Books Librarian.

Library General Holdings. 139,294 volumes (38,062 books; 101,232 journals); 26,836 microforms; 5,189 audiovisual materials; 2,880 current journal subscriptions.

Special Collections

The UAMS Library History of Medicine Division/ Archives contains materials related to Arkansas medical sciences, rare editions, classics in the medical sciences, archives of the University, pamphlets, and photographs. Included among the collections are records of the Pulaski County Medical Society, the Arkansas State Board of Nursing, the Arkansas State Nurses' Association, the Women's Auxiliary of the Pulaski County and the Arkansas Medical Societies, the book collection of Hans G. Schlumberger, M.D., Trinity Hospital, the Basic Science and Healing Arts Board, and the Arkansas Regional Medical Program.

Among the notable manuscript collections are the papers of Roscoe G. Jennings, M.D., the Dibrell Family, and Oliver Clarence Wenger, M.D.

74
University of Central Arkansas
Torreyson Library
Donaghey at Bruce
Conway, Arkansas 72032

Telephone. (501) 329-2931

Institutional Description. The publicly supported university was founded in 1907. Enrollment: 7,066.

Library Administration. Willie Hardin, Director.

Library General Holdings. 390,000 books; 2,500 periodical titles; 750,000 microforms.

Special Collections

Arkansas Room. Contains materials on unique Arkansas subjects and individual works by Arkansas authors.

The library maintains the W.C. and J.P. Faucette Papers and the Heber McAlister Papers.

A **Curriculum Collection, School Library Laboratory Collection,** and the **U.S. Government Documents Collection** are also maintained.

75
University of the Ozarks
Dobson Memorial Library
415 College Avenue
Clarksville, Arkansas 72830

Telephone. (501) 754-3839

Institutional Description. The privately supported liberal arts university is affiliated with the United Presbyterian Church. Enrollment: 632.

Library Administration. Stuart Stelzer, Director.

Library General Holdings. 118,000 volumes; 450 current periodical subscriptions; 4,000 microfilm units.

Special Collections

The library supports the curriculum of the University which offers fields of study in business administration, education, humanities and fine arts, natural sciences and mathematics, and social sciences.

California

76
Academy of Art College
Library
540 Powell Street
San Francisco, California 94108

Telephone. (415) 673-4200

Institutional Description. The privately supported professional college was founded in 1929. It offers programs in advertising and graphic design, illustration, fine arts, and photography. Enrollment: 1,356.

Library Administration. James Van Buskirk, Librarian; Pam Saracino, Slide Librarian.

Library General Holdings. 7,000 volumes; 3,500 periodicals.

Special Collections

The library has special collections of exhibition catalogs, annual reports, paper samples, typeface sample books, and an extensive collection of reference books and slides.

77
Allan Hancock College
Learning Resources Center
800 South College Drive
Santa Maria, California 93454

Telephone. (805) 922-6966

Institutional Description. In 1920, Santa Maria College—later to become Allan Hancock College—was created as an extension of the high school offering courses paralleling those of the lower division of the University of California. The present name was adopted in 1954. Enrollment: 8,157.

Library Administration. Harold Eckes, Director.

Library General Holdings. 45,000 volumes.

Special Collections

A special collection on ethnic studies is maintained by the library.

78
American River College
Kenneth Boettcher Library
4700 College Oak Drive
Sacramento, California 95841

Telephone. (916) 484-8456

Institutional Description. American River College is a publicly supported junior college offering university transfer programs, general and vocational programs, and certificate programs to assist those already employed. Enrollment: 19,271.

Library Administration. James F. Carlson, College Librarian.

Library General Holdings. 75,000 volumes; 500 newspapers; strong microform and non-book items within Learning Center.

Special Collections

Weaving/Textile Collection. A specialized collection of books; weaving samples; oral history tapes; media kits; slide/tape/video presentations; artifacts; pamphlets; periodicals. Collection draws significant interlibrary loan activity throughout the West Coast area.

Books and Oral History Collection. In process/development; to be housed within the *California American* grouping room. The collection will focus upon Japanese sector and the Internment period of World War II.

California Collection. Specialized grouping of books; some journals and serials based upon California history.

79
Armstrong University
College Library
2222 Harold Way
Berkeley, California 94704

Telephone. (415) 848-2500

Institutional Description. The privately supported school of business and teacher education grants associate, baccalaureate, and master's degrees. Enrollment: 427.

Library Administration. Margaret Sederoff, Librarian.

Library General Holdings. 18,000 volumes; 225 cur-

rent periodical subscriptions.

Special Collections

The books in the library are closely coordinated with the college's programs and provide strong support for study in the fields of accounting, finance, management, marketing, and international business. There is a selection of books in the humanities and social sciences as well as a special biography collection. The library also has a small, varied record collection which includes classical, opera, country, and Christmas music.

80
Art Center College of Design
James Lemont Fogg Memorial Library
1700 Lida Street
Pasadena, California 91103

Telephone. (818) 584-5013

Institutional Description. The Art Center College of Design is a privately supported, nonprofit institution offering degree programs in painting, illustration, communications design, photography and film, and industrial design. Enrollment: 1,191.

Library Administration. Elizabeth Galloway, Director of Library.

Library General Holdings. 28,885 bound volumes (includes 4,000 periodical volumes); 543 current periodical titles; 41,000 slides; 528 videos; 125 films.

Special Collections

The library has specialized holdings in commercial art, advertising art, illustration (including children's book illustration); graphics/packaging; industrial design; photography; fine arts; printing and typography.

Other special collections include the Archives of Art Center College of Design, an Ansel Adams portfolio, 100 portfolios of artists' works; and a small collection of pop-up books.

81
Azusa Pacific University
Marshburn Memorial Library
Citrus Avenue and Alosta
Azusa, California 91702

Telephone. (818) 969-3434

Institutional Description. The privately supported liberal arts university was formed by the merger of Azusa College and Los Angeles Pacific College in 1965. Enrollment: 2,174.

Library Administration. Edward Peterman, Director.

Library General Holdings. 380,000 items; 600 current periodical subscriptions.

Special Collections

Special collections include the **Azusa Foothill Citrus Collection;** the MacNeil family's personal historical material; the **Clifford M. Drury Collection** on the missionary in the American West; the **Monsignor Francis J. Weber Collection** of American Catholic Church history; the **Irving Stone Collection of Lincolniana;** and the **George E. Fullerton Collection** of Western Americana.

82
Bethany Bible College
Library
800 Bethany Drive
Scotts Valley, California 95066

Telephone. (408) 438-3800

Institutional Description. The privately supported professional college is affiliated with the Assemblies of God Church. A three-year diploma program is offered in the areas of religious education, ministry, and music. Enrollment: 448.

Library Administration. Arnold McLellan, Head Librarian.

Library General Holdings. 60,000 volumes; 350 current periodical subscriptions.

Special Collections

The library supports the goals of Bethany Bible College which aim to prepare students for dynamic Christian living, for ministry in the church, and for service to mankind in the Biblical perspective. The resources reflect the Christian emphasis.

83
Biola University
Rose Memorial Library
13800 Biola Avenue
La Mirada, California 90639

Telephone. (213) 944-0351

Institutional Description. The privately supported liberal arts and professional university is an interdenominational Christian institution. It requires at least 30 units of Biblical studies and theology of all students. Enrollment: 2,577.

Library Administration. A. Lawrence, Marshburn, Director.

Library General Holdings. 185,000 books and bound periodicals; 1,120 current periodical subscriptions.

Special Collections

Special features of the University Library include an extensive index file of sermon outlines and illustrations, an excellent collection of bilbiographic tools and journal indexes, and a number of special collections including Bibles, evangelical Christianity, and theology.

84
Brooks Institute of Photography
Library
801 Alston Road
Santa Barbara, California 93108

Telephone. (805) 969-2291

Institutional Description. The privately supported institution offers programs in photography, business, photojournalism, and multi-media presentations. It grants associate, baccalaureate, and master's degrees. Enrollment: 943.

Library Administration. Isabelle Higgins, Librarian; James B. Maher, Librarian.

Library General Holdings. 6,000 volumes.

Special Collections

The entire collection of the library relates to the field of photography, graphics, art, and design.

85
Cabrillo College
College Library
6500 Soquel Drive
Aptos, California 95003

Telephone. (408) 499-6451

Institutional Description. The college began classes in 1959 and occupied the present Aptos campus in 1962. Enrollment: 9,730.

Library Administration. John MacPherson, College Librarian.

Library General Holdings. 60,000 volumes; 500 magazine and newspaper titles.

Special Collections

The Cabrillo College Library maintains a special collection of local history and Santa Cruz County.

86
California Baptist College
College Library
8432 Magnolia Avenue
Riverside, California 92504

Telephone. (714) 689-5771

Institutional Description. The privately supported liberal arts college is affiliated with the Southern Baptist Church. Enrollment: 527.

Library Administration. William Stanley, Director.

Library General Holdings. 91,000 volumes; 400 current periodical subscriptions; 3,000 microforms.

Special Collections

The **Wallace Collection** contains Protestant evangelical materials.

87
California College of Arts and Crafts
Meyer Library
5121 Broadway
Oakland, California 94618

Telephone. (415) 653-8118

Institutional Description. The privately supported college was founded in 1907. Its three main functions are the training of professional artists, the developing of art teachers for elementary and secondary schools, and the supplying of supplemental art training for nondegree students. Enrollment: 955.

Library General Holdings. 30,000 volumes.

Special Collections

The major emphasis of the Meyer Library's collection is in the visual arts. There is a substantial periodicals list, clipping files, reproductions, original prints, and recordings. There is a special collection entitled the **Jo Sinel Collection of Industrial Design.**

88
California Institute of Integral Studies
Library
765 Ashbury Street
San Francisco, California 94117

Telephone. (415) 753-6100

Institutional Description. The privately supported institution offers courses on the graduate level only. Programs concentrate on the concepts of human development presented through Eastern and Western psychologies, philosophies, religions, culture, and literature. Enrollment: 262.

Library Administration. Sara Oechsli, Librarian.

Library General Holdings. 27,000 titles

Special Collections

The library's collection is particularly strong in the fields of psychology and counseling, philosophy and religion, East-West comparative studies, social and cultural anthropology, various facets of an integral world view, and the perennial wisdom. The library has received support from the Kern Foundation and the Jewish Chautauqua Society and many other institutional and individual donors.

89
California Institute of Technology
Robert A. Millikan Memorial Library
1201 East California Boulevard
Pasadena, California 91125

Telephone. (818) 356-6811

Institutional Description. The privately supported technological university was founded in 1891 as Throop Institute, designed to feature engineering and scientific research, but emphasizing the humanities as important to the education of engineers and scientists. Enrollment: 1,839.

Library Administration. Glenn Brudvig, Director of Information Resources.

Library General Holdings. 396,021 volumes; 6,450 journal subscriptions.

Special Collections

The Millikan Library includes the collections of biology, chemistry, mathematics, physics, engineering, and humanities and social sciences, each of which is organized as an individual unit complete with books, periodicals, reference works, and card catalog. The library collections that are located elsewhere on campus include aeronautics, applied physics and electrical engineering, astrophysics, chemical engineering, computer science, earthquake engineering, environmental engineering, geology, management, and public affairs. Special collections include the **Robert A. Millikan Collection,** the **Theodore von Karman Collection,** and the **George E. Hale Collection.**

90
California Institute of the Arts
Library
24700 McBean Parkway
Valencia, California 91355

Telephone. (805) 253-7885

Institutional Description. California Institute of the Arts is a privately supported arts institute, composed of the Schools of Art, Dance, Film and Video, Music and Theater. Enrollment: 826.

Library Administration. Frederick B. Gardner, Librarian; Joan T. Anderson, Rare Books Librarian.

Library General Holdings. 66,814 volumes; 11,626 scores; 12,279 recordings; 4,557 performance music; 837 films; 906 video cassettes/discs; 9,211 exhibition catalogs; 79,332 slides; 746 periodical subscriptions; 14,144 periodical volumes on microfilm (6,975 physical, 7,169 bibliographical).

Rare Book Collections

MCA Collection. Materials dating from the 1500s on scientific recreations, the magic lantern, lantern projection photography; histories of the mathematics, optics, and technology leading to the moving picture.

91
California Lutheran University
Pearson Library
60 West Olsen Road
Thousand Oaks, California 91360

Telephone. (805) 492-2411

Institutional Description. The privately supported liberal arts university is affiliated with the American Lutheran Church and the Lutheran Church in America. It grants baccalaureate and master's degrees. Enrollment: 1,790.

Library Administration. Kenneth Flueger, Director of Library Services.

Library General Holdings. 100,000 volumes; 550 current periodical subscriptions; 13,000 microforms.

Special Collections

The library maintains a special collection on Scandinavians and Lutherans in the West.

92
California Maritime Academy
Library
Foot of Maritime Academy Drive
P.O. Box 1392
Vallejo, California 94590

Telephone. (707) 648-4265

Institutional Description. The publicly supported institution prepares men and women for service as officers in the American Merchant Marine. Enrollment: 403.

Library Administration. Paul W. O'Bannon, Senior Librarian.

Library General Holdings. 25,000 volumes; 500 periodical titles; 30 newspapers; 10,000 technical reports on microfiche.

Special Collections

The Library of the California Maritime Academy includes materials on ships and shipping: design, construction, operation, management, economics, history, folklore of the sea, etc.

Rare Book Collections

Archives. Includes photographs, letters and documents, yearbooks, catalogs, and other materials dealing with the history of the Academy since its founding in 1929. Some archival material is included on the history of Morrow Cove (site of the Academy) in South Vallejo on the Carquinez Straits.

93
California Polytechnic State University, San Luis Obispo
Robert E. Kennedy Library
San Luis Obispo, California 93407

Telephone. (805) 756-2344

Institutional Description. California Polytechnic State University is a publicly supported technological university composed of the Schools of Agriculture, Architecture and Environmental Design, Business, Communicative Arts and Humanities, Engineering, Professional Studies and Education, Science and Mathematics. Enrollment: 14,660.

Library Administration. David B. Walch, Dean of Library Services; Nancy E. Loe, Head of Special Collections/University Archives.

Library General Holdings. Over two million items including 600,000 books and 3,000 periodical subscriptions.

Special Collections

Julia Morgan Collection. The personal and professional papers, drawings, sketches, and photographs of one of America's first and foremost architects. Morgan is best known for her monumental work on the estate of William Randolph Hearst at San Simeon.

California History. More than 500 volumes about the history, growth, and development of the state, from the Mission era through the Depression.

Children's Literature. Over 300 examples of American, British, and French primers from the mid-seventeenth century to the present, including a definitive sampling of children's classics.

Fairs. The administrative records, legislative and policy documents and ephemeral material pertaining to the growth and development of state and county fairs in California.

Fine Printing and Graphic Arts. More than 2,500 examples of letterpress printing, handmade paper, and fine binding produced by American bookmakers from the nineteenth century to the present, including the work of Henry Nash, Kelmscott and Ashendene Presses, the Roycrofters, and the Yolla Bolly Press.

Puppetry. 75 volumes describing the history of puppetry, the crafting of puppets, folk puppetry, and marionettes, including several examples of nineteenth century Punch and Judy books.

University Archives. Contains materials documenting the history of the university from its beginnings in 1903 to the present; a photographic collection of over 15,000 images depicts campus activities and historic events.

94
California School of Professional Psychology
2152 Union Street
San Francisco, California 94123

Telephone. (415) 346-4500

Institutional Description. The privately supported graduate school, whose administrative office is in San Francisco, has campuses in Berkeley, Fresno, Los Angeles, and San Diego. Enrollment: Total at the 4 campuses is 1,108.

95
California School of Professional Psychology - Berkeley
Library
1900 Addison Street
Berkeley, California 94704

Telephone. (415) 548-5415

Institutional Description. This institution is a branch campus of the California School of Professional Psychology whose central administrative office is in San Francisco. Enrollment: 294.

Library Administration. Johanna Peterson, Librarian.

Library General Holdings. 17,000 volumes; 300 journal subscriptions. The center for instructional materials for the branch campuses is housed here.

Special Collections

The library's collection of materials in the field of psychology reflects the curriculum of the School. The library maintains a special collections in clinical psychology, psychotherapy, and assessment. There is also a collection of psychological tests.

96
California School of Professional Psychology - Fresno
Library
1350 M Street
Fresno, California 993721

Telephone. (209) 486-8420

Institutional Description. This institution is a branch campus of the California School of Professional Psychology whose central administrative office is in San Francisco. Enrollment: 161.

Library Administration. Inge Kauffman, Librarian.

Library General Holdings. 14,000 volumes; 200 current periodical subscriptions.

Special Collections

The collection of the library is strong in psychology reference works and bibliography.

97
California School of Professional Psychology - Los Angeles
Library
2235 Beverly Boulevard
Los Angeles, California 90057

Telephone. (213) 483-7034

Institutional Description. This institution is a branch campus of the California School of Professional Psychology whose central administrative office is in San Francisco. Enrollment: 339.

Library Administration. Tobeylynn Birch, Librarian.

Library General Holdings. 17,000 volumes; 230 journal subscriptions.

Special Collections

The collection of the library is focused primarily on the clinical practice of psychology with increasing holdings in industrial organizational psychology, health psychology, minority mental health and community psychology within the clinical psychology field. Areas of emphasis include child psychology and family therapy, sex roles, and women's issues, and sexuality.

98
California School of Professional Psychology - San Diego
Library
6212 Ferris Square
San Diego, California 92121

Telephone. (619) 452-1664

Institutional Description. This institution is a branch campus of the California School of Professional Psychology whose central administrative office is in San Francisco. Enrollment: 314.

Library Administration. Ada Burns, Librarian.

Library General Holdings. 18,501 volumes; 339 current periodical subscriptions.

Special Collections

The particular strength of the collection is in psychology and related disciplines.

99
California State Polytechnic University, Pomona
University Library
P.O. Box 3088
Pomona, California 91768

Telephone. (714) 869-3090

Institutional Description. California State Polytechnic University places emphasis on a career-oriented curriculum to prepare both undergraduate and graduate students for professional and occupational roles in the community. Enrollment: 14,159.

Library Administration. Harold B. Schleifer, University Librarian; Walter H. Roeder, Archives/Special Collections Librarian.

Library General Holdings. 500,000 volumes; 3,500 periodical subscriptions; 42 newspaper subscriptions; 653,303 microcards; 600,000 microfiche; 32,000 films; 8,-500 maps.

Special Collections

W.K. Kellogg Arabian Horse Library. A collection of Arabian horse materials located in the University Library; contains approximately 2,100 books and 324 bound periodical volumes as well as numerous pamphlets, brochures, newsletters, videotapes, photographs, letters, reports, and manuscripts; also includes the W.K. Kellogg Ranch papers.

First Edition Collection. First editions (500 volumes) of 20 selected American and English contemporary authors.

California State Polytechnic University Archives Collection. Traces the history of the University since it was founded in 1938; contains 5,000 items including books, pamphlets, reports, student newspapers, photographs, audio and video tapes.

Rare Book Collections

Humphrey Mycology Collection. Contains 107 volumes which were the private collection of Dr. Clarence J. Humphrey who was mycological and plant pathological researcher at the University of Wisconsin, Bureau of Science in Manila (Philippines), and the Soil and Conservation Service at Safford, Arizona.

100
California State University, Bakersfield
Library
9001 Stockdale Highway
Bakersfield, California 93311

Telephone. (805) 833-3172

Institutional Description. The publicly supported state university was established in 1970. Enrollment: 2,-669.

Library Administration. Rodney Hersberger, Librarian; Jim Segesta, Special Collections Coordinator.

Library General Holdings. 300,000 bound volumes; 2,500 subscriptions; 70,000 government publications.

Special Collections

Specialized collections of the library include Kern County oral history, a collection on tape of over 100 interviews with local old-timers; the California Odyssey Project, an oral history of the Dust Bowl migration into the southern San Joaquin Valley.

101
California State University, Chico Meriam Library First and Hazel Streets Chico, California 95929

Telephone. (916) 895-6342

Institutional Description. California State University, Chico is serves the northeastern region (twelve counties) of California and offers both graduate and undergraduate Enrollment: 12,892.

Library Administration. Judith Sessions, University Librarian; William A. Jones, Special Collections/Rare Books Librarian.

Library General Holdings. 600,000 bound volumes; 4,500 current periodicals; 450,000 government documents; 100,000 maps; local government records; curriculum library; photographs; manuscripts.

Special Collections

Northeastern California Collection. Serves as a regional information center for the University's 12-county service region (counties of Siskiyou, Modoc, Trinity, Shasta, Lassen, Tehama, Plumas, Glenn Butte, Colusa, Sutter, Yuba); includes books and periodicals, manuscripts, oral history interviews, historical photographs, maps, environmental impact reports, indexes, Butte County Public Records. The collection covers a wide range of historical and contemporary topics of local interest: agriculture, education, business, history, geography, health care, local planning, city and county government, historic preservation and architecture, environmental issues, transportation, lumbering, mining. Thousands of old photographs, many dating from the nineteenth century; may be accessed by subject, geographic location, or by names of individuals (processing charge for prints).

University Archives. Published works by members of the University community have been acquired, including books written by faculty and student publications; guides and pamphlets relating to the campus and its environs; unpublished records of the University are divided into record groups (archival units).

Rare Book Collections

The rare book collection includes books on a wide variety of subjects, but focuses on rare, limited, and special editions of Northeastern Californiana.

Alfred Storm Bible Collection. Includes a *Biblia Latina,* printed by Johann Froben in 1498 and a Baskerville Bible printed in 1769.

102
California State University, Dominguez Hills University Library 1000 East Victoria Street Carson, California 90747

Telephone. (213) 516-3700

Institutional Description. California State University, Dominguez Hills is composed of the Schools of Humanities and Fine Arts, Sciences, Mathematics and Technology Management, Social and Behavioral Sciences, Education, and University College. Enrollment: 5,450.

Library Administration. Betty J. Blackman, University Librarian; Jacquelyn K. Sundstrand, Archivist, Special Collections Librarian.

Library General Holdings. 349,422 bound volumes; 3,325 periodicals; 474,815 microforms; 590 software titles.

Special Collections

Buckner Collection of American Best Sellers. Represents American popular taste in reading from 1607 to the present; emphasis on the late nineteenth and early twentieth centuries; collection is based on a significant gift by former faculty member Dr. Claudia Buckner.

Local History Collection. Brings together published materials that pertain to the Rancho San Pedro and South Bay areas in particular, and greater Los Angeles and Southern California in general.

103
California State University, Fresno Henry Madden Library Shaw and Cedar Avenues Fresno, California 93740

Telephone. (209) 294-2595

Institutional Description. California State University, Fresno is composed of the Schools of Agriculture and Home Economics, Business and Administrative Sciences, Education, Engineering, Division of Health Professions, Humanities, Natural Sciences, Professional Studies, Social Sciences, Social Work, and Graduate Studies. Enrollment: 13,904.

Library Administration. Lillie S. Parker, University Librarian; Ronald J. Mahoney, Head, Department of Special Collections.

Library General Holdings. 750,000 bound books and periodicals; 4,000 periodical subscriptions; 290,000 government documents.

Special Collections

University Archives. All publications by or about the University, its faculty or students; copies of masters theses, school newspapers, minutes of meetings, photographs of the University.

Fine Arts Collection. Publications relating to art and

artists, especially strong in Oriental arts and graphics.

Special Collections. Books, pamphlets, broadsides, and ephemera on all subjects in many languages from 1474 to the present; included are atlases, early imprints (pre-1800), modern poetry, a William Blake collection, rare books, the printing arts, ichthyology, etc.

Enology Collection. Grapes, wines and wine making, raisins; worldwide coverage in all languages.

Saroyan Collection. Material by and about William Saroyan.

Joseph A. Lowande Collection of Worldwide Rationing. Twentieth century ration material from Germany and the United States (uncatalogued).

Mineral King Collection. Material relating to the history and preservation of the Mineral King area of Sequoia National Forest (uncatalogued).

San Joaquin Valley Farm Workers Collection. Mainly Chavez and Mexican-American to 1970 (uncatalogued).

Expositions Collection. International exhibitions and fairs, 1851-1940; material in all languages relating to exhibitions of international scope (uncatalogued).

Alexander Pronin Collection of Russian Postcards. Approximately 1,500 postcards, ca. 1890-1920 (uncatalogued).

Homan Memorial Stamp Collection. United States postage stamps from 1847 to 1956.

Harold G. Schutt Collection of Tulare County History. Basically olives and lumbering.

The Karl Falk Collection of German Inflation Money. Small display collection of approximately 150 items.

The National Land for People Collection. Federal irrigation water use restrictions.

Rare Book Collections

Manuscript collections include: (1) letters, maps, diaries, newspapers, and promotional literature about the Credit Foncier, a utopian colony at Topolobampo, Sinaloa, Mexico; also, other material relating to North American colonization schemes in Mexico, Mexican commercial and agricultural exploitation by North American and Mexican railroads; (2) business records of Hanford Hardware Company and Central Lumber Company of Hanford; (3) Miller-Lux lands—a small collection of correspondence regarding the New Columbia Division, 1909-1915; (4) selected Fresno City and County records, 1856-1966; (5) Chester Harvey Rowell (1867-1948) Collection of correspondence, 1882-1938; Mr. Rowell was editor of the Fresno Republican from 1898 to 1920; (6) Torontoy Estate—an attempt to develop a vast tract of land in Peru which was claimed to have been the source of the Inca wealth, 1881-1884.

104
California State University, Fullerton
University Library
800 North State College Boulevard
Fullerton, California 92634

Telephone. (714) 773-2714

Institutional Description. California State University, Fullerton is a liberal arts institution offering graduate and undergraduate programs. Enrollment: 16,652.

Library Administration. Richard Pollard, University Librarian; Sharon K. Perry, Special Collections Librarian.

Library General Holdings. 650,000 books; 4,000 current periodical subscriptions (including newspapers); 300,000 government documents; 800,000 microforms.

Special Collections

Roy V. Boswell Collection for the History of Cartography (Pre-1901). Includes over 1,500 maps and a related collection of 2,000 books.

Fictions of Popular Culture. Twentieth-century American genre fiction with a strong emphasis in science fiction manuscripts and periodicals.

Kerridge Angling Collection. Consists of over 3,500 books and 3,200 periodical issues with some folders of emphemera and realia.

Twentieth-Century Press and Fine Printing Collection. Strong emphasis on California printing; 3,000 books and 1,052 pamphlets.

Freedom Center of Political and Social Ephemera, Periodicals, and Books. 4,000 catalogued volumes; 4,000 periodical issues; 300 current subscriptions; 2,000 folders of ephemera from grass roots organizations.

University Archives. 756 linear feet of document boxes and other material.

American Trade Bindings. The collection contains over 5,000 books of the late nineteenth century and early twentieth century.

Local History Ephemera. Focuses on California and Orange County consisting of 504 linear feet of document boxes and other materials.

105
California State University, Hayward
University Library
Hayward, California 94542

Telephone. (415) 881-3000

Institutional Description. The publicly supported liberal arts university was established in 1959. Its Moss Landing Marine Lab offers programs in marine sciences. Enrollment: 9,460.

Library Administration. Melissa Rose, Director.

Library General Holdings. 728,485 volumes including bound periodicals; 2,651 current periodical subscriptions; 19 newspaper subscriptions; 515,516 microforms;

16,805 phonorecords; 15,000 maps; 130,000 federal, state, and international documents.

Special Collections

The major special collections include the **Jensen Family Papers,** a collection of Bay Area poetry, and fine press books of the western United States.

106
California State University, Long Beach
University Library and Learning Resources
1250 Bellflower Boulevard
Long Beach, California 90840

Telephone. (213) 498-4047

Institutional Description. California State University, Long Beach is a liberal arts university offering undergraduate and graduate programs. Enrollment: 23,376.

Library Administration. Jordan M. Scepanski, University Librarian; John B. Ahouse, Special Collections Librarian.

Library General Holdings. 681,373 volumes.

Special Collections

Special Collection Library. Contains materials concerned with the Long Beach area and the history of California, rare and first editions, the Abolition Movement, and the archives of the University. Individual collections are devoted to Robinson Jeffers, Mary Austin, Upton Sinclair, Richard Armour, and Charles Bukowski. Also housed are photography (200 items) and art print (400 items) collections, as well as the "Dick" Whittington Collection of Los Angeles Historical Photography. Transcripts and tapes of the Oral History Center are also deposited in the Library.

Pasadena Playhouse Collection. The holdings of this collection document theater in Los Angeles.

Dorothy Ray Healey Collection. Consists of materials relating to radical politics in southern California.

Jan Law and Darrell Neighbors Collections. Covers geological subsidence in Long Beach.

Gerald Locklin Collection. Includes contemporary poetry in Los Angeles.

Rare Book Collections

Manuscript collections include the papers of State Assemblyman Vincent Thomas, Representative Richard Hanna, Representative Mark Hannaford, and the Fred H. Bixby family of Long Beach.

107
California State University, Los Angeles
John F. Kennedy Memorial Library
5151 State University Drive
Los Angeles, California 90032

Telephone. (213) 224-0111

Institutional Description. The publicly supported state university was established in 1947. Enrollment: 13,919.

Library Administration. Morris Polan, University Librarian.

Library General Holdings. 820,000 books and bound periodicals; 4,500 current periodicals, scholarly journals, and newspapers; 115,000 bound backfiles of periodicals.

Special Collections

Among the library's special collections are the **Perry Long Memorial Collection on Printing and Engraving** containing more than 2,000 items; **Public Officials Papers** donated by local and regional public officials; and the **Roy Harris Archives** containing the papers of the twentieth-century American composer.

108
California State University, Northridge
University Libraries
18111 Nordhoff Street
Northridge, California 91330

Telephone. (818) 885-1200

Institutional Description. The publicly supported state university was founded as San Fernando Valley State College. Special services are offered for the deaf. Enrollment: 20,701.

Library Administration. Norman E. Tanis, Director; Joseph A. Gardener, Special Collections and Rare Books Librarian.

Library General Holdings. 900,000 bound volumes.

Special Collections

Among the special collections of the University Library are holdings in local history, California fine printing, and Assyriana.

Instructional Materials Laboratory. Contains K-12 textbooks, curriculum guides, and audiovisual materials supporting various education programs in the University and providing a resource for the surrounding four-county community of public school educators.

National Center on Deafness Library. Contains materials on the history, education, and rehabilitation of the deaf. The collection of books, reports, periodicals, pamphlets, and signed or captioned media serves educators, interpreters, deaf students, the community-at-large, and students from many departments who use the materials for papers and projects relating to deafness.

University Archives. Consists primarily of theses and various materials published by California State University, Northridge.

109
California State University, Sacramento
University Library
2000 Jed Smith Drive
Sacramento, California 95819

Telephone. (916) 278-6466

Institutional Description. California State University, Sacramento is a liberal arts university offering undergraduate and graduate programs. The Library collection is divided into four reference departments: Education and Psychology, Humanities, Science and Technology, and Social Science and Business Administration. Enrollment: 18,161.

Library Administration. Charles Martell, University Librarian; Georgiana White, Archivist.

Library General Holdings. 880,683 volumes; 6,000 magazines, technical and scholarly journals, and newspapers.

Special Collections

Curriculum Collection. 26,000 educational materials related to preschool through grade 12 including textbooks, juvenile literature, and curricular materials.

Slide Collection. 70,000 slides pertaining primarily to the history of art, but including strong collections of American and Canadian history and the history of costume.

U.S.G.S. Geologic Atlas of the United States. Folio edition, numbers 1-227 (1894-1945).

X-Ray Powder Diffraction File. Organic and inorganic.

University Archives. Contains Charles Mathias Goethe (Sacramento philanthropist) personal correspondence diaries, publications; architectural papers of Julia Morgan who designed the Goethe Sacramento residence now owned by the University; Sacramento Peace Center papers, 1962-date; Women's Studies Collection, 1967-date; Oral History Collection (Sacramento); Dissent and Social Change Collection, 1880-date; Port of Sacramento Working Papers donated by the first Port Director, Melvin Shore, ca. 1963-1986; U.S. Congressman John E. Moss' Legislative Collection, ca. 1955-1978; California State Senator Albert Rodda Papers, ca. 1965-1980.

110
California State University, San Bernardino
Pfau Library
5500 State University Parkway
San Bernardino, California 92407

Telephone. (714) 887-7201

Institutional Description. The publicly supported state university was founded in 1965. Enrollment: 4,909.

Library Administration. Arthur Nelson, Director.

Library General Holdings. 430,000 books and bound periodicals; 3,100 periodical and newspaper subscriptions; 191,200 microforms.

Special Collections

The major special collections of the Pfau Library include materials on the Mojave Desert and a collection of items on railroads and trains.

111
California State University, Stanislaus
Library
800 Monte Vista Road
Turlock, California 95380

Telephone. (209) 667-3232

Institutional Description. California State University, Stanislaus is a liberal arts university offering undergraduate and graduate programs. Enrollment: 34,127.

Library Administration. John Amrhein, Library Director.

Library General Holdings. 277,000 volumes; 4,000 periodicals and serial subscriptions; 775,000 microforms.

Special Collections

Syad Collection of Assyriana. Consists of books in the Syriac dialect of modern Assyrians, often called Nestorians, who are natives of northwestern Iran; other books in English relating to the modern Assyrians are also in the collection along with books on Mesopotamian civilizations.

112
California Western School of Law
Library
350 Cedar Street
San Diego, California 92101

Telephone. (619) 239-0391

Institutional Description. California Western School of Law is a private, independent law school. Enrollment: 667.

Library Administration. Chin Kim, Director of the Law Library and Professor of Law.

Library General Holdings. 108,048 volumes; 884 journals; 10 newspapers; 302,823 microfiche units; 1,741 microfilms; 503 audiovisual tapes.

Special Collections

The Law Library supports the curriculum of the school and the research of the faculty, staff, and students.

Particular areas of strength include international and comparative law, space law, and law of the Pacific Rim countries.

113
Chapman College
Thurmond Clarke Memorial Library
333 North Glassell Street
Orange, California 92666

Telephone. (714) 997-6806

Institutional Description. The privately supported liberal arts college was founded by the Christian Church (Disciples of Christ). Enrollment: 4,143.

Library Administration. Mary Sellen, Librarian; Susan Schlager, Director of Technical Services.

Library General Holdings. 147,847 books; 24,734 periodical volumes; 1,000 current periodical subscriptions; 7,103 audiovisual items.

Special Collections

Albert Schweitzer Collection. This collection was presented to the College in 1978 by Mr. and Mrs. Lee Ellerbrock, encouraged by Mrs. John Scudder. It is an extensive collection of letters, books, pamphlets, manuscripts, articles, newspaper clippings, photographs, and African artifacts collected by the Ellerbrocks over some 30 years beginning in 1949.

Disciples Collection. This collection is comprised of materials related to the theology and history of the Disciples of Christ Church.

114
Christ College Irvine
Library
1530 Concordia
Irvine, California 92715

Telephone. (714) 854-8002

Institutional Description. The privately supported liberal arts college grants associate and baccalaureate degrees. It is affiliated with the Lutheran Church-Missouri Synod. Enrollment: 419.

Library Administration. Dale W. Hartmann, Director of Library Service.

Library General Holdings. 61,000 volumes; 420 current periodical subscriptions; 3,400 microforms; 2,400 audiovisual materials.

Special Collections

The library's collection is strong in the area of religion and theology with emphasis in evangelism and missions. There is a special collection of 3,000 books on Lutheran history and theology.

115
Christian Heritage College
Library
2100 Greenfield Drive
El Cajon, California 92021

Telephone. (619) 440-3043

Institutional Description. The privately supported Christian liberal arts college was founded in 1970. It is affiliated with the Scott Memorial Baptist Church, but provides a nondenominational, Christian approach to education. Enrollment: 372.

Library Administration. Margarette C. Hills, Library Director.

Library General Holdings. 65,000 volumes; 900 periodical subscriptions.

Special Collections

The holdings of the library include collections on theology, Biblical studies, psychology, and education. Also maintained is the **Institute for Creation Research Collection.**

116
Citrus College
Hayden Memorial Library
1000 West Foothill Boulevard
Glendora, California 91740

Telephone. (818) 914-8640

Institutional Description. Citrus College is a publicly supported community college. It was the first community college in Los Angeles County and the fifth in California. Enrollment: 8,641.

Library Administration. John R. Thompson, College Librarian.

Library General Holdings. 58,103 books; 510 periodical titles; 350 films; 703 videos; 2,118 audio recordings; 527 other audiovisual materials.

Special Collections

Hayden Collection. Contains materials by and about Floyd S. Hayden, founder and first president of Citrus College, 1915-1946. Primarily consists of material relating to the history of the college including photos and manuscript for a history of the college.

Schlesinger Collection. Includes materials from the personal library of Dr. Frank Schlesinger, early twentieth century astronomer; includes Dr. Schlesinger's personal diaries and photo albums.

Citrus College Archives. Consists of materials relating to the history of both the Citrus Union High School and the College; consists of such materials as minutes from Board meetings, accreditation reports, college catalogs, schedules, and annuals.

117
City College of San Francisco
Alice Statler Library
50 Phelan Avenue
San Francisco, California 94112

Telephone. (415) 239-3308

Institutional Description. The City College of San Francisco was established in 1935 as an integral part of the San Francisco Unified School District. Enrollment: 23,-205.

Library Administration. Annie McMillian Young, Librarian.

Library General Holdings. 6,000 volumes; 80 current periodicals; 7,000 pamphlets; 1,000 bound periodicals.

Special Collections

The library has an extensive collection of menus, newsletters, and other professional materials relating to the hotel and restaurant field.

118
Claremont Colleges
Honnold Library
Claremont, California 91711

Telephone. (714) 621-8000

Institutional Description. The Claremont Colleges constitute a cluster of individual institutions in the city of Claremont. Comprising the cluster are: Claremont Graduate School, Claremont McKenna College, Harvey Mudd College, Pitzer College, Pomona College, and Scripps College. Enrollment: See the individual colleges.

Library Administration. Patrick T. Barkey, Director of Libraries.

Library General Holdings. 1,600,000 volumes; 4,873 periodicals; 2,855 serial titles; 1,050,000 microforms; 615,-000 government documents. In 1952, individual book collections assembled by each of the Claremont Colleges (Claremont Graduate School, Claremont McKenna College, Harvey Mudd College, Pitzer College, Pomona College, Scripps College) were integrated into one large collection housed in Honnold Library. Smaller collections at the individual colleges serve specialized needs.

Special Collections

There are numerous special collections in the libraries. Among them are the **Oxford Collection** which includes books about Oxford University and the city of Oxford and the **Renaissance Collection** which contains volumes on Italian Renaissance focusing on the life and work of Angelo Poliziano. Three collections complement one another in providing important materials on northern Europe and Scandinavia: the **de Hass Collection** on the Netherlands, and the **Westergaard** and **Bjork Collections** emphasizing Scandinavia and the Baltic area.

Western Americana and Californiana are represented in several collections: **William Smith Mason Collection,** the **Wagner Collection of History and Cartography of the North Pacific,** the **William F. McPherson Collection of Western Americana,** and a collection of materials on the water resources of Southern California. The **Robert Burton Collection** includes various editions of his *Anatomy of Melancholy* and most of the sources cited in his work. The **John Dryden Collection** features early editions of Dryden's plays, poetry, criticism, and translations.

The **McCutchan Collection** assembles many rare books on American hymnology. The **Irving Wallace Collection** includes much of the research and manuscript materials for his writings.

119
Claremont Graduate School
Educational Resource and Information Center
150 East Tenth Street
Claremont, California 91711

Telephone. (714) 621-8000

Institutional Description. The privately supported institution offers graduate programs only. Founded in 1925, it is a member of the Claremont Colleges. Enrollment: 749.

Library Administration. Doty Hale, Director.

Library General Holdings. The library resources of the Claremont Graduate School are combined with collections of other Claremont Colleges in the Honnold Library. *See also* **Claremont Colleges.**

Special Collections

The **Educational Resource and Information Center** contains pamphlets, periodicals, courses of study, textbooks, and indexes in the field of education, and the **Marguerite Brydegaard Collection** relating to the development of creativity in children. The **George G. Stone Center for Children's Books** contains about 16,500 children's books and related publications.

120
Claremont McKenna College
500 East 9th Street
Claremont, California 91711

Telephone. (714) 621-8088

Institutional Description. The privately supported liberal arts college was founded in 1946. It offers an emphasis on economics and political science. It is a member of the Claremont Colleges. Enrollment: 827.

Library General Holdings. The library holdings of Claremont McKenna College are combined with those of other Claremont Colleges in the Honnold Library and the Seely Wintersmith Mudd Library. *See also* **Claremont Colleges.**

Special Collections

The focus in Claremont McKenna's curriculum is on economics and political science.

121
Cogswell College
Library
10420 Bubb Road
Cupertino, California 95014

Telephone. (408) 252-5550

Institutional Description. Cogswell College is an independent technical college offering programs leading to the bachelor's degree in engineering technology. Enrollment: 171.

Library Administration. Maria F. Kramer, Librarian.

Library General Holdings. 12,000 volumes; 500 current periodical subscriptions.

Special Collections

The library maintains collections of electronic data manuals and resources in electronics and mechanical engineering.

122
Coleman College
Library
7380 Parkway Drive
La Mesa, California 92041

Telephone. (619) 465-3990

Institutional Description. The privately supported senior college of business grants associate and baccalaureate degrees. Enrollment: 1,512.

Library Administration. Martha McPhail, Librarian.

Special Collections

The book collection is substantial in the humanities and social sciences and contains an extensive data processing collection, including recommended reading for the Certified Data Processor (CDP) examination.

123
College for Developmental Studies
Laura Ellis Memorial Library
563 North Alfred Street
Los Angeles, California 90048

Telephone. (213) 852-1321

Institutional Description. The privately supported, independent college provides programs in early childhood education, educational therapy, psychology, and teacher training. Enrollment: 37.

Library Administration. Janice M. Eastman, Librarian.

Library General Holdings. 9,000 volumes; 120 current periodical subscriptions.

Special Collections

The library maintains a comprehensive collection of books, records, posters, and magazines appropriate for children two to twelve years of age. There also collections on early childhood and special education, child psychology, and developmental psychology.

124
College of Notre Dame
College Library
Belmont, California 94002

Telephone. (415) 593-1601

Institutional Description. The privately supported liberal arts college was founded in 1868. It is affiliated with the Roman Catholic Church. Enrollment: 760.

Library Administration. Sister Catherine Pelletier, Director.

Library General Holdings. 97,000 volumes; 570 current periodical subscriptions.

Special Collections

Archives of Modern Christian Art. The Archives is a special collection of publications and audiovisual materials which document the history of Christian art and architecture in the modern world.

The library also maintains a special collection of books by writers of the period between World War I and World War II.

125
College of Osteopathic Medicine of the Pacific
Medical Library
352 Pomona Mall E.
Pomona, California 91766

Telephone. (714) 623-6116

Institutional Description. The privately supported professional college grants professional degrees in osteopathy. Enrollment: 236.

Library Administration. Ursula H. Stevenson, Director of Medical Libraries.

Library General Holdings. 10,000 volumes; 415 current periodical subscriptions.

Special Collections

The library has special holdings which include medical reference resource materials and a collection of rare and out-of-print osteopathic books and journals.

126
College of San Mateo
College Library
1700 West Hillsdale Boulevard
San Mateo, California 94402

Telephone. (415) 574-6100

Institutional Description. San Mateo Junior College, the predecessor of the College of San Mateo, opened in 1922. The present college, part of a three-college community college district, opened in 1963 at its present site. Enrollment: 13,503.

Library Administration. Gregg T. Atkins, Coordinator.

Library General Holdings. 60,000 books; 300 magazine and newspaper subscriptions.

Special Collections

The College Library has a rare book collection of 300 volumes.

127
College of the Sequoias
COS Library
915 South Mooney Boulevard
Visalia, California 93277

Telephone. (209) 733-2050

Institutional Description. The publicly supported junior college offered the first post-high school instruction to students of this area in 1926. The college moved to its present 55-acre campus in 1940. Enrollment: 7,909.

Library Administration. Margaret Ann Heater, Head Librarian.

Library General Holdings. 76,150 volumes; 400 magazine and scholarly journal subscriptions.

Special Collections

The library has an extensive reference collection of 12,000 volumes, including an outstanding section of legal materials. Another special feature of the reference area is the Library of American Civilization containing microfiche reproductions of several thousand classic volumes on the development of the United States through the end of the nineteenth century.

128
Columbia College
College Library
Sawmill Flat Road
P.O. Box 1849
Columbia, California 95310

Telephone. (209) 533-5100

Institutional Description. The college was founded in 1968 as Columbia Junior College. The present name was adopted in 1978. Enrollment: 2,309.

Library Administration. Raymond L. Steuben, Director of Library Services.

Library General Holdings. 31,989 volumes; 305 periodicals; 6,508 pamphlets; 4,500 recordings.

Special Collections

The library maintains the **History of the Mother Lode Collection.**

129
Columbia College
Library
925 North La Brea Avenue
Hollywood, California 90038

Telephone. (213) 851-0550

Institutional Description. The privately supported technical college offers professional programs in television and motion picture arts and sciences. Enrollment: 425.

Library Administration. David Nowinson, Librarian.

Library General Holdings. 4,100 volumes; 62 current periodical subscriptions.

Special Collections

The library has a special collection of screenplays and teleplays; the **Vandenecker Collection** of costumes through the ages; and a television production collection.

130
Compton Community College
Library
1111 East Artesia Boulevard
Compton, California 90221

Telephone. (213) 637-2660

Institutional Description. Compton Community College is a two-year college founded in 1927. Enrollment: 3,543.

Library Administration. Floyd Smith, College Librarian.

Library General Holdings. 45,000 volumes; 300 periodical and newspaper subscriptions.

Special Collections

The Library maintains a special collection of 3,000 volumes on Black history and the Black experience. A special collection of legal resources is also available.

131
Cosumnes River College
Library
8401 Center Parkway
Sacramento, California 95823

Telephone. (916) 686-7265

Institutional Description. Cosumnes River College is a junior college granting associate degrees and offering certificate programs. Enrollment: 7,867.

Library Administration. Terry Kastanis, College Librarian; Rosalie Amer, Special Collections Librarian.

Library General Holdings. 55,000 volumes; 400 current periodical subscriptions.

Special Collections

American West Collection. Contains 100 volumes treating the American West; 100 volumes (books and folios) of fine western printing were given to the College by the Holmes Book Company during the first year the Cosumnes Library was open, 1970-71.

132
Cuesta College
Library
P.O. Box 8106
San Luis Obispo, California 93403

Telephone. (805) 544-2943

Institutional Description. The college was organized as a public community college within the California system in 1964. Enrollment: 6,635.

Library Administration. Jack N. Kanbara, Librarian.

Library General Holdings. 40,377 books; 302 periodical subscriptions; 1,360 audiovisual materials.

Special Collections

The library has a special collection on nursing.

133
De Anza College
Learning Center
21250 Stevens Creek Boulevard
Cupertino, California 95014

Telephone. (408) 996-4761

Institutional Description. The college is one of two community colleges in the Foothill-De Anza Community College District which was formed in 1957. Enrollment: 26,127.

Library Administration. James M. McCarthy, Director of Library Services.

Library General Holdings. 77,000 volumes; 500 periodical subscriptions.

Special Collections

The library maintains the **Transportation Library** of of 1,000 items. The **California History Center,** located on the campus, provides students with a unique opportunity to "encounter the historic site, document, or experienced individual, and personally interpret and recreate a period in history." Student research papers on almost every aspect of Santa Clara Valley's development are on file, along with a growing collection of taped oral history interviews, photographs, letters, news clippings, and historical pamphlets.

134
Diablo Valley College
College Library
321 Golf Club Road
Pleasant Hill, California 94523

Telephone. (415) 685-1230

Institutional Description. The college was established in 1950 and originally was named East Contra Costa Junior College. The present name was adopted in 1958. Enrollment: 17,147.

Library Administration. Hettie Bortz, Librarian.

Library General Holdings. 80,000 volumes; 450 magazine and newspaper titles.

Special Collections

The library maintains a special collection of Californiana.

135
Dominican College of San Rafael
Archbishop Alemany Library
1520 Grand Avenue
San Rafael, California 94901

Telephone. (415) 457-4440

Institutional Description. The privately supported liberal arts college was founded in 1890. It is affiliated with the Roman Catholic Church. Enrollment: 628.

Library Administration. Sister Margaret Diener, O.P., Library Director.

Library General Holdings. 88,000 volumes; 470 current periodicals.

Special Collections

The library has a special curriculum collection, an art history slide collection, English literature collection, and the extensive resources of the American Music Resource Center.

136
Fashion Institute of Design and Merchandising
Resource and Research Center
818 West Seventh Street
Los Angeles, California 90017

Telephone. (213) 624-1200

Institutional Description. Founded in 1969 to prepare

students for professions in the fashion industry, the Institute has experienced consistent growth in its expansion to 4 campuses. Enrollment: 3,205.

Library Administration. Kaycee Hale, Director.

Library General Holdings. 14,000 volumes; 150 periodicals; 8,000 slides; 300 videotapes.

Special Collections

The library maintains a collection of textile resource materials and a Costume Museum with over 1,500 historical garments.

137
Fresno Pacific College
Hiebert Library
1717 South Chestnut Avenue
Fresno, California 93702

Telephone. (209) 251-7194

Institutional Description. The privately supported liberal arts college is related to the Mennonite Brethren Church. It was founded in 1944 to train workers for the Church. Enrollment: 708.

Library Administration. Steven Brandt, Director.

Library General Holdings. 112,000 volumes; 892 periodical subscriptions; 6,000 non-print items.

Special Collections

Center for Mennonite Brethren Studies. Includes the records of the Mennonite Brethren Church and its history plus materials to support research on the Anabaptist-Mennonite tradition. The collection is the only one of its kind in the western United States; includes 7,500 volumes, 175 periodicals, and archival material. An additional special collection of 1,000 volumes covers the Radical Reformation.

138
Fuller Theological Seminary
McAlister Library
135 North Oakland Avenue
Pasadena, California 91101

Telephone. (818) 449-1745

Institutional Description. The privately supported institution is a multidenominational seminary offering programs at the graduate level. It was founded in 1947. Enrollment: 1,445.

Library Administration. John Dickason, Director.

Library General Holdings. 141,000 volumes; 850 periodical subscriptions; 700 monographic serials.

Special Collections

The McAlister Library contains a collection with emphasis in the fields of religion, theology, philosophy, and missiology. The collection includes the libraries of Professor Everett Harrison, Robert Bower, and George Eldon Ladd, and Dr. Wilbur Smith, which were donated to the Seminary.

Seminary Archives. Recordings of the "Old Fashioned Revival Hour" with Dr. Charles E. Fuller and tapes from the radio broadcast "The Joyful Sound" with Dr. David Alan Hubbard are housed in the archives along with the *Fuller Theological Seminary Bulletin,* catalogs, and memorabilia.

Christian Formation and Discipleship Resource Center. Contains a wide selection of curriculum materials from many denominations and publishing houses as well as other resources for activities and programs.

Rare Book Collections

Rare Book Room. Contains leather-bound books from the sixteenth through the nineteenth centuries.

139
Gavilan College
College Library
5055 Santa Teresa Boulevard
Gilroy, California 95020

Telephone. (408) 848-4812

Institutional Description. Gavilan College is a community college with a varied program of activities serving the citizens of southern Santa Clara and San Benito Counties. Enrollment: 3,058.

Library Administration. Kathryn A. Young, College Librarian.

Library General Holdings. 50,000 volumes; 370 serial subscriptions.

Special Collections

Hispanic Collection. Contains materials on Hispanic culture, language, and literature.

140
Golden Gate Baptist Theological Seminary
Library
Strawberry Point
Mill Valley, California 94941

Telephone. (415) 388-8080

Institutional Description. The privately supported seminary, founded in 1944, is affiliated with the Southern Baptist Convention. It has three divisions: Theology, Religious Education, and Church Music. Enrollment: 464.

Library Administration. William Hair III, Librarian; J. Craig Kubic, Special Collections Librarian; Deborah Peek, Rare Books Librarian.

Library General Holdings. 177,000 books and microforms; 600 journals; 20,000 music scores.

Special Collections

The library has specialized collections on Baptist history and religious publications from the Southern Baptist Convention; religious tracts; archives of the institution and Western resource for the denomination; Baptist material from 1880-present; Western Baptist material from 1940-present.

141
Golden Gate University
General and Law Libraries
536 Mission Street
San Francisco, California 94105

Telephone. (415) 442-7000

Institutional Description. The privately supported university was founded in 1901. It is composed of the College of Business and Public Administration, the Graduate College, and the School of Law. Enrollment: 5,657.

Library Administration. Ann Coder, Director, General Library Services.

Library General Holdings. General Library: 218,564 volumes; 2,500 periodical subscriptions; Law Library: 180,000 volumes; 750 legal periodicals and journals.

Special Collections

The emphasis of the collection of the General Library is in the field of business. The Law Library has major strengths in taxation, labor law, and individual rights.

142
Graduate Theological Union
Flora Lamson Hewlett Library
2400 Ridge Road
Berkeley, California 94709

Telephone. (415) 649-2400

Institutional Description. The Graduate Theological Union is both a graduate school and a consortium of schools. Participating members are: American Baptist Seminary of the West; Church Divinity School of the Pacific; Dominican School of Philosophy and Theology; Franciscan School of Theology; Jesuit School of Theology at Berkeley; Pacific Lutheran Theological Seminary; Pacific School of Religion; San Francisco Theological Seminary; Starr King School for the Ministry. Enrollment: 293.

Library Administration. John Baker-Batsel, Library Director; Diane Choquette, Head of Public Services and Special Collections.

Library General Holdings. 352,154 volumes; 1,800 serial subscriptions; 180,000 microforms; 2,800 audio cassettes; 1,900 phonodiscs.

Special Collections

New Religious Movements Research Collection. Covers non-Judeao-Christian religious groups in the United States that have begun since 1960 or have grown significantly since that time; includes 3,000 books, 830 periodical titles, 500 audio cassettes; files on 830 organizations; 300 papers; types of groups included are Buddhist, Sikh, Sufi, Hindu, Neo-Pagan, New Age, occult, and anticult.

143
Grossmont Community College
Learning Resource Center
8800 Grossmont College Drive
El Cajon, California 92020

Telephone. (714) 465-1700

Institutional Description. The first college classes of Grossmont College convened in 1961 on a high school campus. The present campus was officially dedicated in 1964. Enrollment: 13,472.

Library Administration. Thomas U. Foster, Director.

Library General Holdings. 97,000 books; 597 current periodicals.

Special Collections

Special collections of materials include U.S. and California law, career information pamphlets and books, college catalogs, and a sculpture art print collection.

144
Hartnell College
College Library
156 Homestead Avenue
Salinas, California 93901

Telephone. (408) 758-8211

Institutional Description. Formerly known as Salinas Junior College (founded in 1920), the school was renamed Hartnell College in 1948. It is a publicly supported community college offering university-transfer, vocational, and general education programs. Enrollment: 5,630.

Library Administration. Esta Lee Albright, Librarian.

Library General Holdings. 70,000 volumes; 400 current periodical subscriptions.

Special Collections

The **O.P. Silliman Memorial Library** portion of the college library offers one of the finest collections of books on ornithology and natural history on the Pacific Coast. It includes many rare volumes on birds and early explorations of the Pacific area.

145
Harvey Mudd College
Norman F. Sprague Memorial Library
Claremont, California 91711

Telephone. (714) 621-8000

Institutional Description. The privately supported college of science and engineering was founded in 1955. It is a member of the Claremont Colleges. Enrollment: 564.

Library Administration. Nancy Waldman, Librarian.

Library General Holdings. 100,000 volumes; 2,000 periodical subscriptions. Students also have access to the library resources the other Claremont Colleges which were combined in 1952. *See also* **Claremont Colleges.**

Special Collections

The famous **"De Re Metallica" Library** of President and Mrs. Herbert Hoover is a special collection of the Sprague Library as well as the **Carruthers History of Aviation Library.** The main collection is comprised of reference works in engineering, science, and mathematics.

146
Hebrew Union College - Jewish Institute of Religion
Frances-Henry Library
3077 University Avenue
Los Angeles, California 90007

Telephone. (213) 749-3424

Institutional Description. Hebrew Union College - Jewish Institute of Religion offers upper division and graduate study only. It is a branch campus of Hebrew Union College in Cincinnati, Ohio. An arrangement exists between the College and the University of Southern California whereby students may enroll simultaneously in both institutions. Enrollment: 59.

Library Administration. Harvey P. Horowitz, Librarian.

Library General Holdings. 80,000 bound volumes; 375 periodical and newspaper subscriptions; 5,000 reels of microfilm; 1,000 albums of Jewish musical recordings.

Special Collections

The Frances-Henry Library is a specialized collection of books, pamphlets, periodicals, microfilms, and other materials basic to the fields of Jewish and Hebrew studies. The Library is especially strong in the areas of Bible (Old Testament), Hebrew language and literature, Jewish Communal Studies, and American Jewish history. As the west coast branch of the American Jewish Archives and the American Jewish Periodical Center, it contains a substantial collection on microfilm of early documents and newspapers pertaining to the American Jewish experience. The Library also houses a collection of 1,000 record albums covering every phase of Jewish music, including synagogue melodies, Yiddish folk songs, and modern Israeli pop music.

Rare Book Collections

The Library contains a collection of sixteenth- to eighteenth-century Hebrew imprints from the early centers of Hebrew publishing such as Venice, Mantua, Rivad, Trento, Constantinople, Amsterdam, Cracow, and Berlin.

147
Holy Names College
Paul J. Cushing Library
3500 Mountain Boulevard
Oakland, California 94619

Telephone. (415) 436-0111

Institutional Description. The privately supported Roman Catholic liberal arts college was chartered in 1880; lay students were admitted in 1916. Baccalaureate and master's degrees are granted. Enrollment: 435.

Library Administration. Sister Helen Clare Howatt, Library Director.

Library General Holdings. 105,000 volumes; 620 current periodicals; 34,000 microforms.

Special Collections

The music library contains a folk music collection that represents the major and many minor regions and ethnic groups of the United States. This special collection is uniquely organized according to melodic and rhythmic elements and have proved invaluable to teachers who come to select songs for teaching music skills through singing. The library also maintains the **John of Salisbury Humanities Collection.**

148
Humboldt State University
Library
Arcata, California 95521

Telephone. (707) 826-3011

Institutional Description. The publicly supported state university is composed of 5 colleges and 2 divisions, granting baccalaureate and master degrees. Enrollment: 5,809.

Library Administration. David Oyler, Librarian.

Library General Holdings. 356,218 books; 2,200 current periodical subscriptions; 430,114 microforms.

Special Collections

The collection of the library is strong in the fine arts, humanities, environmental engineering, and the sciences. There are specialized collections in natural resources and Northwest Coast history.

149
John F. Kennedy University
Robert M. Fisher Library
12 Altarinda Road
Orinda, California 94563

Telephone. (415) 254-0200

Institutional Description. The private, independent, nonprofit institution provides upper division, professional, and graduate study only, primarily serving adult students. Enrollment: 1,290.

Library Administration. Ann Patterson, Director.

Library General Holdings. 45,115 volumes; 459 current periodical subscriptions (includes the Walnut Creek Center Library, the Joy Feinberg Library at the Center for Museum Studies in San Francisco, Fiberworks Center Library, and the Western Design Library).

Special Collections

The collection of the Robert M. Fisher Library has strengths in counseling and psychology, management, women's issues, parapsychology, holistic health, career education, and gerontology. The Fisher Library houses a small collection of Bay Area small press publications as well as pamphlets, annual reports, and audio- and videotapes.

Career Resource Library. Primarily a reference collection which provides information about occupations, the labor market, career planning, job placement, and educational opportunities.

Walnut Creek Center Library. Maintains a 17,500-volume core collection of California, federal, and U.S. law materials.

Joy Feinberg Library. 350 volumes on all facets of museum studies.

150
Loma Linda University
Del E. Webb Memorial Library
Loma Linda, California 92350

Telephone. (714) 824-4300

Institutional Description. The privately supported university occupies two campuses; the second is in Riverside, California. The university, founded in 1909, is owned and operated by the Seventh-day Adventist Church. Enrollment: 3,750.

Library Administration. H. Maynard Lowry, Director.

Library General Holdings. 629,747 books, bound periodicals, and audiovisual materials; 4,058 periodical subscriptions. There are two main libraries: the La Sierra Campus Library and the Loma Linda Campus Library.

Special Collections

La Sierra Campus. This campus library is a general liberal arts collection with concentraitons in history, religion, English, and education. A collection of nineteenth-century Seventh-day Adventist books and pamphlets is in the **Heritage Collection.** Here also are the Ellen G. White source materials, the University Archives, and a collection of published and unpublished works pertaining to the early Adventist movement.

Del E. Webb Memorial Library. The acquisitions of this library on the Loma Linda Campus are in medicine, dentistry, allied health professions, and graduate programs. Some rare materials in the history of medicine (nineteenth-century health reform) are included in the holdings.

151
Los Angeles College of Chiropractic
Seabury McCoy Library
920 East Broadway
Glendale, California 91205

Telephone. (213) 240-7686

Institutional Description. The privately supported professional college was founded in 1911. Enrollment: 862

Library Administration. Robin Lober, Director, Library Services.

Library General Holdings. 20,000 volumes; 350 periodical subscriptions.

Special Collections

The library's collection is related to chiropractic health care and serves as the most comprehensive center of chiropractic literature in the western United States. There are special collections on chiropractic history, nutrition, homeopathic medicine, and sports medicine.

152
Los Angeles Mission College
Learning Resources Center/Library
1212 San Fernando Road
San Fernando, California 91340

Telephone. (818) 365-8271

Institutional Description. Los Angeles Mission College provides two-year academic, vocational, and community service programs that respond to the diversity of the population in the north San Fernado Valley of Los Angeles. Enrollment: 8,035.

Library Administration. Rayma Greenberg, Chairperson, Learning Resources.

Library General Holdings. 45,000 volumes; 430 periodical subscriptions.

Special Collections

Special collections include career materials, college catalogs, magazines on microfilm, and children's literature.

153
Los Angeles Southwest College
Learning Resources Center
1600 West Imperial Highway
Los Angeles, California 90047

Telephone. (213) 777-2225

Institutional Description. The college was founded in 1967 and offers both transfer programs and vocational subjects leading to the associate degree. The college emphasizes developmental education in English and mathematics. Enrollment: 2,873.

Library Administration. Minnie L. Shaw, Special Collections.

Library General Holdings. 55,000 volumes; 600 periodical subscriptions.

Special Collections

The library has the **Rare Book Afro-American Collection** (microfiche) and the **Black Man in America Collection.**

154
Los Angeles Valley College
College Library
5800 Fulton Avenue
Van Nuys, California 91401

Telephone. (818) 781-1200

Institutional Description. The publicly supported community college offers associate degree and certificate programs. Enrollment: 17,701.

Library Administration. David May, Chairperson.

Library General Holdings. 115,000 books; 400 magazine and newspaper subscriptions.

Special Collections

The library has an extensive microfilm and microfiche collection. The **Los Angeles Valley College Historical Museum,** located on the campus, contains documents, photographs, and artifacts relating to the San Fernando Valley.

155
Loyola Marymount University
Charles Von der Ahe Library
Loyola Boulevard at West 80th Street
Los Angeles, California 90045

Telephone. (213) 642-2700

Institutional Description. The privately supported university was founded in 1865. A merger in 1973 of Loyola University of Los Angeles and Marymount College created the present institution. The Roman Catholic school offers liberal arts and professional studies. Enrollment: 5,461.

Library Administration. Betty Blackman, University Librarian.

Library General Holdings. 270,000 books and bound periodicals; 2,000 current periodical subscriptions; 35,000 microforms.

Rare Book Collections

Frank Sullivan Rare and Special Books Room. Houses major collections on Thomas More, Oliver Goldsmith, Spanish Culture and Civilization, and German and American Philosophy.

156
Menlo College
Bowman Library
1000 El Camino Real
Atherton, California 94025

Telephone. (415) 323-6141

Institutional Description. The privately supported college features business administration, computer information, and mass communication. Enrollment: 641.

Library Administration. Donald V. Drury, Director of Libraries.

Library General Holdings. 53,000 volumes; 320 current periodicals.

Special Collections

The Bowman Library's special collections include the **Frank H. Tuban Memorial Tax Library;** a **Middle East Collection;** and the **Alva H. Griffin Library of Management Essentials.**

157
Mennonite Brethren Biblical Seminary
Hiebert Library
4824 East Butler at Chestnut
Fresno, California 93727

Telephone. (209) 251-8628

Institutional Description. The privately supported graduate seminary, established by the Mennonite Brethren Church, was founded in 1955. Enrollment: 119.

Library Administration. Steven Brandt, Director.

Library General Holdings. 112,000 volumes; 892 periodical subscriptions; 6,000 non-print items. The Hiebert Library also serves the students of Fresno Pacific College.

Special Collections

Center for Mennonite Brethren Studies. Includes the records of the Mennonite Brethren Church and its history plus materials to support research on the Anabaptist-Mennonite tradition. The collection is the only one of its kind in the western United States; includes 7,500 volumes, 175 periodicals, and archival material. An additional special collection of 1,000 volumes covers the Radical Reformation.

158
Merritt College
Library/Learning Resources Center
12500 Campus Drive
Oakland, California 94619

Telephone. (415) 531-4911

Institutional Description. Merrit College is a public, comprehensive, two-year college maintained by the Peralta Community College District in Alameda Country. The college was established in 1955 and occupied its present campus in 1971. Enrollment: 6,023.

Library Administration. Al Fleischman, Librarian.

Library General Holdings. 57,000 volumes; 937 periodical subscriptions; 4,000 pamphlets.

Special Collections

The library maintains special collections in oral history and Black studies.

159
Mills College
Library
2515 Hillegass Street
Berkeley, California 94704

Telephone. (415) 841-1905

Institutional Description. Mills College is a private, independent, nonprofit college for women. Enrollment: 936.

Library Administration. Steven P. Pandolfo, College Librarian.

Library General Holdings. 195,000 volumes; 553 current periodical subscriptions; 8,085 microforms; 2,549 audiovisual materials.

Special Collections

The library is housed in a building originally designed by California architect Julia Morgan. The collection is general in nature and supports the liberal arts curriculum with areas of emphasis in literature, the social sciences, history, art, and music.

Special collections include the **Jane Bourne Parton Dance Collection** which includes materials on ballet, ballroom, and modern dance from the sixteenth century to the present and the **Darius Milhaud Music Collection** which includes scores and recordings of the music of the twentieth-century French composer.

Rare Book Collections

Albert M. Bender Collection. Consists of 12,000 rare books and 10,000 manuscripts; broadly based in the humanities with major emphases in nineteenth- and twentieth-century British and American literature.

160
Monterey Institute of International Studies
William Tell Coleman Library
425 Van Buren
Monterey, California 93940

Telephone. (408) 649-3113

Institutional Description. The privately supported institution was founded in 1955. It is dedicated to the understanding of other nations, and features intensive foreign language courses. Enrollment: 473.

Library Administration. Keith Brehmer, Director.

Library General Holdings. 50,000 volumes; 375 current periodical subscriptions.

Special Collections

The library has holdings in eight languages, including books, pamphlets, theses, periodicals, and microforms. Resources are in the areas of international policy studies; French, Hispanic, Chinese, German, Russian, and Japanese studies; economics; North American studies; history; political science; American studies; computer languages; and interdisciplinary studies.

161
Mount St. Mary's College
Charles Willard Coe Memorial Library
12001 Chalon Road
Los Angeles, California 90049

Telephone. (213) 476-2237

Institutional Description. Mount St. Mary's College is a privately supported, liberal arts Roman Catholic college for women. Men may participate in undergraduate music, nursing, extended day, and graduate division programs. Enrollment: 1,055.

Library Administration. Mary L. Sedgwick, Acting Library Director.

Library General Holdings. 133,390 volumes; 653 periodicals; 18 index services; 8 newspapers; 272 microform titles (97 books, 175 periodicals); 3,095 media (films, filmstrips, videos, audiotapes).

Special Collections

Cardinal John Henry Newman/Oxford Movement. Includes books, microfilms, facsimiles, and memorabilia.

Mills Music Company Collection. Includes the output of the company including many of its subsidiaries; bound volumes of sheet music issued from the 1890s until the second half of the twentieth century. The Mills Music Company held at one time or another the publication rights for many small companies and includes a great number of the popular songs turned out during a sixty-year period by many of the successful popular song writers, introduced by many of the popular artists performing during those years. It also includes large numbers of songs that were published and were *not* successful.

162
Mt. San Antonio Community College
Learning Resources Center
1100 North Grand Avenue
Walnut, California 91789

Telephone. (714) 594-5611

Institutional Description. The two-year community college was founded in 1945 and offers university-parallel and career-oriented programs. Enrollment: 20,659.

Library Administration. Tula Demas, Librarian.

Library General Holdings. 90,000 volumes; 500 periodical subscriptions; 5,000 microforms; 9,585 sound recordings.

Special Collections

A California history collection is maintained by the library.

163
National University
Library and Learning Resources
4141 Camino del Rio South
San Diego, California 92108

Telephone. (800) NAT-UNIV

Institutional Description. The privately supported university offers intensive work-related courses designed for mid-career executives who wish to upgrade their management positions. Degrees are granted. Enrollment: 8,-536.

Library Administration. Anne-Marie Secord, Director.

Library General Holdings. 31,525 volumes; 394 current periodical subscriptions; 2,125 microforms; 468 audiovisual materials.

Special Collections

The major strengths of Library and Learning Resources are in the fields of business, counseling, law, and psychology.

164
Naval Postgraduate School
Dudley Knox Library
Monterey, California 93943

Telephone. (408) 646-2341

Institutional Description. The Naval Postgraduate School is a publicly supported technological graduate school serving officers of the U.S. Navy, other U.S. Armed Forces, and Allied Armed Forces; and civilian employees of the United States Government who are eligible to attend. Enrollment: 1,754.

Library Administration. Paul Spinks, Director of Libraries; Roger M. Martin, Special Collections Librarian.

Library General Holdings. 260,000 bound volumes; 1,824 periodical and newspaper subscriptions; 511,000 research reports (paper and microfiche); 71,000 microforms (general); 19,000 vertical file items; 225 video recordings.

Special Collections

Buckley Collection. A collection of 8,000 volumes focusing on naval history and the sea.

165
Northrop University
Alumni Library
5800 West Arbor Vitae Street
Los Angeles, California 90045

Telephone. (213) 337-4439

Institutional Description. Northrop University is a privately supported university composed of the College of Engineering, School of Law, and Aviation Technician School. Enrollment: 1,003.

Library Administration. Dr. Jerome Halpin, University Librarian; Bradford Miller, Special Collections Librarian.

Library General Holdings. 40,000 books; 400 periodical subscriptions; 61,000 bound periodical volumes; 125,-000 microfiche.

Special Collections

American Hall of Aviation History. This special collection related to the history of aviation includes 4,000 volumes and 50,000 photographs plus pamphlets, periodicals, and memorabilia.

166
Occidental College
Mary Norton Clapp Library
1600 Campus Road
Los Angeles, California 90041

Telephone. (213) 259-2852

Institutional Description. Occidental College is a privately supported liberal arts college. Enrollment: 1,630.

Library Administration. Jacquelyn M. Morris, College Librarian; Michael C. Sutherland, Special Collections Librarian.

Library General Holdings. 400,000 volumes; 1,800 periodical and newspaper titles; 300,000 government documents from the United States, California, and the United Nations. The main collection interests of the Special Collections Department lie in the areas of fine printing, history, literature, modern fiction, and rare books.

Special Collections

Starred Collection. This is a very large collection of individual gifts and purchases acquired over the years which are shelved together and flagged with an asterisk above their call numbers—thus the name "Starred" Collection. These books represent just about all subject areas and contain all books received by Special Collections which are not part of one or another of the Department's various named collections.

Aviation Collection. A gift to the College by trustee Richard W. Millar in memory of aviation pioneer John K. Northrop, the collection consists of several hundred titles which combine to illustrate the history and development of the aviation industry in Southern California.

Beigelman Collection. Consists of first editions, illustrated books, landmarks in the fields of European, British, and American literature, the classics, and the history of science. It was given to the College by the late M.N. Beigelman, M.D. over a period of years beginning in the late 1950s. Dr. Beigelman's son, Paul M. Beigelman, M.D., is continuing his father's interest in book collecting by adding worthwhile gifts from time to time.

Bryan Collection. Small collection of books by and about former statesman William Jennings Bryan; manuscript letters to and from William Jennings Bryan.

Cleland Collection. Named for former Occidental College professor and historian Robert Glass Cleland; collection is devoted to history of Latin America.

Doheny Collection. Archival record of research and the sponsoring foundation formed by E.L. Doheny which sent a team of experts in several fields to Mexico to search for oil deposits and analyze the economic, political, and social climate of the country; uncatalogued collection of typewritten reports and studies on all aspects of Mexican political, economic, and social life prior to 1917.

Finch Collection. Deposited in the Occidental College Library's Special Collections Departments by Robert Finch, a graduate of Occidental and former Lieutenant Governor of California under Ronald Reagan, and Secretary of Health, Education, and Welfare during the Nixon Administration; contains a record of some of the concerns which faced California government and the Federal government during the 1960s; access restricted and may be achieved only through the written authorization of Mr. Finch, currently a lawyer practicing in Pasadena.

Guymon Mystery and Detective Fiction Collection. A collection of first editions, manuscripts, film scripts, photographs, and other materials which relate to the genre of mystery and detective fiction dating from 1592 through 1975; numbers approximately 18,000 volumes.

Max and Virginia Hayward Californiana Collection. A collection of early narratives and histories which deal with the early settlement of California.

Jeffers Collection. Poet Robinson Jeffers was a graduate of Occidental College in 1905. The Library has concentrated on building a collection of his works which date from before he was a student at the College through the most recent reprintings of his works; the collection also contains many Jeffers manuscripts and other published material related to Jeffers.

John Lloyd-Butler Railroadiana Collection. An extensive collection of works dealing with the development of the American railroads from 1846 on. In addition to nearly 2,000 published books, the collection contains ephemeral material and railroad periodicals.

Occidentalia Collection. This collection represents the Occidental College Archives; contains books published by faculty, alumni, and other persons connected with the college since its founding in 1887; also includes photographs, films, yearbooks, catalogs, and various serial publications issued by the College.

Risdon Collection. Collection of books about Abraham Lincoln and the Civil War; rich in pamphlet material; contains a section of memorabilia with past U.S. presidents and presidential campaigns.

Ritchie Collection. Publications issued by the Ward Ritchie Press and the press of Anderson, Ritchie and Simon. Ward Ritchie, an alumnus of Occidental College (1928), now retired; continues to publish under the imprint Laguna Verde Imprenta.

Sinclair Collection. A collection of works by Upton Sinclair in many different languages; collected and donated to the library by Dr. Elmer Belt.

Weller Collection of Romantic Literature. Centers on the works of John Keats, but includes other poets who were his contemporaries; collected and donated to the library by Earle V. Weller, son of one of the founders of Occidental College.

Western Americana Collection. A collection of personal narratives concerning the settlement of the West.

Bill Henry Room. Collection of Mr. Henry's personal books and papers; the Olympic materials provide a historical record of the Olympic Games from 1932 to the present.

Braun Room. Resembles an English country manor house library; books represent the development of the art of printing and are examples of fine printing; contains miniature books, incunabula, fore-edge paintings, fine editions of works in literature, science, religion, philosophy, and art.

Rounce and Coffin Club Archives. A collection of past Western Books Exhibitions.

167
Ohlone College
Learning Resources Center
43600 Mission Boulevard
Fremont, California 94539

Telephone. (415) 659-6000

Institutional Description. The college is named for the Ohlone Indians of the Costanoan Tribe who once inhabited the area. The college was founded in 1965. Enrollment: 7,805.

Library Administration. Hans L. Larsen, Assistant Dean, Learning Resources Center.

Library General Holdings. 55,000 volumes; 425 periodical titles.

Special Collections

The library's special collections are on the Ohlone Indians, oral history, law, and materials for the hearing-impaired.

168
Orange Coast College
Norman E. Watson Library
2701 Fairview Road
Costa Mesa, California 92626

Telephone. (714) 432-0202

Institutional Description. Founded in 1947, the two-year community college first opened its doors in 1948. The campus was built on the de-activated Santa Ana Army Base. Enrollment: 22,589.

Library Administration. Donald A. Ackley, Director.

Library General Holdings. 100,000 titles, including books, pamphlets, periodicals, and microfilms.

Special Collections

The **Consumer Resource Center** provides consumer information, counseling, and referrals in many consumer areas. The Center's other activities include seminars by experts on consumer issues, opportunities for work-study projects relating to consumer problems, and information displays giving current, useful consumer information.

169
Otis Art Institute of the Parsons School of Design
Library
2401 Wilshire Boulevard
Los Angeles, California 90057

Telephone. (213) 251-0500

Institutional Description. The private school, founded in 1918, offers professional, upper division, and graduate programs only. Enrollment: 686.

Library Administration. Cathe Dart, Director.

Library General Holdings. 35,000 volumes; 250 current periodical subscriptions; 75,000 audiovisual materials.

Special Collections

Special Collection. Includes hundreds of rare books, signed first editions, private press books, facsimiles of manuscripts, and early printed books as well as original woodcuts, lithographs, and etchings by both historical and contemporary artists. Included in this collection is the largest assembly of original artists books in the western United States. The **Artists' Book Archive** includes work by such artists as Gilbert and George, Ed Ruscha, Jim Dine, and David Hockney. The Special Collection also contains turn-of-the-century periodicals such as *Harper's Weekly* and *Century Magazine.* The **Periodical Collection** is international in scope and contains more than 600 titles. In addition, the library houses an extensive collection of exhibition catalogs.

Media Center. Currently holds more than 25,000 slides that cover the history of world art, architecture, and design. The record and tape collection includes twentieth-century music, spoken word recordings, and ethnic music. Film and video holdings feature interviews with artists, performance art, abstract animation, and documentation.

170
Pacific Christian College
Hurst Memorial Library
2500 East Nutwood Avenue
Fullerton, California 92631

Telephone. (714) 879-3901

Institutional Description. The privately supported Christian liberal arts college is affiliated with the Christian Churches and Churches of Christ. Enrollment: 397.

Library Administration. Jeffrey L. Wilson, Director.

Library General Holdings. 45,000 volumes; 258 current periodical subscriptions; 3,180 audiovisual materials.

Special Collections

Bible and Christian Church History. Includes approximately 15,000 books and bound periodicals about the Bible and Christian Church history.

Christian Church Restoration Movement. Consists of 2,000 books and historical materials on the nineteenth-century movement.

171
Pacific Oaks College and Children's School
Andrew Norman Library
5 Westmoreland Place
Pasadena, California 91103

Telephone. (818) 795-9161

Institutional Description. The privately supported professional college was founded by the Quakers in 1945. It features programs in early childhood and parent education, elementary teaching, college teaching and administration, human development, and work in clinical settings. It offers upper-division college and graduate studies only. Enrollment: 355.

Library Administration. Marjorie Shore, Librarian.

Library General Holdings. 17,000 volumes; 110 current periodical subscriptions.

Special Collections

The college library houses an outstanding collection in the field of human development as well as a historical collection. The children's library offers a children's collection and books related to children and child rearing for parents.

172
Pacific School of Religion
Badè Institute of Biblical Archaeology
1798 Scenic Avenue
Berkeley, California 94709

Telephone. (415) 848-0528

Institutional Description. The Pacific School of Religion is an independent, interdenominational seminary affiliated with the Graduate Theological Union, a consortium of ten Protestant, Roman Catholic, and Buddhist seminaries, and the University of California, Berkeley. Enrollment: 169.

Library Administration. Jeffrey Zorn, Coordinator, Special Collections.

Library General Holdings. As a member of the Graduate Theological Union consortium, seminarians of the Pacific School of Religion have access to the resources of the GTU Library.

Special Collections

Badè Institute of Biblical Archaeology. Archaeological materials related to the ancient Near East, mainly on the history and material culture of Israel; 3,000 books; 28 sets of current periodicals; 22 sets of discontinued periodicals; 10,000 slides; coverage of the art and architecture of the Old World; field records of archaeological excavations at Tell en-Nasbeh, Israel.

Howell Bible Collection. Contains about 250 rare Bibles and religious works from the time of the invention of the printing press to the present; focus is on the history of the printed English Bible, and the collection contains many first editions from the sixteenth century, Bibles in other European languages, Bibles in "exotic languages" such as Manx, Choctaw, Bengali, and shorthand; facsimiles of early Biblical codices, such as Sinaiticus and Vaticanus; eight fragmentary papyri from the Roman town of Oxyrhynchus in Egypt.

173
Pacific Union College
Nelson Memorial Library
Angwin, California 94508

Telephone. (707) 965-6241

Institutional Description. Pacific Union College is a liberal arts college supported by the Seventh-day Adventist Church. Enrollment: 1,327.

Library Administration. Taylor D. Ruhl, College Librarian; Gary Shearer, Special Collections Librarian.

Library General Holdings. 115,340 volumes; 896 periodical subscriptions; 51,383 microforms; 36,321 nonprint items.

Special Collections

Ellen G. White/Seventh-day Adventist Heritage Collection. A research center on the Millerite Movement of the 19th century, the history and theological development of the Seventh-day Adventist Church, and Ellen G. White, co-founder of the denomination; collection also houses the archives of Pacific Union College; 4,700 volumes; 5,000 microforms; vertical files, photographs and slides; various artifacts of historical interest; collection of books, pamphlets, and articles regarding the history of Sabbath and Sunday.

Pitcairn Islands Study Center. A collection of materials concerning the Mutiny on the Bounty, Captain William Bligh, and Pitcairn Island; consists of books, periodicals, articles, vertical files, stamp collection, films, slides, obituary file, photographs, Pitcairn artifacts; nearly complete set of the *Pilhi and Pitcairn Miscellany.*

174
Palomar College
Library/Media Center
1140 West Mission Road
San Marcos, California 92069

Telephone. (619) 744-1150

Institutional Description. Palomar College is a public, two-year community college which was established in 1945. Enrollment: 16,827.

Library Administration. Judy J. Cater, Director.

Library General Holdings. 150,000 volumes; 1,175 current periodical subscriptions; 20,000 pamphlets.

Special Collections

The library maintains special collections on California history, early California, the Iowa frontier, Indians of North America, and Iceland. A collection of World War I posters is also available.

175
Pasadena City College
Library
1570 East Colorado Boulevard
Pasadena, California 91106

Telephone. (213) 578-7123

Institutional Description. In 1928, Pasadena High School and Pasadena Junior College merged into a four-year junior college with grades 11 to 14, inclusive. In 1947, the official names of the two schools became Pasadena City College and John Muir College. In 1966, the formation of a greater Pasadena Area Junior College District was approved and the institutions merged into the present community college. The current name was adopted in 1970. Enrollment: 20,164.

Library Administration. Joanne Y. Kim, Director of Library.

Library General Holdings. 115,000 volumes; 434 periodical subscriptions; 3,000 pamphlets.

Special Collections

The library has a special collection of art prints and a **Special Services Collection** for the hearing and visually impaired and the learning disabled.

176
Patten College
Library
2433 Coolidge Avenue
Oakland, California 94601

Telephone. (415) 533-8300

Institutional Description. Patten College, known as Patten Bible College and Theological Seminary until 1980, is a private, independent Bible college affiliated with the Christian Evangelical Church. Enrollment: 163.

Library Administration. Patricia Bauer, Librarian.

Library General Holdings. 20,000 volumes; 195 religious and secular journals; 2 daily newspapers.

Special Collections

The library maintains a collection of 5,000 Biblical studies items and 8,000 religious resource materials.

177
Pepperdine University
Payson Library
24255 Pacific Coast Highway
Malibu, California 90265

Telephone. (213) 456-400

Institutional Description. The privately supported Christian liberal arts and professional university was founded in 1937. It is affiliated with the Church of Christ, and has two campuses: Malibu and Los Angeles. Enrollment: 4,924.

Library Administration. Harold E. Holland, Director.

Library General Holdings. 210,000 volumes; 1,400 periodicals.

Special Collections

Specialized collections include **Nineteenth-Century Restoration Movement in the United States; Nineteenth-Century Children's Literature,** and the **Mynarsky Collection** of nineteenth-century French literature.

178
Pitzer College
1050 North Mills Avenue
Claremont, California 91711

Telephone. (619) 621-8129

Institutional Description. The privately supported liberal arts college is one of the Claremont Colleges. It was founded in 1963 as a women's college, but became coeducational in 1970. Enrollment: 696.

Library General Holdings. The library resources of Pitzer College were combined with those of the other Claremont Colleges in 1952. *See* **Claremont Colleges.** The majority of students at Pitzer College major in psychology, sociology, anthropology, and political studies.

179
Point Loma Nazarene College
Ryan Library
3900 Lomaland Drive
San Diego, California 92106

Telephone. (619) 222-6475

Institutional Description. The privately supported liberal arts college was founded in Los Angeles in 1902, and maintains a branch campus in Pasadena. Affiliated with the Church of the Nazarene, the college prepares students for service and leadership in an environment of Christianity. Enrollment: 1,681.

Library Administration. James Newburg, Director of Learning Services.

Library General Holdings. 168,000 volumes; 655 current periodical subscriptions; 22,500 microforms.

Special Collections

Special collections, housed in the Rohr Building, include seventeenth- and eighteenth-century books by Methodist theologians John Wesley and James Arminius. Also housed are books, periodicals, and pamphlets relating to the holiness movement of the nineteenth and twentieth centuries.

180
Pomona College
Seeley G. Mudd Science Library
Claremont, California 91711

Telephone. (714) 621-8000

Institutional Description. The privately supported liberal arts college is a member of the Claremont Colleges. It was founded in 1887. Enrollment: 1,356.

Library Administration. Brian Ebersole, Librarian.

Library General Holdings. Students also have access to the collections of other Claremont Colleges whose resources were combined in 1952. *See also* **Claremont Colleges.**

Special Collections

The Seeley G. Mudd Science Library houses the book and journal collections in botany, biology, chemistry, geology, mathematics, and physics-astronomy. The Alfred O. Woodford Rare Book Room is also housed here.

181
Porterville College
Library Media Center
900 South Main Street
Porterville, California 93257

Telephone. (209) 781-3130

Institutional Description. Porterville College is a publicly supported community college. Enrollment: 2,498.

Library Administration. Janet Noll Naumer, College Librarian.

Library General Holdings. 23,000 volumes targeted to curricular areas; 350 periodical and newspaper subscriptions; 25 microform titles.

Special Collections

Bancroft Collection. The Library has most of the volumes of Hubert Howe Bancrofts's multivolume history covering the Pacific coast and Rocky Mountain regions, British Columbia, Alaska, Mexico, and Central America.

182
Rancho Santiago College
Nealley Library
17th and Bristol
Santa Ana, California 92706

Telephone. (714) 667-3000

Institutional Description. Formerly named Santa Ana College, the public, two-year community college was opened in 1915. It is the fourth oldest community college in California. Enrollment: 21,694.

Library Administration. Rolland Boepple, Director, Library Services.

Library General Holdings. 80,000 volumes; 700 current periodical titles.

Special Collections

The **Orange County Fire Science Library** is maintained by the library.

183
The RAND Graduate School
RAND Library
1700 Main Street
Santa Monica, California 90406

Telephone. (213) 393-0411

Institutional Description. The privately supported institution offers graduate programs only. It was founded in 1970. Enrollment: 60.

Library Administration. Elizabeth Gill, Director.

Library General Holdings. 64,000 books; 2,000 periodical subscriptions; 20,000 bound periodicals; 250,000 reports.

Special Collections

The RAND Library maintains one of the largest special libraries on the West Coast. Its special collections include the **Statistical Reference Collection** and the **Slavic and Oriental Library** which contains 8,000 monographs and 7,000 volumes of bound periodicals pertaining to all aspects of Slavic and Oriental countries.

184
Rio Hondo College
Library
3600 Workman Mill Road
Whittier, California 90608

Telephone. (213) 692-0921

Institutional Description. Rio Hondo College is a public, two-year community college which was formed in 1963. The present campus was completed in 1966. Enrollment: 10,872.

Library Administration. Jon L. Breen, Librarian.

Library General Holdings. 80,000 books; 500 current magazine and newspaper subscriptions.

Special Collections

Special collections of the library include law, art history, Chicano studies, and photography.

185
Saint John's College and Seminary
Edward Laurence Doheny Memorial Library and the Carrie Estelle Doheny Memorial Library
5118 East Seminary Road
Camarillo, California 93010

Telephone. (805) 482-4697

Institutional Description. The privately supported Roman Catholic institution contains a four-year liberal arts college and a graduate theological seminary. Founded in 1927, it is composed mostly of those studying for the priesthood. Enrollment: College, 108; Seminary, 106.

Library Administration. Sister M. Ruth Kent, I.H.M., Librarian.

Library General Holdings. The combined holdings of the Edward Laurence Doheny Memorial Library (College) and the Carrie Estelle Doheny Memorial Library (Seminary) number 125,000 volumes.

Special Collections

Many items of the rare book collection of over 10,000 volumes, known as the **Doheny Collection,** were recently auctioned by the Archdiocese of Los Angeles to raise needed funds. The volumes included English and American first editions, manuscript books dating from the ninth century, early printed books, Californiana, private press books, children's literature, book illustrators, fine bindings, books with fore-edge paintings, a first volume Gutenberg Bible, other rare Bible editions, and reference books pertaining to all of the fine art in the collections. There were four thousand rare manuscripts and letters of historical and literary figures. The ultimate destination of these important items, whether into private collections or other college/university libraries, is unknown at the present time. The auction at Christie's in New York on October 17 and 18, 1988 yielded over $4,000,000. All 662 lots up for bidding were sold. An example of the prices paid is the $49,500 for the novel *Pride and Prejudice,* printed in London in 1813.

186
St. Joseph's College
College Library
Box 7009
Mountain View, California 94039

Telephone. (415) 694-1440

Institutional Description. The privately supported institution, formerly known as St. Patrick's College, is a Roman Catholic liberal arts college offering education of candidates for the priesthood. Enrollment: 109.

Library Administration. Molly M. Lyons, Director of the Library.

Library General Holdings. 49,000 volumes including bound periodicals; 230 current periodicals.

Special Collections

The St. Joseph's College Library has a collection of material in philosophy and undergraduate theology, spirituality, and the history of the Roman Catholic Church, particularly history of the medieval and early twentieth century periods. It also has a special collection in the classics—Greek and Roman language and literature.

187
St. Mary's College of California
St. Albert Hall Library
P.O. Box N
Moraga, California 94575

Telephone. (415) 376-4411

Institutional Description. St. Mary's College of California is a Roman Catholic liberal arts college comprised of the Colleges of Liberal Arts, Economics and Business Administration, and Science. Enrollment: 2,853.

Library Administration. Stephanie Bangert, College Librarian; Andrew Simon, Special Collections Librarian.

Library General Holdings. 155,696 bound volumes; 825 current periodicals; 15 newspaper subscriptions; 29,012 microforms; 800 music scores; 9,129 other learning materials.

Rare Book Collections

John Henry Newman and His Times. 5,000 volumes, including many first editions, about 1,200 tracts, and over 500 volumes of bound periodicals. Works by and about Cardinal Newman (1801-1890); supported by the related subject fields of: the Catholic Emancipation Act (1829); the Oxford Movement; "No-Popery" literature; ritualism in the Church of England, Vatican Council I (1869-1890); Liberal Catholicism; the Old Catholic Movement; Kulturkampf (1871-1890) which involved the Church-State conflict in Germany, Austria, and Switzerland.

Library for Lasallian Studies. Originated as a collection of works by and about Saint John Baptist de La Salle (1651-1719), founder of the Institute of Brothers of the Christian Schools; added material includes writings on French religious and spiritual thought in the 16th to 18th centuries: highlights of this group of over 650 volumes are original editions printed before 1800 on Jansenism, Gallicanism, Quietism, Port Royal, contemporary biblical studies; representative collections of Bossuet, Fenelon, and Pascal.

188
St. Patrick's Seminary
McKeon Memorial Library
320 Middlefield Road
Menlo Park, California 94025

Telephone. (415) 321-5655

Institutional Description. The privately supported Roman Catholic seminary, founded in 1891, prepares candidates for the priesthood. Enrollment: 82.

Library Administration. Rev. John F. Mattingly, S.S., Seminary Librarian; Pamela Nurse, Librarian.

Library General Holdings. 67,000 bound volumes; 275 current periodical subscriptions; 15 newspaper subscriptions; 2,200 microform units; 950 audiovisual materials; 4,000 other items (mostly pamphlets).

Special Collections

The library maintains a collection of books owned by the first Archbishop of San Francisco—Most Reverend Joseph Sadoc Alemany, O.P. (1853-1884). This large group of books is mainly in the field of theology and dates from the eighteenth and nineteenth centuries.

189
San Diego Miramar College
Learning Resource Center
10440 Black Mountain Road
San Diego, California 92126

Telephone. (619) 230-6500

Institutional Description. San Diego Miramar College is a two-year community college located in the north central part of metropolitan San Diego. Enrollment: 6,462.

Library Administration. Carolyn Norman, Head Librarian.

Library General Holdings. 12,000 volumes; 176 periodical subscriptions.

Special Collections

The library maintains the **Roi B. Woolley Memorial Fire Protection Library.**

190
San Diego State University
Malcolm A. Love Library
5402 College Avenue
San Diego, California 92182

Telephone. (619) 265-5200

Institutional Description. The publicly supported state university grants the baccalaureate and master degrees, and in cooperation with some of the other California state universities, the doctorate. Enrollment: 26,156.

Library Administration. Don L. Bosseau, University Librarian.

Library General Holdings. 862,000 volumes including books and bound periodicals; 9,900 periodical and serial titles; 2,300,000 microfiche and micropaque cards; 52,800 reels of microfilm; 141,000 maps; 5,700 phonograph records; 51,700 curriculum items; 1,500 linear feet of archival papers.

Special Collections

Significant research collections in the social sciences and humanities include Asian studies, business, public administration, American Civil War, California, Latin American and Mexican history, Chicano resource materials, the literatures of the United States, Spanish America, Europe, Asia, and Africa, and music. Special strengths are in the Middle Ages, the nineteenth century, dramatic arts, including classic films, philosophy, especially medieval and American. Research collections held in the sciences include chemistry, biochemistry, ecology, biology, mathematics, physics, astronomy, anthropology, entomology, paleontology, geology, geological history of Pacific Ocean invertebrate fauna, and the geology of San Diego County and Baja Californa.

Rare Book Collections

Special collections, among them many rare editions, include science fiction, H.L. Mencken, orchidology, the history of science with emphasis on astronomy and botany, German culture and civilization.

191
San Francisco Art Institute
Anne Bremer Memorial Library
800 Chestnut Street
San Francisco, California 94133

Telephone. (415) 771-7020

Institutional Description. San Francisco Art Institute is a privately supported art college with a dual goal of exhibition and education. Enrollment: 531.

Library Administration. Jeff Gunderson, Institute Librarian.

Library General Holdings. 25,000 volumes; 200 periodical subscriptions.

Special Collections

San Francisco Art Institute Archives. Consists of manuscripts, account books, minutes, photographs, broadsides, clipping files, and ephemera documenting the history of the San Francisco Art Association, California School of Design, Mark Hopkins Institute of Art, California School of Fine Arts, San Francisco Museum of Art, Palace of Fine Arts, and the San Francisco Art Institute. Collection includes art exhibition catalogs from 1877 to the present documenting California and Northern California art; manuscripts and ephemera pertaining to all aspects of art and artists in California and the San Francisco Bay Area from 1871 to the present; material pertaining to Diego Rivera; manuscript material documenting post-World War II development of abstract expressionism; special collection ("Elvis Wall") of correspondence, broadsides, posters, photographs, original art work, postcards, oral history transcripts, maps, documents, cover art, transparencies, and ephemera documenting the popularity of Elvis Presley (1935-1977).

192
San Francisco Conservatory of Music
Bothin Library
1201 Ortega Street
San Francisco, California 94122

Telephone. (415) 564-8086

Institutional Description. The privately supported music conservatory was founded in 1917 and offers training in all musical instruments and related music subjects. Enrollment: 200.

Library Administration. Lucretia Wolfe, Head Librarian.

Library General Holdings. 30,000 volumes; 50 current periodical subscriptions; 7,000 audiovisual materials.

Special Collections

Specialized collections within the Bothin Library are holdings of holographs of American composers; a collection of ethnomusicology materials; and a collection of guitar music and recordings.

193
San Francisco State University
J. Paul Leonard Library
1630 Holloway Avenue
San Francisco, California 94132

Telephone. (415) 338-1856

Institutional Description. San Francisco State University offers undergraduate and graduate programs. Enrollment: 18,413.

Library Administration. Olive C. R. James, University Librarian; Helene Whitson, Archives/Special Collections Coordinator.

Library General Holdings. 606,669 books; 93,306 bound periodicals; 20,095 juvenile works; 18,860 juvenile textbooks; 407,980 government publications; 62,040 photographs; 11,915 maps; 4,777 videocassettes and films/filmstrips/film loops; 26,233 phonodiscs; 29,340 microfilm reels; 892,109 microforms other than microfilm reels.

Special Collections

Special Collections/Archives. Repository for the San Francisco Bay Area Television News Archives devoted to the identification, acquisition, organization, preservation, and dissemination of film and video tape materials relating to the portrayal of San Francisco Bay Area life, including history, culture, political events, and science; established in 1986 with two core collections from KQED and KPIX. Archives include materials relating to University history, including campus newspapers, bulletins, student handbooks, yearbooks, and a collection of papers and ephemeral material created during the 1968-69 student turmoil. Also included in the Archives is a representative collection of Bay Area poets from the late 1950s and 1960s.

194
San Francisco Theological Seminary
Library
2 Kensington Road
San Anselmo, California 94960

Telephone. (415) 453-2280

Institutional Description. The privately supported graduate seminary is affiliated with the Presbyterian Church, U.S.A. Enrollment: 429.

Library General Holdings. The library on the San Anselmo campus, located in Geneva Hall, is a branch of the Flora Lamson Hewlett Library of the Graduate Theological Union in Berkeley. The primary function of the library is to supply books needed by students taking courses taught on the San Anselmo Campus.

Special Collections

Donald Gordon Steward Curriculum Library. Contains a wide variety of resources for church education; includes Protestant and Roman Catholic curriculum materials for all age groups and for teacher/leader education.

195
San Jose Bible College
Memorial Library
790 South 12th Street
P.O. Box 1090
San Jose, California 95108

Telephone. (408) 293-9058

Institutional Description. The privately supported professional institution was founded in 1939. It is affiliated with the Christian Churches and Churches of Christ. It grants baccalaureate degrees. Enrollment: 180.

Library Administration. Kay Llovio, Librarian.

Library General Holdings. 29,000 volumes.

Special Collections

The San Jose Bible College is a Christian school established for the purpose of providing education to students which will prepare them for Christian ministries. The collections of the library reflect this purpose with resources in Biblical studies and the liberal arts.

196
San Jose State University
Robert D. Clark Library and John T. Wahlquist Library
One Washington Square
San Jose, California 95192

Telephone. (408) 924-2700

Institutional Description. San Jose State University is the oldest of the California State system of colleges. Enrollment: 18,862.

Library Administration. Ruth Hafter, University Librarian; Jack Douglas, Head, Special Collections/Archives.

Library General Holdings. As a former teacher's college, the University has strong holdings in education and curriculum materials, devices, etc. 700,000 volumes in the book collection, including over 100,000 bound periodicals; over 180,000 documents, courses of study, and other unbound materials; over 11,000 periodical titles; more than 5,000 maps; 25,000 sound recordings; and over 650,000 microforms. The Special Collections Department has a collection of first editions and fine press editions of West Coast (California) writers and California fine presses such as Grabhorn, Book Club of California, Arion, and Yolla Bolly. The historical collection includes material published by the University since its beginning in 1857, publications by the faculty, master's theses, photographs, and numerous artifacts; selected City and County archives; local history materials; the Sourisseau Academy for State and Local History is an adjunct to the Library.

Special Collections

Jackson Aeronautical Collection. 2,500 items collected by the late Rodney Jackson.

Berthold Collection of Baltic Studies. Several hundred volumes, primarily in Latvian, covering the political and cultural history of the Baltic States.

Lawrence Clark Powell Collection. Autographed editions and papers by the noted librarian donated by Dr. O.C. Williams.

Shephard Whitman Collection. The working library of Whitman materials amassed by the late Dr. Esther Shephard of the SJSU faculty.

Mishoff Librarianship Collection. Early ephemera relating to the history of library science in the United States.

St. David's World War I Collection. One hundred classic works on World War I, formerly the property of Lord St. David.

Ira F. Brilliant Center for Beethoven Studies. Devoted to the life and works of Ludwig van Beethoven; first editions, manuscript letters, and other materials.

Steinbeck Research Center. More than four thousand items, including books, manuscripts, periodicals, literary criticism, portraits, and memorabilia; book collection includes first editions and signed presentation copies of most of Steinbeck's major works.

Chicano Library Resource Center. Bibliographies, books, dictionaries, encyclopedias, literary guides, periodical indexes related to Chicano studies.

197
Santa Clara University
Michel Orradre Library
Santa Clara, California 95053

Telephone. (408) 554-4764

Institutional Description. The privately supported university was founded less than six months after the signing of the Declaration of Independence. It is a Roman Catholic liberal arts and professional institution. Enrollment: 6,214.

Library Administration. Elizabeth Salzer, University Librarian.

Library General Holdings. 432,870 books and periodicals; 3,350 periodical subscriptions; 370,000 microforms; 240,000 government documents.

Rare Book Collections

The **Levertov Collection** of rare books is maintained and the **California Room** houses a special collection of California fiction.

198
Santa Rosa Junior College
Bernard C. Plover Library
1501 Mendocino Avenue
Santa Rosa, California 95401

Telephone. (707) 527-4011

Institutional Description. Santa Rosa Junior College is a public, two-year junior college offering programs in occupational education, community education, and university-parallel studies. Enrollment: 23,282.

Library Administration. William Anthony Pettas, Director.

Library General Holdings. 90,000 volumes; 621 periodical subscriptions.

Special Collections

The **California Historical Collection** contains many old and rare materials on Sonoma County and the region.

199
School of Theology at Claremont Library
1325 College Avenue
Claremont, California 91711

Telephone. (714) 626-3521

Institutional Description. The privately supported graduate theological seminary was founded in 1885 by the Methodist Church. It now serves the United Methodist, Disciples of Christ, and Episcopal Churches. Enrollment: 177.

Library Administration. Caroline Becker Whipple, Director.

Library General Holdings. 127,000 volumes; 567 periodical subscriptions (French, German, Spanish, Italian, and English). A cordial and convenient inter-library relationship exists with the other colleges in Claremont and with the million-volume Honold Library, also in Claremont.

Special Collections

Southern California Western Theological Library Association. The Union Catalog for the member libraries of this association is housed in the School of Theology Library.

Rare Book Collections

There is a notable collection of rare books housed in a climate-controlled room. Some volumes were printed more than 500 years ago. Of special interest to United Methodists is an excellent group of original Wesley letters and publications.

200
Scripps College
Ella Strong Denison Library
1030 Columbia
Claremont, California 91711

Telephone. (714) 621-8149

Institutional Description. The privately supported liberal arts college for women is one of the Claremont Colleges. Enrollment: 602.

Library Administration. Judy Harvey Sahak, Librarian.

Library General Holdings. 89,000 volumes. Students also have access to the library resources of other Claremont Colleges. These resources were combined in 1952. *See also* **Claremont Colleges.**

Special Collections

The **Macpherson Collection** of more than 2,500 books by and about significant women contains many primary source materials for original research. First editions and manuscripts by Elizabeth Barrett Browning in the **Browning Collection** complement the collection on women.

Rare Book Collections

The Rare Book Room has many treasures, including rare manuscripts, incunabula, and books from fine presses.

201
Simpson College
Start Kilgour Memorial Library
801 Silver Avenue
San Francisco, California 94134

Telephone. (415) 334-7400

Institutional Description. Simpson College is the western regional campus of The Christian and Missionary Alliance. Enrollment: 278.

Library Administration. Miles S. Compton, College Librarian.

Library General Holdings. 52,500 volumes with strong emphasis in the area of religion; 350 periodical subscriptions; 6 newspapers; small collection of scores and other learning materials.

Special Collections

A.B. Simpson Memorial Library. Books and historical material relating to the Christian and Missionary Alliance denomination.

202
Skyline College
College Library
3300 College Drive
San Bruno, California 94066

Telephone. (415) 355-7000

Institutional Description. Skyline College opened in 1969 and is one of three community colleges in the San Mateo Community College District. Enrollment: 7,725.

Library Administration. Stella Chan, Librarian.

Library General Holdings. 50,000 volumes; 300 current periodical and newspaper subscriptions; 4,500 microforms.

Special Collections

A special collection on **Women's Studies** is maintained in the library.

203
Sonoma State University
Ruben Salazar Library
1801 East Cotati Avenue
Rohnert Park, California 94928

Telephone. (707) 664-2156

Institutional Description. The publicly supported state university was established in 1960. Enrollment: 3,953.

Library Administration. Ruth Hafter, Library Director.

Library General Holdings. 365,000 volumes; 3,200 current periodical subscriptions; 573,902 microforms; 56,000 government documents; 1,225 audiovisual materials.

Special Collections

The Salazar Library special collections include the **Women Artists Archives** consisting of more than 5,000 items (including slides of women artists); miniature books; fine printing; the **Wallace Collection** of Sonoma County maps, survey field books, and building plans.

204
Southern California College
O. Cope Budge Library
55 Fair Drive
Costa Mesa, California 92626

Telephone. (714) 556-3610

Institutional Description. The privately supported liberal arts college was founded in 1920 as a school for training ministers. Liberal arts curricula have been offered since 1959. It is affiliated with the Assemblies of God Church. Enrollment: 841.

Library Administration. Kenneth L. Tracy, Librarian.

Library General Holdings. 80,000 volumes; 458 periodical subscriptions.

Special Collections

The curriculum of the liberal arts college is offered in an evangelical Christian environment. The library's resources emphasize Biblical studies and the liberal arts.

205
Southern California College of Optometry
M.B. Ketchum Memorial Library
2575 Yorba Linda Boulevard
Fullerton, California 92631

Telephone. (714) 870-7226

Institutional Description. The privately supported professional college was founded in 1904. It grants associate, baccalaureate, and professional (Doctor of Optometry) degrees. Enrollment: 378.

Library Administration. Pat Carlson, Director.

Library General Holdings. 12,500 volumes; 325 current periodical subscriptions.

Special Collections

The library maintains a collection of materials on visual science that is one of the most complete such collections in the United States.

206
Southwestern University School of Law
Law Library
675 South Westmoreland Avenue
Los Angeles, California 90005

Telephone. (213) 380-4800

Institutional Description. The privately supported law school was founded in 1911. It grants the Juris Doctor (J.D.) degree. Enrollment: 1,311.

Library Administration. Linda A. Whisman, Director.

Library General Holdings. 275,000 volumes; 800 periodical titles.

Special Collections

Special attention has been given to the development of the collection in the areas of tax law, freedom of information, and law of the People's Republic of China. The library also maintains the private papers, books, and memorabilia of Justice McComb.

207
Stanford University
University Libraries
Stanford, California 94305

Telephone. (415) 723-2300

Institutional Description. The privately supported university was founded in 1885. The Stanfords' gift of $20 million was perhaps the largest in American education. Enrollment: 12,131.

Library Administration. David C. Weber, Director.

Library General Holdings. 5,447,869 volumes.

Special Collections

The Collection Development Program of the University Libraries includes Latin American Collections, Germanic Collection, U.S. and British History Collections, English and American Literature Collections, Romance Language and Humanities Collections, Art and Architecture Collections, Special Collections, Chicano Collections, Social Science Collections, and Russian and East European Collections. There are the Map Collection, Archive of Recorded Sound, Physics Collection, and a Theatre Collection.

Hoover Institution on War, Revolution, and Peace. Since its founding by Herbert Hoover in 1919 as a special collection dealing with the causes and consequences of World War I, the Hoover Institution on War, Revolution, and Peace has become an international center for documentation, research, and publication on political, economic, social, and educational change in the twentieth century. The library includes one of the largest private archives in the United States, and has outstanding area collections on Africa, East Asia, Eastern Europe, the Soviet Union, Latin America, the Middle East, North America, and Western Europe. The holdings include government documents, files of newspapers and serials, manuscripts, memoirs, diaries, and personal papers of men and women who have played significant roles in the events of this century, the publications of ephemeral societies and of resistance and underground movements, and the publications and records of national and international bodies, both official and unofficial, as well as books and pamphlets, many of them rare and irreplaceable.

208
Starr King School for the Ministry
Rare Book Collection Library
2441 Le Conte Avenue
Berkeley, California 94709

Telephone. (415)845-6232

Institutional Description. The privately supported graduate school is the Pacific Coast Educational Center for the Unitarian Universalist Church. Enrollment: 52.

Library General Holdings. Except for the Rare Book Collection, the School shares the joint library facilities of the Graduate Theological Union in Berkeley.

Rare Book Collections

The Rare Book Collection of approximately 1,700 volumes dates from 1500 through 1850. The collection is comprised of books on the Radical Reformation and historical roots of Unitarianism in Hungary and Eastern Europe, as well as early nineteenth-century historical volumes.

209
Thomas Aquinas College
Library
10000 North Ojai Road
Santa Paula, California 93060

Telephone. (805) 525-4417

Institutional Description. Thomas Aquinas College is a privately supported college affiliated with the Roman Catholic Church. It offers a four year required program of reading and discussions of Great Books: the greatest writings in mathematics, science, literature, history, theology, and philosophy. Enrollment: 134.

Library Administration. Mrs. V.A. Jatulis, College Librarian.

Library General Holdings. 26,000 bound volumes; 40 periodical subscriptions; 2,400 recordings.

Special Collections

Great Books. This collection is specialized within the Great Books of Western Civilization.

Rare Book Collections

A small collection of sixteenth- and seventeenth-century books includes early editions of Francis Bacon's works and the 48-volume 1852 Leonine edition of St. Thomas Aquinas' *Opera Omnia.*

210
United States International University
Walter Library
10455 Pomerado Road
San Diego, California 92131

Telephone. (619) 271-4300

Institutional Description. The privately supported university was founded in 1952 as California Western University; it adopted its present name in 1966. Its programs begin with the junior year of high school and continue through the doctorate degree. Enrollment: 3,488.

Library Administration. Lawrence R. Greene, Librarian.

Library General Holdings. 427,217 items; 1,206 periodical subscriptions.

Special Collections

The major strengths of the library are in business, education, psychology, sociology, and the visual and performing arts. The library maintains the University's dissertation and thesis collection.

211
University of California, Berkeley
Bancroft Library
Berkeley, California 94720

Telephone. (415) 642-3781

Institutional Description. The University of California, Berkeley is the oldest and largest of the University of California campuses. Enrollment: 28,982.

Library Administration. Joseph A. Rosenthal, University Librarian; James D. Hart, Director, Bancroft Library; Anthony S. Bliss, Rare Book Librarian.

Library General Holdings. 6,845,732 volumes; 80,160 government documents; 3,385,553 microforms; 2,746,480 audiovisual materials, 98,496 periodicals. The Bancroft Library is a major center for research on the Berkeley campus of the University of California, consisting of a non-circulating collection of books, manuscripts, pictures, maps, and other materials.

Special Collections

Bancroft Collection. The Library's largest resource, documents the history of western North America, particularly from the western plains states to the Pacific Coast and from Panama to Alaska, with greatest emphasis on California and Mexico.

Mark Twain Project. Houses the author's notebooks, correspondence, autobiography and other manuscripts, first editions, and further special materials; through the University of California Press the Project is publishing a 70-volume edition of previously unpublished writings and of hiterto printed works.

Regional Oral History Office. Tape-recordings of the recollections of persons who have contributed to the development of California; these memoirs typed and indexed, and their original recordings include series on agriculture, the arts, conservation, fine printing, labor, politics, winemaking, and University of California history.

Social Protest Project. Collects leaflets, broadsides, and other ephemera documenting diverse sociopolitical activities of California in recent years.

University Archives. Documents the history of the statewide University of California, as well as the Berkeley campus. The collection includes administrative records, student publications, faculty writings, publications by and about the University, handbills and ephemera, memorabilia, and photographs.

Pictorial Collections. Paintings, drawings, photographs, and other documentary depictions from the earliest recorded images to the present day complement the Library's printed and manuscript collections on California, the Far Western United States, Mexico, and Central America.

Rare Book Collections

Rare Books Collection. Preserves about four hundred incunabula; rare European, English, U.S., and South American imprints; fine printing of all periods and places, with emphasis on modern English and American typography; collections of certain major English, American, and European authors; modern poetry archives; and the publications of Afro-American authors. The Collection also includes fine bindings, medieval manuscripts and documents, and papyri.

History of Science and Technology Program. Manuscripts and rare books emphasizing twentieth-century American Science and science-based technology and the physical sciences before 1800. It also conducts oral history interviews.

Manuscripts. Over 44,000,000 items ranging from 4,000 year-old papyri to current papers. Centering of diverse aspects of California and Mexico, they also include writings of persons prominent in literature, politics, journalism, law, science, business, and other activities of many regions. Original manuscripts are supplemented by many microfilms.

212
University of California, Davis
Peter J. Shields Library
Davis, California 95616

Telephone. (916) 752-1011

Institutional Description. The publicly supported university was founded in 1909 as the University Farm. It is now a multipurpose institution. Enrollment: 19,055.

Library Administration. Marilyn J. Sharrow, University Librarian.

Library General Holdings. 2,000,000 volumes; 48,000 periodical and journal titles; 2,100,000 microforms; 150,-000 maps; 567,000 pamphlets, 13,000 sound recordings.

Special Collections

The Department of Special Collections houses rare books, manuscripts, photographs, and pamphlets that support research in the arts and humanities. Special subject strengths include nineteenth-century British literature, American avant-garde poetry, the performing arts, and the history of agriculture, technology, and rural life. The University Archives includes the UC Davis theses and dissertations, and the **Michael and Margaret B. Harrison Western Research Center,** a 15,000-volume collection that documents the history and development of the trans-Mississippi West from the mid-nineteenth century to the present, with particular emphasis on the American Indian.

213
University of California, Hastings College of Law
Law Library
200 McAllister Street
San Francisco, California 94102

Telephone. (415) 565-4600

Institutional Description. The publicly supported law school is a component of the University of California System. Its first class was held in 1878. It grants the Juris Doctor degree. Enrollment: 1,519.

Library Administration. Dan F. Henke, Director.

Library General Holdings. 305,000 volumes; 125,000 volume-equivalents on microfilm.

Special Collections

The library collection includes virtually all Anglo-American case reports, in addition to a large collection of statutes, treatises, and periodicals. There is a special criminal justice collection and a collection of congressional documents. Special holdings also include the **Roger J. Traynor Memorial Collection.**

214
University of California, Irvine
Main Library
Irvine, California 92717

Telephone. (714) 856-5011

Institutional Description. The publicly supported university is one of the youngest in the University of California System. It was founded in 1965. Enrollment: 12,108.

Library Administration. Calvin J. Boyer, University Librarian.

Library General Holdings. 1,200,000 volumes, including 17,000 current serials subscriptions; 400,000 government documents.

Special Collections

Department of Special Collections. Contains noncirculating holdings of rare books and early printed works, noteworthy or finely printed editions, exceptionally costly or fragile items, and manuscripts. Special subject collections include French literature of the seventeenth and eighteenth centuries, the René Wellek Collection of the history of criticism, California history and literature, British naval history, contemporary poetry, dance, historical costume, political pamphlet literature, and the Emma D. Menninger Collection in horticulture.

University Archives. The official repository for records having permanent value in documenting the history of the UCI campus. Includes publications, manuscripts, photographs, and other records of administrative and academic units, student organizations, and campus support groups.

215
University of California, Los Angeles
University Research Library
Department of Special Collections
405 Hilgard Avenue
Los Angeles, California 90024

Telephone. (213) 825-1201

Institutional Description. The publicly supported branch of the University of California is academically one of the leading universities in the United States. Founded as a state normal school in 1881, UCLA now offers a wide variety of programs, granting baccalaureate, professional, master's, and doctorate degrees. Enrollment: 31,051.

Library Administration. Dr. Russell Shank, University Librarian.

Library General Holdings. 5,486,955 volumes; 88,548 periodicals; 3,835,492 microforms; 65,378 sound recordings. The University Library on the UCLA campus is one of the country's largest and most renowned academic libraries. The 19-branch system consists of the University Research Library, the College Library, the Clark Library, and 16 specialized libraries.

Special Collections

Department of Special Collections. Located in the University Research Library, the Department contains rare books and pamphlets, the University Archives, early maps, and files of early California newspapers. Manuscript collections include the literary papers of Henry Miller and Anais Nin, as well as the private papers of Jack Benny, Charles Laughton, Carey McWilliams, King Vidor, and Nobel Peace Prize winner Dr. Ralph J. Bunche, a UCLA alumnus.

Other significant holdings include the **Michael Sadleir Collection** of nineteenth-century fiction, generally regarded as the finest of its kind, and the **Ahmanson-Murphy Collection of Early Italian Printing** (1471-1550) with a concentration on Aldine imprints. The Department also houses UCLA's **Oral History Program,** a national leader in the field, containing over 400 interviews with prominent individuals since the program was founded in 1959.

Architecture and Urban Planning Library. This library includes materials treating architecture, building technology, city and regional planning, and selected environmental topics.

Art Library. The library supports the department's art design and art history programs. The **Elmer Belt Library of Vinciana** is one of the greatest research centers in the world for the study of Leonardo da Vinci and the Italian Renaissance.

Biomedical Library. Located in the Center for the Health Sciences, the library contains over 440,000 volumes and 7,000 serial subscriptions. It serves all the UCLA health and life science schools and the UCLA Medical Center.

Chemistry Library. The library includes material on chemistry, biochemistry, and molecular biology.

Education and Psychology Library. This library includes material on education, psychology, teaching English as a second language, and kinesiology.

Engineering and Mathematical Sciences Library. Materials for engineering, astronomy, computer science, meteorology, and mathematics are housed here.

Geology-Geophysics Library. The collection includes geoscience, invertebrate paleontology, planetary and space science, and hydrology.

UCLA Law Library. The library has a collection of over 300,000 volumes selected to further the course of instruction in the School of Law and the legal research needs of the UCLA community.

Management Library. This library serves the Graduate School of Management and the various subjects related to business and management.

Map Library. Maps, city plans, nautical charts, technical books, and serials on all aspects of cartography are housed here. The collection is one of the largest of its kind in the western United States.

Music Library. The library houses historical musicology and ethnomusicology materials, musical scores, recordings, and the personal collections of such composers as Henry Mancini, Alex North, and Ernest Toch.

Oriental Library. Materials in Chinese, Japanese, and Korean are housed in this library.

Physics Library. The collection covers all aspects of physics, including acoustics and spectroscopy.

Public Affairs Services. The collections include official publications of the United States government, the State of California, California counties and cities, selected United States state and local governments, foreign nations and selected foreign states and provinces, plus those of the United Nations and some of its specialized agencies. Also housed are current English-language, nongovernmental pamphlets on public affairs, representing a wide spectrum of political and social opinion, with strong emphasis on social welfare, economic, social, and political conditions, and industrial relations.

Theater Arts Library. The library houses many prestigious collections which have been donated to UCLA, such as those of Charlton Heston, Rosalind Russell, director William Wyler, and animator Walter Lantz. The collections include original scripts, contracts, correspondence, and shooting diaries.

University Elementary School Library. The collection contains contemporary materials for children from kindergarten through junior high school age.

William Andrews Clark Memorial Library. This collection includes over 80,000 volumes and 15,000 manuscripts related to English culture of the seventeenth and eighteenth centuries. The **John Dryden Collection** is among the most complete in the world.

Other special collections include:

Grunwald Center for the Graphic Arts. The center houses a collection of over 30,000 prints, drawings, and photographs. The collection includes significant examples from the fifteenth century to the present and is particularly noted for its collection of German impressionist prints formed by Fred Grunwald and comprehensive holdings of Matisse, Picasso, and Goya.

Film Archives. This collection is the largest film center west of the Library of Congress. Among its outstanding collections are 27 million feet of Hearst Metrotone News Film dating back to 1919. Other noteworthy holdings include the nitrate print collection of Twentieth Century Fox, the pre-1948 studio print holdings of Paramount Pictures, more than 600 Warner Brothers prints, and selected nitrate prints from the Columbia Studios collection. The Film Archives is world-renowned for its restoration activities. The restoration of the original full-length "A Star is Born" starring Judy Garland and James Mason was accomplished here.

Radio Archives. These collections contain more than 40,000 broadcasts from the early 1930s to the present. Significant collections include 700 Hallmark Company broadcasts and personal collections featuring Jack Benny, Bing Crosby, and Dick Powell. The **Clete Roberts Collection** and the **Edward R. Murrow Collection** highlight a range of news and documentary material.

Television Archives. Under joint auspices of the Academy of Television Arts and Sciences and UCLA, this assemblage of material constitutes the nation's largest university collection of its kind. It consists of over 25,000 titles, including kinescopes, telefilms, and videotapes spanning television history, with particular emphasis on drama and comedy from 1947 to the present. A special **Collection of Television Technology and Design** includes over 300 historical television cameras and receivers dating from the 1930s. The Television Archives was responsible for the restoration of three long-thought-lost or decayed television shows of Fred Astaire. The first of the specials, "An Evening with Fred Astaire" (originally broadcast in 1958) and the subsequent two specials starring Mr. Astaire, were the subject of the first television restoration project. The restored programs were re-broadcast over the Disney Channel in December 1988 and January 1989.

216
University of California, Riverside
The University Library
P.O. Box 5900
Riverside, California 92517

Telephone. (714) 787-3221

Institutional Description. The publicly supported institution has grown since its founding in 1907 as a state agricultural experimental station. Enrollment: 5,257.

Library Administration. James C. Thompson, Librarian; Clifford R. Wurfel, Special Collections Librarian.

Library General Holdings. 1,329,783 volumes; 13,000 current serial subscriptions; 1,177,325 microforms; 25,239 music scores; 72,284 maps; 20,929 pamphlets; 387,781 government documents.

Special Collections

The University of California, Riverside, Library Special Collections contains materials related to California, especially the Mojave and Colorado desert areas; rare editions, pamphlets, maps, manuscripts; the **Archives of the University;** the **Riverside City Archives;** citri-culture, date culture; and the **Tomas Rivera Archives.**

Among the authors respresented are Ezra Pound, Robert Lowell, Thomas Hardy, Sadakichi Hartmann, Heinrich Schenker, William Blake, Joseph Conrad, Eden Phillpotts, Christopher Morley, B. Traven, Niels Gade, Arnold Bennett, H.G. Wells, John Galsworthy, and Charles Dickens.

The **Eaton Collection of Science Fiction and Fantasy** is also maintained as well as the papers of Gregory Benford, David Brin, and Robert L. Forward.

The library also contains the **Rupert Costo Library of the American Indian,** curriculum materials, and material on subtropical agriculture and trickle irrigation (Bio-Agricultural Library). The library has collected extensive materials on Paraguay (history, literature, geography, and natural history).

217
University of California, San Diego
University Libraries
La Jolla, California 92093

Telephone. (619) 452-2230

Institutional Description. The publicly supported university began as Scripps Institution of Oceanography in the late 1800s. It became part of the University of California in 1912. Enrollment: 14,851.

Library Administration. Dorothy Gregor, University Librarian.

Library General Holdings. 1,760,614 volumes; 32,691 current periodical subscriptions; 1,303,332 microforms; 228,788 audiovisual materials; 346,691 government documents.

Special Collections

Mandeville Department of Special Collections. Encompasses materials in four categories: by area (e.g., Baja California), by authors (e.g., D.H. Lawrence, William Butler Yeats), by subject (e.g., Pacific Voyages, Spanish Civil War), and by form (e.g., Archive for New Poetry). Important holdings include the Kenneth Hill Collection on Pacific Voyages. The Slide Collection includes 135,491 slides covering all periods of art history in architecture, sculpture, painting, and the minor arts.

Biomedical Library. Contains collections in biology and medicine which are especially rich in the journal literature of the basic sciences and clinical medicine, with emphasis on cellular and molecular biology, neurosciences, genetics, and neoplasia.

Science and Engineering Library. Of particular importance are the research materials in aeronautics, astrophysics, atomic energy, chemistry, computer science, electronics, engineering, instrumentation, mathematics, missiles research, physics, space sciences, and nuclear energy.

Scripps Institution of Oceanography Library. Considered to be one of the two great oceanographic libraries in the world.

218
University of California, San Francisco
University Library
520 Parnassus
San Francisco, California 94143

Telephone. (415) 476-8112

Institutional Description. The University of California, San Francisco is a health sciences campus offering programs at the upper division and graduate level only. Enrollment: 3,612.

Library Administration. David Bishop, University Librarian; Whitten Zinn, Head, Special Collections.

Library General Holdings. The Library supports the teaching, research, and patient care activities of the Schools of Medicine, Dentistry, Pharmacy, and Nursing plus graduate students in allied health sciences. 641,780 bound volumes; 4,059 current periodicals.

Special Collections

The general focus of Special Collections is on materials in the history of health sciences, in all formats (books, journals, audio and video tapes, manuscripts and archives, artifacts and illustration, photographs, slides). Some of the special collection intensities include anatomy and physiology (pre-twentieth century), forensic medicine, obstetrics and gynecology, infectious diseases, medical education, Spanish colonial medicine, herbals and pharmacopoeias, dentistry, nursing, and pharmacy.

219
University of California, Santa Barbara
University Library
Santa Barbara, California 93106

Telephone. (805) 961-2311

Institutional Description. The publicly supported university was founded in 1943. Enrollment: 17,415.

Library Administration. Joseph A. Boisse, University Librarian.

Library General Holdings. 1,745,000 books and bound journals; 21,200 current periodical subscriptions; 27,340 audiovisual materials; 2,000,000 microforms; 558,000 government documents.

Special Collections

The UCSB library collection is housed in two buildings, the Main Library and the Arts Library. The main building houses the general collection as well as several specialized units and services. Examples include the Science and Engineering Library, the Government Publications Department, the Map and Imagery Laboratory which maintains the **Land SAT Satellite Imagery Collection,** the Curriculum Laboratory, the Black Studies Unit, and the Colleccion Tloque Nahuaque (Chicano Studies Unit). Also located in the Main Library is the Department of Special Collections which houses rare books and manuscripts as well as several distinguished collections, including the **Wyles Collection on the American West and the Civil War,** the **Skofield Printers' Collection,** and other in-depth research collections.

The Arts Library supports academic programs in art and music. In addition to the book and journal collections, special materials include more than 25,000 phonograph records and a collection of music scores.

Rare Book Collections

Andre L. Simon-Eleanor Lowenstein Collection of Gastronomic Literature. Although currently housed at

UCSB in a vault, this collection has yet to find a permanent home. The collection of French, British, and early American works is among the most important of its kind. The collection is owned by the American Institute of Wine and Food. The original intent was to form a national center of scholarship on cuisine and its history at UCSB. However, faculty resistance and other internal University problems prevented this from happening. The collection of 858 cookbooks and manuscripts from the sixteenth to nineteenth centuries is awaiting a new home. Possible sites include Stanford University, UC Davis, UC San Diego, and Harvard University's Radcliffe College.

220
University of California, Santa Cruz
McHenry Library
Santa Cruz, California 95064

Telephone. (408) 429-0111

Institutional Description. The publicly supported branch of the University of California System was founded in 1965. It is composed of eight small, residential colleges of liberal arts and sciences. Enrollment: 7,616.

Library Administration. Allan J. Dyson, University Librarian.

Library General Holdings. 812,000 volumes; 11,500 periodical titles; 280,000 microforms.

Special Collections

The special collections housed in McHenry Library include the **Norman and Charlotte Strouse Collection** of nineteenth-century English essayist and historian Thomas Carlyle; the **Gregory Bateson Archive;** the **Kenneth Patchen Archive;** the **University Archives,** and a collection of imprints of Trianon Press. Other important collections are the **Regional History Project** which includes documentation of central California history; the **Mary Lea Shane Archives** of the Lick Observatory, a national resource for the history of astronomy; and the **Slide Collection** which emphasizes art history but also includes science and history as well as views of campus sites and wildflowers.

221
University of Judaism
Ostrow Library
15600 Mulholland Drive
Los Angeles, California 90077

Telephone. (213) 476-9777

Institutional Description. The privately supported university specializes in Jewish studies and liberal arts. It attempts to meet the professional needs of Jewish life in America. Enrollment: 113.

Library Administration. Lois Shub, Director.

Library General Holdings. 170,000 volumes; 500 current periodical subscriptions.

Special Collections

The Ostrow Library contains materials on the history of the Jewish people; a collection of rare Bibles; and a documentation center with over 600,000 clippings, brochures, and other sources of information covering aspects of contemporary Jewish life throughout the world.

222
University of La Verne
Elvin and Betty Wilson Library
1950 Third Street
La Verne, California 91750

Telephone. (714) 593-3511

Institutional Description. The privately supported liberal arts and professional university was founded by the Church of the Brethren in 1891. It emphasizes service to humanity through Christian witness. Enrollment: 3,983.

Library Administration. Martin Heckman, Librarian.

Library General Holdings. 135,000 volumes; 650 current journal subscriptions.

Special Collections

The library houses special collections on the history of the University of La Verne, the city of La Verne, and the Church of the Brethren.

223
University of Redlands
Armacost Library
1200 East Colton Avenue
Redlands, California 92373

Telephone. (714) 793-2121

Institutional Description. The privately supported university was founded in 1909 by the American Baptists. It consists of three colleges, one of which experiments with nontraditional learning processes. Enrollment: 2,565.

Library Administration. Fred E. Hearth, Director.

Library General Holdings. 280,055 volumes; 1,025 current periodical subscriptions; 84,170 microforms; 6,900 audiovisual materials; 195,000 government documents.

Special Collections

The library's special collections include the **Vernon and Helen Farquhar Collection of Californiana and the Great Southwest,** the **Florence Ayscough and Harley Farnsworth MacNair Collection on the Far East,** the **Ann Peppers Art Section,** and the **Irvine Map Library.**

224
University of San Diego
Helen K. and James S. Copley Library
Alcala Park
San Diego, California 92110

Telephone. (619) 291-6840

Institutional Description. The privately supported Roman Catholic university was founded in 1949. It is a liberal arts and professional institution. Enrollment: 4,461.

Library Administration. Marian P. Holleman, University Librarian.

Library General Holdings. 465,000 volumes; 1,000 current periodical subscriptions; 76,000 microforms.

Special Collections

Special Collections. Includes a rare and valuable sampling of the world's cultural treasures in the medium of the printed page. Examples range from the medieval period (illuminated manuscripts and incunabula) through the centuries to contemporary fine printing and binding. There is also a collection of liturgical music.

225
University of San Francisco
Gleeson Library
Golden Gate and Parker
Ignatian Heights
San Francisco, California 94117

Telephone. (415) 666-6136

Institutional Description. The privately supported university is administered by the Jesuit Fathers of the Roman Catholic Church, who founded it in 1855. Enrollment: 6,210.

Library Administration. Paul E. Birkel, Dean, Gleeson Library.

Library General Holdings. 482,000 volumes; 2,300 current periodical titles; 75,000 bound periodical volumes; 415,200 microforms.

Rare Book Collections

Donohue Rare Book Room. Includes the St. Thomas More Collection and a valuable related collection on recusant literature. The Albert Sperisen Collection of Eric Gill and the Robert Graves Colleciton are among the best in the United States. In additions, there are growing collections of Richard Le Callienne, A.E. and Laurence Housman, and Robinson Jeffers. The Library collects the literary period of the 1890s, including the works of Oscar Wilde and Max Beerbohm. The Tyrell-Modernist Collection covers this Catholic controversy. The history of the book is also collected. Among the fine presses represented are the Theodore M. Lilienthal Collection of San Francisco's Grabhorn Press and the Norman and Charlotte Strouse Collections of the Book Club of California, the Allen Press, Victor Hammer, and John Henry Nash.

226
University of Southern California
Edward L. Doheny Memorial Library
University Park
Los Angeles, California 90007

Telephone. (213) 743-2311

Institutional Description. The privately supported university contains numerous schools and colleges and provides extensive programs overseas. Enrollment: 23,691.

Library Administration. Charles R. Ritcheson, University Librarian.

Library General Holdings. The university libraries include the general library and 14 departmental libraries housing 2,300,000 bound volumes, 33,000 periodicals, 1,-500,000 microforms.

Special Collections

Outstanding special collections include world affairs, American literature, marine science, philosophy, Latin American affairs, and the Lion Feuchtwanger collection of émigré literature. Other important holdings include the manuscripts of Hamlin Garland; papers of California ex-governor Jerry Brown; and cinema archives consisting of 180 individual collections (including the major studios of Warner Brothers, Universal, Twentieth-Century Fox, and Metro-Goldwyn-Mayer.

227
University of the Pacific
William Knox Holt Memorial Library
3601 Pacific Avenue
Stockton, California 95211

Telephone. (209) 946-2011

Institutional Description. The privately supported university is one of the oldest chartered institutions of higher learning in California. Enrollment: 5,323.

Library Administration. Thomas W. Leonhardt, Dean.

Library General Holdings. 370,000 volumes; 3,000 periodical subscriptions; 277,000 microforms.

Special Collections

Holt-Atherton Center for Western Studies. The primary research facility of the Center is the 45,000-volume Stuart Library of Western Americana which houses the John Muir Papers among other notable collections of books, maps, manuscripts, and photographs.

The J.A.B. Fry Research Collections and Methodist Archives are also maintained by the library.

228
University of West Los Angeles Library
12201 Washington Place
Los Angeles, California 90066

Telephone. (213) 313-1011

Institutional Description. The privately supported institution offers paralegal and law programs. It was founded in 1966. Enrollment: 440.

Library Administration. Dinah Granafel, Librarian.

Library General Holdings. 25,000 volumes.

Special Collections

The specialized law collection of the library consists of California, federal, and Supreme Court reference works, reports, statutes, and digests, as well as a growing collection of leading law reviews and treatises.

229
West Coast Christian College
McBrayer Library
6901 North Maple Avenue
Fresno, California 93710

Telephone. (209) 299-7201

Institutional Description. The privately supported Christian college operates under the auspices of the Church of God, Cleveland, Tennessee. It grants associate and baccalaureate degrees. A main purpose is education for Christian service. Enrollment: 257.

Library Administration. Ed Call, Librarian.

Library General Holdings. 29,000 volumes; 372 current periodicals.

Special Collections

The special collections include a Spanish library containing 2,000 volumes and the **J.H. Hughes Ministerial and Pentecostal Research Library.**

230
West Coast University
WCU Libraries
440 South Shatto Place
Los Angeles, California 90020

Telephone. (213) 487-4433

Institutional Description. The privately supported university features programs in science, engineering, and management. It is an evening school only. There are branches in Orange, San Diego, and Santa Barbara Counties. Enrollment: 1,264.

Library Administration. Nancy Dennis, Director; Emma Gibson, Librarian, Orange County Center.

Library General Holdings. 6,500 volumes; 40 current periodicals.

Special Collections

The collections of the libraries are clustered in the University's major curriculum areas of engineering, computer science, and business.

231
Western State University College of Law (Orange County)
Reis Law Library
1111 North State College Boulevard
Fullerton, California 92631

Telephone. (714) 738-1000

Institutional Description. Western State University College of Law is a privately supported law college offering both full- and part-time study programs. Enrollment: 1,125.

Library Administration. Steven C. Perkins, Librarian.

Library General Holdings. 54,000 bound volumes; 40,000 microform-equivalent volumes; 450 periodical and 24 newspaper subscriptions.

Special Collections

The Law Library has collections of legal materials in all areas of California law since statehood as well as English legal history, principally before 1700.

232
Westmont College
Santa Barbara, California 93108

Telephone. (805) 969-5051

Institutional Description. The privately supported liberal arts college was founded in 1940. It is an independent, evangelical Christian institution. Enrollment: 1,169.

Library Administration. John D. Murray, Director of Learning Resources.

Library General Holdings. 137,000 volumes; 700 current periodical subscriptions; 16,500 microforms.

The special collections include 2,500 volumes of children's and young adult literature; the **Christ and Culture Collection** of over 1,000 books relating to Christian values and cultural concerns; and books, pamphlets, and tapes produced since 1976 by the American Enterprise Institute.

233
Whittier College
Wardman Library
7031 Founders Hills Road
Whittier, California 90608

Telephone. (213) 693-0771

Institutional Description. Whittier College is a privately supported liberal arts college controlled by an independent and self-perpetuating board of trustees, one-third of whom are members of the Society of Friends. Enrollment: 1,493.

Library Administration. Philip O'Brien, College Librarian; Joseph Dmohowski, Special Collections Librarian.

Library General Holdings. 161,819 volumes; 780 periodical subscriptions; 32,000 microforms.

Special Collections

Quaker Library. A collection of historical and current material.

John Greenleaf Whittier Collection. Includes books and ephemera.

Richard Nixon Collection. Consists of published works about Nixon; gifts donated by the former president; memorabilia.

W. Somerset Maugham. Includes Maaugham's first editions.

Jessamyn West. A complete book and manuscript collection of the Quaker author.

Jan de Hartog. A complete book and manuscript collection of the Quaker author.

234
Woodbury University Library
7500 Glenoaks Boulevard
Burbank, California 91510

Telephone. (818) 767-0888

Institutional Description. Woodbury University is an independent, nonsectarian institution. Enrollment: 787.

Library Administration. William T. Stanley, University Librarian.

Library General Holdings. 54,000 books; 500 periodical titles; 43,700 microfiche; 4,200 microfilm reels; 157 audio cassettes, 180 recordings; 2,500 slides; 70 film strips; 8 video tapes.

Special Collections

John C. Hogan Collection. 300 volumes comprised of both business and law as well as Dr. Hogan's own writings; donated by Dr. John C. Hogan, a former Woodbury professor of business.

Alexander Stewart Collection. Contains sheet music, records, and books on music.

Colorado

235
Adams State College
Library
Alamosa, Colorado 81102

Telephone. (303) 589-7341

Institutional Description. The publicly supported state college was founded in 1921 as a teachers college and has added through the years liberal arts, preprofessional, and vocational programs. Enrollment: 1,998.

Library Administration. James B. Hemesath, Director.

Library General Holdings. 191,976 volumes; 53,149 bound periodicals; 8,006 bound documents; 453,013 microforms; 293,293 government documents.

Special Collections

Colorado Room. Contains material on the history of Colorado, the San Luis Valley, and the College.

236
Colorado College
Charles Leaming Tutt Library
1021 North Cascade Avenue
Colorado Springs, Colorado 80903

Telephone. (719) 473-2233

Institutional Description. Colorado College is a private institution offering a distinctive Block Plan, a curricular format which divides the academic year into nine three and one-half week segments, or "blocks," and permits a student to concentrate on one course at a time. Enrollment: 1,965.

Library Administration. John Sheridan, Head Librarian; Barbara L. Neilon, Special Collections Librarian.

Library General Holdings. 350,000 volumes; 1,050 periodical subscriptions; 180,000 government documents.

Special Collections

Special collections include the following: Colorado College Collection (archival material); Colorado Collection (16,000 volumes); Justice Chess Collection (300 volumes); Alice Bemis Taylor collection of historical manuscripts (300 items); Archer Butler Hulter Papers; Charles C. Mierow Papers; Helen Hunt Jackson Papers; William S. Jackson Papers; Donald Jackson Collection of Fine Printing (60 items); Spencer Penrose Papers; Theodore Roosevelt Letters (57 items); Edward Royal Warren Papers; Philip Washburn Papers; Charles Collins Collection of Historical Manuscripts (57 items); Oral History (55 items); Robert W. and Elinor L. Hendee Abraham Lincoln Collection (2,500 volumes); Colorado history (20,000 photographs, 70 feet of ephemera); 1,305 rare books; 3,362 special editions.

237
Colorado School of Mines
Arthur Lakes Library
Golden, Colorado 80401

Telephone. (303) 273-3697

Institutional Description. Colorado School of Mines is a state supported engineering institution. Enrollment: 2,-489.

Library Administration. John Golden, Acting Library Director; Mary L. Larsgaard, Assistant Director for Special Collections; Hartley K. Phinney, Jr., Rare Books Librarian.

Library General Holdings. 307,246 volumes (includes monographs, serials, audiovisuals, microforms); 49,675 periodical volumes (2,000 titles); 200,000 microfiche; 150,-000 maps; 65,000 U.S. government documents.

Special Collections

The Library's special collections are mainly mine reports, archival materials concerning mines (e.g., annual reports, correspondence, etc.), and archives of the Colorado School of Mines; the Map Room specializes in geologic and mining maps, primarily of Colorado and the southwestern United States.

Rare Book Collections

History of Science. Pre-1900 publications illustrating the history of science, especially geology and engineering.

238
Colorado State University
Morgan Library
Fort Collins, Colorado 80523

Telephone. (303) 491-1844

Institutional Description. The publicly supported state university consists of three campuses all located in or near the city of Fort Collins. Enrollment: 18,381.

Library Administration. Joan Chambers, University Librarian; John J. Newman, Special Collections and Rare Books Librarian.

Library General Holdings. 1,119,634 volumes; 18,122 periodical subscriptions; 1,346,139 microforms; 8,238 cassettes, discs, tapes; 438,873 government documents.

Special Collections

Germans from Russia. The collection includes general histories detailing the migration of Germans to Russia's open lands of the lower Volga River beginning in the 1760s, as well as sources covering their Russian sojourn and subsequent move to the United States over one hundred years later. Specialized information on local settlements in the United States and specific works on the Germans from Russian in Colorado make this resource unique. The collection details the early German settlements in Colorado, describes historic Colorado in terms of this ethnic group, and relates the role of Germans from Russia in the early growth of the sugar beet industry.

Imaginary Wars. This collection focuses on novels about imaginary future wars. To be included in the collection, books must deal with future wars, fictional wars in the past, or societies or people who survive such wars. The war must occur among known societies on Earth and must be central to the book. Within these definitions, over 1,000 novels have been found.

Vietnam War Literature. Begun in 1975, this collection contains fictional accounts of Americans fighting in Vietnam. It also includes plays, poetry, sketches, cartoons, and miscellaneous works of the imagination. Excluded are historical, political, and autobiographical reports of the war as well as protest literature set outside Vietnam. The collection now numbers over 1,200 items.

Western American Literature. This collection of Western novels was begun in 1966. An original goal of the collection was for this university library to preserve the literature of the region it serves. Selection for the collection is based on the works of thirty major western writers, including John Steinbeck, Willa Cather, Frank Waters, Owen Wister, Mari Sandoz, and Edward Abbey. In addition to the works of major writers, there is a continuing attempt to acquire works of fiction set in Colorado and nearby in the Rocky Mountain West. Included with Western materials is the Charles F. Lummis Manuscript Collection.

Rare Book Collections

Rare Book Collection. A major addition to rare book holdings was made in 1965 when the Libraries acquired the private library of the Trianon Palace in Colorado Springs. Major strengths among these 10,000 volumes include first and other fine editions of English, French, and American authors; incunabula; bibliography; and accounts of travel throughout the world. In 1974, a systematic program was begun to acquire pieces that represent major periods, media, processes, places, and individuals in the history of the written and printed word. This has led to a collection with an historical range that begins with two cuneiform items over four thousand years old and ends with modern first editions. Among significant holdings are papyrii, medieval manuscripts on parchment and vellum, incunabula (including a leaf from Gutenberg's *Mainz Catholicon,* fine printing and binding from the sixteenth through the twentieth centuries, and fore-edge paintings.

239
Colorado Technical College
Resource Center
4435 North Chestnut Street
Colorado Springs, Colorado 80907

Telephone. (719) 598-0200

Institutional Description. Colorado Technical College is a private, four-year college offering programs in Solar Engineering Technology, Computer Science Biomedical Engineering Technology, and Electronic Engineering Technology. Enrollment: 461.

Library Administration. Susan Doughty Raschke, Librarian.

Library General Holdings. 6,500 volumes; 120 current periodicals.

Special Collections

The Resource Center's collection is specialized and covers the subject areas of electrical and electronic engineering, computer science, and biomedical engineering technology.

240
Community College of Denver
Auraria Library
1111 West Colfax Avenue
Denver, Colorado 80204

Telephone. (303) 556-2411

Institutional Description. The publicly supported community college (also known as Denver Auraria Community College) was founded in 1970 and offers associate degrees. Enrollment: 1,258.

Library Administration. The Community College of

Denver shares library facilities with The University of Colorado at Denver (which administers the library) and Metropolitan State College. *See* **University of Colorado at Denver.**

241
Denver Conservative Baptist Seminary
Carey S. Thomas Library
Box 10,000
Denver, Colorado 80210

Telephone. (303) 761-2482

Institutional Description. The privately supported seminary was established in 1950 by a group of Conservative Baptist leaders. Enrollment: 304.

Library Administration. Sarah Lyons, Librarian.

Library General Holdings. 96,000 volumes; 526 journal subscriptions; 2,325 microforms.

Special Collections

The library has a collection of ancient Middle Eastern history and archaeology.

242
Fort Lewis College
College Library
College Heights
Durango, Colorado 81301

Telephone. (303) 247-7661

Institutional Description. The publicly (state) supported liberal arts college grants associate and baccalaureate degrees. Enrollment: 3,466.

Library Administration. Daniel W. Lester, Director.

Library General Holdings. 155,000 volumes; 1,000 journal subscriptions; 30,000 volumes of microfiche; 8,600 microfilm reels; 4,500 recordings.

Special Collections

Center of Southwest Studies. The holdings of the Center include books, magazines, newspapers, separates, photographs, and records of all kinds. The materials on the American Indians are among the largest in the entire western portion of the United States. Other important collections include mining, railroads, and military records.

243
Iliff School of Theology
Ira J. Taylor Library
2201 South University Boulevard
Denver, Colorado 80210

Telephone. (303) 744-1287

Institutional Description. The privately supported graduate theological school is affiliated with The United Methodist Church. Enrollment: 182.

Library Administration. Sara J. Myers, Library Director.

Library General Holdings. 149,000 volumes; 800 current periodical subscriptions; 27,000 microforms.

Special Collections

The Ira J. Taylor Library is the primary resource of theological materials for the nine-state Rocky Mountain region. It houses the Archives of the Rocky Mountain Conference of the United Methodist Church; Archives of the American Academy of Religion, and the Archives of the Society of Biblical Literature. There are also collections of hymnals (approximately 750 donated by John R. Van Pelt) and church histories of the Rocky Mountain region.

244
Loretto Heights College
May Bonfils Library/Resource Center
3001 South Federal Boulevard
Denver, Colorado 80236

Telephone. (303) 936-8441

Institutional Description. The privately supported liberal arts college instituted one of the first University Without Walls programs and also features selected off-campus programs for students. Enrollment: 507.

Library Administration. Barbara Doyle, Director.

Library General Holdings. 109,000 volumes; 650 current periodicals.

Special Collections

Research Center on Women. The Center houses more than 1,500 books, plus collections of articles, news clippings, government documents, and audiovisual materials on the subjects of women and sex roles. The Center provides information about past and current socially-defined sex roles and examines new attitudes, roles, behavior patterns, and options for women and men.

245
Mesa College
Lowell Helny Library
P.O. Box 2647
Grand Junction, Colorado 81502

Telephone. (303) 248-9376

Institutional Description. The publicly supported state college was founded in 1925 as a junior college and became a four-year institution in 1974. Enrollment: 1,551.

Library Administration. Charles R. Hendrickson, Director.

Library General Holdings. 140,000 volumes; 1,100

periodicals.

Special Collections

Specialized collections include the libraries of UMETCO, DOE/Bendix, AIME, and PARAHO plus other private geology and natural resource-related collections.

246
Metropolitan State College
Auraria Library
1006 11th Street
Denver, Colorado 80204

Telephone. (303) 556-3058

Institutional Description. The publicly supported state liberal arts college was founded in 1963 to provide a multi-purpose urban-type college of quality education. Enrollment: 10,104.

Library Administration. Metropolitan State College shares library facilities with The University of Colorado at Denver (which administers the library) and the Community College of Denver. *See* **University of Colorado at Denver.**

247
The Naropa Institute
Library
2130 Arapahoe
Boulder, Colorado 80302

Telephone. (303) 444-0202

Institutional Description. The Naropa Institute, founded in 1974, has developed an approach to education that joins intellect and intuition. Training is contemplative and meditative disciplines are available to interested students. Enrollment: 289.

Library Administration. Stephanie Clement, Librarian.

Library General Holdings. 20,000 bound volumes; 100 periodical subscriptions.

Special Collections

The library's collection is specialized and material is selected to support the educational programs of the school. Strengths of the collection include holdings in psychology, Buddhist studies, Tibetan and Sanskrit texts, contemporary American poetry. The library houses an audiotape collection of classes and other events held at the Institute, particularly in the area of poetics. The library also owns an 8,000-slide collection, begun by a gift from Jose Arguelles, and organized according to his own geographical "pulse" theory.

248
Nazarene Bible College
Trimble Library
1111 Chapman Drive
Colorado Springs, Colorado 80916

Telephone. (719) 596-5110

Institutional Description. The privately supported two-year Bible college was founded in 1967. It is affiliated with the Church of the Nazarene. Enrollment: 436.

Library Administration. Roger M. Williams, Library Administrator.

Library General Holdings. 42,000 volumes; 230 current periodical and newspaper subscriptions; 2,000 microform titles; extensive cassette library of sermons.

Special Collections

The library contains a large collection of missionary books, theological books, and Christian education books dealing chiefly with the Church of the Nazarene.

Rare Book Collections

Wesley Room. The library has an extensive collection of rare first edition monographs and memorabilia of John and Charles Wesley, the founders of Methodism. Also included are the works by and about Francis Asbury and other early fathers of Methodism (bound periodicals and pamphlets). There is also a collection of rare and first edition books of American Methodist and early Church of the Nazarene authors.

249
Northeastern Junior College
Learning Resource Center
100 College Drive
Sterling, Colorado 80751

Telephone. (303) 522-6600

Institutional Description. The two-year college was founded in 1944 as Sterling Junior College. The present name was adopted in 1950. Enrollment: 1,644.

Library Administration. Carole Salsman, Director.

Library General Holdings. 41,000 volumes.

Special Collections

The library maintains a special collection on Colorado.

250
Regis College
Dayton Memorial Library
3539 West 50th Parkway
Denver, Colorado 80221

Telephone. (303) 458-4100

Institutional Description. The privately supported liberal arts college was founded in the New Mexico Territory in 1877 by the Jesuits of the Roman Catholic Church, who still operate it. Enrollment: 2,898.

Library Administration. Sharon Iowa Goad, Associate Professor, Librarian.

Library General Holdings. 130,000 volumes; 650 periodicals in paper format, 600 periodicals in microfilm cassettes.

Special Collections

The library provides the Regis community with a significant collection of resources for research in all areas of the liberal arts and various career programs. Regis is a depository for government documents and also offers a growing collection of audiovisual materials.

251
United States Air Force Academy
Academy Library
Colorado Springs, Colorado 80840

Telephone. (303) 472-4674

Institutional Description. The federally supported academy has the mission of producing Air Force career officers. Enrollment: 4,532.

Library Administration. Lt. Col. Reiner H. Schaeffer, USAF, Librarian; Duane J. Reed, Archivist and Chief, Special Collections; Donald J. Barrett, Rare Books Librarian.

Library General Holdings. 320,000 books; 3,600 periodical subscriptions; 90 newspaper subscriptions; 98,000 bound periodical volumes; 160,000 U.S. government and United Nations documents; 4,500 recordings; 15,000 microfilm rolls; non-shelf listed items include 475,000 report literature titles.

Special Collections

The Special Collections Branch of the Academy Library serves as the USAF Academy archives for significant historical documentation. Documents preserved within the Branch reflect the origin, establishment, construction, growth, and operation of the Academy.

The Manuscript Section of the Branch contains a significant body of personal papers proffered to the Academy by general officers and civilians who were instrumental in the development and implementation of air power. Certain correspondence, reports, diaries, photographs, printed matter, and personal papers provide graphic historical insights into man's early attempts to master flight as well as the evolution of contemporary American air power and doctrine. The Branch also serves as the repository for the Academy Oral History Collection which is generated by the USAFA Department of History and the Office of Air Force History. The majority of the interviews have been conducted with individuals prominent in the development of air power and relate to the origin and development of civil and military aeronautics in the United States.

Rare Book Collections

Falconry Collection. Publications are designated to be housed within the collection by nature of edition, unique binding, autograph, or relationship to falconry. With holdings dating from the seventeenth century, the falconry collection is considered to be one of the most extensive in the nation.

Colonel Richard Gimbel Aeronautical History Collection. This collection came to the Academy in 1971 from the estate of Colonel Gimbel. The collection's primary emphasis is aeronautics history to the beginning of powered flight. There are approximately 20,000 items in the collection, with over 7,500 books, 5,000 prints, and other materials in every medium except motion picture film. The oldest materials are seals which date to about 2700 B.C. The earliest book in the collection was published in 1489. Non-book items include medallions, china, glassware, ceramics, dime novels, newspapers back to 1783, toys, balloon monte, letters from aviation figures, philatelic items, and sheet music. Subjects covered include man's dreams of flight, early experiments with wings, kites, balloon flights, pyrotechnics, first parachute experiments, concepts of lunar flight, and the development of heavier-than-air flying machines.

252
University of Colorado at Boulder
Libraries
Campus Box 184
Boulder, Colorado 80309

Telephone. (303) 492-7511

Institutional Description. The University of Colorado at Boulder is a state institution. Enrollment: 20,220.

Library Administration. James Williams, University Librarian; Nora Quinlan, Head of Special Collections; Jack Brennan, Western History/Archives Librarian.

Library General Holdings. 4 million books, periodicals, microforms, and related materials.

Special Collections

Department of Special Collections. 35,000 volumes and several hundred feet of manuscript material; English and American literature from the eighteenth century to the present; other areas include illustrated books, natural history, and the arts; mountaineering; Epsteen Collection of children's literature; original photographs and literature by Colorado writers; books by the mystery writer John D. MacDonald; collection on the history of metallurgy; fine press books; material illustrating the history of the book and the book arts.

Western Historical Collections/University Archives. Repository for original historical materials pertaining to Colorado, the West, and the University of Colorado; manuscript collections and rare pamphlets, maps, early Colorado newspapers, and photographic prints and negatives.

Archives of the Western Federation of Miners and International Union of Mine, Mill and Smelter Workers. Official archives of the union comprising 500 boxes of correspondence, records, files, and publications as well as an extensive labor library.

Musicology Collection. Comprehensive holdings of complete editions and historical anthologies including copies of Renaissance manuscripts from England and Italy.

Ben Gray Lumpkin Colorado Folklore Collection. Western and Colorado folksong.

Popular Sheet Music Collection. This collection has been recently organized.

253
University of Colorado at Denver Auraria Library Lawrence at 11th Street Denver, Colorado 80204

Telephone. (303) 556-2805

Institutional Description. The publicly supported university is a campus of the University of Colorado System. It was founded in 1912 as an extension division and became a separate campus of the System in 1972. Enrollment: 2,812.

Library Administration. The Auraria Library is administered by the University of Colorado at Denver and also serves Metropolitan State College and the Community College of Denver. Patricia Senn Breivik, University Librarian; Rutherford Witthus, Head of Archives and Special Collections.

Library General Holdings. 473,139 monographs; 36,-473 bound periodicals; 1,855 current periodical titles; 124 current newspaper titles; 75,781 microforms; 4,780 music scores; 36,979 audiovisual materials.

Special Collections

The library maintains **InfoColorado,** a collection of monographic materials covering business and economic development for the State of Colorado and its municipalities.

Rare Book Collections

Archives and Special Collections Department. Contains the Murray Seasongood Library (formerly part of the National Civic League), including materials on state and local government, municipal charters, state constitutional convention studies, and reapportionment studies; the Lester Thonssen Rhetoric Collection (eighteenth- and nineteenth-century works); the National State Policy Repository of state and local policy studies; and biographies and institutional histories relating to the Denver Metropolitan area. The archives of the University of Colorado at Denver, Metropolitan State College, and the Community College of Denver provide primary source materials for the study of a multi-institutional campus.

Among the manuscript collections are the papers of Donald Sutherland, noted literary critic, librettist, translator, and Gertrude Stein scholar; Minoru Yasui, Japanese-American lawyer and activist; Edgar Wahlberg, minister and social activist; and Colorado Senator John A. Carroll's public papers. Included in the collections are materials on the Amache Relocation Camp for Japanese-Americans and alternative newspapers from the 1960s and 1970s.

254
University of Colorado Health Sciences Center Denison Memorial Library 4200 East Ninth Avenue Denver, Colorado 80262

Telephone. (303) 492-7682

Institutional Description. The publicly supported state university consists of the Schools of Medicine, Dentistry, and Nursing. Enrollment: 1,454.

Library Administration. Charles Bandy, Director.

Library General Holdings. 143,000 bound volumes; 2,000 current subscriptions.

Special Collections

The library supports the specialized curricula of the health sciences (medicine, dentistry, and nursing). The library maintains a special collection of 6,000 volumes on the history of medicine.

255
University of Denver Penrose Library 2350 East Evans Avenue Denver, Colorado 80208

Telephone. (303) 871-2007

Institutional Description. The University of Denver is a private university affiliated with the United Methodist Church. Enrollment: 5,222.

Library Administration. Morris Schertz, Director; Steven Fisher, Curator of Archives/Special Collections.

Library General Holdings. 1,097,205 volumes; 9,669 periodical titles; 895,411 microforms; 525,960 government documents.

Special Collections

Margaret Husted Culinary Collection. 7,000 volumes on cookery, gastronomy; spans 1600s to the present.

Miller Civil War Collection. 1,000 volumes; strong in regimental histories.

Judaic Collection. 1,000 volumes; strong in items from 1500 to 1800s.

Mormon Collection. 500 volumes.

History of the Book and Printing. 1,000 volumes.

Western Americana and Colorado Collection. 1,000 volumes.

William Barrett Collections. manuscripts, papers, and all published works of the author of *Lillies of the Field, Left Hand of God,* etc.

Colorado Political Papers. Includes papers of Wayne Aspinwall, John Love, Peter Dominick, Byron Rogers, Michael McKevitt.

256
University of Northern Colorado
James A. Michener Library
Greeley, Colorado 80639

Telephone. (303) 351-2121

Institutional Description. The publicly supported university was founded in 1890, offering a two-year course; in 1911, it expanded to a four-year curriculum as a state teachers college. It is now a full university, offering degrees through the doctorate. Enrollment: 8,312.

Library Administration. Claude J. Johns, Jr., Dean, Library Services.

Library General Holdings. 1,200,000 units of hardbound volumes, periodicals, monographs, government documents, filmstrips, slides, maps, phonograph records, and tapes.

Special Collections

Laboratory School Library. Provides approximately 24,000 volumes plus additional learning media focused on literature for children and young adults.

Music Library. Contains comprehensive holdings including scores and recordings.

257
University of Southern Colorado
Library
2200 Bonforte Boulevard
Pueblo, Colorado 81001

Telephone. (719) 549-2361

Institutional Description. The publicly supported university was founded in 1933. Enrollment: 3,415.

Library Administration. Beverly A. Moore, Librarian; Daniel Sullivan, Acquisitions Librarian.

Library General Holdings. 22,441 volumes; 1,312 current periodical subscriptions; 2,521 periodical titles held; 6,341 microforms; 240,707 government documents.

Special Collections

The library has two strong separately classified areas within the general collection: a 3,475-volume children's literature area and approximately 1,725 music scores with performance parts.

Rare Book Collections

Rare Book Room. This room contains a small selection of eighteenth- and nineteenth-century print materials in English and Spanish. The bulk of the 1,150-volume collection is devoted to Colorado and the Rocky Mountain West. There are a small number of primary source documents given by local families.

Gornick Slavic Heritage Collection. Comprises approximately 800 catalogued items and some local and regional source documents. The collection's focus is Yugoslavia and particularly the history and experience of Yugoslav immigrants to the United States.

258
Western State College
Lesli J. Savage Library
Gunnison, Colorado 81230

Telephone. (303) 943-2053

Institutional Description. The publicly supported state college, established in 1901, is the state's oldest institution of higher learning west of the Continental Divide. Enrollment: 1,982.

Library Administration. Margaret Landrum, Librarian; Ethel Rice, Technical Services/Special Collections Librarian.

Library General Holdings. 100,000 volumes; 800 periodical and newspaper subscriptions.

Special Collections

Helen A. Jensen Western Colorado Room. The room houses materials dealing with Colorado in general but with an emphasis on the western slope of Colorado.

College Archives. Materials pertaining to all aspects of the College since it was founded; includes both written and photographic materials.

Rare Book Collections

Rare books and manuscripts housed in the library pertain to Colorado history.

Connecticut

259
Albertus Magnus College
College Library
700 Prospect Street
New Haven, Connecticut 06511

Telephone. (203) 773-8850

Institutional Description. The privately supported Roman Catholic liberal arts college was founded in 1925 by the Dominican Sisters of Saint Mary of the Springs. It grants associate and baccalaureate degrees. Enrollment: 440.

Library Administration. Sister Wilma Lynch, O.P., Head Librarian.

Library General Holdings. 93,665 volumes; 293 current periodical subscriptions.

Special Collections

The library's special collections include the archival materials of the late Samuel F. Bemis. a noted American historian, and strong holdings of materials on Connecticut.

260
Central Connecticut State University
Elihu Burritt Library
1615 Stanley Street
New Britain, Connecticut 06050

Telephone. (203) 827-7524

Institutional Description. Central Connecticut State University is a state supported institution, founded in 1849 as New Britain Normal School. It is the oldest of Connecticut's publicly supported institutions of higher learning, and in 1947 became the first teachers college in New England to be accredited by the New England Association of Schools and Colleges. Enrollment: 13,510.

Library Administration. William Aguilar, Library Director; Francis J. Gagliardi, Associate Library Director.

Library General Holdings. 328,091 volumes; 70,408 bound periodicals; 2,070 current periodical subscriptions; 249,486 microfiche; 1,200 music scores; 1,363 phonograph recordings.

Special Collections

Polish Heritage Collection. Over 6,000 volumes on everything about Poland to Polish Americans.

Oriental Language Collections: All subjects in Korean, Chinese, and Japanese. Includes uncataloged books, periodicals, and newspapers.

Curriculum Library. 36,000 volumes. Materials for teachers-in-service and teachers-in-training. Curriculum guides, educational software, children's book collection, 100,000-item picture file, periodicals, kits, and games.

Rare Book Collections

Walter Hart Blumenthal Collection. 1886-1969. Books, letters, and manuscripts.

Elihu Burritt Collection. 1810-1879. The Learned Blacksmith Books, manuscripts, letters, documents. Also Elijah Burritt letters and books.

Bruce Rogers Collection. 1870-1957; book designer. Over 300 titles designed or printed by Rogers.

Daniel Webster Collection. 1782-1852. Over 150 volumes.

Frederic Goudy Collection. 1865-1947; type designer and printer. Over 400 books, broadsides, and pamphlets.

World's Fair Collection. Spans the period from the 1867 Paris exposition to New Orleans 1984.

Thomas Hardy Collection. 1840-1928. 200 volumes, primarily first editions.

Connecticut Polish American Archive and Manuscript Collection. 500 linear feet of personal and organizational papers.

University Archives. 500 linear fee; 1849 to the present; includes student and faculty publications, photographs, memorabilia, department publications.

261
Connecticut College
Charles E. Shain Library
Mohegan Avenue
New London, Connecticut 06320

Telephone. (203) 447-1911

Institutional Description. The privately supported liberal arts college was founded in 1911 as the first private college for women in the state. It became coeducational in 1969, and awards baccalaureate and master's degrees. Enrollment: 1,911.

Library Administration. Brian D. Rogers, College Librarian.

Library General Holdings. 410,000 books and bound periodicals; 2,000 periodical and serial subscriptions; 240,000 government documents.

Special Collections

The library maintains special collections of Eugene O'Neill first editions and manuscripts; the Gildersleeve Collection of early children's literature; New London County history.

262
Eastern Connecticut State University
J. Eugene Smith Library
Wiilimantic, Connecticut 06226

Telephone. (203) 456-2231

Institutional Description. The publicly supported liberal arts and teachers university was founded in 1889 for the education of elementary school teachers. Enrollment: 3,873.

Library Administration. 117,000 volumes; 575 current periodical subscriptions; 249,000 microforms; 15,000 government documents.

Special Collections

Center for Connecticut Studies. The Center was established in 1970 to foster quality instruction in the fields of Connecticut history and culture. The Center houses a broad range of materials dealing with Connecticut/New England society from the seventeenth century to the present.

Archives. This resource center makes information available about the University and its total operations. Catalogued for reference are history, organizations, affiliations, policies, programs, plans, committees, publications, staff, student affairs, and memorabilia.

263
Greater Hartford Community College
Arthur C. Banks, Jr. Library
61 Woodland Street
Hartford, Connecticut 06105

Telephone. (203) 549-4200

Institutional Description. The college was opened in the fall of 1967 in the Colt Park section of Hartford and remained there until 1974 when it moved to its present site. Enrollment: 3,430.

Library Administration. Jean F. Hart, Director of Library Services.

Library General Holdings. 36,000 volumes; 3,500 media resources.

Special Collections

The library maintains specialized collections in early childhood and nursing.

264
Greater New Haven State Technical College
College Library
222 Maple Avenue
North Haven, Connecticut 06743

Telephone. (203) 789-7725

Institutional Description. The college is a non-residential institution located in a suburb of New Haven. Classes began at the college in 1977. Enrollment: 875.

Library Administration. Michele N. Cone, Librarian.

Library General Holdings. 10,000 volumes; 385 current periodical subscriptions.

Special Collections

The library maintains a special collection of manufacturers' catalogs and annual reports.

265
Hartford Graduate Center
Graduate Center Library
275 Windsor Street
Hartford, Connecticut 06120

Telephone. (203) 549-3600

Institutional Description. The privately supported institution offers graduate-level programs only. Founded in 1955 by the Renssalaer Polytechnic Institute, it now offers a wide range of professional development programs. Enrollment: 2,239.

Library Administration. Laura Dalton LaBelle, Librarian.

Library General Holdings. 28,000 volumes; 325 current periodicals.

Special Collections

The Graduate Center Library has specialized collections in the areas of computer science, engineering, business, and management studies. It maintains special collections of corporate annual reports and Securities and Exchange Commission Form 10K reports for the Fortune 500 companies, top retail companies, and companies incorporated within the state of Connecticut. There is also a special collection of technical computer manuals.

266
Hartford Seminary
Hartford Seminary Library
77 Sherman Street
Hartford, Connecticut 06105

Telephone. (203) 232-4451

Institutional Description. The privately supported graduate-level seminary, founded in 1834, is interdenominational. Enrollment: 110.

Library Administration. William Peters, Librarian.

Library General Holdings. 68,731 volumes; 240 current periodical subscriptions; 6,255 microforms; 200 audiovisual materials.

Rare Book Collections

Arabic Manuscripts. This collection of 1,200 pieces dates from the ninth to the nineteenth century. They cover a wide variety of topics from magic and alchemy to Qur'anic interpretations.

Macdonald Collection. This collection is comprised of most of the personal library of Duncan Black Macdonald, the Seminary's premier Islamic scholar until his retirement in 1932. The collection is fully catalogued and classified. The rarer pieces and most of the Islamic material are non-circulating, as is the world-famous collection (1,300 volumes) of editions and translations of the *Arabian Nights.* A number of items from this collection were on loan to the Semitic Museum of Harvard University in 1986-87 as part of an exhibit to celebrate Harvard's 350th anniversary.

Also maintained by the library is the **A.C. Thompson Collection** of nineteenth-century missiological materials. A collection of papers of early New England theologians is also housed here.

267
Mattatuck Community College
Learning Resources Center
750 Chase Parkway
Waterbury, Connecticut 06708

Telephone. (203) 575-8044

Institutional Description. The two-year community college was established in 1967 and is a major compoent of the Central Naugatuck Valley Higher Education Center. Enrollment: 4,496.

Library Administration. Patrick DeAngelis, Director.

Library General Holdings. 32,000 volumes; 190 periodical subscriptions; 15,000 microforms.

Special Collections

The library maintains the **Helen Fuld Nursing Collection.**

268
Norwalk Community College
Everett I.L. Baker Learning Resources Center
333 Wilson Avenue
Norwalk, Connecticut 06854

Telephone. (203) 853-2040

Institutional Description. The two-year college was founded in 1961 and was the first community college in Connecticut. It became a state college in 1966. Enrollment: 3,357.

Library Administration. Carmen Bayles, Director.

Library General Holdings. 50,000 books and pamphlets; 200 current magazine and newspaper titles; 6,000 audio- and videotapes.

Special Collections

Special collections include the Human Relations Area Files, the Library of American Civilization, and the Library of English Literature (microform).

269
Paier College of Art, Inc.
Library
Six Prospect Court
Hamden, Connecticut 06511

Telephone. (203) 777-3851

Institutional Description. The privately supported college of art, founded in 1946, offers baccalaureate degrees as well as certificates and diplomas. Enrollment: 391.

Library Administration. Gail J. Nachin, Librarian.

Library General Holdings. 7,757 volumes; 83 current periodical subscriptions; 23,200 audiovisual materials.

Special Collections

The specialized library of Paier College of Art supports the curriculum of the school in the areas of fine arts, graphic design, illustration, interior design, and photography.

270
Post College
Travis Library and Learning Resources Center
800 Country Club Road
Waterbury, Connecticut 06708

Telephone. (203) 755-0121

Institutional Description. Founded in 1890, Post College is a private, coeducational, nondenominational, nonprofit college of business and liberal arts. Enrollment: 1,507.

Library Administration. Darby O'Brien, Library Director.

Library General Holdings. 37,000 volumes; 450 serial subscriptions; 6 newspaper subscriptions.

Special Collections

The Tax Institute of Post College has been instrumental in raising the funds to establish and maintain a specialized collection devoted to taxation research.

271
Quinnipiac College
Instructional Resources Center
Mt. Carmel Avenue
Hamden, Connecticut 06518

Telephone. (203) 288-5251

Institutional Description. The privately supported liberal arts and professional college was founded in 1929. Many programs offered are in the field of health sciences. Enrollment: 3,139.

Library Administration. Norma F. Lang, Director.

Library General Holdings. 142,000 volumes; 900 current periodical subscriptions.

Special Collections

The library maintains a special collection on the history of the State of Connecticut.

272
Sacred Heart University
University Library
Box 6460
Bridgeport, Connecticut 06606

Telephone. (203) 371-7900

Institutional Description. The privately supported liberal arts college was founded in 1963 by the Roman Catholic Church. Enrollment: 5,014.

Library Administration. Dorothy M. Kijanka, Director.

Library General Holdings. 135,000 volumes; 900 periodical titles.

Special Collections

The University Library supports the liberal arts curriculum of the institution. The library reflects the the ecumenical vision of the founder of Sacred Heart University, the Most Reverend Walter W. Curtis, Bishop of Bridgeport.

273
St. Alphonsus College
Library
1762 Mapleton Avenue
Suffield, Connecticut 06078

Telephone. (203) 668-7393

Institutional Description. The privately supported theological seminary prepares candidates of the Roman Catholic Congregation of the Most Holy Redeemer for the priesthood. Enrollment: 52.

Library Administration. Jean DuBois, Librarian.

Library General Holdings. 34,000 volumes; 150 current periodical subscriptions.

Special Collections

Although general cultural materials are adequately represented, special attention is necessarily given to religion and philosophy because of the purpose of the College.

274
Southern Connecticut State University
Hilton C. Buley Library
501 Crescent Street
New Haven, Connecticut 06515

Telephone. (203) 397-4000

Institutional Description. The publicly supported university was founded in 1893 as the New Haven Normal School; it now offers programs leading to associate, baccalaureate, master's, and professional degrees. Enrollment: 10,733.

Library Administration. Kenneth Walter, Director of Library Services.

Library General Holdings. 447,913 volumes; 1,480 current periodical subscriptions; 463,000 microforms; 3,440 audiovisual materials.

Special Collections

The Connecticut Room holds a collection of books, papers, and documents on the state's history. The **Carolyn Sherwin Bailey Collection,** a unique storehouse of children's literature, is housed in the Rare Book Room. There is a collection of early American textbooks and a special collection on India. The **Curriculum Library** is a special resource center, containing the latest instructional material.

275
Trinity College
Library
300 Summit Street
Hartford, Connecticut 06106

Telephone. (203) 527-3151

Institutional Description. The privately supported liberal arts college was founded by the Episcopal Church in 1823 as Washington College. It is now nonsectarian. Enrollment: 2,158.

Library Administration. Ralph S. Emerick, Librarian.

Library General Holdings. 599,000 volumes; 1,900 current periodical subscriptions; 115,000 microforms; 145,000 government documents.

Special Collections

Special collections include the **Enders Ornithology Collection** of 6,000 volumes; the **Watkinson Library,** a collection of nineteenth-century Americana; and the **Moore Collection** of materials relating to the Far East.

276
Tunxis Community College
Elizabeth H. Joyner Learning Center
Farmington, Connecticut 06032

Telephone. (203) 677-7701

Institutional Description. Tunxis Community College first opened for classes in 1970 to serve the Bristol-New Britain and Farmington Valley areas. Enrollment: 3,043.

Library Administration. Judith S. MacLean, Director.

Library General Holdings. 48,000 volumes; 250 periodical subscriptions.

Special Collections

Special collections of the library are on art, criminal justice, and literature.

277
United States Coast Guard Academy Library
New London, Connecticut 06320

Telephone. (203) 444-8444

Institutional Description. The federally supported academy was founded in 1876 to train students to become career commissioned officers in the United States Coast Guard. The baccalaureate degree is awarded. Enrollment: 790.

Library Administration. William A. Temple, Librarian.

Library General Holdings. 150,000 volumes; 885 current periodical subscriptions; 40,000 microfiche; 1,500 videocassettes.

Special Collections

Subjects represented in the library's holdings reflect the strengths of the Academy's curriculum with particular emphasis on marine studies and engineering.

278
University of Bridgeport
Magnus Wahlstrom Library
University Avenue
Bridgeport, Connecticut 06602

Telephone. (203) 576-4000

Institutional Description. The privately supported university was founded in 1927 as a junior college. It attained university status in 1947. Enrollment: 6,337.

Library Administration. Judith Lin Hunt, University Librarian.

Library General Holdings. 355,000 volumes; 1,700 current periodical subscriptions; 350,000 microforms.

Special Collections

Center for Educational Resources. Provides audio, video, and computer resources for research and study. Within the Center is the Helene Fuld Learning Resources Center, an individualized and self-paced facility for nursing and health science students.

279
University of Connecticut
Homer Babbidge Library
Storrs, Connecticut 06268

Telephone. (203) 486-2524

Institutional Description. The University of Connecticut is a state supported institution, founded in 1881 as the Storrs Agricultural School. It has undergraduate branches in Hartford, Waterbury, Avery Point, Stamford, Torrington. Enrollment: 23,486.

Library Administration. Dr. Norman D. Stevens, University Librarian; Richard H. Schimmelpfeng, Director for Special Collections.

Library General Holdings. 2,042,180 volumes; 12,174 current subscriptions, 497 subscriptions in Government Publications Department; 151,000 maps; 10,200 linear feet of archives.

Special Collections

Alternative Press Collection. This collection contains thousands of periodicals, newspapers, pamphlets, books, and ephemeral items reflecting aspects of the political right and left and alternative movements from the 1960s to the present. At its beginning the APC represented the antiwar, the counter-culture, the Black liberation, and student movements of the late 1960s. Over the years it has gradually changed to incorporate material on women's liberation, environmentalism, radical professionals, and antinuclear and other contemporary social and political movements. A collection of American communist and socialist pamphlets of the 1930s and 40s in an important adjunct to the APC.

Literary Manuscripts and Archives. Literary manuscripts of post-modern writers, principally the poet Charles Olson and his associates. Other writers whose manuscripts are owned by the library are Bill Berkson, Tom Clark, Robert Creeley, Fielding Dawson, Ed Dorn, Robert Duncan, Frank O'Hara, Joel Oppenheimer, Tom

Raworth, Michael Rumaker, Ed Sanders, and John Wieners, as well as those of naturalist Edwin Way Teale. Press archives are represented by the papers of Bookstore Press, the Giligia Press, the Oyez Press, and the First Casualty Press, the latter reflecting the Vietnam experience.

Hispanic Studies. A number of special collections in Latin American and Hispanic studies are available in addition to those volumes in the general collection of the library. The Chilean Collection and the Puerto Rican Collection contain the largest number of volumes. Mexico is represented through rare pamphlets, broadsides, and manuscripts. The Madrid Collection offers a wide range of materials in all aspects of that city, while the collection of Spanish periodicals and newspapers (all printed in Spain) forms a rare and important source of information for all of the Spanish empire, principally Latin America.

Graphic and Book Arts. Numerous examples of original graphics, hand-colored sets of rare French 19th century satirical periodicals, a collection of several thousand bookplates, a small collection of origami books, and a small collection of contemporary photographs. Specimens of medieval illuminated manuscript leaves, 15th century printing, etchings, engravings, and woodcuts.

Children's Literature. Appoximately 1,000 American and British children's books published between 1830 and 1930 form a core collection for the study of children's literature.

Americana. The Pierce Welch Gaines Collection of Americana, acquired in 1977, relates to the Federalist period of 1789-1809 and contains more than 4,500 items, chiefly American imprints, including broadsides, pamphlets, and books of the period and works from the libraries of George Washington, John Adams, Thomas Jefferson, and other early political leaders.

Little Magazines. This collection of ephemeral but important often short-lived, literary periodicals was started in the 1920s. The department has a large collection of these little magazines in several languages. These holdings form an important part of the literary archives, along with first editions of modern writers.

Natural History. Since its inception as an agricultural school, the University has amassed a collection of agricultural, botanical, and natural history books with an emphasis on medical botany (or herbals), ornithology, and lepidoptera. Most of the volumes are rare with fine illustrations, frequently hand-colored. The collections include books from the Storrs brothers and from T.S. Gold, an early trustee who operated Cream Hill Farm in Cornwall, Connecticut. A fine collection of materials relating to horses and horsemanship was recently acquired.

Jaime Homero Arjona Collection. 200 volumes devoted to the Spanish dramatist and poet, Lope de Vega.

Camoes Collection. A gathering of editions, translations, and works concerning the 16th century Portuguese poet, Luis de Camoes, especially his epic, *The Lusiad.* 350 volumes.

Paul Laumonier Collection of French Renaissance Literature. A collection of several hundred volumes from sixteenth and seventeenth century France in French, with emphasis on Pierre Ronsard and the Pléiade.

Other Collections. American and British First Editions; Belgian Revolution Collection (1830-1839); French political pamphlets; Italian Risorgimento; Jose Toribio Medina Collection; Powys Collections; Robert W. Stallman Collection of the Writings of Stephen Crane; Richard E. Maynard Memorial Collection of Turkish Books; University of Connecticut Doctoral and Masters' Theses; Ice Skating Collection; Albert E. Waugh Collection of Sundials, Clocks, and Astronomy.

280
University of Hartford
William H. Mortensen Library
200 Bloomfield Avenue
West Hartford, Connecticut 06117

Telephone. (203) 243-4100

Institutional Description. The privately supported university grew from the merger of Hillyer College, Hartt College of Music, and Hartford Art School. Enrollment: 7,611.

Library Administration. John Mcgavern, University Librarian.

Library General Holdings. 335,000 volumes, musical scores, and recordings; 2,300 periodicals and scholarly journals.

Special Collections

The **Rabbi Morris Silverman Judaica Collection,** the Curriculum Laboratory of the College of Education and Allied Services, and the **Black Literature Collection** are housed in the library.

Mildred P. Allen Memorial Library. Included in the collection of over 54,000 catalogued volumes are scores and performance materials representative of all musical media. The 25,000-piece music collection includes standard works and a growing number of historical sets and scholarly editions. Works from all periods and national schools of composition are among the library's holdings. There are over 16,000 phonorecords and 1,000 audio tapes of Hartt School of Music performances.

Anne Bunce Cheney Memorial Library. Houses a large collection of books, periodicals, and reproductions in the various fields of visual arts.

281
University of New Haven
Marvin K. Peterson Library
300 Orange Avenue
West Haven, Connecticut 06516

Telephone. (203) 932-7000

Institutional Description. The privately supported

university was founded in 1920 by the YMCA as a branch of Northeastern University. It was incorporated in 1926. Enrollment: 7,762.

Library Administration. Samuel M. Baker, Jr., University Librarian.

Library General Holdings. 273,000 volumes; 1,400 periodical subscriptions; 115,000 government documents; 10,000 record albums.

Special Collections

The library supports the curriculum of the University's six schools: Graduate School; School of Arts and Sciences; School of Business; School of Engineering; the School of Hotel, Restaurant and Tourism Administration; and the School of Professional Studies and Continuing Education.

282
Wesleyan University
Olin Memorial Library
High Street
Middletown, Connecticut 06457

Telephone. (203) 347-9411

Institutional Description. The privately supported university was founded in 1831 to prepare students for the ministry and professions. It has long been a nondenominational institution and now offers baccalaureate, master's, and doctorate degrees. Enrollment: 3,252.

Library Administration. J. Robert Adams, Director.

Library General Holdings. 1,000,000 volumes; 3,100 periodicals received annually; 83,000 government documents.

Special Collections

Special Collections of the Olin Memorial Library include the George Davison Rare Book Collection; Hymnology Collection; and the Henry Bacon Architectural Drawings.

283
Western Connecticut State University
Ruth A. Haas Library
181 White Street
Danbury, Connecticut 06810

Telephone. (203) 797-4347

Institutional Description. The publicly supported liberal arts and teachers college was founded in 1903 as a normal school. Enrollment: 5,778.

Library General Holdings. 200,000 books, bound periodicals, microforms, scores, and audiovisual items.

Special Collections

The Haas Library supports the liberal arts and sciences, business, career preparation, and professional studies curricula of the University. The Westside Campus houses the Robert S. Young Business Library which contains 5,000 books, including a replication of the core collection of the Harvard Business School Baker Library.

284
Yale University
Beinecke Rare Book and Manuscript Library of the Yale University Library
1603-A Yale Station
New Haven, Connecticut 06520

Telephone. (203) 436-4771

Institutional Description. Yale University was founded in 1701 and was the first university in the United States to award the Ph.D. degree. The privately supported university is composed of 12 schools and colleges. It became coeducational for the first time in its history in 1969. Enrollment: 10,920.

Library Administration. Rutherford D. Rogers, University Librarian; Donald B. Engley, Associate University Librarian; Louis L. Martz, Director of The Beinecke Rare Book and Manuscript Library; Kenneth M. Nesheim, Associate Director.

Library General Holdings. The entire Beinecke Library is Yale's rare book department. Within the Beinecke there is a general collection—with its special emphases—as well as four separate special collections: American Literature, German Literature, Osborn, and Western Americana. For an excellent, detailed, illustrated description of the Beinecke, the reader should consult *The Beinecke Rare Book and Manuscript Library, A Guide to Its Collections,* New Haven: Yale University Library, 1974. The information below was extracted from this publication by permission. Contributors to the various articles contained therein are cited below.

Rare Book Collections

General Collection of Rare Books and Manuscripts. "The handful of books contributed by ten ministers who met in 1701 to found a college in the Colony of Connecticut was the beginning of Yale's rare book collection." (Herman W. Liebert, Librarian Emeritus and Marjorie G. Wynne, Research Librarian.) The outstanding general collection of the Beinecke is strong in British literature and history, continental European literature and history, Latin American history, English poetical miscellanies, British economic tracts, the history of education, books relating to the city and university of Oxford, shorthand, theology, travel and exploration, and newspapers and periodicals, especially British serials of the seventeenth and eighteenth centuries. Many British authors are represented by strong collections. Major collections with the general collection include material on Sir James Matthew Barrie, John Baskerville, William Beckford, James Boswell, Congregationalism, Joseph Conrad, Walter Crane, Daniel Defoe, Charles Dickens, Norman Douglas, Jonathan Edwards, George Eliot and George Henry Lewes, Elizabethan Club, Henry Fielding, French Illustrated Books, George Gissing, Greek and Latin Literature, Thomas Hardy, Incunabula, Japan, James Joyce, Judaica, D.H. Lawrence, George MacDonald, William McFee, Near Eastern Manuscripts, Manuscripts (Pre-1600), John Masefield, Mellon Collection of Alchemy and the Occult, George Meredith, Ornithology, Paleography, Papyrus Collection, Pequot Library (discovery and early history of America), Playing Cards, Cole and Linda Porter Collection (modern English, American, and French literature), Bruce Rogers, John Ruskin, Russian Collection, Sporting Books, Robert Louis Stevenson, Ezra Stiles, Taylor Collection (science and technique of navigation and the discovery and exploration of the coasts and lands of America), Tibetan Collection, Tinker collection (eighteenth- and nineteenth-century English literature), Vanderbilt Collection (early American history), Dame Rebecca West, Yale Association of Japan Collection (Japanese culture), Yale Library in 1742.

Collection of American Literature. This collection "came into existence as the result of the gift to Yale in 1911 by Owen F. Aldis, 1874, of his collection of first and other notable editions by American writers of *belle lettres.* It was part of the original agreement between Mr. Aldis and the University that the collection should be kept separate, with a curator, and that it should not be known by his name so that other friends of Yale might be willing to add their books and manuscripts to his." (Donald Gallup, Curator.) The development of the collection since 1911 has followed to a large extent the principles of Aldis. The largest of the collections, strong in manuscript material, include Léonie Adams, Leonard Bacon, Joel Barlow, Philip Barry, Stephen Vincent Benét, William Rose Benét, Rachel Carson, Barrett H. Clark, Samuel Langhorne Clemens, James Fenimore Cooper, *Dial,* Laura Woodworth (Stedman) Gould Dies, Hilda Doolittle, Muriel Gurdon (Sanders) Draper, Katherine S. Dreier, Arthur Davison Ficke, Vardis Fisher, John Gould Fletcher, Paul Leicester Ford, Hermann Hagedorn, Hutchins and Neith (Boyce) Hapgood, Marsden Hartley, John Hersey, Paul Horgan, *Hound & Horn,* Joseph N. Ireland, Washington Irving, Robinson Jeffers, James Weldon Johnson Memorial Collection of Negro Arts and Letters, Eva LeGallienne, Sinclair Lewis, Mabel (Ganson) Evans Dodge Sterne Luhan, Archibald MacLeish, Norman Macleod, John Phillips Marquand, F.O. Matthiessen, H.L. Mencken, Robert Nathan, Eugene O'Neill, James Gates Percival, William Lyon Phelps, Phoenix Theatre, Anna Marble Pollock Memorial Library of Books About Cats, Ezra Pound, James Purdy, Gertrude Stein, Leo Stein, Donald Ogden Stewart, Alfred Stieglitz, Pavel Tchelitchew, Theatre Guild Archive, Carl Van Vechten, Robert Penn Warren, Edith Wharton, Walt Whitman, Thornton Wilder, William Carlos Williams, Edmund Wilson, *Yale Review.*

Collection of Western Americana. This collection was made available to the public in 1952 and represented a consolidation of previous efforts in the field of Western Americana and the beginning of a new period. "This great step forward was made possible by the gift from the late William Robertson Coe, 1949 Hon., of his collection of rare books, maps, and manuscripts relating to the Trans-Mississippi West." (Archibald Hanna, Jr., Curator.) Yale's resources in Western Americana had up to that time been the result of acquisition of materials as they were published in the late eighteenth and early nineteenth centuries and contributions of the University's distinguished faculty. Alumni also contributed; a major addition was the Henry Raup Wagner collection of materials relating to his native Texas and the Middle-West. Another alumnus, Winlock Miller, Jr., collected sources of the history of the Pacific Northwest. This collection came to Yale in 1950. Walter McClintock, Yale 1891, bequested a fund for the purchase of books relating to American Indians. His collection of photographs and notes has been transformed into a body of material relating to all aspects of American Indian life. The collection of Thomas W. Streeter of Morristown, New Jersey was acquired in 1957 through the generosity of friends of the Yale Library.

German Literature Collection. This "assembly of books is not really a single collection so much as an amalgamation of large and small collections from various sources, welded together to span five centuries of German literature." (Christa A. Sammons, Librarian.) Among the acquisitions throughout the years were the William A. Speck Collection of Goetheana, the Ehrhardt Faust collection, the Carl Berg collection of prints, the George Alexander Kohut collection of materials relating to the poet Heinrich Heine, the papers of Karl Gottfried Theodor Winkler, the von Faber du Faur collection of seventeenth-century German literature, and the Kurt Wolff archive.

Osborn Collection. The Osborn Collection "originally focused on English poetry, especially manuscript verse of the seventeenth and eighteenth centuries, although it contained some significant earlier poems. Over the years, the scope has broadened to include letters and manuscripts of literary figures, and also historical documents. Today the collection encompasses nearly every aspect of English literature and history from the reign of Mary Tudor to that of Victoria." (Stephen Parks, Curator.)

Delaware

285
Delaware State College
William C. Jason Library-Learning Center
1200 Dupont Highway
Dover, Delaware 19901

Telephone. (302) 736-5201

Institutional Description. The publicly supported liberal arts and teachers college offers associate and baccalaureate degree programs. Enrollment: 2,327.

Library Administration. Daniel E. Coons, Director.

Library General Holdings. 150,000 volumes; 870 current periodicals; 228,000 microforms.

Special Collections

The library maintains special collections on Black Americans and the State of Delaware.

286
Goldey Beacom College
J. Wilbur Hirons Library
4701 Limestone Road
Wilmington, Delaware 19808

Telephone. (302) 998-8814

Institutional Description. The privately supported business college was founded in 1886. It offers associate and business degrees. Enrollment: 1,768.

Library Administration. Mary Rose Beach, Director.

Library General Holdings. 18,250 volumes; 275 current periodical subscriptions; 10,500 microforms.

Special Collections

The emphasis of the Hirons Library is on business subjects and computer science.

287
University of Delaware
Hugh M. Morris Library
Newark, Delaware 19716

Telephone. (302) 451-2000

Institutional Description. The publicly supported university was founded in 1743. It now offers associate, baccalaureate, professional, master's, and doctorate degrees. Enrollment: 18,631.

Library Administration. Susan Brynteson, Director; T. Stuart Dick, Associate Librarian, Special Collections.

Library General Holdings. 1,700,000 volumes; 20,500 journal subscriptions; 400,000 government documents; 1,-100,000 microforms; 90,000 maps.

Special Collections

Special books and manuscript holdings include the works of William Butler Yeats, George Bernard Shaw, John Steinbeck, and Nathaniel Hawthorne. Also included are collections in ornamental horticulture, landscape architecture, chemistry, and the history of science. The George Messersmith Diplomatic Papers are also maintained.

288
Wesley College
Robert H. Parker Library
120 North State Street
Dover, Delaware 19901

Telephone. (302) 736-2300

Institutional Description. The privately supported liberal arts college is affiliated with the United Methodist Church. Enrollment: 1,057.

Library Administration. Paul B. Lawless, Librarian.

Library General Holdings. 53,000 volumes; 350 periodical subscriptions.

Special Collections

The emphases of the library's collection are in the fields of business, social sciences, and literature.

289
Wilmington College
College Library
320 Dupont Highway
New Castle, Delaware 19720

Telephone. (302) 328-9401

Institutional Description. The privately supported liberal arts college, founded in 1967, features career-oriented programs. Enrollment: 1,227.

Library Administration. Mary Lou Ponsell, Library Director.

Library General Holdings. 65,000 volumes; 300 periodical subscriptions.

Special Collections

Learning Skills Center. Provides programmed learning machines and materials for the study of basic English and mathematics.

District of Columbia

290
American University
University Library
Massachusetts and Nebraska Avenues, N.W.
Washington, District of Columbia 20016

Telephone. (202) 885-1000

Institutional Description. The privately supported university was founded in 1893 and is affiliated with the United Methodist Church. Enrollment: 11,096.

Library Administration. George D. Arnold, Librarian.

Library General Holdings. 450,000 volumes; 2,600 periodical titles received each year; 460,000 microforms.

Special Collections

Special Collections include the **Artemus Martin Collection** of rare materials on mathematics; the **Spinks Collection** of rare Japanese and other Asian materials; and the **Esther Ballou Memorial Collection** on music.

291
Catholic University of America
John K. Mullen of Denver Memorial Library
Fourth Street and Michigan Avenue, N.E.
Washington, District of Columbia 20064

Telephone. (202) 635-5100

Institutional Description. The privately supported Roman Catholic university was founded in 1887 as a postgraduate school only, but soon added undergraduate programs. Enrollment: 6,661.

Library Administration. Adele Chwalek, Director.

Library General Holdings. 1,200,000 volumes; 8,000 periodical subscriptions; 518,300 microforms; 14,720 audiovisual materials.

Special Collections

The Special Collections of the library include a Semitics Collection, American Labor Papers, and the Lima Library of Brazilian materials.

292
Corcoran School of Art
Corcoran Library
17th Street and New York Avenue, N.W.
Washington, District of Columbia 20006

Telephone. (202) 628-9484

Institutional Description. The privately supported school grants Associate and Baccalaureate degrees and diplomas. Enrollment: 804.

Library Administration. Ann Maginnis, Librarian.

Library General Holdings. 11,000 volumes; 140 periodical subscriptions.

Special Collections

The library supports a Bachelor of Fine Arts program and maintains a collection strong in art history, fine arts, graphic design, and photography.

Rare Book Collections

There is a collection of 500 rare books dating from the eighteenth century, 250 eighteenth-century journals, and other manuscripts.

293
Dominican House of Studies
Dominican College Library
487 Michigan Avenue, N.E.
Washington, District of Columbia 20017

Telephone. (202) 529-5300

Institutional Description. The privately supported graduate-level theological seminary is a Roman Catholic institution. It was founded in 1834 in Somerset, Ohio, and moved to Washington, DC in 1905. Enrollment: 50.

Library Administration. Rev. J. Raymond Vandegrift, O.P., Librarian.

Library General Holdings. 49,000 volumes; 325 current journal subscriptions; 13,000 bound periodical volumes; 125 microfiche; 135 sound cassettes.

Special Collections

Dominican Collection. The Dominicans, founded by St. Dominic in 1216, are a worldwide religious order of preachers, teachers, missionaries, theologicans, mystics, and prelates of the Roman Catholic Church. The Order had its own rite until 1968. The collection, currently numbering over 3,700 volumes, contains histories of the Order and its provinces as well as the writings of its men, the acts of their chapters, letters of superiors, catalogs of libraries, published copies of documents in their archives, copies of their liturgical books, descriptions of their buildings. Periodicals contain articles on the Order and its history. Newsletters and journals edited by Dominicans have been collected from all the provinces. There is a section of dissertations by and about Dominicans. The collection also includes some materials on the Dominican contemplative cloistered communities of women, the Dominican lay people, and the Dominican sisters. The collection also includes biographies and lives of saints.

Thomas Aquinas Collection. The collection, currently numbering over 2,500 volumes, contains many different editions of the works of Saint Thomas Aquinas together with research tools such as the *Index Thomisticus* of Busa, bibliographies, and dictionaries. The editions range from early (sixteenth century to the nineteenth century) printed copies through the critical edition being edited and published by the Leonine Commission to modern editions and versions in English and other European languages. The collection contains the works of the commentators on the *Summa Thologicae;* nineteenth- and twentieth-century pamphlets; doctoral dissertations; the works of Thomistic philosophers and theologians; scholarly journals; acts of the Thomistic congresses; manuals of scholastic philosophy; histories of Thomism.

Rare Book Collections

Rare Book Collection. The bulk of the collection consists of the works of Saint Thomas Aquinas or his commentators, and works by and about Dominicans. There are some incunabula in the collection.

294
Gallaudet University
Library
800 Florida Avenue, N.E.
Washington, District of Columbia 20002

Telephone. (202) 651-5000

Institutional Description. The private university receives extensive support from the federal government. It is a liberal arts institution for the deaf. Enrollment: 1,982.

Library Administration. John Day, College Librarian.

Library General Holdings. 180,000 volumes, including print and non-print materials; 1,400 periodicals received each year.

Special Collections

The library's internationally known special collection of materials on deafness covers the period from 1546 to the present. It includes books, journals, pamphlets, reports from schools for the deaf, school papers, yearbooks, doctoral dissertations and master's theses, and other reports based on research, as well as an extensive archival collection.

295
George Washington University
Gelman Library
2130 H Street, N.W.
Washington, District of Columbia 20052

Telephone. (202) 994-7549

Institutional Description. The privately supported university was founded in 1821, inspired by George Washington's desire for a national university in the federal city. Enrollment: 18,711.

Library Administration. Sharon J. Rogers, University Librarian; William B. Keller, Special Collections Librarian; Suellen Towers, Rare Books Librarian.

Library General Holdings. 1,510,000 volumes; 15,000 serials; 703,421 microforms; 4,745 audiovisual materials.

Special Collections

Within the Gelman Library there are several specialized collections. In the area of diplomacy and international relations, the library holds the **Carnegie Endowment for International Peace Collection.** The library also houses the **Sino-Soviet Information Center,** which has specialized materials in the field of Chinese, Soviet, and Eastern European studies.

George Coffin Papers. Contains many late nineteenth-century pen and ink political cartoons.

Samuel Shaffer Papers and the Frederick Kuh Papers. Reflects the two twentieth-century journalists who chronicled events at the federal as well as the global level.

Murray Latimer Papers and Eli L. Oliver Papers. Contributes to the study of the labor movement in the modern United States.

Washingtoniana. Includes printed, manuscript, and graphic collections documenting the economic, social, political, and cultural history of the District of Columbia. All chronological periods of the history of the District are included. Geographical emphasis is placed on the District of Columbia's present borders (and Alexandria until 1846); the collections include materials pertaining to regional issues such as transportation and planning. The social history of the District of Columbia is also documented by biographical, sociological, and historical publications concerning the District. There is also a broad range of resources about the political history of the District of Columbia. Also collected are cultural, literary, and fine and performing arts-related publications. Of special interest are publications treating historic preservation and architecture.

George Washington University Archives. The Archives serves as the corporate memory of the George Washington University. The records, papers, and memorabilia of the University community chronicle the University's history and contribute to the study of the historical development of the District of Columbia and the Washington region.

Rare Book Collections

Rare Books Collection. Includes literary first editions; books from the early years of the printing press and from twentieth-century fine printing presses; books which are significant because of special characteristics such as prominent former owners or extraordinary illustrations.

296
Georgetown University
Joseph Mark Lauinger Memorial Library
Box 37445
Washington, District of Columbia 20013

Telephone. (202) 687-7444

Institutional Description. Georgetown University is a privately supported, Roman Catholic, coeducational university. Founded in 1789, Georgetown was the first American college to receive a university charter from the federal government. Enrollment: 11,967.

Library Administration. Joseph E. Jeffs, University Librarian; George M. Barringer, Special Collections Librarian.

Library General Holdings. The Lauinger Library houses over 600 special collections. "The formation of the Georgetown University Library Associates in 1975 was one of the seminal events in the development of the Library's special collections. The Associates, untiring in their identification and donation of books, manuscripts, and other library materials for Georgetown, have been equally generous in their giving of funds. Over the past decade this generosity has permitted the acquisition of many rare books and manuscripts available only by purchase." (Joseph E. Jeffs, University Librarian, *Special Collections at Georgetown,* Washington, D.C.: Georgetown University Library, 1985.)

Special Collections

Political Science. This subject has occupied an important place in the curriculum of Georgetown University. Among the collections are the Senator Robert F. Wagner Papers, Senator Earle B. Mayfield Papers, Harry L. Hopkins Papers, Lloyd W. Bowers Papers, John W. Davis Papers, Emily Smith Warner Collection (papers of Al Smith, Governor of New York and unsuccessful Democratic presidential candidate), Robert Low Bacon Papers, McCarthy Historical Project Archive, Archives of the American Political Science Association, Archives of the Fair Campaign Practices Committee, Archives of the Center for the Public Financing of Elections, Samuel Lubell Papers, William J. Walsh Collection (political campaigning), Editorial Cartoon Collections, MacNeil Collection (6,000 monographs, serials, pamphlets, and government documents related to the history of the United States Congress, Barnes Collection (photographs and capsule biographies of members of Congress during the latter part of the nineteenth century).

Diplomacy, International Affairs, and Intelligence. Collections in these areas emphasize American involvement overseas.

AMERICAN DIPLOMATS: Richard T. Crane Papers, Robert F. Kelley Papers, Hamilton King Papers, George C. McGhee Papers, Joseph John Jova Papers, and other diplomatic holdings (diaries and journals of Hugh McCormick Smith, papers of George Van Ruis Horton, and the archives of George S. Roper, Sr.).

INTERNATIONAL AFFAIRS: Franco-American Alliance Collection, James Brown Scott Papers, Edwin Emerson Papers, Rev. Edmund A. Walsh, S.J., Papers, James D. Mooney Papers, Laurence D. Egbert Papers, Dino Grandi Papers, Archives of the American Committee on United Europe, Archives of the Carlucci Commission on Security and Economic Assistance, Archives of the Society for Historians of Foreign Relations, Chauncey Brewster Chapman Papers, and other international affairs holdings (correspondence relating to Rear Admiral Thomas Tingey Craven, letters of Frederic A. Delano, papers of John Hall Brett, and papers of Alvin J. Cottrell).

PANAMA AND THE CANAL: Tomás Herrán Papers, Earl Harding Papers, Panama Canal Subcommittee Papers, Capt. Miles P. DuVal, Jr. Papers, and other Panama collections (papers of Rep. Daniel J. Flood, papers of Harry W. Frantz (UPI correspondent), papers of William R. McCann, papers of Senator Thomas E. Martin, papers of Representative Leonor K. Sullivan, and papers of Representative Clark W. Thompson).

INTELLIGENCE: Russell J.Bowen Collection (spying, covert activities, and related phenomena), Martin F. Herz Papers (leaflets used in propaganda warfare during World War II and the Vietnam War).

American History. Georgetown has acquired a wide range of collections covering virtually every phase of American history. The collections include sixteenth-century printed and manuscript materials but the major strengths are in collections from the nineteenth and twentieth centuries.

THE COLONIAL PERIOD: Shea Collection (Canada and the Spanish Southwest, American Catholic nineteenth-century pamphlets, American Indian history), South America (Jesuit missionary activity in Peru, Chile, and Brazil), Early Maryland History, the John Gilmary Shea Papers (early history of the Catholic Church in America).

THE NINETEENTH CENTURY: Parson Collection (works by Catholic authors printed in the U.S. between 1720 and 1830), Santa Anna Collection (Mexican President and General), David Rankin Barbee Papers (focuses on Lincoln and the Civil War), other nineteenth-century printed materials (state statutes and session laws, Catholic newspapers), E.H. Swaim Collection (career of John Wilkes Booth), the Civil War, various military collections, O'Connor Railroad Collection, Richard X. Evans Collection, Henry G. Hunt - William B. Chilton Collection, Martin I. J. Griffin Papers, John Mullan Papers (military engineer and explorer in the Far West), Ewing-Sherman Family Papers (supplements the collection of family papers at the University of Notre Dame), Levy Collection of Papers of Robert G. Ingersoll (atheist lawyer).

THE TWENTIETH CENTURY: Janet Richards Papers (lecturer and columnist), Ernest Larue Jones Collection (photographs relating to the history of American aviation), Edythe Patten Corbin Papers (international affairs), Margaret Mead Papers, Carl Coan Collection, Archives of Dag Hammarskjöld College (Columbia, Maryland), the Kennedy Assassination, Gene Basset Collection (American political figures from 1960 onward).

LOCAL HISTORY (GEORGETOWN AND WASHINGTON, D.C.): This series of collections includes Printed Books, Early Social and Economic History, Crawford Family Papers, Archives of Holy Trinity Church (Georgetown), Shoemaker Family Papers, Hinckley-Werlich Family Papers, Virginia Murray Bacon Papers, George H. O'Connor Papers, William J. Hughes Papers, Archives of the D.C. Federation of Citizens Association, Robert M. Weston Papers, Rev. Horace B. McKenna, S.J., Papers.

Jesuits in America. This group of collections is the strongest and most comprehensive of its kind and deals with activities of the Society of Jesus in the eastern part of the United States and especially in Maryland.

EUROPEAN BACKGROUND: The Woodstock Theological Library maintains one of the largest collections of works by early Jesuit authors. The collection numbers over 160,000 volumes and within the collection is a rare book section of more than 10,000 volumes. The Georgetown College Library Collection contains more than 2,500 volumes of this early institution and they have been reassembled and shelved according to their original European press-mark schemes; many were written by Jesuits or concerned with various aspects of the history of the Society of Jesus. Other collections touching on European background are the Levins Collection, Jesuit School manuscripts, and the Talbot Collection.

SEVENTEENTH AND EIGHTEENTH CENTURIES: These collections include the Archives of the Maryland Province of the Society of Jesus, American Catholic Sermon Collection, and Early Maryland Jesuits' Papers.

NINETEENTH AND TWENTIETH CENTURIES: Woodstock College Archives; Nineteenth Century Jesuits' Papers; Rev. J. Havens Richards, S.J., Papers; Rev. Francis A. Barnum, S.J., Papers; Rev. John LaFarge, S.J., Papers; Rev. Wilfrid Parsons, S.J., Papers; Rev. John Courtney Murray, S.J., Papers; Rev. Gustave Weigel, S.J., Papers; Rev. John Brosnan, S.J., Collection; Lukas - Teilhard de Chardin Collection; Barbour Collection (by and about Teilhard du Chardin); Granger-Teilhard de Chardin Collection.

European History. This group of collections includes: Scheuch Collection (medieval and early modern documents of the Sala family), Chioccarelli Collection, George C. McGhee Library (Turkish people and the Ottoman Empire), Viti Collection (history of heraldry and chivalric orders, genealogy of selected English and Italian families); Abell Napoleonic Collection, Gonzaga Family Papers, Alexis Carrel Papers, Haggerty Collection (World War I British regimental unit histories and personal narratives), Kalina Collection (Czechoslovakian and Eastern European history), Carroll Quigley Papers, de Garczynski Family Papers (Polish history), Karski Collection, Mrs. Walter R. Benjamin Papers, Goetz A. Briefs Papers, Rodney Loomer Mott Papers - Richard Van Wagenen/OMGUS Collection, Eric F. Menke Map Collection, Snyder Numismatic Collection.

Literature and Linguistics. Emphases in the collections are the works of major English and American Catholic authors of the nineteenth and twentieth centuries.

ANGLO-AMERICAN CATHOLIC AUTHORS: Newman Collections, the *America* Archives, Riedel Collection (works of G.K. Chesterton, Hilaire Belloc, Eric Gill, Msgr. Ronald Knox), Gallery of Living Catholic Authors, Theodore Maynard Papers, Papers of Sister Miriam, R.S.M., Kilmer Family Papers, Rev. John Bannister Tabb Collection, Douglas Woodruff Papers, Sir Shane Leslie Papers, Evelyn Waugh Collections, Christopher Sykes Papers, Graham Greene Papers, Bruce Marshall Papers.

ENGLISH LITERATURE: These collections began in 1934 with the gift by Mrs. Nicholas Brady of the literary manuscripts and first editions collected by her late husband. The various collections include English Romantics, Ziegler Dickens Collection, Frank Kurt Cylke Collection of Arthur Ransome, Grant Richards Papers, James Laver Papers; other English literature holdings include works of W.B. Yeats, W.H. Auden, Max Beerbohm, Joseph Conrad, John Galsworthy, T.S. Eliot, Dylan Thomas, Kingsley Amis, and George Bernard Shaw.

AMERICAN LITERATURE: Georgetown's significant holdings in American literature are of recent acquisition, but it has been the repository of two of the most famous of American literary manuscripts—the holograph manuscript of *The Adventures of Tom Sawyer,* and one of five known autograph drafts of Francis Scott Key's "The Star-Spangled Banner." Collections include: Hawthorne-

Bennoch Collection (letters written by Nathaniel Hawthorne's son, novelist Julian Hawthorne), Flaccus-Masters Archive (research files of poet Kimball Flaccus in the course writing a biography of Edgar Lee Masters), Fulton Oursler Memorial Collection, H.L. Mencken Collection, Murray Marshall Collection, Marguerite Tjader Harris Papers (editorial files and correspondence about the *Direction* magazine), William Peter Blatty Papers (novels and screenplays), Biddle Collection (twentieth-century American poetry), George Santayana Collection, Philip Barry Collection; other holdings of works by James Fenimore Cooper, F. Scott Fitzgerald, Henry David Thoreau, Walt Whitman, Theodore Dreiser, John Steinbeck, Robert Frost, Edwin Arlington Robinson, Marianne Moore, Robinson Jeffers, William Everson, Henry James, and Hart Crane.

JOURNALISM: Georgetown does not offer a degree in journalism, but several collections do offer insight into the profession, namely the papers of Michael Amrine, William R. Downs, Riley Hughes, André Visson, Fulton Oursler, Edwin Emerson, Richard Billings, and others.

LINGUISTICS: These collections support the University's School of Languages and Linguistics and include American Indian Languages; Zalles Celtic Collection, Albert Marckwardt Papers, American Heritage School Dictionary Corpus (records on the development of the dictionary, the first to utilize computer technology).

Bibliography and Allied Subjects. The library's collections is these areas include bibliographic reference, medieval manuscripts and facsimiles, non-European manuscripts (Arabic, Persian, Indian), early printed books, bookbindings, and modern fine printing.

Visual Arts. The various collections include Printed Books (illustrated), Doniger Piranesi Collection, Murphy Collection (American printmakers, 1930-1855), Menke Print Collection, Lynd Ward-May McNeer Papers, Isac Friedlander Papers (Latvian-born printmaker and illustrator), John W. Thomason Collection, Poster Collections, Editorial Cartoons (John Baer, Gene Basset, Oscar Cesare, Robert Clark, Bill Crawford, John Stampone, Bill Talburt), Quigley Photographic Archive (photo "morgue" of Quigley Publications), Quiqley Deposit Collection *(Motion Picture Herald, Motion Picture Daily, International Motion Picture/Television Almanac, Fame),* Department of Defense Film Collection, Lawrence Suid Collection (Hollywood film industry's relations with the Armed Services).

University Archives. Official records of the University from its founding in 1789.

297
Howard University
Founders Library
2400 Sixth Street, N.W.
Washington, District of Columbia 20059

Telephone. (202) 636-6100

Institutional Description. The privately supported university was founded in 1867 by a federal charter. It is composed of 18 schools and colleges. Enrollment: 11,121.

Library Administration. Juanita W. Portis, Deputy Director.

Library General Holdings. 1,841,893 volumes; 24,966 periodicals; 2,266,115 microforms; 56,330 audiovisual materials.

Special Collections

Channing Pollock Theatre Collection. Contains materials on the performing arts and documents the Black experience in that area.

Bernard Fall Southeast Asian Collection. Built around a nucleus of material on North and South Vietnam from the personal library of Dr. Bernard Fall, former Howard University professor and expert on Southeast Asia. The Fall Collection also documents the involvement of Blacks in the Vietnam war.

Moorland-Spingarn Research Center. The world's most comprehensive collection of materials on Africa and persons of African descent is found in this Center. The collection consists of the Jesse E. Moorland Collection, the Arthur B. Spingarn Collection, the Howard University Archives, and the Howard University Museum. The Center's book collections focus on Black life, literature, and history, and include works by Black authors from the sixteenth century to the present. The library also houses the Paul Robeson Papers.

Rare Book Collections

Treasure Room. Contains several collections and individual items that are rare or otherwise valuable.

298
Mount Vernon College
Library
2100 Foxhall Road, N.W.
Washington, District of Columbia 20007

Telephone. (202) 331-0400

Institutional Description. The privately supported liberal arts college for women offers associate and baccalaureate degrees in ten interdisciplinary programs. Enrollment: 468.

Library Administration. Lucy Cocke, Director.

Library General Holdings. 45,000 volumes; 300 periodical subscriptions.

Special Collections

The library houses both print and nonprint collections on art, interior design, and women's studies.

299
Southeastern University
University Library
501 Eye Street, S.W.
Washington, District of Columbia 20024

Telephone. (202) 488-8162

Institutional Description. The privately supported institution offers a variety of business education programs, granting associate, baccalaureate, and master's degrees. Enrollment: 1,226.

Library Administration. Allan Mussehl, Director.

Library General Holdings. 20,000 books; 250 periodicals.

Special Collections

The emphasis of the library's collection is on business and related fields such as accounting, business law, computer science, economics, information systems, management, marketing, public administration, and taxation.

300
Strayer College
Wilkes Library
1100 Vermont Avenue, N.W.
Washington, District of Columbia 20005

Telephone. (202) 467-6966

Institutional Description. The privately supported business college awards certificates, diplomas, and associate and baccalaureate degrees. Enrollment: 1,929.

Library Administration. David Moulton, Director.

Library General Holdings. 16,200 volumes; 100 current periodical subscriptions.

Special Collections

The library houses the 32 volumes of official government documents of the Watergate investigation proceedings. There is also a collection of business management materials.

301
Trinity College
Sister Helen Sheehan Library
125 Michigan Avenue, N.E.
Washington, District of Columbia 20017

Telephone. (202) 939-5000

Institutional Description. The privately supported liberal arts college for women was founded in 1897. It is affiliated with the Sisters of Notre Dame de Namur of the Roman Catholic Church. Enrollment: 964.

Library Administration. Karen Leider, Librarian.

Library General Holdings. 160,000 volumes; 600 current periodicals.

Special Collections

The library maintains a slide collection of art history. A small Rare Book Room houses a collection which includes incunabula, fine bindings, and first editions.

302
University of the District of Columbia
Division of Learning Resources
4200 Connecticut Avenue, N.W.
Washington, District of Columbia 20008

Telephone. (202) 282-7300

Institutional Description. The publicly supported (federal) university was formed in 1977 by the merger of the District of Columbia Teachers College, Federal City College, and the Washington Technical Institute. Enrollment: 11,098.

Library Administration. Albert J. Casciero, Director.

Library General Holdings. 446,000 volumes; 1,890 periodical subscriptions; 521,000 microforms; 75,000 government documents.

Special Collections

The library's special collections include the **Atlanta University Black Culture Collection** in microform; the **Human Relations Area Files,** and the **Water Resources Collection.**

303
Wesley Theological Seminary
Library
4500 Massachusetts Avenue, N.W.
Washington, District of Columbia 20016

Telephone. (202) 885-8600

Institutional Description. The privately supported theological seminary, affiliated with the United Methodist Church, offers graduate degree programs only. Enrollment: 354.

Library Administration. Allen W. Mueller, Director.

Library General Holdings. 110,000 volumes; 600 periodical subscriptions.

Special Collections

The most important special collections include the **John and Charles Wesley Collection** and the records of the former Methodist Protestant Church.

Florida

304
Baptist Bible Institute
Ida J. McMillan Library
1306 College Drive
Graceville, Florida 32440

Telephone. (904) 263-3261

Institutional Description. The privately supported college is owned and operated by the Florida Baptist Convention, in affiliation with the Southern Baptist Church. It offers theological studies to those preparing for careers in church leadership. Enrollment: 329.

Library Administration. William E. Jones, Librarian.

Library General Holdings. 49,000 volumes; 375 current periodical subscriptions.

Special Collections

A substantial collection of associational minutes and state convention annuals is maintained in addition to Southern Baptist Convention annuals. There is also the **Hudson Collection** of letters and memorabilia.

305
Barry University
Monsignor William Barry Memorial Library
1300 N.E. Second Avenue
Miami Shores, Florida 33161

Telephone. (305) 758-3392

Institutional Description. The privately supported liberal arts university was founded in 1940. It is affiliated with the Roman Catholic Church. Enrollment: 4,600.

Library Administration. Hugh W. Ribply, University Librarian.

Library General Holdings. 175,000 items; 1,700 current periodical titles.

Special Collections

The library maintains a special collection of 2,000 volumes on Catholic Church history and theology.

306
Bethune-Cookman College, Inc.
Carl Southwick Swisher Library
640 Second Avenue
Daytona Beach, Florida 32015

Telephone. (904) 255-1401

Institutional Description. The privately supported college is affiliated with the United Methodist Church. Cookman Institute of Jacksonville, founded in 1872, and the Daytona Normal and Industrial Institute for Girls, founded in 1904, merged in 1923 to form the present institution. Enrollment: 1,739.

Library Administration. Gladys Greene, Chief Librarian.

Library General Holdings. 126,519 volumes; 560 current periodical subscriptions; 19,000 microforms; 10,000 audiovisual materials.

Special Collections

Archives. This is the repository for documentary, photographic, and other materials of historic value to Bethune-Cookman College.

Special collections available in the library are the **Mary McLeod Bethune Papers,** books on Abraham Lincoln, and the **Black History Collection.**

307
Daytona Beach Community College
Learning Resources Center
1200 Volusia Avenue
P.O. Box 1111
Daytona Beach, Florida 32015

Telephone. (904) 255-8131

Institutional Description. The first classes of this two-year community college were held in the Princess Issena Hotel from 1958 to 1960. The present campus was occupied in 1960. Enrollment: 11,331.

Library Administration. Yvonne Newcombe-Doty, Acting Director.

Library General Holdings. 60,000 volumes; 500 periodical titles; 5,100 microforms.

Special Collections

The library maintains a special collection of Floridiana and a collection on early United States history. A collection of 200 expensive and out-of-print titles is also maintained.

308
Edward Waters College
Centennial Library
1658 Kings Road
Jacksonville, Florida 32209

Telephone. (904) 355-3030

Institutional Description. The privately supported liberal arts and teachers college is affiliated with the African Methodist Episcopal Church. It was founded in 1866. Enrollment: 828.

Library Administration. Jean S. Jones, Director.

Library General Holdings. 122,000 volumes; 164 current periodical titles.

Special Collections

The **Afro-American Collection** and **Centennial Archives** contain 1,800 volumes and selected periodical titles by and about Afro-Americans. There is also material which reflects the history and development of Edward Waters College. The **Obi Collection,** a permanent exhibit of African art and ethnographic objects is also housed in the library.

309
Embry-Riddle Aeronautical University
Jack R. Hunt Memorial Library
Star Route, Box 540
Bunnell, Florida 32010

Telephone. (904) 673-3180

Institutional Description. The privately supported technical university operates from two main campuses (Daytona Beach, FL and Prescott, AZ), and an International Campus operating on selected military sites and aviation centers worldwide. Enrollment: 7,655.

Library Administration. Sarah K. Thomas, Head Librarian.

Library General Holdings. 54,000 volumes; 835 current periodical subscriptions; 112,000 microforms; 11,000 audiovisual materials.

Special Collections

The Hunt Library has a comprehensive aviation collection. The special collections of the library include NACA and NASA documents, National Transportation Safety Board documents; and a historical aviation collection.

310
Flagler College
Louise Wise Lewis Library
King Street
P.O. Box 1027
St. Augustine, Florida 32085

Telephone. (904) 829-6481

Institutional Description. The privately supported liberal arts college was founded in 1963. Special programs include overseas studies and work at the Florida School for the Deaf and Blind. Enrollment: 1,102.

Library Administration. Robert C. Frost, Director of Library Services.

Library General Holdings. 74,000 volumes; 378 current periodical subscriptions; 12 newspaper subscriptions; 15,102 microfilms; 933 records and cassettes.

Special Collections

The library supports the liberal arts academic program of the college. Cooperation between Flagler College's Education Department and the Florida School for the Deaf and the Blind, the largest institution of its kind in the United States, offers opportunities to students in the areas of general and special education.

311
Florida Agricultural and Mechanical University
Coleman Learning Resources Center
Martin Luther King, Jr. Boulevard
Tallahassee, Florida 32307

Telephone. (904) 599-3000

Institutional Description. The publicly supported state university was founded in 1887. Special programs include the overseas Nigeria project and an academic cooperative plan with the Florida State University. Enrollment: 5,101.

Library Administration. Saiyed A. Ahmad, University Librarian.

Library General Holdings. 411,329 volumes; 2,735 periodicals; 5,000 recordings.

Special Collections

Learning Resources Center. Consists of three elements which make up a comprehensive instruction support center: Instructional Media Services, Instructional Development Services, and Library Services. The Library Services element acquires and processes print and nonprint resources to meet the instructional and research needs of students and faculty.

312
Florida Atlantic University
S.E. Wimberly Library
500 Northwest 20th Street
Boca Raton, Florida 33431

Telephone. (305) 393-3000

Institutional Description. The publicly supported (state) university offers upper level and graduate programs only. It was founded in 1961. Enrollment: 9,879.

Library Administration. Harry R. Skallerup, Director.

Library General Holdings. 1,0000,000 bibliographic items.

Special Collections

In addition to its traditional book and journal holdings, the library's collection contains state and federal government documents, microform backfiles, maps, and business reports. The **Theodore Pratt Collection** is also maintained.

313
Florida College
Chatlos Library
119 Glen Arven Avenue
Temple Terrace, Florida 33617

Telephone. (813) 988-5131

Institutional Description. Florida College is a private, liberal arts junior college founded by the Church of Christ in 1946, but is today independent of any church affiliation. Enrollment: 368.

Library Administration. Harold Tabor, College Librarian; Joy Huffman, Assistant Librarian.

Library General Holdings. 34,183 bound volumes; 327 periodical subscriptions; 1,383 recordings and tapes; 400 books on microform; 1,869 Library of Congress microfiche, 276 COMCAT, and 3,843 MARC; 4 newspaper subscriptions.

Special Collections

Restoration Movement. This collection includes 173 volumes (19th century); 158 reels of microfilm (periodicals); and 453 books (sermons, history, biography, commentaries).

Creation/Evolution Controversy. Emphasis on creationism publications; 270 books.

314
Florida Community College at Jacksonville
(See individual campus listings below)
501 West State Street
Jacksonville, Florida 32202

Telephone. (904) 632-3000

Institutional Description. Florida Community College at Jacksonville was founded in 1965 and now has four campuses (see individual campus listings below). Enrollment: 14,883.

Library Administration. (See individual campus listings below)

Downtown Campus
Downtown Campus Library
101 West State Street
Jacksonville, Florida 32202

Telephone. (904) 633-8169

Library Administration. Kenneth LeRoy Puckett, Jr., College/Special Collections Librarian.

Library General Holdings. 40,000 bound volumes; 73,000 audiovisual items; 460 periodical and newspaper subscriptions; 400 microform titles.

Special Collections

The Downtown Campus Library has in its reference collection the publications of the American Welding Society (AWS). These publications are donated by the local chapter of the AWS and total approximately 200 titles in addition to the regular collection on welding. AWS members are assured access to these publications even though they may not be directly associated with the college.

Fred A. Kent Campus
Fred A. Kent Campus Library
3939 Roosevelt Boulevard
Jacksonville, Florida 32205

Telephone. (904) 387-8222

Library Administration. Dr. Gwendolyn J. Chandler, College Librarian.

Library General Holdings. The library holdings support the curriculum of the Kent Campus and include 63,053 books; 776 bound periodical volumes; 334 current periodical subscriptions; 10 current newspaper subscriptions; 11,710 reels of microfilm; 8,258 microfiche.

Special Collections

Home Economics. Holdings include volumes on the subjects of interior decoration, fashion, beauty culture, cosmetics, hairdressing, food service, nutrition, and cookery.

Business. The major areas of real estate business and management are covered.

North Campus
North Campus Learning Resources Center
4501 Capper Road
Jacksonville, Florida 32218

Telephone. (904) 766-6711

Library Administration. Willie Lee Lucas, Department Chairperson/Reference Librarian; J. Wayne Baker.

Library General Holdings. The overall collection includes 76,204 volumes of books; 746 periodical titles; 35 newspaper subscriptions; 4,935 audiovisual titles (72,063 items); 428 microform titles (32,972 items). This collection is augmented by an extensive collection of vertical file materials, art reprints, maps, globes, and models.

Special Collections

Health-Related Professions. There is a combined total of 8,599 print and audiovisual titles in the Health-Related collection and 67 subscriptions to major health journals with appropriate indexes. This collection provides curriculum support materials for student research and faculty planning for the disciplines of nursing, nursing-related (e.g., surgical technology and medical assisting), dental, emergency medicine, medical laboratory technology, and respiratory therapy. Collection development policies provide for an on-going process of materials evaluation as a basis for maintaining a collection that gives functional support to the Health-Related areas.

South Campus
South Campus Learning Resources Center
11901 Beach Boulevard
Jacksonville, Florida 32216

Telephone. (904) 646-2173

Library Administration. Theodore Grimes, Department Chairman/Reference Librarian.

Library General Holdings. 63,609 bound volumes; 350 current periodical subscriptions; 33 newspaper subscriptions; 18,371 microfiche; 10,927 reels microfilm; small collection of music scores; non-print media collection of 44,000 items including film, tapes, slides, and video.

315
Florida Institute of Technology
Evans Library
150 West University Boulevard
Melbourne, Florida 32901

Telephone. (305) 768-8000

Institutional Description. The privately supported technological institute was founded in 1958 as the Brevard Engineering College, offering evening courses. Day programs were instituted in 1962. Enrollment: 5,354.

Library Administration. L.L. Henson, Director

Library General Holdings. 167,000 volumes; 1,200 current periodical subscriptions.

Special Collections

Special collections include the **Medaris Collection** which contains the personal papers and memorabilia of Major General John B. Medaris and the **Aerospace Collection** of 500 volumes including some autographed editions.

316
Florida International University
University Libraries
Tamiami Trail
Miami, Florida 33199

Telephone. (305) 554-2000

Institutional Description. The publicly supported state liberal arts university offers upper-division studies only. Enrollment: 10,986.

Library Administration. Lawrence A. Miller, Director; Salvador Miranda, Assistant Director for Collection Development.

Library General Holdings. 673,761 volumes; 5,100 journal and serial subscriptions; 1,041,217 microforms; 56,000 audiovisual materials.

Special Collections

Special collections of the University Libraries include the **Narot Collection,** the **International Collection,** and the **Latin American-Caribbean Collection.**

317
Florida Memorial College
College Library
15800 N.W. 42nd Avenue
Miami, Florida 33054

Telephone. (305) 625-4141

Institutional Description. The privately supported liberal arts college is affiliated with the American Baptist Church. Enrollment: 1,758.

Library Administration. Laban Connor, Head Librarian.

Library General Holdings. 75,000 volumes; 250 current periodical subscriptions.

Special Collections

The library maintains the College Archives and a collection on Black studies.

318
Florida Southern College
Roux Library
111 Lake Hollingsworth Drive
Lakeland, Florida 33801

Telephone. (813) 680-4100

Institutional Description. The privately supported liberal arts college, founded in 1885, is affiliated with the United Methodist Church. Enrollment: 2,304.

Library Administration. G. Lawrence Stallings, Director.

Library General Holdings. 177,000 volumes; 755 current periodical subscriptions; 12,000 microforms.

Special Collections

The Roux Library maintains the **Methodist Archives** and the papers of Congressman James A. Haley.

319
Florida State University
Robert Manning Strozier Library
Copeland Avenue
Tallahassee, Florida 32306

Telephone. (904) 644-3271

Institutional Description. The state supported university was authorized in 1851 and is one of the state's oldest universities. Enrollment: 19,876.

Library Administration. Charles E. Miller, University Librarian; Susan Hamburger, Associate University Librarian; Adeline Wilkes, Special Collections Librarian.

Library General Holdings. 1,624,138 bound volumes; 2,727,460 microforms; 564,424 government documents; 150,570 maps. In addition to the special collections described below, the University also has collections of the works of Thomas Hardy, William Butler Yeats, Frank Norris, Richard Harding Davis, Thomas Percy, and Thomas Taylor; Confederate imprints sheet music (Music Library), and Christmas greetings books.

Special Collections

Florida Collection. The Florida Collection is a rich collection of books and periodicals by Florida authors and about Florida topics. The collection is strong in information on Florida subjects ranging from history, natural environment, guidebooks, and indiginous people to current material on government and industry. An extensive vertical file of pamphlets and newspaper clippings containing material of Florida issues, people, and localities provides additional access to information often found only in such ephemeral forms.

Manuscripts and Historical Papers. Florida and local history is brought to life through the resources available in this collection. Here one can find plantation and land grant records; documents from lumber, shipping, railroad and utility companies; papers on the Indian Wars and treaties; family records and personal correspondence which provide an informal picture of life in Tallahassee and Leon County in the early days.

Shaw Poetry Collection. This collection consists of thousands of volumes of English and American poetry, criticism, biography, and reference. It was assembled as the lifetime leisure activity of John Mackay Shaw. All the great poets, and hundreds of minor poets of all periods, are represented in first or early editions. The collection also includes numerous nineteenth and early twentieth century American and British periodicals showing the first printing of the works of major and minor poets.

Mildred and Claude Pepper Collection. The Pepper Collection contains the official and personal papers, photographs, recordings, and memorabilia of Congressman Claude Pepper.

Napoleon and the French Revolution. Currently containing 12,600 items, the collection includes letters, journals, diaries, memoirs, and documents published during the last century and a half. The collection includes works published in the United States as well as many volumes acquired from the private libraries of King Ernest-August of Hanover, and Revolutionary scholars Octure Aubry, Jacques Anna, General Jean Regnault, as well as the Napoleonic bibliophile Marie-Antoinette Pardee.

Carothers Memorial Collection. One or the more recently acquired collections is the Julia Stove and Milton Washington Carothers Collection of Bibles and Rare Books.

McGregor Collection. This Americana collection of 355 volumes, includes works of discovery and exploration, the Colonial period, the Revolutionary and Post Revolutionary period, travel literature, works on the history of the American Indians, early Florida history, and bibliographies.

Louise Richardson "The Night Before Christmas" Collection. This collection of various editions and versions of the Clement C. Moore poem "The Night Before Christmas" was donated to the Strozier Library in 1963 by the family of Louise Richardson, former librarian of the Florida State College for Women and Florida State University. Included in the collection are finely illustrated editions by such artists as Arthur Rackham and Grandma Moses, dime-store versions, clippings about the poem, musical arrangements, Christmas cards, and many humorous parodies.

Louise Richardson Herbal Collection. A second noteworthy Richardson collection is the sixteenth-, seventeenth-, and eighteenth-century works on herbals. These works contain descriptions of the many plants valued for their medicinal, savory, or aromatic qualities.

Lois Lenski Collection. Lois Lenski, author and illustrator of over ninety books of prose, poetry, and plays for children, presented the Library with a collection of her books, original drawings, and articles.

Nancy Bird Fore-Edge Paintings. This collection includes both single fore-edge paintings and double fore-edge paintings.

Scottish Collection. The works in this collection relate to the Highlands and Islands of Western Scotland and provide the basis for research on the Scottish heritage and its influence in North Florida.

Kelmscott Press Books. This collection is a complete set of the fifty-three titles issued by the Kelmscott Press.

University Archives. The University Archives houses both current and historical information about Florida State University.

320
Jacksonville University
Carl S. Swisher Library
2800 University Boulevard, North
Jacksonville, Florida 32211

Telephone. (904) 744-3950

Institutional Description. The privately supported university graduated its first class in 1959. Featured programs include music, art, and education. Enrollment: 1,-898.

Library Administration. Thomas H. Gunn, Director.

Library General Holdings. 350,000 books and bound journals; 577 current periodical subscriptions; 27,000 microforms; 120,000 government documents; 30,000 audiovisual materials.

Special Collections

Special collection within Swisher Library are the **Treasure Room** of rare books, the **Florida Collection,** the **Delius Collection,** the **Jacksonville University Archives,** and the **Library of the Jacksonville Historical Society.** The Music Library has a wide range of recordings from the classics to more popular forms of music.

321
Lake-Sumter Community College
Library
Highway 441, South
Leesburg, Florida 32788

Telephone. (904) 787-3747

Institutional Description. The two-year college was founded in 1962. The present campus was occupied in 1970. Enrollment: 1,448.

Library Administration. Denise E. Stein, Head Librarian.

Library General Holdings. 56,000 volumes; 400 current periodical titles; 37,000 government documents.

Special Collections

Lake-Sumter Community College is one of three Florida community colleges serving as Federal Depositories for United States Government Publications. The library also maintains a special collection of Floridiana.

322
Miami Christian College
College Library
2300 N.W. 135th Street
Miami, Florida 33167

Telephone. (305) 685-7431

Institutional Description. The privately supported professional college is interdenominational. It grants associate and baccalaureate degrees. Enrollment: 211.

Library Administration. Barbara Roberts, Librarian.

Library General Holdings. 40,000 volumes; 215 current periodical subscriptions.

Special Collections

The library maintains special collections of material on Florida, elementary education reference resources, and a music file.

323
Miami-Dade Community College
Libraries
11011 S.W. 104th Street
Miami, Florida 33176

Telephone. (305) 596-1211

Institutional Description. Miami-Dade Community College is a public, two-year college which serves the complete Dade County community on four campuses. It was created in 1960. Enrollment: 29,461.

Library Administration. Mildred E. Dewar, Director of Library Services.

Library General Holdings. 336,000 titles; 3,600 periodical subscriptions; 25,000 multimedia items.

Special Collections

Special collections are maintained on nursing and allied health, Dade County information files, Spanish language popular reading, and career planning. The **McNaughton Collection** consists of best sellers. The **Miami-Dade Archives** are also maintained.

324
Nova University
Albert and Birdie Einstein Library
3301 College Avenue
Fort Lauderdale, Florida 33314

Telephone. (305) 475-7300

Institutional Description. The privately supported liberal arts and professional university was founded in 1964. Enrollment: 6,299.

Library Administration. Robert Bogorff, Director.

Library General Holdings. 136,952 books; 5,228 current periodicals; 766,000 microforms; 18,000 government documents.

Special Collections

The library contains a collection of books and periodicals in the disciplines of the behavioral sciences, education, public administration, computer sciences, business administration, public communications, and the humanities. The library maintains a collection of United Nations documents and international law materials.

325
Okaloosa-Walton Junior College
Learning Resources Center
100 College Boulevard
Niceville, Florida 32578

Telephone. (904) 678-5111

Institutional Description. Founded in 1963, the college began its first classes in August 1964 on a temporary campus in Valparaiso, Florida. The present permanent site was occupied in 1965. Enrollment: 2,720.

Library Administration. Lucy Warren, Head Librarian.

Library General Holdings. 74,000 books; 616 magazine subscriptions; 23 newspaper subscriptions; 46,447 audiovisual items.

Special Collections

The learning resource center's special collections include **Florida Authors and Books About Florida** and an oral history collection by local residents.

326
Orlando College
Orlando College Library
5500 Diplomat Circle
Orlando, Florida 32810

Telephone. (407) 628-5870

Institutional Description. The privately supported business college was formerly known as Jones College. Enrollment: 1,559.

Library Administration. Martha Petty, Librarian.

Library General Holdings. 10,000 volumes; 60 periodical subscriptions; 10 newspaper subscriptions; 100 audiovisual materials.

Special Collections

The library is oriented toward business, medical, and legal materials. The most important special holdings include collections on accounting, management, and marketing. There is also a special collection of 600 dictation and court reporting tapes on cassette.

327
Palm Beach Atlantic College
E.C. Blomeyer Library
1101 South Olive Avenue
West Palm Beach, Florida 33401

Telephone. (305) 833-8592

Institutional Description. Palm Beach Atlantic College is a private liberal arts institution operating under the auspices of the Palm Lakes Baptist Association. It was founded in 1968. Enrollment: 1,143.

Library Administration. Fred W. Youngs, Librarian.

Library General Holdings. 53,000 volumes of book, pamphlet, and periodical holdings, including microfilm backfiles of journals and newspapers.

Special Collections

The library maintains the **Strouse Theatre Collection.** The Elizabeth Etelman Memorial Music Listening Laboratory and a music library containing numerous scores and recordings are housed in the Music Department.

328
Palm Beach Junior College
Library Learning Resources
4600 Congress Avenue
Lake Worth, Florida 33461

Telephone. (305) 439-8000

Institutional Description. Founded in 1933, Palm Beach Junior College was originally housed in the Palm Beach High School. After several moves, the present site was occupied in 1956. Enrollment: 6,029.

Library Administration. Wiley C. Douglass, Director.

Library General Holdings. 134,965 volumes; 6,830 periodicals; 51,753 microforms; 29,634 pamphlets.

Special Collections

Special collections of the library include the **Civil War Collection** and the **Florida Collection.**

329
Polk Community College
Library
999 Avenue H, N.E.
Winter Haven, Florida 33881

Telephone. (813) 294-7771

Institutional Description. The two-year college was established in 1963 and serves Polk County. Enrollment: 4,301.

Library Administration. Patricia S. Deniston, Director.

Library General Holdings. 79,000 volumes; 380 periodical subscriptions.

Special Collections

The library maintains a special **Children's Literature Collection.**

330
Ringling School of Art and Design
Verman Kimbrough Memorial Library
1111 27th Street
Sarasota, Florida 33580

Telephone. (813) 351-4614

Institutional Description. The privately supported art college was founded in 1931 by circus magnate John Ringling and Verman Kimbrough. Enrollment: 373.

Library Administration. Yvonne L. Morse, Director of Library Services.

Library General Holdings. 13,000 volumes; 165 current art journal and other magazine subscriptions; 26,000 audiovisual materials.

Special Collections

The library is one of the finest visual resource centers in the region. Its special collections include the **Duff-Stevens Collection** of seventeenth- and eighteenth-century prints; the **Jackson Collection** of Japanese art books and prints; and the **Simmen Collection** of portraits of eighteenth-century rulers and statesmen.

331
Rollins College
Olin Library
1000 Holt Avenue
Winter Park, Florida 32789

Telephone. (305) 646-2676

Institutional Description. Rollins College is a private, liberal arts institution. Founded in 1885, Rollins offered the first college-level curriculum in Florida. It now offers Bachelor and Master degrees. Enrollment: 2,797.

Library Administration. George C. Grant, College Librarian; Kathleen J. Reich, Head, Archives and Special Collections.

Library General Holdings. 62,142 volumes (Dewey); 152,200 volumes (Library of Congress); 42,087 government documents; 2,671 media titles; 37,444 microform titles; 30 newspaper subscriptions; 1,368 periodical subscriptions; 6,000 reference books.

Special Collections

Floridiana. This collection covers a period of four and a half centuries and includes materials that were written in Latin, Spanish, Portuguese, French, German, English, Italian, and Dutch. The largest part of the collection relates to the period during which Florida has been a part of the United States.

Holt Papers. The papers of Hamilton Holt (President of Rollins College for 24 years) consists of scrapbooks, correspondence, manuscripts, and files on Peace, International Organization, Journalism, and Education; complete set of *The Independent* magazine.

William Elder Marcus Jewelry Books. This reference collection on jewelry was donated by William Elder Marcus, formerly head of Marcus & Company, jewelers of New York. It contains fourteen catalogs of the original drawings of Marcus' jewelry designs which cover a period of 85 years. In addition he gave 53 other books on jewelry and precious stones.

Nehrling Collection. In 1930 Rollins College acquired the personal library of Henry Nehrling, the noted horticulturist and ornithologist. It includes more than 1,700 books, manuscripts, periodicals, pamphlets, and other records in English and German.

Jesse B. Rittenhouse Collection of Poetry. This collection of more than 1,200 volumes includes many works of such poets as Byron, Shelly, and Poe.

Walt Whitman Collection. The collection consists of 1,300 cataloged books of scholarly nature; a complete file of the *Conservator* magazine, bound volumes of the *Democratic Review,* the *Galaxy Magazine, The Critic, Nation,* and the *American Magazine,* all of which contain writings by Whitman; 141 issues of the *Walt Whitman Fellowship Papers;* 28 editions of *Leaves of Grass,* including the rare first issue of the first edition; many critical writings about Whitman. The collection was begun in 1933 when William Sloane Kennedy, the last of Walt Whitman's circle of close personal friends, willed a small Whitman collection of 22 volumes and 94 miscellaneous items of Whitmaniana to Rollins College with an endowment fund. This fund has made possible many additions to the collection.

332
St. John Vianney College Seminary
Maytag Memorial Library
2900 S.W. 87th Avenue
Miami, Florida 33165

Telephone. (305) 223-4561

Institutional Description. The privately supported college offers programs for men preparing to train for the Roman Catholic priesthood. It grants associate and baccalaureate degrees. Enrollment: 65.

Library Administration. Diane Maguire, Librarian.

Library General Holdings. 46,000 volumes; 200 current periodical subscriptions.

Special Collections

The library has one of the largest collections in the South of philosophy works in Spanish and English. Other special collections include the **Antiphonary of Gregorian Chant,** a collection of Spanish histories and ecclesiastical and civil law books; and a collection of the personal papers of Archbishop Coleman F. Carroll.

333
St. Johns River Community College
B.C. Pearce Learning Resources Center
5001 St. Johns Avenue
Palatka, Florida 32077

Telephone. (904) 328-1571

Institutional Description. The two-year college was established as a public institution in 1958 to serve the counties of Clay, Putnam, and St. Johns. Enrollment: 1,020.

Library Administration. Carmen M. Cummings, Director of Library Services.

Library General Holdings. 41,000 volumes; 6,200 bound periodicals; 70,000 government documents; 1,200 recordings; 200 filmstrips; 250 microfilm reels.

Special Collections

The library maintains a **Florida Collection.**

334
St. Leo College
Daniel A. Cannon Memorial Library
P.O. Box 2187
St. Leo, Florida 33574

Telephone. (904) 588-8200

Institutional Description. The privately supported liberal arts and teachers college is affiliated with the Roman Catholic Church. Enrollment: 4,288.

Library Administration. Sister Dorothy Neuhofer, O.S.B., Director.

Library General Holdings. 90,000 volumes; 650 current periodical subscriptions; 25,000 microforms.

Special Collections

The library has a collection on the history of the Catholic Church in Florida.

335
St. Petersburg Junior College
Michael M. Bennett Library
P.O. Box 13489
St. Petersburg, Florida 33733

Telephone. (813) 546-0021

Institutional Description. The college was founded in 1927 as a private, nonprofit institution. The college changed from private to public status in 1948. Enrollment: 11,120.

Library Administration. Glenn R. Dallman, Director, Library Services.

Library General Holdings. 194,000 volumes; 47,000 non-print items.

Special Collections

The Bennett Library has a **Children's Collection** of 273 volumes and a **Florida Collection** of 1,341 volumes.

336
St. Thomas University
University Library
16400 N.W. 32nd Avenue
Miami, Florida 33054

Telephone. (305) 625-6000

Institutional Description. The privatley supported liberal arts university is administered by the Augustinian Community of the Roman Catholic Church. Enrollment: 2,918.

Library Administration. Margaret Elliston, Director.

Library General Holdings. 125,000 volumes; 650 periodicals.

Special Collections

In addition to the liberal arts, the the University offers other areas of specialization, such as business, education, tourism, hospitality management and international enterprise, sports administration, and human resources. It has recently developed an Institute for Pastoral Ministries to help develop leadership skills for the Catholic Church of America. The collections of the library support these programs.

337
Southeastern College of the Assemblies of God
Steelman Media Center
1000 Longfellow Boulevard
Lakeland, FL 33801

Telephone. (813) 665-4407

Institutional Description. This private Bible college of the Assemblies of God was founded in 1935 and occupied a new campus in 1952. Enrollment: 1,013.

Library Administration. Linda L. Jones, Library Director; Noelia M. Delgado, Special Collections Librarian.

Library General Holdings. 67,000 volumes; 550 periodicals; 4 newspaper subscriptions; 1,359 microfiche; 458 miniature music scores; 922 sound recordings; 22,000 glass slides.

Special Collections

Roe Messner Church Builders Alcove. The collection includes books and blueprints on church architecture.

Curriculum Laboratory. Includes over 5,000 volumes of children's materials; 341 texts including some rare textbooks; religious and church school curricula material designed for private schools and Sunday schools.

338
Stetson University
duPont-Ball Library
North Boulevard
P.O. Box 8358
DeLand, Florida 32720

Telephone. (904) 734-4121

Institutional Description. The privately supported university is affiliated with the Southern Baptist Convention. It was founded in 1883 as the DeLand Academy. Enrollment: 2,612.

Library Administration. Sims D. Kline, Director.

Library General Holdings. 254,265 volumes; 1,051 current periodical subscriptions; 255,000 government documents; 105,000 microforms; 2,600 audiovisual materials.

Special Collections

The library was the first Florida depository for federal government documents. Special collections include the **Florida Baptist Archives** and the **Southern Baptist Archives.**

339
Tampa College
College Library
3319 West Hillsborough Avenue
Tampa, Florida 33614

Telephone. (813) 879-6000

Institutional Description. The privately supported senior college of business was founded in 1890. Enrollment: 2,616.

Library Administration. Madeleine M. Lock, Director.

Library General Holdings. 8,000 volumes; 85 current periodical subscriptions.

Special Collections

The library's collections includes resources in business, economics, computer science, and medical technology.

340
University of Central Florida
Library
P.O. Box 25000
Orlando, Florida 32816

Telephone. (407) 275-2564

Institutional Description. The publicly supported institution is a member of the State University System of Florida. Enrollment: 13,907.

Library Administration. Anne Marie Allison, Library Director; Norbert St. Clair, Special Collections Librarian.

Library General Holdings. 500,000 volumes; 4,500 journal, newspaper, and other serial subscriptions; 400,000 microfiche; 1,700 maps; 3,000 audiovisual tapes.

Special Collections

Bryant West Indies Collection. This is a scholarly special private collection on deposit to the library by Mr. William J. Bryant. It contains books, serials, periodicals, and original handicrafts, artifacts, and paintings from the West Indies and the Caribbean area, including Florida, which pertain to the history, geography, economic and social life of the area. It also includes books on language and literature and some pure sciences of the West Indies. There is a special focus on Haitian art. The collection, consisting of about 2,000 titles and 2,200 volumes, is dated from 1709 to the present.

Limited Editions. Includes first class, deluxe editions with beautiful and unusual bindings, typrographical excellence, and illustrations by noted illustrators. Each copy is numbered and some of the editions are limited to 100 copies or less. Most editions pertain to literature of the world. Philosophical works include the writings of Cicero, Ovidius, Plato, and others. In the field of fine arts is an outstanding 12-volumes work, *Oriental Ceramics,* and *Ansel Adams—Images, 1923-1974.* The collection includes about 200 titles and 400 volumes.

Local History Collection. Includes many books, documents, and photographs relating to central Florida.

Music Collection. At present, the collection is limited to musical scores, including more than 60 major operas by noted composers such as Berlioz, Leoncavallo, Mozart, Puccini, Strauss, Verdi, and Wagner. These works are mainly in the original language, many of them in two or three languages. The collection includes some church music, some in Latin by noted composers, such as Bach, Haydn, and Mozart. The nucleus of this collection was donated by Anne Roselle of Lakeland, Florida. She was previously on the faculty of Florida Southern College and a member of the Royal Hungarian Opera Company before World War II.

UCF Archives. The repository for official documents, publications, public records, and memorabilia of the University of Central Florida. It also houses publications by UCF faculty and staff, the UCF Press, and copies of all master's theses, graduate research reports, and dissertations. The history of the University from its beginnings in 1963 is preserved in the Archives.

Wagar Space Shot Collection. A collection of newspaper clippings which documents the space program and moon shots from 1956 to 1976.

Rare Book Collections

Rare Books Collection. Includes early imprints such as an Italian Bible dated 1546, first editions, and books on special subjects such as biography of Adolf Hitler, written in German, containing privately made photographs never published in any other form. There are books by distinguished authors, autographed and dedicated to the UCF Library, and books on special local subjects and history.

341
University of Florida Libraries
Gainesville, Florida 32611

Telephone. (904) 392-6547

Institutional Description. The publicly supported university traces its beginnings back to before 1845 when Florida joined the Union. It is a combined state university and land-grant college. Enrollment: 35,553.

Library Administration. Sidney E. Ives, University Librarian; Elizabeth Alexander, P.K. Yonge Librarian; Carla Kemp, University Archivist.

Library General Holdings. 1,174,736 volumes and pamphlets; 24,056 periodicals; 2,418,127 microforms; 165,156 audiovisual materials.

Special Collections

Braga Brothers Collection. This collection contains records related to the sugar industry in Cuba and U.S.-Cuban commercial relations from the 1870s through the early 1960s. Included in the collection are records from the Czarnikow-Rionda Company, the Francisco Sugar Company, the Manati Sugar Company, and the Cuba Cane Sugar Corporation. Of particular interest are the executive files of Manuel Rionda y Polledo, president of Czarnikow-Rionda from 1909 to 1943 and a participant in several international conferences and commissions intended to regulate the sugar market.

Isser and Rae Price Library of Judaica. This separately housed Price Library of Judaica contains approximately 42,500 printed volumes covering a wide range of topics within the field of Jewish studies. Founded in 1977, the collection is the largest repository of Judaica, Hebraica, and Yiddica in the southeastern United States. History, rabbinics, Judaism, and Hebrew language and literature are especially well represented. Twentieth-century imprints predominate and with few exceptions, the collection is available to researchers on interlibrary loan.

Isabel Briggs Myers Papers. The personal papers of Isabel Briggs Myers, developer of the Myers Briggs Type Indicator.

P.K. Yonge Library of Florida History. This Library of Florida History is the oldest and the most comprehensive collection of Florida history source materials in existence. Its catalog was published in 1977 by the G.K. Hall Company of Boston. Although the P.K. Yonge Library is a scholarly research collection dedicated to fostering the writing of accurate Florida history, many of the thousands of patrons it serves each year are university students or members of the general public. Currently, the library holds approximately 3,000 boxes of major and miscellaneous manuscripts, 22,000 printed works and typescripts, and 2,300 maps. Of special importance are more than 5,000 reels of microfilm of historic Florida newspapers from 1821 to the present; the manuscript papers of dozens of political leaders; photocopies and microfilm of British Florida documents from the Public Record Office; and microfilm and photostatic copies of over two million pages of Spanish Florida documents from the Archivo General de Indias and other archives.

University Archives. This is the official repository for all university records and imprints of permanent and historical value. Its mission encompasses collection of private materials documenting the university community. The archival collection begins in the late 1880s with records of the University of Florida's predecessor institutions. Other types of holdings include university documents, theses and dissertations, and faculty publications.

Rare Book Collections

Rare Books and Manuscript Collections. The most important collections, of New England authors, were acquired in 1980 when President Robert Marston led a successful fund drive to buy the great Parkman Dexter Howe Library. Comprising authors from the eighteenth through the twentieth century, it includes manuscripts and corrected proofs, newspaper and magazine printings, ephemera, first book and revised printings, and collected works. In fulfillment of the sales contract, the University is publishing descriptions of the collections by nationally known bibliographers, printed at the Stinehour Press in Vermont. The Howe Library Catalogues now in print are: *New England History and Literature to 1800; Henry David Thoreau; Ralph Waldo Emerson; Henry Wadsworth Longfellow; Richard Henry Dana, Jr.; Sarah Orne Jewett; Emily Dickinson; William Cullen Bryant; Edwin Arlington Robinson;* and *John Greenleaf Whittier.* Holmes, Hawthorne, Melville, and Frost are forthcoming.

Author archives of Marjorie Kinnan Rawlings, Zora Neale Hurston, Lillian Smith, and John D. MacDonald include correspondence, holographs, and first editions. The Margaret Dreier Robins papers document her activities in the women's trade union movement; the Rochambeau papers, centered around Haiti and Santo Domingo, are important for the history of the Caribbean.

among other research archives are 10,000 pamphlet publications of theological controversy in nineteenth-century England and a large collection of twentieth-century American Black literature.

Standard strengths include English theology of the seventeenth and eighteenth centuries with emphasis on the evangelicals; Restoration drama, eighteenth-century English literature with special attention to landscape and architecture and the works of Laurence Sterne; writers of the Irish Renaissance; Greek and Latin classics; selected incunabula; natural history; modern British and American poetry; and a collection of modern fine printing by William Morris, Cobden-Sanderson, Eric Gill and others, with types and woodblocks from Joseph Ishill's Oriole Press and a unique gathering of original blocks cut by Alexander Anderson (1775-1870) for book illustration.

The Belknap Library contains scores and libretti of American operas, musicals, and popular songs; programmes and theatre bills; costume drawings; photographs and books detailing stage settings, costumes and lighting; theatre serials; and materials for the history of American stage and screen production.

342
University of Miami
Otto C. Richter Library
Coral Gables, Florida 33124

Telephone. (305) 284-2211

Institutional Description. The privately supported university was founded in 1925; it offers baccalaureate, professional, master's, and doctorate degrees. Enrollment: 12,748.

Library Administration. Frank D. Rodgers, Director of Libraries.

Library General Holdings. 1,552,910 volumes; 21,565 periodical subscriptions; 2,150,000 microforms; 20,000 audiovisual materials.

Special Collections

The Richter Library maintains special collections in marine science, Floridiana, and Caribbean and Latin American publications.

Morton Collectanea. This is a specialized reference and research department devoted to the acquisition, classification, and maintenance of data in the field of economic botany and economic zoology. Its resources include more than 200,000 items of data collated in approximately 30,000 classified subject-files of plant and animal species and of recognized foods and food adjuncts from the arctic and antarctic to the tropical.

Ornithology. Housed in the Department of Biology, the 15,000 specimens comprising these collections provide a diversified basis for instruction and research. The collections are in particular representative of the avifaunas of the southeastern United States, of Central America, sections of South America, and of East Africa, including the Robert E. Maytag Collections from the Lake Rudolf area of Kenya.

343
University of North Florida
Thomas G. Carpenter Library
P.O. Box 17605
Jacksonville, Florida 32216

Telephone. (904) 646-2616

Institutional Description. The publicly supported institution offers upper-division studies only. It was founded in 1965. Enrollment: 6,582.

Library Administration. Andrew Farkas, Librarian; Eileen Brady, Special Collections Librarian; Kathleen Cohen, Head of Reference.

Library General Holdings. 318,035 bound volumes; 2,046 periodical subscriptions; 113,064 government documents; 646,435 microfiche; 18,873 microfilms; 6,310 audio discs; 353 filmloops; 544 kits; 20,256 slides; 5,120 maps.

Special Collections

The library maintains a **Curriculum Collection** (Media Resources Department); **Annual Report Collection,** and a collection of University of North Florida theses.

Local History. These collections include the Senator John E. Mathews Papers (state politician); Eartha M.M. White Papers (Black philanthropist); and the Arthur Sollee Papers (transportation engineer).

University Archives. The collection includes all administrative records of the University.

344
University of South Florida
University of South FLorida Library
Tampa, Florida 33620

Telephone. (813) 974-2731

Institutional Description. When the University of South Florida opened to a charter class of 2,000 freshmen in 1960 it became the first state university in the United States to be totally planned and initiated in this century. The first doctoral program began in 1968. Enrollment: 28,015.

Library Administration. Arthur L. Ketchersid, Director of Libraries; Mr. J. B. Dobkin, Special Collections/Rare Books Librarian; Paul Eugene Camp, Associate Librarian, Special Collections.

Library General Holdings. 1,025,738 volumes; 2,776,491 microform pieces; 12,958 serials; over 5,000 music scores.

Special Collections

The Special Collections Department contains major collections in the areas of nineteenth-century American literature (with emphasis on juvenile literature); twentieth-century American boys', girls', and anthropomorphic animal series books (the Harry K. Hudson Collection); nineteenth-century American school books; American toybooks; pre-1901 American almanacs; the works of English boys' book author George Alfred Henty; Florida History (with emphasis on the Tampa Bay region); dime novels and nickle libraries; Afro-American sheet music; Florida sheet music; nineteenth-century American songsters; Mosher Press books; and acting editions of nineteenth-century British and American plays.

The Department also houses the library's general rare books collection and the University archives. Additionally, the library houses extensive manuscript collections, most relating to its major book collections. Also present are extensive holdings of maps, photographs, nineteenth-century trade and greeting cards, postcards, and cigar industry advertising art and memorabilia.

345
University of Tampa
Merl Kelce Library
401 West Kennedy Boulevard
Tampa, Florida 33606

Telephone. (813) 253-3333

Institutional Description. The privately supported university was founded in 1931. It offers the baccalaureate and master's degrees. Enrollment: 1,745.

Library Administration. Lydia M. Acosta, Director.

Library General Holdings. 200,560 volumes; 1,700 periodical subscriptions; 52,300 microforms.

Special Collections

The special collections of the Merl Kelce Library include old and rare books, first editions, autographed editions, materials on Florida and the Southeast, the **Florida Military Collection,** and the University Archives. The **Stanley Kimball Collection** includes research and manuscripts for the unpublished works "Mr. Lincoln's Washington," "Mr. Davis' Richmond," and the completed work *The Mad Booths of Maryland.* The **William C. Cramer Collection** includes the papers of the Representative from Florida.

346
University of West Florida
John C. Pace Library
1100 University Parkway
Pensacola, Florida 32514

Telephone. (904) 474-2213

Institutional Description. The University is one of nine state universities in Florida. Enrollment: 6,172.

Library Administration. Dean DeBolt, Associate University Librarian/Special Collections.

Library General Holdings. 500,000 volumes; 700,000 microforms; 3,800 periodicals and newspapers; 1,000,000 special collection items.

Special Collections

The Special Collections Department acquires, preserves, and makes available materials concerning the ten-county region of West Florida, its history, development, and people. Collections include manuscript collections (1720s to the present), photographs, newspapers, microforms, books, and related materials. Emphasis is on the colonial Gulf Coast region from the Apalachicola River to New Orleans from the 16th century up to 1821, and the West Florida regions from Florida Territory to the present. Specialized collections include the Papers of the Panton, Leslie & Company, 1785-1875; the watercolors of George Washington Sully (1816-1890); the papers of Florida Governor Sidney F. Catts; and related collections. The University Archives are also housed.

Rare Book Collections

The Rare Book Collection emphasizes primary resources concerning the West Florida region from earliest settlement to the present, including related resources, such as *Gentleman's Quarterly,* 1731-1856. Other collections include the **Eudora Welty Collection,** the **Langston Hughes Collection,** the **H.L. Mencken Collection,** cookbooks and telephone directories of the West Florida region. Other materials in the division include local area genealogies, autographed editions, fine bindings, and a representative selection of editions from the world's small presses.

347
Valencia Community College
Learning Resources Center
P.O. Box 3028
Orlando, Florida 32802

Telephone. (305) 299-5000

Institutional Description. Valencia Community College was founded in 1967 as Valencia Junior College. The present name was adopted in 1971. Enrollment: 8,284.

Library Administration. Donna J. Carver, Librarian.

Library General Holdings. 61,000 volumes; 1,000 periodical subscriptions; 45,000 microforms; 3,600 audiovisual items.

Special Collections

The learning resources center has a special collection of 1,192 recordings for the handicapped.

348
Warner Southern College
Learning Resource Center
5301 U.S. Highway 27 S
Lake Wales, Florida 33853

Telephone. (813) 638-1426

Institutional Description. The privately supported Christian liberal arts college was founded in 1964. It is affiliated with the Church of God. Enrollment: 258.

Library Administration. Arthur F. Tetrick, Director.

Library General Holdings. 70,000 volumes; 350 current periodical subscriptions.

Special Collections

The **Church of God Historical Collection** contains materials relating to the denominational history of the Church of God.

Georgia

349
Abraham Baldwin Agricultural College
Baldwin Library
ABAC Station
Tifton, Georgia 31793

Telephone. (912) 386-3223

Institutional Description. Abraham Baldwin Agricultural College is a two-year, residential, coeducational institution. Located in south central Georgia, the school was established in 1908 and became part of the university system of Georgia in 1933. Enrollment: 1,752.

Library Administration. Mary Emma S. Henderson, College Librarian; Harriett E. Mayo, Special Collections Librarian; Brenda A. Sellers, Rare Books Librarian and Assistant Librarian for Readers' Services.

Library General Holdings. 54,821 book titles; 61,947 volumes; 532 current periodical titles; 2,327 bound periodicals; 5,296 units of microform; audiovisual materials: 36 films; 35 videotapes; 678 audiotapes; 512 multimedia kits; 248 graphic materials.

Special Collections

College Archives. Contains historical materials about the college, college publications, photographs, news clippings, and memorabilia.

Rare Book Collections

Georgiana Collection. Contains materials related to Georgia including county histories, biographies, books by and about Georgians, and books about Georgia.

350
Agnes Scott College
McCain Library
Decatur, Georgia 30030

Telephone. (404) 371-6000

Institutional Description. The privately supported liberal arts college for women was founded in 1889. The enrollment is kept small purposely to insure academic excellence. Enrollment: 510.

Library Administration. Judith Bourgeois Jensen, Librarian.

Library General Holdings. 180,00 volumes; 780 current periodical subscriptions; 20,000 microforms.

Special Collections

Special collections in the library include the original manuscripts and papers of Catherine Marshall; the writings by Walter Posey on the development of religion on the American frontier; and the **Robert Frost Collection** which includes manuscripts, correspondence, personal papers, and autographed first editions.

351
Albany Junior College
Library-Learning Resources Center
2400 Gillionville Road
Albany, Georgia 31707

Telephone. (912) 439-4600

Institutional Description. The two-year college is a public institution established in 1963. The present campus was occupied in 1966. Enrollment: 1,732.

Library Administration. Edward L. Philbin, Director.

Library General Holdings. 67,000 volumes; 800 periodical and 20 newspaper subscriptions; 4,500 microfilm reels.

Special Collections

The library has the special collection of the **American Enterprise Institute.** Other collections in a variety of formats are being developed, including music scores, recordings, and government publications.

352
Albany State College
Margaret Rood Hazard Library
504 College Drive
Albany, Georgia 31705

Telephone. (912) 439-4600

Institutional Description. The publicly supported (state) liberal arts and professional college was founded in 1903. It is a member of the Georgia State University System. Enrollment: 1,911.

Library Administration. Barbara W. Carroll, Interim Head Librarian.

Library General Holdings. 150,000 volumes; 600 periodical titles; 400 serial titles; 380,473 microforms.

Special Collections

Special collections include the **William Reese Medical Collection,** and books written by Dr. Joseph Winthrop Holley, founder and former president of the College. Also maintained are collections on Black literature and French literature.

353
Andrew College
Pitts Library
413 College Street
Cuthbert, Georgia 31740

Telephone. (912) 732-2171

Institutional Description. Andrew College is a two-year United Methodist liberal arts college with a university-parallel curriculum. The college was chartered in 1854. Enrollment: 245.

Library Administration. Richard W. Cruce, Director of Library Services.

Library General Holdings. 35,000 volumes; 100 periodical and 11 newspaper subscriptions.

Special Collections

Two special collections are maintained by Pitts Library—the **Methodist and Religious History Collection** and the **Genealogy and Southern History Collection.**

354
Armstrong State College
Lane Library
11935 Abercorn Street
Savannah, Georgia 31419

Telephone. (912) 927-5332

Institutional Description. Armstrong State College, a publicly supported institution, was founded in 1935 as a junior college. It began offering a four-year program and moved to a new campus in 1965. Enrollment: 2,745.

Library Administration. Jack Dennis, College Librarian; Laurie McClellan, Reference/Special Collections Librarian.

Library General Holdings. 145,108 books; 830 periodical subscriptions; 78,802 microfiche and film units.

Special Collections

The Minis Room in Lane Library houses a special collection of Georgia and Savannah history and authors, including a complete set of Conrad Aiken's publications in first editions. The history of Savannah, coastal Georgia, and colonial Georgia are emphasized.

355
Atlanta Christian College
James A. Burns Memorial Library
2605 Ben Hill Road
East Point, Georgia 30344

Telephone. (404) 761-8861

Institutional Description. The privately supported professional Bible college is affiliated with the Churches of Christ. It grants baccalaureate degrees. Enrollment: 152.

Library Administration. Rachel Howard, Librarian.

Library General Holdings. 43,000 volumes; 150 current periodical subscriptions; 12,000 microforms.

Special Collections

The library maintains the **James A. Burns Collection** of personal papers and other materials; a collection of works by alumni of the College; and the microform Library of American Civilization.

356
Atlanta College of Art
Atlanta College of Art Library
1280 Peachtree Street NE
Atlanta, Georgia 30309

Telephone. (404) 898-1166

Institutional Description. The private, coeducational art college was founded in 1928 as the educational institution of the Atlanta Art Alliance. Enrollment: 329.

Library Administration. Terry L. Fraver, Head Librarian.

Library General Holdings. 22,000 books and exhibition catalogs pertaining to the history, development, and technique of the visual arts.

Special Collections

The contemporary art scene is the focus of the library's collection which includes over 230 current periodical subscriptions on the fine arts, architecture, design, photograph, crafts, video, film, and computer graphics. Art history and studio courses are supported by the library's extensive audiovisual collection. Currently the library houses over 50,000 slides, 950 photographic reproductions, and 450 sound recordings. The library's extensive artists' book collection brings together a uniquely contemporary art genre. Since the 1960s, the library has collected over 1,000 rare and representative pieces by book artists from around the world.

357
Atlanta University
Atlanta University Center Robert W. Woodruff Library
111 James P. Brawley Drive, S.W.
Atlanta, Georgia 30314

Telephone. (404) 522-8980

Institutional Description. The Atlanta University Center is a consortium of six institutions of higher education in the city of Atlanta: two graduate schools (Atlanta University, Interdenominational Theological Center) and four undergraduate colleges (Clark College, Morehouse College, Morris Brown College, Spelman College).

The privately supported Atlanta University, at 223 James P. Brawley Drive, S.W., was founded in 1869, offering a liberal arts, Christian education. In 1930, undergraduate courses were discontinued in favor of graduate programs only, in connection with its affiliation with other schools in the consortium. It now grants master's and doctorate degrees. Enrollment: 623.

Library Administration. Guy C. Craft, Atlanta University Center Librarian; Minnie H. Clayton, Head, Division of Archives and Special Collections.

Library General Holdings. The Atlanta University Center Robert W. Woodruff Library was achieved in 1982 by the merger of the libraries of the six participating institutions in a new facility on a 3.66-acre site. The library building covers an area equal to two city blocks. *See* **Atlanta University Center, Inc.**

358
Atlanta University Center, Inc.
Robert W. Woodruff Library
111 James P. Brawley Drive, S.W.
Atlanta, Georgia 30314

Telephone. (404) 522-8980

Institutional Description. Atlanta University Center is a consortium of four private undergraduate colleges: Clark, Morehouse, Morris Brown, and Spelman; a graduate school, Atlanta University; and a theological school, the Interdenominational Theological Center, consisting of seven seminaries. Each school is autonomous, but they are located on adjoining campuses in Atlanta and they share many academic programs and facilities, including the Robert W. Woodruff Library.

Library Administration. Guy C. Craft, Librarian; Minnie H. Clayton, Head, Division of Archives and Special Collections.

Library General Holdings. 104,264 bound volumes; 45,923 bound periodicals; 1,314 periodical subscriptions; 232,386 microforms; 104,264 government documents; 13,038 Atlanta University Center theses/dissertations. The library's holdings include those of participating institutions of the Atlanta University Center (see above).

Special Collections

Association of Southern Women for the Prevention of Lynching Collection. Original papers covering the period 1930-1943.

Atlanta University Archives. Dates from 1865, including charter, administrative, faculty, alumni, and student papers/publications.

Clarence A. Bacote Collection. Correspondence, office, and professorial files of the Atlanta University history professor; covers the 1930s-1940s.

John Brown Collection. Letters and papers of John Brown, American abolitionist (1814-1859).

Clark College Archives. Dates from 1869; administrative, departmental, faculty, alumni, and student papers/publications.

Thomas Clarkson Collection. Items relating to the English abolitionist (1785-1871).

Commission on Interracial Cooperation Collection. Includes the papers created and collected by the organization (founded to reduce racial tensions during post-World I in the South), 1929-1943.

Countee Cullen/Harold Jackman Memorial Collection of Literary Manuscripts. Manuscripts and memorabilia of Afro-Americans in writing and the performing arts, mainly 1930-1970.

Hoyt W. Fuller Memorial Collection. Correspondence, manuscripts, office research files, personal library of books; includes memorabilia and photographs; created and collected during Fuller's career as college and university professor, editor of *Negro Digest* and *Black World;* founder, editor, publisher of *First World* (international journal of Black thought) and world lecturer/traveler.

John and Lugenia Burns Hope Papers. A collection of official and personal correspondence, manuscripts, photographs, memorabilia, and printed materials documenting the life and career of the couple as President of Morehouse College, President of Atlanta University; and wife and founder of The Neighborhood Union of Atlanta, Georgia (microfilm).

Interdenominational Theological Center Archives Collection. Includes administrative, faculty, student, and alumni papers created and collected by the ITC and its component seminaries including Morehouse School of Religion (Baptist); Gammon Theological Seminary (Methodist); Turner Theological Seminary (African Methodist Episcopal); Phillips School of Theology (Colored/Christian Methodist Church); Johnson C. Smith Seminary, Inc. (Presbyterian); and Charles H. Mason Theological Seminary (Church of God in Christ); also includes these denominational church memorabilia, photographs, and publications.

Maud Cuney Hare Music Collection. A collection formerly belonging to Hare and consisting of sheet music manuscripts and related materials of Afro-American music and musicians.

Charles Eric Lincoln Collection. Personal and career

materials including correspondence, manuscripts, photographs, pamphlets, and other related materials created as a writer, lecturer, minister, professor, world traveler, and authority on Black Muslims and Afro-American religion.

Morehouse College Archives. Administrative, departmental, faculty, alumni, student papers/publications and memorabilia.

Morris Brown College Archives. Administrative, departmental, faculty, alumni, student papers/publications and memorabilia.

Neighborhood Union Collection. Correspondence, publications, other printed materials and memorabilia tracing the founding and activities of this early private social welfare agency in Atlanta, organized by Negroes for assistance to Negroes revealing much about its founder Lugenia Burns Hope.

Henry P. Slaughter Collection. Manuscripts and related materials of the early history of the Negro in the U.S.

Southern Conference for Human Welfare Collection. Mainly official files of SCHW including correspondence, drafts of speeches, publications and related printed materials and personal files of Clark Foreman as President and office holder of the organization from its inception.

Southern Education Foundation Archives. Records and papers (1910-1970) of SEF and its component organizations from its inception in 1937 including correspondence, studies, reports, minutes, financial records, projects, project reports, and learned publications in education.

Southern Regional Council Archives. Successor organization to the Commission on Interracial Cooperation working toward equality of Afro-Americans; consists of correspondence, internal records, reports, project files, publications, and related materials.

Spelman College Archives. Includes materials initially collected by librarians at Atlanta University, Trevor Arnett Library including some presidents' annual reports, treasurers' reports, catalogs, yearbooks, memorabilia; administrative, departmental, faculty, student and alumni publications; and related materials.

Anna Chittenden Thayer/Abraham Lincoln Exhibit Collection. A collection of over 300 items of U.S. President Abraham Lincoln memorabilia and artifacts collected and donated to Atlanta University in 1953 by Mrs. Anna Chittenden Thayer.

George Alexander Towns Collection. Correspondence, literary works, and notes of Towns as a graduate of Atlanta University and Harvard University, faculty member of Atlanta University and Fort Valley State College; collection is strong in correspondence to him from various literary associates.

359
Augusta College
Reese Library
Walton Way
Augusta, Georgia 30901

Telephone. (404) 737-1744

Institutional Description. Augusta College is a state supported, four-year arts and sciences college, and is part of the University System of Georgia. It offers bachelor and master's degrees. Enrollment: 3,388.

Library Administration. A. Ray Rowland, College Librarian; D. Charlynn Clayton, Assistant Librarian and Special Collections Librarian.

Library General Holdings. 430,000 bound volumes; 1,024,000 microforms; 233,000 government documents; 2,500 periodicals and other serials.

Special Collections

The Special Collections Department houses many documents and monographs related to Augusta and Richmond County, Georgia.

360
Bainbridge Junior College
Library
Highway 84 East
P.O. Box 953
Bainbridge, Georgia 31717

Telephone. (404) 246-7642

Institutional Description. The two-year public college was created in 1970. Classes began in 1973. Enrollment: 522.

Library Administration. Edwin L. Holton, Library Director.

Library General Holdings. 28,000 volumes; 190 periodical subscriptions.

Special Collections

Approximately 75,000 manuscripts make up the archives section of the library. Former Georgia Governor S. Marvin Griffin's papers are a valuable addition to this collection. The papers of Colonel John E. Donalson, founder of Donalsonville and Faceville and a former mayor of Bainbridge, are also included.

361
Brenau College
Library
One Centennial Circle
Gainesville, Georgia 30501

Telephone. (404) 534-6299

Institutional Description. The privately supported lib-

eral arts college was founded in 1878. It offers programs in liberal arts, fine arts, nursing, and teacher education. Enrollment: 1,745.

Library Administration. Caroline E. Alday, Director.

Library General Holdings. 60,000 volumes; 400 current periodical subscriptions.

Special Collections

Special collections include the **James Quillian Classical Recording Collection** of 2,500 recordings; the **Tom Watson Collection** of historical books; and an archival and rare books collection. The Nursing Library contains approximately 5,000 volumes.

362
Brunswick Junior College
Clara Wood Gould Memorial Library
Alabama at Fourth Street
Brunswick, Georgia 31523

Telephone. (912) 264-7235

Institutional Description. Brunswick Junior College was founded by the regents of the University System of Georgia in 1961. Enrollment: 1,502.

Library Administration. Allen Spivey, Head Librarian.

Library General Holdings. 48,000 volumes; 28,000 units of microfilm and microfiche.

Special Collections

The library maintains the **Coastal Georgia Collection.**

363
Clark College
Atlanta University Center Robert W. Woodruff Library
111 James P. Brawley Drive, S.W.
Atlanta, Georgia 30314

Telephone. (404) 522-8980

Institutional Description. The Atlanta University Center is a consortium of six institutions of higher education in the city of Atlanta: two graduate schools (Atlanta University, Interdenominational Theological Center) and four undergraduate colleges (Clark College, Morehouse College, Morris Brown College, Spelman College).

Clark College, at 240 Chestnut Street, S.W., is a privately supported liberal arts college affiliated with the United Methodist Church. It was founded in 1869 by the Freedmen's Aid Society of the Methodist Church. Enrollment: 1,814.

Library Administration. Guy C. Craft, Atlanta University Center Librarian; Minnie H. Clayton, Head, Division of Archives and Special Collections.

Library General Holdings. The Atlanta University Center Robert W. Woodruff Library was achieved in 1982 by the merger of the libraries of the six participating institutions in a new facility on a 3.66-acre site. The library building covers an area equal to two city blocks. *See* **Atlanta University Center, Inc.**

364
Columbia Theological Seminary
John Bulow Campbell Library
701 Columbia Drive, South
Decatur, Georgia 30031

Telephone. (404) 378-8821

Institutional Description. The privately supported theological seminary is affiliated with the Presbyterian Church (U.S.A.). It offers graduate-level programs only. Enrollment: 261.

Library Administration. James A. Overbeck, Librarian.

Library General Holdings. 87,000 books.

Special Collections

The collection of the library is strong in Biblical studies, Biblical archaeology, patristics, the Reformation, pastoral counseling, and Presbyterianism. Reformation sources include the Calvin and Melanchthon sections of the *Corpus Reformatorum* and the Weimar edition of Luther.

365
Columbus College
Simon Schwab Memorial Library
Columbus, Georgia 31993

Telephone. (404) 568-2042

Institutional Description. Columbus College was founded as a junior college, the result of a community endeavor in 1958. The College was approved as a senior liberal arts college in 1966 and operates as a publicy controlled institution. Enrollment: 3,696.

Library Administration. Merryll S. Penson, College Librarian; Craig Lloyd, Archivist.

Library General Holdings. 220,000 bound volumes; 1,400 periodical/newspaper subscriptions; 166,000 government documents; 475,000 microforms; 1,000 films; 450 videotapes; 5,500 audiocassettes; 9,900 slides/graphics; 970 kits.

Special Collections

The Library's circulating collection contains three specialized collections: curriculum materials (700 volumes) and numerous audiovisual items; a children's literature collection of over 3,000 volumes, most published after 1960; approximately 2,900 musical scores (classical/

semi-classical).

Columbus College Archives. Contains material related to the history of the College. Materials include yearbooks, catalogs, committee minutes, and student papers.

Chattahoochee Valley Historical Collections. Material includes manuscripts and books relating to the history of Columbus and the surrounding area; papers of Absalom H. Chappell (1801-1878), Alva C. Smith (1883-1965), and former Congressman Jack T. Brinkley. There is also a photograph file of over 1,500 pictures and a large collection of local newspapers.

366
Dalton College
Library Resource Center
213 North College Drive
Dalton, Georgia 30720

Telephone. (404) 272-4527

Institutional Description. The publicly supported junior college was chartered in 1963 and is a unit of the University System of Georgia. Enrollment: 1,371.

Library Administration. Marilyn S. Lary, College Librarian and Director.

Library General Holdings. 82,000 volumes; 1,500 periodicals; government document depository.

Special Collections

The Library Resource Center maintains a small special collection of materials, primarily books, on Georgia authors.

367
Emmanuel College and School of Christian Ministry
Shaw-Leslie Learning Resources Center
P.O. Box 128
Franklin Springs, Georgia 30639

Telephone. (404) 245-7226

Institutional Description. The privately supported junior and professional college was founded in 1919. Affiliated with the Pentecostal Holiness Church, it grants associate and baccalaureate degrees. Enrollment: 346.

Library Administration. Rachel Howard, Librarian.

Library General Holdings. 32,000 volumes; 220 periodical subscriptions; 4,000 microforms.

Special Collections

The library supports the School of Christian Ministry with resources in Biblical studies and the International Pentecostal Holiness Church.

368
Emmanuel County Junior College
Library
237 Thigpen Drive
Swainsboro, Georgia 30401

Telephone. (912) 237-7831

Institutional Description. The college was founded in 1973 by the Regents of the University System of Georgia. The present campus was occupied in 1974. Enrollment: 361.

Library Administration. James E. Dorsey, Librarian.

Library General Holdings. 37,000 volumes; 400 periodical and 40 newspaper subscriptions.

Special Collections

The library has a collection of manuscripts on local and regional history.

369
Emory University
University Libraries
1380 South Oxford Road, N.E.
Atlanta, Georgia 30322

Telephone. (404) 727-6123

Institutional Description. The privately supported university is affiliated with the United Methodist Church. Enrollment: 7,838.

Library Administration. Herbert F. Johnson, Director.

Library General Holdings. 1,700,000 volumes; 17,000 periodical and serial subscriptions; 1,143,000 microforms; 30,000 reels of microfilm; 3,896 linear feet of manuscripts.

Special Collections

The Special Collections Department of the Robert W. Woodruff Library houses rare books, university archives, manuscripts, and several notable collections, including English literature of the eighteenth and nineteenth centuries; English and French history; the history, culture, and art of the Low Countries; the Irish Literary Renaissance; and various aspects of Atlanta and Georgia history, including business, politics, the women's movement, and the Civil War.

The Candler Library has a collection of over 35,000 volumes which consists primarily of library and information science books and journals. The Pitts Theology Library contains over 385,000 volumes with extensive material on Southern Methodist history, Wesleyana, the Reformation, and the Third World. Included within the Pitts Library is the acclaimed Hartford Seminary Collection.

370
Fort Valley State College
Henry A. Hunt Memorial Library and Learning Resource Center
805 State College Drive
Fort Valley, Georgia 31030

Telephone. (912) 825-6342

Institutional Description. The publicly supported college was founded in 1895; its first four-year college class graduated in 1941. Enrollment: 2,127.

Library Administration. Carota R. Taylor, Library Director.

Library General Holdings. 181,789 bound volumes; 1,180 current periodicals; 50 newspaper subscriptions; 176,015 microforms; 10,500 curriculum materials; 5,338 government documents (separate collection).

Special Collections

The Library houses the Fort Valley State College Archives.

371
Georgia College
Ina Dillard Russell Library
Milledgeville, Georgia 31061

Telephone. (912) 453-5573

Institutional Description. The publicly supported liberal arts college granted its first degree in 1921; a graduate program was initiated in 1958. Enrollment: 3,552.

Library Administration. Janice C. Fennell, College Librarian; Nancy Davis Bray, Special Collections Associate.

Library General Holdings. 141,703 bound volumes; 1,120 current subscriptions; 384,004 microforms; 60,447 other materials.

Special Collections

Flannery O'Connor Collection. In addition to manuscripts, the collection contains O'Connor's personal library of over 700 books and journals.

James C. Bonner Collection. A primary source collection for nineteenth century Georgia; includes letters, legal documents, business documents, and agriculture.

U. Erwin Sibley Collection. Presents an overview of the middle Georgia area during the period 1900-1978. Includes personal and legal correspondence of Mr. Sibley.

372
Georgia Institute of Technology
Price-Gilbert Memorial Library
225 North Avenue, N.W.
Atlanta, Georgia 30332

Telephone. (404) 894-2000

Institutional Description. The publicly supported state technological institute was founded in 1885. It grants baccalaureate, master's, and doctorate degrees. Enrollment: 10,609.

Library Administration. Miriam Drake, Director.

Library General Holdings. 2,096,000 volumes; 28,557 current serials and periodicals; 2,007,000 microtexts; 545,-22 government documents; 137,415 maps.

Special Collections

The library's collection includes scientific, engineering, and management materials, as well as the largest collections of patents in the Southeast. The library acquires research reports from the National Technical Information Service, the U.S. Department of Energy, and the National Aeronautics and Space Administration. It is a depository for publications issued by the U.S. Defense Mapping Agency, Topographic and Aerospace Centers, U.S. Geological Survey, and the U.S. National Ocean Survey.

373
Georgia Southern College
Zach S. Henderson Library
Landrum Box 8074
Statesboro, Georgia 30460

Telephone. (912) 681-5115

Institutional Description. The publicly supported state college was established in 1906 as one of ten district agricultural and mechanical schools. Enrollment: 6,834.

Library Administration. Julius Ariail, Director of Libraries; Edna Earle G. Brown, Associate Director of Libraries.

Library General Holdings. 388,511 bound volumes; 383,187 government documents; 22,199 microform units; 593,872 microfiche units; 10,850 other microform units; 2,756 graphic units; 4,940 audio units; 471 film units; 355 video units; 648 multimedia kits; 65 machine-readable units; 459 linear feet of manuscript/archival collection; 3,316 current periodical titles.

Special Collections

The Special Collections section of the Zach S. Henderson Library contains rare editions, letters written by Margaret Mitchell, some Civil War era letters from both sides of the conflict, and tax records from Bulloch, Effingham, and Liberty counties. It also houses the papers of Congressmen Ronald "Bo" Ginn and Billy Evans, Lt. Governor Peter Zack Geer, Under Secretary of the Treasury Bette Anderson, and some of the letters, films, and memorabilia of Commander William M. Rigdon.

374
Georgia Southwestern College
James Earl Carter Library
Glessner Street
Americus, Georgia 31709

Telephone. (912) 928-1279

Institutional Description. The publicly supported (state) liberal arts college was founded in 1906 as as agricultural and mechanical school. It is a member of the Georgia State University System. Enrollment: 2,268.

Library Administration. Gwendolyn Creswell, Acting Director.

Library General Holdings. 143,000 volumes; 825 current periodical subscriptions; 148,000 government documents; 163,000 microforms.

Special Collections

Library holdings are carefully selected and designed to serve not only the varied needs of undergraduate students, but also the special needs of graduate students engaged in research. An emphasis is on the the field of education including early childhood education, middle grades education, reading, special education, and secondary education.

375
Georgia State University
William Russell Pullen Library
University Plaza
Atlanta, Georgia 30303

Telephone. (404) 658-2000

Institutional Description. The publicly supported state university was founded in 1913 with a specialty in business. It now offers associate, baccalaureate, master's, and doctorate degrees in many diverse fields. Enrollment: 18,372.

Library Administration. Ralph E. Russell, University Librarian; Leslie Hough, Special Collections Librarian; Laurel Bowen, Rare Books Librarian.

Library General Holdings. 1,000,000 volumes; 6,000 periodical subscriptions; 600,000 microforms.

Special Collections

The Special Collections Department of the library houses the **Johnny Mercer Collection,** begun with a gift by Mrs. Johnny Mercer in 1981, containing primary source material for research into the life and work of the late Johnny Mercer. The **Southern Labor Archives** is a collection of records of unions and professional organizations and personal papers, totaling more than 500 linear feet of shelf space in more than 100 record groups describing the development of organizations of workers in the South. The **University Archives** includes materials of importance to the history of the University. The **Georgia Government Documentation Project** collects manuscripts, especially oral history, relating to the history and government of Georgia.

Rare Book Collections

The **Rare Book Collection** contains many rare items and includes those related to labor and popular music. The library also as a photograph collection, also related to labor and popular music as well as the South.

376
The Interdenominational Theological Center
Atlanta University Center Robert W. Woodruff Library
111 James P. Brawley Drive, S.W.
Atlanta, Georgia 30314

Telephone. (404) 522-8980

Institutional Description. The Atlanta University Center is a consortium of six institutions of higher education in the city of Atlanta: two graduate schools (Atlanta University, Interdenominational Theological Center) and four undergraduate colleges (Clark College, Morehouse College, Morris Brown College, Spelman College).

The Interdenominational Theological Center, 671 Beckwith Street, S.W., was created in 1958 and is composed of six member seminaries: Gammon Theological Seminary (United Methodist), Charles H. Mason Theological Seminary (Church of God in Christ), Morehouse School of Religion (Baptist), Phillips School of Theology (Christian Methodist Episcopal), Johnson C. Smith Theological Seminary (Presbyterian Church U.S.A.), Turner Theological Seminary (African Methodist Episcopal). It offers graduate-level programs only. Enrollment: 293.

Library Administration. Guy C. Craft, University Center Librarian; Minnie H. Clayton, Head, Division of Archives and Special Collections.

Library General Holdings. The Atlanta University Center Robert W. Woodruff Library was achieved in 1982 by the merger of the libraries of the six participating institutions in a new facility on a 3.66-acre site. The library building covers an area equal to two city blocks. *See* **Atlanta University Center, Inc.**

377
Kennesaw College
College Library
P.O. Box 444
Marietta, Georgia 30061

Telephone. (404) 429-2700

Institutional Description. The publicly supported (state) liberal arts college was founded in 1963. It is a member of the Georgia State University System. Enrollment: 5,656.

Library Administration. Robert J. Greene, Librarian.

Library General Holdings. 243,000 volumes; 1,350 periodicals; 386,000 microforms.

Special Collections

Serving as a federal depository for the Seventh District, the library has more than 58,000 government documents and publications on file. A large art galley features periodic exhibits by visiting and faculty artists, and a special collection room houses the rare book collection.

378
LaGrange College
William and Evelyn Banks Library
601 Broad Street
LaGrange, Georgia 30240

Telephone. (404) 882-2911

Institutional Description. The privately supported liberal arts college was founded in 1831 as the LaGrange Female Academy. It became coeducational in 1953. LaGrange College is affiliated with the United Methodist Church. Enrollment: 864.

Library Administration. Frank R. Lewis, Librarian.

Library General Holdings. 86,000 volumes; 475 current periodical subscriptions.

Special Collections

The Irene W. Melson Room houses many first editions, as well as the **Lafayette Collection** of manuscripts, papers, and pamphlets on the life of Marquis de Lafayette. Also include are the **Florence Grogan Collection** of papers and first editions of outstanding publications of LaGrange College alumni and students. Other endowed special collections include the **Bascom Anthony Book Collection,** the **Hubert T. Quillian Book Collection,** and the **Bannister R. Bray Book Collection.**

379
Medical College of Georgia
Medical College of Georgia Library
Fifteenth Street
Augusta, Georgia 30912

Telephone. (404) 721-3444

Institutional Description. The publicly controlled medical college was founded in 1828 as the Medical Academy, and is the oldest school of medicine in Georgia. Enrollment: 1,887.

Library Administration. Thomas G. Basler, College Librarian; Dorothy H. Mims, Librarian for Special Collections.

Library General Holdings. 140,000 volumes (55,000 monographs and bound journals); 10,000 audiovisual materials; 2,600 microforms; 1,623 current journal subscriptions. Subject areas selectively acquired are in education and the social sciences, chiefly in support of the nursing education program.

Special Collections

Institutional Publications. Includes the publications and reports of the Medical College of Georgia and those of the Board of Regents of the University System of Georgia.

Nineteenth Century Library. This collection consists of 1,600 titles, most of which comprised the nineteenth-century library of the Medical College of Georgia. It contains a number of the significant works which shaped the medical thinking of the period, as well as those which reflected the typical thought and practice of the time. The earliest work is a 1608 Latin translation of the Arabian physician Avicenna. The collection also includes runs of several of the scientific and medical journals of the early nineteenth century.

Landmarks in Modern Medicine. This collection is comprised of out-of-print classics from the late nineteenth and early twentieth centuries which were significant in the development of modern medicine.

380
Mercer University, Atlanta
Monroe F. Swilley, Jr. Library
3001 Mercer University Drive
Atlanta, Georgia 30341

Telephone. (404) 458-5904

Institutional Description. The privately supported university was founded in 1968 as the Atlanta Baptist College. In 1972, it joined with and became a branch of Mercer University, Atlanta. It is affiliated with the Southern Baptist Church. Enrollment: 1,951.

Library Administration. Nancy Fennel Williams, Director, Swilley Library; Elizabeth Christian Jackson, Head Librarian, Naylor Library.

Library General Holdings. 63,000 volumes; 19,000 volumes on microforms; 625 current periodical subscriptions; 228,500 microforms; 1,250 musical scores; 2,400 items of audiovisual materials.

Special Collections

The Swilley Library supports the varied curriculum of Mercer University in Atlanta. The Naylor Library houses a collection of 6,000 volumes and 130 periodicals in the subject areas of pharmacy, medicine, chemistry, biological science, and nursing.

381
Mercer University, Macon
Eugene W. Stetson Memorial Library
1400 Coleman Avenue
Macon, Georgia 31207

Telephone. (912) 744-2700

Institutional Description. The privately supported university, founded in 1833, is affiliated with the Southern Baptist Church. Enrollment: 2,569.

Library Administration. Mary Howard, Director.

Library General Holdings. 242,000 volumes; 2,122 periodical subscriptions; 78,405 microforms; 4,625 audiovisual materials.

Special Collections

A special collections room contains the Mercer and Georgia Baptist Convention archives. The Eugene W. Stetson Room houses Mr. Stetson's library on economics and other memorabilia. The library collection also includes 12,000 volumes which once comprised the Mercer Theological Library. Also available is the library of the late Dr. Albert H. Newman which contains several hundred volumes of Baptist history and theology, as well as books of general interest.

Presented to the library by the families of owners are the Albert T. Spaulding, the Judge George Hillyer, the T.C. Nolan, the Rufus W. Weaver, the George Rosser, and the O.P. Gilbert Collections. The collections range in size from several hundred books to more than a thousand. The papers of James H. Kilpatrick are also housed.

Included in the library's holdings and of great importance in the field of English literature are the Percy Bysshe Shelley and the Robert Burns collections. The **Shelley Collection,** containing several hundred volumes, is among the richer Shelley collections in the United States. The **Burns Collection** consists of more than 800 volumes by and about Robert Burns, the Burns country, and Scotland in the Burns era. It was collected by Dr. Joseph Jacobs and was a gift to Mercer from Edward Shorter, an alumnus and former trustee. It is the most extensive collection in the South and probably one of the largest in the United States.

382
Morehouse College
Atlanta University Center Robert W. Woodruff Library
111 James P. Brawley Drive, S.W.
Atlanta, Georgia 30314

Telephone. (404) 522-8980

Institutional Description. The Atlanta University Center is a consortium of six institutions of higher education in the city of Atlanta: two graduate schools (Atlanta University, Interdenominational Theological Center) and four undergraduate colleges (Clark College, Morehouse College, Morris Brown College, Spelman College).

Morehouse College, 830 Westview Drive, S.W., a privately supported liberal arts college for men, was founded in 1867 as the Augusta Institute. It grants baccalaureate degrees. Enrollment: 2,159.

Library Administration. Guy C. Craft, Atlanta University Center Librarian; Minnie H. Clayton, Head, Division of Archives and Special Collections.

Library General Holdings. The Atlanta University Center Robert W. Woodruff Library was achieved in 1982 by the merger of the libraries of the six participating institutions in a new facility on a 3.66-acre site. The library building covers an area equal to two city blocks. *See* **Atlanta University Center, Inc.**

383
Morris Brown College
Atlanta University Center Robert W. Woodruff Library
111 James P. Brawley Drive, S.W.
Atlanta, Georgia 30314

Telephone. (404) 522-8980

Institutional Description. The Atlanta University Center is a consortium of six institutions of higher education in the city of Atlanta: two graduate schools (Atlanta University, Interdenominational Theological Center) and four undergraduate colleges (Clark College, Morehouse College, Morris Brown College, Spelman College).

Morris Brown College, 634 Martin Luther King, Jr. Drive, S.W., is a privately supported liberal arts college. It is affiliated with the African Methodist Episcopal Church, and was founded in 1881. Enrollment: 1,252.

Library Administration. Guy C. Craft, Atlanta University Center Librarian; Minnie H. Clayton, Head, Division of Archives and Special Collections.

Library General Holdings. The Atlanta University Center Robert W. Woodruff Library was achieved in 1982 by the merger of the libraries of the six participating institutions in a new facility on a 3.66-acre site. The library building covers an area equal to two city blocks. *See* **Atlanta University Center, Inc.**

384
North Georgia College
Stewart Library
Dahlonega, Georgia 30597

Telephone. (404) 864-3391

Institutional Description. The publicly supported (state) liberal arts and teachers college was founded in 1873. It is a member of the Georgia State University System. Enrollment: 1,870.

Library Administration. Valentine Dobbs, Director.

Library General Holdings. 120,000 volumes; 1,000 newspapers, magazines, and journals.

Special Collections

The library maintains special collections on military history and children's literature. Also housed in the library is the microfilm collection of the daily *New York*

Times from September 1851 to the present.

385
Oglethorpe University
University Library
4484 Peachtree Road, N.E.
Atlanta, Georgia 30319

Telephone. (404) 261-1441

Institutional Description. The privately supported liberal arts university was founded in 1835 by a group of Georgia Presbyterians. Today a nonsectarian institution, it grants baccalaureate and master's degrees. Enrollment: 841.

Library Administration. John A. Ryland, Librarian.

Library General Holdings. 190,000 items including books, periodicals, microforms, and audiovisual materials; 300 current periodical subscriptions.

Special Collections

The R.L. Dempsey Special Collections room includes materials on James Edward Oglethorpe and Georgia; Sidney Lanier (an Oglethorpe alumnus); and other collections of autographed books and unique volumes. The **Sears Collection of Children's Literature** contains over 2,000 volumes of children's books which help support the graduate program of elementary education. The **Japanese Collection** consists of books in the English language and other materials on Japanese history and culture. A collection of Walt Whitman is also maintained.

386
Oxford College of Emory University
O'Kelley Memorial Library
Hamill Street
Oxford, Georgia 30267

Telephone. (404) 786-7051

Institutional Description. Oxford College was founded in 1836 and is a two-year liberal arts division of Emory University. It is affiliated with the United Methodist Church. Enrollment: 550.

Library Administration. Margaret McPherson, Librarian.

Library General Holdings. 56,000 volumes; 311 periodical subscriptions.

Special Collections

The library maintains the **Dillard R. Lasseter Special Collection** which includes Emoryana, Confederate histories, and Methodist histories. The **Ogletree Lewis Special Collection** contains predominantly American poetry (particularly the Poets Laureate of Georgia), and Southern authors.

387
Paine College
Warren A. Candler Memorial Library
1235 15th Street
Augusta, Georgia 30910

Telephone. (404) 722-4471

Institutional Description. The privately supported liberal arts college was founded in 1883. It is affiliated with the United Methodist Church and the Christian Methodist Episcopal Church. Enrollment: 667.

Library Administration. Millie Parker, Head Librarian.

Library General Holdings. 80,000 volumes; 300 periodical and serial subscriptions.

Special Collections

Three special collections of the library include the **Frank Yerby Collection** which includes autographed editions; the **Martin Luther King, Jr. Collection;** and the **Howard Thurman Meditation Collection.**

388
Piedmont College
E. Louise Patten Memorial Library
165 Central Avenue
Demorest, Georgia 30535

Telephone. (404) 778-8301

Institutional Description. The privately supported liberal arts college was founded in 1897 by the Congregational Churches of the United States. Now independent, it grants baccalaureate degrees. Enrollment: 370.

Library Administration. David S. Pratt, Librarian.

Library General Holdings. 91,000 volumes; 225 current periodical subscriptions.

Special Collections

The library maintains the **Piedmont College Archives** and the **Phil Landrum Collection** of congressional papers.

389
Savannah State College
Asa Gordon Library
Savannah, Georgia 31404

Telephone. (912) 356-2240

Institutional Description. The publicly supported state college was founded in 1890 to serve the educational needs of Black students; today it offers all students associate, baccalaureate, and master's degrees. Enrollment: 1,735.

Library Administration. Andrew J. McLemore, Director, Library and Media Services.

Library General Holdings. 264,274 volumes; 813 cur-

rent periodicals subscriptions; 30 newspaper subscriptions; 335,000 microforms.

Special Collections

There is an extensive collection of materials by and about Black Americans.

390
Shorter College
Livingston Library
Shorter Avenue
Rome, Georgia 30161

Telephone. (404) 291-2121

Institutional Description. Shorter College is a private liberal arts college controlled by the Georgia Baptist Convention. The College was founded in 1873 as the Cherokee Baptist Female College. Enrollment: 676.

Library Administration. Mary Mac Mosley, Director of Library Services.

Library General Holdings. 100,500 bound volumes; 1,200 periodical titles; 6,000 phonograph recordings; 7,000 music scores; 2,000 microforms.

Special Collections

The Livingston Library has local Baptist association minutes on microfilm.

391
Southern College of Technology
Southern College of Technology Library
1112 Clay Street
Marietta, Georgia 30060

Telephone. (404) 424-7275

Institutional Description. Southern College of Technology, a publicly supported coeducational unit of the University System of Georgia, offers both two-year associate and four-year bachelor degrees in several areas of engineering technology as well as an associate degree in textile management. Enrollment: 3,043.

Library Administration. John W. Pattillo, Library Director.

Library General Holdings. 93,742 volumes; 1,408 current subscriptions; 23,297 microforms; 17,750 miscellaneous materials.

Special Collections

In a sense, the entire library is a special collection. Aside from a small core liberal arts collection, the library's holdings are all in areas of engineering technology—architecture, apparel/textile, computer, electrical, industrial, civil, construction, and mechanical. It is the only collection devoted to engineering technology within the State of Georgia.

Rare Book Collections

The library's rare books fall primarily into the areas of architecture and building construction. Included are the works of early architects, builders' manuals, trade catalogs, lithographs, photographs, drawing implements, and related miscellaneous materials.

392
Spelman College
Atlanta University Center Robert W. Woodruff Library
111 James P. Brawley Drive, S.W.
Atlanta, Georgia 30314

Telephone. (404) 522-8980

Institutional Description. The Atlanta University Center is a consortium of six institutions of higher education in the city of Atlanta: two graduate schools (Atlanta University, Interdenominational Theological Center) and four undergraduate colleges (Clark College, Morehouse College, Morris Brown College, Spelman College).

Spelman College, 350 Spelman Lane, S.W., is a privately supported liberal arts college for women. Founded in 1881 as the Atlanta Baptist Female Seminary, it now grants baccalaureate degrees. Enrollment: 1,667.

Library Administration. Guy C. Craft, Atlanta University Center Librarian; Minnie H. Clayton, Head, Division of Archives and Special Collections.

Library General Holdings. The Atlanta University Center Robert W. Woodruff Library was achieved in 1982 by the merger of the libraries of the six participating institutions in a new facility on a 3.66-acre site. The library building covers an area equal to two city blocks. *See* **Atlanta University Center, Inc.**

393
Toccoa Falls College
Seby Jones Library
Toccoa Falls, Georgia 30598

Telephone. (404) 886-6831

Institutional Description. The privately supported professional Bible college was established in 1907 to offer preparation for Christian ministries. Now granting associate and baccalaureate degrees, it is affiliated with the Christian and Missionary Alliance. Enrollment: 618.

Library Administration. Ruth M. Good, Head Librarian.

Library General Holdings. 65,000 volumes.

Special Collections

A memorial room houses the personal library of Richard A. Forrest, founder of the College.

394
University of Georgia
Hargrett Rare Book and Manuscript Library
Athens, Georgia 30602

Telephone. (404) 542-7123

Institutional Description. The publicly supported institution is one of the oldest chartered universities in the United States, having been founded in 1785. Enrollment: 25,005.

Library Administration. Thomas E. Camden, Head, Hargrett Library; Mary Ellen Brooks, Rare Books Librarian.

Library General Holdings. 2,510,730 volumes; 54,531 periodicals; 3,375,262 microforms; 445,827 audiovisual materials.

Special Collections

The mission of the Special Collections Division is to maintain and service the University Libraries' research collections. Most of the current special collections have been in existence for a number of years. The largest holdings are in **Georgiana** which are spread throughout the Division.

Georgia Collection. The primary objective of the Georgia collection is to develop and maintain the variety of materials necessary for scholarly research and reference. In addition to books, newspapers, periodicals, and pamphlets, Georgia-related non-book materials are acquired, including microforms, phonograph recordings, photographs, slides, posters, maps, and ephemera. Excluded are videocassettes and computer software.

The basic goal of the Georgia Collection is to acquire, as comprehensively as feasible, a collection of published materials wholly or substantially concerning the state of Georgia: its history, people, organizations, and institutions. Collection interests fall into three categories: works by Georgians, works about Georgia or Georgians, and works published in Georgia.

Richard B. Russell Memorial Library. This Library serves as the center for twentieth-century Georgia political studies. The collections comprise the papers, audiovisual materials, oral histories, and memorabilia of Georgia political figures, political organizations, and activist groups.

Department of Archives and Records Management. The mission of this Department is the collection, preservation, and administration of the University's official and organizations records.

Rare Book Collections

Rare Books and Manuscripts. This Department's materials currently have a heavy concentration of Georgiana. There are collections of Georgia authors and artists, businessmen, dramatists and cartoonists, journalists and ministers, business records, religious, social and cultural groups, family papers, and genealogical material. The Manuscripts Sections has a large collection of photographs taken in Georgia and an extensive postcard collection. The Rare Books Section holds early Georgia imprints including monographs, newspapers, periodicals, maps, broadsides, pamphlets, and prints. General rare books are strong in natural history, Southern travels, and nineteenth-century literature. The strength of the Rare Books and Manuscripts Department rests with its subject collections which include primary and secondary printed works, manuscripts, ephemera, and graphics. It is within these subject collections that most research is done. As mentioned, the Georgiana materials are large and strong. In addition, there are extensive holdings in literature, fine printing, theater, music, journalism, and history. The collection of Confederate imprints includes books, newspapers, periodicals, broadsides, sheet music, and maps published in the Confederate States between 1861 and 1865.

Literature Collections. Georgia author collections include: Conrad Aiken, Erskine Caldwell, James Dickey, Julian Green, Carson McCullers, Don Marquis, Margaret Mitchell, Flannery O'Connor, Lillian Smith, Calder Willingham, Donald Windham. Non-Georgia author collections include the works of: James Agee, Hervey Allen, Stephen Vincent Benet, Truman Capote, Eudora Welty, Katherine Anne Porter, William Styron, Robert Penn Warren, Tennessee Williams, and Stark Young. British collections have been established for John Fowles, A.L. Rowse, and Robert Louis Stevenson.

Private Press Collection. Includes representative samples of contemporary private presses in the United States and England. The Rare Book and Manuscript Department is responsible for collecting fine printing in Georgia and collects exhaustively the publications of the following private presses: Beehive (Savannah), Ashantilly (Darien), Bozart (Atlanta), and Pigeonhole (Savannah). The Department also holds a complete run of the University of Georgia Press titles together as a press. The Department collects works of other private presses throughout the United States and some foreign.

Theater History. In the area of theater, the holdings include European theater as well as American, and a growing collection of toy theater. Especially valuable is a collection of costume and set designs. The **Paris Music Hall Collection** consists of nearly 7,000 original costume drawings and set designs. Printed matter such as programs and photographs are acquired. A large collection of playbills is worldwide in scope although the emphasis is on American theater. American radio, television, stage, and moving picture scripts are actively sought. Personal papers of twentieth-century Georgia actors and dramatists are also collected. The **Charles Coburn Collection** and the **Cary Bynum Collections** are two of the important collections of personal papers of Georgia actors.

Graphics. This collection includes all varieties of photography. The Darrah collection of 30,000 stereoptic views provides a generous cross-sampling of photographers, stereoptic publishing companies, and subject matter.

History. The content of the History collections is generally Southern, based on the strengths of the **DeRenne Collection** and the many gifts of Felix Hargrett. Specifically materials for the study of Georgia history and that of the Confederate states are extensive. The **British Local History Collection** consists of books acquired from the library of the British historian A.L. Rowse.

Music. Two major manuscript collections, the **Olin Downes Collection** and the **Guido Adler Collection** are comprehensive and international in scope. An extensive sheet music collection consists of approximately 15,000 pieces comprised primarily of popular music of the nineteenth century.

Journalism. There are three major journalism archives: Arbitron, a national marketing survey for radio and television; the WSB (Channel 2, Atlanta) radio archive; and the Peabody Institute Award written entries. Collections of distinguished journalists, including cartoonists, are acquired on a selective basis to complement the John W. Drewry, the Medora Field Perkerson, and the Alfred Brewerton papers.

395
Valdosta State College
Library
North Patterson Street
Valdosta, Georgia 31698

Telephone. (912) 333-5800

Institutional Description. The publicly supported state college was founded in 1913 as South Georgia State Normal College for Young Ladies. The College became coeducational and changed its name in 1950. Enrollment: 5,592.

Library Administration. David L. Ince, Director.

Library General Holdings. 275,000 volumes; 2,400 current periodicals; 500,000 microforms.

Special Collections

The library houses the **Archives of Contemporary South Georgia History.**

396
Wesleyan College
Willet Memorial Library
4760 Forsyth Road
Macon, Georgia 31297

Telephone. (912) 477-1110

Institutional Description. The privately supported liberal arts college for women was founded in 1836 with the first state charter for granting degrees to women. It grants baccalaureate degrees. Enrollment: 359.

Library Administration. Hasseltine Roberts, Librarian.

Library General Holdings. 118,000 volumes; 490 current periodical subscriptions; 8,000 microforms; 5,000 recordings.

Special Collections

The Georgia Room houses the library's special collections. The nucleus of the collection is the 1,500-volume library of Georgiana presented in 1931 by the late Judge Orville A. Park of Macon. In this room are also items of rare Americana, books by Georgia authors, and memorabilia of college significance. The library also has a collection of Wesleyana.

397
West Georgia College
Irvine Sullivan Ingram Library
Carrollton, Georgia 30118

Telephone. (404) 836-6495

Institutional Description. In 1933 the Board of Regents of the University System of Georgia established the school as a junior college member of the System. Since becoming a senior college in 1957, the College has been among the fastest growing institutions of higher education in the South. It now grants the associate, bachelor, specialist, and master's degrees. Enrollment: 6,773.

Library Administration. Charles E. Beard, College Librarian; Myron W. House, Reference/Special Collections Librarian.

Library General Holdings. 260,000 bound volumes; 135,000 U.S. government documents; 18,000 reels of microfilm; 742,000 microforms; 14,000 maps and charts. Special collections number 17,000 manuscripts, photographs, and other items.

Special Collections

West Georgia College History. Includes materials documenting the history of the College and its programs.

West Georgia College Curriculum. Manuscript collections that support faculty and student research within the framework of the curriculum of the college.

West Georgia Area. A collection of books and related materials on the West Georgia area (defined as Polk, Haralson, Paulding, Carroll, Douglas, Coweta, and Heard Counties). Includes family histories, photographs, and church records.

Sacred Harp Music. A collection of materials of music related historically to the geographic area; also materials dealing with the history of American psalmody, but most especially those treating the origin and practice of shaped note singing.

398
Young Harris College
Duckworth Libraries
P.O. Box 98
Young Harris, Georgia 30582

Telephone. (404) 379-3111

Institutional Description. The college began as a mission school of the Methodist Church in 1886. Enrollment: 393.

Library Administration. Robert J. Richardson, Director of Library Services.

Library General Holdings. 48,000 volumes; 360 periodical subscriptions.

Special Collections

The library maintains the **Merle B. Mann Indian Artifact Collection** and the **Byron Herbert Reece Collection.**

Hawaii

399
Brigham Young University - Hawaii
Joseph F. Smith Library
55-220 Kulanui
Laie, Hawaii 96762

Telephone. (808) 293-3850

Institutional Description. This private liberal arts college was founded in 1955 by the Church of Jesus Christ of Latter Day Saints as the Church College of Hawaii. More than one-fourth of its students are from foreign countries and an international atmosphere prevails at the college. Enrollment: 1,863.

Library Administration. Rex Frandsen, College Librarian; Riley Moffat, Reference Librarian.

Library General Holdings. 140,000 books; 1,050 periodical subscriptions; 40 newspaper subscriptions; 25,000 reels of microfilm; 500,000 pieces of microfiche; 19,000 pieces of ultrafiche; 5,000 media titles; 80,000 government documents on paper and 50,000 on microfiche; 10,000 maps.

Special Collections

The Joseph F. Smith Library has a specialized research collection of Pacific Island materials covering Polynesia, Micronesia, Melanesia, New Zealand, and Australia though highlighting Hawaii and other island groups of Polynesia. There is also a significant collection of materials related to Mormons and Mormonism—its theology, history, and culture. In the Library there is a separately maintained Curriculum Library with texts, teacher's guides, educational kits and games, and educational computer programs for the use of a strong Education Division.

Rare Book Collections

The Library houses the University's Archives. There is a significant restricted collection of early Pacific Islands and Mormonism materials including voyages, explorations, early scientific studies and research in the Pacific Islands, journals of early Latter Day Saints missionaries in the Pacific Islands, early Mormon periodical literature, and a collection of photographs related to LDS church history in Hawaii in the Laie area. In the Archives Department is a collection of several hundred eighteenth and nineteenth century Polynesian artifacts in stone, wood, woven and beaten fibers, feathers, etc. There is also a collection of scrimshaw from the whaling period of Pacific history.

400
Chaminade University of Honolulu
Sullivan Library
3140 Waialae Avenue
Honolulu, Hawaii 96816

Telephone. (808) 735-4711

Institutional Description. The privately supported liberal arts and professional university is affiliated with the Roman Catholic Church. Enrollment: 1,474.

Library Administration. Marian Hubbard, Head Librarian.

Library General Holdings. 60,000 volumes; 475 magazine and newspaper subscriptions.

Special Collections

The library has a special collection of Hawaiiana and maintains the **Julius J. Nodel Judaica Collection.**

401
Hawaii Loa College
Atherton Memorial Library
45-045 Kamehameha Highway
Kaneohe, Hawaii 96744

Telephone. (808) 235-3641

Institutional Description. The privately supported liberal arts college was founded in 1963. It was founded by, and is affiliated with, four Protestant denominations: Episcopal, United Church of Christ, United Methodist, and United Presbyterian. Enrollment: 428.

Library Administration. Dr. James V. DiGiambattista, Head Librarian.

Library General Holdings. 51,000 volumes; 300 periodical subscriptions.

Special Collections

The **Boyd MacNaughton Pacific Resources Room** houses a collection of bookstand periodicals related to the Pacific Islands.

402
Hawaii Pacific College
Meader Library
1166 Fort Street
Honolulu, Hawaii 96813

Telephone. (808) 544-0200

Institutional Description. The privately supported college was founded in 1965 and offers associate, baccalaureate, and master's degrees. Enrollment: 2,618.

Library Administration. Barbara Burton Hoefler, Head Librarian.

Library General Holdings. 28,000 bound volumes; 500 current newspapers, magazines, and journals.

Special Collections

Special collections include Hawaiian-Pacific books and periodicals; United States commercial and Federal Reserve Bank System bank newsletters conveying present and future economic trends; current pamphlet files of both a general nature and those related to Hawaii and the islands of the Pacific; selected audiovisual materials and rare books. Highly specialized collections in accounting, political science, profit sharing, and corporate planning are augmented by interested local professional associations.

403
Honolulu Community College
Library
874 Dillingham Boulevard
Honolulu, Hawaii 96817

Telephone. (808) 845-9211

Institutional Description. Honolulu Community College traces its origin to the establishment in 1920 of the Territorial Trade School located on the grounds of the Old Chinese Hospital in Palama. Under the Community College Act of 1964, the college was incorporated into the University of Hawaii System. Enrollment: 4,535.

Library Administration. Ronald F. Chapman, Head Librarian.

Library General Holdings. 50,197 books; 280 periodical and magazine titles.

Special Collections

The library maintains a **Hawaii/Pacific Collection.**

404
Maui Community College
Library Learning Resource Center
310 Kaahumanu Avenue
Kahului, Hawaii 96732

Telephone. (808) 244-9181

Institutional Description. The college is an ougrowth of the Maui Vocational School established in 1931. It was incorporated into the Community College System in 1965 under the jurisdiction of the University of Hawaii. Enrollment: 1,962.

Library Administration. Bill Lindstrom, Head Librarian.

Library General Holdings. 35,000 books.

Special Collections

The **Hawaiiana Collection** is maintained by the library.

405
University of Hawaii at Hilo
Edwin H. Mookini Library
1400 Kapiolani Street
Hilo, Hawaii 96720

Telephone. (808) 961-9444

Institutional Description. The publicly supported (state) university is a member of the University of Hawaii System. It is composed of the College of Arts and Crafts, the College of Agriculture, and the Hawaii Community College. Enrollment: 2,578.

Library Administration. Kenneth R. Herrick, Director of Libraries.

Library General Holdings. 180,000 volumes; 1,400 periodical and newspaper subscriptions; 220,000 government documents; 25,000 microforms.

Special Collections

The library's special collections are in Hawaiiana materials.

406
University of Hawaii at Manoa
Hamilton Library
2550 The Mall
Honolulu, Hawaii 96822

Telephone. (808) 948-7923

Institutional Description. The publicly supported university was founded in 1907. It became a university in 1920 when the College of Arts and Sciences was added. Enrollment: 15,250.

Library Administration. John R. Haak, University Librarian; Eleanor C. Au, Head, Special Collections.

Library General Holdings. 2,164,497 bound volumes; 32,989 current periodical and newspaper subscriptions; 2,350,040 microforms; 122,212 maps; 625,732 government documents.

Special Collections

Jean Charlot Collection. This collection is an archive of material about the muralist who was on the faculty of the University of Hawaii. It includes his library books, correspondence, some of his paintings, and material on persons closely associated with him, e.g., his printer, Lynton Kistler.

Hawaiian Collection. A regional collection of publications by and about the State of Hawaii, comprehensive in scope, including all languages. Special resources include publications by and about the University of Hawaii; its dissertations and theses; and early voyages to the Hawaiian Islands.

Pacific Collection. A regional collection of material about Polynesia, Micronesia, and Melanesia, including the Maori of New Zealand. Special resources include government publications of Pacific Island governments, Pacific linguistics and vernacular texts, and the Trust Territory Archives master microfilm.

Tsuzaki Reinecke Pidgin Creole Collection. Material on creole languages of the world, collected to produce a comprehensive bilbiography of creole languages. Includes reprints, books, pamphlets, and correspondence.

Rare Book Collections

Rare Book Collection. Books for which printing, date, cost, edition, scarcity, or provenance require special handling. Rare Hawaiian and rare Pacific items are included in the collection.

Idaho

407
Boise State University
Boise State University Library
1910 University Drive
Boise, Idaho 83725

Telephone. (208) 385-1234

Institutional Description. Boise State University was established in 1932 as a community college; it progressed into a four-year university in 1967 and became a part of the state system in 1969. Enrollment: 10,962.

Library Administration. Timothy A. Brown, University Librarian; Ralph W. Hansen, Associate Librarian; Alan Virta, Special Collections Librarian.

Library General Holdings. 295,000 volumes; 4,000 current periodicals, newspapers, and other serials; 111,000 maps; 144,000 government publications.

Special Collections

Senator Frank Church Papers. Consists of speeches, correspondence with constituents, agency files, campaign files, trip files, research materials on wilderness and foreign affairs, films, videotapes, and photographs spanning the Senator's life.

Senator Len B. Jordan Collection. Consists of correspondence with Idaho constituents on a variety of topics —most notably the Vietnam War. The collection also contains background material on contemporary issues and proposed legislation, and copies of legislation that Jordan authored or supported.

408
College of Idaho
N.L. Terteling Library
East Cleveland Boulevard
Caldwell, Idaho 83605

Telephone. (208) 459-5011

Institutional Description. The privately supported liberal arts college was founded in 1891. Although affiliated with the United Presbyterian Church, it maintains a nonsectarian atmosphere. Enrollment: 1,264.

Library Administration. Dale I. Corning, Librarian.

Library General Holdings. 125,000 volumes; 535 current periodical titles; 75,000 government documents; 35,-000 microforms.

Special Collections

Strengths of the library are in the fields of business and education. An elementary and secondary text book collection is maintained.

409
Idaho State University
Eli M. Oboler Library
P.O. Box 8089
Pocatello, Idaho 83209

Telephone. (208) 236-2997

Institutional Description. The state supported Idaho State University was founded in 1901 as the Academy of Idaho, and assumed its present name in 1963. The University's continuing education program includes three off-campus centers. Enrollment: 7,031.

Library Administration. Peter Watson, University Librarian; Gary Domitz, Reference/Archives Librarian (Special Collections and Rare Books Librarian).

Library General Holdings. 331,446 books; 3,269 current subscriptions; 26,139 microfilm reels; 1,010,342 microfiche; 41,153 maps.

Special Collections

Intermountain West Collection. Contains approximately 3,000 volumes on the history of Idaho and the contiguous states.

Map Collection. Contains approximately 40,000 maps (most are USGS and DMATC depository maps); also much of the NCIC and USGS historic map collectons on microfilm (over 130,000 maps).

Rare Book Collections

The rare book collection contains 750 volumes, including the **Glenn Tyler Collection** of approximately 300 titles on the history of science.

University Archives. Contains the historic records of Idaho State University and its predecessors.

Manuscript Collections. Contains unpublished

material pertaining to Idaho history (personal papers, manuscripts, and letters). Among the collections are the papers of Fred T. Dubois, Idaho's first Senator; papers of Dr. Minnie Howard, local historian; and the Lemhi Indian Agency papers.

410
Lewis-Clark State College Library
8th Avenue and 6th Street
Lewiston, Idaho 83501

Telephone. (208) 746-2341

Institutional Description. The publicly supported state college was founded in 1893 to train teachers; it became a four-year institution in 1965. Enrollment: 2,022.

Library Administration. Paul Krause, Director.

Library General Holdings. 72,000 volumes; 556 periodical subscriptions; 6,000 microforms; 2,900 audiovisual materials.

Special Collections

Special collections include Pacific Northwest materials; children's and young adult's literature; elementary and secondary school textbooks; and the Library of American Civilization, a microfiche collection that covers all phases of United States history and culture through 1914.

411
North Idaho College
Kildow Memorial Library
1000 West Garden Avenue
Coeur d'Alene, Idaho 83814

Telephone. (208) 667-7422

Institutional Description. The two-year community college was founded in 1933 as Coeur d'Alene College. Its present name was adopted in 1971. Enrollment: 2,235.

Library Administration. Keith H. Sturts, Head Librarian.

Library General Holdings. 37,000 volumes; 585 serial subscriptions.

Special Collections

The special collections of the Kildow Library are the **Veeder Collection of Pacific Northwest History and Indian Affairs** and the **McEwing Collection of Original Bagpipe Music and Piping Memorabilia.**

412
Northwest Nazarene College
John E. Riley Library
Nampa, Idaho 83651

Telephone. (208) 467-8777

Institutional Description. The privately supported liberal arts college was founded in 1913 as an elementary school; degrees were first awarded in 1917. The college is affiliated with the Church of the Nazarene. Enrollment: 1,178.

Library Administration. Edith Lancaster, Head Librarian.

Library General Holdings. 124,000 volumes; 710 current periodical subscriptions; 41,000 microforms.

Special Collections

The **Annie Laurie Bird Collection** contains materials on Nampa, Idaho. The library also has materials on the Church of the Nazarene.

413
University of Idaho
University Library
Moscow, Idaho 83843

Telephone. (208) 885-7951

Institutional Description. The state supported University of Idaho was founded in 1889. Enrollment: 8,586.

Library Administration. Eileen Hitchingham, Dean of Library Services; Herman Ronnenberg, Head, Special Collections and Archives (Special Collections and Rare Books Librarian).

Library General Holdings. 1,039,558 volumes; 219,403 microforms; 2,177 audiovisual materials; 12,314 current periodical subscriptions. The Special Collections Department includes those materials which, because of subject coverage, rarity, source, condition, or form, are best handled separately from the General Collection.

Special Collections

Day-Northwest Collection. This comprehensive collection of over 11,500 volumes consists of published materials for the study of Idaho and the Pacific Northwest. Some of the notable items in this collection are the original manuscript of the *Bozeman Trail* by Hebard and Brininstool, Captain John Mullan's own copy of his report on Colonel Wright's Campaign against the Indians in Oregon and Washington Territories, and three Lapwai imprints from the press of Reverend Henry Spalding dating back to 1839.

Basque Collection. This collection of material relating to the history and culture of the Basque people was begun in 1964 because of the large population in Idaho and because of the scarcity of material on their culture in this country. There are over 3,400 volumes in this collection.

Idaho Documents Collection. This collection consists of printed, mimeographed, and other near-print publications of the State and its subdivisions including the University; includes a complete set of the territorial session laws and the journals of the territorial council and House of Representatives.

Scott Collection. This collection of first editions of the works of Sir Walter Scott, along with books relating to him, was presented to the University Library by Earl Larrison, Professor of Zoology, in 1962. Since that date many volumes by or about the British writer have been added to the collection which now numbers over 1,200 volumes.

Picture Collection. This collection consists mainly of photographs of the University and its many activities and of the State of Idaho. On of the most valuable segments of this collection consists of the negatives given to the Library by the heirs of the late Nellie Stockbridge of Wallace. These pictures are an almost complete photographic record of Wallace and the surrounding Coeur d'Alene mining districts from 1894-1965. There are over 90,000 photographic prints in the picture collection.

Pound Collection. In 1973 the Library began to collect works by and about Ezra Pound, American man of letters who was born in Hailey, Idaho in 1885. The Pound Collection now contains over 280 titles including first edition, signed copies, transcripts of FBI files on Pound, and complete runs of *Agenda* and *Paideuma.*

Caxton Collection. This is a collection of all titles issued by Caxton Printers, Ltd. of Caldwell, Idaho. It presently numbers over 1,000 volumes.

Idaho Theses Collection. This collection consists of the first or file copies of nearly 4,000 theses and dissertations submitted for advanced degrees at the University of Idaho.

Historical Maps. These are early maps that include the area now known as Idaho, covering the period up to 1900. There are over 650 maps in this collection.

Yearbook Collection. This collection of Idaho High School and College yearbooks is added to by gifts from the Journalism Department. There are over 600 volume in this collection.

Oral History Collection. The University of Idaho library is a repository for the tapes and transcripts generated by the Latah County Historical Society Oral History Program.

Personal Papers and University Archives. Among the primary source materials in the Department of Special Collections are personal and organizational papers, and records and University archives. Totaling nearly 3,000 cubic feet, the material covers nearly all facets of life in Idaho and the Pacific Northwest. A large group of materials reflect Idaho's major industries. Also in the collection are records of Idaho's only home-grown mail-order religion: Psychiana, and its founder Frank B. Robinson.

Rare Book Collections

Day Collection of Fine Bindings. This collection of books, notable for its distinguished bindings, has been presented to the Library by Mrs. Lucy Day, widow of Jerome J. Day. It consists of over 1,365 volumes of rare editions, some bound in leather and hand tooled in gold by Italian craftsmen. Included are 40 volumes of Shakespeare printed on rag paper; the Lenor edition of the complete works of Edgar Allen Poe, printed on Japanese vellum and limited to 10 signed and numbered sets of which this is number one; plus multi-volume sets of the works of Hawthorne, Stevenson, Burns, Dumas, and many others.

The **Rare Book Collection** includes early imprints, such as incunabula; significant works from famous presses; volumes with exceptional bindings or illustrations; and first editions of landmark books, such as Charles Dickens' *Little Dorritt* as issued in 20 parts from 1825 through June 1857. There are approximately 1,500 volumes in this collection.

Illinois

414
American Conservatory of Music
Hattstaedt Library
116 South Michigan Avenue
Chicago, Illinois 60605

Telephone. (312) 263-4161

Institutional Description. The privately supported professional conservatory organizes its courses on a collegiate basis and awards baccalaureate, master's, and doctorate degrees. It was founded in 1886. Enrollment: 339.

Library Administration. Janice Das, Librarian.

Library General Holdings. 9,392 volumes; 5,895 scores; 2,000 recordings.

Special Collections

Special collections include Bach Gesellschaft Ausgabe, Nene Bach Ausgabe, Nene Mozart Ausgabe, Haydn Werke.

415
The Art Institute of Chicago
Ryerson and Burnham Libraries
Michigan Avenue at Adams Street
Chicago, Illinois 60603

Telephone. (312) 443-3666

Library Administration. Jack Perry Brown, College Librarian; Susan Glover Godlewski, Associate Director (Special Collections Librarian).

Library General Holdings. 162,000 volumes; 1,500 periodical subscriptions; 15,000 microforms; 310,000 slides. The holdings of the libraries concentrate on the history of art and architecture of all periods, all nationalities.

Special Collections

Special collections include: seventeenth-, eighteenth-, and nineteenth-century architectural treatises; printed and archival material on Chicago and Midwestern architecture (Daniel H. Burnham Papers, Ludwig K. Hilberseimer Archives, Louis Sullivan's System of Ornament, Marion Mahoney Griffin's Magic of America, Frank Lloyd Wright's Jacobs House and Dwight Bank, Howard Van Doren Shaw, etc.); Japanese and Chinese woodblock books (Ryerson Collection); Russian folk art (Ernest Hamill Collection); James McNeill Whistler (Walter Brewster Collection); and Surrealism (Mary Reynolds Collection).

Rare Book Collections

The library houses archival records and manuscripts of various artists and architects, including: Ivan Lorraine Albright Collection (53 journals dated from 13 January 1923 to 25 May 1981; also 3 scrapbooks dating from 1918-1983); Georges Rouault Collection (1946-1976); Daniel H. Burnham Papers (1846-1912); 900 North Michigan Avenue Buidling, Jarvis Hunt, Architect; Herbert and Katherine Jacobs House, Frank Lloyd Wright, Architect; Mies van der Rohe correspondence, 1947-1969; Richard M. Skinner House, 1878; Sullivaniana Collection (papers, photographs, and letters of Louis Henry Sullivan, 1974-1924; Chicago Architectural Exhibition League (minutes of the Board of Directors (1924-1953); First National Bank of Dwight (Illinois), Peter Bonnett Wight Collection, 1884-1916; E.H. Bennett Papers, 1906-1950s; Howard Van Doren Shaw Collection, 1893-1926; The Kalo Shop, notebook of designs by Mildren B. Bevis (c.1910-1913); Bagley Cottage, Frank Lloyd Wright, Architect; Marion Mahony Griffin, The Magic of America; Ludwig Karl Hilberseimer Archives, 1906-1967.

416
Augustana College
Denkmann Memorial Library
639 38th Street
Rock Island, Illinois 61201

Telephone. (309) 794-7208

Institutional Description. The privately supported liberal arts college was founded in 1860 as the first Scandanavian college in America. It is affiliated with the Lutheran Church in America. Enrollment: 2,035.

Library Administration. John Caldwell, Director.

Library General Holdings. 286,400 volumes; 1,490 current periodical titles; 44,000 microforms.

Special Collections

Swenson Swedish Immigration Research Center. Includes books, manuscripts, microfilms, and periodicals dealing with the development of Swedish culture in the U.S. beginning in the 1860s; also includes historical material about the Augustana Lutheran Synod.

Hauberg Upper Mississippi Valley History Collection. Contains local and Indian history from the mid-1800s to the mid-1900s.

Charles XV Collection. Includes materials on eighteenth-century French radicalism with original source materials and books dating from 1789 to 1848.

Rare Book Collections

A rare book collection, including first editions of Milton and Spenser, as well as hundreds of volumes of Mississippiana, is displayed in a special room.

417
Aurora University
Charles B. Phillips Library
347 South Gladstone Avenue
Aurora, Illinois 60507

Telephone. (312) 892-6431

Institutional Description. The privately supported liberal arts college was founded in 1893 as Mendota Seminary. Although an independent institution, it is affiliated with the Advent Christian Church. Enrollment: 1,335.

Library Administration. Susan L. Craig, Director.

Library General Holdings. 115,000 volumes; 600 current periodical subscriptions; 10,000 microforms.

Special Collections

Special collections include the **Jenks Collection of Adventual Materials,** (Advent Christian Church); the **University Archives;** and the **Prouty Shakespeare Collection.**

418
Barat College
College Library
700 East Westleigh Road
Lake Forest, Illinois 60045

Telephone. (312) 234-3000

Institutional Description. The privately supported liberal arts college was founded in 1919. It is affiliated with the Roman Catholic Church. Enrollment: 435.

Library Administration. Alan Barney, Director.

Library General Holdings. 84,000 volumes; 624 periodicals.

Special Collections

Special collections include a collection of nineteenth-century women's rights periodicals; a collection on Roman Catholic theology and philosophy; and a **Middle English Literature Collection.**

419
Bethany Theological Seminary
Seminary Library
Butterfield and Meyers Roads
Oak Brook, Illinois 60521

Telephone. (312) 620-2214

Institutional Description. Bethany Theological Seminary is the only graduate school of theology for the Church of the Brethren, and is one of seven institutions of higher education affiliated with the denomination. Immediately adjacent to the Northern Baptist Theological Seminary, Bethany shares library facilities with the other seminary. Enrollment: 74.

Library Administration. Kenneth Shaffer, Director.

Library General Holdings. 141,452 bound volumes; 2,900 audiovisual items; 600 current periodicals. These resources represent the combined libraries of Bethany and Northern Baptist Theological Seminaries. Special strengths are in Baptist history, Church of the Brethren history, peace studies, Pietism, and psychological journals.

Special Collections

The Special Collections contain the **Abraham H. Cassel Collection** of sixteenth- through nineteenth-century theological books and pamphlets and a nearly complete collection of American Tract Society publications; the **Ora Huston Collection** of over four hundred volumes of English Bibles; Baptist Association records; Danish and Norwegian Baptist Seminary material; the **Donald Dayton Collection** of nineteenth-century evangelicalism; and the **Olmstead Collection in Ancient and Near Eastern Languages and Literature.**

420
Black Hawk College - East Campus
Gust E. Lundberg Learning Resources Center
Junction Routes 34 and 78
Kewanee, Illinois 61443

Telephone. (309) 852-5671

Institutional Description. In 1967, major efforts on the part of the citizens of Kenwannee and surrounding communities resulted in the annexation of nine school districts to the Black Hawk College District and the establishment of the East Campus. The present campus was occupied in 1978. Enrollment: 590.

Library Administration. Marg M. Rogers, Director.

Library General Holdings. 16,000 volumes; 300 periodical subscriptions.

Special Collections

The library is the depository for the **Archives of Phi Delta Kappa.**

421
Black Hawk College - Quad Cities Campus Library
6600 34th Avenue
Moline, Illinois 61625

Telephone. (309) 796-1311

Institutional Description. In 1946, the college was founded as an extension to the University of Illinois. In 1948, it became known as Moline Community College. In 1961, the college became the first junior college in the State of Illinois and became known as Junior College District #1 and assumed the name Black Hawk College. Enrollment: 3,151.

Library Administration. Caroline Barnes, Librarian.

Library General Holdings. 70,000 books; 500 current periodical subscriptions.

Special Collections

The library maintains the area **Belgian Culture Collection,** a rare book collection, the College Archives, and a collection of law books, and selected, award-winning children's books.

422
Blackburn College
Lumpkin Library
700 College Avenue
Carlinville, Illinois 62626

Telephone. (217) 854-3231

Institutional Description. The privately supported liberal arts college was founded in 1837. Affiliated with the United Presbyterian Church, the college conducts an on-campus work program whereby all students work 15 hours per week to aid in expenses. Enrollment: 404.

Library Administration. Robert L. Underbrink, Head Librarian.

Library General Holdings. 77,000 volumes; over 400 periodical subscriptions.

Special Collections

The library maintains special collections on botany, religion, and eighteenth-century literature.

423
Bradley University
Cullom-Davis Library
1501 West Bradley Avenue
Peoria, Illinois 61625

Telephone. (308) 677-2850

Institutional Description. The privately supported university was founded in 1987 by Mrs. Lydia Moss Bradley in memory of her husband and children as a nonsectarian, nonpolitical, nonpartisan, privately-endowed educational institution. Enrollment: 4,161.

Library Administration. Betty Hendrickson, Acting Director; Charles Frey, Special Collections and Rare Books Librarian.

Library General Holdings. 950,000 items including over 285,000 circulating books, 190,000 government documents, and 351,000 microforms; 2,060 serial subscriptions; 11,000 music scores; 8,000 recordings.

Special Collections

Baldwin Collection. Over 3,000 volumes collected by a prominent turn-of-the century newspaper publisher in Peoria. Almost all are examples of fine printing and include a wide range of historical and literary works, both classical and modern. Among the more unusual items is a complete run of *Punch* from volume one in 1848 to volume 73 in 1913.

Merrill Bothamley Collection. Approximately 1,500 volumes focusing primarily on American business. Especially rich in histories of specific firms; the collection also includes many biographies and autobiographies of business leaders.

Library of American Civilization. A microbook collection of over 6,500,000 pages relating to all aspects of American life from the beginnings to the outbreak of World War I.

Library of English Literature. A microbook collection containing more than 1,500,000 pages on English literature from the beginnings through the Restoration of Charles II to the death of Dr. Johnson.

Archives of Maryland. Seventy-volume set representing historical records from 1636 to 1784 with emphasis on the colonial court and assembly.

Archives of New Jersey. Forty-seven volumes with cumulative index reprinting historical records from 1631 to 1813.

Pennsylvania Archives. One hundered thirty-five indexed volumes reprinting historical records from 1644 to 1902.

Curriculum Materials Center. Contains approximately 4,200 items including textbooks, curriculum guides, and books on teaching.

Rare Book Collections

Bennett Collection. One of Bradley's original faculty members and a pioneer in the industrial education movement, Charles Alpheus Bennett also founded the Manual Arts Press, now the Bennett Publishing Company, a division of Macmillan. In the later 1930s, Bennett donated to the school his personal library of approximately 1,000 books and 6,000 pamphlets. The collection can be divided roughly into four categories: (1) books acquired to complete research for his two books, *History of Manual and Industrial Education Up To 1870* and *History of Manual and Industrial Education, 1870 to 1917;* (2) ephemeral material gathered during his forty years as editor of *Industrial Education Magazine;* (3) technical books and course outlines published during the early years of the Manual Training Movement in Sweden, England, France, German, and America; (4) books on art instruction published prior to the mid-nineteenth century. Within these categories, the collection also provides a good deal of information about Bennett and his activities in the Peoria area.

Lincoln Collections. These groupings total approximately 2,500 items and include several original Lincoln letters and a notebook kept by Lincoln in 1855 while a candidate for the U.S. Senate. The principal body of material is contained in the Martin L. Houser Collection which consists of about 1,000 volumes and 300 pamphlets. Mr. Houser was regarded as the foremost authority on the books the self-educated Lincoln read from his earliest childhood. Houser collected duplicates of every book Lincoln was known to have studied, and always in the same edition. The collection also includes general works about Lincoln, the Civil War, and personalities of the period, many in limited editions.

Chase Collections. Materials pertaining to Philander Chase (1775-1852), first Episcopal bishop of Illinois and founder of Jubilee and Kenyon colleges. The heart of the collection is a group of 2,400 manuscript letters from Bishop Chase and his family.

Peoria Historical Society Library. On deposit at the University Library since 1980, this collection holds over 7,000 items, including 1,700 books, pertaining to the history of Peoria and central Illinois. In addition to vertical file material, the collection contains Civil War diaries, letters, and camp records; a collection of over 200 works by Peoria authors; and 12,000 photographic images of early Peoria.

Illinois APCO Collection. The Associated Public-Safety Communications Officers is the nation's oldest and largest public safety radio user group. The Illinois Chapters files and records, along with all the records from the state chapter, proceedings of the Annual Conferences from 1944 through 1952, and one of the most complete runs of the *APCO Bulletin* are in the collection.

424
Catholic Theological Union
Catholic Theological Union Library
5401 South Cornell Avenue
Chicago, Illinois 60615

Telephone. (312) 324-8000

Institutional Description. The Catholic Theological Union is a school of ministry in the Roman Catholic tradition, begun in 1968 by a number of religious communities of men who combined resources in order to educate more creatively for priesthood. It grants graduate degrees. Enrollment: 260.

Library Administration. Kenneth O'Malley, C.P., Library Director and Special Collections Librarian.

Library General Holdings. 110,000 volumes. The collection is primarily English language materials dealing with Roman Catholic theology. The collection is especially strong in Roman Catholic scripture, missiology, and spirituality.

Special Collections

Sufi Mystics Collection. A 450 volume work.

425
Chicago State University
Paul and Emily Douglas Library
95th Street at King Drive
Chicago, Illinois 60628

Telephone. (312) 995-2400

Institutional Description. The publicly supported state university offers liberal arts, business administration, allied health, nursing, and teacher education programs. Enrollment: 4,835.

Library Administration. William C. Prigge, Dean of Library and Learning Resources.

Library General Holdings. 270,000 volumes; 1,692 current periodicals; 47,500 government documents; 379,000 microforms; 6,700 audiovisual materials.

Special Collections

Special collections include the Schomburg Collection and the American Periodical Series.

426
Chicago Theological Seminary
Hammond Library
5757 South University Avenue
Chicago, Illinois 60637

Telephone. (312) 752-5757

Institutional Description. The privately supported graduate seminary is affiliated with the United Church of Christ. It was founded in 1855. Enrollment: 102.

Library Administration. Rev. Neil W. Gerdes, Library Director.

Library General Holdings. 102,000 volumes; 220 current journal subscriptions. Subject strengths are in the areas of English-language Bibles, church history, theology, Christian education, ethics, pastoral theology, psychology, social sciences, Hebraica, and Judaica.

Special Collections

The library has a special collection in the area of the Congregational Church, its history and institutional relations. It contains materials from the continent but more especially in England and America. Church records and histories of midwestern Congregational Churches and organizations (such as the Community Renewal Society in Chicago) are also on file. Religious education curriculum materials as well as pamphlets and tracts from the Congregational Church and its successor, the United Church of Christ, are also collected.

Rare Book Collections

Rare books from early American church history in colonial New England and in the later settlement of the Midwest are housed with similar European church histories from the post Reformation period; some early books in Hebrew are being kept. The Manuscript Collection includes those of Presidents of the Chicago Theological Seminary as well as Anton Boisen, a founder of Clinical Pastoral Education.

427
College of DuPage
Learning Resources Center
22nd Street and Lambert Road
Glen Ellyn, Illinois 60137

Telephone. (312) 858-2800

Institutional Description. The two-year community college was founded in 1965. Enrollment: 11,772.

Library Administration. Bernard Fradkin, Director.

Library General Holdings. 115,000 volumes; 780 periodical subscriptions.

Special Collections

The learning resource center maintains a **Planning and Information Center for Students,** the **College Archives,** the **Juvenile Collection,** and the **Library of American Civilization** (microform).

428
College of Lake County
John C. Murphy Memorial Library
19351 West Washington
Grayslake, Illinois 60030

Telephone. (312) 223-6601

Institutional Description. This is a public (district) community college. In addition to the main campus, the college operates facilities in Waukegan and Highland Park. Enrollment: 4,684.

Library Administration. Tom Buchta, College Librarian; Robert Finnegan, Librarian.

Library General Holdings. 100,000 books; 511 periodical subscriptions; 260,000 microforms (including ERIC documents, 1978-); 5,190 audiovisual sets.

Special Collections

Pat Gill Jazz Collection. Consists of 600 albums.

429
Columbia College
College Library
600 South Michigan Avenue
Chicago, Illinois 60605

Telephone. (312) 663-1600

Institutional Description. The privately supported liberal arts college grants baccalaureate and master's degrees. Enrollment: 4,618.

Library Administration. Mary Schellhorn, Director.

Library General Holdings. 65,000 volumes; 48,000 slides; 700 videotapes and films; 16,000 microfilms; 815 periodical titles.

Special Collections

The **George S. Lurie Fine Arts Collection** is a significant resource of film, photography, and arts materials. In addition, the Arts, Entertainment, and Media Management's Resource Center provides unique materials to support the curriculum in that field. Other special collections include the **Black American Literature Collection** which contains first editions of contemporary black authors. There is also a Center for the Study of Black Music.

430
Concordia College
Klinck Memorial Library
7400 West Augusta
River Forest, Illinois 60305

Telephone. (312) 771-8300

Institutional Description. The private liberal arts college and graduate school is supported by the Lutheran Church—Missouri Synod. Its purpose is to provide Christian Education for students interested in careers within the Church and/or within business and society. Enrollment: 1,039.

Library Administration. Henry R. Latzke, Director of Library Services.

Library General Holdings. 145,000 bound volumes;

395,000 microforms; 550 periodical subscriptions; 1,000 music scores.

Special Collections

Various collections include the Curriculum Collection (9,000 textbooks and other curriculum material; 6,000 volumes of juvenile literature; complete ERIC Microfiche Collection; 560 volumes of hymnals and choral books; 36 sets of historical music sets (collected editions and monuments to 1800); Migne's *Patrologia*, writings of the Church Fathers in Greek and Latin; complete writings of Martin Luther, Weimar German edition and American English edition; Melanchton's complete works in German.

431
DePaul University
University Library
2323 North Seminary
Chicago, Illinois 60614

Telephone. (312) 341-8088

Institutional Description. The privately supported Roman Catholic university was founded in 1898 by the Vincentian Fathers. Enrollment: 9,244.

Library Administration. Doris Brown, University Librarian; Kathryn DeGraff, Special Collections Librarian.

Library General Holdings. 295,365 volumes; 2,498 current periodical titles; 95,971 bound periodicals; 16,747 microforms.

Special Collections

The library of DePaul University has specialized collections in philosophy (Continental nineteenth- and twentieth-century philosophers); business, economics, and the U.S. Civil War. The University Archives contain materials relating to the history of DePaul University. The Archives of the Lincoln Park Conservation Association are also maintained. The various special collections of the library include:

Charles Dickens Collection. Contains 590 volumes and includes numerous editions of Dickens' works in the original publisher parts, first complete editions, first American editions, and special editions. Books about Dickens and a complete run of *The Dickensian* are also a part of the collection. Non-monograph material such as prints, posters, and china figurines depicting characters from Dickens' works are included.

Napoleonic Collection. Contains over 4,000 volumes including materials depicting the era of Napoleon through correspondence, memoirs, and biographies of Napoleon and his family. Histories of France and Europe are included in the collection that reflect the social, political, and military situations of the time. The collection is rich in contemporary literary works such as pamphlets, broadsides, military maps, and atlases.

Stuyvesant Peabody Sports Collection. Numbers over 900 volumes including a complete collection of *The Sporting Magazine,* 1792-1870. The collection reflects the sports of the British aristocracy of the late eighteenth to the late nineteenth centuries. The focus is primarily on field sports, especially fox hunting and horse racing. There are novels, rule-books, and collections of sporting songs and verse. Included in this collection are some of the most renowned sporting books in first editions.

Verrona Derr Collection of African-American Studies. The purpose of the collection is to contribute to research and scholarship and to lead to better racial understanding. The collection includes novels, monographs, anthologies, poetry, and periodicals such as *The Journal of Negro History.*

Rare Book Collections

Rare Book Collection. Consists of 2,000 volumes, including ten incunabula and notable editions of English literature from the sixteenth through the twentieth centuries. Many of these books are first editions or special printings with unique bindings. There are also such non-book materials as portraits, illustrations, and autographs of historical or literary significance.

Manuscript Collection. Includes a variety of documents. Letters written by St. Vincent DePaul and a letter written by Queen Isabella I of Spain are particularly noteworthy. A decorated vellum document, dated 1669 and dedicated to the city of Nuremburg, displays the text of the Book of Wisdom written in fine, interweaving circles. Hand drawn and hand colored maps, some of which are the work of sixteenth-century cartographers, are a rich resource for study.

432
Dr. William M. Scholl College of Podiatric Medicine
Library
1001 North Dearborn Street
Chicago, Illinois 60610

Telephone. (312) 280-2910

Institutional Description. The privately supported professional college was founded in 1912. It grants the Doctor of Podiatric Medicine degree. Enrollment: 547.

Library Administration. Richard Klein, Director, Library Services.

Library General Holdings. 15,000 volumes; 300 current periodical titles.

Special Collections

Both the book and journal collections are well represented by podiatric medicine, orthopedics, dermatology, biomechanics, diagnostic medicine, sports medicine, and the basic sciences.

433
Eastern Illinois University
Booth Library
Charleston, Illinois 61920

Telephone. (217) 581-2223

Institutional Description. The publicly supported state university was founded in 1895 as the Eastern Illinois State Normal School. It now includes over 32 departments including teacher education. Enrollment: 9,845.

Library Administration. Wilson Luquire, Library Services Assistant.

Library General Holdings. 536,000 volumes; 2,590 current periodical subscriptions; 1,281,000 microforms; 36,000 audiovisual materials; 206,000 government documents.

Special Collections

The library serves as a depository for selected publications of the United States Government and for maps issued by the U.S. Army Map Service. A publishers' exhibit of textbooks for elementary and secondary schools is also provided. A collection of books for children of all ages is available for the students who study children's literature.

434
Elmhurst College
A.C. Buehler Library
190 Prospect Avenue
Elmhurst, Illinois 60126

Telephone. (312) 279-4100

Institutional Description. The privately supported liberal arts college is affiliated with the United Church of Christ. The college was founded in 1871 as a normal school and became a senior college in 1924. Enrollment: 2,384.

Library Administration. Esther Bullock, Librarian.

Library General Holdings. 179,000 volumes; 810 current periodical subscriptions; 10,450 microforms; 3,500 audiovisual materials.

Special Collections

The library has special collections in nursing and annual reports of associations and corporations. There is also a display of outstanding art work, primarily of the Chicago Imagist school.

Rare Book Collections

A collection of 230 hymnals and hymnology books date from the late eighteenth century and are mostly in German.

435
Eureka College
Melick Library
300 East College Avenue
Eureka, Illinois 61530

Telephone. (309) 467-3721

Institutional Description. The privately supported liberal arts college is affiliated with the Christian Church (Disciples of Christ). It was founded in 1855. Enrollment: 447.

Library Administration. Nancy Blomstrom, Director.

Library General Holdings. 82,000 volumes; 356 current periodical subscriptions.

Special Collections

The library houses the **Hinkhouse Collection of Art** and the **Ronald Reagan Memorabilia Collection.** President Reagan was a member of the Class of 1932. The library also has a special collection of nineteenth-century English literature and materials relating to the history of the Disciples of Christ (Christian Church).

436
Felician College
Library
3800 West Peterson Avenue
Chicao, Illinois 60659

Telephone. (312) 539-1919

Institutional Description. Felician College was chartered in 1926 and operated as an extension of Loyola University until 1953. From 1953 to 1967 the college served the Felician Order to educate its members. It was opened to lay students (primarily women) in 1967 and to male students in 1974. Enrollment: 197.

Library Administration. Sister Mary Inez Moch, Director of Library Services.

Library General Holdings. 60,000 books, records, filmstrips, tapes, and other items; 200 periodical and newspaper subscriptions.

Special Collections

The library maintains special collections in art and architecture; ethnic studies, history, and religious studies. The **Polish History and Literature Collection** is also maintained.

437
Garrett-Evangelical Theological Seminary
United Library
2121 Sheridan Road
Evanston, Illinois 60201

Telephone. (312) 866-3900

Institutional Description. The privately supported theological seminary is affiliated with the United Methodist Church. It offers graduate-level programs of preparation for various vocations of Christian ministry. Enrollment: 286.

Library Administration. Alva A. Caldwell, Librarian.

Library General Holdings. 262,960 volumes; 1,027 periodical subscriptions; 7,100 microforms.

Special Collections

Special collections of the library include Methodistica (monographs, manuscripts, biographies, and official documents of the Methodist Church in England and the United States, including information on major church leaders and figures associated with the Seminary; the Paul Edwin Keene Bible Collection including examples of the English Bible (Matthews Bible (1537) and a King James Bible (1611); and a Patristic Collection of monographs about the Church Fathers and translations of their works.

438
Governors State University
University Library
University Park, Illinois 60466

Telephone. (312) 534-5000

Institutional Description. The publicly supported state university was founded to furnish upper-level and graduate programs for the increasing number of junior college graduates in the state. Thus it enrolls only juniors, seniors, and graduate students. Enrollment: 2,377.

Library General Holdings. 242,000 volumes; 28,000 media items; 2,400 periodical subscriptions; 600,000 microforms.

Special Collections

The library has a collection of Black literature and maintains the **Kuper Collection** of plays of the twentieth century. The **Materials Center** collection contains curriculum materials, textbooks, and juvenile literature in support of the teacher education program.

439
Greenville College
Ruby E. Dare Library
315 East College Avenue
Greenville, Illinois 62246

Telephone. (618) 664-1840

Institutional Description. The privately supported liberal arts college was founded in 1892 as Almira College to provide college courses within a Christian atmosphere. It is affiliated with the Free Methodist Church. Enrollment: 595.

Library Administration. Jane L. Hopkins, Acting Director.

Library General Holdings. 95,500 books; 400 periodical and newspaper titles; 1,200 recordings.

Special Collections

The Media Center and the Educational Resources Center provide faculty and students with a wide array of audiovisual equipment and services, and teacher education materials normally found in the public schools.

440
Harrington Institute of Interior Design
Design Library
410 South Michigan Avenue
Chicago, Illinois 60605

Telephone. (312) 939-4975

Institutional Description. This is a private institution offering a three-year associate program. Enrollment: 372.

Library Administration. Adeline Schuster, Head Librarian.

Library General Holdings. The 10,000 volume collection supports all aspects of the Institute's interior architecture curriculum, the single major offered here. 90 current periodical subscriptions from 3 continents indexed in specialized art and architecture indices; 12,000 slides include art and architecture, historical images, works of contemporary designers and architects, and representations of student work.

Special Collections

Approximately 1,000 current catalogs representing manufacturers of furniture, plumbing fixtures and equipment, architectural hardware, lamps and lumieres, institutional furnishings and architectural materials; included also are photographs, specifications, and current prices.

441
Illinois Benedictine College
Theodore F. Lownik Library
5700 College Road
Lisle, Illinois 60532

Telephone. (312) 960-1500

Institutional Description. The privately supported liberal arts college was founded in Chicago in 1887 and moved to its present location in 1901. It is supported by the Roman Catholic Benedictine Monks of Saint Procopius Abbey. The Abbey is located adjacent to the college. Enrollment: 1,494.

Library Administration. Bert A. Thompson, Director of Library Service.

Library General Holdings. 137,000 volumes; 915 current periodical titles; 30,000 government documents; 14,000 microforms.

Special Collections

In addition to a rare book collection, the library maintains the **Abraham Lincoln Collection** and a collection of materials on the Czech heritage.

442
Illinois College
Schewe Library
1101 West College Avenue
Jacksonville, Illinois 62650

Telephone. (217) 245-7126

Institutional Description. The privately supported liberal arts college was founded in 1829. It is affiliated with the United Presbyterian Church and the United Church of Christ. Enrollment: 724.

Library Administration. Richard L. Pratt, Librarian.

Library General Holdings. 110,000 volumes; 700 current periodicals; 3,100 microfilm reels; 1,600 phonorecords.

Special Collections

A collection of Lincolniana was the gift of Mr. Roy D. Packard and a collection of books on the Civil War has been established by the Civil War Round Table of Springfield, Illinois, as a memorial to Benjamin P. Thomas, Lincoln scholar and former trustee of the College. The Special Collection Area also contains books by faculty, students, and alumni of Illinois College as well as rare books and incunabula.

443
Illinois College of Optometry
Carl F. Shepard Memorial Library
3241 South Michigan Avenue
Chicago, Illinois 60616

Telephone. (312) 225-1700

Institutional Description. The privately supported professional college was founded in 1872. It offers programs on the upper-division and graduate levels only. Enrollment: 969.

Library Administration. Gerald Dujsik, Director.

Library General Holdings. 17,000 volumes; 190 current periodical titles.

Special Collections

The library's collection includes the topics of optometry, ophthalmology, and vision science.

444
Illinois Institute of Technology
Paul V. Galvin Library and Chicago-Kent Library
3300 South Federal Street
Chicago, Illinois 60616

Telephone. (312) 567-3001

Institutional Description. The privately supported technological university was formed in 1940 by a merger of Armour Institute of Technology (founded in 1892) and Lewis Institute (founded in 1896). Enrollment: 4,445.

Library Administration. David K. Dowell, Director of Libraries.

Library General Holdings. 327,618 volumes; 20,000 microforms.

Special Collections

Galvin Library. Supports undergraduate instruction in all disciplines with strong collections in engineering, science, technology, business, economics, architecture, and psychology.

Chicago Kent Library. Houses all essential books, treatises, periodicals, and materials necessary to the study of law. Also there is the unique Library of International Relations which supports research in international law, international business, and international relations.

445
Illinois State University
Milner Library
Normal, Illinois 61761

Telephone. (309) 438-2111

Institutional Description. The publicly supported state university was founded in 1857 as the first state institution of higher education in Illinois. Enrollment: 19,040.

Library Administration. Fred M. Peterson, Librarian.

Library General Holdings. 1,001,945 books; 332,270 government documents; 58,750 reels of microfilm; 1,382,950 microcards, microfiche, and microprint; 21,800 recordings; 413,500 maps; 5,500 current periodical subscriptions.

Special Collections

Among the special collections maintained by the library are a collection of twentieth-century English and American authors; a collection of private press books; and a collection on the history of the circus and allied arts.

446
Illinois Valley Community College
Jacobs Library
2578 East 350th Road
Oglesby, Illinois 61348

Telephone. (815) 224-2720

Institutional Description. The college is the second oldest in downstate Illinois and traces its history to 1924 when it was established as LaSalle-Peru-Oglesby Junior College. The present name was adobted in 1966. Enrollment: 2,252.

Library Administration. Betty Jo Hanson, Head Librarian.

Library General Holdings. 47,000 volumes; 590 current periodical subscriptions.

Special Collections

The library is a depository for Nuclear Regulatory Commission publications as well as for state and federal documents.

447
Illinois Wesleyan University
Sheean Library
P.O. Box 2899
Bloomington, Illinois 61702

Telephone. (309) 556-3172

Institutional Description. Illinois Wesleyan University is a privately supported liberal arts university affiliated with the United Methodist Church. Enrollment: 1,750.

Library Administration. Clayton Highum, University Librarian; Robert Frizzell, Social Science and Special Collections Librarian.

Library General Holdings. 155,000 volumes; 900 current periodicals; 25,000 government documents; 1,600 audiovisual items; 12,000 music scores.

Rare Book Collections

The Dr. John T. Gernon Collection. Includes nineteenth- and twentieth-century first editions, Americana, Western Americana, art books, and a colleciton of American and British mystery novels numbering some 300 titles.

448
John A. Logan College
Library
Centerville, Illinois 62918

Telephone. (618) 985-3741

Institutional Description. The two-year public college was founded in 1967. The present campus was occupied in 1982. Enrollment: 2,189.

Library Administration. Linda Barrette, Librarian.

Library General Holdings. 35,000 volumes; 300 periodical titles; 2,500 microforms; 7,000 audiovisual materials; 2,500 pamphlets.

Special Collections

The library maintains the **Logan Memorial Collection.**

449
John Marshall Law School
Library
315 South Plymouth Court
Chicago, Illinois 60604

Telephone. (312) 427-2737

Institutional Description. The privately supported law school was founded in 1899 as a nonprofit educational institution, and grants Juris Doctor degrees. Enrollment: 1,651.

Library Administration. Randall T. Peterson, Director of Library Services.

Library General Holdings. 220,000 volumes; 4,057 serial and periodicals; 379 audiovisual titles.

Special Collections

The library provides a collection of relevant and timely materials important to the study of law and to legal research.

450
Judson College
Benjamin P. Browne Library
1151 North State Street
Elgin, Illinois 60123

Telephone. (312) 695-2500

Institutional Description. The privately supported Christian liberal arts college grew from the 1920 college division of the Northern Baptist Theological Seminary of Chicago. It is affiliated with the American Baptist Churches in the U.S.A. Enrollment: 446.

Library Administration. Dennis E. Read, Director.

Library General Holdings. 72,000 volumes; 27,000 microfiche; 400 current periodical subscriptions.

Special Collections

The **Jeffersonian Americana Collection** and the **Social History of England Collection** are a resource of 23,500 volumes reduced and reproduced on separate microfiche cards. The collection covers all aspects of American life and literature from the exploration of America to the beginning of World War I. A similar collection of English literature has been added. In addition, the library has the **Donald G. Peterson Collection** on Baptist history and missions. The **Schofield Music Collec-**

tion represents the largest collection of music resources in the Elgin Area.

451
Kendall College
Library
2408 Orrington Avenue
Evanston, Illinois 60201

Telephone. (312) 866-1300

Institutional Description. The privately supported liberal arts college was founded in 1934 as a junior college. It now grants associate and baccalaureate degrees. The college is affiliated with the United Methodist Church. Enrollment: 333.

Library Administration. Stephanie Rapp, Director.

Library General Holdings. 37,000 volumes; 190 current periodical titles.

Special Collections

Special collections in the areas of culinary arts and business are maintained by the library. There is also a collection on American Indian culture.

452
Knox College
College Library
Galesburg, Illinois 61401

Telephone. (309) 343-0112

Institutional Description. The privately supported liberal arts college was founded in 1837. It grants baccalaureate degrees. Enrollment: 952.

Library Administration. Douglas Lawson Wilson, Director.

Library General Holdings. 224,000 volumes; 750 current periodical subscriptions.

Special Collections

Special collections maintained by the library include the **Ernest Hemingway Collection;** a collection of rare early maps; the **Finley Collection** on the Old Northwest; the **Smith Collection** on the Civil War; and an extensive collection of materials on the Mississippi River.

453
Lake Forest College
Donnelley Library
Lake Forest, Illinois 60045

Telephone. (312) 234-3100

Institutional Description. The privately supported liberal arts college was founded in 1857. It is affiliated with the United Presbyterian Church. Enrollment: 1,146.

Library Administration. Arthur H. Miller, Librarian.

Library General Holdings. 201,000 volumes; 1,270 current periodical titles; 117,000 government documents; 64,000 microforms.

Special Collections

Special Collections complement the core holdings and off-campus sources by providing access to significant primary source materials for students and faculty rsearchers. Larger collections donated by friends, faculty, and alumni include: **Scotiana Collection** of 3,000 volumes for the study of Scottish history, art, literature, music, genealogy, and printing; and the **Garrett Leverton Library** of nearly 5,000 volumes of plays and material on the development of the theatre in the United States.

Collections on railroad history, over 8,000 items in all, include the library of Elliott Donnelley, the collection of Munson Paddock, and recent gifts from Mr. James Sloss. The **O'Kieffe Collection** contains over 1,500 volumes of Americana, language, literature, and rare books. The papers and library (170,000 sheets and 1,000 volumes) of Captain Joseph Medill Patterson, founder of the *New York Daily News* and grandson of the College's first president, are also housed. Other substantial collections include the **Richard Templeton Collection** of modern art.

Rare Book Collections

The **Hamill Collection** of contains over 6,000 rare books in the humanities.

454
Lewis and Clark Community College
Library
Godfrey Road
Godfrey, Illinois 62035

Telephone. (618) 466-3411

Institutional Description. The first classes of the two-year community college were held in 1970. In 1971, the college purchased the campus of Monticello College. Enrollment: 2,589.

Library Administration. Beverly Humphries, Librarian.

Library General Holdings. 34,000 volumes.

Special Collections

The **Law Enforcement Collection** is maintained by the library.

455
Lewis University
Lewis University Library
Route 53
Romeoville, Illinois 60441

Telephone. (815) 838-0500

Institutional Description. The privately supported institution was founded in 1932 as a technical school. Now a Roman Catholic liberal arts university, Lewis is directed by the Brothers of the Christian Schools. Enrollment: 2,-312.

Library Administration. Fredereike A. Moskal, Library Director.

Library General Holdings. 100,265 volumes; 19,376 bound periodical volumes; 520 current periodical subscriptions; 6 newspaper subscriptions; 4,499 microfilm reels (periodicals); 24,078 volumes on microfiche; 2,000 audiovisual titles.

Special Collections

Illinois and Michigan Canal National Heritage Corridor. Materials collected and organized by Professor John Lamb, a member of the History Department at Lewis University.

A collection of orchestral scores and parts was donated to the library. The Music Department is working to organize the collection, after which it will be made available for use by orchestras in the Lewis University area.

456
Lincoln Christian College
Jessie C. Eury Library
P.O. Box 178
Lincoln, Illinois 62656

Telephone. (217) 732-3168

Institutional Description. The privately supported Christian Bible college was founded in 1944. Affiliated with the Church of Christ, it offers preparation for seminary studies as well as programs leading to church service. Enrollment: 269.

Library Administration. Thomas Tanner, Librarian.

Library General Holdings. 77,000 bound and microtext volumes; 400 journal subscriptions.

Rare Book Collections

The **Enos E. Dowling Rare Book Room** contains 1,000 volumes of Greek and Hebrew manuscripts and early Restoration Movement journals and documents, as well as a collection of 2,000 rare hymnbooks (800 of which are directly related to the Restoration Movement).

457
Lincoln College
McKinstry Memorial Library
300 Keokuk Street
Lincoln, Illinois 62656

Telephone. (217) 732-3155

Institutional Description. Lincoln college is a two-year private, independent college in central Illinois. It was founded in 1865 by the Cumberland Presbyterian Church as Lincoln University and was the only college named for Abraham Lincoln during his lifetime. The college became indpendent in 1929 and a two-year college in 1932. Enrollment: 1,180.

Library Administration. Preston Gilson, Librarian.

Library General Holdings. 35,000 volumes.

Special Collections

The nationally famed **Lincoln Museum** is housed in the library as well as the **McKinstry Rare Books Room,** and the **Museum of the Presidents.** The Museum's collection of Lincolniana includes several signatures of Abraham Lincoln and the desk Lincoln used when he served in the Illinois State Legislature. Documents signed by every President of the United States are exhibited in the Museum of the Presidents, along with pictures, commemorative medals, and signatures of most First Ladies.

458
Lincoln Land Community College
Learning Resource Center
Shepherd Road
Springfield, Illinois 62708

Telephone. (217) 786-2273

Institutional Description. The two-year community college was estalished in 1968. Enrollment: 3,427.

Library Administration. Elijah Singley, Librarian; Helen Ruth Dillow, Librarian.

Library General Holdings. 70,000 volumes.

Special Collections

The library has special collections on faculty development and nursing.

459
Loyola University of Chicago
University Libraries
820 North Michigan Avenue
Chicago, Illinois 60611

Telephone. (312) 670-2900

Institutional Description. The privately supported university was founded in 1870 by the Society of Jesus as Saint Ignatius College. The Roman Catholic institution became a university and adopted its present name in 1909. Enrollment: 10,742.

Library Administration. Ellen J. Waite, Director.

Library General Holdings. 924,477 volumes; 5,625 current periodicals; 856,000 microforms; 21,850 audiovisual materials.

Special Collections

Special collections located in the Cudahy Library at the Lake Shore Campus include the Samuel Insull Papers, the Catholic Extension Society Papers, and the Loyola University Archives. The major strengths of the Julia Deal Lewis Library at the Water Tower Campus are in education and business administration.

460
MacCormac Junior College Library
615 North West Avenue
Elmhurst, Illinois 60126

Telephone. (312) 941-1200

Institutional Description. The college is the oldest of the City Colleges of Chicago. It was founded in 1911. The college has an urban campus in the financial district of Chicago and a suburban setting which opened in in Elmhurst in 1977. Enrollment: 446.

Library Administration. Marilyn S. Luebbing, Librarian.

Library General Holdings. 12,000 volumes; 77 periodical subscriptions.

Special Collections

The library maintains an **Art History Slide Collection** and the **Antique Typewriter Collection.**

461
MacMurray College
Henry Pfeiffer Library
East College at Lurton
Jacksonville, Illinois 62650

Telephone. (217) 245-6151

Institutional Description. The privately supported liberal arts college was founded in 1846. It grants baccalaureate degrees. Enrollment: 810.

Library Administration. Ronald Daniels, Head Librarian.

Library General Holdings. 145,000 volumes; 300 current periodical titles; 200,000 government documents.

Special Collections

Special collections include the **Lincoln Collection;** the **Birdseye Pepys Collection** of books by and about the seventeenth-century British diarist, Samuel Pepys; and the **Austin-Ball Collection** on singing and voice instruction.

462
McCormick Theological Seminary
Jesuit-Krauss-McCormick Library
5555 South Woodlawn Avenue
Chicago, Illinois 60637

Telephone. (312) 241-7800

Institutional Description. The privately supported theological seminary is affiliated with the Presbyterian Church (U.S.A.). It offers graduate-level programs only. Enrollment: 286.

Library Administration. Caroline B. Whipple, Director.

Library General Holdings. 450,000 items; 1,200 periodical titles.

Special Collections

McCormick's library dates from 1829 when the earliest portions of its collection were founded as part of Lane Theological Seminary. Under the leadership of its first librarian, Charles Evans (later to become one of America's greatest bibliographers) and successor librarians, McCormick has contributed a number of initiatives nationally to theological library development. The library at the present time includes a collection belonging to the Chicago and Detroit Provinces of the Society of Jesus.

463
McKendree College
College Library
701 College Road
Lebanon, Illinois 62254

Telephone. (618) 537-4481

Institutional Description. The privately supported liberal arts college was founded in 1828 as Lebanon Seminary. It now grants baccalaureate degrees and has branch campuses at Belleville Area, Kaskaskia, Lewis and Clark, Matoon, Olney, and Rend Lake Colleges; Scott Air Force Base; and in Kentucky at Fort Knox/Elizabethtown, and Louisville. It is affiliated with the United Methodist Church. Enrollment: 647.

Library Administration. Helen E. Gilbert, Head Librarian.

Library General Holdings. 65,000 volumes; 365 current periodical titles; 36,000 microforms.

Special Collections

The library maintains the archives of the Southern Illinois Conference of the United Methodist Church.

464
Meadville/Lombard Theological School
The Library
5701 South Woodlawn Avenue
Chicago, Illinois 60637

Telephone. (312) 753-3196

Institutional Description. The privately supported theological school is a Unitarian-Universalist, coeducational, graduate institution. It was founded in 1844. Enrollment: 36.

Library Administration. Neil W. Gerdes, Library Director.

Library General Holdings. 97,000 volumes; 86 retrospective serials; 124 current periodical subscriptions. The Library specializes in advanced religious studies, but focuses on liberal religion and related fields such as science and religion, environmental ethics, and comparative religions.

Special Collections

Pamphlet File. An extensive file of seventeenth-, eighteenth-, and nineteenth-century materials relating to Unitarianism and Universalism as well as other liberal religions and issues. New England and the Midwest are areas particularly covered.

Rare Book Collections

The Manuscript Collection includes the personal and professional papers of Jenkin Lloyd Jones, A. Powell Davies, Jack Mendelsohn, and others, as well as original manuscript sermons of William Ellery Channing. A hymnody collection made up of those put together by Kenneth Patton and Vincent B. Silliman is shelved separately. Church and ministry records from the Central Midwest Unitarian Universalist Association are also on file.

465
Millikin University
Staley Library
1184 West Main Street
Decatur, Illinois 62522

Telephone. (217) 424-6210

Institutional Description. The privately supported university was founded in 1901 as the Decatur College and Industrial School. Together, with nearby Lincoln College, they were known for 50 years as the James Millikin University. Now a separate institution, Millikin University is affiliated with The Prebyterian Church (U.S.A.). Enrollment: 1,494.

Library Administration. Charles E. Hale, Librarian.

Library General Holdings. 154,000 volumes; 890 current periodical subscriptions; 7,500 microforms.

Special Collections

Special collections include the **Carlyle Baer Bookplate Collection,** the **Civil War Memorial Collection,** and the **Alice in Wonderland Collection.**

466
Moody Bible Institute
Institute Library
820 North La Salle Drive
Chicago, Illinois 60610

Telephone. (312) 329-4000

Institutional Description. The privately supported interdenominational professional institute was founded in 1886 to train students in the Bible and practical Christian work. It grants baccalaureate degrees. Enrollment: 1,330.

Library Administration. Richard G. Schock, Librarian.

Library General Holdings. 115,000 volumes.

Special Collections

The library houses a special collection on Christian education as well as the Moodyana and historical collection.

467
Mundelein College
Learning Resource Center
6363 Sheridan Road
Chicago, Illinois 60660

Telephone. (312) 989-5406

Institutional Description. The privately supported liberal arts college was founded in 1929 by the Sisters of Charity of the Blessed Virgin Mary of the Roman Catholic Church. Enrollment: 820.

Library Administration. Patricia A. Donohoe, Director.

Library General Holdings. 142,167 volumes; 636 periodical subscriptions; 11,000 audiovisual materials.

Special Collections

Educational Materials Center. Houses the children's and adolescents' literature collection, textbooks and curriculum materials, and a variety of kits in various disciplines.

Mundelein Center for Religious Education. The Center offers a complete collection of materials for religious education for all ages, as well as special collections on justice and peace education, the Hispanic ministry, and various interfaith projects.

468
National College of Chiropractic
Sordoni-Burich Library
200 East Roosevelt Road
Lombard, Illinois 60148

Telephone. (312) 629-2000

Institutional Description. The privately supported professional college was founded in 1906. It offers upper-level and graduate programs only. Enrollment: 793.

Library Administration. Joyce E. Whitehead, Director, Learning Resource Center.

Library General Holdings. 13,000 books; 450 journal subscriptions.

Special Collections

Special emphases of the library's collections are on chiropractic, nutrition, orthopedics, neurology, radiology, and sports medicine.

469
National College of Education
N. Dwight Harris College Library Center
2840 Sheridan Road
Evanston, Illinois 60201

Telephone. (312) 256-5150

Institutional Description. The privately supported college was founded in 1886 to meet the demand for teachers in Chicago. The College maintains two additional campuses: the Urban Campus in Chicago and the Lombard (IL) Campus. Enrollment: 2,398.

Library Administration. Marilyn Lester, Director, Learning Resources.

Library General Holdings. 150,000 volumes; 800 journal subscriptions.

Special Collections

Robert R. McCormick Children's Library and Media Center. Maintains a collection of 10,000 volumes, 30 periodicals, and 3,000 non-print materials. Microcomputers for children are also provided.

470
North Central College
Oesterle Library
30 North Brainard Street
Naperville, Illinois 60566

Telephone. (312) 420-3434

Institutional Description. The privately supported liberal arts college is affiliated with the United Methodist Church. Founded in 1861, it offers extensive after-hours programs and grants baccalaureate and master's degrees. Enrollment: 1,668.

Library Administration. Edward W. Meachen, Director.

Library General Holdings. 105,000 volumes; 615 current periodical subscriptions.

Special Collections

The library maintains the archival papers and photographs of North Central College; the **Leffler Lincoln Collection,** and the **Sang Jazz Collection.**

471
North Park College and Theological Seminary
Wallgren Library; Mellander Library
3225 West Foster Avenue
Chicago, Illinois 60625

Telephone. (312) 583-2700

Institutional Description. The privately supported Christian college and seminary, founded in 1891, is owned and operated by the Evangelical Covenant Church of America. Enrollment: 1,330.

Library Administration. Dorothy-Ellen Gross, Director.

Library General Holdings. 170,000 volumes; 875 periodicals.

Special Collections

The Wallgren Library maintains a **Scandinavian Collection** (includes the Jenny Lind Collection); **Abraham Lincoln Collection;** and a rare books collection.

Mellander Library. A collection of materials in the field of religion and related subjects consisting of 66,700 volumes as well as microforms and audiovisual materials. The goal of collection development is to collect on an advanced study level in order to support the curriculum of the Seminary. The holdings are extensive in terms of the Evangelical Covenant Church with the heaviest subject concentration in Biblical studies. This reflects the evangelical and pietistic concern for the Bible as well as the distribution of published materials available.

Swedish-American Historical Society and Archives. A collection of Swedish Americana.

Covenant Archives and Historical Library. Official correspondence, minutes and reports from various departments of the Evangelical Covenant Church, manuscripts, diaries, and person records, as well as 4,000 photographs. Much of the material written before 1925 is in Swedish. The holdings also include literature in the fields of Swedish history, Swedish Americana, and other denominations of Swedish origin. Among its treasures is a copy of the Gustav Vasa Swedish Bible published in 1541.

472
Northeastern Illinois University
Ronald Williams Library
5500 North St. Louis Avenue
Chicago, Illinois 60625

Telephone. (312) 583-4050

Institutional Description. The publicly supported liberal arts and teacher education university was founded in 1961. It grants baccalaureate and master's degrees. Enrollment: 6,348.

Library Administration. John D. Gabowry, University Library.

Library General Holdings. 500,000 volumes; 600,000 educational support items such as recordings, microfilms, maps, documents, filmstrips, pamphlets, and periodicals.

Special Collections

The library's major strength is in the field of education. Special collections include the **Chicago and Cook County Archives** and the **Afro-American Studies Collection.**

473
Northern Baptist Theological Seminary
Bethany/Northern Seminary Library
660 East Butterfield Road
Lombard, Illinois 60148

Telephone. (312) 620-2105

Institutional Description. The privately supported theological seminary, founded in 1913, is affiliated with the American Baptist Churches, USA. It offers graduate programs only. Enrollment: 148.

Library Administration. Kenneth Shaffer, Library Director; Hedda Barnbaugh, Catalog and Special Collections Librarian.

Library General Holdings. 141,452 bound volumes; 2,900 audiovisual items; 600 current periodicals. These resources represent the combined libraries of Bethany and Northern Baptist Theological Seminaries. Special strengths are in Baptist history, Church of the Brethren history, peace studies, Pietism, and psychological journals.

Special Collections

The Special Collections contain the Abraham H. Cassel Collection of sixteenth- through nineteenth-century theological books and pamphlets and a nearly complete collection of American Tract Society publications, the Ora Huston Collection of over four hundred volumes of English Bibles; Baptist Association records, Danish and Norwegian Baptist Seminary material, the Donald Dayton Collection of nineteenth-century evangelicalism, and the Olmstead Collection in Ancient and Near Eastern Languages and Literature.

474
Northern Illinois University
Founders Memorial Library
DeKalb, Illinois 60115

Telephone. (815) 753-1271

Institutional Description. The publicly supported (state) university was founded in 1895 as the Illinois State Normal School. It now grants baccalaureate, master's, and doctoral degrees. Enrollment: 20,154.

Library Administration. Theodore F. Welch, Director.

Library General Holdings. 1,100,000 volumes; 859,000 government documents; 1,500,000 microforms; 184,368 maps; 34,000 recordings; 4,689 films; 4,198 linear feet of manuscript and archive material; 5,140 current periodical subscriptions.

Special Collections

The major special collections of the library include the **Afro-American Studies Collection;** the **Chicago and Cook County Archives,** and an education collection. The Faraday Library serves faculty and students in the disciplines of chemistry and physics; the Music Library serves the music curriculum; the Map Library contains maps and atlases vital to research in geography; and the Instructional Materials Center complements the Outdoor Education Program at Loarado Taft Field Campus.

475
Northwestern University
Charles Deering Library
Evanston, Illinois 60201

Telephone. (312) 491-3741

Institutional Description. The privately supported university was founded in 1851. It is now one of the country's largest independent educational institutions. Enrollment: 14,065.

Library Administration. John P. McGowan, University Librarian.

Library General Holdings. 3,124,863 volumes; 25,474 periodicals; 1,432,758 microforms.

Special Collections

Core Collection. This collection is designed especially for undergraduates and contains more than 47,000 key books in all disciplines.

Curriculum Collection. Contains elementary and secondary teaching materials, courses of study, and children's literature.

Map Collection. Contains 173,500 map sheets and 2,330 volumes, including atlases and reference books relating to cartography.

Melville J. Herskovits Library of African Studies. A special collection of international repute containing 139,-

160 volumes on every aspect of Africa.

Music Library. The rare books and manuscripts collection includes a portion of the Moldenhauer Archive. Special collections include Twentieth Century Music; Fritz Reiner Library; John Cage Notation Collection; John Cage Archive; manuscripts of Jean Martinon; Ricordi Collection; ethnomusicological recordings emphasizing African music.

Poetry/Listening Facility. Includes a non-circulating collection emphasizing contemporary American and British poetry, a listening center with a collection of folk, rock, jazz, and blues records; spoken-word recordings of poetry and drama; and film and slide projection rooms.

Special Collections Department. The collections number some 185,000 volumes in a number of distinguished collections. Included are the Twentieth Century Collections, the Herskovits Library of African Studies, rare books, manuscripts, limited editions and fine bindings, underground press publications, and women's movement literature.

Transportation Library. Specializes in all the socioeconomic and operational aspects of all modes of transport, and includes an important collection on highway and police administration.

University Archives. Contains the publications and historical records of the University.

476
Olivet Nazarene University
Benner Library and Learning Resource Center
P.O. Box 527
Kankakee, Illinois 60901

Telephone. (815) 939-5011

Institutional Description. The privately supported university, founded in 1907, is affiliated with the Church of the Nazarene. It offers associate, baccalaureate, and master's degrees, as well as certificates. Enrollment: 1,561.

Library Administration. Allan L. Wiens, Director.

Library General Holdings. 137,000 volumes plus 55,000 other items (government documents, maps, audiovisual materials, records, sheet music, microfilm); 800 periodical subscriptions.

Rare Book Collections

John Wesley Collection. Includes original manuscripts and pamphlets of the English founder of Methodism. The library also has a special collection of the theological writings of James Arminius.

477
Principia College
Marshall Brooks Library
Elsah, Illinois 62028

Telephone. (618) 374-2131

Institutional Description. Principia College is privately supported institution affiliated with the Christian Science Church. Enrollment: 682.

Library Administration. Daphne Selbert, College Librarian; Marsha Burruss, Associate Director and Special Collections/Rare Books Librarian.

Library General Holdings. 151,000 bound volumes; 1,000 periodicals/newspapers; 160,000 microforms; 5,000 phonograph records; 8,000 audiotapes; 470 videotapes.

Special Collections

Curriculum Materials. Include Bible studies; Christian Science; Wurtz Collection on fresh water biology; selective depository for U.S. Government Documents.

Rare Book Collections

The collection of rare books includes book and pamphlets on Christian Science; books and manuscripts concerned with Baja California; fore-edge paintings; children's literature; eighteenth-century British and American authors; early European maps, illustrations, and bibliography; dime novels—in the **Harvey Feurborn Collection;** the **Florence Bade Collection** of autographed works of modern poets; and World War II propaganda.

478
Quincy College
Brenner Library
1800 College Avenue
Quincy, Illinois 62301

Telephone. (217) 222-8020

Institutional Description. The privately supported liberal arts college was founded in 1860. It is conducted by the Franciscan Friars of the Roman Catholic Church. Enrollment: 873.

Library Administration. Rev. Victor Kingery, O.F.M., Director.

Library General Holdings. 200,000 volumes; 870 journal titles; 99,000 microtext items.

Special Collections

Instructional Materials Center. A collection of print and non-print materials supporting the teacher education programs.

Special collections include a Spanish-American Collection and an English Literature Collection.

Rare Book Collections

The library has a rare book collection of 4,000 volumes including books from the twentieth century.

479
Rend Lake College
Learning Resource Center
Rural Route 1 - Ken Gray Parkway
Ina, Illinois 62846

Telephone. (618) 437-5321

Institutional Description. The two-year college was founded in 1955. The present campus was occupied in 1970. Enrollment: 1,562.

Library Administration. David Patton, Director.

Library General Holdings. 30,000 volumes; 450 periodical and 12 newspaper subscriptions.

Special Collections

The library maintains a collection of materials on southern Illinois history and archaeology.

480
Roosevelt University
University Library
430 South Michigan Avenue
Chicago, Illinois 60605

Telephone. (312) 341-3515

Institutional Description. The privately supported university was founded in 1945. Enrollment: 3,154.

Library Administration. Adrian Jones, Director of Libraries.

Library General Holdings. 400,000 volumes; 1,478 periodicals.

Special Collections

The library has the microbook Library of American Civilization. The Music Library houses 10,000 records and music scores as well as 20,000 books.

481
Rosary College
Rebecca Crown Library
7900 West Division Street
River Forest, Illinois 60305

Telephone. (312) 366-2490

Institutional Description. The privately supported liberal arts college traces its origins to Sinsinawa Academy, founded in 1848. It is conducted by the Roman Catholic Sisters of Saint Dominic of Sinsinawa, Wisconsin. Enrollment: 958.

Library Administration. Kay Beaudrie, Chief Librarian.

Library General Holdings. 209,000 volumes; 1,100 current periodical and newspaper titles; 87,000 government documents.

Special Collections

Special collections are maintained in the fields of library science and English literature.

482
Rush University
University Library
1653 West Congress Parkway
Chicago, Illinois 60612

Telephone. (312) 942-5000

Institutional Description. The privately supported professional institution offers baccalaureate, master's and doctorate degrees in the health sciences. Enrollment: 1,056.

Library Administration. Trudy A. Gardner, Director.

Library General Holdings. 52,776 books, 64,641 bound serial volumes; 2,207 current periodical subscriptions.

Special Collections

The library is the oldest health sciences library in Chicago and serves the entire University and Medical Center. Special holdings include books by and about Dr. Benjamin Rush; books and pamphlets on cholera and cholera epidemics of the nineteenth century; and books on sixteenth- and seventeenth-century medicine.

483
St. Augustine College
Library
1333 West Argyle
Chicago, Illinois 60640

Telephone. (312) 878-8756

Institutional Description. The purpose of the college is to provide junior college instruction in the liberal arts and sciences and applied sciences to minority adults with special emphasis on those of Hispanic descent. Enrollment: 855.

Library General Holdings. 5,000 volumes; 126 periodical subscriptions.

Special Collections

The library maintains a special collection of over 400 volumes in the Spanish language.

484
St. Mary of the Lake Seminary
Feehan Memorial Library
Mundelein, Illinois 60060

Telephone. (312) 566-6401

Institutional Description. The privately supported theological seminary grants professional and master's degrees. It is affiliated with the Roman Catholic Church. Enrollment: 227.

Library Administration. Gloria Sieben, Librarian.

Library General Holdings. 140,000 books; 400 periodical subscriptions.

Special Collections

The library is especially strong in its sections covering philosophy, patristic studies, theology, and Catholic Church history.

485
Sangamon State University
Brookens Library
Shepherd Road
Springfield, Illinois 62794

Telephone. (217) 786-6597

Institutional Description. The publicly supported institution is an upper-division state university, offering the last two years of baccalaureate study and master's degrees. Enrollment: 2,046.

Library Administration. Brian Alley, University Librarian; Thomas J. Wood, University Archivist and Head of Special Collections.

Library General Holdings. 440,000 volumes; 2,700 periodical subscriptions; 100,000 volumes government documents; 80,000 microforms; 600 films and videotapes.

Special Collections

The Sangamon State University Archives/Special Collections Unit contains the archives of the university; personal papers of faculty, students, and alumni; manuscript collections relating to community, grassroots, and political action organizations in the Springfield area; and other collections relating to the history and culture of Central Illinois.

Notable collections include the Richard Phillips Collection of photographs of Illinois vernacular architecture; records of the Women's International League for Peace and Freedom (Springfield Chapter); the William Di Marco Collection of Railroad memorabilia; and the Handy Writers' Colony Collection which includes papers and manuscripts of novelist James Jones.

Rare Book Collections

The Special Collections Unit contains rare, fragile, and other non-circulating library materials, including a collection of early editions of Walt Whitman's *Leaves of Grass.* As a member of the Illinois Regional Archives Depository (IRAD) System, the SSU Archives holds county and municipal records dating from 1817 to the present from a 14-county area of Central Illinois.

486
Southeastern Illinois College
Learning Resource Center
Rural Route 4, College Drive
Harrisburg, Illinois 62946

Telephone. (618) 252-4411

Institutional Description. The college was founded in 1960 as an extension of the Harrisburg High School where it was housed until 1971. Enrollment: 1,582.

Library Administration. Melba Patton, Director.

Library General Holdings. 30,000 units (books, periodicals, pamphlets, audiotapes, phonorecords, maps, filmstrips, filmloops, multimedia kits).

Special Collections

The library maintains a collection of materials on southern Illinois.

487
Southern Illinois University - Carbondale
Delyte W. Morris Library
Carbondale, Illinois 62901

Telephone. (618) 453-2522

Institutional Description. The publicly supported university is a multipurpose institution. Founded in 1869, it now consists of several separate and diverse campuses, including a medical center in Springfield. Enrollment: 20,237.

Library Administration. Kenneth G. Peterson, Dean of Libraries; David V. Koch, Curator, Special Collections; Shelley Cox, Rare Books Librarian.

Library General Holdings. 2,000,000 volumes; 14,946 periodical subscriptions; 2,247,340 microforms.

Special Collections

Modern American Philosophy. Includes the papers and library of John Dewey, the archives of the Open Court Press, archives of *Christian Century* magazine; archives of the Library of Living Philosophers; papers of Henry Nelson Wieman, James K. Feibleman, Paul Weiss, John Childs, George Counts.

Harley K. Croessmann James Joyce Collection. Contains papers, letters, and books, including papers of James Joyce's biographer Herbert Gorman, and translator George Goyest; all printings of all editions of James Joyce's works.

First Amendment Freedoms. Includes the Ralph E. McCoy Freedom of the Press Collection; the papers and library of Theodore Schroeder; the papers of John Howard Lawson; correspondence between Henry Miller and his defense attorney Elmer Gertz; books and papers by and about Robert Ingersoll.

Southern Illinois History. Includes the papers of John W. Allen.

Ulysses S. Grant. Books, correspondence, and manuscripts.

American and British Expatriate Writers. Books, manuscripts, and correspondence of twentieth-century American and British authors, primarily between 1920-1950—the "Expatriates" and others of their generation, including D.H. Lawrence, Richard Aldington, Kay Boyle, Lawrence Durrell, Robert Graves, and Henry Miller.

Irish Renaissance Writers. Books, manuscripts, and correspondence of Irish writers, 1890-1950; "the Irish Renaissance" including W.B. Yeats, Lennox Robinson, Katharine Tynan Hinkson, *The Envoy* magazine, and Dublin's Abbey Theater and Gate Theater.

Printing in the Twentieth Century. Particularly American presses, but also the Cuala Press in Ireland, Hogarth Press, Hours Press, and American presses in Europe.

488
Southern Illinois University - Edwardsville
Elijah P. Lovejoy Library
Edwardsville, Illinois 62026

Telephone. (618) 692-2720

Institutional Description. The publicly supported university includes the Edwardsville campus of Southern Illinois University, The School of Dental Medicine at Alton, and East St. Louis Center. Enrollment: 8,354.

Library Administration. Gary N. Denue, Director; Louisa Bowen, Archivist.

Library General Holdings. 768,000 volumes; 36,400 periodical subscriptions; 600,000 microforms; 41,400 audiovisual titles; 485,000 government documents; 300,000 other material in research and map collections.

Special Collections

The library's special collections include music (especially jazz); materials on the Illinois region of the United States; and materials relating to the architect, Louis Sullivan.

489
Spertus College of Judaica
Norman Asher and Helen Asher Library
618 South Michigan Avenue
Chicago, Illinois 60605

Telephone. (312) 922-9012

Institutional Description. The privately supported liberal arts and teachers college was founded in 1925. It provides programs in Bible, Hebrew language and literature, Talmud, history, philosophy, communal service, and teacher education. Enrollment: 185.

Library Administration. Richard W. Marcus, Director and Head Librarian.

Library General Holdings. 75,000 volumes; 600 current periodical subscriptions; 1,500 microforms.

Special Collections

The Asher Library is one of the largest circulating libraries of Judaica in the Midwest. Its resources include extensive collections in Judaica and Hebraica; a distinguished rare book collection housed in the Katzin Memorial Rare Book Room; Israeli publications; the Badona Spertus Library of Art in Judaica; and the Chicago Jewish Archives which hold the archives of the Jewish Federation of Metropolitan Chicago.

The library has developed the Levin microfilm and microfiche collection of Jewish newspapers and journals.

490
Spoon River College
Learning Resource Center
Rural Route 1
Canton, Illinois 61520

Telephone. (309) 647-4645

Institutional Description. Spoon River College grew out of Canton Community College which was founded in 1959. The current name was adoped in 1968. Enrollment: 1,112

Library Administration. Wayne Gudzinskas, Librarian.

Library General Holdings. 34,000 volumes; 320 periodical subscriptions.

Special Collections

Special collections are maintained on agricultural machinery, visual communications, energy conservation, and Fulton County history.

491
State Community College of East St. Louis
Senator Kenneth Hall Learning Resource Center
Governor James R. Thompson Boulevard
East St. Louis, Illinois 62201

Telephone. (618) 274-6666

Institutional Description. Founded in 1969, the publicly supported community college is located in the urban area of East St. Louis, Illinois. Enrollment: 887.

Library Administration. W. J. van Grunsven, Director; Bettye Brown, Librarian.

Library General Holdings. 30,000 volumes. Collections support the curriculum of vocational educational development, allied health, business education, industrial management, communication and humanities, social science/human services, mathematics and science. Audiovisual center is college- and community-oriented.

Special Collections

The learning resource center maintains a special collection on Black studies.

492
Trinity Christian College
College Library
6601 West College Drive
Palos Heights, Illinois 60463

Telephone. (312) 597-3000

Institutional Description. The privately supported liberal arts college was founded in 1959 by the Christian Reformed Church. It grants baccalaureate degrees. Enrollment: 444.

Library Administration. Hendrik Sliekers, Director of Library Services.

Library General Holdings. 54,000 volumes; 300 current periodical subscriptions; 19,000 microforms.

Special Collections

The library maintains the **Dutch Heritage Collection.**

493
Trinity Evangelical Divinity School
James E. Rolfing Memorial Library
2065 Half Day Road
Deerfield, Illinois 60015

Telephone. (312) 945-8800

Institutional Description. The privately supported seminary is governed by the Evangelical Free Church of America. It provides graduate-level programs only. Enrollment: 830.

Library Administration. Brewster Porcella, Librarian.

Library General Holdings. 116,000 volumes; 1,000 current periodicals.

Special Collections

The resources of the Rolfing Library include the addition of the personal libraries of two outstanding evangelican scholars, the late Dr. Wilber M. Smith and that of Dr. Carl F.H. Henry. The library has a growing collection of microfilm materials, including University Microfilms' *Short-Title Catalogue of Early English Books* (Series 1 & 2: 1475-1700). This collection now includes more than 64,000 volumes of fifteenth-, sixteenth-, and seventeenth-century works. The Divinity School archives are also maintained by the library.

Rare Book Collections

Archives of the Evangelical Free Church of America. This collection of historical data includes publications dating from the earliest days of the immigrant churches in the United States.

494
University of Chicago
Joseph Regenstein Library
1100 East 57th Street
Chicago, Illinois 60637

Telephone. (312) 702-8705

Institutional Description. The privately supported university was founded in 1891 by numerous donors including the American Baptist Education Society, Marshall Field, and John D. Rockefeller. Enrollment: 9,145.

Library Administration. Martin Runkle, University Librarian; Robert Rosenthal, Special Collections Librarian.

Library General Holdings. 4,460,683 bound volumes; 47,796 periodical subscriptions; 114,544 microcards; 1,139,846 microfiche; 83,060 microfilms; 74,471 microprints; 9,000 sound recordings; 295,000 maps.

Special Collections

Distinctive collections within the general library stacks include the holdings of the former John Crerar Library (for science and technology), as well as collections on Far Eastern and South Asian studies, children's literature, and modern poetry.

The University of Chicago Library Department of Special Collections has extensive holdings in medieval and Renaissance philosophy, French and British neoclassical drama, German *Almanache* and nineteenth century popular literature, children's literature, American drama, modern poetry, and literary first editions, as well as theology and British Bibles.

Noteworthy history concentrations document Greek and Roman civilization, Judaica, English Civil War, French Revolution, early life in Kentucky and the Ohio River Valley, and Lincolniana.

The University Archives contains administrative records as well as collections on the Chicago School sociologists, Willaim Rainey Harper, Edith and Grace Abbott, S. Chandrasekhar, Enrico Fermi, James Franck, Amos Alonzo Stagg, Robert Maynard Hutchins, and George Herbert Mead.

Rare Book Collections

The John Crerar Library's rare book collection recently augmented existing strengths in the history of science and medicine. Byzantine manuscripts of the New Testament, English manorial records, and the files of *Poetry* magazine highlight the manuscript collection, which includes late Renaissance northern Italian notarial documents and records of the Atomic Scientists' Movement.

495
University of Health Sciences - The Chicago Medical School
Learning Resources Center
3333 South Green Bay Road
North Chicago, Illinois 60664

Telephone. (312) 578-3000

Institutional Description. The privately supported medical school was founded in 1912, and moved to the grounds of the Veterans Administration Hospital in 1980. Enrollment: 824.

Library Administration. Nancy Garn, Director.

Library General Holdings. 72,076 bound volumes and microfilm reels; 1,300 periodical subscriptions.

Special Collections

The special collections of this health sciences library include a Magnetic Resonance Imaging Collection; AIDS Collection; and a Grants Collection.

496
University of Illinois at Chicago
University Library
801 South Morgan
Chicago, Illinois 60680

Telephone. (312) 996-0998

Institutional Description. The publicly supported state university offers extensive programs leading to baccalaureate, professional, master's, and doctorate degrees. Enrollment: 21,777.

Library Administration. Beverly P. Lynch, University Librarian.

Library General Holdings. 1,474,784 volumes; 14,202 current periodical subscriptions; 1,449,924 microforms; 235,000 audiovisual materials; 492,308 government documents.

Special Collections

The University Library consists of the Main Library, the Architecture and Art Library, the Library of the Health Sciences, the Mathematics Library, and the Science Library. These collections provide students with materials in all curricular areas, for graduate programs, and for faculty research.

Special Collections Department. Concentrates on books, documents, and papers relating to the history and development of Chicago. It is also responsible for maintaining the University Archives; the **Jane Addams Memorial Collection;** the **Robert Hunter Middleton Design Printing Collection;** and the **Corporate Archives of the Chicago Board of Trade.**

497
University of Illinois at Urbana-Champaign
University of Illinois Library at Urbana-Champaign
1408 West Gregory Drive
Urbana, Illinois 61801

Telephone. (217) 333-0791

Institutional Description. The publicly supported university has accreditation in at least 33 specialties including teacher education and several categories of engineering. Enrollment: 33,274.

Library Administration. David F. Bishop, University Librarian; Norman Brown, Special Collections Librarian; Nancy Romero, Rare Books Librarian; Carl W. Deal, Director of Library Collections.

Library General Holdings. 7,190,443 volumes; 93,973 current serials and newspaper subscriptions; more than 3,000,000 microform units.

Special Collections

Specialized collections of the University of Illinois Library are listed below under the library in which they are housed.

Classics Library:

Dittenberger-Vahleu Pamphlet Collection. Mostly classical philology and accessible through an alpha file.

Communications Library:

D'Arcy Collection. Advertisements between 1890 and 1970. This collection is being microfilmed.

Education and Social Science Library:

Arms Control, Disarmament and International Security (ACDIS). Materials in the fields of arms control, disarmament, and international security including annuals, yearbooks, bibliographes, databooks, digests, newsletters, maps, directories, and journals.

Professional Collection. Core collection of serials and monographs for immediate research needs of the high school faculty emphasizing education for the gifted.

S - Collection. Literature and non-fiction written for children and young adults.

Merton J. Mandeville Collection in Occult Sciences. Materials in the occult sciences.

Journal Supplement Abstract Service in Psychology. Fugitive materials such as technical reports, invited addresses, bibliographies, literature reviews, reports on research in progress and proceedings. *Psychological Documents* is the index to this collection.

Odell Test Collection. Over 7,000 educational and psychological tests dating from 1914-present.

General Stacks:

Mexican Pamphlets. A collection consisting of 1,476 titles of Mexican imprints published mostly in the early nineteenth century.

Spanish Drama. A collection comprised of 13,000 titles (eighteenth- through early twentieth-century).

Geology and Earth Sciences Library:

Geological Documents. Includes documents of the state Geological Surveys, U.S. Geological Survey, and the Canada Geological Survey.

Geological Maps. Includes maps of Illinois geology, topographic maps of Illinois and surrounding states.

Manuscripts. Unpublished manuscripts on Illinois geology.

History Library:

Cavagna Collection. Italian local history.

Illinois Historical Survey:

Collection of books, periodicals, maps, and manuscripts relating to the history of Illinois.

Law Library:

Briefs - Illinois Supreme Court. Coverage from ca. 1962 to ca. 1976.

Briefs - U.S. Court of Appeals for the Seventh Circuit. Arranged by docket number (file not complete).

Roman Law Manuscripts. A collection of sixteenth- to eighteenth-century legal dissertations.

Lincoln Room:

Lincoln Collection. Material on and by Abraham Lincoln including newspapers, sound recordings, graphic materials, manuscripts, etc.

Maps and Geography Library:

Aerial Photography. Sequential coverage of Illinois since 1936.

Cavagna Collection. Early European and Italian maps.

County Atlases of Midwestern States. Nineteenth and twentieth centuries.

Freeman Collection. Early maps of America.

Lybyer Collection. Early maps of the Near East.

Schmidt Collection. Collection of various editions of the Lewis Evans maps of the Middle British Colonies and Ohio Valley.

Modern Languages and Linguistics Library:

Linguistic Atlases. Presently consists of 160 quarto and folio volumes published since the 1920s in the area of Romance and Germanic languages.

Newspaper Library:

Over 1,000 titles of single issues of short run original newsprint from early 1700 to the present.

Rare Book Collections

The **Rare Book and Special Collections Library** collects materials by and about John Milton; seventeenth- and eighteenth-century English literature; maps; celestial atlases; works on the history of science; Confederate imprints; incunabula; Bibles; early English drama; Shakespeare; books and pamphlets relating to the literary, political, and religious life of the seventeenth century; newsletters printed before 1700; sixteenth- and seventeenth-century catechisms; the correspondence of Marcel Proust, W.S. Merwin, H.G. Wells, Robert Browning; works by and about Rainer Maria Rilke; first editions of major nineteenth-century English authors; Italian history and civilization; works of Mark Twain and Carl Sandburg; works on freedom of expression; and American humor. The various collections are too numerous to mention; a select list follows below.

Baskette Collection on Freedom of Expression, 16th century-1960. Contains ca. 15,000 items on civil liberties and freedom of expression in the United States.

Cavagna Library, 1116-1910. Ca. 30,000 items, 450 volumes of manuscripts, and 138 portfolios of miscellaneous items. Contains books on genealogy, biography, local history, law, economics; manuscripts on local history mainly relating to Italian cities and towns.

Harwell Collection of Confederate Imprints. Ca. 2,100 items (1,200 Confederate imprints and 900 Civil War publications).

Hollander Economic Library, 1574-1937. Contains ca. 4,500 items which document the development of economics. Includes works by Adam Smith, Malthus, Thornton, J.B. Say, Lord Lauderdale, James and John S. Mill, Robert Torrens, and David Ricardo; letters by Adam Smith, Jeremy Bentham, Malthus, Ricardo, James and John S. Mill.

Mayer Collection. 2,000 items of the works by and about Rainer Maria Rilke, including rare and special editions, translations into major languages, major and minor works of criticism, and letters.

Meine Collection in Folklore, Local Color, and Humor. Ca. 9,000 items of American humor in all forms, e.g., satire, joke books, humorous ballads, reminiscences of famous comedians, cartoons, comic almanacs, and humor magazines.

Meine Mark Twain Collection. Contains ca. 3,000 items including 300 first editions of Twain's books and many variant editions; foreign translations, as well as manuscripts, memorabilia, newspaper and magazine contributions by and about Twain, and many biographical and critical volumes.

Merwin Collection. An archive of unpublished works, notes, letters, ideas for poems, personal correspondence, and other literary papers and major published works.

Motley Collection of Theatre Design. Contains 3,000 items including original drawings of set and costume designs for more than 300 productions in London, New York, and Stratford-upon-Avon from 1932-1976.

Proust Collection. Ca. 2,000 letters from and to Marcel Proust, many of which have never appeared in printed form. Includes manuscripts, proof sheets from various Proust works, assorted documents of the Proust family, and published Proust works.

Sandburg Collection. The private papers and library of the Illinois-born poet; manuscripts, recordings, and transcriptions of Sandburg's radio broadcasts and lectures, many articles and newspaper clippings by and about Sandburg, and photographs.

H.G. Wells Archives. Ca. 60,000 letters to Wells and

2,000 from Wells to others. Contains manuscripts, correspondence, editions of Wells' works, miscellaneous documents, family and business records, photographs, diaries, periodical articles by and about Wells, newspaper clippings, 40 full-length books in typescript or manuscript format in several drafts with handwritten corrections, and 1,000 volumes of Wells' copies of his printed works (including first editions, revisions, and translations).

Baldwin Collection. Ca. 5,800 volumes containing material for the study of Shakespeare and other Elizabethan figures, especially works on Shakespeare's education; sixteenth-, seventeenth-, and eighteenth-century texts of classical authors with commentaries, rhetorics, histories, Bibles, and prayerbooks.

Nickell Collection. 2,000 volumes of eighteenth-century English literature. Contains original editions of Daniel Defoe, Jonathan Swift, Henry Fielding, Alexander Pope, Oliver Goldsmith, Samuel Johnson, James Boswell, Joseph Addison, Tobias Smollett, and others.

Music Library. Catalogued books and music housed in the Music Library's Special Collections area: Approximately 2,500 books and 5,000 music editions, largely eighteenth and twentieth century, together with rare or expensive twentieth-century materials; as well as items requiring special protections because of format, size, or physical condition. Strengths include eighteenth-century British music editions; hymnology; nineteenth-century Americana, including numerous song collections as well as several hundred songsters; pre-World War II college song books; nineteenth-century European opera scores; books on organ construction; pedagogical works of various types; over 80 unpublished motion picture scores by Hollywood composer Frank Skinner; miscellaneous music manuscripts.

University of Illinois Archives. Established in 1963, the Archives includes 14,060 cubic feet of office records, publications, and personal papers from the University and the Urbana-Champaign campus. Its collections include hundreds of manuscript collections and the archives of about thirty professional associations. Among the personal papers in the Archives are those of chemist Roger Adams, historian Arthur Bestor, alumnus Avery Brundage, dean of men Thomas A. Clark, agriculturalist Eugene Davenport, political scientist John Fairlie, alumnus Stewart Howe, businessman Wayne Johnston, physicist Frederick Seitz, sculptor Lorado Taft, electrical engineer Joseph Tykociner, football coach Bob Zuppke, and the presidents of the University. The Archives contains about 500,000 photographs and 3,500 sound recordings.

498
VanderCook College of Music
Harry Ruppel Memorial Library
3209 South Michigan Avenue
Chicago, Illinois 60616

Telephone. (312) 225-6288

Institutional Description. The privately supported professional college was founded in 1909. It grants baccalaureate and master's degrees. Enrollment: 100.

Library Administration. Dean Jensen, Director.

Library General Holdings. 18,898 volumes; 24,260 scores; 68 current periodical titles; 1,840 microfiche titles; 1,875 record albums; 2,538 discs.

Special Collections

The library has a special collection of instrumental, band, and orchestral method books.

499
Western Illinois University
University Libraries
900 West Adams Street
Macomb, Illinois 61455

Telephone. (309) 298-1891

Institutional Description. The publicly supported university was founded in 1899 as a normal school. It now offers a greatly expanded curriculum. Enrollment: 10,090.

Library Administration. Gordana Rezab, Rare Books and Special Collections Librarian.

Library General Holdings. 600,000 volumes; 4,000 current journal subscriptions; 10,000 periodical titles.

Special Collections

The special collections area of the library houses such unique collections as Tom Railsback's Congressional papers, the Center for Icarian Studies, and papers of other noted individuals, both scholars and celebrities. Includes the Burl Ives Collection and the Center for Regional Authors.

500
Wheaton College
Buswell Memorial Library
Wheaton, Illinois 60187

Telephone. (312) 260-5705

Institutional Description. The privately supported Christian liberal arts college is interdenominational and offers baccalaureate and master's degrees. Enrollment: 2,-475.

Library Administration. P. Paul Snezek, College Librarian; Mary Dorsett, Special Collections/Rare Books Librarian.

Library General Holdings. 295,767 volumes; 303,005 nonprint resources (microforms, charts, audiovisual), 1,-675 current periodical subscriptions.

Special Collections

Jonathan Blanchard and Charles Albert Blanchard Collection. The former (father) and the latter (son) were the first two presidents of Wheaton College. Both men were prolific authors and their library contains copies of their own publications, as well as many volumes depicting nineteenth-century American culture and society. The issues of slavery and freemasonry were of particular interest to the Blanchards.

Dr. V. Raymond Edman (1900-67). Fourth president of Wheaton College; his library includes many devotional and inspirational volumes, as well as several commentaries and theological texts which Dr. Edman used during his missionary and academic careers.

Alumni-Faculty Fine Arts Collection. Consists of scholarly or artistic productions by Wheaton College alumni, trustees, and past and present faculty members.

John B. Russell Collection. A library of over 1,000 titles providing a glimpse into the field of nineteenth-century educational history and methods.

John Danforth Nutting. The volumes in this collection cover both sides of the Mormon issue and a wide range of topics from general histories of the area and biographies of Mormon leaders to hymnals.

Stephen Barabas Keswick Collection. Contains over 800 books and pamphlets about the Keswick Holiness Movement which began in England in the mid-nineteenth century; includes extensive works and almost complete run of *Keswick Week.*

Hymnal Collection. Over 2,000 hymnals dating from the early 1800s.

Elizabeth Green Papers. Books, correspondence, notes, and other materials documenting the career and personal life of Elizabeth Green, teacher of stringed instruments and orchestra conductor.

Margaret Clarkson Papers. Includes the materials of the noted author and hymnwriter.

Commercial Collection. Approximately 2,500 television commercials document one twenty-four hour day (January 5, 1975) on a VHF network station.

Richard Crabb Papers. Papers and manuscripts of the journalist, author, and longtime observer of Illinois culture and politics.

Everett Mitchell Papers. Mr. Mitchell was a pioneer in the early days of radio, remembered as the host of NBC's "National Farm and Home Hour." His collection contains books, papers, and some memorabilia.

Lottie Holman O'Neill Collection. Memorabilia of the first woman sworn into the Illinois General Assembly (1923).

Gerald R. Weeks Collection. Papers and memorabilia of the Chairman of the DuPage County Board and active member of the local Republican Party.

Harold "Red" Grange Collection. Material documenting the career of Mr. Grange, charter member of the Professional Football Hall of Fame who played for the University of Illinois and the Chicago Bears.

Betsy Palmer Collection. Known as a star from the "Golden Age" of television and also for numerous roles on the stage, Miss Palmer has donated her collection of scrapbooks, playbills, memorabilia, and photographs.

American Scientific Affiliation. Founded in 1941 to "investigate any area relating Christian faith and science and to make known the results of such investigations for comment and criticism by the Christian Community and by the scientific community." Material includes minutes, correspondence, bound journals, books, membership records, and abstracts of papers presented at annual meetings.

Malcolm Muggeridge Papers. Letters, papers, and manuscripts of the English author, critic, media personality, and Christian commentator.

Other Collections. Papers, manuscripts, letters, and other materials are collected on Stephen Schofield, Hans Rookmaaker, Dr. Kenneth P. Taylor, Robert Siegel, Frederick Buechner, and Madeleine L'Engle.

Rare Book Collections

William S. Akin Collection. Contains over 4,000 titles and includes many first editions, illustrated editions, and elaborately bound volumes of literature. Mr. Akin, a long-time friend of Wheaton College, collected these volumes as the result of a childhood experience which instilled in him a deep love and appreciation for acquiring rare books. The collection highlights the works of various authors including: John Bunyan—over 200 different copies of *Pilgrim's Progress,* Lewis Carroll, Samuel Johnson, James Boswell, and Charles Dickens. Holdings for Miquel de Cervantes Saavedra, Herman Melville, Daniel DeFoe, and others are less comprehensive but important.

Indiana

501
Anderson College
Wilson Library; Byrd Memorial Library
1100 East Fifth Avenue
Anderson, Indiana 46012

Telephone. (317) 649-9071

Institutional Description. The privately supported liberal arts college and graduate school of theology was founded in 1917. A Christian college, Anderson is affiliated with the Church of God. Enrollment: 1,789.

Library Administration. Karen Nelson, Director, Learning Resources Center; Harold Boyce, Director, Byrd Memorial Library.

Library General Holdings. 138,000 volumes; 610 current periodicals.

Special Collections

An important collection of the Wilson Library's holdings is the collection of papers of Charles E. Watson, former U.S. Secretary of Defense.

Byrd Memorial Library. The School of Theology's Byrd Memorial Library contains a specialized collection of periodicals and books supporting graduate programs. It houses 58,000 volumes. The library is the official depository for the archives of the Church of God. The Warner Memorial Historical Collection is a considerable resource for ministers and scholars who wish to do research in the heritage of the Church of God. There is a significant and growing collection of artifacts from ancient cultures of the Near East.

502
The Associated Mennonite Biblical Seminaries
Library
3003 Benham Avenue
Elkhart, Indiana 46517

Telephone. (219) 296-3726

Institutional Description. The privately supported graduate theological seminary is composed of two units. In 1958, two seminaries within the organization of the General Conference of the Mennonite Church (The Mennonite Biblical Seminary in Chicago, IL and the Goshen Biblical Seminary in Goshen, IN) joined to form the Associated Mennonite Biblical Seminaries in Elkhart. Enrollment: 175.

Library Administration. Eileen K. Saner, Librarian.

Library General Holdings. 101,362 volumes; 545 current periodical subscriptions; 1,015 microforms; 575 audiovisual materials.

Rare Book Collections

Studer Bible Collection. This collection totals over 2,000 books and items including major divisions of English and non-English translations of the Bible. There are sub-divisions of Abridged Bibles, Illustrated Bibles, Bible Stories, Miniatures, Summaries, and Concordances. Related also is a library of significant books about the Bible, its preservation, printing, translation, and distribution as well as Apocrypha and Pseudoscriptures. Accompanying the library are several file drawers of clippings, pamphlets, etc. related to the collection.

503
Ball State University
Alexander M. Bracken Library
2000 University Avenue
Muncie, Indiana 47306

Telephone. (317) 289-1241

Institutional Description. The publicly supported state university was founded in 1918. Enrollment: 16,138.

Library Administration. Michael B. Wood, Dean; David Tambo, Special Collections Librarian.

Library General Holdings. 1,180,000 volumes; 4,207 current periodical subscriptions; 97,000 government documents; 172,422 microforms; 414,000 audiovisual materials.

Special Collections

John Steinbeck Collection. In honor of Elizabeth Otis, Steinbeck's friend and literary agent, this collection consists of more than 800 works by and about Steinbeck including first editions, autographed copies, original manuscripts and letters, galley proofs, and posters of various movie adaptations of his works.

Sir Norman Angell Collection. Contains 2,300 books, periodicals, and personal papers.

The library also maintains special collections of American poetry and the famous Middletown Studies.

504
Butler University
Irwin Library
4600 Sunset Avenue
Indianapolis, Indiana 46208

Telephone. (317) 283-9227

Institutional Description. The privately supported university was founded in 1855 and is dedicated to undergraduate liberal arts education of students pursuing courses of general and professional study. Enrollment: 2,782.

Library Administration. The Irwin Library System consists of: The Irwin Library; Science Library; Music and Fine Arts Library; Curriculum Resource Center.

John P. Kondelik, University Librarian; Gisela S. Terrell, Rare Books and Special Collections Librarian.

Library General Holdings. 307,560 volumes; 73,450 government documents; 12,000 microforms; 12,500 audiovisual materials; 1,555 current periodical subscriptions. In addition to the special collections highlighted below, the University Archives are maintained as well as smaller collections including a collection of nineteenth- and early twentieth-century American primers, grammars, and other textbooks; special print and manuscript specimen collections; a collection of twentieth-century American poetry centered around Alice Bidwell Wesenberg; and the United States Blind Athletes Association archives.

Special Collections

William F. Charters South Seas Collection. 2,700 titles pertaining to the discovery and exploration of the Pacific Islands; early circumnavigators' reports; missionary activities; European settlements; anthropology, ethnology; native cultures; natural sciences; current political and socioeconomic developments. The collection includes many bibliographic rarities as well as modern research materials.

Harold E. Johnson Sibelius Collection. Scores, recordings, and secondary sources. The scores include unpublished and unperformed materials; the sound recordings include all early recordings; secondary materials in all languages. This is the largest and most important Sibelius collection anywhere outside of Finland.

National Track and Field Hall of Fame Historical Research Library. Includes books, periodicals, programs, organizational archives, clippings, annuals, statistics, etc. for all track and field events, coaching and training methods, competitive events (Olympics, world, international, national); historical and current materials; more than 15,000 items.

Gaar Williams/Kin Hubbard Collection. Includes original drawings, sketch books, published books, letters, manuscripts, clippings, and memorabilia.

Jeanette Siron Pelton Botanical Print Collection. Consists of fifteenth- to nineteenth-century original prints illustrating the development of early modern science. Augmented by a similar collection of zoological prints

Lincoln Collection. Nineteenth-century pamphlets, newspapers, booklets, and manuscripts illustrating the life and times of Abraham Lincoln.

505
Calumet College
College Library
2400 New York Avenue
Whiting, Indiana 46394

Telephone. (219) 473-4333

Institutional Description. The privately supported liberal arts college is affiliated with the Roman Catholic Church. It grants associate and baccalaureate degrees. Enrollment: 508.

Library Administration. Jon L. Iglar, Librarian.

Library General Holdings. 100,000 volumes; 550 current periodical titles.

Special Collections

The special collections of the library include 3,000 volumes on the North American Indian including nineteenth-century and out-of-print editions; 10,000 items dealing with contemporary theology; and 8,000 items on education.

506
Christian Theological Seminary
Seminary Library
1000 West 42nd Street
Indianapolis, Indiana 46208

Telephone. (317) 924-1331

Institutional Description. The privately supported theological seminary offers graduate-level programs only. Affiliated with the Christian Church (Disciples of Christ), the seminary traces its beginnings to Butler University, where, in 1899, it was the Bible Department. Enrollment: 194.

Library Administration. Leslie R. Galbraith, Librarian.

Library General Holdings. 101,000 volumes; 510 periodical subscriptions.

Special Collections

In 1901, Dr. Jabez Hall, Dean of Butler College of the Bible, instituted a special program of collecting books, manuscripts, photographs, tracts, periodicals, and other materials dealing with the history of the Christian Church (Disciples of Christ) and related movements. This collection has increased through the years and is one of the primary such collections in existence. Students of Discipliana will find ample resources for special studies. The library also has a collection of rare Bibles.

507
Concordia Theological Seminary Library
6600 North Clinton Street
Fort Wayne, Indiana 46825

Telephone. (219) 482-9611

Institutional Description. The privately supported theological seminary was founded in 1846. Offering graduate-level programs only, it is affiliated with the Lutheran Church—Missouri Synod. Enrollment: 476.

Library Administration. Cameron A. MacKenzie, Director of Library Services.

Library General Holdings. 120,000 items including books, periodicals, and microforms.

Special Collections

The most important special holdings of the library are 4,000 volumes of primary source material on sixteenth- and seventeenth-century Lutheranism.

508
DePauw University
Roy O. West Library
Greencastle, Indiana 46135

Telephone. (317) 658-4500

Institutional Description. The privately supported liberal arts university was established in 1837. Enrollment: 2,316.

Library Administration. Kathy Davis, Acting Director; Wesley Wilson, Coordinator of Archives and Special Collections.

Library General Holdings. 199,928 bound volumes; 831 microform titles; 3,000 linear feet of manuscripts and archives; 937 sound recording titles; 25,000 photographs and slides; 1,100 current periodical subscriptions.

Special Collections

Archives of DePauw University and United Methodism. Includes not only records of both institutions, but also manuscripts of 19th century Indiana Methodist preachers, DePauw faculty administrators and alumni including Charles and Mary Bear, John Jakes, Max Ehrman, David Lilienthal, and Thomas Bond Wood.

Curriculum Materials. Includes textbooks in use and used by Putnam County, Indiana public schools.

Note: The Special Collections Department was established in 1987 and incorporated the former rare book section of the Library and the books from the Archives. New additions include the Society of Professional Journalists/Sigma Delta Chi Records (1920-1980). Holdings include the Governor James C. Whitcomb Collection, the Bret Harte Collection; George B. Manhart World War II Collection, and books on the history of bookmaking.

509
Earlham College
Lilly Library
Richmond, Indiana 47374

Telephone. (317) 983-1269

Institutional Description. Earlham College is an independent liberal arts college affiliated with the Quakers (Society of Friends). Enrollment: 1,058.

Library Administration. Evan I. Farber, College Librarian; Philip D. Shore, Associate Librarian; Bridget Bower, Rare Books Librarian.

Library General Holdings. 320,000 volumes (including 92,000 documents); 118,000 microforms; 1,340 current periodical subscriptions.

Special Collections

The Earlham College Library contains a special collection of materials on the Society of Friends. This includes an estimated 10,000 books, pamphlets, and bound magazines. There are also some microfilms of early printed materials and also of various manuscript collections. An important subset is over 1,000 volumes of genealogical works focused on Quaker families.

Rare Book Collections

The **Earlham College Archives** contains not only the college archives, but also manuscript collections of several people important to the history of the college and the Society of Friends. There is also a collection or rare books about the Society of Friends plus several thousand pamphlets, broadsides, and ephemeral materials. An important part of the collection is about 75 linear feet of manuscript records of local Friends Meetings in Indiana.

510
Franklin College of Indiana Library
501 East Monroe
Franklin, Indiana 46131

Telephone. (317) 736-8441

Institutional Description. The privately supported liberal arts college was founded in 1834 by Baptist pioneers, and today maintains an affiliation with the American Baptist Churches in the U.S.A. Enrollment: 676.

Library Administration. Vicco von Stralendorff, Head Librarian.

Library General Holdings. 122,500 volumes; 400 current periodical subscriptions.

Special Collections

Special collections include the **David Demaree Banta Collection** of Indiana history; the **Indiana Baptist Collection,** and the papers of Roger D. Branigin.

511
Goshen Biblical Seminary
3003 Benham Avenue
Elkhart, Indiana 46517

Telephone. (219) 295-3726

Institutional Description. The privately supported theological seminary shares a campus with the Mennonite Biblical Seminary, and together they are known as the Associated Mennonite Biblical Seminaries. It is affiliated with the Mennonite Church. Enrollment: 91.

Library Administration. The library facilities are administered by the parent seminary. *See* **Associated Mennonite Biblical Seminaries.**

512
Goshen College
Library
1700 South Main Street
Goshen, Indiana 46526

Telephone. (219) 533-3161

Institutional Description. The privately supported liberal arts college was founded in 1894 and is affiliated with the Mennonite Church. Enrollment: 994.

Library Administration. Devon J. Yoder, Librarian.

Library General Holdings. 120,000 volumes; 780 periodical subscriptions; 48,000 microforms.

Special Collections

The library supports the liberal arts curriculum of the college and the goals of the Mennonite Church.

513
Grace College
Betty Zimmer Morgan Library
200 Seminary Drive
Winona Lake, Indiana 46590

Telephone. (219) 372-5101

Institutional Description. The privately supported liberal arts college was established in 1948 as a collegiate division of Grace Theological Seminary, founded in 1937. It is affiliated with the Fellowship of Grace Brethren Churches. Enrollment: 653.

Library Administration. William E. Darr, Assistant Director of Libraries.

Library General Holdings. 126,000 volumes; 800 current periodical titles; 35,000 microforms. The library of Grace Theological Seminary is housed with the Grace College Library.

Special Collections

Special collections include materials relating to the evangelist Billy Sunday; a Middle East map collection; a slide archive of Holy Land pictures; and a collection of materials relating to the Grace Brethren Church. The McClain Alcove contains the personal library of Alva J. McClain, first president of Grace Schools.

514
Hanover College
Duggan Library
Hanover, Indiana 47243

Telephone. (812) 866-2151

Institutional Description. The privately supported liberal arts college was founded in 1827, and as such, is the oldest of the four-year private colleges in Indiana. It is affiliated with the United Presbyterian Church. Enrollment: 1,090.

Library Administration. Walter D. Morrill, Director of College Libraries.

Library General Holdings. 300,000 volumes; 120,000 microforms.

Special Collections

The most important special collections maintained by the Duggan Library include the archives of many Indiana Presbyterian churches; the First Editions Collections of local authors (Edward Eggleston, George Cary Eggleston, and David Graham Phillips); and the Charles J. Lynn Rare Book Collection. These are housed in the Archives/Special Collections Room which also includes the Hanover College Archives.

515
Huntington College
RichLyn Library
Huntington, Indiana 46750

Telephone. (219) 356-6000

Institutional Description. This privately supported liberal arts college is controlled by the Church of the United Brethren in Christ. The theological seminary of Huntington College grants the Master's and Associate degrees. Enrollment: 446.

Library Administration. Robert Kaehr, Director of Library Services; Jane Mason, Rare Books Librarian.

Library General Holdings. 65,000 volumes; 10,000

bound periodical titles; 425 current periodical subscriptions; 8,000 microform volumes; 9,500 government documents; 500 classical recordings.

Special Collections

Curriculum Materials Center. Serves the Education Department and houses textbooks (elementary and secondary), kits/media, junior fiction/biography, computer disks, and reference and nonfiction collections.

Rare Book Collections

The library maintains the archives of Huntington College and the United Brethren in Christ.

516
Indiana Institute of Technology
McMillen Library
1600 East Washington Boulevard
Fort Wayne, Indiana 46803

Telephone. (219) 422-5561

Institutional Description. The privately supported technological institute grants baccalaureate degrees. Enrollment: 415.

Library Administration. Jean Hickling, Librarian.

Library General Holdings. 46,000 volumes; 200 current periodicals.

Special Collections

The library maintains a collection of NASA special publications and reports.

517
Indiana State University
Cunningham Memorial Library
Terre Haute, Indiana 47809

Telephone. (812) 237-3700

Institutional Description. This publicly supported state university enrolled its first class in 1865. It is a general, multi-purpose institution. Enrollment: 9,211.

Library Administration. Ronald G. Leach, University Librarian; David E. Vancil, Head, Rare Books and Special Collections Department.

Library General Holdings. 1,040,607 bound volumes; 6,001 serial subscriptions; 658,830 microforms; 47,805 audiovisual materials.

Special Collections

Warren N. and Suzanne B. Cordell Collection of Dictionaries. Dictionaries and other word books from the manuscript period to the present; emphasis on pre-1901 materials; English and Western European languages receive the main focus and account for 85 percent of the collection; over 250 issues and editions of Samuel Johnson dictionaries; 20 incunables and many unique items; 12,000 volumes.

Eugene V. Debs Collection. 3,600 letters, 3,800 pamphlets, 1,200 books; materials by Debs, written to Debs, by his associates, or about the labor movement during the period in which Debs was active, 1880-1930.

Indiana Collection. Books by Indiana authors or pertaining to the history and culture of Indiana from the first writings to the present time; 4,500 volumes.

Cunningham Collection. Emphasizes classic books on theory and methodology in American education, including particularly important early textbooks; 1,000 volumes.

Floyd Family Collection. Public schoolbooks published or used in Indiana schools from circa 1840-1940, a formative period in Indiana and one which illustrates the change in teaching methodology, content, etc.; 700 volumes.

Walker Collection. Early school textbooks; 300 volumes.

Faculty Publications Collection. 1,000 offprints; 450 volumes, all edited or written by faculty members while employed at Indiana State University.

Rare Book Collections

Rare Book Collection. Emphasizes travel and discovery, literature, bindings, and printings; also includes expensive facsimile reprints; 90 percent of the collection is pre-twentieth century; 6,000 volumes.

518
Indiana University at South Bend
IUSB Library
1700 Mishawaka Avenue
P.O. Box 7111
South Bend, Indiana 46634

Telephone. (219) 237-4220

Institutional Description. The publicly supported campus of the University of Indiana System grants associate, baccalaureate, and master's degrees. Enrollment: 2,-809.

Library Administration. James L. Mullins, Director.

Library General Holdings. 250,000 volumes; 1,750 serial titles; 100,000 microforms.

Special Collections

The library maintains the **James Lewis Casaday Theatre Collection** and the **Christianson Lincoln Collection.**

519
Indiana University - Bloomington
Lilly Library
Bloomington, Indiana 47405

Telephone. (812) 337-4602

Institutional Description. The publicly supported state university was founded in 1820, and is now the state's largest institution of higher learning. The Bloomington campus of Indiana University is a national and international center of education and research in the sciences, humanities, and professions. Enrollment: 27,891.

Library Administration. William Cagle, Rare Books Librarian.

Library General Holdings. 4,513,000 volumes; 22,586 current periodical titles; 1,829,000 microforms; 514,000 audiovisual units.

Special Collections

The Lilly Library combines the two functions of rare book library and department of special collections within the Indiana University system. There are nearly 6,000,000 manuscripts, 360,000 printed books, and 100,000 pieces of music. The Lilly Library does not circulate its books or manuscripts but makes them available to all readers in the library's Reading Room. A number of special aids are available in this room. The chronological file lists the early printed books in the library by year of publication, a useful tool for the student of seventeenth- or eighteenth-century history. There are separate files describing maps, prints, and bindings, as well as a printers and presses file listing finely printed books from the fifteenth through the twentieth centuries. There is also a new acquisitions card file in which the reader will find all the recently acquired books before they are catalogued.

While the Lilly Library is primarily a research library designed to meet the needs of scholars and advanced students in the humanities, it should be emphasized that its collections are open to all who wish to use them. The collections are a memorial to the achievement of many private and professional collectors and serve, in their areas of specialization, an international clientele.

Because the breadth and scope of the Lilly Library's holdings are vast, the special collections can be described only in the broadest terms. The various collections are summarized under the headings below. The information was obtained, through the courtesy of the Lilly Library, from a brochure entitled "Lilly Library of Indiana University," published by the Lilly Library with funds from the Wendell L. Willkie Educational Trust administered by the Indiana University Foundation.

For a detailed description of the development of the Lilly Library, see *The Lilly Library: The First Quarter Century 1960-1985* (The Lilly Library, Indiana University, Bloomington, Indiana, 1985).

History of Printing. The Lilly Library collection of incunabula now numbers over 700 titles and is being added to on a selective basis, primarily in the major works of the humanities and sciences. Presses from the sixteenth century to the present are well represented, and to aid the user there is a separate printers and presses file which will lead to the major books of all periods from Gutenberg to Grabhorn. It is a selective rather than a comprehensive collection.

Bibles and Religion. There is a fine collection of printed versions of the Bible from the Gutenberg New Testament to the most recent ecumenical text. Holdings include, among others, the Biblia Germanica (Strassburg 1466), which is the first Bible in a vernacular language, the Coverdale Bible, the Ostrog Bible published in Church Slavic in 1581, the first printing of the King James Authorized Version, the Eliot Indian Bible (first and second editions), the Sauer and Aitken Bibles, several Polyglot Bibles, and the Bruce Rogers Lectern Bible. There are also substantial holdings of doctrinal and controversial works by Catholic and Protestant authors, including some significant writings by Martin Luther and other Reformation figures. Catholic materials include large manuscript holdings relating to the Church in the Spanish colonies, with much material of the Inquisition and the Church's relations with Latin American Indians.

European Expansion and Latin American History. The 40,000 printed pieces and 26,000 manuscripts comprising the Latin American collections came largely from the library formed by Dr. Bernardo Mendel. The printed items begin with the first and second Latin printings of the third Columbus letter announcing the discovery of America (Rome 1493 and 1494). From discovery through the period of independence, with special emphasis on Mexico and Peru, this collection is rich in primary source material. It is supported by a fine collection of early atlases and accounts of voyages of exploration.

The acquisition of the library of Dr. Charles Boxer added extensive resources on the Dutch and Portuguese colonial empires to the already strong collections on the Spanish colonies. The purchase of the W.E.D. Allen library provided resources on the eastward expansion of Russia, with materials on Russo-Turkish and Sino-Russian relations through the nineteenth century.

British History. The Lilly's in-depth holdings in British history begin with the events leading to the Civil War (1642-1649) and continue through the end of Walpole's administration (1745). Anglo-American relations prior to the American Revolution are also strongly documented in contemporary pamphlets and other publications. The emphasis, beginning with the nineteenth century, shifts from political to social history as represented by the Sadlier collection of London low-life materials and numerous works relating to the social and economic conditions of the times.

United States History. There are strong holdings in several areas of United States history, among which should be mentioned Anglo-American relations leading to the American Revolution, the period of the Revolution, the history of the U.S. Constitution, the War of 1812, and westward expansion through the Ohio Valley and over the plains and Rocky Mountains to the Pacific. More than 5,000 printed volumes and 7,000 manuscript items relating to the settlement of the continent may be found in the Library's Ellison, Service, and Harding collections. There are books on desperados, scouts, Indian wars, fur, and cattle industries, railroads, and local Western history. There are both printed and manuscript overland accounts and a collection of gold rush newspapers.

Lincoln materials, both primary and secondary, are extensive. Modern U.S. politics is represented by the papers of, among others, Charles Fairbanks, Wendell L. Willkie, Charles Halleck, and Birch Bayh.

To document Indiana history, the Lilly Library's holdings include business and commercial records such as the papers of the Howard Shipyards in Jeffersonville for the period 1874-1941, the Indiana Cotton Mills records for 1852-1947, and the Edward Aloysius Rumely papers for 1888-1965. Collections relating to the state's political history include the papers of Governors Samuel Ralston and Paul McNutt and of lawyer John Barron Niles. The state is also well represented pictorially by such collections as the Frank Hohenberger photographic collection, which records daily life in southern Indiana during the second quarter of this century, and the Lefevre Cranstone watercolors done in 1859 and 1860.

British Literature. The earlier periods of British literature are represented in the Lilly Library only by high spots such as the editions of Chaucer, and Gower printed by William Caxton in the fifteenth century, first editions of Spenser, Donne, and William Lily, and the four seventeenth-century Shakespeare folios. Beginning with John Milton, the Lilly has numerous comprehensive author collections, among the most notable of which are Daniel Defoe, Laurence Sterne, and William Wordsworth. The Lilly's nineteenth-century holdings are strong in fiction and poetry but are especially so in drama, where the collection numbers more than 16,000 plays, with extensive supporting materials.

The collection of works by twentieth-century authors, both major and minor, is too broad to attempt a list of specific names, though special mention might be made of both W.B. Yeats and Joseph Conrad, whose works have been collected in every discoverable form. Among the many authors represented in the manuscript collections are J.M. Barrie, Arnold Bennett, Joseph Conrad, John Galsworthy, D.H. Lawrence, J.M. Synge, George Russell ("A.E."), W. Somerset Maugham, Richard Hughes, Vita Sackville-West, Harold Nicolson, Dylan Thomas, Stephen Spender, Harold Pinter, Ted Hughes, and Ian Hamilton Finlay. Also housed are the archives of the British publishing firm Calder and Boyars, which included Samuel Beckett among its authors. The study of modern British literature is further supplemented by a collection of more than 800 BBC radio scripts—drama, interviews, poetry—from the archives of Douglas Cleverdon, Lancelot Sieveking, and D.G. Bridson.

United States Literature. Both Indiana University and Mr. Josiah Lilly collected widely in the field of American literature; thus it is a principal area of strength. Beginning with Anne Bradstreet's *The Tenth Muse Lately Sprung up in America* (London 1650) and her *Several Poems* (Boston 1678), the collection moves forward in both prose and verse. Coverage is excellent for the era of Cooper, Hawthorne, Emerson, and Poe and is equally strong for the age of Twain, Howells, and Henry James. Indiana authors are well represented in both books and manuscripts, including extensive manuscript holdings for James Whitcomb Riley and Lew Wallace, plus smaller collections for Meredith Nicolson, Booth Tarkington, George Ade, and Theodore Dreiser. The nineteenth-century holdings are further supplemented by the publishing files of Appleton-Century (1848-1900) which include material on several authors, among them Edith Wharton and Stephen Crane.

Holdings in twentieth-century American literature are extensive. The manuscript materials include the principal archives of Upton Sinclair, Max Eastman, Sylvia Plath, Galway Kinnell, and others, as well as smaller collections for Edith Wharton, F. Scott Fitzgerald, Ezra Pound, Ernest Hemingway, William Carlos Williams, and several more recent writers. The archives of Bobbs-Merrill, Capra Press, and number of little magazines have added substantially to the records of modern publishing and the authors represented in their files. In printed books, first and other significant editions of twentieth-century American authors now number approximately 20,000 titles.

Science fiction, including long runs of the more important "pulps," and detective fiction also are well represented. It also should be noted that there are several hundred scripts for film, radio, stage, and television productions and also the personal archives of Orson Welles and of John Ford.

Children's Literature. The Lilly Library holds nearly 10,000 children's books, most of them from the Elisabeth W. Ball collection. The emphasis is on English language works of the eighteenth and nineteenth centuries but also include a large number of twentieth-century books and representative works in French and German. There are hornbooks, mechanical books, thumb Bibles, miniature libraries, Newbery and Marshall imprints, and a good selection of original art by children's book illustrators—Kate Greenaway, Walter Crane, Randolph Caldecott, and Ernest Shepard among them.

French Literature. The French literature collection has its roots in Mr. Lilly's interest in Jules Verne and Anatole France but has grown far beyond that interest. There are now holdings of works by most notable nineteenth- and twentieth-century French authors. The collection is especially strong in contemporary French poetry, where the printed material is supported by a small but interesting group of manuscripts.

Medicine, Science, and Technology. The first appearances in print of great medical and scientific discoveries was an area of strength in Mr. Lilly's library, which contained such works as William Harvey's *De Motu Cordis*

(Frankfurt 1628); Vesalius' great 1543 anatomy; and first editions of the principal works of Copernicus, Galileo, and Kepler. The materials range in date from Pliny's *Historia Naturalis* (1469) to Alexander Fleming's *On the Antibacterial Action of Cultures of a Penicillium* (1944), and the reports of the Apollo II moon landing in 1969. There is a strong collection in the history of genetics, including the papers of Nobel prize winning geneticist Herman J. Muller, Tracy M. Sonneborn, and others in this field. The Vaclav Hlavaty papers in mathematics include a long correspondence with Albert Einstein concerning the mathematical proofs for Einstein's theories.

Music. Soon after he arrived at Indiana University in 1956, David Randall purchased for the Library a small but choice group of musical scores by great composers which he had assembled as head of Scribner's Rare Book Department. To this core have been added several individual pieces and collections. Among these are the collection of scores by George Frederick Handel formed by his bibliographer, William S. Smith; Carroll Wilson's Gilbert and Sullivan Collection; a large group of nineteenth-century operas in both full scores and piano-vocal scores; and the vast Starr American Sheet Music Collection, which numbers approximately 100,000 pieces and ranges from the eighteenth century to the present. The library was chosen as the repository for the annotated scores of the renowned German conductor, Fritz Busch.

Other Fields. There are many other collections of significance including those in German literature, especially for the eighteenth and early nineteenth centuries, Voltaire, the French Revolution, Lafayette, U.S. almanacs of the eighteenth and nineteenth centuries, London street cries, the Panama and Suez Canals, early printing in Turkey, and contemporary fine printing and binding.

520
Manchester College
Funderburg Library
North Manchester, Indiana 46962

Telephone. (219) 982-2141

Institutional Description. The privately supported liberal arts college was founded in 1860; it merged with Mount Morris College of Illinois in 1932. Manchester College is affiliated with the Church of the Brethren. Enrollment: 903.

Library Administration. J. Allen Willmert, Director.

Library General Holdings. 161,500 volumes; 800 periodical titles; 4,200 audio recordings.

Special Collections

The library maintains the **Church of the Brethren Collection** and three separate collections on peace studies.

521
Marian College
Mother Theresa Hackelmeier Memorial Library
3200 Cold Spring Road
Indianapolis, Indiana 46222

Telephone. (317) 929-0341

Institutional Description. The privately supported liberal arts college was founded in 1851 as a women's college by the Sisters of St. Francis, Oldenberg, and became coeducational in 1954. Enrollment: 879.

Library Administration. Susan A. Stussy, Head Librarian.

Library General Holdings. 113,000 volumes; 500 periodicals; 20 newspaper subscriptions; 3,000 audiovisual items.

Special Collections

The library maintains a collection of materials documenting Marian College history and the papers of Archbishop Paul Schulte.

Rare Book Collections

Rare books include a collection dealing with Indiana and Midwest Catholic history donated by Archbishop Schulte.

522
Marion College
Library
4201 South Washington Street
Marion, Indiana 46953

Telephone. (317) 674-6901

Institutional Description. The privately supported liberal arts college is affiliated with the Wesleyan Methodist Church. It grants baccalaureate and master's degrees. Enrollment: 869.

Library Administration. Harold Boyce, Director of Library Services.

Library General Holdings. 113,500 volumes; 410 current periodical subscriptions.

Special Collections

The library maintains a strong collection on nursing and a **Wesleyana Collection.**

523
Mennonite Biblical Seminary
3003 Benham Avenue
Elkhart, Indiana 46517

Telephone. (219) 295-3726

Institutional Description. The privately supported

theological seminary shares a campus with the Goshen Biblical Seminary, and together they are known as the Associated Mennonite Biblical Seminaries. It is affiliated with the Mennonite Church. Enrollment: 84.

Library Administration. The library facilities are administered by the parent seminary. *See* **Associated Mennonite Biblical Seminaries.**

524
Oakland City College
Founder's Memorial Library
100 Lucretia Street
Oakland City, Indiana 47660

Telephone. (812) 749-4781

Institutional Description. The privately supported liberal arts college was founded in 1855. It is affiliated with the Baptist Church and grants baccalaureate and master's degrees. Enrollment: 532.

Library Administration. Martin H. Gallas, Director.

Library General Holdings. 68,000 volumes; 325 periodical and newspaper subscriptions.

Special Collections

Special collections include the Baptist General Association minutes (1891 to the present) and the minutes of the Liberty Association of General Baptists (1891 to the present).

525
Purdue University
University Libraries
West Lafayette, Indiana 47907

Telephone. (317) 494-1776

Institutional Description. The publicly supported state university was founded in 1869 as a technical school offering courses in engineering and agriculture. It now provides a wide diversity of programs. Enrollment: 30,693.

Library Administration. Joseph M. Dagnese, Director of Libraries.

Library General Holdings. 1,695,000 volumes; 18,000 serial titles; 1,530,000 microforms.

Special Collections

The University Libraries house their holdings in 15 school and departmental libraries. These libraries cover the fields of aviation technology; biochemistry; chemistry; consumer and family sciences; engineering; geosciences; humanities, social science, and education; management and agricultural economics; life sciences; mathematical sciences; pharmacy, nursing and health sciences; physics; psychological sciences; undergraduate studies; and veterinary medicine.

A few of the important special collections include the Krannert Collection on the history of economics and economic thought; the Gilbreth Library of Industrial Management; and the Goss Library of Engineering History.

526
Purdue University - Calumet
Library
2233 171st Street
Hammond, Indiana 46323

Telephone. (219) 844-0520

Institutional Description. The publicly supported (state) campus of Purdue University provides liberal arts and professional programs. Enrollment: 4,444.

Library Administration. Bernard H. Holicky, Director.

Library General Holdings. 166,000 volumes; 1,200 current periodical titles; 338,355 microform units.

Special Collections

The library maintains a special collection on Black history and literature, Purdue University Calumet archival materials, and a collection of Northwest Indiana historical material.

527
Rose-Hulman Institute of Technology
John A. Logan Library
5500 Wabash Avenue
Terre Haute, Indiana 47803

Telephone. (812) 877-1511

Institutional Description. The privately supported science and engineering institute for men grants baccalaureate and master's degrees. Enrollment: 1,307.

Library Administration. Herman Cole, Jr., Librarian.

Library General Holdings. 66,000 volumes; 550 current periodical titles.

Special Collections

The strengths of the library are in the various fields of engineering. The library maintains the **Institute Archives** and the **Tri Kappa Collection** of works by Indiana artists.

528
Saint Joseph's College
College Library
Rensselaer, Indiana 47978

Telephone. (219) 866-7111

Institutional Description. The privately supported liberal arts college is affiliated with the Roman Catholic Church. It grants baccalaureate and master's degrees. Enrollment: 804.

Library Administration. Robert J. Vigeant, Head Librarian.

Library General Holdings. 180,000 volumes; 800 current periodical titles; 100,000 government documents.

Special Collections

The library has strong English literature and Catholic collections. The library also has some excellent resources in the areas of non-Western cultures such as Africa, Asia, and India.

529
Saint Mary-of-the Woods College Library
Saint Mary-of-the-Woods, Indiana 47876

Telephone. (812) 535-5151

Institutional Description. The privately supported liberal arts college for women was founded in 1840 by the Roman Catholic Sisters of Providence. Enrollment: 511.

Library Administration. Emily Walsh, S.P., Administrator of Library.

Library General Holdings. 144,000 volumes; 450 current periodical titles.

Special Collections

Special collections include the **Gladys McKenney Molony Collection** of fore-edge paintings; the original library of the Sisters of Providence dating from 1840; and the **Samuel Taylor Coleridge Collection.**

530
Saint Mary's College
Cushwa-Leighton Library
Notre Dame, Indiana 46556

Telephone. (219) 284-4328

Institutional Description. The privately supported liberal arts college is primarily for women. It is affiliated with the Roman Catholic Church. Enrollment: 1,765.

Library Administration. Sister Bernice Hollenhorst, Director.

Library General Holdings. 172,000 volumes; 800 current periodical titles.

Rare Book Collections

The **Rare Book Room** contains an outstanding Dante collection and the College Archives.

531
St. Meinrad College and School of Theology Library
St. Meinrad, Indiana 47577

Telephone. (812) 357-6611

Institutional Description. The privately supported liberal arts college and school of theology are conducted by the Benedictine Monks of the Roman Catholic Church. The college prepares men for entrance into the seminary which further prepares the candidates for the priesthood. Enrollment: 159 in the College, 123 in the School of Theology.

Library Administration. Rev. Simeon Daly, O.S.B., Librarian.

Library General Holdings. 130,000 volumes; 550 current periodical subscriptions.

Special Collections

The library supports the liberal arts program of the college with emphasis on the spiritual, social, and cultural development of the student whose ultimate goal is Roman Catholic priesthood.

532
Taylor University
Zondervan Library
Reade Avenue
Upland, Indiana 46989

Telephone. (317) 998-5201

Institutional Description. The privately supported liberal arts college was founded by the Methodist Episcopal Church in 1846. Now an interdenominational Christian institution, it grants baccalaureate degrees. Enrollment: 1,472.

Library Administration. David C. Dickey, Director.

Library General Holdings. 142,500 volumes; 685 current periodical subscriptions.

Special Collections

The **Taylor University Archives** include materials relating to the history of Taylor University and the local community. Other special materials include collections on computer and information sciences, English literature, the Bible, and Christianity.

533
Tri-State University
Perry T. Ford Memorial Library
Angola, Indiana 46703

Telephone. (219) 665-3141

Institutional Description. The privately supported business and engineering university was founded in 1884. It grants baccalaureate degrees in a wide variety of programs. Enrollment: 947.

Library Administration. Enriqueta G. Taboy, Director.

Library General Holdings. 113,000 volumes; 500 cur-

rent periodical subscriptions; 31,000 government documents.

Special Collections

Special collections include curriculum materials for elementary education and technical publications issued by NASA, AGARD, and NATO.

534
University of Evansville Clifford Memorial Library 1800 Lincoln Avenue Evansville, Indiana 47722

Telephone. (812) 477-6241

Institutional Description. The privately supported university was founded in 1854 and is affiliated with the United Methodist Church. Enrollment: 2,708.

Library Administration. P. Grady Morein, University Librarian.

Library General Holdings. 170,000 bound books and journals; 12,000 periodical volumes in microform; 105,000 microformats; 3,000 audiovisual items.

Special Collections

The special collections of the library include the **James L. Clifford Collection** of eighteenth-century British literature; **Johnsoniana;** editorial cartoons of K.K. Knecht; the Library of American Civilization; and the Library of English Literature.

535
University of Indianapolis Krannert Memorial Library 1400 East Hannah Avenue Indianapolis, Indiana 46227

Telephone. (317) 788-3368

Institutional Description. The privately supported university was founded in 1902 and is affiliated with the United Methodist Church. Enrollment: 1,851.

Library Administration. Florabelle Wilson, Librarian; H. Merrill Underwood, Curator/Archivist.

Library General Holdings. 200,000 volumes; 1,020 current periodical subscriptions; 5,500 microforms; 2,000 audiovisual materials.

Special Collections

The most important holdings of the library are the Krannert Collection of rare books and fine bindings; United Brethren Church books and resource materials; and the University Archives which includes documents and artifacts of importance to the history of the institution.

536
University of Notre Dame University Libraries Notre Dame, Indiana 46556

Telephone. (219) 239-5000

Institutional Description. The privately supported university operates under the auspices of the Roman Catholic Church. Enrollment: 9,674.

Library Administration. Robert C. Miller, Director; David E. Sparks, Special Collections Librarian.

Library General Holdings. 1,500,000 volumes; 14,300 general and specialized research journals; 500,000 microforms; 35,000 audiovisual materials.

Special Collections

The University has nine libraries on its campus designed to meet the research needs of the various schools and colleges in the fields of architecture, chemistry/physics, earth sciences, engineering, life sciences, law, mathematics, and radiation technology.

The important special collections include Medieval Studies; materials on Dante; and Catholic Americana.

537
University of Southern Indiana Library Evansville, Indiana 47712

Telephone. (812) 464-1756

Institutional Description. The publicly supported state university offers associate, baccalaureate, and master's degrees in technical and teacher education programs. Enrollment: 3,027.

Library Administration. Bette J. Walden, Director of Library Services.

Library General Holdings. 158,000 volumes; 805 current periodicals; 66,000 government documents; 153,000 microforms; 3,00 audiovisual materials.

Special Collections

Among the specialized collections are the large **Mead Johnson & Company Archives** and the **Jeanne Suhrheinrich Theatre Collection** which contains press kits for more than 800 movies, theatre programs, and photographs of Hollywood and worldwide stars. Also included is the Center for Communal Studies which collects information on historic and contemporary communal societies. The **University Archives** collects, preserves, and services materials related to the past, present, and future of the tri-state region.

538
Valparaiso University
Henry F. Moellering Memorial Library
Valparaiso, Indiana 46383

Telephone. (219) 464-5364

Institutional Description. This privately supported university is related to the Lutheran Church—Missouri Synod, and operates within the Lutheran tradition. It was founded in 1859 as a pioneer in coeducational enrollment. Enrollment: 3,458.

Library Administration. Margaret Perry, Director of Libraries.

Library General Holdings. 245,000 bound volumes; 88,000 microforms; 1,300 current periodicals; 251,000 government documents; 92,000 maps; 4,300 recordings and tapes.

Special Collections

The Library maintains special collections on Nazism; religious materials from the fifteenth century onward; Lutheranism; and Indiana.

539
Vincennes University
Lewis Historical Collections Library
LRC-22 Vincennes University
Vincennes, Indiana 47591

Telephone. (812) 885-4330

Institutional Description. Vincennes University, a publicly supported junior college, is the oldest institution of higher education in Indiana. It was founded as Jefferson Academy in 1801. A branch center is located in Jasper, IN. Enrollment: 5,658.

Library Administration. Robert Slayton, University Librarian; Robert R. Stevens, Director, Lewis Historical Collections Library.

Library General Holdings. 55,000 volumes; 475 periodical subscriptions.

Special Collections

The Lewis Library is a comprehensive historical collections library consisting of books, documents, manuscripts, newspapers, and other materials. A special area is the collection of those items pertaining to the early midwest and more particularly the Northwest Territory and the Indiana Territory.

Regional History Collection. A collection of documents, letters, and records pertaining to the historic area of southwestern Indiana and southeastern Illinois. Of particular interest are those papers of figures instrumental in the formation of the Indiana Territory 1800-1816.

540
Wabash College
Lilly Library
301 West Wabash
Crawfordsville, Indiana 47933

Telephone. (317) 362-1400

Institutional Description. The privately supported liberal arts college for men was founded in 1832. The college features an academic cooperative program with Columbia and Washington Universities. Enrollment: 772.

Library Administration. Larry J. Frye, Head Librarian.

Library General Holdings. 228,000 volumes; 987 periodicals; 97,000 government documents.

Special Collections

The most important special collections of the Lilly Library are collections of the classics; early American and British history; and the Wabash College Archives.

Iowa

541
Buena Vista College
Ballou Library
College and West 4th Streets
Storm Lake, Iowa 50588

Telephone. (712) 749-2103

Institutional Description. The privately supported Christian liberal arts college has branch campuses in eight locations throughout the state. It is affiliated with the United Presbyterian Church. Enrollment: 2,127.

Library Administration. Barbara Palling, Head Librarian.

Library General Holdings. 83,000 volumes; 400 current periodical subscriptions.

Special Collections

The **Curriculum Library** contains elementary and secondary school textbooks, teaching aids, and a representative collection of library materials such as would be found in a school library. The collection contains over 6,500 volumes.

542
Central University of Iowa
Geisler Learning Resource Center
Pella, Iowa 50219

Telephone. (515) 628-5219

Institutional Description. The privately supported liberal arts college is affiliated with the Reformed Church in America. Enrollment: 1,565.

Library Administration. Robin E. Martin, Library Director; Madeline Vanderzyl, Special Collections Librarian.

Library General Holdings. 145,000 volumes; 835 current periodical and newspaper subscriptions.

Rare Book Collections

Archives Collection. This collection is the depository for manuscripts, records, and documents regarding the history and traditions of the city of Pella and of Central College. The majority of Pella documents are the papers and letters of Dominie Hendrik Pieter Scholte, the founder of Pella. Many of these documents are letters to Dominie Scholte from the leaders of provincial congregations in the Netherlands at the time of the secession of these congregations from the Netherlands Reformed Church in 1834. Others are papers regarding the emigration from the Netherlands, introducing Scholte to persons in the United States, documents regarding the founding of Pella, records of the purchase of government land and its division, financial records of the colonists, and early town and church proceedings.

The Central College documents consist of financial administration and records, faculty and committee minutes, general correspondence, papers of former presidents, and publications of students and faculty. There is a photograph collection, and programs of significant college events.

There is also a small collection of printed material covering the secession of the Scholte group from the Netherlands Reformed Church, records of emigration from Holland to America, histories of Pella, Central University of Iowa, and Iowa county histories. The Archives also contain church records, a newspaper collection, pamphlets, and a clipping file of information concerning Pella and Pella residents.

543
Coe College
Stewart Memorial Library
1220 First Avenue
Cedar Rapids, Iowa 52402

Telephone. (319) 399-8686

Institutional Description. The privately supported liberal arts college is affiliated with the United Presbyterian Church. It grants baccalaureate degrees. Enrollment: 973.

Library Administration. Richard Doyle, Director of Library Services.

Library General Holdings. 157,000 volumes; 840 current periodical and serial subscriptions; 33,000 microforms.

Special Collections

The published works and notes of William L. Shirer, Coe class of 1925, are in the College Archives of the library; they include over 3,000 pages of manuscript material for the book, *The Rise and Fall of of the Third Reich.* The works of Iowa poet, Paul Engle, Class of 1931, are also housed. The seven Grant Wood murals—The Fruits of Iowa—are on permanent display in the lobby of the library.

544
Cornell College
Cole Library
Mount Vernon, Iowa 52314

Telephone. (319) 895-8811

Institutional Description. The privately supported liberal arts college was founded in 1853. It is affiliated with the United Methodist Church. Enrollment: 1,168.

Library Administration. Thomas M. Shaw, Director of Library Services.

Library General Holdings. 180,000 volumes; 600 current periodical subscriptions.

Special Collections

The library has a special collection on the subject of ornithology and maintains holdings on the Middle East. Library endowments support collections in American history, English literature, missions and missionaries, Bible study and religious literature, chemistry, humanities, juvenile literature, psychology, and education.

545
Drake University
Crowles Library
25th and University Avenue
Des Moines, Iowa 50311

Telephone. (515) 271-2199

Institutional Description. The privately supported university was founded in 1881. Enrollment: 4,463.

Library Administration. William A. Stoppel, Director of Libraries.

Library General Holdings. 460,000 volumes; 2,400 periodical and newspaper subscriptions; 505,000 microforms; 89,000 government documents; 2,0000 audiovisual materials.

Special Collections

Special collections include a collection of Iowana.

Curriculum Library. This collection of the College of Education includes textbooks, children's literature, courses of study and units of work; 5,000 volumes are in the collection.

Pharmacy. A collection of approximately 2,600 volumes is maintained in the field of pharmacy.

546
Graceland College
Frederick Madison Smith Library
Lamoni, Iowa 50140

Telephone. (319) 784-5000

Institutional Description. The privately supported liberal arts college is sponsored by the Reorganized Church of Jesus Christ of Latter Day Saints. Founded in 1895, it grants baccalaureate degrees. Enrollment: 888.

Library Administration. Diane Sheton, Director.

Library General Holdings. 106,084 books; 660 periodical and newspaper subscriptions; 5,800 pamphlets; 63,-000 government documents; 1,038 recordings.

Special Collections

Graceland is the location of a special collection of books, documents, pictures, manuscripts, oral history tapes, and administrative records dealing with the history of the Reorganized Church of Jesus Christ of Latter Day Saints, the community of Lamoni, and Graceland College. The collection is housed in the DuRose Rare Books Room.

547
Grand View College
College Library
1351 Grandview Avenue
Des Moines, Iowa 50316

Telephone. (515) 263-2877

Institutional Description. The privately supported college, founded in 1896, is affiliated with the Lutheran Church in America. Enrollment: 1,080.

Library Administration. Barbara Burn, Library Director.

Library General Holdings. 82,000 volumes; 600 periodical and newspaper subscriptions; 11,700 microform units; 3,500 audiovisual materials; 8,700 pamphlet file; 350 curriculum items.

Special Collections

Danish Immigrant Archives. This collection includes information by and about the Danish immigrant to America. It consists of books, periodicals, letters, documents, memoirs, pictures, obituaries, tapes, and memorabilia from the U.S. and Canada, mostly in Danish. It is also the home of the Danish Immigrant Archival Listing (DIAL) project which is a comprehensive listing of archival holdings in the U.S., Canada, and Denmark. The library has an extensive collection of over 200 books and periodicals (mostly in Danish) by and about N.F.S. Grundtvig, the father of the Danish folk high schools. Due to the interest and efforts of a former instructor who first came to the U.S. as a prisoner-of-war, the library has a small collection (about 150 titles) on Nazi Germany.

548
Grinnell College
Burling Library
Grinnell, Iowa 50112

Telephone. (515) 236-2500

Institutional Description. The privately supported liberal arts college, founded in 1846, offers extensive overseas programs (including the Junior Year Abroad) as well as a large academic cooperative program with other colleges and universities. Enrollment: 1,260.

Library Administration. Christopher McKee, Librarian.

Library General Holdings. 286,000 volumes; 1,725 current periodical subscriptions; 10,000 sound recordings; 5,000 reels of microfilm; 5,500 linear feet of government documents.

Special Collections

The Burling Library maintains the **James Norman Hall Collection** of manuscripts and books.

549
Iowa State University of Science and Technology
The William Robert Parks and Ellen Sorge Parks Library
Ames, Iowa 50011

Telephone. (515) 294-1442

Institutional Description. The publicly supported university is organized into eight colleges. Enrollment: 24,482.

Library Administration. Warren B. Kuhn, University Librarian; Stanley M. Yates, Head, Department of Special Collections.

Library General Holdings. 1,723,000 volumes; 21,500 current serials, periodicals, and newspapers; 1,988,000 microforms; 108,000 maps and aerial/sky atlas photographs; 38,900 audiovisual materials.

Special Collections

The Parks Library has extensive holdings of serial publications of European academies of science, agricultural experiment stations, and U.S. Department of Agriculture serial publications.

Rare Book Collections

There are strong holdings in botany, entomology, ornithology, early scientific expeditions, early scientific serials, underground comics, and Little Blue Books.

Among the notable manuscript collections are the papers of Roswell Garst, Henry Gilman, Jay Lush, Earl Heady, and Norman Borlaug. There are also the Archives of American Agriculture, the Archives of American Veterinary Medicine, the Statistics Archive, the Evolution/Creation Archive, and the American Archives of the Factual Film (over 10,000 non-Hollywood films).

550
Iowa Wesleyan College
J. Raymond Chadwick Library
Mount Pleasant, Iowa 52641

Telephone. (319) 385-8021

Institutional Description. The privately supported liberal arts college was founded in 1842. It is affiliated with the United Methodist Church. Enrollment: 484.

Library Administration. Patricia Newcomer, Librarian.

Library General Holdings. 106,000 volumes; 565 current periodical subscriptions; 17,250 microforms; 5,000 audiovisual materials.

Special Collections

The College Archives and the Iowa United Methodist Conference Archives are housed in the library as well as the collection on German Americans and a collection of contemporary graphic artists' prints and books.

Rare Book Collections

Herman Miller Memorial Rare Book Room. Contains the Iowa Collection consisting of materials of significance on the history and culture of Iowa, the Robert Lincoln Collection, and other rare and useful materials.

551
Kirkwood Community College
Learning Resource Center
6301 Kirkwood Boulevard, S.W.
Cedar Rapids, Iowa 52406

Telephone. (319) 398-5411

Institutional Description. Kirkwood Community College was formally established in 1966. The college offers transfer, vocational/technical, and continuing education programs. Enrollment: 4,553.

Library Administration. Maude W. Jahncke, Director.

Library General Holdings. 46,000 volumes; 400 periodical titles.

Special Collections

The library maintains the **American History Collection,** the **Black History Collection,** and the **Van Vechten Collection.**

552
Loras College
Wahlert Memorial Library
14th and Alta Vista Streets
Dubuque, Iowa 52001

Telephone. (319) 588-7164

Institutional Description. The privately supported liberal arts college is affiliated with the Roman Catholic Church. Enrollment: 1,777.

Library Administration. Robert Klein, Librarian.

Library General Holdings. 240,000 volumes; 1,059 periodical subscriptions; 31,942 microfiche; 89,079 U.S. government documents; 15,355 microfiche of state depository documents; 4,527 maps.

Special Collections

Center for Dubuque History Collection. Contains manuscript material dating from the beginning of white settlement in 1833. Fifty-six linear feet of manuscript petitions and reports to the city government from 1883-1970; also includes County of Dubuque records, primarily manuscript ledgers, e.g., Tax Lists from 1853-1900; 500 images in a photograph collection of Dubuque area scenes and people.

Rare Book Collections

First Editions Collection. Includes the works of Virginia Woolf, William Faulkner, Frederick Rolfe (Baron Corvo), James Joyce, Charles Dickens (his novels in parts), Sir Walter Scott.

Horace Howard Furness Collection. A collection of Latin poet Quintus Horatius Flaccus; 811 books dating from 1482 to present; mostly various editions of the poet's works.

Torch Press Imprints Collection. 550 printed books, mostly limited editions of private presses.

The library also houses 57 incunabula dating from 1471-1500; 14 codex manuscripts including a twelfth-century Gospel of Mark, a twelfth-century complete Bible, and three copies of the *Book of Hours;* 1,300 manuscript letters, wills, etc., dealing with the Italian church, dating from the fourteenth to nineteenth centuries, mostly in Latin; 800 charters, wills, and indentures from England of the Elizabethan to Victorian periods in Latin and English.

553
Luther College
Preus Library
Decorah, Iowa 52101

Telephone. (319) 387-1001

Institutional Description. The privately supported liberal arts college became coeducational in 1936, after 75 years of being a men-only institution. It is affiliated with the American Lutheran Church. Enrollment: 2,063.

Library Administration. Leigh Jordahl, Head Librarian.

Library General Holdings. 270,000 volumes; 800 current periodical subscriptions; 10,000 microforms.

Special Collections

There is a manuscript library of 443 collections containing more than 27,000 items. These include papers and historical materials about Norwegian-American Lutheranism in the nineteenth century and papers of nineteenth- and twentieth-century Norwegian-American church leaders. The library maintains a microfilm collection of Norwegian-American newspapers covering the period from the nineteenth century to the present.

554
Maharishi International University
MIU Library
Fairfield, Iowa 52556

Telephone. (515) 472-5031

Institutional Description. The privately supported liberal arts university grants baccalaureate, master's, and doctoral degrees. It was founded in 1972 in California, and moved two years later to Iowa. Required courses include the Science of Creative Intelligence and Transcendental Meditation. Enrollment: 754.

Library Administration. Gloria Watterson Foster, Librarian.

Library General Holdings. 86,000 volumes; 1,240 current periodical subscriptions; 32,000 microforms.

Special Collections

The **Science of Creative Intelligence Collection** offers more than 6,500 video and audio tapes, including lectures, conferences, and symposia on the Science of Creative Intelligence as it is expressed in all fields of study. The video tapes include Maharishi Mahesh Yogi and others discussing the mechanics of consciousness and its relationship to academic disciplines. The library maintains special interest collections in business, education, psychology, physiology, and physics.

555
Morningside College
Hickman-Johnson-Furrow Library
1501 Morningside Avenue
Sioux City, Iowa 51106

Telephone. (712) 274-5246

Institutional Description. The privately supported liberal arts college was founded by The United Methodist Church in 1894. It continues to maintain its relationship with the Church. Enrollment: 1,222.

Library Administration. Charles LeMaster, Librarian; Christopher J. Feider, Reference/Archives Librarian.

Library General Holdings. 120,000 volume; 609 periodicals; 9 newspapers; 14,116 microcard titles; 432 microfilm titles; 54,887 microfiche titles; 300 ultrafiche titles; 315 videocassettes; 31 audiocassettes; 1,725 music scores.

Special Collections

Peace Studies Collection. Donated by Joanne Soper, this collection totals 180 volumes.

Indian Studies Collection. Includes 1,200 volumes and supports the Indian Studies Department on campus; the collection also serves the Native American population of the area.

Rare Book Collections

Rare Books and Archives Collections. The Rare Books Collection includes 825 monographs (first editions). The Archives materials deal with the history of Morningside College and its predecessors (Charles City College and the University of the Northwest). Faculty publications are also included in the Archives.

556
Mount Mercy College
Lundy Library
1330 Elmhurst Drive N.E.
Cedar Rapids, Iowa 52402

Telephone. (319) 363-8213

Institutional Description. The privately supported liberal arts college is affiliated with the Roman Catholic Church. Enrollment: 1,034.

Library Administration. Marilyn J. Murphy, Director of Library Services.

Library General Holdings. 73,000 volumes; 415 periodical subscriptions.

Special Collections

The library maintains a collection of the papers of Joan Lipsky, a former Iowa legislator.

557
Mount Saint Clare College
College Library
400 North Bluff Boulevard
Clinton, Iowa 52732

Telephone. (319) 242-4023

Institutional Description. The privately supported liberal arts college is affiliated with the Roman Catholic Church. It grants associate and baccalaureate degrees. Enrollment: 284.

Library Administration. Flora Lowe, Library Director.

Library General Holdings. 29,000 volumes; 480 periodical titles; 26,500 microforms.

Special Collections

Special collections include materials in the **Durham Collection of Theology and History** and the **DaMour Collection of Literature and Fine Arts.**

558
Northwestern College
Ramaker Library
101 7th Street
Orange City, Iowa 51041

Telephone. (712) 737-4821

Institutional Description. The privately supported liberal arts and teachers college was founded in 1882. A Christian college, it is affiliated with the Reformed Church in America. Enrollment: 817.

Library Administration. Arthur G. Hielkema, Director.

Library General Holdings. 96,000 volumes; 500 current periodical titles; 35,000 government documents.

Special Collections

The library's special collections include the **Dutch Heritage Collection;** a collection of 8,000 volumes of commentary on mainstream Protestantism; and an extensive collection of modern literature.

559
Palmer College of Chiropractic
David D. Palmer Health Sciences Library
1000 Brady Street
Davenport, Iowa 52803

Telephone. (319) 326-9600

Institutional Description. The privately supported professional college offers courses at the upper and graduate levels only. It grants professional degrees. Enrollment: 1,591.

Library Administration. John Budrew, Director.

Library General Holdings. 39,000 volumes; 750 current periodical subscriptions.

Special Collections

The circulating and reference collection is strong in chiropractic education with over 24,000 titles. There is also an extensive osteological collection which includes a large number of abnormal bone specimens showing many of the common and uncommon pathologies found in the skeletal structure of the human body. A collection of radiographic case studies numbers over 1,300.

560
St. Ambrose University
McMullen Library
Davenport, Iowa 52803

Telephone. (319) 383-8800

Institutional Description. The privately supported liberal arts university is affiliated with the Roman Catholic Church. It grants baccalaureate and master's degrees. Enrollment: 1,699.

Library Administration. Corinne J. Potter, Director.

Library General Holdings. 125,000 volumes; 700 current periodical titles.

Special Collections

The library maintains specialized collections in business, economics, management, and religious studies.

561
Simpson College
Dunn Library
701 North C Street
Indianola, Iowa 50125

Telephone. (515) 961-1663

Institutional Description. The privately supported liberal arts college was founded in 1860, and is affiliated with The United Methodist Church. Enrollment: 1,033.

Library Administration. Cynthia M. Dyer, Director of Library Services.

Library General Holdings. 130,534 bound volumes; 504 current periodicals; 6,631 microforms.

Special Collections

Avery O. Craven Collection. Avery O. Craven (1885-1980) was a well-known American historian who specialized in mid-nineteenth-century American history, particularly the Antebellum South. The Craven collection includes his personal library of over 2,000 volumes, notes, manuscripts, correspondence with historian Frederick Jackson Turner and others, and memorabilia.

562
Southeastern Community College Libraries
1015 South Gear Avenue
West Burlington, Iowa 52655

Telephone. (319) 752-2731

Institutional Description. The two-year community college offers university-parallel and vocational/technical programs. The college was founded in 1966. Enrollment: 2,110.

Library Administration. Elizabeth A. Gardner, Librarian (South Campus); Angela Hotze, Librarian, (North Campus).

Library General Holdings. 40,000 volumes; 300 periodical and 12 newspaper subscriptions.

Special Collections

The library maintains a collection of rare books and offers the Iowa Public Employment Relations Board Information Service. A College Archival staff assigned to the library is responsible for collecting and preserving documents and artifacts of historical value to the institution. A primary objective is to promote knowledge and understanding of the origins, aims, programs, and goals of the institution.

563
University of Dubuque
Ficke-Laird Library
2000 University Avenue
Dubuque, Iowa 52001

Telephone. (319) 589-3223

Institutional Description. The privately supported liberal arts university and theological seminary is affiliated with the United Presbyterian Church. Enrollment: 763.

Library Administration. Duncan Brockway, Director of Libraries.

Library General Holdings. 133,000 volumes; 850 current periodical subscriptions; 30,000 microforms.

Special Collections

The library houses the Theological Seminary Library which is a collection of resources in the fields of theology and philosophy. The collections of materials includes Reformed and Methodist tradition, medical ethics, other religions, and Biblical studies.

564
University of Iowa
University of Iowa Libraries
Iowa City, Iowa 52242

Telephone. (319) 335-5299

Institutional Description. The publicly supported university was founded in 1847 and now consists of ten colleges. Enrollment: 24,713.

Library Administration. Sheila Creth, University Librarian; Robert A. McCown, Head, Special Collections; David Schoonover, Rare Books Librarian.

Library General Holdings. 2,839,825 volumes; 26,986 current periodical subscriptions; 3,905,683 microforms.

Special Collections

The Special Collections Department of the University of Iowa Libraries has four divisions: books, manuscripts, a map collection, and the archives of the

University.

BOOKS. Special resources include:

Leigh Hunt Collection. Consists of over 2,000 manuscripts and manuscript letters written by Hunt or to him, over 100 association volumes, and over 600 editions of Hunt's writings.

French Revolution Collection. Contains more than 8,000 pamphlets from the years 1788-1799.

John Springer Collection. Includes 2,300 volumes on typography.

Typography Laboratory Collection. Consists of 300 books on printing.

Bollinger-Lincoln Collection. Contains over 4,100 volumes on Abraham Lincoln.

Harvey Ingham Collection. Includes over 500 volumes of Western Americana.

History of Hydraulics Collection. Consists of 500 volumes of historic writings on the science of hydraulics.

Edmund Blunden Collection. Includes 650 volumes of poetry, biography, and criticism plus manuscripts and letters relating to the English poet Edmund Blunden.

Mabbott-Poe Collection. Contains over 750 books relating to Edgar Allan Poe.

John Martin Collection. Includes over 2,000 books on the history of medicine.

Szathmary Family Culinary Collection. Contains over 1,400 books.

Iowa Authors Collection. Over 10,000 volumes by over 2,000 authors are included in this collection.

Mark Ranney Memorial Collection. Contains 3,700 volumes of limited editions in fine bindings and art books.

Social Documents Collection. Consists of a large assemblage of printed materials published by right wing, conservative, and libertarian organizations in the United States.

"X" Collection. A gathering of early, rare, or special works on diverse subjects, including books of the fifteenth and sixteenth centuries, early Americana, Roxburghe Club publications, private press books, dime novels, children's literature, the Dada movement, and selected modern first editions (especially Mark Twain, Baron Corvo, Walt Whitman, Harriet Beecher Stowe, Robert Frost, Iris Murdoch, and Angus Wilson).

MANUSCRIPT COLLECTION. Includes more than 10,000 individually catalogued letters or manuscript items of English and American authors or historical figures, principally of the nineteenth and twentieth centuries. Historical manuscripts include materials on agriculture, labor, U.S. Vice President Henry A. Wallace and his era, journalism, railroads, women's activities and organizations, popular culture, politics, and the American Civil War. At present there are over 450 collections of personal papers and corporate records including **Redpath Chautauqua and Lyceum** records, the **Levi O. Leonard Collection** on the construction of the Union Pacific Railroad, the **Jay N. "Ding" Darling Collection** of papers and cartoons, the **Twentieth Century Fox Film Corporation Script Collection,** the **Keith/Albee Collection** of vaudeville records, and the **John P. Vander Maas Collection of Railroadiana.** The major literary manuscripts are the Leigh Hunt, Iris Murdoch, and Angus Wilson collections.

MAP COLLECTION. Contains more than 136,000 maps, nearly 100,000 aerial photographs, 4,000 books and atlases, and 4,800 microfiche.

ARCHIVES. This collection includes material pertaining to the University that is of permanent historical, administrative, fiscal, or legal value.

565
University of Northern Iowa
Donald O. Rod Library
23rd and College
Cedar Falls, Iowa 50614

Telephone. (319) 273-2281

Institutional Description. The publicly supported state university was founded as a normal school in 1876. It now consists of five colleges and a graduate school. Enrollment: 9,785.

Library Administration. Barbara M. Jones, Director.

Library General Holdings. 633,000 volumes; 2,895 current periodical subscriptions; 211,000 government documents; 567,000 microforms; 33,373 maps.

Special Collections

Youth Collection. A representative collection of elementary and secondary school library material; 16,081 volumes.

Other special collections include American fiction of the 1960s and 1970s.

566
University of Osteopathic Medicine and Health Sciences
Medical Library
3200 Grand Avenue
Des Moines, Iowa 50312

Telephone. (515) 271-1430

Institutional Description. The University is a privately supported medical college. Enrollment: 1,053.

Library Administration. Larry D. Marquardt, Library Director.

Library General Holdings. 8,000 books; 432 journal titles; 17,000 bound journals.

Special Collections

The Medical Library contains specialized collections in the fields of osteopathic and podiatric medicine.

Rare Book Collections

Historical Collection of Medical Textbooks. This specialized collection of medical textbooks of the late nineteenth and early twentieth century contains early works in osteopathic medicine, including several by the founder of the field, Dr. Andrew Taylor Still.

567
Upper Iowa University
Henderson-Wilder Library
Box 1858
Fayette, Iowa 52142

Telephone. (319) 425-5270

Institutional Description. The privately supported liberal arts institution was founded by The United Methodist Church, but separated from denominational support in 1928. Enrollment: 960.

Library Administration. Becky S. Wadian, Library Director.

Library General Holdings. 87,327 volumes; 157 current periodicals; 8 newspaper subscriptions; 2,421 microforms; 175 films, filmstrips, videos; 1,313 slides; 148 audiotapes; 1,366 audio recordings.

Special Collections

NASA Collection. This collection includes approximately 1,000 pieces of ephemera collected in the 1960s-1970s on manned and unmanned space projects; consists of tapes, patches, banners, photographs, and slides.

568
Waldorf College
Voss Memorial Library
South 6th Street
Forest City, Iowa 50436

Telephone. (515) 582-2450

Institutional Description. Founded in 1903, Waldorf College is affiliated with the American Lutheran Church and offers transfer and general education programs leading to the associate degree. Enrollment:

Library Administration. Mary Ann Bartz, Librarian.

Library General Holdings. 42,000 volumes; 300 current periodical subscriptions.

Special Collections

The Voss Library has a special collection of Bibles and and miscellaneous Norwegian antiquarian books.

569
Wartburg College
Englebrecht Library
222 9th Street N.W.
Waverly, Iowa 50677

Telephone. (319) 352-8200

Institutional Description. The privately supported liberal arts college is affiliated with the American Lutheran Church. Enrollment: 1,265.

Library Administration. Donavon M. Schmoll, Director.

Library General Holdings. 130,000 volumes; 900 current periodicals.

Special Collections

The library maintains a special collection on peace and justice and houses materials donated by Kathryn Koob, a Wartburg alumna, who withstood 444 days of captivity as an Iranian hostage in 1980-81. The Curriculum Library contains 10,910 items including textbooks, children's literature, curriculum materials, and printed resources used in teaching.

570
Wartburg Theological Seminary
Reu Memorial Library
333 Wartburg Place
Dubuque, Iowa 52001

Telephone. (319) 589-0200

Institutional Description. The privately supported theological seminary offers graduate-level programs only. It is owned and operated by the American Lutheran Church. Enrollment: 206.

Library Administration. Duncan Brockway, Director.

Library General Holdings. 87,200 volumes. The library operates under a unified management with the Ficke-Laird Library and the Couchman Memorial Library on the University of Dubuque campus. The arrangement is under the Library of the Schools of Theology in Dubuque (Wartburg Theological Seminary and the University of Dubuque Theological Seminary).

Rare Book Collections

The library has a rare book collection of Lutheran materials.

571
Westmar College
Charles W. Mock Library
1002 3rd Avenue S.E.
Le Mars, Iowa 51031

Telephone. (712) 546-7081

Institutional Description. The privately supported liberal arts college is affiliated with the United Methodist Church. Enrollment: 469.

Library Administration. Boyd F. Plumley, Director.

Library General Holdings. 90,000 volumes; 375 cur-

rent periodical subscriptions.

Special Collections

The library has a special collection of rare Bibles and a collection of books by Iowa authors. A curriculum library contains over 2,500 books and pamphlets.

572
William Penn College
Wilcox Library
Trueblood Avenue
Oskaloosa, Iowa 52577

Telephone. (515) 673-8311
Institutional Description. The privately supported liberal arts college was founded in 1873 by Quakers and is still affiliated with the Society of Friends. Enrollment: 510.
Library Administration. Edward A. Goedeken, Librarian.
Library General Holdings. 72,000 volumes.

Special Collections

The library maintains a **Quaker Collection** of over 4,000 volumes covering Quaker history.

Kansas

573
Baker University
Collins Library
Baldwin City, Kansas 66006

Telephone. (913) 594-6451

Institutional Description. The privately supported liberal arts college was founded in 1858 by the Kansas-Nebraska Conference of the Methodist Church. It is now affiliated with the United Methodist Church. Enrollment: 807.

Library Administration. John Forbes, Director.

Library General Holdings. 98,000 volumes; 325 periodical subscriptions.

Special Collections

Baker University's special collections range in form from artifacts and paintings to illuminated manuscripts and published works of scholarship.

The **Eugene Collins Pulliam Collection,** representing memorabilia of a distinguished Arizona-Indiana journalist who had attended Baker University's academy, includes originals of photographs of many personalities significant in public life. The **William Alfred Quayle Collection** of rare Bibles exemplifies the work of medieval scribes as well as modern printers.

The **United Methodist Collection** deals with the history of the denomination both abroad and in America. It includes materials related to the Evangelical Association and United Brethren in Christ, as well as the Methodist Episcopal Church. Smaller collections are those that relate to missions, Sunday schools, and temperance reform as well as hymnody.

The **Kansas History Collection** emphasizes early settlement. The **Nelson Case Collection** focuses on the political development of the United States in the first hundred years of independence. The **Warren Baldwin Cochran-Merton Stacher Rice Collection** on Lincolniana has both primary and secondary sources. The **Thomas Henry Coole Collection** contains coins of China during the dynastic era.

574
Bethany College
Wallerstedt Learning Center
235 East Swensson
Lindsborg, Kansas 67456

Telephone. (913) 227-3311

Institutional Description. The private liberal arts college was founded in 1881 and is controlled by the Lutheran Church in America. Enrollment: 700.

Library Administration. Dixie M. Lanning, Library Director.

Library General Holdings. 111,000 volumes; 503 periodical and newspaper subscriptions; 1,497 titles on audiovisual materials; 46 microcomputer programs.

Special Collections

Special collections include books in the Swedish language (most pre-1930 imprints); Swedish Bibles; books on Swedish immigration or used by early Swedish immigrants.

Other collections include the letters and papers of Carl A. Swenson, founder and second president of Bethany College; a small collection of letters and poems of Carl Sandburg, also including poetry and history books written and autographed by Carl Sandburg.

575
Bethel College
Mennonite Library and Archives
300 East 27th Street
North Newton, Kansas 67117

Telephone. (316) 283-2500

Institutional Description. The private college was founded in 1887 by the Mennonite Church. Enrollment: 631.

Library Administration. Dale R. Schrag, Director of Library; David A. Haury, Special Collections Librarian.

Library General Holdings. The Mennonite Library and Archives is a treasure-house of information on the story of Mennonite people—particularly those who settled in the prairie states. It is a resource for the appreciation of the Anabaptist-Mennonite heritage. It includes more than 22,000 volumes on Mennonite, Anabaptist, and related topics; a collection of 2,000 manuscripts on Mennonite and Anabaptist subjects; the Schowalter Oral History Collection of 500 tapes of interviews on World War I and II, missions, and other experiences; a collection of more than 10,000 color slides; several hundred Fraktur—documents illuminated by folk artists.

576
Central Baptist Theological Seminary
Central Seminary Library
Seminary Heights
Kansas City, Kansas 66102

Telephone. (913) 371-1544

Institutional Description. The Seminary, a graduate school of theology, was founded in 1901, and is affiliated with the American Baptist Churches in America. Enrollment: 84.

Library Administration. Larry Blazer, Seminary Librarian; Arel T. Lewis, Assistant Librarian.

Library General Holdings. 76,461 bound volumes; 295 periodical subscriptions; 513 microforms; 6,638 units of audiovisual material (filmstrips, slides, audio and video cassettes, phonograph records), 495 pamphlets.

Special Collections

Fred E. Young Qumran Collection. Dr. Fred E. Young, Dean of Central Baptist Seminary, has prepared a two-volume bibliography on Qumran containing 10,000 titles from 1947-1987. The titles are in various languages of the world. At the present time, 5,000 of the 10,000 titles are in the library collection. It is the intent of Dr. Young eventually to secure all 10,000 titles for the Library.

577
Coffeyville Community College
Learning Resource Center
Eleventh and Willow Streets
Coffeyville, Kansas 67337

Telephone. (316) 251-4350

Institutional Description. The college was the seventh Kansas junior college founded in 1923. Dormitories were available in 1975. Enrollment: 773.

Library Administration. Rosemary Henderson, Director.

Library General Holdings. 26,000 volumes.

Special Collections

The special collections of the library are on women's studies, marriage, and family life. There is also a special collection of Civil War materials.

578
Emporia State University
William Allen White Library
1200 Commercial
Emporia, Kansas 66801

Telephone. (316) 343-1200

Institutional Description. This state college has led all other Kansas institutes of higher learning in the certification of teachers for Kansas schools every year since 1948. Its first graduating class was in 1867. Enrollment: 4,344.

Library Administration. Henry R. Stewart, University Librarian; Mary E. Bogan, Special Collections Librarian.

Library General Holdings. 448,550 volumes; 2,005 current periodical subscriptions; 248,935 government documents; 18,410 audiovisual materials.

Special Collections

William Allen White Collection. Contains letters and telegrams exchanged between Mr. White and members of his family and such national figures as Herbert Hoover, Calvin Coolidge, Theodore Roosevelt, Franklin D. Roosevelt, William Dean Howells, William Howard Taft, Robert Taft, and many others. Magazine articles written by and about Mr. White as well as hundreds of newspaper editorials, stories and features by and about Mr. White are in the collection. The manuscripts of Mr. White's published books and some unpublished works are housed in the collection. The manuscripts of many speeches, editorials, poems, songs, and his personal diary, written during his college years, are included. The realia section of the collection includes original illustrations from books by W.A. White, scrapbooks and materials from world-wide travels. The collection's photograph section contains numerous photos of Mr. White and his family and the many national figures with whom he associated and corresponded. In commemoration of the 100th anniversary of Mr. White's birth, Emporia State University published a two-volume annotated and illustrated bibliography of William Allen White materials in this collection in 1969.

Lois Lenski Collection. Lois Lenski wrote and illustrated children's books from the 1920s through 1969. The collection includes photographs and other background material, rough sketches, notes, correspondence, manuscripts, dummies, and galley proofs for *Shoo-Fly Girl,* a regional story about the Amish in Lancaster County, Pennsylvania. Similar, although less extensive material is included in the collection for *Auto Worker's Son,* a Round-About America Series story, which was set in Detroit. This collection also includes books, original art work for many of Lois Lenski's works as well as music, sound recordings, pamphlets, articles and other materials.

Normaliana. In 1863, the Kansas State Normal School (now Emporia State University) was established. Material published by this institution and about this institution since it was a normal school is located in this collection. Materials include books, college catalogs, yearbooks, class schedules, student directories, and periodicals. A photograph collection pictorially chronicles the development of this institution from Kansas State Normal School to Emporia State University.

Elizabeth Yates Collection. This collection honors Elizabeth Yates, the distinguished author of *Amos Fortune, Free Man,* which received the first William Allen White Children's Book award and *Prudence Crandall, Woman of Courage,* which was on the 1957-1958 White Award Master List. The collection includes background information, the handwritten and typed manuscripts, and galley proofs of the author's works.

Historical Children's Literature Collection. Includes books as well as periodicals important in the history of Children's Literature in the English language in the nineteenth and twentieth centuries. Rare and valuable children's books including some eighteenth century publications are in the collection. Children's books related to Kansas are also included in the collection.

Mary White Collection. Mary White's tragic death in 1921 at the age of sixteen was memorialized by her father, William Allen White, in the "Mary White" editorial which has been widely reprinted in newspapers as well as high school and college literature books. A framed copy of this editorial is displayed on the west wall of the Mary White Room. The collection includes school books and notebooks which belonged to Mary White. There are also photographs, albums, letters, a copy of the typescript for the "Mary White" editorial, five other manuscripts, clippings, a scrapbook, yearbooks, and other personal belongings of Mary White's. Most of the materials deal with Mary's life in Emporia from 1904-1921. Some materials such as the clippings date from the period following her death.

May Massee Collection. This collection is a memorial to Miss Massee, one of the foremost editors of children's books. The collection contains books, original art work, manuscripts, galley proofs, audiovisual materials, correspondence, and memorabilia—all related to Miss Massee's work at Doubleday and The Viking Press, emphasizing the role of the editor in the publishing of children's books.

Ruth Garver Gagliardo Collection. Ruth Garver Gagliardo, a specialist in children's literature, established the William Allen White Children's Book Award as the first statewide reader's choice award program. The collection contains books from her personal library which included rare and valuable books, including many copies inscribed to her by the authors and illustrators.

William Allen White Children's Book Award Collection. Includes the books which have appeared on the White Award Master Lists since 1952. Many of the books are autographed copies. There are business records, correspondence, ballots, voting report forms, photographs, publicity, and other materials related to the Award. The archives contain original art work, audiotapes, videotapes, information about authors, master lists, bookmarks, and tally sheets.

Rare Book Collections

Rare and Valuable Book Collection. This collection contains rare books including incunabula such as *Divina Providentia* which was printed in Paris about 1495. Also included in this collection are valuable books by such early printers as Froben and Christopher Plantin. Facsimile reproductions of such famous works as the "Gutenburg Bible," the *Lorsch Gospels, The Rabbula Gospels,* and various examples of Books of Hours are also found in this collection. The collection also includes periodicals such as *Gentleman's Magazine,* (1731-1870).

579
Fort Hays State University
Forsyth Library
600 Park Street
Hays, Kansas 67601

Telephone. (913) 628-4431

Institutional Description. The state assisted university was founded in 1900 when the federal government enacted legislation granting the land of the abandoned Fort Hays Military Reservation to the State of Kansas for a state university. Enrollment: 4,277.

Library Administration. Karen Cole, Library Director; Esta Lou Riley, Assistant Library Director and Special Collections/Rare Books Librarian.

Library General Holdings. 314,000 bound volumes; 675,000 federal and state government documents; 1,155,000 microfilms; 2,000 audiovisual items (kits, filmstrips, audiotapes). Instructional Resources Center houses 10,761 books and 415 non-book items.

Special Collections

Ethnic Studies Collection. Contains a variety of materials relating to the various ethnic groups that settled in Kansas. While the collection is particulary rich in documents and published works relating to the history of the Germans from Russia, other immigrant groups such as the Czechs, Germans, Scandinavians, French, English, Mexican, and Dutch are also represented.

Harsh Collection of Literature for Children and Young Adults. A collection of 10,000 volumes of books for children and young adults, selected over a number of years by Donna Harsh for use in teaching her Children's Literature classes at Fort Hays State University. More than 1,000 are foreign books, most in English translation, collected on literature tours around the world.

Military History Microfilm Collection. Includes the official army records of Fort Hays, Kansas (and its predecessor, Fort Fletcher) covering the period 1866-1889; the medical records of Fort Zarah, Kansas, 1864-1869. The

Fort Hays records constitute a valuable resource for the study of old Fort Hays and of army life on the frontier. The collection also contains the World War II newspaper of the Walker Army Air Field, Walker, Kansas, entitled *The Walker-Talker,* published 1942-46. The microfilm includes a short history of the field.

Western Collection. This collection contains Kansas material, primary emphasis Western Kansas (history, biography, description, and travel) including fiction and non-fiction about Kansas from its beginning to the present time. The collection also contains fiction and non-fiction covering cowboys, and the cattle industry of the Great Plains from the industry's beginnings to pre-World War I. There is also a collection of reprints, selected by Elam Bartholomew from scientific journals, covering plant rusts and related materials for the time period from 1880 to 1933.

Restricted Collection. This collection has been separated from the library's general collections because of scarcity, physical condition, or exceptional format. Among the interesting items are books published in limited editions of from 100 to 1,200 copies, some bearing autographs of authors or illustrators, and several religious books published in Ephrata, Lancaster, or other Pennsylvania locations in the late 1700s or early 1800s in German.

University Archives. Includes records and publications of the university, photographs, movies, videocassettes, posters, scrapbooks, and other miscellaneous materials relating to the history of the institution. Important collections in the Archives include the Jean Stouffer Collection (Dean of Women and Foreign Student Advisor from 1955 to 1976); the Lyman Dwight Wooster Collection (instructor, department chairman, and president 1909 to 1961); the Folklore Collection (written and tape-recording materials including reminiscences, poetry, beliefs, superstitions, jump rope rhymes, songs, music, tall tales, riddles, jokes, and recipes); and the Oral History Collection.

580
Friends University
Edmund Stanley Library
2100 University
Wichita, Kansas 67213

Telephone. (316) 261-5880

Institutional Description. This private, Christian, liberal arts college was founded by the Kansas Yearly Meeting of Friends. It is located on the property that was formerly Garfield University. Enrollment: 849.

Library Administration. Sharon M. Ailslieger, Library Director; Elaine Maack, Special Collections/ Rare Books Librarian.

Library General Holdings. 90,000 volumes; 550 current periodical titles (plus 95 titles on microfilm); 2,000 phonograph records; 5,000 media items; curriculum lab (educational materials); computer lab.

Special Collections

Quaker Collection. A collection of materials by and about Quakers and Quakerism (Society of Friends). Housed in the collection are yearly minutes, journals, pamphlets and books, some of which date back to the 1600s. Also included are materials on peace and peace movements.

581
Haskell Indian Junior College
Academic Support Center
P.O. Box H-1305
Lawrence, Kansas 66044

Telephone. (913) 749-8470

Institutional Description. Haskell Indian Junior College was established in 1884 and is an institution for the education of American Indians. Enrollment: 819.

Library Administration. Milton S. Overby, Director.

Library General Holdings. 17,000 volumes.

Special Collections

A collection on the **American Indians** is maintained by the library.

582
Independence Community College
Learning Resources Center
College Avenue and Brookside Drive
Independence, Kansas 67301

Telephone. (316) 331-4100

Institutional Description. The college was founded in 1925 as grades 13 and 14 of the Independence Public School System. A new campus was built and occuped for the first time in 1970. Enrollment: 560.

Library Administration. Del Singleton, Director of Learning Resources.

Library General Holdings. 31,000 volumes; 165 current periodical subscriptions.

Special Collections

The **William Inge College** is housed in the ICC library. This special collection includes the private book and record collection of the famous playwright and some original manuscripts and memorabilia. Inge was born and attended schools in Independence including ICC.

583
Kansas State University
Farrell Library
Manhattan, Kansas 66506

Telephone. (913) 532-5616

Institutional Description. The publicly supported state university was founded in 1863 under the Morrill Act, by which land-grant colleges came into being. Enrollment: 15,851.

Library Administration. Brice G. Hobrock, Dean; John Vander Velde, Special Collections/Rare Books Librarian; Virginia M. Quiring, Associate Dean, Library Development.

Library General Holdings. 1,058,610 volumes; 2,050,-253 microforms; 8,914 serial titles; 43,812 audiovisual and other format items.

Special Collections

Charles Stratton Music Collection. The collection, a bequest from the estate of Professor Charles W. Stratton, reflects a wide range of interests. The piano—its composers, music, history, and techniques—was Professor Stratton's forte, and the collection reflects this emphasis. The collection has many works about other instruments and virtually the entirety of musical forms.

Cookery Collection. Embraces all aspects of foods, nutrition, and cookery as well as early treatises on household economy, including recipes, home remedies, and other information vital to setting up and maintaining a household. Imprints date from the mid-sixteenth century. Contains the rare first edition and over twenty subsequent editions of Hannah Glasse's *Art of Cookery.*

Donald Von Ruysdael Drenner Book and Manuscript Collection. A variety of subjects is represented. All reflect a high degree of editorial excellence with attention to the details of printing and typography that exemplify the art of the private press.

Equine Collection. Primarily English language works about the horse, treatment of its diseases, and tack.

Frank Harris Oriental Art Collection. This gift collection contains predominantly English language works on Chinese and Oriental art, with emphasis on Chinese paintings, sculpture, procelain, tombs, temples, and textiles.

Fred H. and Jeannette Higginson James Joyce Collection. Contains secondary materials and is considered a working collection. Although the works by Joyce are reflected in the collection, there is an equal number of works about Joyce and his times including Dublin and its life.

Fred H. and Jeannette Higginson Robert Graves Collection. Contains many first editions and many autographed by Graves. Variant editions and printings are also included for all the major works.

Farming Systems Research. Published and unpublished literature in English, Spanish, and French; includes materials concerning the small farmer. A related Rural Third World collection includes a wider range of topics from adult education to land ownership and small business.

Gordon Parks Collection. Contains works by and about Parks and includes several foreign language translations of *The Learning Tree* and *A Choice of Weapons.*

Historic Costume and Textile Collection. Focuses on clothing styles of many nationalities and ethnic groups from ancient times to the modern era.

James and Jean Mathews Private Press Collection. Includes private press printings of poetry, calendars, avant garde publications, catalogs, and books about private presses.

Leonora Hering Memorial Poultry Collection. This collection is a bequest collected for over forty years by a prominent poultry fancier. Focuses on the chicken and its breeding, including rare breeds. There are also books and lithographs depicting the chicken and other fowl in art.

Louis Von Trebra Germanic Collection. A group of German language works, printed during the nineteenth century, that focus on the history and literature of Germany.

Mackenzie Linnaeana Collection. Reflects the writings of Linnaeus, his associates, and his students. The collection is rich in theses, dissertations, and printed lectures by Linnaeus's students at the University of Uppsala. Most of the items in the collection were published between 1730 and 1850.

Norman Nadel Performing Arts Collection. Formed in 1983 when Nadel, a New York drama critic, donated his collection of 612 playbills and theatrical programs.

Objectivist Poetry Collection. Contains first editions of varying rarity of writings from American and English poets in the Objectivist School; some are extremely limited printings.

Rex and Lucille Anderson Abraham Lincoln Collection. The earliest book in the collection was published in 1860; the latest in 1980. There are several rarities, including volumes with Lincoln medals, and limited editions. About fifteen percent of the collection consists of books on the Civil War.

Rhetoric Collection. Historical texts, all in English, on all aspects of rhetoric and oratory.

Theological Collection. The collection is ecumenical as well as eclectic and focuses on the history of religion in theory and in practice.

Alice C. Nichols Papers. Correspondence, typescripts, and printed materials 1922-1961, including papers associated with writing and publishing *Bleeding Kansas* in 1954.

Arthur W. Hershberger Papers. Collection documents Hershberger's career as a Wichita attorney and a member of the Kansas Board of Regents, 1951-57, as well as materials spanning the years 1908-75.

Clementine Paddleford Papers. A collection of correspondence, scrapbooks, printed material, 1925-67; a compilation of food articles and recipes as editor for *Farm and Fireside, New York Herald Tribune,* and *This Week.*

Harold R. Fatzer Papers. Major portion of the collection associated with Fatzer's service as Justice of the Supreme Court of Kansas, 1956-77.

James C. Carey Papers. Papers generated by Dr. Carey during his employment as a professor in the Department of History at Kansas State University, 1848-81.

Dan D. Casement Papers. Correspondence, typescripts, press releases, photographs, 1795-1959, relating to the cattleman, writer and farm organization leader, Dan Casement, and his father, John S. Casement, Union Army officer in the Civil War.

Far-Mar-Co Records. Collection documents the activities of cooperatives in Kansas, Nebraska, Colorado, and Missouri and the involvement of Far-Mar-Co on the national and international level.

Nels A. Tornquist Papers. Collection of military papers saved by Tornquist during his service in the United States Army. Documents his activities in the Spanish American War, Punitive Expedition into Mexico against Pancho Villa, and World War I.

Photograph Collection. Covers the period 1880 to the present; 20,000 prints; 1,250 negatives; subjects include buildings, campus views, events and activities, students, faculty, administrators, and alumni.

Third World Women. Covers a variety of areas—socioeconomic participation, women and migration, health/nutrition/fertility and family planning, and communications.

University Archives. Records of Kansas State University, 1863 to the present.

Velma L. Carson Papers. Literary manuscripts, correspondence, printed material, 1924-83, related to her writing career.

Wendell Lady Papers. Correspondence, reports, surveys, minutes, legal documents, printed materials, 1969-82; papers document terms as a member of the Kansas House of Representatives, 1969-82.

William F. Danenbarger Papers. Majority of collection is associated with Danenbarger's activities as member of Kansas Council on Economic Education, 1962-75 and Kansas Board of Regents, 1961-65 and 1970-74.

William R. Roy Papers. Correspondence, legal documents, reports, printed material, 1971-74 of Roy as a U.S. Congressman.

The Jerry Wexler Collection. A group of nearly 2,000 recordings in the Audiovisual Department donated by alumnus Jerry Wexler, co-owner of Atlantic Records in the 1950s. Consists of recordings from the mid-1960s through the 1970s and into the 1980s and reflects the professional and personal interests of their donor. The collection represents a panorama of sound that illuminates an important corner of American popular music and culture.

Rare Book Collections

General Rare Book Collection. Contains 10,011 books and printed materials. Embraces a wide variety of subjects and includes books, pamphlets, atlases about Kansas and the Great Plains. Also contains examples of beautiful printing and fine binding such as those from John Baskerville and William Morris's Nonesuch Press. Imprints range from the sixteenth century to date.

584
Kansas Wesleyan University
Memorial Library
100 East Claflin
Salina, Kansas 67401

Telephone. (913) 827-5541

Institutional Description. The privately supported university was founded by the Methodist Episcopal Church in 1886. It is a liberal arts institution offering undergraduate courses leading directly to professional and vocational opportunities as well as preparation for graduate studies. Enrollment: 570.

Library Administration. Linda Strandberg, University Librarian; Donna Werhan, Assistant to the Librarian/Government Documents Librarian.

Library General Holdings. 71,532 volumes; 230 periodicals; 9 newspaper subscriptions (microfilm editions of *The New York Times* and *The Salina Journal;* 1,262 audiovisual titles.

Special Collections

The "W" Collection. Consists of books on or about the college and its history, the Methodist Church, the Kansas West Conference of the Methodist Church, and the Wild West.

Government Documents. The University receives twenty-four percent of the documents the Government Printing Office has available from which federal depositories may choose; older issues of the Area Handbooks issued by the GPO are retained; these older issues contain information which is not in the current Country Study Handbooks.

585
Marymount College
College Library
East Iron and Marymount Road
Salina, Kansas 67401

Telephone. (913) 825-2101

Institutional Description. The privately supported liberal arts college was founded in 1922 as the first four-year college for women in Kansas. It has been coeducational since 1965. It is affiliated with the Roman Catholic Church. Enrollment: 397.

Library Administration. Sister Bernadine Pachta, Director of Library Services.

Library General Holdings. 91,000 volumes; 300 current periodical titles.

Special Collections

The library maintains special collections on Catholicism, ethnic studies (Black, Chicano, Indian), and alcoholism and drug abuse. A special collection of ethnic newspapers and periodicals is also available.

586
McPherson College
Miller Library
1600 East Euclid
P.O. Box 1402
McPherson, Kansas 67460

Telephone. (316) 241-0731

Institutional Description. An independent liberal arts institution, McPherson College was founded in 1887. It is related to the Church of the Brethren. Enrollment: 446.

Library Administration. Rowena Olsen, College Librarian.

Library General Holdings. 62,644 volumes (including 2,383 in microformat); 2,962 nonprint materials; 30,285 pamphlets; 601 periodical titles.

Special Collections

Brethren Collection. Consists of materials by and about the Church of the Brethren and McPherson College and their people. Includes rare book materials.

Juvenile Collection. Contains textbooks, children's literature, and educational pamphlet material.

587
Mid-America Nazarene College
Mabee Library
P.O. Box 1776
Olathe, Kansas 66062

Telephone. (913) 782-3750

Institutional Description. The privately supported liberal arts college, an institution of the Church of the Nazarene, was founded in 1968. Enrollment: 899.

Library Administration. Ray L. Morrison, Library Director.

Library General Holdings. 75,000 bound volumes; 400 periodical subscriptions; 25,000 other items.

Rare Book Collections

The library maintains a rare book collection of books by or about American and European authors published in the 1700s, 1800s, and early 1900s. It contains over 900 volumes including such authors as Robert Burns, Sir Francis Drake, and others.

588
Ottawa University
Library
10th and Cedar
Ottawa, Kansas 66067

Telephone. (913) 242-5200

Institutional Description. The privately supported liberal arts university was founded in 1865; it is affiliated with the American Baptist Church. Enrollment: 664.

Library Administration. J. Marion Roth, Librarian.

Library General Holdings. 84,000 volumes; 380 periodical subscriptions.

Special Collections

The library maintains a collection of 2,000 rare and scholarly books on Chinese art and ceramics.

589
Pittsburg State University
Leonard H. Axe Library
Pittsburg, Kansas 66762

Telephone. (316) 231-7000

Institutional Description. Pittsburg State University is a multi-purpose state university. Enrollment: 4,682.

Library Administration. Robert A. Walter, University Librarian; Gene DeGruson, Special Collections Librarian.

Library General Holdings. 199,000 volumes; 1,462 current subscriptions; 275,000 microforms; 50,000 music scores; 20,000 other learning materials.

Special Collections

Appeal to Reason Collection. Consists of variant editions of the Socialist newspaper, publications of the Appeal to Reason publishing house and its business records, and correspondence of its founding editor, J. A. Wayland (1854-1912) and of managing editor Fred D. Warren (1872-1959).

E. Haldeman-Julius Collection. Contains the periodical publications, Little Blue Books, and Big Blue Books of E. Haldeman-Julius Publications, as well as the publisher's correspondence, business records, and private library.

Eva Jessye Collection. Contains the music and correspondence of the conductor/composer, as well as personal correspondence and library. Included among her papers are three leaves of the *Porgy and Bess* manuscript.

Ida Hayman and Phil H. Callery Collections. Contains the correspondence and photographs of the Socialist lawyers who represented the 14th District of the United Mine Workers of America.

Margaret E. Haugawout Collection. Consists of the feminist's diaries, correspondence, and private library.

Zula Bennington Greene Collection. Consists of books and pamphlets published by Kansas authors.

James Tate Collection. Consists of books and correspondence of the poet.

Anne Tedlock Books Collection. Contains the correspondence and publications of the children's author.

The Vance Randolph Collection. Materials pertaining to folklore of the southeast Kansas and Ozarks regions.

Albert Bigelow Paine Collection. Consists of books written by the author.

Joe Saia Collection. Consists of correspondence of the southeast Kansas Democratic political leader.

Joe Skubitz Collection. Scrapbooks and correspondence of the U.S. House of Representatives members.

Walter Pennington Collection. Consists of books pertaining to Irish and Old French literature.

Southeast Kansas Collection. Books, pamphlets, newspapers, maps, and correspondence pertaining to the fourteen counties of southeast Kansas.

Martha Pate Collection. Consists of organ music.

Harold Bell Wright Collection. Writings and clippings pertaining to his career in Pittsburg, Kansas, 1898-1903.

Sam Roper Collection. Romance and adventure novels written by the Girard legislator.

William Inge Collection. Consists of plays and clippings pertaining to his teaching career in Columbus, Kansas.

Bertie Cole Bays Collection. Contains the manuscripts of the last poet laureate (1937-1972) of Kansas.

Ted Watts Collection. Consists of correspondence, business records, art work, and publications of the sports artist.

590
Saint Mary College
De Paul Library
4100 South 4th Street Trafficway
Leavenworth, Kansas 66048

Telephone. (913) 682-5151

Institutional Description. The Roman Catholic liberal arts college for women was founded by the Sisters of Charity of Leavenworth in 1858. First named Saint Mary Academy, the school became a junior college in 1923. Now known as Saint Mary College, it is a four-year institution which grants baccalaureate degrees. Enrollment: 453.

Library Administration. Sr. Anna Rose Hanne, SCL, College Librarian; Sr. Therese Deplazes, SCL, Special Collections Librarian.

Library General Holdings. 119,000 volumes; 460 current magazine and newspaper subscriptions; 38,363 microforms; 5,715 audiovisual units; music scores and records, housed in the Music Department.

Special Collections

Abraham Lincoln Collection. Consists of 1,200 fully catalogued volumes (many rare or out-of-print), 110 photographic prints, 54 framed portraits or documents, 700 rare pamphlets, 300 post cards, sheet music and song sheets, stamps, and memorabilia.

Kansas Collection. History (state, Leavenworth, Fort Leavenworth, Catholic Church), authors, textbooks of Territorial days, Sisters of Charity of Leavenworth, Saint Mary College.

Manuscript Documents. Includes Americana: deeds of sale, official appointments, wills, slave papers of early American historical periods; holograph letters of Col. Philip G. Marsteller (one of George Washington's pall bearers) and of his son, Samuel Arell Marsteller; of the Edward Cutts family; of the William Ellery (signer of the Declaration of Independence) family: Christopher Ellery (first Jeffersonian senator from Rhode Island), Frank Ellery, Midshipman; of Mary "Polly" Carter; and a few modern authors.

Scripture Collection. The Sir John J. and Mary Craig Scripture Collection consists of more than 2,000 fully catalogued volumes of Scripture, Theology, Liturgy and Ritual, and Spiritual Life. The collection spans the second to twentieth centuries. Two manuscripts, a scroll of the Hebrew Book of Ruth and a codex of the Gospels of the New Testament (72 leaves), date from the early thirteenth century; in addition there are 43 separate other vellum or parchment manuscripts dating from 1150, and early printed leaves, totaling about 135, as well as facsimiles and transcriptions of early codices; incunabula volumes and many rare volumes printed after 1500 are included.

Rare Book Collections

William Shakespeare Collection. Contains about 100 volumes considered rare or unusual: the earliest printing of a single work of Shakespeare, *Coriolanus,* 1743; the complete set edited by Samuel Johnson, George Stevens, and F. Malone, 1792; facsimile of the first folio of 1623; scrapbooks, theatre programs, actors, actresses, prints, memorabilia.

Charles Dickens. Includes 60 rare items; three titles in the original monthly parts in wrappers: *Dombey and Son,* 1848; *Little Dorritt,* 1857; *Our Mutual Friend,* 1865; eleven editions of *A Christmas Carol,* including a facsimile page of the author's manuscript and a tape by Lionel Barrymore; three first editions; two rare print collections; memorabilia.

591
Southwestern College
Memorial Library
100 College Street
Winfield, Kansas 67156

Telephone. (316) 221-4150

Institutional Description. The privately supported liberal arts college was founded in 1886. It is affiliated with the United Methodist Church. Enrollment: 551.

Library Administration. Daniel L. Nutter, Librarian.

Library General Holdings. 122,000 volumes; 565 current periodicals.

Special Collections

The special collections of the library include 250 drawings and paintings by Arthur Covey, a twentieth-century Kansas artist; the **Ludwig Walker Collection** of 300 volumes on Afro-American history; the **Watumull India Collection** of 350 volumes on the literature and history of Southeast Asia and India. There is also an Archives and History Room of the Kansas West Conference of the United Methodist Church.

592
Tabor College
College Library
400 South Jefferson
Hillsboro, Kansas 67063

Telephone. (316) 947-3121

Institutional Description. The privately supported liberal arts college was founded in 1908. It is affiliated with the Mennonite Brethren Churches. Enrollment: 360.

Library Administration. Bruce Entz, Head Librarian.

Library General Holdings. 70,000 volumes; 450 current periodical subscriptions.

Special Collections

The library collects the works of Aleksandr Solzhenitsyn, C.S. Lewis, and James Michener. There is also a collection on Mennonite Brethren history.

593
University of Kansas
Kenneth Spencer Research Library
Lawrence, Kansas 66045

Telephone. (913) 864-4334

Institutional Description. This state supported university was founded in 1864 and had its first class in 1866. Enrollment: 25,531.

Library Administration. James Ranz, University Librarian; Alexandra Mason, Spencer Librarian and Special Collections/Rare Books Librarian.

Library General Holdings. Main Library: 2,177,159 volumes; 23,573 serials; 1,322,985 microfiche; 784,746 documents; 57,102 reels of microfilm; 257,788 maps; 1,-550,000 photographs, glass negatives; 20,000+ linear fee of manuscripts and archives; 73,243 sound recordings. Kenneth Spencer Research Library: 190,000 volumes printed matter (books, magazines, etc.); ca. 1,250 running feet of manuscripts; ca. 85 antiquarian maps.

Special Collections

The Kenneth Spencer Research Library is the rare books, manuscripts, and archives library of the University of Kansas. Its three departments are the Department of Special Collections, the Kansas Collection, and the University Archives. For detailed description of the Spencer Library and its collections, see Alexandra Mason, *A Guide to the Collections,* 4th edition, The Department of Special Collections, Kenneth Spencer Research Library, University of Kansas, Lawrence, Kansas, 1987.

Printed Books. The collections in this category include:

RENAISSANCE AND EARLY MODERN IMPRINTS: The Summerfield Renaissance Collection, The Aitchison Collection of Vergil, The Cervantes Collection, The Clubb Anglo-Saxon Collection (books in Anglo-Saxon typefaces).

EIGHTEENTH-CENTURY COLLECTIONS: The Edmund Curll Collection, The English Poetical Collection, The Realey Collection of Sir Robert Walpole, The Bond Periodical and Newspaper Collection, Eighteenth-Century Pamphlet Collections, The Brodie of Brodie Collection, The Horn Collection of Marlborough, The Melvin French Revolutionary Collection.

NINETEENTH- AND TWENTIETH-CENTURY AUTHOR AND LITERARY COLLECTIONS: The Paden Collection of Tennyson, The Rilke Collection, The Joyce Collection, The Yeats Collection, The Lawrence Collection, The Treadway Collection of Churchill, The Mencken Collection, The New American Poetry Collections, The Science Fiction Collections.

SUBJECT AND GENRE COLLECTIONS: The Boehrer Luso-Brazilian Collection, The Children's Literature Collection, The Gerritsen History of Women Collection, The Gilbert First Issue Collection (magazine history), The Griffith Guatemalan Collection, The Howey Economic History Collection, The O'Hegarty Irish Library, Voyages and Travel.

SCIENTIFIC AND TECHNOLOGICAL COLLECTIONS: The Ellis Ornithology Collection, The Fitzpatrick Botany Collection, The Linnaeus Collection (taxonomy), Scientific Offprint Collections, The Willett-Pashley Architectural Library, The Frank Lloyd Wright Collection.

Manuscripts. The Department's manuscripts are much more numerous than the printed books and cover a much longer span of time. By far the majority of them come from Great Britain and western Europe although they concern all parts of the globe. A large part of the manuscript holdings consists of collections—over a thousand—of historical papers. The subject areas covered by the Manuscripts Division include Mediaeval and Early Renaissance Manuscripts (see below), Collections of Letters, Economics and Commerce, Family and Estate Papers, Political Papers, Literary Papers, Theatrical Papers, Intellectual Life, Music, Voyages and Travels, Latin America, History of Science and Technology, History of Writing, Scholar's Notes, and Donors' Archives.

Kansas Collection. This collection preserves and makes available materials which document the economic, social, cultural, and political history of Kansas and the Great Plains region. Diaries, letters, and records constitute 5,000 feet of manuscript materials. Supplementing these are 120,000 books, periodicals, and newspapers which provide researchers with original source materials and the latest in contemporary scholarship. Graphic materials include over 700,000 photographs, as well as historical maps and original art for published cartoons.

Archives of Recorded Sound. Housed in the Music Library; includes ca. 80,000 phonodiscs, cylinders, etc., from the history of opera and jazz.

University Archives. Repository for the history of the University, both present and past, including the official papers of the chancellors and other administrative records, records of student and faculty activities, papers of alumni, photographs, blueprints and architectural drawings, videotapes, newspapers, faculty and alumni publications, and one of the country's foremost collections of sports photographs.

Rare Book Collections

General Rare Book Collection. One of the largest and most important collections in the Department is one without unifying principle or name. Commonly called the general collection or the rare books collection and including over 22,000 titles, this is the basic workhorse collection. It is the repository of all departmental holdings which do not fall into one of the separate "named" collections. It includes most of the Department's sixteenth- and seventeenth-century English books, many eighteenth-century English, Continental, and American imprints, nineteenth-century imprints, and modern literature. It is strong in botany, voyages and travels, typography, eighteenth-century French history, nineteenth- and twentieth-century English literature, English history, and economics; beyond that it includes lesser holdings on a multitude of subjects.

Medieval and Early Renaissance Manuscripts. The Department collects medieval manuscripts primarily for their texts and the information they convey about the way books were published before the invention of printing.

594
University of Kansas Medical Center
The Clendening History of Medicine Library and Museum
39th and Rainbow Boulevard
Kansas City, Kansas 66103

Telephone. (913) 588-7040

Institutional Description. The publicly supported University of Kansas was founded in 1864. The Medical Center consists of the School of Medicine, the School of Allied Health, and the School of Nursing. Enrollment: 25,531 (for the whole university).

Library Administration. Susan B. Case, Rare Books Librarian.

Library General Holdings. 22,000 volumes.

Special Collections

The Logan Clendening collection of books on the history of medicine is one of the most notable collections of its kind in the United States. The collection was bequeathed by Dr. Clendening to his alma mater, the University of Kansas School of Medicine. This library contains special collections in radiology, hematology, plastic surgery, and anesthesiology and "there is no outstanding medical classic of which there is not a copy in the Clendening collection, and not merely editions but outstanding editions, for Logan Clendening was a most intelligent bibliophile who was not only familiar with the contents of the book but highly sensitive to the beauties of printing and binding." (Dr. Ralph Major, Professor Emeritus of Medicine and of the History of Medicine, University of Kansas.) Dr. Clendening (1884-1945) was the author of the *Human Body,* a national bestseller. He later became a successful health columnist during the Depression years and the early 1940s.

The Thor Jager Collection of Rudolf Virchow Manuscripts was donated to the Kansas University Endowment Association in 1970. Jager and Clendening were friendly competitors in the quest for pertinent items in the history of medicine.

Several other notable collections within the Library are: The Edward Holman SkQinner Collection on Electricity, Radiology, and Radium; The Russell Landram Collection on the History of Dermatology and Microscopy; The Paul Herrington Collection on Orthopedic Surgery; The Darrel Thomas Shaw Collection (consists of 4,050 items and includes handwritten letters, portraits, and signatures).

595
Washburn University of Topeka
Mabee Library
17th and College Streets
Topeka, Kansas 66621

Telephone. (913) 295-6300

Institutional Description. The publicly supported university was founded in 1865 as a Congregational school. It became a public institution in 1941. Enrollment: 4,721.

Library Administration. Wilma Rife, Director.

Library General Holdings. 220,000 volumes; 1,200 current periodical titles.

Special Collections

Within many departments of the College of Arts and Sciences are specialized collections. Among these are the Karl Menninger Reading Room in the Corrections and Criminal Justice department which contains criminal justice administration manuals and private collections of books in corrections; the Art and Theatre Arts department which has a viewing room containing 50,000 slides exemplifying oriental and western painting, sculpture, and architecture; and the Education department which maintains an extensive curriculum library containing primary and secondary school textbooks, professional books, and children's story books.

596
Wichita State University
The Ablah Library
Box 68
Wichita, Kansas 67208

Telephone. (316) 689-3586

Institutional Description. The publicly supported state university traces its origins to Fairmont College, founded by the Congregational Church in 1895. In 1926 Fairmont became a municipal institution; it was added to the Kansas state system of higher education in 1964. Enrollment: 10,719.

Library Administration. Jasper Schad, University Librarian; Michael T. Kelly, Curator, Special Collections.

Library General Holdings. 777,023 bound volumes; 3,811 current periodicals; 641,364 microforms.

Special Collections

American Studies Department Student Papers. These student research papers cover many aspects of American, and particularly of Kansas, history. Among the topics pertinent to Kansas are agriculture, the cattle trade, architecture, art, music, literature, military posts, county and township histories, industries, and special events. There are also numerous papers on American Indians.

Americanization Movement Collection. Comprised of xeroxed copies of correspondence and a transcript of the proceedings of a conference, attended by State Governors, of the National Bureau of Education and the National Committee of One Hundred. This conference was held just prior to America's entry into World War I, and reflected the unease of Americans at the Communist Revolution in Russia and the Kaiser's dominance in much of Europe.

Anti-Slavery Collection. Consists of broadsides and correspondence penned by some of the most prominent men in the anti-slavery movement.

Founding of Arkansas City, Kansas. Documents relating to the founding of Arkansas City in September, 1870.

Nurse Bidwell Collection: Panama Canal. Consists of personal and general correspondence of Louise C. Bidwell while she was a nurse at a Panama Canal hospital in Ancon.

Bimetallism and the National Currency System Pamphlets. Pamphlets published between 1877 and 1928, addressing the issue of coinage and the monetary system.

Papers Relating to the British Seizure of American Ships, 1793-1801. Contains correspondence relating to British seizure of American ships between 1793 and 1801 under the British Admiralty's Rule of 1756.

Alys McKey Bryant Collection. Correspondence, photographs, slides, clippings, and memorabilia of Aly Harrison McKey, popular aviatrix who took up flying in 1912.

Papers of Walter E. Burnham. Includes correspondence, engineering drawings, photographs, financial documents, and memorabilia relating primarily to Burnham's professional career as an aviation engineer.

Chicago and Pacific Railroad Collection. This collection, taken from the personal files of George S. Bowen, deals with the efforts of the Chicago and Pacific Railroad Company to raise money to complete its line from Chicago to the Mississippi River after the Panic of 1873. A related collection is comprised of items concerning the construction of a trunk railroad from Arlington, Nebraska, to St. John, Kansas.

Congressional Papers. Separate collections of congressional papers related to congressional sessions, political campaigns, speeches, and specific committees of Congressmen from Kansas as well as other states.

Papers of the Federal Writers' Project of the WPA for Kansas. The WPA Federal Writers' Project for Kansas was established to provide employment to writers and researchers who were unemployed and needy during the 1930s and early 1940s. This particular collection represents 50 out of 105 counties in Kansas.

E.M. Forster Collection. All correspondence in this collection is written to Siegfried Sassoon and covers a span of 41 years from 1918 to 1959.

Eunice McIntosh Merrill Collection of William Lloyd Garrison Papers. This collection includes manuscripts and family correspondence from the years 1845 to 1875, relating to William Lloyd Garrison and the anti-slavery movement.

German Pamphlet Collection. Relates to all aspects of German life and culture beginning with pre-1933 pamphlets. Most are written in German.

Ben F. Hammond Collection. Contains editorial cartoons drawn by Ben Hammond who was a cartoonist with the *Wichita Eagle.*

The Television and Radio Scripts of Kathleen Hite. Spans the years 1946-1978. This time period includes scripts for such popular western shows as Gunsmoke, Guns of Will Sonnett, Laramie, and Wagon Train. Ms. Hite's writings also include scripts for dramas such as The

Alfred Hitchcock Show, The Jane Wyman Show, The General Electric Theatre, The Waltons, and Apple's Way.

A.E. Howse Papers. Includes legislative material on water resources development, papers from Howse's term as mayor of Wichita, other city government reports from 1955 to 1962, papers of the Municipal Research Crime Commission, and ephemeral material.

Papers of Edwin Markham. Primarily correspondence from 1890 to 1950, the collection also contains poetry, clippings, and memorabilia relating to Markham.

Daniel McCormick Collection. Contains published and unpublished cartoons, correspondence, and clippings.

Mid-Arkansas Valley Development Association, Inc. Material concerns the Mid-Arkansas Valley Development Association, Inc. from 1967 to 1973, including the project to extend the navigation of the Arkansas River from Tulsa, Oklahoma to Wichita, Kansas, and to build a water port in Wichita.

Papers of T.B. Miskimon. The papers of T.B. Miskimon, inspector for General Goethals during the building of the Panama Canal, describe the problems on non-construction activities at the site of the Canal, 1906-1911.

Mylai Incident. The collection contains the transcript of the proceedings of the court martial against Captain Ernest Medina. Also included are photographs and miscellaneous court rulings.

Ben Santos Collection. Diaries, lectures, drafts of stories and poems relating to the literary career of the Filipino writer.

University Archives. Included in the archives collection are records of Fairmount College, the University of Wichita, Wichita State University, papers of William Jardine, Hugo Wall, Sidney J. Brick, Harry F. Corbin, Emory Lindquist, and the Legislative Effort—Wichita State University, 1957-1964.

Thomas Wolfe Papers. These papers consist of xerox copies of miscellaneous correspondence form 1920 to 1938. Correspondents include his parents and other members of his immediate family.

World War I Pamphlet Collection. This collection touches on many aspects of the Great War.

World War II Pamphlet Collection. Covers all aspects of the conflict.

Other Collections: The E.H. Byington Collection; Diary of Doris Caesar; Laiten Camien Collection; Cheney Reservoir Photograph Collection; Civil War Letters; Papers of George A. Crawford; John Denning Collection; Depression ERA Relief Collection; Letters to D.B. Dyers; Fair Play Township (Marion County, Kansas) Collection; Farming Account Books; Royal Flying Corps; Royal Naval Air Service; Margarita Fischer Collection; Fedonia Photograph Collection; Autobiography of James Grant Gilchrist; John W. Gladding, U.S. Patent Collection; Letter Hon. John Guthrie; Papers of Edward Everett Hale; Milton Edward Earle Hampton II Collection; Press Releases of George Hart, Kansas; Papers of Omah Scott Horton; Huerfans Valley Ditch and Reservoir Company; The Herbert Jones Collection; KAKE-TV News Archives; Papers of the Kansas Governor's Commission on the Status of Women; Kansas Land Documents; Kansas-Nebraska Bill Pamphlets; Kansas Territory—Letters from Mound City, 1859; Kansas Water Resources Board Papers; The Chester I. Long Papers; Henry Malone Collection; Papers of Russell E. McClure; Papers of J. Hudson McKnight; Marcellus M. Murdock papers; Nicaragua and Isthmian Canal Commission Papers, 1899-1904; Panama Collection; The Photo-Journal Collection; Papers of Timothy Pickering; Harry Pollard Collection; Populist Period Pamphlets Collection; Prohibition Pamphlet Collection; The Papers of Herb Rawdon; Papers of William L. Riley; The Paul Robeson Concert Police Documents; The Papers of Edward S. Safford; Stanley Spencer Collection; Standard Nuclear Unit Power Plant Preliminary Safety Analysis Report; Clayton H. Staples Collection; Floyd B. Streeter Collection; Richard H. Sullivan Papers, Kansas Audubon Society; William Sulzer Papers; Alexander Telford's Catalog of Books; Admiral John G. Walker Collection of Family Papers.

Rare Book Collections

Robert T. Aitchison Collection. Contains examples of important printers and styles of printing from the fifteenth century to the present.

Maurice M. and Jean H. Tinterow Collection. The Tinterow Collection contains a comprehensive collection of books, dating from the eighteenth century, on the history of hypnotism.

Kentucky

597
Alice Lloyd College
McGaw Library and Learning Center
Pippa Passes, Kentucky 41844

Telephone. (606) 368-2101

Institutional Description. The privately supported liberal arts college was founded in 1923. It grants associate and baccalaureate degrees. Enrollment: 528.

Library Administration. Charlotte Madden, Librarian.

Library General Holdings. 45,000 volumes; 300 periodicals.

Special Collections

Photographic Archives. Old photographs of the Central Appalachian region are being actively collected, copied, and indexed as a scholarly collection in order to preserve the visual history of the region.

Oral History. This project is administered by Alice Lloyd College and includes the participation of three other colleges in Kentucky, Virginia, and North Carolina. Students conduct audio-tape interviews with long time residents of the area.

598
Asbury College
Morrison-Kenyon Library
201 North Lexington Avenue
Wilmore, Kentucky 40390

Telephone. (606) 858-3511

Institutional Description. The privately supported liberal arts and teachers college was founded in 1890 as a church school. It operates on the doctrinal standards of John Wesley, but is an interdenominational Christian institution. Enrollment: 966.

Library Administration. William Abernathy, Director of Library Services.

Library General Holdings. 122,000 volumes; 618 periodical subscriptions.

Special Collections

Special collections include the **Asa Mahan Collection** of books by and about the nineteenth-century philosopher, educator, and president of Oberlin College; and the **Bishop J. Waskom Pickett Collection** of books, correspondence, and miscellaneous papers.

599
Asbury Theological Seminary
B.L. Fisher Library
204 North Lexington Avenue
Wilmore, Kentucky 40390

Telephone. (606) 858-3581

Institutional Description. The privately supported theological seminary operates within the Wesleyan-Arminian tradition, although it is interdenominational. Enrollment: 681.

Library Administration. David William Faupel, Director.

Library General Holdings. 151,000 volumes; 805 current periodical titles.

Special Collections

The **Heritage Room** is designed for the preservation of mementos related to the history of the Seminary, and other old and historically significant materials. Specific emphasis has been placed on securing an extensive research collection in the area of Biblical studies. In harmony with the Wesleyan emphasis in the seminary's program, a constant effort is also made to strengthen holdings in the areas of Wesleyana, Methodistica, and holiness movements. Attention has also been given to strengthening the Missions and Evangelism Collection to service the E. Stanley Jones School of World Mission and Evangelism.

600
Bellamarine College
College Library
2001 Newburg Road
Louisville, Kentucky 40205

Telephone. (502) 452-8211

Institutional Description. The privately supported liberal arts college was formed in 1968 by the merger of Bellarmine (founded 1950) and Ursuline (founded 1938) Colleges. It is affiliated with the Roman Catholic Church. Enrollment: 1,731.

Library Administration. Joan E. Wettig, Director.

Library General Holdings. 120,000 books, periodicals, and non-print media.

Special Collections

Thomas Merton Center. The Center is dedicated to preserving the works and furthering the concerns of Thomas Merton. The collection contains 40,000 items, including Merton's literary estate, published works by and about Merton, and several hundred volumes from Merton's own library. It is the largest Merton collection in the world, incorporating Merton items translated into twenty-four languages.

Data Courier Collection. The library is the repository for journals and periodicals indexed and abstracted in the ABI/INFORM database.

The library also maintains the **John Lyons Kentucky Catholic History Collection.**

601
Berea College
Hutchins Library
Berea, Kentucky 40404

Telephone. (606) 986-9341

Institutional Description. Berea College is devoted to the advancement of the people of the southern Appalachian Mountain Region, and 80 percent of its students are from this area. The private liberal arts college grew from a nonsectarian religious community founded in 1855. Enrollment: 1,523.

Library Administration. Tom Kirk, College Librarian; Gerald Roberts, Head of Special Collections.

Library General Holdings. 255,000 volumes; 1,180 current newspaper and periodical subscriptions; 400 microfilm titles; 500 music scores; 3,700 sound recordings.

Special Collections

Weatherford-Hammond Mountain Collection. 12,000 volumes of books and printed sources on southern Appalachia; the nation's oldest Appalachian collection.

John A. Shedd Lincoln Collection. 1,600 volumes on the life and career of Abraham Lincoln. The nucleus of the collection was given to the Berea College Library in 1925 from the estate of New York attorney John A. Shedd.

Berea Collection. 1,700 volumes on the history of Berea College and the Berea community; books by Berea faculty, staff, and alumni.

Southern Appalachian Archives. Records and manuscripts relating to the history and culture of southern Appalachia.

Berea College Archives. Documents the history and mission of Berea College.

Historical Collections. Materials of general historical interest, including local history.

Rare Book Collections

Rare Book Collection. 10,000 volumes, including 8 incunabula, a rare Bible collection, eighteenth-century English literature, American literature, ballad collection, and anti-slavery materials.

602
Brescia College
College Library
120 West 7th Street
Owensboro, Kentucky 42301

Telephone. (502) 685-3131

Institutional Description. The privately supported liberal arts college was founded in 1925 as a women's junior college by the Ursuline Sisters of Mount St. Joseph. Now a four-year coeducational institution, it is affiliated with the Roman Catholic Church. Enrollment: 541.

Library Administration. Sister Judith Nell Riney, Director of Library Services.

Library General Holdings. 76,000 volumes; 740 current periodical titles.

Special Collections

The library has a collection of books and other published materials by and about Kentucky authors as well as a collection of materials on eighteenth- and nineteenth-century Kentucky culture and history.

603
Campbellsville College
Montgomery Library
200 College Street West
Campbellsville, Kentucky 42718

Telephone. (502) 456-8158

Institutional Description. The four-year liberal arts college functions under the auspices of the Kentucky Southern Baptist Convention. Originally founded as Russell Creek Academy in 1906, the college developed into a junior college and then instituted a four-year program in 1959. Enrollment: 603.

Library Administration. Irvin Murrell, Director of the Library.

Library General Holdings. 88,700 volumes; 2,685 microforms; 3,375 government documents; 465 current periodical subscriptions.

Special Collections

Kentuckiana Collection. Contains Kentucky documents, works pertinent to the local area, Kentucky history, works about Kentucky industries; college archival materials.

Education Curriculum Laboratory. Contains curriculum materials actually used in local public schools; books about education (Dewey 370s, LC "L"; juvenile collection; children's story collection; student projects pertaining to teacher education.

Baptist Research Collection. Contains works pertinent to Baptist work in Kentucky and elsewhere.

604
Centre College of Kentucky
Grace Doherty Library
College and Walnut Streets
Danville, Kentucky 40422

Telephone. (606) 236-6064

Institutional Description. The privately supported liberal college was founded by the Presbyterian Church in 1819. It is now independently governed. Enrollment: 799.

Library Administration. Stanley Richard Campbell, Director of Libraries.

Library General Holdings. 135,000 volumes; 650 periodical subscriptions; 10,000 government documents; 30,000 microforms; 10,000 audiovisual materials.

Special Collections

Archives. Houses the college's official records, various rare documents, Centre publications, oral history interviews, photographs, and materials from the old Kentucky College for Women and the old Central University.

The most important special collections include the **Dante Collection** of nineteenth-century editions, criticism, and commentary; the **Kentucky History Collection** which includes religious and church history; and the **Le Compte Davis Collection** of nineteenth- and twentieth-century popular fiction and history of the American West.

605
Eastern Kentucky University
John Grant Crabbe Library
University Drive
Richmond, Kentucky 40475

Telephone. (606) 622-1778

Institutional Description. Founded in 1906, the publicly supported university contains nine colleges and a graduate school. Enrollment: 11,784.

Library Administration. Ernest E. Weyhrauch, University Librarian; Ken Barksdale, Coordinator, Collection Development. Special Collections Librarians: Jerry Dimitrov, Townsend Room; Charles Hay, Archives; Elizabeth Baker, Music; Verna Casey, Law Enforcement; Marilee Gabbard, Learning Resources Center.

Library General Holdings. 792,344 volumes; 1,039,713 microformats (fiche/film); 4,013 periodical subscriptions; 87 newspaper subscriptions.

Special Collections

Law Enforcement Library. Special collection of criminal justice materials including police administration, correctional services, security and loss prevention, traffic safety, and fire technology and services. The collection contains 17,654 bound volumes including textbooks, periodicals, theses, and other materials to support the curriculum.

Learning Resources Center. Provides educational services to students and faculty; sources of learning and teaching materials to strengthen the curriculum; accredited 12-grade library for the Library Science classes and Teacher Education.

John Wilson Townsend Collection. Books, letters, maps, pictures, journals, clippings, microforms, and pamphlets by Kentucky authors and about Kentucky; many of the literary works are signed first editions; holdings include 18,684 books; genealogy and photographic collections.

Music Library. Contains collected works of composers, historical sets, several several facsimiles of works by John Jacob Niles; archival music resource materials for teachers; extensive collection of jazz monographs and jazz recordings.

Rare Book Collections

University Archives. Contains the Archives of the University including photographs, athletic contest films, and papers of faculty members; records of Central University; records of Madison County and Richmond business, governmental, professional and civic organizations; some Madison County church records from 1790; Civil War letters (including Abraham Lincoln correspondence); association and conference papers; oral history.

606
Georgetown College
Cooke Memorial Library
College Street
Georgetown, Kentucky 40324

Telephone. (502) 863-8011

Institutional Description. The privately supported liberal arts college was founded in 1829, and as such, is the third oldest Baptist college in the country. It grants baccalaureate and master's degrees. Enrollment: 1,322.

Library Administration. William Terry Martin, Director of Library Services.

Library General Holdings. 105,000 volumes including 25,000 bound periodicals.

Special Collections

Special collections include the **Thompson Collection of Biblical Literature,** the **Spears Collection of American Literature,** and the **Smith Law Library.** A special feature of the library is the Georgetown College Room which houses the **College Archives.**

607
Hopkinsville Community College Library
North Drive
P.O. Box 2100
Hopkinsville, Kentucky 42240

Telephone. (502) 886-3921
Institutional Description. The two-year community college began instruction in 1965. It is a member institution of the University of Kentucky Community College System. Enrollment: 688.
Library Administration. Peggy Myers, Librarian.
Library General Holdings. 45,000 volumes.

Special Collections

The library has a special collection of 546 items on law.

608
Kentucky State University
Blazer Library
East Main Street
Frankfort, Kentucky 40601

Telephone. (502) 227-6852
Institutional Description. The publicly supported liberal arts and teachers education university was founded in 1866. Enrollment: 1,693.
Library Administration. Donald A. Lyons, Director of Libraries.
Library General Holdings. 283,286 volumes.

Special Collections

Topics in special collections of the Blazer Library include Afro-American and African history and culture; materials relating to Kentucky State University, including records, correspondence, and publications; history of Black people in Kentucky; papers and memorabilia of Rufus Atwood and Whitney M. Young, Sr.; records of the Kentucky High School Athletic League. Materials date from the 1800s to the present and include 500 linear feet of manuscripts and archives; 1,500 rare books and periodicals; 800 photographic images; 12 rolls of microfilm; 75 oral history interviews; and miscellaneous museum artifacts.

609
Kentucky Wesleyan College
Library Learning Center
3000 Frederica Street
Owensboro, Kentucky 42301

Telephone. (502) 926-3111
Institutional Description. The privately supported liberal arts college was founded in 1858. It is affiliated with the United Methodist Church. Enrollment: 707.
Library Administration. Douglas D. Oleson, Director.
Library General Holdings. 170,000 books, periodicals, government documents, audiovisual materials, and other resources; 575 current periodical subscriptions.

Special Collections

Heritage Room. Houses materials for the Kentucky Methodist Heritage Center; the official records of the Louisville Conference of the United Methodist Church; a Kentuckiana collection; and the **Dr. and Mrs. M. David Orrahood Collection** of nineteenth- and twentieth-century English literature.

610
Lexington Theological Seminary
Bosworth Memorial Library
631 South Limestone Street
Lexington, Kentucky 40508

Telephone. (606) 252-0361
Institutional Description. The privately supported theological seminary offers programs on the graduate level only. It is affiliated with the Christian Church (Disciples of Christ). Enrollment: 103.
Library Administration. Phillip Dare, Director.
Library General Holdings. 100,000 volumes; 1,000 current periodical titles.

Special Collections

The library's holdings reflect the mission of the Seminary—to offer professional training essential to preparation for Christian ministry. The collections include all of the Disciples of Christ publications and the major religious journals of the world.

611
Louisville Presbyterian Theological Seminary
Seminary Library
1044 Alta Vista Road
Louisville, Kentucky 40205

Telephone. (502) 895-3411

Institutional Description. The privately supported theological seminary was founded in 1853. Both professional and theological programs are offered at the graduate level only. It is affiliated with the Presbyterian Church, U.S.A. Enrollment: 184.

Library Administration. Ernest M. White, Librarian.

Library General Holdings. 100,000 volumes.

Special Collections

Special collections are in support of disciplines within theological education, especially those of concentration in areas of specialization in the Doctor of Ministry program.

612
Madisonville Community College
Learning Resource Center
University Drive
Madisonville, Kentucky 42431

Telephone. (502) 821-2250

Institutional Description. The college is a member institution of the University of Kentucky Community College System. The college began in the fall of 1960. Enrollment: 741.

Library Administration. Emily Alward, Librarian.

Library General Holdings. 24,000 volumes; 160 current periodical subscriptions.

Special Collections

The special collections of the library are in dental hygiene, mining, and land reclamation.

613
Morehead State University
Camden-Carroll Library
Morehead, Kentucky 40351

Telephone. (606) 783-2829

Institutional Description. The publicly supported state university was founded in 1922 as a normal school. Enrollment: 4,570.

Library Administration. Larry Besant, University Librarian; Carrie Back, Special Collections Librarian.

Library General Holdings. 1,067,183 items including 453,003 books; 53,393 bound periodicals; 20,679 microcards; 420,990 microfiche; 18,151 recordings (disk and tape); 12,240 microfilm reels; 3,663 curriculum guides; 2,697 pictures, art objects, models, and displays; 1,341 maps, charts, games; 3,318 kits; 76,377 films, filmstrips, slides, videotapes; 1,331 teaching aids; 1,990 active periodical title subscriptions; 22 newspaper subscriptions.

Special Collections

Appalachian/Kentucky Collection. Consists of materials drawn from almost all subject areas of the library. These items reflect the Appalachian Region as a whole and what information the library has about the Appalachian Mountains in other states. Includes state and local government reports, biography, fiction, and other subject areas.

James Still, Jesse Stuart, and Roger Barbour Rooms. Each room houses materials about and by the three famous Kentucky writers.

Morehead State University Archives. This collection consists of non-book historical and research material relating to the University.

Rare Book Collections

Rare Book Collection. Some books from the Appalachian/Kentucky Collection are old, rare, or valuable for other reasons and are housed along with similar items in Special Collections. Included among the collection are first editions, rare editions, and a complete set of the *War of the Rebellion* (1901). Among the notable manuscript collections are the papers of Ione Chapman, Robert Hawkins, Inez Faith Humphrey, Pearl L. McBrayer, Buddie Knipp, Otto L. Nickell, Allie Young, and George Young.

614
Murray State University
Forrest C. Pogue Special Collections Library
Murray, Kentucky 42071

Telephone. (502) 762-6152

Institutional Description. The publicly supported state university was founded as Murray State Teachers College in 1923. Enrollment: 6,327.

Library Administration. Coy L. Harmon, Dean of Libraries; Keith M. Hein, Head, Special Collections, Pogue Library.

Library General Holdings. 420,900 volumes; 375,130 government documents; 116,137 volumes equivalent of microforms; 36,000 audiovisual materials; 2,140 current periodical subscriptions.

Special Collections

Western Kentucky and Neighboring States. Materials relating to the history and culture of western Kentucky and neighboring states, and the areas from which most of the early settlers came: Tennessee, North Carolina, South Carolina, Virginia, Georgia, Maryland, and Pennsylvania; materials ranges widely from histories of Civil War units, defunct railroads, religion, and pioneer music to how to make burgoo.

Genealogy and Local History. Reference materials and other resources in genealogy and history, including passenger and immigration lists, census records, family histories and thousands of other records.

Manuscript Collection. Papers of Governor Edward T. Breathitt and Lieutenant Governor Harry Lee Waterfield; papers of Jesse Stuart, Kentucky author; papers of Congressmen Ollie James, Voris Gregory, Noble Gregory, and Frank Albert Stubblefield; papers of Robert "Fats" Everett of Tennessee; papers of C.L. Timberlake, Black educator and civil rights leader; United Daughters of the Confederacy Collection; memorabilia of Alney Norell, actress.

615
Northern Kentucky University W. Frank Steely Library Louie B. Nunn Drive Highland Heights, Kentucky 41076

Telephone. (606) 572-5456

Institutional Description. The publicly supported university is one of Kentucky's newest, having been founded in 1968. It grants associate, baccalaureate, master's, and professional degrees. Enrollment: 6,415.

Library Administration. Mary Ellen Rutledge, Director.

Library General Holdings. 235,000 volumes; 1,670 current periodical subscriptions; 320,000 government documents; 410,000 microforms.

Special Collections

The Steely Library maintains the University Archives which contains **Kentuckiana;** the **Shonert Collection** of political and Civil War memorabilia; presidential signatures; more than 1,500 literary works of Kentucky history, the Civil War, and Abraham Lincoln; and a developing collection of oral history interviews with prominent Northern Kentucky figures. The library also maintains collections of the Confederate and Tuskegee Institute imprints. Materials in the collections date from 1784 to the present.

616
Paducah Community College Library P.O. Box 7380 Paducah, Kentucky 42001

Telephone. (502) 442-6131

Institutional Description. Paducah Community College was founded in 1932 and is an institutional member of the University of Kentucky Community College System. Enrollment: 1,258.

Library Administration. Jennie S. Boyarski, Library Coordinator.

Library General Holdings. 22,000 volumes.

Special Collections

The library has special collections on the history of western Kentucky and the history of Paducah.

617
Southern Baptist Theological Seminary James P. Boyce Centennial Library 2825 Lexington Road Louisville, Kentucky 40280

Telephone. (502) 897-4011

Institutional Description. The privately supported theological seminary offers graduate-level programs only. Courses are designed to equip men and women for leadership in all aspects of Christian ministry. Enrollment: 2,-077.

Library Administration. Ronald F. Deering, Librarian; Martha C. Powell, Church Music Librarian.

Library General Holdings. 284,378 bound volumes; 1,272 periodical subscriptions; 23,000 microforms; 39,000 audiovisual materials.

Special Collections

Billy Graham Collection. Includes materials relating to the crusades of the famous evangelist.

Other special collections include a Baptist historical collection and a collection of church music.

618
Spalding University Library and Learning Resources Center 851 South Fourth Street Louisville, Kentucky 40203

Telephone. (502) 585-9911

Institutional Description. The privately supported liberal arts university was founded in 1814 by the Sisters of Charity of Nazareth. Now an independent institution, it is affiliated with the Roman Catholic Church. Enrollment: 752.

Library Administration. Lucille W. Fitzpatrick, Library Director.

Library General Holdings. 107,000 volumes; 580 current periodical subscriptions.

Special Collections

The library maintains the **Flaget Collection** of religious and other books, named for an early Catholic Kentucky Bishop. There is also a collection of nursing resources and a children's literature collection.

619
Thomas More College Learning Resources Center 2771 Turkey Foot Road Crestview Hills, Kentucky 41017

Telephone. (606) 341-5800

Institutional Description. The privately supported lib-

eral arts college was founded in 1921 as Villa Madonna College. Affiliated with the Roman Catholic Church, the college grants associate and baccalaureate degrees. Enrollment: 1,167.

Library Administration. Robert Nichols, Director.

Library General Holdings. 109,500 volumes; 535 current periodical titles.

Special Collections

The library has a special collection of several hundred volumes by and about Thomas More. There is also a collection of Kentuckiana.

620
Transylvania University
J. Douglas Gay Jr. Library; Frances Carrick Thomas Library
300 North Broadway
Lexington, Kentucky 40508

Telephone. (606) 233-8120

Institutional Description. The privately supported liberal arts institution was founded in 1780. It has been affiliated with the Christian Church (Disciples of Christ) since 1865. Enrollment: 829.

Library Administration. Kathleen C. Bryson, Director.

Library General Holdings. 122,000 volumes; 385 current periodical subscriptions.

Special Collections

The library complex of the Gay Library and Thomas Library houses the University Archives, the special collections of the Farris Rare Book Room, the Old Medical Library (pre-1850), and special collections of Kentuckiana including the **J. Winston Coleman Collection.**

621
Union College
Abigail E. Weeks Memorial Library
College Street
Barbourville, Kentucky 40906

Telephone. (606) 546-4151

Institutional Description. The privately supported liberal arts college was founded in 1879. It is affiliated with the United Methodist Church. Enrollment: 906.

Library Administration. Virginia B. Saddler, Head Librarian.

Library General Holdings. 80,000 volumes; 350 current periodical subscriptions.

Special Collections

The **Lincoln Civil War Collection** contains over 1,000 volumes including rare books and memorabilia. There is also a curriculum library for the Department of Education and a music library with a collection of more than 3,500 recordings and music scores.

622
University of Kentucky
Margaret I. King Library
Euclid Avenue and Rose Street
Lexington, Kentucky 40506

Telephone. (606) 257-8611

Institutional Description. The publicly supported state university was established in 1865 as the Agricultural and Mechanical College. It now provides a wide variety of programs. Enrollment: 17,585.

Library Administration. Paul A. Willis, Director of Libraries.

Library General Holdings. 2,890,000 volumes; 22,242 periodical and serial titles; over 3,000,000 microforms; 25,000 audiovisual materials.

Special Collections

The Department of Special Collections and Archives maintains a collection of Kentuckiana; materials on Appalachia; English, American, and Victorian literature; Miltoniana; musicology, Mexicana; modern political papers; University archives; audiovisual archives (tapes and films); oral history; history of women; local and family history; history of printing and the fine press; King Library Press imprints.

Rare Book Collections

Materials date from 1153 to the present and include 13,000 linear feet of manuscripts and archives; 90,000 rare books and periodicals; 300,000 photographic images; 2,100 oral history interviews; 35,000 other audiovisual materials; and miscellaneous museum artifacts.

623
University of Louisville
University Libraries
2301 South Third Street
Louisville, Kentucky 40292

Telephone. (502) 588-6761

Institutional Description. The publicly supported university was founded in 1798 as Jefferson Seminary. In 1846 it became a university with an Academic Department, Medical School, and School of Law. Enrollment: 15,255.

Library Administration. Martha A. Bowman, University Librarian.

Library General Holdings. 962,324 volumes; 6,225 current periodicals.

Special Collections

Materials in the special collections of the University Libraries include Kentucky and United States historical and fine art photographs; regional government, politics, social movements and agencies; business and transportation history; biography; culture; the arts; Irish and Kentucky literature; Louisville neighborhoods; ethnic and family history; papers of Justices Louis D. Brandeis and John M. Harlan; history of mathematics; natural and health sciences; and University of Louisville history.

Rare Book Collections

The collections include 7,500 linear feet of manuscripts and archives; 31,550 rare books and periodicals; 1,020,000 photographic images; 1,000 rolls of microfilm; 1,250 oral history interview; and 3,100 miscellaneous museum artifacts. Materials date from the tenth century to the present.

624
Western Kentucky University
Western Kentucky Library
Bowling Green, Kentucky 42101

Telephone. (502) 745-2592

Institutional Description. The publicly supported university was founded in 1906 as Western State Normal School. Established as a university in 1966, it contains five colleges and a graduate school. Enrollment: 9,374.

Library Administration. Michael Binder, University Librarian; Riley D. Handy, Department Head/Special Collections.

Library General Holdings. 866,000 volumes; 6,500 periodical titles; 440,247 microforms; 28,300 audiovisual materials.

Special Collections

Kentucky Library. A non-circulating collection of Kentuckiana containing more than 30,000 bound volumes, as well as thousands of maps, broadsides, photographs, sheet music, newspapers, scrapbooks and other non-book items.

Kentucky Museum. The Museum documents regional history and houses thousands of Kentucky and non-Kentucky artifacts.

Rare Book Collections

Manuscript Division. Holdings are chiefly nineteenth and twentieth century materials, relating mainly to Bowling Green, Warren County, and south central Kentucky. Materials from many regions and on many topics are represented because of Kentuckians' varied activities. Among the literary collections are those of A.L. Crabb, Janice Holt Giles, William S. Hays, Willard R. Jillson, David Morton, Lida Calvert Obenchain, Alice Hegan Rice, Cale Young Rice, and Jesse Stuart.

Louisiana

625
Centenary College of Louisiana
John F. Magale Memorial Library
2911 Centenary Boulevard
P.O. Box 4188
Shreveport, Louisiana 71131

Telephone. (318) 869-5011

Institutional Description. The privately supported liberal arts college was founded in 1825. It is affiliated with the United Methodist Church. Enrollment: 794.

Library Administration. James G. Volny, Director of Library Services.

Library General Holdings. 159,000 volumes; 875 current periodical subscriptions; 156,000 microforms.

Special Collections

The library maintains the archives of the Louisiana Conference of the United Methodist Church. There are also specialized collections in religion, geology, and business/economics.

626
Dillard University
Will W. Alexander Library
2601 Gentilly Boulevard
New Orleans, Louisiana 70122

Telephone. (504) 283-8822

Institutional Description. The privately supported university was formed by a merger of Straight College (United Church of Christ) and New Orleans University (United Methodist Church), both of which were founded in 1869. Enrollment: 1,194.

Library Administration. Carole R. Taylor, Librarian.

Library General Holdings. 133,000 volumes.

Special Collections

The Alexander Library supports the curriculum of the college with emphases in business administration, education, humanities, natural sciences, nursing, and the social sciences.

627
Grambling State University
A.C. Lewis Memorial Library
P.O. Box 3
Grambling, Louisiana 71245

Telephone. (318) 274-2220

Institutional Description. The publicly supported state university was founded as an industrial school in 1901. It is now a diverse institution with several component colleges. Enrollment: 4,640.

Library Administration. Pauline W. Lee, Director of the Library; Vernice S. Attuquayefio, Special Collections Librarian.

Library General Holdings. 243,268 volumes; 26,563 bound periodicals; 1,301 current periodical subscriptions; 52 newspaper subscriptions; 22,266 book titles in microform; 91,619 periodicals in microform.

Special Collections

Afro-American Collection. Includes resources by and about Black Americans, peoples of Africa, and the Caribbean. There are 7,386 volumes in this collection including reference and non-reference books, magazines, journals, newspapers, newsletters, and newspaper clippings. The collection is enhanced by an extensive microform collection.

Rare Book Collections

Black Culture Collection. This collection consists of 1,428 titles. It is augmented by a collection of 27 titles from the Schomburg Center for Research in Black Culture.

Western States Black Research Center Collection. The library has acquired a special rare book collection from the holdings of the Western States Black Research Center of Los Angeles, California. There are 152 items in this collection. Most of the items are books, usually first editions, and many of them are scarce or one of a kind and were written in the nineteenth and early twentieth centuries.

628
Louisiana College
Richard W. Norton Memorial Library
1140 College Drive
Pineville, Louisiana 71360

Telephone. (318) 487-7011

Institutional Description. The privately supported liberal arts college was founded in 1906, and now consists of 15 academic departments. It is affiliated with the Southern Baptist Church (Louisiana Baptist Convention). Enrollment: 949.

Library Administration. C. Landrum Salley, Director.

Library General Holdings. 112,000 volumes; 500 current periodical titles.

Special Collections

The library has a collections of rare books, children's literature, and music scores.

629
Louisiana State University
Middleton Library
Baton Rouge, Louisiana 70803

Telephone. (504) 388-6977

Institutional Description. The publicly supported university was founded in 1860 as the Louisiana State Seminary; the Louisiana State Agricultural and Mechanical College was founded in 1874. The two institutions merged in 1877. Enrollment: 26,344.

Library Administration. Sharon A. Hogan, Director, Middleton Library.

Library General Holdings. 2,147,840 volumes; 24,140 current periodical subscriptions; 2,271,965 microforms; 4,500,000 manuscripts.

Special Collections

The special collections of the Middleton Library have been greatly enriched through the acquisition of several private collections. These include the **David S. Blondheim Collection** of romance philology materials; the **Richard T. Ely Collection** on economics and related subjects; the **Jules M. Burguieres Sugar Collection,** a fine collection on sugar culture and sugar technology; the **Judge Oliver P. Carriere Collection** on poker materials; the **Klaus Berger Collection** on art history; the **Clarence J. Laughlin Collection** of art, photography, and related subjects; the **Rendell Rhoades Collection** on crawfish; and the **T. Harry Williams Collections** of Civil War and American history materials.

The **Troy H. Middleton Collection of Memorabilia** includes items depicting Middleton's life from boyhood through his retirement in 1962 as president of LSU. A book collection on military history and strategy is also contained within this special room.

Special collections housed in the Hill Memorial Library include:

Warren L. Jones Lincoln Collection. A collection of approximately 5,000 items includes all of the great Lincoln books and pamphlets, special editions of some of the outstanding works and many publications contemporaneous with Lincoln's own lifetime.

E.A. McIlhenny Collection. The original ornithological collection has been greatly expanded to cover the entire field of natural history.

Louisiana Collection. Contains an outstanding research and reference collection devoted to printed materials relating to Louisiana. Included are rare and early imprints pertaining to exploration and colonization of the Lower Mississippi Valley, books on Louisiana subjects, books by Louisianians, journals, maps, sheet music, parish and municipal documents, and an extensive vertical file of clippings on numerous Louisiana subjects. The Louisiana Collection is a complete historical depository for Louisiana state documents.

Rare Book Collections

Rare Book Collection. Contains books and pamphlets from all fields of knowledge and human experience except that of natural history. There are representative works ranging from incunabula to publications of modern special presses. Among its largest special collections are the **Bruce Rogers Imprints Collection,** the **Limited Editions Club Books,** and the **Richard T. Ely Collection.** Other notable groups of items include facsimiles of codices, books published in English before 1720, Confederate imprints, major works on North American Indians, books with fore-edge paintings, and modern first editions.

Manuscripts Collection. Consists of over 4,500,000 items and volumes of historical manuscripts, University archives, and related unpublished materials providing a record of contemporary life in the Lower Mississippi Valley for over 200 years. The collection is an important body of primary source material for advanced research in political and social history, cultural geography, agriculture, education, American and Louisiana French literature, speech, sociology, music and other arts, business and economics, steamboat transportation, and other fields in the social sciences and humanities. The collection consists of personal, professional, business, and organizational records, including letters, diaries and other writings, account books, scrapbooks, historical photographs, ephemera, and oral history interviews; personal and official papers of University presidents and related University archives; and unpublished inventories and research materials of two former federal archival projects in Louisiana.

630
Louisiana State University at Eunice
Arnold LeDoux Library
P.O. Box 1129
Eunice, Louisiana 70535

Telephone. (318) 457-7311

Institutional Description. The two-year college was authorized by the 1964 Legislature as a basic and integral part of the University System to extend additional facilities and opportunities to southwest Louisiana. The college opened in 1967. Enrollment: 1,181.

Library Administration. James L. Forester, Head Librarian.

Library General Holdings. 72,000 microforms; 2,000 microforms.

Special Collections

The library has a collection of genealogical materials and a collection on Louisiana.

631
Louisiana State University in Shreveport
Library
8515 Youree Street
Shreveport, Louisiana 71115

Telephone. (318) 797-5203

Institutional Description. The publicly supported branch of the Louisiana State University was opened in 1964 as a two-year commuter college. It began four-year programs in 1972, and now grants associate, baccalaureate, professional, and master's degrees. Enrollment: 3,389.

Library Administration. Malcolm G. Parker, Director.

Library General Holdings. 190,000 volumes; 2,210 current periodical titles.

Special Collections

LSUS-Archives. Contains a collection of unpublished primary sources documenting the heritage of northwest Louisiana; includes oral history tapes and transcripts of interviews with individuals significant in regional history and provides materials for research in area history, government, politics, economics, geography, and other fields.

Louisiana Collection. Contains books, journals, and other publications by regional authors.

Pioneer Heritage Center. Contains primary sources such as original letters, diaries, ledgers, successions, and other documents from the 1830s to the early twentieth century, together with archival materials such as folklore interviews, photographs, plantation records, and studies in folk architecture.

Faculty Collection. Comprised of books, articles, theses, dissertations, and other papers written by the LSU in Shreveport faculty.

632
Louisiana State University Medical Center at New Orleans
Library
1440 Canal Street
New Orleans, Louisiana 70112

Telephone. (504) 568-4800

Institutional Description. The publicly supported (state) medical center was founded in 1931. It is part of the Louisiana State University System. Enrollment: 2,474.

Library Administration. Judith Caruthers, Director.

Library General Holdings. 290,000 volumes; 2,750 periodical titles.

Special Collections

The library maintains a special collection of materials on yellow fever and a collection on Louisiana medical history.

633
Louisiana Tech University
Prescott Memorial Library
P.O. Box 3186 Tech. Sta.
Ruston, Louisiana 71272

Telephone. (318) 257-0211

Institutional Description. The publicly supported (state) university was founded in 1894 as the Industrial Institute and College of Louisiana. It is now comprised of six colleges and four schools. Enrollment: 9,646.

Library Administration. W. Walter Wicker, Director.

Library General Holdings. 303,000 volumes; 1,965 current periodical subscriptions; 628,000 government documents; 174,000 microforms.

Special Collections

The library provides the resources and services that undergird all of the academic endeavors for the teaching and research programs of the colleges of Administration and Business, Arts and Sciences, Education, Engineering, Home Economics, and Life Sciences. Prescott Memorial Library is a designated depository of federal and State of Louisiana government publications.

634
Loyola University
University Library
6363 St. Charles Avenue
New Orleans, Louisiana 70118

Telephone. (504) 865-2011

Institutional Description. The privately supported

Roman Catholic university is administered by the Society of Jesus. In 1912, the merger of Loyola College and the College of the Immaculate Conception formed Loyola University. Enrollment: 4,081.

Library Administration. Mary Lee Sweat, University Librarian.

Library General Holdings. 317,620 volumes; 1,631 periodical and journal subscriptions; 112,170 microforms; 41,995 state and federal government documents; 1,193 media titles.

Special Collections

Noteworthy among the special collections are the rare holdings of Spanish and French colonial archival documents on microfilm. Other special microform holdings include the 20,000-volume Library of American Civilization containing books, periodicals, and documents prior to 1914; the 3,000 volume Library of English Literature with materials from the beginning to 1660; and extensive holdings in Jesuitica.

635
McNeese State University
Frazar Memorial Library
Box 91445
Lake Charles, Louisiana 70609

Telephone. (318) 475-5716

Institutional Description. The publicly supported state university was founded in 1939 as a division of Louisiana State University offering only the first two years of higher education. It advanced to four-year status and separated from LSU in 1950. Enrollment: 6,540.

Library Administration. Richard H. Reid, Director of Library Services; Kathie Bordelon, Archivist and Special Collections/Rare Books Librarian.

Library General Holdings. 350,000 bound volumes; 437,650 microforms; 1,624 periodicals; 794,000 government documents.

Special Collections

The only specialized collections within the general stacks of the library are books about Louisiana, books by Louisiana authors, and an outstanding mathematics collection.

Rare Book Collections

McNeese Room. Houses several rare book collections of moderate size including first editions of twentieth-century American fiction authors, books with fore-edge paintings, books by and about Lafcadio Hearn, a facsimile of the Gutenberg Bible, and a growing collection of southwest Louisiana historical material.

636
New Orleans Baptist Theological Seminary
John T. Christian Library
4110 Seminary Place
New Orleans, Louisiana 70126

Telephone. (504) 282-4455

Institutional Description. The privately supported seminary was the first such institution established by the Southern Baptist Convention. It was known as the Baptist Bible Institute from its founding in 1917 to 1946 when its present name was adopted. Enrollment: 1,181.

Library Administration. Paul Gericke, Director of the Library.

Library General Holdings. 178,801 bound volumes; 1,102 current periodicals; 14,916 microforms; 14,392 audio recordings; 7,357 audiovisual materials; 17,891 unbound music scores and anthems.

Special Collections

The library is a depository for Baptist materials and contains specialized book collections, manuscripts, and memorabilia from outstanding church leaders. The library houses the 5,000 volumes of the personal library of Dr. Robert G. Lee, an outstanding pulpit orator. The J.D. Grey Missionary Home houses the library of Dr. J.D. Grey.

A collection of music materials has been developed and includes 9,000 books, reference works, and bound periodicals; 9,500 scores; 1,500 hymnals and psalters; 3,000 recordings; and several thousand anthems and larger classical works. The **Edmond D. Keith Collection** of 5,000 books, hymnals, and scores is a special feature of this collection.

Rare Book Collections

Bible Manuscripts. Includes original manuscripts of the Bible since the sixteenth century, photocopies of fourth- to sixth-century documents, and second- and third-century papyrii.

637
Nicholls State University
Allen J. Ellender Memorial Library
University Station
Thibodaux, Louisiana 70301

Telephone. (504) 446-8111

Institutional Description. The publicly supported liberal arts and teachers university was formed in 1948 as a junior college branch of the Louisiana State University. Becoming a four-year institution in 1956, it now grants associate, baccalaureate, and master's degrees. Enrollment: 6,412.

Library Administration. Randall A. Detro, Director.

Library General Holdings. 300,000 volumes; 1,500

current periodical titles; 124,000 government documents; 321,500 microforms.

Special Collections

Special collections include the **Allen J. Ellender Archives** and the **Nicholls State University Presidents' Archives** as well as numerous local history collections. Notable are the **J. Wilson Lepine Laurel Valley Plantation Collection,** the **Litt Martin Collection,** the **Martin-Pugh Collections** and the **Lafourche [Parish] Heritage Society "Face of Lafourche" Photograph Collection.**

638
Northeast Louisiana University
Sandel Library
700 University Avenue
Monroe, Louisiana 71209

Telephone. (318) 342-2011

Institutional Description. The publicly supported (state) university was founded as a junior college in 1931 and became a four-year institution in 1950. It now grants associate, baccalaureate, master's, and doctorate degrees. Enrollment: 9,856.

Library Administration. Larry D. Larason, Director.

Library General Holdings. 342,000 volumes; 2,890 current periodical titles; 122,500 government documents; 380,000 microforms (volumes).

Special Collections

The **Otto E. Passman Library** on the second floor of the Sandel Library houses the Passman Congressional papers. Other special collections include an **Historic Cartographic Collection** for the U.S. Corp of Engineers and the **Griffin Studio Photographic Collection.**

639
Northwestern State University of Louisiana
Eugene P. Watson Memorial Library
College Avenue
Natchitoches, Louisiana 71497

Telephone. (318) 357-4585

Institutional Description. The publicly supported state university was founded in 1884 as a two-year normal school; it became a four-year institution in 1918. Enrollment: 4,382.

Library Administration. Ada Jarred, University Librarian; Carolyn M. Wells, Archivist, Special Collections/Rare Books Librarian.

Library General Holdings. 284,550 volumes; 29,850 government documents; 53,325 microfoms; 5,664 audiovisual materials; 1,907 current periodical subscriptions.

Special Collections

The major collections include the **Melrose Plantation Collection,** the **Caroline Dorman Collection,** and **C.F. Gauss Collection.** Includes authors, journalists, and poets of the nineteenth and twentieth centuries; native, naturalized, and garden plants and conservation (1930 to the present); medical books and materials (1760 to 1950s); official reports, letters, memoirs, news and editorials, diaries of the Reconstruction Period; World War II; Riverboats and steamboats (1847 to 1890s); Ireland; Great Depression; business (1780-1916); diaries, journals, and memoirs (early nineteenth century to the present); agriculture (1781-1934); education, schools, and teachers (1819 to the present); travel (1780 to the present); Russia (1910-1970); various biographical subjects.

640
Our Lady of Holy Cross College
College Library
4123 Woodland Drive
New Orleans, Louisiana 70114

Telephone. (504) 394-7744

Institutional Description. The privately supported liberal arts college was founded in 1917 as a two-year normal school. In 1938, the Roman Catholic institution became a four-year teachers college. Enrollment: 435.

Library Administration. Sister H. Fontenot, Director.

Library General Holdings. 37,000 volumes; 415 current periodical titles.

Special Collections

The library has a **Louisiana Collection** and collections of children's and adolescent literature.

641
Saint Joseph Seminary College
Pere Rouquette Library
Saint Benedict, Louisiana 70457

Telephone. (504) 892-1800

Institutional Description. The privately supported seminary for men is conducted by the Benedictine Monks of St. Joseph Abbey. It was established in 1891 and grants the baccalaureate degree. Enrollment: 109.

Library Administration. Fr. Timothy J. Burnett, O.S.B., Director of Library.

Library General Holdings. 70,000 volumes; 200 periodical titles; subscriptions to all Catholic diocesan papers of the state of Louisiana. Undergraduate library specializing in history, literature, philosophy, and religion.

Special Collections

Natchez Episcopal Library. An uncataloged collection.

Rare Book Collections

Several rare books and manuscripts mainly found in connection with the Natchez Episcopal Library.

642
Southeastern Louisiana University
Linus A. Sims Memorial Library
100 West Dakota Avenue
Hammond, Louisiana 70402

Telephone. (504) 549-2280

Institutional Description. The publicly supported liberal arts and professional university was founded in 1925. It began its four-year program in 1937. Enrollment: 7,784.

Library Administration. F. Landon Greaves, University Librarian.

Library General Holdings. 276,320 volumes; 1,800 serial titles; 114,000 government documents; 385,000 microforms; 41,000 audiovisual materials.

Special Collections

The special collections of the library include the papers of Congressman James Morrison and the **Kennedy Assassination Papers.** The music library maintains a collection of music scores and the Regional Film Library has a collection of 12,000 filmstrips and 5,000 16mm films. A curriculum library for the Department of Education is maintained in the Learning Resource Center.

643
Southern University at Baton Rouge
John B. Cade Library
Baton Rouge, Louisiana 70813

Telephone. (504) 771-4500

Institutional Description. The publicly supported university, founded in 1881, has two branch campuses, located in New Orleans and Shreveport. Enrollment: 8,898.

Library Administration. Georgia W. Brown, Librarian.

Library General Holdings. 451,762 items including 392,890 circulating materials; 7,000 reference sources; 20,569 microforms; 58,862 government documents; 30,144 bound periodicals; 2,410 current newspaper and periodical titles.

Special Collections

Special collections include the **Black Heritage Collection** of works by and about Blacks, the **Rodney G. Higgins Memorial Collection of Political Science Literature,** the **Nursing Collection,** the **John Brother Cade Manuscript Collection** the **J.S. Clark Papers,** and University archival material.

644
Southern University in New Orleans
Leonard Washington Memorial Library
6400 South Press Drive
New Orleans, Louisiana 70126

Telephone. (504) 282-4401

Institutional Description. The publicly supported (state) university was founded in 1956. It is a campus of the Southern University and Agricultural and Mechanical College System. Enrollment: 2,461.

Library Administration. Eddiemae Young, Library Director.

Library General Holdings. 90,000 volumes.

Special Collections

The library has a special collection of Afro-French literature and a **Black Collection,** and the **Kellogg Business Collection.**

645
Southern University - Shreveport
Library
3050 Martin Luther King Drive
Shreveport, Louisiana 71107

Telephone. (318) 674-3300

Institutional Description. The two-year college was founded in 1964 and opened for instruction in 1967. Enrollment: 726.

Library Administration. Orella R. Brazile, Head Librarian.

Library General Holdings. 37,081 volumes; 387 periodical subscriptions; 614 microfilms; 8,394 microfiche; 559 cassettes; 339 filmstrips; 293 record albums; 4,578 slides; 120 transparencies; 28 videotapes.

Special Collections

The library houses two special collections: the **Black Collection** of books by and about Black people and the **Louisiana Collection** of books by and about Louisianans.

646
Tulane University
Howard-Tilton Memorial Library
New Orleans, Louisiana 70118

Telephone. (504) 865-5131

Institutional Description. The private, nonsectarian university is composed of 11 schools and colleges and four research centers. Enrollment: 8,894.

Library Administration. Philip E. Leinbach, University Librarian; Wilbur E. Meneray, Special Collections Librarian; Sylvia V. Metzinger, Rare Books Librarian.

Library General Holdings. 1,125,000 volumes; 1,600,-

000 government documents; hundreds of thousands of microforms, manuscripts, photographs, recordings, and other items; more than 50,000 new titles are added each year.

Special Collections

Louisiana Collection. Materials pertaining to the history and development of Louisiana from colonial times to the present; the Carnival Collection, dating back to 1857, includes such items as watercolor parade float and costume designs, ball invitations, programs, dance cards, and posters; general vertical file; art vertical file; print file; over 1,000 maps, originals and copies, dating back to 1513 and 1718.

Latin American Library. An extensive collection of books and periodicals on all Latin American countries in almost every subject area; over 150,000 volumes of history, social sciences and general materials; traditional focus for research materials has been on Mexico, Central America, and the Caribbean, particularly in the history, archaeology, and anthropology of these areas; 5,500 rare books and manuscripts; Codex Tulane, map collection; Merle Greene Robertson collection of 500 original rubbings of relief sculpture, stone carvings, and plaster and stucco work from Maya archaeological sites in Mexico and Guatemala; Latin American Photographic Archive.

William Ransom Hogan Jazz Archive. Holdings include oral history tapes, music recordings, sheet music, photographs, scrapbooks, documents, and memorabilia, as well as a research collection of books and serials pertaining to jazz.

Southeastern Architectural Archive. Contains one of the country's larger and more important architectural research collections with over 150,000 original drawings, manuscripts, specifications, maps, and books. The major emphasis of the collection is on Louisiana, and New Orleans in particular. Collection dates from 1835 to the present.

The **New Orleans Academy of Science Collection** and the microfiche collection of the standards of the American Society for Testing and Materials (ASTM) are housed in the Library's Science-Engineering Division.

Rare Book Collections

Rare Books, Manuscripts, and University Archives. Rare Books contains over 45,000 volumes, dating from a leaf from the Gutenberg Bible to recent first editions of contemporary authors; major author collections include William Faulkner and Lafcadio Hearn, Edward Gorey, Robert Southey, Huey P. Long, and Stendhal. The Manuscripts Section holds over 3,500 individual manuscript collections, relating primarily to New Orleans, the Gulf South, and the Mississippi Valley; the University Archives houses the official records of Tulane University.

647
University of New Orleans
Earl K. Long Library
Lake Front
New Orleans, Louisiana 70148

Telephone. (504) 286-6000

Institutional Description. The publicly supported institution is a member of the Louisiana State University System, and was opened in 1958. Enrollment: 12,770.

Library Administration. Donald D. Hendricks, Dean, Library Services.

Library General Holdings. 1,000,000 books and periodocals (one-half in microforms); 5,500 current serial subscriptions.

Special Collections

Special collections include the **Crabites Collection of Egyptology;** an urban studies collection; a comprehensive collection of material by and about William Faulkner; and the **Supreme Court of Louisiana Collection** (1816-1921). The latter is representative of a number of important archival collections with strength in material that reflects the city's twentieth-century urban aspects and especially its ethnic groups and labor and business organizations. The library also maintains a collection on Marcus Christian, the Black poet and historian.

648
University of Southwestern Louisiana
Dupre Library
USL PO Box 40199
Lafayette, Louisiana 70504

Telephone. (318) 231-6396

Institutional Description. The publicly supported university was founded in 1898 as the Southwestern Louisiana Industrial Institute. It became a senior college in 1921 and adopted its present name in 1960. Enrollment: 14,199.

Library Administration. Donald L. Saporito, University Librarian; I. Bruce Turner, Head, Archives and Special Collections.

Library General Holdings. 605,387 volumes; 4,707 periodicals and newspapers; 1,419,269 microform units; 5,000 phonograph recordings, videotapes.

Special Collections

Louisiana Room. Books, serials, state documents, maps, microforms—related to Louisiana; especially strong in law, Acadian and Cajun history and development, geology, and literature.

Rare Book Collections

Special strengths in seventeenth century Italian architecture, eighteenth century French literature, and nineteenth century British and U.S. horticulture.

Southwestern Archives and Manuscripts Collection. Includes the University Archives and individuals' papers; strengths of the collection are in politics, literature and architecture, economy, and women's studies. The Manuscripts Collection focuses on the Acadiana region of Louisiana.

649
Xavier University of Louisiana
Xavier University Library
7325 Palmetto Street
New Orleans, Louisiana 70125

Telephone. (504) 483-7304

Institutional Description. The privately supported university was founded in 1925 by the Sisters of the Blessed Sacrament; it is now operated by a joint lay-religious board of trustees. Enrollment: 1,797.

Library Administration. Robert E. Skinner, University Librarian; Sr. Roberta Smith, Chief Archivist.

Library General Holdings. 100,000 volumes; 700 periodical subscriptions; 500 music scores; large collection of disc recordings; media collection holds a wide variety of reel-to-reel and cassette tapes, videocassettes, and 16mm films.

Rare Book Collections

The largest part of Special Collections is devoted to Afro-American history and culture. The most important collection is the **Heartmann Collection** of letters, records, and other documentary material relating to the history of Blacks in the United States. Aspects of both free and enslaved negroes in the eighteenth, nineteenth, and twentieth centuries are included in this collection; another important collection is the **A.P. Bedou Photographic Collection,** possibly the largest single collection of work by the Black photographer.

Smaller collections include pamphlets and broadsides concerning slavery printed during the eighteenth and nineteenth centuries, sheet and manuscript music by Black composers, and manuscripts of published works by Black writers and novelists. Subsidiary collections include books published in New Orleans and other items related to the history of the city, rare books and archival materials relating to the Civil War, and old and rare children's books. A small but steadily growing collection consists of autographed first printings by Southern novelists including James Jones, Walker Percy, and Eudora Welty.

Maine

650
Bangor Theological Seminary
Moulton Library
300 Union Street
Bangor, Maine 04401

Telephone. (207) 942-6781

Institutional Description. Bangor Theological Seminary was founded in 1814 and is affiliated with the United Church of Christ. Its primary purpose is to provide professional training for the pastoral ministry. Enrollment: 123.

Library Administration. Clifton G. Davis, Librarian; Sally A. Kaubris, Assistant Librarian.

Library General Holdings. 83,678 volumes including 12,500 bound periodicals; 744 microform units; 832 audiovisual units; 2,000 pamphlets (mostly eighteenth- and nineteenth-century sermons).

Special Collections

The library's major holdings are in the field of religion covering general history, natural theology, Bible, theology, devotional, pastoral theology, church work, church history, churches and sects, and other religions.

651
Bates College
George and Helen Ladd Library
Lewiston, Maine 04240

Telephone. (207) 786-6255

Institutional Description. The privately supported liberal arts college has been coeducational since its founding in 1855. It grants baccalaureate degrees. Enrollment: 1,-519.

Library Administration. Joseph Jensen Derbyshire, Librarian.

Library General Holdings. 450,250 volumes; 1,620 current periodical subscriptions; 171,300 microforms.

Special Collections

The library's special collections include nearly 2,000 rare books; one of the strongest collections in America of early Baptist publications; the **Stanton Natural History Collection,** the **Phelps Collection** of signed first editions, the **Marsden Hartley Collection,** the **David Berent Collection of Judaica,** and archival material relating to the College and its history.

652
Bowdoin College
Bowdoin College Library
Brunswick, Maine 04011

Telephone. (207) 725-3280

Institutional Description. Privately supported, Bowdoin College was founded in 1794 by a charter from the General Court of Massachusetts. It became coeducational in 1970. Enrollment: 1,399.

Library Administration. Arthur Monke, College Librarian; Dianne M. Gutscher, Curator of Special Collections.

Library General Holdings. 695,000 volumes; 2,000 periodical subscriptions; 30 newspaper subscriptions; 10,-500 microfilm reels; 37,500 microtexts; 7,200 sound recordings; 250 videotapes.

Special Collections

Vance Bourjaily Papers. The literary archives of the prominent contemporary American novelist, a member of the Class of 1944.

Bowdoin Collection. This collection contains approximately 2,100 volumes from the library of James Bowdoin III, 565 volumes that belonged to Governor James Bowdoin II, and about 1,000 pamphlets.

Charles Brockden Brown Papers. Contains 159 letters and manuscripts relating to America's first professional novelist.

Nathaniel Hawthorne Collection. Contains approximately 700 volumes by and about Hawthorne, 113 manuscripts, and numerous scrapbooks and ephemeral items.

Huguenot Collection. A collection of 800 volumes of contemporary works concerning the Huguenots from the sixteenth to the eighteenth centuries.

Elijah Kellogg Collection. Contains more than 50 volumes of Kellogg's adventure stories for boys and 1,500 manuscript sermons and pieces of correspondence.

Henry Wadsworth Longfellow Collection. All of

Longfellow's first and subsequent editions and translations are included; correspondence and original manuscripts of several of his poems.

Maine Collection. Books and manuscripts relating to the state of Maine; all books, pamphlets, broadsides, newspapers, etc. printed in Maine before 1836; Maine authors such as Kenneth Roberts, Sara Orne Jewett, Mary Ellen Chase, Harriet Beecher Stowe, John Neal, Edwin Arlington Robinson, Robert P.T. Coffin, and others.

Franklin Pierce Collection. Includes twenty-nine manuscripts and documents, including eleven letters written by Pierce to his Bowdoin classmate Horatio Bridge.

Kate Douglas Wiggin Collection. Consists of the personal library of Kate Douglas Wiggin and includes books, manuscripts, clippings, and ephemeral items.

Marguerite Yourcenar Collection. This collection of more than 100 volumes includes first and subsequent editions and translations of the writings of Marguerite Yourcenar and the manuscripts of *Theater I* and *L'Oeuvre au Noir.*

Other special collections include the Abbott Memorial Collection (Abbott family); Jesse Appleton Papers (clergyman's career); Atlantic and St. Lawrence Railroad Papers; Robert A. Bartlett Papers (Arctic explorer); Beston Family Papers; Susan Dwight Bliss Collection (fine arts, French and English history and literature, and travel); Thomas Carlyle Collection; Joshua L. Chamberlain Papers; Chase-Johnson Papers; Parker Cleaveland Papers (Bowdoin professor of chemistry); Cuala Press Collection (Anglo-Irish literary revival of the early twentieth century); Fessendon Family Papers; Alfred Otto Gross Collection (Bowdoin ornithologist); Edward Chipman Guild Papers (clergyman's career); Richard B. Harwell Collection (Bowdoin's librarian from 1961-1968, personal interests in Southern history and the Confederacy); Oliver Otis Howard Papers (Class of 1850); Roger Howell Papers (Bowdoin President); Hubbard Family Papers; McArthur Family Papers; Donald B. MacMillan Collection (Arctic explorer); Frederic Wilson Main Collection (art of printing and bookmaking); Mellen Papers (New England history); Mosher Press Collection; Picard Collection (Limited Editions Club publications); Joseph Priestley Collection (Anglo-American educator); Thomas Brackett Reed Papers (U.S. Congressman, 1877-1899); Kenneth C.M. Sills Collection (Bowdoin's eighth president); Southworth-Anthoensen Press Collection (Portland printing house); Charles Asbury Stephens Collection; Thomas C. Upham Collection (Bowdoin professor of philosophy, 1824-1867); Vaughan Collection (eighteenth- and early nineteenth-century scientific books and periodicals); Thomas Wallcut collection (books printed in the sixteenth, early eighteenth centuries); William Willis Papers (former mayor of Portland and president of the Maine Historical Society).

Rare Book Collections

American Imprints. All books and pamphlets printed in the English colonies and the United States before 1821; contains more than 2,500 volumes of political, religious, economic, and social importance, including both the first and second editions of the famous John Eliot *Indian Bible,* (Cambridge, 1661, 1680).

British Imprints. Books printed in England, Scotland, Wales, and Ireland before 1701 and works relating to British history in general.

653
Colby College
Miller Library
Waterville, Maine 04901

Telephone. (207) 872-3284

Institutional Description. Privately supported, Colby College was founded in 1813. It is a residential college of liberal arts. Enrollment: 1,696.

Library Administration. Suanne Muehlner, College Librarian; J. Fraser Cocks, III, Curator, Special Collections.

Library General Holdings. 400,000 volumes; 79,335 microforms; 7,000 audiovisual materials; 1,780 current periodical subscriptions.

Special Collections

Edwin Arlington Robinson Collection. Books, manuscripts, and letters pertaining to American and British poetry and prose, 1850 to the present; Robinson's published works, as well as books from his library, manuscripts, and over 1,000 of his letters.

Thomas Hardy Collection. Contains all editions of Hardy's titles, a library of secondary works pertaining to him, and a substantial number of Hardy's manuscripts and letters; includes letters of Hardy's wives, Florence and Emma.

Fine Presses. This collection contains a complete run of William Morris' Kelmscott Press which includes the famous *The Works of Geoffrey Chaucer;* also includes a very nearly complete collection of Maine's Mosher Press.

Bern Porter Collection of Contemporary Letters. Contains over 1,500 volumes of books and periodicals published by American and European avant-garde presses and experimental writers, many of Porter's own writings and productions, and an extensive file of his correspondence with Maine writers and poets.

James Augustine Healy Collection of Nineteenth- and Twentieth-Century Irish Literature. Includes 6,000 primary and critical sources representing the Irish Literary Renaissance, 1880-1940; contains a complete run of William Butler Yeats' Cuala Press productions.

Other collections include the works of many important New England writers, including Sarah Orne Jewett,

Kenneth Roberts, Mary Ellen Chase, William Dean Howells, Henry James, Celia Thaxter, and Ben Ames Williams.

Colby College Archives. Contains the historical records of Colby College, 1813 to the present; books by Colby authors; Senior Scholar theses; runs of the student newspaper, *The Echo,* the *Alumnus,* and the student annual, *The Oracle,* are on file.

654
College of the Atlantic
College Library
Eden Street
Bar Harbor, Maine 04609

Telephone. (207) 288-5015

Institutional Description. The privately supported liberal arts college was founded in 1969. It features ecology programs, granting baccalaureate degrees. Enrollment: 132.

Library Administration. Marcia L. Dworak, Director.

Library General Holdings. 19,500 volumes; 370 current periodical subscriptions.

Special Collections

The library's special collections include the **R. Amory Thorndike Humanities Collection,** the **Philip Darlington Evolution Collection;** and the **Dorcas Crary Natural History and Horticulture Collection.**

655
Husson College
College Library
One College Circle
Bangor, Maine 04401

Telephone. (207) 945-5641

Institutional Description. The privately supported four-year business and professional college was founded in 1898. It grants certificates and diplomas as well as associate, baccalaureate, and master's degrees. Enrollment: 1,516.

Library Administration. Berneice E. Thompson, Librarian.

Library General Holdings. 35,000 volumes; 430 current periodical titles.

Special Collections

The specialized collections of the library include materials in accounting, business, nursing, and the liberal arts.

656
Maine Maritime Academy
Nutting Memorial Library
Battle Avenue
Castine, Maine 14421

Telephone. (207) 326-4311

Institutional Description. The publicly supported institution is maintained by the State of Maine with the aid of the federal government. It offers courses to equip its students with the knowledge to qualify as officers of the U.S. Merchant Marine. Enrollment: 600.

Library Administration. Marjorie T. Harrison, Librarian.

Library General Holdings. 55,000 volumes; 800 periodicals.

Special Collections

Allie Ryan Maritime Collection. Includes 60,000 items relating to the maritime history of the nineteenth and twentieth centuries, particularly memorabilia from the local area. The collection was created by Allie Ryan of South Brooksville, Maine. The Collection is a satellite branch of the Maine State Museum.

657
Portland School of Art
Portland School of Art Library
619 Congress Street
Portland, Maine 04101

Telephone. (207) 775-5153

Institutional Description. The privately supported college was founded in 1882, and grants the Bachelor of Fine Arts degree. Enrollment: 400.

Library Administration. Joanne Waxman, Librarian.

Library General Holdings. 17,000 volumes; 38,000 slides (art and art history); over 5,000 vertical file items; 94 art periodical subscriptions.

Special Collections

The Art Library contains 17,000 volumes of art history, studio art, photography, and crafts in support of the School's curriculum.

658
St. Joseph's College
Wellehan Library
White's Bridge Road
Windham, Maine 04062

Telephone. (207) 892-6766

Institutional Description. The privately supported liberal arts college was founded in 1915 as a women's college. The Roman Catholic institution, conducted by the Sisters of Mercy, became coeducational in 1971. Enrollment: 4,-358.

Library Administration. Sister Fleurette Kennon, Director.

Library General Holdings. 51,000 volumes; 486 current periodical titles.

Special Collections

The library maintains the **Maine Collection,** an **Irish Collection,** and the **Bishops' Collection** of periodicals, papers, and books.

659
Southern Maine Vocational-Technical Institute
SMVTI Library
Fort Road
South Portland, Maine 04106

Telephone. (207) 799-7303

Institutional Description. The publicly supported two-year technical college was founded in 1946. Enrollment: 1,018.

Library General Holdings. 10,000 books; 200 magazine and technical journal subscriptions.

Special Collections

The library has special collections on marine technology, electronics, criminal justice, horticulture, culinary arts, and automotive technology.

660
Thomas College
Marriner Library
West River Road
Waterville, Maine 04901

Telephone. (207) 873-0771

Institutional Description. The privately supported liberal arts and business college was founded in 1894 as a pioneer in business education. It grants associate, baccalaureate, and master's degrees. Enrollment: 832.

Library Administration. Richard A. Boudreau, Librarian.

Library General Holdings. 21,000 volumes; 225 current periodical titles.

Special Collections

The library's collection is complemented by many business reference works.

661
Unity College
College Library
RR 78 - Box 1
Unity, Maine 04988

Telephone. (207) 948-3131

Institutional Description. The privately supported liberal arts college was founded in 1965 with the purpose of emphasizing studies in environmental science and outdoor recreation. It grants associate and baccalaureate degrees. Enrollment: 283.

Library Administration. Dorothy Quimby, Head Librarian.

Library General Holdings. 42,000 volumes; 400 current periodical subscriptions.

Special Collections

The special collections of the library include the **American Indians Collection** and the **Environmental Studies Collection.**

662
University of Maine at Augusta
Learning Resources Center
University Heights
Augusta, Maine 04330

Telephone. (207) 622-7131

Institutional Description. The publicly supported state university was founded in 1965, offering associate and baccalaureate degrees. Enrollment: 3,368.

Library Administration. Kirk Rau, Coordinator Director of Library Services.

Library General Holdings. 39,00 books; 280 current periodicals.

Special Collections

Learning Resources Center. Serving a commuter college with no dormitories, the Center maintains materials to support the curriculum in the fields of art and graphic arts, business administration, criminal justice, jazz and contemporary music, computer information systems, medical laboratory science, nursing, and photography.

Career Resource Center. The Center has an extensive collection of books, pamphlets, and periodicals to assist with career planning and effective job search techniques.

663
University of Maine at Farmington
Mantor Library
41 High Street
Farmington, Maine 04938

Telephone. (207) 778-3501

Institutional Description. Founded in 1864 to prepare teachers for public schools, the University of Maine at Farmington was the first state-supported college in Maine. Enrollment: 2,140.

Library Administration. Richard C. Holmes, Library Director.

Library General Holdings. 104,228 volumes; 4,945 bound periodicals; 7,951 other print materials (excluding vertical file); 29,773 microform pieces; 4,306 nonbook materials (excluding maps); 761 current subscriptions.

Special Collections

Curriculum Resource Center. Contains 9,310 items including textbooks, audiovisual materials, and indexed vertical file material, plus unindexed material and recordings for children.

Juvenile Books. Collection contains 6,117 volumes.

U.S. Geological Survey Reports. In series, housed in the regular collection, consists of about 8,250 volume; related collection of maps and charts containing 5,716 pieces.

Archives. University records and a collection of Franklin County, Maine, historical material, containing 1,311 cataloged volumes, extensive vertical files, and some realia.

664
University of Maine at Orono
Raymond H. Fogler Library
Orono, Maine 04469

Telephone. (207) 581-1686

Institutional Description. The publicly supported university was founded originally as the State College of Agriculture and Mechanical Arts under provisions of the Morrill Act of 1862. Enrollment: 11,180.

Library Administration. Elaine M. Albright, University Librarian; Eric S. Flower, Head, Special Collections Department.

Library General Holdings. 668,691 volumes; 996,000 microform pieces; 24,585 audiovisual items; 1,427,270 government documents; 5,200 periodical subscriptions.

Special Collections

State of Maine Collection. Includes 15,000 volumes on Maine's history and literature.

Clinton L. Cole Maritime History Collection. Contains 4,500 volumes; strong in New England and North Atlantic history.

Ronald B. Levinson Collection. 2,000 volumes on philosophical topics.

Ezekial Holmes Library. The University of Maine's original book collection; principally agriculture.

Taylor Collection of Modern History, War, and Diplomacy. Contains 1,200 volumes.

Maine State Documents Collection. Extensive collection of 7,000 titles comprising some 46,800 documents is made up of agency publications beginning with those from 1820.

University Collection. Archives of the University; included are the records and publications of academic and administrative departments, publications of individual faculty members, honors and masters theses, as well as doctoral dissertations.

Manuscript Collections. The Fogler Library maintains an extensive array of manuscript collections, ranging from Maine family papers (Hamlin Family) to Maine businesses (Androscoggin and Kennebec Railroad Company) to those of native authors (Stephen King).

665
University of Maine at Presque Isle
University Library
181 Main Street
Presque Isle, Maine 04769

Telephone. (207) 764-0311

Institutional Description. The publicly supported university was originally founded as a state college in 1903; it became part of the University of Maine System in 1968. A multi-purpose institution, it offers A.A., B.A., and B.S. degrees. Enrollment: 1,210.

Library Administration. John Vigle, University Librarian; Anna Mcgrath, Special Collections Librarian.

Library General Holdings. 65,000 monographs; 6,000 bound periodical volumes; 900 periodical titles; 18,000 maps; 20,000 fine arts slides; 500 phonograph recordings; 50,000 government documents (microfiche equivalent and hard cover).

Special Collections

Aroostook Collection. Aroostook County authors; town, city, county histories; oral tapes of Aroostook characters, newspapers, maps, photographs, scrapbooks, memorabilia, phonograph recordings.

Maine Collection. Maine authors; nonfiction about Maine.

Rare Book Collections

Rare Books Collection. Books on education, history, and literature in English and foreign languages, published prior to 1900.

666
University of New England
Library
605 Pool Road
Biddeford, Maine 04005

Telephone. (207) 283-0171

Institutional Description. The privately supported university specializes in career-oriented programs. It was established in 1953 as a liberal arts college, has added numerous professional programs, and now grants baccalaureate and professional degrees. Enrollment: 934.

Library Administration. Andrew Golub, Librarian.

Library General Holdings. 97,000 volumes; 630 periodical subscriptions; 3,000 microforms; 485 audiovisual aids.

Special Collections

There are special collections in the fields of osteopathy and allied health. The library also maintains the personal papers of Booth Tarkington, American novelist and playwright (1869-1946).

667
University of Southern Maine
University Library
38 College Avenue
Gorham, Maine 04103

Telephone. (207) 780-4480

Institutional Description. The publicly supported unit of the University of Maine has two campuses: one in Gorham and one in Portland. The University of Maine Law School is located on the Portland campus. Enrollment: 8,769.

Library Administration. George Parks, Librarian.

Library General Holdings. 700,000 items including nearly 3,000 current subscriptions to scholarly journals, magazines, newspapers, and yearbooks; 280,000 microfilms; 67,000 international, United States, and state documents.

Special Collections

University Archives. Includes materials of importance to the history of the University dating back to 1878.

Anthoenson Collection of Fine Printing. The library maintains this special collection illustrative of fine printing throughout the history of the art.

Rare Book Collections

The **Smith Collection** includes maps, atlases, globes, and geographies from the period 1513-1800.

668
Westbrook College
College Library
716 Stevens Avenue
Portland, Maine 04103

Telephone. (207) 797-7261

Institutional Description. The privately supported liberal arts college was founded in 1831. It grants associate and baccalaureate degrees. Enrollment: 1,138.

Library Administration. Todd S. Trevorrow, Library Director.

Library General Holdings. 36,500 volumes; 290 current periodical titles.

Special Collections

The library has a **Maine Women Writer's Collection** of 5,000 items, including first editions, manuscripts, clippings, and memorabilia, some dating back to the early eighteenth century.

Maryland

669
Allegany Community College Library Willowbrook Road Cumberland, Maryland 21502

Telephone. (301) 724-7700

Institutional Description. The publicly supported two-year college was founded in 1961. It offers both day and evening classes in academic and vocational-technical areas. Enrollment: 1,944.

Library Administration. Ellen Abar, Coordinator of Library Service.

Library General Holdings. 45,000 books; 400 periodical subscriptions; subject area emphases of the Library include health, forestry, food services management, and criminal justice.

Special Collections

Appalachian Collection. The book collection forms the backbone of this collection. A wide range of topics are included dealing with the history of Allegany County and its environs (from biography to industrial history; from manners and customs to social conditions). The collection also contains oral history recordings, pamphlets, photographs, and genealogies.

670
Baltimore Hebrew College Joseph Meyerhoff Library 5800 Park Heights Avenue Baltimore, Maryland 21215

Telephone. (301) 578-6900

Institutional Description. The privately supported college offers teacher preparatory and professional programs in Judaic and Hebraic studies. Enrollment: 214.

Library Administration. Jesse Mashbaum, Director.

Library General Holdings. 40,000 volumes; 250 current periodical subscriptions; 2,000 microfiche; 600 microfilm reels.

Special Collections

The Joseph Meyerhoff Library is the central resource in the Baltimore area for research in Judaica. All aspects of Jewish life and history are covered, including ancient Near Eastern history, Biblical literature, rabbinics, Jewish languages and literature, Jewish philosophy and mysticism, medieval and modern Jewish history, sociology of Jewish life, modern Middle Eastern Affairs, and State of Israel and international relations.

Rare Book Collections

The library contains over 600 rare books which date from the sixteenth to the eighteenth centuries. Included are texts of the Biblical and Talmudic commentaries and supercommentaries and law codes and collections. Many of these volumes were rescued from the rubble of European synagogues by the United States Army after World War II and later distributed among several important Judaica libraries in the United States.

In recent years, the library has received several outstanding collections. Dr. Louis L. Kaplan contributed over 1,000 volumes in Hebraica and Judaica from his personal library, including rare sixteenth- and seventeenth-century works. Other private library contributions were made by the Honorable Simon F. Sobeloff, former Solicitor General of the United States and a past Chairman of the Board of Trustees of the college, by the family of the late Mr. Hyman Silver, and by Professor Leo J. Kanner.

Since 1979, the books of the B'nai B'rith International Four Freedoms Library have been housed in the library on permanent loan. This collection of 4,000 volumes, which includes materials in history, politics, and Judaica, constitutes one of the best known collections of materials on human rights assembled by American Jewry.

671
Bowie State College Thurgood Marshall Library Bowie, Maryland 20740

Telephone. (301) 464-3400

Institutional Description. The publicly supported

state college owes its founding to a bequest left by Nelson Wells to be used to establish a school for training Black teachers. The school was founded in 1865 and provided only teacher training until 1963; it now offers various baccalaureate majors and a graduate school. Enrollment: 2,902.

Library Administration. Mrs. Courtney H. Funn, Director; William A. Peniston, Special Collections Librarian.

Library General Holdings. 119,000 volumes; 1,500 periodical titles; 6,200 microfilms; 300,000 microfiche.

Special Collections

North Star Collection. A circulating collection with some reference materials and some rare books on Afro-American affairs. It also includes information on Africa south of the Sahara.

Maryland Collection. Contains materials on the history, politics, economy, law, and culture of Maryland.

Rare Book Collections

The rare books of the Thurgood Marshall Library are an eclectic collection of materials, most of which date from the nineteenth century and most of which are in the fields of history and literature.

Afro-Americans
Africa

672
Capitol Institute of Technology
Learning Resources Center
11301 Springfield Road
Laurel, Maryland 20708

Telephone. (301) 953-0060

Institutional Description. The privately supported four-year technological college was founded in 1964. It grants associate and baccalaureate degrees. Enrollment: 1,026.

Library Administration. Kay Brodie, Director of Learning Resources.

Library General Holdings. 30,000 volumes; 200 periodical subscriptions.

Special Collections

The **Chesapeake Room** of the Learning Resources Center houses a specialized collection of works by Eastern Shore authors and materials relating to Eastern Shore culture. In addition to the 6,000 volumes, the collection also includes a pamphlet file, videotapes, slides, and various Eastern Shore artifacts.

673
Charles County Community College
Learning Resource Center
Mitchell Road
P.O. Box 910
La Plata, Maryland 20646

Telephone. (301) 934-2251

Institutional Description. The two-year community college was founded in 1958. The present campus was opened in 1968. Enrollment: 4,553.

Library Administration. Elaine Ryan, Dean, Division of Learning Resources.

Library General Holdings. 29,155 volumes; 235 periodical titles; 3,000 microforms; 6,000 audiovisual materials.

Special Collections

The **Southern Maryland Rooms** of the learning resources center provides an opportunity for students and the community to research the history and culture of the southern Maryland region.

674
Chesapeake College
Chesapeake College Learning Resource Center
Box 23
Wye Mills, Maryland 21679

Telephone. (301) 822-5400

Institutional Description. The publicly supported junior college was founded in 1965. Enrollment: 2,018.

Library Administration. Kay Brodie, Library Administrator; Harold Jopp, Curator.

Library General Holdings. 35,000 volumes; 6,000 reels of microfilm; audiovisual, computer, and curriculum support materials.

Special Collections

Chesapeake Room Collection. Contains books and pamphlets about the Eastern Shore of Maryland.

675
College of Notre Dame of Maryland
Loyola-Notre Dame Library
4701 North Charles Street
Baltimore, Maryland 21210

Telephone. (301) 435-0100

Institutional Description. The privately supported liberal arts college, primarily for women, was founded in 1873. It is affiliated with the Roman Catholic Church. Enrollment: 1,886.

Library Administration. Sister Mary Ian Stewart,

S.S.N.D., Director.

Library General Holdings. 231,000 volumes; 1,680 current periodical titles; 259,000 microforms.

Special Collections

The library has a special collection of the first editions of Henry James; the **Knott Collection** of fore-edge paintings; and the **Gerard Manley Hopkins Collection.**

676
Columbia Union College
Theofield G. Weis Library
7600 Flower Avenue
Takoma Park, Maryland 20912

Telephone. (301) 270-9200

Institutional Description. The privately supported liberal arts college is affiliated with the Seventh-day Adventist Church. It offers degree programs primarily for the Columbia Union Conference. Enrollment: 1,184.

Library Administration. Margaret J. von Hake, Director.

Library General Holdings. 116,000 volumes.

Special Collections

Curriculum Library. This collection supports the teacher education programs of the college.

677
Coppin State College
Parlett Longworth Moore Library
2500 West North Avenue
Baltimore, Maryland 21216

Telephone. (301) 333-5990

Institutional Description. The publicly supported state teachers college was founded in 1900 as a school for teacher education. It now also features nursing and social work. Enrollment: 2,315.

Library Administration. Mary Wanza, Director.

Library General Holdings. 123,000 volumes; 85,000 microforms.

Special Collections

The library has special collections such as the Library of American Civilization (microform), the **Maryland Collection,** the **Juvenile Collection,** and the **Helene Fuld Collection** on nursing.

678
Frostburg State University
Library
Frostburg, Maryland 21532

Telephone. (301) 689-4889

Institutional Description. The publicly supported university was founded as a normal school in 1902. It is now a diverse liberal arts institution. Enrollment: 3,716.

Library Administration. David M. Gillespie, Librarian; MaryJo A. Price, Map/Special Collections Librarian.

Library General Holdings. 168,323 monographs; 1,200 periodical subscriptions; 22 newspaper subscriptions; 96,888 documents; 38,164 maps; 30,106 audiovisual materials; 4,499 curriculum materials; 8,998 microfilms; 139,325 microforms; 1,700 music scores.

Special Collections

World War II Collection. Materials collected by John W. Davis during his career teaching history at Frostburg State, 1970-1980.

Coal Mining Collection. These materials were collected by Dr. John J. Rutledge while he was Chief Mining Engineer of the Maryland Bureau of Mines, 1922-1952; includes maps, periodicals, memorabilia, and monographs on mining in western Maryland.

J. Glenn Beall, Jr. Papers. Includes papers collected by Beall while he was a U.S. Representative (1967-71) and a U.S. Senator (1971-1977).

John Kennedy Lacock Papers. Maps, photographs, and personal papers collected by Lacock from 1871-1933 while he conducted research on foot of the Braddock Military Road (Cumberland, Maryland to Braddock, Pennsylvania), the Forbes Military Road (Bedford, Pennsylvania to Pittsburgh, Pennsylvania), and Fort Necessity from 1908-1912.

Charles Sager Collection. Includes the books and vocal scores acquired by Charles Sager while he was a professor of voice at Frostburg State from 1954-1977.

The library acquires as much information as possible on all aspects of Western Maryland history, geography, economics, etc., including all available information on Frostburg State University from its beginning to the present.

679
Goucher College
Julia Rogers Library
Dulaney Road
Towson, Maryland 21204

Telephone. (301) 337-6000

Institutional Description. The privately supported liberal arts college for women was founded in 1885, and grants baccalaureate and master's degrees. Enrollment: 843.

Library Administration. Betty Ruth Kondayan, Librarian.

Library General Holdings. 251,000 volumes; 970 periodical subscriptions; 97,000 government documents; 57,448 slides; 8,218 microforms.

Special Collections

The Rogers Library's important special collections include the **Jane Austen Collection** of first editions, memorabilia, and collateral material; the **Mark Twain Collection** of American and English first editions and biographies; and the **H.L. Mencken Collection** of books, manuscripts, pamphlets, periodicals, and photographs.

680
Hood College
Joseph Henry Apple Library
Rosemont Avenue
Frederick, Maryland 21701

Telephone. (301) 663-3131

Institutional Description. The privately supported liberal arts college for women was founded in 1893. It is affiliated with the United Church of Christ. Enrollment: 1,967.

Library Administration. Lloyd Wagner, Director.

Library General Holdings. 152,000 volumes; 953 current periodicals; 202,500 microforms; 13,500 audiovisual aids; 1,900 music scores.

Special Collections

The Apple Library maintains the **Irving M. Landauer Civil War Collection;** the **Hood College Archives** which includes the Frederick Female Seminary Papers, 1841-1893; and the **Samuel Cole Hogarth Prints Collection.**

681
The Johns Hopkins University
Milton S. Eisenhower Library
3400 North Charles Street
Baltimore, Maryland 21218

Telephone. (301) 338-8325

Institutional Description. The privately supported university was founded in 1876. Matriculated students may take courses at several American and foreign educational institutions through a cooperative arrangement. Enrollment: 8,214.

Library Administration. Susan K. Martin, University Librarian; Ann S. Gwynn, Associate Director for Special Collections; Judy Gardner-Flint, Gannett Librarian; Cynthia Regvardt, Manuscript Librarian; Robert Bartram, Peabody Librarian.

Library General Holdings. 2,564,700 volumes; 1,441,-800 microforms; 7,145 audiovisual materials. special collections total approximately 75,000 rare books including 192 incunabula.

Special Collections

Abram G. Hutzler Collection of Economic Classics. Over 5,000 printed titles and more than 1,000 manuscripts in the fields of economic history and thought, principally in English and mostly from the time of Adam Smith to John Stuart Mill. The full range of the collection is from the sixteenth to the twentieth century.

American Literature. The collections of American literature include the works of Sidney Lanier, Oliver Wendell Holmes, Henry James, Edith Wharton, and Louis Zukofsky.

American Revolution. A collection of books on the American Revolution and preceding events; early editions of Thomas Paine's *Common Sense* include one published in 1776 in London which left blank those passages that might have offended British readers.

Anti-Slavery Collection. Rare pamphlets and periodicals from the eighteenth century through the Civil War to about 1868.

History of Graduate Education. The papers in this collection are a significant resource for the history of higher education in the United States, especially graduate programs, in which The Johns Hopkins University was a pioneer.

Lester S. Levy Collection. Consists of over 30,000 pieces of sheet music relating to a wide variety of subjects and forming a social commentary on nearly two hundred years of American history.

Oscar Wilde Collection. The collection contains 6 manuscripts and approximately 50 books, including *Ravenna,* the author's first book.

Sidney Lanier Collection. Original manuscripts of his compositions as well as music by other composers which belonged to Lanier.

Rare Book Collections

Bible Collection. Julius Hofmann gave the University a collection of Bibles, including the four-volume Bible printed by Koberger in Nuremberg in 1497. To this collection was added the Polyglot Psalter, the "September Bibel" of Martin Luther, and Eliot's Indian Bible, the first edition of the first complete Bible printed in the New World.

Byron and Contemporaries. The 900 volumes of this collection include all of Byron's works in as many editions as it has been possible to obtain.

English Literature. The sixteen and seventeenth century English literature collection is a blend of books collected by the Garrett family and by the Tudor and Stuart Club of Johns Hopkins. The collection includes rare editions of Shakespeare, Johnson, Fletcher, Bacon, Spenser, Milton, Chaucer, Donne, Drayton, Dryden, Evelyn, and others.

Fowler Collection of Early Architectural History. The original Fowler Architectural library was made up of four hundred forty-eight items featuring Vitruvius, Alberti, Serlio, Palladio, Vignola, and Scamozzi, as well as works of English, French, and German architects. This collection is fully described in *The Fowler Architectural*

Collection of The Johns Hopkins University compiled by Laurence Hall Fowler and Elizabeth Baer (Baltimore: The Evergreen House Foundation, 1961).

John Work Garrett Collection. Approximately 30,000 rare books and several hundred manuscripts includes incunabula, sixteenth and seventeenth century English literature, natural history, Americana, and New World exploration and travel.

German Literature. The Kurrelmeyer Collection, Collitz Collection, and the Loewenberg Collection are included in the eighteenth and nineteenth century German literature books and manuscripts.

Thomas G. Machen Collection of Incunabula and Fine Printed Books. This collection, gathered together by Thomas G. Machen and given to the University by his widow in 1980, consists of a hundred volumes, fifty-two of which are incunabula.

Other collections of rare books, manuscripts, and archival materials at Johns Hopkins include the Archives Project at the Applied Physics Laboratory; the Alan Mason Chesney Medical Archives at the School of Medicine; the Ferdinand Hamburger, Jr. Archives in the Milton S. Eisenhower Library; the Institute of the History of Medicine at the Welch Medical Library; the Nightingale Room (Collection of Nursing Material) at the Welch Medical Library; and the Music Library of the Peabody Institute.

682
Loyola College
Loyola/Notre Dame Library
4501 North Charles Street
Baltimore, Maryland 21210

Telephone. (301) 323-1010

Institutional Description. The privately supported liberal arts college, affiliated with the Roman Catholic Church, is conducted in the Jesuit tradition. Baccalaureate and master's degrees are granted. Enrollment: 5,228.

Library Administration. Sister M. Ian Stewart, Director.

Library General Holdings. The libraries of Loyola College and the College of Notre Dame of Maryland are combined and operated as one unit. *See* **College of Notre Dame of Maryland.**

683
Maryland Institute, College of Art
Decker Library
1300 West Mt. Royal Avenue
Baltimore, Maryland 21217

Telephone. (301) 669-9200

Institutional Description. The privately supported professional college grants baccalaureate and master's degrees. Enrollment: 1,248.

Library Administration. John Stoneham, Librarian.

Library General Holdings. 45,000 volumes; 200 current periodical subscriptions.

Special Collections

The holdings of the library are related not only to art and art history, but to the whole spectrum of the humanities. There is a slide library housing over 75,000 slides.

684
Montgomery College - Germantown
Germantown Campus Library
20200 Observation Drive
Germantown, Maryland 20874

Telephone. (301) 972-2000

Institutional Description. Founded in 1946 in a local high school, Montgomery College is the largest community college in Maryland, with three campuses in Takoma Park, Rockville, and Germantown. Enrollment: 2,611.

Library Administration. Polly-Ann Proett, Assistant Director.

Library General Holdings. 50,000 volumes; 525 periodical titles; 20,000 microfiche; 15,000 miscellaneous items.

Special Collections

The special collections of the library include a **Children's Collection** of over 3,000 items; a **Science Fiction Collection** of over 1,500 items; and the Library of American Civilization (microform).

685
Morgan State University
Soper Library
Hillen Road and Cold Spring Lane
Baltimore, Maryland 21239

Telephone. (301) 444-3488

Institutional Description. The publicly supported liberal arts college was founded in 1867 as the Centenary Biblical Institute. In 1939, it joined the state system as Morgan State College. It now grants baccalaureate, master's and doctorate degrees. Enrollment: 3,751.

Library Administration. Karen Robertson, Director.

Library General Holdings. 445,000 volumes; 2,075 current periodical subscriptions; 155,000 government documents; 82,000 microforms.

Special Collections

The **Beulah Davis Room** of the library contains one of the largest Afro-American collections in the United States.

686
Mount St. Mary's College and Seminary
Phillips Library
Emmitsburg, Maryland 21727

Telephone. (301) 447-6122

Institutional Description. The privately supported liberal arts and theology college was founded in 1808. Affiliated with the Roman Catholic Church, both the college and the seminary were established at the same time. Enrollment: 1,769.

Library Administration. D. Stephen Rockwood, Director.

Library General Holdings. 160,000 volumes; 800 literary, scientific, and professional journals.

Special Collections

The library maintains special collections of Marylandia, early Catholic Americana, and theology.

687
Peabody Institute of The Johns Hopkins University
Music Library
1 East Mount Vernon Place
Baltimore, Maryland 21202

Telephone. (301) 659-8100

Institutional Description. The privately supported institution is often referred to as The Peabody Conservatory of Music. It was founded in 1868 and grants baccalaureate, master's, and doctorate degrees in the musical arts. Enrollment: 472.

Library Administration. Edwin A. Quist, Jr., Librarian.

Library General Holdings. 56,000 volumes; 15,000 recordings.

Special Collections

The Peabody Conservatory libraries contain strong collections of performance materials, music reference materials, scholarly editions, and periodicals.

Rare Book Collections

Notable among the rare items owned by the Conservatory Libraries are a collection of sixteenth-century Venetian *laudi;* the Enrico Caruso and John Charles Thomas collections of memorabilia; a small collection of early American sheet music, and several early editions of scores and orchestral parts of Hector Berlioz. A collection of the works of composers associated with the Peabody includes manuscripts of Asger Hamerik, Gustav Strube, Louis Cheeslock, Franz Bornschein, Howard Thatcher, George Boyle, Theodore Hemberger, Robert L. Paul, and others.

The main library building houses the **George Peabody Collection** of The Johns Hopkins University. Formerly the Peabody Research and Reference Library, which was part of the Enoch Pratt Free Library system of Baltimore, this library's collections are internationally renowned and still accessible to the general public as well as to Peabody students.

688
St. John's College
Library
60 College Avenue
Annapolis, Maryland 21401

Telephone. (301) 263-2371

Institutional Description. The privately supported liberal arts college was founded in 1696 as King William's School; it was chartered in 1784 using its present name. A sister college, using the same name and also featuring the liberal arts, was founded in Santa Fe, New Mexico, in 1964. Enrollment: 419.

Library Administration. James M. Benefiel, Librarian.

Library General Holdings. Annapolis campus: 85,000 volumes; 130 current periodical subscriptions. Santa Fe campus: 50,000 volumes.

Special Collections

Both libraries of St. John's College hold interesting special collections. Annapolis has the **Reverend Thomas Bray Collection** dating from 1696, known as the "first public library in America," and the **Peter Huntington Jackson Collection,** and the **Henry Lee Bowen Collection** of mythology, symbolism, and architecture. The **Witter Bynner Collection** and the **Edgar Allan Poe Collection** in Santa Fe contain first editions of each poet as well as other *belles lettres.* In addition, the Santa Fe library contains several distinguished music collections, including the Amelia White, the Grumman, the Schmidt, and the Holzman collections.

689
St. Mary's College of Maryland
College Library
St. Mary's City, Maryland 20686

Telephone. (301) 862-0200

Institutional Description. The publicly supported (state) liberal arts college was founded in 1839 and became the state's first junior college in 1927. It now grants baccalaureate degrees. Enrollment: 1,426.

Library Administration. John G. Williamson, Director.

Library General Holdings. 110,000 volumes.

Special Collections

The **Maryland Collection** includes materials on the history of Maryland.

690
St. Mary's Seminary and University Library
5400 Roland Avenue
Baltimore, Maryland 21210

Telephone. (301) 323-3200

Institutional Description. The privately supported Roman Catholic institution is administered by the Priests of St. Sulpice. Offering graduate-level programs only, it provides education mainly for the priesthood, but includes other offerings as well. Enrollment: 452.

Library Administration. David P. Siemsen, Director of Library Services.

Library General Holdings. 100,000 volumes; 320 periodical titles; 16,000 bound periodicals.

Special Collections

The collection of the library reflects the original purpose of the founding Sulpicians which is to train young men for the Roman Catholic priesthood. Subjects include theology, philosophy, church history, sacraments, liturgy, canon law, pastoral works, and scripture.

The scripture collection was richly enhanced in the 1950s through a gift of the late Edward P. Arbez, a priest of the Society of St. Sulpice. Father Arbez's donation consisted of his personal library of 25,000 volumes. In 1981, the liberal arts collection added 15,000 books from the library of St. Charles College in Catonsville upon its closure.

691
Salisbury State University
Blackwell Library
College and Camden Avenues
Salisbury, Maryland 21801

Telephone. (301) 543-6130

Institutional Description. The publicly supported state university was established in 1925, offering a two-year course for the preparation of elementary school teachers. The baccalaureate program was initiated in 1953. Enrollment: 4,708.

Library Administration. James R. Thrash, University Librarian; Keith R. Vail, Associate Director of Library.

Library General Holdings. 210,000 volumes; 1,750 periodical and newspaper subscriptions; various microfiche collections; depository for U.S. documents and Maryland publications.

Special Collections

Educational Resources Collection. Consists of textbooks, curriculum guides, multimedia learning kits, unit files, picture files.

Maryland Room Collection. Contains books, periodicals, and vertical files dealing primarily with the history and culture of Maryland.

692
Towson State University
Albert S. Cook Library
Baltimore, Maryland 21204

Telephone. (301) 321-2000

Institutional Description. The publicly supported state university, founded in 1866, is the oldest of Maryland's public colleges. It was originally a teacher training institution, but since has added a variety of programs. Enrollment: 15,410.

Library Administration. Thomas E. Strader, Director.

Library General Holdings. 964,000 items; 2,500 periodicals.

Special Collections

The library has a U.S. Government Documents Depository; Maryland State Documents Depository; collections of textbooks and curriculum guides for elementary and secondary education; a collection of educational resource documents (ERIC); a collection of early English literature; a strong women's studies collection; a Black studies collection; and a collection of early American periodicals.

693
Uniformed Services University of the Health Sciences
Learning Resource Center
4301 Jones Bridge Road
Bethesda, Maryland 20814

Telephone. (301) 295-3100

Institutional Description. The publicly supported professional university was founded by the Federal government in 1972 to provide medical training for members of the armed forces. It grants professional, master's, and doctorate degrees. Enrollment: 736.

Library General Holdings. 88,000 volumes.

Special Collections

The Learning Resource Center is affiliated with the National Library of Medicine Regional Medical Library Program for the mid-Atlantic area. The Center's holdings include a collection on military medicine.

694
United States Naval Academy
The Nimitz Library
Annapolis, Maryland 21402

Telephone. (301) 267-2220

Institutional Description. Founded in 1845, the publicly supported U.S. Naval Academy is the undergraduate college of the U.S. Navy. Bachelor of Science degrees are awarded, as are commissions in the U.S. Navy and U.S. Marine Corps. Enrollment: 4,685.

Library Administration. Richard A. Evans, Academy Librarian; John P. Cummungs, Associate Librarian; Alice S. Creighton, Special Collections Librarian.

Library General Holdings. 500,000 volumes; collection supports all parts of the undergraduate curriculum and is particularly strong in history and naval science.

Special Collections

The Nimitz Library Special Collections contain materials related to naval history and seapower, the United States Navy, and the United States Naval Academy, and includes rare and historically significant books, manuscripts, photographs, and oral history transcripts.

Annapolis Collection. Contains the volumes which made up the original 1845 Naval Academy Library.

Park Benjamin Collection. Rare books and early works on electricity and magnetism.

Harry F. Guggenheim Collection. First editions of Charles Dickens, early aviation and natural history, and a typescript copy of Robert H. Goddard's rocketry research notebooks.

Paul H. Wiedorn Collection. Contains color plate books, chiefly nineteenth century.

Manuscript Collections. Includes, among others, the papers of Captain Joel Abbot, USN (1793-1855), Rear Admiral Daniel Vincent Gallery, USN (1901-1977), Rear Admiral William Adger Moffett, USN (1869-1933), Albert Abraham Michelson (1852-1931), and Ambassador William J. Sebald (1902-1980). The Manuscripts Collections also include ships' logs, letterbooks, journals, and watch-station-quarter bills, 1759-1943.

Picture File. Includes nineteenth- and twentieth-century prints and photographs related to naval officers, ships, shore stations and shipyards, chiefly American and British.

Edward J. Steichen Collection. Includes World War II combat prints, Farm Security Administration prints, photographs by Ansel Adams, Edward and Brett Weston, Margaret Bourke-White, and other American photographers, plus photographically illustrated books, chiefly American.

695
University of Baltimore
Langsdale Library
1420 Maryland Avenue
Baltimore, Maryland 21201

Telephone. (301) 625-3135

Institutional Description. The publicly supported university was founded in 1925. It is composed of three main divisions: College of Liberal Arts, School of Law, School of Business. Enrollment: 5,020.

Library Administration. William Newman, University Librarian; Gerry Yeager, Director of Special Collections.

Library General Holdings. 403,976 volumes; 122,102 government documents; 1,285 current periodicals.

Special Collections

American Civil Liberties Union. Files, publications, and programs, 1947-1978.

Baltimore City Department of Planning. Cartographic records, case files, federal grant applications, housekeeping records, working papers related to all phases of the city planning process.

Baltimore Neighborhood Heritage Project. Written history of neighborhood included; oral history interviews on tapes; written outlines of information on tapes. Topics include: migration, immigration, racial and ethnic identity, national and local events, neighborhood family life, work, and religion.

Belvedere Hotel Corporation. Correspondence, minutes, contracts, financial records, appraisals and operational records (includes guest ledgers, banquet records, personnel files, purchasing records, etc.) of the Belvedere Hotel Corporation and the Sheraton-Belvedere Corporation, 1904-1970.

Commission on Government Efficiency and Economy. Scrapbooks containing newspaper clippings from the "Sunpapers" on such subjects as city and state finances, elections, education, and civic matters, 1930-1960.

Herwood Accounting Collections. Representative collection of accounting literature beginning with Lucca Paccioli's Treatise published in 1494, to the end of the 19th century.

Independent Order of Odd Fellows. Minutes, correspondence, membership records, officer's roles, membership register, question book, black book, financial records, dues, annual reports, and regalia, 1819-1970.

Lyric Theatre. News clippings, correspondence, announcements, prospectus, 1917-1966.

Maryland Council of Churches. Minutes, correspondence, annual reports, studies, staff reports, juvenile court cases, maps, photographs, posters, books, file cards, accounting ledgers and other housekeeping records, slides and tapes, 1964-1971.

Steamship Historical Society of America. Collection

devoted entirely to steamships and steamship history; includes approximately 60,000 photographs, 25,000 negatives, over 100 journals, and over 4,000 books on vessels and shipping, maritime maps, charts, ship plants, blueprints, and reference books; post cards, ship logs, and artifacts, 1790 to the present.

Other collections include the A.S. Abell Film Collection; American Lung Association of Maryland; American Society of Pension Actuaries; Baltimore Economic Development Corporation; Baltimore Neighborhoods, Incorporated; Baltimore Room Books; Baltimore Typographical Union; Baltimore Urban Renewal and Housing Agency; Blakeslee Lane, Inc., Christ Evangelical Church; Citizens League of Baltimore; Chamber of Commerce of Metropolitan Baltimore; Clinton Railroad Company; Leven J. Colsten; Poe Society; Swann Collection (sketches of historical houses of Baltimore); YMCA of Greater Baltimore.

696
University of Maryland at College Park
Theodore R. McKeldin Library
College Park, Maryland 20742

Telephone. (301) 454-5550

Institutional Description. The publicly supported state university was founded in 1856, and is now a campus of the University of Maryland's state system. Enrollment: 38,639.

Library Administration. H. Joanne Harrar, Director; Donald Farren, Director for Special Collections.

Library General Holdings. The libraries on the College Park Campus include over 1,600,000 volumes; 2,300,-000 microfilm units; 19,800 current periodicals and newspapers; 566,000 government documents; 91,000 maps; 36,000 phonorecords; films and filmstrips; slides; prints; and music scores. The McKeldin Library supports the graduate and research programs of the University and is also open to undergraduates.

Special Collections

The McKeldin Library has special collections that include the **Katherine Anne Porter Collection,** the **East Asia Collection** containing the Gordon W. Prange Collection of Japanese language materials from the period of the Allied Occupation of Japan (1945-1949); and Maryland-related books and manuscripts. The library also contains U.S. government publications, publications of the United Nations, the League of Nations, and other international organizations; agricultural experiment station and extension service publications, maps from the U.S. Army Map Service and U.S. Geological Survey; files on the Industrial Union of Marine and Shipbuilding Workers of America, and other industrial and craft unions.

The Music Library contains such special collections as the **Wallenstein Collection** of musical scores, research collections of the American Bandmasters Association, the Music Educators National Conference, the National Association of College Wind and Percussion Instructors, and the International Piano Archives at Maryland.

697
University of Maryland, Baltimore County
Albin O. Kuhn Library
5401 Wilkens Avenue
Catonsville, Maryland 21228

Telephone. (301) 455-1000

Institutional Description. The publicly supported branch campus of the University of Maryland was established in 1963. It grants baccalaureate, master's, and doctorate degrees. Enrollment: 9,267.

Library Administration. Cyril Feng, Director.

Library General Holdings. 416,000 volumes; 3,435 current periodical titles; 84,500 microforms; 143,000 government documents.

Special Collections

The Kuhn Library's Special Collections houses one of the nation's major photographic archives. Here one can find the works of Lewis Hine,, the photographs and negatives of Edward L. Bafford, Phillipe Halsman, Alfred Steiglitz, William Henry Jackson, Ansel Adams, Lotte Jacobi, Alexander Garner, Timothy O'Sullivan and many others. The Special Collections Department also contains the **Archives of the American Society for Microbiology,** the **Edward G. Howard Collection of Marylandia,** the **Edgar Merkle Collection of English Graphic Satire,** the **Azriel Rosenfeld Science Fiction Research Collection,** and several other collections of rare books.

698
University of Maryland, Eastern Shore
Frederick Douglass Library
Princess Anne, Maryland 21853

Telephone. (301) 651-2200

Institutional Description. The publicly supported branch campus of the University of Maryland was founded in 1886 as the Delaware Conference Academy. It now grants baccalaureate, master's, and doctorate degrees. Enrollment: 1,331.

Library Administration. Jessie C. Smith, Director.

Library General Holdings. 136,000 volumes; 900 literary, scientific, scholarly, and popular periodicals.

Special Collections

Among the special collections are the **Curriculum Library** of textbooks and courses of study, the **Maryland Collection,** the **Black Collection,** and the **Juvenile Collection.** Publications of the United Nations and its agencies are received regularly.

699
Villa Julie College
Learning Resources Center
Green Spring Valley Road
Stevenson, Maryland 21153

Telephone. (301) 486-7000

Institutional Description. The college opened in 1947 as a one-year professional medical secretarial school. It became a two-year institution in 1952. Enrollment: 1,141.

Library Administration. Mary S. Dagold, Head Librarian.

Library General Holdings. 38,356 volumes; 314 periodical subscriptions; 2,221 audiovisual materials.

Special Collections

The library has a strong collection of legal reference materials. There is also a cassette tape collection for court reporters and a children's book collection cataloged and arranged as a laboratory library for child development students.

700
Washington Bible College
Oyer Memorial Library
6511 Princess Garden Parkway
Lanham, Maryland 20706

Telephone. (301) 552-1400

Institutional Description. The privately supported interdenominational Bible college was founded in 1938 to prepare students for Christian ministries and church vocations. Enrollment: 389.

Library Administration. Carol A. Satta, Director of Library Services.

Library General Holdings. 50,000 volumes.

Special Collections

Two newly-developed satellite libraries are the Children's Literature and Curriculum Library and the Christian Service Library.

701
Washington College
Clifton M. Miller Library
Washington Avenue
Chestertown, Maryland 21620

Telephone. (301) 778-2800

Institutional Description. The privately supported liberal arts college was founded in 1782 and now grants baccalaureate and master's degrees. Enrollment: 797.

Library Administration. William J. Tubbs, Librarian.

Library General Holdings. 140,000 volumes; 660 current periodical subscriptions.

Special Collections

The **Maryland Collection** and the **College Archives** are housed in the Miller Library.

702
Washington Theological Union
The Union Library
9001 New Hampshire Avenue
Silver Spring, Maryland 20903

Telephone. (301) 439-0551

Institutional Description. The privately supported Roman Catholic school of theology offers graduate programs only. It was formed in 1968 as the Washington Theological Coalition, and represents 7 Roman Catholic groups. Enrollment: 352.

Library Administration. Carol R. Lange, Librarian.

Library General Holdings. 126,000 volumes; 355 periodicals. The seminaries sponsored by diverse religious communities decided to pool their resources and function as one school; these were Augustinian College, Capuchin College, Holy Name College, Holy Trinity Mission, and Whitefriars Hall. The Union is now one of the largest fully-accredited Roman Catholic schools of theology.

Special Collections

The Union Library is located at Holy Trinity Missionary Seminary. Its concern is to support and extend classroom instruction with carefully selected collections of pertinent literature. The library contains basic theological reference works required by the curriculum.

703
Western Maryland College
Hoover Library
Westminster, Maryland 21157

Telephone. (301) 848-7000

Institutional Description. The privately supported liberal arts college was founded in 1867 by the former Methodist Protestant Church. Now independent and nondenominational, it grants baccalaureate and master's degrees. Enrollment: 1,654.

Library Administration. Margaret Woods Denman-West, Senior Librarian.

Library General Holdings. 145,000 volumes; 1,075 current periodical titles; 189,500 government documents; 54,500 microforms.

Special Collections

The Hoover Library maintains the **College Archives** and a collection of rare books. The **Davis Collection** contains historical materials.

Massachusetts

704
American International College
James A. Shea Memorial Library
100 State Street
Springfield, Massachusetts 01109

Telephone. (413) 737-7000

Institutional Description. The privately supported liberal arts and professional college offers programs in teacher education, arts and sciences, business administration, and nursing. Enrollment: 1,873.

Library Administration. F. Knowlton Utley, Librarian.

Library General Holdings. 106,500 volumes; 520 current periodical subscriptions; 12,800 microforms.

Special Collections

An important special collection of the library is the **Garland Library of War and Peace.** Other collections include an education curriculum library for teacher training.

705
Amherst College
Amherst College Library
Amherst, Massachusetts 01002

Telephone. (413) 542-2212

Institutional Description. The privately supported liberal arts college was founded in 1821. Originally a college for men, it is now coeducational. Amherst participates in a five-college cooperative program with Mount Holyoke College, Smith College, Hampshire College, and the University of Massachusetts. Enrollment: 1,554.

Library Administration. Willis E. Bridegam, College Librarian; John Lancaster, Curator of Special Collections; Daria D'Arienzo, Archivist of the College and Special Collections Coordinator.

Library General Holdings. 668,967 volumes; 3,634 serials (of which 2,235 are periodicals); 259,116 microform units; 10,373 music scores (included in total volumes); 38,351 government documents.

Special Collections

Printed Books. Against a background collection representing most aspects of early and modern printing (from incunabula to modern fine printing and small presses), several areas stand out. **The Van Nostrand Theatre Collection** consists of ca. 40,000 acting editions of nineteenth- and twentieth-century plays, chiefly the archival collection of the firm of Samuel French (and its predecessors), joined by many business records of the firm, and a wide range of theatre memorabilia; it is complemented by the **Plimpton Collection** of plays (some 5,000) and the **William Britton Stitt Collection** of the works of Eugene O'Neill (including some manuscript material) and other theatrical authors. English-language poetry of the nineteenth and twentieth centuries is heavily represented with particularly large collections of the Georgian poets (England ca. World War I), Robert Frost, Walt Whitman, James Merrill, Richard Wilbur, Emily Dickinson, Ezra Pound, T. S. Eliot, along with much modern small-press poetry. Important modern fine printing is found in the **Harbor Press Collection** (Roland Wood was a graduate of the College, and gave the Press' own working collection), the Cunningham Press, Ronald Gordon's Oliphant Press (and his work as designer and printer for others), and Francis Fobes' Snail's Pace Press. **The Ralph M. Williams Collection** of eighteenth-century material focuses on Mark Akenside, John Dyer (whose biography Williams wrote), and James Thomson; the Akenside material includes the bulk of the poet's surviving manuscripts. **The John Updike Collection** built by Jack W. C. Hagstrom contains not only a comprehensive run of books by and contributed to by Updike, but a nearly complete collection of his periodical appearances and much ephemera, as well as some manuscripts. Early printing (to 1876) in the town of Amherst and neighboring villages is collected exhaustively. The works of Samuel G. Goodrich ("Peter Parley") are collected in depth, including books published by him, and the many imitations and piracies here and abroad. O.S. Fowler, a graduate of the College, was a partner in the publishing firm of Fowlers and Wells, in which Amherst has an extensive and growing collection. **The Cornelius Howard Patton Collection** of William Wordsworth is comprehensive in scope and extends to many peripheral aspects of Wordsworth's life; manuscript material is included. There are many other smaller but substantial collections.

Manuscripts. Amherst holds the primary collection of papers of Louise Bogan and Richard Wilbur, as well as major collections of the papers of Emily Dickinson, Robert Frost, Rolfe Humphries, and George Bellows. There are many nineteenth-century playscripts and some scores of early twentieth-century musicals among the theatre collections noted below; also ca. 9 linear feet of Augustin Daly promptbooks and several Clyde Fitch manuscripts are included. Ca. 20 pre-1600 manuscripts, both secular and liturgical, are in the collection. Slavic interests are represented by the diaries of Elena Roerich and the Russian émigré collection of George Ivask. In the College Archives, the papers of Dwight Morrow are the most extensive among many papers of alumni and faculty, which include literary figures (Talcott Williams), scientists (Edward Hitchcock), and educators (Alexander Meiklejohn).

706
Andover Newton Theological School
Franklin Trask Library
210 Herrick Road
Newton Centre, Massachusetts 02159

Telephone. (617) 964-1100

Institutional Description. The privately supported theological seminary was founded in 1807 as the Andover Theological Seminary; it merged in 1931 with the Newton Theological Institution which was founded in 1825. It is affiliated with the United Church of Christ and the American Baptist Church. Offering graduate programs only, Andover Newton grants professional, master's, and doctoral degrees. Enrollment: 449.

Library Administration. Ellis E. O'Neal, Jr., Librarian.

Library General Holdings. 206,500 volumes; 560 current periodical titles (not including continuations and publications of learned societies).

Special Collections

The campus library has special collections including the **Bible Collection** of nearly 1,000 volumes given by the American Board of Commissioners for Foreign Missions; a significant collection of Jonathan Edwards manuscripts; and the library of the Backus Historical Society, comprising nearly 5,000 pamphlets, many manuscripts, and church records relating to New England Baptist history. The Department of Pastoral Psychology and Clinical Studies has an excellent collection of both published and unpublished works in the field of analytical psychology.

707
Assumption College
Library
500 Salisbury Street
Worcester, Massachusetts 01609

Telephone. (617) 752-5615

Institutional Description. Assumption College is a privately supported, Roman Catholic liberal arts institution founded (1904) by and conducted under the auspices of the Augustinians of the Assumption. Enrollment: 1,885.

Library Administration. Philippe L. Poisson, Librarian.

Library General Holdings. 172,000 volumes; 1,110 current periodical titles.

Special Collections

The major special collections of the library are the holdings in the **Ecumenical Institute of Religious Studies.**

708
Atlantic Union College
G. Eric Jones Library
South Lancaster, Massachusetts 01561

Telephone. (617) 365-4561

Institutional Description. The privately supported liberal arts college, founded in 1882, is affiliated with the Seventh-day Adventist Church. Enrollment: 617.

Library Administration. Lee Parson, Director of the Library.

Library General Holdings. 101,350 books and bound periodicals; 661 periodical subscriptions; 16 newspaper subscriptions; 6,433 microforms; 22 drawers of pamphlets; 2,202 audiovisual titles; 800 music scores.

Special Collections

African Studies Collection. Includes books on Africa housed in the general stacks.

Ellen G. White Collection. Comprised of books by and about Ellen G. White, one of the founders of the Seventh-day Adventist Church.

Edwin Markham Collection. Includes books from the library of the American poet.

Reavis Reading Area Collection. Includes books and booklets in the field of education provided by the Phi Delta Kappa Foundation.

Music Phonograph Collection. Includes approximately 6,000 phonodiscs of manual recordings covering all periods of music.

Literary Criticism. Extensive holdings of literary criticism on English and American literature, but also includes other European and non-European literature as well.

Women's Studies. Emphasis on women and theology.

Curriculum Materials Center. A separate facility of the Education Department containing textbooks, curriculum materials, and teaching aids in various formats.

Rare Book Collections

Historical Materials Collection Room. Houses a photograph collection and artifacts relating to the history of the college and Seventh-day Adventists.

Oscar R. Schmidt Heritage Room. Houses books, periodicals, microforms, and pamphlet files relating to Seventh-day Adventist history and doctrine. This includes an Ellen G. White collection and faculty thesis and dissertations; included also are scrapbooks of news clippings related to Atlantic Union College, ephemera such as alumni and graduation weekend programs, and other historical material.

Special Collections Room. Houses books, periodicals, pamphlet files, photographs of historical/cultural interest; includes local history, faculty theses and dissertations on non-Seventh-day Adventist topics; selected bound Adult Degree Program units; and other materials.

709
Babson College
Horn Library
Babson Park, Massachusetts 02157

Telephone. (617) 239-4471

Institutional Description. The privately supported college was founded in 1919 as a business school for men; it became coeducational in 1968. It is now a professional institution offering programs of study in business management at both the baccalaureate and graduate levels. Enrollment: 3,180.

Library Administration. James Boudreau, College Librarian; Elizabeth Tate, Rare Books Librarian; Patricia V. Maguire, Assistant Director, User Services.

Library General Holdings. 110,000 volumes; 1,020 periodical and newspaper subscriptions; 233,472 microforms; 64 films; 313 videos; 4,774 slides; 1,411 audiocassettes.

Special Collections

Sailing. The library has a collection of 450 books on sailing given by Edward B. Hinckley, President of Babson Institute, 1946-1956.

Rare Book Collections

Sir Isaac Newton Collection. The core of the collection is a library of over 1,000 volumes, including every important edition (both English and foreign) of Newton's works. Several of these are from Newton's personal library and contain annotations and corrections in his hand. This collection is augmented by biographies of Newton and related scholarly works, autographed manuscripts, portraits, maps, medals, and other Newton memorabilia.

710
Bentley College
Solomon R. Baker Library
Beaver and Forest Streets
Waltham, Massachusetts 02154

Telephone. (617) 891-2000

Institutional Description. The privately supported accounting college was founded in 1917 as the Bentley School of Accounting and Finance. It now grants associate, baccalaureate, and master's degrees. Enrollment: 8,-085.

Library Administration. Sherman L. Hayes, Director.

Library General Holdings. 147,000 volumes; 1,200 periodical subscriptions; 135,000 microforms.

Special Collections

Specialized holdings of the library include microfiche annual 10K reports for over 8,000 companies, a complete collection of college catalogs, a large **Career Collection,** and a collection of historical accounting resources.

711
Berklee College of Music
Library of Berklee College
150 Massachusetts Avenue
Boston, Massachusetts 02115

Telephone. (617) 266-1400

Institutional Description. The privately supported college was founded in 1945. It grants the Bachelor of Music degree in composition, music education, and applied music. The music education program offers teacher certification in Massachusetts. Enrollment: 2,425.

Library Administration. John Voigt, Librarian.

Library General Holdings. 47,485 volumes; 60 periodical subscriptions; 3,000 microforms; 21,000 music scores.

Special Collections

The Music Library contains 16,000 books, primarily in the field of music; recordings of over 5,000 jazz and pop LPs, 1,000 classical LPs, and 2,000 Berklee concerts and recitals. The Library is equipped with 50 reel-to-reel tape decks. Materials are acquired to support the curriculum, as well as to address the needs in the reference, independent study, and recreational reading and listening areas. The Berklee Ensemble Library contains works by noted professional arrangers as well as those by faculty members. All musical styles are represented.

712
Berkshire Christian College
Dr. Linden J. Carter Library
Box 826
94-96 Winter Street
Haverhill, Massachusetts 01240

Telephone. (413) 637-0401

Institutional Description. The privately supported four-year institution is an evangelical Christian College, emphasizing the development of the whole person. Enrollment: 100.

Library Administration. Oral Collins, Acting Librarian.

Library General Holdings. 50,000 (bound volumes, books, periodicals, microforms).

Special Collections

Adventist Collection. The official depository for the Advent Christian denomination; rich in books and periodicals of the nineteenth century Adventist (Millerite) Movement, including complete files of its principal organs and other deposits from the original editorial libraries.

713
Boston Architectural Center
Shaw and Stone Library
320 Newbury Street
Boston, Massachusetts 02115

Telephone. (617) 536-9018

Institutional Description. The privately supported institution specializes in architecture; the program is available in evening classes. Enrollment: 1,361.

Library Administration. Susan Lewis, Head Librarian.

Library General Holdings. 20,000 volumes; 150 periodical titles; collection emphasizes architecture, design, architectural history, solar energy, photography, and graphic design.

Special Collections

The Memorial Library contains 2,000 titles concerning architecture; most titles were published in France, Italy, Germany, and England in the 1800s; most of the items were purchased by architects on the "Grand Tour," in the Beaux Arts tradition.

714
Boston College
John J. Burns Library of Rare Books and Special Collections
140 Commonwealth Avenue
Chestnut Hill
Newton, Massachusetts 02167

Telephone. (617) 552-3282

Institutional Description. Boston College, a privately supported institution, is one of 23 Jesuit colleges and universities in the United States. It has the largest full-time enrollment of any Catholic university in the country. Enrollment: 14,208.

Library Administration. Mary I. Cronin, College Librarian; Robert K. O'Neill, Special Collections/Rare Books Librarian.

Library General Holdings. 987,167 volumes; 117,508 government documents; 1,364,558 microforms; 8,425 audiovisual materials; 10,308 periodical subscriptions. The Burns Library contains over 90,000 books and 3 million manuscripts.

Special Collections

Banking Archives. Archives of several banks, including the Hibernia Savings Bank, the Union Warren, The Provident Institutions for Savings, and the Yankee Bank for Finance and Savings. Also included is the Savings Banks Association of Massachusetts.

Hilaire Belloc Collection and Archives, 1870-1953. The world's most complete assemblage of materials dealing with the British Catholic critic, historian, essayist, journalist, novelist, poet, and politician. Includes his personal library, all published works, and most of his correspondence and manuscripts.

British Catholic Authors. Books, archives, letters, etc. of prominent nineteenth and twentieth century writers: Maurice Baring, George Barker, Robert Hugh Benson, Pamela Frankau, Graham Greene, Ronald Knox, Peter Levi, Cardinal Newman, James Spencer Northcote, Evelyn Waugh, and many others.

Gilbert Keith Chesterton Collection, 1874-1936. Extensive collection of the British writer's books, reviews, drawings, and correspondence.

Citywide Coordinating Council Archives. Complete records of the council formed to desegregate the Boston school system.

The Rev. Robert F. Drinan, S.J. Papers. The collection represents an extensive record of Fr. Drinan's service in the U.S. House of Representatives from 1970 to 1980. He was the first Roman Catholic priest ever elected to Congress.

Fine Print Collection. Representative collections from modern limited press editions: Foulis Press, Golden Cockerel, Nonesuch, Oriole Press (Ishill), Peppercannister, St. Dominic's, and Stanbrook Abbey.

Irish Collection. The collection represents the periods 1790-1810 and 1850-1885. Included also are samplings of the Irish literary renaissance poets and playwrights, such as Seamus Hearney, and writers and private presses of Ireland today.

Rita Kelleher Collection. In recognition of her twenty-five years of service to the School of Nursing, including twenty years as Dean, this collection contains archival, historical, research, and other significant materials in nursing.

Liturgy and Life, 1825-1975. Books, ephemera, and the personal papers of the twentieth century pioneer liturgists documents the life of the Church in American in the pre-Vatican II era.

Meynell Family Collection. Includes correspondence, first editions, and works about the poet Alice Meynell, her publisher husband Wilfred, and their children Francis, the proprietor of the Nonesuch Press, and Viola.

Thomas P. O'Neill, Jr. Papers. Includes the papers and memorabilia of the former Speaker of the U.S. House of Representatives dating from his election to Congress in 1952 to his retirement from politics in 1986. The collection contains extensive correspondence on the American military buildup in Southeast Asia and provides an overview of Democratic party politics over three decades.

Rex Stout Collection and Archives, 1886-1975. Famed creator of the Nero Wolfe mysteries, Stout is represented by his personal manuscripts, correspondence, editions, and secondary sources, together with his own library.

Francis Thompson Collection, 1859-1907. The most complete body of material by Francis Thompson, one of the foremost poets of the British Catholic literary renaissance. Includes autographed manuscripts, 1,500 frames of microfilm of hitherto unknown manuscripts and first editions; also material by and about Coventry Patmore.

Typography and Design. Collection of books, woodblocks, prints, etc. from such artists as Eric Gill, David Jones, Bruce Rogers, and George F. Trenholm.

Nicholas M. Williams Collection. A collection assembled by Joseph Williams, S.J., in honor of his father. The emphasis on Jamaica and its black culture is supplemented by West African roots and South American parallelisms. Includes the Anansi Folktale Archives.

Other special collections include: Maurice Baring Collection; Bookbuilders of Boston Archives; Burns, Oates and Washbourne Collection; Annie Christitch (Christic) papers; Charlotte Louisa Hawkins Dempster Collection; Eleanor Early papers; Eire Society of Boston Archives; Fatherless Children of France Memorial Volume Records; Eric Gill Collection; David Goldstein Papers; Graham Greene Collection; Peter Levi Collection of Papers; Joseph McCarthy Papers; Thomas Merton Collection; Morrisey Collection of Japanese Prints; Music Manuscripts of American Popular Songs; Nonesuch Press Collection; James Spencer Northcote Collection; Bruce Rogers Collection; Salem, Massachusetts, First Church of Christ Library (including the library of John Prince); Joseph Coolidge Shaw Collection; Edith Sitwell Collection; McNiff Collection of Stanbrook Abbey Press; Playbill Collection; George Francis Trenholm Papers; Evelyn Waugh Collection.

Special nursing collections in the O'Neill Library include the Boston College Guild of St. Luke of Boston Health Ethics Collection and the National Health Planning Information Center.

Rare Book Collections

Jesuitana Collection, 1543-1773. Includes rare works dealing with missionary letters written from the Far East in the sixteenth and seventeenth centuries; works of science; and works on Biblical exegis and classical scholarship.

715
Boston Conservatory
Albert Alphin Music Library
8 The Fenway
Boston, Massachusetts 02215

Telephone. (617) 536-6340

Institutional Description. The privately supported conservatory was founded in 1867, and is one of the first such schools to offer professional training in the three performing arts: music, drama, and dance. It awards baccalaureate and master's degrees. Enrollment: 420.

Library Administration. Reginald A. Didham, Director.

Library General Holdings. 40,000 volumes.

Special Collections

The complete works of major composers and a broad representation of minor and contemporary composers are represented through the 1,700 volumes of editions of *Gesamtausgaben,* collections of study scores, performing editions, and sound recordings. Performing editions include repertoire for orchestra, string orchestra, chamber orchestra, concert band, chamber ensembles, stage band, chorus, and solo instruments (notably keyboard and guitar). An extensive collection of opera scores and libretti, including many rare editions, along with scores for *lieder* and art songs, form the vocal repertoire collection. Also housed are the compositions of Boston Conservatory faculty and composition majors, along with Boston Conservatory masters degree theses in music education.

Rare Book Collections

A noteworthy collection is the **Jan Veen-Katrine Amory Hooper Memorial Collection** containing many rare and foreign books on dance and art. Within the dance section, which contains books on dance history, biography, dance forms, and choreography, is a special collection on the subject of dance notation. Represented here is the chronological development of the Sutton Movement Shorthand. Created by former faculty member Valerie Sutton, it is an innovative system of movement notation for dance in use nationally with a broad range of applicability, such as working with the deaf. Visual aids include video tapes of faculty and student choreography and performances, and slides on dance and art history.

716
Boston University
Mugar Memorial Library
121 Bay State Road
Boston, Massachusetts 02215

Telephone. (617) 353-2300

Institutional Description. The privately supported university was founded in 1839 as a theological seminary. By 1874 a wide variety of programs and a graduate school were available. Enrollment: 27,397.

Library Administration. John P. Laucus, University Librarian.

Library General Holdings. 1,500,000 volumes; 26,517 periodicals; 7,000 recordings; 2,063,280 microforms.

Special Collections

The Special Collections Department includes the **Twentieth-Century Archives** which contain the personal papers of over 1,200 public figures in literature, journalism, theatre, film, music, politics, and diplomacy. Among these figures are Martin Luther King, Jr., Bette Davis, Alistair Cooke, Max Ascoli, John W. McCormack, Danilo Dolci, Isaac Asimov, Irwin Shaw, and Rosalyn Tureck. Other collections include materials on Lincoln, Pascal, Franz Liszt, colonial America, military history, nursing, and book arts.

717
Bradford College
College Library
320 South Main Street
Bradford, Massachusetts 01830

Telephone. (617) 372-7161

Institutional Description. The privately supported liberal arts college was founded in 1803. Originally established by the Congregational Church, Bradford is now nondenominational, and grants associate and baccalaureate degrees. Enrollment: 403.

Library Administration. Thomas E. Sweda, Director.

Library General Holdings. 58,200 volumes; 190 current periodical subscriptions.

Special Collections

The library has a strong collection on nineteenth-century history; extensive holdings in Shakespearean criticism, and a collection of Bradfordiana which includes historical materials on Bradford College and alumni.

718
Brandeis University
Brandeis University Libraries
Waltham, Massachusetts 02254

Telephone. (617) 736-4700

Institutional Description. The privately supported nonsectarian university was founded in 1948 by the American Jewish Congregations. Enrollment: 3,476.

Library Administration. Bessie K. Hahn, University Librarian; Charles Cutter, Acting Head, Special Collections.

Library General Holdings. 799,000 volumes (526,397 book titles); 4,176 periodical subscriptions; Music Department houses 16,500 recordings and scores; extensive microform collection.

Special Collections

Spanish Civil War Collection. A multimedia collection of materials relating to the armed conflict in Spain from 1936-1939; included in the collection are 7,000 books and pamphlets and the archives of the Abraham Lincoln Brigade.

Vito Volterra Collection on the History of Science and Mathematics. A collection of more than 5,000 titles in science and mathematics written in the period from the sixteenth to twentieth centuries plus journals and offprints.

Leonardo da Vinci Collection. Consists of over 1,000 volumes dealing with all aspects of da Vinci's life, art, and engineering feats.

Dime Novel and Juvenile Literature Collection. Contains nineteenth and early twentieth century children's literature by such authors as Horatio Alger, Harry Castleman, Oliver Optic; numerous volumes of Dime Novels.

Victor Young Collection. Consists of 39 linear feet of musical manuscripts, phonodiscs, and memorabilia.

In addition, Special Collections houses manuscript materials relating to the works of such noted authors as Irving Wallace, Joseph Heller, Ludwig Lewisohn, and John Cheever. Also, correspondence to Daniel Webster and from Justice Louis D. Brandeis and his wife Alice are housed.

719
Bridgewater State College
Clement C. Maxwell Library
Bridgewater, Massachusetts 02324

Telephone. (617) 697-1200

Institutional Description. The publicly supported (state) liberal arts and teachers college was founded in 1840. It grants baccalaureate and master's degrees. Enrollment: 7,914.

Library Administration. Owen Thomas Paul McGowan, Director.

Library General Holdings. 200,000 volumes; 1,500 periodical subscriptions.

Special Collections

Special collections include an extensive children's collection; the **Theodore Roosevelt Collection** and the **Horatio Alger Collection** (both donated by Dr. Jordan Fiore, Professor of History); a 20,000-volume (ultrafiche) Library of American Civilization; a 6,000-volume (ultrafiche) Library of English Literature; a collection of books by Bridgewater authors; a **Charles Dickens Collection** and a collection of early American textbooks.

720
Cape Cod Community College
Library-Learning Resources Center
Route 132
West Barnstable, Massachusetts 02668

Telephone. (617) 362-2131

Institutional Description. The two-year college began classes in 1961 in the renovated buildings of the former Normal School in downtown Hyannis. In 1970, the college opened on the new campus in West Barnstable. Enrollment: 4,586.

Library Administration. Greg M. Masterson, Director.

Library General Holdings. 51,283 volumes; 475 periodical subscriptions; 23,723 microforms; 14,105 audiovisual materials.

Special Collections

The **Cape Cod History Collection** includes over 5,300 volumes, manuscripts and audio- and videotapes.

721
Clark University
Robert Hutchings Goddard Library
950 Main Street
Worcester, Massachusetts 01610

Telephone. (617) 793-7711

Institutional Description. The privately supported university was established in 1887 as a graduate school. Undergraduate programs were added in 1909. Extensive evening, part-time and graduate programs are available. Enrollment: 3,226.

Library Administration. Susan S. Baughman, University Librarian.

Library General Holdings. 500,000 volumes (including microform volumes); 225,000 monograph titles; 2,300 periodical subscriptions.

Special Collections

The library's special collections include the **Robert H. Goddard Papers** and the **G. Stanley Hall Papers.**

Guy H. Burnham Map and Aerial Photograph Library. One of five federal depositories for maps and charts, the collection consists of over 147,000 maps, charts, atlases, aerial photographs, and globes.

Center for Environment, Technology, and Development (CENTED) Library. A specialized research collection that is coordinated with the University's central library and contains book and reference materials on some 93 technological hazards and subscriptions to 150 journals and newsletters.

722
College of Our Lady of the Elms
Alumnae Library
291 Springfield Street
Chicopee, Massachusetts 10113

Telephone. (413) 598-7561

Institutional Description. The privately supported liberal arts college for women was established in 1928 by the Sisters of Saint Joseph. Enrollment: 909.

Library Administration. Mary E. Brennan, S.S.J., College Librarian; Patricia Bombardier, Special Collections Librarian; Mary E. Gallagher, S.S.J., Rare Books Librarian.

Library General Holdings. 84,375 books; 35 newspaper subscriptions; 66,671 microforms; 19,181 audiovisual materials (includes phonodiscs, audio and video cassettes, kits); 624 periodicals; 34,903 government documents.

Special Collections

Curriculum Library. Provides a collection of textbooks, teachers' materials, audiovisual matter, and tests numbering 4,945 volumes.

Bellamy Collection. Photographs, correspondence, first editions, and other memorabilia of Edward Bellamy (1850-1898).

Fenton Collection. Some of the rare books from his personal library; a small reflection of his lifelong endeavor to build a viable and extensive collection in ecclesiology.

Indian Clay Statues from Chengail, India. Authentic clay artifacts that are more than 60 years old; the clothing represents the occupation of each figure.

Medals and Coinage. Vatican City and Papal State Coins; Franklin Mint; National Museum of History and Technology Medals.

Paralegal Collection. Includes 550 titles, many of which are multivolume sets.

Theology Collection. Contains 9,600 volumes.

Rare Book Collections

Barry Collection. A collection of rare books, dating from 1485 through the 1800s; includes voyages and travel, Latin classics, theology, Johnsoniana.

Ursula Toomey Collection. Framed illuminated manuscripts from the third century B.C. to the fifteenth century.

723
College of the Holy Cross
Dinand Library
1 College Street
Worcester, Massachusetts 01610

Telephone. (617) 793-2011

Institutional Description. The privately supported liberal arts college was founded in 1843. A Roman Catholic institution, it is directed by the Jesuits, and grants baccalaureate and master's degrees. Enrollment: 2,548.

Library Administration. James E. Hogan, Director.

Library General Holdings. 380,000 volumes; 2,400 professional and scholarly journals.

Special Collections

The Special Collections consist of incunabula, sixteenth- and seventeenth-century Jesuitiana, Americana books, Newman letters and first editions, Louise Imogen Guiney correspondence and books, the Senator David I. Walsh and James M. Curley collections, and the Holocaust collection.

724
Curry College
Louis R. Levin Memorial Library
1071 Blue Hill Avenue
Milton, Massachusetts 02186

Telephone. (617) 333-0500

Institutional Description. The privately supported liberal arts and teachers college was founded in 1879. The Perry School for teacher training has become part of the college. Baccalaureate and master's degrees are granted. Enrollment: 1,244.

Library Administration. Catherine B. King, Acting Director.

Library General Holdings. 100,000 books; 1,000 serial title subscriptions.

Special Collections

The library houses the College Media Center, the Curriculum Library and Education Resource Center, the Essential Skills Center, and the Computer Laboratory. The Curriculum Library and Education Center are designed to aid the student of education in field experiences and student teaching, and to provide instructional materials for courses in methods of teaching.

725
Dean Junior College
E. Ross Anderson Library
99 Main Street
Franklin, Massachusetts 02038

Telephone. (617) 528-9100

Institutional Description. The privately supported institution was founded in 1865 by the Universalist Church. Originally known as the Dean Academy, it has operated as a junior college since 1957. Enrollment: 2,354.

Library Administration. Jerald K. Dachs, Head Librarian.

Library General Holdings. 50,000 volumes; 340 periodical subscriptions; 7,500 microform pieces; 22,500 ultrafiche.

Special Collections

Encyclopaedia Britannica Library of Civilization. This is a large collection of early American literature and nonfiction on ultrafiche.

726
Eastern Nazarene College
Nease Library
23 East Elm Avenue
Quinct, Massachusetts 02170

Telephone. (617) 773-6350

Institutional Description. The privately supported liberal arts college grants associate, baccalaureate, and master's degrees. It is affiliated with the Church of the Nazarene. Enrollment: 951.

Library Administration. Susan Watkins, Head Librarian.

Library General Holdings. 105,000 volumes; 620 current periodical subscriptions.

Special Collections

A special collection of the library is the **Gould Library** which contains materials on religion.

727
Emerson College
College Library
100 Beacon Street
Boston, Massachusetts 02116

Telephone. (617) 578-8500

Institutional Description. Emerson College, a privately supported institution, offers a comprehensive undergraduate and graduate curricula in the communication arts and sciences and the performing arts. Enrollment: 2,295.

Library Administration. Michael Ann Moskowitz, Director.

Library General Holdings. 94,000 volumes; 725 current periodical titles; 7,700 microforms; 11,100 audiovisual units.

Special Collections

The **College Archives,** located in the library, house a collection of historical materials relating to Boston theatre and to Emerson College.

728
Emmanuel College
Cardinal Cushing Library
400 The Fenway
Boston, Massachusetts 02115

Telephone. (617) 277-9340

Institutional Description. The privately supported liberal arts college for women was founded in 1919. A Roman Catholic institution, Emmanuel is conducted by the Sisters of Notre Dame de Namur. Enrollment: 958.

Library Administration. Judith K. Ritter, Acting Director.

Library General Holdings. 131,000 volumes; 490 current periodical subscriptions.

Special Collections

The Cardinal Cushing Library offers students the use of extensive reference and circulating collections as well as a periodical room with indices, journals, microfilm, and the Deadline Data on World Affairs.

729
Endicott College
Fitz Memorial Library
376 Hale Street
Beverly, Massachusetts 01915

Telephone. (617) 927-0585

Institutional Description. The privately supported junior college for women offers programs in the liberal and professional arts. Enrollment: 1,047.

Library Administration. Rebecca F. Duschatko, Library Director.

Library General Holdings. 40,000 volumes; 206 periodical subscriptions; microfilm collection.

Special Collections

Wahlstrom Lincoln Library and Museum. A collection of Lincolniana donated to the College by the late Honorable Carl E. Wahlstrom, an early trustee; consists of approximately 1,200 books and 1,700 pamphlets and documents, as well as prints, photographs, statues, medals, stamps, and china devoted to Abraham Lincoln and the Civil War.

730
Episcopal Divinity School
EDS/ Weston Libraries
99 Brattle Street
Cambridge, Massachusetts 02138

Telephone. (617) 868-3450

Institutional Description. The privately supported divinity school was formed in 1974 by a merger of the Philadelphia Divinity School (founded in 1857) and the Episcopal Theological School (founded in 1867). A cooperative relationship exists with Harvard University. Enrollment: 130.

Library Administration. James Warren Dunkly, Director of Libraries.

Library General Holdings. 250,000 volumes; 1,000 periodical titles. The libraries of the Episcopal Divinity School and Weston School of Theology form a single operation under a common staff.

Special Collections

New Testament Abstracts. A Weston enterprise that deposits both its periodical exchanges and its review copies with the library, thus supplying each year virtually all significant international publications in New Testament and related fields.

English Christianity. This field is especially well-served, since the two institutions enrich the whole collection from both Anglican (Episcopal Divinity School) and Catholic (Weston School of Theology) perspectives.

Islam and the Arab World. This Weston special collection includes some 4,000 volumes.

731
Fitchburg State College
College Library
Fitchburg, Massachusetts 01420

Telephone. (617) 345-2151

Institutional Description. The publicly supported state college was established in 1894 as a normal school, became a state teachers college in 1933, and a state college in 1962. It grants baccalaureate and master's degrees. Enrollment: 6,692.

Library Administration. William Casey, Librarian.

Library General Holdings. 152,000 books; 1,170 current periodical titles; 262,000 microfiche.

Special Collections

Special collections include the **College Archives,** the **Robert Cormier Collection,** a children's literature collection of 7,000 volumes, and the **Fitchburg-Leominster Sentinel and Enterprise Collection.**

732
Framingham State College
Henry Whittemore Library
Framingham, Massachusetts 01701

Telephone. (617) 620-1220

Institutional Description. The publicly supported state college was founded in 1839. It features liberal arts and teacher education. Enrollment: 3,258.

Library Administration. Stanley M. McDonald, Jr., Director of Library Services; Sarah Phillips, Special Collections Librarian.

Library General Holdings. 150,000 bound volumes; 1,200 current periodicals; 400,000 microforms.

Special Collections

Special collections include the Curriculum Library and unique materials housed in the Archives and Poetry Rooms.

733
Gordon College
Winn Learning Resources Center
255 Grapevine Road
Wenham, Massachusetts 01984

Telephone. (617) 927-2300

Institutional Description. The privately supported Christian liberal arts college was founded in 1899 as the Boston Bible and Missionary Training School. Now an interdenominational institution, it grants baccalaureate degrees. Enrollment: 1,073.

Library Administration. John Beauregard, Director.

Library General Holdings. 117,000 volumes; 645 current periodical subscriptions; 77,000 government documents; 70,000 microforms; 10,000 audiovisual units.

Special Collections

Specialized collections include the **Vining Rare Book Collection,** the **College Archives,** and a **Temperance Collection.**

734
Gordon-Conwell Theological Seminary
Burton L. Goddard Library
130 Essex Street
South Hamilton, Massachusetts 01982

Telephone. (617) 468-7111

Institutional Description. The privately supported interdenominational theological seminary was formed in 1969 by the merger of Gordon Divinity School and Conwell School of Theology. Enrollment: 864.

Library Administration. Roger R. Nicole, Curator of the Library.

Library General Holdings. 114,000 books and bound periodicals; 1,000 current periodical subscriptions.

Special Collections

The core strength of the Seminary's collection is in Biblical and theological studies and other classic disciplines of theological study. Special emphases in recent years have been given to extending the collection in missiology, Christian social ethics, pastoral psychology and counseling, and preaching/communication arts.

Rare Book Collections

Rare Book Room. This room houses an important collection of Bibles which belonged previously to Roger Babson and the Open Church Foundation. Two other collections are noteworthy: 2,000 Assyro-Babylonian volumes from the personal library of the late Samuel A.B. Mercer and the Edward Payson Vining Collection of rare Bibles, manuscripts and linguistic studies maintained at nearby Gordon College.

735
Greenfield Community College
College Library
One College Drive
Greenfield, Massachusetts 01301

Telephone. (413) 774-3131

Institutional Description. The publicly supported junior college was established in 1962. Enrollment: 2,350.

Library Administration. Margaret E.C. Howland, Library Director and Curator, Archibald MacLeish Collection; Carol G. Letson, Special Collections Librarian.

Library General Holdings. 50,140 volumes; 14,434 units of nonbook materials; 375 periodical subscriptions.

Special Collections

Archibald MacLeish Collection. This collection is the only authorized collection in the world devoted solely to the purpose of advancing the knowledge and understanding of Archibald MacLeish, the man, his life, his works, and his times. It is a private nonprofit research facility housed in the Greenfield Community College Library and contains over 4,000 items including books, periodicals, and manuscripts, oral and visual materials and memorabilia such as his desk and chair, his medals and citations, and his personal library.

Pioneer Valley Resource Center. The PVRC is devoted to the study of all aspects of the Pioneer Valley which is defined as that area surrounding the Connecticut River in Western Massachusetts, and includes Franklin, Hampshire, and Hampden counties. The collection is rich in the areas of art and architecture, economics, geology, and history of the Valley, as well as in local anthropology, folk-life, women's history, and Valley writers. The collection contains 3,000 units of print and nonprint material, including over 2,000 books that are both current and rare (published prior to 1900), oral histories and slide-tape presentations (37), motion pictures and video recordings (15 titles), and the Howes Brothers Photographic Collection of over 20,000 photos on microfilm together with 200 study prints. A vertical file of clippings, booklets, and student papers is available for research, as well as federal census data on Massachusetts. Back issues of local newspapers and periodicals (16 titles) are available in hard copy and on microfilm.

736
Hampshire College
Harold F. Johnson Library Center
West Street
Amherst, Massachusetts 01002

Telephone. (413) 549-4600

Institutional Description. The privately supported liberal arts college was founded in 1970. It was established by a joint effort of Amherst, Mount Holyoke, and Smith Colleges and the University of Massachusetts, all of whom continue an interest in its programs through a consortium. Enrollment: 1,000.

Library Administration. Gai Carpenter, Director.

Library General Holdings. 90,000 volumes; 800 current periodicals; 5,000 microforms; 25,000 audiovisual materials.

Special Collections

The Natural Science Reading Room has a collection of scientific books and periodicals on microbiology, genetics, chemistry, the environment, women in science, energy, and general science. Special collections also include environmental studies, Caribbean literature, and reproductive rights.

737
Harvard University
Houghton Library
Harvard Yard, Harvard University
Cambridge, Massachusetts 02138

Telephone. (617) 495-2114

Institutional Description. The privately supported university was founded in 1636. Enrollment: 24,848.

Library Administration. Ms. Y.T. Feng, Librarian of Harvard College; Lawrence Dowler, Librarian of Houghton Library; Roger E. Stoddard, Curator of Rare Books.

Library General Holdings. 11,000,000 volumes. Harvard is the oldest university in the United States and has the largest university library collection in the world.

Special Collections

Houghton Library, since 1942 the principal center of special collections of Harvard, reflects the instincts, ambitions, and generosities that produced the Harvard Library. Originating in 1639 with John Harvard's gift of some four hundred books, mainly theological in character, the Harvard Library grew in numbers and complexity until it was reduced to basics by the fire of 1764. The way of recovery and growth has ever since been marked out by the names of great collectors, donors, and librarians. Their efforts and successes can be seen, dramatically if only partially, in the books and manuscripts now housed and studied in Houghton.

The scope and significant surprises of the Houghton's collections make it impossible adequately to characterize the library's holdings. A thirteenth-century Japanese kakemono scroll containing a Buddhistic painting on vellum; a sixteenth-century manuscript copy of Chüan 981 of *Yung Lo Ta Tien,* the Chinese encyclopedia; *Inkanyezi yokusa* (Port Natal, 1850), the first periodical in Zulu Kaffir—it is arresting to come upon such finds in Houghton, a library whose strengths are in the study of Western Civilization, but whose scholarly curiosity and appetite reach across the planet.

The following paragraphs suggest only the kinds of material to be found in the stacks of Houghton. For further information, see *Houghton Library: Printed Books and Ephemera* and *Houghton Library: Manuscripts,* (Harvard University Press, n.d.). Information included here was obtained by permission from *Houghton Library: The Collection and Reading Room,* also published by Harvard University.

American History and Literature. In both printed and manuscript materials, Houghton is magnificently rich in material documenting American cultural, social, and political history. The library houses important collections of New England primers and catechisms, works by members of the Mather family, and books owned by Presidents of the United States. There are extensive, if scattered, numbers of colonial and early nineteenth-century American newspapers; a large group of American broadsides; a fully catalogued collection of prints, mainly political cartoons from the nineteenth century; and a large collection of Audubon drawings.

Houghton manuscripts bear on the classic episodes and eras of American history. For the Revolution through the early Republic: the Loammi Baldwin papers; the Dearborn Collection; the Joseph Dennie papers; the correspondence of General William Hull; the Arthur Lee papers; the Sparks collection; the Charles Stewart papers; the William Whipple papers. For the Civil War and its long prelude: the Francis William Bird papers; the correspondence of Robert Carter; the W.W. Clapp papers; the Dearborn Collection; the John Murray Forbes papers; the Manning Ferguson Force papers; the Edward William Hooper papers; the papers of the Garrison family; the

Charles Greely Loring papers; the Charles Lowell Nightingale papers; the John Anthony Quitman papers; the Robert Gould Shaw papers; the Siebert collection on the Underground Railroad; the Charles Sumner papers.

The library has many files of correspondence and diaries of figures in various areas of public enterprise during the nineteenth and twentieth centuries: the artist and naturalist, John James Audubon; the reformer, Dorthea Dix; the churchman, Phillips Brooks; the journalist, railway promoter, and financier, Henry Villard; the newspapermen, E.L. Godkin and Lewis Stiles Gannett; Theodore Roosevelt (and the records of the Progressive Party); David Franklin Houston, Secretary of Agriculture and Secretary of the Treasury under Wilson; and the politician and statesman, Christian Herter. For American diplomacy, there are important manuscripts by or pertaining to Joel Barlow, William R. Castle, Ellis Loring Dresel, W. Cameron Forbes, Roger Sherman Green, Joseph Grew, William Jones Hoppin, Abbott Lawrence, William Woodville Rockhill. The experiences of Americans abroad in America are preserved in travel accounts, diaries, and letters home. The magician's world is documented in papers of Harry Houdini; the publisher's, in the Ticnor and Fields/ Houghton Mifflin records; the sailor's, in the log books of American whaling ships; the airport engineer's, in the S.S. Hanks papers.

Aspects of American intellectual and academic life are preserved in the papers of Scott Buchanan, Francis James Child, the Dante Society, J.T. Fields, William James, John Livingston Lowes, F.O. Matthiessen, C.E. Norton, Arthur Stanley Pease, C.S. Pierce, George Sarton, and F.R. Wulsin. For modern American architecture, the papers of Walter Gropius and the papers and drawings of H.H. Richardson are important. The names Gropius, Sarton, and Jaeger point up another subject of the Houghton collections—the continuing Europeanization of American thought, the latest episode in the scurrying of the learned westwards, a theme rich with Polybian and Byzantine echoes.

The papers of the American Board of Commissioners for Foreign Missions, a heavily used archive that is important across many disciplines within American studies, provide testimony on the American Indian, the Near East and Far East, Africa, and the Sandwich islands. The Papers record American encounters with the peoples of such areas and the response of the latter to Americans. These materials are of the first importance for nineteenth- and twentieth-century American social, cultural, diplomatic, religious, and ecclesiastical history.

Houghton has many collections of photographs—for example, those that supplement the James Family and John Reed papers. There are extensive collections of Civil War photographs and a set of *The North American Indian* by Edward S. Curtis, which contains 1,500 photographs of American tribal life.

Houghton is strong in Canadiana, especially from the period of Canada's early settlement. The stacks hold a nearly complete run of Jesuit *Relations;* a collection of material relating to Canadian local history; the **Chadenat Collection** on the history of New France; the James Wolfe papers, which relate to the British conquest of Canada. For more recent times, the library possesses the papers of Joseph Howe, the nineteenth-century Canadian statesman.

Latin America is covered by some important collections: The **Radepont Collection** of material for the years 1850-1864 pertaining to the French expedition to Mexico; the Escoto Papers, which relate to the history of Cuba; a collection of seventeenth- and eighteenth-century ecclesiastical treatises, encyclicals, bulls, and proclamations, partly in manuscript, relating to the Spanish colonies, chiefly Mexico and Peru; and a collection of papers relating to Haiti for the years 1784-1830.

To place the works of T.S. Eliot at one end of a shelf and those of Richard Harding Davis at the other is to set an image of the range of Houghton's collections in the literature of America—bedrock collections for serious research into the lives and works of many authors. In addition to printed editions, the library has major holdings of manuscript materials, particularly of the classic writers of New England, and it possesses personal libraries of many authors. Among large collections of papers of American writers: Bronson Alcott, Louisa May Alcott, Edward Bellamy, Gamaliel Bradford, John Mason Brown, Witter Bynner, e.e. cummings, Emily Dickinson, T.S. Eliot, Ralph Waldo Emerson, Margaret Fuller, John Hawkes, Oliver Wendell Homes, William D. Howells, Alice James, Henry James, William James, Sarah Orne Jewett, Edward Knoblock, Henry Wadsworth Longfellow, James Russell Lowell, Amy Lowell, Robert Lowell, Herman Melville, Edward Arlington Robinson, Richard Jay Selig, Robert Sherwood, L.E. Sissman, John Updike, Jones Very, John Greenleaf Whittier, and Thomas Wolfe. The **New Directions Collection** includes manuscripts of American, British, and continental writers of the twentieth century.

The Early Period. In addition to collections of ostraca and papyri, Houghton possesses over a thousand manuscripts from the period before 1600. Among the oldest and most noteworthy is a ninth-century manuscript in Carolingian minuscule that includes commentaries on Scripture by Jerome, Augustine, and Gregory the Great, as well as a life of Jerome by Sebastian of Monte Casino. Many manuscripts, especially from the fourteenth and fifteenth centuries, are illuminated. The **Riant Collection** is particularly striking for items, manuscript and printed, relating to the history of the Crusades and to life and travel in the Near East.

Harvard's 2,600 incunabula, most of which are housed in Hougton, document the earliest history of western printing and are the very stuff and substance of modernity, products of the intersection of new technology with old and new intellectual traditions. *Editiones principes* of Greek authors and many works of science suggest the fifteenth-century riches preserved in this collection.

English History and Literature. Harvard's collection of early English printed books to 1640 ("STC" books) is one of the major such collections in the United States. Some of the books are unique copies, many others the only copies in this country. Most of these Harvard books are housed in Houghton. Though especially strong in literary works of the late sixteenth and early seventeenth centuries, Houghton also has good depth in religious, historical, and scientific publications, as well as in many other areas of English Renaissance life and culture. The **Bute Collection of Broadsides** covers the period of English history from 1560 to 1748.

For the period of the Civil War and Commonwealth, there is a very strong gathering of pamphlets, broadsides, and newspapers. The Orrery Papers tell much of eighteenth-century England's culture, finances, and relations with the Continent. They also cast light on the state of Ireland. The White Family Papers deal with Gilbert White of Selborne (1720-1793).

For the nineteenth century, there are the following indexed collections: The **Tegg Caricatures** collection; the papers of Lord Nelson and Lady Hamilton; the journals and correspondence of Benjamin Robert Haydon; and The **John F. Glaser Collection** of historical autograph letters and manuscripts. Drawings and books by Cruikshank and Rowlandson (many of which are in the **Harry Elkins Widener Collection** report on the mores and matérialités of society. The Upcott-Evelyn-Pepys papers cover parts of the seventeenth, eighteenth, and nineteenth centuries.

Sidney, Donne, Herbert, Johnson, Blake, Shelley, Thackeray, George MacDonald, Lewis Carroll, Henry Kingsley, Conrad, Masefield—much longer would be the list that approximately suggested the scope of the library's printed and manuscript holdings in the field of English literature. Houghton collections are critical to research into several authors, including the following: Keats, Tennyson, Coleridge, Edward Lear, Lewis Carroll, T.E. Lawrence, and Max Beerbohm. Special mention should be made of over three hundred books owned and annotated by Thomas Carlyle for his research on Cromwell and Frederick the Great, as well as of a twenty-eight volume set of the *Oeuvres* of Voltaire, which Carlyle borrowed and also annotated. For the late nineteenth century and the first decades of this century, the Rohtenstein Papers preserve a large amount of literary correspondence.

European History. Evidence of the beliefs, ideas, and politics that made for energy and restlessness in modern Europe survive in Houghton Books and manuscripts. Editions of Thomas à Kempis and Machiavelli are particularly impressive examples, as are collections of Neo-Latin literature and works of the New Learning. The Reformation—impulses to advance, to avoid, and to counter it—is documented in editions of Luther, Erasmus, More, Sadoleto, and others.

The acrimony and acrobatics of continental public life following the sixteenth-century reshuffling of certainties and allegiances are richly suggested in a large collection of seventeenth-century French Civil War tracts (the Mazarinades), in material from the pamphlet war of Jansenists and Jesuits during the same century, and in printed and manuscript materials from a collection of French civil and ecclesiastical trials of the seventeenth and eighteenth centuries. Mirabeau manuscripts reflect France on the eve and during the first years of revolution. Published proclamations of the government offer official glimpses of the Revolution in power and in action. The life of revolutionary times also appears in religious tracts of the period. The manuscript journal of the Russian general Michael Andreas Barclay de Tolly gives one angle of vision on the campaign of 1812. The aftermath of revolution shows through the Houghton collection of *European Prints and Drawings of the Eighteenth and Nineteenth Centuries,* many of which comment on the Napoleonic enterprise and fate. The researches and writings of François Alphonse Aulard fix a steadier, more reflective gaze on the ways of revolution.

Other collections recall other scenes of the century: a collection of 1848 Austrian revolutionary ephemera; manuscripts and printed documents from the Paris Commune of 1871; seventeen bound volumes of photographs dealing with the siege and ruins of Paris in 1870-71 and one volume showing the siege of Strasbourg; and an extensive collection of manuscripts, printed books, and ephemera produced by the Dreyfus Affair. Related to the latter, but in fact spanning much of modern European history, is the **Lee M. Friedman Collection of Judaica.** Of similarly wide range, extending from the fifteenth to the nineteenth centuries in its coverage, is The **Leichtenstein Collection** of engraved maps. The papers of Fernando Palha cover several centuries of Portuguese history.

A group of twentieth century manuscripts in the **My Life in Germany Collection** describes daily life at the turn from Weimar to Hitlerian Germany. The roots and results of revolution, one of the great topical strengths of Houghton, are clearly documented in other nineteenth- and twentieth-century materials: the papers of the Second International; the archives of the Republic of Georgia; the papers of John Reed; a collection of Russian revolutionary ephemera; the correspondence of Feliks Vadimovich Volkhovskii; the Rev. J.J. Yarkovsky collection of material on the Czech legion in Siberia during World War I; the documents of the Sokolov Investigation of the assassination of the Russian imperial family; the papers of Leon Trotsky; and ephemera from the ephemeral resuscitation of civic life in Czechoslovakia before and during the spring of 1968 and from the more recent doings of Solidarity in Poland.

European Literature. Most of the classic authors of continental literature are represented in strong collections of printed editions. Impressive representatives of national literatures are works of Dante and Machiavelli, CamÓks and Cervantes, Montaigne, Molière, Bossuet, Pascal, Restif de la Bretonne, Jules Verne, Heine, Rilke, and Hofmannsthal. **The Kilgour Collection** brings together important examples of Russian belles lettres from the eighteenth century to the twentieth.

In the manuscript collections, the German holdings are important: The **W.R. Schweizer Collection of German Literary Autographs;** manuscripts of Heine, Brecht, and Rilke; the papers of Hofmannsthal and Beer-Hofmann. Iberian letters are represented by the holograph of Benito Pérez Galdós's *Fortunata y Jacinta* (a manuscript of over 4,000 pages) and the papers of Pedro Salinas and Jorge Guillén. There are important individual manuscripts and small collections of manuscripts of the classic French authors, particularly of the nineteenth and twentieth centuries. Finally, papers of Antoine Henri Becquerel, Franz Brentano, J.F.W. Herschel, Werner Jaeger, and George Sarton provide suggestive tracks through the modern history of philosophy, scholarship, and science.

Printing and Graphic Arts. The Department of Printing and Graphic Arts concentrates on illustrated books, fine printing, and illuminated and calligraphic manuscripts. Particular strengths are illustrated books of sixteenth-century England and France, and *livres de peintres* of the twentieth century. The collection includes a large group of type specimen books, a section of writing manuals, and a section of press books. Two special collections are landscape watercolors, nonsense drawings, and books by Edward Lear and architectural drawings by H.H. Richardson and his firm. A special field of emphasis is drawings for book illustration, with a large collection of western European and American examples from the seventeenth century to the twentieth century.

Harvard Theatre Collection. This collection, founded in 1901, is housed in Pusey Library. The collection encompasses all aspects of the history of performance throughout the world, especially the English and American stage and the history of dance. The areas of cinema and popular entertainment, such as fairground, circus, minstrel, and vaudeville, also are well represented. In addition to manuscripts, printed books, journals, and newsclippings, the collection is estimated to contain over three million playbills and programs, about 650,000 photographs, 250,000 engraved portraits and scenes, 15,000 scenery and costume designs, and nearly 5,000 promptbooks, in addition to manuscripts, printed books, journals, and newsclippings.

738
Hebrew College
Jacob and Rose Grossman Library
43 Hawes Street
Brookline, Massachusetts 02146

Telephone. (617) 232-8710

Institutional Description. The privately supported college offers Judaic studies. It was founded in 1921. Enrollment: 219.

Library Administration. Maurice S. Tuchman, Director of Library Services and Special Collections Librarian; Shalva Siegel, Rare Books Librarian.

Library General Holdings. 90,000 volumes; 250 periodical subscriptions; 2,500 microforms; 600 phonograph records; 250 cassettes, filmstrips, games, kits, realia, and slides; 100 maps and charts. The collection is divided mainly between Hebrew and English (43% in English, 42% in Hebrew, 15% spread among German, French, Yiddish, and Russian).

Special Collections

The library has the following specialized collections: **Harry A. and Beatrice C. Savitz Jewish Medical Ethics Collection** of 1,000 items; **Herman and Peggy Vershbow Pedagogic Center** with 2,500 items in Jewish education (curriculum guides, student textbooks, teachers guides); large print books of Jewish interest (100 items); and the **Dr. Gerald Wohlberg Middle East and Israeli Affairs** collection of 5,000 items.

Rare Book Collections

The library has a Rare Books and Manuscript Collection in Hebrew and Jewish studies. The great majority of the items are in the fields of Rabbinics, Bible, Hassidism and Kabbalah, Jewish history, and Jewish and Hebrew literature.

Among the rare books are two incunabula: a Hebrew commentary on the Biblical books of Judges and Samuel I and II published in 1485 and Maimonides commentary on the *Tractate Avot,* published in 1492.

The Library contains some 200 items from the sixteenth century, 250 items from the seventeenth century, and 800 items from the eighteenth century and later. Included in the later books in the rare book collection are autographed copies of works by noted Jewish political and literary figures. The Library also has 72 manuscripts, the great bulk being in the field of Rabbinics, Bible, Hassidism, and Kabbalah. The oldest manuscript dates from the late fourteenth century. Included in the manuscript collection is a DP newspaper (Displace Persons) written in 1946 in the DP camps of Europe. Almost all of the manuscripts are in Hebrew.

739
Lesley College
Main Library
29 Everett Street
Cambridge, Massachusetts 02238

Telephone. (617) 868-9600

Institutional Description. The privately supported teachers college for women grants associate, baccalaureate, and master's degrees. The graduate school is coeducational. Enrollment: 3,762.

Library Administration. James J. Slattery, Director of Libraries.

Library General Holdings. 72,000 volumes; 530 current periodical titles; 90,000 microforms.

Special Collections

Elementary education, psychology, special education, and art therapy are particular areas of strength in the library. The Kresge Center, a center for teaching resources, contains juvenile books, teaching aids, instructional kits, recordings, films, tapes, and other materials designed for use with children. It is considered one of the best collections of its kind in the northeastern United States.

740
Massachusetts College of Art
College of Art Library
621 Huntington Avenue
Boston, Massachusetts 02115

Telephone. (617) 232-1555

Institutional Description. The publicly supported (state) teachers and professional college was founded in 1873 as the Massachusetts Normal School of Art. It grants baccalaureate and master's degrees. Enrollment: 3,330.

Library Administration. George Morgon, Librarian.

Library General Holdings. 85,000 volumes; 450 current periodical subscriptions; 65,000 slides; 525 films; 150 videotapes.

Special Collections

The holdings of the library include special collections on early art education in the United States and the history of the College.

741
Massachusetts College of Pharmacy and Allied Health Sciences
Sheppard Library
179 Longwood Avenue
Boston, Massachusetts 02115

Telephone. (617) 732-2800

Institutional Description. The privately supported college was founded in 1823 and now offers associate, baccalaureate, master's, and doctorate degree programs. Enrollment: 1,161.

Library Administration. Mark J. Gazillo, Pharmacy Librarian.

Library General Holdings. 64,000 volumes; 688 current periodical subscriptions; 6,000 microforms.

Special Collections

The Sheppard Library acts as a pharmaceutical information center for students, faculty, alumni and health scientists, particularly pharmacists, physicians, nurses, and other persons in the community with a serious scientific purpose. Books, journals, pamphlets, and audiovisual materials are acquired in such subject areas as medicinal chemistry, all phases of pharmacy, drug composition, drug abuse, medicinal and poisonous plants, administration of community and hospital pharmacies, and pharmaceutical statistics. The library houses and cooperates with the New England Drug Information Service.

742
Massachusetts Institute of Technology
The Libraries, MIT
Institute Archives and Special Collections
14N-118 MIT
Cambridge, Massachusetts 02139

Telephone. (617) 253-5136

Institutional Description. The privately supported science-based university was founded in 1861. It is organized into five schools and one college. Enrollment: 9,577.

Library Administration. Jay K. Lucker, Director, MIT Libraries; Helen W. Samuels, Head, Institute Archives and Special Collections; Kathy Marquis, Reference Archivist.

Library General Holdings. 2,000,000 volumes; 21,200 current periodicals; 1,500,000 microforms; 1,151,000 audiovisual materials.

Special Collections

Institute Archives. The Archives collects and preserves records which document MIT's history and the people who have been a part of that history. It gathers unpublished material including the official records of the Institute, personal and professional papers of the faculty, staff, and students, published material about the Institute, and MIT theses and technical reports. The collections chronicle the founding and growth of the five school and their course. The Archives houses significant material about MIT's programs in architecture, management, and humanities. The development of science and engineering education and research is particularly well documented.

The Institute Archives includes material revealing the Institute's wide role in contemporary society. The Archives has a strong interest in documenting the evolution of modern science and engineering and its impact on society. The papers of Norbert Wiener, Robert J. Van de Graaff, the Magnetic Core Memory (Whirlwind) Project, and the Recombinant DNA History Collection are rich resources in this area. Emphasis has also been placed on the role of scientists and engineers in the formation of science policy. Diverse contributions are illustrated by the papers of Karl T. Compton, Vannevar Bush, James R. Killian, Jr., Jerome B. Wiesner, Frank Press, Carroll Wilson, Bernard T. Field, and many other faculty members who have served the government or taken public stands on science issues. The activities of private organizations are represented by such collections as the records of the Union of Concerned Scientists and the Citizens League Against the Sonic Boom.

Rare Book Collections

Rare Books. Included in the MIT Libraries Special Collections are rare books, pamphlets, prints, and photographs. Notable are the Vail Collection which contains many early works on telecommunications, electricity, ballooning, aeronautics, and animal magnetism. The Gaffield Collection on glass and glassmaking and the Bryant, Clark and Forbes Collections on early navigation and shipbuilding are also included. The Derr and I. Austin Kelly Collections contain significant monuments of science, technology, and printing; and the Baldwin Collection contains works on nineteenth-century civil engineering. The William Barton Rogers Collection comprises the personal library of MIT's founder. The Roman Jacobson Collection on Linguistics is also maintained.

743
Montserrat College of Art
Paul M. Scott Library
Dunham Road, Box 62
Beverly, Massachusetts 01915

Telephone. (617) 922-8222

Institutional Description. Montserrat College of Art is a privately supported four-year professional school, granting baccalaureate degrees and diplomas. Enrollment: 112.

Library Administration. Gordon B. Arnold, Library Director.

Library General Holdings. 12,000 print items including books, periodicals, catalogues, exhibition announcements, manuscript materials, art reproductions; slide collection of approximately 14,000 slides.

Special Collections

A significant portion of the library's holdings is comprised of a specialized collection of books, slides, and periodicals in the field of visual arts, including such areas as contemporary art, graphics, photography, and art history.

Paul M. Scott Manuscripts and Papers. The library houses the papers and manuscripts of the late artist/art educator Paul M. Scott. Included in the collection are many teaching materials developed by Mr. Scott.

744
Mount Holyoke College
Williston Memorial Library
South Hadley, Massachusetts 01075

Telephone. (413) 538-2000

Institutional Description. The privately supported liberal arts college for women was founded in 1836, and as such is one of the oldest continuing institutions of higher learning for women in the country. Enrollment: 1,996.

Library Administration. Anne Carey Edmonds, College Librarian.

Library General Holdings. 503,367 volumes; 1,834 periodical subscriptions.

Special Collections

The library maintains a special collection on the history of Mount Holyoke College and the College Archives.

Dante Collection. This collection includes illustrated editions of Dante's *Divine Comedy.*

745
New England College of Optometry
College Library
424 Beacon Street
Boston, Massachusetts 02115

Telephone. (617) 266-2030

Institutional Description. The privately supported professional college of optometry was founded as the Klein School of Optics in 1894. It now grants the degrees Bachelor of Science in Optometry, Doctor of Optometry, Doctor of Ocular Science, and Doctor of Humane Letters. Enrollment: 382.

Library Administration. F. Eleanor Warner, Head Librarian.

Library General Holdings. 8,760 volumes; 215 current periodical titles.

Special Collections

The library houses an extensive collection of materials relating to vision care in both print and nonprint materials.

746
New England Conservatory
Harriet M. Spaulding Library
33 Gainsborough Street
Boston, Massachusetts 02178

Telephone. (617) 262-1120

Institutional Description. The privately supported conservatory of music offers the diploma as well as undergraduate and graduate degrees. Enrollment: 741.

Library Administration. Jean Morrow, Director of

Libraries.

Library General Holdings. 60,000 volumes of music scores and books; 250 current periodical titles; 18,000 sound recordings. The Idabelle Firestone Audio Library is located at 290 Huntington Avenue in Boston.

Special Collections

John A. Preston Collection. Nineteenth-century letters (including some by Beethoven, Berlioz, Liszt, Mendelssohn, Schumann, and Wagner).

"Voice of Firestone" Collection. Includes instrumental and vocal arrangements, recordings, and kinescopes from radio and television broadcasts, sponsored by the Firestone Tire and Rubber Company from 1928 to 1958.

Vaughn Monroe Collection. Contains orchestrations and recordings.

New England Conservatory Concert Tape Collection. Contains tapes of all New England Conservatory faculty recitals.

Other various collections include eighteenth-century books on singing, psalmody, and glees; autographed manuscript scores and parts by the "Boston classicists" (e.g., Edward Ballantine, Amy Beach, Frederick Converse, George Chadwick, Arthur Foote); manuscript works for saxophone commissioned between 1901 and 1914 by Elise Coolidge Hall, including holographs by Charles M. Loeffler, Andé Caplet, and Claude Debussy.

747
Nichols College
Library
Dudley, Massachusetts 01570

Telephone. (617) 943-1560

Institutional Description. The privately supported business college was founded in 1815. An all-male college until 1972, it grants associate, baccalaureate, and master's degrees. Enrollment: 1,655.

Library Administration. Cheryl S. Nelson, Library Director.

Library General Holdings. 67,000 volumes; 460 current periodical subscriptions.

Special Collections

The library maintains the Nichols Academy and Nichols College Archives. Also available are video recordings of the Institute of American Values Symposia. The Institute provides a forum for the free exchange of ideas.

748
North Adams State College
Eugene Lawrence Freel Library
Church Street
North Adams, Massachusetts 01247

Telephone. (413) 664-4511

Institutional Description. The publicly supported teachers college was founded in 1894 as the State Normal School. It now grants baccalaureate and master's degrees. Enrollment: 505.

Library Administration. Gary Lewis, Director of Library Services.

Library General Holdings. 146,000 volumes; 694 current journals and newspapers; 200,000 units of microtext.

Special Collections

The Special Collections Room houses materials on the Northern Berkshire area of Massachusetts. The Teacher Resources Center contains 9,000 items including a file of standardized tests.

749
Northeastern University
Dodge Library
360 Huntington Avenue
Boston, Massachusetts 02115

Telephone. (617) 437-2000

Institutional Description. The privately supported university, founded in 1898, seeks innovative ways to meet community needs through educational programs. One such program is cooperative education, whereby students work outside the academic environment during alternate terms in fields allied with their majors, and receive academic credit. Enrollment: 39,191.

Library Administration. Alan R. Benenfeld, Dean and Director.

Library General Holdings. 546,000 volumes; 4,000 periodical and newspaper subscriptions; 250,000 government documents.

Special Collections

The University Libraries include seven facilities of which Dodge Library, on the Boston campus, is the main library. Dodge houses the materials that support the University's programs in the humanities, social sciences, fine arts, education, engineering, criminal justice, nursing, business, and at the undergraduate level, in the sciences.

Important special collections of the library include the **John A. Volpe Collection;** the **Glen Gray Collection;** and the **Horace Mann Collection.** A special collection on international aspects of higher education is housed in the Center for International Higher Education Documentation (CIHED). The CIHED collection is unique to the Boston area.

University Archives. Serves as a depository for the historical records of the University. Faculty publications as well as student yearbooks, newspapers, and Northeastern dissertations are also housed in the Archives.

750
Radcliffe College
Arthur and Elizabeth Schlesinger Library
Cambridge, Massachusetts 02138

Telephone. (617) 495-8637

Institutional Description. The privately supported liberal arts college for women was founded in 1879. It is an affiliate of Harvard University and its classes are taught by the Harvard Faculty of Arts and Sciences. Radcliffe's students are students of Harvard University.

Library Administration. Patricia Miller King, Director.

Library General Holdings. 25,000 volumes.

Special Collections

History of Women in America. The Schlesinger Library maintains a collection covering the history of women in America. The major emphasis is on the period from 1800 to the present. There are more than 560 manuscript collections which document virtually all of women's contribution to American life. Also maintained are the records of the National Organization for Women, the Women's Equity Action League, and the Association of Commissions on Women. There are more than 25,000 books covering the same area as the manuscript collections and also including an outstanding collection of cookbooks.

751
Regis College
Regis College Library
235 Wellesley Street
Weston, Massachusetts 02193

Telephone. (617) 893-1820

Institutional Description. The privately supported liberal arts college for women provides a Catholic education. Founded in 1927, it is conducted by the Congregation of the Sisters of Saint Joseph of Boston, and is affiliated with the Catholic University of America. Enrollment: 1,240.

Library Administration. Elizabeth L. Keenan, Director of the Library.

Library General Holdings. 129,000 volumes; 802 periodical subscriptions; 7,000 units of microfilm; 12,800 units of microfiche; 3,100 phonodiscs and cassettes.

Special Collections

Cardinal John Henry Newman Collection. Includes the writings by and about Cardinal Newman, numbering 2,500 volumes and including five manuscript letters of the Cardinal and one manuscript letter of Cardinal Henry E. Manning.

Education Curriculum Collection. Contains approximately 3,700 items, including textbooks, children's and young adult literature, curriculum materials, and kits.

752
St. Hyacinth College and Seminary
Kolbe Memorial Library
66 School Street
Granby, Massachusetts 01033

Telephone. (413) 467-7191

Institutional Description. The privately supported college and seminary for men prepares students for training for the Roman Catholic priesthood. Conducted by the Order of Friars Minor Conventual, it grants baccalaureate degrees. Enrollment: 41.

Library Administration. Brother Christian M. Katusz, Librarian.

Library General Holdings. 57,000 volumes; 165 current periodical subscriptions.

Special Collections

Special collections include Franciscan works; books, articles, and memorabilia relating to Saint Maximilian Kolbe; and a collection of Polish materials and pre-1800 volumes.

753
Salem State College
College Library
352 Lafayette Street
Salem, Massachusetts 01907

Telephone. (617) 741-6000

Institutional Description. The publicly supported state liberal arts and professional college was founded in 1854. It offers a wide variety of professional and liberal arts programs, granting baccalaureate and master's degrees. Enrollment: 8,654.

Library Administration. Neil B. Olson, Director.

Library General Holdings. 200,000 volumes; 1,100 current periodical titles.

Special Collections

There is a special collection of nineteenth-century textbooks. The library also maintains the papers of Representative Michael Harrington.

754
School of the Museum of Fine Arts
Library
230 The Fenway
Boston, Massachusetts 02115

Telephone. (617) 267-9300

Institutional Description. The privately supported professional art school awards diplomas and certificates, and, in affiliation with Tufts University, grants baccalaureate and master's degrees. Enrollment: 602.

Library Administration. Carol Bjork, Librarian.

Library General Holdings. 9,500 volumes; 83 current periodical subscriptions.

Special Collections

The library maintains a collection of 66,000 slides on art of the twentieth century.

755
Simmons College
Simmons College Libraries
300 The Fenway
Boston, Massachusetts 02115

Telephone. (617) 738-3141

Institutional Description. The privately supported college for women accepts men into its graduate programs only. It was chartered in 1899 and is nonsectarian. Enrollment: 3,138.

Library Administration. Artemis Kirk, Director of Libraries; Megan Suiffin-Marinoff, College Archivist/Special Collections Librarian.

Library General Holdings. 225,000 volumes (includes 31,000 bound periodicals); 1,762 periodical subscriptions; 1,232 microfilm units; 1,498 media items. The Archives houses 1,500 linear feet of records, papers, and photographs and 4,000 volumes of rare books.

Special Collections

Colonel Miriam E. Perry Goll Archives. Established in 1974 to collect, preserve, and organize materials which reflect the history and development of Simmons College; named for the late Colonel Goll (Simmons College 1930) who led a long and distinguished career in the field of dietetics in the Armed Forces (Col. Goll was the first dietitian to achieve the rank of Colonel in the U.S. Air Force); collection includes a photograph collection of approximately 50,000 images.

Historical Book Collections. The historical book collections at Simmons College reflect the strong professional orientation of the college curriculum. Represented are mostly nineteenth and twentieth century works relating to public health nursing, social welfare, children's literature, household economics, and the history of the book. The **Knapp Collection of Early Children's Books** contains over 1,200 nineteenth-century and early twentieth-century juvenile books by American, English, and some European authors such as Jacob Abbot, Juliana Horatia Ewing, Louisa May Alcott, Martha Finley, and Horatio Alger. The runs of *Saint Nicholas* and *Youth's Companion* are typical of periodicals also found in the collection. The **Donald Moreland and Robert Ramsey Collections** of late eighteenth, nineteenth, and early twentieth century European and American works include the topics of philanthropy, slum life and poverty, child labor and welfare, medical care of the mentally ill, crime, and slavery. The **Boston Children's Aid Society Annual Report Collection** contains annual reports of private charities, public welfare agencies, and hospitals throughout Boston and Massachusetts dating from 1826.

Social Work Collection. The largest portion of the Simmons College Archives' holdings, approximately forty percent, documents the development of the social work profession in general, in addition to the educational activities, professional work, and personal lives of the faculty and students of The Simmons College School of Social Work, the first academically affiliated school of social work in the United States.

Horn Book Collection. Includes the historical records of *The Horn Books,* the first magazine published with a concern entirely for children's books and reading; the records on deposit include correspondence, illustrations, manuscripts, photographs, scrapbooks, and printed material dating from 1916.

756
Simon's Rock of Bard College
Library
Alford Road
Great Barrington, Massachusetts 01230

Telephone. (413) 528-0771

Institutional Description. The privately supported liberal arts college was founded in 1966. It is affiliated with Bard College of Annandale-on-Hudson, New York, and grants associate and baccalaureate degrees. Enrollment: 305.

Library Administration. David Tipple, Head Librarian.

Library General Holdings. 53,000 volumes; 350 current periodical titles; 11,000 microforms.

Special Collections

The library houses three special collections. The **Adolf A. Berle Collection,** from the library of one of the twentieth century's most influential scholars and public servants, was donated to Simon's Rock by his widow in 1977. A collection of books related to Black history and the Black experience is dedicated to historian and sociologist W.E.B. DuBois, who grew up in Great Barrington. The **Bernard Krainis Collection of Early Chamber Music,** includes fifteenth- to seventeenth-century musical scores.

757
Smith College
William Allan Neilson Library
Northampton, Massachusetts 01063

Telephone. (413) 584-2700

Institutional Description. The privately supported liberal arts college for women was founded in 1875. Its graduate school is coeducational. Enrollment: 2,485.

Library Administration. Billie Rae Bozone, College Librarian.

Library General Holdings. 978,415 volumes; 3,033 periodicals; 150,296 microforms; 70,360 photos and facsimiles; 44,861 recordings and tapes.

Special Collections

Sophia Smith Collection. This collection is a women's history archive and includes materials on Margaret Sanger and the Garrison Family.

Rare Book Collections

Rare Book Room. This collection of over 15,000 books, manuscripts, and ephemera includes the works of Sylvia Plath, Virginia Woolf, and early lithography.

758
Southeastern Massachusetts University
Library Communications Center
Old Westport Road
North Dartmouth, Massachusetts 02747

Telephone. (617) 999-8675

Institutional Description. The publicly supported university was created in 1960 as the Southeastern Massachusetts Technological Institute. Enrollment: 5,618.

Library Administration. Janet Freedman, Dean of Library Services; Helen Koss, Special Collections/Rare Books Librarian; Bruce Barnes, Collection Development Librarian.

Library General Holdings. 300,000 volumes; 2,500 periodical subscriptions; extensive audiovisual and microform holdings.

Special Collections

Robert F. Kennedy Assasination Archives. This collection is the national focal point for the release of government documents concerning this tragic historical event. Under the Freedom of Information Act, the Archive has collected 100,000 pages of formerly sealed Federal and California files on this case. The collection also includes a supporting collection of books, audiovisuals, and other secondary sources.

759
Springfield Technical Community College Library
Armory Square
Springfield, Massachusetts 01105

Telephone. (413) 781-7822

Institutional Description. The two-year technical college was founded in 1967 on the site of the deactivated Springfield Armory. Enrollment: 6,762.

Library Administration. Tamson M. Ely, Director of Library Services.

Library General Holdings. 47,000 books; 360 journal titles; 12,000 pamphlets and documents.

Special Collections

The library has a Career Center with specialized collections in health and technical fields.

760
Stonehill College
Cushing-Martin Library
Washington Street
North Easton, Massachusetts 02357

Telephone. (617) 238-1081

Institutional Description. The privately supported liberal arts college was founded in 1948. It is affiliated with the Roman Catholic Congregation of the Holy Cross. Enrollment: 2,786.

Library Administration. Carol Fraser, Director.

Library General Holdings. 138,000 volumes; 1,000 current periodical titles; 149,000 government documents; 20,000 microforms.

Special Collections

A study room in the library houses the papers and memorabilia of Speaker of the House of Representatives Joseph W. Martin, Jr. Also maintained are the **Arnold Tofias Industrial Archives,** and the papers of Michael Novak.

761
Suffolk University
Mildred F. Sawyer Library
41 Temple Street
Boston, Massachusetts 02114

Telephone. (617) 723-4700

Institutional Description. The privately supported university was founded in 1906. It includes the Suffolk Law School and the Colleges of Liberal Arts, Journalism, and Business Administration. Enrollment: 6,124.

Library Administration. Edmund G. Hamann, Director.

Library General Holdings. 245,000 volumes; 3,885 current periodicals; 481,000 microforms.

Special Collections

Special collections include annual reports of American corporations and the **Afro-American Literature Collection.** This latter collection includes poetry, drama, fiction, and non-fiction prose of important Black American writers from the eighteenth century to the present in both book and periodical form. It contains related critical, historical, biographical, and bibliographical works by writers of all races. Of special interest is the Collection of Afro-American writers associated with New England.

Microtexts in the library include a history of American business and nineteenth-century Americana.

762
Tufts University
Nils Yngve Wessell Library
Medford, Massachusetts 02155

Telephone. (617) 628-5000

Institutional Description. The privately supported university was founded in 1852. Its College of Liberal Arts is for men, its Jackson College is for women, and its other units are coeducational. Tufts' School of Medicine is located in Boston. Enrollment: 5,967.

Library Administration. David C.R. Heisser, Librarian.

Library General Holdings. 385,000 volumes; 2,000 current periodicals; 270,000 government publications; 75,000 maps; 500,000 microforms; 2,500 sound recordings.

Special Collections

Wessell Library, the principal library of the University, has basic resources in the humanities, social sciences, biological sciences, and earth sciences. The collections are especially strong in illustrated books and fine arts including books about stained glass.

Special collections include the libraries of Hosea Ballou and Charles Gott; the **Ritter Collection of Sixteenth to Nineteenth Century Music;** the **Theatre Collection of Plays;** the **Tufts Author Collection,** and other rare books and manuscripts. The **University Archives** contain documents, memorabilia, and publications relating to the history of the university and archival copies of Tufts University theses. The **Curriculum Laboratory** contains sample textbooks for elementary and secondary schools, children's fiction, pamphlets, sample tests, workbooks, and curriculum guides.

Edward Ginn Library, Fletcher School. The Ginn Library contains collections in international studies, law and diplomacy, and supporting collections. Special collections, totaling 110,000 items, include the **Edward R. Murrow Collection** of the personal library, papers, and memorabilia donated by Mrs. Murrow to the Edward R. Murrow Center of Public Diplomacy; the **John Moors Cabot Collection** of papers; and the **Philip Kingsland Crowe Collection** of books, papers, and memorabilia.

Health Sciences Library. Special collections include a history of medicine collection, with 100 antique medical prints donated by Dr. Robert Lurie, the **Berlinger Periodontal Collection,** and the **Domeshek Library in Hematology.**

763
University of Lowell
University Libraries
1 University Avenue
Lowell, Massachusetts 01854

Telephone. (617) 452-5000

Institutional Description. The publicly supported state university was formed in 1975 by the merger of Lowell State College and Lowell Technological Institute. Enrollment: 16,586.

Library Administration. Joseph V. Kopycinski, Director, Alumni/Lydon Library; Charles R. Meehan, Director, O'Leary Library.

Library General Holdings. 300,000 books and periodicals.

Special Collections

Special collections of the University Libraries include the collections of the American Association of University Women (Greater Lowell Chapter); Boston and Maine Railroad Historical Society; Lowell Historical Society; Lowell Museum; Manning Family; Middlesex Canal Association; Proprietors of the Locks and Canals on Merrimack River; University Archives; and a collection of regional histories. Other resources include New England maps published by the Geological Survey, and educational media.

764
University of Massachusetts at Amherst
University Library
Amherst, Massachusetts 01003

Institutional Description. The publicly supported university was founded in 1863 as the Massachusetts Agricultural College. Enrollment: 27,156.

Library Administration. Richard J. Talbot, University Librarian; John D. Kendall, Head, Special Collections & Rare Books.

Library General Holdings. 1,590,000 volumes; 1,385,000 microforms; 14,200 current periodicals.

Special Collections

The Department of Special Collections and Rare Books makes available for research and study books and other materials requiring special conditions for their preservation and/or interpretation. Items are selected for inclusion in the department's holdings on the basis either of their individual intrinsic value as artifacts or as objects of intellectual interest, or their value in relation to other items in the collections in facilitating research and study of a particular topic. Many items have been added to the collections through the corporate generosity of Friends of the Library, or as gifts of individual donors. The holdings of Special Collections and Rare Books comprise some

12,500 volumes and 2,500 calendared pamphlets and other items. Holdings include many early works on agriculture, gardening, botany, and zoology, especially entomology, reflecting the earliest mission of the University and the library's responses to it; a collection of Medieval and Renaissance illuminated manuscript leaves, twelfth to sixteenth centuries; a set of the Diderot *Encyclopédie* with its *Supplément* and plates, 35 volumes in folio, 1761-1777; a collection of papers of the first fourteen Federal Congresses; and works illustrative of the history and culture of the United States from the Crash to Pearl Harbor. Individual collections include:

Russell K. Alspach Yeats Collection. First and other significant editions, including prefaces, contributions to collective works, and periodical appearances, of the works, 1889-1966, of W.B. Yeats gathered by Russell K. Alspach in preparing the variorum editions of Yeat's poems and of his plays and the second and third editions of Allan Wade's *Bibliography of the Writings of W.B. Yeats.*

Anti-Slavery Pamphlet Collection. Principally United States with emphasis on anti-slavery movements in New England, especially Massachusetts, 1725-1911; includes speeches, sermons, proceedings of meetings, and publications of societies, including the American Colonization Society; some pro-slavery items.

Collection Binet (Révolution Française). Books, pamphlets, and manuscripts relating to the French Revolution, its immediate antecedents, and the early Empire, collected by Dr. Maurice Emmanuel Hippolyte Binet, M.D. (b. 1877) of Vichy; mostly contemporary with the events.

Broadside Press Collection. A nearly complete collection of the publications of the Broadside Press, Detroit, 1965-76, conducted by Dudley Randall and publishing Black poets; includes books, broadsides, cassettes, posters, press releases, other publicity and advertising, and *Broadside News.*

F. Lauriston Bullard Sacco-Vanzetti Collection. Scrapbooks of clippings on the Sacco-Vanzetti case collected and mounted by F. Lauriston Bullard (1866-1952), chief editorial writer (1919-1943) of the *Boston Herald,* winner of a 1926 Pulitzer Prize in journalism for his editorial on the case entitled "We Submit"; clippings from North American and European newspapers and periodicals; includes some pamphlets.

F. Lauriston Bullard Teapot Dome Collection. Clippings, pamphlets, etc., 1927-1929, relating to the oil scandals and trials subsequent to the Teapot Dome disclosures, gathered and originally mounted in ring binders by F. Lauriston Bullard.

Federal Land Bank Collection. Former cartographic reference library of Region 1 (New England, New York, and New Jersey) of the Federal Land Bank/Farm Credit Banks system; comprising county atlases (mostly ca. 1865-1890), bound U.S.G.S. and A.M.S. topographical sheets, and wall maps.

Robert Francis Collection. Publications in book form and in periodicals of the post-1936 works of poet Robert Francis (1901-), together with published works of other poets presented to Francis.

Literary Translation Collection. Works illustrative of the art of literary translation by the distinguished practitioners Ralph Manheim, from French and German literature, mainly contemporary; and Gregory Rabassa, from Spanish and Portuguese Latin American literature.

Harold J. Gordon Collection. Books and pamphlets of politics, history, and propaganda documenting, as primary sources, the German Revolution of 1918, the Weimar Republic, and the National Socialist period, especially the activities of the *Freikorps,* the establishment of the *Reichswehr,* the effects of the Versailles Treaty, the Kapp Putsch, and the rise of the Nazis; 1918-1946.

Archibald MacLeish Collection. First and other important editions, some signed, some inscribed for presentation, of the works of poet Archibald MacLeish (1892-1982); some periodical appearances, correspondence; 1917-1982.

William Manchester Collection. First and other editions of the works of William Manchester (Massachusetts State College 1946), including translations into other languages, notable *The Death of a President* and *The Arms of Krupp.*

Massachusetts Pamphlet Collection. Miscellaneous pamphlets, mainly by or about Massachusetts persons 1729-1902, including election, ordination, installation, dedication, fast-day, mission, farewell, and funeral sermons; Fourth of July orations; and addresses to or sponsored by some 45 Massachusetts societies, etc.

Massachusetts Town Boundary Atlas Collection. Atlases produced by the Massachusetts Topographic Survey Commission (pre-1901), later by the Massachusetts Harbor and land Commission, presenting minutely detailed cartographic representations of the boundaries of every municipality in the Commonwealth (through 1915) with each of its neighbors, together with descriptions of boundaries as originally laid down, triangulation data, and descriptions (occasionally accompanied by photographs) of corners.

William Morris Collection. Works of English poet, artist, designer, printer, and social reformer William Morris (1834-1896), often in first editions, some printed by him, some signed; 1858-ca. 1930. Includes Morris's holograph manuscript of *The Friendship of Amis and Amile.*

Nineteenth-Century Cartographic and Geographical Materials. Includes atlases, wall maps, folding pocket maps, and gazetteers of states, regions, counties, and cities in the Northeast ca. 1850 to ca. 1920 (main emphasis on New England, but including New York and New Jersey); also includes strong representation of Massachusetts cities and towns.

John P. Roche Collection. Political pamphlets collected by John P. Roche, political scientist, professor, government consultant, and journalist (1923-); emphasis on the left in the United States during the 1930s and 1940s but including items from the political right, from Eastern and Western Europe, and from the late nineteenth century to the 1950s; publications representing some 120 publishers, mostly political and social interest groups: political parties (especially various Socialist and Communist parties), *ad hoc* committees, labor unions, educational organizations, religious bodies, and official and unofficial Communist and Marxist publishing houses, 1866-ca. 1955.

Santerre Collection. Books and pamphlets, 1872-1962, documenting the experience of Franco-Americans, primarily of Quebec origin, in New England; includes statistical and biographical compilations, bibliographies, publications of social organizations, local and ecclesiastical histories, and some literary works; collected by Richard Santerre.

Wallace Stevens Collection. Books owned (some annotated) by, including some presentation copies to, poet Wallace Stevens; periodical issues including poems or prose by him; articles, correspondence, and minor memorabilia, 1900-1954.

Paul Theroux Collection. Editions, some signed, of the works of Paul Theroux (University of Massachusetts 1963), novelist and travel writer 1968-1984.

Transportation, Travel, and Tourism in the Northeast. Books and pamphlets, ca. 1820-ca. 1920, documenting the development of transportation with emphasis on New England, but including New York and New Jersey; travel literature; tourist guides; resort ephemera, including railroad and trolley brochures; and view books.

Archives and Manuscripts Department. The subject areas of the major manuscript collections are: Black studies, business, crosscultural and ethnic studies, labor, literary and fine arts, local history, natural sciences, peace and social action groups, politics and diplomacy, religion and theology, rural life and agriculture, social service agencies, and women's studies.

765
University of Massachusetts at Boston
Joseph P. Healey Library
100 Arlington Street
Boston, Massachusetts 02125

Telephone. (617) 929-7000

Institutional Description. The publicly supported (state) university was founded in 1965, and recently incorporated Boston State College. It is a branch campus of the University of Massachusetts System, granting baccalaureate and master's degrees. Enrollment: 11,496.

Library Administration. Donald Grose, Director.

Library General Holdings. 453,500 volumes; 3,320 current foreign and domestic newspapers and journals; 484,000 microforms.

Special Collections

The Healy Library maintains special collections in the fine arts, music, and the sciences. Paintings, drawings, books, and manuscripts of historical interest and examples of the printer's art are on display in exhibition areas. Other special collections include materials on the German Bauhaus movement, anti-war material of the Vietnam era, and nineteenth-century Boston settlements. A small collection, designed specifically for the students and faculty at the College of Public and Community Service, is located at the Downtown Center. Students and instructors have access to the John F. Kennedy Presidential Library which stands on the coastal edge of the Boston Harbor campus.

766
Wellesley College
Margaret Clapp Library
Wellesley, Massachusetts 02181

Telephone. (617) 235-0320

Institutional Description. The privately supported liberal arts college for women was established in 1875. Enrollment: 2,170.

Library Administration. Eleanor Gustafson, Librarian; Anne Anninger, Special Collections Librarian.

Library General Holdings. 614,626 volumes; 2,793 current periodical subscriptions; 169,477 microforms; 118,759 government documents; 13,440 audiovisual materials.

Special Collections

Alcove of North American Languages. This collection was presented in 1887 by Eben Norton Horsford, son of a missionary among the Senecas. The collection of 280 volumes includes 5 Micmac manuscripts by the Reverend Silas Rand as well as printed books including dictionaries, vocabularies, grammars, and translations of the Bible in Indian language.

Book Arts Collection. Covering all aspects of book production papermaking, printing, illustrating, bookbinding, this collection of 4,600 volumes also includes over 1,300 fine printing specimens from the late eighteenth century to the present.

Durant Collection. A collection of 10,000 volumes presented at the opening of the College by its founders, Mr. and Mrs. Henry Fowle Durant. These volumes originally formed the nucleus of the general collection and represent a record of Victorian taste, both English and American.

Elbert Collection. Presented in 1938 by Ella Smith Elbert, this collection holds works on slavery, emancipation, and Reconstruction. The 800 volumes include personal narratives, autobiographies, tracts and pamphlets, poetry, novels, and folklore.

English Poetry Collection. This collection of 12,000

volumes and 15 linear feet of manuscripts and autographs includes English and American poets, from Chaucer to Eliot and from Anne Bradstreet to Sylvia Plath. There are strong holdings of autograph, manuscript, and printed material by and about Elizabeth Barrett and Robert Browning.

Juvenile Collection. Includes 1,000 volumes of primers, songbooks, folk tales, fairy tales of the nineteenth and twentieth centuries.

Ruskin Collection. A 900-volume collection presented in 1920 by Charles Eliot Goodspeed. It is a comprehensive collection including first editions of Ruskin's works, rare pamphlets, ephemera, autographs, and original watercolors.

Rare Book Collections

Rare Books Collection. The collection of 12,000 volumes covers a variety of fields: early illuminated manuscripts, incunables, early English Bibles, seventeenth- and eighteen-century cookbooks, early editions of the classics, and first editions of major authors.

Plimpton Collection. The 1,200 volumes in this collection were presented in 1904 by George Arthur Plimpton in memory of his wife, Frances Taylor Pearsons Plimpton. The collection illustrates the history of Italian literature from the fourteenth to the seventeenth centuries. It includes Renaissance manuscripts, early editions of Boccaccio, Dante, and Petrarch, and substantial holdings of Romances of Chivalry.

767
Western New England College
D'Amour Library
1215 Wilbraham Road
Springfield, Massachusetts 01119

Telephone. (413) 782-3111

Institutional Description. The privately supported liberal arts, business, and professional college was founded in 1919 as the Springfield Division of Northeastern University. In 1951, the present name was adopted. Enrollment: 5,140.

Library Administration. Glenn H. Johnson, Jr., Director.

Library General Holdings. 108,00 volumes; 1,100 periodical titles.

Special Collections

The library maintains the **Saex Judaica Collection.** The S. Prestley Blake Law Center's library has a collection on tax, labor, and insurance.

768
Weston School of Theology
Library
3 Phillips Place
Cambridge, Massachusetts 02138

Telephone. (617) 492-1960

Institutional Description. The privately supported graduate-level school of theology prepares students for ministry in the Roman Catholic Church. A coeducational institution, it is conducted by the Jesuits. Enrollment: 181.

Library Administration. James Dunkly, Director of Libraries.

Library General Holdings. 250,000 volumes; 800 periodical titles. The libraries of Weston School of Theology and the Episcopal Divinity School form a single operation under a common staff.

Special Collections

New Testament Abstracts deposits both its periodical exchanges and its review copies with the library, thus supplying each year virtually all significant international publications in New Testament and related fields. The history of English Christianity is especially well served, since the two institutions (Weston and Episcopal Divinity School) enrich the whole collection from both Catholic and Anglican perspectives. Continental European theology is a particular strength of the Weston Library. Special attention is given to maintaining an outstanding reference collection, particularly in bibliography and ecclesiastical documentation. Some 4,000 volumes pertaining to Islam and the Arab world comprise a special Weston collection.

769
Wheaton College
Madeleine Clark Wallace Library
Norton, Massachusetts 02766

Telephone. (617) 285-7722

Institutional Description. The privately supported college for women was founded in 1834 as an undergraduate seminary for women. It now grants baccalaureate degrees. Enrollment: 1,191.

Library Administration. Sherrie S. Bergman, College Librarian.

Library General Holdings. 258,000 volumes; 1,200 periodical titles.

Special Collections

The Wallace Library maintains special collections on Wheaton College authors; the Wheaton College Archives; the Lucy Larcom Collection; and private press books.

770
Wheelock College
Wheelock College Library
132 The Riverway
Boston, Massachusetts 02215

Telephone. (617) 734-5200

Institutional Description. The privately supported liberal arts college is primarily for women. Founded in 1888 with a one-year program for kindergarten teachers, it now features professional training for nursery school and kindergarten. Baccalaureate and master's degrees are offered. Enrollment: 1,706.

Library Administration. Andrea Hoffman, College Librarian; Audrey Potter, Assistant Director.

Library General Holdings. 70,000 volumes; 500 periodical titles; complete ERIC microfiche collection; materials for students to use with children (picture story books, fiction and nonfiction, recordings, cassettes, filmloops, study prints, textbook series, kits, and curriculum guides).

Special Collections

E.A. Liddle Collection and **Martha Wheatland Ingraham Children's Literature Collection.** Both collections include children's books of the late eighteenth and early nineteenth centuries.

771
Williams College
College Library
Williamstown, Massachusetts 01267

Telephone. (413) 597-2233

Institutional Description. The privately supported liberal arts college was founded in 1793. It grants baccalaureate and master's degrees. Enrollment: 2,131.

Library Administration. Phyllis L. Cutler, College Librarian.

Library General Holdings. 600,000 volumes; 3,000 current periodicals; 55,000 government documents; 165,-000 microforms; 18,000 audiovisual materials.

Special Collections

The library maintains the Paul Whiteman Collection.

Rare Book Collections

The **Shaker Collection** includes 1,300 volumes of eighteenth-century rare books, diaries, and letters; the **Chapin Library of Rare Books** consists of 35,000 volumes including incunabula.

772
Worcester Polytechnic Institute
George C. Gordon Library
100 Institute Road
Worcester, Massachusetts 01609

Telephone. (617) 793-5000

Institutional Description. The privately supported technological institution, founded in 1865, prepares its students for careers in engineering, science, and management. Enrollment: 3,810.

Library Administration. Albert G. Anderson, Jr., Head Librarian.

Library General Holdings. 246,000 bound books and periodicals; 1,300 current periodical subscriptions; 700,000 microfiche.

Special Collections

The Gordon Library maintains the collection of diaries of Theo Brown (1890-1977), an alumnus of Worcester Polytechnic Institute and a major designer of agricultural machinery; and the Alden Hydraulic Laboratory Records (1900-1960).

773
Worcester State College
Learning Resources Center
486 Chandler Street
Worcester, Massachusetts 01602

Telephone. (617) 793-8027

Institutional Description. The publicly supported state college, founded in 1874, offers baccalaureate and master's degree programs. Enrollment: 7,106.

Library Administration. Bruce Plummer, College Librarian; Bill Piekarski, Special Collections Librarian.

Library General Holdings. 163,515 volumes; 1,005 current periodical titles; 10 newspaper subscriptions; 9,-399 reels of microfilm; 10,000 nonprint items.

Special Collections

Education Resources. Consists of over 10,000 items including 7,000 textbooks, curriculum guides, transparencies, study prints, games/charts, instructional materials, professional tests.

Children's Collection. Includes 11,000 volumes covering picture books through junior high school; juvenile reference material.

Michigan

774
Adrian College
Shipman Library
Adrian, Michigan 49221

Telephone. (517) 265-5161

Institutional Description. The privately supported liberal arts college was founded in 1845 by the Wesleyan Methodists at Leoni, Michigan. Today it continues its Protestant Christian heritage and is related to the United Methodist Church. Enrollment: 1,117.

Library Administration. James A. Dodd, Library Director.

Library General Holdings. 132,215 volumes including 17,184 bound periodicals; 778 current periodical subscriptions; 21 newspaper subscriptions; 31,156 microfiche; 1,892 phonograph recordings; 126 art prints; 72 microfiche titles; 33 microfilm titles.

Special Collections

Lincoln Collection. Consists of 763 books; 362 periodicals; 23 folders; 2 catalogues; 27 pictures; 8 newspapers; 4 sheet music; 5 miniature books; 157 pamphlets.

775
Albion College
Mudd Learning Center/Stockwell Memorial Library
611 East Porter Street
Albion, Michigan 49224

Telephone. (517) 629-5511

Institutional Description. The privately supported liberal arts college was founded in 1835. It is affiliated with the United Methodist Church. Enrollment: 1,579.

Library Administration. Michael A. VanHouten, Acting Director.

Library General Holdings. 250,000 volumes; 1,000 periodical subscriptions.

Special Collections

The library houses a rare book collections and archives that include the historical collection of the United Methodist Church's West Michigan Conference.

776
Alma College
Alma College Library
614 West Superior
Alma, Michigan 48801

Telephone. (517) 463-7227

Institutional Description. The privately supported liberal arts college was founded in 1886 by the Presbyterian Church of Michigan. Engineering students may participate in an academic cooperative plan with the University of Michigan. Enrollment: 975.

Library Administration. Peter Dollard, College Librarian; Lawrence Hall, Reference, Archives, and Special Collections Librarian.

Library General Holdings. 173,000 volumes; 1,049 current periodical subscriptions; 9,920 microforms.

Special Collections

The library contains historical sources from eighteenth-century British and American Colonial/early national period; Japanese foreign affairs documents (1868-1945); local interest holdings include **Michigan Pioneer and Historical Collections** (1874-1929), local newspapers (1885-present), U.S. 7th Census (1850) for Michigan, and U.S. Geological Survey maps (1:24,000) of Michigan; collection of 5,000 classical, popular, and folk phonograph recordings.

Rare Book Collections

Longyear Bible Collection. Contains Bibles in 103 languages and dialects.

Other rare book and manuscript collections include nineteenth century pamphlets; published works and manuscripts of Alma College and local writers. The **Alma College Archives** (1886-1987) include the manuscript sermons of John Wert Dunning and the papers of Robert D. Swanson.

777
Andrews University
James White Library
Berrien Springs, Michigan 49104

Telephone. (616) 471-3100

Institutional Description. The privately supported liberal arts and professional university was founded in 1874 as Battle Creek College. A consolidation with Emmanuel Missionary College in 1959 resulted in the present institution. Affiliated with the Seventh-day Adventist Church, the university includes a theological seminary. Enrollment: 2,475.

Library Administration. Marley H. Soper, Director.

Library General Holdings. 658,000 volumes; 3,460 current periodical subscriptions; 268,500 microforms.

Special Collections

Heritage Room. Houses the Seventh-day Adventist Archive and Research Center which holds material on the history and development of the Advent Movement and the Seventh-day Adventist Church since 1844. Among these publications are 13,499 books, 9,646 pamphlets, and an extensive file of 1,500 titles of periodicals in more than 100 languages. In addition, it houses the **Advent Source and Conditionalist Faith Collections** made up of several thousand items dealing with the origins of Adventists and history of the doctrine of conditional immortality. Besides the published material, there is approximately 500 linear feet of collections of private papers, such as diaries, correspondence, sermons of some of the denominational pioneers and contemporary workers, early S.D.A. congregational records, and pictures of denominational interest. An obituary file of over 80,000 names of Seventh-day Adventists, 2,459 theses and term papers by Andrews students, and artifacts are among other resources available. A growing collection of Bibles and rare books from the fifteenth to the seventeenth centuries is also housed. Among these are the **George B. Suhrie Bible Collection** and several original editions of Martin Luther's smaller works.

Ellen G. White Research Center. The Center contains copies of letters and manuscripts of Ellen G. White, along with 4,600 of her published articles and thousands of pages of other documents related to the history and early development of the Adventist Church.

778
Aquinas College
Woodhouse Learning Resource Center
1607 Robinson Road, S.E.
Grand Rapids, Michigan 49506

Telephone. (616) 459-8281

Institutional Description. The privately supported liberal arts college was founded in 1886 by the Roman Catholic Dominican Sisters of Marywood. It grants baccalaureate and master's degrees. Enrollment: 1,794.

Library Administration. Larry W. Zysk, Director.

Library General Holdings. 93,000 volumes; 925 current periodical subscriptions; 16,500 microforms.

Special Collections

The library maintains a business collection modeled after the collection of the Harvard Business School Library; the **Mother Goose Collection** which includes early and foreign language editions; and a collection of works in religion.

779
Calvin College
Calvin Library
3207 Burton Street, S.E.
Grand Rapids, Michigan 49506

Telephone. (616) 957-6000

Institutional Description. The privately supported liberal arts college was founded in 1876 as a two-year college. It added a baccalaureate program in 1921, and later a master's program. The college is affiliated with the Christian Reformed Church. Enrollment: 4,016.

Library Administration. Marvin Monsma, Director; Peter De Klerk, Theological Librarian and Curator of the H. Henry Meeter Calvinism Research Collection.

Library General Holdings. 386,000 volumes; 2,575 current periodicals; 36,000 microforms.

Special Collections

Several special collections are housed in the library. The **H.H. Meeter Calvinism Research Collection** is one of the most extensive collections of books and articles on John Calvin and Calvinism available anywhere. The **Colonial Origins Collection,** which consists of manuscripts, archives, and other records of the Christian Reformed Church, its leaders, its Dutch origins, and closely related institutions, is also housed in the library.

780
Calvin Theological Seminary
Calvin Library
3233 Burton Street, S.E.
Grand Rapids, Michigan 49506

Telephone. (616) 949-2494

Institutional Description. The privately supported seminary was founded in 1876 as the theological school of the Christian Reformed Church. It grants professional and master's degrees. Enrollment: 235.

Library Administration. Peter De Klerk, Theological Librarian and Curator of the Calvinism Research Collection.

Library General Holdings. The library of the Seminary is combined with that of Calvin College. *See* **Calvin College.**

781
Central Michigan University
Charles V. Park Library
Mount Pleasant, Michigan 48859

Telephone. (517) 774-3131

Institutional Description. The publicly supported state university was founded in 1892 as the Central Michigan Normal School and Business Institute. It now offers a wide variety of programs. Enrollment: 15,725.

Library Administration. John Weatherford, Director of Libraries.

Library General Holdings. 659,237 volumes of books, periodicals, and documents; 5,500 periodicals and newspapers.

Special Collections

Clarke Historical Library. contains 60,000 volumes of books, periodicals, and extensive collections of manuscripts, maps, newspapers, photographs, and broadsides relating to the history of Michigan, the Old Northwest Territory, and the Great Lakes area. The collection also includes the **Lucile Clarke Memorial Children's Library,** the **American Presidential Campaign Biographies Collection,** the **Wilbert Wright Collection of Americana and Afro-Americana,** and the **George Armstrong Custer Collection.** The core of the library was given to the University by Dr. Norman E. Clarke, Sr., Class of 1913.

782
Concordia College
Library
4090 Geddes Road
Ann Arbor, Michigan 48105

Telephone. (313) 665-3691

Institutional Description. The privately supported liberal arts college, founded in 1962, is affiliated with the Lutheran Church—Missouri Synod. Enrollment: 411.

Library Administration. Roy O. Kronsbein, Director.

Library General Holdings. 96,000 volumes; 200 current periodical subscriptions; 13,000 microforms; 1,200 audiovisual titles.

Special Collections

The library maintains a 22,000-volume special collection in religion as well as a collection in language and literature.

783
Cranbrook Academy of Art
Library
500 Lone Pine Road
Box 801
Bloomfield Hills, Michigan 48013

Telephone. (313) 645-3355

Institutional Description. The privately supported professional school was formed in 1927; it grew and was chartered to grant degrees in 1942. Enrollment: 134.

Library Administration. Judy Dyki, Director, Library Services.

Library General Holdings. 30,000 volumes.

Special Collections

The focus of the library's collection is to provide practicing artists with a wealth of visual resources in book form rather than in duplicating existing art historical research collections. The library maintains a wide selection of periodicals, slides, vertical file materials, exhibition catalogues, and tapes of Academy lectures. The library maintains the **George G. Booth Collection** of fine art folios and a collection of Cranbrook Press books.

784
Eastern Michigan University
University Library
Ypsilanti, Michigan 48197

Telephone. (313) 487-1849

Institutional Description. The publicly supported university was founded by the state of Michigan in 1849. It features teacher education, business, and technology. Enrollment: 15,426.

Library Administration. Morell D. Boone, Dean, Learning Resources and Technologies.

Library General Holdings. 500,000 volumes; 400,000 microforms; 135,000 government documents.

Special Collections

Special collections include an Instructional Materials Center in conjunction with the educational and psychology holdings, a map library in the science and technology unit, government documents, and the University Archives.

Michigan Consumer Education Center. Houses the nation's leading collection of consumer education resources.

785
Ferris State College
Ferris Library
South State Street
Big Rapids, Michigan 49307

Telephone. (616) 796-0461

Institutional Description. The publicly supported state college was founded in 1884 as the Big Rapids Industrial School. It continues to provide professional and technical programs. Enrollment: 10,542.

Library Administration. Mary M. Bower, Director.

Library General Holdings. 290,000 volumes; 1,790 periodicals; 2,750,000 microforms; 54,000 government documents; 9,890 audiovisual materials.

Special Collections

The **Michigan Collection** includes materials relating to the history of Michigan and its people.

786
GMI Engineering and Management Institute
GMI Library
1700 West Third Avenue
Flint, Michigan 48502

Telephone. (313) 762-9864

Institutional Description. The privately supported technological institute operates on a cooperative plan which uses alternate work and study periods for its programs in engineering and management. Baccalaureate degrees are awarded. Enrollment: 3,092.

Library Administration. Emily R. Mobley, Library Director.

Library General Holdings. 54,000 volumes; 815 current periodical titles; 15,000 microforms; 3,000 government documents; 800 recordings.

Special Collections

The library's collection includes all ground vehicle papers of the Society of Automotive Engineers; all papers of the Society of Manufacturing Engineers; and all papers and transaction series from the American Society of Mechanical Engineers.

787
Grand Rapids Junior College
Learning Resource Center
143 Bostwick Street, N.E.
Grand Rapids, Michigan 49503

Telephone. (616) 456-4895

Institutional Description. Grand Rapids Junior College was founded in 1914. It is now and has been since its founding a part of a K-12 large urban school district. Enrollment: 3,178.

Library Administration. Bernice Whitley, Director.

Library General Holdings. 52,000 volumes; 524 periodical titles.

Special Collections

A special **Abraham Lincoln Collection** is maintained in the library.

788
Grand Valley State College
James H. Zumberge Library
College Landing
Allendale, Michigan 49401

Telephone. (616) 895-6611

Institutional Description. The publicly supported liberal arts college was founded by the State of Michigan in 1960. It grants baccalaureate and master's degrees. Enrollment: 5,768.

Library Administration. Stephen Ford, Director.

Library General Holdings. 355,000 volumes; 1,900 periodical subscriptions; 14,000 microfilm reels.

Special Collections

The library has specialized collections dealing with regional history. There is also a curriculum materials library for use of students studying to be teachers.

789
Great Lakes Bible College
College Library
P.O. Box 40060
Lansing, Michigan 48901

Telephone. (517) 321-0242

Institutional Description. The privately supported Bible college prepares students for effective Christian service, granting associate and baccalaureate degrees. It is affiliated with the Church of Christ. Enrollment: 155.

Library Administration. Nancy Jean Olson, Librarian.

Library General Holdings. 26,200 volumes; 198 current periodical subscriptions.

Special Collections

Special collections include *Restoration History* publications (Churches of Christ/Christian Churches); the Library of Religion in America (microform); and a microfilm collection of the *Christian Standard* covering the period 1866 to 1966 and a hardcopy collection from 1966 to the present.

790
Hillsdale College
Carr Memorial Library
33 East College Street
Hillsdale, Michigan 49242

Telephone. (517) 437-7341

Institutional Description. The privately supported liberal arts college was founded in 1844. It grants baccalaureate degrees. Enrollment: 1,032.

Library Administration. Dan Joldersma, Librarian.

Library General Holdings. 120,000 volumes; 1,025 current periodical subscriptions.

Special Collections

The library houses the historical collection of the College. The **Ludwig von Mises Collection** includes 5,000 volumes of the personal library of the economist; the **Wilber J. Carr Collection** contains materials on international relations; and the **Manion Forum Tape Collection** includes World War II era tapes.

791
Hope College
Van Wylen Library
Holland, Michigan 49423

Telephone. (616) 394-7790

Institutional Description. This privately supported liberal arts college emphasizes the historic Christian faith, incorporating freedom, openness, and creativity. It has an independent board of trustees and is affiliated with the Reformed Church in America. Enrollment: 2,299.

Library Administration. David Jensen, College Librarian; Linda Visscher, Technical Services Coordinator.

Library General Holdings. 241,000 volumes; 1,475 current periodicals; 39,500 microforms; 3,150 sound recordings; 2,600 cassettes; 8,900 publications of the U.S. Bureau of the Census.

Special Collections

The Van Wylen Library maintains a collection of the **U.S. Bureau of the Census** publications; a **Curriculum Library** containing 5,200 items including materials used in elementary and secondary classrooms; a collection on peace donated from the personal collection of A.J. Muste and materials ordered by the Library; a collection of materials on the Reformed Church in America and the Dutch in Michigan; the Library of American Civilization collection of 19,000 volumes on ultrafiche. The Library also has a Nuclear Regulatory Commission Local Public Document Reading Room with material on the Palisades Nuclear Power Plant.

792
Kalamazoo College
Upjohn Library
Thompson and Academy Streets
Kalamazoo, Michigan 49007

Telephone. (616) 383-8481

Institutional Description. The privately supported liberal arts college was founded in 1833. It is affiliated with the American Baptist Church. Enrollment: 1,103.

Library Administration. Eleanor H. Pinkham, Director of Libraries and Media Services.

Library General Holdings. 250,000 volumes; 1,000 journal titles; microforms, spoken-word recordings, audiotapes, videotapes, maps, and pamphlets are also included in the collection.

Special Collections

College Archives. Serves as the repository for materials tracing the history of Kalmazoo College since its founding in 1833 and for documents relating to the history of Baptists in Michigan. Included are the personal papers of many individuals who have had close associations with the college. Among the notable collections are those of T.Z.R. Jones, an early missionary in Michigan; E.J. Fish, a nineteenth-century Baptist minister and a long-term president of the Michigan Baptist Convention; Maynard Owen Williams, chief of the foreign staff of *National Geographic* from 1930 t0 1953; and Preston C. Hammer, a scholar in the field of applied mathematics and a pioneer in computer science education.

Rare Book Collections

A.M. Todd Rare Book Room. Houses a distinctive collection of rare and unusual books and manuscripts. Subject areas of note include English and American literature with first editions of Milton, Shelley, Thoreau, Longfellow, and others; scientific works, including the first publications of Boyle's Law, Priestley's discovery of oxygen, and Lavoisier's chemical nomenclature; ornithology, with many hand-colored folio volumes by John Gould, Daniel Eliot, and R. Bowdler Sharpe. Numerous fine editions of the Latin and Greek classics and works illustrating the history of printing and book production, from Gutenberg to William Morris and Lucien Pissarro, are additional strengths in the collection.

793
Kellogg Community College
Emory W. Morris Learning Resource Center
450 North Avenue
Battle Creek, Michigan 49016

Telephone. (616) 965-3931

Institutional Description. The two-year community college, founded in 1956, separated from the public school system of Battle Creek and became a separate college district in 1970. Enrollment: 1,162.

Library Administration. Clara Stewart, Librarian.

Library General Holdings. 44,600 volumes; 500 periodical titles; 8,250 audiovisual materials.

Special Collections

The **Kellogg Memorial Collection** and a collection of materials on the Civil War is maintained in the library.

794
Kendall College of Art and Design
Frank and Lyn Van Steenberg Learning Resource Center
111 Division Avenue North
Grand Rapids, Michigan 49503

Telephone. (616) 451-2787

Institutional Description. The privately supported professional art college was founded in 1928. Enrollment: 693.

Library Administration. Ruth Hornbach, Librarian.

Library General Holdings. 13,000 volumes; 100 periodical subscriptions; 8 newspaper subscriptions; 36,000 slides.

Special Collections

The Steenberg Learning Resource Center houses materials supporting the art and design curriculum of the college. There are specialized collections on graphic design and furniture designer's original sketches and drawings.

Rare Book Collections

The library has a collection of 1,000 rare and out-of-print books on furniture design.

795
Kirtland Community College
Library
Route 4
Roscommon, Michigan 48653

Telephone. (517) 275-5121

Institutional Description. Kirtland Community College was established in 1966 and provides transfer, career, and continuing education programs. Enrollment: 840.

Library Administration. Stuart E. Lawrence, Director.

Library General Holdings. 34,000 volumes; 300 current periodical subscriptions; 2,400 reels of back periodicals on microfilm; 210 bound periodical volumes.

Special Collections

The library has special collections on career planning and children's literature.

796
Lake Superior State College
College Library
Sault Sainte Marie, Michigan 49783

Telephone. (906) 635-2202

Institutional Description. The publicly supported state liberal arts college was established in 1946. Enrollment: 2,311.

Library Administration. Fredrick Michels, Director.

Library General Holdings. 125,000 volumes of books; 15,000 bound periodical volumes; 75,000 microforms; 1,100 current periodical subscriptions.

Special Collections

Special collections include the **Osborn Collection** of materials of Governor Osborn dating from the early 1900s; the **Marine Collection** of historical texts and scrapbooks about the Great Lakes; and the **Michigan Collection** containing materials about the Upper Peninsula area, the Hiawatha legend, Sault Ste. Marie, and American Indians.

797
Lansing Community College
Department of Library Information Services
419 North Capitol Avenue
P.O. Box 40010
Lansing, Michigan 48901

Telephone. (517) 483-1852

Institutional Description. The two-year college was founded in 1957. Enrollment: 9,392.

Library Administration. Ellen Person, Chairperson.

Library General Holdings. 100,000 book and audiovisual titles; 1,000 periodical titles.

Special Collections

Special collections of the library include the **Professional Resource Center Collection,** the **Western Michigan University Public Administration Collection,** and an **Easy Reading Browsing Collection.**

798
Lawrence Institute of Technology
Library
21000 West Ten Mile Road
Southfield, Michigan 48075

Telephone. (313) 356-0200

Institutional Description. The privately supported professional and technological institution was founded in 1932 as a college of engineering. It grants associate and baccalaureate degrees. Enrollment: 4,298.

Library Administration. Gary Cocozzoli, Director.

Library General Holdings. 70,000 books and periodicals.

Special Collections

Albert Kahn Collection. This collection, on permanent loan from Albert Kahn Associates, Inc, architects and engineers, consists of about 3,000 books acquired by Mr. Kahn before his death in 1943, and many photographs of structures designed by Mr. Kahn and his associates. The collection is housed in the original walnut cabinetry in two rooms carefully reconstructed to resemble Mr. Kahn's Detroit offices.

799
Madonna College
Library
36600 Schoolcraft Road
Livonia, Michigan 48150

Telephone. (313) 591-5000

Institutional Description. The privately supported liberal arts college was incorporated as a senior college in 1947. It is conducted by the Felician Sisters of the Roman Catholic Church. Enrollment: 2,482.

Library Administration. Sister Mary Lydia Miodzianowski, Director of Library Services.

Library General Holdings. 105,000 books; 950 current periodical subscriptions.

Special Collections

The library maintains the **Polish Collection** of materials relating to the Polish ethnic group. The Livonia Bar Association Law Library, deeded to the library, constitutes a special resource for students studying law-related courses.

800
Marygrove College
Marygrove Library
8425 West McNichols Road
Detroit, Michigan 48221

Telephone. (313) 862-8000

Institutional Description. The privately supported liberal arts college was founded in 1846 as St. Mary Academy by the Roman Catholic Congregation of the Sisters, Servants of the Immaculate Heart of Mary. Enrollment: 954.

Library Administration. Anna Mary Waickman, I.H.M, Director.

Library General Holdings. 182,000 books and reference volumes; 750 current periodical subscriptions; 16,500 microforms.

Special Collections

A special collections in the fine arts is maintained as well as the **Vatican Collection** of Roman Catholic religious materials.

Rare Book Collections

The **Rare Book Room** contains signed publications of the alumni and faculty.

801
Michigan Christian College
Muirhead Library
800 West Avon Road
Rochester, Michigan 48063

Telephone. (313) 651-5800

Institutional Description. The privately supported Christian college is affiliated with the Church of Christ. It grants the Bachelor of Religious Education degree. Enrollment: 257.

Library Administration. Laureen Ilasenko, Director of Library Services.

Library General Holdings. 32,000 volumes; 220 current periodical subscriptions; 14,000 microforms.

Special Collections

The library has the microbook Library of American Civilization of over 11,000 rare volumes.

802
Michigan State University
University Libraries
East Lansing, Michigan 48824

Telephone. (517) 355-2344

Institutional Description. The publicly supported state university offers a wide diversity of programs and curricula. Enrollment: 38,925.

Library Administration. Richard E. Chapin, Director of Libraries; Beth J. Shapiro, Deputy Director of Libraries; Jeanette Fiore, Special Collections/Rare Books Librarian.

Library General Holdings. 2,431,942 bound volumes; 19,175 current periodical subscriptions; 160,488 maps; 28,044 non-print materials; 600,000 government documents; 2,307,304 microforms; 200 pieces of computer software.

Special Collections

American Radicalism Collection. Incorporates books, pamphlets, periodicals, posters, and emphemera covering a wide range of viewpoints on political, social, and economic issues in American life.

Illuminated Manuscript Facsimile Collection. Includes facsimile reproductions of European manuscripts from the sixth through the fifteenth centuries.

Printing Collection. Includes works on the history of printing and the book arts, a fine collection of type specimen books, and a major archive for the history of printing in the United States—the papers of Douglas C. McMurtrie.

Russel B. Nye Popular Culture Collection. One of two major archives in the United States that makes available for research a wide range of popular reading materials in subjects including comic books and strips, mass market fiction, popular information materials, and materials relating to mass media.

Rare Book Collections

Rare Books Collection. The collections are especially rich in areas of the natural sciences and in early agriculture, cookery, and related subjects. The **Veterinary Medicine Collection** is among the finest collections of early works on this subject in the world. There is a small but important collection of early works in apiculture. Holdings in early agriculture, horticulture and landscape gardening, botany, entomology, and ornithology are strong. The **Mary Ross Reynolds Collection** in cookery and domestic arts and the **Charles and Ruth Schmitter Fencing Collection** are outstanding resources.

Other subjects of importance include toxicology and early European criminology and legal history. English-eighteenth century life in all its aspects and British local history, topography and antiquities are areas of significant strengths. Other emphases in European studies include a major collection in the history of the French monarchy and Revolution and works of the Italian Risorgimento period. There are significant collections of literary first editions, notably of writers of the Irish Literary Renaissance, selected American and English authors of the nineteenth century, and a number of American expatriate writers of the twentieth century. Works of the expatriate press in Paris between the two World Wars and twentieth-century American small press poetry are well represented, and there is a nearly comprehensive collection of works of Argentine writer Jorge Luis Borges. The Canadian Northwest Territory, especially the Red River Settlement and the life of Canadian rebel Louis Riel, is another important collecting focus, as is early travel literature, especially accounts of European travellers in Africa and descriptions of travels in North America.

803
Michigan Technological University
University Library
Houghton, Michigan 49931

Telephone. (906) 487-1885

Institutional Description. The publicly supported state university was founded in 1885 as a mining college. It now offers a widely diverse curriculum in the technologies, and grants associate, baccalaureate, master's, and doctorate degrees. Enrollment: 6,120.

Library Administration. Leroy J. Lebbin, Director.

Library General Holdings. 800,000 items including books, bound periodicals, documents, and microforms.

Special Collections

The major strengths of the library are in the fields of engineering, science, and technology. The library maintains a special collection of the Upper Michigan Peninsula/Keweenaw and the University Archives.

804
Mid Michigan Community College
Charles A. Amble Library
1375 South Clare Avenue
Harrison, Michigan 48625

Telephone. (517) 386-7792

Institutional Description. The two-year community college was established in 1965. A new campus was occupied in 1969. Enrollment: 1,111.

Library Administration. Pat Pinaire, Librarian.

Library General Holdings. 20,123 volumes; 262 periodical titles.

Special Collections

The **Clare County Picture Collection** of 2,134 items is maintained by the library.

805
Montcalm Community College
Learning Resources Center
1464 West Sidney Road
Sidney, Michigan 48885

Telephone. (517) 328-2111

Institutional Description. The two-year college was established by popular vote in 1965. Enrollment: 1,054.

Library Administration. John Carlson, Director.

Library General Holdings. 22,000 volumes; 200 current periodical titles.

Special Collections

The library maintains a pamphlet file on Michigan.

806
Northern Michigan University
Lydia M. Olson Library
Marquette, Michigan 49855

Telephone. (906) 227-2242

Institutional Description. The publicly supported state university was founded in 1899 as a teacher training institute. It now offers a wide diversity of programs. Enrollment: 6,340.

Library Administration. Rena Fowler, Director.

Library General Holdings. 425,000 volumes, including books and journals; 528,000 microfilms; 220,000 government documents; 34,000 maps.

Special Collections

The library houses a **Finnish-American Collection.** There are over 27,000 historical monographs and dozens of historical or historically-related periodicals and journals. Primary sources available to student and faculty include the State Department, Office of Indian Affairs, Bureau of Census, and governmental records on microfilm, microcard, or microfiche, plus major European collections such as the Nuremburg Trial Records and Foreign Office Records. The **Moses Coit Tyler Collection** consists of Mr. Tyler's personal library holdings.

807
Northwestern Michigan College
Mark Osterlin Library
1701 East Front Street
Traverse City, Michigan 49684

Telephone. (616) 922-1010

Institutional Description. Northwestern Michigan College was founded as a two-year college in 1951. Enrollment: 1,985.

Library Administration. Bernard Rink, Head Librarian.

Library General Holdings. 50,000 volumes.

Special Collections

The Osterlin Library has a collection of 215 Eskimo carvings and 265 Eskimo prints.

808
Northwood Institute
Strosacker Library
3225 Cook Road
Midland, Michigan 48640

Telephone. (517) 832-4273

Institutional Description. Northwood Institute is a private, independent business and management-oriented college with three campuses: Midland (Michigan), West Palm Beach (Florida), and Cedar Hill (Texas). Enrollment: 2,771.

Library Administration. Catherine W. Chen, Director of Libraries; James C. MacCampbell, Director of the Margaret Chase Smith Library Center.

Library General Holdings. 40,000 volumes; 540 periodical titles.

Special Collections

Collection development concentrates on acquiring materials for a well rounded education with emphasis on business management and economics. Special curriculum collections include accounting, advertising, automotive management, executive secretarial, fashion merchandising, and hotel and restaurant management.

Margaret Chase Smith Library Center. This Center is located in Skowhegan, Maine and is a private library open to serious students, educators, government representatives, researchers, and business and and industrial leaders who are interested in the compatible, constructive coexistence of government and the private sector. The library, in addition to its collection of political and government documentation, serves as an arena for free discussion of the economic ideas and ideals upon which the nation is founded.

809
Oakland University
Kresge Library
Walton and Squirrel Road
Rochester, Michigan 48309

Telephone. (313) 370-2481

Institutional Description. This is a publicly supported university, granting baccalaureate and graduate degrees. Enrollment: 9,142.

Library Administration. Suzanne Frankie, University Librarian; Robert Gaylor, Curator and Special Collections/Rare Books Librarian.

Library General Holdings. 1,276,845 pieces of library material, plus unprocessed manuscripts, memorabilia, and museum pieces. Included are 745,546 microforms; 13,362 records and phonotapes; 51,735 periodical volumes; 283,-793 cataloged circulating and reference books.

Special Collections

The special collections in the Kresge Library include the **James Collection** of folklore; the **William Springer Collection** of Lincolniana; **Hicks Collection** of seventeenth to nineteenth century books; various books, artifacts, photographs, and manuscripts; women in literature; and local and regional historical materials.

810
Olivet College
Main Library
Main Street
Olivet, Michigan 49076

Telephone. (616) 749-7608

Institutional Description. The privately supported liberal arts college is affiliated with the United Church of Christ. It grants baccalaureate degrees. Enrollment: 699.

Library Administration. Marjorie Stevens, Director.

Library General Holdings. 92,500 volumes; 600 current periodical subscriptions; 11,000 microforms.

Special Collections

The library has a special collection of materials on the Antarctic and maintains the Olivet College Archives.

811
Sacred Heart Seminary College
Ward Memorial Library
2701 Chicago Boulevard
Detroit, Michigan 48206

Telephone. (313) 868-2700

Institutional Description. The privately supported liberal arts and professional college was founded in 1919 to prepare candidates to train for the Roman Catholic priesthood. Enrollment: 83.

Library Administration. Arnold Rzepecki, Librarian.

Library General Holdings. 60,000 volumes; 250 current periodical subscriptions.

Special Collections

Special collections include the **Cardinal Mooney Collection** of papers relating to the institutional church and church and state relations; the **Monsignor Canfield Collection** of early editions; and a collection of material on the Roman Catholic Church in Michigan.

812
Saginaw Valley State College
Melvin J. Zahnow Library
2250 Pierce Road
University Center, Michigan 48710

Telephone. (517) 790-4042

Institutional Description. The publicly supported liberal arts state college was established in 1964. It grants baccalaureate and master's degrees. Enrollment: 3,303.

Library Administration. Clifton H. Jones, Director.

Library General Holdings. 135,000 volumes; 1,025 periodical titles; 22,000 microform items; 4,500 pamphlets.

Special Collections

The **Career Information Center** contains 2,600 books, brochures, and leaflets, as well as college catalogs of national and international institutions of higher learning. The library also maintains a collection of Saginaw area history which includes personal narratives and diaries.

813
St. John's Provincial Seminary
Seminary Library
4401 Five Mile Road
Plymouth, Michigan 48170

Telephone. (313) 453-6200

Institutional Description. The privately supported professional theological seminary offers programs on the graduate level only. It is affiliated with the Roman Catholic Church, and prepares candidates for the priesthood. Enrollment: 267.

Library Administration. Jean McGarty, Librarian.

Library General Holdings. 72,000 volumes; 400 current periodical titles; 1,700 cassette tapes.

Special Collections

The **Gabriel Richard Room** houses special materials on the early Catholic Church in Michigan, including several hundred volumes from the personal library of the pioneer missionary, Michigan educator, and legislator, Father Gabriel Richard, S.S., and the seminary's collection of rare books and fine printings.

814
St. Mary's College
Alumni Memorial Library
Commerce and Indian Trail Roads
Orchard Lake, Michigan 48033

Telephone. (313) 682-1885

Institutional Description. The privately supported Roman Catholic liberal arts college offers programs for those preparing for the priesthood as well as for those seeking a liberal arts curriculum. Enrollment: 166.

Library Administration. Sister Mary Ellen Lampe.

Library General Holdings. 61,500 volumes; 340 current periodical titles.

Special Collections

Special collections of the library include sociological papers and books on Polish-Americans; Roman Catholic theology; **Polish-Americana, 1860-Present** which includes books, periodicals, and personal papers; and **Polonica,** a collection of rare books.

815
University of Detroit
Main Library
4001 West McNichols
Detroit, Michigan 48221

Telephone. (313) 927-1070

Institutional Description. The privately supported university was founded in 1877 and reorganized in 1911.

It is a Catholic institution conducted by the Jesuit Fathers. Baccalaureate and graduate degrees are offered. Enrollment: 4,015.

Library Administration. Margaret E. Auer, Director of Libraries; Ann Walaskay, Head of Reference.

Library General Holdings. 439,000 volumes; 1,200 periodical subscriptions; 13,500 audiovisuals; depository for U.S. Government Documents. Major strengths in the areas of architecture, American folklore, medieval history, philosophy, theology, eighteenth and nineteenth British and American literature.

Special Collections

The library has special collections of instructional materials which include elementary and secondary textbooks, young adult and children's literature, tests, and curriculum guides for the metropolitan Detroit area schools.

816
University of Michigan
University Libraries
Ann Arbor, Michigan 48109

Telephone. (313) 764-7433

Institutional Description. The publicly supported state university was founded in 1817. It is now one of the nation's largest institutions of higher education with a wide, diverse curriculum. Enrollment: 32,535.

Library Administration. Richard M. Dougherty, Director of the University Libraries.

Library General Holdings. 5,000,000 volumes; 40,000 periodicals; 1,500,000 microfilms. The University Library System includes the Harlan Hatcher Graduate Library, the Undergraduate Library, and many special collections. Four major libraries on the Ann Arbor campus are administered separately from the main library system: the Law Library, the William L. Clements Library of Americana, the Michigan Historical Collections/Bentley Library, and the library of the School of Business Administration.

Special Collections

Law Library. One of the largest legal research libraries in the United States; is especially rich in materials on foreign law and jurisprudence.

William L. Clements Library of Americana. The Clements Library consists of an invaluable collection of books, newspapers, maps, manuscripts, and prints relating to early American history. It is especially notable for its manuscripts from the British side of the American Revolution.

Michigan Historical Collections/Bentley Library. The collections are concerned with manuscript and printed materials relating to the history of the state and its people. They are housed in the Bentley Historical Library and contain over 4,000 manuscript collections.

Business Amdinistration Library. Contains over 171,000 volumes.

Gerald R. Ford Presidential Library. This collection is part of the National Archives and is located on the North Campus near the Bentley Library.

Library Science Library. Contains over 37,000 volumes and 3,000 microfilms; books about books, bibliography, encyclopedias, atlases, and other reference materials in the field of library science.

Other important special collections include the **Meyers Collection on Germany** which covers the period 1933-1934 and contains earlier materials on the Ludenorff, Nazi, and other political groups; a **Papyri Collection** which is chiefly Greek and Latin texts, and the scholarly literature supporting their study; the **Labadie Collection** on radical political and social movements of the late nineteenth century to the present.

817
University of Michigan - Flint
Library
Flint, Michigan 48502

Telephone. (313) 762-3410

Institutional Description. A publicly supported unit of the University of Michigan. Enrollment: 3,721.

Library Administration. David W. Palmer, Librarian; Paul M. Gifford, Archivist.

Library General Holdings. 135,749 books; 1,023 periodical subscriptions; 18,177 bound periodicals; 312,455 microforms; 100,480 government documents.

Special Collections

The Genesee Historical Collections Center. Contains manuscript and published material on the history of Flint and Genesee County and the archives of the University of Michigan - Flint. Manuscript collections include those of Flint industrialist Arthur Giles Bishop; industrial psychologist Orlo Crissey; the Urban League of Flint; and the International Institute of Flint.

818
Walsh College of Accountancy and Business Administration
College Library
3838 Livernois Road
P.O. Box 7006
Troy, Michigan 48007

Telephone. (313) 689-8282

Institutional Description. The privately supported professional college was founded in 1922. Baccalaureate degrees are granted in accountancy and in business administration; master's degrees are granted in taxation, finance, and professional accountancy. Enrollment: 1,144.

Library Administration. Gloria B. Ellis, Director.

Library General Holdings. 17,000 volumes; 350 periodicals and newsletters.

Special Collections

The College Library maintains one of the most extensive tax collections in Michigan, either public or private. The overall collection reflects specialized topics in accounting, business law, communications, data processing, economics, finance, marketing, management, and statistics.

819
Washtenaw Community College Learning Resource Center 4800 East Huron River Drive P.O. Box D-1 Ann Arbor, Michigan 48106

Telephone. (313) 973-3300

Institutional Description. Founded in 1965, the two-year college began classes in 1966 in Willow Run. The college moved to its permanent campus in 1970. Enrollment: 3,701.

Library Administration. Kathleen Scott, Librarian.

Library General Holdings. 58,000 books; 500 magazine and 20 newspaper subscriptions; 10,000 pamphlets and clippings.

Special Collections

The library maintains the **Washtenaw Community College Archives,** the **Washtenaw Genealogical Society Collection;** and a collection of Michigan quadrant maps.

820
Wayne State University Wayne State University Libraries 5244 Cullen Mall Detroit, Michigan 48202

Telephone. (313) 577-4020

Institutional Description. The publicly supported university offers undergraduate and graduate degrees as well as certificates and specialist degrees. Enrollment: 18,516.

Library Administration. Peter Spyers-Duran, Dean, University Librarian.

Library General Holdings. 2,200,000 volumes; 25,000 current periodical subscriptions; 1,900,000 microforms.

Special Collections

Ashcom Collection. Donated by Prof. Benjamin Ashcom; includes 255 Spanish plays printed from the late seventeenth century to about 1825; over 800 volumes of Spanish literary texts supplemented by 1,500 general interest items on the Spanish Golden Age.

Berg Collection. A collection of books, posters, photos, programs, clippings, and memorabilia on dance, emphasizing dance in Detroit.

Ciardi Collection. Nine cartons of poetry and prose manuscripts (unprocessed) of the poet John Ciardi.

Depression Novel Collection. 125 American novels written about the Depression during the Depression.

French Belles-Lettres. 8,000 volumes from the period between the two world wars.

Graf Collection. A small collection of manuscript materials by the German author Oscar Maria Graf.

Hesse Collection. Manuscript materials by the German author Herman Hesse.

Heusler Collection. Andreas Heusler was a Swiss philologist specializing in the Nordic epic; includes selected titles from the residue of his collection remaining after the bulk of the materials were shared between several Swiss universities.

Howard/Lincoln/Civil War Collection. Frank Howard was a Detroit Lincoln buff of the 1930s. His collection was purchased by the Kresge Foundation and given to WSU. The collection centers on Lincoln but is rich in biographies of military and political figures, anti-slavery material, Civil War military campaigns, and diaries.

Kasle Collection. A collection of Judaica (much in Hebrew).

Kemeny Collection. A collection of a Hungarian poet and literary editor who published a newspaper in Detroit in the first third of this century.

Machen Collection. Letters and manuscripts by Arthur Machen.

Ordon Collection. Over 3,000 items in Polish on various topics.

Ramsey Collection. Over 10,000 items about and representing the history of children's literature. This is supplemented by a large current collection of children's literature; includes a number of rare volumes.

River Rouge Collection. Contains books, documents, reports, and other materials pertaining to environmental pollution in the Detroit-River Rouge complex.

Samuel Cox Hooker Collection. 21,000 volumes brought to WSU in 1944 by means of a grant from the Kresge Foundation; these volumes formed the nucleus of the present Science Library. Dr. Hooker was a chemist who privately collected works on chemistry and related subjects.

Simons Collection. Between 1,000 and 1,500 items relating to the discovery and exploration of the Great Lakes area and settlement of the Old Northwest Territory, emphasizing Detroit or Michigan; items are leather bound.

Symonds Collection. Letters and manuscript material by John Addington Symonds.

System on Automotive Safety Information Collection. Contains almost 200,000 items in the areas of motor vehicles, traffic engineering and science, accident analysis, air pollution, and drivers. Forms of materials include newspaper and journal articles, technical papers, foundation reports, radio and television transcripts, private correspondence and memoranda, books, chapters from books, internal reports and government documents.

Webber Collection. Periodicals on the field of retailing donated by a family related to the Hudson family.

Whitmer Collection. 2,000 to 2,500 titles purchased from a collector specializing in nineteenth century English fiction; the collection is of minor popular novelists influential as a body on the development of the novel form during its most prolific period.

821
Western Michigan University
Dwight B. Waldo Library
Kalamazoo, Michigan 49008

Telephone. (616) 383-1600

Institutional Description. The publicly supported state university offers baccalaureate, master's, and doctorate degrees. Enrollment: 15,415.

Library Administration. Carl H. Sachtleben, Director.

Library General Holdings. 2,400,000 volumes; 10,000 periodical and serial titles; 750,000 microforms.

Special Collections

Ann Kercher Memorial Collection. An extensive collection of materials on Africa south of the Sahara.

Southern Asia. Library holdings on Southern Asia are another area of special strength. Together with the Kercher Collection, they help support the University's commitment to area studies.

Medieval Period. Includes the history, religion, philosophy, and culture of the medieval period; these materials support the programs of the University's Medieval Institute.

Randall Frazier Memorial Collection. A collection honoring a notable alumnus which includes a wealth of material on the history and culture of Black America.

Regional History Collection. Includes a unique group of items of the thirteen counties of southwest Michigan. In addition to books, this collection contains manuscripts of early residents of this area.

C.C. Adams Ecological Collection. Consists of the personal collection of books and papers of the pioneer American ecologist.

Cistercian Studies Library. The library is a collection of books in the areas of monastic history, spirituality, and general church history which supports the research and programs of the Institute of Cistercian Studies and the area of medieval studies at the University. The collection includes rare books, manuscripts, and incunabula, most of which are on an indefinite loan to Western Michigan University from the Abbey of Gethsemane. Over 400 of the some 6,000 volumes in the library are rare items of interest to medieval scholars from all over the world.

Rare Book Collections

A rare book from Michigan history, William Beaumont's *Physiology of Digestion with Experiments on the Gastric Juice,* was acquired in 1977 as the one-millionth volume in Western's libraries. The work, considered a milestone in medicine, was written by a military surgeon stationed at Ft. Michilimackinac (now Mackinaw City) in 1822. The two-millionth volume, acquired in 1982, was an exact reproduction of *The History of Kalamzaoo County, Michigan,* first published in 1880.

822
Western Theological Seminary
Beardslee Library
86 East 12th Street
Holland, Michigan 49423

Telephone. (616) 392-8555

Institutional Description. The privately supported professional theological seminary is affiliated with the Reformed Church in America. Programs are on the graduate level only; degrees are professional and master's. Enrollment: 180.

Library Administration. Leslie Burke, Librarian; Elaine R. Cline, Librarian.

Library General Holdings. 85,000 volumes; 500 current periodical subscriptions.

Special Collections

The **Kohlman Memorial Archives** preserve letters and papers which document the history of the Reformed Church in America and of Western Seminary, as well as the lives and labors of men and women influential in the mission and ministry of the church.

823
William Tyndale College
Johnston Library
35700 West Twelve Mile Road
Farmington Hills, Michigan 48018

Telephone. (313) 553-7200

Institutional Description. The privately supported liberal arts and professional college, formerly known as the Detroit Bible College, is interdenominational. It offers church service as well as conventional liberal arts programs. Enrollment: 336.

Library Administration. Anne Frohlich, Librarian.

Library General Holdings. 55,000 volumes; 190 current periodical subscriptions.

Special Collections

The library maintains collections of pamphlets, Christian education material, tapes, records, flannelgraphs, slides, and filmstrips.

Minnesota

824
Augsburg College
George Sverdrup Library
731 21st Avenue South
Minneapolis, Minnesota 55454

Telephone. (612) 330-1001

Institutional Description. The privately supported liberal arts college is affiliated with the American Lutheran Church. Enrollment: 1,541.

Library Administration. Margaret Anderson, Head Librarian.

Library General Holdings. 160,00 volumes; 626 periodical subscriptions; 3,000 government documents; 5,175 audiovisual materials.

Special Collections

Augsburg Archives. The Archives house historical materials relating to the history and development of the college.

825
Bemidji State University
A.C. Clark Library
1500 Birchmont Drive NE
Bemidji, Minnesota 56601

Telephone. (218) 755-2955

Institutional Description. The publicly supported state university was founded in 1919 as a normal school. It now offers undergraduate and graduate degrees. Enrollment: 3,839.

Library Administration. Deane A. Kishel, University Librarian; Ardis Wilander, Special Collections Librarian.

Library General Holdings. 150,000 volumes; 800 current periodical subscriptions; partial depository for U.S. Government Documents (keeping latest 5 years); 20,000 titles in children's books and sample teaching materials (audiovisual and textbooks).

Special Collections

American Indian Collection. Includes about 3,500 items at all levels from picture books for children to scholarly materials; areas of concentration in order of importance to the collection are the Ojibwa and Sioux of Minnesota, Indians of the Upper Midwest, and the remainder of North America (including Eskimos); houses the National Indian Education Association Collection, formerly based in Minneapolis.

Special Collection Room. Includes materials by local authors (most signed) with a few manuscripts; local historical material; and examples of sixteenth to nineteenth century printing. The Bemidji State University Archives and a branch collection of the Minnesota Historical Society are also housed.

826
Bethel College
Library
3900 Bethel Drive
St. Paul, Minnesota 55112

Telephone. (612) 638-6400

Institutional Description. The privately supported four-year college was founded in 1871 and is owned and operated by the Baptist General Conference of America. Enrollment: 1,722.

Library Administration. Norris A. Magnuson, Library Director.

Library General Holdings. 118,000 books; 750 current periodicals; 6,000 audiocassette tapes; 1,500 microforms.

Special Collections

The Library has a strong collection of materials by and about Baptists, as well as by and about the larger Evangelical movement.

Lundquist-Nelson Collection. Consists of material on Christian spirituality.

Rare Book Collections

Skarstedt Collection in Pietisic Literature. Consists of about 3,000 volumes from the seventeenth through the mid-nineteenth centuries; collected by Professor C.W. Skarstedt of Lund University (Lund, Sweden), procured, and donated to Bethel Seminary about 1920 by Professor

Emanuel Schmidt of Bethel Seminary.

Klingberg Collection of Puritan Literature. Includes more than 100 editions of Bunyan's *Pilgrim's Progress,* and about 150 additional volumes of Puritan writings from the sixteenth through the eighteenth centuries. Collected by J.E. Klingberg and Haddon Klingberg, Swedish Baptist pastors. The Klingberg Collection is part of a larger collection of more than 500 largely Puritan volumes from pre-1800 reflecting the evangelical heritage.

Scandinavian Hymnody. Includes about 200 titles from the seventeenth through the nineteenth centuries.

827
Bethel Theological Seminary
Seminary Library
3949 Bethel Drive
St. Paul, Minnesota 55112

Telephone. (612) 638-6182

Institutional Description. The privately supported graduate seminary was founded in 1871 and occupies a campus jointly with the four-year liberal arts Bethel College. It is owned and operated by the Baptist General Conference of America. Enrollment: 339.

Library Administration. Robert C. Suderman, Director.

Library General Holdings. The Seminary Library is combined with the Bethel College Library. *See* **Bethel College.**

828
Brainerd Community College
Library
College Drive at SW 4th Street
Brainerd, Minnesota 56401

Telephone. (218) 828-2525

Institutional Description. Established in 1938, the college became part of the Minnesota Community College System in 1964. Enrollment: 703.

Library Administration. Larry M. Kellerman, Librarian.

Library General Holdings. 24,000 volumes; 150 periodical titles; 10,500 microforms.

Special Collections

The library has a special collection of child development materials and a licensed practical nursing film strip training program. There are also collections on art and physics.

829
Carleton College
Carleton Library
Northfield, Minnesota 55057

Telephone. (507) 663-4000

Institutional Description. The privately supported liberal arts college was founded in 1866 by the General Conference of the Congregational Churches of Minnesota. Today it is a nondenominational institution. Enrollment: 1,854.

Library Administration. T. John Metz, College Librarian.

Library General Holdings. 389,000 volumes; 1,430 current periodicals; 143,000 government documents; 53,000 microforms.

Special Collections

Special collections in the Carleton Library include the **Arctic and Antarctic Collection;** the **Warming Orchid Books Collection,** and **the Donald Beaty Bloch Collection of Western Americana.**

830
College of Saint Benedict
Clemens Library
College Avenue South
Saint Joseph, Minnesota 56374

Telephone. (612) 363-5505

Institutional Description. The privately supported liberal arts college for women is a coordinate college with St. John's University for men, in nearby Collegeville. Both are affiliated with the Roman Catholic Church. Enrollment: 1,913.

Library Administration. Michael Kathman, Director of Libraries.

Library General Holdings. The libraries at the College of Saint Benedict and Saint John's University serve the combined student body with a joint staff and coordinated programs and services. Joint holdings of the two libraries are 400,000 volumes, 1,800 periodical subscriptions, 110,000 government documents, and 20,000 microforms.

Special Collections

The Clemens Library's collection is particularly strong in the fields of literature, religion, women's studies, education, fine arts, and nursing. The resources of the Education Department Curriculum Library and Music Library of the Benedicta Arts Center are also available. *See also* **St. John's University (Minnesota).**

831
College of St. Catherine
College Library
2004 Randolph Avenue
St. Paul, Minnesota 55105

Telephone. (612) 690-6525

Institutional Description. The privately supported liberal arts college for women was founded in 1905. It is affiliated with the Roman Catholic Church, and grants baccalaureate degrees. Enrollment: 2,546.

Library Administration. Janet Kinney, Director.

Library General Holdings. 211,200 volumes; 1,000 current periodical and newspaper subscriptions.

Special Collections

The library's maintains a special collection of 3,500 titles on women's studies and and a collection of books, records, and tapes on the performing arts.

832
College of St. Catherine - St. Mary's Campus Library
2500 South Sixth Street
Minneapolis, Minnesota 55454

Telephone. (612) 332-5521

Institutional Description. The privately supported junior college was established in 1964 under the auspcies of the Roman Catholic Church. Enrollment: 600.

Library Administration. Janet S. Kinney, Director.

Library General Holdings. 25,000 volumes.

Special Collections

The library maintains a collection of the National League for Nursing pamphlets.

833
College of St. Scholastica Library
1200 Kenwood Avenue
Duluth, Minnesota 55811

Telephone. (218) 723-6033

Institutional Description. The privately supported Roman Catholic liberal arts college grants baccalaureate and master's degrees. Enrollment: 1,294.

Library Administration. Mary Jane Kumsha, Director of Libraries.

Library General Holdings. 95,000 volumes; 620 current periodical titles.

Special Collections

The library maintains special collections for **American Indian Studies** and children's and young adult literature.

American Indian Cultural Resource Center. The Center serves as a hub for the many Indian educational programs and activities at St. Scholastica.

834
College of St. Thomas
O'Shaughnessey Library
2115 Summit Avenue
St. Paul, Minnesota 55105

Telephone. (612) 647-5212

Institutional Description. The privately supported liberal arts college for men was founded in 1885. Its graduate school is coeducational. The college is affiliated with the Roman Catholic Church. Enrollment: 5,818.

Library Administration. Karl L. Ozolins, Director.

Library General Holdings. 250,000 books; 1,500 scholarly journals.

Special Collections

The library's special **Celtic Collection** includes 6,000 titles (some in Gaelic) in literature and political science.

Rare Book Collections

The rare book collections of the library contain eighteenth- and nineteenth-century pre-Revolutionary French literature and history, including over 500 diaries plus 1,000 rare books in first editions and autographed copies.

835
Concordia College - Moorehead
Carl B. Ylvisaker Library
Moorehead, Minnesota 56560

Telephone. (218) 299-3000

Institutional Description. The privately supported liberal arts college is affiliated with the American Lutheran Church. Enrollment: 2,512.

Library Administration. Verlyn D. Anderson, Librarian.

Library General Holdings. 265,000 books; 1,300 journal subscriptions; 48 newspaper subscriptions.

Special Collections

Career Information Center. Includes materials useful to students in planning careers.

Rare Book Collections

The special collections area of the library houses rare books such as early pioneer memoirs from the days of the first Red River Valley settlements.

836
Concordia College - St. Paul
Buenger Memorial Library
Hamline and Marshall Avenue
St. Paul, Minnesota 55104

Telephone. (612) 641-8211

Institutional Description. The privately supported liberal arts and teachers college was founded in 1893 with a three-year classical and normal preparatory course. It is affiliated with the Lutheran Church—Missouri Synod. Enrollment: 897.

Library Administration. Glenn W. Offermann, Librarian.

Library General Holdings. 99,000 volumes; 440 current periodical subscriptions; 6,900 microforms; 15,000 audiovisual materials.

Special Collections

Special collections include a hymnbook collection, Lutheran and Reformation-related materials, and a historical textbook collection.

837
Dr. Martin Luther College
DMLC Library
New Ulm, Minnesota 56073

Telephone. (507) 354-8221

Institutional Description. The privately supported teachers college was founded in 1884 to offer theological training. It grants baccalaureate degrees and is affiliated with the Wisconsin Evangelical Lutheran Synod. Enrollment: 484.

Library Administration. Gerald J. Jacobson, Librarian.

Library General Holdings. 87,000 volumes; 355 current periodical subscriptions.

Special Collections

The library's most significant special collection contains major editions of the works of Martin Luther. The library also has a children's literature section and a curriculum library.

838
Gustavus Adolphus College
Folke Bernadotte Memorial Library
St. Peter, Minnesota 56082

Telephone. (507) 931-7556

Institutional Description. This private liberal arts college is supported by the Minnesota and Red River Valley Synods of the Lutheran Church in America. Originally supported by the Minnesota Conference of the Augustana Lutheran Church, it is one of the oldest (1862) educational institutions in Minnesota. Enrollment: 2,172.

Library Administration. Michael Haeuser, College Librarian; Edith Thorstensson, Special Collections Librarian; Marita Karlisch, Visiting College Archivist.

Library General Holdings. 215,000 books; 1,320 periodical subscriptions; 11,500 audiovisual materials; 28,500 microforms; 60,000 U.S. Government Documents.

Special Collections

The Folke Bernadotte Memorial Library holds specialized collections of materials related to Selma Lagerlog, Swedish writer and Nobel prize winner in the **Nils Sahlin Collection; The Barnwell Collection** of children's literature; Swedish-American books, periodicals and other publications in the **Historical Archives Collection;** and a collection of Korean porcelain and Japanese prints in the **Oriental Art Collection.** The library also has extensive holdings in Scandinavian literature.

Rare Book Collections

Rare books and manuscripts held in the Folke Bernadotte Memorial Library include several hundred Bibles, Testaments, and Psalmbooks published in languages other than English (many Scandinavian) during the sixteenth to nineteenth centuries; first edition works by regional authors; and the political cartoons of Gene Basset.

839
Hamline University
Bush Memorial Library
1536 Hewitt Avenue
St. Paul, Minnesota 55104

Telephone. (612) 641-2202

Institutional Description. The privately supported liberal arts college was founded in 1854. Affiliated with the United Methodist Church, it includes a law school. Enrollment: 1,736.

Library Administration. Jack King, University Librarian.

Library General Holdings. 170,000 volumes; 640 current periodical subscriptions.

Special Collections

Special collections include the **Burke Collection of South Asia,** the **Jewish Studies Collection,** the Minnesota Jewish Historical Society Collection, and the **Methodist Church Collection.** Hamline's collection of brass rubbings is also displayed in the library.

840
Luther Northwestern Theological Seminary
Luther Northwestern Seminary Library
2375 Como Avenue
St. Paul, Minnesota 55108

Telephone. (612) 641-3224

Institutional Description. The privately supported seminary traces its origin to the Chicago Lutheran Divinity School begun in 1920. Through a series of mergers covering more than half a century, the seminary represents the consolidation of what at one time were six separate institutions. The seminary is affiliated with The American Lutheran Church and The Lutheran Church in America. Enrollment: 558.

Library Administration. Norman G. Wente, Library Director.

Library General Holdings. 191,515 volumes; 2,165 microforms; 5,450 audiovisual materials; 747 current periodical subscriptions.

Special Collections

Lutheran Brotherhood Foundation Reformation Library. During the "Luther Year" of 1983 which marked the 500th birthday of Martin Luther, the Lutheran Brotherhood Insurance Company based in Minneapolis announced the formation of a microfilm library of prime resource materials from the Reformation era. All important documents books, *flugschriften,* etc., pertaining to the Reformation were to be filmed and copies made available to scholars, researchers, interested laity and clergy.

A pilot filming project was immediately initiated in the Rare Book Room of Luther Northwestern Seminary in St. Paul and one hundred sixteenth-century books were selected for microfilming. A unique collection of 19 letters written by George Spalatin recently acquired by Lutheran Brotherhood was also filmed. Eventually, pertinent films were also acquired from the Hill Monastic Manuscript Library in Collegeville, Minnesota. To this original core of materials has been added research materials from the libraries of Oxford and Cambridge Universities and from the Herzog August Bibliothek in Wolfenbuettel, Germany.

The library also maintains the **Doving Hymnal Collection** and the **Tanner Catechism Collection.**

841
Mankato State University Memorial Library Mankato, Minnesota 56001

Telephone. (507) 389-1822

Institutional Description. The publicly supported state university offers liberal arts and professional programs. Enrollment: 11,814.

Library Administration. Thomas Peischl, Dean of the Library.

Library General Holdings. 680,000 volumes; 2,500 periodical subscriptions.

Special Collections

The library has large collections of microtexts, maps, aerial photographs, records, tapes, periodicals, newspapers, films, videotapes, and other audiovisual materials. Music materials are housed in the Music Library. The library is the site of the Center for Minnesota Studies.

842
Minneapolis College of Art and Design Library 133 East 25th Street Minneapolis, Minnesota 55404

Telephone. (612) 870-3161

Institutional Description. The privately supported professional visual arts college grants baccalaureate degrees. Enrollment: 538.

Library Administration. Richard Kronstedt, Head Librarian.

Library General Holdings. 50,000 volumes; 1,000 audio- and videocassettes; 170 art and design publications.

Special Collections

The library maintains an extensive picture file and 75,000 slides of art works from all historical periods. The majority of the library's collection is devoted to the visual arts.

843
Moorehead State University Livingston Lord Library Moorehead, Minnesota 56560

Telephone. (218) 236-2922

Institutional Description. The publicly supported state university was established as a two-year normal school in 1885. In 1921, it became a four-year college, and in 1975, adopted its present name. Enrollment: 5,654.

Library Administration. Darrel M. Meinke, Dean of Instructional Resources; Carol Hanson Sibley, Curriculum Librarian; Terry Shoptaugh, Archives Librarian.

Library General Holdings. 231,500 bound volumes; 1,405 periodical subscriptions.

Special Collections

Curriculum Materials Center. Contains 37,300 items including juvenile books, textbooks, curriculum guides, audiovisual materials, and reference books used in teaching preschool through secondary levels.

Northwest Minnesota Historical Center. The Center is a special archives collection housing manuscripts, documents, maps, photographs, oral histories, and other materials concerning the history and culture of the northwestern part of the state. Among the 500 linear feet of materials in the collection are the papers of pioneer lawyer Solomon Comstock, 1,100 photographs of early photographer Haakon Bjornaas, and the papers of many state legislators, businesses, and organizations.

844
North Central Bible College
T.J. Jones Memorial Library
910 Elliot Avenue, S.
Minneapolis, Minnesota 55404

Telephone. (612) 332-3491

Institutional Description. The privately supported professional Bible college was founded in 1930. It is affiliated with the Assemblies of God Church, and grants associate and baccalaureate degrees. Enrollment: 1,031.

Library Administration. Clyde Root, Director.

Library General Holdings. 45,000 volumes; 287 periodical titles.

Special Collections

Because North Central Bible College is part of the unique Pentecostal movement, the library has organized those books which deal with Pentecostal phenomena into the **Archive Collection.** This collection is comprised of material that deals specifically with the Baptism in the Holy Spirit, Glossalalia, Spiritual Gifts, the spread of the Pentecostal message, the Rivivaltime Pulpit, and various theological works by some of the Assembly of God founders, such as Myer Pearlman, E.S. Williams, F.M. Boyd, and others.

845
Northwestern College
McAlister Library
3003 North Snelling Avenue
St. Paul, Minnesota 55113

Telephone. (612) 631-5241

Institutional Description. This is a privately supported Christian college of the Bible, arts, sciences, and vocational education. It prepares students for Christian vocations. Enrollment: 942.

Library Administration. Sheila Carblom, College Librarian; Mary Lou Hovda, Associate Librarian and Special Collections Librarian.

Library General Holdings. 70,000 volumes; 530 periodicals; 3,500 microforms; 3,300 phonodiscs; 4,000 audiovisual materials.

Special Collections

The McAlister Library maintains the **W.B. Riley Collection** consisting of manuscripts, scrapbooks, pamphlets, correspondence, periodicals.

846
Northwestern College of Chiropractic Library
2501 West 84th Street
Bloomington, Minnesota 55431

Telephone. (612) 888-4777

Institutional Description. The privately supported professional college was founded in 1941. It grants the Doctor of Chiropractic degree. Enrollment: 542.

Library Administration. Cheryl A. Bjerke, Head Librarian.

Library General Holdings. 12,000 volumes; 385 current periodical subscriptions.

Special Collections

The library houses a collection which consists of books in the basic and clinical sciences and in the areas of chiropractic and radiology.

847
St. Cloud State University
Learning Resources Services
3rd Avenue South
St. Cloud, Minnesota 56301

Telephone. (612) 255-0121

Institutional Description. St. Could State University was founded in 1869. Enrollment: 13,588.

Library Administration. John Berling, Dean, Learning Resources Services.

Library General Holdings. 708,000 volumes; 3,700 periodical titles; 1,131,000 microforms; 22,000 audiovisual materials; 53,000 maps; 83,000 microbook units.

Special Collections

The special collection efforts of Learning Resources Services include the areas of children's literature and manuscripts of Minnesota authors.

Central Minnnesota Historical Center. The purpose of the Center is to collect primary and secondary sources of history of central Minnesota in order to preserve these materials and to make them available for the use of students, scholars, and interested citizens.

848
Saint John's University
Alcuin Library
Collegeville, Minnesota 56321

Telephone. (612) 363-2011

Institutional Description. The privately supported Roman Catholic university for men is comprised of a liberal arts college, a school of divinity, a graduate school in theological studies, and an institute for advanced ecumenical studies. Enrollment: 1,903.

Library Administration. Michael D. Kathman, Director of Libraries and Media.

Library General Holdings. 298,000 volumes; 1,300 periodical subscriptions; 27,000 microforms; 160,000 government documents; 5,000 audiovisual materials.

Special Collections

Strengths in the area of special collections are theology and history with emphasis on Catholic liturgy.

Hill Monastic Manuscript Library. The library has the dual purpose of preserving handwritten manuscript treasures on film and making them available to scholars. Since it was established in 1964 as a sponsored program of Saint John's University, complete collections of manuscripts have been microfilmed systematically in libraries and archives throughout Europe and Africa. The manuscripts now preserved on microfilm were largely written by hand and have been preserved by Benedictine and other monastic libraries. Through the production of catalogues and other tools of access, the Library has become a national resource for the documentation and study of the periods presented. This "collection of collections" at Saint John's houses more than 20,000,000 pages of documentation.

849
St. Mary's College
Fitzgerald Library
Winona, Minnesota 55987

Telephone. (507) 457-1503

Institutional Description. The privately supported liberal arts college was founded in 1912. It is operated by the Roman Catholic Church's Christian Brothers. Enrollment: 1,663.

Library Administration. Br. Paul Ostendorf, F.S.C., Head Librarian.

Library General Holdings. 100,000 volumes; 658 current periodical subscriptions.

Special Collections

The library has special collections of works by James Joyce, Henry David Thoreau, and Paul Clandel.

850
St. Olaf College
Rolvaag Memorial Library
Northfield, Minnesota 55057

Telephone. (507) 663-3000

Institutional Description. The privately supported liberal arts college is affiliated with the American Lutheran Church. It was founded in 1874. Enrollment: 3,108.

Library Administration. Forrest E. Brown, Librarian.

Library General Holdings. 367,000 volumes; 1,350 periodicals.

Special Collections

The collections are especially strong in the fields of religion and Scandinavian literature and history. The library is one of the few places where extensive materials can be found for the study of the culture and church life of Norwegian-Americans. The library maintains a collection of books on Lutheran theology in the sixteenth through the eighteenth centuries.

Kierkegaard Library. This library is one of the major research libraries in the world for the study and thought of Soren Kierkegaard.

St. Olaf College Archives. The materials in the Archives provide historical information about the Board of Regents, the faculty, the student body, alumni, academic departments, administrative offices, campus services, college organizations, and campus activities.

Norwegian-American Historical Foundation. This Association has been sheltered by St. Olaf College since 1925. The NAHA publishes on a regular basis scholarly books that treat topics related to Norwegian migration to America. The Archives of NAHA consist of books, periodicals, and manuscripts. The manuscript collections range from personal papers to organizational records, from diaries and journals to unpublished book-length manuscripts.

851
St. Paul Bible College
Library
Bible College, Minnesota 55375

Telephone. (612) 446-1411

Institutional Description. The privately supported liberal arts and professional Bible college is affiliated with the Christian and Missionary Alliance Church. It grants associate and baccalaureate degrees. Enrollment: 605.

Library Administration. Marcelyn J. Smid, Director of Library and Media Services.

Library General Holdings. 78,000 volumes; 360 current periodical titles.

Special Collections

A curriculum library of 9,500 children's books is maintained for the Elementary Education program. The library also contains archival material about the Christian and Missionary Alliance and the St. Paul Bible College.

852
Southwest State University
University Library
Marshall, Minnesota 56258

Telephone. (507) 537-6272

Institutional Description. The publicly supported state university was established in 1963 as a four-year college featuring liberal arts and technical programs. Enrollment: 2,206.

Library Administration. John M. Bowden, Director.

Library General Holdings. 139,000 volumes; 670 current periodicals; 23,000 microforms; 11,000 non-book items.

Special Collections

Curriculum Library/Instructional Media Laboratory. Supports the teacher education programs of the University.

Southwest Minnesota Historical Center. This is one of several such centers in the state and is operated by the History/Political Science Department. It collects personal, corporate, and organizational papers of historical interest as well as oral histories of particular interest to southwestern Minnesota.

853
United Theological Seminary of the Twin Cities
Library
3000 Fifth Street, N.W.
New Brighton, Minnesota 55112

Telephone. (612) 633-4311

Institutional Description. The privately supported professional theological seminary was formed in 1962 by the merger of Mission House Theological Seminary of Wisconsin and the Yankton School of Theology of South Dakota. It offers programs on the graduate level only, and is affiliated with the United Church of Christ. Enrollment: 115.

Library Administration. Arthur Merrill, Director of Library Services.

Library General Holdings. 61,000 volumes; 298 current periodical subscriptions.

Special Collections

The library maintains a collection geared to its curriculum and has special holdings in theology, women and religion, and Evangelical and Reformed Church history.

854
University of Minnesota - Duluth
Library and Learning Resources Service
2400 Oakland Avenue
Duluth, Minnesota 55812

Telephone. (218) 726-8000

Institutional Description. The publicly supported state university is a campus of the University System of Minnesota. It was founded in 1947. Enrollment: 6,825.

Library Administration. Donald J. Pearce, Director.

Library General Holdings. 280,000 volumes; 2,600 periodicals.

Special Collections

Important special holdings of the library include the Ramseyer-Northern Bible Society museum collection and the Voyageur Collection of northeastern Minnesota history. The library also maintains the campus Archives.

Northeast Minnesota Historical Center. Operated jointly with the St. Louis County Historical Society, the Center collects books, papers, pamphlets, and other materials relating to the history of northeastern Minnesota.

855
University of Minnesota - Morris
Rodney A. Briggs Library
Morris, Minnesota 56267

Telephone. (612) 589-2211

Institutional Description. The publicly supported branch campus of the University of Minnesota was established in 1960, offering liberal arts and teacher education. Enrollment: 1,665.

Library Administration. Russell E. DuBois, Head Librarian.

Library General Holdings. 137,000 volumes; 810 current periodical subscriptions; 16,000 microforms.

Special Collections

The library houses the West Central Minnesota Historical Research Center.

856
University of Minnesota - Twin Cities
University Libraries
100 Church Street Southeast
Minneapolis, Minnesota 55455

Telephone. (612) 625-5000

Institutional Description. The publicly supported state university offers of a wide variety of programs, colleges, and schools. It consists of five campuses: the main campus at Minneapolis-St. Paul, Duluth, Crookston, Waseca, and Morris. Enrollment: 45,630 (main campus).

Library General Holdings. 4,000,000 volumes. The resources of the University of Minnesota - Twin Cities Libraries system, one of the largest American university libraries, includes more than 20 library units, including the Biomedical Library (health sciences collections), Institute of Technology Libraries (engineering, architecture, mathematics, and physical sciences collections), St. Paul Libraries (agriculture, biological sciences, and veterinary medicine collections), and Walter and Wilson Libraries (social sciences, humanities, archives, and special collections).

Special Collections

Areas of particular strength include British history, English and American literature, agriculture, biological sciences, engineering technology, Scandinavian studies, South Asia, history of European expansion, and history of medicine. Of particular importance are the **James Ford**

Bell Library on European expansion before 1800; the **Kerlan Collection of Children's Literature;** and the **Wongensteen Historical Library of Biology and Medicine.**

857
Winona State University
Maxwell Library
Johnson and Sanborn
Winona, Minnesota 55987

Telephone. (507) 457-2017

Institutional Description. The publicly supported liberal arts and teacher education university was founded in 1858 as the State Normal School in Winona. Today, a wide variety of programs is offered. Enrollment: 5,032.

Library Administration. Robert Wilson, Department Chairperson.

Library General Holdings. 202,000 volumes; 1,305 periodicals; 834,000 microforms.

Special Collections

The library maintains special holdings in the field of education, nursing, and paralegal studies.

Mississippi

858
Alcorn State University
John Dewey Boyd Library
Lorman, Mississippi 39096

Telephone. (601) 877-3711

Institutional Description. Alcorn State University is a state institution and land-grant college. Enrollment: 2,329.

Library Administration. Epsy Y. Hendricks, Director.

Library General Holdings. 178,000 volumes; 1,000 periodical subscriptions; 49,936 microforms; 4,565 audiovisual titles; 184,959 government documents.

Special Collections

The library maintains a collection of materials on Black studies.

859
Coahoma Junior College
Library
Route 1, Box 16
Clarksdale, Mississippi 38614

Telephone. (601) 627-2571

Institutional Description. By establishing Coahoma County Agricultural High School in 1924, Coahoma County became the first county in Mississippi to provide an agricultural high school for Blacks. The junior college curriculum was added in 1949 and the present name was adopted. Enrollment: 1,617.

Library Administration. Laura Wilkins, Librarian.

Library General Holdings. 12,000 volumes.

Special Collections

The library maintains a **Black Collection** of 759 items and a **Professional Collection** of 223 career-oriented items.

860
Copiah-Lincoln Junior College
Evelyn Oswalt Library
P.O. Box 457
Wesson, Mississippi 39191

Telephone. (601) 643-5101

Institutional Description. The two-year college was established in 1928. It offers courses in vocational/technicial and academic areas for terminal and transfer programs. Enrollment: 1,825.

Library Administration. Willie May Dunn, Librarian.

Library General Holdings. 35,000 volumes; 265 magazine and 13 newspaper subscriptions.

Special Collections

A **Mississippi Collection** is housed in the library.

861
Delta State University
W.B. Roberts Library
Highway 8 West
Cleveland, Mississippi 38733

Telephone. (601) 846-4000

Institutional Description. The university is a state institution founded in 1924. Enrollment: 3,294.

Library Administration. Myra Faye Macon, Director of Library Services.

Library General Holdings. 248,000 volumes; 1,300 current periodicals; 390,000 microforms; 57,000 government documents; 15,000 audiovisual materials.

Special Collections

Mississippi Room. Houses materials on the history of Mississippi. The library also maintains the papers of Walter Sillers.

862
East Mississippi Junior College
Tubb-May Memorial Library
P.O. Box 158
Scooba, Mississippi 39358

Telephone. (601) 476-8442

Institutional Description. The two-year college was founded in 1927. A branch campus is located in Mayhew. Enrollment: 775.

Library Administration. Myra Faye Macon, Director of Library Services.

Library General Holdings. 22,000 volumes.

Special Collections

The library's collection supports the curriculum of the college with emphases in the humanities, music education, and pre-professional fields.

863
Hinds Junior College
Learning Resources Services
Raymond, Mississippi 39154

Telephone. (601) 857-5261

Institutional Description. The two-year college was founded in 1917 and offers academic, technical, vocational, and continuing education programs. Enrollment: 6,669.

Library Administration. Alma Fisher, Administrative Librarian.

Library General Holdings. 110,000 books; 100,000 items of non-print materials; 800 periodical titles.

Special Collections

The library is a depository for Nuclear Regulatory Commission publications.

864
Holmes Junior College
Library
Hill Street
Goodman, Mississippi 39079

Telephone. (601) 472-2312

Institutional Description. The two-year college evolved from the Holmes County Agricultural High School which had its beginnings in 1911. College work was added in 1928. Enrollment: 1,176.

Library Administration. Eugenia Collins, District Librarian.

Library General Holdings. 37,000 volumes; 250 periodical titles.

Special Collections

The **Mississippi Juvenile Literature Collection** is housed in the library.

865
Itawamba Junior College
Learning Resources Center
Fulton, Mississippi 38843

Telephone. (601) 862-3101

Institutional Description. The curriculum of the two-year college is based on the training needs of business and industry. Enrollment: 4,004.

Library Administration. Brenda J. Edmonson, Librarian.

Library General Holdings. 46,000 volumes; 496 periodical titles; 45,000 microfiche.

Special Collections

The special collection of Mississippiana contains over 680 items.

866
Jackson State University
H.T. Sampson Library
1400 J.R. Lynch Street
Jackson, Mississippi 39217

Telephone. (601) 968-2123

Institutional Description. The publicly supported state university was founded in Natchez in 1877. It was originally a private church school and for 53 years was supported by the American Baptist Home Mission Society. It became a teachers college of the State of Mississippi in 1940. Enrollment: 6,425.

Library Administration. Lelia G. Rhodes, Librarian; Bernadine McClain, Reference and Special Collections Librarian.

Library General Holdings. 700,000 items.

Special Collections

Afro-American Collection. Contains books by and about Blacks (including first editions and autographed copies), newspaper clippings, selected periodicals, photographs, pamphlets, bills of sale for slaves, recordings, manuscripts and bound transcriptions of the *Black Women Oral History Project.*

Margaret Walker Alexander Collection. Includes a copy of each book written by the author, newspaper clippings, galley proof of *Jubilee,* an uncorrected copy of *Poetic Equations: Conversations Between Nikki Giovanni and Margaret Walker,* foundation file of the Institute for the Study of Life, History and Culture of Black People, recordings, tapes, speeches, letters, photographs, programs, and a bronze bust of Phillis Wheatley sculptured especially for Jackson State University.

Mississippi Collection. Contains a limited number of books by and about Mississippians, Mississippi State publications, newspaper clippings, a file of original accrediting reports of Mississippi elementary junior and senior high schools for Blacks prior to desegregation, Magnolia State High School Activities Association and Mississippi Big Eight Conference files, the original set (minus volumes 1 and 10) of the Centenary Series of the Publications of the Mississippi Historical Society, and a representative number of the early laws of Mississippi.

Bolton C. Price Collection. Scientific books, magazines, bulletins, notes, and photographs comprise this collection.

Other special collections include the University Archives, the Raymond I. Johnson Music Collection, and the microfilm titles of the Schomberg Center for Research in Black Culture.

867
Meridian Junior College
L.O. Todd Library
5500 Highway 19N
Meridian, Mississippi 39305

Telephone. (601) 483-8241

Institutional Description. The two-year college opened in 1937 and moved to its present site in 1965. Enrollment: 3,619.

Library Administration. Scott R. Johnson, Director.

Library General Holdings. 42,446 volumes; 700 current periodical subscriptions; 250,000 microforms.

Special Collections

The library supports the curriculum of the college with emphases in business, health education, and technology.

868
Millsaps College
Millsaps-Wilson Library
Jackson, Mississippi 39210

Telephone. (601) 354-5201

Institutional Description. Millsaps College is a private college affiliated with the United Methodist Church. Enrollment: 1,358.

Library Administration. James F. Parks, Jr., College Librarian; Kathryn A. Holden, Associate Librarian for Collection Development.

Library General Holdings. 200,000 volumes; 700 periodical subscriptions.

Special Collections

Special collections are: the **Lehman Engel Collection** of books and recordings, the **Mississippi Methodist Archives,** the **Kellogg Collection** of juvenile books and curriculum materials; the **Eudora Welty Collection;** the **Millsaps Archives,** and a rare book collection.

869
Mississippi College
Leland Speed Library
P.O. Box 127
Clinton, Mississippi 39056

Telephone. (601) 925-3438

Institutional Description. The privately supported liberal arts and comprehensive college is owned and operated by the Mississippi Baptist Convention. It is one of the oldest and largest Baptist colleges in the United States, having been chartered in 1826, and is the oldest institution of higher learning in Mississippi. Enrollment: 2,191.

Library Administration. J.B. Howell, College Librarian; Alice G. Cox, Special Collections Librarian.

Library General Holdings. 215,000 volumes; 772 periodical and newspaper subscriptions; 6,000 microforms; 3,227 audio recordings; 1,559 audiocassettes; 2,000 videocassettes.

Special Collections

Mississippi Baptist Historical Collection. A collection of 1,200 volumes and 2,500 other items consisting of church records, minutes of Baptist associations, early newspapers, periodicals published by the denomination, and a number of rare books which tell the Baptist story in Mississippi, 1836 to the present.

Alumni Publications Collection. This collection consists of 600 books, which were written, edited, or compiled by Mississippi College graduates, 1880 to the present; also includes copies of journal articles, reprints, and recordings.

Rare Book Collections

Mississippi

870
Mississippi State University
University Library
Mississippi State, Mississippi 39762

Telephone. (601) 325-2323

Institutional Description. This state institution and land-grant college was founded in 1878. Enrollment: 11,-474.

Library Administration. George R. Lewis, Director of Library Services.

Library General Holdings. 1,092,688 volumes; 7,459 current periodical subscriptions; 268,000 government documents; 1,740,000 microforms.

Special Collections

Special collections contain materials of historical value, including many manuscript collections, church and business records, the papers of a number of public figures of importance to Mississippi—most notable those of U.S. Senator John C. Stennis, Hodding Carter, and Turner Catledge—and the archives of the University.

871
Mississippi University for Women Library Columbus, Mississippi 39701

Telephone. (601) 329-4750

Institutional Description. The publicly supported (state) liberal arts and teachers university for women was founded in 1884. The first male students were admitted in 1982. Associate, baccalaureate, and master's degrees are granted. Enrollment: 1,850.

Library Administration. David L. Payne, Director of Library Services.

Library General Holdings. 371,475 volumes; 1,595 current periodical subscriptions; 413,000 microforms; 206,000 government documents.

Special Collections

Special holdings of the library include a collection of Mississippiana which includes books by and about local authors.

872
Mississippi Valley State University James Herbert White Library Itta Bena, Mississippi 38941

Telephone. (601) 254-9041

Institutional Description. This state university was founded in 1946. Enrollment: 2,133.

Library Administration. Robbye R. Henderson, Chief Librarian.

Library General Holdings. 101,591 volumes; 545 current periodical subscriptions; 156,000 microforms; 7,500 audiovisual materials.

Special Collections

The **University Archives** and **Oral History Collection** are housed in the Mississippi Room.

873
Reformed Theological Seminary Library 5422 Clinton Boulevard Jackson, Mississippi 39209

Telephone. (601) 922-4988

Institutional Description. The privately supported theological seminary provides professional education on the graduate level, especially for the Presbyterian and Reformed denominations. Enrollment: 218.

Library Administration. Thomas G. Reid, Jr., Library Director.

Library General Holdings. 75,000 volumes (including bound periodicals); 665 periodical subscriptions; 2,200 microfilm; 31,000 microfiche; 5,000 audiocassettes; 500 other media.

Special Collections

George A. Blackburn Memorial Library. Covers Southern Presbyterianism to 1959; includes 1,100 book volumes; numerous periodicals, minutes, articles, and papers.

John L. Girardeau Papers. Papers and class notes of John L. Girardeau, Southern Presbyterian pastor, seminary professor, theologian, and writer.

Southern Presbyterian Collection. This collection of about 200 volumes complements the Blackburn Library (see above).

874
Southwest Mississippi Junior College Library/Learning Resources Center Summit, Mississippi 39666

Telephone. (601) 684-0411

Institutional Description. The two-year college offers a college transfer program along with vocational/technical programs. Enrollment: 1,062.

Library Administration. Jo Ann Young, Librarian.

Library General Holdings. 30,333 volumes; 134 periodical titles; 2,933 non-print items.

Special Collections

The **Mississippi Room** contains a special collection of Mississippiana.

875
Tougaloo College L. Zenobia Coleman Library Tougaloo, Mississippi 39174

Telephone. (601) 956-4941

Institutional Description. The privately supported college offers teacher preparatory and professional programs in Judaic and Hebraic studies. Enrollment: 214.

Library Administration. Jeannetta Cole-Roach, Head Librarian.

Library General Holdings. 107,000 volumes; 450 periodical subscriptions.

Special Collections

Special collections include the **Black Collection** containing more than 3,000 rare and special titles by and about Blacks. The **Tougaloo Archives Collections** include rare books, faculty and alumni publications, photographs, programs, speeches, artifacts, and other historical information related to the College.

876
University of Mississippi
John Davis Williams Library
University, Mississippi 38677

Telephone. (601) 232-7408

Institutional Description. The publicly supported university was founded in 1848. The University of Mississippi Medical Center is located in Jackson. Enrollment: 8,896.

Library General Holdings. 624,665 volumes; 7,029 current periodical subscriptions; 1,048,053 government documents; 171,772 microforms; 30,411 audiovisual materials.

Special Collections

Afro-Americana Collection. Consists of books, journals, and sheet music relating to Afro-American culture and history.

Archives and Manuscripts. The University Archives holds official and unofficial records of The University of Mississippi, including Board of Trustee and faculty minutes, papers of chancellors, faculty papers, student letters, and photographic collections.

The manuscripts collections include over three hundred collections of private and corporate papers and records. A notable collection is the lumber archives, documenting the lumber industry of southern Mississippi from the 1830s to the 1950s. A manuscript collection of international significance is the "Rowan Oak Papers." One of the most important manuscript finds of this century, the Rowan Oak Papers contain over eighteen hundred pages of early William Faulkner literary manuscripts. In 1983, the Wynn Collection of William Faulkner Poetry Manuscripts, including previously unknown literary works, was donated to the department. In addition to the litrary manuscripts of Faulkner, Barry Hannah, Will D. Campbell, and Beth Henley, the manuscipts unit includes a wide variety of personal papers, diaries, letters, legal documents, Congressional and Senatorial papers.

Brickell Collection. Includes modern Southern fiction with strengths in first editions, review and presentation copies, and correspondence from Margaret Mitchell and Eudora Welty.

Latham Collection. Contains early printed books and eighteenth-century French books concerning pre-revolutionary France.

Mississippi Collection. This collection is the core printed book collection. Established in 1927 as a gift to the University from Judge Stone Deavours, the collection is now one of the largest dedicated collections of books concerning Mississippi and Mississippians. The collection includes holdings of early works on Mississippi as well as comprehensive author collections of Mississippi writers William Faulkner, Eudora Welty, Tennessee Williams, and Richard Wright. The Faulkner Collection now ranks as one of the strongest research collections on Faulkner in the world.

Mississippi State Documents. The library has been a depository for state documentary materials since 1966.

Sterling Plumpp Collection of Afro-American Fiction and Verse. The emphasis of this collection is on the urban experience of Afro-Americans.

877
University of Southern Mississippi
Joseph Anderson Cook Memorial Library
Hattiesburg, Mississippi 39406

Telephone. (601) 266-4241

Institutional Description. The publicly supported university was founded in 1912 as a normal school. It now offers a wide variety of programs, granting baccalaureate, master's, and doctorate degrees. Enrollment: 11,444.

Library Administration. Onva K. Boshears, Director.

Library General Holdings. 709,000 volumes; 5,000 current periodical subscriptions; 702,000 microforms; 309,000 government documents.

Special Collections

William David McCain Library and Archives. The Library, which opened in 1976, contains the University's special collections of manuscripts, books, and memorabilia and the University Archives. These collections are maintained primarily to support research in selected areas. Among the special collections, the most prominent are: **Mississippiana; Genealogy;** the **de Grummond Children's Literature Collection;** the **Woods Collection** of rare books; the papers of William M. Colmer, Theodore G. Bilbo, Paul Johnson, Richard S. Lackey, and M.M. Roberts; the **Walen Collection on the Confederacy and the Civil War;** and the distinguished **Cleanth Brooks Collection** of *belles lettres.*

878
Wesley College
Wesley College Library
P.O. Box 70
Florence, Mississippi 39073

Telephone. (601) 845-2265

Institutional Description. The privately supported Bible and liberal arts college is affiliated with the Congregational Methodist Church. Enrollment: 71.

Library Administration. Janice G. Perker, College Librarian.

Library General Holdings. 21,000 volumes; 84 periodical and newspaper subscriptions.

Special Collections

The Wesley College Library has the following three specialized collections: **Religious Materials,** including Methodist Church disciplines, holiness materials, Bible commentaries, and other research aids; **Cult Materials,** including primary and secondary sources on a wide variety of cults; and **Literature Materials,** including sets of books by American and English authors.

879
William Carey College
I.E. Rouse Library
Tuscan Avenue
Hattiesburg, Mississippi 39401

Telephone. (601) 582-5051

Institutional Description. The privately supported liberal arts college was founded in 1906 as a women's college. It became coeducational in 1953. Affiliated with the Southern Baptist Church, it grants baccalaureate and master's degrees. Enrollment: 1,027.

Library Administration. Marilyn M. Pound, Director of Libraries.

Library General Holdings. 110,000 volumes; 600 periodical subscriptions.

Special Collections

The **Clarence Dickinson Collection** is centered around church music. It contains 5,600 items which include books, scores, manuscripts, microforms, phonodiscs, tapes, paintings, and memorabilia. The **Otis Seal Ministerial Library** forms another special collection of more than 2,000 items consisting of books, tapes, and other materials that assist ministerial students in the preparation of sermons.

880
Wood Junior College
Learning Resource Center
Route 2, Box C
Mathiston, Mississippi 39752

Telephone. (601) 263-8128

Institutional Description. Wood Junior College was founded in 1886 and is affiliated with the United Methodist Church. Enrollment: 332.

Library Administration. Rosabelle J. Land, Librarian.

Library General Holdings. 32,000 volumes; 155 periodical subscriptions; 5,000 pamphlets.

Special Collections

The **Historical Journals and Minutes of the North Mississippi Conference of the United Methodist Church** are housed in the learning resource center.

Missouri

881
Aquinas Institute
Library
3642 Lindell Boulevard
St. Louis, Missouri 63108

Telephone. (314) 658-3882

Institutional Description. The privatley supported professional theological seminary offers programs at the graduate level only. It is located on the campus of St. Louis University, and is affiliated with the Roman Catholic Church. Enrollment: 51.

Library Administration. Henry Baldwin, F.S.C., Librarian.

Library General Holdings. 35,000 volumes; 230 current periodical titles.

Special Collections

The library has special strengths in philosophy, systematic theology, and Dominican materials.

882
Assemblies of God Theological Seminary
Cordas C. Burnett Library
1445 Boonville Avenue
Springfield, Missouri 65802

Telephone. (417) 862-3344

Institutional Description. The privately supported professional theological seminary offers programs on the graduate level only. It is affiliated with the Assemblies of God Church, and grants professional and master's degrees. Enrollment: 326.

Library Administration. Joseph F. Marics, Librarian.

Library General Holdings. 53,500 volumes; 860 periodicals; 45,000 microforms.

Special Collections

The **Assemblies of God Archives** provide a wealth of information on the history of the Pentecostal Movement.

883
Calvary Bible College
Kroeker Library
15800 Calvary Road
Kansas City, Missouri 64147

Telephone. (816) 322-0110

Institutional Description. The privately supported independent Bible college grants Associate, Bachelor and Master's degrees. Enrollment: 322.

Library Administration. John Hartog, College Librarian.

Library General Holdings. 48,000 volumes (mostly of theology and Bible or of a religious nature); 300 periodicals; 2 daily newspaper subscriptions; 1,100 microforms; 100 music scores; 450 other learning materials.

Rare Book Collections

The Library has approximately 1,300 rare books; about 60 percent are of a religious nature and 40 percent of various areas; some of the books were donated by Dr. Walter Wilson, a medical doctor, author, and one of the founders of Calvary Bible College.

884
Central Christian College of the Bible
College Library
1111 Urbandale Drive, E.
Moberly, Missouri 65270

Telephone. (816) 265-3900

Institutional Description. The privately supported professional Bible college is affiliated with the Christian Church (Disciples of Christ), and grants associate and baccalaureate degrees. Enrollment: 85.

Library Administration. Patty Agee, Assistant Librarian.

Library General Holdings. 23,500 volumes; 158 current periodical subscriptions.

Special Collections

A distinctive feature of the library is the addition of the missionary files collected by the Walter Cobles of Garrett, Indiana. This collection is one of the most complete files on independent missions to be found anywhere.

885
Central Methodist College
College Library
Fayette, Missouri 65248

Telephone. (816) 248-3391

Institutional Description. The privately supported liberal arts college was founded in 1854. Affiliated with the United Methodist Church, it grants baccalaureate degrees. Enrollment: 632.

Library Administration. Robert Yontz, Head Librarian.

Library General Holdings. 100,000 volumes; 400 periodical subscriptions.

Special Collections

The library's record collection consists of over 3,000 recordings, including the Clifford Collection. It is also the official depository of the Missouri West Conference of the United Methodist Church Commission on Archives and History and of the Boonslick Historical Society.

886
Central Missouri State University
Ward Edwards Library
Warrensburg, Missouri 64093

Telephone. (816) 429-4111

Institutional Description. The publicly supported state university was founded in 1871 as a state normal school. It now offers liberal arts curricula as well as teacher education. Enrollment: 8,060.

Library General Holdings. 615,000 volumes; 2,650 periodical subscriptions; 625,000 items in microprint.

Special Collections

Special collections include materials on safety, U.S. Civil War history, and teacher education.

887
Cleveland Chiropractic College
Dr. Ruth Cleveland Memorial Library
6401 Rockhill Road
Kansas City, Missouri 64131

Telephone. (816) 333-8230

Institutional Description. The privately supported professional college was founded in 1922. It grants professional degreees in chiropractic. Enrollment: 361.

Library Administration. Marcia M. Thomas, Library Director.

Library General Holdings. 99,000 volumes; 200 journal subscriptions.

Special Collections

The library's holdings are a specialized collection of chiropractic and health science works which support the college's curriculum and promote independent study. Standard indexing and abstracting services, such as the *Abridged Index Medicus* and the **Chiropractic Research Archive Collection** are available for the student and researcher.

888
Conception Seminary College
Conception Abbey and Seminary Library
Conception, Missouri 64433

Telephone. (816) 944-2211

Institutional Description. The privately supported Roman Catholic seminary for men was established in 1883 by the Benedictine Monks of Conception Abbey. Attendance is limited to candidates preparing for the priesthood. Enrollment: 83.

Library Administration. Aidan McSorley, O.S.B., Librarian.

Library General Holdings. 91,155 books; 18,483 bound periodicals; 308 current periodical subscriptions; 2,755 phonograph recordings; 13,166 art slides; 671 microforms; 54 incunabula; 38 manuscript leaves.

Rare Book Collections

The Rare Books Collection consists of about 2,600 volumes, derived from the parent institution, Engelberg Abbey, founded in the eleventh century in Switzerland. The Abbey sent its collection to the United States to escape a threatened confiscation at the hands of an antimonastic government. This accounts for the large number of fifteenth-century books and the fact that the books have not passed through different owners or bookdealers. The books have remained in good condition, being passed from one monastery to the present monastery.

Of the books in the collection, 15 percent was printed in the 1500s, 24 percent in the 1600s, 54 percent in the 1700s. The main subject areas covered are Benedictine Order, Ascetics, Bible, Law, Philosophy, Church History, and Liturgy. Smaller numbers of books are in the areas of Literature, Moral Theology, Patrology, and Hagiography.

Also part of the collection are leaves from manuscripts from the ninth to sixteenth centuries, for the most part from liturgical and biblical books.

889
Concordia Seminary
Seminary Library
801 DeMun Avenue
St. Louis, Missouri 63105

Telephone. (314) 721-5934

Institutional Description. The privately supported theological seminary was founded in 1839. It is affiliated with the Lutheran Church—Missouri Synod, and offers graduate-level programs only. Enrollment: 463.

Library Administration. David P. Daniel, Director of Library Services.

Library General Holdings. 165,000 volumes; 1,080 current periodicals; 39,000 microforms; 14,000 audiovisual materials.

Special Collections

Special collections include the personal libraries of many of the founding fathers of The Lutheran Church—Missouri Synod and its theology professors, e.g., C.F.W. Walther, Georg Stoeckhardt, F. Pieper, E.A. Krauss, and others. Alumni and interested individuals have frequently given unusual and rare materials to the library, e.g., the **Hemmeter Collection** which contains over 1,300 dissertations and pamphlets published before 1800 and the incunabula given by C.A. Graebner. Other special collections include the **Maier Collection** of medical and Reformation publications; the **Haffenreffer Collection** of works by or about Johannes Brenz; and the **Luther and Lutheran Reformation Collection.**

890
Cottey College
Blanche Skiff Ross Memorial Library
225 South College
Nevada, Missouri 64772

Telephone. (417) 667-8187

Institutional Description. The privately supported junior college for women was founded in 1884. It features the liberal arts and is owned by the P.E.O. Sisterhood. Enrollment: 340.

Library Administration. Rebecca Kiel, Interim Library Director.

Library General Holdings. 60,000 volumes; 184 periodical titles; microforms; music scores; audiovisual media.

Special Collections

Women's Collection. Contains 1,500 books about women, including relationships of women to other areas of society, historical works, and works of women artists. Many of the newer books are purchased with funds given by the International Chapter of P.E.O. Sisterhood.

Children's Literature Collection. Consists of 1,300 juvenile books and a collection of 18,000 art slides used to support courses in children's literature and in art history.

891
Covenant Theological Seminary
J. Oliver Buswell, Jr. Library
12330 Conway Road
St. Louis, Missouri 63141

Telephone. (314) 434-4044

Institutional Description. The privately supported graduate seminary has as its primary purpose the preparation of qualified candidates for the gospel ministry. It is the official seminary of The Reformed Presbyterian Church in America. Enrollment: 111.

Library Administration. Joseph H. Hall, Librarian; Ian M. Tate, Curator.

Library General Holdings. 50,530 volumes; 360 current periodical subscriptions; 2,950 microforms; 715 audiovisual aids.

Rare Book Collections

Tait Puritan and Rare Book Collection. The library of Covenant Theological Seminary has been the fortunate recipient of a generous gift which has made possible the purchase of the remarkable personal collection of Puritan and rare books of the Reverend Doctor Ian M. Tait of England. This collection has been designated "one of the finest private collections of Puritan works and rare books in either England or the United States." It has been joined by other Puritan and rare books already on the shelves and a collection recently purchased from Covenant College. Of over 2,000 volumes in the collection, most are out of print and difficult to obtain. A few are collector's items: Aristotle's *De Physico* published in Venice in 1540 with its original vellum binding. Erasmus' *De Copia Verborum* printed in 1555 and Philip Melanchton's *Responsiones Scriptae* published at Wittenberg in 1559 with heavily embossed vellum covers and decorated with a watercolor painting on the front edge of its pages.

There are numerous sets of collected, complete, or select works. One of the most prized works in the collection is *Opera Omnia* of John Calvin published in Latin in Amsterdam in 1671 in nine folio volumes bound in vellum. The 56-volume set of the works of the reformers published by the Parker Society is part of the collection.

892
Culver-Stockton College
Carl Johann Memorial Library
Canton, Missouri 63435

Telephone. (314) 288-5221

Institutional Description. The privately supported liberal arts college was founded in 1853. Affiliated with the Disciples of Christ Church, it grants baccalaureate degrees. Enrollment: 761.

Library Administration. Sharon K. Upchurch, Librarian.

Library General Holdings. 116,500 volumes; 300 current periodical subscriptions.

Special Collections

The special collections of the library include the **Kermit Murdock Collection** of American and English literature and the **Johann Midwest Americana Collection.**

893
DeVry Institute of Technology
James A. Lovan Library
11224 Holmes Road
Kansas City, Missouri 64131

Telephone. (816) 941-0430

Institutional Description. The privately supported institute offers programs in computer science and electronics engineering technology. It grants associate and baccalaureate degrees. Enrollment: 2,141.

Library Administration. Connie Migliazzo, Director, Learning Resource Center.

Library General Holdings. 6,890 volumes; 140 periodical subscriptions; 26 annuals and looseleaf services; 24,425 microfiche.

Special Collections

Electronics Manufacturers Data Book Collection. This collection includes over 600 data books from the manufacturers of electronic components.

894
Drury College
Walker Library
900 North Benton Avenue
Springfield, Missouri 65820

Telephone. (417) 865-8731

Institutional Description. The privately supported liberal arts college is affiliated with the United Church of Christ (Congregational) and the Christian Church (Disciples of Christ). Its School of Religion has been in existence since 1909. Enrollment: 1,841.

Library Administration. Judith G. Armstrong, Director.

Library General Holdings. 160,000 volumes; 895 current periodical titles; 14,000 microforms; 40,000 government documents.

Special Collections

The library has original manuscripts and first editions of the nineteenth-century Irish author George Moore. The **John F. Kennedy Assasination Memorial Collection** is also maintained. The personal library of Major T.P. Walker, a 1908 alumnus and former trustee of the college, consists of first editions and rare books which are housed in the Rare Book Room.

895
East Central College
Library
Highway 50 and Prairie Dell Road
P.O. Box 529
Union, Missouri 63084

Telephone. (314) 583-5193

Institutional Description. East Central College is a comprehensive community college offering two-year liberal arts and professional programs. Enrollment: 1,618.

Library Administration. Rebecca I. Grady, Assistant Librarian.

Library General Holdings. 20,100 volumes; 300 periodical titles.

Special Collections

The library has a collection of math tapes for algebra, trigonometry, and calculus.

896
Eden Theological Seminary
Luhr Library
475 East Lockwood Avenue
Webster Groves, Missouri 63119

Telephone. (314) 961-3627

Institutional Description. The privately supported theological seminary was founded in 1850. It is affiliated with the United Church of Christ and offers graduate-level programs only. Enrollment: 106.

Library Administration. Karen M. Luebbert, Director.

Library General Holdings. Eden Seminary and Webster University share a common library of over 177,000 volumes; 800 French, German, and American journals; 11,000 microforms; 29,000 audiovisual materials.

Special Collections

James I. Good Collection. Consists of 5,000 items, including catechisms, liturgies, and other materials of the Reformed Church of the United States; the **Evangelical Synod Archives** which includes records, correspondence, and files from the Evangelical Synod of North America, a denomination which existed from 1850 until it merged in 1934 with the Reformed Church.

897
Fontbonne College
Fontbonne College Library
6800 Wydown Boulevard
St. Louis, Missouri 631105

Telephone. (314) 862-3456

Institutional Description. The privately supported college was established in 1917. It is a coeducational institution under the sponsorship of the Roman Catholic Sisters of St. Joseph of Carondelet. Enrollment: 716.

Library Administration. Sr. Alberta Ruys, Library Director.

Library General Holdings. 97,000 volumes; 470 current periodicals; 7 newspaper subscriptions; 21,022 audiovisual materials.

Special Collections

Curriculum Library. Includes 5,000 items; besides the textbooks used in most Missouri schools, there are housed various kits and teaching aids as well as the subject guides for teachers which are required by the State Department of Education.

Rare Book Collections

The Library has a few rare books, including the *Official Record of the Union and Confederate Navies 1862-1865.*

898
Hannibal-LaGrange College
L.A. Foster Library
Palmyra Road
Hannibal, Missouri 63401

Telephone. (314) 221-3675

Institutional Description. The privately supported liberal arts college was founded in 1858. It is affiliated with the Southern Baptist Church. Enrollment: 522.

Library Administration. Vivian Rasmussen, Director.

Library General Holdings. 57,200 volumes; 480 current periodical subscriptions.

Special Collections

The library maintains the **Missouri Collection,** the **College Archives,** and a rare book collection.

899
Harris-Stowe State College
College Library
3026 Laclede
St. Louis, Missouri 63103

Telephone. (314) 533-3366

Institutional Description. The publicly supported state teachers college was founded in 1857 as Harris Teachers College. It merged with Stowe Teachers college in 1954. Harris-Stowe grants baccalaureate degrees. Enrollment: 772.

Library Administration. Martin Knorr, Director, Library Services.

Library General Holdings. 88,000 volumes; 340 current periodical subscriptions; 24,000 microforms.

Special Collections

Urban Education Specialist/Multi-cultural Education Collection. This collection consists of books, materials, models, and films relating to both the Urban Education Specialist Degree Program and the Multi-Cultural Education Program.

Juvenile Literature Collection. This collection is devoted entirely to written and graphic material suited for young readers.

The library also maintains the **Proceedings and Reports of the St. Louis Public Schools** covering the period 1851 to the present.

900
Kansas City Art Institute
Art Institute Library
4415 Warwick Boulevard
Kansas City, Missouri 64111

Telephone. (816) 561-4852

Institutional Description. The privately supported professional school was chartered in 1887 as the Fine Arts Institute. It now grants baccalaureate degrees. Enrollment: 446.

Library Administration. May Gamer, Director.

Library General Holdings. 35,000 volumes; 115 current periodical titles.

Special Collections

The library is a specialized collection of volumes for the visual arts and liberal arts curriculum. The **Slide Library** contains 60,000 slides of subjects ranging from prehistoric artifacts to contemporary works of art. The primary function of this collection is instruction support for art history courses, but it also serves as a visual resource for all faculty and students.

901
Kemper Military School and College
Library
701 3rd Street
Boonville, Missouri 65233

Telephone. (816) 882-5623

Institutional Description. The two-year private college for men was founded in 1923. Enrollment: 162.

Library Administration. Sara L. Rohrs, Librarian.

Library General Holdings. 20,000 volumes; 135 periodical subscriptions; 3,500 microfiche.

Special Collections

The **McNeely Collection of Military History** is maintained by the library.

902
Kenrick Seminary
Charles L. Souvay Memorial Library
7800 Kenrick Road
St. Louis, Missouri 63119

Telephone. (314) 644-0266

Institutional Description. The privately supported theological seminary was founded in 1818. Affiliated with the Roman Catholic Church, it offers graduate-level programs only. Enrollment: 70.

Library Administration. Jacquelin M. Page, Director; Dorothy Kaiser, Archivist.

Library General Holdings. 73,000 volumes; 350 current periodical subscriptions.

Special Collections

The present library is the product of fusion of two principal collections: the St. Louis Archdiocesan collection, or St. John's Library, assembled by Bishop Rosati and by Archbishop Kenrick and given to the Seminary at its foundation in 1893; and the St. Catherine Library Association collection, originally placed at St. Vincent's College, Cape Girardeau, Missouri, where diocesan students for the priesthood received their education prior to 1893. Since 1900, these two basic collections have been developed in numerous ways by gifts, bequests, and purchases to form the present basically theological library.

The library has acquired its special tone and character also from the fusion of various personal libraries, such as the St. Louis Catholic Historical Society Collection, the former separately maintained Faculty Library of Kenrick, the personal library of John Cardinal Glennon, a number of gifts from His Eminence, John Joseph Cardinal Carberry of St. Louis and the Most Reverend Albert R. Zuroweste of Belleville, Illinois. The library also has acquired much of the personal library of Monsignor Martin B. Hellriegal who collected a wealth of liturgical material.

The library has a collection of the writings of Thomas Merton. In addition to books, there is a 22-volume set compiled by Father Thomas J. Nelson, C.M., an alumnus of Kenrick, which consists of the writings of Merton found in periodical literature, poetry, pamphlets, and books with contributions, including some unpublished manuscripts. The library also has a set of cuneiform tablets given principally to Father Souvay, whose name now graces the library.

Rare Book Collections

The 1,800 rare and special books range from a 1495 Bible, the earliest of the Bibles in the collection, to some area histories of the Church in the United States, a number of diocesan synods before 1930, yearbooks of the Archdiocese of St. Louis, and most of the works of the two Archbishops Kenrick, Peter Richard of St. Louis, and Francis Patrick of Philadelphia.

903
Kirksville College of Osteopathic Medicine
A. T. Still Memorial Library
800 West Jefferson
Kirksville, Missouri 63501

Telephone. (816) 626-2345

Institutional Description. The privately supported college was established in 1892. Degrees granted are professional in osteopathic medicine. Enrollment: 544.

Library Administration. Lawrence W. Onsager, Library Director.

Library General Holdings. 62,000 volumes; 840 current periodical subscriptions.

Special Collections

The A.T. Still Memorial Library supports the curriculum with major emphasis on the field of osteopathy.

904
Lincoln University
Inman E. Page Library
820 Chestnut Street
Jefferson City, Missouri 65101

Telephone. (314) 681-5501

Institutional Description. The publicly supported state liberal arts and professional university was founded in 1866 as Lincoln Institute. It has been a state school since 1879. Enrollment: 2,106.

Library Administration. Elizabeth A. Wilson, Reference Librarian.

Library General Holdings. 150,000 volumes; 800 current periodical subscriptions; 46,000 non-book materials.

Special Collections

Special areas of concentration include the Library of American Civilization, an ultrafiche library of American history and the **Black Collection** which includes a slavery microfiche collection of documents concerned with slavery and the slave trade, the nineteenth-century Black newspapers, and an extensive grouping of books by and about Blacks.

905
Logan College of Chiropractic
Learning Resources Center
1851 Schoettler Road
P.O. Box 1065
Chesterfield, Missouri 63006

Telephone. (314) 227-2100

Institutional Description. The privately supported chiropractic college was founded in 1935. It offers programs on the graduate level only. The curriculum is based on the belief that the chiropractic student should be liberally educated in addition to being completely trained in the sciences and chiropractic skills. Enrollment: 605.

Library Administration. Rosemary E. Buhr, Director, Learning Resources Center.

Library General Holdings. 12,000 volumes; 225 current periodical titles; audiovisual collection consisting of videotapes and slide/sound programs.

Special Collections

Included in the Learning Resources Center is a collection of osseous material (full skeleton, spines, and individual bones); anatomical models; current information on chiropractic legislation from state legislatures, chiropractic associations, and other chiropractic organizations. Records and other historical material are housed in the Archives of the college.

906
Maryville College
Father Edward J. Dowling Library
13550 Conway Road
St. Louis, Missouri 63141

Telephone. (314) 576-9510

Institutional Description. The privately supported liberal arts college was founded as an academy in 1827. It is now an independent, career-oriented institution, granting associate, baccalaureate, and master's degrees. Enrollment: 1,598.

Library Administration. Tony C. Krug, Director.

Library General Holdings. 101,000 volumes; 600 current periodical subscriptions; 25,000 government documents; 150,000 microforms.

Special Collections

The library maintains curriculum materials and a juvenile literature collection in the Education Center. In addition, the **Father Edward J. Dowling Collection** contains materials on Catholicism, political science, alcoholism, and mental illness. The **Maryville Archives** contains materials on the history of the college and the **Hutig Chapel Collection** includes works on religion and personal counseling.

907
Mineral Area College
Learning Resources Center
Flat River, Missouri 63601

Telephone. (314) 756-6701

Institutional Description. The two-year public college was created in 1965 as a successor to Flat River Junior College. Enrollment: 1,536.

Library Administration. Chris William, Director.

Library General Holdings. 27,000 books; 175 magazine subscriptions.

Special Collections

The **Webster College Collection** of 148 volumes is maintained in the library.

908
Missouri Baptist College
College Library
12542 Conway Road
St. Louis, Missouri 63141

Telephone. (314) 434-1115

Institutional Description. The privately supported liberal arts college was founded as an extension center of Hannibal-LaGrange College in 1957. Now merged with its parent institution, it grants baccalaureate degrees. It is affiliated with the Southern Baptist Church. Enrollment: 467.

Library Administration. Stephen Gateley, Director of Library Services.

Library General Holdings. 98,700 volumes; 400 periodical titles.

Special Collections

The library maintains a curriculum library for church leadership and the publications of the Southern Baptist Convention.

909
Missouri Southern State College
George A. Spiva Library
Newman and Duquesne Roads
Joplin, Missouri 64801

Telephone. (417) 625-9386

Institutional Description. The publicly supported state college includes liberal arts and teacher training. Enrollment: 3,290.

Library Administration. Charles Nodler, Librarian and Archivist.

Library General Holdings. 175,000 volumes; 1,300 current periodicals; 26 newspaper subscriptions; 38,000 volumes on microfilm; 378,000 microfiche.

Special Collections

The Spiva Library maintains the **Gene Taylor Congressional Papers,** the **Tri-State Mining Collection** (maps and drill logs); the **Arrel Morgan Gibson Literary Manuscripts;** and the College Archives and historical material.

910
Missouri Western State College Library 4525 Downs Drive St. Joseph, Missouri 64507

Telephone. (816) 271-4200

Institutional Description. The publicly supported liberal arts and teachers college was founded in 1915 as St. Joseph Junior College. Enrollment: 3,005.

Library Administration. Helen J. Wigersma, Dean, Learning Resources Center.

Library General Holdings. 150,000 volumes; 1,100 journals.

Special Collections

The library's collections reflect a blend of the traditional liberal arts subjects and career-oriented programs. These include agriculture, business and economics, criminal justice and legal studies, education, physical education and recreation, nursing, secretarial science, allied health, and technology.

911
Nazarene Theological Seminary William Broadhurst Library 1700 East Meyer Boulevard Kansas City, Missouri 64131

Telephone. (816) 333-6254

Institutional Description. The privatley supported theological seminary offers programs on the graduate level only. Affiliated with the Church of the Nazarene, it provides courses to prepare students for various phases of the Christian ministry. Enrollment: 457.

Library Administration. William C. Miller, Librarian.

Library General Holdings. 71,000 volumes; 460 current periodical subscriptions.

Special Collections

Among the collections of the library are excellent sections on the doctrine of holiness as perpetuated in the Wesleyan tradition and on the history of the Church of the Nazarene. Through the generosity of Mr. and Mrs. E.H. Land, a major collection relating to the theological and historical sources of the holiness movement has been acquired and designated as the **James P.McGraw Memorial Wesleyana-Methodistica Collection** in honor of Dr. McGraw, late professor of preaching.

912
Northeast Missouri State University Pickler Memorial Library Kirksville, Missouri 63501

Telephone. (816) 785-4526

Institutional Description. The publicly supported state university was founded in 1867. Originally a normal school and commercial college, it is now a liberal arts and teacher education institution. Enrollment: 5,944.

Library Administration. George Hartje, Library Director; Odessa Ofstad, Special Collections Librarian and Archivist.

Library General Holdings. 285,039 volumes (including bound periodicals and newspapers); 1,802 current periodical subscriptions; 44 newspaper subscriptions; 997,405 microfilms; 11,751 curriculum materials; 58,493 U.S. and Missouri documents.

Special Collections

The Curriculum Library houses 11,751 textbooks, curriculum guides, and related materials of use in training teachers. A laboratory collection of children's literature includes another 6,065 volumes.

The Music/Media Library contains the following types of materials of universal subject matter: 5,449 phonograph recordings; 2,529 scores; 51,457 slides; 1,068 film loops; 7,403 cassettes; 3,018 filmstrips; and 2,505 videos.

The Audio-Visual Department administers 1,192 16mm films. The Library is a selective depository for federal government documents and a full depository of Missouri documents. There are also 4,890 documents of the Rand Corporation.

Missouriana. Books about Missouri, by Missourians, or published in Missouri. Mark Twain holdings are especially strong, supplemented by the **Brashear-Henderson Mark Twain Collection,** containing many first editions; also strong in regional history.

Fred D. and Ethel Schwengel Abraham Lincoln Collection. A collection of books, art works, and artifacts concerning Abraham Lincoln and the Civil War; approximately 2,000 items.

Glenn Frank Collection. The papers of Glenn Frank, editor of *Century Magazine* and President of the University of Wisconsin.

University Archives. Contains normal archival records and papers. Notable among presidential and former faculty papers: John R. Kirk, Eugene Violette, James. M. Greenwood, Marie Turner Harvey.

Central Wesleyan Archives. Records of defunct institution (1864-1941) of Warrenton, Missouri.

Harry Laughlin Collection. Manuscript collection of eugenics expert.

The library also houses a collection of 78rpm recordings of past years and the **E. Wilder Spaulding Austrian Collection.**

Rare Book Collections

Rare Book Collection. Contains examples of rare editions, fine bindings, and signed copies of universal subject matter.

913
Northwest Missouri State University
B. D. Owens Library
Maryville, Missouri 64468

Telephone. (816) 562-1193

Institutional Description. The publicly supported liberal arts and teachers university functioned as a normal school from its founding in 1905 until 1919. Enrollment: 4,237.

Library Administration. Nancy Dumont, University Librarian; Thomas Carneal, Archivist.

Library General Holdings. 255,414 volumes; 2,194 periodical subscriptions; 61 newspaper subscriptions; 365,017 microforms; 7,653 audiovisual materials; 15,418 pamphlet file pieces.

Special Collections

Among the specialized collections in the Library is a collection of first editions and autographed editions of Willa Cather, noted regional author; more than 800 books on the Vietnam War and the military and decision-making processes behind the fighting; a collection of 700 Civil War books including the Official Records of the Union and Confederate Armies and Navies; and the Luke L. Boone Curriculum Materials Center which contains textbooks and curricular materials. The Library is also a depository for federal documents and collects Missouri state documents.

Missourian Collection. This collection constitutes a research center and teaching laboratory for Missouri history and government, social, economic and cultural development with emphasis on the northwestern area of the state. It acts as a depository for family papers, diaries, documents, public and private records, newspapers, books, and other printed matter. Notable among these are the papers of Governor Albert P. Morehouse, Governor of Missouri, 1887-1889, and the collection of books completed by the students of Susan Blow, originator of the first kindergarten in the United States in St. Louis.

University Archives. Contains memorabilia and records connected with the school, and the non-official records of Horace Mann High School, the former laboratory school of campus.

914
St. Louis College of Pharmacy
O.J. Cloughly Alumni Library
4588 Parkview Place
St. Louis, Missouri 63110

Telephone. (314) 367-8700

Institutional Description. The privately supported professional college was founded in 1864. It grants baccalaureate, professional, and master's degrees. Enrollment: 725.

Library Administration. Helen Silverman, Librarian.

Library General Holdings. 34,000 volumes; 420 current periodical subscriptions; 10,000 microforms.

Special Collections

The library's holdings include the **Drug Information Collection.** The general holdings include resources in medical and pharmaceutical literature.

915
St. Louis Conservatory of Music
Whitaker Library
560 Trinity Avenue
St. Louis, Missouri 63130

Telephone. (314) 863-3033

Institutional Description. The privately supported professional college was founded in 1923. It grants baccalaureate and master's degrees. Enrollment: 106.

Library Administration. Marion Sherman, Librarian.

Library General Holdings. 10,000 volumes; 80 current periodical subscriptions; 2,000 microforms.

Special Collections

The Whitaker Library is especially designed for the needs of the performing musician. Editions of all the major chamber works, accompanied by study scores and recordings, are generally available to all students. The large listening library contains a wide selection from the standard repertoire for solo instruments, chamber groups and orchestra, as well as one of the nation's largest collections of opera recordings. The library also contains tapes of visiting artists, faculty and student concerts and recitals for student listening.

916
St. Louis University
University Libraries
221 North Grand Boulevard
St. Louis, Missouri 63103

Telephone. (314) 658-2500

Institutional Description. The privately supported Roman Catholic university was founded in 1818. It is governed jointly by laymen and the Society of Jesus. Enrollment: 6,339.

Library General Holdings. 1,238,487 bound volumes and government documents; 11,412 continuations. The libraries of the University are: Pius XII Memorial Library, the Divinity Library, the Jeanette L. Windegger Library of the School of Social Service, the Omer Poos Law Library, the Medical Center Library, and the Parks College Library.

Special Collections

The major special collections include the **Vatican Manuscripts Microfilm Library** and collections of Western Americana and Jesuitica.

917
St. Paul School of Theology
Dana Dawson Library
5123 Truman Road
Kansas City, Missouri 64127

Telephone. (816) 483-9600

Institutional Description. The privately supported professional theological seminary was founded in 1959. Affiliated with the United Methodist Church, it offers programs on the graduate level only. Enrollment: 165.

Library Administration. William S. Sparks, Librarian.

Library General Holdings. 62,000 volumes; 375 current periodical titles.

Special Collections

Strong collections are being developed in Afro-American and Native American studies, feminism, and gerontology. An extensive curriculum laboratory for use in Religious Education functions as part of the library operations. A growing collection of regional church historical source materials is housed in the Heritage Room.

918
School of the Ozarks
Library
Point Lookout, Missouri 65726

Telephone. (417) 334-6411

Institutional Description. The privately supported Christian liberal arts college provides free tuition, room, and board in return for four hours of work each day by the student. Affiliated with the Presbyterian Church U.S.A., it was founded in 1906. Enrollment: 1,047.

Library Administration. Robert E. Anderson, Head Librarian.

Library General Holdings. 100,000 volumes; 600 periodicals; 3,000 reels of microfilm.

Special Collections

The library of the School of the Ozarks supports a liberal arts curriculum which is offered in a Christian environment.

919
Southeast Missouri State University
Kent Library
Cape Girardeau, Missouri 63701

Telephone. (314) 651-2000

Institutional Description. The publicly supported state university was founded as Missouri Normal School in 1873. It now offers a wide variety of programs at the associate, baccalaureate, and master's levels. Enrollment: 7,685.

Library Administration. 350,000 volumes; 2,600 current periodical subscriptions; 65,000 microforms.

Library General Holdings. James Zlak, University Librarian.

Rare Book Collections

Rare Book Room. Houses the **Charles I. Harrison Collection** and additional vintage items which require special care for their preservation. The Harrison Collection contains over 800 rare and unusual books and manuscripts. Also housed is the **Louis Daniel Brodsky Collection,** an internationally acclaimed private collection of works by and about William Faulkner. Access to the Brodsky Collection is by special arrangement with the curator of the collection.

920
Southwest Baptist University
Estep Library
1601 South Springfield
Bolivar, Missouri 65613

Telephone. (417) 326-5281

Institutional Description. The privately supported liberal arts institution was founded by the Baptists of Southwest Missouri in 1878. It is now affiliated with the Southern Baptist Church. Enrollment: 1,899.

Library Administration. Betty Van Blair, Director, Library Services; Coleen Rose, Special Collections/Rare Books Librarian.

Library General Holdings. 98,993 bound volumes; 41,961 microforms; 1,142 current periodical and newspaper subscriptions; 1,548 music scores; 5,412 audiovisual materials.

Special Collections

Butler Baptist Heritage Library. Included in this collection are microfilmed copies of original source materials on the Anabaptists in the 1500s in England.

American materials date from the very beginning of the colonial United States. Present-date materials are being added.

Library of American Civilization. The materials in this core collection relate to all aspects of American life and literature up to the outbreak of World War I (1914). It is contained in a 12,000-volume microbook format.

SBC Resource Lab. A comprehensive collection of denominational study material provided by the Sunday School Board, Woman's Missionary Union, and the Brotherhood Commissions. Material in the lab consists of learning resources (both print and non-print) in a variety of subjects (church polity and organization, missions, music) used to support and implement the curriculum plan.

The library also houses the archives of the University, several stamp album collections, several rare Bibles, older works on Missouri Baptists and Baptists in general. It also contains the minutes of some Missouri and Illinois Baptist Associations.

921
Southwest Missouri State University
Duane G. Meyer Library
901 South National
Springfield, Missouri 65804

Telephone. (417) 836-5000

Institutional Description. The publicly supported state liberal arts and teachers university was founded in 1905 to train teachers. It now offers a wide variety of programs. It has a branch in West Plains. Enrollment: 12,413.

Library Administration. John M. Meador, Jr., Dean, Library Services.

Library General Holdings. 450,000 volumes; 4,310 current periodical and serial subscriptions; 600,000 documents.

Special Collections

A curriculum laboratory houses a children's literature collection, a textbook collection, a collection of curriculum guides, and special learning materials. Special collections include the personal papers of poet Robert Wallace and the archives of his Bits Press. The **William J. Jones Rimbaud Collection** is the largest collection in the United States of materials by and about Jean Arthur Rimbaud, the French poet. Other special collections deal with Michel Butor and Stephane Malarme.

922
State Fair Community College
Library and Learning Resources Center
1900 Clarendon Road
Sedalia, Missouri 65301

Telephone. (816) 826-7100

Institutional Description. The publicly supported junior college was founded in 1966. Enrollment: 1,092.

Library Administration. Arja Crampton, Head Librarian.

Library General Holdings. 34,000 books; 1,000 audiovisual kits; 900 cassettes; 260 videotapes; 200 magazine titles; 2,000 bound periodicals; 13 newspaper subscriptions; 8,500 microforms; 668 records.

Special Collections

Missouri Collection. Books and materials pertaining to Missouri history, state and local government, biography, fiction and works by Missouri authors.

Central Missouri Ragtime Collection. An archives for Central Missouri ragtime music featuring Scott Joplin, Blind Boone, C.L. Woolsey, Arthur Marshall, Tom Ireland plus other musical greats of the area. Books, sheet music (original editions), and memorabilia are included.

923
Stephens College
Hugh Stephens Library
Broadway at College Avenue
Columbia, Missouri 65215

Telephone. (314) 876-7181

Institutional Description. The privately supported liberal arts college for women was founded in 1833 as the Columbia Female Academy. It grants associate and baccalaureate degrees. Enrollment: 1,005.

Library Administration. Marguerite Mitchel, Director.

Library General Holdings. 122,000 volumes; 465 current periodical titles.

Special Collections

The library maintains a special **Women's Studies Collection** and has significant holdings in political science and literature.

924
University of Missouri - Columbia
Ellis Library
Lowry Mall, University of Missouri
Columbia, Missouri 65201

Telephone. (314) 882-7461

Institutional Description. The publicly supported university was established in 1839. It was the first state university in the Louisiana Territory and west of the Mississippi. Enrollment: 19,437.

Library Administration. Thomas W. Shaughnessy, University Librarian; Margaret A. Howell, Head, Special Collections/Rare Books.

Library General Holdings. 2,365,235 volumes; 17,407 periodical and newspaper subscriptions; 4,198,365 microforms.

Special Collections

Special Collections include the **Thomas Moore Johnson Collection** of Plato and the Neoplatonists; the **Frank Luther Mott Collection of American Best Sellers,** and the **Anthony DeBellis Collection of Italian Renaissance Literature.** Special Collections also contain a fine press collection, illustrated books from the sixteen through nineteenth centuries, and seventeenth- to nineteenth-century British political and religious tracts.

The University of Missouri - Columbia Libraries have extensive collections of academic publications dating from the eighteenth century to the present, acting editions of American and English Plays, and Reformation history and literature.

The microform collection ranks sixth in size in the U.S. and Canada. Special strengths in this collection are U.S. history, energy, education, and U.S. newspapers.

925
University of Missouri - Kansas City
General Library
5100 Rockville Road
Kansas City, Missouri 64110

Telephone. (816) 276-1531

Institutional Description. The publicly supported campus of the University of Missouri System was founded in 1933 as the privately supported University of Kansas City. It joined the State System in 1963. Enrollment: 7,-703.

Library Administration. Ted P. Sheldon, Director.

Library General Holdings. 421,234 volumes; 5,081 current serial subscriptions.

Special Collections

The special collections include the **Snyder Collection of Americana** (20,000 volumes) and the **Kansas City Ecumenical Library** (7,500 volumes). Among other special collections are the **Kansas City Chapters of American Institute of Architects;** the **Producers Council and Construction Specifications Institute;** the **Architectural Collection,** the **Mila and Thomas Baker Collection** in literature; the **Chancellor Carleton E. Schofield Collection** in psychology; and the **Edgar Snow Memorial Collection.** The many memorials include those in the names of David Benjamin, Rudolf K. Bernard, Elizabeth Ann Boyle, S. Herbert Hare, Eugenia Reisner, Joseph H. Tedrow, and Joseph L. Wolff. The **Institute for Studies in American Music Collection** is housed in the Music Library as well as the **Western Historical Manuscript Collection** of 500 volumes.

926
University of Missouri - Rolla
Curtis Laws Wilson Library
Rolla, Missouri 65401

Telephone. (314) 341-4227

Institutional Description. The publicly supported university was founded in 1870 as the University of Missouri School of Mines and Metallurgy. Enrollment: 4,964.

Library Administration. Ronald G. Bohley, University Librarian; Susan Singleton, Collection Development.

Library General Holdings. 402,799 volumes; 2,117 periodical subscriptions; 411,530 microforms.

Special Collections

The Library has large collections of the United States Geological Survey and Bureau of Mines publications; series from these agencies from the beginning of their publication to the present. Also available are the NASA and IEEE publications.

927
University of Missouri - St. Louis
USMSL Libraries
8001 Natural Bridge Road
St. Louis, Missouri 63121

Telephone. (314) 553-5252

Institutional Description. The publicly supported university is a campus of the University of Missouri, headquarted in Columbia. It was founded in 1963 as a junior college, and added the baccalaureate program two years later. Enrollment: 7,315.

Library Administration. Ronald Krash, Director; Anne R. Kenney, Associate Director.

Library General Holdings. 686,000 volumes, including 4,000 periodical subscriptions, more than 268,000 government documents, and 1,150,000 items in microform.

Special Collections

The **Archives** contains official records, campus publications, student newspapers, photographs, and other material on the history of UMSL. The **Western Historical Manuscript Collection,** contains primary source materials for research in many fields, including local history, the environment, women's history, politics, and Black history. The library also maintains collections of materials on utopian societies and art history.

928
Washington University
John M. Olin Library
St. Louis, Missouri 63130

Telephone. (314) 889-5400

Institutional Description. The privately supported university was founded in 1853 as the Eliot Seminary. Today it is composed of 10 schools. Enrollment: 9,399.

Library Administration. Nicholas Burckel, Acting Director; Holly Hail, Special Collections Librarian.

Library General Holdings. 2,000,000 volumes; 15,400 serial and periodical subscriptions.

Special Collections

Outstanding collections in the Olin Library include English history, Germanic languages and literature, Latin Americana, modern English and American authors, Romance languages and literature, and urban research. Special collections include the **Isador Mendle Collection** on the history of printing; the **Ernst Krohn Musicological Collection;** the **History of the Russian Revolution Movement,** the **John M. Wolfing Collection** on classical archaeology and numismatics; the **History of Architecture Collection,** and various author collections including Samuel Beckett, Conrad Aiken, James Dickey, Robert Creely, and Ford Maddox Ford.

Rare Book Collections

The library maintains the **George N. Meissner Rare Book Collection.**

929
Webster University
Luhr Library
470 East Lockwood Avenue
St. Louis, Missouri 63119

Telephone. (314) 968-6900

Institutional Description. The privately supported liberal arts university was founded in 1915. It operates educational facilities on numerous armed forces bases, at ten graduate centers throughout the U.S., and in 4 foreign countries. Enrollment: 4,689 (St. Louis campus).

Library General Holdings. The Luhr Library, shared by Webster University and Eden Theological Seminary, is located on Eden's campus. *See* **Eden Theological Seminary.**

930
Westminster College
Reeves Memorial Library
7th and Westminster Avenue
Fulton, Missouri 65251

Telephone. (314) 642-3361

Institutional Description. The privately supported liberal arts college was founded in 1851 as Fulton College. It is affiliated with the Presbyterian Church, U.S.A. Enrollment: 627.

Library Administration. W.E. Marquardt, Head Librarian.

Library General Holdings. 71,000 volumes; 359 current periodical subscriptions; 7,700 microforms; 5,300 audiovisual materials.

Special Collections

Winston Churchill Memorial and Library. The national landmark to Sir Winston Churchill is housed in the Church of St. Mary, Aldermanbury, originally a twelfth-century English church. The church was destroyed in the Great Fire of London in 1666, rebuilt by Sir Christopher Wren, and partially destroyed again by an incendiary bomb during World War II. In the mid-1960s the church was dismantled in London, shipped stone-by-stone to Fulton, and reconstructed on the Westminster campus. Today it serves as the Westminster College chapel and commemorates Sir Winston's 1946 visit to the college, where he delivered his famous "Sinews of Peace" (Iron Curtain) address. The library houses materials on Churchill and Anglo-American relations.

931
William Jewell College
Charles F. Curry Library
Liberty, Missouri 64068

Telephone. (816) 781-4120

Institutional Description. The privately supported liberal arts college is affiliated with the Southern Baptist Church. It was founded in 1849. Enrollment: 1,682.

Library Administration. John P. Young, Director.

Library General Holdings. 175,000 volumes; 690 periodicals; 41,000 microforms; 15,140 audiovisual materials.

Special Collections

The special collections of the Curry Library include the private library of Charles H. Spurgeon, the great English preacher; the **Dr. Louis Mertins Collection** of signed manuscripts, first editions, and holographs; the **Ted Malone Collection of Poetry;** the famous **Hubmaier Collection** of the great Anabaptist reformer; and the **William E. Partee Center for Baptist Historical Studies** sponsored by the college and the Missouri Baptist Historical Society, a collection of thousands of Baptist papers and other important historical material. Other collections include a collection of Western Americana which contains historical and contemporary works on Missouri, material on the Pony Express, and other aspects of the settling of the West; and a collection of old hymnals and material written by early Puritans.

932
William Woods College
Dulaney and Reeves Libraries
Fulton, Missouri 65251

Telephone. (314) 642-2251

Institutional Description. This private, nonsectarian liberal college for women is related to the Christian Church (Disciples of Christ). Enrollment: 737.

Library Administration. Helen Renaud, Librarian.

Library General Holdings. 160,000 volumes; 750 periodical subscriptions.

Special Collections

Special Collections include the Educational Materials Collection; Equestrian Science Resources; and music scores and discs.

Montana

933
Carroll College
Carroll College Library
North Benton Avenue
Helena, Montana 59625

Telephone. (406) 442-3450

Institutional Description. The privately supported liberal arts college was founded in 1909. It is affiliated with the Roman Catholic Church. Enrollment: 1,409.

Library Administration. Lois Fitzpatrick, Library Director.

Library General Holdings. 93,000 volumes; 470 current periodical titles.

Special Collections

The library maintains special collections in theology and the health sciences. Some of the periodical titles have holdings dating from 1850.

934
College of Great Falls
Library
1301 20th Street South
Great Falls, Montana 59405

Telephone. (406) 761-8210

Institutional Description. The privately supported coeducational institution is a Catholic college conducted by the Sisters of Providence. It is open to students of every race and creed, and grants associate, baccalaureate, and master's degrees. Enrollment: 1,160.

Library Administration. Una M. Koontz, College Librarian.

Library General Holdings. 66,500 volumes; 450 periodical subscriptions; 11,346 bound periodicals; 35,633 periodicals in microform; 1,545 musical scores; 2,467 audiovisual materials.

Special Collections

Bertsche Collection. A collection of Montana materials including many of the local history books from all over the state. Many of these works were locally published and printed and not widely distributed. Also included in the collection is the Montana Bureau of Agriculture, Labor, and Industry Yearbooks for the 1890s and the early part of this century.

Microbook Library of American Civilization is a microfiche set of American books, periodicals, and other materials on all aspects of American life and literature from their beginnings until World War I.

935
Eastern Montana College
College Library
1500 North 30th Street
Billings, Montana 59101

Telephone. (406) 657-2011

Institutional Description. The publicly supported (state) liberal arts and teachers college was founded in 1927. It grants baccalaureate and master's degrees. Enrollment: 4,478.

Library Administration. Edward Neroda, Librarian.

Library General Holdings. 145,000 volumes; 1,000 current periodical subscriptions; 220,000 government documents; 480,000 microforms.

Special Collections

The Special Collection Division maintains the **Elizabeth B. Custer Collection** of memorabilia and letters of General George Armstrong Custer covering his career from West Point to Little Big Horn. This collection is integrated with material on the Indian wars and the 7th Cavalry collection. The **Dora White Memorial Collection** consists of 2,000 volumes, prints, and photographs of the early West and includes material on travel and exploration, fur trade, the homestead period, and the Indian frontier and Indian culture. The **Barstow Collection of Indian Drawings** includes drawings by Medicine Crow recording his trip to Washington, D.C. in 1880. The **Billings [Montana] Mayoral Collection** is also maintained.

936
Flathead Valley Community College
College Library
Kalispell, Montana 59901

Telephone. (406) 755-5222

Institutional Description. The two-year college was founded in 1967. Enrollment: 1,954.

Library Administration. Michael J. Ober, College Librarian.

Library General Holdings. 11,000 volumes; 350 periodical titles. Combined with the Flathead County Library, students have access to over 143,000 volumes.

Special Collections

A special collection on Montana built jointly with Flathead County Library contains over 9,500 volumes.

937
Montana College of Mineral Science and Technology
Library
Butte, Montana 59701

Telephone. (406) 496-4101

Institutional Description. Montana College of Mineral Science and Technology is a state institution founded in 1893. The college is referred to as Montana Tech. Enrollment: 1,932.

Library Administration. Joanne V. Lerud, Head, Library.

Library General Holdings. 68,000 volumes; 673 periodical subscriptions; 65,000 government documents.

Special Collections

The special collections include a geology collection which features volumes dating back to 1830 and international and state geological documents; materials on early Montana history, including diaries, letters, and journals; and a mining engineering collection including volumes dating back to 1846 on all aspects of mining and metallurgy.

Roger V. Pierce Memorial Art Collection. Sponsored by Montana Tech Alumni Association, this collection contains 93 oil paintings by Raul de la Peno depicting the history of mining in Mexico.

938
Montana State University
University Libraries
Bozeman, Montana 59717

Telephone. (406) 994-4242

Institutional Description. The publicly supported state university was founded in 1893 as an agricultural college. Enrollment: 10,151.

Library Administration. Noreen S. Alldredge, Dean of Libraries.

Library General Holdings. 500,000 volumes; 7,871 current periodical and newspaper subscriptions.

Special Collections

The collection strengths of the Special Collections/Archives include sources on Yellowstone National Park, agriculture, pioneer history, mining, architecture, American Indians, and the Gallatin Valley. Among the more than 30,000 books and 1,600 manuscript collections are:

Haynes Collection. Contains the complete business files of the F. Jay Haynes family, operators of the exclusive photographic concession in Yellowstone Park from 1881-1968. These files, complemented by the Haynes family library and numerous brochures and books about the park, contain 3,000 volumes and 110 linear feet of other material.

Yellowstone National Park Archives, 1884-1917. A microfilm collection of 45 reels.

M.L. Wilson Agricultural Collection. Papers of M.L. Wilson who served as Chairman of MSU's Department of Agricultural Economics in the 1920s, Under Secretary of Agriculture under President Franklin D. Roosevelt, and Director of the Federal Agricultural Extension Service under Presidents Franklin Roosevelt and Harry Truman; 1,508 volumes.

Alexander Leggat Collection. Books and pamphlets on Montana and Northwest history; 2,223 volumes.

Abraham Lincoln Collection. Books and pamphlets; 1,503 volumes.

Architectural Drawing Collection. A collection of 1,000 drawings of Montana buildings.

Works Progress Administration Collection. WPA files for Montana including Federal Writers Project and Historical Records Survey. The most extensive materials relate to livestock history, but the files also contain guidebook manuscripts and encyclopedia manuscripts; 34 linear feet.

University Archives. Collects and preserves the organized body of permanent records in connection with the transaction of University affairs.

939
Northern Montana College
Vande Bogart Library
P.O. Box 751
Havre, Montana 59501

Telephone. (406) 265-3221

Institutional Description. Northern Montana College is a state college founded in 1913. Enrollment: 1,788.

Library Administration. Terrence A. Thompson, Director.

Library General Holdings. 100,000 volumes; 700 cur-

rent periodical titles; 380,000 microfiche.

Special Collections

Western Americana. Includes books on the history of Montana, the western United States, and western Canada; emphases on Western art and literature; and Indian art, culture, and history.

Lucke Photograph Collection. Includes photographs showing the history and development of the city of Havre, Montana from the nineteenth century.

940
Rocky Mountain College
Paul Adams Memorial Library
1511 Poly Drive
Billings, Montana 59102

Telephone. (406) 657-1085

Institutional Description. The privately supported liberal arts college was founded in 1878. It is affiliated with The United Presbyterian Church of the U.S.A., The United Church of Christ, and The United Methodist Church. Enrollment: 425.

Library Administration. Jan Jelenik, College Librarian.

Library General Holdings. 65,000 volumes; 275 current periodical and newspaper subscriptions; large collections of records and music scores, filmstrips, and slides.

Special Collections

The library contains almost complete serial publications of the Geological Society of America, the American Association of Petroleum Geologists, and the United States Geological Survey.

941
University of Montana
University Libraries
Missoula, Montana 59801

Telephone. (406) 243-6266

Institutional Description. The University of Montana is a state institution founded in 1893. Enrollment: 8,840.

Library Administration. Ruth J. Patrick, Dean.

Library General Holdings. 711,673 volumes; 4,800 periodicals; 988,000 microforms.

Special Collections

Significant holdings of Montana history are found in archives and special collections. Represented are rare books, pamphlets, papers, manuscripts, and photographs. These reflect important literary and political figures, as well as business and industry, in Montana. The Montana state documents collection contains those books and periodicals issued by state agencies. The papers of Senator Mike Mansfield are housed in the library's special collections.

942
Western Montana College
College Library
710 South Atlantic Street
Dillon, Montana 59725

Telephone. (406) 683-7011

Institutional Description. Western Montana College is a state institution and a land-grant college established as a State Normal School in 1893. Enrollment: 970.

Library Administration. James B. Hemesath, Librarian.

Library General Holdings. 80,000 volumes; 500 current periodicals; 25,000 microforms.

Special Collections

Montana Room. Contains a collection of 1,500 books by Montana authors or about Montana.

The library also has the Library of American Civilization in microform and the **Emerick Art Collection.**

Nebraska

943
Bellevue College
F. Hoyte Freeman Library
Wright Way at Galvin Road
Bellevue, Nebraska 68005

Telephone. (402) 291-8100

Institutional Description. The privately supported liberal arts college grants baccalaureate degrees. Enrollment: 1,457.

Library Administration. Karen Kozak, Director.

Library General Holdings. 97,225 volumes; 665 current periodical subscriptions; 29,000 microforms.

Special Collections

The library maintains the Human Relations Area File (microfiche, 5,234 volumes); the New York Times plus indices for 1899-1919 and 1945-1974 (microfilm); and the **Barbara Miller Memorial Collection,** consisting of 250 volumes on the subject of economics.

944
Chadron State College
College Library
Tenth and Main
Chadron, Nebraska 69337

Telephone. (308) 432-4451

Institutional Description. Chadron State College is a state institution chartered in 1910. Enrollment: 2,240.

Library Administration. Terrence Brennan, Director of Library Services.

Library General Holdings. 160,000 volumes; 850 periodicals.

Special Collections

The library maintains special collections in the curriculum library, the young people's collection, and the Historical Center. The **Mari Sandoz Heritage Society Collection** is housed in the library.

945
College of St. Mary
Library
1901 South 72nd Street
Omaha, Nebraska 68124

Telephone. (402) 399-2400

Institutional Description. The privately supported liberal arts college for women was founded in 1923. It operates under the Roman Catholic Religious Sisters of Mercy. Enrollment: 653.

Library Administration. Robert Lehr, Librarian.

Library General Holdings. 52,000 volumes; 470 current periodical titles; 18,000 audiovisual items.

Special Collections

The College of St. Mary is the only women's college and the only single-sex institution of higher education in the state of Nebraska. Concomitantly, the library's most important special collection is in the field of women's studies.

946
Concordia Teachers College
Link Library
800 North Columbia
Seward, Nebraska 68434

Telephone. (402) 643-3651

Institutional Description. The privately supported college is affiliated with the Lutheran Church—Missouri Synod, and furnishes training for parish school teachers. It was founded in 1894. Enrollment: 775.

Library Administration. Glenn Ohlmann, Director of Library Services.

Library General Holdings. 166,000 volumes; 750 current periodical subscriptions; 11,000 audiovisual materials.

Special Collections

The most significant special collection of the Link Library is the **Renata Koschmann Memorial Collection,** consisting of 13,000 children's books.

947
Creighton University
Carl M. Reinert Alumni Memorial Library
2500 California Street
Omaha, Nebraska 68178

Telephone. (402) 280-2703

Institutional Description. Creighton University is a private, independent, nonprofit institution founded in 1878. It is operated by the Jesuits in the traditions of that Catholic religious order. Enrollment: 5,903.

Library Administration. Raymond B. Means, Director.

Library General Holdings. 298,000 volumes (Alumni Library); 144,098 volumes (Law Library); 82,070 volumes (Health Sciences Library); 250,000 microforms; 13,500 audiovisual materials; 2,991 current periodicals; 41,300 government documents.

Special Collections

Important special collections include the **Joseph Gold International Monetary Fund Collection,** a current and historical theology collection; and the **National Football League Collection on Autism.**

948
Grace College of the Bible
Library
1515 South 8th Street
Omaha, Nebraska 68108

Telephone. (402) 449-2893

Institutional Description. The privately supported professional Bible college was founded in 1943. It grants associate and baccalaureate degrees. Enrollment: 281.

Library Administration. Norma McWilliams, Director.

Library General Holdings. 55,000 volumes; 270 magazine and periodical titles.

Special Collections

A wide selection of visual aid materials is available for various Christian Service ministries.

949
Kearney State College
Calvin T. Ryan Library
Kearney, Nebraska 68849

Telephone. (308) 234-8544

Institutional Description. The publicly supported state college was founded in 1903. Law and medical students may participate in an academic cooperative plan with the University of Nebraska. Enrollment: 6,534.

Library Administration. John Mayeski, College Librarian; John G. Lillis, Reference/Archives Librarian.

Library General Holdings. 200,000 volumes.

Special Collections

Nebraska History. A collection on Nebraska history partially funded by an endowment from the Gene Hamaker Fund; 1,915 cataloged items.

Kearney State College Archives. Includes 14,678 uncataloged and 620 cataloged items.

The library is a selective depository for federal government documents and a full depository for documents from the State of Nebraska.

950
Metropolitan Technical Community College
Instructional Resource Center
P.O. Box 3777
Omaha, Nebraska 68103

Telephone. (402) 449-8417

Institutional Description. Metropolitan Technical Community College is a publicly supported two-year postsecondary institution which serves four Nebraska counties. Enrollment: 6,835.

Library Administration. Paul Marsh, Director of Instructional Resources/Technologies.

Library General Holdings. 40,000 volumes; 396 current periodical titles.

Special Collections

Special collections are maintained on Nebraska authors, children's literature, photography, electronics, dentistry, and respiratory therapy.

951
Midland Lutheran College
Luther Library
900 North Clarkson Street
Fremont, Nebraska 68025

Telephone. (402) 721-5480

Institutional Description. The privately supported liberal arts college is affiliated with the Lutheran Church in America. It was established in 1883. Enrollment: 763.

Library Administration. Thomas E. Boyle, Library Director; Martha Peters, Special Collections Librarian.

Library General Holdings. 116,000 items; 550 current periodicals; over 5,000 nonprint media.

Special Collections

Library of Biblical Literature. A collection of approximately 2,000 items related to the Bible as a form of literature; includes a large number of Bibles in various languages, studies of the history of the Bible, and works on the literary content of the Bible.

College Archives. Consists of the records of Midland Lutheran College as well as the colleges which joined to make the present institution—Midland College in Atchenson, Kansas; Luther College in Wahoo, Nebraska; Fremont College in Fremont, Nebraska. The Archives also hold much of the print records from the Nebraska Synod of the Lutheran Church in America and its earlier bodies.

952
Nebraska Wesleyan University
Cochrane-Woods Library
5000 St. Paul Avenue
Lincoln, Nebraska 68504

Telephone. (402) 466-2371

Institutional Description. Nebraska Wesleyan University is a private, liberal arts institution affiliated with the United Methodist Church. Enrollment: 1,347.

Library Administration. John M. Robson, Librarian.

Library General Holdings. 185,000 books and bound periodicals; 700 current periodical subscriptions.

Special Collections

The library supports the liberal arts curriculum of the University which is offered in a Christian environment.

953
Peru State College
Library
Peru, Nebraska 68421

Telephone. (402) 872-3815

Institutional Description. The publicly supported liberal arts and teachers college was founded in 1867. It grants associate and baccalaureate degrees. Enrollment: 1,118.

Library Administration. Faye M. Brandt, Librarian.

Library General Holdings. 100,000 volumes; 720 current periodical subscriptions; 19,000 microforms.

Special Collections

Special collections include materials on Southeastern Nebraska; and collections named for Marion Marsh Brown, Dr. Ruth Crone, Ellsworth P. Conkle, and Louise Mears.

954
Union College
Library
3800 South 48th Street
Lincoln, Nebraska 68506

Telephone. (402) 488-2331

Institutional Description. The privately supported liberal arts college was founded in 1891. Affiliated with the Seventh-day Adventist Church, it grants associate and baccalaureate degrees. Enrollment: 593.

Library Administration. Lawrence Onsager, Director.

Library General Holdings. 113,500 volumes; 745 current periodical titles.

Special Collections

The library maintains the **Union College Archives;** a collection of material on Seventh-day Adventist theology and history; and a collection of monographs on frontier history.

955
University of Nebraska - Lincoln
Libraries
Lincoln, Nebraska 68588

Telephone. (402) 472-2526

Institutional Description. The publicly supported university was established in 1869 as a land-grant institution. Today it consists of 9 colleges and 4 schools. Enrollment: 20,901.

Library Administration. Kent Hendrickson, University Librarian; Joseph Svoboda, University Archivist.

Library General Holdings. 1,725,730 volumes; 19,261 current periodical subscriptions; 1,887,560 microforms; 12,151 music scores.

Special Collections

Sadtler Standard Spectra. Five series of the Sadtler Standard Spectra are housed in the Chemistry Library Collection: (1) infrared grating, (2) proton nuclear magnetic resonance, (3) carbon-13 nuclear magnetic resonance, (4) ultraviolet, and (5) 100 MHz nuclear magnetic resonance. The spectra contain valuable data for identifying and characterizing a large number of chemical compounds. The collection currently contains 219,888 spectra and is housed in the Mathematics Library.

Topographic Maps. The Geology Library has a collection of 80,000 topographic maps covering all mapped areas of the United States. The library also has a comprehensive collection of publications issued by the Nebraska Conservation and Survey Division, including bulletins, educational circulars, resource reports, and water survey papers.

Dentistry. Monographs relating to outstanding leaders and pioneers in the various fields of dentistry and histories of the development of dentistry in the United States are housed in the Dental Library.

Entomology Collection. This collection is housed in the Agricultural Library and includes extensive and thorough serial runs. Monographs are equally impressive. The Acarina or mites area is likely the strongest of the holdings.

Czech Heritage Collection. The heart of this collection relates to the activity of Czech Americans from all parts of the United States but stresses Nebraska and the Midwest.

Mari Sandoz Collection. In January 1966, two months before her death, Mari Sandoz decided to give her collection accumulated during her literary career to the University of Nebraska. She determined that her documentary material remain west of the Mississippi River. In her opinion, too much western material has already gravitated to the East. She frequently commented on the irony that such great sources as the Coe and Streeter collections at Yale and the Rollins collection at Princeton were located along the Atlantic coast. The location of such sources as these was one of the reasons that prompted her to leave Nebraska and move to New York City. The collection now is located on the Lincoln campus of the University of Nebraska. It occupies more than two hundred linear feet of shelving space and contains most of the author's files, her vast accumulation of notes and interviews, documents, letters, maps, and a cross index to use the material.

Virginia Faulkner Collection. This collection of one of Nebraska's distingusihed writers and scholars contains over 2,000 titles. Although the content of the collection is eclectic—ranging from Renaissance plays to geological surveys and cookbooks—it is especially strong in twentieth-century writers and in University of Nebraska press publications.

The University Archives/Special Collections unit of the UN-L Libraries contains Archives of the University including papers of outstanding professors such as Charles E. Bessey; about 20,000 rare books; World War I pamphlets; a World War II psychological warfare collection; rare maps; first editions of books by Willa Cather; Sterling Morton Collection of early U.S. pamphlets (1800-1850); Fred Morrow Fling Collection of French Revolutionary books; Anatole Mazour Collection of Russian History and Culture; Latvian Collection; and Benjamin Botkin's Collection of folklore consisting of 12,000 volumes of books, author's correspondence, and collected research materials. Other specialized collections housed in the Music Library include:

Ruth Etting Collection. Contains approximately 700 items, including recordings, scores, sheet music covers, filmstrips, photographs, movie stills, Ruth Etting's personal scrapbook (oversized), miscellaneous unsorted papers, letters, invoices, and some personal effects.

Labaree Jazz Collection. Contains 380 45rpm recordings of jazz and pop music (various performers in the 1950s).

Richard White Louis Armstrong Record Collection Library. Contains 47 33-1/3rpm albums featuring Louis Armstrong.

Vernon Guenther Passion Collection. Contains 313 items, including scores of oratorios, cantatas and motets, and settings of the Seven Last Words of Christ on the Cross, sound recordings, books and dissertations, and reprints of periodical articles.

Lawbaugh Organ Collection. Contains 892 items, a high percentage of which are foreign publications, including books, pamphlets, and journal backfiles on organ building and design.

956
University of Nebraska - Omaha
University Library
60th and Dodge Streets
Omaha, Nebraska 68182

Telephone. (402) 554-2640

Institutional Description. The publicly supported institution came under the control of the Nebraska State University System in 1968. It was founded in 1908 as the Municipal University of Omaha. Enrollment: 9,870.

Library Administration. Robert S. Runyon, University Librarian; Robert Nash, Collection Development Librarian.

Library General Holdings. 445,753 books; 111,045 bound periodicals; 403,258 government documents; 3,893 periodical subscriptions; 1,095,876 microforms; 3,759 audiotapes; 650 videotapes; 15,012 maps and charts.

Special Collections

The most significant collection in Special Collections at the University of Omaha is the **Arthur Paul Afghanistan Collection** which consists of books, periodicals, newspapers, maps, microforms, documents, collections of papers, and oral history tapes on Afghanistan.

Other major collections include the **Mary L. Richmond Cummington Press Collection;** the **Nebraska Authors and History;** the **Omaha Federal Writers Project (WPA) Papers;** the **Icarian Collection;** and the **University of Nebraska at Omaha Faculty Monograph Collection.**

957
Wayne State College
U.S. Conn Library
Wayne, Nebraska 68787

Telephone. (402) 375-2200

Institutional Description. Wayne State College is a state institution established in 1909 as the Nebraska State Normal School. Enrollment: 2,948.

Library Administration. Jack L. Middendorf, Director of Information Services.

Library General Holdings. 160,000 volumes; 1,100 periodicals; 50,000 government documents; 300,000 microforms; 3,500 audiovisual materials.

Special Collections

The **Teacher/Learning Center** houses resource materials for the teacher education programs.

Nevada

958
Northern Nevada Community College Learning Resources Center 901 Elm Street Elko, Nevada 89801

Telephone. (702) 738-8493

Institutional Description. The two-year college began as Elko Community College in 1967. State governance began in 1969 and the present name was adopted in 1973. Enrollment: 1,928.

Library Administration. Juanita Karr, Director.

Library General Holdings. 25,000 volumes; 285 current periodical titles; 14,285 audiovisual titles.

Special Collections

Special collections are maintained on the American Indian, Basque culture, and Nevada.

959
Sierra Nevada College MacLean Library Box 4269 Incline Village, Nevada 89450

Telephone. (702) 831-1314

Institutional Description. The privately supported liberal arts college grants baccalaureate degrees. Enrollment: 285.

Library Administration. Margaret Solomon, Library Director.

Library General Holdings. 16,000 volumes; 100 print and microfiche periodical subscriptions.

Special Collections

The library has a circulating topographic map collection, a non-circulating **Lake Tahoe Research Collection** and bibliography, and an extensive music collection. Emphases in other areas of collection are in environmental science and alternative energy.

960
University of Nevada, Las Vegas James R. Dickinson Library 4505 Maryland Parkway Las Vegas, Nevada 89154

Telephone. (702) 739-3252

Institutional Description. The publicly supported university was started in 1957 as a coordinate campus of the University of Nevada, established in 1864 in Elko. Enrollment: 9,838.

Library Administration. Mary Dale Deacon, University Librarian; Susan M. Jarvis, Special Collections Librarian.

Library General Holdings. 508,000 volumes; 718,000 microforms; 226,000 government documents; 58,000 nonbook materials (including records, tapes, cassettes, and films); 6,000 periodical subscriptions.

Special Collections

Beckley Nevada Collection. The collection encompasses the development of Southern Nevada from its beginnings to the present; includes information pertaining to mining activities, railroads, water and land use, environment, agriculture, tourism, geology, anthropology and archaeology, recreation, gaming, politics, and the economy of Clark, Esmeralda, Lincoln, and Nye Counties. Major emphasis is given to Hoover Dam and Colorado River Water Rights, Nellis Air Force Base, and the Nevada Test Site.

Gaming Collection. A comprehensive research collection on gambling and related activities. With the earliest volume dated 1559, the collection includes all formats of information: monographs, journals, photographs, pamphlets, posters, publicity releases, audio and video cassettes, and recorded discs. Supporting the collection are select volumes on risk, probabilities, and associated legal and illegal activities. The collection is an excellent resource on nineteenth century studies on the moral and religious aspects of gambling and recent studies on the behavior and treatment of pathological gamblers.

Map Collection. Although comprised primarily of modern items, the collection contains nineteenth century maps from military reconnaissance expeditions and Geographical and Geological Survey explorations. There are many U.S. Geological Survey topographic maps, general highway and road maps, and railroad maps. The emphasis is on a comprehensive history of the Las Vegas area.

Archives and Manuscripts. University of Nevada, Las Vegas archives and private archives created by organizations, institutions, families, and individuals. The subjects covered include Southern Nevada history, Hoover Dam, Nellis Air Force Base, and the Nevada Test Site.

Menu Collection. The menus contained in the **Bohn-Bettoni Collection,** purchased by the University in 1970, form the core of this specialized collection. Primarily supporting the College of Hotel Administration, pre-1870, award-winning menus, special occasion menus and menus with unique formats are a valuable information resource for students of the culinary arts.

Photographic Collection. Approximately 25,000 images. The forms include black and white, color, negatives, some glassplate and nitrate negatives, color tansparencies, and photos contained in albums. The photographs are a visual documentation of the historic development of the four Southern Nevada counties: Clark, Esmeralda, Lincoln, and Nye.

961
University of Nevada, Reno
Noble H. Getchell Library
Ninth and Center Streets
Reno, Nevada 89557

Telephone. (702) 784-6865

Institutional Description. The publicly supported state university was founded in 1864 in Elko, and moved in 1886 to Reno. Enrollment: 10,245.

Library Administration. Harold G. Morehouse, Director of Libraries.

Library General Holdings. 777,000 volumes; 1,900,000 microforms; 5,700 current periodicals.

Special Collections

Among the library's extensive collections are the **Nevada History Collection;** the **Modern Authors Collection;** the **Basque Collection,** and the **Great Basin Indians Collection.**

Desert Research Institute. The Institute has specialized collections in the water resources and atmospheric sciences.

New Hampshire

962
Colby-Sawyer College
Susan Colgate Cleveland Library
Main Street
New London, New Hampshire 03257

Telephone. (603) 526-2010

Institutional Description. The privately supported college for women was founded in 1837. It grants associate and baccalaureate degrees. Enrollment: 468.

Library Administration. Loretta Kelner, Director.

Library General Holdings. 65,000 volumes; 450 current periodical titles.

Special Collections

The library maintains the **College Archives** consisting of historical and other materials relating to Colby-Sawyer College.

963
Daniel Webster College
Library
University Drive
Nashua, New Hampshire 03063

Telephone. (603) 883-3556

Institutional Description. The privately supported technical college was founded in 1965 as the New England Aeronautical Institute, which remains as a division of the college. It now offers aeronautical and business degrees. Enrollment: 1,127.

Library Administration. Patience K. Jackson, Library Director.

Library General Holdings. 24,000 volumes; 600 periodical titles.

Special Collections

Special collections in the fields of aeronautics, computer sciences, and business are tailored to meet the needs of the College's curricula.

964
Dartmouth College
The Libraries
Hanover, New Hampshire 03755

Telephone. (603) 646-1110

Institutional Description. Dartmouth College is a private, independent, nonprofit college established in 1769. Enrollment: 4,627.

Library Administration. Margaret Amelia Otto, Librarian.

Library General Holdings. 1,643,692 volumes; 20,052 periodicals; 1,802,000 microforms; 44,500 audiovisual materials. Included in the library system are seven specialized branch libraries with extensive collections in art, English, music, biomedical sciences, business and engineering, physical sciences, and mathematics. Most of the permanent collection is in the Baker Memorial Library.

Special Collections

Important special collections include the **Vilhjalmur Stefansson Collection** of 5,000 books, 440 linear feet of manuscripts, and artifacts pertaining to the arctic explorer; the **History of Printing Collection** covering the period from 1500 to the present; and the **Robert Frost Collection** of 1,300 printed items concerned with the famous American poet.

Among the features of particular interest in the Baker Memorial Library are the famous frescoes by José Clemente Orozco that adorn the walls of the Reserve Corridor; a number of special rooms located throughout the building; a display area devoted to the history of the College, and extensive provision for exhibitions relating principally to resources of the Libraries.

965
Franklin Pierce College
Library Resource Center
College Road
Rindge, New Hampshire 3461

Telephone. (603) 899-5111

Institutional Description. Franklin Pierce College is a

private, independent, nonprofit college established in 1962.

Library Administration. Robert W. Chatfield, Director.

Library General Holdings. 37,500 books; 400 periodical titles.

Special Collections

The library maintains a special newspaper collection from the era of the Franklin Pierce presidency and a collection in English literature.

Noteworthy is the library's membership in the Human Relations Area File (HRAF). This is a collection of some 50,000 pieces of microfiche containing descriptive ethnographic data, mainly on non-Western cultures. It is designed as a tool for cross-cultural and comparative research in anthropology, economics, sociology, politics, and history.

966
Hawthorne College
Silver Library
Antrim, New Hampshire 03440

Telephone. (603) 588-6341

Institutional Description. The privately supported liberal arts college was founded in 1962. Granting associate and baccalaureate degrees, it offers programs in business, aeronautics, aviation management, computer science, criminal justice, and engineering. Enrollment: 636.

Library Administration. Joan MacFarlane, Director.

Library General Holdings. 40,000 volumes.

Special Collections

Emphases of the library's collection are in aviation and aeronautics, recreation management, criminal justice, and computer technology.

967
Keene State College
Wallace E. Mason Library
229 Main Street
Keene, New Hampshire 03431

Telephone. (603) 352-1909

Institutional Description. The publicly supported state college offers the liberal arts as a division of the University of New Hampshire. Enrollment: 3,512.

Library Administration. C. Paul Vincent, College Librarian; Robert J. Madden, Special Collections/Reference Librarian.

Library General Holdings. 166,000 volumes; 950 periodical subscriptions; 25 newspaper subscriptions; 400,000 microforms; 17,000 items in Learning Resource Center.

Special Collections

The Wallace E. Mason Library special collections include education materials (curriculum materials and ERIC microfiche); the Envirofiche collection; legal materials; selected New Hampshire documents; Library of American Civilization (microfiche); Library of English Literature (microfiche); Phonefiche; and a collection of college catalogs (microfiche). The library also maintains a collection of the works of New Hampshire authors, including some manuscripts and galleys of Elizabeth Yates.

Rare Book Collections

Harry B. Preston Collection. Consists of New Hampshire history, authors, and imprints; contains about 3,500 volumes of which about 20 percent deal with the history of New Hampshire and its counties and towns. Most of these date from the nineteenth century.

968
New England College
H. Raymond Danforth Library
Henniker, New Hampshire 03242

Telephone. (603) 428-2211

Institutional Description. The privately supported liberal arts college grants baccalaureate and masters degrees. It maintains a fully-accredited campus in Arundel, Sussex, England. Enrollment: 1,260.

Library Administration. Mary K. Wirth, Director.

Library General Holdings. 98,250 volumes; 565 periodical subscriptions; 28,500 microforms.

Special Collections

The library maintains the papers of Styles Bridges, a former New Hampshire governor and U.S. Senator; the **Adams Shakeskpeare Collection;** and a collection of materials relating to New Hampshire.

969
New Hampshire College
Harry A.B. and Gertrude C. Shapiro Library
2500 North River Road
Manchester, New Hampshire 03104

Telephone. (603) 668-2211

Institutional Description. The privately supported college maintains an active continuig education division. The college grants associate, baccalaureate, and master's degrees. Enrollment: 7,619.

Library Administration. Richard Pantano, Library Director.

Library General Holdings. 73,000 volumes; 900 current periodical subscriptions; 121,000 microforms.

Special Collections

Collection development is aimed at meeting research needs of undergraduate and graduate level business and human services students. The library has a microfiche collection of 55,000 company financial and annual reports. The library also supports the curriculum of the Culinary Institute of New Hampshire College.

970
New Hampshire Technical Institute
Paul E. Farnum Library
Fan Road
Concord, New Hampshire 03301

Telephone. (603) 271-2531
Institutional Description. New Hampshire Technical Institute opened in 1965 with three academic programs in engineering technology. Nursing and several health sciences programs began in 1970. Enrollment: 2,077.
Library Administration. Wm. John Hare, Coordinator of Learning Resources.
Library General Holdings. 27,000 volumes; 300 periodical subscriptions.

Special Collections

The Farnum Library's collection is specialized in the fields of the Institute's programs in the health sciences, engineering, data processing and allied subjects, with supporting materials in English and the physical and social sciences. The library also maintains the College Archives and a special collection of nursing novels.

971
Notre Dame College
Library
2321 Elm Street
Manchester, New Hampshire 03104

Telephone. (603) 669-4298
Institutional Description. The privately supported liberal arts college for women is administered by the Roman Catholic Sisters of the Holy Cross. It grants associate, baccalaureate, and master's degrees. Enrollment: 772.
Library Administration. Sister Gertrude Gagnier, C.S.C., Librarian.
Library General Holdings. 48,000 volumes; 250 current periodical titles.

Special Collections

A signifcant special collection of the library is the **McInnich Collection** consisting of materials in the field of economics. The general collection supports the college's divisions of humanities, allied health and natural science, and social sciences.

972
Plymouth State College
Herbert H. Lamson Library
Summer Street
Plymouth, New Hampshire 03264

Telephone. (603) 536-1550
Institutional Description. The publicly supported state college, founded in 1871, was one of the first teachers colleges in New England to gain accreditation. Enrollment: 3,577.
Library Administration. Philip C. Wei, Director of Library Services.
Library General Holdings. 241,496 volumes; 457,415 non-print pieces and serials totalling 1,663 titles.

Special Collections

The special collections of the Lamson Library include the **George H. Browne Collection** of Robert Frost's poetry; materials on state and local history; and the **Ernest L. Silver Collection** of early textbooks.

973
Rivier College
Regina Library
429 South Main Street
Nashua, New Hampshire 03060

Telephone. (603) 888-1311
Institutional Description. The privately supported liberal arts college primarily for women was founded in 1933. It is affiliated with the Roman Catholic Church. Enrollment: 2,257.
Library Administration. Sister Albina Marie Gazaille.
Library General Holdings. 110,000 volumes; 900 current periodical titles; 15,000 microforms; 6,000 audiovisual materials.

Special Collections

The library's collection has emphases in education (early childhood, special education, counseling, general education); business; and French literature, including the **Corinne Rocheleau-Rouleau Collection.**

974
St. Anselm College
Joseph H. Geisel Library
St. Anselm's Drive
Manchester, New Hampshire 03102

Telephone. (603) 669-1030
Institutional Description. The privately supported liberal arts college was founded by the Roman Catholic Order of St. Benedict in 1889. It grants associate and

baccalaureate degrees. Enrollment: 1,917.

Library Administration. James P. Kennedy, Librarian.

Library General Holdings. 164,000 volumes; 15,000 periodical titles; 47,000 volumes of microfilms; 6,300 audio records, tapes, and cassettes.

Special Collections

The Geisel Library has special collections on Catholic theology, nursing, and New England.

975
University of New Hampshire
Dimond Library
Durham, New Hampshire 03824

Telephone. (603) 862-2714

Institutional Description. The publicly supported university began as the New Hampshire College of Agriculture and the Mechanic Arts in 1866, as a part of Dartmouth College. Enrollment: 13,602.

Library Administration. Donald Vincent, University Librarian; Timothy Dodge, Special Collections Librarian.

Library General Holdings. 890,544 volumes; 6,379 current periodicals; 611,400 microforms; 5,134 audiovisual materials; 2,501 audiotapes; 85,650 maps; 170 art reproductions.

Special Collections

New Hampshire Collection. Consists of over 20,000 books and pamphlets on New Hampshire.

University Archives. The repository of documents generated by the University and some of the documents associated with the town of Durham, New Hampshire.

Manuscript Collections. Acoustical Recordings; Adams Family; Balch Family; Shirley Barker; Amy C. Beach, composer; Boston and Maine Railroad; Bostwick Portraits; William Bronk, poet; Alice Brown; Burning Deck Press; Witter Bynner; Robert P. Tristram Coffin; Norris Cotton; Cotton Mills of Dover, New Hampshire; John Duncan, children's literature author; Epping Brick Company; William B. Ewert, publisher; Farrington Early Medical Practice; Daniel Ford, author; Robert Frost; Grant Stereoscopic Slides of China; Friedrich Grosshut, German exile author; George W. Haven;; Lance Hidy, artist; Johan A. Hogan, UNH Professor; Nonny Hogrogian and David Kherdian, children's literature author and illustrator; Howell-Day Family; Margaret C. Hubbard, journalist; Robert Huff, poet; Humanalo, Science Fiction Society of New Hampshire; Isles of Shoals, items and manuscripts; Robert E. Jones, set designer; Kent State, papers; Jack Kerouac, pamphlets and broadsides; Edward MacDowell, papers; Thomas J. McIntyre, U.S. Senator; Robert J. Manton, composer; Movie Stills; New England Calendar; New Hampshire Writers Photos; New Hampshire newspapers; Northwood Photographs; Eric Partridge, correspondence; Perkins Family, papers; Gerda Peterich, photographer; Portsmouth Naval Shipyard Photographs; Kenneth Roberts, papers; Edwin Arlington Robinson, papers; Rye Project, photographs; Sceptre Press, papers; Henry Shute, children's author; Martin Snow-Civil War Mementos; J. Duane Squires, UNH Professor; Samuel Swasey, N.H. House of Representatives; Thompson Family and Durham, N.H. history; Today's Women: An Oral History; Towle U.N.H. Writers Conference, papers; Typographeum/R.T. Risk (Press); Van Ackeren Family, papers; W.P.A. Federal Art Project, N.H., photographs; W.P.A. Historical Records Survey, N.H., papers; James B. Wallace - George Kimball, abolitionists; White Mountains Photographs; and William Yale, UNH Professor.

Rare Book Collections

Special Books. Over 10,000 rare, early printing, private press, limited and first edition, and inscribed books. Included here are books by New Hampshire-related authors (Robert Frost, Edwin Arlington Robinson) and the **Milne Angling Collection** of over 2,000 books on fishing. Two uncataloged collections are the **Lamson Genealogy** of around 1,500 volumes and the **Stark Collection of Early New Hampshire Imprints** of over 800 volumes.

976
White Pines College
Library
Chester Street
Chester, New Hampshire 03036

Telephone. (603) 887-4401

Institutional Description. The private junior college was founded in 1965. Enrollment: 64.

Library Administration. Darlette Smith, Head Librarian.

Library General Holdings. 20,000 volumes; 100 periodical subscriptions.

Special Collections

A special collection of children's literature was begun in 1975. The core of this library is the **Lindquist Collection** which consists of over 600 books for children given to the College by Miss Jennie Lindquist, former editor of the *Horn Book Magazine.* The **President's Collection** of 450 volumes was added to the children's literature library in 1977. New award-winning volumes are acquired each year to update and expand this collection.

The **Social Work Resource Collection** is one of the most extensive holdings in this subject area in New Hampshire. It includes periodicals, monographs, abstracts, and pamphlets. A collection of **Career Development Resources** contains a core of volumes designed to aid students in making post-graduation plans.

New Jersey

977
Bloomfield College
College Library
467 Franklin Avenue
Bloomfield, New Jersey 07003

Telephone. (201) 748-9000

Institutional Description. The privately supported liberal arts college was founded in 1868 as a German theological school. Its sponsorship by the United Presbyterian Church began in 1958, and it now offers a full four-year curriculum. Enrollment: 1,406.

Library Administration. Imre Gal, Head Librarian.

Library General Holdings. 134,000 volumes; 500 periodical subscriptions.

Special Collections

Special collections include the **Administrative Reserve,** consisting of 400 volumes on all aspects of higher education; the **Abraham Lincoln Collection,** including 150 volumes of Lincoln's life; and a **Black and Urban Studies Collection** of 200 volumes which are multidisciplinary in nature and focus on the years 1960 to 1970.

978
Brookdale Community College
Learning Resources Center
Newman Springs Road
Lincroft, New Jersey 07738

Telephone. (201) 842-1900

Institutional Description. The two-year college was founded in 1967. Enrollment: 10,573.

Library Administration. Elinor Ebeling, Director, Learning Resources.

Library General Holdings. 128,115 volumes.

Special Collections

Special collections include the **New Jersey Collection,** the **Play Collection,** and the **Brookdale Community College Archives.**

979
Caldwell College
College Library
Ryerson Avenue
Caldwell, New Jersey 07006

Telephone. (201) 228-4424

Institutional Description. The privately supported liberal arts college primarily for women was founded in 1939 by the Roman Catholic Sisters of St. Dominic. It grants baccalaureate degrees. Enrollment: 744.

Library Administration. Sister Patricia Hodge, Library Director.

Library General Holdings. 92,000 volumes; 360 current periodical subscriptions.

Special Collections

The library maintains the **Grover Cleveland Collection of American History.**

980
Camden County College
Wolverton Learning Resources Center
Little Gloucester Road
P.O. Box 200
Blackwood, New Jersey 08012

Telephone. (609) 227-7200

Institutional Description. The publicly-supported, comprehensive, two-year college was founded in 1967. It has its main campus in Blackwood, and a branch in Camden. Enrollment: 8,127.

Library Administration. Joan Getaz, Library Director.

Library General Holdings. 80,000 volumes; 500 subscriptions; some periodical holdings in microfilm; 1,000 sound recordings; 1,000 filmstrips; 200 videotapes; uncataloged art slides.

Special Collections

The Library houses materials in all media related to the college curriculum in Animal Science, Dental Hygiene, Laser Technology, and Computer-Integrated

Manufacturing.

981
Centenary College
Learning Resources Center
400 Jefferson Street
Hackettstown, New Jersey 07840

Telephone. (201) 852-1400

Institutional Description. The privately supported college primarily for women offers two-year and four-year programs, granting associate and baccalaureate degrees. Enrollment: 1,215.

Library Administration. Carol Nolde Steen, Director.

Library General Holdings. 47,000 volumes.

Special Collections

Special collections include the **George Wyckoff Cummins Collection** consisting of archaeological and historical books, documents, and artifacts of North American Indians dating from the late 1700s; the **William Lewis Lancey Abraham Lincoln Collection** of over 100 volumes, photographs, busts, a daguerrotype, and a run of the *Lincoln Lore Newsletter* from 1858 to the present.

982
College of Saint Elizabeth
Mahoney Library
Convent Station, New Jersey 07961

Telephone. (201) 292-6476

Institutional Description. The privately supported institution was one of the first Roman Catholic Colleges for women to be established in the United States. It features the liberal arts and is conducted by the Sisters of Charity of Saint Elizabeth. Enrollment: 997.

Library Administration. Sr. Marie Rousek, Library Director and Special Collections/Rare Books Librarian.

Library General Holdings. 176,000 volumes; 1,094 current periodicals and serials; 18,000 microforms.

Special Collections

The Mahoney Library has fairly extensive collections in various aspects of women's studies and in gerontology. It is a selective depository for federal government documents and has picture files emphasizing art history and costume. A collection of books, pamphlets, and ephemera of the pre-1962 Catholic Church is maintained.

Young People's Collection. Consists of 4,800 volumes in fiction treating of minorities and special children.

Rare Book Collections

Rare Books and Manuscripts Collection. Includes the Doris and Yisrael Mayer collection on the history of women in the U.S.; the Helen C. Phillips collection of of atlases; Elizabeth and John St. George collection of madonnas in several media; the Florence E. Wall collection on the history of chemistry; and the Henry C. and Ann Fox Wolfe collection of literary and first editions.

983
Cumberland County College
Library
P.O. Box 517
Vineland, New Jersey 08360

Telephone. (609) 691-8600

Institutional Description. Founded in 1963, the two-year college opened in 1966 as the first New Jersey community college to begin classes on its own campus. Enrollment: 2,232.

Library Administration. James L. Luther, Director of Library Services.

Library General Holdings. 50,000 volumes; 215 periodical titles; 4,134 microfilm reels.

Special Collections

The library has a special collection of materials about New Jersey.

984
Drew University
University Library
36 Madison Avenue
Madison, New Jersey 07940

Telephone. (201) 377-3000

Institutional Description. The privately supported university was founded as the Drew Theological Seminary in 1866. The present name was adopted in 1928. It is affiliated with the United Methodist Church. Enrollment: 1,341.

Library Administration. Arthur E. Jones, Jr., Director.

Library General Holdings. 431,000 bound volumes; 1,720 periodical subscriptions; 187,000 microforms.

Special Collections

Wesleyana Collection. Contains 22,000 items pertaining to the lives and works of founders of the Methodist movement, John and Charles Wesley, including their books and some original manuscripts.

Pamphlet Collections. Material from the eighteenth and nineteenth centuries in the Luke Tyerman and George Osborne Collection.

Theology Collection. A collection of more than 250,000 volumes is one of a relatively small number of especially strong collections in North America and contains books and manuscripts of high value for scholarly research. Resources are exceptional in Biblical scholarship, patristics, Reformation, and nineteenth-century and American theology.

Archives and History Center of the United Methodist Church. The materials housed here plus Drew's own substantial Methodist resources give access to the world's largest collection of Methodistica.

Other collections include Will Herberg, Carl Michalson, and Fred Maser collections; the **David Creamer Hymnology Collection;** subject collections on slavery, the Civil War, and the Reformation. There is a vast collection of Methodistica which, when combined with the materials brought to Drew in 1982 under the United Methodist Commission on Archives and History, resulted in a Methodist collection of unparalleled world importance for use of both denonimational and secular historians.

Rare Book Collections

John McClintock Rare Book Collection. Includes 2,000 volumes, primarily rare books from the sixteenth and seventeenth centuries, concentrating on the English dissenting tradition and the humanistic tradition in Europe.

Gibbons Family Papers. A collection of 10 linear feet of family records and correspondence between Thomas Gibbons and his son William pertaining to their Georgia rice plantations and their steamboat interests; covers the period 1780-1850.

985
Fairleigh Dickinson University
Messler Library
Montrose Avenue
Rutherford, New Jersey 07070

Telephone. (201) 460-5074

Institutional Description. The privately supported university opened its first campus in 1942 in Rutherford, and later added branch campuses in Teaneck and Madison. Enrollment: 13,632.

Library Administration. Ruth Schwartz, University Librarian; Richard Goerner, Rare Books Librarian.

Library General Holdings. 650,510 volumes; 4,545 current periodical subscriptions; 40,000 audiovisual materials; 412,000 microforms; 11,700 government documents.

Special Collections

New Jersey Room. A special collection of approximately 25,000 titles, 1,200 rare books, 140 manuscript collections, 900 rare maps, 540 rolls of microfilm of U.S. and New Jersey census material; and 340 periodical subscriptions. As a full depository for New Jersey state documents, the collection regularly receives published reports and public hearings of the New Jersey Legislature and its various commissions and committees, and of the annual and irregular reports of the executive agencies, as well as Supreme and Superior Court reports. Business-related documents include statistics on economic indicators, population, labor markets, employment and unemployment insurance, among others. There are directors for state and local officials, industrial parks, realtors, factory outlet stores and trade and vocational schools in the state. The collection also includes early reports of state agencies.

There is much printed published historical literature. This includes maps (such as the Gordon "Bergen Meadows"), published genealogies, and state and local histories. The manuscript collection includes a number of original colonial laws and deeds as well as Rutherford-Watts-Russell, Hobart and Schultze papers. It contains the largest collection of the Hackensack Meadowlands Development Commission in the state, and the personal papers of former State Senator Fairleigh S. Dickinson, Jr.

The Messler Library also houses the **Outdoor Advertising Association of America Archives** and the **Harry Chesler Collection** of original comic art and illustration.

986
Felician College
College Library
260 South Main Street
Lodi, New Jersey 07644

Telephone. (201) 778-1190

Institutional Description. The privately supported liberal arts college for women was founded as a normal school, and now offers a variety of programs. Men are admitted to evening and summer programs. Enrollment: 557.

Library Administration. Sister Mary Mericia Liszewski, Director.

Library General Holdings. 72,500 volumes; 510 current periodical subscriptions.

Special Collections

Recordings of music and literary masterworks are housed in the Listening Room and a curriculum library serves as a resource center for the Teacher Education Programs. A special collection of Polish books is housed in Marian Hall.

987
Georgian Court College
Farley Memorial Library
Lakewood Avenue
Lakewood, New Jersey 08701

Telephone. (201) 364-2200

Institutional Description. The privately supported liberal arts college primarily for women was founded in 1908. Evening programs and the graduate school are coeducational. It is affiliated with the Roman Catholic Church. Enrollment: 1,773.

Library Administration. Barbara J. Hutchison, Director.

Library General Holdings. 88,000 volumes; 1,150 periodical titles.

Special Collections

The Farley Library maintains a special collection on New Jersey history as well as collections of materials in education and religious studies.

988
Glassboro State College
Savitz Library
Glassboro, New Jersey 08028

Telephone. (609) 863-6101

Institutional Description. The publicly supported state college began as a two-year normal school in 1923. It continues to emphasize teacher education. Enrollment: 8,662.

Library Administration. Sandor Szilassy, College Librarian; Clara M. Kirner, Special Collections Librarian.

Library General Holdings. 356,153 volumes; 68,207 microform units; 46,361 government documents in microform; 2,135 periodical titles.

Special Collections

Stewart Collection. The collection was willed to the college by Frank H. Stewart in 1948. It is the only comprehensive research collection of New Jersey history in southern New Jersey. The collection presently numbers some 15,000 books and pamphlets, 5,000 documents and manuscripts, photostats, 500 early West Jersey deeds, maps, newspapers, and periodicals. Emphases in the collection are primarily South Jersey history, the Revolutionary War period, Quaker history, the Old United States Mint, and Indian lore. The significant source material includes: letters, diaries, deeds, slavery documents, legal papers, business records, handwritten archives and military records.

Satterthwaite Genealogical Collection. This collection contains the working papers, letters, and genealogies amassed by Elizabeth Satterthwaite during her more than twenty years as a professional genealogist. Approximately one hundred families from New Jersey (many from Central and Southern Jersey) are represented.

Bole Summit Papers. Dr. Robert Bole, professor emiritus of Glassboro State College and author of the book *Summit at Holly Bush* amassed a voluminous collection of press releases and personal interviews during the time of the Kosygin-Johnson meeting. The material includes news articles, editorials, and pictures from world newspapers and periodicals.

Charles A. Wolverton Papers. Included in this collection are scrapbooks of the New Jersey Congressman which were kept during his many terms of office; also included are copies of the speeches which he made.

Nineteenth Century Textbook Collection. Approximately two hundred elementary and secondary school texts for almost every subject give an interesting view into the type of textbook which was used in schools during the early 1800s. The oldest is an arithmetic text printed in Dublin, 1777.

Tighe Collection. Over three hundred eighteenth and nineteenth century children's books are contained in this collection. Included are chapbooks, toy books, shape books, alphabet books, and nursery rhymes.

College Archives. Publications of Glassboro State College including annual reports, college catalogs, press releases, faculty and departmental publications, masters theses, and a few artifacts relating to the history of the college.

Ankenbrand Collection. A book and pamphlet collection of Frank Ankenbrand; includes first editions, autographed copies, and some of Ankenbrand's own publications.

The oldest book in the Special Collections at Glassboro is an incunabulum published in Latin in 1499 entitled *Epigrammatum Libri Quattuor* (and other verses) by Renaissance poet Pamfilo Sasso.

989
Jersey City State College
Forrest A. Irwin Library
2039 Kennedy Boulevard
Jersey City, New Jersey 07305

Telephone. (201) 547-6000

Institutional Description. The publicly supported state liberal arts and teachers college was founded in 1929. It grants baccalaureate, professional, and master's degrees. Enrollment: 7,020.

Library Administration. Robert S. Nugent, Director.

Library General Holdings. 263,000 volumes; 1,580 current periodical subscriptions; 58,000 government documents.

Special Collections

Important holdings of the library are in art history, social service, and music. The Curriculum Materials Center is well stocked with courses of study, textbooks, pamphlets, juvenile encyclopedias and reference works. The library also has over 500,000 microforms of particular interest to students investigating special topics in education, American studies, anthropology, sociology, and criminal justice.

990
Kean College of New Jersey
Nancy Thompson Library
Morris Avenue
Union, New Jersey 07083

Telephone. (201) 527-2017

Institutional Description. The publicly supported college, founded in 1855, features liberal arts, sciences, preprofessional, and teacher preparation programs. Enrollment: 12,938.

Library Administration. Barbara Simpson, Library Director; Eleanor McKnight, Rare Books Librarian.

Library General Holdings. 250,000 volumes; 1,500 periodical and newspaper subscriptions.

Special Collections

The Nancy Thompson Library maintains a collection of the American Welding Society publications; microcard editions of Early American Imprints; Three Centuries of Drama - English; and English and American Drama of the Nineteenth Century (1500-1800). The microfilm *Catalog of the Schomburg Center for Research in Black Culture* is available. The Library is a selective depository for federal government documents and a selective regional depository for New Jersey state documents.

Curriculum Materials Center. Curricula publications, textbooks, software, and a wide range of teaching aids; it is supplemented by an extensive collection of children's literature.

New Jersey Collection. Over 1,200 volumes related to the history of New Jersey; contains many rare items.

Florence Dwyer Collection. An extensive collection of Congresswoman Dwyer's papers.

Archives. Documents and records relevant to the history of the college.

991
Monmouth College
Guggenheim Memorial Library
Cedar Avenue
West Long Branch, New Jersey 07764

Telephone. (201) 571-3400

Institutional Description. The privatley supported liberal arts college was founded in 1933. It grants associate, baccalaureate, and master's degrees. Enrollment: 4,442.

Library Administration. Robert Brooks, Library Director.

Library General Holdings. 233,000 volumes; 1,820 periodicals; 69,000 government documents; 223,000 microforms.

Special Collections

The library maintains a special collection of materials pertaining to the state of New Jersey which includes over 2,000 books, microforms, and miscellaneous items.

992
Montclair State College
Harry A. Sprague Library
Upper Montclair, New Jersey 07043

Telephone. (201) 893-4000

Institutional Description. The publicly supported liberal arts and teachers college was founded in 1909 as a normal school. In 1966, liberal arts programs were started. Enrollment: 12,922.

Library Administration. Blanche W. Haller, Director, Library Services.

Library General Holdings. 350,000 books; 3,100 periodical subscriptions; 30,000 government documents; 860,-000 non-print items.

Special Collections

Sullivan Collection. Consists of 1,200 volumes of modern American poetry, including first editions.

Webster Memorial Collection. Includes 350 volumes of mostly American twentieth-century poetry; many first editions and some signed by notable poets.

William Carlos Williams Collection. Contains 110 volumes of poetry and criticism, including first editions, from the library of the twentieth-century American poet.

993
New Brunswick Theological Seminary
Gardner A. Sage Library
21 Seminary Place
New Brunswick, New Jersey 08901

Telephone. (201) 828-1526

Institutional Description. The privately supported seminary is an institution of the Reformed Church in America. It was founded in 1784. Enrollment: 133.

Library Administration. Renee S. House, Library Director; Russell Gasero, Denominational Archivist.

Library General Holdings. 150,000 volumes; 300 current periodical subscriptions.

Special Collections

Classics Collection. Contains 2,000 Greek and Latin language volumes published 1830-1920; includes such major sets as Migne and Loeb.

Leiby Collection. The core of this 600-volume collection is made up of the library of Dr. Adrian Leiby, historian of the Revolutionary War in New Jersey and surrounding areas; focus is on the Revolutionary War Period and fifty years following in New Jersey and New York.

Reformed Church in America Archives. Includes unpublished manuscripts, letters, diaries, important papers of individuals connected with the Reformed Church of America engaged in missions or ministry; official records of the denomination and its various institutions; local church records.

Vedders Art Collection. A collection of secondary sources (1,300 titles) on the fine arts and architecture; largely focused on religious art and architecture.

Rare Book Collections

Dutch Collection. Include 800 rare Dutch language imprints, published in the Netherlands between 1610 and 1750 (a few items published as late as 1890); covers a broad range of subjects—political science, geography, science, literature, philology, economics, history—but two-thirds of the collection is Dutch theology and Biblical studies.

Dutch Colonial Collection. Primary and secondary sources concerning the Reformed Church of America—its local congregations (records, sermons), institutions, general history and liturgy, published denominational proceedings, including Dutch roots; inclusive 1628 to the present.

Rare Books Collection. An eclectic collection of 2,-000 titles published from the 1470s to 1790s; primarily theological treatises in Latin and English; collection of Dutch "Staten General" Bibles, including family genealogy; a few early New Jersey imprints.

994
New Jersey Institute of Technology Robert W. Van Houten Library 323 Martin Luther King, Jr. Boulevard Newark, New Jersey 07102

Telephone. (201) 596-3000

Institutional Description. The publicly supported (state and city) technological university was founded in 1881. It was formerly known as Newark College of Engineering. The day and evening Undergraduate Division is supplemented by the New Jersey School of Architecture, the Division of Technology, the Division of Continuing Education, and the Graduate Division. Enrollment: 7,591.

Library Administration. Morton Snowhite, Librarian.

Library General Holdings. 130,000 volumes; 1,350 periodical subscriptions.

Special Collections

Memorial gifts from the personal libraries of people formerly associated with the Institute have been received by the Van Houten Library. Foremost among these gifts are books and periodicals from the collections of charter trustee Dr. Edward Weston and State Senator Roy V. Wright. The **Edward C. Molina Collection** contains 1,300 books about mathematics, probability, astronomy and related subjects. The Architecture Library contains more than 1,200 books and 65,000 slides.

995
Northeastern Bible College Lincoln Memorial Library 12 Oak Lane Essex Fells, New Jersey 07021

Telephone. (201) 226-1074

Institutional Description. The privately supported professional Bible college, founded in 1950, is interdenominational. It offers specialized curricula for those training for the ministry. Enrollment: 211.

Library Administration. Shirley N. Wood, Director of Library Services.

Library General Holdings. 54,000 volumes; 600 periodical titles.

Special Collections

The library recently received, from the family of the Rev. Edward N. Cleaveland, a most significant donation of over 6,000 books dealing with Judaistics and Jewish Evangelism.

996
Princeton Theological Seminary Robert E. Speer Library Mercer Street Princeton, New Jersey 08540

Telephone. (609) 921-8300

Institutional Description. The privately supported theological seminary is affiliated with the Presbyterian Church (U.S.A.). Founded in 1812, it now offers graduate programs only. Enrollment: 854.

Library Administration. Louis Charles Willard, James Lennox Librarian.

Library General Holdings. 322,000 volumes; 1,390 current periodical subscriptions; 3,700 microforms.

Special Collections

In addition to a renowned theological collection, the library maintains the **Louis F. Benson Collection of Hymnology** which numbers over 10,000 hymnals and books about hymnology; the **Grossert Library of Puritan and Nonconformist Theology,** acquired in 1885 and augmented regularly, now contains over 5,000 volumes; and the **Sprague Collection** of an unusually large collection of early theological pamphlets. Over 2,000 volumes and 3,-000 pamphlets dealing with the controversy regarding the proper form of baptism are in the **Agnew Baptist Collection.** The Alumni Alcove, supported substantially by the donations of authors, preserves their published works as a testimony to the influential position of Seminary graduates and faculty in theological and general literature.

997
Princeton University
University Library
Princeton, New Jersey 08544

Telephone. (609) 452-3000

Institutional Description. The privately supported university had its beginnings in 1746 when John Hamilton established it as the College of New Jersey. The original trustees of the university were leaders in the evangelical wing of the Presbyterian Church. Enrollment: 6,293.

Library Administration. Donald W. Koepp, University Librarian. Curators: Dale Roylance, Graphic Arts; Jean Preston, Manuscripts; Mary Schmidt, Marquand Art Library; Brooks Levy, Numismatics; Ann Hanson, Papyrology; Alexander Wainwright, Parrish Collection of Victorian Novelists and the Robert H. Taylor Collection; Stephen Ferguson, Rare Books; Alfred Bush, Historic Maps Collection; Janet Ing, Scheide Library; Nancy Bressler, Twentieth Century Manuscripts in American Statecraft and Public Policy; Alfred Bush, Western Americana; Mary Ann Jensen, William Seymour Theatre Collection.

Library General Holdings. 3,856,700 volumes; 43,000 linear feet of manuscripts and archives.

Special Collections

The Department of Rare Books and Special Collections includes thirteen divisions, each supervised by its own curator.

Rare Book Collections

General Rare Books Collections. These collections contain rare and historically significant publications in non-Oriental languages representing most fields in which the Princeton University Library acquires books as well as various special collection materials. The outstanding strengths are in the fields of American history and literature and English history and literature. There are also large numbers of early printed Continental books. The collections total approximately 140,000 volumes and about 1,000 broadsides and slip ballads. Most of the books are arranged in two continuous sequences. In addition, separately arranged special collections include the following:

Sylvia Beach Collection, 1,800 volumes

Carton Hunting Collection, 1,300 volumes

Grover Cleveland Library, 216 volumes

College of One Collection of Sheilah Graham, 360 volumes

Cook Chess Collection, 2,100 volumes

Meirs Collection of George Cruikshank, 1,440 volumes

Derrydale Press Collection and the Sporting Books of Eugene V. Connett, 475 volumes

Jonathan Edwards Library, 360 volumes

J. Harlin O'Connell Collection of English Literature of the 1890s, 575 volumes

Kenneth McKenzie Fable Collection, 700 volumes

Hall Handel Collection, 500 volumes

Incunabula, over 500 volumes

Otto von Kienbusch Angling Collection, 2,400 volumes

Charles Scribner Collection of Charles Lamb, 150 volumes

Robert F. Metzdorf Collection of Victorian bookbindings, 1,050 volumes

Harry B. Vandeventer Poetry Collection, 650 volumes

Orlando F. Weber Collection of Economic History, 1,335 volumes

Goertz Collection, 3,300 volumes

Laurence Hutton Collection, 1,010 volumes

Miriam Y. Holden Collection on the History of Women (rare books section only), 650 volumes

Grenville Kane Collection of Americana, 750 volumes

Stanley Lieberman Memorial Collection of Hero Fiction, 780 volumes

Cyrus McCormick Collection of Americana, 300 volumes

William Nelson Collection of New Jerseyana, 470 volumes

New Jersey Imprints, over 200 volumes

Morris L. Parrish Collection of Victorian Novelists, 6,500 volumes

Princeton Borough Collection, 220 volumes

Princeton Borough Agricultural Association, 75 volumes

Princetoniana Collection, 45 volumes

Pitney Collection on International Law and Diplomacy, 150 volumes

Robert Patterson Collection of Horace, 1,730 volumes

Kenneth H. Rockey Angling Collection, 900 volume

Julius Spencer Morgan Collection of Vergil, 1,300 volumes

John Shaw Pierson Civil War Collection, 4,575 volumes

John Witherspoon Library, 1,080 volumes

Woodrow Wilson Collection, 1,335 volumes

Manuscripts. The collections of manuscripts include codices, autograph letters, deeds, literary works, diaries, publishers' and corporate archives, English and American history and literature, Princetoniana, Persian and Arabic manuscripts, examples of writing and the book in different formats, day tablets, papyri. Dates range from ca. 6th century B.C. to today. Languages range from ancient Sumerian, Babylonian, Assyrian, Egyptian through Greek, Latin, Coptic, Arabic, Indic, Armenian, Syriac,

Turkish to Italian, French, German, Spanish, etc. Several million manuscripts and papers include ca. 1,000 cuneiform tables, ca. 250 Babylonian cylinder and stamp seals, ca. 600 papyri, ca. 400 medieval codices, ca. 10,000 deeds, ca. 10,000 Arabic manuscripts, as well as regular English language manuscripts and papers.

Important collections include the Garrett collection of medieval codices; the Garrett collection of Islamic manuscripts; the Parrish Collection of Victorian authors; the Rollins collection of Western Americana; publishers' archives such as Scribners, Henry Holt, Harper and Company; collections of Princeton alumni, such as James Madison, Aaron Burr, F. Scott Fitzgerald, and astronomer Henry Norris Russell; and artists' collections such as Beardsley, Cruikshank, and the Pre-Raphaelites. For detailed information regarding the manuscript collections at Princeton, see Alexander P. Clark, *The Manuscript Collections of the Princeton University Library. An Introductory Survey,* Princeton: 1960 and the *Princeton University Library Chronicle,* Vol. XIX, Nos. 3 & 4 (Spring & Summer, 1958).

Marquand Art Library. Covers the history of art and architecture; archaeology and includes 140,000 monographs and bound periodicals; 9,000 art exhibition catalogs; 12,000 art auction catalogs.

Twentieth-Century Manuscripts in American Statecraft and Public Policy. Subject areas include political, economic, social, and legal history; the papers of Bernard Baruch, Allen W. Dulles, John Foster Dulles, James V. Forrestal, John Marshall Harlan, George F. Kennan, David E. Lilienthal, H. Alexander Smith, Adlai E. Stevenson, and about 125 others as well as the archives of the American Civil Liberties Union, Common Cause, and other groups. For further detailed information about this collection, see Nancy Bressler, "The Seeley G. Mudd Manuscript Library: A Home Fit for a Statesman," *Princeton University Library Chronicle,* XXXIX, No. 1 (Autumn, 1977), pp. 1-10 and also Nancy Bressler, *A Descriptive Catalogue of the Papers in the area of Twentieth Century American Statecraft and Public Policy,* Princeton: 1972; revised, 1974).

Historic Maps. Pre-1919 maps from and of all parts of the world, especially Europe and the Americas; 40,000 flat-sheet maps and charts; 1,000 monographs in historical cartography; some journal subscriptions.

Western Americana. The area of collecting interest is the history and culture of the American states west of the Mississippi, especially the Rocky Mountain states and the Southwest; Western Canada, Mexico, and Central America whose history is intimately attached to the history of these states. Mormonism is strongly collected and is one of the largest such collections on the East Coast outside of Church repositories. American Indian history and culture is collected as well, especially American Indian newspapers. Includes manuscripts, imprints, paintings, photographs, objects, ephemera, broadsides, from the collections of Philip Ashton Rollins, Class of 1889, and others. For detailed information about the collection, see Alfred Bush, "The Princeton Collections of Western Americana," *Princeton University Library Chronicle,* Vol. XXXIII, No. 1 (Autumn, 1971), pp. 1-17.

Numismatics. Coinage and currency of all nations and cultures, ancient to modern, with particular emphasis on Greek (ca. 2,000), Roman (ca. 6,000), and American coinage; on American colonial, Continental, and Confederate currency. Medals are also collected and include those of World War I and the Arthur Newman collection of over 1,000 medals commemorating the history of aviation.

Papyri. The Rare Book Department preserves some 600 Greek papyri, largely from the Rome and Byzantine periods in Egypt. The collection also contains a few Latin papyri, likewise from Greco-Roman Egypt, as well as individual items written in hieroglyphics, Demotic characters, Coptic, and Arabic.

Parrish Collection of Victorian Novelists. Includes 6,500 volumes and many manuscripts covering twenty-four authors; strongest in Lewis Carroll, Charles Dickens, Thomas Hardy, Robert Louis Stevenson, William Thackeray, Anthony Trollope. For further information regarding this collection, see Alexander D. Wainwright, "The Morris L. Parrish Collection of Victorian Novelists: A Summary Report and an Introduction," *Princeton University Library Chronicle,* Vol. XVII, No. 2 (Winter, 1956), pp. 59-67.

The Scheide Library. This Library, which has been assembled by three generations of book collectors, was moved in 1959 from its original location in Titusville, Pennsylvania, to Princeton and the home of William H. Scheide, the present owner and grandson of the founder. The library is housed in Firestone Library in a room constructed with funds provided by Mr. Scheide. Although still a private library, it is available to scholars. The collection consists of essential books which have deeply influenced the developments of Western culture: the Bible, incunabula, voyages and travels, literature, and Americana. For more detailed information, see "The Scheide Library," a special issue of the *Princeton University Library Chronicle,* Vol. XXXVIII, No. 2 (Winter, 1976).

Robert H. Taylor Collection. This collection consists of over 7,000 rare books and numerous manuscripts illustrating in their wide range the scope of English literature. For detailed information about this collection, see Robert J. Wickenheiser, "The Robert H. Taylor Collection," *Princeton University Library Chronicle,* Vol. XXXVIII, No. 2 and 3 (Winter-Spring, 1976-77).

Graphic Arts. Covers the subject areas of paper, printing, book arts, print making, photography, artists' books, private press books; 5,000 specimens of printing; 8,000 prints; 4,000 photographs. For details on the collection, see the Winter, 1981 number of the *Princeton University Library Chronicle* which includes a cumulative subject index to articles on the American graphic arts appearing in the *Chronicle* between 1939 and 1980.

Theatre. This collection covers theatre, film, circus, and dance; 9,000 monographs and bound periodicals; Princeton theatrical archives, playbills, broadsides, scrapbooks, photographs, engravings, and other prints; piano-vocal scores, cassettes of musical shows, correspondence, posters, promptbooks and acting scripts, set and costume designs, route books. For detailed information about the collection, see Mary Ann Jensen, "The William Seymour Theatre Collection, Princeton University Library," *Special Collections,* Vol. 1, No. 1 (Fall, 1981), pp. 41-51.

998
Ramapo College of New Jersey
College Library
505 Ramapo Valley Road
Mahwah, New Jersey 07430

Telephone. (201) 529-7500

Institutional Description. The publicly supported (state) liberal arts college was founded in 1971. The college is divided into several smaller schools in order to offer more individualized attention. Enrollment: 3,858.

Library Administration. Norma Yueh, Director of Library Services.

Library General Holdings. 156,000 volumes; 1,370 current periodicals; 102,000 government documents.

Special Collections

Special holdings of the library include Bergen County (New Jersey) government documents and Mahwah Township (New Jersey) publications. The library also maintains the **Holocaust Collection** and the **Genocide Studies Collection.**

999
Rider College
Franklin F. Moore Library
2083 Lawrenceville Road
Lawrenceville, New Jersey 08648

Telephone. (609) 896-5111

Institutional Description. The privately supported college was founded as the Trenton Business College in 1865. In 1956 it purchased 306 acres of rolling farmland not far from Trenton and began building a modern, carefully designed campus. Enrollment: 5,027.

Library Administration. Ross Stephen, Director of Library Services; Henry Halpern, Special Collections Librarian.

Library General Holdings. 325,000 volumes; 1,800 current subscriptions; 25,000 microfilm reels; 400,000 microfiche; 250 audiovisual items.

Special Collections

Alan C. Lloyd Historical Collection of Typewriting Materials. Contains over 900 items pertaining to the history of the teaching of typewriting. Includes student textbooks, instructors' manuals; programs for military personnel, selected journals, slide programs, and other pedagogical materials; spans the years 1889 to 1984.

History of Rider College Collection. Includes catalogs, yearbooks, floor plans, architectural drawings, photographs, documents, and early model typewriters, dating from the late 1880s to the present.

Kendrick C. Hall Collection. Contains over 200 volumes on shorthand and bookkeeping, dating from 1855 to 1915.

1000
Rutgers, The State University of New Jersey
Rutgers University Libraries
College Avenue
New Brunswick, New Jersey 08903

Telephone. (201) 932-7739

Institutional Description. The publicly supported university, founded in 1766, consists of 10 day-time and 3 evening-time colleges located in New Brunswick, Camden, and Newark. Enrollment: 33,969 (New Brunswick campus); 4,959 (Camden campus); 9,611 (Newark campus).

Library Administration. Joanne Euster, University Librarian; Halina R. Rusak, Head of the Art Library; Pennt B. Page, Center of Alcohol Studies Librarian; Don Luck, Institute of Jazz Studies Librarian; Dan Morgenstern, Head, Special Collections, Institute of Jazz Studies.

Library General Holdings. 2,000,000 volume equivalents; the University's collection of archives, rare books, and manuscripts totals more than 2,400,000 items. Each Rutgers campus houses a library and students have access to any library in the system.

Special Collections

Art Library. The Art Library, located in Voorhees Hall on the College Avenue Campus in New Brunswick, houses 50,000 bound volumes, 120 current periodical subscriptions, 17,000 microfiche, and a pamphlet file of 5,000 items. The **Louis E. Stern Collection** of books on modern art contain plates designed by Chagall. The collection consists of 3,000 volumes and came from the estate of a prominent art collector. The **Mary Bartlett Cowdrey Collection** includes over 1,000 art monographs, exhibition catalogs, and brochures on American art. The collection was donated by a distinguished scholar in the area of nineteenth-century American art and an alumna of the Douglass College, Class of 1933. The **Howard Hibbard Collection** on Italian Renaissance and Baroque art came from the estate of Howard Hibbard, art historian, author, and teacher at Columbia University.

Institute of Jazz Studies. This collection consists of 2,000 volumes; 90 current periodical subscriptions; 4,000 bound and unbound journal backfile volumes; 75,000 discs, 1,000 tapes, 100 compact discs; plus clipping files, photographs, videos, motion pictures, oral histories, microforms, sheet music, and arrangements. The Institute, administratively attached to the Newark Dana Library, contains a large collection of materials on jazz periodicals (including the Flakser collection), and is probably the largest in the world. The collection of sound recordings (including non-commercial tapes and transcriptions), the clipping files, the photo files, and the oral history files are very extensive. Some of the archival materials collections are those of Ed Kirkeby, Mary Lou Williams, Marshall Sterns, and George Duvivier. The Institute publishes the *Annual Review of Jazz Studies,* and the monograph series in jazz (with Scarecrow Press).

Center of Alcohol Studies Library. This Center, located in Smithers Hall of the Busch Campus in Piscataway, New Jersey, contains over 8,000 volumes, 200 current periodical subscriptions, 1,700 microforms, and 50,000 reprints of research and professional materials dealing with all aspects of alcohol use and alcohol problems (from social and psychological to biomedical). The Center houses the **Ralph G. Connor Alcohol Research Reference Files,** a collection of 500 survey instruments that have been used in alcohol-related research projects. Many of these instruments are not published or available from other distributors.

There is also the Classified Abstract Archive of the Alcohol Literature, one of the earliest and most unique documentation and retrieval tools in the alcohol studies field. It contains over 16,000 abstracts of alcohol research literature from 1935-1976.

The Center also houses the National Association of Lesbian and Gay Alcoholism Professionals (NALGP) collection on alcoholism and homosexuality, collected and donated by NALGAP in 1987. The collection contains over 900 items.

Rare Book Collections

Special Collections and Archives. Contains manuscripts, rare books, pamphlets, almanacs, maps, broadsides, pictorial materials, the archives of the University, and the **Donald A. Sinclair Reference Collection** of printed works related to New Jersey. Topics included are Westerners in the Orient, history of science and technology, the consumer movement in the United States, twentieth-century Latin American politics and society, women's studies, social welfare, public policy, history of etymology, New Jersey congressional and senatorial papers, and Puritanism.

Among the notable manuscript collections are the papers of William Cobbett, Walter Weyl, William Dean Howells, Walt Whitman, Arthur Waley, General J.F.C. Fuller, William Elliot Griffis, the Roebling family, contemporary scores of Handel's anthems, the Synmington collection of manuscripts and letters of nineteenth-century British authors, most notably Algernon Charles Swinburne. The rare book collection has strengths in the following areas: the reports and observations of Westerners in the Orient (sixteenth to nineteenth centuries); dictionaries and grammars (British, American, European); botanies, herbals, and agricultural treatises (sixteenth to eighteenth centuries) as well as seventeenth- to eighteenth-century British and American political tracts and the works of Milton, Cobbett, and Defoe.

1001
Seton Hall University
McLaughlin Library
400 South Orange Avenue
South Orange, New Jersey 07079

Telephone. (201) 761-9000

Institutional Description. The privately supported Roman Catholic university was founded in 1856. It contains six colleges and schools. Enrollment: 7,451.

Library Administration. Rev. James C. Sharp, University Librarian.

Library General Holdings. 360,000 titles; 2,000 periodicals; 2,500 phonodiscs.

Special Collections

Asian Studies Collection. This collections includes 4,000 volumes on Chinese, Japanese, and Korean history, political science, and literature.

McManus Collection. Contains 3,000 volumes of Irish history and literature.

New Jersey Catholic Historical Commission Records. Contains historical materials on the Catholic Church in New Jersey, including diaries, correspondence, and personal papers of bishops and archibishops of the Newark diocese.

Other special collections include the Dr. Helen B. Warrin Curriculum Room which offers the latest in education philosophies; the Falk Rare Book Room; the Visceglia Room; and the Gerald Murphy Civil War Room.

1002
Stevens Institute of Technology
Samuel C. Williams Library
Castle Point
Hoboken, New Jersey 07030

Telephone. (201) 420-5198

Institutional Description. The privately supported college of engineering was founded by Edwin Stevens in 1870. Programs are offered at both the undergraduate and graduate levels. Enrollment: 3,303.

Library Administration. Richard P. Widdicombe, Librarian; Jane G. Hartye, Associate Curator.

Library General Holdings. 105,000 volumes; 850 current periodicals; 5 newspaper subscriptions.

Special Collections

Frederick Winslow Taylor Collection. The only existing collection of materials on the "father of scientific management," including his private papers totaling 3,000 items and 1,000 volumes with first editions of all of his books.

Colonel John Stevens Family Papers. Microfilm copies include those of Edwin Augustus Stevens who founded the Institute; also extensive reference materials on the family including articles, books, photographs, slides, and genealogy.

The library also has 100 original drawings of the U.S.S. Monitor by draftsman Charles MacCord.

Rare Book Collections

John Lieb Leonardo da Vinci Collection. Consists of 1,500 volumes, including facsimiles of da Vinci's *Codex Leicester* and other notebooks, prints, and many rare books and first editions dating from 1504.

1003
Stockton State College
Stockton College Library
Pomona, New Jersey 08240

Telephone. (609) 652-1776

Institutional Description. The publicly supported state liberal arts college was founded in 1971. It features personally-designed curricula. Enrollment: 5,071.

Library Administration. Eileen Dubin, Director of Library Services.

Library General Holdings. 156,000 volumes; 1,400 periodical subscriptions; 262,000 government documents; 122,000 microforms.

Special Collections

Stockton is a depository library for selected New Jersey, Atlantic County, and U.S. Government publications and U.S. Geological Survey maps. It has an extensive collection of material relating to the New Jersey Pine Barrens. The college archives are located in the library and important documents related to the governance of Stockton, including Board of Trustees materials, union agreements, the college budget, and charters may be found there.

1004
Trenton State College
Roscoe L. West Library
Hillwood Lakes CN 4700
Trenton, New Jersey 08650

Telephone. (609) 771-1855

Institutional Description. The publicly supported state liberal arts and professional college was founded in 1855. It offers a wide range of programs. Enrollment: 8,179.

Library Administration. Richard P. Matthews, Special Collections Librarian.

Library General Holdings. 520,000 volumes; 1,750 current periodical subscriptions; 550,000 microforms.

Special Collections

The **Felix Hirsch Reference Collection** of 18,000 volumes includes leading encyclopedias, dictionaries, atlases, and a variety of subject handbooks in several languages. The library also has special collections of old textbooks, New Jersey materials, the College Archives, and an **Oral History Collection.**

1005
University of Medicine and Dentistry of New Jersey
George F. Smith Library of the Health Sciences
30 Twelfth Avenue
Newark, New Jersey 07103

Telephone. (201) 456-4580

Institutional Description. The publicly supported health sciences institution is composed of three medical schools, a school of dentistry, a graduate school of biomedical sciences, and a school of health related professions. It was founded in 1954. Enrollment: 3,712.

Library Administration. Philip Rosenstein, Librarian; Barbara S. Irwin, Special Collections Librarian/Archivist.

Library General Holdings. 60,248 books; 2,354 current journal titles; 69,405 journal volumes; 3,621 media titles; 100 software titles.

Rare Book Collections

Morris H. Saffron Collection. Includes 212 rare books on historical medicine.

History of Medicine. Consists of 550 titles of nineteenth-century editions and Americana; includes serials.

New Jersey Medical History Collection. Contains rare books, pamphlets, emphemera, vertical files (subject and geographical), and oral histories.

New Jersey Medical History Manuscript Collections. Papers of individuals and organizations including photographs.

UMDNJ-University Archives. Includes oral histories and photographs; papers of Harrison Martland, M.D., Rita Finkler, M.D., and Sam Berg, M.D.

1006
Upsala College
College Library
Prospect Street
East Orange, New Jersey 07019

Telephone. (201) 266-7000

Institutional Description. The privately supported liberal arts college was founded in 1893. It is affiliated with the Lutheran Church in America. Enrollment: 1,366.

Library Administration. David L. Murray, Director.

Library General Holdings. 150,000 volumes; 950 serials.

Special Collections

Lincoln Collection. This collection contains duplicates of 350 books from the library of Abraham Lincoln.

1007
Westminster Choir College
Talbott Library-Learning Center
Hamilton at Walnut
Princeton, New Jersey 08540

Telephone. (609) 921-7100

Institutional Description. The privately supported professional college of music was founded in 1926. Academic cooperative programs are available with Rider College and Princeton University. Enrollment: 340.

Library Administration. Sherry L. Vellucci, Director.

Library General Holdings. 48,000 volumes; 135 current periodical titles; 7,900 sound recordings.

Special Collections

The Talbott Library-Learning Center memorializes Katherine Houk Talbott, one of the leading benefactors of the college during its earliest days in Dayton, Ohio. The **Music Education Resource Center,** a collection of current materials in various media for the classroom music teacher is located in the library. The **Performance Collection,** comprises some 300,000 multiple copies of 3,300 titles of choral music compositions.

1008
William Paterson College of New Jersey
Sarah Byrd Askew Library
300 Pompton Road
Wayne, New Jersey 07470

Telephone. (201) 595-2116

Institutional Description. The publicly supported liberal arts and teachers college was founded as a city normal school in 1855. Enrollment: 9,232.

Library Administration. Robert L. Goldberg, College Librarian; Michele T. Ruhlin, Special Collections Librarian; Amy G. Job, Catalog Librarian.

Library General Holdings. 296,000 volumes; 1,500 periodical subscriptions; 2,500 music scores; 672,783 microforms; partial depository for New Jersey state documents.

Special Collections

New Jersey Collection. Approximately 1,500 titles and a vertical file covering the state but with emphasis on northern New Jersey; specific attention is focused on Paterson and Passaic, with a number of rare and older titles detailing labor history.

Curriculum Materials Collection. Contains 16,000 textbooks, juvenile titles, teacher's aids, and reference materials as well as an extensive collection of curriculum guides.

Music Scores. Contains 2,500 music scores, primarily classical but includes a sizeable collection of contemporary composers, particularly those written by Hugh Aitken.

The library maintains a collection of approximately 1,000 first and limited editions of nineteenth- and twentieth-century American and British authors (some autographed).

Rare Book Collections

William Paterson Papers. The professional papers of William Paterson, purchased for the college by the Alumni Association, are a collection of over 700 pages of letters, ledgers, and legal notes handwritten by Paterson and his family. They constitute approximately one-third of the Paterson papers known to exist.

New Mexico

1009
College of Santa Fe
Fogelson Library Center
St. Michaels Drive
Santa Fe, New Mexico 87501

Telephone. (505) 473-6234

Institutional Description. The privately supported liberal arts college was founded in 1874 as the College of the Christian Brothers of New Mexico. It continues its affiliation with the Roman Catholic Church. Enrollment: 1,182.

Library Administration. Brother Brendan Wilkinson, F.S.C., Head Librarian.

Library General Holdings. 98,000 volumes; 300 current periodical subscriptions.

Special Collections

The **Southwest Collection** contains over 8,000 volumes on local culture and folklore dating from the early nineteenth century. The collection also includes works by New Mexico authors.

1010
College of the Southwest
Scarborough Memorial Library
6610 Lovington Highway
Hobbs, New Mexico 88240

Telephone. (505) 392-6561

Institutional Description. The privately supported liberal arts college is an independent Christian institution. It was founded by a small group of Baptist laymen as Hobbs Baptist College in 1956. Enrollment: 178.

Library Administration. Richard Tubesing, College Librarian and Special Collections Librarian.

Library General Holdings. 34,050 volumes; 10,000 microforms; 405 current periodical subscriptions; 285 audiovisual materials.

Special Collections

Thomas A. Webber Heritage Collection. Includes 4,000 volumes on all aspects of New Mexico, West Texas, Eastern Arizona, and the "Four Corners" history, literature, anthropology, geography, and culture; emphasis on southeastern New Mexico.

New Mexico State Textbook Adoption Center. Consists of 10,000 textbook and media titles on the New Mexico State Textbook Adoption List.

1011
Eastern New Mexico University
Golden Library
Portales, New Mexico 88130

Telephone. (505) 562-2624

Institutional Description. The publicly supported state university began as a junior college in 1934. In 1940 upper-level programs were added. There are branches in Roswell, Clovis, Artesia, Hobbs, and Tucumcari. Enrollment: 3,186.

Library Administration. C. Edwin Dowlin, Library Director; Mary Jo Walker, Special Collections Librarian.

Library General Holdings. 272,000 volumes; 1,187 current periodicals; 665,000 microforms; 43,000 audiovisual materials. Rare books, maps, newspapers, magazines, government documents, photographs, oral histories, and original manuscripts pertaining to the fields of science fiction, southwestern and local history, postmodern literature, lyric theatre and dance, as well as official university records, comprise the main body of the Special Collections and Archives.

Special Collections

Jack Williamson Science Fiction Library. This collection was officially dedicated in 1982 "in honor of our world-renowned pioneer science fiction writer, teacher, student and benefactor." The collection actually began in 1967 when Williamson made his first donation of materials. It currently spans a period of 70 years or more with approximately 10,000 books and many thousands of specialty magazines, manuscripts, letters, and memorabilia from established writers.

Southwest Collection. Includes rare, out of print, and current materials, in both published and unpublished form, pertaining to the Southwest. Particular emphasis is placed on New Mexico and contiguous states with indepth holdings for Portales and Roosevelt County.

Local and State History Archives. Photographs of early days, oral histories recorded with early settlers, maps, government documents, and files of records from individual donors and organizations. The **Father Stanley Crocchiola Papers,** supplementing the work of a man who has written over 200 books about the region, comprise a unique part of this group.

Miscellaneous smaller subject collections include the post-modern innovative literature group which features a variety of ephemeral "little" magazines. The lyric theatre and dance group of materials contains rare printed materials pertaining to theatres and touring companies in the United States and abroad.

1012
Grants Branch Community College Learning Resource Center 1500 Third Street Grants, New Mexico 87020

Telephone. (505) 287-7981

Institutional Description. Grants Branch Community College is a two-year state school and is a branch of the New Mexico State University. Enrollment: 485.

Library Administration. Frederic Wilding-White, Coordinator of Learning Resource Center.

Library General Holdings. 28,533 volumes.

Special Collections

A special collection of the learning resource center is the **Law Library.**

1013
Institute of American Indian Arts Library St. Michaels Drive Santa Fe, New Mexico 87501

Telephone. (505) 988-6670

Institutional Description. The Institute of American Indian Arts is devoted to the arts education of the native American Indians. It offers a liberal arts program leading to the associate degree which is transferable to four-year colleges/universities. The Institute is situated on the campus of the College of Santa Fe. Enrollment: 208.

Library General Holdings. 15,000 volumes.

Special Collections

The library's specialized collection emphasizes art education. There is a collection of American Indian music and photographs and the **American Indian Collection.**

1014
New Mexico Highlands University Donnelly Library National Avenue Las Vegas, New Mexico 87701

Telephone. (505) 425-7511

Institutional Description. The publicly supported state university offers undergraduate and graduate programs in liberal arts and teacher training. It was founded in 1893. Enrollment: 1,823.

Library Administration. Raul Herrera, University Librarian; John McCance, Head, Technical Services.

Library General Holdings. 150,000 volumes; 1,300 periodical titles.

Special Collections

The Donnelly Library special collections include the Westphall Collection of 450 volumes covering the history of Blacks; a Genealogy Collection of 90 volumes; and the William S. Gray Collection in Reading of 10,000 titles in microfiche. Other microfiche collections include a Core Collection of Literature (330 volumes; and Books for College Libraries (600 volumes). *The Schomburg Collection in U.S. History* of 544 microfilm reels and *The Schomburg Center for Research in Black Culture Collection* of 50 microfilm reels are also available.

Rare Book Collections

Arrott Collection of Western Americana. Consists of 600 volumes.

The Library also has 238 file folders of manuscripts of nineteenth-century and early twentieth-century New Mexico military history and the Fort Union Archives.

1015
New Mexico Institute of Mining and Technology Martin Speare Memorial Library Campus Station Socorro, New Mexico 87801

Telephone. (505) 835-5614

Institutional Description. The publicly supported state institute has four divisions: the College, the State Bureau of Mines and Mineral Resources, the Petroleum Recovery Research Center, and the Research and Development Division. It was founded in 1889. Enrollment: 1,019.

Library Administration. Betty Reynolds, Library Director.

Library General Holdings. 130,000 volumes; 850 current periodical subscriptions; 85,000 government documents in print, 37,000 in microform; 10,000 maps.

Special Collections

The Martin Speare Memorial Library supports a strong collection of materials in the geological sciences specializing particularly in the publications and maps of the U.S. Geological Survey dating from the Survey's earliest days.

1016
New Mexico Military Institute
Library
1600 North Main
Roswell, New Mexico 88201

Telephone. (505) 622-6250

Institutional Description. New Mexico Military Institute was founded in 1891 as Goss Military College. The present name was adopted by the territorial legislature in 1893. Enrollment: 427.

Library Administration. Kathy Flanary, Librarian.

Library General Holdings. 68,000 volumes; 275 periodical titles.

Special Collections

The library maintains the **Paul Horgan Collection** and the **Napoleonic Archival Collection.**

1017
New Mexico State University
University Library
University Park
Las Cruces, New Mexico 88003

Telephone. (505) 646-1508

Institutional Description. The publicly supported state university was founded in 1888 as Las Cruces College. It was established as a land-grant college the next year. The university includes 2-year branches in Grants, Alamagordo, Carlsbad, and Dona Ana (Las Cruces). Enrollment: 13,223.

Library Administration. Hiram Davis, Dean and Director.

Library General Holdings. 771,000 volumes; 6,920 current periodicals; 369,000 government documents; 765,000 microforms.

Special Collections

Rio Grande Historical Collection. Consists of personal papers, organization records, photographs, tape recordings, and other documented material related to the Southwest and New Mexico.

1018
St. John's College
Library
Camino Cruz Blanco
Santa Fe, New Mexico 87501

Telephone. (505) 982-3691

Institutional Description. St. John's College is a nonsectarian, private, independent college and a branch of St. John's College in Annapolis, Maryland. Enrollment: 332.

Library Administration. James M. Benefiel, Director.

Library General Holdings. 51,000 volumes; 226 current periodical subscriptions.

Special Collections

The special collections in the library include the **Witter Bynner Collection** and the **Edgar Allan Poe Collection,** each containing first editions of each poet as well as other *belles lettres.* In addition, the library contains several distinguished music collections, including the Amelia White, the Grumman, the Schmidt, and the Holzman collections. The Music Library, located in the Music and Fine Arts Building, includes 7,725 records and tapes.

1019
San Juan College
Learning Resources Center
4601 College Boulevard
Farmington, New Mexico 87401

Telephone. (505) 326-3311

Institutional Description. The two-year college was founded in 1956 as the Farmington Branch of New Mexico College of Agriculture and Mechanic Arts. In 1981, the institution, then known as the San Juan Branch of New Mexico State University, became an independent instituion and the present name was adopted. Enrollment: 1,265.

Library Administration. Richard Harris, Director.

Library General Holdings. 37,000 volumes; 205 current periodical titles.

Special Collections

The library maintains a special collection on the Southwest.

1020
University of New Mexico
General Library
Albuquerque, New Mexico 87131

Telephone. (505) 277-4241

Institutional Description. The publicly supported university was established in 1889 as a normal school. Enrollment: 17,271.

Library Administration. Robert Migneault, Dean of Library Services; William Tydeman, Head, Special Collections; Kathleen Ferris, Archivist.

Library General Holdings. Over 1,000,000 volumes; 10,000 current journals, magazines, and newspapers.

Special Collections

Western Americana Collection. Consists of over 7,000 books and several hundred pamphlets on Western Americana and Native American ethnology and history. The core of the collection, including many rare volumes, was donated by the late Senator Clinton P. Anderson, an avid scholar of Western regional history.

New Mexicana. Materials dealing with the historical, political, social, and cultural development of New Mexico, including Indian affairs, land grants, folklore, family history, anthropology, education, and history. Some important materials are: thousands of copies of New Mexico documents from the Archivo General de las Indias and the the Archivo General de la nacion; various censuses of New Mexico; church records; historic maps; thousands of books, fiction and nonfiction, relating to New Mexico and the Spanish borderlands.

John Gaw Meem Archive of Southwest Architecture. A regional collection of drawings, specifications, plans, renderings, correspondence, photographs, and models from many important Southwest architects, including John Gaw Meem who was influential in the retention and development of the Spanish-Pueblo style of architecture. Other architectural firms represented are Burk and Burk, Frank Standhardt, W.C. Kruger and Associates, and Van Dorn Hooker. There are also the papers of art historian Bainbridge Bunting and his students.

Photoarchives. Photographs, slides, lantern slides, and postcards depicting the culture and environment of New Mexico, the Southwest, and Latin America. Some of the photographers represented are A. Briquet, W.H. Cobb, Edward Curtis, Marc Ferrez, G.W. James, Charles Lummis, F.H. Maude, Henry A. Schmidt, and G.B. Waite.

Rare Book Collections

Rare books include publications on the history and politics of New Mexico, first editions by such authors as Henry James, Edwin Arlington Robinson, and D.H. Lawrence, and the fine press collections from the Grabhorn Press and John Henry Nash.

Approximately 500 collections are maintained including video tapes, oral history tapes, institutional records, family papers and manuscripts; focus is on the history and culture of New Mexico and the work of well-known New Mexicans. Among the collections are business records, organizational records, ranch records and land grant records. The papers of New Mexico political figures include Thomas Catron, Miguel Otero, and Albert Fall, as well as more recent Congressional and Senatorial papers. Local literary figures represented include Mary Austin, D.H. Lawrence, Paul Horgan, Erna Fergusson, John Sinclair, and Frank Waters.

1021
Western New Mexico University
J. Cloyd Miller Library
College Avenue at C Street
Silver City, New Mexico 88061

Telephone. (505) 538-6106

Institutional Description. The publicly supported liberal arts and professional university was founded in 1893 as a normal school. It now is a multipurpose institution. Enrollment: 1,234.

Library Administration. Louise Leon, Librarian.

Library General Holdings. 123,000 volumes; 270,000 volumes in microformats; 750 current periodicals; 7,300 audiovisual materials.

Special Collections

The library maintains a special collection of local newspapers on microfilm covering pre-1900 to the present and the 19,000 microform volumes of the Library of American Civilization.

New York

1022
Adelphi University
University Libraries
South Avenue
Garden City, New York 11530

Telephone. (516) 663-1032

Institutional Description. The privately supported university was the first degree-granting liberal arts institution on Long Island, New York, having been founded in 1896 in Brooklyn as Adelphi College. Enrollment: 10,727.

Library Administration. Eugene Neely, Dean of Libraries; Donald V.L. Kelly, Special Collections Librarian; Erica Doctorow, Fine Arts/Rare Book Librarian.

Library General Holdings. 570,000 volumes; 2,800 current periodicals; 532,000 microforms; 34,000 audiovisual materials.

Special Collections

The major strengths of the Libraries' collections are in the areas of social work, psychology, mathematics, history, and English.

Special collections include: William Cobbett; William Blake; Americana; Gerhart Hauptmann; Cuala Press; Expatriate Writers; Spanish Civil War; Christopher Morley; Walt Whitman; Richard Stoelzer Collection of music scores and instruments; University Archives.

1023
Adirondack Community College
Library
Bay Road
Glens Falls, New York 12801

Telephone. (518) 793-4491

Institutional Description. Officially established in 1960, the two-year college opened in 1961 in Hudson Falls, New York. In 1967, the college moved to its present campus north of Glens Falls. Enrollment: 2,783.

Library Administration. Francis R. Warrick, Librarian.

Library General Holdings. 52,782 volumes; 365 current periodical titles; 2,832 microforms; 5,277 audiovisual materials.

Special Collections

The library maintains the **William H. Hill Local History Collection** consisting of materials by the noted authority and writer on the history of the Adirondack area and especially of Washington County, New York.

1024
Albany College of Pharmacy
Library
106 New Scotland Avenue
Albany, New York 12208

Telephone. (518) 445-7211

Institutional Description. The privately supported college of pharmacy was founded in 1881. It prepares students for state board examinations in any state in the U.S., and grants baccalaureate degrees. Enrollment: 630.

Library Administration. Irene-Marie Petzinger Kaplan, Librarian.

Library General Holdings. 11,000 volumes; 155 current periodical subscriptions.

Special Collections

The collection of the library is mainly in the subject areas of pharmacy and those basic sciences supporting pharmacy. Special areas of collection are in the history of pharmacy. The Throop Pharmacy Museum is maintained on the campus.

1025
Albany Medical College
Schaffer Library of the Health Sciences
47 New Scotland Avenue
Albany, New York 12208

Telephone. (518) 445-5544

Institutional Description. The privately supported medical college was founded in 1839. It grants professional, master's, and doctorate degrees. Enrollment: 601.

Library Administration. Ursula H. Poland, Librarian.

Library General Holdings. 102,500 volumes; 1,200 current medical periodical subscriptions; 1,000 audiovisual programs.

Special Collections

The library serves not only medical students and faculty but also Albany College of Pharmacy, the Albany Medical Center Hospital Staff, the Medical Center School of Nursing, the Capital District Psychiatric Center, and physicians and hospitals in neighboring communities. It is also a source of the less common books and periodicals for the affiliated Veterans Administration Hospital. Special holdings include the papers of Alden March, M.D., founder of the Albany Medical College and a complete run of *Albany Medical Annals.*

1026
Alfred University
Herrick Memorial Library
Alfred, New York 14802

Telephone. (607) 871-2184

Institutional Description. The privately supported university includes the publicly supported State University of New York College of Ceramics as well as the privately endowed: College of Liberal Arts and Sciences, College of Nursing, College of Business and Administration, Graduate School, and Summer School. Enrollment: 2,431.

Library Administration. Arolana M. Meissner, University Librarian; Norma B. Higgins, University Archivist and Special Collections Technical Specialist.

Library General Holdings. 216,801 volumes; 34,573 documents; 1,354 periodical titles; 19 newspaper subscriptions; 570 serials; 40,297 audiovisual materials; 17,062 microfiche; 7,733 microfilm reels.

Special Collections

Alfredana Collection. Serving as the corporate memory of an institution, the Alfred University archives include faculty and alumni-authored books; university masters' theses, senior, and honors papers; university history (from 1836), catalogs, directories, handbooks, and newsletters; programs from athletic events, plays, concerts, and other extracurricular happenings; student papers, letters, yearbooks, and memorabilia; photographs, drawings, deeds, and histories of the campus and its buildings; articles and addresses by and about faculty and alumni.

Bergren Collection. This collection of theological books, donated by his family, is the personal library of the late Dr. Richard V. Bergren, Alfred University professor from 1962 to 1974. It consists of about 900 volumes and pamphlets with an emphasis on Old Testament history and theology.

Hillel Collection. Named for the national Jewish student association which has had an active chapter at Alfred University since 1950, this 1,600 collection includes books on Jewish culture, religious rituals, historical movements, music, art, and literature.

Howells/Fréchette Collection. An extensive collection of letters and memorabilia of the family of William Cooper Howells; donated by Dr. Van Derck Freéchette, member of the New York State College of Ceramics faculty.

Local History Collection. A limited local history collection of the Alfred region of western New York. Among the materials available are genealogies, directories, newspapers, photographs, diaries, ledgers, club minutes, letters, clippings, maps of Alfred village and town, Allegany County and nearby counties since the 1820s.

Nineteenth Century Collection. Consists of 1,250 volumes with emphasis on early travel, education, children and young adult literature, and the issues of slavery, abolition, suffrage, and temperance.

Openhym Collection of Modern British Literature and Social History. Dates from 1890 and consists of 6,000 volumes; core collection of the Bloomsbury Group, W.H. Hudson, and Henry James. The collection is largely first editions of which 200 are considered rare. There is a large contemporary criticism section (clippings and periodicals as well as books) and 370 letters and other pieces by 99 authors.

Seventh Day Baptist Collection. Unique in its founding by and long association with the tiny, once fiercely liberal Seventh Day Baptist denomination, the University retains a core colleciton of works concerning this Sabbath-keeping sect.

Waid Collection. Consists of about 600 books published for ordinary citizen consumption in the Germany of the 1930s and 1940s. These materials are largely of the kind which would have been found in an average German home during this pre-war period; provides a picture of the growth of Nazism in Germany, showing through illustrations and texts the strong antisemitic and pro-Nazi propaganda that helped World War II erupt.

Rare Book Collections

Rare Books Collection. Many languages and centuries (1511 to 1968) are represented in this collection of old and valuable books. Some are signed first editions while others have outstanding characteristics such as unique subject matter, illustration, or special construction. A few representative examples include Appianus of Alexandria's *Romanarum Historiarum de Bellis Punicis Liber Basileae,* Froben, 1554; and John Heckewelder's *A Narrative of the Mission of the United Brethren among the Delaware and Mohegan Indians* (1820).

1027
Bank Street College of Education
Library
610 West 112th Street
New York, New York 10025

Telephone. (212) 663-7200

Institutional Description. The privately supported teachers college offers programs at the graduate level only. Founded in 1916, the college features experimental programs and conducts a school for children. Enrollment: 603.

Library Administration. Eleanor R. Kulleseid, Director.

Library General Holdings. 96,000 volumes; 935 current periodical subscriptions; 183,000 microforms.

Special Collections

The library's special collections are in children's literature and textbooks.

1028
Bard College
Hoffman and Kellogg Libraries
Annandale-on-Hudson, New York 12504

Telephone. (914) 758-6822

Institutional Description. The privately supported liberal arts college was founded by the Episcopal Church in 1860. It is now nonsectarian. Enrollment: 800.

Library Administration. Richard Wiles, Director of Libraries; David Tipple, Head Librarian.

Library General Holdings. 170,000 volumes; 600 periodical titles.

Special Collections

In addition to collections supporting each of the academic disciplines taught at Bard, the resources of the library include special collections of note. These include the personal library of the late Dr. Hannah Arendt, political theorist and philosopher, and her husband, the late Heinrich Bluecher who taught philosophy for many years at Bard. The Bard family papers are housed with the rare book collection. The library has received substantial gifts from the estates of Marius Bewley, noted literary critic, and Olin Dowes, a painter in the federal art project.

1029
Barnard College
Wollman Library
606 West 120th Street
New York, New York 10027

Telephone. (212) 280-5262

Institutional Description. The privately supported college for women was founded in 1889 and is an affiliate of Columbia University. Enrollment: 2,162.

Library Administration. Elizabeth Corbett, Director of Libraries.

Library General Holdings. 158,000 volumes; 12,300 microforms.

Special Collections

Special collections in the library include the **Barnard Archives,** a historical colleciton of official and student publications, documents, letters, and photographs from Barnard's founding in 1889 to the present; the **Alumnae Collection** of works by former Barnard students; the personal library of Nobel Prize-winning Chilean poet Gabriela Mistral; the **Overbury Collection** of 3,300 books and manuscripts by and about American women authors; and a small rare book collection. The library has an especially strong collection in women's studies, supplemented by the Women's Center resource collection.

1030
Bernard Baruch College of the City University of New York
Baruch College Library
17 Lexington Avenue
New York, New York 10010

Telephone. (212) 725-3000

Institutional Description. The publicly supported college, founded in 1968, features programs in business and public administration. Enrollment: 16,124.

Library Administration. Stanton F. Biddle, Chief Librarian.

Library General Holdings. 275,000 volumes; 2,000 current periodical titles; 300,000 microforms.

Special Collections

The most important special collections include business, economics, and industrial and labor relations.

1031
Boricua College
Boricua College Library
3755 Broadway
New York, New York 10032

Telephone. (212) 865-9000

Institutional Description. The privately supported liberal arts college features nontraditional programs. A branch is located in Brooklyn. It grants associate and baccalaureate degrees. Enrollment: 1,125.

Library Administration. Aurora Gomez, Director, Library and Learning Resources.

Library General Holdings. 110,000 volumes; 380 current periodical subscriptions.

Special Collections

Puerto Rican and Hispanic Studies Collection. Boricua maintains this specialized collection for research by Puerto Rican and Hispanic scholars and students. The collection deals with United States, Puerto Rican and Hispanic-related issues of a local, national, and international nature. Some of the subjects it contains are: bilingualism, biculturalism, Puerto Rican and Hispanic culture, education, bilingual education, human-social services, civil rights, manpower census, and health-related issues.

Badillo Collection. Herman Badillo's congressional papers have been given to Boricua College as a gift. Mr. Badillo's papers are the basis for an important archive showing his significant and important contributions to America as an identified leader of the Hispanic Community. As the number of Hispanics in the United States increases, the Badillo papers will provide documentation and information of earlier activities of Hispanics.

American Geographical Society Map Collection A gift of the AGS, the collection contains over 40,000 hard cover texts, pamphlets, newsletters, folios, and maps related to the geography of the world.

1032
Brooklyn College of the City University of New York
Brooklyn College Library
Bedford Avenue and Avenue H
Brooklyn, New York 11210

Telephone. (718) 780-5485

Institutional Description. The publicly supported liberal arts college was founded in 1930. It was the first coeducational liberal arts college in the city of New York. Enrollment: 14,628.

Library Administration. Philip Tompkins, Chief Librarian.

Library General Holdings. 830,000 volumes; 3,346 periodical subscriptions; 14,373 audiovisual materials.

Special Collections

Special collections include the **Women's Studies Collection,** the major collection of its kind in the New York metropolitan area; the **Brooklyniana Collection;** the **Historical Manuscripts Collection** which includes materials of Oscar Handlin, Sam Levenson, Lauretta Bender, Paul F. Schilder, Laura Benet, Dorothy Salisbury Davis, Francis E. Dorn, James M. Pettit, Roy D. Richardson, and Paul Windell; the **Norman Cousins Papers,** the **Oral History Archives,** the college archives (partial), and rare and uncommon items, including three incunabula. Special concentrations also exist in African studies and Judaic studies.

Coates Memorial Classics Library. Contains more than 1,000 volumes of Greek and Latin texts donated by the late Professor Procope S. Costas and other members of the Classics Department.

1033
Brooklyn Law School
Henry L. Ughetta Memorial Library
250 Joralemon Street
Brooklyn, New York 11201

Telephone. (718) 780-7900

Institutional Description. The privately supported professional law school was founded in 1901. It grants the Juris Doctor (J.D.) degree. Enrollment: 1,310.

Library Administration. Sara Robbins, Law Librarian.

Library General Holdings. 253,000 volumes; 850 current law-related periodical titles; 79,000 microforms.

Special Collections

The Ughetta Library has one of the largest collections of legal materials in the New York metropolitan area. The library collection includes the latest annotated statutes of the 50 states; reported decisions of all state courts prior to the National Reporter System; the complete National Reporter System; multiple copies of New York official and unofficial reports; New York State and federal administrative decisions, opinions and rulings; specialized looseleaf services; digests; citators; and encyclopedias. The library also houses an extensive international law collection which supports the academic curriculum and the research needs of the *Brooklyn Journal of International Law.* There are also special holdings in Anglo-American legal materials.

1034
Broome Community College
Cecil C. Tyrrell Learning Resources Center
P.O. Box 1017
Binghamton, New York 13902

Telephone. (607) 771-5045

Institutional Description. The publicly supported two-year college was founded in 1946 as the New York State Institute of Applied Arts and Sciences at Binghamton. Broome County became the school's sponsor in 1953. Enrollment: 5,887.

Library Administration. James D. Baker, Director of the Learning Resources Center.

Library General Holdings. 65,000 volumes; 677 periodical and serial subscriptions; 5,000 microforms; 2,000 audiovisual kits and recordings; 11,000 items in pamphlet files.

Special Collections

Community College Education. Several hundred books and twenty journals devoted to community college education in the United States.

1035
Bryant and Stratton Business Institute - Syracuse
Library
400 Montgomery Street
Syracuse, New York 13202

Telephone. (315) 472-6603

Institutional Description. Bryant and Stratton is a two-year institution whose purpose is to provide business education. Campuses are located at various locations in the United States. Its origin can be traced to 1852 when H.B. Bryant, J.C. Bryant, and H.D. Stratton organized Bryant and Stratton Mercantile College in Cleveland, Ohio. Enrollment: 1,715.

Library General Holdings. 3,000 volumes; 95 current periodical titles.

Special Collections

The library maintains a special collection on **Women in Business** and has a collection of information on health care.

1036
Canisius College
Andrew Bouwhuis Library
2001 Main Street
Buffalo, New York 14208

Telephone. (716) 883-7000

Institutional Description. The privately supported liberal arts college was founded by German Jesuits from the famous University of Innsbruck, in 1870. Enrollment: 4,-250.

Library Administration. George Telatnik, Director of the Library; Karen Bordonaro, Reference Librarian and Special Collections/Rare Books Librarian.

Library General Holdings. 260,000 volumes; 1,250 current periodicals; 2,214 microforms.

Special Collections

Although not maintained as separate collections, the Canisius College Library does collect heavily in the following subject areas: all facets of business; Irish history, literature, and culture; and the Catholic Church.

Rare Book Collections

Special Collections Room. Contains materials relating mainly to the study of Jesuitica (early theological and philosophical tracts). Also included are early Bibles (from the fifteenth century on), the Book of Hours, a collection of Irish literature, the Charles A. Brady Papers, and some historical items on early Buffalo, New York.

1037
Cayuga County Community College
Norman F. Bourke Memorial Library
Franklin Street
Auburn, New York 13021

Telephone. (315) 255-1743

Institutional Description. The two-year college was founded in 1953 as Auburn Community College. The college was transferred to county sponsorship in 1975 and the current name was adopted. Enrollment: 2,697.

Library Administration. Douglas O. Michael, Director.

Library General Holdings. 68,000 volumes; 660 and 20 newspaper periodical subscriptions.

Special Collections

Special collections include juvenile literature, local history, law, and the College Archives.

1038
Christ the King Seminary
Seminary Library
711 Knox Road
P.O. Box 607
East Aurora, New York 14052

Telephone. (716) 652-8900

Institutional Description. The privately supported theological seminary is affiliated with the Roman Catholic Church. It grants professional and baccalaureate degrees. Enrollment: 124.

Library Administration. Rev. Bonaventure F. Hayes, O.F.M., Library Director.

Library General Holdings. 100,000 volumes; 400 current periodical subscriptions.

Special Collections

Although primarily a research collection for theology and related areas, the collection contains standard works in other disciplines, especially in philosophy. The library houses the **Monsignor James Bray Collection** of 750 volumes dealing with the history of the Niagara Frontier and French Canada.

1039
City College of the City University of New York
Morris Raphael Cohen Library, North Academic Center
Convent Avenue and 138th Street
New York, New York 10031

Telephone. (212) 690-5367

Institutional Description. The publicly supported college was founded in 1847 and is the only school in the CUNY system with a complex of professional schools. It is its oldest school, as well. Enrollment: 12,784.

Library Administration. Ann Randall, Chief Librarian; Barbara Dunlap, Chief, Archives and Special Collections.

Library General Holdings. 1,023,831 volumes (501,-206 book titles); 3,608 periodical subscriptions; 119,342 microforms; 13,199 audiovisual materials; 9,000 phonograph albums; 10,780 score titles.

Special Collections

Archives. The College Archives collects, preserves, and makes available materials (both printed and manuscript) concerning the history of The City College from its founding in 1847 to the present day.

Rare Book Collections

Special Collections (Rare Books and Manuscripts) contains a comprehensive collection of English Civil War Pamphlets and of printed editions of the works of William Butler Yeats as well as a strong collection of books on dress and costume. The **Russell Sage Collection** on the history of social welfare contains over 100,000 printed items documenting the work of social welfare institutions between 1880 and 1940. While the emphasis is on the United States, Great Britain is also well represented. Over 300 individual editions of Restoration, eighteenth-century and Regency plays are supplemented by all the major collected editions (such as Bell's British Theatre).

Significant manuscript collections include the diplomatic papers of Townsend Harris (first U.S. Minister to Japan), over 200 broadcast, radio, and television scripts by Ira Marion. The **Phonographic Library of Contemporary Poets** consists of over 100 recordings of American poets of the inter-war period reading their works; it is supplemented by autographed editions of individual volumes of poems. The master tapes of the Hatch-Billops Oral History Collection of Black Arts (interviews with playwrights and performance artists) is also housed here.

1040
City University of New York
Central Office Library and Archives
535 East 80th Street
New York, New York 10002

Telephone. (212) 794-5510

Institutional Description. The publicly supported university is composed of nineteen undergraduate and graduate colleges spread through the five boroughs of New York City. It is the largest municipal university system in the United States. Enrollment: 185,937.

Library Administration. Paul Perkus, Librarian and Archivist.

Library General Holdings. 5,278,981 volumes; 5,254,-476 microforms; 89,900 audiovisual materials; 27,699 current periodical subscriptions. See individual campuses for special/rare book collections.

Special Collections

The Central Office Library collects publications of the offices of the central administration of The City University of New York. These include annual reports, financial reports, program reviews, institutional research. There is a separate file dealing with Open Admissions at CUNY covering 166-1974. Included also are the minutes and other documents of the Board of Trustees. The Archives contain administrative documents of the Board of Trustees and the Central Administration from 1929 to 1985.

1041
Clarkson University
Andrew S. Schuler Educational Resources Center
Potsdam, New York 13676

Telephone. (315) 268-6590

Institutional Description. The privately supported technological university grants baccalaureate, master's, and doctorate degrees. Enrollment: 3,905.

Library Administration. Richard Valente, Director.

Library General Holdings. 350,000 print and microform items; 1,200 journal subscriptions.

Special Collections

Specialized collections include NASA technical reports and ENERGYFICHE, an extensive collection of articles, reports, and proceedings in the field of energy.

1042
Clinton Community College
Leroy M. Douglas Memorial Learning Resource Center
Route 9S
Plattsburgh, New York 12901

Telephone. (518) 561-6650

Institutional Description. The publicly supported two-year college was opened in 1969. Enrollment: 1,615.

Library Administration. Gail M. Staines, Assistant Librarian for Print Materials.

Library General Holdings. 50,000 volumes; 320 current periodical and newspaper subscriptions; 2,300 microform titles.

Special Collections

Adirondack Collection. Includes print materials related to the Adirondacks, the North Country, and

Northern Vermont; included within this collection are books by local North Country authors.

The College houses photographic prints and historical documents pertaining to Hotel Champlain (now the site of Clinton Community College), the grand resort for U.S. Presidents in the years before the Great Depression of the 1920s.

The Learning Resources Center is in the process of acquiring the Northern New York American Canadian Genealogical Society Collection. This collection contains genealogical documents of North Country, northern Vermont, and southern Quebec family histories.

1043
Colgate University Libraries
Hamilton, New York 13346

Telephone. (315) 824-1000

Institutional Description. Colgate University is a private, independent, nonprofit institution established in 1819. Enrollment: 2,696.

Library Administration. Judith Gibson Green, University Librarian.

Library General Holdings. 405,000 volumes; 2,465 current periodicals; 52,000 government documents; 237,000 microforms.

Special Collections

Everett Needham Case Library. This library serves the humanities and the social sciences at the University. The University Archives, Special Collections, rare books, and manuscripts are housed here. Important special collections include the **Ernest Gann Collection** which contains a complete collection of his manuscripts; the **Chambers Collection;** the **Joseph Conrad Collection,** including first editions, manuscripts, and letters; and the **Powys Family Papers** which consists of letters, manuscripts, and first editions.

1044
Colgate-Rochester Divinity School Ambrose Swasey Library 1100 Goodman Street
Rochester, New York 14620

Telephone. (716) 271-1320

Institutional Description. The privately supported interdenominational theological seminary, established in 1817, is affiliated with the University of Rochester, Crozer Theological Seminary, Bexley Hall, and St. Bernard's Institute. Enrollment: 231.

Library Administration. Norman J. Kansfield, Director of Library Services.

Library General Holdings. 325,000 volumes.

Special Collections

During the last two decades, with the formation of a consortium of theological schools on one campus, the Swasey Library has experienced massive infusions of new materials. The Bexley Hall Collection not only brought a strong Episcopal emphasis, but also included a sizeable group of polyglot and foreign language Bibles, a variety of hymnals, and copies of works of Erasmus. The Crozer Library was distinguished by a large number of books of European Biblical scholarship, the patristics, materiasls by and about Dwight L. Moody, the Morgan Edwards' materials about Baptists in Colonial America, and a unique selection of sixteenth-century tracts, similar in nature to the Karpinski Collection of Colgate-Rochester.

In 1981, a major core of the St. Bernard's Seminary Library was transferred to Colgate-Rochester. In 1984, the full integration of the 45,000 volumes was begun. These materials, including journals and audio cassettes, provide rich resources in Roman Catholic theology and spirituality, liturgics, patristics, and other topics of Roman Catholic interest. Of special significance are the Archbishop Fulton J. Sheen archives which contain audiovisual and printed materials by and about the late Archbishop.

American Baptist Historical Society. This is one of the oldest denominational study centers of its kind. The collection consists of the **Samuel Colgate Baptist Historical Library** of 20,000 volumes; national Baptist archives, manuscript collections, and artifacts relating to the Baptist movement worldwide. The Society is the official archives of American Baptist-related national societies and organizations. Thousands of original records have been placed with the Society, covering foreign and home missions, educational enterprises, the American Baptist Churches, USA, and related agencies. The archives also house the records of the Danish-Norwegian Baptist Conference, the Freewill Baptist General Conference, and significant holdings of the Baptist General Conference (Swedish) and the North American Baptist Conference (German). Recent acquisitions include a large collection of the official documents of the Baptist World Alliance and the North American Baptist Fellowship.

Local church records exist for thirty-one states and cover the period 1680-1981. Regional organizational records have been deposited for New York, New England, New Jersey, Pennsylvania, Ohio, Illinois, Michigan, South Dakota, Colorado, and Oregon. The largest extant file of Baptist periodical literature supports this set of records.

The Society provides various collections of personal papers and manuscripts. The largest single collection is the **Walter Rauschenbusch Papers,** now totalling several hundred linear feet.

1045
College of Aeronautics
Library
LaGuardia Airport Station
Flushing, New York 11371

Telephone. (212) 429-6600

Institutional Description. The College of Aeronautics is a junior college devoted to the education of men and women for technical careers in the aviation, aerospace, electronics, and related industries. Enrollment: 1,054.

Library Administration. Jo Ann Jayne, Librarian.

Library General Holdings. 57,164 volumes; 326 periodical titles; 91,543 microforms.

Special Collections

The library maintains a collection of 25,000 special reports and technical data comprised of aircraft manuals and NASA, SAE, FAA, and NACA reports.

1046
The College of Insurance
Kathryn and Shelby Cullon Davis Library
One Insurance Plaza
101 Murray Street
New York, New York 10007

Telephone. (212) 962-4111

Institutional Description. The privately supported college was founded by the Insurance Society of New York in 1962. It offers associate, baccalaureate, and master's degrees. Enrollment: 1,002.

Library Administration. Beverly Rosignolo, Chief Librarian.

Library General Holdings. 155,755 items including books, bound periodicals, vertical file items, microfilm reels, microfiche; 438 periodical subscriptions; 10 newspaper subscriptions.

Special Collections

The Insurance Society of New York Library contains materials on all aspects of insurance and actuarial science. The **Winter Marine Collection** contains books specifically on marine insurance; the **Heber B. Churchill Earthquake Collection** consists of materials on earthquakes.

The library also houses the papers, claims records, and investigative information on the Black Tom Island (New Jersey) explosion which occured around World War I. Various insurance treatises and insurance policies going back to the seventeenth and eighteenth centuries, both domestic and foreign, are also maintained. The Association of Average Adjusters (U.S.) Library is also part of the Library's collection.

1047
College of Mount St. Vincent
Library
263rd Street and Riverdale Avenue
Riverdale, New York 10471

Telephone. (212) 549-8000

Institutional Description. The privately supported liberal arts college was founded in 1847 by the Sisters of Charity of New York. It includes Malcolm-King: Harlem College Extension. Enrollment: 1,016.

Library Administration. Mary Hernandez, Director.

Library General Holdings. 135,000 volumes; 596 current periodical subscriptions.

Special Collections

Special collections include the **Irish Collection** of 450 items by Celtic authors on Celtic philosophy and genealogy, dating from the fifteenth century; a rare book collection including Bibles and other literature dating from the sixteenth century; and a collection of first editions, signed copies and other items primarily by nineteenth-century authors. The library is the repository for the works of Joseph Tusiani, internationally known poet and translator of Italian classics.

1048
College of New Rochelle
Gill Library
Castle Place
New Rochelle, New York 10805

Telephone. (914) 632-5300

Institutional Description. The privately supported liberal arts college was founded in 1904 as a college for women. Now coeducational, it is affiliated with the Roman Catholic Church. Enrollment: 4,265.

Library Administration. Gloria T. Greco, Library Director.

Library General Holdings. 180,00 volumes of print and non-print resources; 1,142 current periodicals.

Special Collections

Special collections of note are the **Thomas More Collection** of rare and original works; the **Ursuline Collection,** and the **Career Resources Collection.**

1049
Columbia University
Columbia University Libraries
535 West 114th Street
New York, New York 10027

Telephone. (212) 280-2271

Institutional Description. The privately supported

university traces its beginnings to a charter granted by George II of England in 1754 for the founding of King's College to teach "...the Learned Languages and the Liberal Arts and Sciences." Enrollment: 17,523.

Library Administration. Patricia M. Batten, University Librarian; Kenneth Lohf, Rare Book and Manuscript Librarian.

Library General Holdings. 6,000,000 volumes; 39,000 government documents; 2,135,000 microforms; 18,000 audiovisual materials; 25,000 current periodicals.

Special Collections

In addition to the collections of the Rare Book and Manuscript Library, distinctive collections at Columbia University include the Avery Architectural and Fine Arts Library, the C.V. Starr East Asian Library, the Augustus Long Health Sciences Library, the Law and International Law Library, and the School of Library Service Library. All of these libraries within the Columbia University Libraries include special collections and archival material unique to the subject area indicated by their titles. For a detailed description of the Columbia University Libraries, see Barbara A. Chernow, *Guide to the Research Collections of the Columbia University Libraries,* Columbia University: New York, 1984. Information below by courtesy of Academic Information Services Group, Columbia University in the City of New York.

Rare Book Collections

The Rare Book and Manuscript Library contains over 500,000 rare books and 22,000,000 manuscripts in almost two thousand separate collections. It houses material in all disciplines, except law, art and architecture, health sciences, and East Asian languages and literature. These areas are covered by the libraries listed above.

Park Benjamin Collection of Knickerbocker Literature. Consists of New York imprints between 1840 and 1865; includes extensive holdings of first editions of the works of Washington Irving, Charles Fenno Hoffman, Nathaniel Parker Willis, and Timothy Shay Arthur.

Book Arts Collection. Covers all phases of book production; contains more than 150,000 volumes of books dealing with information about book production and books that are examples of fine printing and illustration.

Samuel S. Dale Library of Weights and Measures. Consists of 1,000 volumes tracing the development of standard measures in all countries dating from the fifteenth century.

Dramatic Museum and Library. Includes the 5,000-volume Brander Matthews Dramatic Collection which is strong in English and American drama, nineteenth-century acting editions of plays, works by and about Molière, and materials relating to Augustin Daly. The museum contains nearly 80,000 autograph letters, manuscripts, prints, photographs, pamphlets, clippings, playbills, and programs dealing mainly with nineteenth-century American and English theater. It also houses the Joseph Urban theater models and a number of models representing both historic and contemporary stage design.

Solton and Julia Engel Collection. A collection of more than 500 books, manuscripts, and original drawings; most of the volumes are association books and first editions. Includes such items as the writings of Jeremy Bentham; works by Poe, Whitman, and Kipling; and two variant states of the first American edition of *Alice in Wonderland,* published in 1866.

Edward Epstean Collection. Includes 300 books on the history of photography and its application to the reproduction of type, pictures, and objects. The holdings are strong in the specialized fields of printing processes, color and orthochromatic photography, and the chemistry of photography.

Historical Collection of Children's Literature. Consists of 8,000 books and 450 periodicals, primarily printed in English between the eighteenth and twentieth centuries.

Holland Society Library. Deals with Dutch settlement in New York in the early seventeenth century.

Bronson Howard Collection. Consists of 1,500 volumes on the theater including biographies of theatrical people as well as editions of many plays.

Incunabula. This collection is one of the finest collections of incunabula in the United States. The titles are especially strong in editions of classical authors, humanist texts, and fine printing. Among the more famous items are the "Book of Revelations" from the Gutenberg Bible, ca. 1454-1455, and the 1458 *Canon Missae,* one of the three recorded copies and the single most important volume in the library.

Joan of Arc Collection. Consists of 1,700 volumes dealing with Joan of Arc and the period in which she lived. It is one of the outstanding collections of its kind in the world and includes several fifteenth- and sixteenth-century manuscripts, as well as books of poetry, fiction, and drama centering on Joan of Arc.

Edwin P. Kilroe Collection of Tammaniana. A collection of 104,338 items on the history of Tammany Hall.

Gonzalez Lodge Collection. A collection of 2,000 volumes of books by Greek and Roman classical authors printed between the fifteenth and nineteenth centuries. Includes the first collected edition of Homer's works published in Florence around 1488.

Stephen Whitney Phoenix Collection. Consists of 4,000 volumes of literature, the classics, emblem books, illustrated books, and books on travel. Many of the books are notable for their bindings.

George A. Plimpton Library. A collection of 16,000 volumes and 300 medieval and Renaissance manuscripts; a gift in 1936 of a successful publisher who was interested in tracing the development of subjects taught in schools and universities; one of the most complete sections is on arithmetic.

Jack Harris Samuels Library. Books and manuscripts collected by Mr. Samuels; nearly 3,000 volumes include first editions, association books, and manuscripts covering English and American literature from the sixteenth to the twentieth centuries.

Edwin R. A. Seligman Library. A collection of 55,000 items including manuscripts, broadsides, pamphlets, and first editions on economics and banking from the earliest printed books to the 1920s.

David Eugene Smith Collection. A collection of 10,000 books and pamphlets that record the development of mathematics from earliest times to the beginning of the twentieth century; includes 3,000 portraits of mathematicians and 275 mathematical and astronomical instruments.

Baruch Spinoza Collection. The collection contains seventeenth- and eighteenth-century editions of works by Spinoza; 3,933 volumes.

Middle Eastern Collections. Near and Middle Eastern manuscripts as well as cuneiform tablets, epigraphy specimens, and papyri.

Other collections include American Institute of Graphic Arts Fifty-Books-of-the-Year; Hector Berlioz Collection; Arthur Billings Hunt Collection of American Music; Samuel and William Samuel Johnson Library (Columbia's first and third presidents); Mary Queen of Scots Collection; Isidore Witmark Collection of Autographed Books and Music Scores; Historical Map Collection; Rockwell Kent Collection of drawings and paintings; William Barclay Parsons Collection of Railroad Prints; Arthur Rackham Collection of original drawings, paintings, and sketchbooks; and the papers of Robert Wilson, theatrical artist.

Manuscript Collections. The Manuscript Department is the University's major repository for collections of original papers, letters, manuscripts, and documents. It now contains more than twenty-two million manuscripts in nearly 2,000 separate collections. Subjects covered include authors, business records, economics, fine arts and graphic arts, history, journalism and publishing, language and literature, librarians, medicine and psychology, organizations, performing arts, philosophy/religion, political leaders, political science, science, and sociology and social work. The various letters, papers, and manuscripts for these subject areas are indexed in this volume by name of author, organization, etc.

Oral History Collection. The collection, founded by the distinguished historian Allan Nevins, covers topics of interest to scholars in all disciplines; over 5,000 interviews fill more than 500,000 transcribed pages.

Bakhmeteff Archive of Russian and East European History and Culture. Collection contains over 1.2 million items in 900 collections dating from the seventeenth through the twentieth centuries.

Columbiana. Contains 20,000 books and vertical files important to Columbia's history from its founding in 1754 to the present.

Herbert H. Lehman Papers. The personal and professional papers of Herbert H. Lehman; includes 1,250,000 items in a multimedia archive. Housed in the Hebert H. Lehman Suite, it also contains the papers of Lehman's wife, Edith Altschul Lehman, and some of his associates.

1050
The Cooper Union Library
41 Cooper Square
New York, New York 10003

Telephone. (212) 254-6300

Institutional Description. The privately supported college offers programs in art, architecture, engineering, and fine arts. It was founded in 1859. Enrollment: 975.

Library Administration. Elizabeth A. Vajda, Chief Librarian.

Library General Holdings. 95,000 volumes; 350 periodicals; 45,000 slides.

Special Collections

An important special collection of the Cooper Union Library consists of the published and unpublished materials relating to the founder of the institution, Peter Cooper, and his son-in-law, Abram Hewitt.

1051
Cornell University
University Libraries
Ithaca, New York 14853

Telephone. (607) 255-4144

Institutional Description. The privately supported university was founded in 1856 and now contains 13 undergraduate and graduate schools and colleges. Enrollment: 18,446.

Library Administration. Alain Seznec, University Librarian.

Library General Holdings. 5,010,000 volumes; 4,000,000 microforms; 55,000 audiovisual materials.

Special Collections

The John M. Olin Library, devoted more sppcifically to graduate and faculty research, houses many special collections of books and manuscripts, among them rare books. Collections include the **Wason Collection** on China and the Chinese; the **Echols Collection** on Southeast Asia, the **Icelandic Collection,** the **History of Science Collections,** and the archives of the University, maps, microfilms, and newspapers.

F.M. Wells Memorial Slide Collection. Housed in the Fine Arts Library, this collection consists of extensive files of architectural history slides and a large and growing collection of slides of art and architecture from all parts of the world. The library now includes approximately

300,000 slides.

1052
The Culinary Institute of America
Library
Route 9
Rhinebeck, New York 12358

Telephone. (914) 452-9600

Institutional Description. As a store front operation, The Culinary Institute began in 1946 as the New Haven Restaurant Institute located in New Haven, Connecticut. At inception, it was a vocational training school for returning World War II veterans. In 1946, the school exapnded to a 40-room mansion adjacent to Yale University and changed its name to The Culinary Institution of Connecticut. In 1952, it became known as The Culinary Institute of America. In 1970, the Institute purchased the 75-acres of land overlooking the Hudson River where it is currently located. Enrollment: 1,806.

Library Administration. Henry Woods, Director of Learning Resources.

Library General Holdings. 26,573 volumes; 165 periodical titles.

Special Collections

The specialized library of the Culinary Institute of America is devoted to the culinary arts and gastronomy. There is a special collection of menus.

1053
Dowling College
Learning Resources Center
Idle Hour Boulevard
Oakdale, New York 11769

Telephone. (516) 244-3000

Institutional Description. The privately supported liberal arts college was founded in 1959. In addition to the traditional liberal arts programs, Dowling offers an aeronautics program, preparing students for careers in corporate aviation, air transport, and airways management. Pilot license training is also offered. Enrollment: 3,063.

Library Administration. Wendell Guy, Director of Learning Resources.

Library General Holdings. 107,000 volumes; 760 current periodicals; 27,000 government documents; 310,000 microforms.

Special Collections

Special collections include books and manuscripts dealing with Long Island history and the **Fogle Collection** of nineteenth-century British romantic poetry.

1054
Dutchess Community College
Library
Pendell Road
Poughkeepsie, New York 12601

Telephone. (914) 471-4500

Institutional Description. The two-year community college was founded in 1957. Enrollment: 6,336.

Library Administration. Michael J. Pope, Director.

Library General Holdings. 90,960 volumes; 650 current periodical titles; 14,741 microfilm reels.

Special Collections

The library maintains a **History of Technology Collection** and a collection of art history and archaeology slides.

1055
Elizabeth Seton College
Learning Resources Center
1061 North Broadway
Yonkers, New York 10701

Telephone. (914) 969-4000

Institutional Description. The two-year college was established as a women's college controlled by the Sisters of Charity of New York. In 1970, the college became independent and a lay Board of Trustees asssumed control. Enrollment: 1,087.

Library Administration. Loretta M. Hauser, Director.

Library General Holdings. 50,000 volumes.

Special Collections

The library maintains special collections on Irish history and literature, art history, English literature, and Americana.

1056
Elmira College
Gannett-Tripp Learning Center
Park Place
Elmira, New York 14901

Telephone. (607) 734-3911

Institutional Description. The privately supported liberal arts college grants associate, baccalaureate, and master's degrees. Enrollment: 1,975.

Library Administration. James D. Gray, Director.

Library General Holdings. 267,000 volumes; 760 current periodical subscriptions.

Special Collections

Mark Twain Collection. A special area has been provided on the second floor of the Learning Center for this collection. It has facilities for students and visiting scholars who are conducting research on the world-famous author. The marble floor, wood ceiling, and cast iron sculpture, donated by Nicky and Tuffe Yunis, were once part of the Klapproth Saloon which Twain frequented during his stays in the city of Elmira. The Mark Twain Study, given to the college in 1952, once stood on East Hill near Quarry Farm, where the Clemens family spent many summers. There Twain wrote his most famous books, including *The Adventures of Huckleberry Finn* and *Tom Sawyer.* The octagonal building is a mecca for visitors from around the world. Mark Twain is buried nearby in Woodlawn Cemetery.

The library also maintains a **Women's History Collection** and a collection of New York State history.

1057
Erie Community College - South Campus
South Campus Library
4140 Southwestern Boulevard
Orchard Park, New York 14127

Telephone. (716) 658-5400

Institutional Description. Erie Community College is a multi-campus community college. It was established in 1946. The South Campus was added in 1974. Enrollment: 3,406.

Library Administration. Judith A. Geer, Librarian, South Campus Library.

Library General Holdings. 150,000 volumes; 1,000 periodical subscriptions.

Special Collections

The South Campus Library houses the **H.L. Mencken Collection.**

1058
Fashion Institute of Technology
Shirley Goodman Research Center Library
227 West 27th Street
New York, New York 10001

Telephone. (212) 760-7660

Institutional Description. The publicly supported professional institute of art, design, business, and technology was formed to provide professionally trained men and women for the fashion and related industries. Founded in 1944, it grants associate and baccalaureate degrees, and is administered by the State University of New York. Enrollment: 11,774.

Library Administration. Barbara Jones, Director of the Library.

Library General Holdings. 105,000 volumes; 675 current periodicals; 10,000 microforms.

Special Collections

Special Collections is an outstanding collection of rare books and materials pertinent to the library's specialized areas. Opened in April 1982, Special Collections contains all titles in the Library's book collection that predate 1860. In addition, it holds selected titles from 1860 to the present that are singled out for their rarity, value, aesthetic qualities, or fragile condition. Special Collections also houses original fashion sketches, scrapbooks containing biographical material on designers, and companies, archives, portfolios of plates, and photographs.

Some of the highlights of the Special Collections are: W.P.A. scrapbooks of picture sources; periodicals such as *Vogue* (1916-1939), *Harper's Bazaar* (1867-1939), *Gazette du Bon Ton* (1912-1925); and *Les Ideés Nouvelles de la Mode* (1922-1932); sketches by Muriel King (ca. 1932-45, including costumes designed for Katherine Hepburn, Ginger Rogers, and Margaret Sullavan), Lady Duff-Gordon (ca. 1908-1919, known as Lucille, an early fashion designer with an international business and the first titled individual to achieve top rank in the field of fashion), Whittingham and Humphreys (1888-1914), Frederick Milton, Sophie Gimbel, Max Meyer, Bill and Hazel Haire, Harriet Meserole, Florence Schatken, Cardinal Fashion Studios, Berley Studio, Davidow, Joseph Love Inc., and Bergdorf Goodman; scrapbooks compiled by Adele Simpson, Jo Copeland, Herbert Sondheim, Joseph Love Inc., Joseph Whitehead, Claire McCardell, and Mainbocher; archives including an F.I.T. historical collection, David Dubinsky, B.H. Wragge Inc., and *Esquire* archives.

Special Collections materials cover such subjects as regional costume, dressmaking and tailoring, fashion, textile design, art, architecture, decoration and ornament, interior decoration, erotica, and historical works on textile science and the textile industry.

1059
Fordham University
Duane Library
Fordham Road
Bronx, New York 10458

Telephone. (212) 579-2414

Institutional Description. The privately supported university was founded under Roman Catholic auspices, and through the years has been conducted by the Jesuits. It now has a lay board of trustees. Enrollment: 12,256.

Library Administration. Anne M. Murphy, University Librarian; Joseph A. LoSchiavo, Rare Books and Special Collections Librarian.

Library General Holdings. 1,413,331 volumes; 4,875 current periodical subscriptions; 1,295,833 microforms; 456 audiovisual materials.

Rare Book Collections

Barberini Collection. Consists of printed books, archival records, and thousands of codices representing an extremely rich collection of materials for Medieval Studies. The collection was privately owned before it was incorporated into the Vatican Library in 1902. The microfilmed portion owned by Fordham consists of a large number of the approximate 10,000 Latin codices made available through the filming project of the Knights of Columbus Film Library at St. Louis University.

Charles Allen Munn Collection of Rare Americana. Includes 151 items relating to Colonial America and the early history of the United States. Along with rare printed books, the collection includes manuscripts and letters in the autographs of George Washington, John Trumbull, Lafayette, William Penn and others of equal and lesser importance. The collection also includes 37 drawings by the American artist John Trumbull (1756-1843).

Cobbett Collection. A collection of 81 books and 20 manuscripts written by and relating to the journalist William Cobbett (1763-1835) who used the pseudonym "Peter Porcupine."

Givernaud Collection. More than one thousand items relating to the French Revolution, given to Fordham by Joseph Givernaud. Many of the imprint dates are contemporary with events of the revolutionary period.

Hopkins Collection. Religious pamphlets donated by Mr. Joseph Hopkins; 79 items in 21 volumes.

Incunabula. Books printed during the earliest days of printing, 1450-1500 A.D. The collection is comprised of 25 titles contained in 20 volumes.

Jesuitica. Most areas of Humanistic study are represented in this collection of 431 printed books by Jesuit authors dating from 1500 to the twentieth century.

Manuscripta Collection. Microfilms of rare and out-of-print books produced at St. Louis University. The collection consists of filmed sets of reference and source materials of fundamental importance for various types of historical research. Areas covered, so far, include Medieval and Renaissance poetry, philosophy and theology of the Middle Ages, incunabula of works of the vernaculars.

Manuscripts. Consists of 50 items dating from the thirteenth to the twentieth centuries, including 28 documents on vellum, many of which related to the Augustinian Brotherhood at Gemunde.

MacLees Collection. The library of William A. MacLees, including more than 700 book and 165 volumes of journals, all relating to Gaelic language and literature.

Rare Books. This collection includes 536 volumes dating from 1500 to the twentieth century; consists of rare editions, unique copies, and autographed first editions. There are no facsimiles in this collection. Subject areas include literature, history, philosophy, theology, classical studies, and the arts.

Works of Art. These works, exclusive of those in the Munn Collection, include 19 items, principally drawings by Edmund Woerndle von Adelsfried (Austrian, 1827-1906) depicting scenes from the Parsifal epic.

1060
The General Theological Seminary
St. Marks Library
175 Ninth Avenue
New York, New York 10011

Telephone. (212) 243-5150

Institutional Description. The privately supported theological seminary was founded in 1817. It is a graduate-level institution and is affiliated with the Episcopal Church. Enrollment: 161.

Library Administration. David Green, Director; Clifford Urr, Head of Public Services.

Library General Holdings. 205,000 volumes; 500 journal subscriptions.

Special Collections

The St. Marks Library has a large amount of nineteenth-century theological literature, especially of the Episcopal Church; most literature of Episcopal Church Conventions from most dioceses; and hundreds of tracts and pamphlets.

Rare Book Collections

Bible Collection. This is the largest collection of Latin Bibles in the United States, many dating back centuries.

Early English Theology. Includes fifteenth- to eighteenth-century Anglican Episcopal theological materials. Includes the papers of Samuel Seabury and other Episcopal Church fathers.

Clement Clarke Moore Collection. The author of *The Night Before Christmas* donated land and taught at the Seminary.

Manuscripts. The Library maintains an extensive collection of manuscripts of many Episcopal Church priests and leaders.

1061
Graduate School and University Center of the City University of New York
Mina Rees Library
33 West 42nd Street
New York, New York 10036

Telephone. (212) 790-4395

Institutional Description. The publicly supported unit of the City University of New York combines resources from the university's various campuses to provide quality doctorate, master's, and research programs. Enrollment: 3,769.

Library Administration. Jane Ross Moore, Chief Librarian.

Library General Holdings. 185,000 volumes; 1,600 current periodicals; 328,000 microforms; 145,000 audiovisual materials.

Special Collections

Special collections of the Mina Rees Library include the **Art Slide Collection,** especially for nineteenth- and twentieth-century American art; **Utopian Communities Collection,** the **U.S. Presidential Papers;** the **Human Relations Areas Files** (HRAF); and the CUNY doctoral dissertations. The library also includes the **William H. and Gwynne K. Crouse Library for Publishing Arts.**

1062
Hamilton College
Daniel Burke Library
Clinton, New York 13323

Telephone. (315) 859-4011

Institutional Description. The privately supported liberal arts college was founded in 1812. It grants baccalaureate degrees. Enrollment: 1,685.

Library Administration. Ralph H. Stenstrom, Librarian.

Library General Holdings. 411,000 volumes; 2,000 current periodical subscriptions; 235,000 microforms.

Special Collections

Among the library's special collections are the **Rare Book Collection;** the **Ezra Pound Collection** of 3,200 items including first editions and letters; the **McIntosh Collection** of 1,500 items dealing with the Women's Suffrage Movement and including rare books, first editions, and manuscripts; the **Walter Beinecke, Jr. Collection** of 1,250 items relating to the pre-history and settlement of the Lesser Antilles and including rare books, maps, and personal papers; the **Alumni Collection** of books written by and about graduates of the college.

1063
Hartwick College
Hartwick College Library
Oneonta, New York 13820

Telephone. (607) 432-4200

Institutional Description. The privately supported liberal arts college is an outgrowth of Hartwick Seminary, affiliated with the Luthern Church, and founded in 1797. The College was established in 1928, and has been independent since 1968. Enrollment: 1,465.

Library Administration. Eric von Brockdorff, Director of Libraries.

Library General Holdings. 195,000 volumes; 1,070 periodical subscriptions; 43,000 microforms.

Special Collections

Hartwick Seminary Collection. Consists of 400 volumes and includes classical authors and works on theology, church history and the Bible, most published in the seventeenth through early nineteenth centuries. Many of the books are in Greek, Latin, and German and many belonged to Johann Christopher Hartwick, Lutheran pastor and missionary who died in 1796.

Indians of North America. About 9,000 items, mostly books but also microforms on the Indians of North America, particularly those of the eastern woodlands and New York. The collection has its origin in the books on Indians collected by Willard E. Yager, an Oneonta businessman, amateur archeaologist and author. While the bulk of the collection is on the open shelves, Mr. Yager's books, augmented by rare and expensive books acquired as gifts or by purchase, are kept in the Rare Books Room.

1064
Hebrew Union College - Jewish Institute of Religion
Klau Library
One West 4th Street
New York, New York 10012

Telephone. (212) 674-5300

Institutional Description. The privately supported school of religious studies is a branch campus of the parent institution headquartered in Cincinnati, Ohio. It is affiliated with the Union of American Hebrew Congregations. Enrollment: 101.

Library Administration. Philip E. Miller, Librarian.

Library General Holdings. 115,000 volumes; 300 current periodical subscriptions.

Special Collections

The Klau Library's collection of modern Hebrew literature is especially strong. The library also houses a branch of the microfilm collections of the American Jewish Archives and of the American Jewish Periodical Center.

1065
Herkimer County Community College
Library
Reservoir Road
Herkimer, New York 13350

Telephone. (315) 866-0300

Institutional Description. Herkimer County Community College was established in 1966 and is a unit of the State University of New York. Enrollment: 2,041.

Library Administration. Michael J. McLane, Librarian.

Library General Holdings. 74,000 volumes; 623 cur-

rent periodical titles; 11,300 microforms; 4,200 audiovisual materials.

Special Collections

The library maintains a **Polish Culture Room** and a **Peace and Non-Violence Library.**

1066
Hobart and William Smith Colleges
Warren Hunting Smith Library
337 Pulteney Street
Geneva, New York 14456

Telephone. (315) 789-5500

Institutional Description. The privately supported colleges share facilities but maintain separate campuses. Hobart College, for men, was founded in 1822. It is affiliated with the Episcopal Church. William Smith College, for women, was founded in 1908. Enrollment: 1,973.

Library Administration. Paul William Crumlish, Librarian.

Library General Holdings. 230,000 volumes; 1,600 magazines and professional journals; 30 newspapers; 42,000 microforms.

Special Collections

The special collections of the Smith Library include 5,000 original issues of various Geneva (NY) newspapers published from 1806 to 1894; the **Potter Historical Collection** which includes 287 monographs pertaining to France during the seventeenth and eighteenth centuries; and the **Douglas Collection** of nineteenth-century manuscripts, correspondence, journals, and other materials of a prominent Geneva family, including the only existing original sketches of bridges on the Erie Canal. The **Geneva Local History Collection** includes 4,700 monographs and 7,300 other items, including manuscripts, journals, and photographs relating to the history of the colleges and the region, dating from the early nineteenth century.

1067
Hofstra University
Joan and Donald E. Axinn Library
1000 Fulton Avenue
Hempstead, New York 11550

Telephone. (516) 560-5092

Institutional Description. The privately supported liberal arts university was founded in 1935. Enrollment: 12,060.

Library Administration. Dean Charles Andrews, University Librarian; Barbara M. Kelly, Curator, Special Collections.

Library General Holdings. 1,145,342 volumes; 1,098,075 microforms; 7,015 current periodical subscriptions; 168,820 government documents; 1,165 audiovisual materials.

Special Collections

Long Island Studies Institute. A cooperative venture of Hofstra University and the Nassau County Division of Museum Services, the Institute combines Hofstra's New York State History Collection (the James N. MacLean Memorial Library, supported by the American Legion in Nassau County) and the Nassau Country Museum Reference Library. These resources constitute a major research center for the study of Long Island local and regional history.

Utopian Communities Collection. This collection is composed of materials relating to several Utopian Communities, particularly those based within New York State (Oneida, Shakers, Quakers).

Weingrow Avant-Garde Collection. This collection consists of some 4,000 original illustrated books, manifestoes, periodicals, catalogs, posters, prints, manuscripts, photographs, film, and records, which represent the Dada, Surrealist, and Expressionist movements. Also included are samples of many other movements of the late nineteenth and early twentieth centuries as well as selections from the second avant-garde of the late 1960s, and the movement known as New Realism.

German Fascist Collection. Books, manuscripts, and posters developed by the German right-wing political movement during the periods of the Weimar Republic and the Nazi regime.

Art of the Book. Books related to the history of print, of binding, illustration, etc. Examples of early books, rare books, and book art. Facsimiles of world famous examples of illuminated manuscripts.

Private Presses. Books issued from private presses; some are hand set and hand printed in limited editions. Private presses represented include William Morris' Kelmscott Press, Black Sparrow Press, Golden Cockerel Press, Hogarth Press, Mosher Press, Nonesuch Press, Limited Editions, Heritage Press, and Overbook Press.

Nila Banton Smith Historical Collection in Reading. Primers, readers, manuals, and textbooks related to the teaching of reading from the colonial times to the present.

Macready-Meyer Theatrical Collection. Based on the career of William Charles Macready, an early nineteenth-century Shakespearian actor, this collection includes biographies, photographs, playbills, and scripts relating to the nineteenth-century theatre.

Harold E. Yuker Collection on the History of Psychology. This collection, a gift of Hofstra University Psychology Professor Harold E. Yuker, contains nineteenth and twentieth century materials related to the history of psychology with special emphasis on works produced in the period between 1900 and 1930.

Paul Radin Collection on Anthropology and Philosophy. The Radin collection was the personal library of the

American anthropologist Paul Radin. The collection is representative of Radin's work as an ethnographer, with special strengths in the culture of the native Americans and the history of religion.

Blaise Pascal Collection. Materials related to the life and work of the early mathematician/philosopher, Blaise Pascal.

1068
Houghton College
Willard J. Houghton Library
Houghton, New York 14744

Telephone. (716) 567-2211

Institutional Description. The privately supported liberal arts college was founded in 1883 by the Wesleyan Methodist Church of America. It includes music and religion programs. Enrollment: 1,268.

Library Administration. Joyce Moore, Director.

Library General Holdings. 160,000 volumes; 633 journal subscriptions; 7 newspaper subscriptions; 5,240 microforms; 3,500 audiovisual materials.

Special Collections

The library maintains a special collection of **Wesleyana** and the Houghton College Archives.

1069
Hunter College of the City University of New York
Jacqueline Grennan Wexler Library
695 Park Avenue
New York, New York 10021

Telephone. (212) 772-4000

Institutional Description. The publicly supported liberal arts unit of CUNY was established in 1870 as a teacher training institution for women. It became coeducational in 1964, and now offers a variety of programs. Enrollment: 19,577.

Library Administration. David O. Lane, Chief Librarian; William Omelchenko, Special Collections and Rare Books Librarian.

Library General Holdings. 555,000 volumes; 3,950 current periodical subscriptions; 32,500 government documents; 765,000 microforms; 10,000 audiovisual materials.

Special Collections

The most important special collections of the Wexler Library are the **Stonehill Collection** of English novels; a collection of recent Cuban history; and education books and related teacher education materials. The library of the **Center for Puerto Rican Studies** is also located in the Wexler Library.

1070
Iona College
Ryan Library
715 North Avenue
New Rochelle, New York 10801

Telephone. (914) 633-2000

Institutional Description. The privately supported liberal arts college was founded by the Roman Catholic Congregation of Christian Brothers in 1940. It is open to students of all denominations. Enrollment: 5,904.

Library Administration. Patrick J. Larkin, Chief Librarian.

Library General Holdings. 210,000 volumes; 1,360 current periodical subscriptions; 47,000 microforms.

Special Collections

The Ryan Library has a collection of rare books and maintains an **Irish Collection.**

1071
Ithaca College
Library
Danby Road
Ithaca, New York 14850

Telephone. (607) 274-3013

Institutional Description. The privately supported liberal arts and teachers college offers both baccalaureate and master's degrees. Enrollment: 5,757.

Library Administration. R. Robert Woerner, Director.

Library General Holdings. 300,000 volumes of books and periodicals; 124,000 microforms; 14,000 phonograph records.

Special Collections

The Music Special Collections consist of the **Gustav Haenschen and Donald Voorhees Broadcast Music Libraries;** the **Roberta Peters Collection** of memorabilia; and the **Milton Cross Collection.** Pulitzer Prize-winning composer Karel Husa has designated the library as the repository for the complete collection of recordings and scores of all his music.

1072
Jefferson Community College
Melvil Dewey Library
Watertown, New York 13601

Telephone. (315) 782-5250

Institutional Description. Founded by public referendum in 1961, the two-year college opened in 1963 and moved to its present campus in 1965. Enrollment: 1,870.

Library Administration. Suzon O. Kister, Librarian.

Library General Holdings. 52,438 volumes; 346 periodical titles; 4,722 microforms.

Special Collections

An Archives containing material about Jefferson County and the North Country is maintained by the library.

1073
The Jewish Theological Seminary of America
Seminary Library
3080 Broadway
New York, New York 10027

Telephone. (212) 678-8075

Institutional Description. The privately supported seminary was established in 1886 as a rabbinical school. It has grown to a university complex of five schools and is the academic and spiritual center of the Conservative Movement in Judaism. Enrollment: 389.

Library Administration. Mayer Rabinowitz, Seminary Librarian; Rabbi Jerry Schwarzbard, Reference Librarian, Special Collections.

Library General Holdings. 273,911 volumes; 699 current periodical subscriptions; 6,215 microforms.

Special Collections

The Jewish Theological Seminary Library contains one of the largest and most exhaustive collections of Hebraica and Judaica in the world. It has been assembled over generations and preserved through many vicissitudes of Jewish life, including the great fire which attacked the library in 1966. The Library is rich in primary sources for research in Bible and its Jewish commentaries, rabbinics, Jewish philosophy, liturgy, history, and medieval and modern Hebrew literature. The manuscript division has several hundred codices and scrolls of the Bible and an extremely valuable collection of medieval Hebrew commentaries to Scripture. The library includes one of the major collections of fragments from the Cairo Geniza, a mine of primary research material. In addition, there are monographs and studies in related fields such as ancient Near Eastern history and Semitic philology.

The Cantors Institute has a collection of 1,400 albums of classical music and a unique library of Jewish recorded music. Among the 1,000 records in this collection are many rare items. For purposes of instruction and research, the Cantors Institute reprints standard hazzanic and Jewish music materials not otherwise obtainable. An outstanding collection of tapes of authentic folk materials recently gathered in the Middle East is being regularly increased.

1074
John Jay College of Criminal Justice of the City University of New York
Library
444 West 56th Street
New York, New York 10019

Telephone. (212) 489-3500

Institutional Description. The publicly supported unit of CUNY offers programs in criminal justice, fire science, public administration, forensic science, and forensic psychology. Enrollment: 6,679.

Library Administration. Eileen Rowland, Chief Librarian.

Library General Holdings. 260,000 books, periodicals, microforms, and cassette tapes.

Special Collections

The library holds a number of unique research collections directly related to the College's central mission. Trial transcripts from the New York criminal courts from the late 1890s through the post-World War I years are among the holdings as well as an extensive collection of police department annual reports from all over the United States. There are also personal papers of individuals who have made significant contributions to the field, such as the **Warden Lewis E. Lawes Papers** (warden of Sing Sing prison, 1920-1941). There are also microfilmed archives of social, political, and investigative agencies.

1075
The Juilliard School
Lila Acheson Wallace Library
Lincoln Center Plaza
New York, New York 10023

Telephone. (212) 799-5000

Institutional Description. The privately supported school of music was established in 1905; its graduate school, in 1924. It now offers training in all the performing arts, granting baccalaureate, master's, and doctorate degrees. Enrollment: 906.

Library Administration. Jane Gottlieb, Librarian.

Library General Holdings. 65,000 volumes on music, dance, drama, and the humanities; 47,000 music performance and study scores; 14,000 phonographs, cassette tapes, and reel-to-reel tape recordings.

Special Collections

There are many rare scores, first editions and limited edition books, manuscripts, and scholarly editions of the complete sets of works by many composers. The School's orchestral library has a complete collection of the standard repertoire in full scores and performing parts. Nearly 1,000 titles that form the core of the School's orchestral performances are available to students for study and audition preparation.

The orchestral library also houses the School's collection of some 100 instruments, ranging from contrabassoons and piccolos to strings and percussion.

1076
The King's College
College Library
Lodge Road
Briarcliff Manor, New York 10510

Telephone. (914) 944-5543

Institutional Description. The privately supported liberal arts college grants associate and baccalaureate degrees. Enrollment: 580.

Library Administration. Esther Scaman, Director.

Library General Holdings. 90,000 volumes; 600 current periodical subscriptions.

Special Collections

The major special collection in the library is collection of books by Dr. Robert A. Cook who was associated with Scripture Press prior to becoming president of The King's College in 1962.

1077
Laboratory Institute of Merchandising
Learning Resource Center
12 East 53rd Street
New York, New York 10022

Telephone. (212) 752-1530

Institutional Description. The privately supported college offers programs in fashion merchandising, retailing, promotion, and advertising. It grants associate and baccalaureate degrees. Enrollment: 276.

Library Administration. George Sanchez, Director.

Library General Holdings. 7,000 volumes; 110 current periodical subscriptions; 4,300 slides.

Special Collections

The library maintains a comprehensive collection pertaining to fashion merchandising and related fields.

1078
Le Moyne College
Le Moyne College Library
Le Moyne Heights
Syracuse, New York 13214

Telephone. (315) 445-4325

Institutional Description. The privately supported college is a Roman Catholic liberal arts institution conducted by the Jesuits. It was founded in 1946. Enrollment: 2,133.

Library Administration. James J. Simonis, College Librarian; Annette M. Monaco, Special Collections/Rare Books Librarian.

Library General Holdings. 157,246 volumes of books; 21,946 bound volumes of periodicals; 1,262 current periodical subscriptions; 15,556 microform units.

Special Collections

Teaching Materials Collection. Consists of 400 volumes including teaching syllabi and guides.

Irish Literature Collection. A collection of 300 books of modern Irish literature covering the period from 1880 to 1950.

Jesuitiana. Collection of 110 books covering the history of Jesuits in central New York from the seventeenth century to the present.

McGrath Music Collection. Includes 500 manuscripts and published works; choral and instrumental works of Joseph McGrath (1889-1968), composer of sacred and secular music.

Rare Book Collections

The Library has a collection of 3,500 rare books on Catholic Church history and American and English literature.

1079
Lehman College
Lehman College Library
Bedford Park Boulevard West
Bronx, New York 10468

Telephone. (212) 960-8577

Institutional Description. The publicly supported liberal arts college, founded in 1931, is a member of the City University of New York. Enrollment: 9,366.

Library Administration. Larry E. Sullivan, Chief Librarian; Janet Munch, Special Collections Librarian.

Library General Holdings. 447,000 volumes; 1,800 current periodicals; 465,000 microforms.

Special Collections

The library also maintains a special collection of children's books; a **Bronx History Archive,** the **Fordham Manor Church Records,** and the **Riverdale Neighborhood House Records.** The **Fine Arts Room** contains holdings in art, architecture, music, and the dance.

1080
Long Island University, C. W. Post Campus
B. Davis Schwartz Memorial Library
Northern Boulevard
Brookville, New York 11548

Telephone. (516) 299-0200

Institutional Description. The privately supported liberal arts campus of Long Island University was founded in 1954. Among its several schools and colleges, C. W. Post contains the Palmer Graduate Library School. Enrollment: 9,670.

Library Administration. Donald Ungarelli, Director of Libraries.

Library General Holdings. 700,000 books and periodicals; 4,430 current periodical subscriptions.

Special Collections

Special collections include the **Franklin B. Lord, Sr. Library of Sports,** one of the outstanding collections of its kind and of particular historical interest to the North Shore of Long Island; the **H.T. Lindeberg Collection** in the fields of architecture and fine arts; the **Dudley Field Underhill Collection** of Quaker history; the **M. Demerec Biological Collection;** the Floyd M. McCaffree Library of history and political science; the private library of Eugene and Carlotta O'Neill, the gift of ex-Chancellor John H.G. Pell; the **Harry Kurz Collection** in language and literature; the collection of naval history given in memory of Admiral Richard Lansing Conolly by Mr. Charles K. Post; **Theodore Roosevelt Association Collection,** representing 2,000 books and pamphlets about the life, times, and writings of Theodore Roosevelt; a naval history library; and a presidential library. The **Christine B. Gilbert Collection of Children's Literature,** named in honor of a former professor of the Palmer School; and the government and state documents collection of the late Congressman William K. Macy, presented by Mr. and Mrs. Quentin Mohr of Islip, New York.

1081
Manhattan College
Cardinal Hayes Library
Manhattan College Parkway
Riverdale, Bronx, New York 10471

Telephone. (212) 920-0100

Institutional Description. The privately supported liberal arts and professional college was founded in 1853 by the Roman Catholic Christian Brothers. It grants associate, baccalaureate, and master's degrees. Enrollment: 4,-339.

Library Administration. Harry E. Welsh, Director of Libraries.

Library General Holdings. 239,000 volumes; 1,530 journals, magazines, and newspapers; 230,000 microforms; 6,000 audiovisual materials.

Special Collections

The library's special collections include the **Thomas More Collection,** the **Slattery Dante Collection,** and the **De Coursey Fales Collection** of English and American literature.

1082
Manhattan School of Music
Frances Hall Ballard Library
120 Claremont Avenue
New York, New York 10027

Telephone. (212) 749-2802

Institutional Description. The privately supported professional college of music was founded in 1917. It grants baccalaureate, master's, and doctorate degrees. Enrollment: 778.

Library Administration. Richard Presser, Reference Librarian.

Library General Holdings. 75,000 volumes; 85 current periodical subscriptions.

Special Collections

The major emphasis of the library is on music and music education. The score collection emphasizes performance materials and includes study scores and scholarly editions. The H. Mott Brennan Listening Library contains a collection of more than 15,000 recordings. The **Heckscher Children's Library** serves the needs of the Preparatory Division and was donated by the Heckscher Foundation for Children.

1083
Manhattanville College
Library
Purchase Street
Purchase, New York 10577

Telephone. (914) 694-2200

Institutional Description. The privately supported liberal arts college was founded in 1841 by the Roman Catholic Academy of the Sacred Heart. Now independent, it grants baccalaureate and master's degrees. Enrollment: 1,495.

Library Administration. Stefania Koren, Reference Librarian.

Library General Holdings. 247,000 volumes; 1,015 periodical subscriptions; 42,000 microforms.

Special Collections

The library maintains the **Zigmund Cerbu Collection** on Buddhism and Hinduism.

Rare Book Collections

The rare book collection contains 1,700 items varying from incunabula and other early printed books to manuscripts and letters of the nineteenth and twentieth centuries. Of special interest are Civil War manuscripts, U.S.

Catholic history, liturgical music, and early American textbooks.

1084
Mannes College of Music
Harry Scherman Library
150 West 85th Street
New York, New York 10024

Telephone. (212) 580-0210

Institutional Description. The privately supported college, founded in 1916, grants the baccalaureate and master's degrees. Enrollment: 203.

Library Administration. Deborah G. Davis, Head Librarian.

Library General Holdings. 6,100 volumes; 55 periodical subscriptions; 23,800 volumes of music scores; 5,000 recordings.

Special Collections

The Library has two specialized collections: **The Salzedo Collection** consisting of harp music annotated by Carlos Salzedo and the **Mannes Collection** consisting of compositions and arrangements by Leopold Damrosch Mannes.

1085
Marist College
College Library
82 North Road
Poughkeepsie, New York 12601

Telephone. (914) 471-3240

Institutional Description. The privately supported liberal arts college grants baccalaureate and master's degrees. Enrollment: 4,315.

Library Administration. Barbara Brenner, Director of Library Services.

Library General Holdings. 120,000 volumes; 680 periodical subscriptions.

Special Collections

Special collections include a local history collection containing material by and about the Marist Brothers; material about Dutchess County and the six surrounding counties and including county annuals, legislative proceedings, and rare books; historical documents and annals of St. Anne's Hermitage, the first Marist house of studies in the United States.

1086
Maryknoll School of Theology
Library
Maryknoll, New York 10545

Telephone. (914) 941-7590

Institutional Description. The Maryknoll School of Theology is a graduate and professional school whose purpose is to serve the needs of the Catholic Foreign Mission Society of America (Maryknoll) and the Roman Catholic Church in the United States in the areas of theological education and formation for priesthood and other ministries. Enrollment: 94.

Library Administration. Rev. Arthur E. Brown, Librarian.

Library General Holdings. 98,000 volumes; 650 current periodical subscriptions.

Special Collections

Special collections include area studies of Africa, Asia, China, Japan, Philippines, and Latin America. The library also maintains a collection of materials on foreign missions (Catholic).

1087
Marymount College
Gloria Gaines Memorial Library
Tarrytown, New York 10591

Telephone. (914) 631-3200

Institutional Description. The privately supported liberal arts college for women was founded in 1919 by the Roman Catholic Religious of the Sacred Heart of Mary. It grants baccalaureate degrees. Enrollment: 1,258.

Library Administration. Virginia McKenna, R.S.H.M., Director.

Library General Holdings. 114,000 volumes; 500 current periodicals.

Special Collections

The special collections of the library include the **Thomas More Collection** of books by and about More, including incunabula and first editions; the **Mussolini Papers** which includes his personal papers and official records on 316 reels of microfilm; a collection of *Catholic News,* the publication of the Archdiocese of New York covering the period 1888-1965.

1088
Marymount Manhattan College
Thomas J. Shanahan Library
221 East 71st Street
New York, New York 10021

Telephone. (212) 517-0400

Institutional Description. The privately supported liberal arts college, primarily for women, was founded in 1936. Serving the greater New York City area, it offers a full range of programs for part-time students. Enrollment: 1,551.

Library Administration. Lynn S. Mullins, Head Librarian.

Library General Holdings. 95,000 volumes; 12,000 microforms; 800 current periodical subscriptions.

Special Collections

Special collections include the **Geraldine A. Ferraro Papers,** a collection in the social sciences and humanities, and a **Women's Studies** collection.

1089
Mater Dei College
Augsbury Memorial Library
Riverside Drive
Ogdensburg, New York 13669

Telephone. (315) 393-5930

Institutional Description. The privately supported two-year junior college was founded in 1960 by the Roman Catholic Sisters of St. Joseph of Watertown, New York. Enrollment: 606.

Library Administration. Sr. Mary Joseph Meichelbeck, College Librarian; Sally E. Rusaw, Associate Librarian and Special Collections Librarian.

Library General Holdings. 55,000 volumes; 275 current periodical subscriptions; 2,100 microfilm units; 3,700 audiovisual and video materials; vertical file of clippings, pamphlets, and documents.

Special Collections

Alcoholism and Chemical Dependency. A collection of 650 bound volumes, 8 current periodicals, 35 audiovisual titles, 37 microform units, and a vertical file of clippings, government documents, and pamphlets on alcoholism and chemical dependency with the current emphasis on alcoholism. The growing collection began with a grant from the New York State Division of Alcoholism and Alcohol Abuse in 1983 and is intended to serve students in the Alcohol and Chemical Dependency Program and professionals in the field in northern New York.

1090
Medaille College
Scholastica Library
18 Agassiz Circle
Buffalo, New York 14214

Telephone. (716) 884-3281

Institutional Description. The privately supported liberal arts, teachers, and career college was founded in 1875. It grants associate and baccalaureate degrees. Enrollment: 967.

Library Administration. Ilona Middleton, Director.

Library General Holdings. 50,000 volumes; 500 periodical subscriptions.

Special Collections

The library maintains special collections in education/reading, business management, and human services.

1091
Medgar Evers College - CUNY
College Library
1150 Carroll Street
Brooklyn, New York 11225

Telephone. (718) 735-1854

Institutional Description. The publicy supported campus of the City University of New York provides two-year and four-year programs in professional studies. From its founding in 1971 it has been attentive and responsive to the needs of the surrounding community in Brooklyn. Enrollment: 5,169.

Library Administration. Robert B. Ford, Jr., Chief Librarian.

Library General Holdings. 76,000 volumes; 515 current periodical subscriptions.

Special Collections

A collection of microforms in excess of 25,000 includes the **Schomburg Collection for Research in Black Culture** and other collections supporting research in American studies.

1092
Mercy College
Mercy College Libraries
555 Broadway
Dobbs Ferry, New York 10522

Telephone. (914) 693-4500

Institutional Description. The privately supported liberal arts college was founded in 1950 to train women for the Religious Sisters of Mercy. Today, coeducational and nondenominational, it grants associate, baccalaureate, and master's degrees. Enrollment: 3,881.

Library Administration. Larry Earl Bone, Director.

Library General Holdings. 314,000 volumes; 1,900 current periodical subscriptions; 416,000 microforms; 44,000 government documents.

Special Collections

The special collections of the library include the **Millbrook Hunt Collection** in the equestrian arts; the **Ernst Dichter Papers,** the **Vander Peel Art Print Collection;** and the **Peter Goldmark Record Collection.**

1093
Mohawk Valley Community College Library 1101 Sherman Drive Utica, New York 13501

Telephone. (315) 797-9530

Institutional Description. The two-year college was founded in 1946 as the New York Institute of Applied Arts and Science. In 1950, it became a constituent unit of the State University of New York. The present name was adopted in 1960. Enrollment: 6,146.

Library Administration. Alice B. Griffith, Director.

Library General Holdings. 70,000 volumes; 800 periodical titles.

Special Collections

The library houses a **Women's Resource Center.**

1094
Mount Saint Mary College Curtin Memorial Library Powell Avenue Newburgh, New York 12550

Telephone. (914) 561-0800

Institutional Description. The privately supported liberal arts college was founded in 1954 by the Roman Catholic Sisters of the Order of St. Dominic. It grants baccalaureate and master's degrees. Enrollment: 1,114.

Library Administration. Roberta Singer, Director.

Library General Holdings. 102,000 volumes; 510 current periodical subscriptions; 17,000 microforms.

Special Collections

Special collections include the **Monihan Collection** on Newburgh and local history and a **Curriculum Materials Center** which houses textbooks on the elementary and secondary levels as well as syllabi and teaching aids.

1095
Mount Sinai School of Medicine - CUNY Gustave L. and Janet W. Levy Library One Gustav L. Levy Place New York, New York 10029

Telephone. (212) 650-6500

Institutional Description. The publicly supported professional medical unit of the City University of New York was founded in 1963. It grants professional and doctorate degrees. Enrollment: 483.

Library Administration. Lynn Kasner Morgan, Director.

Library General Holdings. 120,000 bound volumes; 2,000 current journal subscriptions; 2,500 audiovisual materials.

Special Collections

The Levy Library exists as a major biomedical informational resource serving primarily the educational, research, and clinical programs of the medical center and the clinical practice and continuing education needs of its staff.

1096
Nassau Community College A. Holly Patterson Library Stewart Avenue Garden City, New York 11530

Telephone. (516) 222-7400

Institutional Description. The two-year college was created in 1959 by Nassau County as part of the State University of New York. Enrollment: 19,363.

Library Administration. Arthur Friedman, Chairman.

Library General Holdings. 150,000 volumes; 1,000 periodical titles; 40,000 audiovisual items.

Special Collections

The library has the **New York State Health Film Collection** of 864 titles on 2,300 reels; the "Round Pages" of taped books for the blind; and a rare book collection. Also maintained are the **G. Wilson Knight Interdisciplinary Society** and the **Dozenal Society** collections.

1097
Nazareth College of Rochester Lorette Wilmot Library 4245 East Avenue Rochester, New York 14610

Telephone. (716) 586-2525

Institutional Description. The privately supported liberal arts college was formed as a college for women in 1924 and became coeducational in 1973. It grants baccalaureate and master's degrees. Enrollment: 2,811.

Library Administration. Richard Matzek, Library Director.

Library General Holdings. 225,000 volumes; 1,780 current serials; 185,000 microforms; 1,290 music scores; 10,600 records, tapes, films.

Special Collections

Thomas Merton Collection. Contains 192 titles, 280 volumes; contains growing number of books by and about Thomas Merton in foreign languages; some manuscript material; collection support made possible through a donation by Monsignor William H. Shannon, a noted Merton scholar.

Rare Book Collections

Hendrick Papers. A small collection of letters and notes of Bishop Thomas Augustine Hendrick (1849-1909) who served briefly in the Philippine Islands.

Rare book collections include those on G.K. Chesterton, 300 titles; Maurice Baring, 42 titles; Hilaire Belloc, 150 titles; Sitwell, 136 titles; and Auburn Imprints, 60 titles (mid-nineteenth century books published chiefly in Auburn, New York).

1098
New School for Social Research
Raymond Fogelman Library
66 West 12th Street
New York, New York 10111

Telephone. (212) 741-5600

Institutional Description. The privately supported specialized university was founded in 1919 by such notable scholars as John Dewey, Charles Beard, and Thorstein Veblen. It offers upper division and graduate studies only. The Parsons School of Design is included under its auspices. Enrollment: 6,252.

Library Administration. 112,000 volumes; 658 current periodicals.

Library General Holdings. The Raymond Fogelman Library is rich in resources related to the social sciences. The Graduate Faculty also houses the Husserl Archives and students have access to the unusual art collections in the New School's Gimbel Library.

1099
New York Chiropractic College
Library
P.O. Box 167
Glen Head, New York 11545

Telephone. (516) 626-2700

Institutional Description. The privately supported professional college, founded in 1919, grants professional degrees. Enrollment: 749.

Library Administration. Michele L. Barrett, Chief Librarian.

Library General Holdings. 4,000 volumes; 110 current periodicals.

Special Collections

The New York Chriopractic College is a participant in a unique library partnership with the New York Institute of Technology and C.W. Post College. Students of NYCC have full access to the holdings of their libraries. In addition to this material, NYCC maintains a special chiropractic collection which includes the works of B.J. Palmer and other books of current and historic relevance to chiropractic, particularly in the sacro-occipital technique and applied kinesiology.

1100
New York City Technical College - CUNY
Main Library
300 Jay Street
Brooklyn, New York 11201

Telephone. (718) 643-4900

Institutional Description. The publicly supported unit of the City University of New York is composed of the Divisions of Commerce, Liberal Arts and Sciences, Health and Natural Sciences, and Technology. Enrollment: 10,-812.

Library Administration. Catherine T. Brody, Department Chair.

Library General Holdings. 150,000 volumes; 600 magazines and newspaper subscriptions.

Special Collections

The library's holdings reflect the institution's urban technical education programs. From four career programs in 1946, "City Tech's" offerings have expanded to include more than 40 two-year degrees, options, and one-year certificate programs, as well as New York City's only four-year degree in Hotel and Restaurant Management. In addition to supporting these various programs, the library maintains a special collection of menus.

1101
New York Institute of Technology
Schure Hall Library
Wheatley Road
Old Westbury, New York 11561

Telephone. (516) 686-7754

Institutional Description. The privately supported technological university, founded in 1955, has branch campuses in New York City and Central Islip. Featured programs include engineering, architecture, and interior design. The New York College of Osteopathy is a member of the Institute. Enrollment: 13,916.

Library Administration. C. Woo, Librarian.

Library General Holdings. 156,000 volumes; 2,100 current periodicals; 230,000 microforms.

Special Collections

The library maintains collections on architecture, energy, engineering and technology, labor and industrial relations; and the natural sciences.

1102
New York Law School
Library
57 Worth Street
New York, New York 10013

Telephone. (212) 966-3500

Institutional Description. The privately supported professional college was founded in 1891. It grants the degree Juris Doctor (J.D.). Enrollment: 1,528.

Library Administration. Joyce Saltalamachia, Library Director.

Library General Holdings. 270,000 volumes.

Special Collections

The library's collection contains the court reports and statutes of all jurisdictions in the United States as well as those of Great Britain. There are also extensive holdings of legal periodicals and treatises and loose-leaf services in major subject specialties. The library has one of the largest microform collections among law school libraries in the state which offers access to rare and extremely important reference documents. Of particular interest is the Communications Library which is a specialized collection of material related to the Media Law clinic at New York Law School. Other special collections include labor law, human rights, international law, and alternative dispute resolution.

1103
New York Medical College
Medical Sciences Library
Valhalla, New York 10595

Telephone. (914) 993-4200

Institutional Description. The privately supported professional medical college was founded in 1860. It grants professional, master's, and doctorate degrees. Enrollment: 1,157.

Library Administration. Donald E. Roy, Director.

Library General Holdings. 127,000 volumes; 1,450 journal titles.

Special Collections

The library maintains the **Westchester Academy of Medicine Collection,** the Alexander Van Heuven Collection, and the **Haas Collection.** There is a History of Medicine reading room.

1104
New York School of Interior Design
Library
155 East 56th Street
New York, New York 10022

Telephone. (212) 753-5365

Institutional Description. The privately supported school grants the associate degree. Enrollment: 713.

Library Administration. Malcolm E. Scheer, Library Director.

Library General Holdings. 3,300 volumes; 600 periodicals; 800 slides.

Special Collections

The entire library is a special collection of books and materials relating to interior design (art, architecture, design, etc.).

1105
New York Theological Seminary
Seminary Library
5 West 29th Street
New York, New York 10001

Telephone. (212) 532-4012

Institutional Description. The privately supported, interdenominational theological seminary offers programs on the graduate level only. Degrees granted are professional, master's, and doctorate. Enrollment: 240.

Library Administration. Eleanor Soler, Librarian.

Library General Holdings. 15,000 volumes. *See also* **General Theological Seminary.**

Special Collections

The primary research facility for NYTS graduate students is the St. Marks Library at General Theological Seminary, just 16 blocks from NYTS. In addition, the Seminary maintains a 15,000-volume, program-centered library in religion and social science, with concentrations in Bible, doctrinal and practical theology, counseling, religious education, the Black church, and women in the church. About 200 volumes are in Spanish.

1106
New York University
Elmer Holmes Bobst Library
100 Washington Square
New York, New York 10012

Telephone. (212) 998-2440

Institutional Description. The privately supported university, founded in 1831, now includes 21 colleges and schools at 6 major centers in New York City. It operates the Institute of Environmental Medicine on a 1,000-acre site in Sterling Forest near Tuxedo, NY. Enrollment: 45,-975.

Library Administration. Carleton C. Rochell, Dean of Libraries.

Library General Holdings. 3,000,000 volumes; 33,000 current periodicals; 2,100,000 microforms; 462,000 audiovisual materials.

Special Collections

Among the noteworthy resources of the Bobst Library are the collections in American and English literature and history, economics, education, science, music,

United Nations documents, Near Eastern and Ibero-American languages and literatures, and Judaica and Hebraica. There is also the **Tamiment Institute/Ben Josephson Library** on the history of radicalism in the United States, the **Robert F. Wagner Archives** on the history of the New York City labor movement; the **Fales Library** of English and American Literature since 1750; the **Robert Frost Library,** the **Berol Collection** of Lewis Carroll materials, and numerous rare books and manuscripts.

Rare Book Collections

John and Bertha E. Waldmann Memorial Library. Located at the Dental Center, this library contains one of the largest collections of rare books on dentistry in the United States, including the **Weinberger Collection,** the **Blum Collection,** and the **Mestel St. Apollonia Collection.**

1107
North Country Community College
Library
20 Winona Avenue
Saranac Lake, New York 12983

Telephone. (518) 891-2915

Institutional Description. The two-year college is cosponsored by Franklin and Essex Counties. A new campus was occupied in 1979. Enrollment: 1,580.

Library Administration. Patrick McIntyre, Director.

Library General Holdings. 37,043 volumes.

Special Collections

The **Adirondack Collection** is maintained by the library.

1108
Orange County Community College
Library
115 South Street
Middletown, New York 10940

Telephone. (914) 343-1121

Institutional Description. Founded in 1950, Orange County Community College was the first community college in New York State. Enrollment: 4,933.

Library Administration. Christina D. Baum, Director of Learning Resources.

Library General Holdings. 88,500 books and periodicals.

Special Collections

The **Orange County History and Heritage Collection** is maintained in the library.

1109
Pace University
Library
Pace Plaza
New York, New York 10038

Telephone. (212) 488-1667

Institutional Description. The privately supported liberal arts and professional university was founded in 1906 to prepare students for the accounting profession. The university now includes 6 schools plus campuses in Pleasantville and White Plains. Enrollment: 24,651.

Library Administration. Henry Birnbaum, University Librarian; Mel Isaacson, Librarian.

Library General Holdings. 323,000 volumes; 1,450 periodicals.

Special Collections

The library's collection includes much material in the business and accounting fields. The library maintains special collections of children's and young adult literature; vocational literature; and catalogs from colleges and universities throughout the United States.

1110
Parsons School of Design
Adam and Sophie Gimbel Design Library
66 Fifth Avenue
New York, New York 10011

Telephone. (212) 741-8910

Institutional Description. The privately supported college offers programs in art and design. Founded in 1896, the school is affiliated with the New School for Social Research. In 1979, Parsons merged with the Otis Art Institute of Los Angeles. Enrollment: 2,688 (New York).

Library Administration. Sharon Chickanzeff, Director.

Library General Holdings. 30,000 volumes in the art and design fields; 230 periodicals; 500 exhibition catalogs received annually.

Special Collections

The special collections in the Gimbel Library include the original sketchbooks of fashion designer Claire McCardell (a Parsons alumna), and several hundred rare books. The picture collection holds over 35,000 mounted plates arranged by subject.

1111
Paul Smith's College
Frank Cubley Library
Paul Smiths, New York 12970

Telephone. (518) 327-6211

Institutional Description. Paul Smith's College was established in 1937 and is a private insitution offering programs in business, liberal arts, and technical fields. Enrollment: 702.

Library Administration. Theodore D. Mack, Librarian.

Library General Holdings. 43,000 volumes; 500 periodicals; 6,543 audiovisual materials.

Special Collections

The library maintains specialized collections on forestry, hotel and restaurant management, outdoor recreation, and surveying. Among the most recent gifts to the library are the personal collections of the late Colonel Gordon A. Rust and Gertrude Massey Barse. The Trudeau Foundation has given a collection in history, psychology, and literature. A scientific collection on the subject of wildlife was received from Mr. Lang Elliott. The Adirondack-Smith Alcove contains a pictorial history of the tradition established by the Smith family and its relationship to the area.

1112
Polytechnic University University Libraries 333 Jay Street Brooklyn, New York 11201

Telephone. (718) 643-5000

Institutional Description. The privately supported liberal arts and technological university has a branch campus in Farmingdale and a Westchester Graduate Center in White Plains. Enrollment: 5,030.

Library Administration. Richard Sweeney, Dean of Libraries and Information Services.

Library General Holdings. 272,000 volumes; 1,290 current periodical subscriptions.

Special Collections

The collections of the University Libraries include the areas of engineering and technology, telecommunications, digital systems, imaging sciences, operations research, polymer research, transportation, and fire research.

1113
Pratt Institute Library 200 Willoughby Avenue Brooklyn, New York 11205

Telephone. (718) 636-3600

Institutional Description. The privately supported professional school contains the Schools of Architecture, Art and Design, Liberal Arts and Sciences, Engineering; the Graduate School of Library and Information Science; and the Phoenix School of Design. Enrollment: 3,614.

Library Administration. George Lowy, Dean of Libraries.

Library General Holdings. 185,000 volumes; 680 periodical and newspaper subscriptions; 50,000 slides; 135,000 pictures; 22,000 microforms; 130,000 government documents.

Special Collections

The collection of the Pratt Library is especially strong in art and architecture, and in library and information science. Special collections include examples of early children's books and materials on the history of printing.

1114
Queens College of the City University of New York Paul Klapper Library 65-30 Kissena Boulevard Flushing, New York 11367

Telephone. (718) 520-7000

Institutional Description. The publicly supported liberal arts college is a member of the City University of New York. Enrollment: 15,827.

Library Administration. Matthew J. Simon, Chief Librarian.

Library General Holdings. 550,000 books; 4,000 current periodicals.

Special Collections

Important special collections include historical documents of Queens County through the mid-1880s; a collection of theater playbills and memorabilia; and a collection of colonial newspapers in microformat.

1115
Rensselaer Polytechnic Institute Richard G. Folsom Library 8th Street Troy, New York 12180

Telephone. (518) 266-6000

Institutional Description. The privately supported technological university consists of the schools of Architecture, Engineering, Humanities and Social Sciences, Management, and Science; the Graduate School; and Division of Research. Enrollment: 6,821.

Library Administration. Barbara Lockett, Director.

Library General Holdings. 352,000 volumes; 4,500 current periodicals; 740,000 microforms; 30,000 government documents; 59,000 audiovisual materials.

Special Collections

The Institute Archives and Department of Special Collections contain much information on the history of Rensselaer through the correspondence, photographs, and campus publications which are generated by its students, faculty, staff, and alumni. Also available are rare books and the personal papers of alumni and faculty which relate to the history of American science and technology. The **John A. Roebling Collection** includes books, manuscripts, and original drawings (1840-1880) from the designer of the Brooklyn Bridge; a collection of books and correspondence from the mid-1800s by and about the inventor, chemist, and botanist Eben N. Horsford; and the libraries of Amos Eaton and James Hall.

Architecture Library. The library includes a data file of classified photographs, plates, journal extracts, and government and commercial publications on design, the history of architecture, art and sculpture, city planning, structures, building materials and construction, and mechanical and electrical equipment.

1116
Roberts Wesleyan College
Kenneth B. Keating Library
2301 Westside Drive
Rochester, New York 14624

Telephone. (716) 594-9471

Institutional Description. The privately supported liberal arts and sciences college is affiliated with the Free Methodist Church. Enrollment: 688.

Library Administration. Alfred C. Krober, Director of Library Services.

Library General Holdings. 89,000 volumes; 545 current periodical subscriptions.

Special Collections

The Keating Library maintains the **Benjamin Titus Roberts Collection** which includes materials of the founder of the Free Methodist Church.

1117
Rochester Institute of Technology
Wallace Memorial Library
1 Lomb Memorial Drive
Rochester, New York 14623

Telephone. (716) 475-2557

Institutional Description. The privately supported institution offers specialized study in professional and technical areas. Enrollment: 13,387.

Library Administration. Patricia A. Pitkin, Librarian; Gladys M. Taylor, Archivist/Special Collections Librarian.

Library General Holdings. 286,408 bound volumes; 4,983 current periodical subscriptions; 21 newspaper subscriptions; 20,087 microfilm reels; 250,000 microfiche.

Special Collections

The library holdings include: 986 European and American posters 1890-1960s; several hundred contemporary artists' books; 1,584 original cartoons by Messner; 4,758 titles related to the deaf and deafness; 54 books and journals in braille (Center for Visually Impaired).

Rare Book Collections

Archives and Special Collections. Includes the archives of the Institute; 115 rare books with fore-edge paintings; 55 rare miniature books; a small collection of rare books and journals pertaining to the history of photography and printing.

1118
Rockefeller University
University Libraries
York Avenue and 66th Street
New York, New York 10021

Telephone. (212) 570-8086

Institutional Description. The privately supported graduate school and research center was founded by John D. Rockefeller in 1901. It offers preparation for careers in research and teaching in physics, chemistry, biology, philosophical psychology, and environmental and behavioral sciences. The Ph.D. degree is granted.

Library Administration. Sonya W. Mirsky, University Librarian.

Library General Holdings. 248,000 volumes; 1,942 current periodical subscriptions.

Special Collections

The most important specialized holdings of the libraries are in the field of biomedical sciences.

1119
Russell Sage College
James Wheelock Clark Library
45 Ferry Street
Troy, New York 12180

Telephone. (518) 270-2346

Institutional Description. The privately supported liberal arts college for women traces its origins to a female seminary established in 1814. The College was founded in 1916. Enrollment: 3,253.

Library Administration. Donald L. Ryan, Director of Libraries.

Library General Holdings. 187,995 volumes; 1,141 current periodical subscriptions; 6,902 microforms; 42,339 audiovisual materials.

Special Collections

The Library has a special collection of source materials on women's history in New York State (donated by Dorothy Thomas). It is supported by over 5,000 volumes of books and periodicals on women's studies.

Also, there is a collection of the papers of Ian Hamilton Finlay and the archives of Something Else Press, as well as about 7,000 volumes of twentieth-century poetry, many of which are autographed. Emphasis of the poetry collection is on the avant-garde and concrete poetry of the 1960s and women poets of the 1970s and 1980s.

1120
St. Bonaventure University
Franciscan Institute Library
St. Bonaventure, New York 14778

Telephone. (716) 357-2337

Institutional Description. The privately supported university was founded in 1859 by the Roman Catholic Franciscan Fathers, Province of the Most Holy Name of the Order of Friars Minor. Enrollment: 2,739.

Library Administration. Paul J. Spaeth, Franciscan Institute Librarian.

Library General Holdings. 20,000 volumes; 3,000 bound periodical volumes; 150 current periodical subscriptions; 350 photostatic copies of manuscripts; 700 microfilmed manuscripts; 100 manuscripts; 200 incunabula; 10,000 rare books (imprint dates 1501-1850).

Special Collections

The Franciscan Institute Library contains the most extensive collection of materials in the United States covering the history and thought of all branches of the Franciscan Order. The collection is also rich in medieval studies in general, especially in the areas of medieval philosophy, medieval theology, and scholasticism. The collection is made up of materials which have historically belonged to the Institute along with a great many titles which have come from Holy Name College (Washington, D.C.).

1121
St. Francis College
McGarry Library
180 Remsen Street
Brooklyn, New York 11201

Telephone. (718) 522-2300

Institutional Description. The privately supported liberal arts college was established in 1858. It grants associate and baccalaureate degrees. Enrollment: 2,143.

Library Administration. Joan Torrone, Head Librarian; Arthur Konop, Director, James A. Kelly Institute for Local Historical Studies.

Library General Holdings. 148,000 volumes; 840 current periodical subscriptions.

Special Collections

James A. Kelly Institute for Local Historical Studies. Names for the late Brooklyn Borough Historian, the Institute was created in 1973 and is housed in the basement of the Science Building. The Institute contains one of New York's largest collections of primary source records of local history, including original charters of the Dutch and English governors, Indian deeds, and town records.

The Congressman John Rooney, Congressman Eugene Keogh, and Alderman Peter McGuiness Collections, Francis Sinnott papers, and a number of political scrapbooks and memorabilia are preserved here. The papers of former City Councilman Tom Cuite, an alumnus of St. Francis College, are also in the collection. The total number of documents numbers more than 3,000,000 items.

1122
Saint John Fisher College
Charles J. Lavery Library
3690 East Avenue
Rochester, New York 14618

Telephone. (716) 385-8000

Institutional Description. The privately supported liberal arts college is now nondenominational, but was founded by the Roman Catholic Basilian Fathers in 1948. It grants baccalaureate and master's degrees. Enrollment: 3,353.

Library Administration. Robert J. Gullo, Director.

Library General Holdings. 150,000 items; 800 subscription titles.

Special Collections

Special collections in the Lavery Library include the **Reverend Alexander Stewart Collection** of papers, original correspondence, books, and documents about seventeenth-century Jesuit missionaries and their contact with the Indians of western New York; a **Grand Army of the Republic Collection** of correspondence by and published materials and films about local Union Army veterans and their families from 1866-1945; and the **George Decker Collection** of documents of the Rochester lawyer who in the early 1900s represented the six nations of the Iroquois Confederacy. The Rochester-Genesee County Room houses rare books and special materials on local history.

1123
St. John's University
St. Augustine Library
Grand Central and Utopia Parkways
Jamaica, New York 11439

Telephone. (718) 990-6161

Institutional Description. The privately supported Roman Catholic institution, founded in 1870, is sponsored by the Congregation of the Mission (Vincentian Fathers). Enrollment: 19,211.

Library Administration. Sr. Marie Melton, University Librarian; Szilvia E. Szmuk, Special Collections Librarian.

Library General Holdings. 606,715 bound volumes; 4,189 current periodical and newspaper subscriptions; 250,901 microforms; 15,783 learning materials.

Special Collections

Baxter Collection. John E. Baxter donated 311 volumes of first editions representing almost all the published works of four American authors: Thomas Bailey Aldrich, William Dean Howells, Henry Van Dyke, and Edith Wharton. There are approximately a dozen inscribed or presentation copies among these volumes bearing the author's signature.

James Buckley Collection. Senatorial papers, clippings, press releases, correspondence; material for 1970 campaign including audio and video tapes.

Hugh L. Carey Collection. Contains the bulk of Governor Carey's congressional papers, beginning with his first year as a congressman in 1961 and ending with 1974, the last year he served as congressman from the 15th Congressional District, Brooklyn, New York. In addition, the university has the personal files of his Governor's Papers, 1975-1982.

Carofano Collection. In 1969, Mrs. Edward Carofano donated two sixteenth-century Venetian majolica jars to St. John's University. Several years later followed 49 books on apothecary pottery and on history of pharmacology. The entire collection of 400 majolica jars and pharmacy-related artifacts came to SJU in 1987.

Children's Historical Collection. The primary emphasis of this 250-volume collection donated by Anne Thaxter Eaton is children's books of the nineteenth century. There are examples of original Caldecott picture books, McGuffey's readers, as well as first editions of fables and stories illustrated by Arthur Rackham.

William M. Fischer Lawn Tennis Collection. William M. Fischer, an accountant by profession, was an avid tennis enthusiast. Starting in 1897 he built a varied collection of over 2,500 items including books, periodicals, yearbooks, newspaper clippings, photographs, souvenir programs, and memorabilia. The collection's emphasis is on material through the early part of the century up to 1955.

Halpern Collection. Congressman Seymour Halpern's gift of 40 autograph letters written by pope and saints of the Catholic Church.

Heller Collection. This collection of Saul Heller consists of eighteenth- and nineteenth-century English and American textbooks representing both the practical and theoretical aspects of stenography and shorthand.

King Jazz Collection. Housed in the Media Center, the collection covers up to the mid-1970s and includes 1,000 phonograph recordings by major jazz artists.

Limited Editions. Some of the more unusual items in this collection are art exhibit catalogues and folders containing original lithographs and etchings. The *Colophon* (1932-1938) and the *New Colophon* (1948-1950) are examples of limited editions periodicals.

Myer Collection. Consists of 187 monographs, journals, and ledgers on the theory, history, and practice of accounting. Publication dates span four centuries. The strength of this collection is primarily seventeenth- and eighteenth-century Continental and nineteenth-century American books on methods of bookkeeping and business procedures.

James J. Needham Papers. Speeches and news clippings concerned with the Chairman of the New York Stock Exchange.

Paul O'Dwyer Collection. Papers of City Councilman Paul O'Dwyer, especially material dealing with the Irish in America.

Cormac O'Malley Collection. Covers Irish and Irish-American affairs.

Special Collection. The Special Collection within Special Collections contains volumes of no specific designation but of special interest. In this group are autographed copies of John Kennedy's *The Strategy of Peace;* William White's biography of Lyndon B. Johnson *The Professional;* a complete run of *The Yellow Book;* as well as expensive facsimile volumes, original color-plates, fragile, or unusual publications.

Rare Book Collections

Rare Books. Most of the collection consists of transfers from the general circulating collection and donations from parish, seminary, and private clerical libraries. As a result, there are several sixteenth- and seventeenth-century editions of works of the Church Fathers and eighteenth- and nineteenth-century writing of missionaries. The library owns one of the ten extant copies of the third edition of the first German Bible printed in America.

1124
St. Joseph's Seminary
Corrigan Memorial Library
201 Seminary Avenue
Yonkers, New York 10704

Telephone. (914) 968-6200

Institutional Description. The privately supported theological seminary prepares candidates for the Roman Catholic priesthood. The graduate-level seminary operates under the sponsorship and control of the Archdiocese of New York. Enrollment: 99.

Library Administration. Sr. Ellen E. Gaffney, RDC,

Library Director.

Library General Holdings. 103,553 volumes; 426 current periodicals and newspapers; 945 microforms.

Special Collections

The Corrigan Memorial Library maintains special collections in church architecture, sacred music, and liturgy. Among the items in the collection are incunables; Irish imprints (1700-1895); *Acta Sanctorum* (seventeenth century); Recusant literature; decretals and papal bulls (fifteenth to the nineteenth centuries); Bibles (fifteenth to the twentieth centuries); writings on the Oxford Movement; controversial literature of the Catholic Church; and Catholic Americana (eighteenth to nineteenth centuries).

1125
St. Lawrence University
Owen D. Young Library
Park Street
Canton, New York 13617

Telephone. (315) 379-5451

Institutional Description. The privately supported university was nondenominational and coeducational from its founding in 1856. Enrollment: 2,449.

Library Administration. Richard J. Kuhta, University Librarian; Lynn Ekfelt, University Archivist and Curator of Rare Books and Special Collections.

Library General Holdings. 358,329 volumes; 2,445 current periodicals; 18 newspaper subscriptions; 255,058 microforms; 174,000 government documents. The *Guide to Historical Resources in St. Lawrence County New York Repositories* (New York: Cornell University Libraries, 1987) gives current information on the manuscript holdings of the Special Collections room.

Special Collections

In addition to the manuscripts (family papers, correspondence, etc.) listed in the Cornell University publication cited above, the library houses collections of the first editions of Irving Bacheller, Marietta Holley, Nathaniel Hawthorne, Edwin Arlington Robinson, and Frederic Remington as well as critical material on these authors. Also housed separately are collections on the history of the Adironondack region, of the history of the North Country, of North Country imprints, and of Adirondack fiction.

University Archives. Includes papers and documents relating to the history of the University. In addition, the papers of graduate Owen D. Young (1874-1962, Class of 1894) are maintained as well as those of Henry Reiff who was instrumental in the founding of the United Nations and the writing of the International Law of the Sea.

1126
St. Vladimir's Orthodox Theological Seminary
Fr. Georges Florovsky Library
575 Scarsdale Road
Crestwood, New York 10707

Telephone. (914) 961-8313

Institutional Description. The privately supported seminary prepares candidates for the priesthood in the Orthodox Church, for missionary work, teaching, and other forms of service in the church. This graduate-level institute was founded in 1938 by the Russian Orthodox Greek Catholic Church of North America. Enrollment: 80.

Library Administration. V. Rev. Paul N. Taraza, Acting Librarian; Eleana Silk, Assistant to the Librarian for Circulation; Michael Sochka, Assistant to the Librarian for Cataloging.

Library General Holdings. 55,000 volumes; 330 journal and serial subscriptions; 400 volumes of dissertations; 600 sound recordings; 1,290 titles on microfilm/microfiche.

Special Collections

The Florovsky Library collection is especially strong in the areas of Orthodox history, theology, philosophy, and culture. Through the acquisition of Archimandrite Anthony Repella's library in 1956, Metropolitan Makary's in 1957, and Fr. Florovsky's in 1979, the collection is unique in the field of Russian theological literature. Acquisition of the Kolchin collection of Russian liturgical music in 1973 and copies of the Ladd Johnson collection of sound recordings in 1979 has bolstered the Seminary's holdings in these areas.

1127
Sarah Lawrence College
Esther Raushenbush Library
1 Meadway Road
Bronxville, New York 10708

Telephone. (914) 337-0700

Institutional Description. The privately supported liberal arts college was founded in 1926 as a college for women. It became coeducational in 1968. It grants the baccalaureate and master's degrees. Enrollment: 1,083.

Library Administration. Rose Anne Burstein, Librarian.

Library General Holdings. 194,000 volumes; 939 current periodicals; 75,000 government documents; 90,000 audiovisual materials.

Special Collections

Special subject collections of the library include the **Genevieve Taggard Emily Dickinson Collection,** the Bessie **Schonberg Dance Collection,** and the **John W. Nields Law Collections.**

Music Library. 3,500 books and a collection of 7,250 pieces of music for piano, voice, and stringed instruments, as well as opera, choral, and orchestral scores. The collection of music records numbers over 15,000.

Slide Library. Located in the Performing Arts Center, this collection has approximately 62,000 slides on world art, decorative art, and architecture.

1128
Skidmore College
Lucy Scribner Library
Saratoga Springs, New York 12866

Telephone. (518) 584-5000

Institutional Description. The privately supported liberal arts college was founded in 1903. It grants baccalaureate degrees. Enrollment: 2,180.

Library Administration. David H. Eyman, Head Librarian.

Library General Holdings. 300,000 volumes; 1,500 journal and periodical subscriptions.

Special Collections

Special collections of the Scribner Library include the **Frances Steloff Collection** of autographed first editions named for the founder of the famous Gotham Book Mart in New York City; and the **Edna St. Vincent Millay Collection.** The library also houses a collection of more than 6,000 phonograph records and cassettes, approximately 60,000 slides in the area of art and art history, and a growing collection of videotapes.

1129
State University of New York at Albany
University Libraries
1400 Washington Avenue
Albany, New York 12054

Telephone. (518) 442-3542

Institutional Description. The publicly supported state university was founded in 1844, and is the oldest of the four university centers of the state system. Enrollment: 16,112.

Library Administration. Joseph Nitecki, University Librarian; Don C. Kemer, Head, Special Collections and Archives; Mary Osielski, Rare Books Librarian.

Library General Holdings. 1,150,000 volumes; 2,850,000 microforms.

Special Collections

German Intellectual Emigré Collection. Papers and other materials pertaining to émigré writers, social scientists, and artists who left Nazi-dominated Europe in the 1930s and 1940s.

Archives of Public Affairs and Policy. Papers and records pertaining to New York State politics and policy issues, especially since 1950.

University Archives. Records of the University and its predecessor institutions since 1844.

Rare Book Collections

Rare Book Collection. Includes Pre-1800 European imprints; the Elsevier Imprint Collection (seventeenth-century Dutch); nineteenth-century English illustrated books; Historical Children's Literature Collection (chiefly 1855-1950 American series); Kosover Collection (sixteenth- to nineteenth-century Judaica); twentieth-century social and economic movements (pamphlets); business ephemera including nineteenth- and twentieth-century trade catalogs and other materials on American business and industry.

1130
State University of New York at Binghamton
Glenn G. Bartle Library
Vestal Parkway East
Binghamton, New York 13901

Telephone. (607) 777-4841

Institutional Description. This is a publicly supported state university. Enrollment: 12,306.

Library Administration. Albert A. Dekin, Jr., Acting University Librarian; Marion Hanscom, Assistant Director for Special Collections and Fine Arts.

Library General Holdings. 1,282,663 volumes; 12,041 journal and serial subscriptions; 848,242 microforms; 75,500 sound recordings; 6,500 exhibition catalogs; 125 films; 101,443 maps; 331,572 documents.

Special Collections

Holocaust Collection. Consists of 450 volumes, both fiction and nonfiction titles, dealing with the Nazi destruction of six million Jews. The collection was a gift of the Margolis family in memory of Belle Margolis and of her 32 relatives who died in the Holocaust.

William J. Haggerty Collection of French Colonial History. Formerly the library of the Central Committee for France overseas, known in France as *La Bibliothèque du comité Central Francais pour l'Outre Mer,* containing approximately 12,250 volumes and pamphlets and 135 periodical titles. Subject areas include colonial history and biography, law and politics, education, race relations, tropical medicine, health and nutrition in addition to other Africana and Asia materials.

Rare Book Collections

Max Reinhardt Archive. Contains over 250,000 papers, personal letters, documents, and original prompt books; a photograph and negative collection in excess of 14,000 items; extensive material on scene design; and Max Reinhardt's personal library.

Frances R. Conole Archive of Recorded Sound. A large and extensive disc and tape collection devoted to preservation of twentieth century vocal art as recorded over the last ninety years. More than 3,000 singers are represented in the holdings along with 4,000 complete performances of over 400 operas.

Film Collection. A small but important collection of creative film-making containing study prints of classic films and examples of American independent avant-garde films.

A small rare book collection is maintained and is composed of early European, English and American imprints, some fifteenth-century incunabula, limited editions, and examples of fine printing. University archives and Broome County, New York and surrounding area resources are also included. Among the notable manuscript collections are the papers of Padraic and Mary Colum, Mary Lavin, and the papers of three local luminaries: Edwin A. Link (1904-1981), inventor, industrialist, pioneer in the fields of aviation simulation, underwater archaeology, and ocean engineering; Lamont Montgomery Bowers (1847-1941) manufacturer and business man who achieved national importance through his association with Rockefeller corporate interests; David Bernstein (1915-1974) journalist, editor publisher, civic leader.

1131
State University of New York at Buffalo University Libraries 3435 Main Street Buffalo, New York 14214

Telephone. (716) 636-2820

Institutional Description. The publicly supported university is the largest single unit and most comprehensive graduate center of the State University. It was founded in 1846 as the University of Buffalo. Enrollment: 23,977.

Library Administration. Barbara von Wahlde, Director.

Library General Holdings. 2,250,000 volumes; 22,660 serials; 13,000 periodicals. The University Libraries system is among the leading research libraries in North America. The major units are: Architecture and Environmental Design Library; Chemistry Library; Health Sciences Library, Law Library, Lockwood Memorial Library, the Music Library, the Science and Engineering Library, and the Oscar A. Silverman Undergraduate Library.

Special Collections

Important special collections include the **Courier Express Collection,** the **Lois Lenski Collection,** and the **Selig-Adler Jewish Archives of Greater Buffalo.**

Rare Book Collections

The Health Sciences Library houses a collection of rare materials in the **History of Medicine Collection.**

1132
State University of New York at Stony Brook Frank Melville, Jr. Memorial Library Stony Brook, New York 11794

Telephone. (516) 689-6000

Institutional Description. The publicly supported liberal arts and engineering branch of the State University of New York grants baccalaureate, professional, master's, and doctorate degrees. Enrollment: 14,527.

Library Administration. John Brewster Smith, Director of Libraries.

Library General Holdings. 1,522,368 volumes; 19,117 periodicals; 2,049,066 microforms; 17,922 audiovisual materials.

Special Collections

The Melville Library's collections serve the social sciences, fine arts, music, and humanities. These collections are strong in English, Western European, and Latin literature, as well as in modern Western history and Latin American history. Special collections of the Melville Library include the **William Butler Yeats Archives,** the **Institute for Advanced Studies of World Religions,** particularly Asian systems; the **Senator Jacob K. Javits Collection** of private papers and memorabilia, 200 million items establishing one of the nation's leading archives of twentieth-century congressional papers.

1133
State University of New York College at Brockport Drake Memorial Library Brockport, New York 14420

Telephone. (716) 395-2140

Institutional Description. The publicly supported college was established by the Baptist Church in 1836 as an institute to train teachers and ministers. In 1866 title to the college passed to the state and it became Brockport State Normal School. Enrollment: 7,724.

Library Administration. Mrs. Raj Madan, Librarian; Virginia A. Papandrea, Special Collections Librarian; Judith Bloch, Rare Books Librarian; Judith Jennejahn, Head of Acquisitions.

Library General Holdings. 380,000 volumes; 82,000 journals; 1,600,000 microtexts; 37,605 media items; 1,985 journal subscriptions.

Special Collections

Special Materials Collection. Contains 37,605 items including textbooks, children's literature, curricular materials, printed resources used in teaching, standardized tests, and audiovisual materials (slides, filmstrips, audio cassettes, phonograph records, transparencies, video tapes, film loops, models, games and kits).

Rare Book Collections

Archives Collection. Contains various official publications of the College at Brockport from its beginnings as a Baptist village Academy in the 1830s to the present; materials include bulletins, yearbooks, newsletters, as well as copies of masters' theses by Brockport students.

Local History Collection. Includes materials on western Monroe, Orleans, and Genesee Counties, including the towns of Ogden, Sweden, Hamlin, Clarkson, Gates-Chili, Parma, and Wheatland.

Edwards Collection. Contains materials printed in the United States before 1866 and elsewhere before 1801; no subject restrictions.

Mary Jane Holmes Collection, 1928-1907. Contains her novels, miscellaneous uncataloged items, and personal effects.

D.S. Morgan Papers. 1950-; records of the company which manufactured agricultural implements; includes photographs, drawings, patents, business records, legal documents.

John Sutphin Collection of Civil War Papers. Records of Company H, 3rd New York Calvary Regiment.

William H. Heyen Collection. Contains contemporary American poetry material in book, broadside, Christmas card, and correspondence form; also included are Heyne's own manuscripts and collection of magazines and books in which his work has appeared. Dr. Heyen is a noted poet and professor of English at SUNY College at Brockport and has been an avid bibliophile for many years.

1134
State University of New York College at Buffalo
E.H. Butler Library
1300 Elmwood Avenue
Buffalo, New York 14222

Telephone. (716) 878-6304

Institutional Description. This publicly supported undergraduate college grants the baccalaureate degree. Enrollment: 12,011.

Library Administration. G. Charles Newman, Librarian; Sr. Martin Joseph Jones, Archives/Special Collections Librarian.

Library General Holdings. 428,378 volumes; 2,206 current periodical and newspaper subscriptions; 89,837 bound periodical volumes; 5,491 microfilm reels; 460,887 microfiche and ultrafiche; 105,041 microcards;

Special Collections

Lois Lenski Collection. Consists of 241 titles, first edition and autographed; some in various languages; also 310 original illustrations representing 44 titles; original manuscripts, notes, research, dummies, photos, etc. representing 36 titles; articles by and about the author.

Hertha Ganey Children's Books Collection. Approximately 500 titles of classics in children's literature with special emphasis on historical development of such books.

Kempke/Root Collection. Covers early textbooks of most fields including readers, mathematics, history, geography, civics, and spellers.

Paul G. Reilly Seneca Indians Land Claims. Xerox copies of all treaties/agreements between Iroquois/Seneca Nations and early colonists, later the states, then the national government. Items date from the mid-1600s to mid-1800s.

The Buffalo Courier Express Library. Contains approximately one million clips and one hundred thousand photographs arranged and filed by subject and person. The newspaper, dating from 1840-1982 is on microfilm, but the clippings and photographs include dates 1950-1982, important years of change and redevelopment on the Niagara Frontier.

Creative Studies Foundation Collection. Over 3,000 items, most of which are monographs; the most comprehensive collection in this field in the world; content deals with creativity as an aspect of psychology and its application in various problem-solving techniques, education, management, the arts, and technology. Also includes collected research (especially on gifted) of John Curtis Gowen, 1950s-1970s.

1135
State University of New York College at Cortland
College Memorial Library
Graham Avenue
Cortland, New York 13045

Telephone. (607) 753-2001

Institutional Description. The publicly supported college of liberal arts and teacher education was founded in 1868. Enrollment: 6,702.

Library Administration. Bonn I. Thomas, Librarian.

Library General Holdings. 250,000 volumes; 1,300 periodicals.

Special Collections

Teaching Materials Center. Houses more than 23,000 items including textbooks, educational kits, curriculum guides, picture files, slides, records, and the complete indexing services of the Educational Resources Information Center (ERIC). The Center's materials represent those that are useful in grades from kindergarten through 12. The Center also houses a collection of children's literature.

1136
State University of New York College at Fredonia
Reed Library
Fredonia, New York 14063

Telephone. (716) 673-3111

Institutional Description. The publicly supported college of the State University of New York was founded in 1826 and has continued, throughout its existence, the preparation of elementary and music teachers. Enrollment: 4,926.

Library Administration. John P. Saulitis, Director.

Library General Holdings. 361,000 volumes; 2,100 serial titles; 800,000 microforms; 14,000 microfilm reels.

Special Collections

The library maintains several special collections to aid faculty and student research. The **Local History Collection** contains materials pertaining to Chautauqua and Cattaraugus Counties; the **Stefan Zweig Collection** of print and manuscript materials; and the **Archives** which includes materials relating to the history of the college. The music collection contains over 14,000 recordings and more than 29,300 scores.

1137
State University of New York College at Geneseo
Milne Library
Geneseo, New York 14454

Telephone. (716) 245-5210

Institutional Description. The publicly supported college of arts and sciences was founded in 1871. It joined the State University of New York in 1948. Enrollment: 5,333.

Library Administration. Richard C. Quick, Director of Libraries.

Library General Holdings. 380,000 volumes; 2,500 periodical and serial titles; 640,000 government documents; 153,000 microforms.

Special Collections

Milne Library's special collections include the **College Archives,** the **Genesee Valley Historical Collection,** the **Wadsworth Family Papers** (1790-1950); and various compilations, such as the distinguished **Aldous Huxley Collection** and the **Carl F. Schmidt Collection** in historical architecture. The library also houses a collection of nineteenth- and twentieth-century juvenile and young adult books and a collection of rare books.

1138
State University of New York College at New Paltz
Sojourner Truth Library
New Paltz, New York 12561

Telephone. (914) 257-2121

Institutional Description. The publicly supported college of liberal arts and sciences was founded in 1828. Enrollment: 7,608.

Library Administration. William E. Connors, Director.

Library General Holdings. 350,000 books; 1,500 periodicals; 250,000 microforms.

Special Collections

The college library is named in honor of Sojourner Truth, an ex-slave from New Paltz whose outstanding speaking ability and militancy on behalf of freedom made her one of the outstanding figures of the Civil War period.

Curriculum Resources Center. Maintains a collection of both print and non-print materials for teaching.

1139
State University of New York College at Oneonta
James M. Milne Library
Oneonta, New York 13820

Telephone. (607) 431-2723

Institutional Description. The publicly supported liberal arts and teachers college was established as a normal school in 1889. Enrollment: 5,610.

Library Administration. Richard D. Johnson, Library Director; Diane A. Clark, Special Collections Librarian.

Library General Holdings. 478,109 volumes; 2,328 current periodicals; 72 current newspaper subscriptions; 498,064 microform units; 32,075 audiovisual units; 70,442 government document items.

Special Collections

Early Textbook and Educational Theory Collections. Primarily nineteenth- and early twentieth-century materials.

Martha C. Chambers Collection. Popular fiction of the nineteenth century and early twentieth century, primarily American romantic fiction, mysteries, and westerns.

Press Collections. Including examples from Mosher Press, Roycroft Press, Folio Society, and contemporary local presses, as well as examples of fine modern press editions from European and American firms.

New York State Collection. Includes materials on local and state history.

New York State Verse Collection. Consists of versifiers from or writing about New York State during the nineteenth and early twentieth centuries.

Archival Collection. Includes committee minutes, student publications, faculty papers, the college yearbook, photographs, scrapbooks, lantern slides, and other memorabilia.

1140
State University of New York College at Oswego
Penfield Library
Oswego, New York 13126

Telephone. (315) 341-3110

Institutional Description. This publicly supported college of arts and sciences was one of the charter members of the State University System in 1948. It had been founded in 1861 as the Oswego Normal School. Enrollment: 8,449.

Library Administration. Judy Wellman/Lois Stolp, Special Collections Librarians.

Library General Holdings. 326,000 volumes; 3,398 periodicals; 874,000 microforms; 59,505 recordings.

Special Collections

College Archives. The College Archives is responsible for the collection, preservation, and housing of the papers, records, photographs, and other significant evidential material of permanent value generated by the College, students, and personnel for the legitimate use and scholarly research of the campus and community.

Local and Regional Historical Collections. Special Collections has the responsibility for the collection, preservation, organization, and use of printed, manuscript, photographic, and oral records pertaining to the history of Oswego and the surrounding region. Within the local community, Special Collections seeks to cooperate with other local agencies and individuals in preservation of local historical source records of significance. Within the context of Penfield Library and the college community, Special Collections assumes the specific responsibility for the collection, preservation, and use of those printed and non-printed materials necessary to student and scholarly inquiry into the history of Oswego and the surrounding region.

Millard Fillmore Papers. Includes the papers of Millard Fillmore, President of the United States from 1851-1853 and a native of central New York.

Oral History Program of Oswego County. Jointly sponsored by the Oswego County Historical Society and the State University of New York College at Oswego. The purpose of the program is the collection and preservation of oral testimony relating to the history of Oswego County. It sponsors periodic training workshops, maintains the tape library, and in specified instances, lends equipment and tapes to groups who undertake their own interviewing projects.

Rare Book Collections

Rare Book Collection. The rare book collection comprises a wide range of printed materials exclusive of those in the local history collection that require special protections and restricted usage due to their inherent uniqueness and irreplaceability as well as extreme fragility or other special value.

1141
State University of New York College at Plattsburgh
Feinberg Library
Plattsburgh, New York 12901

Telephone. (518) 564-2000

Institutional Description. The publicly supported college of arts and science is part of the New York State University System. Enrollment: 6,196.

Library Administration. Robert E. Burton, Director of Libraries.

Library General Holdings. 300,000 volumes; 1,700 periodicals.

Special Collections

The most important special collection of the Feinberg Library is a collection of materials on North Country history.

Rockwell Kent Gallery. The Gallery features a special collection of the artist's original works.

1142
State University of New York College at Potsdam
Frederick W. Crumb Memorial Library
Pierrepont Avenue
Potsdam, New York 13676

Telephone. (315) 267-2000

Institutional Description. The publicly supported college of arts and science was founded in 1816 as the St. Lawrence Academy. In 1942 it became a teachers college; in 1948 it joined the state university system. Enrollment: 4,301.

Library Administration. Germaine C. Linkins, Library Director; Margaret N. Weitzmann, Archives Librarian.

Library General Holdings. 332,000 volumes; 1,584 periodicals; 333,000 microforms.

Special Collections

Curriculum Library. 2,100 guides and syllabi; 6,700 textbooks and teaching materials; 4,673 maps; 1,936 slides; plus films, sound recordings, videocassettes.

Northern New York History Collection. Includes books and documents on the subject of northern New York, the St. Lawrence Valley.

Bertrand Snell Papers. Correspondence, speeches, scrapbooks, etc. 1902-1960 relating to U.S. Congressional legislation and local business.

Potsdam Normal School/SUNY Potsdam Archives. Includes materials dating from 1867.

Crane School of Music Archives. Contains the papers of Julia Crane, founder of the School; papers of Helen Hosmer, Dean and Director of the School, 1930-1966. The Crane Music Library contains 12,100 books on music and music history.

1143
State University of New York College at Purchase
Library
Purchase, New York 10577

Telephone. (914) 253-5085

Institutional Description. The publicly supported college opened on a regular basis in 1971. Enrollment: 3,989.

Library Administration. Robert W. Evans, College Librarian and Special Collections Librarian.

Library General Holdings. 220,000 volumes; 1,500 current periodical subscriptions; 9,000 microfilm reels; 200,000 microfiche; 75,000 U.S. government documents; 70,000 slides; 300 films and videos; 10,000 audio recordings.

Special Collections

Noah Greenberg Collection of the New York Pro Music Antiqua. Contains performance scores and other materials relating to medieval and Renaissance music. The performance scores include complete editions of individual composers' works and national series, as well as manuscript copies of works that have not been published in modern editions. The special strengths of the book collection are books about musical instruments in the Middle Ages and Renaissance books concerning theatrical history, methods and production techniques of those periods.

Gerald D. McDonald Collection of Cinema Materials. Consists of approximately 1,400 books about the film industry in this country and abroad; long runs of major periodicals; files of press releases, reviews, and plot summaries; around 10,000 photographic stills; 300 hand-tinted glass slides of early movies; approximately 4,000 pieces of music, including parts for theater orchestra; and miscellaneous film memorabilia.

Rare Book Collections

Peter Pauper Press Collection. Contains approximately 300 titles; the Library attempts to collect all of the imprints of Peter Pauper Press which is located on the SUNY/Purchase campus.

1144
State University of New York College of Environmental Science and Forestry
F. Franklin Moon Library and Learning Resources Center
Syracuse, New York 13210

Telephone. (315) 470-6716

Institutional Description. The publicly supported primarily upper-division and graduate college was founded in 1911. Enrollment: 1,485.

Library Administration. Donald F. Webster, Librarian; Flora May Nyland, College Archivist.

Library General Holdings. 90,000 items; 900 current journal subscriptions.

Special Collections

The collection of the Moon Library and Learning Resources Center constitutes a specialized information source for the forestry, environmental science, and landscape architecture programs of the college. It has concentrations in such areas as botany and plant pathology, biochemistry, chemical ecology, forest chemistry, polymer chemistry, economics, entomology, environmental studies, landscape architecture, environmental design, management, paper science and engineering, photogrammetry, silviculture, soil science, water resources, world forestry, wildlife biology, wood products engineering, and zoology.

Rare Book Collections

The Moon Library Special Collections is located with the Terence J. Hoverter College Archives in the lower level of F. Franklin Moon Library. Collections include the Thomas M. Cook *History of Papermaking,* featuring hand made paper, watermarks, and books by Dard Hunter; a manuscript collection of American landscape architect Fletcher Steele (1886-1971) including 21 linear feet primarily of photographs of his client's gardens; the photo library of the Roosevelt Wildlife Forest Station, a field research program dedicated to the conservationist and 26th President of the United States.

Other collections relating to forestry, forestry education, the geographic regions in New York State, and environmental issues are Empire State Forest Products Association, Great Lakes-St. Lawrence Winter Navigation Season Extension Project, National Resources Council of Onondaga County, New York Forest Owners Association, Inc., New York State Forestry and Park Association, Society of American Foresters—New York Section, and Water Resources Council.

1145
State University of New York College of Optometry
Harold Kohn Vision Science Library
100 East 24th Street
New York, New York 10010

Telephone. (212) 420-5085

Institutional Description. The publicly supported professional college was founded in 1971. Enrollment: 250.

Library Administration. Margaret S. Lewis, Librarian and Special Collections Librarian.

Library General Holdings. 28,000 volumes; 539 current periodical subscriptions; 1,800 audio tapes; 300 slide programs; 150 video programs; 100 computer programs; CD-ROM searching on ERIC and MEDLINE available.

Special Collections

The primary focus of the library is on all aspects of vision. This includes the optics of vision, the physiology of vision, and all medical and optometric aspects of the subject. There is also a collection on learning disabilities and aging as they relate to visual problems.

1146
State University of New York College of Technology
Library
811 Court Street
P.O. Box 3050
Utica, New York 13504

Telephone. (315) 792-3450

Institutional Description. The publicly supported technological college was founded in 1966. It is a branch of the State university of New York, granting baccalaureate and master's degrees. Enrollment: 2,471.

Library Administration. Bruce I. Keeney, Director, Library and Learning Resources.

Library General Holdings. 135,000 volumes; 2,100 journal titles and backfiles on 9,000 titles; 384,000 microforms; 50,000 government documents.

Special Collections

Specialized collections of the library include the Educational Resources Information Center microfiche collection, robomatrix literature, Fortune 500 annual reports, and the Library of American Civilization (19,000 titles in a microbook collection).

1147
State University of New York Health Science Center at Syracuse
Library
750 East Adams Street
Syracuse, New York 13210

Telephone. (315) 473-5540

Institutional Description. The publicly supported Health Science Center of the State University of New York is composed of the College of Medicine, the College of Graduate Studies, and the College of Health-Related Professions. It grants associate, baccalaureate, professional, master's, and doctorate degrees. Enrollment: 926.

Library Administration. Evelyn L. Hoey, Director.

Library General Holdings. 147,000 volumes; 1,615 current periodical titles.

Rare Book Collections

The library maintains a collection of 2,200 rare books including the library of the Geneva Medical College, early American medical imprints, and an archival collection containing numerous artifacts pertaining to the history of the Medical Center and of medicine in Syracuse.

1148
State University of New York Health Sciences Center at Brooklyn
Medical Research Library of Brooklyn
450 Clarkson Avenue
Brooklyn, New York 11203

Telephone. (718) 270-1000

Institutional Description. The publicly supported health science center is a member of the State University of New York. It was founded in 1860 and is composed of the Colleges of Health Related Professions, Medicine, Nursing, School of Graduate Studies, and the State University Hospital. Enrollment: 1,404.

Library Administration. Kenneth E. Moody, Director of Libraries.

Library General Holdings. 253,000 volumes; 1,420 current periodical titles. The collections of the Academy of Medicine of Brooklyn and the SUNY Health Science Center are combined.

Special Collections

The most significant special collections include the **Gamble-Curran Medical History Collection** and the **Brooklyn Medical Archives.**

1149
State University of New York Maritime College
Stephen B. Luce Library
Fort Schuyler
Bronx, New York 10465

Telephone. (212) 409-7200

Institutional Description. The publicly supported maritime college was founded in 1874. It is now a member of the State University of New York, and prepares students for the civilian license as an officer for the United States Merchant Marine. Baccalaureate degrees are awarded in engineering, science, computer science, or business. Enrollment: 881.

Library Administration. Richard H. Corson, Librarian.

Library General Holdings. 72,000 volumes; 545 current periodical titles; 30,000 microforms.

Special Collections

Special collections of the Luce Library include **Maritime History,** a collection of texts on nautical education and historical treatises on marine engineering, marine transportation, maritime labor, the merchant marine, and naval architecture. The **Robert W. Gove Collection of Professional Literature** is a circulating collection of books designed to stimulate a love of the sea and foster a better understanding of the seagoing profession and life at sea.

Archival collections include the **College Archives** which include institutional records, and publications, historical materials on Fort Schuyler, a photo collection, and papers of notable alumni. The **Marine Society of New York Archives** include journals of proceedings, minutes of the Standing Committee, treasurer's account, minutes of the annual meetings, and other documents dating from 1769 to 1967. **The Sailor's Snug Harbor Archives** include institutional records for the period 1797-1972. The **Archives of the Sandy Hook Pilot Association** include pilotage books, day books, and logs for the period 1855-1964.

1150
Syracuse University
Syracuse University Library
222 Waverly Avenue
Syracuse, New York 13244

Telephone. (315) 423-2574

Institutional Description. The privately supported university was founded in 1870 by the Methodist Episcopal Church with financial help from the city of Syracuse. Enrollment: 21,120.

Library Administration. David H. Stam, University Librarian; Amy S. Doherty, Acting Head and University Archivist; Mark F. Wimer, Rare Books Librarian; Carolyn A. Davis, Manuscript Librarian; Jeffrey Horrell, Assistant University Librarian for Planning.

Library General Holdings. 2,217,231 bound volumes; 22,299 current periodicals; 3,146,128 microforms; 251,891 slides; 140,289 maps; 314,229 phonograph records.

Special Collections

George Arents Research Library for Special Collections. Consists of materials related to New York history, art history, history of the book, public communications, Methodist history of central New York, American history, adult and continuing education, science fiction, American literature, mass communications, and business history. Included among the manuscript collections are the papers of photojournalist Margaret Bourke-White, journalist Dorothy Thompson, pediatrician and civil activist Benjamin Spock, science fiction writer and editor Hugo Gernsback, and sculptors Anna Hyatt Huntington and James Earle Fraser.

Syracuse University Archives. Includes papers of many prominent faculty members and administrators as well as the records of University offices, departments, schools, colleges, buildings, and people and events.

Rare Book Collections

Rare Book Division. Includes general runs of fifteenth-, sixteenth-, seventeenth-, and eighteenth-century imprints; early American imprints; collections of finely printed and privately printed books; finely illustrated books; fine bindings; and strong nineteenth- and twentieth-century literary collections. Areas of strength include the Leopold Von Ranke Library, the Stephen Crane Collection, the Kipling Collection, the William Hobart Royce Balzac Collection, the Oneida Community Collection, the L. Frank Baum Collection, and the Albert Schweitzer Collection.

1151
Teachers College of Columbia University
Milbank Memorial Library
525 West 120th Street
New York, New York 10027

Telephone. (212) 678-3000

Institutional Description. The privately supported graduate school of education was founded in 1887. It became affiliated with Columbia University in 1898. Enrollment: 4,069.

Library Administration. Jane P. Franck, Director.

Library General Holdings. 405,000 volumes; 1,550 current periodicals; 255,000 microforms; 9,100 audiovisual materials. The Milbank Library contains the largest and richest collection of education materials in the world. It consists of original documents; historical and contemporary textbooks; early catalogs and histories of academies, schools, and colleges; administrative reports of school systems; surveys; and curriculum guides. The collection is comprehensive in American elementary and secondary education.

Special Collections

The Milbank Library houses a number of collections of both contemporary and historical children's literature: a representative collection of twentieth-century fiction and nonfiction for children; the **Harvey Darton Collection,** one of the finest collections of British juveniles published prior to 1850; the **"W" Collection** of eighteenth- and nineteenth-century children's books; and the **Annie E. Moore Collection** showing the development of children's book illustration from the middle of the eighteenth century.

Rare Book Collections

Rare book holdings include important collections of works on education dating from the fifteenth to nineteenth centuries; American textbooks published before 1900; international, elementary, and secondary-level textbooks; and early children's books. The **Adelaide Nutting Historical Nursing Collection** contains books, pamphlets, manuscripts, and other materials on the history of nursing. Personal letters and works of Florence Nightingale and a group of French manuscripts and documents relating to hospitals are included.

The manuscript and archival collections cover a wide range of educational topics and include personal papers as well as the records of such major organizations as the National Council for Social Studies, the Board of Education of the City of New York, and the National Kindergarten Association. The voluminous archives of the Department of Nursing Education constitute the nation's most valuable single collection of primary source materials dealing with the development of nursing education in the United States.

1152
Touro College
Touro College Library
30 West 44th Street
New York, New York 10036

Telephone. (212) 575-0190

Institutional Description. The privately supported liberal arts and science college grants associate, baccalaureate, professional, and master's degrees. It has a branch campus in Huntington, Long Island. Enrollment: 4,901.

Library Administration. Max Celnik, Director of Libraries.

Library General Holdings. 140,000 volumes; 750 journal subscriptions.

Special Collections

Touro College was established to imbue in the lives of contemporary students a sense of meaning and purpose based on the Maimonidean ideal of intellectual and moral synthesis in an atomosphere conducive to the transmission of the values of the Jewish heritage and Western culture. The collection of the library supports these ideals and values with an emphasis in the collection on Jewish studies and well-balanced resources relating to the other academic disciplines pursued by the student body.

1153
Ulster County Community College
MacDonald DeWitt Library
Stone Ridge, New York 12484

Telephone. (914) 687-7621

Institutional Description. The publicly supported two-year college was founded in 1962, and is sponsored by the County of Ulster. Enrollment: 3,012.

Library Administration. David Oettinger, Director of Library Services; Patricia Carroll, Special Collections/Local History Librarian.

Library General Holdings. 71,400 volumes; 519 periodical titles; 104 titles on microfilm; 6,270 bound periodical volumes; 7,220 microforms; 2,480 audio disks and cassettes.

Special Collections

Local History Collection. Consists of material pertaining to Ulster County and nearby areas of the Hudson Valley in the state of New York; includes various books and journals from the nineteenth century relating to the areas.

1154
Union College
Schaffer Library
Union Street
Schenectady, New York 12308

Telephone. (518) 370-6000

Institutional Description. The privately supported liberal arts college was founded in 1795 and maintains a branch campus in Poughkeepsie. It grants baccalaureate, master's, and doctorate degrees. Enrollment: 3,124.

Library Administration. Ann M. Seemann, Director.

Library General Holdings. 457,000 volumes; 2,130 current periodical subscriptions; 243,000 microforms.

Special Collections

Within the library are several of Union College's most prized possessions, including an "elephant folio" edition of Audubon's *Birds of America,* which the College purchased directly from the artist; the original Ramée drawing for the campus; the Trianon editions of William Blake's works; the first books bought for the library in 1795; and the original College charter. The library also maintains the a collection of materials on American history.

1155
Union Theological Seminary
Burke Library
3041 Broadway
New York, New York 10027

Telephone. (212) 662-7100

Institutional Description. The privately supported theological seminary prepares students for every type of Christian ministry. Offering graduate programs only, it has a reciprocal arrangement with Columbia University, granting master's and doctorate degrees in religion. Enrollment: 392.

Library Administration. Richard Dwight Spoor, Director.

Library General Holdings. 600,000 items. The Burke Library is a major national and international resource for theological study and research.

Special Collections

Archives. Includes the historical records of Union Theological Seminary and Auburn Theological Seminary, and the papers of many organizations, scholars, pastors, laypersons, and others connected with the church.

Auburn Collection. Includes some 12,000 volumes acquired from Auburn Theological Seminary in 1939.

Bonhoeffer Collection. A distinguished collection of primary and secondary source materials, including dissertations and papers related to the life, thought, and works of Dietrich Bonhoeffer.

Missionary Research Collection. Consists of tens of thousands of books, pamphlets, periodicals, reports, minutes, and archival materials originally collected by a group of American Protestant mission boards and now continued by the Burke Library. The collection constitutes an invaluable record of the Protestant missionary enterprise throughout the world and provides an array of materials related to the geographic, sociopolitical, religious, and cultural settings in which it occurred. Following its establishment at Union in 1929, the collection was merged with the Library's Charles Cuthbert Hall Collection.

Religious Education Collection. Consists of books, pamphlets, and curricular materials in the fields of education, psychology, and religion.

Sacred Music Collection. Includes scores, musicological works, theses, and dissertations. A constituent part of this collection is the noteworthy body of 1,500 hymnals originally collected by the Hymn Society of America.

Rare Book Collections

Americana Collection. Consists of a considerable body of early American imprints, ca. 1680-1800, including sermons, essays, histories, biographies, books of poetry, prayer books, and sacred music.

Gillett Collection of American History and Theology. Consists of a large body of original pamphlets, tracts, sermons, general and local histories, and biographies from the period ca. 1750-1850.

McAlpin Collection of British History and Theology. This emminent collection consists of some 18,000 sixteenth- and seventeenth-century imprints, sources critical to an understanding of the political, theological, and ecclesiastical climate of this important period.

Reformation Tracts Collection. This is a significant body of original imprints bearing on Martin Luther and the Protestant Reformation.

Thompson Collection. This collection is rich in Bibles and prayer books; it is particularly valuable for the study of bindings and illustrations in early printed books.

Van Ess Collection. Include some 13,000 pieces, consisting of manuscripts and early printed books, including many incunabula.

Manuscript Collection. Consists of numerous western medieval and renaissance manuscripts, as well as Greek, Hebrew, Arabic, Turkish, Armenian, Ethiopic, and Syriac materials. The collection of Syriac manuscripts is one of the largest to be found in the Western Hemisphere.

1156
United States Merchant Marine Academy
Schuyler Otis Bland Memorial Library
Steamboat Road
Kings Point, New York 11024

Telephone. (516) 773-5864

Institutional Description. The publicly supported technological institution is maintained by the U.S. Department of Transportation, granting the Bachelor of Science Degree and the commission of Ensign in the Naval Reserve. Enrollment: 959.

Library Administration. George J. Billy, Librarian; Esther W. Bovarnick, Reader Services Librarian/Special Collections Librarian; Martin Goldberg, Special Collections Librarian; Stephen Wiist, Rare Books Librarian.

Library General Holdings. 160,000 bound volumes; 1,200 periodical titles (including newspapers); 90,000 microfiche; 4,000 films; 250 audiocassettes; 170 videocassettes; 200 recordings; 300 items of computer software.

Special Collections

Specialized collections within the general stacks of the library include maritime transportation, diesel engineering, nautical science, and sea charts. There is also a collection of documents relating to the nuclear ship *Savannah.*

Rare Book Collections

Maritime History Collection. Along with its modern collection of materials concerning nautical science and marine engineering the Academy Library has a collection of approximately 1,250 rare books devoted to marine topics. The collection contains the early editions of Nathaniel Bowditch's *New American Practical Navigator,* a classic work on navigation, beginning with the first edition of 1802. There is an 1846 edition of a seaman's manual authored by Richard Henry Dana. Other items of interest concern naval history. There is an extensive collection of ships' pictures and newspaper clippings in the Academy's vertical file collection concerning vessels of both sail and steam periods.

1157
United States Military Academy
United States Military Academy Library
Jefferson and Cullum
West Point, New York 10996

Telephone. (914) 938-2230

Institutional Description. The publicly supported, coeducational professional college, established in 1802, is under the general direction of the Department of the Army. Enrollment: 4,487.

Library Administration. Kenneth Hedman, Librarian; Alan C. Aimone, Assistant Librarian for Special Collections; Gladys Calvetti, Rare Books Librarian.

Library General Holdings. 600,000 volumes; 2,223 periodical and newspaper subscriptions; 150,000 government documents; 209,000 microforms; 3,900 linear feet of USMA Archives; 21,000 audiovisual items.

Special Collections

The Academy Library maintains special collections on military art and science, fortifications, West Point history, West Point graduates, nineteenth-century periodicals, military handbooks, and early architectural books. The library also maintains papers of graduates, including the General Omar Bradley Papers.

1158
University of Rochester
Rush Rhees Library
Rochester, New York 14627

Telephone. (716) 275-4461

Institutional Description. The privately supported university consists of eight schools and colleges. It was founded in 1850. Enrollment: 8,762.

Library Administration. James F. Wyatt, University Librarian; Peter Dzwonkoski, Head, Department of Rare Books and Special Collections; Mary M. Huth, Assistant Head, Department of Rare Books and Special Collections.

Library General Holdings. Over 2,000,000 volumes; 12,000 current periodicals; 500,000 volumes of government documents; over 2,000,000 microform items; 35,000 volumes in central reference collection.

Rare Book Collections

The Department of Rare Books and Special Collections of some 75,000 volumes range from incunabula (books printed before 1501) to modern first editions. Within a broad representative collection of British and American literature are strengths in English drama (particularly John Dryden and Samuel Foote), works of selected authors (Robert Southey, Benjamin Disraeli, Alfred Tennyson, Henry James, John Masefield, John Ruskin, Christopher Morley, Sean O'Casey, John Gardner), early American children's books, filmed books, Tauchnitz editions, and the Roycroft Press. Other book collections with significant holdings include the history of law and political theory, seventeenth-century English theology and politics, Leonardo da Vinci, Victorian edition bindings, books illustrated with original photographs, and local history.

The Department houses more than 300 manuscript collections as well as several thousand single manuscript items such as letters, diaries, and account books. Although there are representative examples of medieval, renaissance, and other early manuscripts, the collection's strength is in nineteenth- and twentieth-century material. Included in the literary manuscript collections are local writers Adelaide Crapsey, Hyam Plutzik, and Henry Clune; British authors Robert Southey and Colin Maclnnes; and contemporary writers Frederick Exley, John Gardner, Jerre Mangione, John A. Williams, and Thomas McGuane. Several manuscript collections in nineteenth century British and American theatre include the papers of J.L. Toole, Arthur Wing Pinero, George Alexander, Clement William Scott, Leon Marks Lion, Edwin Booth, and Lillian Russell.

The collection of historical manuscripts is especially strong in nineteenth-century American political figures, particularly William Henry Seward, Thurlow Weed, Susan B. Anthony, and Frederick Douglass. Twentieth-century political history is represented in the papers of Thomas E. Dewey, Kenneth B. Keating, and Marion B. Folsom. The papers of others prominent in industrial history (George Eastman), social sciences (Lewis Henry Morgan, Henry Augustus Ward) and the arts (Claude F. Bragdon) are also in the Department.

The history of Rochester and upstate New York is represented in books, manuscripts, prints, photographs, and maps. The manuscript collections include the papers of individuals and families important in the political, cultural, religious, and business affairs of the area. Many of the collections reflect the reform activities prevalent in upstate New York during the nineteenth century. The papers of Amy and Isaac Post include letters from their associates in the abolition, women's rights, temperance, and spiritualist movements. The Ellwanger and Barry Papers document Rochester's important place in the history of horticulture, while the Michaels Stern Papers are a record of the city's clothing industry. The archives of charitable institutions such as the Rochester Orphan Asylum (now Hillside Children's Center) and the Rochester Home for the Friendless (now the Rochester Friendly Home) are also represented in the collections.

The Department houses the archives of the University of Rochester. These printed and manuscript records include the papers of past University presidents, official and student publications, photographs, architectural drawings, and museum pieces.

1159
Vassar College
Vassar College Library
Poughkeepsie, New York 12601

Telephone. (914) 452-7000

Institutional Description. The privately supported liberal arts college, founded in 1865, was a women's college until it became coeducational in 1968. Enrollment: 2,317.

Library Administration. David L. Paulus, Librarian; Nancy S. MacKechnie, Curator of Rare Books and Manuscripts.

Library General Holdings. 623,978 bound volumes; 3,000 periodicals, serials, and newspapers; 353,760 microforms.

Rare Book Collections

The Special Collections in the Vassar College Library contain an extensive rare book collection with notable examples of incunabula and fine printing; first editions of important English and American literary and historical works; collections of antiquarian household manuals, cookbooks, and etiquette and courtesy books from the seventeenth to the twentieth centuries; the Latin and German editions of Hartman Schedel's *Weltchrnik;* and the double elephant folio edition of Audubon's *Birds of America.* Other significant book collections include children's literature from the eighteenth to the twentieth centuries; rare atlases and maps; books and periodicals by and about Robert Owen; and Village Press books and ephemera.

Among the notable manuscript collections are the papers of Mary McCarthy, Elizabeth Bishop, Ruth Benedict, Maria Mitchell, Hallie Flanagan Davis, and Lucy Maynard Salmon; as well as materials on women's history and the suffrage movement. Special Collections is also the repository for the journals of John Burroughs and the Jean Webster McKinney Family Papers which include a collection of manuscripts and letters of Samuel Clemens, Mrs. McKinney's great-uncle. The Vassariana Collection includes various materials relating to the history and development of Vassar College.

1160
Villa Maria College of Buffalo
Library
240 Pine Ridge Road
Buffalo, New York 14225

Telephone. (716) 896-0700

Institutional Description. The two-year college was founded by the Congregation of Sisters of St. Felix (Felician Sisters) as a training center for its Sisters in the field of education as an affiliate of Catholic University of America. Admission was extended to lay women in 1965 and it became coeducational in 1968. Enrollment: 601.

Library Administration. Sister Mary Terenita Dobrzynski, Director of Library Services.

Library General Holdings. 56,000 volumes; 296 periodical titles; 16 newspaper subscriptions.

Special Collections

The library maintains the **Polish Collection** and a **Children's Literature Collection.**

1161
Wadhams Hall Seminary-College
Library
RD 4
Riverside Drive
Ogdensburg, New York 13669

Telephone. (315) 393-4231

Institutional Description. The privately supported seminary/college was founded in 1924. It prepares men for graduate studies leading to the Roman Catholic priesthood, granting baccalaureate degrees. Enrollment: 50.

Library Administration. Rev. Richard S. Sturtz, Head Librarian.

Library General Holdings. 97,582 volumes.

Special Collections

The library has particular strength in its works on Scripture and its material in the fields of philosophy, Greek and Latin classics, French literature, and the fine arts. It has the entire 382-volume microcard set of Greek and Latin Church Fathers edited by Jacque Migne.

Rare Book Collections

A rare book collection includes special editions of the works of Augustine and Aquinas.

1162
Wagner College
August Horrmann Library
631 Howard Avenue
Staten Island, New York 10301

Telephone. (718) 390-3100

Institutional Description. The privately supported liberal arts college, founded in 1883, is affiliated with the Lutheran Church in America. Enrollment: 2,927.

Library Administration. Y. John Auh, Director.

Library General Holdings. 275,000 bound volumes; 1,000 periodical titles.

Special Collections

Edwin Markham Collection. Named for the American poet, the collection consists of 10,000 volumes and 25,000 items. It reflects not only Markham's interest in poetry, other literature, religion, and social issues, but also the character of the literature of the period.

Rare Book Collections

Thomas Harris Collection. Consists of 1,000 volumes including many rare books, from the library of the American man of letters.

1163
Webb Institute of Naval Architecture
Livingston Library
Crescent Beach Road
Glen Cove, New York 11542

Telephone. (516) 671-2213

Institutional Description. The privately supported technological college, established in 1889, is the oldest school of its kind in the nation. The Bachelor of Science in Naval Architecture and in Marine Engineering are granted. Enrollment: 87.

Library Administration. David J. Zaehringer, Librarian.

Library General Holdings. 42,000 volumes; 195 current periodical subscriptions.

Special Collections

Special collections include a substantial selection of books in marine history and rare or unusual works on naval architecture and marine engineering, naval and shipbuilding history.

1164
Wells College
Louis Jefferson Long Library
Aurora, New York 13026

Telephone. (315) 364-3360

Institutional Description. The privately supported liberal arts college for women was founded in 1868. It grants baccalaureate degrees. Enrollment: 404.

Library Administration. Marina Brown, Librarian for Acquisitions.

Library General Holdings. 201,000 volumes; 640 periodical and newspaper subscriptions.

Special Collections

The Long Library maintains a special collection of memorabilia, documents, and correspondence concerning the early express companies that helped to open the West in the mid-nineteenth century. The founder of the College, Henry Wells, played a major role in these ventures as a pioneer of the Wells Fargo stagecoach lines and the American Express Company. The library also has a collection of the papers of Emily Howland, early feminist and close friend of Susan B. Anthony.

1165
Westchester Community College
Library
75 Grasslands Road
Valhalla, New York 10595

Telephone. (914) 285-6600

Institutional Description. The two-year college was founded in 1946 as the New York State Institute of Applied Arts and Sciences in White Plains, New York. The college is a unit of the State University of New York. Enrollment: 7,493.

Library Administration. John Kager, Dean, Learning Resources.

Library General Holdings. 80,000 volumes; 600 periodical titles.

Special Collections

The library maintains a **College and Career Collection** and a reference collection which contains pamphlets, clippings, corporate reports, and police department reports.

1166
Yeshiva University
University Libraries
500 West 185th Street
New York, New York 10033

Telephone. (212) 960-5400

Institutional Description. The privately supported university, founded in 1886, is one of the nation's oldest and largest universities under Jewish auspices. It has four teaching centers in New York City. Enrollment: 4,245.

Library Administration. Frederic S. Baum, Dean of

University Libraries.

Library General Holdings. 850,000 volumes, periodicals, and other materials in all branches of the arts and sciences and Judaica.

Special Collections

The **Mendel Gottesman Library of Hebraica-Judaica,** the **Strauss Collection of Hebraica;** the archives of the Central Relief Committee and the Vaad Hatzalah; and the rare book and manuscript room constitute the special collections housed in the Mendel Gottesman Library at Yeshiva University.

1167
York College of the City University of New York
Library
94-20 Guy R. Brewer Boulevard
Jamaica, New York 11451

Telephone. (718) 262-2000

Institutional Description. The publicly supported liberal arts and teachers college of the City University of New York, founded in 1967, offers baccalaureate degrees. Enrollment: 4,267.

Library Administration. Gladys W. Jarrett, Chief Librarian.

Library General Holdings. 170,000 volumes; 1,362 periodical titles; 25,280 equivalent volumes in microforms; 8,900 volumes of government documents.

Special Collections

Special collections in the library include the **Human Relations Area File** (HRAF); the Library of American Civilization; a scholarly collection of Hebrew and Yiddish works in religion and literature; Discussion Papers of the Institute for Research on Poverty; American Federation of Labor Records; the **John L. Lewis Papers;** the **Morris Hilquit Papers;** the **Papers of the NAACP;** and the **United Negro College Fund Archives.**

North Carolina

1168
Appalachian State University
Carol Grotnes Belk Library
Boone, North Carolina 28608

Telephone. (704) 262-2000

Institutional Description. Appalachian State University was established as Watauga Academy in 1899. Enrollment: 10,419.

Library Administration. Richard I. Barker, University Librarian.

Library General Holdings. 448,000 volumes; 3,920 current periodicals; 208,000 government documents; 511,000 microforms; 15,000 audiovisual materials.

Special Collections

W.L. Eury Appalachian Regional Collection. Contains books, pictures, and artifacts primarily concerned with the Appalachian region.

Justice-Query Instructional Materials Center. Houses the Curriculum Library, the Young People's Collection, the Film Library, and the Microforms Collection.

1169
Atlantic Christian College
Willis N. Hackney Library
West Lee Street
Wilson, North Carolina 27983

Telephone. (919) 237-3161

Institutional Description. Atlantic Christian College is a private college affiliated with the Christian Church (Disciples of Christ). Enrollment: 1,278.

Library Administration. Jeanette Woodward, Library Director.

Library General Holdings. 100,000 volumes; 600 current periodical subscriptions.

Special Collections

Carolina Discipliana Collection. This collection is housed in the Hardy Center and contains a rich and unique research source pertaining to the Disciples of Christ and related religious movements.

1170
Belmont Abbey College
Abbot Vincent Taylor Library
Belmont, North Carolina 28012

Telephone. (704) 825-3711

Institutional Description. The privately supported liberal arts college was founded in 1876. It is operated by the Roman Catholic Order of St. Benedict, and grants baccalaureate degrees. Enrollment: 1,674.

Library Administration. Marjorie C. McDermott, Director of Learning Resources.

Library General Holdings. 115,000 books, periodicals, and microfilms; 485 periodical subscriptions.

Special Collections

The library maintains the **Benedictine Collection** which includes monastic material and incunabula; a special collection of first editions; and the **Carolina Collection.**

1171
Bennett College
Thomas F. Holgate Library
900 East Washington Street
Greensboro, North Carolina 27420

Telephone. (919) 273-4431

Institutional Description. The privately supported liberal arts college for women was founded in 1873. It is affiliated with the United Methodist Church. Enrollment: 566.

Library Administration. Ednita Bullock, Head Librarian.

Library General Holdings. 83,000 volumes; 400 periodical and newspaper subscriptions.

Special Collections

Included in the library's collection are several special holdings: the **Bennett College Archives** which contains reports, letters, papers, photographs, books, newspaper clippings, scrapbooks, and other memorabilia relating to the history of the College. The **Afro-American Women's**

Collection contains nearly 450 primary and secondary materials by or about the Black woman from the eighteenth century to the present. The **Norris Wright Cuney Collection** contains the personal and business correspondence, diaries, and newspaper clippings of Norris Wright Cuney, a Black Texas Republican who lived during the late 1800s.

Rare Book Collections

The **Rare Book Collection** is a small collection of out-of-print books dating back to the early 1800s.

1172
Campbell University
Carrie Rich Memorial Library
P.O. Box 127
Buie's Creek, North Carolina 27506

Telephone. (919) 893-4111

Institutional Description. The privately supported liberal arts university is affiliated with the Southern Baptist Church. Founded in 1887, it grants associate, baccalaureate, master's, and professional degrees. Enrollment: 2,975.

Library Administration. K. David Weeks, Director of Library Services.

Library General Holdings. 160,500 volumes; 910 current periodical subscriptions; 85,000 government documents; 118,000 microforms.

Special Collections

Special collections include **Berry's Geology Collection;** the Southern Baptist Convention papers; and the papers of James Archibald Campbell, Leslie H. Campbell, and Gilbert Stephenson.

1173
Catawba College
College Library
Salisbury, North Carolina 28144

Telephone. (704) 637-4448

Institutional Description. The privately supported liberal arts college is supported by the United Church of Christ. It was founded in 1851 to educate men for the ministry, but became coeducational in 1890. Enrollment: 840.

Library Administration. Betty Sell, Director of Library Services.

Library General Holdings. 135,874 volumes; 1,073 current periodical subscriptions; 5,707 audiovisual materials; 47,268 microforms; 19,924 government documents.

Special Collections

Evangelical and Reformed/United Church of Christ Archives, Southern Chapter. The archival collection of the Southern Chapter of the Historical Society of the UCC (United Church of Christ, formerly Evangelical and Reformed Church) contains material related chiefly to the German Reformed Church and the Evangelical and Reformed Church of North Carolina. The collection of over 5,000 items consists of books, manuscripts, information about individual churches, periodicals, photographs; and North Carolina Classis, Southern Synod, and Southern Conference minutes.

1174
Central Piedmont Community College
Richard Hagemeyer Learning Resources Center
1201 Elizabeth Avenue
Charlotte, North Carolina 28235

Telephone. (704) 342-6633

Institutional Description. In 1963, the creation of a statewide system of community and technical colleges resulted in the merger of Mecklenburg College and the Central Industrial Education Center to establish Central Piedmont Community College. Enrollment: 12,872.

Library Administration. Susan Melson, Technical Services Librarian.

Library General Holdings. 76,039 volumes; 433 periodical titles; 29,979 microforms.

Special Collections

The library has a special collection of law materials for paralegal students.

1175
Chowan College
Whitaker Library
Murfreesboro, North Carolina 27855

Telephone. (919) 398-4101

Institutional Description. The college was founded in 1848 as a four-year college for women. It became a coeducational institution in 1931 and a junior college in 1937. Enrollment: 954.

Library Administration. Geraldine L. Harris, Head Librarian.

Library General Holdings. 80,000 volumes; 387 periodical titles; 56,000 government documents.

Special Collections

The Antiquities Room of Whitaker Library houses a collection of old and rare books as well as the **Creech Baptist Collection.**

1176
Cleveland Technical College
Learning Resources Center
137 South Post Road
Shelby, North Carolina 28150

Telephone. (704) 484-4000

Institutional Description. Cleveland Technical College is a commuter college offering two-year programs. It was established in 1965. Enrollment: 1,707.

Library Administration. Haley C. Dedmond, Dean of Learning Resources.

Library General Holdings. 31,880 volumes; 205 current periodicals; 4,868 sound recordings.

Special Collections

The library maintains a special collection of 200 volumes on genealogy.

1177
College of the Albemarle
Learning Resources Center
North Road Street
P.O. Box 2327
Elizabeth City, North Carolina 27909

Telephone. (919) 335-0821

Institutional Description. Originally chartered in 1960 as a junior college, College of the Albemarle became the first comprehensive community college in the North Carolina Community College system in 1963. Enrollment: 1,375.

Library Administration. C. Donald Lee, Director.

Library General Holdings. 49,912 volumes; 250 periodicals; 6,000 microfiche; 4,500 audiovisual materials.

Special Collections

A special collection of 500 volumes on North Carolina is maintained by the learning resources center.

1178
Craven Community College
R.C. Godwin Memorial Library
Race Track Road
New Bern, North Carolina 28560

Telephone. (919) 638-4131

Institutional Description. The two-year college began in 1965 as the Craven County Industrial Education Center. The name was changed to Craven County Technical Institute in 1968 and the present name was adopted in 1973. Enrollment: 2,322.

Library Administration. Vance Harper Jones, Director.

Library General Holdings. 25,500 volumes; 296 current periodical titles; 15,875 microforms; 2,682 sound recordings.

Special Collections

The Craven Community College learning resources center maintains a special collection on North Carolina.

1179
Davidson County Community College
Library
P.O. Box 1287
Lexington, North Carolina 27292

Telephone. (704) 249-8186

Institutional Description. The two-year college was chartered in 1958 and was first named Davidson County Industrial Education Center. It became the Davidson County Community College in 1965. Enrollment: 3,623.

Library Administration. Mary A. Hamil, Director of Library Services.

Library General Holdings. 45,354 books; 250 current periodical titles; 11,529 microforms; 1,600 pamphlets; 8,643 sound recordings.

Special Collections

Special collections include over 500 children's books, law, genealogy, and local history. Some of the latter material is housed in the Davidson Room along with some of the books and manuscripts of Richard Walser.

1180
Davidson College
E.H. Little Library
P.O. Box 1837
Davidson, North Carolina 28036

Telephone. (704) 892-2000

Institutional Description. The privately supported liberal arts college was established in 1837 by the Presbyterians of North Carolina. Enrollment: 1,397.

Library Administration. Leland M. Park, Library Director; Chalmers G. Davidson, College Archivist.

Library General Holdings. 340,000 volumes; 1,600 periodical subscriptions; 90 newspaper subscriptions; 200,000 government documents items.

Special Collections

The Davidsoniana Room. Includes books and articles written by Davidson faculty, administration, students, and alumni (e.g., William Styron, Woodrow Wilson); college publications (annuals, newspapers, magazines, announcement sheets, programs); Mecklenburg Declaration of Independence (1775; this event occurred in Mecklenburg County and works about this as well as annual celebrations publications since that time are maintained);

memorabilia connected with the history of the college; first library of the college; Peter Stuart Ney research and publications (legendary Marshal Ney of France).

Rare Book Collections

Old and rare items in the Library's collection include incunabula; Bruce Rogers/printer; William P. Cumming Map Collection; Robert Burns Collection; publications of the fifteenth to nineteenth centuries; and an autograph collection.

1181
Duke University
William R. Perkins Library
Durham, North Carolina 27706

Telephone. (919) 684-2263

Institutional Description. Duke University is a private, independent, nonsectarian institution associated with the United Methodist Church. Enrollment: 15,552.

Library Administration. Jerry Campbell, Librarian; John Sharpe, Rare Books Librarian; Robert Byrd, Manuscripts Librarian.

Library General Holdings. 3,460,000 volumes; 10,000 periodicals; 14,000 serials; 166 newspapers; 7,500,000 manuscripts; 87,000 maps; 39,000 music scores; 1,214,000 rolls or sheets of microtext.

Special Collections

Newspaper Collection. This collection, with nearly 220,500 reels of microfilm, has several long eighteenth-century files, strong holdings of nineteenth-century New England papers, and antebellum and Civil War papers from North Carolina, South Carolina, and Virginia, as well as many European and Latin American papers.

Manuscript Collection. The collection is particularly strong in all phases of the history, politics, and social and economic life of the South Atlantic region and contains approximately 7,500,000 items. It also includes significant papers in English and American literature.

Several treatise collections are housed in the School of Law Library. These include the **George C. Christie Collection** on jurisprudence and the **Floyd S. Riddick Collection** of autographed senatorial material. The foreign law collection is extensive in coverage, with concentrations in European law and business law materials. The international law collection is strong in primary source and treatise material on both private and public international law topics.

University Archives. As the official archival agency of the University, the Archives collects, preserves, and administers the records of the University which have continuing administrative or historical value, including published material, photographs, papers of student groups and faculty, and selected memorabilia.

Rare Book Collections

Rare Books Collection. Contains many scarce and valuable materials covering a broad range of fields, and the Latin and Greek manuscripts constitute one of the outstanding collections of its kind in the United States. The collection of Confederate imprints is the largest in the country.

History of Medicine Collections. These collections are housed in the Medical Center Library, including the **Josiah C. Trent Collection,** and consist of rare books and manuscripts and a supporting group of histories, biographies, bibliographies, pictures, and ephemeral materials. The collections also include the **Duke Authors Collection** which preserves an archival copy of each book published by a member of the Duke medical faculty.

1182
East Carolina University
Joyner Library
Greenville, North Carolina 27858

Telephone. (919) 757-6514

Institutional Description. The publicly supported state university was established as a two-year teachers college in 1907; in 1920 it became a four-year institution offering teacher education; by 1960 it had become the state's third largest educational institution. Enrollment: 13,400.

Library Administration. Ruth Katz, University Librarian; Donald R. Lennon, Special Collections Librarian; Bobbie L. Collins, Reference Librarian.

Library General Holdings. 815,000 volumes; 5,200 serial titles; 1,000,000 microforms; 354,000 international and federal documents. The Music Library, a branch of Joyner Library, contains 45,000 books, scores, periodicals, and sound recordings of musical compositions representative of all types of music.

Special Collections

Curriculum Materials Center. Contains 12,585 items, including textbooks and other teaching materials for grades K-12. The K-6 Collection houses over 15,000 books for young people.

University Archives. Contains more than 2,000 linear feet of records reflecting the development of East Carolina University since its establishment in 1907.

East Carolina Manuscript Collection. Contains approximately 2,800 linear feet of letters, diaries, scrapbooks, photographs, reports, and other unpublished materials concentrated in the history of North Carolina since 1715; military affairs (1776-present); tobacco history (1890s-1960s); and missionary service (1850s-present) in various parts of the world.

Hoover Collection on International Communism. Consists of 500 linear feet of monographs, documentary volumes, journals, newspapers, and pamphlets dealing in some fashion with international Communism.

1183
Elizabeth City State University
G.R. Little Library
Parkview Drive
Elizabeth City, North Carolina 27909

Telephone. (919) 335-3230

Institutional Description. Elizabeth City State University was established in 1891 and offers comprehensive programs in the sciences, humanities, social sciences, business, technology, education, and other areas of study. Enrollment: 1,533.

Library Administration. Claude W. Green, Administrative Librarian.

Library General Holdings. 116,647 volumes.

Special Collections

Curriculum Materials Laboratory. Provides a wide variety of book and non-book instructional materials in the academic areas and at levels ranging from pre-primary through high school.

University Archives. The Archives preserves historical and administrative records of the University.

1184
Elon College
Iris Holt McEwen Library
Haggard Avenue
Elon College, North Carolina 27244

Telephone. (919) 584-2338

Institutional Description. The privately supported liberal arts college was founded in 1889. It is affiliated with the United Church of Christ. Enrollment: 2,672.

Library Administration. Plummer Alston Jones, Jr., Head Librarian.

Library General Holdings. 160,000 volumes; 171,000 microforms.

Special Collections

Special collections of the library include the **Johnson Collection** of North Carolina authors; the **Spence Collection** covering the liberal arts; and the **Church History Collection** which includes the archives of the Southern Conference of the United Church of Christ.

1185
Fayetteville State University
Charles Waddell Chesnutt Library
1200 Murchison Road
Newbold Station
Fayetteville, North Carolina 28301

Telephone. (919) 486-1613

Institutional Description. The publicly supported state university was established as a two-year normal school in 1887 and became a four-year institution in 1969. Enrollment: 2,638.

Library Administration. Richard Griffin, University Librarian; Ellen Anderson-McEachern, Archivist/Special Collections Librarian.

Library General Holdings. 150,000 books; 12,000 bound periodical volumes; 2,000 periodical subscriptions; 11,000 government documents.

Special Collections

The major special collection is one of materials by and about Blacks. It includes biographies, autobiographies, and significant books and other publications by and about Blacks. There are numerous books on politics and politicians, education and educators, slavery, emancipation, and post-slavery and documentation on developments, movements, theories, customs, and practices, and the existing views on these subjects through historical periods. There are also 60 selected titles of journals and newspapers related to Afro-American history dating from 1925.

University Archives. A collection of official records and materials of significant historical value related to Fayetteville State University.

1186
Gardner-Webb College
John R. Dover Memorial Library
Boiling Springs, North Carolina 28017

Telephone. (704) 434-2361

Institutional Description. Gardner-Webb College ia a private college owned by the Baptist State Convention of North Carolina. Enrollment: 1,882.

Library Administration. Thomas Hutchins, Library Director.

Library General Holdings. 300,000 books, bound periodicals, audiovisual materials, phonograph recordings, and microforms.

Special Collections

The special collection holdings include the writings and personal library of the post-Civil War author Thomas R. Dixon; the diaries and scrapbooks of Fay Webb Gardner, wife of O. Max Gardner, former North Carolina governor, advisor to Franklin Delano Roosevelt, and ambassador to the Court of Saint James.

1187
Gaston College
Library
Highway 321 South
Dallas, North Carolina 28034

Telephone. (704) 922-3136

Institutional Description. The two-year college was chartered in 1963 and serves Gaston and Lincoln counties. Enrollment: 3,447.

Library Administration. David L. Hunsucker, Director.

Library General Holdings. 44, 385 volumes; 225 current periodical titles; 9,113 microforms; 3,362 sound recordings.

Special Collections

The library maintains a special collection of U.S. Civil War books.

1188
Greensboro College
James Addison Library
815 West Market Street
Greensboro, North Carolina 27401

Telephone. (919) 272-7102

Institutional Description. The privately supported liberal arts college was founded in 1838. It is affiliated with the United Methodist Church. Enrollment: 533.

Library Administration. Susan McClintock Jones, Director.

Library General Holdings. 81,000 volumes; 400 current periodical titles.

Special Collections

The library has a collection on Methodism in North Carolina and a collection of secondary source materials on Napoleon Bonaparte.

1189
Guilford College
Guilford College Library
5800 West Friendly Avenue
Greensboro, North Carolina 27410

Telephone. (919) 292-5511

Institutional Description. The privately supported liberal arts college was founded in 1837. Dual degree programs are available in selected subjects with Duke University, Bowman Gray School of Medicine, and Georgia Institute of Technology. Enrollment: 1,470.

Library Administration. Herbert L. Poole, College Librarian; Damon D. Hickey, Curator; Carol Treadway, Quaker Bibliographer.

Library General Holdings. 155,000 volumes; 784 periodical subscriptions; 20 newspaper subscriptions; 17,000 microforms; 182 music scores; 948 maps; 2,200 audiovisual materials.

Special Collections

Special collections within the library include works on Quaker history and thought, peace and justice, science fiction, North Caroliniana, and the Civil War.

Rare Book Collections

Friends Historical Collection. Includes records of the Society of Friends (Quakers) in the Carolinas, Georgia, and Tennessee from 1680 to the present; private papers of Quakers and Quaker organizations, primarily in the South; records of New Garden Boarding School and its successor, Guilford College.

1190
Isothermal Community College
Library
P.O. Box 804
Spindale, North Carolina 28160

Telephone. (704) 286-3636

Institutional Description. The publicly supported junior college was founded in 1963. Enrollment: 2,218.

Library Administration. Susan Vaughan, Librarian; Glenna Womick, Library/Special Collections Clerk.

Library General Holdings. 33,496 volumes; 280 periodicals and newspapers; 1,690 microforms; 1,154 graphics; 950 audios; 407 films; 208 videos; 933 other materials.

Special Collections

Old Tryon Historical Collection. Researchers from all over the United States have found this collection to be one of the finest sources in western North Carolina for the study of local, regional, and state history. The collection includes practically every type of publication on the region. Over 1,200 books line the shelves, ranging from fiction by North Carolinians to histories of the state, its counties, and its families; from government manuals to travel guidebooks; from ghost stories to geology. Rare books dating from the 1850s are available for use. There are also state and regional magazines such as the *North Carolina Historical Review, The State,* and *Appalachian Journal.* An extensive file of pamphlets and clippings from local and regional newspapers is an important supplement to the collection.

Microfilm in the collection comprises some 2,000 reels, including census records of the two Carolinas from 1790 to 1910, and county records such as wills, deeds, and court proceedings. Extensive records are available for the counties of Rutherford and Polk, as well as selected records for thirty-six other counties of North Carolina and three in South Carolina. Newspapers of Rutherford and Polk Counties are available on microfilm, dating from 1830. This collection is updated periodically.

In addition to local and regional history, the Collection contains items that document the founding and subsequent growth and development of Isothermal Community College.

1191
John Wesley College
Perry Memorial Library
2314 North Centennial Street
High Point, North Carolina 27260

Telephone. (919) 889-2262

Institutional Description. The privately supported, independent, professional Bible college is interdenominational. Founded in 1932, it provides training for pastors, missionaries, evangelists, and other workers in Christian service. Enrollment: 73.

Library Administration. Geneva Temple, Librarian.

Library General Holdings. 26,000 volumes; 85 current periodical titles.

Special Collections

The **John Wesley Collection** and a collection of Christian education materials are maintained by the library.

1192
Johnson C. Smith University
James B. Duke Memorial Library
100 Beatties Ford Road
Charlotte, North Caolina 28216

Telephone. (704) 378-1029

Institutional Description. The privately supported liberal arts and education institution was founded in 1867. Affiliated with the Presbyterian Church (U.S.A.), it grants baccalaureate degrees. Enrollment: 1,252.

Library Administration. Shirley Wilkins, Director.

Library General Holdings. 103,000 volumes; 900 current periodical subscriptions.

Special Collections

Special collections of the library include the **Earl A. Johnson Collection** of Black studies, Judaica, and art; the **Calvin Hoover Collection** of governmental biography and history.

1193
Lees-McCrae College
James H. Carson Library
P.O. Box 128
Banner Elk, North Carolina 28604

Telephone. (704) 898-5241

Institutional Description. Lees-McCrae College is a private, two-year college affiliated with the Presbyterian Church (U.S.A). It was founded in 1900. Enrollment: 668.

Library Administration. Richard Jackson, Librarian.

Library General Holdings. 61,475 volumes.

Special Collections

The library maintains the **Stirling Collection of Appalachian Materials.**

1194
Lenoir Community College
Learning Resources Center
P.O. Box 188
Kinston, North Carolina 28501

Telephone. (919) 527-6223

Institutional Description. The two-year college was began in 1960 with the establishment of the Lenoir County Industrial Education Center. It became a community college in 1966. Enrollment: 3,311.

Library Administration. Mildred Mathis, Dean of Learning Resources.

Library General Holdings. 50,000 volumes; 355 periodical subscriptions; 6,500 microforms.

Special Collections

The library maintains special collections on local history and genealogy, aviation education resources, and Small Business Administration reports.

1195
Lenoir-Rhyne College
Carl Augustus Rudisill Library
P.O. Box 7163
Hickory, North Carolina 28603

Telephone. (704) 328-1741

Institutional Description. The privately supported liberal arts college was founded in 1891. It is affiliated with the Lutheran Church in America, and grants baccalaureate and master's degrees. Enrollment: 1,323.

Library Administration. A. Curtis Paul, Director of Learning Resources.

Library General Holdings. 122,000 volumes; 740 current periodical subscriptions; 200,000 microforms.

Special Collections

The library maintains a collection on Lutherans in Catawba County, works by Martin Luther, and the **Quetzalcoatl Collection.**

1196
Livingstone College
Andrew Carnegie Library
701 West Monrow Street
Salisbury, North Carolina 28144

Telephone. (704) 633-7960

Institutional Description. The privately supported college includes the College of Liberal Arts and the Hood Theological Seminary. The College was founded in 1879 and is largely supported by the African Methodist Episcopal Zion Church. Enrollment: 630.

Library Administration. Ms. G. Hicks, Librarian; Millard J. Wallace, Assistant Librarian.

Library General Holdings. 61,501 volumes; 495 periodicals; 10,914 microforms; 1,983 sound recordings.

Special Collections

African Methodist Episcopal Zion Collection. An extensive collection of materials and artifacts (general conference minutes, Bishop's archives and books, eighteenth century tracts on Methodism).

African-American Experience. Materials pertaining to and describing the African-American experience in the Carolinas (North and South) as well as the southern United States.

1197
Mars Hill College
Memorial Library
Mars Hill College, North Carolina 28754

Telephone. (704) 689-1141

Institutional Description. The privately supported liberal arts college was founded in 1856. It is affiliated with the Southern Baptist Church and grants associate and baccalaureate degrees. Enrollment: 1,310.

Library Administration. David Dean Cadle, Special Collections Librarian.

Library General Holdings. 85,000 volumes; 450 periodical and serial titles.

Special Collections

Appalachian Room. This room houses books and other resources related to the southern mountain region. Notable among the manuscript collection is the **Bascom Lamar Lansford Folk Music Collection** which includes scrapbooks, pictures, sound recordings, and other memorabilia.

Other special collections include the **Southern Appalachian Photographic Archives,** the **Gertrude M. Ruskin Collection** of Cherokee Indian artifacts and materials; the **Long Collection** of Baptist records including associational minutes and church histories; and the **College Archives** including papers relating to the history of Mars Hill College.

1198
Martin Community College
Martin Community College Learning Resources Center
Kehukee Park Road
Williamston, North Carolina 27892

Telephone. (919) 792-1521

Institutional Description. The publicly supported two-year college, founded as a technical institute in 1968, became a community college in 1976. Enrollment: 849.

Library Administration. Peggy T. Cherry, Dean, College Resources and Services.

Library General Holdings. 21,998 volumes; 188 periodicals; 8 newspaper subscriptions; 625 microforms.

Special Collections

Learning Resources Center. Special collections of physical therapy and equine technology materials.

Rare Book Collections

Francis M. Manning History Room. Contains historical materials of Martin County (North Carolina) and genealogical information of Martin County families. Materials in this room were donated by the family of the late Francis M. Manning, editor and owner of the local newspaper, *The Enterprise* (Williamston, North Carolina).

1199
Mayland Technical College
Learning Resources Center
P.O. Box 547
Spruce Pine, North Carolina 28777

Telephone. (704) 765-7351

Institutional Description. The two-year College was established 1971 and a new campus was occupied in 1977. Enrollment: 2,198.

Library Administration. Joyce B. Orndoff, Director.

Library General Holdings. 16,420 volumes; 205 periodical titles.

Special Collections

The **Appalachian Room** contains a specialized collection of books, pamphlets, magazines, and microfilm pertaining specifically to the area of Spruce Pine, North Carolina. Materials to help both the beginning and more advanced researcher are available. There are three separate collections: the North Carolina Collection, the Appalachian Studies Collection, and the Genealogy Collection.

1200
Methodist College
Davis Memorial Library
Raleigh Road
Fayetteville, North Carolina 28301

Telephone. (919) 488-7110

Institutional Description. The privately supported liberal arts college was founded in 1960. It is affiliated with the United Methodist Church, and grants associate and baccalaureate degrees. Enrollment: 1,077.

Library Administration. Norma C. Womack, Director of Library Services.

Library General Holdings. 75,000 volumes; 510 current periodical subscriptions; 7,600 microforms.

Special Collections

The main library contains a number of special collections. The **Lafayette Room** houses books, documents, letters, and other materials relating to General Lafayette, for whom the City of Fayetteville is named. The **North Carolina Room** contains materials about North Carolina history and fiction by North Carolina authors such as Thomas Wolfe. Among the items in the library's manuscript collection are letters of Mrs. Stonewall Jackson, Mrs. Verina (Jefferson) Davis, and George Washington Lee (the son of Robert E. Lee.

Rare Book Collections

The library also houses a rare Bible collection donated by the Reverend Allen C. Lee.

1201
Montreat-Anderson College
L. Nelson Bell Library
Montreat, North Carolina 28757

Telephone. (704) 669-2382

Institutional Description. The privately supported junior college operated as a normal school from its founding in 1916 until it became a junior college in 1933. It was established by members of the Presbyterian Church. Enrollment: 379.

Library Administration. Elizabeth Pearson, Librarian.

Library General Holdings. 55,000 volumes; 379 current periodical and newspaper subscriptions; 2,895 audiovisual units (videotapes; audiotapes; slides, films).

Special Collections

Dr. L. Nelson Bell Collection. Contains memorabilia of Dr. L. Nelson Bell, an outstanding Christian layman, missionary, and surgeon; includes photographs, awards, Bibles, plaques, and reports.

Crosby-Adams Collection. A collection of books, music scores, photographs, newspaper clippings, and some letters concerning the work and lives of Mr. and Mrs. Crosby Adams, musicians who lived and taught in Montreat, North Carolina.

Howard Kester Papers. A microfilm edition including material relating to Kester's work in the Southern Tenant Farmer's Union; reports, correspondence, and writing by and about Kester. Mr. Kester was active with the Southern Tenant Farmer's Union from 1935-41.

1202
North Carolina Agricultural and Technical State University
Ferdinand Douglass Bluford Library
1601 East Market Street
Greensboro, North Carolina 27411

Telephone. (919) 334-7500

Institutional Description. The University was chartered in 1890 as the A and M College for the Colored Race. It changed its name to the Agricultural and Technical College of North Carolina in 1915 and adopted its present name in 1967. Enrollment: 5,865.

Library Administration. Alene C. Young, Director.

Library General Holdings. 327,000 volumes; 1,572 serial subscriptions; 152,000 government documents.

Special Collections

The library maintains special collections in Black studies, teacher education, and chemistry. The University Archives are also maintained.

1203
North Carolina Central University
James E. Shepard Memorial Library
1801 Fayetteville Street
Durham, North Carolina 27707

Telephone. (919) 683-6475

Institutional Description. North Carolina Central University was was established in 1909. Enrollment: 4,-747.

Library Administration. Floyd C. Hardy, Director.

Library General Holdings. 375,000 volumes; 3,093 current serial titles.

Special Collections

Special collections are maintained by the School of Library Science and the Curriculum Materials Center.

The Treasure Room Collection contains materials on Negro life and culture including the **Martin Collection on Minorities.**

1204
North Carolina State University at Raleigh D.H. Hill Library Campus Box 7111 Raleigh, North Carolina 27695

Telephone. (919) 737-2843

Institutional Description. The publicly supported state university was founded in 1887 as North Carolina College of Agriculture and Mechanic Arts, a land-grant institution. It now offers a wide variety of programs. Enrollment: 22,846.

Library Administration. Susan K. Nutter, Director.

Library General Holdings. 1,154,000 volumes; 8,000 journals and magazine titles; 714,000 government documents; 1,560,000 microforms.

Special Collections

The collections of the D.H. Hill Library and its branches are particularly strong in the biological and physical sciences, engineering, agriculture, forestry, textiles, and architecture. Five special libraries serve the needs of their respective schools: the Burlington Textiles Library, the Harrye B. Lyons Design Library, the School of Forest Resources Library, the Veterinary Medical Library, and the Curriculum Materials Center. Noteworthy special collections are the Smith, Tipman, and Metcalf Collections in entomology.

1205
North Carolina Wesleyan College College Library 3400 Wesleyan Boulevard Rocky Mount, North Carolina 27804

Telephone. (919) 977-7171

Institutional Description. The privately supported liberal arts college is related to The United Methodist Church; it grants the baccalaureate degree. Enrollment: 831.

Library Administration. Anne B. Wilgus, Director of the Library; Leverett Tyrell Smith, Curator, Black Mountain College Collection.

Library General Holdings. 73,000 volumes; 700 periodical subscriptions; 18 newspaper subscriptions; 5,000 music scores; 8,000 recordings.

Special Collections

Black Mountain College Collection. A collection of interesting volumes from the library of Black Mountain College. Valuable items are housed in a separate collection; others are included in the stacks. Dr. Smith continues to obtain works by or about one-time teachers or students at Black Mountain College.

1206
Pembroke State University Mary Livermore Library Pembroke, North Carolina 28372

Telephone. (919) 521-4214

Institutional Description. Pembroke University was established in 1887 and is a member of the North Carolina Southeastern Consortium for International Education. Until 1945, only Robeson County Indians were eligible for admission to Pembroke. Enrollment: 2,339.

Library Administration. Robert C. Hersch, Director of Library Services.

Library General Holdings. 186,000 books; 1,000 periodical subscriptions.

Special Collections

Native American Resource Center. The Center is comprised of authentic Indian artifacts, handicrafts, art, books, cassettes, record albums, and filmstrips about Native-Americans with emphasis on the Lumbee Indians of Robeson County.

1207
Queens College Everett Library 1900 Selwyn Avenue Charlotte, North Carolina 28274

Telephone. (704) 337-2200

Institutional Description. The privately supported liberal arts college for women was founded in 1857. Now included are the degree-granting New College and the graduate school, both coeducational. Enrollment: 1,148.

Library Administration. Judith Abner, Administrative Librarian.

Library General Holdings. 114,000 volumes; 580 current periodical subscriptions.

Special Collections

The Special Collections Room houses a collection of Charlotte imprints, books on the history of Mecklenburg County, and materials relating to the history of Queens College. Also maintained is a collection of materials on Presbyterian history.

1208
Richmond Technical College Library Highway 74 P.O. Box 1189 Hamlet, North Carolina 28345

Telephone. (919) 582-1980

Institutional Description. The two-year public college was established in 1964 as the Richmond Technical Institute. The present name was adopted in 1980. Enrollment: 1,681.

Library Administration. Emily U. Hartzell, Director.

Library General Holdings. 27,000 books; 200 periodical titles; 4,000 pamphlets; 2,750 audiovisual materials.

Special Collections

The library maintains the **Railroadiana, Automobiliana,** and the **North Caroliniana** collections.

1209
Roanoke Bible College
College Library
P.O. Box 387
Elizabeth City, North Caolina 27909

Telephone. (919) 338-5191

Institutional Description. The privately supported professional Bible college is affiliated with the Christian Churches and Churches of Christ. It grants associate and baccalaureate degrees. Enrollment: 125.

Library Administration. Patricia S. Griffin, Librarian.

Library General Holdings. 34,000 volumes.

Special Collections

The library has special collections on Christian education, the deaf, and the mentally retarded.

1210
Rockingham Community College
Learning Resources Center
Wrenn Memorial Drive
Wentworth, North Carolina 27375

Telephone. (919) 342-4261

Institutional Description. The two year comprehensive community college was established in 1966. Enrollment: 1,504.

Library Administration. Robert J. Foeller, Director.

Library General Holdings. 30,000 books; 200 magazine and newspaper subscriptions.

Special Collections

Of growing interest for both the classroom student and for the independent researcher in local history and genealogy is the collection of materials including deeds, wills, trusts, marriage notices, and similar documents. Old newspapers, local histories, and architectural surveys are also materials which have been increasingly popular in the Special Collections Room. The **Local History Collection** is a project of the Rockingham Community College Foundation.

1211
St. Andrews Presbyterian College
De Tamble Library
Laurinburg, North Carolina 28352

Telephone. (919) 276-3652

Institutional Description. The privately supported liberal arts college was founded by the Synod of North Carolina, Presbyterian Church in the United States. Enrollment: 721.

Library Administration. Elizabeth Holmes, Librarian.

Library General Holdings. 101,000 volumes; 600 serial subscriptions; 50,647 microfilm reels.

Special Collections

St. Andrews Collection. A collection of books and papers written by St. Andrews faculty, current and past.

Abrams Collection. Consists mostly of playbills and recordings from on and off Broadway productions from the 1960s on and comprising 1,500 items (located in the Music Library).

Rare Book Collections

The Scottish and Rare Book Collection. Contains books dealing primarily with Scottish literature and history, and rare books covering a wide variety of subjects.

Mishima Collection. Contains the complete works of the Japanese writer in their original Japanese, a gift to the college from the author's wife.

1212
Saint Mary's College
Sarah Graham Kenan Library
900 Hillsborough Street
Raleigh, North Carolina 27603

Telephone. (919) 839-4039

Institutional Description. The privately supported junior college for women was founded in 1842. Owned and operated by the Protestant Episcopal Church, it is now a combined high school and junior college. Enrollment: 296.

Library Administration. Martha M. Smith, College Librarian; Christine L. Thomson, Reference Librarian/Special Collections Librarian.

Library General Holdings. 40,000 volumes; 300 current periodical subscriptions; 7 newspaper subscriptions.

Special Collections

Thomas Wolfe Collection. Includes first editions, secondary materials, photographs, manuscripts, and letters.

St. Mary's Archives. Contains memorabilia, official papers, private collections of faculty and student papers, volumes typical of a library collection of the 1800s, and photographs.

The Sarah Graham Kenan Library also has special collections on women's studies and Shakespearean studies.

1213
Salem College
Dale H. Gramley Library
Salem Station
Winston-Salem, North Carolina 27108

Telephone. (919) 721-2600

Institutional Description. The privately supported liberal arts college for women was founded in 1772. It is affiliated with the Moravian Church, and grants baccalaureate degrees. Enrollment: 613.

Library Administration. Rose Simon, Director of Libraries.

Library General Holdings. 114,000 volumes; 500 current periodical subscriptions.

Special Collections

The **Siewers Room** houses special collections devoted to the history of the Moravian Church and of Salem Academy and College.

Rare Book Collections

The **Clarence E. Clewell Rare Book Room** houses a collection of rare books and early imprint material.

1214
Shaw University
Library/Learning Resources Center
118 East South Street
Raleigh, North Carolina 27602

Telephone. (919) 755-4800

Institutional Description. Shaw University is a private institution affiliated with the Baptist Church. Enrollment: 1,736.

Library Administration. Clarence Toomer, Director.

Library General Holdings. 83,000 volumes; 445 periodical subscriptions; 16,000 audiovisual materials.

Special Collections

Special collections within the library are the **Yergen Collection,** a collection of books largely of 1,400 African titles; the **Indian Collection,** a collection of books and monographs on the culture of the North American Indian; and the **Gilmour Collection,** a collection of books on philosophy, language, literature, and history of religion. Print and non-print materials on the history of the Afro-American are extensive and rich with sources for research and general information. Included in this group of materials are the microfilm collections Series I and II of the Schomburg Center for Research in Black Culture.

1215
Southeastern Baptist Theological Seminary
Seminary Library
Wake Forest, North Carolina 27587

Telephone. (919) 556-3101

Institutional Description. The Seminary is a private institution affiliated with the Southern Baptist Convention. Enrollment: 1,099.

Library Administration. H. Eugene McLeod, Librarian.

Library General Holdings. 225,000 items including books, periodical volumes, music scores, music recordings, audiovisual materials, and microforms.

Special Collections

The microforms collection includes early American and early British materials including important Baptist history resources.

1216
University of North Carolina at Asheville
D. Hilden Ramsey Library
One University Heights
Asheville, North Carolina 28804

Telephone. (704) 251-6600

Institutional Description. The University was established in 1927 as Buncombe County College. It became a part of the University of North Carolina in 1969. Enrollment: 2,929.

Library Administration. Malcolm Eugene Blowers, University Librarian.

Library General Holdings. 150,000 volumes; 1,517 current periodicals; 50,000 government documents; 180,000 microform volumes.

Special Collections

Southern Highlands Research Center. The Center collects, organizes, and makes accessible a wide variety of source materials related to the culture, society, and history of the Southern Highlands. As part of the Center, the Jewish Studies Center provides a focal point for the study of southeastern Jewish history and culture and sponsors outreach programs dealing with the broad areas of Jewish history and culture.

1217
University of North Carolina at Chapel Hill
Wilson Library
Chapel Hill, North Carolina 27514

Telephone. (919) 962-1345

Institutional Description. The publicly supported state university was provided for in the state constitution in 1776 and chartered in 1789. It was the first state university in the U.S. to award state university diplomas. Enrollment: 21,228.

Library Administration. James Govan, University Librarian; Marcella Grendler, Associate University Librarian for Special Collections; Richard Shrader, Acting Curator of Manuscripts; Charles McNamara, Rare Books Librarian.

Library General Holdings. 3,301,751 volumes; 9,879,-184 manuscripts; 218,215 maps; 2,342,370 microfiche, cards, prints; 131,637 microfilms; 158,268 newspaper clippings; 1,778,371 pamphlets; 38,425 pictures, prints, photos; 36,716 recordings; 29,141 other audiovisual materials.

Special Collections

General and Literary Manuscripts. A component of the Manuscripts Department, this Collection includes private manuscripts not related to the South or to Southerners. Among the holdings are materials related to George Bernard Shaw, John Ruskin, George Cruikshank, Augustus Thomas, and Washington Irving; and a large group of family papers from Popayan, Colombia.

North Carolina Collection. This Collection has been called the "Conscience of North Carolina," for it seeks to preserve for present and future generations all that is published *about* the state and its localities and people or *by* North Carolinians, regardless of subject. A North Carolinian is defined as one who is born in the state, or whose name becomes indelibly associated with the state, or who publishes while a citizen of the state. In this mission the Collection's clientele is broader than the University community; indeed, it is the entire citzenry of North Carolina. Its acquisitions are made possible by gifts and private endowment funds; thus it also represents the respect that North Carolinians have for their heritage.

Southern Folklore Collection. This Collection is also a component of the Manuscripts Department. It includes the John Edwards Memorial Collection, the Folk Music Collection, field tapes, slides, movie film, and other materials related to study and research in the field of folklore, with emphasis on the folklore of the Southern United States.

Southern Historical Collection. This is the largest and best known component of the Manuscripts Department. The University began acquiring North Carolina manuscripts in the 1840s, broadened its policies in the 1920s to seek manuscripts from the entire South, and established the Southern Historical Collection in 1930. The Collection is a center for research on the South, with important holdings from all of the Southern states. The manuscripts are private papers of individuals and families or records of private organizations or institutions, not official government records. The Collection preserves letters, diaries, printed items, but not museum objects or general published works.

University Archives. The Archives are the official unpublished records of the University created since its charter in 1789 and include such basic documentation as Trustees Minutes, Faculty Journals, administrative correspondence, student records, and records of the two student debating societies.

Rare Book Collections

Rare Book Collection. The scope of this collection is wide. There are two dozen special collections among which are the Hanes Foundation for the Study of the Origin and Development of the Book and the Whitaker collections of British authors. These holdings span nearly the entire range of man's recorded history: from clay tablets of the Third Ur Dynasty (dating from approximately 2100 B.C.) to illuminated medieval manuscripts and incunabula to modern books published by private presses. The resources of the Collection support the work of scholars, students, and collectors. Researchers in fields such as art history, bibliography, textual studies, history, book illustration, and literary criticism rely on the collection's books, which are primary documentary source materials.

1218
University of North Carolina at Charlotte
J. Murrey Atkins Library
Charlotte, North Carolina 28223

Telephone. (704) 547-2221

Institutional Description. The publicly supported university was founded in 1946 as the Charlotte Center of the University of North Carolina, to provide instruction for returning veterans of World War II. In 1965, it became a campus of the state university. Enrollment: 9,148.

Library Administration. Raymond A. Frankle, University Librarian; Robin Brabham, Special Collections Librarian.

Library General Holdings. 409,049 volumes; 5,296 periodical subscriptions; 650,658 microforms; 59,500 audiovisual materials; 522,499 manuscripts and archives material.

Special Collections

Manuscript Collection: Documents the social, political, and architectural history of the Metrolina region of North Carolina, with particular emphasis on Charlotte and Mecklenburg County. The collection is particularly strong in the subject of civil rights and includes the papers of *Carolina Israelite* publisher Harry Golden; of national NAACP chairman Kelly Alexander; and of rival attorneys in the precedent-setting Swann vs. Charlotte/Mecklenburg Board of Education busing case. The collection also includes papers of Benjamin Gitlow, a founder of the Communist Party in the U.S. and substantial material by and about Carl Sandburg.

Photograph Collection. Includes photographs relating to the University and to the history of the region.

University Archives. Includes the non-current, permanently valuable official records of the University and theses.

Rare Book Collections

Rare Book Collection. Collecting emphasis is on American literature and children's books of the nineteenth and early twentieth centuries. The collection is also strong in English literature and history, especially the drama of the seventeenth to nineteenth centuries and the works of John Wolcot. Other subjects collected include architecture, North Carolina, and erotica.

1219
University of North Carolina at Greensboro
Walter Clinton Jackson Library
1000 Spring Garden Street
Greensboro, North Carolina 27412

Telephone. (919) 334-5000

Institutional Description. The University of North Carolina at Greensboro was founded in 1891. Enrollment: 10,382.

Library Administration. James H. Thompson, Director.

Library General Holdings. 1,700,000 items, including 360,000 federal and state documents and 650,000 items in microtext; 6,500 newspaper, periodical, and serial subscriptions.

Special Collections

Special collections include the **Homans-Wellesley College Collection in Physical Education;** the **Luigi Silva Collection** of cello music; the **Randall Jarrell Collection** of manuscripts, tapes, and books; the **Lois Lenski Collection;** the **Woman's Collection;** and collections devoted to dance, the books as an art form, and modern private presses. There is also a notable collection of rare books.

1220
University of North Carolina at Wilmington
William Madison Randall Library
601 South College Road
Wilmington, North Carolina 28403

Telephone. (919) 395-3760

Institutional Description. The publicly supported state university was founded as a county educational institution in 1947. In 1947 it became a four-year senior college. Enrollment: 5,829.

Library Administration. Lana D. Taylor, Special Collections Librarian.

Library General Holdings. 231,722 volumes; 4,731 serial subscriptions; 336,955 U.S. and North Carolina state government documents; 446,651 microforms; 11,944 audiovisual materials.

Special Collections

Curriculum Materials Center. Includes textbooks and computer software for grades K-12, curriculum guides, diagnostic tests, and the ERIC database on compact disc (CD-ROM).

Rare Book Collections

Helen Hagan Rare Book Room. Contains material related to southeastern North Carolina, rare editions, Confederate imprints, broadsides, pamphlets, maps, the University Archives, and the North Carolina Visual Arts and Artists Collection (NCVAA). Included among the rare books are first editions of Thomas Wolfe and Robert Ruark.

1221
Wake Forest University
Z. Smith Reynolds Library
P.O. Box 7305
Winston-Salem, North Carolina 27109

Telephone. (919) 761-5000

Institutional Description. Wake Forest University is a private institution affiliated with the North Carolina Baptist Convention.

Library Administration. Merrill G. Berthrong, Director of Libraries.

Library General Holdings. 773,902 volumes; 666,171 microforms; 30,014 microfilm reels; 84,380 volumes of United States government documents; 11,573 current periodical and serial subscriptions.

Special Collections

Special collections cover the works of selected late nineteenth and early twentieth century English and American writers, and include pertinent critical material. Among the special collections are a **Mark Twain Collection**, a **Gertrude Stein Collection**, and the **Ethel Taylor Crittenden Collection in Baptist History.**

Artom Collection. This collection is a clipping file which covers major national and international events from 1948 to the present.

Rare Book Collections

The acquisition of the **Charles H. Babcock Collection of Rare and Fine Books** represents an important addition to the resources of the Z. Smith Reynolds Library.

1222
Wake Technical College
Library
9101 Fayetteville Road
Raleigh, North Carolina 27603

Telephone. (919) 772-0551

Institutional Description. The publicly supported two-year technical school was founded as Wake Technical Institute in 1963. It awards the associate degree. Enrollment: 4,351.

Library Administration. James Gray, Librarian.

Library General Holdings. 32,623 volumes; 264 periodical subscriptions; 566 microforms; 1,746 pamphlets.

Special Collections

Vocational Collection. Includes materials on plumbing, welding, automotive repair, heavy equipment repair, electrical installation and maintenance, computer operations, and electronic servicing.

Business Collection. Contains materials on business administration, accounting, secretarial science, and business computer programming.

Allied Health Collection. Consists of books on nursing, medical laboratory technology, radiologic technology, and emergency medical technology.

Other areas of emphasis are engineering technology (electronics, chemical, mechanical, industrial, architectural, pharmaceutical, civil); criminal justice, postal service, and child care.

1223
Warren Wilson College
Martha Ellison Library
Warren Wilson Road
Swannanoa, North Carolina 28778

Telephone. (704) 298-3325

Institutional Description. Warren Wilson College is a private college affiliated with the United Presbyterian Church (U.S.A.). Enrollment: 498.

Library Administration. Jean Hutton, Director.

Library General Holdings. 83,000 books; 550 periodicals.

Special Collections

Intercultural Resource Center. This Center maintains a growing collection of artifacts and print materials representing such global areas as Africa, South America, and Asia, and includes objects as well as museum quality artifacts and prints.

The library also maintains the **Jamie Clark Papers,** a collection of art books and exhibition catalogs, and the College Archives.

1224
Western Carolina University
Hunter Library
Cullowhee, North Carolina 28723

Telephone. (704) 227-7307

Institutional Description. The publicly supported state university became part of the state university system in 1972. Prior to that, it was founded as a semipublic school in 1889; in 1905 it became a normal and industrial school, and in 1929, a senior college. Enrollment: 5,191.

Library Administration. William Kirwan, University Librarian; Lewis Miller, Special Collections Librarian.

Library General Holdings. 320,532 books; 60,649 bound periodicals; 37,807 microfilm reels; 1,092,242 microforms; 107,251 government documents; 2,203 periodical subscriptions; 816 serial subscriptions.

Special Collections

The Special Collections of Hunter Library contain materials related to southern Appalachian culture and natural history, western North Carolina history, Cherokee Indians, the Great Smoky Mountains National Park, and the archives of Western Carolina University. These topics are most strongly developed and also include spider behavior.

Notable manuscript collections include: William Holland Thomas (1805-1893), businessman, politician, and Indian agent to the Cherokee Indians; Horace Kephart (1862-1931), author and observer of Appalachian life and culture and of outdoor recreational activities; Cherokee Documents in Foreign Archives, a microfilm collection relating to Cherokee Indians from depositories in Great Britain, Canada, France, Mexico, and Spain (821 reels).

1225
Western Piedmont Community College
Learning Resources Center
1001 Burkemont Avenue
Morganton, North Carolina 28655

Telephone. (704) 437-8688

Institutional Description. The two-year college was chartered by the North Carolina Board of Education in 1964 as a member institution of the North Carolina Community College System. Enrollment: 2,779.

Library Administration. Winston Lear, Dean of Learning Resources.

Library General Holdings. 30,000 volumes; 250 periodical titles.

Special Collections

Special collections include the **Grace DiSanto Poetry Collection** and the **Chidnes Prehistoric Indian Artifacts Collection.**

1226
Wilkes Community College
Learning Resources Center
P.O. Box 120
Wilkesboro, North Carolina 28697

Telephone. (919) 667-7136

Institutional Description. The two-year college was founded in 1964 and occupied a new campus in 1969. Enrollment: 2,890.

Library Administration. I. Fay Bird, Director, Division of Learning Resources.

Library General Holdings. 50,000 volumes; 150 current periodical titles.

Special Collections

The library is building an extensive collection on local and area history, including writings of Wilkes County authors, microfilm of Wilkes County records, and media concerning northwest North Carolina people and events. The **James Larkin Pearson Library** contains over 4,000 volumes on Wilkes County, North Carolina.

1227
Wingate College
Ethel K. Smith Library
Wingate, North Carolina 28174

Telephone. (704) 4061

Institutional Description. The privately supported liberal arts college was founded in 1896. It is affiliated with the Southern Baptist Church. Enrollment: 1,497.

Library Administration. Michael J. LaCroix, Head Librarian.

Library General Holdings. 102,000 volumes; 350 current periodical subscriptions; 190,000 microforms.

Special Collections

The **Mary Ann Kincaid Children's Literature Collection** is maintained by the library. Other collections include materials on the history of Wingate College, business, and economics.

1228
Winston-Salem State University
C.G. O'Kelly Library
Winston-Salem, North Carolina 27110

Telephone. (919) 761-2011

Institutional Description. Winston-Salem State University was established in 1892 as the Slater Industrial Academy. Enrollment: 2,590.

Library Administration. Mae H. Rodney, Director, Division of Library Services.

Library General Holdings. 152,000 volumes; 1,000 current periodicals. The collection supports the curricular and reference needs of the university as well as materials for the cultural and general reading interests of student and faculty.

Special Collections

Educational Media Center. The Center is a centralized pool of teaching-learning resources for faculty and students.

North Dakota

1229
Dickinson State University
Mathilda Stoxen Library
Dickinson, North Dakota 58601

Telephone. (701) 227-2135

Institutional Description. The publicly supported state university was founded in 1918 as a college of education. It was formerly known as the State University of North Dakota at Dickinson. Enrollment: 1,227.

Library Administration. Bernnett G. Reinke, Library Director.

Library General Holdings. 74,000 volumes; 560 current periodical subscriptions; 15 current newspaper subscriptions; 10,000 microfilm reels (periodicals); 3,700 audiovisual materials.

Special Collections

Theodore Roosevelt Collection. Consists of over 200 books written by and about Theodore Roosevelt.

1230
Jamestown College
Raugust Library
Box 6070 Jamestown College
Jamestown, North Dakota 58401

Telephone. (701) 252-3467

Institutional Description. The privately supported liberal arts college is the oldest such institution in North Dakota, having been established in 1884. Enrollment: 559.

Library Administration. Phyllis Ann K. Bratton, Librarian.

Library General Holdings. 67,000 volumes; 380 periodical subscriptions; 9 newspaper subscriptions; 7,750 audiovisual materials; 16,000 microforms; 900 non-print materials.

Special Collections

Alec Bond Foklore Archive. Contains manuscripts and papers dealing with North Dakota folklore/folklife, including photographs, recipes, jokes, customs, and oral history cassettes.

Mary Young Collection. Papers of a local historian who is a descendant of original settlers in Jamestown and who has collected diaries and primary information for the last sixty years.

1231
Mayville State College
Library
Mayville, North Dakota 58257

Telephone. (701) 786-2301

Institutional Description. The publicly supported state liberal arts and teachers college was founded in 1889. It also offers programs in business. Enrollment: 657.

Library Administration. Betty J. Karaim, Director of Library Services.

Library General Holdings. 80,000 volumes; 500 current periodical subscriptions.

Special Collections

The **North Dakota Collection** is a special collection in the library.

1232
Minot State University
Memorial Library
Ninth Avenue Northwest
Minot, North Dakota 58701

Telephone. (701) 857-3300

Institutional Description. The publicly supported liberal arts and teachers college grants associate, baccalaureate, and master's degrees. Enrollment: 2,774.

Library Administration. Larry Greenwood, Director.

Library General Holdings. 145,000 volumes.

Special Collections

Special collections include children's literature, U.S. Government and State of North Dakota publications, and a North Dakota collection that includes materials on Indians of the north central states.

1233
North Dakota State College of Science Library
Wahpeton, North Dakota 58075

Telephone. (701) 671-1130

Institutional Description. The two-year college was founded in 1903. Its first trade and technical programs began in 1922. Enrollment: 2,822.

Library Administration. Jerald K. Stewart, Head Librarian.

Library General Holdings. 90,000 volumes.

Special Collections

The library maintains a collection of trade and technical manuals and reference books which is one of the largest in the region.

1234
North Dakota State University Library
1301 Twelfth Avenue North
Fargo, North Dakota 58105

Telephone. (701) 237-8011

Institutional Description. The University is a state institution and land-grant college. Enrollment: 10,473.

Library Administration. Kilbourn L. Janecek, Director.

Library General Holdings. 385,000 volumes; 5,000 current serial titles; 250,000 government documents; 70,000 maps.

Special Collections

Institute for Regional Studies. Houses the University Archives, manuscripts, and regional histories.

1235
North Dakota State University - Bottineau Branch and Institute of Forestry
Fossum Foundation Library
First and Simrall Boulevard
Bottineau, North Dakota 58318

Telephone. (701) 228-2277

Institutional Description. The publicly supported two-year state college was founded in 1907. It offers the first two years of a college curriculum plus one- and two-year programs in business, forestry, agriculture, wildlife, parks and recreation, horticulture. Enrollment: 375.

Library Administration. Janice Wopothi, Librarian.

Library General Holdings. 30,000 volumes.

Special Collections

Fossum Foundation Library. M. Truman Fossum, a nationally recognized figure in the fields of horticulture and agricultural economics, established with his family the Fossum Foundation Library. The first gift of the foundation was the personal library of Fossum, who since graduation from the College in 1933 has been engaged in professional research and who has accumlated a collection reflecting many interests.

1236
Trinity Bible College
Graham Library
Ellendale, North Dakota 58436

Telephone. (701) 349-3621

Institutional Description. The privately supported professional Bible college is affiliated with the Assemblies of God Church. It grants associate and baccalaureate degrees. Enrollment: 506.

Library Administration. Esther L. Zink, Librarian.

Library General Holdings. 60,000 volumes; 360 current periodical subscriptions.

Special Collections

The library maintains the **Trinity Bible College Archive Collection,** the **Bible and Theology Collection,** and the **Juvenile Collection.**

1237
University of North Dakota
Chester Fritz Library
Grand Forks, North Dakota 58202

Telephone. (701) 777-2011

Institutional Description. The University of North Dakota is a state university with a branch campus offering associate degrees at Williston. Enrollment: 10,763.

Library Administration. Edward Warner, Director of Libraries.

Library General Holdings. 500,000 books and periodicals; 1,000,000 items in report, document, and microform collections; 3,110 current periodical subscriptions.

Special Collections

The Department of Special Collections preserves all unique, non-book, or special book collections not available for general circulation, with primary emphasis on regional and North Dakota historical material. These include five separate, but homogeneous collections: the **Orin G. Libby Manuscript Collection,** the **North Dakota Book Collection,** the **University Archives;** the **North Dakota State Documents;** and the **Fred G. Aandahl Collection of Books on the Great Plains.**

Rare Book Collections

Rare Book Collection. The Department also maintains a rare book collection featuring a significant gift from Frank and Elvira Jestrab. Established in 1980, the **Family History-Genealogy Room** is an integral part of the Department of Special Collections.

1238
Valley City State College
Allen Memorial Library
Valley City, North Dakota 58072

Telephone. (701) 845-7100

Institutional Description. The publicly supported liberal arts and teachers college was founded in 1890. It grants baccalaureate degrees. Enrollment: 974.

Library Administration. Richard Holmes, Director.

Library General Holdings. 79,000 volumes; 400 current periodical subscriptions.

Special Collections

The library maintains the **Woiwode Collection** of manuscripts.

Ohio

1239
Antioch College
Olive Kettering Library
Yellow Springs, Ohio 45387

Telephone. (513) 767-7331

Institutional Description. The privately supported college of liberal arts and sciences adopted the cooperative plan in 1920, whereby students gain certain college credits by working on the job. Antioch has many branch campuses throughout the United States. Enrollment: 3,116.

Library Administration. Joseph J. Cali, Librarian; Kim Iconis, Rare Books Librarian; Nina D. Myatt, Curator of Antiochiana.

Library General Holdings. 256,000 volumes; 1,050 periodicals; 20 newspapers; 43,200 microforms; 1,200 music scores; 4,300 sound recordings; 200 audiovisual materials.

Special Collections

The Bessie Totten Room. Houses a small collection of anti-slavery books, tracts, periodicals, and pamphlets assembled by a nineteenth century physician, Adams Jewett of Dayton, Ohio.

Rare Book Collections

The Antiochian Collection. Consists of historical and archival records of Antioch College and Antioch University; materials relating to the Christian Church, founders of Antioch College (1852) including periodicals (1808-); biographies of early Christian ministers; the Robert L. Straker Collection on Horace Mann, first president of Antioch College; the Peabody Sisters; Antioch College history (1852-1920) in manuscripts, letters, photographs; Arthur E. Morgan Papers, president of Antioch College 1920-1936 and first director of the Tennessee Valley Authority; Eleanor C. Lewis Papers.

1240
Ashland College
Ashland College Library
401 College Avenue
Ashland, Ohio 44805

Telephone. (419) 289-4142

Institutional Description. The privately supported liberal arts college includes a graduate school, the Ashland Theological Seminary. The College was founded by members of the German Baptist Brethren Church in 1878; the Seminary was added in 1930. Enrollment: 2,861.

Library Administration. Darwyn J. Batway, Librarian; Faith Greene, Rare Books Librarian; Patricia Brown, Administrative Assistant.

Library General Holdings. 180,880 volumes; 11,411 pamphlets; 22,472 periodicals; 80,000 microforms; 5,516 sound recordings.

Rare Book Collections

Dr. Harold E. Andrews Collection of Special and Rare Books. Consists of books on American history and literature, English literature, the fine arts, and first editions. The core of the collection was purchased from the Andrews estate. Gifts have been responsible for further acquisitions such as the books donated by Mr. and Mrs. Orrin B. Wentz on early American history with emphasis on the Lewis and Clark expeditions. The Lulu L. Wood collection of rare and unusual children's books was received from her estate. Recently received was a collection of first editions and original manuscripts of the writings of Jack Matthews, a current Ohio author. A first edition collection of works of the late Louis Bromfield is a part of the collection. A miscellaneous assortment of maps, books, plates, and memorabilia round out the collection.

1241
Baldwin-Wallace College
Ritter Library
275 Eastland Road
Berea, Ohio 44017

Telephone. (216) 826-2424

Institutional Description. The privately supported liberal arts college was formed by a merger of Baldwin University and German-Wallace College in 1913. It is affiliated with the United Methodist Church. Enrollment: 3,032.

Library Administration. Patrick J. Scanlan, Director.

Library General Holdings. 200,000 volumes; 860 cur-

rent periodical subscriptions; 205,000 microforms.

Special Collections

Important special collections include the **Riemenschneider Bach Institute Collection,** of original Bach works; the **Reidenhauer Folk Song Collection,** and the **United Methodist Historical Collection.**

1242
Bluffton College
Mennonite Historical Library
Bluffton, Ohio 45817

Telephone. (419) 358-8015

Institutional Description. The privately supported liberal arts and sciences college was established as an academy; gradually, college-level courses were added. It was founded in 1899 as a Mennonite institution although it has always welcomed students regardless of religious affiliation. Enrollment: 553.

Library Administration. Delbert Gratz, Librarian.

Library General Holdings. 106,700 volumes.

Special Collections

The Mennonite Historical Library. The collection contains approximately 5,000 books, files of about 250 Mennonite periodicals, 8,000 frames of microfilm, and other materials such as maps and clippings. The Library is particularly strong on Swiss, south German, and eastern American Mennonite materials, as well as Mennonite family histories. The collection includes any material relating to the Mennonite Church, including the Amish, Hutterian Brethren, Brethren in Christ, and Apostolic Christian Church. Selected materials that relate to similar groups that are allied historically or doctrinely to the Mennonite Church, such as the Church of the Brethren, Quakers, Schwenckfelders are also included.

1243
Bowling Green State University
William T. Jerome Library
Bowling Green, Ohio 43403

Telephone. (419) 372-7914

Institutional Description. The publicly supported state university grants baccalaureate, master's, specialist, and doctorate degrees. Enrollment: 16,031.

Library Administration. Rush Miller, Dean of Library and Learning Resources; Nancy Steen, Rare Books Librarian.

Library General Holdings. 1,422,889 volumes; 14,150 current periodical subscriptions; 1,354,978 microforms; 486,819 audiovisual materials; 697,812 maps, charts, and photographs; 432,331 government documents.

Special Collections

Center for Archival Collections. Contains materials on northwest Ohio, the University Archives, and Rare Books and Special Collections. It also houses the Sam Pollock Labor Collection.

The Curriculum Resource Center contains materials supporting grades K-12 teacher education.

The Nationally known Popular Culture Library contains the Ray and Pat Browne Collection as well as numerous other materials related to American popular culture.

The Music Library maintains a collection of sound recordings in the field of popular music.

Rare Book Collections

Rare Books Division. Contains works of the fifteenth to twentieth centuries with emphasis on English, Irish, and American literature of the nineteenth and twentieth centuries. Included are books, manuscripts, galleys, broadsides, ephemera, and autographs. Important collections are the works of William Dean Howells, Ray Bradbury, Walt Whitman, and Maxfield Parish. Notable manuscript collections are the Ray Bradbury Collection, the Robert Aickman Collection, and the Jan Wahl Collection.

The Thomas F. Eckman Memorial Collection and the Stranahan Poetry Collection together form a strong collection of English and American poetry from the nineteenth and twentieth centuries.

The Ockuly FDR Collection is a comprehensive collection of books and periodicals and ephemera relating to Franklin D. Roosevelt's life and times.

1244
Capital University
University Libraries
2199 East Main Street
Columbus, Ohio 43209

Telephone. (614) 236-6908

Institutional Description. The privately supported liberal arts and professional university, founded in 1830, is the oldest university in central Ohio and the oldest educational institution of the American Lutheran Church. Enrollment: 2,284.

Library Administration. Albert F. Maag, Director.

Library General Holdings. 145,000 volumes; 1,050 current periodical subscriptions; 45,000 microforms.

Special Collections

The library maintains the **Lois Lenski Collection** of manuscripts, medals, and a complete collection of her books. The **University Archives** are also housed.

1245
Case Western Reserve University
University Libraries
11161 East Boulevard
Cleveland, Ohio 44106

Telephone. (216) 368-2992

Institutional Description. The privately supported university is a combination of two old and respected institutions. Western Reserve College, established in 1826, and Case Institute of Technology, established in 1880, joined in 1967 to form an institution including two undergraduate colleges, eight professional schools, and a graduate school. Enrollment: 6,700.

Library Administration. Susan Cote, Director of Libraries; Sue Hanson, Head of Special Collections/Rare Books.

Library General Holdings. 1,432,560 volumes; 10,322 periodical subscriptions; 353,544 bound documents; 82,-533 microcards; 386,353 microfiche; 20,651 microfilms.

Special Collections

History of the Book Collection. Includes a variety of materials: a cuneiform tablet, fragments of papyri, medieval manuscripts, incunabula, and books from early printing houses such as Aldus Manutius, Elzevier, and Plantin. Also, there are books from private and fine press publishers: Strawberry Hill, Kelmscott, Doves, Roycrofters, Nonesuch, Hogarth, Cuala, Black Sun, Bits.

Literature Collections. There are literature collections such as the Wilhelm Scherer collection of German literature with first editions of German authors and early periodicals such as *Der Deutsche Markur,* the Haskell collection of Illustrated Victorian Literature with books illustrated by Cruikshank, Browne, Rackham, and Tenniel, the Bailey collection of Henry David Thoreau with first editions of Thoreau's works including over forty editions of *Walden.*

History of Science and Technology. Includes first and early editions of major works of science: *De Fabrica* by Vesalius, *Opticks* by Newton, and important early German, French, English, and American journals. The Natural History collection includes 220 plates of Audubon's *Birds of America,* Catesby's *The Natural History of Carolina, Florida, and the Bahama Islands,* and *Travels of Lewis and Clark.*

Fine Arts Collections. Examples of medieval music manuscripts, early printed works such as *Musica Transalpina, L'Art du Facteur d'Orgues, Histoire de la Notation Musicale.* There are also important books of plates, woodcuts, engravings, and etchings and original works of art by William Sommer, Frank Wilcox, Abraham Warshawsky, Malvina Hoffman, and William McVey.

Collections of local interest would include Hart Crane, Black writers Charles Chesnutt and Langston Hughes, papers of the firms of Warner and Swasey and Charles F. Brush and the Ernest J. Bohn Housing and Planning Library. Other book collections include books from the personal library of Henry Adams with a presentation copy of *Mont Saint Michel and Chartres.* The Western Reserve College Library Collection of 1850 was reconstructed with over eighty percent of the books that had been in the library in Hudson, Ohio.

A fine collection of manuscripts representing mostly British and American literary, political, and historical figures has been received from a number of donors. There are letters from Mme. de Sévigné, Voltaire, George III, Oscar Wilde, Virginia Woolf, and John Steinbeck, among others.

1246
Central State University
Hallie Q. Brown Memorial Library
Wilberforce, Ohio 45384

Telephone. (216) 777-3151

Institutional Description. Central State University was founded in 1887. Enrollment: 2,680.

Library Administration. George T. Johnson, Librarian.

Library General Holdings. 146,000 volumes; 900 periodicals; 250,000 microforms.

Special Collections

The library houses three special collections: a collection of books by and about Black Americans; the **Hopping Collection** of newspapers of early Greene County, Ohio; and the memorabilia of Hallie Q. Brown, the renowned educator after whom the library is named.

1247
Cincinnati Bible College and Seminary
G.M. Elliott Library
2700 Glenway Avenue
Cincinnati, Ohio 45204

Telephone. (513) 244-8197

Institutional Description. The privately supported institution was founded in 1924 by the consolidation of two previously-established schools: McGarvey Bible College of Louisville, Kentucky and Cincinnati Bible Institute of Cincinnati, Ohio. Every teacher and trustee must be a member of the Church of Christ. Enrollment: 560.

Library Administration. James H. Lloyd, Library Director.

Library General Holdings. 63,000 volumes; 3,000 bound periodicals; 370 periodical subscriptions; 2,500 microforms; 8,000 audiovisual materials; 62,000 music scores; 4,000 curriculum materials.

Special Collections

The G.M. Elliott Library specializes in Biblical and theological works in general and materials of the Restoration Movement in particular.

1248
Circleville Bible College
Melvin Maxwell Library
P.O. Box 458
Circleville, Ohio 43113

Telephone. (614) 474-8896

Institutional Description. The privately supported professional Bible college was founded in 1948 to prepare persons for Christian service. It is affiliated with the Church of Christ in Christian Union. Enrollment: 180.

Library Administration. Louis Bailey, Librarian.

Library General Holdings. 50,000 volumes.

Special Collections

The library houses the **Stout Bible Collection** of over 225 Bibles and Bible portions in a variety of editions from the 1660s to the present.

1249
Cleveland Institute of Music
CIM Library
11021 East Boulevard
Cleveland, Ohio 44106

Telephone. (216) 791-5165

Institutional Description. The privately supported professional music conservatory was founded in 1920, and grants baccalaureate, master's, and doctoral degrees. It also grants diplomas on both the undergraduate and graduate levels. Enrollment: 338.

Library Administration. Karen Griffith, Director.

Library General Holdings. 45,400 books and scores.

Special Collections

The sound recording collection numbers 11,400 items and includes the Jean Bassett Loesser Tape Library.

1250
Cleveland State University
Main Library
Euclid Avenue at East 24th Street
Cleveland, Ohio 44115

Telephone. (216) 687-2000

Institutional Description. Cleveland State University was founded in 1923 as Fenn College. Enrollment: 17,951.

Library Administration. Bruce E. Langdon, Director, University Libraries.

Library General Holdings. 662,000 volumes; 6,545 periodicals; 518,000 microforms; 8,150 audiovisual materials.

Special Collections

Special collections of the library include the Cleveland City Club Tapes and the Library of American Civilization.

University Archives. The Archives preserve official records, correspondence, publications, photographs, audio-recordings, motion pictures, and other artifacts pertinent to the history and development of the University.

1251
College of Mount St. Joseph
Archbishop Alter Library
5701 Delhi Pike
Mount St. Joseph, Ohio 45051

Telephone. (513) 244-4232

Institutional Description. The privately supported liberal arts college primarily for women was founded in 1920. It is affiliated with the Roman Catholic Church. Enrollment: 1,241.

Library Administration. Cheryl Albrecht, Director.

Library General Holdings. 80,000 volumes; 550 current periodical subscriptions; 7,000 titles in non-print format.

Special Collections

The library maintains a children's literature collection, primarily for the use of students in the elementary and junior high teacher-training program.

1252
College of Wooster
Andrews Library
Wooster, Ohio 44691

Telephone. (216) 263-2152

Institutional Description. The privately supported liberal arts college was founded in 1866. It is affiliated with the United Presbyterian Church. Enrollment: 1,675.

Library Administration. Patricia Rom, Director; Lowell Coolidge, Special Collections Librarian.

Library General Holdings. 740,200 items including books, periodicals, microforms, recordings, audiovisual materials, journals, newspapers, and United States government documents.

Special Collections

Special collections include the **McGregor Collection of Americana;** the **Homer E. McMaster Lincoln Collection;** the **Wallace Notestein Library** of English history; the **Paul O. Peters Collection** of American politics; the **Gregg D. Wolfe Memorial Library of the Theatre,** and other rare books and manuscripts.

1253
Cuyahoga Community College
Learning Resource Center
700 Carnegie Avenue
Cleveland, Ohio 44115

Telephone. (216) 241-5966

Institutional Description. Cuyahoga Community College is comprised of three modern campuses locatede in downtown Cleveland, Parma, and Warrensville Township. Enrollment: 12,117.

Library Administration. Margaret Barron, Librarian.

Library General Holdings. 30,000 volumes; 300 periodical titles; 3,000 pamphlets; 4,000 microforms.

Special Collections

Special collections on **Black Studies** and oral history are maintained.

1254
Defiance College
Anthony Wayne Library
701 North Clinton Street
Defiance, Ohio 43512

Telephone. (419) 784-4010

Institutional Description. The privately supported liberal arts college was founded in 1886. It is affiliated with the United Church of Christ. Enrollment: 808.

Library Administration. Maxie J. Lambright, Director.

Library General Holdings. 90,000 volumes; 520 periodicals; 9,500 microforms.

Special Collections

Special collections include the **Indian Wars Collection** and an **Afro-American Collection.**

Eisenhower Room. Contains a rare book collection and mementos of the Eisenhower administration.

1255
Dyke College
Library Resource Center
112 Prospect Avenue
Cleveland, Ohio 44115

Telephone. (216) 696-9000

Institutional Description. The privately supported college concentrates on business and business-related fields of study. It grants associate and baccalaureate degrees and diplomas. Enrollment: 913.

Library Administration. Darwyn J. Batway, Director.

Library General Holdings. 12,500 volumes; 135 current periodical subscriptions.

Special Collections

Special collections include samples of writing and calligraphy of Spencerian College founder Platt R. Spencer and his students. A business reference collection is also maintained.

1256
Findlay College
Shafer Library
1000 North Main Street
Findlay, Ohio 45840

Telephone. (419) 422-8313

Institutional Description. The privately supported liberal arts college was founded in 1882. It is affiliated with the Churches of God in North America. Enrollment: 1,-328.

Library Administration. Robert Schirmer, Director.

Library General Holdings. 100,000 books; 600 periodicals.

Special Collections

The library maintains the congressional papers of Tennyson Guyer (1951-1973) and Jackson Betts (1951-1973). The College Archives are also preserved by the library.

1257
Franklin University
University Library
201 South Grant Avenue
Columbus, Ohio 43215

Telephone. (614) 224-6237

Institutional Description. The privately supported liberal arts and technical college grants associate and baccalaureate degrees. Enrollment: 2,863.

Library Administration. William E. Snyder, Head Librarian.

Library General Holdings. 148,000 items; 1,200 current periodical subscriptions.

Special Collections

Specialized collections available include an extensive product information file and the most extensive tax information center in central Ohio.

1258
Hebrew Union College - Jewish Institute of Religion
Library
3101 Clifton Avenue
Cincinnati, Ohio 45220

Telephone. (513) 221-1875

Institutional Description. The privately supported institution was formed by a merger, in 1950, of two old and respected institutes of higher learning: The Hebrew Union College (the rabbinic school of Reform Judaism in America founded in 1875) and The Jewish Institute of Religion (founded in 1922). Enrollment: 157.

Library Administration. Herbert C. Zafren, Librarian; Arnona Rudavsky, Coordinator of Special Collections.

Library General Holdings. 350,000 volumes; 2,000 periodical and newspaper subscriptions; 15,500 microfilm reels; 18,600 microfiche; 2,500 music records and cassettes; 2,000 manuscript codices and many thousands of manuscript pages; numerous archival collections.

Special Collections

The emphasis of the library's collection is on Judaica, Hebraica, and Bible studies. Within these areas, the special collections include a recorded music collection and song index to this collection; filmstrips and slides; maps from the fifteenth century to the present, primarily of the Holy Land; over 500 titles on microfilm of American Jewish periodicals, housed in the American Jewish Periodical Center; the Cuneiform Studies Room Collection which brings together basic texts and reference works for the study of languages written in cuneiform script; ephemeral material relating to Jewish institutions; Rabbinic Resource Center vertical file; and manuscripts on microfilm from other library collections such as the Vatican Library.

Rare Book Collections

Hebrew Union College Library Rare Book Collection. Contains some 14,000 printed books and over 2,000 manuscript codices as well as many thousands of manuscript pages. Among the printed books are: Hebrew and non-Hebrew incunabula; 1,300 volumes of sixteenth-century Hebrew books; Josephus and Spinoza collections; British Judaica; Jewish Americana dating to 1875; and Inquisition sermons. Among the manuscripts are: 52 Hebrew manuscripts from Kaifeng, China; illuminated manuscripts, including the fifteenth-century Cincinnati Haggadah; and fifty Samaritan manuscripts. Other collections include: Broadsides Collection; Jewish Theater Collection; Eduard Birnbaum Manuscript Collection in Jewish music; Moses Marx's unpublished *History and Annals of Hebrew Printing;* stamp collections; Bookplate Collection; as well as other inventoried collections.

1259
Heidelberg College
Beeghly Library
10 Greenfield Street
Tiffin, Ohio 44883

Telephone. (419) 448-2104

Institutional Description. The privately supported college, founded in 1850, is affiliated with the United Church of Christ. It sponsors student exchange programs with the University of Heidelberg (Germany), and cooperative programs with Ohio State University, Duke University, Case Western Reserve University, and several hospitals. Enrollment: 965.

Library Administration. Janice Strickland, Director of Library Services.

Library General Holdings. 152,850 volumes; 715 periodical and newspaper subscriptions; 9,185 microform volumes.

Special Collections

Besse Collection. Includes 7,152 volumes of published letters, primarily English and American authors; approximately 800 are considered rare book material.

Other collections include the **Pohlable Ballet Collection** and the **Scott Collection of American First Editions.**

1260
Hiram College
Teachout-Price Memorial Library
Hiram, Ohio 44234

Telephone. (216) 569-5359

Institutional Description. The privately supported liberal arts college's fundamental aim is to encourage scholarship and citizenship. It was founded by the Christian Church (Disciples of Christ) in 1850. Enrollment: 1,189.

Library Administration. Gorman L. Duffett, Librarian; Joanne M. Sawyer, Archivist and Special Collections/Rare Books Librarian.

Library General Holdings. 165,000 volumes; 800 periodical subscriptions; 25 newspaper subscriptions; 7,800 microfilm reels (mostly newspaper backfiles); 34,000 microfiche (mostly periodical backfiles); 114,000 federal government documents; 20,000 Ohio documents; 5,300 sound recordings; 2,200 music scores.

Special Collections

Archives. Contains the archives and related photographic collections of Hiram College and the local area.

Harold E. Davis Collection. Contains World War I propaganda pamphlets and a collection of World War I sheet music.

Maurice and Ethlynn Fox Collection. Includes antique regional maps, atlases, gazeteers, travel diaries, and country histories.

James A. Garfield Collection. Contains manuscripts, newspapers, books, and ephemera relating to the twentieth President of the United States.

Nicholas Vachel Lindsay Collection. Original manuscripts and drawings, publications, and criticism; among the notable manuscripts are those of Burke A. Hinsdale, John S. Kenyon, Robert A. Liston, Eugene H. Peters, Grace E. Pickford, and Edmund B. Wakefield.

The library also contains special collections of Regional Studies monographs pertaining to Ohio's Western Reserve area; Church History, especially the Christian Church (Disciples of Christ); and the published works of Hiram authors.

1261
John Carroll University
Grasselli Library
University Heights
Cleveland, Ohio 44118

Telephone. (216) 397-4711

Institutional Description. The privately supported Roman Catholic university was founded in 1886 by the Society of Jesus, and known as St. Ignatius College. The present name was adopted in 1923. Enrollment: 2,943.

Library Administration. John S. Piety, Director; Marcy Milota, Librarian; Laurie R. Nalepa, Rare Books Librarian.

Library General Holdings. 323,055 books; 1,320 periodical titles; 139,213 microforms; 31 items of software; 46 films/videocassettes; 394 filmstrips; 3,431 slides; 2,412 recordings; 263 audiotapes.

Rare Book Collections

G.K. Chesterton Room. The primary focal point of the special collections housed in this room is the Robert John Bayer Chesterton Collection. Gilbert Keight Chesterton (1874-1936) was a poet, critic, essayist, and humorist who attained much renown during his time; his works are still studied all over the world. The collection contains over 1,000 items written by or about G.K. Chesterton—first editions of all 111 of his books and pamphlets; volumes as well as manuscripts, drawings, and a fine collection of microfilmed material which comes from the manuscripts and notebooks of Miss Dorothy Collins, Chesterton's daughter by adoption, secretary, and literary executrix.

1262
Kent State University
Kent State University Libraries
Kent, Ohio 44242

Telephone. (216) 672-2962

Institutional Description. The publicly supported state university includes seven regional campuses. It awards baccalaureate, master's, and doctorate degrees, and provides research facilities. Enrollment: 16,565.

Library Administration. Don L. Tolliver, University Librarian; Alex Gildzen, Curator of Special Collections.

Library General Holdings. 1,600,000 volumes; 7,000 serial subscriptions; 20,300 music scores; 9,800 film/video titles.

Special Collections

The strengths of the Department of Special Collections are in nineteenth- and twentieth-century American and British literature and history with significant holdings in cryptography, graphic design, motion pictures, parapsychology, and printing.

The primary specialized collections within the general stacks are the **Ethnic Collection** (15,000 titles in Latvian, Lithuanian, Polish, Rumanian and other Baltic languages), **Children's Literature** (11,800 titles), and the **Three Rivers Collection** of 500 titles on water resource management.

Rare Book Collections

Among collections in the rare books and manuscript division are the archives of the Open Theater, Saalfield Publishing Company, *Prose* magazine, Broadcast Designers Association and University and College Design Association, papers of actor-director Joseph Chaikin, playwright Jean-Claude van Itallie, fantasy writer Stephen R. Donaldson, poet-playwright Marc Kaminsky, and film historians Gerald Mast and James Robert Parish. Among collections in the archives division is the May 4th Collection, the Betsy Mix Cowles papers, and the records of the Catholic Diocese of Youngstown and the International Brotherhood of Pottery and Allied Workers.

1263
Kenyon College
Olin Chalmers Memorial Library
Gambier, Ohio 43022

Telephone. (614) 427-5186

Institutional Description. The privately supported liberal arts college was founded in 1824, as Ohio's first private college. It is affiliated with the Episcopal Church. Enrollment: 1,518.

Library Administration. Haslen Marley, Acting Director.

Library General Holdings. 340,000 volumes; 1,000 current periodical subscriptions; 200,000 microforms.

Special Collections

The library maintains special collections of the papers of poet James Wright, a graduate of Kenyon College; first and variant editions of the works of William Butler Yeats; and books on and works from fine printing presses and typeface designers. The **Philander Chase Letters** and the Charles Pettit McIlvaine Letters are also maintained.

1264
Lake Erie College
Lincoln Library
391 West Washington Street
Painesville, Ohio 44077

Telephone. (216) 352-3361

Institutional Description. The privately supported liberal arts college for women was founded in 1856. As well as the traditional liberal arts curricula, the college offers career-oriented programs including pre-professional and professional studies. Enrollment: 489.

Library Administration. Terry G. Hancox, Director.

Library General Holdings. 95,000 volumes; 400 periodical titles.

Special Collections

The **Thomas Harvey Collection** includes the library of the nineteenth-century American grammarian.

1265
Lourdes College
Duns Scotus Library
6832 Convent Boulevard
Sylvania, Ohio 43560

Telephone. (419) 885-3211

Institutional Description. The privately supported liberal arts college is conducted by the Roman Catholic Sisters of St. Francis. It was Founded in 1958. Enrollment: 420.

Library Administration. Sr. Mary Thomas More (Ruffing), Librarian.

Library General Holdings. 49,000 volumes; 280 current periodicals; 13 newspaper subscriptions; 7,900 microforms; 800 audiovisual items.

Special Collections

The library has a special collection of Franciscan Order books collected over the years by the Sisters of St. Francis, the founding corporation of the College; a large collection of Bibles (English and foreign language); dictionaries, especially various English language publications; a collection of Shakespeare references; and a collection of ancient maps papered to the walls of a special reading/stack room.

Rare Book Collections

The library maintains a separate unit of materials of rare editions, foreign (European, Middle East, Orient, and American) dating from ca. 1500. There are antiphonies and hand-printed manuscripts, special Bible editions, special Shakespeare editions, various facsimiles, first editions, limited editions, and unique printings.

1266
Malone College
College Library
515 25th Street N.W.
Canton, Ohio 44709

Telephone. (216) 489-0800

Institutional Description. The privately supported liberal arts college was founded in 1892. It is affiliated with the Evangelical Friends Church. Enrollment: 891.

Library Administration. R. Stanford Terhune, Jr., Director of Library Services.

Library General Holdings. 95,000 volumes; 51,500 government documents; 8,400 microforms.

Special Collections

The library maintains a collection of 1,552 volumes in Quaker history.

1267
Marietta College
Dawes Memorial Library
Marietta, Ohio 45750

Telephone. (614) 374-4757

Institutional Description. The privately supported liberal arts college grants baccalaureate and first-professional degrees. Enrollment: 1,140.

Library Administration. Robert Cayton, College Librarian.

Library General Holdings. 280,588 volumes (including 5,539 microfilm; 16,422 microfiche; 6,076 audiovisual items); 918 current periodical and newspaper subscriptions.

Special Collections

The Special Collections, presently numbering 35,000 volumes and 32,000 manuscripts, contain materials related to the Old Northwest Territory; the city of Marietta; three incunabula; rare editions; nineteenth-century textbooks and travel; American literature; Ohio Company of Associates records; nineteenth-century Americana (Indian, Civil War, slavery, abolition); Marietta College (1835-) archives; science fiction; maps; photographs; and oral history tapes. Included among the collections are the Fischer and Hoag collections of photographs. Among the notable manuscript collections are the papers of Samuel P. Hildreth, the Cutler Collection of correspondence, and papers of Ephraim and William Parker Cutler; the Dawes Collection of autographed letters and documents of internationally known men and women of the past 400 years; papers of the Putnam family, the Frances Macmillan family, and Edward B. Manley.

1268
Methodist Theological School in Ohio
The John W. Dickhaut Library
P.O. Box 1204
Delaware, Ohio 43015

Telephone. (614) 363-1146

Institutional Description. The privately supported theological school admitted its first class in 1960. It is affiliated with The United Methodist Church. Enrollment: 168.

Library Administration. M. Edward Hunter, Librarian; Julia Foster, Reference Librarian.

Library General Holdings. 85,000 volumes; 329 periodical subscriptions.

Special Collections

Philip Gatch Manuscripts. Manuscripts by and related to Philip Gatch, early Methodist circuit rider. Includes autobiographical and biographical materials, including many primary sources; correspondence; unpublished and/or partial manuscripts; photographs and information about relatives and descendants; documents regarding churches begun or influenced by Philip Gatch. Much of the material relates to general early Methodistica, including controversial issues from the 1970s.

McCleary Colllection. Includes books and manuscript materials donated by Rev. Paul McCleary which includes several smaller collections. Major divisions include:

World Council of Churches. Covers major WCC Central Committee meetings; WCC Assemblies from 1955-1984 with primary and working documents from many of the same; extensive information on Unit II from late 1970s/early 1980s; some information on Units I and III, EDCS; transcripts and correspondence regarding "Reader's Digest" and "60 Minutes" controversies.

National Council of Churches. Governing Board information and minutes, working papers, etc., from 1975-1983; participation in WCC.

Latin America. Cuban church issues and Cuban refugee exodus of the early 1970s; journal articles on Latin American politics and economics; Board of Global Ministries activities in Latin America; and materials on Methodist Church activities in Bolivia.

Vietnam. Includes information on Kampuchea and China; wheat shipments to Vietnam; general politics.

World Division UMC. 1969-1970 Quadrennial emphasis.

Church World Service. Committee meeting files, 1975-1984.

Structure Study Commission. Extensive documents from early surveys and consultants' recommendations; various questionnaires; SSC meeting minutes and working papers; 1972 General Conference material.

1269
Miami University
King Library
Oxford, Ohio 45056

Telephone. (513) 529-3323

Institutional Description. The publicly supported university was founded in 1824. There are branches in Middletown and Hamilton. Enrollment: 18,025.

Library Administration. Judith Sessions, University Librarian; Helen Ball, Curator, Special Collections.

Library General Holdings. 1,126,000 volumes; 6,000 current periodical and newspaper subscriptions; 140,000 federal government publications; 1,850,000 microforms; 85,000 maps.

Special Collections

The overall, generalized strength of specialized collections within the stacks of the library are in nineteenth century material.

Rare Book Collections

Various rare material collections include regional history (including manuscripts); antiquarian children's books (1535 to 1930s); school books (nineteenth century, mostly American—large collection of McGuffey readers; McGuffey letters); Americana; author collections (William Dean Howells, James Farrell, George Orwell, Mark Twain, Eugene O'Neill); Russia (pre-revolutionary); regimental histories; private press books.

1270
Mount Union College
College Library
1972 Clark
Alliance, Ohio 44601

Telephone. (216) 821-5320

Institutional Description. The privately supported liberal arts college was founded in 1846. It is affiliated with the United Methodist Church. Enrollment: 1,055.

Library Administration. William E. Coleman, Jr., Director.

Library General Holdings. 209,500 volumes; 850 current periodicals; 5,000 slides and photographic reproductions of works of art.

Rare Book Collections

Samuel Austin English Bible Collection. Contains several sixteenth-century Bibles; there are a number of other rare and unusual Bibles included with the collection such as the Bruce Rogers World Bible and a facsimile reproduction of the Gutenberg Bible.

Sutherin Classical Collection. A collection of rare and early editions of Greek and Latin classics and facsimiles of Biblical codices.

1271
Mount Vernon Nazarene College
Library
800 Martinsburg Road
Mount Vernon, Ohio 43050

Telephone. (614) 397-1244

Institutional Description. The privately supported liberal arts college was founded in 1966 as the official college of the East Central education zone of the Church of the Nazarene. Enrollment: 945.

Library Administration. Richard L. Schuster, Director.

Library General Holdings. 95,000 volumes; 500 current periodical subscriptions.

Special Collections

The library supports the liberal arts curriculum of the college which is offered in a Christian environment.

1272
Muskingum Area Technical College
College Library
1555 Newark Road
Zanesville, Ohio 43701

Telephone. (614) 454-2501

Institutional Description. The two-year technical college was founded in 1969. The present campus, shared with Ohio University-Zanesville, was occupied in 1972. Enrollment: 929.

Library Administration. Roberta M. Armstrong, Librarian.

Library General Holdings. 14,000 volumes; 240 current periodical subscriptions; 2,000 pamphlets; 1,780 recordings.

Special Collections

The library maintains a collection of local genealogical materials.

1273
Muskingum College
College Library
New Concord, Ohio 43762

Telephone. (614) 826-8115

Institutional Description. The privately supported liberal arts college was founded in 1837. It is affiliated with the United Presbyterian Church in the U.S.A. Enrollment: 1,036.

Library Administration. Richard M. Cochran, Director.

Library General Holdings. 178,000 volumes; 780 periodical subscriptions; 45,000 federal government documents; 7,000 Ohio documents; 25,000 bound periodicals; 60,000 microforms.

Special Collections

Special collections housed in the library include materials on Ohio history; British history; and the papers of Muskingham College presidents.

1274
North Central Technical College
Learning Resources Center
2441 Kenwood Circle
Mansfield, Ohio 44901

Telephone. (419) 747-4999

Institutional Description. The two-year technical college offers university-parallel and career program. The college was established in 1968. Enrollment: 1,169.

Library General Holdings. 126,125 volumes; 466 current periodical titles; 2,500 microforms; 15,000 audiovisual materials.

Special Collections

The library maintains the **Louis Bromfield Collection** of manuscripts, first editions, photographs, and personal materials.

1275
Northeastern Ohio Universities College of Medicine
Oliver Ocasek Regional Medical Information Center
P.O. Box 95
Rootstown, Ohio 44272

Telephone. (216) 325-2511

Institutional Description. The publicly supported medical college was founded in 1973. Enrollment: 379.

Library Administration. G. Thomas Osterfield, Archivist.

Library General Holdings. 28,049 monographs; 1,051 serial titles (659 journal subscriptions); 2,597 audiovisual items; 698 computer diskettes.

Special Collections

Although the Ocasek Information Center is a general purpose medical school library with emphasis on the basic medical sciences, it also has significant holdings in "home remedies" and human values in medicine. The Center also collects general items about the Western Reserve area of Ohio.

The special collections include the archives of the College of Medicine and its Foundation; medical curriculum materials; oral history tapes about the College and about health care in the Western Reserve; office records and personal files of local health care providers; and medical and surgical instruments illustrating the development of local health care primarily in this century.

1276
Oberlin College
College Library
Mudd Center
Oberlin, Ohio 44074

Telephone. (216) 775-8285

Institutional Description. The privately supported liberal arts college was founded in 1833, one of the world's first coeducational colleges. There are two divisions: College of Arts and Sciences, and the Conservatory of Music. Enrollment: 2,805.

Library Administration. William A. Moffett, Librarian; Dina Schoonmaker, Special Collections Librarian; Roland M. Baumann, Archivist; Eric J. Carpenter, Collection Development Librarian.

Library General Holdings. 889,724 volumes; 2,656 current periodicals; 86 newspaper subscriptions; 271,819 microforms; 61,470 music scores; 31,547 musical disc recordings.

Special Collections

American Communist Party Pamphlets. 786 items from the papers of House Committee on Un-American Activities investigator Michael A. Ondreyco, acquired in 1983. Mainly pamphlets published by the Communist Party of the United States of America's New Century Publishers, Workers Library Publishers, and International Publishers. Also includes U.S. Government documents and pamphlets from the Communist Party of Great Britain.

Antislavery. Over 2,500 abolitionist books and pamphlets published prior to the Emancipation Proclamation. Most of the collection has been reprinted on microcards which are available for public use in the Library.

Early Imprints. American titles published prior to 1821 and English and European titles published prior to 1801.

Oberliniana. Materials written by and about Oberlin and Oberlinians, including books from the Oberlin Collegiate Institute Library.

Spanish Drama. Approximately 8,000 Spanish language plays dating from the last quarter of the seventeenth century to 1924.

History of the Book. Many examples of fine printing and binding, including manuscripts, incunabula, and limited and private press editions.

Violin Society of America/Goodkind. Over 4,500 books, journals, articles, and auction catalogs relating to the making and playing of violins and other stringed instruments, and to the people who made and played them.

Oberlin College Archives. Includes records relating to the College of Arts and Sciences and the Conservatory of Music; records of the Graduate School of Theology, 1835-1966; official records of eleven college presidents, 1843-1981; general files of the Office of the Provost, 1961-1983; files of college departments, organizations and committees; faculty and student publications; catalogues and yearbooks.

Both Special Collections and the College Archives are strong in black history, women's history, coeducation, liberal arts education, women's suffrage, temperance, abolitionism, missionary work in Far East, and women's rights. Other notable materials include books with important illustrations or plates, pamphlets on women's concerns, and collections of American dime novels, popular sheet music, War of 1812 materials, and Edwin Arlington Robinson books.

Other areas of interest are architecture and landscape gardening (housed in the Art Library); nineteenth century American Protestant Evangelicalism: church history, sermons, tracts, and missionary activities (especially in Asia); travel literature related to nineteenth century American Protestant missionary activity abroad; East Asian Collection of 16,000 volumes in Chinese and Japanese (works in humanities and some social sciences).

1277
Ohio Dominican College
Spangler Library
1216 Sunbury Road
Columbus, Ohio 43219

Telephone. (614) 253-2741

Institutional Description. The privately supported liberal arts college was founded in 1911 as the College of St. Mary of the Springs. It is affiliated with the Roman Catholic Church. Enrollment: 884.

Library Administration. Sister Rosalie Graham, O.P., Director.

Library General Holdings. 102,000 volumes; 600 periodicals.

Special Collections

The collection of the Spangler Library is especially strong in the areas of philosophy, theology, sociology, and education. It includes 8,000 volumes donated by a noted Biblical scholar.

1278
Ohio State University
William O. Thompson Memorial Library
1800 Cannon Drive
Columbus, Ohio 43210

Telephone. (614) 422-2424

Institutional Description. The publicly supported state university was founded in 1870 as the Ohio Agricultural and Mechanical College. It now includes 17 colleges and a graduate school. There are 9 schools within the colleges. Enrollment: 52,039.

Library Administration. Robert A. Tibbitts, Rare Books and Special Collections Librarian; Raimund Goerler, University Archivist.

Library General Holdings. 4,000,000 volumes; 30,000 periodicals; 530,000 government documents; 2,650,000 microforms; 12,000 audiovisual materials. The Ohio State University library system is one of the 17 largest library systems in the United States. Included are the Main Library (William O. Thompson Memorial Library) and more than 30 department and other libraries. The latter are libraries specializing in particular subjects or groups of related subjects, such as agriculture, biological sciences, commerce, education, geology, music, and physics. The Main Library contains the collections pertaining to most of the disciplines of the humanities and social sciences, a general reference service, the microform and newspaper collections, and the rare book collection.

Special Collections

Various reading rooms in the Main Library are organized for specialized study and research in English, communication and theatre, history, philosophy and political science, classics, German, Romance languages and linguistics, international studies, Black studies, and women's studies.

Several of the important special collections are the **William Charvat Collection of American Fiction;** the **James Thurber Collection,** and the Hilander Research Library.

The library maintains the archives of the American Association of Editorial Cartoonists and records of the American Plywrights' Theatre. The **Richard E. Byrd Papers** and the **Floyd and Marion Rinhart Collection** of daguerrotypes are also housed. There are also collections of Australiana, Reformation history, bookplate literature, little magazines, science fiction magazines, and Oriole Press imprints.

1279
Ohio State University - Mansfield Campus
Louis Bromfield Resources Center
1660 University Drive
Mansfield, Ohio 44906

Telephone. (419) 755-4321

Institutional Description. The Mansfield Campus of The Ohio State University offers programs leading to the associate and baccalaureate degrees. Enrollment: 1,141.

Library Administration. David Cheltham, Director.

Library General Holdings. 47,000 volumes; 446 periodical subscriptions.

Special Collections

The **Louis Bromfield Papers** are maintained by the Resources Center. Bromfield was a native of Ohio and resided on a one-thousand acre farm in the Mansfield area. The farm was made famous in *Pleasant Valley* (1945), *Malabar Farm* (1948), *Out of the Earth* (1950), and *From My Experience* (1955).

1280
Ohio University
Vernon R. Alden Library
Park Place
Athens, Ohio 45701

Telephone. (614) 593-2703

Institutional Description. The publicly supported university features a University Honors Tutorial College which permits academically- and creatively-gifted students to study on a one-to-one basis with faculty tutors. The university was founded in 1804. Enrollment: 16,214.

Library Administration. Hwa-Wei Lee, University Librarian; George W. Bain, Head, Department of Archives and Special Collections; Sheppard Black, Rare Books Librarian.

Library General Holdings. 1,300,000 volumes (including 260,800 government documents); 1,400,000 microforms; 10,000 current periodicals.

Special Collections

Southeast Asia Collections. Focuses on the ASEAN nations; 90,000 volumes and 5,000 serials; resources are particularly rich in materials of nineteenth- and twentieth-century Indonesia, contemporary Malaysia, Singapore, and Brunei; includes materials on Sumatra and South Java.

Fine Arts Library. 40,000 volumes; 175 periodicals; especially strong in photography, film criticism, film history, and film theory.

Health Sciences Library. 80,000 volumes; 1,478 periodicals; particular strengths in osteopathic medicine, cardiovascular physiology, neuromuscular physiology, and exercise physiology.

Music/Dance Library. 30,000 volumes; 10,000 recordings; 130 periodicals; particular emphasis on music history, music theory, and jazz. The Library houses the **Richard D. Wetzel Collection** of printed sheet music (1790-1900) and American communal music.

Rare Book Collections

The Archives and Special Collections Department. Houses both archival and rare book materials. The book collections include Ohioana collection with a southeastern Ohio emphasis; the Morgan Collection in the History of

Chemistry; the Osteopathic Medicine collection; the Edmund Blunden library of Romantic and Georgian literature; and collections for the authors Arnold Bennett, Thomas Campbell, William Combe, William Cowper, George Crabbe, Charles Dickens, Samuel Foote, John Galsworthy, Lafcadio Hearn, Maurice Hewlett, Thomas Hood, Leigh Hunt, Rudyard Kipling, Arthur Machen, George Moore, Samuel Rogers, John Ruskin, Alfred Tennyson, and H.G. Wells.

Archival records and manuscripts collections include the University archives (1804-present); local government records for eighteen southeastern Ohio counties; faculty papers collections including psychologist Harvey Lehman, biographer Paul M. Kendall, musician Eusebia Hunkins, and writer Charles Allen Smart; manuscript collections including Cornelius Ryan (war books research files); a presidential campaign artifacts collection (1824-1980); two recent Congressional papers collections; labor history collections including United Mine Workers-District 6, and two Oil, Chemical and Atomic Workers locals; and local collections such as the Athens chapter, League of Women Voters.

1281
Ohio Wesleyan University
Leon A. Beeghly Library
Delaware, Ohio 43015

Telephone. (614) 369-4431

Institutional Description. The privately supported liberal arts college was founded in 1842. It is affiliated with the United Methodist Church. Enrollment: 1,453.

Library Administration. Kathleen Weibel, Director.

Library General Holdings. 412,000 volumes; 1,165 current periodicals; 11,500 microfiche; 46,000 government documents.

Special Collections

Important special collections in the Beeghly Library include the **Gonsaulus Browning Collection** of manuscripts and artifacts from the poets Elizabeth Barrett and Robert Browning; the **Bayley Walt Whitman Collection;** and the regional history of Methodism in the United Methodist Archives.

1282
Otterbein College
Courtright Memorial Library
West College Avenue
Westerville, Ohio 43081

Telephone. (614) 898-1215

Institutional Description. The privately supported liberal arts college was founded in 1847. It is affiliated with the United Methodist Church. Enrollment: 1,601.

Library Administration. Alberta Mackenzie, Director.

Library General Holdings. 150,000 volumes; 890 current periodicals; 62,500 government documents; 59,000 microforms; 8,200 audiovisual materials.

Special Collections

Special collections include the historical records of the United Methodist Church and Otterbein College.

1283
Pontifical College Josephinum
A.T. Wehrle Memorial Library
7625 North High Street
Columbus, Ohio 43085

Telephone. (614) 885-5585

Institutional Description. The privately supported seminary college was founded in 1888. Its main purpose is to prepare students for the Roman Catholic priesthood. Baccalaureate, professional, and master's degrees are granted. Enrollment: 211.

Library Administration. Peter G. Veracka, Director.

Library General Holdings. 87,000 books; 13,000 bound periodicals; 415 periodical titles; 2,000 audiovisual items.

Special Collections

The Special Collections area houses archival material, rare books, and incunabula in theology and philosophy.

1284
Raymond Walters General and Technical College
Library
9555 Plainfield Road
Cincinnati, Ohio 45236

Telephone. (513) 745-4200

Institutional Description. Raymond Walters General and Technical College is one of eighteen colleges and divisions of the University of Cincinnati. It was founded in 1967 and offers two-year career, transfer, and general education programs. Enrollment: 3,108.

Library Administration. Lucy Wilson, College Librarian.

Library General Holdings. 41,153 volumes; 610 current periodical titles; 1,500 microforms; 2,500 audiovisual materials.

Special Collections

The library has a special collection on dental hygiene.

1285
Trinity Lutheran Seminary Library
2199 East Main Street
Columbus, Ohio 43209

Telephone. (614) 235-4136

Institutional Description. The privately supported theological seminary was founded in 1930. In 1978, the seminary consolidated with the Hamma School of Theology. Trinity Lutheran Seminary is affiliated with the American Lutheran Church and the Lutheran Church in America. Enrollment: 278.

Library Administration. Donald L. Huber, Librarian.

Library General Holdings. 90,000 volumes; 525 current periodicals.

Special Collections

The library supports the theological mission of the Seminary.

1286
United Theological Seminary
Memorial Library
1810 Harvard Boulevard
Dayton, Ohio 45406

Telephone. (513) 278-5817

Institutional Description. The privately supported graduate seminary was founded in 1871, and took its present name in 1954 as the result of the union of the Bonebrake Theological Seminary and the Evangelical School of Theology. It is a seminary of The United Methodist Church. Enrollment: 219.

Library Administration. Rev. Elmer J. O'Brien, Librarian; Rev. Richard R. Berg, Assistant Librarian and Special Collections/Rare Books Librarian.

Library General Holdings. 110,000 volumes; 400 current periodical and newspaper subscriptions; 500 microfilm reels; 1,500 microfiche sheets, plus videocassettes, audiocassettes, filmstrips, and kits.

Special Collections

E.S. Lorenz Hymnal Collection. Comprises some 300 volumes of hymn and tune books from the early nineteenth century to the present.

Rare Book Collections

The library contains materials related to the former Evangelical United Brethren Church and its antecedents, the Church of the United Brethren in Christ, the Evangelical Association of North America, The United Evangelical Church, and the Evangelical Church. Included among the collections are 7,000 volumes consisting of books by denominational officials in the area of doctrine, polity, history, theology, Biblical studies; official publications of the denominations including disciplines, General Conference proceedings, Board and judicatory minutes, annual conference proceedings, and newspapers.

Among the manuscript collections are the papers of Dr. Paul H. Eller, including the Hyman Commission of the Evangelical United Brethren Church; Bishop Grant D. Batdorf (1874-1954); Bishop Wesley Matthias Stanford (1846-1923); Bishop Paul M. Milhouse (1910-); Miss Mary McLanachan (1905-1985); Rev. Lloyd Mignery, including Anti-Saloon League materials, World War II chaplaincy materials, and general church correspondence; Schuyler Colfax Enck (1868-1963); Rev. Joseph Graham; Otterbein Thomas Deever; Emerson Bragg; Louis Odon; Rev. and Mrs. Walter Schutz. Also included in the collection are the archives of United Theological Seminary (1871-) and many of its faculty, most notably: Dr. Walter Roberts, Dr. Merl Harner, Dr. George A. Funkhouser, Dr. John Knecht, Dr. Irvin W. Batdorf, Dr. Harriet L. Miller, Dr. J. Arthur Heck, Dr. Arthur C. Core, and others.

1287
University of Akron
Bierce Library
302 East Buchtel Avenue
Akron, Ohio 44325

Telephone. (216) 375-7497

Institutional Description. The publicly supported state university was originally founded as the Buchtel College by the Ohio Universalist Convention. It became a public institution in 1913. Enrollment: 17,535.

Library Administration. George V. Hodowanec, Director.

Library General Holdings. 1,935,000 volumes; 6,415 periodical subscriptions; 396,000 government documents; 771,000 microforms.

Special Collections

Major special collections include the **Archives of the History of American Psychology;** the **Herman Muehlstein Rare Book Collection;** and the **University Archives.** The **American History Research Center** is also on the campus.

1288
University of Cincinnati
University Libraries
Cincinnati, Ohio 45221

Telephone. (513) 475-2218

Institutional Description. The publicly supported state university includes the Evening College, the University College, and the Ohio College of Applied Science. Enrollment: 24,962.

Library Administration. Linda J. Cain, Dean and University Librarian.

Library General Holdings. 1,500,000 volumes; 19,650 current periodicals; 2,100,000 microforms.

Special Collections

Important special collections include a **Modern Greek Collection,** a collection of eighteenth-century English literature, the **McNamara Collection** of American labory history, and a collection of German-Americana. Also housed are the **Elliston Poetry Collection,** the **D.H. Lawrence Collection,** the **Cincinnati Observatory Collection,** the **Dorbell Collection** of eighteenth-century British anonymous poetical pamphlets; and the **Oesper Collection** on the history of chemistry.

1289
University of Dayton
Roesch Library
300 College Park Avenue
Dayton, Ohio 45469

Telephone. (513) 229-4221

Institutional Description. The privately supported Roman Catholic university was founded over a century ago by the Catholic teaching order of the Society of Mary. Enrollment: 9,000.

Library Administration. Edward Garten, University Librarian; Cecilia Mushenheim, Special Collections Librarian; Raymond H. Nartker, Rare Books Librarian; Thomas Thompson, S.M., Special Collections Librarian for the Marian Library; William Fackovec, S.M., Librarian for the Marian Library.

Library General Holdings. 533,594 bound volumes; 2,450 periodical subscriptions; 253,221-volume equivalent of microforms; 183,883 government documents.

Special Collections

The Roesch Library maintains a Curriculum Materials Center housing children's literature and other curriculum materials.

Marian Library. The Marian Library is a special division of the Roesch Library of the University of Dayton. It is the world's largest collection of printed materials whose focus is the Blessed Virgin Mary. It houses over 72,000 books and pamphlets from all five centuries of printing history and written in over 50 languages. A general reference collection on the Bible, Church history, patristic studies, liturgy, Christian art, and general bibliography forms a base for the Marian works: theological tracts, collections of prayers, histories of shrines, biographies of Marian devotees, works on Marian organizations. There is a collection of newspaper clippings and other ephemera (52,000 items) as well as thousands of postcards (shrines and art works), photographs, devotional pictures, medals, albums of Marian stamps, and slides.

Rare Book Collections

Rare Book Collection. This collection of 7,200 volumes includes first editions of nineteenth- and early twentieth-century English and American literature; works of Paul Laurence Dunbar, Booth Tarkington, Charles Craddock, George McCutcheon; Lincoln and the Civil War; Limited Editions books; theology; church history; and canon law.

1290
University of Toledo
William S. Carlson Library
22801 West Bancroft
Toledo, Ohio 43606

Telephone. (419) 472-4480

Institutional Description. The publicly supported state university contains eight colleges. Enrollment: 15,-833.

Library Administration. Leslie W. Sheridan, University Librarian; Richard W. Oram, Director, Canaday Center for Special Collections.

Library General Holdings. 600,000 volumes; 6,000 periodical subscriptions; 140,000 maps.

Special Collections

Ward M. Canaday Center for Special Collections. The Center maintains collections in the following areas: Women's Social History (American, 1840-1920), including American gift books and annuals, birth control materials, health and marriage manuals, etiquette books; twentieth-century Afro-American literature, including Harlem Renaissance first editions, postwar poetry (especially by women), and the papers of Etheridge Knight; corporate archives of Libbey-Owens-Ford Corporation (glass manufacturing), including minute books, photographs; scrapbooks, advertising, and publications; manuscript collections and photographs relating to Toledo and northwest Ohio. Author collections include Ezra Pound (first editions, books from Pound's library, periodicals, and some manuscript material; also Pound's sources, including Egyptian texts and Social Credit Movement; T.S. Eliot (first editions, periodicals, and some manuscript materials; William Faulkner (first editions); William Dean Howells (first editions); Leigh Hunt (first editions); and Scott Nearing (first editions, ephemera, materals relating to "Nearing case").

1291
Urbana University
Swedenborg Memorial Library
College Way
Urbana, Ohio 43078

Telephone. (513) 652-1301

Institutional Description. The privately supported liberal arts college is affiliated with the Swedenborgian Church. It grants baccalaureate degrees. Enrollment: 650.

Library Administration. Lois H. Ward, Head Librarian.

Library General Holdings. 58,000 volumes; 300 periodical subscriptions.

Special Collections

The library maintains the **Swedenborg Collection** of 2,036 titles; the **Curriculum Collection** of 1,924 titles; and a **Sheet Music Collection** of 1,747 titles.

1292
Ursuline College
Ralph M. Besse Library
2550 Lander Road
Pepper Pike, Ohio 44124

Telephone. (216) 449-4200

Institutional Description. The privately supported Roman Catholic college was founded in 1871 by the Ursuline Nuns of Cleveland. The first chartered women's college in Ohio, Ursuline is now coeducational. Enrollment: 1,021.

Library Administration. Betsey Belkin, Library Director.

Library General Holdings. 104,173 volumes; 661 current periodicals; 6,434 curriculum volumes; 31,775 audiovisual items.

Special Collections

Art Therapy Collection. A comprehensive special area collected for the graduate program.

Curriculum Materials. Includes 6,434 volumes for education students.

Global Collection. Special collection on peace, nonviolence, Third World development; collection is in memory of Sr. Dorothy Kazel, an Ursuline nun killed in El Salvador in 1980.

Ralph Besse Notebook Collection. Includes thousands of picture clippings of current local and world topics.

Rivers Room. Special collection on rivers donated by Ralph M. Besse, for whom the library is named.

1293
Wilberforce University
Rembert E. Stokes Learning Resources Center Library
Wilberforce, Ohio 45384

Telephone. (513) 376-2911

Institutional Description. The privately supported university was founded in 1856. Since 1863, it has been under the auspices of the African Methodist Episcopal Church. Enrollment: 786.

Library Administration. Jean K. Mulhern, Chief Librarian; Jacqueline Brown, Special Collections Librarian.

Library General Holdings. 52,000 volumes; 350 current periodical subscriptions; 6,060 microforms; 1,600 audiovisual materials.

Special Collections

The Special Collections were formed in the early 1920s with the acquisition of materials concerning the African Methodist Episcopal Church. These collections contain the history of the development of the A.M.E. Church, the oldest Black American religious denomination. The collections consists of the Archives and Minutes, and the personal papers of Bishop Reverdy E. Ransom (founder of The Niagara Movement, now known as the National Association for the Advancement of Colored People), William S. Scarborough (includes memorabilia from such persons as Booker T. Washington, W.E.B. DuBois, and Frederick Douglass), Dr. Milton S.J. Wright, and Dr. Charles L. Hill.

University Archives. Contains faculty records, course offerings, catalogs, publications, information on campus organizations, memorabilia, and other records important to Wilberforce University history. These materials trace the history of America's oldest historically Black owned and operated University.

Rare Book Collections

Archives Library. Consists of 10,000 volumes on Black topics focusing on books about Wilberforce University or the the A.M.E. Church, or books by authors connected with either institution. It also includes a strong collection of Black poetry.

1294
Wilmington College
S. Arthur Watson Library
Pyle Center Box 1227
Wilmington, Ohio 45177

Telephone. (513) 382-6661

Institutional Description. The privately supported liberal arts college was founded by the Religious Society of Friends in 1870. An academic cooperative plan with the University of Chicago is available for social science students. Enrollment: 1,188.

Library Administration. Ina E. Kelley, Archivist and Special Collections Librarian.

Library General Holdings. 109,000 volumes; 562 periodical subscriptions.

Special Collections

Quaker Collection. Contains 7,000 volumes covering all aspects of Quaker history, thought, philosophy, and practice; emphasizes history, biography, education, and peace; some fiction, poetry, and children's books are also included. This collection is the repository for the official records, ca. 1800-present, of the Wilmington Yearly Meeting and the Ohio Valley Meeting, of the Religious Society of Friends (Quakers). The records include Monthly Meeting minutes, membership lists, committee minutes, and financial records. The records cover southwestern Ohio and parts of Indiana and Tennessee. Genealogists should direct inquiries to the Clinton County Historical Society, P.O. Box 529, Wilmington, Ohio 45177.

College Archives. This collection preserves historical material about Wilmington College from 1870-present. The Archives include Board of Trustee minutes, college publications, yearbooks, student newspapers, and several thousand photographs. The Archives also hold some records of National Normal University, Lebanon, Ohio.

1295
Wittenberg University
Thomas Library
Springfield, Ohio 45501

Telephone. (513) 327-7916

Institutional Description. The privately supported Christian liberal arts college was founded in 1845. It is affiliated with the Lutheran Church in America. Enrollment: 2,121.

Library Administration. Imre Meszaros, Director.

Library General Holdings. 285,000 volumes; 1,225 periodicals; 54,500 microforms; 16,000 audiovisual materials.

Special Collections

The Thomas Library has special collections of materials on Martin Luther and the Protestant Reformation which includes writings, original letters, and rare books; the **Cyril dos Passos Collection** on lepidoptera which includes specimens and journals; and the writings and paintings of the local artist, Walter Tittle.

1296
Wright State University
University Library
Colonel Glenn Highway
Dayton, Ohio 45435

Telephone. (513) 873-2380

Institutional Description. The publicly supported state university was established in 1964. Enrollment: 12,-209.

Library Administration. Ritchie D. Thomas, Librarian; Patrick B. Nolan, Head of Archives and Special Collections.

Library General Holdings. 400,000 volumes; 4,000 periodical subscriptions; 700,000 microforms.

Special Collections

Children's Literature. The core of this collection was donated by the late Dr. Mary Harbage, Professor of Education at Wright State, and consists of over 100 rare children's books illustrated by the famous late nineteenth- and early twentieth-century English illustrator, Arthur Rackham.

Early Aviation History. This collection focuses on early aeronautics and stems naturally from the University being a living memorial to Orville and Wilbur Wright, the two Dayton brothers who invented powered flight at the turn of the century. In 1975, the Wright family chose Wright State University as the repository for a rich collection of Wright Brothers personal, family and technical papers, journals, diaries, photographs, books, and memorabilia. Comprising over 6,000 items, this research collection is one of the most complete records of the Wrights' life and work.

In addition to the Wright Brothers Collection, the archives holds over thirty-five other manuscript collections relating to the history of flight. These collections include the Clayton Bruckner Papers (1928-1972) which consist of the business records of the WACO Aircraft Company; the Peter B. Kline Papers (1922-1986) which cover a wide variety of aeronautical subjects; and the International Cyclopedia of Aviation Biography Records (1925-1939) which include files on over 3,000 individuals prominent in aviation in the early twentieth century. In addition to these manuscript materials, the aviation reference collection consists of over 2,500 books and periodicals pertaining to aeronautics and the history of early flight.

Local and Regional History. The Department of Archives and Special Collections is the designated repository for local government records and historical manuscript materials from an eleven-county area in central southwestern Ohio. The Archives preserves and makes available to researchers a wide range of individual and family papers, business and labor union records, as well as the papers of civic, cultural, and fraternal organizations, churches, special districts, and women's organizations.

University Archives. Records preserved in this collection include presidential papers, minutes and reports of administrative committees and boards, university publications, annual budgets, university and community events files, faculty governance records, and the records of university offices.

1297
Xavier University
McDonald Memorial Library
Dana Avenue and Victoria Parkway
Cincinnati, Ohio 45207

Telephone. (513) 745-3000

Institutional Description. The privately supported Roman Catholic university was founded in 1831. There are two campuses: the Main Campus, and Edgecliff College. Enrollment: 3,906.

Library Administration. Paula Warnken, Director.

Library General Holdings. 250,000 volumes; 1,750 periodicals; 300,000 microforms; 3,000 recordings.

Special Collections

Special collections include incunabula, rare books, manuscripts of literary and historical figures, and the University Archives. There are collections which include manuscripts and the complete works of Fr. Francis Finn, S.J.; Bibles; and Jesuitica.

1298
Youngstown State University
William F. Maag, Jr. Library
410 Wick Avenue
Youngstown, Ohio 44555

Telephone. (216) 742-3101

Institutional Description. The publicly supported state university was originally founded by the Young Men's Christian Association as the School of Law of the Youngstown Association School. It joined the State University System in 1967. Enrollment: 11,077.

Library Administration. David C. Genaway, University Librarian.

Library General Holdings. 528,000 volumes; 3,440 periodicals; 739,000 microforms; 128,000 government documents.

Special Collections

Special collections in the Maag Library include the **Pacific Northwest Railroad Service Collection;** a collection of Americana; and a reproduction of a page from the *Nuremberg Chronicle.*

Oklahoma

1299
Cameron University
University Library
2800 West Gore Boulevard
Lawton, Oklahoma 73505

Telephone. (405) 248-2200

Institutional Description. The publicly supported (state) university was founded in 1908 as a school of agriculture. It became a junior college in 1927 and a senior college in 1966, granting associate and baccalaureate degrees. Enrollment: 3,727.

Library Administration. Robert S. Phillips, Director of Library Services.

Library General Holdings. 193,000 volumes; 2,500 serial titles; 213,000 microforms; 2,338 non-print media.

Special Collections

Special collections of the library are on Indian history, Western history, and sociology.

1300
Central State University
University Library
Edmond, Oklahoma 73060

Telephone. (405) 341-2980

Institutional Description. The publicly supported state university was founded in 1890 as the Territorial Normal School. It now features teacher education and nursing. Enrollment: 8,802.

Library Administration. John L. Lolley, Director.

Library General Holdings. 700,000 volumes; 4,500 serial and periodical subscriptions.

Special Collections

Special collection in the library are the map collection; the juvenile literature collection; the curriculum collection of state adopted texts; the Oklahoma collection of archives and Oklahoma historical documents (includes townsite cases); the papers of Lloyd Rader.

1301
East Central University
Linscheid Library
Ada, Oklahoma 74820

Telephone. (405) 332-8000

Institutional Description. The publicly supported university was established in 1909 as a state normal school. It now offers arts and sciences as well as teacher education, and grants the Certificate, Bachelor and Master degrees. Enrollment: 3,533.

Library Administration. John A. Walker, University Librarian; Louise S. Robbins, Special Collections Librarian.

Library General Holdings. 200,000 volumes; 1,000 current periodical subscriptions; 10 newspaper subscriptions.

Special Collections

Admire Collection. The papers, maps, and letters of James L. Admire (1896-1956) who operated a successful farm management service in Hugo, Oklahoma. This collection provides insight into agriculture in southeastern Oklahoma since the 1920s.

Jack Conn Watch Collection. The substantial part of the Conn collection is composed of American railroad watches.

Crawford Collection. A Ponotoc County district judge, Johnson Tal Crawford was a member of the Military Tribunal which conducted the Nazi War Crimes Trials at Nuremburg. In addition to photographs and transcripts, his papers include his multi-volume set of the trial proceedings.

Dale Collection. George Dale was a telegrapher at the Frisco Railroad Station in Francis, Oklahoma and his records include time rolls, service manuals, and union agreements.

Hauan Collection. A gift from distinguished alumnus Martin Hauan, this collection includes political advertising on tape, videotape, and film, as well as printed speeches, memorabilia, and books, all associated with the campaigns of various Oklahoma and nationally-known politicians.

Leaders of World War I Collection. This unique collection includes letters and autographed photographs of many world leaders of the World War I era, collected by former ECU faculty member, E.A. MacMillan.

University Archives. The Archives is the official depository of ECU publications and records of historical and research value. Included are the papers of long-time librarian Casper Duffer; the typescript of a book by tramp poet, Welborn Hope; and oral history materials about the University.

Rare Book Collections

Rare Books Collection. The centerpiece of this collection is a facsimile of the famous Gutenberg Bible, the first book printed with moveable type and therefore the keystone event in the history of the book. The facsimile, made to be an exact replica of the Cardinal Mazarin Bible, or 42-line Bible, is a gift of Norma English Walker. Other books in this collection include some rare Americana, such as Schoolcraft's early record of life among the Indian tribes and early twentieth-century first editions, with an emphasis on books about the American Southwest. Examples of fine printing and binding and autographed books are also in the collection.

1302
Flaming Rainbow University
Learning Resources Center
419 North Second Street
Stilwell, Oklahoma 74960

Telephone. (918) 696-3644
Institutional Description. The privately supported institution was established in 1972. Enrollment: 189.
Library Administration. Mary Fulk, Librarian.
Library General Holdings. 4,075 volumes; 54 periodical subscriptions; 31,700 microforms.

Special Collections

The Learning Resource Center of this small University acquires materials that relate to the Cherokee Indians.

1303
Mid-America Bible College
Charles Ewing Brown Library
3500 S.W. 119th Street
Oklahoma City, Oklahoma 73170

Telephone. (405) 691-3800
Institutional Description. The privately supported professional college is designed to prepare men and women for the Christian ministry and other aspects of Church work. It is affiliated with the Church of God. Enrollment: 187.
Library Administration. Ronald Kriesel, Librarian.
Library General Holdings. 37,652 volumes; 222 current periodicals; 1,008 bound periodicals; 12,000 microforms.

Special Collections

The **Charles Ewing Brown Collection** emphasizes items of historical significance to the Church of God Movement.

1304
Murray State College
Library/Learning Resource Center
Tishomingo, Oklahoma 73460

Telephone. (405) 371-3500
Institutional Description. The two-year public college was established in 1908. Enrollment: 842.
Library Administration. James W. Kennedy, Librarian.
Library General Holdings. 20,000 volumes; 250 current periodical subscriptions; 2,000 microforms; 2,400 recordings.

Special Collections

A special collection on Oklahoma history is maintained in the library.

1305
Northeastern State University
John Vaughan Library/Learning Resources Center
Tahlequah, Oklahoma 74464

Telephone. (918) 456-5511
Institutional Description. The publicly supported state university was founded in 1846 when the Cherokee National Council provided for the National Male Seminary and the National Female Seminary. Through various developments the Female Seminary became first a state teachers college and then part of the Oklahoma State System. Enrollment: 6,171.
Library Administration. Delores T. Sumner, Special Collections Librarian.
Library General Holdings. 181,974 volumes; 2,167 current periodicals; 221,028 government documents; 178,688 microforms; 4,492 audiovisual materials.

Special Collections

Special Collections contains particular materials relating to the history and culture of the Cherokee Indians, other tribes of Oklahoma, and the state of Oklahoma, with emphasis on the northeastern Oklahoma region. Materials are housed relating to the history and founding of Northeastern State University which has roots in early Cherokee education. T.L. Ballenger, former NSU history professor (1883-1987) wrote and published many books on the history of NSU Seminary Hall (the dormitory/school for Cherokee women in the late 1800s to early 1900s), the Cherokee Nation, and on the towns of Tahlequah and Park Hill. His book collection is housed in Special Collections.

The book collection includes *Niles Weekly Register,* Cherokee laws, Kappler's laws and treaties, American State papers, tribal publications, dictionaries, primers and grammar books of many Native American languages, H.R. Schoolcraft's *History of the Indian Tribes of the United States,* and books by Oklahoma authors and Indian Territory Reports.

As the book collection covers publications concerning the Cherokee Nation and Native Americans, so does the microfiche collection which includes U.S. Bureau of American Ethnology (1846-), U.S. Commission of Indian Affairs-Annual Reports, American State papers (1832-1861), the oral history programs "Listening to Indians," and the Indian-Pioneer Papers (1860-1935).

The microfilm collection includes U.S. Reports of the Commissioner of Indian Affairs; letters received by the Office of Indian Affairs (1824-1880); letters sent by the Office of Indian Affairs (1824-1881); the *Cherokee Phoenix* (1828-1829); *Muskogee Phoenix* (1894-1899); the *Indian Missionary;* the *Cherokee Advocate* (1844); and many other early newspapers of the northeastern Oklahoma area.

Rare Book Collections

Rare materials include those related to Oklahoma and the Cherokee Nation, rare editions, Native American language books, Bibles and hymnals of the Five Civilized Tribes dating from the early 1800s, pamphlets, maps, and Oklahoma state publications. The collections housed are: Lola Bowers, W.W. Hastings, John Ross Letters, Stand Watie Letters, John T. Drew, Jr. (1877-1910), and the Nave Papers. These materials relate to the early history of the northeastern area of Oklahoma and the Cherokees.

1306
Oklahoma Baptist University
Mabee Learning Center
500 West University
Shawnee, Oklahoma 74801

Telephone. (405) 275-2850

Institutional Description. The privately supported liberal arts and professional university was founded in 1910. It is affiliated with the Southern Baptist Church. Enrollment: 1,359.

Library General Holdings. 155,000 volumes; 650 periodicals; 75,000 microforms.

Special Collections

Oklahoma Baptist Collection. Contains archival and printed materials pertaining to Oklahoma Baptist history, as well as the archives of the University, including the yearbook, the *Yahnseh,* and the student newspaper, *The Bison.*

Rare Book Collections

W.B. Bizzell Collection. Consists of 3,000 volumes of literature and history. Other significant personal collections include the **E.C. Routh Library of Missions** and the **J.W. Storer Collection** on the Civil War and World War II.

1307
Oklahoma Christian College
Mabee Learning Center
Oklahoma City, Oklahoma 73111

Telephone. (405) 478-1661

Institutional Description. The privately supported liberal arts college was founded in 1950 and became a four-year college in 1960. It is affiliated with the Church of Christ. Enrollment: 1,413.

Library Administration. Brad Robison, Director.

Library General Holdings. 106,000 volumes; 450 current periodicals; 22,000 microforms; 5,200 audiovisual materials.

Special Collections

The Mabee Learning Center's holdings emphasize the College's goals of career preparation and spiritual growth. A clipping file of the *Daily Oklahoman* (1907-1981) is maintained.

1308
Oklahoma City University
Dulaney-Browne Library
2501 North Blackwelder
Oklahoma City, Oklahoma 73106

Telephone. (405) 521-5000

Institutional Description. The privately supported university was founded in 1904. It is affiliated with the United Methodist Church. Enrollment: 2,308.

Library Administration. Susan McVey, Director.

Library General Holdings. 245,000 volumes.

Special Collections

George Shirk Oklahoma History Center. Contains one-of-a-kind photographs, books, and maps and a rare collection of related books on the history of Oklahoma City, the State of Oklahoma, and the region of the Southwest.

1309
The Oklahoma College of Osteopathic Medicine and Surgery
College Library
1111 West 17th Street
Tulsa, Oklahoma 74107

Telephone. (918) 582-1972

Institutional Description. The publicly supported college was founded in 1972. It grants the degree Doctor of Osteopathy. Enrollment: 259.

Library Administration. Linda L. Roberts, College Librarian; Dave Money, Assistant Librarian for Media.

Library General Holdings. 20,249 volumes; 1,185 bound periodicals; 547 journal subscriptions; 9 audiovisual subscriptions; 181 active serial titles; 4 newspaper subscriptions; 22,695 microfiche; 871 microfilm reels; 2,694 audiovisual programs (includes 1,600 videocassettes; 1,300 slide sets; 800 anatomical models; 100 Apple CAI disks).

Special Collections

The library is primarily a medical collection emphasizing osteopathic medicine. In addition to the materials described above, the Library maintains 800 plastic and papiermache anatomy models, real bone and plastic skeletons, cross-sectional tissue specimens embedded in acrylic, and patient simulator modes such as Resusci-Annie.

1310
Oklahoma Panhandle State University
Marvin E. McKee Library
Box 430
Goodwell, Oklahoma 73939

Telephone. (405) 349-2610

Institutional Description. The publicly supported liberal arts, teachers, and technological university was founded in 1909. It grants baccalaureate degrees. Enrollment: 1,011.

Library Administration. Edward F. Bryan, Jr., Director.

Library General Holdings. 73,500 volumes; 455 current periodical subscriptions.

Special Collections

Special collections include the **Howsley Poetry Collection** which consists primarily of the works of Chaucer and Shakespeare including many first editions of critical works, commentaries, and biographies. The **Curriculum Collection** contains samples of textbooks, workbooks, curriculum guides, and a collection of materials suitable for elementary and secondary schools. A collection of children's literature is also maintained.

1311
Oklahoma State University
University Library
Stillwater, Oklahoma 74078

Telephone. (405) 624-6384

Institutional Description. The publicly supported state university was founded in 1890. It offers a wide selection of programs. Enrollment: 18,175.

Library Administration. Roscoe Rouse, University Librarian.

Library General Holdings. 1,400,000 volumes; 14,000 journals; 1,400,000 microforms; 180,000 maps.

Special Collections

Special collections in the University Library include the Finnell papers on soil conservation, the **McBride Collection** on water resources; and the gubernatorial and personal papers of former Governor Henry Bellmont.

1312
Oklahoma State University Technical Institute
Library
900 North Portland
Oklahoma City, Oklahoma 73107

Telephone. (405) 947-4421

Institutional Description. Prior to the creation of the Institute in 1961, Oklahoma City University had technical education as part of its educational mission. A decision was made by the City University to allow Oklahoma State University to assume this technical education function in Oklahoma City, thus founding the Institute. Enrollment: 1,666.

Library Administration. Merle R. Long, Director of Learning Resources.

Library General Holdings. 11,000 books and nonbook items; 230 magazine and newspaper titles.

Special Collections

The library has special collections in fire protection, horticulture, computer programming, and electronics.

1313
Oral Roberts University
Holy Spirit Research Center
7777 South Lewis Avenue
Tulsa, Oklahoma 74171

Telephone. (918) 495-6898

Institutional Description. The privately supported, Christian liberal arts university was founded by the Oral Roberts Evangelistic Association in 1963. Enrollment: 4,664.

Library Administration. William Jernigan, Librarian; Karen Jermyn, Director of the Holy Spirit Research Center.

Library General Holdings. 12,000 volumes; 2,000 bound periodicals; 500 current periodical subscriptions; 1,800 audiocassettes; 90 videocassettes; vertical file of unpublished papers, newsletters, pamphlets, news articles, tracts, and an in-house indexing system to the collection's periodicals.

Special Collections

The purpose of the Holy Spirit Research Center is to collect and care for the historical accounts of events, spiritual truths, and secular studies concerning the Pentecostal-Charismatic movement, with the broadest of all possible coverages. The Center has a large collection on divine healing; a large collection of William Branham sermons on audiocassettes; the Bishop Daniel T. Muse collection of letters, manuscripts, sermons, and books; and a collection of Edward Irving books and Catholic Apostolic Church pamphlets.

1314
Phillips University
Zollars Memorial Library
Box 2400 University Station
Enid, Oklahoma 73702

Telephone. (405) 237-4433

Institutional Description. The privately supported Christian university is composed of an undergraduate college, a seminary, and a division of graduate studies. It was founded in 1907 and operates with the cooperation of the Christian Church (Disciples of Christ). Enrollment: 764.

Library Administration. John R. Sayre, Library Director.

Library General Holdings. 166,168 volumes; 733 current periodical subscriptions; 28,610 microforms; 11,989 audiovisual materials.

Special Collections

Living Legends Collection. An oral history collection consisting of 200 cassette interviews conducted by students in oral history seminars of long-time residents of Enid and Garfield Counties. Many interviews refer to the Land Run of 1893 (Cherokee Outlet), early life in Enid, Garfield County, and northwest Oklahoma, including the history of Phillips University and other institutions and businesses.

Rare Book Collections

Rare Book Room. Includes a collection of rare and historical manuscripts of T.W. Phillips and his family donated by H.H. Phillips of San Antonio, Texas, a grandson of T.W. Phillips for whom the University was named. The collection includes 37 autographed letters, documents, and bits of famous works mounted in frames for display. Among them is a letter written by the noted divine Wendel Phillips, and the first stanza of the original "Excelsior" by Longfellow. One of the oldest pieces is a letter signed by George III, King of England, dated 1785.

1315
Southeastern Oklahoma State University
Henry G. Bennett Memorial Library
Durant, Oklahoma 74701

Telephone. (405) 924-0121

Institutional Description. The publicly supported state university was established in 1909. Enrollment: 3,-004.

Library Administration. Kay Parham, Library Director.

Library General Holdings. 152,000 volumes; 790 current periodical subscriptions; 152,000 microforms; 2,236 maps; 61,000 U.S. government documents; 240 sound recordings.

Special Collections

Curriculum Materials. This collection consists of approximately 11,500 volumes including elementary and secondary textbooks, workbooks, tests, curriculum guides, reference materials, and early childhood education materials.

Indians of North America and Oklahoma History. There are strong collections on these subjects within the general collection.

Todd Downing Collection. This collection includes several hundred mystery/detection novels and also Latin American titles.

1316
Southern Nazarene University
The R. T. Williams Learning Resources Center
4115 North College
Bethany, Oklahoma 73008

Telephone. (405) 491-6350

Institutional Description. The privately supported institution, until recently known as Bethany Nazarene College, was founded in 1899. It is affiliated with the Church of the Nazarene. Enrollment: 1,080.

Library Administration. Shirley Pelley, Librarian; Joy Pauley, Special Collections Librarian.

Library General Holdings. 105,514 volumes; 620 current periodical subscriptions; 184,782 microfiche; 203 videotapes; 117 audiotapes; 1,973 phonograph recordings; 171 microcomputer software; 1,471 other materials.

Special Collections

Archives Collection. Consists of historical materials of the University, the city of Bethany, and other archival materials.

Holiness Collection. Contains books written by authors who hold to the Arminian theological position.

John E. Moore Letter Collection. A collection of signatures of famous political figures, hymnwriters, and churchmen; donated to the University by the Rev. Bernie Smith.

Hymnological Collection. Consists of hymn books, denominational and non-denominational; includes books of history and criticism of hymns.

R.T. Williams, Sr. Collection. The family of Dr. R.T. Williams, Sr. donated these volumes of his books, sermons, letters, and other artifacts relating to the years he served as minister and General Superintendent of the Church of the Nazarene.

Rare Book Collections

Ross Hayslip Bible Collection. This is a collection of Bibles given by Rev. Ross Hayslip; includes rare, polyglot, and contemporary texts.

1317
Tulsa Junior College
Learning Resources Center
6111 East Skelly Drive
Tulsa, Oklahoma 74135

Telephone. (918) 664-5620

Institutional Description. The two-year college is an urban, multi-campus comprehensive community college offering occupational, career, and university-parallel programs. The college was established in 1970. Enrollment: 6,260.

Library Administration. Michael Rusk, Dean, Learning Resources Center.

Library General Holdings. The library has a collection of the **Gilcrease Tapes** consisting of 950 audiocassette tapes on American history.

1318
University of Oklahoma
University Libraries
401 West Brooks
Norman, Oklahoma 73019

Telephone. (405) 325-2611

Institutional Description. The publicly supported university was founded in 1890, before Oklahoma became a state. It now consists of 15 colleges. Enrollment: 19,466.

Library Administration. Sul H. Lee, Dean of Libraries; Wilbur Stolt, Director, Library Public Services.

Library General Holdings. 2,200,000 volumes; 17,000 serial subscriptions; 1,600,000 government documents; 2,-500,000 microforms; 127,000 maps.

Rare Book Collections

History of Science Collections. These Collections are a teaching and research library of 76,000 volumes. The core of the Collections is the printed writings of scientists in both monographic and periodical form dating from the beginning of printing to the twentieth century. Supporting materials include scientific textbooks and popular works on science, encyclopedias, dictionaries, bibliographical works, bibliographies of scientists, history of science journals, histories of science, histories of individual sciences, and histories of scientific institutions; also first editions of most notable books in science—and frequently all editions—are found in the Collections. The printed *Catalogue of the History of Science Collections* (London: Mansell, 1976) describes bibliographically the first 40,000 volumes and short-title catalogs issued in microfiche and lists all current holdings.

Western History Collections. These Collections include published works, manuscripts, sound recordings, and photographs relating to the history of the American West and the development of Native American cultures. There are collections on the life and career of George A. Custer, the Louisiana Purchase, the St. Louis World's Fair, and Abraham Lincoln. The Manuscripts Division includes papers of early Cherokee leaders, Stand Watie and Elias Budinet; official records of the Cherokee and Choctaw Nations; files of the Oklahoma State Federation of Labor; letters of Patrick Hurley, American ambassador to China; and recordings of the Doris Duke Indian Oral History Collection. The Photographic Archives are a major source of information about the American Indian, the Oklahoma Land runs, western life, and the petroleum industry.

Harry W. Bass Collection. Notable acquisitions in this collection include Johannes Nider's *De Contractibus Mercatorum* (1468) and Luc Pacioli's *Summa de Arithmatica, geometria, proportioni, et proportionalita* (1523). The archives of the J. & W. Seligman and Company, one of America's oldest financial houses, is also in the collection.

1319
University of Oklahoma Health Sciences Center
Health Sciences Center Library
P.O. Box 26901
Oklahoma City, Oklahoma 73190

Telephone. (405) 271-2285

Institutional Description. The publicly supported health sciences center is a branch of the University of Oklahoma. The medical school was founded in 1900 and moved from Norman to Oklahoma City in 1910 to merge with the Epworth Medical Center. It now is comprised of the Colleges of Nursing, Allied Health, Dentistry, and Pharmacy. Enrollment: 3,160.

Library Administration. C.M. Thompson, Director.

Library General Holdings. 175,000 books, journals, and audiovisuals.

Special Collections

The library has two special collections. The **Indian Health Collection** is made up of books of a historical nature as well as reports of current research related to the health and well-being of the American Indian.

Rare Book Collections

The **Rare Book Collection** contains books and journals that are rare or are anticipated to be of value. Included in this collection are manuscripts and archives related to the Health Sciences Center and health care in Oklahoma.

1320
University of Tulsa
McFarlin Library
600 South College Avenue
Tulsa, Oklahoma 74104

Telephone. (918) 592-6000

Institutional Description. The privately supported university was founded in 1894, at Muskogee, Indian Territory, by the Presbyterian Board of Home Missions. Enrollment: 4,110.

Library Administration. Robert Patterson, University Librarian; Sidney Huttner, Special Collections/Rare Book Librarian; Lori N. Curtis, Assistant Curator, Special Collections.

Library General Holdings. 1,879,790 volumes; 1,505,-820 microforms; 5,391 audiovisual materials; 4,547 current periodical subscriptions. For a detailed description of materials housed in the Rare Books and Special Collections of McFarlin Library, see *A Guide to Literary and Related Materials* (The University of Tulsa: 1987).

Special Collections

Cyril Connolly Library. Includes over 8,000 books (many rare editions), 1,100 issues of literary periodicals, and numerous letters from such major literary figures as Stephen Spender, T.S. Eliot, W.H. Auden, John Betjeman, Evelyn Waugh, and others.

Edmund Wilson Library. This collection comprises over 10,000 volumes collected by the noted author and critic. Contained in the library are Wilson's copies of the books of Vladimir Nabokov, with whom Wilson maintained a famous literary friendship and feud. Many of the books are inscribed, including works published in Russia prior to Nabokov's emigration to the United States. The Library also includes the handprinted first editions of Anais Nin's *Winter of Artifice* and *Under a Glass Bell.*

Martin Secker Collection. This collection reflects the publishing history of Martin Secker's publishing company formed before World War I. It contains virtually every book published by Secker and includes such volumes as D.H. Lawerence's *Women in Love,* Compton Mackenzie's *Sylvia Scarlet,* Conrad Aiken's *Bring! Bring!,* and Hugh Walpole's *Fortitude* and *The Dark Forest.*

Henneke Archives of Performing Arts. Named for Ben Graf Henneke, former president of The University of Tulsa and long-time drama faculty member, these collections are composed of various materials pertaining to the performing arts. The Stanley Swift Collection is the cornerstone of the Henneke Archives and establishes McFarlin Library as one of the centers for certain types of theatre research in the United States. The collection contains over 4,000 playbills, programs, and clippings relating to activities in English and American theatres in London, New York, Philadelphia, Boston, Detroit, and Chicago. In addition, it includes over 200 files on individual actors and actresses from the nineteenth century, many of whom played before Abraham Lincoln. Another part of the Henneke Archives is a collection of over 700 items documenting circus life. In the area of recorded performance, a group of over 6,000 original recordings given to the University in 1977 includes forms of musical recording from Edison's rolls to the long-playing record. All genres of American music are present, with almost every significant performing artist represented in depth. The Henneke Archives also hold motion picture scripts for figures better known for their literary production, such as F. Scott Fitzgerald, Ernest Hemingway, John Steinbeck, and John Fowles.

Harriet Shaw Weaver Joyce Collection. This collection was acquired in 1977 from the National Book League in England. Through Miss Weaver's editorial connections with the magazine *The Egoist,* she was associated with such figures as Wyndham Lewis, Ezra Pound, and T.S. Eliot, but she is better known for her relationship with James Joyce. The collection is the center of the Joyce holdings at McFarlin Library. It consists of more than 200 volumes of works by and about Joyce. Also present are numerous subsequent editions and translations of Joyce's writings and various critical studies which had been given to Miss Weaver by other publishers and authors.

Kenneth Hopkins Collection. For almost forty years the British poet and scholar Kenneth Hopkins collected eighteenth- and nineteenth-century English poetry. The result of his dedication is found in the collection of 5,000 volumes of English poetry from the past two centuries. There are over 300 eighteenth-century imprints in the Hopkins collection.

Nineteenth-Century Fiction. In 1982, McFarlin Library added a most unusual collection of nineteenth-century fiction formed at the time the books were being published. In the early 1820s the merchants and wine-traders who had come from Britain and settled in Oporto, Portugal, felt the need for a library of English books to serve the increasing number of British families living in and near the city. A librarian was appointed who also used an agent in London to supply books as they were published. A fiction library was established at an early date, the titles being chosen either by the librarian, by the agent, or in response to the wishes of the readers. The number of titles was considerably increased to 1,000 over the following 70 years. In time the local population of readers decreased Gradually, the "old" fiction library was forgotten. This intact circulating library formed between 1820 and 1890 was discovered just a few years ago and has now been moved to The University of Tulsa. It was started when the three-volume (or "three-decker") novel was supplanting the Gothic four-volume novel. The collection ended in the 1890s when the three-decker was at its last gasp and the one-volume novel had finally replaced it. The library also includes one- and two-volume titles published at the same time and in its entirety numbers 2,500 volumes. This collection provides insights into the reading tastes of a British community living abroad in the nineteenth century.

Joyce Bell Witt Collection of California Fine Printing. The cornerstone of this collection is a complete holding of the publications from the Book Club of California. From its origin in 1913 to the present day, it has published over 160 books that reflect not only historical and literary developments in the West but also represent many of the finest accomplishments in printing and typography in California.

Edwardian Fiction. This collection goes beyond the acknowledged masters of the period—such figures as Wells, Chesterton, Galsworthy, and Forster—and includes a substantial body of fiction which is less famous. The collection is a gauge of what the public was reading at the time.

The Great War. This collection includes holdings of writers such as Rupert Brooke, Isaac Rosenberg, Siegfried Sassoon, Wilfred Owen, Robert Graves, Edmund Blunden, David Jones, and Henri Barbusse. These writings by actual participants in the fighting of World War I are complemented by over 1,500 books written on the war.

Native American Literature. One of the most recently identified areas of strength in McFarlin Library includes the work of American Indian authors such as Lynn Riggs, N. Scott Momaday, John Joseph Matthews, Carter Revard, and John Rollin Ridge. Other forms of Indian writing include manuscripts of Cherokee medicine formulas written in verse in Sequoyah's syllabary. Related material is found in tape recordings of oral legends and the massive Indian Pioneer Papers now on microfilm.

La Cour Collection of Popular Fiction. A collection of detective novels, western novels, science fiction, and other works which would be classified as "entertainments." The authors represented range from P.G. Wodehouse, Robert Coover, and Arthur Conan Doyle to Agatha Christie, Dashiell Hammett, and Ian Fleming; from Zane Grey, O.Henry, and Mark Twain to Arthur Clarke, Robert Heinlein, and Fredrick Pohl.

Pataphysical and Surrealist Collection. This collection was acquired in 1974 from Simon Watson Taylor. An editor-anthologist, translator, and authority on the avant-garde in modern French literature. Taylor was a distinguished member of the College de Pataphysique founded in 1949. Taylor's collection of publications, documents, and memorabilia emanating from the College is supplemented by his working library of texts by and about Alfred Jarry (1873-1907), founder of the science of Pataphysics.

Proletarian Collection. This collection of over 2,000 items includes plays, poetry, anthologies, emphemeral and fugitive pieces of proletarian writing, music, and periodicals. The original collection of proletarian literature was based on Walter Rideout's *The Radical Novel in the United States, 1900-1954.*

Greenslade Collection. This collection of eighteenth- and nineteenth-century first editions and related volumes was an early gift to McFarlin Library. Some of the authors represented by first editions in this collection are Sir Walter Scott, Charles Dickens, George Eliot, Herman Melville, Nathaniel Hawthorne, William Makepeace Thackeray, Henry Fielding, and Samuel Richardson.

Modern Author Collections. As the concept of special collections began to grow at The University of Tulsa, part of the focus fell naturally on modern authors whose works are studied in the academic programs and whose writings might still be sufficiently available to assemble complete holdings. The books of these writers became known as the Modern Authors Collection in which approximately 40 figures were included. In recent years the scope has been enlarged to include in-depth collecting of more authors. Among the authors collected are: Erskine Caldwell, Stephen Crane, Edward Dahlberg, John Dos Passos, T.S. Eliot, William Faulkner, F. Scott Fitzgerald, John Fowles, The Fugitive Poets (Walter Clyde Curry, Donald Davidson, William Yandell Elliott, Sidney Hirsch, Andrew Lytle, Merrill Moore, John Crowe Ransom, Alan Tate, and Robert Penn Warren), Robert Frost, Robert Graves and Laura Riding, Graham Greene, L.P. Hartley, Ernest Hemingway, James Joyce, D.H. Lawrence, Doris Lessing, Malcolm Lowry, Katherine Mansfield, Ezra Pound, Anthony Powell, Jean Rhys, Dorothy Richardson, Siegfried Sassoon, Stevie Smith, Gertrude Stein, John Steinbeck, James Stephens, Wallace Stevens, James Thurber, Evelyn Waugh.

Manuscripts and Correspondence. The extent of the manuscripts and correspondence in the Department of Rare Books and Special Collections is enormous and includes such literary luminaries as Logan Pearsall Smith, Enid Bagnold, T.S. Eliot, E.M. Forster, Edith and Osbert Sitwell, Nancy Mitford, John Lehmann, Sonia Orwell, Anthony Hobson, Christopher Isherwood, Sherwood Anderson, F. Scott Fitzgerald, Waldo Frank, W.K. Magee, Ernest Hemingway, Eugene O'Neill, William Carlos Williams, Thornton Wilder, Flannery O'Connor, Margaret Drabble, John Updike, Gregory Corso, William Trevor, Anna Kavan, David Gascoyne, Paul Scott, David Plante, and Edward Charles.

Alice Robertson Collection. Composed of letters, articles, photographs, newspapers, books, and artifacts that span approximately 116 years of Indian Territory and Oklahoma history along with three generations of the Worcester-Robertson family. Most of the family years were spent as missionary-teachers among the Cherokee and Creek Indians.

John W. Shelppey Collection. Includes over 6,000 items including books, manuscripts, periodicals, and government documents related to American Indian historical studies; includes a rare first edition of Thomas McKenney and James Hall, *History of the Indian Tribes of North America* (Philadelphia: 1837), and a copy of James Adair, *The History of the American Indian (London: 1775).*

Oregon

1321
Bassist College
Bassist College Library
2000 SW Fifth Avenue
Portland, Oregon 97201

Telephone. (503) 228-6528

Institutional Description. The privately supported junior college specializes in retail management, apparel design, and interior design. It was founded in 1963. Enrollment: 217.

Library Administration. Norma Bassist, Librarian. Staff: Joseph Schiwek, Jr. and Nancy Thurston.

Library General Holdings. 11,000 volumes; 102 periodical subscriptions.

Special Collections

The Bassist College Library holdings cover the fields of accounting, advertising, apparel production, architecture, art, building construction, business, costume history, display, fashion coordination, fashion designers, fashion illustration, fashion manufacturers, furniture, interior design, management, marketing, merchandising, retail management, selling, stores, and textiles.

Rare Book Collections

Costume History. The Library maintains a collection of rare books in costume history. Bound volumes date from the 1600s and bound periodicals from the 1800s.

1322
Blue Mountain Community College
College Library
2411 NE Carden Avenue
Pendleton, Oregon 97801

Telephone. (503) 276-1260

Institutional Description. Blue Mountain Community College is a community-oriented, two-year postsecondary institution whose primary mission is to provide quality education and training opportunities to all persons who reside with the College District (Umatilla and Morrow Counties). Enrollment: 1,569.

Library Administration. Mary Bates, Director of Library Services.

Library General Holdings. 45,000 volumes; 400 periodical and 28 newspaper subscriptions.

Special Collections

The **Kilkenny Collection** includes material on Irish history and historical materials on Umatilla and Morrow Counties.

1323
Central Oregon Community College Library
College Way
Bend, Oregon 97701

Telephone. (503) 382-6112

Institutional Description. Founded in 1949, the two-year college began as a night school which used the local high school facilities until its present campus was completed in 1964. Enrollment: 2,126.

Library Administration. Margaret Mason, Director.

Library General Holdings. 30,000 books; 300 periodical titles; 15 newspaper subscriptions.

Special Collections

The **Oregon Collection** provides materials related to the history and culture of the people of central Oregon.

1324
Columbia Christian College
College Library
9101 East Burnside
Portland, Oregon 97216

Telephone. (503) 257-1365

Institutional Description. The privately supported liberal arts college was founded in 1956. It is affiliated with the Church of Christ, and grants baccalaureate degrees. Enrollment: 251.

Library Administration. Richard Chi-ho Lee, Head Librarian.

Library General Holdings. 33,000 volumes; 210 cur-

rent periodical titles; 26,500 microforms.

Special Collections

Special collections include literature on the Protestant Restoration Movement and religious studies.

1325
Eastern Oregon State College
Walter M. Pierce Library
8th and K Avenue
La Grande, Oregon 97850

Telephone. (503) 963-1540

Institutional Description. The publicly supported college was established in 1929 as a normal school. It is now a liberal arts college with an emphasis on teacher education. Enrollment: 1,900.

Library Administration. Douglas D. Oleson, Director of Libraries.

Library General Holdings. 105,000 bound volumes; 1,250 serial subscriptions; 25 newspaper subscriptions; 35,941 microforms; 139,932 government documents; 28,-870 audiovisual items.

Special Collections

Curriculum Library. This collection contains examples of the full Oregon public school textbook list, test files, games, and ephemeral materials on teaching.

Rare Book Collections

The library holds a specialized collection of Oregon materials with an emphasis on the eastern Oregon region. Included are only works about Oregon, by Oregon authors, and a comprehensive local genealogy collection.

1326
George Fox College
Shambaugh Library
Newberg, Oregon 97132

Telephone. (503) 538-8383

Institutional Description. The privately supported liberal arts college was founded in 1891. It is affiliated with the Society of Friends, and grants baccalaureate degrees. Enrollment: 582.

Library Administration. Merrill I. Johnson, Director of Library Services.

Library General Holdings. 80,000 volumes; 525 periodical subscriptions.

Special Collections

The library maintains the **Quaker Collection** of basic Quaker authors, pamphlets, periodicals, and artifacts. The archives of Northwest Yearly Meeting of Friends Church and of George Fox College, dating from the 1890s, are also housed in the library. A special business and economics collection is housed in the Kershner Center of the Hoover Academic Building. The John C. Brougher Memorial Museum houses artifacts of George Fox College history, Quaker history and missions, and early Northwest Americana. The Shambaugh Library maintains the **Peace Collection** and resource materials on Herbert Hoover.

1327
Lewis and Clark College
Aubrey Watzek Library
0615 S.W. Palatine Hill Road
Portland, Oregon 97219

Telephone. (503) 293-2650

Institutional Description. The privately supported liberal arts college was founded in 1867. It is affiliated with the United Presbyterian Church, and grants baccalaureate, professional, and master's degrees. Enrollment: 2,160.

Library Administration. 217,000 volumes; 1,100 current periodical subscriptions; 41,000 microforms; 26,000 government documents; 9,000 audiovisual materials.

Library General Holdings. Randall Collver, Director.

Special Collections

College Archives. Houses the formal and informal records generated by the college since its beginning in Albany, Oregon.

Rare Book Collections

Chuinard Collection. Includes materials on the Lewis and Clark Expeditions.

1328
Linfield College
Northrup Library
McMinnville, Oregon 97128

Telephone. (503) 472-4121

Institutional Description. The privately supported liberal arts college provides a variety of overseas programs for students. It was founded in 1849. Enrollment: 1,770.

Library Administration. Lynn Chmelir, Librarian; Mary Margaret Benson, Technical Services Librarian.

Library General Holdings. 118,000 volumes; 850 current subscriptions to newspapers, magazines, and journals; 10,000 microfilm volume equivalents supplement the periodicals collection; 12,000 music scores.

Special Collections

Joiner Collection of Northwest Americana. The gift of Truman Joiner in 1985, this collection includes over 1,000 monograph and serial volumes on the history of the

Northwest.

Cookbooks. The Library has a special collection of cookbooks, donated by Antoinette Kuzmanich Hatfield (Mrs. Mark Hatfield), who in 1971 received an honorary doctorate of science from Linfield College.

Rare Book Collections

Northwest Baptist History Collection. Includes early manuscript church records for many of Oregon's Baptist churches, as well as a monograph and periodical collection of works on Oregon and Northwest Baptist church history.

1329
Linn-Benton Community College
Learning Resource Center
6500 S.W. Pacific Boulevard
Albany, Oregon 97321

Telephone. (503) 967-6100

Institutional Description. The two-year community college was established in 1966. The present campus was occupied in 1970. Enrollment: 10,933.

Library Administration. Stanley N. Ruckman, Director.

Library General Holdings. 43,000 volumes; 400 periodical and newspaper subscriptions.

Special Collections

Special collections maintained by the library include the **Women's Studies Collection,** the **Nursing Collection,** and a collection of materials on the history of Linn and Benton Counties.

1330
Marylhurst College for Lifelong Learning
College Library
Marylhurst, Oregon 97036

Telephone. (503) 636-8141

Institutional Description. The privately supported liberal arts college offers programs for adults, with courses in the evenings and on weekends. It is affiliated with the Roman Catholic Church. Enrollment: 903.

Library Administration. Paula Hamilton, Library Director.

Library General Holdings. 100,000 volumes; 300 current periodical titles.

Special Collections

The library maintains specialized materials on Western and contemplative thought; art and music; and career resources.

1331
Mount Angel Seminary
Mount Angel Abbey Library
St. Benedict, Oregon 97373

Telephone. (503) 845-3292

Institutional Description. The privately supported seminary trains candidates for the Roman Catholic Priesthood. Founded in 1887, it is conducted by the Benedictine Monks of Mount Angel Abbey. Enrollment: 146.

Library Administration. Rev. Hugh Feiss, O.S.B., Library Director and Special Collections Librarian; Rev. Martin Pollard, O.S.B., Rare Books Librarian.

Library General Holdings. 135,000 volumes; 600 current periodical subscriptions; 20,000 microforms.

Special Collections

Roman Catholic theology is the strongest special collection; overlapping this and also a specialty is Pateistic and Latin Christian literature. Other strong areas include philosophy, American Civil War, and Africana.

Rare Book Collections

The library has a collection of 2,500 rare books including six illuminated manuscripts and a few incunabula. The majority of the books are sixteenth to eighteenth century works, mostly in Latin.

1332
Northwest Christian College
Learning Resource Center
828 East 11th Avenue
Eugene, Oregon 97401

Telephone. (503) 343-1641

Institutional Description. The privately supported liberal arts college was founded in 1895 as the Eugene Divinity School. It is sponsored by the Christian Church (Disciples of Christ), and provides training for church service. Enrollment: 255.

Library Administration. Margaret Sue Rhee, Director.

Library General Holdings. 58,000 volumes; 400 serials and periodicals.

Special Collections

A museum collection features African and Oriental artifacts donated by missionaries as well as American Indian and pioneer items. Materials on the early history of the Northwest and fine editions of printed books are in the **Northwest Collection** and the **Turnbull Collections.** The records of memorabilia of Northwest Christian College and its predecessor institutions dating from 1895 and history of the Disciples churches in the Northwest are located in the Archives. A unique hymnbook collection is also a part of the special collections.

Rare Book Collections

Rare Book and Bible Collection. Includes rare Bibles, incunabula, facsimile copies, early manuscripts, and other rare books.

1333
Oregon Health Sciences University
OHSU Library
3181 S.W. Sam Johnson Park Road
Portland, Oregon 97201

Telephone. (503) 279-8026

Institutional Description. The publicly supported professional university is a campus of the Oregon State Higher Education System. It is composed of the Schools of Dentistry, Medicine, and Nursing. It grants all levels of degrees, from associate to doctoral. Enrollment: 1,263.

Library Administration. James Morgan, Director.

Library General Holdings. 181,000 volumes; 2,665 current periodical titles.

Special Collections

The library maintains special collections in the history of dentistry and the history of medicine.

1334
Oregon State University
William Jasper Kerr Library
Corvallis, Oregon 97331

Telephone. (503) 754-3411

Institutional Description. The publicly supported state university was founded as Corvallis College and was designated as the agricultural college of the state in 1868. It now includes 12 colleges and schools plus a Graduate School. Enrollment: 15,379.

Library Administration. Melvin George, University Librarian; Clifford Mead, Head of Special Collections.

Library General Holdings. 1,047,823 volumes; 12,390 current periodicals; 770,957 microforms; 379,361 government documents.

Special Collections

Linus Pauling Papers. The collection includes all of Pauling's personal and scientific papers, notebooks, and correspondence from 1916 to the present. There are over 125,000 items plus Dr. Pauling's books, medals, research models, and memorabilia.

1335
Pacific University
Harvey W. Scott Memorial Library
Forest Grove, Oregon 97116

Telephone. (503) 357-6151

Institutional Description. The privately supported university began in 1842 and received its charter in 1849. Affiliated with the United Church of Christ, it grants baccalaureate, professional, master's, and doctoral degrees. Enrollment: 1,275.

Library Administration. Ronald Johnson, Director of Library Services.

Library General Holdings. 161,000 volumes; 890 current periodical subscriptions; 23,000 microforms.

Special Collections

The library maintains special collections in the fields of optometry and clinical psychology.

1336
Portland Community College
Library Media Center
12000 S.W. 49th Avenue
Portland, Oregon 97219

Telephone. (503) 244-6111

Institutional Description. The two-year college has four campuses and serves over 700,000 residents. It was established in 1961. Enrollment: 15,640.

Library Administration. Barbara J. Swanson, Librarian.

Library General Holdings. 78,000 books; 900 periodical titles.

Special Collections

The library has a special collection of 1,000 volumes on genealogy.

1337
Portland State University
Branford P. Millar Library
P.O. Box 751
Portland, Oregon 97207

Telephone. (503) 229-4433

Institutional Description. The publicly supported state university was founded in 1955. It has grown rapidly and is now composed of 8 schools and colleges and 7 specialized centers. Enrollment: 15,640.

Library Administration. C. Thomas Pfingsten, Director.

Library General Holdings. 700,000 volumes; 11,000 serial subscriptions.

Special Collections

Special Collections Room. Among the special collections of the Millar Library housed here are included the special holdings in Middle East studies.

1338
Reed College
Eric V. Hauser Memorial Library
3203 S.E. Woodstock Boulevard
Portland, Oregon 97202

Telephone. (503) 771-1112

Institutional Description. The privately supported liberal arts and teachers college was founded in 1909. It grants baccalaureate and master's degrees. Enrollment: 1,218.

Library Administration. Luella Rebecca Pollock, Librarian.

Library General Holdings. 300,000 books; 1,400 periodicals; 80,000 government documents.

Special Collections

Special collections are maintained in biology, chemistry, physics, and mathematics.

Rare Book Collections

Rare and irreplaceable materials are kept in the Cornelia Marvin Pierce Rare Book Complex. These include the **Thomas Lamb Eliot Papers,** consisting of manuscripts, notebooks, journals, correspondence, sermons, and miscellaneous personal papers of the nineteenth-twentieth-century educator, Unitarian minister, and civic leader instrumental in founding Reed College; the **Lloyd Reynolds Collection** of more than 300 volumes of books, letters, miscellaneous papers on the history of calligraphy, printing, and book manufacturing; and the **Simeon Garnet Reed Papers** which include business records and letters of the nineteenth-century transportation and mining magnate who financed the founding of The Reed Institute.

1339
Southern Oregon State College
Library
Ashland, Oregon 97520

Telephone. (503) 482-6445

Institutional Description. The publicly supported state college was founded in 1926. It now functions as a multipurpose institute. Enrollment: 4,727.

Library Administration. Sue Burkholder, Librarian; Harold Otness, Acquisitions/Serials/Special Collections Librarian.

Library General Holdings. 235,000 volumes; 2,000 periodical subscriptions; 200,000 U.S. and Oregon state government documents; 550,000 microforms.

Special Collections

The library collects materials on Oregon history with an emphasis on southern Oregon.

Rare Book Collections

The Margery Bailey Renaissance Collection. Contains over 6,000 volumes by and about William Shakespeare and his times. There are approximately 300 volumes published prior to 1800, including a second edition of Holinshed's *Chronicles* (1584), a second Shakespeare folio (1632), a fourth Shakespeare folio (1685), the first and second Ben Jonson folios (1616 and 1640), and the first and second Beaumont & Fletcher folios (1647 and 1679). Major editions of the collected plays of Shakespeare are included from the eighteenth century to the present. Also included are photocopies of the directors' promptbooks of the Oregon Shakespearian Festival Association and other publications concerning that organization, including festival publicity.

1340
Southwestern Oregon Community College
Learning Resource Center
1988 Newmark Avenue
Coos Bay, Oregon 97420

Telephone. (503) 888-3234

Institutional Description. The two-year community college was established in 1961. Enrollment: 4,713.

Library Administration. Dartha McCarthy, Director.

Library General Holdings. 52,598 volumes; 476 periodical titles; 9,976 record albums.

Special Collections

The library of the learning resource center has a special collection on William Shakespeare.

1341
Treasure Valley Community College
College Library
650 College Boulevard
Ontario, Oregon 97914

Telephone. (503) 889-6493

Institutional Description. Treasure Valley Community College was founded in 1962. Classes began in the local high school and moved to the college's own campus in 1964. Enrollment: 1,806.

Library Administration. Clark Hamer, Director of Library Services.

Library General Holdings. 31,500 books; 200 periodical titles.

Special Collections

The library is responsible for the **Horace and Roa Arment Indian Artifact Collection.** The collection consists of arrowheads, stone tools, and other artifacts of Indian culture.

1342
University of Oregon
University of Oregon Library
15th and Kinkaid Streets
Eugene, Oregon 97403

Telephone. (503) 686-3056

Institutional Description. The publicly supported university was established in 1872, concentrating on classical and literary subjects. Today there are 9 colleges offering a wide variety of subject areas. Enrollment: 17,142.

Library Administration. George W. Shipman, University Librarian; Kenneth W. Duckett, Special Collections Librarian; Timothy Pyatt, Rare Books Librarian; Hilary Cummings, Manuscripts Curator, Special Collections.

Library General Holdings. 1,713,832 volumes; 17,986 current periodical subscriptions; 1,397,148 microforms; 220,100 audiovisual materials.

Special Collections

Oregon Collection. Contains more than 30,000 volumes representing state and local history, Oregon city telephone directories, Oregon periodicals, and fiction by Oregon authors. Notable authors collected include Ken Kesey, Damon Knight, Ursula Le Guin, William Stafford, and Kate Wilhelm.

Manuscript Collection. Materials in the nearly 2,000 different manuscript collections emphasize the political, social, economic, and literary history of the United States in the twentieth century. Special strengths include Oregon history, politics, and culture; authors and illustrators of children's literature; the conservative and libertarian movement in the mid-twentieth century; popular literature with an emphasis on western fiction; missionaries to foreign countries, especially the Far East; and women in society, particularly those in nontraditional occupations, feminists and anti-feminists, and women writers, especially of fantasy and science fiction.

Photograph Collection. This collection contains more than 125,000 images depicting life and scenes from Appalachia to the Arctic with an emphasis on the Pacific Northwest. Notable are the Doris Ulmann, Lee Moorhouse, and Angelus Studio collections.

Rare Book Collections

Rare Book Collection. Contains nearly 40,000 volumes of literary first editions, fine press works, early imprints, and Western Americana. The collection contains 70 incunabula and nearly 40 Medieval and Renaissance manuscripts. Notable collections include the Edward S. Burgess Collection of Rare Books and Early manuscripts, the Gertrude Bass Warner Library of Oriental Art, the Pauline Potter Homer Collection of Beautiful Books, and the George A. Connor Collection of works written in the artificial language Esperanto.

Also housed in the Rare Book Collection is the Robert F. Lane Collection, which contains one of the largest collections in North America of works printed by the eighteenth century Italian typographer, Giambattista Bodoni. Other areas of note are eighteenth- and nineteenth-century British literature and fine books produced in Oregon.

1343
University of Portland
Wilson W. Clark Memorial Library
5000 North Wilamette Boulevard
Portland, Oregon 97203

Telephone. (503) 283-7111

Institutional Description. The privately supported university was founded by the Roman Catholic Congregation of the Holy Cross, a society of priests and brothers, in 1901. It is now governed by regents who represent many religious denominations. Enrollment: 2,610.

Library Administration. Joseph P. Browne, Director.

Library General Holdings. 300,000 volumes of books and periodicals; 191,000 microforms; 14,000 government documents.

Special Collections

Significant special collections include the **David Wheeler Hazen Collection** of approximately 4,000 volumes in American history and Lincolniana; the **Daniel Buckley Memorial Forestry Collection** of over 1,100 volumes on the forestry industry in the Pacific Northwest; a **Canadian Collection** which includes materials on Canadian literature, history, education, and politics; the **Salvador Macias Collection** of Spanish literature; and the **Rev. Anthony J. Juliano Collection** of theatre and drama materials.

1344
Warner Pacific College
College Library
2219 S.E. 68th Avenue
Portland, Oregon 97215

Telephone. (503) 775-4368

Institutional Description. The privately supported liberal arts college was founded in 1937 as Pacific Bible College. Now granting associate, baccalaureate, and master's degrees, it is affiliated with the Church of God (Anderson, Indiana). Enrollment: 382.

Library Administration. Bernice Wood, Library Administrator.

Library General Holdings. 52,000 volumes; 250 current periodical titles.

Special Collections

The library maintains a special religion collection and the **Church of God Archives.**

1345
Western Baptist College
Library-Media Center
5000 Deer Park Drive, S.E.
Salem, Oregon 97301

Telephone. (503) 581-8600

Institutional Description. The privately supported liberal arts, professional, and Bible college is affiliated with the General Association of Regular Baptist Churches. It grants associate and baccalaureate degrees. Enrollment: 257.

Library Administration. J. Richard Muntz, Librarian.

Library General Holdings. 56,000 items; 340 current periodical titles.

Special Collections

The library's collection in the field of religion represents 42 percent of its total holdings and supports the core curriculum in Bible and theology.

1346
Western Conservative Baptist Seminary
Cline-Tunnell Library
5511 S.E. Hawthorne Boulevard
Portland, Oregon 97215

Telephone. (503) 233-8561

Institutional Description. The privately supported theological seminary was founded in 1927. It is affiliated with the Conservative Baptist Church, and grants professional, master's, and doctorate degrees. Enrollment: 633.

Library Administration. Robert Allen Krupp, Library Director.

Library General Holdings. 60,000 volumes; 900 journal titles.

Special Collections

A significant special collection includes books and periodicals on Baptist history.

1347
Western Evangelical Seminary
George Hallauer Memorial Library
4200 SE Jennings Avenue
Portland, Oregon 97267

Telephone. (503) 654-5182

Institutional Description. The privately supported seminary was founded in 1945 as an interdenominational graduate school of theology. Enrollment: 172.

Library Administration. Gary Metzenbacher, Director of the Library.

Library General Holdings. 50,000 volumes; 430 current periodical subscriptions; 10,000 microfiche; 300 microfilm reels.

Special Collections

The library's collection focuses on theology, Christian education, counseling, marriage and family therapy, church history, missions, and Biblical studies.

Free Methodist Church Historical Collection. Contains about 1,000 volumes covering some aspect of the history of the denomination. The library is the depository for the archives of the Evangelical Church and holds over 2,500 volumes relating to the history of this denomination.

Curriculum Library. Contains 5,000 items including texts, teacher's manuals, audiovisual materials, and teaching helps.

E.J. Petticord Music Collection. Contains 25,000 items including music scores, choir pieces, and hymn arrangements.

Rare Book Collections

Archives. Contains 20,000 items including pamphlets, tracts, letters, and books relating to the nineteenth- and early twentieth-century Wesleyan/Holiness movement in America. Archival materials also include 500 volumes relating to the founding of the Northwest Yearly Meeting of the Friends Church.

1348
Western Oregon State College
Library
Monmouth, Oregon 97361

Telephone. (503) 838-1220

Institutional Description. The publicly supported state college has been involved in teacher training and educational research since its inception in 1861 as Monmouth University. Enrollment: 4,802.

Library Administration. Clarence C. Gorchels, Director.

Library General Holdings. 179,000 volumes; 1,600 serials; 270,000 microforms; 70,000 government documents.

Special Collections

Learning Activities Resources Center. A collection of more than 20,000 items of print and nonprint material covering subjects taught in Oregon elementary and secondary schools, including materials for the handicapped and severely handicapped. The collection includes a curriculum library of more than 4,500 elementary and secondary textbooks and about 1,200 courses of study used in Oregon and elsewhere.

1349
Western States Chiropractic College
W.A. Budden Library
2900 N.E. 132nd Avenue
Portland, Oregon 97230

Telephone. (503) 256-3180

Institutional Description. The privately supported professional college was founded in 1907. It grants the Doctor of Chiropractic Degree. Enrollment: 408.

Library Administration. Kaye Irvine, Director.

Library General Holdings. 15,000 volumes; 450 current periodical subscriptions; 2,500 microforms; 1,000 audiovisual materials.

Special Collections

Special resource materials are maintained in the historical chiropractic and alternative healing collection.

Pennsylvania

1350
Academy of the New Church Swedenborg Library 2815 Huntingdon Pike Bryn Athyn, Pennsylvania 19009

Telephone. (215) 938-2547

Institutional Description. The privately supported liberal arts college includes a seminary. The college provides associate and baccalaureate degrees designed to train students in the doctrine and philosophy of the General Church of the New Jerusalem. The theological school educates candidates for the ministry of the Church. Enrollment: 135.

Library Administration. Carroll C. Odhner, Library Director.

Library General Holdings. 85,000 volumes; 295 serial titles; 1,500 microforms; 900 audiovisual materials.

Special Collections

The Special Collections include the works of Swedenborg, New Church collateral literature, books and periodicals of the seventeenth and eighteenth centuries known by Swedenborg or giving the thought of his age, and the archives which contain material dealing with the Academy and the General Church of the New Jerusalem.

Rare Book Collections

A rare book and periodical collection includes a copy of *The True Christian Religion,* 1st edition in Latin, 1771, in which Swedenborg's handwritten list of gifts given to him by angels is found. Also, there is one of only three copies known to exist of the *Arcana Coelestia,* English translation, 1750, volume 2, a translation which Swedenborg saw through publication.

1351
Albright College Gingrich Library P.O. Box 15234 13th and Exeter Streets Reading, Pennsylvania 19612

Telephone. (215) 921-2381

Institutional Description. The privately supported liberal arts college was founded as Union Seminary in 1856 by the Central Pennsylvania Conference of the Evangelical Association of New Berlin, Pennsylvania. Now affiliated with The United Methodist Church, Union Seminary moved to Reading and adopted its present name. Enrollment: 1,961.

Library Administration. William Hannaford, Librarian; Fianna D. Holt, Head of Technical Services.

Library General Holdings. 148,500 volumes; 1,002 current periodical subscriptions; 10 current newspaper subscriptions; 100 abstract and index titles; 15,000 microforms and audiovisual materials (includes 3,300 recordings).

Special Collections

Norse-American Collection. Contains information on the Viking exploration of America. The collection, put together by Fred C. Bauer, includes books, manuscripts, notes, and newspaper clippings.

The Dick Collection. Includes most of the fine editions published by the Limited Editions Club. Included are the finest illustrators of the 1930s and 1940s.

J. Bennett Nolan Collection. This collection of books was owned by noted author, historian, and attorney J. Bennett Nolan (1877-1964). It includes local (Reading and Berks County) and Pennsylvania history as well as sheet music of local composers, local genealogical materials, and works by Nolan himself.

Albright College. A special collection of the history and ongoing work of Albright College and its predecessors (including Albright College at Myerstown, Pennsylvania and Schuylkill Seminary at Reading, along with other institutions merged into the present day college). The material also includes works by faculty and alumni.

1352
Allegheny College Lawrence Lee Pelletier Library Meadville, Pennsylvania 16335

Telephone. (814) 724-3100

Institutional Description. The privately supported lib-

eral arts college was founded in 1815. It is affiliated with the United Methodist Church. Enrollment: 1,900.

Library Administration. Margaret Louise Moser, Librarian.

Library General Holdings. 379,000 volumes; 915 current periodical subscriptions; 168,000 government documents; 99,000 microforms.

Special Collections

The Special Collections Area of the library contains the **Original Library** of the college collected by Timothy Alden; the **College Archives;** the **Ida M. Tarbell Collection** of Miss Tarbell's papers, her personal library, and her Lincoln Collection; and the **Americana Collection.**

1353
Allentown College of St. Francis de Sales Library Station Avenue Center Valley, Pennsylvania 18034

Telephone. (215) 282-1100

Institutional Description. The privately supported liberal arts college was founded in 1965. It is conducted by the Roman Catholic Oblate Fathers of St. Francis de Sales. Enrollment: 1,462.

Library Administration. Brother James P. McCabe, O.S.F.S., Library Director.

Library General Holdings. 112,000 volumes; 775 current periodical titles.

Special Collections

The library maintains special collections in nursing, theatre, and Salesian philosophy of Christian humanism.

1354
Alvernia College College Library Bernardine Street Reading, Pennsylvania 19607

Telephone. (215) 777-5411

Institutional Description. The privately supported liberal arts college was founded in 1961. It is affiliated with the Roman Catholic Church. Enrollment: 877.

Library Administration. Sister Mary Carlanita, Director, Library Services.

Library General Holdings. 80,000 volumes; 806 periodical and serial subscriptions.

Special Collections

The library maintains a **Polish Collection.**

1355
Annenberg Research Institute for Judaic and Near Eastern Studies Library Merion, Pennsylvania 19066

Telephone. (215) 667-1830

Institutional Description. The privately supported specialized institute was founded in 1907 as Dropsie College for Hebrew and Cognate Learning. Offering programs at the graduate level only, the institute grants master's and doctorate degrees. Enrollment: 47.

Library Administration. Mcihael Terrig, Bibliographic Services; Claudia Bloom, Technical Services.

Library General Holdings. 150,000 volumes; 800 current periodical subscriptions.

Special Collections

Special collections include the **Geniza Fragment Collection;** collections of works on Jewish education, history, and Hebrew literature; rare Bibles; a collection on Poland and Hungary; a collection of medieval Hebrew documents; the **History of Philadelphia Collection,** and materials on the Jewish labor movement.

1356
Berean Institute Learning Resources Center 1901 West Girard Avenue Philadelphia, Pennsylvania 19130

Telephone. (215) 763-4833

Institutional Description. The Berean Institute was founded in 1899 by Dr. Matthew Anderson, also founder and pastor of the Berean Presbyterian Church. Enrollment: 339.

Library Administration. Barbara Clarke, Librarian.

Library General Holdings. 3,000 volumes; 35 periodical titles.

Special Collections

The **Edyth Ingraham Black Experience Collection** is maintained in the library.

1357
Bloomsburg University of Pennsylvania Harvey A. Andruss Library Main and Penn Streets Bloomsburg, Pennsylvania 17815

Telephone. (717) 389-4000

Institutional Description. The publicly supported liberal arts, business, and teachers university was founded as a private academy in 1839. In 1916, it became part of the state educational system. Enrollment: 6,737.

Library Administration. William V. Ryan, Director.

Library General Holdings. 300,000 volumes; 1,085,-000 microforms; 850 current periodical subscriptions; 7,-600 pamphlets; 5,600 phonograph records.

Special Collections

A special collection of books contains first editions, autographed copies, and illustrated books.

1358
Bryn Mawr College
Mariam Coffin Canaday Library
Bryn Mawr, Pennsylvania 19010

Telephone. (215) 645-5000

Institutional Description. The privately supported liberal arts college for women was founded in 1885 by the Society of Friends. The graduate programs are coeducational. Enrollment: 1,794.

Library Administration. James Tanis, Director.

Library General Holdings. 728,000 volumes; 2,575 current periodicals; 106,000 government documents; 62,-000 microforms; 220,000 slides. The collections for the humanities and social sciences are largely in the Canady Library, except for art and archaeology which are housed in the M. Carey Thomas Library.

Special Collections

M. Carey Thomas Library. Books and other study materials of the Departments of Classical and Near Eastern Archaeology, History of Art and the Department of Visual Resources are housed here.

The library maintains a collection of the works of the poet, Marianne Moore.

Rare Book Collections

Rare Book Room. The Marjorie Walter Goodhart Medieval Library provides basic texts of the late Middle Ages and the emerging Renaissance. The Louise Bulkley Dillingham Collection of Spanish-American books ranges from sixteenth-century exploration and settlement to contemporary Spanish-American life and culture. Important and and extensive collections of early material on Latin America, Africa, and Asia are to be found in the Dillingham, McBride, and Plass collections. The Castle and Adelman collections expand the opportunities for the study of the graphic arts in books. In addition to these special collections are numerous rare books and manuscripts.

1359
Bucknell University
Ellen Clarke Bertrand Library
Lewisburg, Pennsylvania 17837

Telephone. (717) 524-1557

Institutional Description. The privately supported university, founded in 1846, features liberal arts, sciences, management, and engineering. Enrollment: 3,453.

Library Administration. Ann de Klerk, Director of Library Services.

Library General Holdings. 475,226 volumes; 2,479 current periodical titles; 280,093 government publications; 424,890 microforms.

Rare Book Collections

The Special Collections of the Bertrand Library is comprised of approximately 5,000 bound volumes and 40 linear feet of letters and manuscripts. These include rare and finely printed books in many fields of interest, but the primary strength of the collection lies in the field of Irish literature. There are numerous letters of Oliver St. John Gogarty, George Bernard Shaw, Lord Dunsany, George Russell, and William Butler Yeats, as well as several manuscripts of Gogarty and D.H. Lawrence. First editions and important later editions of these authors' works also are available to the researcher.

1360
Cabrini College
Holy Spirit Library
King of Prussia Road
Radnor, Pennsylvania 19087

Telephone. (215) 687-2100

Institutional Description. The privately supported liberal arts college for women was founded in 1957. It is conducted by the Roman Catholic Missionary Sisters of the Sacred Heart. Enrollment: 970.

Library Administration. Anita Johnson, Director.

Library General Holdings. 79,239 volumes; 320 current periodical subscriptions.

Special Collections

The library maintains a special collection on Franklin Delano Roosevelt and the College Archives.

1361
California University of Pennsylvania
Louis L. Manderino Library
California, Pennsylvania 15419

Telephone. (412) 938-4096

Institutional Description. The publicly supported institution provides teacher education as well as liberal arts, science, and technology. Enrollment: 5,460.

Library Administration. William L. Beck, Dean of Library Services; Janet DeStefon, Special Collections Clerk.

Library General Holdings. 278,000 volumes; 1,550

periodical subscriptions; 1.3 million microforms; 59,000 audiovisual materials; 5,000 U.S. and Pennsylvania government documents.

Special Collections

The library maintains a collection of curriculum materials, a historical collection of Industrial Arts textbooks, and the University Archives.

1362
Carlow College
Grace Library
3333 Fifth Avenue
Pittsburgh, Pennsylvania 15213

Telephone. (412) 578-6000

Institutional Description. The privately supported liberal arts college for women was founded in 1929 as Mount Mercy College. It is affiliated with the Roman Catholic Church. Enrollment: 1,120.

Library Administration. Joan Mitchell, Director of Library Services.

Library General Holdings. 107,600 volumes; 425 current periodical subscriptions; 6,400 audiovisual materials; 12,000 microforms.

Special Collections

Special collections include those in peace studies, Black studies, career resources, and the College Archives.

1363
Carnegie-Mellon University
University Libraries
5000 Forbes Avenue
Pittsburgh, Pennsylvania 15213

Telephone. (412) 268-2000

Institutional Description. The privately supported university is composed of the College of Fine Arts, Mellon College of Science, Carnegie Institute of Technology, College of Humanities and Social Sciences, School of Urban and Public Affairs, and Graduate School of Industrial Administration. Enrollment: 6,752.

Library Administration. Thomas Michalak, Director; Robert W. Kiger, Director, Hunt Institute.

Library General Holdings. 675,000 volumes; 3,000 periodical subscriptions; 100,000 slides; 399,100 microforms.

Special Collections

The Special Collections Department maintains manuscripts and university archives, CMU yearbooks, and the Drama Department's "prompt books." The collection of 100,000 slides includes a wide variety of subjects, with emphasis on the fields of art and architecture. Other special collections include materials on fine arts, robotics, engineering, science, and computer science.

Hunt Institute for Botanical Documentation. The Hunt Institute is devoted to the history of botany and allied fields. Its program embraces research, documentation, publication, exhibition, and reference service involving botanical literature, biography, iconography, and art and illustration, as well as the practice of the science itself. This work is supported by the Institute's rich collections of herbals and early modern botanical, horticultural, agricultural, and travel literature, of original botanical artworks of old and modern, of manuscripts and other archival materials, and of portraiture.

1364
Cedar Crest College
Cressman Library
Cedar Crest Boulevard
Allentown, Pennsylvania 18104

Telephone. (215) 437-4471

Institutional Description. The privately supported liberal arts college for women was founded in 1867. It is affiliated with the United Church of Christ, but welcomes all students. Enrollment: 1,145.

Library Administration. Patricia Ann Sacks, Director.

Library General Holdings. 113,000 volumes; 757 current periodical subscriptions; 11,000 microforms; 2,900 phonodiscs; 9,000 slides; 825 music scores; 400 audiotapes.

Special Collections

The **Marjorie Wright Miller Poetry Room** houses works of twentieth-century poetry. The library also maintains a **Women's Studies Collection** and the College's archives.

1365
Chatham College
Jennie King Mellon Library
Woodland Road
Pittsburgh, Pennsylvania 15232

Telephone. (412) 365-1100

Institutional Description. The privately supported liberal arts college for women was founded in 1869 as the Pennsylvania Female College. Students may register for courses in 9 local colleges and universities under a reciprocal plan. Enrollment: 602.

Library Administration. Mary Cay Rojitas-Milliner, Technical Services; Irma M. Smith, Information Services.

Library General Holdings. 125,000 volumes; 560 periodical subscriptions.

Special Collections

A significant special collection of the library is the **Snowdon Collection** of materials dealing with the Mayan culture and civilization.

1366
Chestnut Hill College
Logue Library
Germantown and Northwestern Avenues
Philadelphia, Pennsylvania 19118

Telephone. (215) 248-7000

Institutional Description. The privately supported liberal arts college for women was founded in 1924. It is affiliated with the Roman Catholic Church. Enrollment: 924.

Library Administration. Helen Hayes, Director.

Library General Holdings. 113,500 volumes; 1,075 current periodical titles.

Special Collections

The **Irish Collection** and the **Morton Collection** of rare first editions are maintained by the library.

1367
Cheyney University
Leslie Pinckney Hill Library
Cheyney Road
Cheyney, Pennsylvania 19319

Telephone. (215) 399-2245

Institutional Description. The publicly supported college, founded in 1837, offers a number of career-oriented degree programs. Enrollment: 1,507.

Library Administration. Karen Humbert, Acting Director of Library Services.

Library General Holdings. 221,844 bound volumes; 985 periodical subscriptions; 29 newspaper subscriptions; 384,680 microforms.

Special Collections

Ethnic Collection. This collection is comprised of 3,319 books on the Afro-American experience.

1368
Clarion University
Carlson Library
Clarion, Pennsylvania 16214

Telephone. (814) 226-2490

Institutional Description. The publicly supported liberal arts and teachers institution was established in 1867. Enrollment: 6,112.

Library Administration. Gerard B. McCabe, Library Director; Roger Horn, Collections Librarian.

Library General Holdings. 360,000 volumes; 1,650 periodical subscriptions; 1,500,000 units in various formats.

Special Collections

The special collection of the library is currently being reduced to only those items in need of special care and/or protection. Special holdings in local history are being eliminated by putting some in the general stacks and donating other material to the local and other historical societies.

1369
College Misericordia
Francesca McLaughlin Memorial Library
Lake Street
Dallas, Pennsylvania 18612

Telephone. (717) 675-2181

Institutional Description. The privately supported liberal arts college primarily for women was founded in 1924. It is affiliated with the Roman Catholic Church. Enrollment: 1,118.

Library Administration. Mary Sharon Gallagher, R.S.M., Director.

Library General Holdings. 73,500 volumes; 760 current periodical subscriptions.

Special Collections

The library maintains a special collection of ANA and NLN nursing publications and selected award-winning books in children's literature.

1370
Community College of Beaver County
College Library
College Drive
Monaca, Pennsylvania 15061

Telephone. (412) 775-8561

Institutional Description. Founded in 1966, the original campus was located in temporary buildings in Freedom, Pennsylvania. The present campus was completed in 1971. Enrollment: 2,511.

Library Administration. Carol V. Vuckovich, Director.

Library General Holdings. 45,000 volumes; 300 periodical and professional journal subscriptions; 1,200 recordings.

Special Collections

The library has special collections on law and nursing.

1371
The Curtis Institute of Music
The Curtis Institute of Music Library
1726 Locust Street
Philadelphia, Pennsylvania 19103

Telephone. (215) 893-5265

Institutional Description. The privately supported music institute was founded in 1924. It grants diplomas and baccalaureate and master's degrees. Enrollment: 182.

Library Administration. Elizabeth Walker, Head Librarian; Edwin Heilakka, Curator, Leopold Stokowski Collection; Elizabeth Walker and Edwin Heilakka, Special Collections/Rare Books Librarians.

Library General Holdings. 10,000 books; 45 periodical subscriptions; 55,000 music scores; 8,000 sound recordings; 70 microfilm reels.

Special Collections

Special Collections include the personal library of Leopold Stokowski, featuring his orchestral transcriptions, scrapbooks, and memorabilia. These materials are complemented by the Robert Gatewood collection of all recordings made by Stokowski. Other important collections are the personal library of nineteenth century Philadelphia musician Charles H. Jarvis and collections of music, manuscripts, and memorabilia from former faculty members including Lynnwood Farnam, Josef Hofmann, William Kincaid, Carlos Salzedo, Anton Torello, Efrem Zimbalist, Samuel Barber, and Max Rudolf.

Archival Material. Includes photographs, scrapbooks, clippings, programs of all Curtis performances, broadcast student concerts from the 1930s-40s on 350 unique 78rpm discs, Curtis concerts since the 1960s preserved on 2,000 fully indexed and cataloged tapes, archive videotapes of Curtis opera productions, and the published and recorded accomplishments of Curtis alumni, many of whom are well-known performers. There is a fully indexed photograph collection recording primarily the first decade of the school (1924-34) and 250 rolls for mechanical piano and organ.

Rare Book Collections

Rare materials in the Curtis Music Library include important holograph music manuscripts of George Antheil, Samuel Barber, and Carlos Salzedo; holograph music manuscripts of minor works and a small collection of letters of composers and musicians of the eighteenth and nineteenth centuries; first editions of important compositions and books on music; a small collection of books printed in Italy 1570-1870.

1372
Delaware Valley College of Science and Agriculture
Krauskopf Memorial Library
Doylestown, Pennsylvania 18901

Telephone. (215) 345-1500

Institutional Description. The privately supported (state aided) professional college, primarily for men, offers programs in specialized fields in agriculture, biology, chemistry, and business administration. Enrollment: 1,434.

Library Administration. Constance R. Smook, Head Librarian.

Library General Holdings. 80,000 volumes.

Special Collections

Special collections include the **Joseph Krauskopf Collection** which includes his personal library of philosophy and Jewish writing; United States Department of Agriculture, state extension, and related pamphlets.

Poultry Diagnostic Laboratory. This laboratory was established in 1953 by the Commonwealth of Pennsylvania. It is designed to serve the livestock and poultry industries and to assemble and apply the results of the latest research work being done in the field of animal diseases.

1373
Dickinson College
Boyd Lee Spahr Library
150 South College Street
Carlisle, Pennsylvania 17013

Telephone. (717) 243-5121

Institutional Description. The privately supported liberal arts college was founded in 1773. An independent institution by charter, it maintains an historical relationship with the United Methodist Church. Enrollment: 1,-943.

Library Administration. Martha C. Slotten, Librarian and College Archivist.

Library General Holdings. 396,000 volumes; 1,200 current periodicals; 128,500 microfiche; 92,000 government documents; 7,800 microfilm reels; 6,700 music recordings.

Special Collections

The Morris Room of the library houses the Special Collections which include a major collection of tapes and documents pertaining to the Three Mile Island nuclear accident and subsequent investigation; materials of Joseph Priestley, the discoverer of oxygen; and the papers of James Buchanan, the fifteenth President of the United States. The library also maintains materials on the prominent colonial figureheads who were the founders of the

College, such as Benjamin Rush and John Dickinson.

1374
Dickinson School of Law
Sheely-Lee Law Library
150 South College Street
Carlisle, Pennsylvania 17013

Telephone. (717) 243-4611

Institutional Description. The privately supported professional law school was founded in 1834. It grants the professional Juris Doctor (J.D.) and master's degrees. Enrollment: 524.

Library Administration. James R. Fox, Librarian.

Library General Holdings. 215,000 volumes; 800 periodical subscriptions.

Special Collections

The library supports a wide range of legal study and scholarship. Collections of Jewish law, medical jurisprudence, and intellectual property law supplement growing special interests. To complement the School's summer programs in Florence (Italy), Vienna (Austria), and Strasbourg (France), the library has developed a strong collection of international and comparative law materials.

1375
Drexel University
W.W. Hagerty Library
32nd and Chestnut Streets
Philadelphia, Pennsylvania 19104

Telephone. (215) 895-2000

Institutional Description. The privately supported (state aided) university was founded in 1891. Enrollment: 12,494.

Library Administration. Richard L. Snyder, Director of Libraries.

Library General Holdings. 455,000 volumes; current 4,175 periodicals; 117,000 government documents; 572,000 microforms; 32,000 audiovisual materials.

Special Collections

The major strengths of the library's holdings are in the fields of technology, pure science, business, nutrition, design, and library and information science. An important special collection includes materials pertaining to A.J. Drexel and the Drexel family.

1376
Duquesne University
University Library
800 Forbes Avenue
Pittsburgh, Pennsylvania 15282

Telephone. (412) 434-6130

Institutional Description. The privately supported Roman Catholic university was founded in 1878 by the Fathers of the Congregation of the Holy Ghost and of the Immaculate Heart of Mary. Enrollment: 6,757.

Library Administration. Paul J. Pugliese, University Librarian; William B. Spinelli, Assistant University Librarian.

Library General Holdings. 481,401 volumes; 2,100 current journal subscriptions.

Special Collections

The library has extensive holdings in Roman Catholic theology, history and biography, an international collection of music scores; and much material on Africa south of the Sahara, particularly linguistics.

Rare Book Collections

Rabbi Herman Hailperin Collection. The focus of this collection is on Judeo-Christian intellectual religion during the Middle Ages. The collection is rich in works in Hebrew and medieval Latin collected by Rabbi Hailperin on his extensive travels in Europe and the Middle East.

Justice Michael A. Musmanno Collection. The collection houses the personal library and private papers and correspondence of the late Justice. There is extensive and unique material dealing with the Sacco/Vanzetti case, the Nazi War Crimes Trials, the death of Adolf Hitler, and the abolition of the Pennsylvania Coal and Iron Police.

Cardinal Wright Collection. The Cardinal was very much a part of Vatican Council II and the Synods that followed (up to 1977). Here is an abundant source of material covering those deliberations.

Simon Silverman Phenomenology Center. The intent of this collection is to acquire "all the literature on phenomenology—every author, every language, every edition, every scrap of evidence that might shed light on the movement or be useful to scholars." It is also the official branch of the Husserl Archives of the University of Louvain, Belgium. These archives contain 40,000 handwritten sheets (in an esoteric shorthand) and 10,000 typed pages.

1377
East Stroudsburg University of Pennsylvania Library
East Stroudsburg, Pennsylvania 18301

Telephone. (717) 424-3211

Institutional Description. The publicly supported liberal arts and teachers university was founded in 1893 as a private normal school. It now offers a wide variety of programs at the undergraduate and graduate levels. Enrollment: 4,320.

Library Administration. Alvin C. Berger, Director.

Library General Holdings. 360,000 volumes of books

and bound periodicals; 930,000 microforms.

Special Collections

Curriculum Library. This library provides teacher-trainees with a special collection of 5,660 items including a selection of textbooks currently used in schools throughout the country and a comprehensive collection of school courses of study. An assortment of models, globes, transparencies, and other teaching aids is also available.

1378
Eastern Baptist Theological Seminary
Austin K. deBlois Library
City Line and Lancaster Avenue
Philadelphia, Pennsylvania 19151

Telephone. (215) 896-5000

Institutional Description. The privately supported theological seminary was founded in 1925. Affiliated with the American Baptist Churches U.S.A., it offers graduate-level programs only. Enrollment: 385.

Library Administration. Thomas F. Gilbert, Director of Learning Resources.

Library General Holdings. 100,000 volumes.

Special Collections

Special strengths of the library are in the fields of Biblical studies and archaeology, preaching and communication, pastoral counseling, and Baptist History.

1379
Eastern College
Warner Memorial Library
Fairview Avenue
St. Davids, Pennsylvania 19087

Telephone. (215) 341-5957

Institutional Description. The privately supported liberal arts college was founded in 1932 as a department of Eastern Baptist Theological Seminary. Now affiliated with the American Baptist Churches, it became independent in 1932. Enrollment: 1,044.

Library Administration. James L. Sauer, Director of Library.

Library General Holdings. 73,000 books; 740 current subscriptions; 10,000 bound periodicals; 35,000 microforms; 2,000 recordings.

Special Collections

Goebal Collection. Includes fine print books, bookplates, and a significant collection of Bruce Rogers' printing works.

Marcus Aurelius Collection. 200 editions of this Stoic philosopher's works.

Oliver Wendell Holmes Stereoscopic Library. The library of the National Stereoscopic Association; includes a collection of books, magazines, stereoscopes, and over 45,000 stereoscopic slides.

1380
Edinboro University of Pennsylvania
Baron-Forness Library
Edinboro, Pennsylvania 16444

Telephone. (814) 732-2779

Institutional Description. The publicly supported university is the oldest such institution in Pennsylvania west of the Allegheny Mountains. Founded in 1856, it became a four-year college in 1926. Enrollment: 6,014.

Library Administration. Saul Weinstein, University Librarian; John Fleming, Reference Librarian.

Library General Holdings. 400,000 volumes; 1,500 periodical subscriptions; 1,000,000 microforms; 1,200 music scores; 11,000 recordings; 400 videotapes; 200 motion pictures.

Special Collections

Curriculum Materials Collection. Contains approximately 55,000 pieces, including textbooks, curriculum guides, children's literature, media, flat pictures and prints, kits, games, and microfiche materials.

Southeast Asia Collection. Consists of materials on the southeastern Asian nations of Vietnam, Laos, Cambodia, Malaysia, Thailand, Indonesia, and Burma, plus Korea, as mandated by the Commonwealth of Pennsylvania; approximately 2,000 items.

The library's Special Collections area, while not truly a rare book area, includes materials by University professors and a fairly extensive group of American Civil War items.

1381
Elizabethtown College
Zug Memorial Library
One Alpha Drive
Elizabethtown, Pennsylvania 17022

Telephone. (717) 367-1151

Institutional Description. The privately supported liberal arts college was founded by the Church of the Brethren in 1899. Enrollment: 1,692.

Library Administration. Nelson Bard, Librarian; Naomi Hershey, Reference Librarian/Special Collections Librarian.

Library General Holdings. 194,500 volumes; 146,000 volumes in general circulating collection; 9,000 volumes in reference collection; 1,000 current periodicals; 20,000 bound periodicals; 15 cabinets of microforms including back periodicals, books, and documents; 38,704 audiovisual items.

Rare Book Collections

Brethren Collection. 2,000 volumes, including histories of the Church of the Brethren, minutes of Church Boards, church directories, letters, photographs, and rare books; a non-circulating research collection.

1382
Franklin and Marshall College
Shadek-Fackenthal Library
P.O. Box 3003
Lancaster, Pennsylvania 17604

Telephone. (717) 291-4216

Institutional Description. The privately supported liberal arts college is one of the oldest in the nation. Franklin College was established in 1787, Marshall College in 1836. They joined in 1853, and have had a historical relationship with the United Church of Christ. Enrollment: 2,040.

Library Administration. Kathleen Moretto Spencer, Librarian; Charlotte B. Brown, College Archivist/Special Collections Librarian.

Library General Holdings. 204,131 volumes; 1,694 current periodical subscriptions; 15,649 reels of microforms (periodicals); 233,814 federal documents (paper, microfiche, maps).

Special Collections

Institutional Archives. There are seven primary groups of college archives covering the histories of Franklin College, 1787-1852; Marshall College, 1837-1853; and Franklin and Marshall College, 1853 to the present. Included in these files are the records of the Board of Trustees and other boards of control, administrative records, as well as faculty and student files. From the standpoint of Pennsylvania history, the institutional archives contribute in-depth documentation of the growth and development of a liberal arts college and of higher education in general in Pennsylvania from the late eighteenth century to modern times. The roles of prominent Pennsylvanians affiliated with the college are also documented. Included are themes such as the nineteenth-century Protestant Church reform movements, primarily the Mercersburg Reform, and the developments of commerce and culture in south-central Pennsylvania in the decades after the Civil War. Other institutional records of interest are those relating to James Buchanan (1791-1868), President pro-tem and a college trustee; student participation in the Civil War and the effects of the Battle of Gettysburg upon the running of the college; early nineteenth century land records documenting college-owned property in Pennsylvania; World War I Student Army Training Corps and World War II Naval/Marine V-5 and V-12 programs; the development of college athletic programs from the mid-nineteenth century to date; college agent, plus other fund raising activities (ca. 1840-present); student life (ca. 1837-present); and alumni association and biographical files (ca. 1800-present). There are more than 10,000 photographs in the institutional records.

Other special collections include the Gonzalez Lodge Collection of nineteenth-century classics; nineteenth-century theology/classical philosophy; Lancaster County, Pennsylvania imprints; nineteenth-century astronomy and botany; and nineteenth-century U.S. government publications.

Rare Book Collections

German-American Imprint Collection. This collection, consisting of primarily printed materials written in the German language and printed in North America up to 1900, was formerly two collections. Previously known to researchers as the Unger-Bassler Collection and the collection of the Pennsylvania Dutch Folklore Center, these materials have now been combined to form one of the most complete and extensive collections of German-Americana in the United States. This is especially true for items printed before 1830. Of particular note are the collections of printed broadsides (ca.1720-1860) and of the Lancaster County *frakturschriften* manuscripts (ca. 1720-1880).

Manuscript Collections. Personal/family papers of those having affiliation with Franklin College, Marshall College, and Franklin Marshall College; personal papers of south-central Pennsylvania area natural historians (i.e. "Scientifics") of the nineteenth century; personal papers of Pennsylvania German-Americans of the nineteenth century.

Napoleana Collection. Monographs by or about Napoleon and the Napoleonic era with a focus upon military history and anti-Bonaparte writings; primarily nineteenth century imprints.

Reichenbach Collection. A bequest which formed the first library of Franklin College, 1787-1853; mostly classical texts in Greek, Latin, and vernacular, ca. 1753-1770.

Alexander Toth Collection. Includes the works of Walter de la Mare.

1383
Gannon University
Monsignor Wilfred J. Nash Library
University Square
Erie, Pennsylvania 16541

Telephone. (814) 871-7000

Institutional Description. The privately supported Roman Catholic liberal arts university was founded in 1933. Enrollment: 3,952.

Library Administration. Rev. L. Thomas Snyderwine, Director.

Library General Holdings. 200,000 volumes; current 1,150 periodicals.

Special Collections

Significant special collections include the **G.K. Chesterton Collection,** the **John Carney Collection** on Erie history; and the **Archbishop John Mark Gannnon Collection** (founder of the University).

1384
Geneva College
McCartney Library
College Avenue
Beaver Falls, Pennsylvania 15010

Telephone. (412) 846-5100

Institutional Description. The privately supported liberal arts college was founded in 1848. It is affiliated with the Reformed Presbyterian Church, and grants associate and baccalaureate degrees. Enrollment: 1,177.

Library Administration. Gerald D. Moran, Librarian.

Library General Holdings. 134,000 volumes; 660 periodical subscriptions; 61,000 microforms.

Special Collections

The **Coleman Science Collection,** the **Clarence M. Church Classical Record Collection,** the **Covenanter Collection** of materials on the Reformed Presbyterian Church of North America and Scottish genealogy; and memorabilia of Clarence E. McCartney are special collections of the library. The Career and Counsling Library is a specialized collection of occupational and placement resources located in the Student Center.

1385
Gettysburg College
Musselman Library
North Washington Street
Gettysburg, Pennsylvania 17325

Telephone. (717) 337-6000

Institutional Description. The privately supported liberal arts college was founded in 1832 as the first Lutheran college in the United States. It retains its affiliation with the Lutheran Church in America. Enrollment: 1,922.

Library Administration. Willis M. Hubbard, College Librarian.

Library General Holdings. 300,000 volumes; 1,400 periodical subscriptions; 32,000 government documents; 36,000 microforms; 11,500 records.

Special Collections

Important holdings in the special collections are the **John H.W. Stuckenberg Collection,** the **Civil War Collection,** and the **H.L. Mencken Collection.**

1386
Gratz College
Gratz College Library
10th Street and Tabor Road
Philadelphia, Pennsylvania 19141

Telephone. (215) 329-3363

Institutional Description. The privately supported teachers college was founded in 1895. It offers programs in Jewish, Hebraic, and Middle East Studies, and in Jewish Education. Enrollment: 255.

Library Administration. Jack Weinstein, Librarian.

Library General Holdings. 110,000 items; 115 current periodical subscriptions.

Special Collections

The library contains the **Dr. Samuel Pitlik Collection of Hebrew Literature** as well as the collection of the Philadelphia Branch of the Histadrut Ivrit. The library has a growing collection of 45,000 books in the fields of Judaica, Hebraica and general reference. In 1981, the **Gratz College Holocaust Oral History Archive** was established to collect, preserve, and make available to scholars and researchers the testimony of Holocaust survivors currently residing in the greater Philadelphia area. In 1984, Dr. Carl Lampner donated a significant collection of 1,600 books on education, many of which concentrate on special education.

1387
Grove City College
Henry Buhl Library
Grove City, Pennsylvania 16127

Telephone. (412) 458-6600

Institutional Description. The privately supported liberal arts college was founded in 1876. It is affiliated with the Presbyterian Church U.S.A. Enrollment: 2,133.

Library Administration. Diane H. Grundy, Librarian.

Library General Holdings. 148,00 books and bound periodicals; 700 current periodical subscriptions; 112,000 microforms.

Special Collections

The Buhl Library houses several special collections: the **Ludwig von Mises Papers;** the **Leslie Leland Locke Collection** of mathematics books and personal papers; and the **General George B. McClelland Collection** of Civil War books. The libraries of Dr. Isaac C. Ketler, founder of the College, and of Dr. Alexander Ormond, second president of the College, are also maintained.

1388
Gwynedd Mercy College
Lourdes Library
Sumneytown Pike
Gwynedd Valley, Pennsylvania 19437

Telephone. (215) 646-7300

Institutional Description. The privately supported college of arts and sciences is sponsored by the Roman Catholic Sisters of Mercy. Founded in 1948, the College offers associate and baccalaureate degrees and programs for teacher certification. Enrollment: 1,980.

Library Administration. Purima Bagga, Librarian; Evelyn S. Udell, Catalog Librarian/Special Collections Librarian.

Library General Holdings. 83,000 books; 750 periodical subscriptions; 4,500 audiovisual materials.

Special Collections

The Library has a special collection of Irish language, history, and culture containing approximately 950 titles. The majority of materials have been donated by the Irish Cultural Society.

There is also a collection of children's literature (2,000 volumes).

1389
Hahnemann University
Library
230 North Broad Street
Philadelphia, Pennsylvania 19102

Telephone. (215) 448-7184

Institutional Description. The privately supported university provides education in the health sciences. It is composed of the Medical School (founded in 1848), the Graduate School (established in 1949), and the School of Allied Health Professions (organized in 1968). Enrollment: 2,006.

Library Administration. Carol Finichel, Director; Barbara Williams, Archivist.

Library General Holdings. 80,000 volumes; 1,250 current periodical subscriptions. The library has a wide range of current and retrospective literature in biomedical and allied health sciences.

Special Collections

The library's special collections include the **Thomas L. Bradford Collection** of biography and history of homeopathic medicine; and the **Constantine Hering Collection** on Theophrastus Paracelsus.

1390
Haverford College
Magill Library
Haverford, Pennsylvania 19041

Telephone. (215) 896-1161

Institutional Description. The privately supported liberal arts college, founded in 1833, was the first college established by the Society of Friends in the United States. Enrollment: 1,112.

Library Administration. Michael S. Freeman, Librarian; Edwin B. Bronner, Curator, Quaker Collection; Diana Alten, Manuscripts Cataloger; Elisabeth P. Brown, Quaker Bibliographer.

Library General Holdings. 456,196 volumes; 1,236 current periodical subscriptions; 4,735 microforms; 1,500 audiovisual materials; 62,100 government documents.

Special Collections

American Friends Service Committee Archives. Includes archival material from 1917 to the present.

Haverfordiana. The Haverford College History Collection is the most complete part of the collection. It contains material such as photographs, the *News* from 1909 to the present; minutes of the Board of Managers; masters' theses and other materials. The Archives collection consists of publications from the Admissions Office; student yearbooks; President's Reports; alumni magazines; artifacts and memorabilia. The President's Collection is a set of the published works of past and present Haverford Presidents.

J. Rendell Harris Collection. Approximately 100 items of "chiefly Oriental manuscripts" with an emphasis on Semitic languages spanning the thirteenth to nineteenth centuries. It includes Hebrew, Syriac, Latin, Arabic, Coptic, Armenian, and Persian manuscripts.

Rufus M. Jones Collection on Mysticism. During his lifetime, Rufus M. Jones gave the College his personal collection of books on mysticism, nearly 1,000 volumes which he accumulated in connection with his voluminous writing on the subject. The collection now includes 1,400 books from the Renaissance period to the present. The papers of Rufus Jones are also maintained by the library and consist of some 75 linear feet of correspondence, lecture notes, speeches, manuscripts of books, and diaries.

Lockwood Collection. Consists of some 3,000 volumes of works by and about Italian Humanists given to the Library by Dean P. Lockwood, Librarian from 1920 to 1949.

Christopher Morley Collection. Comprises about 1,000 letters and memoranda from his correspondence files. There are autographed letters from more than 100 contemporary authors. Morley, the Class of 1910, was born on the campus of Haverford College.

C.C. Morris Cricket Collection. This collection and library houses several thousand books and memorabilia about the history of cricket.

Roberts Autograph Letters Collection. The collection contains 20,000 letters varying in date from ca. 1400 to the present. It includes a set of the Signers of the Declaration of Independence, letters of the Presidents of the

United States, members of the Constitutional Convention of 1787, letters of officers of the American Revolution, and also large collections of distinguished authors, composers, royalty, scientists, educators, and businessmen. There are many Quaker letters in this collection.

Other collections include the William Pyle Philips Collection of the Signers of the Declaration of Independence and the Nathaniel Peabody Rogers Anti-Slavery Collection.

Rare Book Collections

Collinson-Fothergill Collection. This collection of semi-rare books includes sets of periodicals, encyclopedias, and other publications. Peter Collinson and Dr. John Fothergill were eighteenth-century Quaker scientists who supported American colonial libraries.

French Drama Collection. Consists of several hundred popular plays produced in Paris between 1790 and 1850.

Philips Collection. Consists primarily of rare books and manuscripts, mostly of the Renaissance period; includes first editions of Dante, Copernicus, Spenser, the King James Bible, Milton, Newton, and the four folios of Shakespeare.

Quaker Collection. At Haverford, the Quaker books have always been included in the college Library as part of its regular acquisitions. The 25,000 printed volumes—as distinct from manuscripts—in the collection are housed in the Treasure Room. The addition of the Borton Wing of the Library doubled the Quaker Collection and rare book area. Many other books with Quaker associations are among the volumes on the regular shelves of the Library. The Quaker Collection includes:

William H. Jenks Collection. Includes 1,400 rare Quaker tracts and pamphlets, mostly from the seventeenth century; more than 160 writings of George Fox, 67 by William Penn, 53 by Isaac Pennington, 45 by George Whitehead, and 35 by James Nayler; 22 unbound broadsides. There are 1,600 volumes in the Jenks Collection. These volumes, combined with the other rare seventeenth-century Friends publications, make this the finest collection of early Quaker writings in the United States.

In addition to the seventeenth-century items in the Jenks Collection, the Quaker Collection contains more than 2,000 other seventeenth-century printed works. The collection, however, is not limited to rare and unusual items. There are more than 25,000 cataloged items in the Quaker Collection, not including uncataloged pamphlets, clippings, and other ephemeral material.

Maps, Photographs, and Pictures. The map collection contains maps of early Pennsylvania, New England, and other areas where Quakers have been active. There are hundreds of photographs, pictures, and silhouettes of Friends and their homes and meetinghouses.

Manuscript Collection. This collection now contains more than 250,000 items. In addition to William Penn letters, there are a number of letters and papers written by George Fox, Robert Barclay (microfilm), John Woolman, and many other seventeenth- and eighteenth-century Friends. There are nearly 700 manuscript journals; family papers; and material on Friends and the Indian (papers of the Associated Executive Committee of Friends on Indian Affairs and the Lake Mohonk Conference of Friends of the Indians and Other Independent People), including the papers of Enoch Hoag, John B. Garrett, and Jonathan Richards. The manuscript collection includes many Disciplines of Yearly Meetings of the Society of Friends.

1391
Holy Family College
College Library
Grant and Frankford Avenues
Philadelphia, Pennsylvania 19114

Telephone. (215) 637-7700

Institutional Description. The privately supported liberal arts college was founded in 1954. It is affiliated with the Roman Catholic Church. Enrollment: 1,549.

Library Administration. Joseph A. McDonald, Director of Library Services.

Library General Holdings. 96,000 volumes; 435 current periodical subscriptions.

Special Collections

The library maintains a special collection on radium and its discoverer, Madame Curie; a collection on local Philadelphia history; and a collection of materials on the Polish language and literature.

1392
Immaculata College
College Library
Immaculata, Pennsylvania 19345

Telephone. (215) 647-4400

Institutional Description. The privately supported liberal arts college for women was founded in 1920. It is affiliated with the Roman Catholic Church. Enrollment: 1,904.

Library Administration. Sister Florence Marie, Director.

Library General Holdings. 129,000 volumes; 620 current periodical subscriptions.

Special Collections

The classic works of Catholic literature, as well as important contemporary contributions to Catholic thought, are well represented in the library.

1393
Indiana University of Pennsylvania
Patrick J. Stapleton, Jr. Library
Indiana, Pennsylvania 15705

Telephone. (412) 357-3039

Institutional Description. The publicly supported university began as a normal school in 1875. Enrollment: 13,248.

Library Administration. Larry A. Kroah, Librarian; Phillip J. Zorich, Special Collections Librarian.

Library General Holdings. 568,000 volumes; 4,300 periodical subscriptions; 486,000 microforms.

Special Collections

The Special Collections Division of the library contains the **Pennsylvania Collection,** University Archives, rare books and manuscripts. The library collects significant regional historical manuscripts, especially that relate to the coal mining industry. Manuscript collections include the papers of the Rochester and Pittsburgh Coal Company, United Mine Workers District Two, Congressman John P. Saylor, United Steel Workers Local 1397 (Homestead, PA), and children's author Lois Lenski.

Cogswell Music Library. Contains a broad variety of music materials with especially strong holdings in musicological literature, music monuments, and collected editions. Among the more specialized materials are: (1) a complete set of the Foster Hall reproductions of the works of Stephen Collins Foster, (2) a large representative collection of 78 rpm phonographs records, including the **Otto E. Albrecht Collection** of recordings, (3) the **Albert R. Casavant Research Collection** of marching band and drill team materials, and (4) the collected papers and memorabilia of Edward Melvin Harris.

Rare Book Collections

Notable collections in rare books are those related to Washington Irving, Charles Darwin, John Greenleaf Whittier, and Norman Mailer.

1394
Juniata College
Beeghly Library
Huntingdon, Pennsylvania 16652

Telephone. (814) 643-4310

Institutional Description. The privately supported liberal arts college was founded in 1876. Enrollment: 1,089.

Library Administration. A.M. Jaffurs, Public Services Librarian.

Library General Holdings. 160,000 bound volumes; 826 periodical and newspaper subscriptions.

Special Collections

The library maintains a curriculum library to support the program of the Education Department.

Rare Book Collections

Rare book materials include early Pennsylvania German imprints (mostly eighteenth-century); archives of books and manuscripts related to Church of the Brethren; Pennsylvania county histories; the Henry W. Shoemaker Collection of Pennsylvania folklore; and the Abraham H. Cassel Collection of nineteenth-century pamphlets.

1395
Keystone Junior College
Miller Library
La Plume, Pennsylvania 18440

Telephone. (717) 945-5141

Institutional Description. The two-year college is a private residential junior college that began as an academy in 1868. It became a junior college in 1936. Enrollment: 1,131.

Library Administration. David Schappert, Director.

Library General Holdings. 37,000 volumes; 230 periodical titles.

Special Collections

The **Sol Davidson Slide Collection** of 12,000 items is available in the library.

1396
King's College
D. Leonard Corgan Library
133 North River Street
Wilkes-Barre, Pennsylvania 18711

Telephone. (717) 826-5900

Institutional Description. The privately supported liberal arts college was founded in 1920. It is conducted by the Roman Catholic congregation of the Holy Cross. Enrollment: 2,299.

Library Administration. Judith Tierney, Special Collections Librarian.

Library General Holdings. 143,500 volumes; 735 current periodical titles; 382,000 government documents; 619,000 microforms.

Special Collections

The Special Collections repository of the library contains an extensive collection of original sources relating to the history of northeastern Pennsylvania and regional folklore. Included in this collection are the public and private papers of the Honorable Daniel J. Flood, congressman who served the local district for the last quarter century, as well as the complete collection of the books, tapes, manuscripts, and memorabilia of the late George Korson, the eminent and internationally known folklorist.

1397
Kutztown University
Rohrbach Library
Kutztown, Pennsylvania 19530

Telephone. (215) 683-4480

Institutional Description. The publicly supported liberal arts and teachers college began as the Keystone Normal School in 1866. Baccalaureate and master's degrees are offered as well as preparation for teacher certification. Enrollment: 6,647.

Library Administration. Herbert D. Safford, Director of Library Services; Anita Sprankle, Readers' Services Librarian (includes maps, rare books, etc.); Linda A. Woods, Reference Librarian/University Archivist.

Library General Holdings. 356,376 books; 2,053 periodical and newspaper subscriptions; 995,890 microforms; 20,000 maps; 1,448 teaching aids; 6,666 pamphlets.

Special Collections

Archives Collection. A repository of records that pertain to, or may have research or historical value particular to the University and its unique history. The collection is made up of official University records as well as other materials produced by administrators, faculty, and students. Included in the Archives are books, theses, correspondence, manuscripts, publications, photographs, tapes, drawings, and newspaper clippings.

Curriculum Materials Center. Includes 14,000 items such as textbooks, curriculum guides, resource pamphlets, and other teaching aids.

Map Collection. Contains 20,000 sheets with area specializations in city planning and topographic maps.

Russian Culture Center. Contains 12,000 books and 60 periodical titles (in English and Russian) about Russia and its people, culture, art, geography, and history.

Rare Book Collections

Rare Books Collection. Contains 623 items including old elementary textbooks, facsimiles of *The Book of Kells,* the Gutenberg Bible, and other items.

1398
La Salle University
David Leo Lawrence Memorial Library
20th and Olney Avenue
Philadelphia, Pennsylvania 19141

Telephone. (215) 951-1290

Institutional Description. The privately supported Roman Catholic liberal arts university was founded by the Christian Brothers in 1863. Enrollment: 6,106.

Library Administration. Jean Haley, Librarian; John Baky, Collection Development Librarian.

Library General Holdings. 300,000 volumes; 1,200 serial titles; 15 newspaper titles.

Special Collections

The library has a special collection on imaginative literature generated by the Vietnam War. Material represented spans the years 1956 to the present. The collection is a comprehensive holding of some 1,000 volumes limited to novels, short stories, poetry, and photograph books. It also includes unpublished manuscripts, galley proofs, page proofs, variant editions, and filmscripts.

Also maintained by the library is a special collection concerning American and British fiction writers of the twentieth century who have converted to the Roman Catholic religion. Among the authors represented are Graham Greene, Katherine Anne Porter, Julien Green, and Walker Percy.

Instructional Resource Center. Includes a specialized collection of 10,000 pedagogical texts, realia, filmstrips, and programmed texts.

Rare Book Collections

The library holds rare book collections concerning Graham Greene (100 volumes) including variant editions, manuscripts, correspondence, and criticisms. Collections with identical parameters are also held for Katherine Anne Porter and T.H. White.

1399
Lafayette College
David Bishop Skillman Library
Easton, Pennsylvania 18042

Telephone. (215) 250-5151

Institutional Description. The privately supported liberal arts college was founded in 1826 as a men's college. It became coeducational in 1970 and is affiliated with the Presbyterian Church (U.S.A.). Enrollment: 2,330.

Library Administration. Dorothy Cieslicki, Librarian; Diane Windham Shaw, Special Collections Librarian and College Archivist.

Library General Holdings. 375,000 volumes; 2,200 periodical subscriptions; 62,000 microforms; 5,600 sound recordings; 500 maps.

Special Collections

The library has a special collection on northeastern Pennsylvania history and maintains a computerized bibliography in this subject area. The Kirby Museum includes the Garner Lincolniana Collection.

Lafayette's Special Collections of 16,500 volumes includes materials related to angling, Stephen Crane, the

Marquis de Lafayette, Lafayette College history, and William E. Simon.

1400
Lancaster Bible College
Stoll Memorial Library
901 Eden Road
Lancaster, Pennsylvania 17601

Telephone. (717) 560-8250

Institutional Description. The privately supported, interdenominational Bible college trains students to become pastors, youth workers, ministers of sacred music, or missionaries. The school was founded in 1933. Enrollment: 377.

Library Administration. Stephen L. Robbins, Head Librarian.

Library General Holdings. 42,247 volumes; 377 current subscriptions; 3,083 audiovisual program volumes; 1,794 volumes in microform.

Special Collections

Over forty percent of the library's collection consists of works on the Bible, theology, pastoral theology, and missions.

Curriculum Resource Center. Houses elementary and secondary level textbooks, children's literature, and Christian education curricular materials.

LBC Collection. Consists of 435 volumes of works by present and former students and faculty of the College.

1401
Lancaster Theological Seminary
Philip Schaff Library
555 West James Street
Lancaster, Pennsylvania 17603

Telephone. (717) 393-0654

Institutional Description. The privately supported theological seminary was founded in 1825. Although closely related to the United Church of Christ, the seminary is broadly ecumenical in both students and faculty. Enrollment: 248.

Library Administration. Anne-Marie Salgat, Director of Library Services.

Library General Holdings. 128,000 volumes; 350 periodical subscriptions. Special strengths of the collection include Bible, Reformation church history, and the history of the Reformed Church in the United States.

Special Collections

Raymond F. Albright Collection. Contains 7,000 volumes including a number of rare books and is especially strong in English and American church history and liturgics.

The **Central Archives and Library of the Evangelical and Reformed Historical Society** and the **Archives of the United Church of Christ** are house in the Omwake Room.

1402
Lebanon Valley College
Library
101 North College Avenue
Annville, Pennsylvania 17003

Telephone. (717) 867-6100

Institutional Description. The privately supported liberal arts college, affiliated with the United Methodist Church, was founded in 1866 as the Annville Academy. It now grants baccalaureate degrees. Enrollment: 1,224.

Library Administration. William E. Hough, III, Librarian.

Library General Holdings. 124,000 volumes; 660 current periodical titles; 14,000 volumes.

Special Collections

The library maintains the **Hiram Herr Shenk Collection** and the **C.B. Montgomery Memorial Collection** on Pennsylvania German history and customs.

1403
Lehigh University
E.W. Fairchild-Martindale Library
Bethlehem, Pennsylvania 18015

Telephone. (215) 861-3000

Institutional Description. The privately supported university was founded in 1865. It is comprised of the Colleges of Arts and Science, Business and Economics, Engineering and Physical Science, and Education; also, the Graduate School, and the Research Institute. Enrollment: 6,439.

Library Administration. Berry G. Richards, Director.

Library General Holdings. 859,000 volumes; 9,170 current periodical subscriptions; 299,500 government documents; 1,000,000 microforms; 15,000 audiovisual materials.

Special Collections

The historic Linderman Library serves as a specialized humanities library with a collection of 330,000 volumes encompassing academic strengths in British colonial history and American and English literature.

Rare Book Collections

The Bayer Galleria of Rare Books opened in the fall of 1985 and contains 24,000 volumes in special collections. Included are the university rare books and **Robert B. Honeyman Collections,** which consists of important originals in the history of science, the Renaissance, and American literature. Also included in the 6,000-volume rare book collection is an original edition of John James Audubon's *Birds of America* and three copies of the first edition of Charles Darwin's *Origin of the Species.*

1404
Lincoln University
Langston Hughes Memorial Library
Lincoln University, Pennsylvania 19352

Telephone. (215) 932-8300

Institutional Description. The privately supported, and state related, liberal arts university was founded in 1854. It grants associate, baccalaureate, and master's degrees. Enrollment: 1,323.

Library Administration. Emery Wimbish, Jr., Director; Ella M. Forbes, Special Collections Librarian.

Library General Holdings. 150,000 volumes, including bound periodicals.

Special Collections

The library has a special collection of Afro-American and African literature representing all aspects of the Black experience. The library also houses a part of the **Susan Reynolds Underhill Collection,** and selections from other collections of African art and artifacts.

1405
Lock Haven University
George B. Stevenson Library
North Fairview Street
Lock Haven, Pennsylvania 17745

Telephone. (717) 893-2309

Institutional Description. The publicly supported university offers programs in teacher education, mathematical computer science, management science, and speech communication. Enrollment: 2,725.

Library Administration. Robert S. Bravard, Director of Library Services.

Library General Holdings. 327,596 volumes; 1,269 periodical subscriptions; 55 newspaper subscriptions; 12,-151 reels of microfilm; 406,694 microfiche; 11,503 audiovisual materials.

Rare Book Collections

Archives Room. The collection includes a special collection of works by and about the English author, Eden Phillpotts (1862-1960). There are 195 volumes consisting of first, limited, and autographed editions of Phillpotts; the critical studies and bibliographies covering Phillpotts; and the work of his daughter. In addition, there is 1.5 cubic feet of Phillpotts letters (originals and copies). The Archives Room also contains a small collection of works of local history including nineteenth-century Clinton County history.

1406
Lutheran Theological Seminary at Gettysburg
Abdel Ross Wentz Library
Gettysburg, Pennsylvania 17325

Telephone. (717) 334-6286

Institutional Description. The privately supported theological seminary is designed to prepare men for the Christian ministry, and men and women for Christian education, missionary service, and parish work. It is affiliated with the Lutheran Church in America. Enrollment: 243.

Library Administration. Donald N. Matthews, Librarian.

Library General Holdings. 141,000 volumes; 600 current periodicals. The library's collection has a significant depth in historical materials.

Special Collections

The library is the beneficiary of the collection once belonging to the **Lutheran Historical Society.** The richness and uniqueness of particularly nineteenth-century materials make this collection an important source for the study of the history of Lutheranism in the United States.

Rare Book Collections

Early in the century many old and rare works of literature, history, biography, and fine arts came to the library through the generosity of Reverend Jeremiah Zimmerman.

1407
Lutheran Theological Seminary at Philadelphia
Krauth Memorial Library
7301 Germantown Avenue
Philadelphia, Pennsylvania 19119

Telephone. (215) 248-4616

Institutional Description. The privately supported theological seminary was founded in 1864 to prepare students for the Christian ministry. It is affiliated with the Lutheran Church in America. Enrollment: 343.

Library Administration. Rev. David J. Wartluft, Director.

Library General Holdings. 148,000 volumes; 598 current periodical subscriptions; 13,250 microforms. The collection supports the Lutheran theological mission of the Seminary.

Special Collections

The archives of five supporting synods are housed in the library.

1408
Luzerne County Community College
Instructional Resources Center/Library
Prospect Street and Middle Road
Nanticoke, Pennsylvania 18634

Telephone. (717) 829-7420

Institutional Description. The publicly supported junior college was established in 1967. Enrollment: 4,609.

Library Administration. Robert N. Cohee, Director/ Learning Resources.

Library General Holdings. 54,056 volumes; 400 current periodical and newspaper subscriptions; 15,501 microforms; 2,666 units of various types of media.

Special Collections

The library maintains special collections on dental assisting and dental hygiene, ethnic studies, hotel and restaurant management, nursing, criminal justice, and fire science technology.

1409
Mansfield University of Pennsylvania
Library
Mansfield, Pennsylvania 16933

Telephone. (717) 662-4000

Institutional Description. Mansfield University of Pennsylvania is a state institution established in 1854 as Mansfield Classical Seminary. Enrollment: 2,670.

Library Administration. Larry L. Nesbit, Director.

Library General Holdings. 195,000 volumes; 531,000 micro-volumes; 2,333 current periodicals; 23,000 reels of microfilm; 14,967 media items; over 8,000 music recordings.

Special Collections

The library maintains collections on education, literature, and music.

1410
Mary Immaculate Seminary
Library
300 Cherryville Road
Northampton, Pennsylvania 18067

Telephone. (215) 262-7866

Institutional Description. The privately supported theological seminary was founded in 1939. It is affiliated with the Roman Catholic Church and offers programs on the graduate level only. Enrollment: 46.

Library Administration. Cathleen Kokolus, Director.

Library General Holdings. 69,000 volumes; 405 periodical subscriptions.

Special Collections

Special collections include books and materials from the early nineteenth century concerned with the Vincentian Community inspired by St. Vincent de Paul; includes biographies, history of the movement, and annals of their Chinese mission.

1411
Marywood College
Marywood Library
2300 Adams Avenue
Scranton, Pennsylvania 18509

Telephone. (717) 348-6211

Institutional Description. The privately supported liberal arts college for women was founded in 1915. Men are admitted to graduate classes. It is operated by the Roman Catholic Church. Enrollment: 3,251.

Library Administration. Mary Anne Fedrick, Director.

Library General Holdings. 176,500 volumes; 1,200 periodicals; 25,000 nonprint items.

Special Collections

The library supports the curriculum of the College with strengths in social work, music and music therapy, art and design, nursing, fashion merchandising, and dietetics.

1412
Mercyhurst College
Hammermill Library
501 East 38th Street
Erie, Pennsylvania 16546

Telephone. (814) 825-0200

Institutional Description. The privately supported liberal arts college is affiliated with the Roman Catholic Church. It grants associate, baccalaureate, and master's degrees. Enrollment: 1,847.

Library Administration. Joanne Cooper, Director.

Library General Holdings. 108,000 volumes; 670 current journal and newspaper subscriptions.

Special Collections

The library's special collections include the **Archives of Northwestern Pennsylvania History** and the **Sisters of Mercy Archives.**

1413
Messiah College
Murray Learning Resources Center
Grantham, Pennsylvania 17027

Telephone. (717) 766-2511

Institutional Description. The privately supported liberal arts college was founded in 1909 as the Messiah Bible School and Missionary Training Home. Affiliated with the Brethren in Christ Church, the college now offers over 40 majors through 12 departments. Enrollment: 1,916.

Library Administration. Roger C. Miller, Director of Learning Resources Center.

Library General Holdings. 140,000 books; 100 periodical titles; 15,000 microforms; 25,000 audiovisual items.

Special Collections

The **College Archives** and the **Archives of the Brethren in Christ Church** are maintained by the library. Other special collections are in the fields of seventeenth-century English literature and the history of religion.

1414
Millersville University of Pennsylvania
Ganser Library
Millersville, Pennsylvania 17551

Telephone. (717) 872-3612

Institutional Description. The publicly supported liberal arts and teachers institution was founded as a normal school in 1855. Enrollment: 7,166.

Library Administration. David S. Zubatsky, Dean of the Library and Media Services; Robert E. Coley, University Archivist - Special Collections Librarian; Marjorie Markoff, Rare Books Librarian.

Library General Holdings. 615,000 books, periodicals, microforms, and audiovisual materials; 1,700 current magazine subscriptions.

Special Collections

Millersville Authors Collection. Includes the writings and published works of the faculty, staff, and alumni of the University.

Wickersham Pedagogical Collection. Contains pre-1900 textbooks and books on teaching methods.

Other collections include a research collection of books and related materials about Pennsylvania and local history. Specialties within the collection are pre-1861 Pennsylvania imprints, minibooks, books from private presses in Pennsylvania, signed first editions, books on textiles, and books on the Amish and Mennonites.

Also housed in the Ganser Library are The Leo Ascher Center for the Study of Operetta Music, Living Pennsylvania Composers Collection, the archives of the International Technology Education Association (formerly the American Industrial Arts Association), the Chester Wittell Music papers, the Carl Van Vechten Memorial Collection of Afro-American Arts and Letters, the Richard Gehrnan Papers, and a collection of approximately 10,000 sheet music popular songs from 1890-1955.

1415
Moravian College and Theological Seminary
Reeves Library
Bethlehem, Pennsylvania 18018

Telephone. (215) 861-1541

Institutional Description. The privately supported liberal arts college and seminary serve the Moravian Church. Enrollment: 1,639.

Library Administration. John Thomas Minor, Library Director.

Library General Holdings. 186,000 books; 1,200 periodical and newspaper subscriptions.

Special Collections

Moravian Studies Collection. Reeves Library attempts to collect all materials relating to the life and history of the Moravian Church (Unitas Fratrum). This includes materials on such figures as Hus, Comenius, and Zinzendorf and selected materials on countries and regions where there are now or have been Moravian communities and congregations. The collection currently consists of approximately 3,000 volumes in English, Czech, and German.

Herman Adler Collection. The Music Listening Library maintains this collection of 4,500 Baroque and predominantly German classic and romantic recordings.

Rare Book Collections

Rare Books Room. Contains materials related to the early history of the Moravian Church and the Renewed Moravian Church (1732-) including a number of eighteenth- and nineteenth-century historical studies and hymnals and studies of John Amos Comenius. The room also houses the Alan Herr Collection of Elizabethan Sermons and some materials on the poet H.D.

1416
Mount Aloysius Junior College
Learning Center
William Penn Highway
Cresson, Pennsylvania 16630

Telephone. (814) 886-4131

Institutional Description. Mount Aloysius Junior College is a private liberal arts college operated by the Sisters of Mercy. The college was founded in 1939. Enrollment: 849.

Library Administration. Phoebe Link, Acting Director.

Library General Holdings. 31,232 volumes; 214 current periodical subscriptions; 5,000 pamphlets.

Special Collections

The **Memorabilia Room** contains a collection of 126 rare books. The library participates in a cooperative program with the Laurel Highland Health Sciences Library Consortium. This program gives student access to the collections of three colleges, three hospitals, and other allied services in the area.

1417
Muhlenberg College
John A.W. Haas Library
2400 Chew Street
Allentown, Pennsylvania 18104

Telephone. (215) 433-3191

Institutional Description. The privately supported liberal arts college was founded in 1848. It is affiliated with the Lutheran Church in America. Founded as a men's college, Muhlenberg became coeducational in 1957. Enrollment: 2,309.

Library Administration. Patricia Ann Sacks, Director of Libraries.

Library General Holdings. 295,000 volumes; 1,483 current periodical subscriptions; 19,453 microforms; 83,-520 government documents; 3,000 recordings; 487 motion pictures and filmstrips; 9,500 slides. The Haas Library and Cedar Crest College's Cressman Library operate as a joint system.

Special Collections

Special collections are housed in the Muhlenberg Room and include the **Muhlenberg Papers,** the **Women's Collection;** the **American Women Poets Collection,** and the **Pennsylvania German Collection.**

1418
Northeastern Christian Junior College
Whitworth Library
1860 Montgomery Avenue
Villanova, Pennsylvania 19085

Telephone. (215) 525-6780

Institutional Description. The privately supported junior college, founded in 1959, is affiliated with the Churches of Christ. Enrollment: 207.

Library Administration. Robert S. Brown, Librarian.

Library General Holdings. 30,675 books; 215 current periodicals subscriptions.

Special Collections

Restoration Library. Includes works by and about members of the Churches of Christ, Christian Church, and Disciples of Christ.

Rare Book Collections

The rare book collections includes rare Bibles printed in 1537 (Matthew's), 1591 (Bishop's), 1608 (Geneva), 1610 (Douay), 1812 (King James), 1881 and 1885 (American Revised *New Testament,* and *Old Testament). There are also reprints of the New Testament:* Wycliffe, 1848; Tyndale, 1836; and Coverdale, 1838.

1419
Pennsylvania College of Optometry
Albert Fitch Memorial Library
1200 West Godfrey Avenue
Philadelphia, Pennsylvania 19141

Telephone. (215) 276-6200

Institutional Description. The privately supported professional college offers classes on the graduate level only. Founded in 1919, it now grants the degree Doctor of Optometry as well as master's and doctorate degrees. Enrollment: 607.

Library Administration. Marita J. Krivda, Library Director.

Library General Holdings. 14,500 volumes; 290 health science journal and periodical titles.

Special Collections

The Fitch Library collection's major strength is in the visual sciences with additional holdings in the basic sciences, clinical sciences, public health, psychology, and rehabilitation.

1420
Pennsylvania College of Podiatric Medicine
Charles E. Krausz Library
Eighth at Race Street
Philadelphia, Pennsylvania 19107

Telephone. (215) 629-0300

Institutional Description. The privately supported professional college was founded in 1963. It grants the Doctor of Podiatric Medicine (D.P.M.) and master's degrees. Enrollment: 475.

Library Administration. John C. Harris, Librarian.

Library General Holdings. 19,000 volumes; 330 current periodical titles.

Special Collections

The library maintains an archival collection and special podiatric exhibits for the Center for the History of Foot Care and Foot Ware. The **Dr. Stewart E. Reed Historical Collection** is also housed in the library.

1421
Pennsylvania State University
Pattee Library
University Park, Pennsylvania 16802

Telephone. (814) 865-2112

Institutional Description. The publicly supported state university contains 22 campuses across the state. It was founded in 1855. Enrollment: 35,261.

Library Administration. Stuart Forth, Dean of Libraries; Charles Mann, Special Collections/Rare Books Librarian.

Library General Holdings. 2,530,000 volumes; 25,800 current serials; 1,680,000 microforms; 307,600 maps.

Special Collections

Historical Collections and Labor Archives. HCLA specializes in documents, manuscripts, and photographs of Pennsylvania industrial society from the Civil War to the present. Sources on the history of business and labor in the Commonwealth include records of industrial firms, businessmen's papers, and documents of labor unions and labor leaders. This collection is the official repository for the archive of the United Steel Workers of America and for the tape recordings and transcripts made by the Penn State Oral History Project. HCLA also has collections of papers from politicians and elected officials, journalists, scholars, and professionals in the fields of industrial efficiency, drug enforcement, medicine, and photography. Written documents are complemented by files of photographs, pictures of Pennsylvania towns, newspapers, and microfilm.

Penn State Room/University Archives. Here are preserved materials created by all segments of Penn State University, including official records generated by the University, private papers and publications of faculty members and students, University Press books, and Penn State photographs, films, and audio- and videotapes. Supplementing materials produced by University faculty, students, and staff are items relating to Centre County and to Penn State's campuses throughout the Commonwealth. Biographical and subject indices are maintained for many collections and publications, including the *Daily Collegian* and the *Centre Daily Times.*

Rare Book Collections

Rare Books Room. This collection of imprints and manuscripts encompasses a broad scope of literature and literary endeavors. Outstanding resources include the **Allison-Shelley Collection** of books and manuscripts concerned with the literary and cultural relations between Germany and the English-speaking world; Pennsylvania (county histories, atlases, maps, and rare imprints); and large collections of Australiana, utopian literature, the occult, science fiction, and Freemasonry. Literary manuscripts and correspondence of John O'Hara, John Barth, Arnold Bennett, Jean Giraudoux, George Bernard Shaw, and a number of other authors are also among the the collections.

1422
Pennsylvania State University - Capitol Campus
Richard H. Heindel Library
U.S. Route 20
Middletown, Pennsylvania 17057

Telephone. (717) 948-6000

Institutional Description. The publicly supported branch of the state university is a senior college and graduate center. It grants baccalaureate and master's degrees. Enrollment: 2,888.

Library Administration. Charles T. Townley, Head.

Library General Holdings. 185,000 volumes of books and bound journals; 1,300 periodicals; 800,000 micoroforms.

Special Collections

The library maintains compete sets of ERIC, HRAF, Envirofiche, Energyfiche, and other research materials. The resources of the Pattee Library at the University Park Campus are available through an online integrated library system of the University Libraries.

1423
Pennsylvania State University, Erie, The Behrend College
The Behrend College Library
Station Road
Erie, Pennsylvania 16563

Telephone. (814) 898-6106

Institutional Description. The publicly supported college of the State University System offers programs leading toward the associate, baccalaureate, and master's degrees. Enrollment: 2,378/

Library Administration. Robert F. Rose, Head Librarian.

Library General Holdings. 66,000 books and bound periodicals; 747 periodicals and other serials; 37,000 microforms; 639 recordings.

Special Collections

Ernst Behrend Collection. This collection was the private library of a local industrialist. Its contents range from sets of literary works to the manufacture of paper to works of nineteenth century philosophers. The collection numbers in excess of 1,000 volumes.

Rare Book Collections

Abraham Lincoln Collection. The library has a special collection on Abraham Lincoln, dating from 1860 and collected by Henry True Fowler.

1424
Pennsylvania State University, M.S. Hershey Medical Center
George T. Harrell Library
P.O. Box 850
Hershey, Pennsylvania 17033

Telephone. (717) 531-8626

Institutional Description. The publicly supported medical center of the State University System was founded through a trust created by Milton S. Hershey, the founder of the Hershey Chocolate Company, in 1963. Enrollment: 705.

Library Administration. Lois J. Lehman, Librarian.

Library General Holdings. 95,999 books; 1,683 periodicals.

Special Collections

The George T. Harrell Library supports the curriculum of the M.S. Hershey Medical Center. The main collection includes works on the preclinical sciences and medicine and related subjects.

History of Medicine and Humanities Special Collection. This collection contains materials designed to support the Humanities and Behavioral Science departments of the Medical Center.

Rare Book Collections

Rare Book Room. Contains monographs published before 1835 and leather-bound monographs published before 1900.

1425
Philadelphia College of Bible
Library
Langhorne Manor
Langhorne, Pennsylvania 19047

Telephone. (215) 752-5800

Institutional Description. The privately supported professional Bible college was established in 1951 as the result of a merger of the Bible Institute of Pennsylvania (founded in 1913) and the Philadelphia School of the Bible (founded in 1914). It is designed to prepare students for Christian vocations. Enrollment: 545.

Library Administration. Julius C. Bosco, Director.

Library General Holdings. 55,000 volumes; 510 periodical subscriptions; 18,000 microforms.

Special Collections

The **Jamieson Missionary Research Collection** was dedicated in 1974 in memory of Miss Janet P. Jamieson and Miss Helen T. Jamieson. The library also maintains a collection of early English and American hymnals and a collection of books on the conservative-evangelical tradition in Christianity.

1426
Philadelphia College of Osteopathic Medicine
O.J. Snyder Memorial Library
4150 City Avenue
Philadelphia, Pennsylvania 19131

Telephone. (215) 581-6370

Institutional Description. The privately supported professional college was founded in 1899. The current college is a result of a merger of the Osteopathic Hospital of Phialdelphia and the Osteopathic Foundation of Philadelphia. It grants the Doctor of Osteopathy degree. Enrollment: 833.

Library Administration. Shanker H. Vyas, Director.

Library General Holdings. 51,000 volumes; 700 current periodical titles (77 are osteopathic publications).

Special Collections

The Archival Room of the library contains historic records of PCOM's past, as well as archival materials in medicine and osteopathic medicine.

1427
Philadelphia College of Pharmacy and Science
Joseph W. England Library
43rd Street and Kingsessing Mall
Philadelphia, Pennsylvania 19104

Telephone. (215) 596-8800

Institutional Description. The privately supported professional college was founded in 1821. It grants baccalaureate, mester's, and doctorate degrees. Enrollment: 1,390.

Library Administration. Mignon S. Adams, Director of Library Services.

Library General Holdings. 57,000 volumes; 820 current periodical subscriptions; 31,000 microforms.

Special Collections

The England Library contains one of the largest collections of phamaceutical literature in the United States. The library also maintains a reference service which provides information in areas such as new and old drugs, laboratory procedures, foreign prescriptions, sources of drugs, and nomenclature. Special collections include the **History of Pharmacy Collection,** foreign pharmacy journals, rare and old books on botany, chemistry, and herbs.

1428
Philadelphia College of Textiles and Science
Pastore Library
School House Lane and Henry Avenue
Philadelphia, Pennsylvania 19144

Telephone. (215) 951-2840

Institutional Description. The privately supported professional college was founded in 1884. Known originally as the Philadelphia Textile School of the Pennsylvania Museum of Art, it was founded by the Philadelphia Manufacturers Association. Enrollment: 3,249.

Library Administration. Evelyn Minick, Acting College Librarian; Stanley Gorski, Special Collections Librarian.

Library General Holdings. 70,000 volumes; 1,500 periodical subscriptions; access to OCLC, DIALOG, ORBIT, VU/TEXT.

Special Collections

As the oldest private textile school in the U.S., the library attempts to maintain a comprehensive collection in textile science and all of its applications. This includes a strong business collection focusing on all aspects of the textile marketplace. This emphasis on textiles includes a strong art and design collection.

Rare Book Collections

Textile Industry Historical Collection. This collection encompasses all aspects of the textile industry in the U.S. during the nineteenth and early twentieth centuries. Of special interest is material relevant to the development and vicissitudes of textile commerce in the Middle Atlantic states from colonial times to the present. The collection is oriented toward an in-depth coverage of the Philadelphia textile industry. Besides books, pamphlets, and ephmera, the library actively pursues business records for textile firms, diaries of workers, and business directories. Although the emphasis is on the technical aspects of textile production, materials dealing with labor in the textile industry in the nineteenth and twentieth centuries is sought.

1429
Philadelphia Colleges of the Arts
Clara and William S. Fishman Memorial Library
Broad and Pine Streets
Philadelphia, Pennsylvania 19102

Telephone. (215) 875-4800

Institutional Description. The privately supported professional college was formed by the merger in 1986 of the Philadelphia College of Art and the Philadelphia College of the Performing Arts. Together, they focus on the visual arts as well as music, dance, and theater. Enrollment: 1,041.

Library General Holdings. 55,000 volumes; 150 current periodicals.

Special Collections

The special collections include art exhibit catalogs, reproductions, pictures, and pamphlets.

1430
Pittsburgh Theological Seminary
Clifford E. Barbour Library
616 North Highland Avenue
Pittsburgh, Pennsylvania 15206

Telephone. (412) 362-5610

Institutional Description. The privately supported theological seminary was formed in 1959 by the merger of Pittsburgh-Xenia Theological Seminary and Western Theological Seminary. Affiliated with the Presbyterian Church, the seminary offers graduate programs only. Enrollment: 353.

Library Administration. Dikran Y. Hadidian, Librarian.

Library General Holdings. 207,500 volumes; 858 current periodical subscriptions; 1,700 microforms.

Special Collections

Historical Collections. The archive room of Barbour Library contains materials relating to Associate, Associate Reformed, and United Presbyterian congregations, presbyteries, synods, and general assemblies.

Rare Book Collections

James Warrington Collection of Hymnology. Includes several thousand hymn and song books which came from the estate of James Warrington of Philadelphia; provides research materials for scholars of American and British hymnody.

John M. Mason Memorial Collection. Contains classical theological works dating from the Reformation period.

1431
Point Park College
Helen-Jean Moore Library
201 Wood Street
Pittsburgh, Pennsylvania 15222

Telephone. (412) 391-4100

Institutional Description. The privately supported liberal arts college was founded in 1960. Enrollment: 2,787.

Library Administration. Mary Jane Sunder, Director.

Library General Holdings. 115,871 volumes; 600 periodical subscriptions; 26,000 microforms.

Special Collections

The library maintains the Library of American Civilization on ultra-microfiche and has collections in industrial relations, international business management, journalism, communications, and the performing arts.

1432
Reading Area Community College
Learning Resource Center
10 South Second Street
P.O. Box 1706
Reading, Pennsylvania 19603

Telephone. (215) 372-4721

Institutional Description. The two-year community college was opened in 1971 and moved to its permanent campus in 1978. Enrollment: 1,290.

Library Administration. David M. Lawrence, Director.

Library General Holdings. 20,000 books; 250 periodical titles.

Special Collections

The library maintains a special collection in nursing.

1433
Robert Morris College
College Libraries
Narrows Run Road
Coraopolis, Pennsylvania 15108

Telephone. (412) 5,444

Institutional Description. The privately supported liberal arts college and professional school of business was founded as the Pittsburgh School of Accountancy in 1921. It grants associate, baccalaureate, and master's degrees. Enrollment: 5,444.

Library Administration. Mary Celine Miller, Director.

Library General Holdings. 98,675 volumes; 790 current periodicals; 106,000 microforms; 83,300 government documents; 23,000 audiovisual materials.

Special Collections

The libraries of Robert Morris College contain an extensive collection of corporate annual reports; a **Curriculum Library Collection** for training secondary school business teachers; and a **Business Collection** which has emphases in management, marketing, and taxation.

1434
Rosemont College
Rosemont College Library
Rosemont, Pennsylvania 19010

Telephone. (215) 527-3995

Institutional Description. The privately supported liberal arts college for women was founded in 1922. A Roman Catholic institution, the College was started by the Religious of the Society of the Holy Child Jesus. Enrollment: 597.

Library Administration. Sr. Mary Dennis Lynch, S.H.C.J., Director of Library Services.

Library General Holdings. 148,639 volumes; 23,184 microforms; 8,328 audiovisual items.

Special Collections

Curriculum Collection. A separate collection for the use of education students; includes textbooks, education kits, and audiovisual materials; juvenile literature; and Apple software.

Pennsylvania Collection. Includes *Colonial Records* (microfilm collection of 800 volumes on 26 reels); early laws and statutes; the mine archival series; and books and pamphlets by and about Pennsylvanians and the Commonwealth.

1435
St. Charles Borromeo Seminary
Ryan Memorial Library
Overbrook
Philadelphia, Pennsylvania 19151

Telephone. (215) 667-3394

Institutional Description. The privately supported Roman Catholic theological seminary was founded in 1832. It is owned and operated by the Philadelphia Archdiocese to prepare candidates for the priesthood. The Seminary grants baccalaureate, professional, and master's degrees. Enrollment: 455.

Library Administration. Lorena Filosa Boylan, Director of Libraries; Joseph J. Casino, Archivist.

Library General Holdings. 118,000 bound volumes; 6,700 audiovisual materials; 390 reels of microfilm; 597 current periodical subscriptions.

Special Collections

Archives and Historical Collections. The collections contain 400,000 manuscripts, 45,000 books and pamphlets, 8,000 newspapers, 6,000 prints and photographs, and hundreds of artifacts chronicling and illustrating the development of religion in general, and Catholicism in particular, in the eastern part of the United States from the seventeenth century to the present.

In the Archvies can be found charters of incorporation, lists of subscribers to building funds, deeds, legal and financial papers, and correspondence dealing with the foundation and growth of Catholic institutions in the United States. The institutions represented include parishes, orphanages, hospitals, schools, seminaries, religious orders, and civic and social groups.

The history of Catholic laypersons in the United States is chronicled in a number of collections which include correspondence, diaries, business and legal papers, literary productions, memoirs, memorabilia, and pictorial records. These laypersons include business persons, physicians and medical researchers, soldiers, teachers, immigrants and refugees from other countries, historians and antiquarians, diplomats and political leaders, and converts from other faiths. These records are complemented by other collections.

The Archives contains one of the most complete collections of Catholic directories and almanacs found in the United States covering the period 1822 to the present. There is also a large newspaper collection, concentrated in the nineteenth century. This collection is very strong in, and contains the only extant copies of, many ethnic Catholic newspapers including several early Black Catholic periodicals, such as the *American Catholic Tribune,* 1887-1894, and the *Journal,* 1892, labor-oriented publications, and papers devoted to the concerns of women and youth. The Historical Pamphlet Collection consists of about 6,000 items beginning in 1707 and is richest in nineteenth-century materials. There are also collections of catechisms, prayerbooks, missals, and devotional works which illustrate the development of popular piety in the United States from the seventeenth century to the present.

Rare Book Collections

Rare Book Collection. Consists of 14,750 volumes, including 27 incunabula. The collection's strengths are in sixteenth-, seventeenth-, and eighteenth-century works in theology and philosophy, ecclesiastical history and law, science, literature, geography, history, early Americana, nineteenth-century works in literature, and Irish history. There are also twentieth-century works of special significance to the Seminary and the Philadelphia area.

1436
St. Francis College
Pius XII Memorial Library
Loretto, Pennsylvania 15940

Telephone. (412) 321-8383

Institutional Description. The privately supported liberal arts college was founded in 1847. It is affiliated with the Roman Catholic Church. Enrollment: 1,746.

Library Administration. Margaret Tobin, Head Librarian.

Library General Holdings. 166,000 volumes; 525 current periodical titles.

Special Collections

In support of the teacher education program, the library has a collection of elementary education materials which are housed in a room designated to resemble the rooms used in children's libraries. In addition, a curriculum collection for both elementary and secondary teachers contains over 700 items for use by those preparing to become teachers. The library's other special collections include the **Franciscan Archives,** the **Prince Gallitzin Collection,** and the **Captain Paul Boynton Collection.**

1437
Saint Joseph's University
Francis A. Drexel Library
5600 City Avenue
Philadelphia, Pennsylvania 19131

Telephone. (215) 879-7300

Institutional Description. The privately supported liberal arts university was founded in 1851 by the Jesuits of the Roman Catholic Church. Enrollment: 5,715.

Library Administration. Josephine Savaro, Director.

Library General Holdings. 212,000 volumes; 1,600 periodicals.

Special Collections

Campbell Food Marketing Library. Serves faculty and students with 3,800 titles and 230 periodicals plus extensive corporate information files.

1438
St. Vincent College and Seminary Library
Latrobe, Pennsylvania 15650

Telephone. (412) 539-9761

Institutional Description. The privately supported liberal arts college and theological seminary was founded in 1846. Affiliated with the Roman Catholic Church, it grants baccalaureate, professional, and master's degrees. Enrollment: 1,247.

Library Administration. Chrysostom V. Schlimm, O.S.B., Director.

Library General Holdings. 331,000 volumes; 905 current periodical titles; 98,000 microforms.

Special Collections

The special collections of the library include Benedictiana, Pennsylvaniana, and liturgical works.

1439
Seton Hill College
Reeves Memorial Library
Greensburg, Pennsylvania 15601

Telephone. (412) 834-2200

Institutional Description. The privately supported liberal arts college for women was founded by the Sisters of Charity of the Roman Catholic Church in 1883. Enrollment: 865.

Library Administration. Deborah Pawlik, Director.

Library General Holdings. 85,000 volumes; 11,000 periodical volumes; 390 current periodical subscriptions.

Special Collections

Besides special areas of concentration in fine arts, literature, and women's studies, the collection has been strengthened in its holdings in other cultures such as Latin America, Asia, and Africa through a grant from the National Endowment for the Humanities.

1440
Shippensburg University of Pennsylvania
Library
Shippensburg, Pennsylvania 17257

Telephone. (717) 532-9121

Institutional Description. The publicly supported liberal arts and professional university is a campus of the State System. It was founded in 1871. Enrollment: 6,219.

Library Administration. Eugene R. Hanson, Director of Library and Media Services.

Library General Holdings. 1,500,000 items including 375,000 bound volumes; 1,000,000 microforms; 55,000 government documents; 25,000 audiovisual materials; 1,500 current periodical subscriptions.

Special Collections

Alma Winton Pennsylvania Collection. This 8,000 volume collection is a primary resource for scholars who research the history of central Pennsylvania; includes pamphlets from the 1870s.

Rare Book Collections

The library maintains a rare book collection which includes old German Bibles, early Americana, and autographed first editions of the works of famous Pennsylvania authors.

1441
Slippery Rock University of Pennsylvania
Bailey Library
Slippery Rock, Pennsylvania 16057

Telephone. (412) 794-2510

Institutional Description. The publicly supported liberal arts and teachers university is a campus of the State System, which it joined in 1960. It was founded in 1889 as a normal school. Enrollment: 6,496.

Library Administration. William W. Garton, Director.

Library General Holdings. 454,150 volumes; 1,530 current periodical subscriptions; 132,000 government documents; 874,000 microforms; 89,000 audiovisual items.

Special Collections

The library has a strong collection of library and information science materials as well as in the various fields of education, particularly recreation and sports and physical education. The **Japan Collection** contains materials relating to the Japanese culture and civilization.

1442
Spring Garden College
Library
7500 Germantown Avenue
Philadelphia, Pennsylvania 19119

Telephone. (215) 248-7900

Institutional Description. The privately supported science and technology college was founded in 1950. It offers associate and baccalaureate degrees. Enrollment: 1,558.

Library Administration. Mildred Glushakow, Librarian.

Library General Holdings. 24,000 volumes; 495 current periodical subscriptions.

Special Collections

The library's special collections include the history of Spring Garden Institute from its founding in 1850 to the present and a collection on the history of technology in the United States.

1443
Susquehanna University
Roger M. Blough Learning Center
Selinsgrove, Pennsylvania 17870

Telephone. (717) 374-0101

Institutional Description. The privately supported liberal arts university was founded in 1858 as the Missionary Institute of the Evangelical Lutheran Church. It is now affiliated with the Lutheran Church in America. Susquehanna admitted women in 1873. Enrollment: 1,759.

Library Administration. James B. Smillie, Director.

Library General Holdings. 125,000 bound volumes; 1,150 periodical subscriptions; 25,000 microforms; 7,000 recordings; 2,500 pieces of printed music.

Special Collections

Wilt Collection on Music. Consists of 2,000 volumes of criticism of nineteenth-century European and American music.

1444
Swarthmore College
The Thomas B. and Jeanette E.L. McCabe Library
Swarthmore, Pennsylvania 19081

Telephone. (215) 328-8489

Institutional Description. The privately supported liberal arts college was founded by the Religious Society of Friends in 1864. Enrollment: 1,341.

Library Administration. Michael J. Durkan, College Librarian; Edward Fuller, Special Collections Librarian; Wendy E. Chmielewski, Archivist.

Library General Holdings. 701,000 volumes; 2,850 periodical subscriptions; 14,200 reels of microfilm; 16,889 recordings; 746 videotapes.

Special Collections

Swarthmore College Peace Collection. This collection is an archival repository and research library devoted to the collection and maintenance of the papers of individuals and the records of organizations committed to the establishment of permanent world peace through disarmament, pacifism, conscientious objection, and nonviolent social change. Included are 122 major document groups and approximately 1,500 smaller archival collections maintained in two collection groups. Also included are four special collections.

In addition to archival materials, the Peace Collection maintains a research library consisting of more than 7,500 volumes on such subjects as peace leaders, pacifism, and conscientious objection, disarmament and arms control, conscription and compulsory military service, protests against war and proposals for permanent peace, international arbitration, and the moral, psychological, and economic costs of war. Specialized collections include the **Jane Addams Library,** the **Garland Library of War and Peace,** and the **Horace Alexander Collection** of more than 200 books by and about Mahatma Gandhi. Also housed here are extensive periodical holdings from the nineteenth and twentieth centuries including over 1,800 titles. Approximately 280 periodicals in 11 languages are received from 23 countries.

Other collections maintained by the library include **British Americana** (accounts of British travelers in the U.S.); **Private Press Collection** (a representative sampling of the output of the British and American small presses); **Bathe Collection** (history of technology); **Thomson/Wordsworth Collection,** and the works of W.H. Auden, Seamus Heaney, and Patrick Oliphant (cartoons).

Rare Book Collections

Friends Historical Library. There are some 255 manuscript collections in the Friends Historical Library which include the records of virtually all Quaker meetings in Philadelphia and Baltimore Yearly Meetings from the 1860s onwards. There are also materials on Ohio and Illinois Yearly Meetings (Hicksite) and microfilm records of many meetings in New England, New York, and North Carolina. The varied activities of Quakers in literature, science, abolition, Indian rights, and the women's movement are represented. Among the most important collections are papers of Lucretia Mott (antislavery, feminism); Samuel Janney (history, antislavery, Indian rights); John Greenleaf Whittier (poetry and social reform); Emily Howland (women's rights, social reform); Graceanna Lewis (natural science and art); Moses Sheppard (mental health). The papers of Elias Hicks, Benjamin Terris, Joel Bean, and Samuel Battle related to religious controversies in the mid-nineteenth century. There are manuscripts and drawings of Benjamin West and paintings by West, Edward Hicks, James Sharples, and Howard Pyle. Small collections include materials on famous Quakers such as Anthony Benezet, John Comly, Henry Drinker, John Bright, Elizabeth Fry, Joseph John Gurney, and the Pembertons. The collections includes approximately 35,000 volumes of books, pamphlets, and serials. In 1982 a nine-volume catalog of the collection was published by G.K. Hall.

1445
Temple University
Temple University Libraries
13th and Berks Streets
Philadelphia, Pennsylvania 19122

Telephone. (215) 787-8231

Institutional Description. The privately supported university is state-related. It was founded in 1884 as Temple College. Enrollment: 31,492.

Library Administration. James N. Meyers, University Librarian; Thomas M. Whitehead, Head, Special Collections.

Library General Holdings. 2,000,000 volumes; 5,000 periodical subscriptions; 3,000 continuation subscriptions; 350,000 microforms.

Special Collections

Blockson Afro-American Collection. Contains 30,000 items (printed, manuscript, and photographic); developed from the private collection of the noted historian, Charles L. Blockson. In addition to the General Research and Reference Collections, the Blockson Collection includes a Rare Book Collection, Manuscripts and Archives Collection, and various Special Collections described below.

Slave Narrative Collection. Includes a wide and varied compository of documented slave experiences; more than one hundred narratives make up the collection. Among the representative works are the narratives of Olaudah Equiano, Ignatius Sancho, Prince Lee Boo, Robert the Hermit, Bethany Veney, Ellenor Eldridge, Soujourner Truth, Frederick Douglass, Thomas Cooper, Venture Smith, Benjamin Banneker, Robert Adams, Nancey Prince, and Silvia Dubois.

Underground Railroad Collection. This collection is from the private collection of Charles L. Blockson and is one of the largest in the country. The bulk of the collection contains over a thousand items on the members of the underground railroad as well as historical pamphlets, broadsides, and memoirs of the leading figures of this organization. Among these highly valued materials are the letters of William Still.

Prints and Photographs. The visual arts collection is the repository of hundreds of prints and Black film posters which are annually loaned for exhibit to major museums and historical institutions throughout the country. This collection also contains hundreds of rare slavery broadsides and pamphlets. This section also houses an assortment of rare African and Caribbean maps. The 1985 addition of the John Mosley Photograph Collection of over 500,000 photograph prints and negatives provides a rich visual history of notable Black entertainers, social and political personalities, and general social life of Pennsylvania's African-Americans.

Raymond Trent Oral History Collection. Contains thousands of taped proceedings and radio programs on Afro-American history and culture. The collection is also augmented by additional tape recordings from the private collection of Charles Blockson and the Alpha Boule Society.

Other collections maintained by the Special Collections include:

Conwellana-Templana Collection: The University Archives. The collection provides access to Minutes of the Board of Trustees, Papers of the Presidents and other administrators, the records of various University committees, publications that reflect student life, and many other sources of information on campus activity. Named for the University founder Russell H. Conwell, the collection in recent years has begun to include the personal papers of faculty and alumni.

National Immigration Archives. This Temple-sponsored research program is currently housed at the Balch Institute for Ethnic Studies. In 1977, Special Collections had transferred from the National Archives and Record Service 1,500 cubic feet of original ship passenger manifests from 1820-1902. These manifests, mandated by an 1819 federal law, document arrivals in five American ports: Baltimore, Boston, Philadelphia, New Orleans, and New York. Each manifest identifies the ship, its ports and its passengers with details of name, age, literacy, occupation, hometown, destination, and other information.

Photojournalism Archives. Special Collections is the repository of two photographic media archives: the pre-1973 photograph and negative collection of *The Philadelphia Inquirer* and *The Philadelphia Daily News,* and the 1947-1976 news and documentary film of the local television station WPVI (formerly WFIL) Channel 6.

Urban Archives Center. The Center was founded in 1967 to collect, preserve, and make available to researchers records pertaining to the development of metropolitan Philadelphia and adjoining urban areas since the Civil War. The Center functions as a repository for organizational records and personal papers, and as a research facility for urban studies. Over the past fifteen years the Archives has acquired more than 125 collections, totalling about 4,000 cubic feet of records.

Rare Book Collections

Blockson Rare Book Collection. Includes extensive first edition Afro-American and Caribbean holdings dating back to as early as the sixteenth century. At present an estimated 3,500 volumes comprise the nucleus of the rare book holdings. Among the highly prized works are the complete and authoritative first editions of the writings of Phillis Wheatley, George Washington Williams, Booker T. Washington, Charles Chesnutt, Francis Harper, Joseph Wilson, William Wells Brown, W.E.B. DuBois, Langston Hughes, Richard Wright, Chester Himes, and numerous others which contribute to the outstanding holdings of the collection. The collection also contains one of the more comprehensive repository holdings of the Harlem Renaissance and the Black Power period of the 1960s. Another notable feature of the collection is the assortment of rare African and Caribbean bibles. The **African Bible Collection** contains bibles written in a variety of African languages, including Ibo, Hausa, Twi, Yoruba, Mpongwe, Dikele, Ga, Sechuane (Setlapi dialect), Amharic, and Bulu. The collection also includes several bibles in West Indian Creole. *The Creole Testament* is one of four known copies in the United States. The Manuscripts and Archives Collection within the major Blockson Collection includes the following:

The Alpha Boule Society Papers. Papers of the Sigma Pi Phi Fraternity of Philadelphia consists of programs, social registers, oral historical materials, and private papers of this important Afro-American social fraternity.

John Colton Brown Collection. Provides a variety of memorabilia on John Brown's life and the Abolition Society of Pennsylvania.

Caroline Still-Anderson Papers. Contains many important items on the life and times of William Still.

Caribbean Collection contains many primary source documents, including the *Haitian Presidential Papers,* the *Jamaica Alamanack* and *Register of 1794* and the Christophe manuscripts.

Samuel Holmes Collection. Consists of hundreds of items which document Black Philadelphia social life from slavery to the present. Many other private papers and selective materials comprise specialized units of the Blockson Collection.

Paul Robeson Collection. Contains significant memorabilia, including sheet music, photographs, memoirs, posters, first edition publications and ephemera.

Rhythm Brown Collection. Documents an extensive history of Black tap dancers and the TOBA circuit includes scrapbooks, personal papers and general information on the Black entertainment world.

The Rare Books and Manuscripts collections of Temple University Libraries is the repository and collecting unit for the early, rare, scarce, and valuable printed books, the manuscript and archival collections not collected by other Special Collection units. The Collection actively acquires in the areas of twentieth-century literature, particularly Georgian and Imagist authors, Symbolist literature, Gothic romances, nineteenth- and twentieth-century printing, publishing and bookselling history, business history, eighteenth-century English religious and parliamentary history, lithography, book illustration, and fine printing. Various collections are described below:

Contemporary Culture Collection. The materials included in this collection are those produced by alternative, independent, and small literary publishers, political organizations of the far left and right, social reform and liberation movement organizations, alternative life-style and energy advocates, and radicals in the professions. The collection contains 4,000 journal, newsletter, and newspaper titles and 5,000 books and pamphlets. It was established in 1969 and has grown to include microfilm collections, audiotapes, posters, broadsides, emphera, and manuscript collections. Among its manuscript collections are the records of the Liberation News Service, the Committee of Small Press Editors and Publishers, Youth Liberation, *Seven Days,* and the personal papers of poet Lyn Lifshin.

England (Seventeenth Century). Intellectual, religious, and political history of England in the seventeenth century, based on the Nordell and Simpson Collections.

English Literature (Twentieth Century). In-depth collections of Walter de la Mare and Richard Aldington, with additional collecting of the Georgians and Imagists.

History of Business and Accounting. The "Cochran Collection" of pre-1800 manuscripts (receipts, ledgers, vede mecums, codexes, etc.) and early printed books; ca. 500 manuscripts and 500 printed books.

Printing History and Lithography. Printed and manuscript collections representing the technical and commercial development in the printing, publishing, and allied fields of the nineteenth and twentieth centuries including lithographic manuals, archives of the Directors' files of Constable & Co., London; Thomas Nelson and Sons (U.S.); Leary & Co., booksellers; William J. Campbell Bookseller; manuscripts and halftone collections of William T. Innes and Frederick Eugene Ives; the library of Richard W. Ellis (printer/designer).

Paskow Science Fiction Collection. This collection was established as a research collection in 1972 when the Library received 5,000 books from the personal library of the late David C. Paskow, a graduate of the master's program in education at Temple. The collection now comprises more than 10,000 volumes (including reference works), magazines (pulps, "fanzines," and academic journals), over 100 cubic feet of manuscripts, and selected posters, paintings, drawings, and related materials. Primarily twentieth-century science fiction, the Collection also includes earlier works about imaginary voyages, contemporary editions of works by such authors as Verne and Wells, and some examples in the related genre of fantasy.

Other book collections are the Bush-Brown Horticulture and Landscape Gardening Collection, the Nordell Puritanism Collection, the Ladd Thomas and Frederick Maser Bible Collections, the Maser Collections of Joseph Conrad, John Masefield, and Robert Louis Stevenson. Thirty-five incunabula are held, primarily relating to business and commercial arithmetic.

Manuscript Collections. These collections include the Frances Hirtzel Collection of Sir Richard Owen Correspondence, the Arthur H. Lewis Papers, E.S. Stuart Papers (Pennsylvania Governor), François Joseph Jérôme Niicklès Correspondence (chemistry), Gertrude Traubel Papers, Stanley Richards papers, Morton M. Hunt Papers, and extensive literary manuscripts.

Prints and Drawings. The Library also has the George Tyler War Poster Collection of 2,500 items, the Louis Prang Collection and related graphic arts holdings.

1446
Thiel College
Langenheim Memorial Library
College Avenue
Greenville, Pennsylvania 16125

Telephone. (412) 588-7700

Institutional Description. The privately supported Christian liberal arts college was founded in 1866. It is affiliated with the Lutheran Church in America. Enrollment: 812.

Library Administration. Douglas J. Cerroni, Director.

Library General Holdings. 125,000 books; 941 periodical titles; 202,654 government documents.

Special Collections

The library's collection includes emphases in art history, biological sciences, nursing, and theology.

1447
Thomas Jefferson University
Scott Memorial Library
11th and Walnut Streets
Philadelphia, Pennsylvania 19107

Telephone. (215) 928-7966

Institutional Description. The privately supported university of health sciences was founded in 1824 as a medical school. It now includes the Jefferson Medical College, the College of Graduate Studies, The College of

Allied Health Sciences, and Thomas Jefferson University Hospital. Enrollment: 1,996.

Library Administration. Edward W. Tawyea, Librarian; Samuel A. Davis, Special Collections Librarian.

Library General Holdings. 110,000 bound books and journals; 1,600 journal subscriptions; 705 videocassettes; 65 audiocassettes; 304 slides.

Special Collections

Herbut Papers. These bound volumes contain photocopies of papers, letters, and speeches of the former University president, Peter, A. Herbut.

Jeffersoniana. This collection includes books authored by Thomas Jefferson University faculty.

Rare Book Collections

Bland Collection. A collection of books on obstetrics and gynecology collected and donated by P. Brooke Bland, M.D., former chairman of the department and also former chairman of the library committee. The collection includes books published in Europe before 1800 and books published in the United States before 1820.

1448
United Wesleyan College Library 1414 East Cedar Street Allentown, Pennsylvania 18103

Telephone. (215) 439-8709

Institutional Description. The privately supported professional Bible college was founded in 1921 as the Beulah Park Bible School. Affiliated with the Wesleyan Church, it now grants associate and baccalaureate degrees. Enrollment: 186.

Library Administration. Lois Updegrove, Librarian.

Library General Holdings. 33,000 volumes; 100 current periodical titles.

Special Collections

The special collections of the library include the **Wesleyana Collection,** the **Bible Commentary Collection,** and the periodicals of the Pilgrim Holiness, Wesleyan Methodist, and Wesleyan Church.

1449
University of Pennsylvania University Libraries Philadelphia, Pennsylvania 19104

Telephone. (215) 898-7091

Institutional Description. The privately supported (state aided) university, founded in 1740, offers a wide variety of programs through its numerous colleges and schools. Enrollment: 21,742.

Library Administration. Daniel Traister, Special Collections Librarian.

Library General Holdings. 3,377,000 volumes; 13,000 current periodical subscriptions; 1,972,000 microforms.

Special Collections

Outstanding special collections include the **Lea Library of European Middle Ages,** specializing in legal and ecclesiastical history; the **E.F. Smith Collection** on the history of chemistry; the **Dreiser Papers,** the **Terrick Collection** of Jonathan Swift, and the **Furness Library** of Shakespeare and his contemporaries. Other collections include materials on the Spanish Inquisition, canon law and witchcraft, eighteenth-century English literature, chemistry, early Americana, and American drama.

The library has a collection of Aristotle's tracts and commentaries, the **McClure Collection** of French revolutionary pamphlets, the **Mendelsohn Collection** on cryptography, Italian Renaissance literature, eighteenth- and nineteenth-century French plays, and a collection of Elzevier imprints. The **Marian Anderson Collection** is housed in the library, as well as various author collections including James T. Farrell, Waldo Frank, Washington Irving, Lewis Mumford, Mark Twain, and Walt Whitman.

Leon Levy Library. This library houses one of the world's most complete collections of dental literature. It is especially strong in historical materials, including most of the rare early books on dentistry.

Lippincott Library. This library of the Wharton School is one of the world's largest business libraries. The Peck Corporation Finance Room houses a permanent collection of annual reports issued by 2,500 corporations during the past 130 years, company histories, and numerous directories and reports.

1450
University of Pittsburgh Hillman Library Fifth and Bigelow Streets Pittsburgh, Pennsylvania 15260

Telephone. (412) 648-8190

Institutional Description. The University of Pittsburgh is an independent, nonsectarian, state-related university with four regional campuses in addition to the main campus in the Oakland section of Pittsburgh. It was founded in 1787. Enrollment: 21,742.

Library Administration. 2,583,597 volumes; 26,328 current periodicals; 334,778 government documents; 2,021,116 microforms; 26,933 audiovisual materials.

Library General Holdings. Charles E. Aston, Jr., Head, Special Collections Department; W. Gerald Heverly, Curator, Archives of Scientific Philosophy and General Manuscripts; Frank A. Zabrosky, Curator, Archives of Industrial Society; Dean Root, Curator, Foster Hall Collection. The Special Collections Department was established in 1966 and houses the rare books, general manuscripts, and special collections. The collections now consist of over 52,000 physical volumes, 560 linear feet of manuscripts and archives, 13,000 photographs, 500,000 theatre programs, and various slides, microfilms, posters, recordings, ephemera, and memorabilia. The following information was supplied through the courtesy of the Special Collections Department.

Special Collections

Ant's Forefoot Archive. This collection includes manuscripts, correspondence, graphics, and published issues of an important "little" poetry magazine published between 1967 and 1973 at the Coach House Press in Toronto.

Archive of Popular Culture. Includes over 2,000 paperback science fiction novels, 14 journal titles (over 1,000 issues), and a collection of science fiction fanzines. Also included are over 9,000 inventoried comic books plus collections of fanzines and pulp magazines donated by the Pittsburgh Comix Club and individual donors.

Archives of Scientific Philosophy in the Twentieth Century. Includes the personal papers and manuscripts of three important figures in twentieth-century scientific philosophy.

Rudolf Carnap Collection. The works of Carnap (1891-1970), one of the most influential philosophers of the twentieth century, who was a key figure in the rise of logical positivism. Includes Carnap's working library, his published works, manuscripts, diaries, and correspondence, including correspondence between Carnap and philosophers Karl Popper, Bertrand Russell, and Ludwig Wittgenstein.

Frank Ramsey Papers. Contains an important collection of autograph material by Frank Plumpton Ramsey (1900-1930) consisting of notes, lectures, and unfinished manuscripts (1,500 autograph pages).

Hans Reichenbach Collection. Includes his library, published and unpublished manuscripts, lectures, correspondence, and miscellaneous materials.

Bernard S. Horne Memorial Collection - Isaak Walton's Compleat Angler. This collection contains over 360 editions, issues, and states of Izaak Walton's *Compleat Angler* which were given to the University in 1873 by Mrs. Horne as a memorial to her late husband. Mr. Horne assembled the collection during his lifetime and drew upon it to prepare his *Compleat Angler, 1653-1967, a New Bibliography* published in 1970. It is presumably the largest single collection of *Angler* editions in the United States.

Bollingen Foundation Collection. This collection was donated by the A.W. Mellon Educational and Charitable Trust Foundation and Mr. Paul Mellon in 1980. It is comprised of approximately 300 volumes of the Bollingen Foundation imprints.

Cooperative Movement Collection. Consists of over 680 rare monographs and pamphlets published between 1851-1979 on the Cooperative Movement around the world, with heavy emphasis on Great Britain. Includes publications on agricultural, dry goods, food, housing, manufacturing, and trade union co-ops.

Darlington Memorial Library. The Darlington Library maintains collections of approximately 17,000 volumes of books and journals, over 4,000 pamphlets, various early atlases, 1,000 early maps, and over 45 linear feet of manuscripts, letters, and journal books. Donated by the Darlington family in 1918, the library is especially rich in American history of the colonial period, the French and Indian War, the Revolution, and the War of 1812. The Darlington Collection of Americana emphasizes Western Pennsylvania and the Ohio Valley.

Fidelis Zitterbart Collection. This collection was given to the University by the local composer's family in 1960. Zitterbart was a contemporary of Stephen Foster. The collection includes nearly 1,500 manuscript compositions.

Flora and Norman Winkler Collection. This collection was donated to the University by Dr. Norman Winkler at the time of his death in 1961. It is a collection of over 300 volumes of Spanish, English, and Brazilian literature, including first editions and many fine bindings. There are also microfilm copies of Brazilian literary history and critical studies, many of which relate to the works of Jose Martiniano de Alencar.

Ford E. and Harriet R. Curtis Theatre Collection. Consists of several thousand volumes of playscripts, acting editions, histories, and critical works of the theatre and drama, over 500,000 theatre programs, journals relating to drama, reference works, reviews, articles, posters, 13,000 photographs, miscellaneous data on the contemporary theatre, material on off-Broadway productions, archival records of theatre organizations (e.g., records of the old Pittsburgh Playhouse), and the papers of theatre people (e.g., the papers of producer Michael Ellis). The collection was founded in 1960 by Dr. and Mrs. Ford E. Curtis. Emphasis is on New York and Pittsburgh from the Civil War to the present.

Foster Hall Collection. This collection is housed in the Stephen Foster Memorial and includes approximately 20,000 items divided among three areas:

Research Library. Includes books, periodicals, works of world culture (Japanese music textbooks), Acts of the Kentucky Legislature, guidebooks (from Florida), songbooks, programs, pamphlets, and broadsides.

Museum. Contains musical instruments, posters, portraits, artifacts of nineteenth- and twentieth-century American music, the eyeglasses of Foster's father, account books, The Buchanan Club minutes, items on Foster's person at the time of his death (wallet, coins, scraps of paper), the death telegram, and other times.

Archives. Includes 8,000 sheets of music, first and early editions of Foster's works, 1,000 sound recordings (early 78 RPMs included), manuscripts and correspondence, nineteent-century photographs of musicians and minstrel shows (E.P. Christy), twentieth-century national press clippings, and other items.

Hervey Allen Collection. Includes manuscripts, correspondence, memorabilia, and the personal library of Mr. Allen. Hervey Allen (1889-1949) was a graduate of the University of Pittsburgh.

Lawrence Lee Collection. This collection was donated by Professor Lee's family in 1978, the year of his death. Lee was a short story writer and a published poet. At the time of his death he was a contributing columnist to the *Pittsburgh Press* and he had been a member of the Pitt English Department for 31 years. The collection includes poetry manuscripts and personal correspondence, published books and magazine articles, autographed editions by other contemporary authors, and association copies. *Compiler's Note:* One of the compilers of this book, an alumnus of Pitt, studied sophomore English with Dr. Lee. He is remembered as a man of distinction with impeccable manners who was an inspiration to his students. In those days he was referred to as the "Poet Laureate of Pitt."

Mary Roberts Rinehart Collection. Consists of books, manuscripts, and correspondence; interviews with Mrs. Rinehart; newspaper clippings, pictures, and biographical material and memorabilia about her. Mary Roberts Rinehart (1876-1958) was a native of Pittsburgh.

Nietz Old Textbook Collection. Nearly 15,000 volumes are in the collection and consist of two principal types of publications: (1) old primary and secondary school texts, some of which date back to the sixteenth century, most of which were published before 1900; and (2) books on the history and theory of education and writings of the key figures in the field of education.

Pavlova-Heinrich Dance Collection. Consists of the "Mlle. Anna Pavlova Memorial Ballet Library," formed by Mr. Karl Heinrich in conjunction with the Pittsburgh Civic Ballet; also includes printed books on dance, scrapbooks, original sketches, posters, and choreographic notes.

Ramon Gomez De La Serna Collection. Consists of annotated first editions, clippings, and 60,000 manuscripts by this twentieth-century Spanish author. This collection represents an important resource for the study of modern Spanish literature.

Ripon England Documents. Includes 23 English manuscript documents, mostly from the town of Ripon, England. These documents were donated by the English Nationality Room Committee in 1961. Mostly indentures, the manuscripts include mortgages, deeds, bargain and sale transactions, and marriage settlements from 1636 through 1770, with at least one from the reign of each English monarch during that period. All but one written on parchment.

Robert Watson Collection - Founder's Collection. Comprises the remaining books in the original Watson Collection given to the Western University of Pennsylvania in 1875.

Servicio De Monitoring De Colegio Nacional De Taquifrafos. ("Miami Radio Monitoring Service"—Miramos). A complete 20-year collection of transcripts of monitoring reports of Radio Havana, Cuba, beginning March 20,1963 through June 20, 1982 when the monitoring reports ceased.

Thomas G. Masaryk Papers. Unpublished draft manuscripts by Thomas Garrigue Masaryk (1850-1937), first President of Czechoslovakia, given to the University by the Czechoslovak Nationality Room Committee in 1983. The manuscripts were either written personally by Masaryk or drafted according to his specific instructions during 1918 and 1919. Includes letters, memoranda, and messages later published in finished form, either in English or Czech, and addressed to American and European statesmen during the final phase of World War I and the early period of Czechoslovak independence.

Walter and Martha Leuba Collection. A beginning collection of fine books, private press publications, and first editions donated by the Leubas. It was established in 1976 and includes a separate **George Saintsbury Collection.**

William Steinberg Collection. Comprised of rare and fine books from the library of the late former conductor of the Pittsburgh Symphony (1952-1976). Includes music scores, memorabilia, and photographs.

Wittgenstein Papers. A microfilmed collection of original manuscripts, notebooks, journals, and typescripts written by the philosopher Ludwig Wittgenstein between ca. 1914-1951. The original papers are in England; the original microfilm is owned by Cornell University.

World War II Picture Collection. "The Bombing of London." Donated in 1966, the collection consists of 143 black and white photographs from the Associated Press, London, and the Graphic Photo Union, London, covering the bombing of London in the early 1940s.

Archives Service Center.

In 1966, the **University Archives** was officially established by the Chancellor to function as the corporate memory of the University and to provide a central source of information about University departments, people, events, and buildings. The Archives documents the history of the University since its founding as the Pittsburgh Academy in 1787.

The **Archives of Industrial Society** was established in 1963. It collects and preserves records concerning the development of urban industrial society, with an emphasis upon Pittsburgh and Western Pennsylvania. Core collections are divided into seven sections, some of which contain subunits. These are: Local Public Records; Organizations, Societies, Etc. (Civic, Cultural, Fraternal, and Philanthropic); Institutional Records (Churches, Educational and Scientific); Politics, Government, Political, and Social Activism; Business Records; Labor and Working Class History; and Oral History Collections.

Rare Book Collections

Rare Books and General Manuscripts Collections. Includes materials from both the humanities and the social sciences, including the history of science and technology. These collections contain many unusual or unique items, such as first editions, early imprints, fine bindings, beautifully illustrated books, literary and historical manuscripts, modern small and private press poetry from England and the United States, the "little" poetry magazines, and alternative press publications from the U.S.

1451
University of Pittsburgh at Bradford
UPB Library
Campus Drive
Bradford, Pennsylvania 16701

Telephone. (814) 362-3801

Institutional Description. The regional college of the privately supported (and state aided) University of Pittsburgh was opened in 1963. It grants associate and baccalaureate degrees. Enrollment: 979.

Library Administration. Robert L. Balliot, Director.

Library General Holdings. 65,000 volumes; 490 periodical subscriptions; 9,900 microform items.

Special Collections

The library maintains the **Lowenthal Library of Skepticism** and a collection of French literature including the works of Michel [Eyquem] de Montaigne.

1452
University of Scranton
Alumni Memorial Library
Linden Street and Monroe Avenue
Scranton, Pennsylvania 18510

Telephone. (717) 961-7400

Institutional Description. The privately supported university was founded by the Roman Catholic Church. Established as St. Thomas College in 1888, it is now one of the Jesuit Colleges. Enrollment: 4,789.

Library Administration. Kenneth J. Oberembt, Director.

Library General Holdings. 225,000 volumes; 1,600 periodicals; 38,000 microforms.

Special Collections

Special collections include the **Byzantine and Eastern Christian Studies Collection** and the **Scranton Family Gift Collection.** The offices of the University's semimonthly national book review, *Best Sellers,* are located here.

1453
Ursinus College
Myrin Library
Collegeville, Pennsylvania 19426

Telephone. (215) 489-4111

Institutional Description. The privately supported liberal arts college grants associate and baccalaureate degrees. It is affiliated with the United Church of Christ. Enrollment: 2,293.

Library Administration. Charles A. Jamison, Acting Library Director.

Library General Holdings. 160,000 volumes; 725 current periodical subscriptions; 125,000 microforms; 20,000 audiovisual materials.

Special Collections

Special collections of the library include the **Pennsylvania German Studies Archive** the **Huntington-Wilson Papers** dating from 1897-1913; the **J.H.A. Bomberger Collection** of books, manuscripts, and papers of the founder of Ursinus College dating from 1848-1890.

1454
Valley Forge Christian College
South Campus Library
Charlestown Road
Phoenixville, Pennsylvania 19460

Telephone. (215) 935-0450

Institutional Description. The privately supported professional and theological school is affiliated with the Assemblies Of God Church. It was founded in 1939 for the training of pastors, evangelists, missionaries, and Christian lay workers. Enrollment: 589.

Library Administration. Ann E. Tortorelli, Director of Learning Resources.

Library General Holdings. 42,000 volumes; 400 periodicals; 2,600 pamphlets; 2,500 microforms; 37,000 audiovisual items; 1,000 sound recordings.

Special Collections

The library maintains a special collection on Pentecostalism.

1455
Villa Maria College
College Library
2551 West Lake Road
Erie, Pennsylvania 16505

Telephone. (814) 838-1966

Institutional Description. The privately supported Roman Catholic college was founded in 1925. A liberal arts college for women, it was established by the Sisters of

St. Joseph of Northwestern Pennsylvania. Enrollment: 505.

Library Administration. Loralyn Ann Whitney, Librarian.

Library General Holdings. 43,000 books; 4,700 bound periodicals; 205 current periodical subscriptions; 4,000 media items.

Special Collections

The special strengths in the collection of the main library include nursing and education. There is also a separate curriculum library.

1456
Villanova University
Falvey Memorial Library
Lancaster Pike
Villanova, Pennsylvania 19085

Telephone. (215) 645-4500

Institutional Description. The privately supported university was founded in 1842. It was founded and is operated by the Order of St. Augustine of the Roman Catholic Church. Enrollment: 11,956.

Library Administration. Mary Ann Griffin, Director.

Library General Holdings. 536,000 volumes; 2,590 current periodical subscriptions; 12,800 government documents; 1,050,000 microforms; 25,000 audiovisual materials.

Special Collections

Special collections of the Falvey Memorial Library includes the **Joseph McGarrity Collection** of Irish history and literature.

Center for Concern. The Center is housed in the Office for Social Action Programs and maintains a vertical file of issues and organizations involved with social change.

Rare Book Collections

Augustinian Historical Institute. The Institute maintains a collection of books, manuscripts, reviews, and microcopies pertinent to the allied fields of theology, philosophy, missiology, and biography. The collection includes handwritten manuscripts and literature related to St. Augustine and the Order of St. Augustine.

1457
Washington and Jefferson College
U. Grant Miller Library
South Lincoln Street
Washington, Pennsylvania 15301

Telephone. (412) 222-4400

Institutional Description. The privately supported liberal arts college was founded in 1781. It grants associate, baccalaureate, and master's degrees. Enrollment: 1,329.

Library Administration. Robert E. Connell, Librarian.

Library General Holdings. 186,000 volumes; 640 current periodicals; 9,500 microforms.

Special Collections

Henry P. Walker Memorial Room. Contains the archives and historical records collection of Washington and Jefferson College, Washington County, Western Pennsylvania, and the Upper Ohio Valley.

1458
Waynesburg College
College Library
51 College Street
Waynesburg, Pennsylvania 15370

Telephone. (412) 627-8191

Institutional Description. The privately supported liberal arts college is affiliated with the United Presbyterian Church. Enrollment: 957.

Library Administration. Theresa Viarengo, Librarian.

Library General Holdings. 125,000 volumes; 600 current periodicals.

Special Collections

Special collections include the **Southwestern Pennsylvania History Collection,** established by O.D. Robinson in memory of his wife, Ethel C. Robinson; the **Presbyterian Women's "Opportunity Fund" Collection;** the **Judge Adrian and Howard Suydam Lyon Library,** devoted to history and literature; the **Elizabeth Steele Miller and Mary B. Patterson Collections;** the **Foundation Collection** established by Dr. Charles G. Reigner; and the **Dawn Logan Miller English Literature Memorial Books Collection.**

1459
West Chester University
Francis Harvey Green Library
West Chester, Pennsylvania 19383

Telephone. (215) 436-2747

Institutional Description. The publicly supported liberal arts and teachers university was founded in 1812. Enrollment: 10,498.

Library Administration. Frank Q. Helms, University Librarian; R. Gerald Schoelkopf, Special Collections Librarian.

Library General Holdings. 440,000 volumes; 2,600 journals; 350,000 titles micromedia collection. Music Library: 22,000 music scores; 19,000 recordings.

Special Collections

College Archives. Includes newspapers, catalogs, scrapbooks, minutes from the founding of the University in 1871.

Ehinger Collection. Consists of materials on health and physical education published prior to World War II.

Normal Collection. Includes books written by the University's alumni and faculty.

Rare Book Collections

Chester County Collection. This collection includes materials on the history of Chester County and materials written by Chester County authors; includes books from the libraries of William Darlington (botanist from West Chester) and the Chester County Cabinet of Natural Sciences (largely botanical works from the 1800s).

Philip's Autograph Collection. Consists of autographed books collected by George Morris Philips between 1880-1920.

1460
Westminster College
McGill Memorial Library
New Wilmington, Pennsylvania 16172

Telephone. (412) 946-7330

Institutional Description. The privately supported liberal arts college offers cooperative programs in engineering with Lafayette College and Pennsylvania State University whereby students may obtain an engineering degree from the participating institution and a baccalaureate degree from Westminster. The College is related to the United Presbyterian Church in the U.S.A. Enrollment: 1,306.

Library Administration. Molly P. Spinney, Librarian; Mabel C. Kochner, Special Collections Librarian; Hilton Turner, Special Collections.

Library General Holdings. 215,000 volumes; 1,000 current periodical and newspaper subscriptions; 19,948 volumes on microform.

Special Collections

The McGill Library has a special collection of the books written by Margaret Deland (1857-1942) and Agnes Sligh Turnbull (1888-1982). Both of these writers were born near Pittsburgh in western Pennsylvania. The background of most of their novels and short stories is in the area of Westminster College. Most of the books in the collection are signed first editions.

1461
Westminster Theological Seminary
Seminary Library
Church Road and Willow Grove Avenue
P.O. Box 27009
Philadelphia, Pennsylvania 19118

Telephone. (215) 887-5511

Institutional Description. The privately supported theological seminary was founded in 1929. Affiliated with the Presbyterian Church, Westminster offers programs on the graduate level only. Enrollment: 534.

Library Administration. John R. Muether, Librarian.

Library General Holdings. 95,000 volumes; 500 periodicals.

Special Collections

The library has particular strengths in Reformed theology and in Biblical interpretation and exegesis. The holdings of major collected works of great theological writers include the entire Migne edition of the fathers, the *Corpus Christianorum,* the Weimer edition of Luther, and the *Corpus Reformatorum* edition of Calvin, Zwingli, and Melanchthon.

The Seminary has received valuable portions of the libraries of various professors, including the 1,300 Presbyterian and Reformed classics of the late Principal John Macleod.

Rare Book Collections

The Rare Book Room houses an extensive collection of Latin, Greek, and English Bibles dating from the invention of printing to the present day.

1462
Westmoreland County Community College
Learning Resources Center
Youngwood, Pennsylvania 15697

Telephone. (412) 836-1600

Institutional Description. The two-year community college offers transfer and career education programs. It was established in 1971. Enrollment: 3,595.

Library Administration. Mary J. Stubbs, Dean for Learning Resources.

Library General Holdings. 31,623 volumes; 315 periodical titles; 22,950 microforms; 26,469 government documents.

Special Collections

Specialized collections are available in nursing and the technologies.

1463
Widener University
Wolfgram Memorial Library
14th and Chestnut Streets
Chester, Pennsylvania 19013

Telephone. (215) 499-4000

Institutional Description. The privately supported liberal arts and technological university is composed of Pennsylvania Military College, Penn Morton College, and Crozer Foundation College of Nursing. Affiliated institutions are Brandywine College and Delaware Law School, both in the State of Delaware. Enrollment: 6,257.

Library Administration. Theresa Taborsky, Director.

Library General Holdings. 160,000 volumes; 1,500 periodical subscriptions; 18,000 microforms.

Special Collections

The Wolfgram Library maintains the **Wolfgram Collection of English Literature** and the **Delaware County Historical Society Library.**

1464
Wilkes College
E.S. Farley Library
170 South Franklin Street
P.O. Box 111
Wilkes-Barre, Pennsylvania 18766

Telephone. (717) 824-4651

Institutional Description. The privately supported liberal arts college was founded in 1933. It grants baccalaureate and master's degrees. Enrollment: 3,380.

Library Administration. P. Robert Paustian, Director.

Library General Holdings. 185,000 volumes; 1,250 current journal and newspaper subscriptions; 500,000 microforms.

Special Collections

The library has an extensive collection of research materials in English literature, American cultural history, and the history of science.

1465
Wilson College
John Stewart Memorial Library
Philadelphia Avenue
Chambersburg, Pennsylvania 17201

Telephone. (717) 264-4141

Institutional Description. The privately supported liberal arts college for women was founded in 1869. It is affiliated with the Presbyterian Church (U.S.A.). Enrollment: 444.

Library Administration. Susan Matusak, Librarian.

Library General Holdings. 149,000 volumes; 410 current periodical titles.

Special Collections

The library maintains the archives of the Totem Pole Theater, the **Maria Bashkirtseff Collection** and the **Jean Stapleton Putch Archives.** Miss Stapleton (Mrs. Putch) is the highly acclaimed stage, screen, and television actress.

1466
York College of Pennsylvania
Schmidt Library
Country Club Road
York, Pennsylvania 17403

Telephone. (717) 846-7788

Institutional Description. The privately supported liberal arts college was founded in 1787 as York Academy. It merged in 1927 with York Collegiate Institute (founded in 1883). Enrollment: 4,633.

Library Administration. Susan M. Campbell, Director; Dorothy Lagunowich; Special Collections Librarian.

Library General Holdings. 120,000 volumes; 1,000 current periodicals; 50,000 government documents.

Special Collections

The Special Collections and Rare Books Room of the Schmidt Library includes the **Lincoln Collection;** a collection of nineteenth-century fiction; and the **York County History Collection.** An Oral History Center is also housed in the library.

Puerto Rico

1467
American University of Puerto Rico
American University Library (Bayamon Branch)
Apartado 2037
Bayamon, Puerto Rico 00621

Telephone. (809) 798-2040

Institutional Description. The privately supported institution features liberal arts and business administration. Enrollment: 3,773.

Library Administration. Alberto Hernandez-Banuchi, Head Librarian.

Library General Holdings. The emphasis of the library's collection is in business management, secretarial sciences, and education (special education and educational technology).

Special Collections

Within the general collection the Library has special print and non-print material (books, magazines, newsletters, videotapes, microfiche, software) in the area of recreational management, food marketing management, and the hospitality industry. Also there are special collections in the areas of business communications and desk-top publishing.

1468
Catholic University of Puerto Rico
Encarnacion Valdes Library
Las Americas Avenue
Ponce, Puerto Rico 00732

Telephone. (809) 844-4150

Institutional Description. The privately supported university was founded in 1948. It has been affiliated with the Catholic University in America (in the United States) since its formation. Enrollment: 11,762.

Library Administration. Antonio Matos, Director.

Library General Holdings. 403,000 volumes; 2,480 current periodical subscriptions.

Special Collections

The library maintains the **Monsignor Vicente Murga Collection,** materials on Roman Catholic theology, and a **Puerto Rican Collection.**

1469
Centro de Estudios Avanzados de Puerto Rico y el Caribe
Biblioteca
Del Cristo Street 52
Box 54467
San Juan, Puerto Rico 00904

Telephone. (809) 723-4481

Institutional Description. The privately supported institution offers graduate courses and undergraduate programs in the humanities. Enrollment: 228.

Library Administration. Carmen Sylvia Arroyo, Librarian.

Library General Holdings. 12,500 books; 100 periodical subscriptions.

Special Collections

The library maintains a regional oral history collection on audiocassettes; recordings of the Cerro Maravilla trial; materials on West Indian archaeology; catalogs of art exhibitions; and theses presented by the students of the school.

1470
Inter American University of Puerto Rico
Guayama Regional College Library
P.O. Box 1293
Hato Rey, Puerto Rico 00919

Telephone. (809) 758-8000

Institutional Description. The privately supported university was founded in 1912 as the Polytechnic Institute. It now offers liberal arts, career, and professional programs, and is affiliated with the United Presbyterian Church (U.S.A.). Enrollment: 19,128.

Library Administration. Gilberto Morales Napoleoni, Director.

Library General Holdings. 102,000 volumes; 1,835 current periodical subscriptions.

Special Collections

Special collections of the library include the **Puerto Rico Collection,** the **Emilio S. Belaval Collection,** and the **Jaime Benitez Collection.**

1471
Ponce School of Medicine
Medical Library
Ponce, Puerto Rico 00731

Telephone. (809) 843-8288

Institutional Description. The privately supported professional college grants the M.D. degree. Enrollment: 177.

Library General Holdings. 11,000 volumes; 260 current periodical subscriptions.

Special Collections

The Medical Library has a special collection in anatomy and maintains the **Puerto Rican Collection** and the **Hispanic Periodical Collection.**

1472
University of Puerto Rico, Mayaguez Campus
Mayaguez Campus Library
Mayaguez, Puerto Rico 00709

Telephone. (809) 834-4040

Institutional Description. The publicly supported branch campus of the University of Puerto Rico was founded in 1911. It offers a wide variety of programs at all levels. Enrollment: 10,203.

Library Administration. Grace Quiñones, Acting Director.

Library General Holdings. 246,000 volumes; 1,950 current periodical titles; 459,000 government documents; 311,000 microforms.

Special Collections

The library maintains the **Puerto Rican Collection,** the **Alfred Stern Collection,** the **Marine Sciences Collection,** the **Music and Oral History Collection,** and the **Collection for the Blind.**

1473
University of Puerto Rico, Rio Piedras Campus
Rio Piedras Campus Library
Ponce de Leon Avenue
Rio Piedras, Puerto Rico 00931

Telephone. (809) 764-0000

Institutional Description. The publicly supported branch campus of the University of Puerto Rico is the largest of the several university and college campuses. It was founded in 1900 as a normal school and now offers a wide variety of programs. Enrollment: 22,060.

Library Administration. Haydee Munoz-Sola, Director.

Library General Holdings. 262,000 volumes; 4,310 current periodical titles; 1,675,000 microforms; 1,495,000 government documents.

Special Collections

Special collections of the library are the **Puerto Rican Collection,** the **Caribbean and Latin American Studies Collection,** a **Services for the Blind Collection,** the **Zenobia and Juan Ramon Jimenez Collection,** and an oral history collection.

1474
University of the Sacred Heart
Madre Maria Teresa Guevara Library
Box 12383, Loiza Station
Santurce, Puerto Rico 00914

Telephone. (809) 728-1515

Institutional Description. The privately supported liberal arts and teachers university was founded in 1880. It is affiliated with the Roman Catholic Church. Enrollment: 8,274.

Library Administration. Maria A. Morales de Garin, Director; R.S.C.J. Haydee Vecchini, Special Collections Librarian.

Library General Holdings. 131,000 volumes; 800 current periodical titles; 38,000 microforms.

Special Collections

The library maintains a collection of materials on Puerto Rico.

Rhode Island

1475
Brown University
John Hay Library
20 Prospect Street
Providence, Rhode Island 02912

Telephone. (401) 863-2146

Institutional Description. The privately supported university was founded in 1764. It features a "New Curriculum," emphasizing interdisciplinary majors, independent studies, and small seminar courses; this program eliminates grades and curriculum requirements. Enrollment: 7,198.

Library Administration. Merrily Taylor, University Librarian; Samuel Streit, Assistant University Librarian for Special Collections; John Stanley, Head Special Collections Librarian; Jean Rainwater, Reader Services Librarian; Curators of Special Collections: Richard B. Harrington, Catherine Denning, Mary T. Russo, Rosemary L. Cullen, Mark N. Brown, Jennifer B. Lee; University Archivist, Martha L. Mitchell.

Library General Holdings. 2,000,000 volumes; 15,520 periodical subscriptions; 1,000,000 microforms; 114,000 maps; 500,000 sheet music.

Special Collections

Anne S.K. Brown Military Collection. With over 30,000 books, 60,000 prints, 5,000 miniature soldiers, and numerous drawings, watercolors, and manuscripts, this is one of the world's largest collections devoted to military history and iconography. Because of its international scope and great chronological breadth, the collection also is a valuable source for the study of social and cultural history, architecture, city planning, and the development of printing and book illustration.

Annmary Brown Memorial. This is one of the largest and most important collections of incunabula in the United States. Beginning with Gutenberg, the collection traces the development of printing as it spread across Europe in the second half of the fifteenth century. Many important classical and Renaissance authors are represented in the Memorial's collections in early, often first, printed editions. Subjects range from religion and law to literature and music. In addition to incunabula, the Memorial houses European and American paintings dating from the seventeenth to the nineteenth centuries, and sizeable manuscript holdings relating to the American Revolutionary and Civil Wars, and to the seventeenth century New England witchcraft phenomenon.

Broadside Collection. Contains over 40,000 items, the majority of which are printed on single sheets of paper. While subject scope of the collections is quite broad, there are special strengths in American verse, Rhode Island history, and fine printing. The collection of verse, which complements the Harris Collection of American Poetry and Plays, consists of poetry of every description dating from the eighteenth century to the present. In addition to representing the work of thousands of individual poets, the collection is a valuable resource for the study of American political and social history, literature, music, and theater.

The Sidney S. Rider Collection of Rhode Island Broadsides includes advertisements, programs, posters, playbills, cartoons, and lottery tickets. Perhaps the most significant segment of the collection concerns the Dorr Rebellion of 1842. Other important components of the broadside collection are the 800 World War I and II posters, the 5,500 item Sonia Lustig Bookplate Collection, and large representative collections of postcards, Christmas and St. Valentine's Day cards, and advertising ephemera.

Harris Collection of American Poetry and Plays. The collecting policy for the Harris Collection is to acquire all works of poetry and plays written by Americans or Canadians in any country, in any language, at any time. The resulting 200,000 volumes constitute the world's largest collection in its field. Included are exhaustive holdings of such major figures as Whitman, Poe, Longfellow, Frost, Pound, and O'Neill, along with thousands of volumes by lesser known authors. Subsumed within the collection are important subject areas such as poetry by or about Blacks, Asian-American poetry, thousands of acting scripts, and Yiddish-American literature. In addition to standard editions, the collection also acquires film and television scripts and the output of small and fine presses, and subscribes to over 600 literary journals and magazines. The collection also acquires American verse set to music, including songsters, song sheets, hymnals, scores, folk music, and librettos. Closely associated with the Harris

Collection is a collection of 500,000 pieces of sheet music. Although its holdings date from the eighteenth century, the collection's strength lies in the nineteenth and twentieth centuries. Minstrel music, jazz, Broadway and movie tunes, and rock and roll all find their place in the collection.

Manuscript Collections. There are more than 800 manuscript collections and 500,000 separate items in the John Hay Library's manuscript collections. The principal strengths are in American history and literature since the eighteenth century, although there are notable collections in other areas and periods. Literary manuscripts include large groups of letters and other manuscripts of H.P. Lovecraft, Edgar Lee Masters, Henry David Thoreau, Emile Zola, and John Buchan. Related to the field of American literature are the records of small presses among which are the archives of the Unicorn Press, *December Magazine, Stone Country,* and the *West Coast Poetry Review.*

Historical collections are strongest for the nineteenth century. Important holdings include those relating to the War of 1812, the careers of Abraham Lincoln and John Hay, New England church history and the history of Rhode Island. Scientific and mathematical manuscripts are also acquired by the library. The Lownes History of Science Collection includes important manuscripts by several major European and American scientists, including such figures as Pasteur, Linnaeus, Darwin, and Audubon. Other important scientific papers include those of mathematician Raymond Clare Archibald, inventor George Corliss, engineer Elmer Corthell, and surgeon William Williams Keen.

McLellan Lincoln Collection. The Lincoln Collection, one of the five strongest in the country, provides research opportunities not only in relation to Lincoln's presidency and the Civil War, but also for the entire middle period of American history. The collection contains 15,000 books and newspapers, 5,000 broadsides and leaflets, 7,000 prints and photographs, and over 2,500 manuscript letters and documents of which 950 were written or signed by Lincoln.

University Archives. The vast resources of the University Archives consist of official university records, office and departmental files, photographs and prints, manuscripts and audiovisual materials ranging from academic celebrations to sports events. The Archives support the history of Brown, provide a detailed record of student life from the eighteenth to the twentieth centuries, chronicle the development of American higher education, and supply biographical information on tens of thousands of alumni/ae. **The Pembroke Archives** offer important insights into the history of women at Brown and into women's studies in general.

East Asian Collections. These collections consist of over 79,000 volumes in Chinese and 2,500 volumes in Japanese. Except for reference tools, no Western language materials are included in the collections. The Chinese Collection was founded through the gift of Professor Charles Gardner, a noted Sinologist, and is strong in the cultural, economic, literary, political, and social development of China, especially during the Ch'ing Dynasty (1644-1912). More recent additions to the East Asian holdings have included materials in the fields of linguistics, history, religion, and political science.

Rare Book Collections

Printed Books. The printed book collections are essentially a microcosm of the entire Brown University library system, the principal difference being that the books in Special Collections are rare, fragile, or otherwise unusual. Many of the books are in the general rare book collections, the largest of which are grouped according to subject or as they were formed by collectors who donated them to Brown. Among the 150 named book collections are the Lownes History of Science Collection, one of the largest of its kind in any American library; the Chambers Dante Collection; the Lamont Collection of British literature; the Damon Occult Collection; the Damon Collection of William Blake; the Foster Collection of works by Horace; the Morse Whaling Collection; the Kimball Collection of American and European literature; and the Koopman Collection which contains both European literature and resources for the study of the book arts. In addition to books, Special Collections holds many of Brown's pre-twentieth century serials and, in the Metcalf Collection, a vast number of English and American pamphlets on a wide variety of subjects dating from the seventeenth to the nineteenth centuries.

1476
Bryant College
Edith M. Hodgson Memorial Library
450 Douglas Pike
Smithfield, Rhode Island 02917

Telephone. (401) 232-6100

Institutional Description. The privately supported business college was founded in 1863. It grants associate, baccalaureate, and master's degrees. Enrollment: 6,505.

Library Administration. John P. Hannon, Director.

Library General Holdings. 108,000 volumes; 920 current periodical titles.

Special Collections

Bound periodicals and other holdings total more than 5,000 volumes in the business and investment fields.

1477
Johnson and Wales College
Emilio Capomacchio Library
8 Abbott Park Place
Providence, Rhode Island 02903

Telephone. (401) 456-1000

Institutional Description. The privately supported liberal arts and vocational college was founded in 1914. It grants associate and baccalaureate degrees as well as certificates and diplomas. Enrollment: 8,741.

Library Administration. Richard P. Keogh, Librarian; Margaret A. Thomas, Culinary Arts Librarian.

Library General Holdings. 28,000 volumes.

Special Collections

The library's special resources include books and materials in the fields of accounting, business, culinary arts, data processing, equine studies, hospitality management, and secretarial science.

1478
Providence College
Phillips Memorial Library
Eaton Street and River Avenue
Providence, Rhode Island 02918

Telephone. (401) 865-1000

Institutional Description. The privately supported liberal arts and sciences college was founded in 1917. It is operated by the Dominican Order of the Roman Catholic Church. Enrollment: 5,679.

Library Administration. Joseph H. Doherty, Director.

Library General Holdings. 270,000 volumes; 1,785 current periodicals; 90,500 government documents; 25,000 microforms.

Special Collections

The special collections of the Phillips Memorial Library include the papers of former Senator John O. Pastore (1950-1976); the papers of the former Congressman John E. Fogarty (1942-1967); and the **Bonniwell Collection** of Catholic liturgy.

1479
Rhode Island College
James P. Adams Library
600 Mt. Pleasant Avenue
Providence, Rhode Island 02908

Telephone. (401) 456-8052

Institutional Description. The publicly supported college features liberal arts and teacher preparation. Enrollment: 8,530.

Library Administration. Richard A. Olsen, Librarian; Sally M. Wilson, Assistant Librarian in Special Collections.

Library General Holdings. 325,000 volumes; 2,100 periodical subscriptions; 536,127 microforms; 2,550 sound recordings; 61,742 government publications.

Special Collections

College Archives. Material relating to Rhode Island College; papers and publications which document all aspects of activity at the College.

Archives of the Portuguese Cultural Association of Rhode Island. Includes papers and other materials from 1959 to the present.

Records of the International Institute of Rhode Island. Papers and records covering the period 1930-1950.

Social and Political Materials Collection. Consists of publications of a variety of partisan political organizations, selected to represent a wide range of political and social options.

Nathaniel T. Bacon Collection. Business records, literary papers of Pulitzer Prize winning poet Leonard Bacon; correspondence and papers of the Hazard family.

Honorable Michael DeCiantis Collection. Consists of the papers of a former judge of the Rhode Island Family Court.

Irving Jay Fein Collection. Papers and books of a Providence businessman who was active in local civil rights and fair housing efforts, ca. 1959-1970.

Dr. Charles Russell Gross Collection. Manuscript material of a Providence physician who was the historian of the Black Community in Rhode Island. This collection serves as the nucleus of a broad range of material on Black history and culture.

Nancy Elizabeth Prophet Collection. Photographs, watercolors, and two works of sculpture by a Black artist from Rhode Island.

Charles H. Smith Papers. Nineteenth-century real estate and business records, correspondence, and notebook.

Maurice and Vera Vendettuoli Collection. Papers concerning the busing controversy in a Providence high school, 1965-1975.

Rhode Island Collection. Books, pamphlets, documents, and papers related to various aspects of the history of Rhode Island.

Amy Thompson Collection. Consists of a selection of early children's books.

1480
Rhode Island School of Design
Library
2 College Street
Providence, Rhode Island 02906

Telephone. (401) 331-3511

Institutional Description. The privately supported institution, committed to education in art, architecture, and design, was founded in 1877. Enrollment: 1,838.

Library Administration. Carol S. Terry, Director of Library Services.

Library General Holdings. 74,000 bound volumes; 350 current periodicals; 30,000 art reproductions; 300,000 clippings; 93,700 slides (2x2); 21,000 lantern slides; 150 posters; 785 phonograph recordings.

Special Collections

The library maintains a specialized collection of artists' books (500 volumes) and the Lowthorpe Collection of Landscape Architecture (1,200 volumes).

1481
Roger Williams College
College Library
Old Ferry Road
Bristol, Rhode Island 02809

Telephone. (401) 253-1040

Institutional Description. The privately supported college, founded in 1919, became independent of its parent institution, Northeastern University, in 1956. It features mechanical, electrical, and construction engineering, and business administration. Enrollment: 3,718.

Library Administration. Carol K. DiPrete, Librarian; Wendell B. Pols, Reference/Special Collections Librarian, and Archivist.

Library General Holdings. 99,141 books; 1,022 periodical titles; 37 newspapers; 980 bound periodicals; 8,095 microfilm reels; 9,899 microfiche sheets; 5,366 slides; 3,-147 phonodiscs; 219 maps and charts; 364 musical scores.

Special Collections

State of Rhode Island Collection. The library has a special collection of over 1,320 volumes on the State of Rhode Island and its cities and towns. The collection emphasizes history, arts, architecture, business and industry, politics, science, sociology, and biography.

1482
University of Rhode Island
University Library
Kingston, Rhode Island 02881

Telephone. (401) 792-2594

Institutional Description. The publicly supported university was founded as one of the land grant colleges in 1892. Enrollment: 13,616.

Library Administration. Arthur Young, University Librarian; David C. Maslyn, Head, Special Collections and Rare Books.

Library General Holdings. 789,622 volumes.

Special Collections

Rhode Island Collection. This is a collection of special books of Rhode Island history, authors, and imprints. Most of the items in the collection are historical books, although there are also serials, maps, and early Rhode Island almanacs.

University Archives. The Archives are the official repository for all University records. These records consists of the non-current files generated by the University in the conduct of its business, papers of faculty and staff, records of official and unofficial student organizations, a set of student newspapers and yearbooks, and copies of University publications.

Maps. A member of the Defense Mapping Agency Topographic Center since 1947, the library keeps on deposit approximately 5,000 topographic maps of all parts of the world. Recently the program has been expanded to include aeronautical and hydrographic charts.

Rare Book Collections

Manuscript Collection. This collection of personal and historical material consists primarily of papers and records generated in Rhode Island. Included are early town records, ledgers, journals, and personal papers, as well as the papers of twentieth century political figures.

Rare Books Collection. The collection is divided into two parts: rare books of a general nature and collections by and about specific authors. The oldest rare book in the collection is dated 1515, but there are also facsimile editions of many classic works. The collection contains many books of historical interest on botany (including herbals), zoology, history, and philosophy, as well as collections by and about specific authors: Walt Whitman, Ezra Pound, Edna St. Vincent Millay, Edward Arlington Robinson, and Leonard Bacon.

South Carolina

1483
Baptist College at Charleston
L. Mendel Rivers Library
P.O. Box 10087
Charleston, South Carolina 29411

Telephone. (803) 797-4718

Institutional Description. The privately supported liberal arts college was established in 1965. It is owned and controlled by the South Carolina Baptist Convention. Enrollment: 1,261.

Library Administration. Enid R. Causey, Director of the Library.

Library General Holdings. 116,046 volumes; 500 current periodicals; 10 newspaper subscriptions; 55,013 microforms; 25,414 audiovisual titles; 86,786 government documents.

Special Collections

Baptist Collection. Includes 100 books about Baptist theology and Baptist associations and organizations.

Curriculum Collection. Consists of 4,500 items including textbooks, kits, curricular materials, and printed resources used in teaching.

Government Documents Collection. Includes 87,000 U.S. federal documents and 2,000 South Carolina state publications.

Juvenile Collection. Consists of 4,050 books for children and young adults.

South Carolina Collection. Includes over 1,200 books on the people, history, art, and music of South Carolina plus books written by South Carolinians.

1484
Beaufort Technical College
Learning Resources Center
100 South Ribaut Road
P.O. Box 1288
Beaufort, South Carolina 29902

Telephone. (803) 524-3380

Institutional Description. The two-year college serves four rural counties in the southern coastal area of South Carolina. The school became part of the statewide Technical Education System in 1972. Enrollment: 791.

Library Administration. Helen Fellers, Director.

Library General Holdings. 20,000 volumes; 157 periodical titles; 26,136 microfiche.

Special Collections

The library has special collections on nursing, electronics, and computers. Beaufort Tech has entered into an agreement with the libraries of Beaufort County and of the University of South Carolina at Beaufort by which the borrower's card from any one library is honored at all three.

1485
Benedict College
Benjamin F. Payton Learning Resources Center Library
Harden and Blanding Streets
Columbia, South Carolina 29204

Telephone. (803) 256-4220

Institutional Description. The privately supported Christian liberal arts college was founded in 1870. It grants baccalaureate degrees. Enrollment: 1,363.

Library Administration. Cassandra Norman, Head Librarian.

Library General Holdings. 144,000 volumes; 475 current periodical subscriptions.

Special Collections

The Payton Library's **Afro-American Collection** includes over 11,000 volumes plus picture files and vertical file material.

1486
Central Wesleyan College
Library-Learning Center
Wesleyan Drive
Central, South Carolina 29630

Telephone. (803) 639-2453

Institutional Description. The privately supported evangelical Christian liberal arts and teachers college was founded in 1906. It is affiliated with the Wesleyan Methodist Church, and grants baccalaureate degrees. Enrollment: 367.

Library Administration. Martha S. Evatt, Librarian.

Library General Holdings. 66,000 volumes; 365 current periodical subscriptions.

Special Collections

The **Roy S. Nicholson Collection of Wesleyan Church History** and the **Clayton Genealogical Collection** are maintained in the library.

1487
The Citadel, The Military College of South Carolina
Daniel Library
Charleston, South Carolina 29409

Telephone. (803) 792-5000

Institutional Description. The publicly supported (state) liberal arts and military college was founded in 1842. Citadel is primarily for men, but offers coeducational evening and part-time courses. Enrollment: 2,503.

Library Administration. Lieutenant Colonel Richard J. Wood, Director of Library Services.

Library General Holdings. 250,000 books, bound periodicals, government documents, and pamphlets; 1,400 periodical subscriptions; 450,000 microforms.

Special Collections

General Mark W. Clark Archives. Contains 60,000 manuscripts, 40,000 photographs, and many films, tape recordings, newspapers; newspaper clippings, and artifacts. Invaluable as an original source of documents relating to World War II and the Korean Conflict, the archives has received national attention from archival institutions and historians. The archives also houses the papers of General Hugh P. Harris which contain background material on the development of airborne forces.

1488
Claflin College
Hubert Vernon Manning Library
700 College Avenue, N.E.
Orangeburg, South Carolina 29115

Telephone. (803) 534-2710

Institutional Description. The privately supported liberal arts college was founded in 1869. It is affiliated with the United Methodist Church, and grants baccalaureate degrees. Enrollment: 760.

Library Administration. Louisa Robinson, Head Librarian.

Library General Holdings. 14,000 volumes; 330 current periodical subscriptions.

Special Collections

Located in the library is the **Wilbur R. Gregg Black Collection Center** which housing books and materials by and about Blacks. The Center is named for the late Rev. Wilbur R. Gregg, a former faculty member who contributed to the development of the collection. The library also houses the **Claflin College Archives,** the minutes of the 1866 United Methodist Conference, and the papers of Rev. Matthew McCollum, religious and civic leader.

1489
Clemson University
Clemson University Libraries
Clemson, South Carolina 29634

Telephone. (803) 656-3026

Institutional Description. The publicly supported state university was founded in 1889. Enrollment: 11,770.

Library Administration. Joseph F. Boykin, Jr., University Librarian; Michael F. Kohl, Head, Special Collections.

Library General Holdings. 1,488,658 books; 7,057 periodical subscriptions; 31,449 microcards; 984,714 microfiche; 20,397 microfilms; 26,225 maps.

Special Collections

Manuscript Collections. Special Collections has a number of collections of papers closely related to the University's history. The papers of John C. Calhoun and founder Thomas Green Clemson document the activities of the two distinguished owners of the Fort Hill plantation, now the site of Clemson University. Papers of Clemson alumni, faculty, staff and administrators: Dr. Rupert Fike, the "Father of IPTAY"; James Eleazer, agricultural Extension information specialist; and Professor Alester Holmes, historian—all document Clemson's history. The J.C. Littlejohn Collection ia source of University history compiled by its long-time former business manager.

Other collections of papers of important political leaders from South Carolina include Benjamin R. Tillman, governor and U.S. Senator; James F. Byrnes, Congressman, U.S. Senator, U.S. Supreme Court Justice, U.S. Secretary of State, and Governor; Carroll Campbell, Governor and Congressman; A. Frank Lever, Congressman; Edward Young, Congressman; Edgar Brown, South Carolina Senator; and Paul Quattlebaum, South Carolina Senator. The Senator Strong Thurmond Collection serves as a focus for continued collection efforts in the area of South Carolina political history and will be a major resource for the research programs of the Strom Thurmond Institute of Government and Public Affairs.

Papers documenting conservation and recreational resources include those of Dr. George Aull, former Clemson professor in agricultural economics who was instrumental in the development of the Clemson Forest, and those of former National Park Service directors George Hartzog, Ronald Walker, and Russell Dickerson. There are also a few manuscript collections, such as the Henry Ravenel and the Bernard Behrend Papers related to the history of science and technology. The Papers of Ben Robertson, Clemson graduate and World War II correspondent, and South Carolina author Julia Peterkin are of literary interest. The papers of A. Wolfe Davidson document the life of a noted sculptor whose work is found throughout the University.

University Archives. The Archives holds copies of official records such as the Minutes of the Board of Trustees, University Publications, including its course catalogs, student publications, a newspaper clippings file on University subjects, papers of the University's presidents, and a photograph collection consisting of several thousand images.

Rare Book Collections

Rare Book Collection. This collection offers a resource rich in South Carolina history and the history of science. The collection is based upon the generous donations of local authors and collectors, the use of funds from the William J. Latimer bequest and the gifts of Mrs. Bernard Behrend. The Behrend gifts include a collection of Thackeray's works and some of the world's most significant scientific works. First editions by Galileo, Newton, Priestly, and other great scientist form the basis of this small but valuable collection.

The Rare Book Collection also contains a number of volumes from the Pendleton Farmer's Society, herbals containing fine plates of flowers and other plants, and a variety of other interesting material. These books include portions of the libraries of James F. Byrnes and Benjamin R. Tillman, pamphlets on the nullification and secession controversies, a collection of antebellum women's literature bought by the Class of 1915, and a collection of original Pogo comics.

1490
Coker College
College Library
East College Avenue
Hartsville, South Carolina 29550

Telephone. (803) 332-1381

Institutional Description. The privately supported liberal arts college, primarily for women, purposely keeps a small enrollment to preserve personalized instruction. It grants the baccalaureate degree. Enrollment: 313.

Library Administration. Gordon J. Gourlay, Director.

Library General Holdings. 64,000 books; 330 periodical subscriptions.

Special Collections

The Coker College Library maintains the **Arents Tobacco Collection** and the **Major James Lide Coker Collection** of first edition histories covering the period 1865-1910.

1491
College of Charleston
Robert Scott Small Library
66 George Street
Charleston, South Carolina 29424

Telephone. (803) 792-5507

Institutional Description. The publicly supported (state) liberal arts college grants baccalaureate and master's degrees. Enrollment: 4,416.

Library Administration. David Cohen, Director of Libraries.

Library General Holdings. 293,000 volumes; 2,000 journal and periodical subscriptions.

Special Collections

The principal special collection is the **South Carolina Collection** which includes a large number of pamphlets, manuscripts, and transcripts of other records. Other collections are the **Burnett Rhett Maybank Papers** including documents of the U.S. Senator dating back to 1770 and the **Friendly Moralist Society Minutes** including documents of an antebellum free Black mutual aid society.

The Cooperative Marine Research Facility Library at Fort Johnson consists of the combined marine science holdings of the College of Charleston and the South Carolina Wildlife Resources Department. The collection consists of 10,000 volumes, 220 current periodical subscriptions, and thousands of reprint articles dealing with fishes and fisheries, marine invertebrates, estuarine and marine ecology, water quality, coastal zone management, and other fields in the marine sciences.

1492
Columbia Bible College
Learning Resources Center
7435 Monticello Road
Columbia, South Carolina 29230

Telephone. (803) 754-4100

Institutional Description. The privately supported professional Bible college, although interdenominational, stresses an evangelical Protestant spirit. It grants associate, baccalaureate, and master's degrees. Enrollment: 838.

Library Administration. Ruth Marshall, Director of Media Resources.

Library General Holdings. 90,000 items of print and non-print materials; 650 journal subscriptions.

Special Collections

The library's collection has concentrations in missiological, Biblical, and theological areas.

1493
Columbia College
J. Drake Edens Library
Columbia College Drive
Columbia, South Carolina 29203

Telephone. (803) 786-3716

Institutional Description. The privately supported liberal arts college for women is affiliated with The United Methodist Conference of South Carolina. Founded in 1854, it is one of the oldest women's colleges in the South. Enrollment: 1,062.

Library Administration. John C. Pritchett, Library Director.

Library General Holdings. 125,000 volumes; 760 current periodical and newspaper subscriptions; 10,000 microforms; 15,000 other learning materials.

Special Collections

Instructional Media Center. The Center houses curriculum and audiovisual materials.

The library has a special collection on nineteenth- and twentieth-century religious literature for children. It also collects the works of local authors Peggy Parish and Barbara Johnson.

1494
Converse College
Gwathmey Library
580 East Main Street
Spartanburg, South Carolina 29301

Telephone. (803) 596-9000

Institutional Description. The privately supported liberal arts college, primarily for women, is nondenominational but has a Christian emphasis. Enrollment: 828.

Library Administration. James G. Harrison, Jr., Head Librarian.

Library General Holdings. 150,000 books, records, and scores; 655 periodical subscriptions; 13,000 recordings; 11,000 music scores.

Special Collections

The library maintains the **Elizabeth Boatwright Coker Collection** of South Caroliniana.

1495
Erskine College and Seminary
McCain Library
P.O. Box 308
Due West, South Carolina 29639

Telephone. (803) 379-2131

Institutional Description. The privately supported liberal arts college (coeducational) and theological seminary (for men) was founded in 1839. It is affiliated with the Associate Reformed Presbyterian Church. Enrollment: 598.

Library Administration. John H. Wilde, Librarian.

Library General Holdings. 135,000 volumes; 800 current periodical subscriptions; 75,000 government documents; 24,700 bound periodical volumes.

Special Collections

The library maintains the theological collection of the Erskine Theological Seminary. It also houses a collection of materials on Southern history.

1496
Francis Marion College
James A. Rogers Library
P.O. Box F-7500
Florence, South Carolina 29501

Telephone. (803) 661-1362

Institutional Description. The publicly supported state liberal arts college was founded in 1970. Enrollment: 2,869.

Library Administration. H. Paul Dove, Director.

Library General Holdings. 260,000 volumes (40,000 in microform); 1,500 periodical subscriptions.

Special Collections

The Arundel Room houses significant material about the Pee Dee region of South Carolina, colonial South Carolina, books relating to General Francis Marion, other rare books, and the College Archives.

1497
Furman University
James Buchanan Duke Library
Greenville, South Carolina 29613

Telephone. (803) 294-2191

Institutional Description. The privately supported liberal arts university was founded as a college in 1826; the graduate school was added in 1897. The University is affiliated with the South Carolina Baptist Convention. Enrollment: 2,827.

Library Administration. Edward Alderman Scott, University Librarian; John Glenwood Clayton, Special

Collections Librarian; Kathy Ann Grenga, Archivist of the South Carolina Baptist Historical Collection.

Library General Holdings. 293,999 volumes; 1,500 periodicals; 37,268 microforms.

Special Collections

The Special Collections of Furman University include the **South Carolina Baptist Historical Collection** and the **Furman University Collection.** The major manuscript collections are: Basil Manly, Jr., Edmund Botsford, Oliver Hart, Richard Furman, and Raven I. McDavid, Jr. Other holdings include church histories, the *Baptist Courier* and its predecessors, state associational and State Convention minutes, church records on microfilm, maps, and photographs.

1498
Lander College
Larry A. Jackson Library
Greenwood, South Carolina 29646

Telephone. (803) 229-8366

Institutional Description. The publicly supported college was founded as a Methodist college for women in 1872, and became a part of the South Carolina State System in 1973. It is now coeducational. Enrollment: 1,973.

Library Administration. Ann T. Hare, Library Director; Betty H. Williams, Special Collections Librarian.

Library General Holdings. 192,122 items including 61,170 microforms, 7,145 bound periodicals, 851 periodical subscriptions.

Special Collections

The library maintains a small collection of Welsh literature, language, and history.

1499
Lutheran Theological Southern Seminary
Lineberger Memorial Library
4201 North Main Street
Columbia, South Carolina 29203

Telephone. (803) 786-5150

Institutional Description. The privately supported theological seminary, established in Columbia in 1911, offers graduate level-programs only. It is affiliated with the Lutheran Church in America. Enrollment: 162.

Library Administration. W. Richard Fritz, Librarian.

Library General Holdings. 90,000 volumes; 450 periodicals.

Special Collections

The classics of the Christian faith are shelved with contemporary resources for communicating the gospel. There are growing collections in social problems, human relationships, pastoral care, comparative religion, philosophy, and secular history. The library also houses special collections in Southern Lutheran Church history and seventeenth- and eighteenth-century German pietism.

1500
Medical University of South Carolina
The Health Affairs Library of the Medical University of South Carolina and The Waring Historical Library
171 Ashley Avenue
Charleston, South Carolina 29425

Telephone. (803) 792-2288

Institutional Description. The publicly supported state university was established in 1824 as a medical college, and has added five additional colleges on the same campus to form the present university. Enrollment: 1,892.

Library Administration. Warren C. Sawyer, Director of Libraries; Elizabeth Y. Newsom, Curator of Waring Historical Library.

Library General Holdings. 165,000 volumes; 2,460 current journal subscriptions; 2,300 audiovisual titles. The Waring Historical Library is a part of the Health Affairs Library but is housed separately.

Rare Book Collections

Waring Historical Library. The library was acquired by the Medical University with other properties of the Porter Military Academy, and in 1966 it was repaired and refurbished to become a department of the main library of the University. Through the foresight of the late Joseph I. Waring, M.D., the collection of the Library of the Medical Society of South Carolina in Charleston was obtained to form the nucleus of the library's holdings. Begun in 1791, this collection grew gradually over the years to a fairly considerable size, suffering the depridations in the period of the Civil War and thereafter being neglected for a great many years. Most of the books date from the eighteenth and nineteenth centuries, and there are early journals of the period from England, France, and the United States. A few of the books date back to the sixteenth century. The collection has expanded to approximately 7,000 books, mostly through the generosity of individuals. Dr. Waring himself contributed heavily to the library's growth, providing his own personal collection of books, historical papers, his own research files, and his collection of medical caricatures.

The Library has about 500 miscellaneous museum objects (old instruments, medicine chests, saddle bags), and a number of prescription books and day books. It includes also the handwritten theses of students of the Medical College of South Carolina from 1825 to 1860, early day graduation diplomas, many Edinburgh theses, and a number of lecture notes from South Carolinians who studied at Edinburgh and Pennsylvania. There is a fairly large South Carolina collection including books (old and new) written by South Carolinians and files of biographical and general material bearing on the history of medicine in the state. There is also a collection of valuable papers and documents, mostly of South Carolinians and a microfilm collection.

1501
Newberry College
Wessels Library
2100 College Street
Newberry, South Carolina 29108

Telephone. (803) 276-5010

Institutional Description. The privately supported liberal arts college was founded in 1856. It is affiliated with the Lutheran Church in America, and grants baccalaureate degrees. Enrollment: 575.

Library Administration. Everett J. Dennis, Director of Library and Media Services.

Library General Holdings. 88,000 volumes; 450 current magazine and scholarly journal subscriptions.

Special Collections

The **Special Collections Room** contains historical materials on the Lutheran Church and the Newberry College Archives. There is also a collection of South Caroliniana.

1502
Presbyterian College
James H. Thomason Library
P.O. Box 975
Clinton, South Carolina 29325

Telephone. (803) 833-2820

Institutional Description. The privately supported liberal arts college was founded in 1880. It is affiliated with the Presbyterian Church (U.S.A.), and grants baccalaureate degrees. Enrollment: 931.

Library Administration. Lennart Pearson, Director.

Library General Holdings. 140,000 volumes; 650 periodical and newspaper subscriptions; 1,500 phonorecords.

Special Collections

The library maintains a special collection of South Caroliniana and Presbyteriana displayed in the historically appointed Dillard-Elliott Room. This collection has benefited through the years from numerous gifts of books from private collectors, including the personal library of Founder William Plumer Jacobs.

1503
South Carolina State College
Miller F. Whittaker Library
Orangeburg, South Carolina 29117

Telephone. (803) 536-7000

Institutional Description. The publicly supported state liberal arts and professional college was founded in 1895. Enrollment: 4,164.

Library Administration. Barbara Williams Jenkins, Library Director.

Library General Holdings. 313,000 volumes; 1,430 periodical subscriptions; 39,500 government documents; 386,000 microforms.

Special Collections

The library maintains two special collections: **The Black Collection** of materials by and about Blacks and the **South Carolina State College Historical Collection,** a developing collection emphasizing the history of the college.

1504
University of South Carolina
Thomas Cooper Library
Columbia, South Carolina 29208

Telephone. (803) 777-3142

Institutional Description. The publicly supported university was founded in 1801 as South Carolina College. Today, a very diverse program of studies is offered. Enrollment: 18,096.

Library Administration. George D. Terry, Director of Libraries; Davy-Jo S. Ridge, Associate Director of Libraries; Roger Mortimer, Rare Books Librarian.

Library General Holdings. 1,900,000 volumes; 1,850,000 microforms; 185,000 maps; 9,200 music scores; 6,900 phonodiscs; 3,000 films; 77,000 aerial photographs; 11,000 current periodical subscriptions.

Special Collections

Map Collection. This map collection is the third largest in the Southeast. The collection is limited to twentieth-century material and is a depository for the U.S. Geological Survey and the Defense Map Agency. There is complete topographical coverage of the United States and partial coverage of foreign areas. The collection also includes a large number of out-of-print twentieth-century atlases.

Rare Book Collections

The library's special collections are built around items acquired between 1801 and 1860. At the outbreak of the Civil War, the University owned one of the finest libraries in North America. The books acquired by that time form the nucleus of the present special collections. Many other areas have been developed in response to the institution's research needs. Natural history collections include a fine collection of works by and about John James Audubon (1785-1851). His *Birds of America* (1827-1838) was acquired on publication and the library owns all significant editions of his work. **The Phelps Memorial Collection** of books on the camellia, perhaps the finest in existence, contains every colour-plate book on the subject published between 1819 and 1860. The library also owns fine illustrated horticultural books of the seventeenth century. The early science collections include a group of the rare first editions of the Danish astronomer Tycho Brahe and a group of late eighteenth- and nineteenth-century works on geology and paleontology collected by the University's second president, Thomas Cooper (1759-1839).

American literature includes notable holdings of Whitman, Frost, and Melville. British literature includes extensive holdings of the major eighteenth- and nineteenth-century novelists and poets; Scottish literature of the same period; and the finest extant collection of the Poet Laureate, Robert Bridges (1844-1930). The largest section of the American history collections is an important and extensive group (ca. 5,000 items) of works relating to the Civil War. History of books and printing collections contain a representative cross-section ranging from Babylonian clay tablets, through papyrus and the medieval manuscript, to the printed book, with representative items from the fifteenth century to modern fine printing.

The principal manuscript collection is the papers of Reginald Clfford Allen, Lord Allen of Hurtwood (1889-1939). Allen was a political ally of Ramsay MacDonald and the archive contains significant materials relating to MacDonald's period as coalition Prime Minister. The archive also contains a significant collection of correspondence relating to Allen's attempts to aid political prisoners in Nazi Germany during the late 1930s.

1505
University of South Carolina at Aiken
Gregg-Graniteville Library
171 University Parkway
Aiken, South Carolina 29801

Telephone. (803) 648-6851

Institutional Description. The publicly supported branch of the University of South Carolina was founded in 1961. It grants associate and baccalaureate degrees. Enrollment: 1,532.

Library Administration. Frankie H. Cubbedge, Director.

Library General Holdings. 94,000 volumes; 765 current periodical subscriptions; 12,000 microforms.

Special Collections

The library's special collections include the **May Collection of Southern History** and the historical files of Graniteville County covering the period 1845 to the present.

1506
University of South Carolina at Coastal Carolina College
Kimbel Library
P.O. Box 1954
Conway, South Carolina 29526

Telephone. (803) 347-3161

Institutional Description. The publicly supported branch college of the University of South Carolina was founded in 1954. It offers preparation for the state teachers certificate. Enrollment: 2,246.

Library Administration. Lynne Smith, Director.

Library General Holdings. 96,000 volumes; 845 periodical subscriptions; 20,000 microforms.

Special Collections

The library has special collections on marine science and the Waccamaw region of South Carolina.

1507
Voorhees College
Elizabeth Evelyn Wright Library
Denmark, South Carolina 29042

Telephone. (803) 793-3351

Institutional Description. The privately supported liberal arts college was founded in 1897. It is affiliated with the Protestant Episcopal Church. Enrollment: 612.

Library Administration. Joyce C. Wright, Administrative Librarian.

Library General Holdings. 100,000 volumes; 400 periodical and journal subscriptions.

Special Collections

The library maintains a **Black History Collection** and the Library of American Civilization (microfiche).

1508
Winthrop College
Ida Jane Dacus Library
Oakland Avenue
Rock Hill, South Carolina 29733

Telephone. (803) 323-2211

Institutional Description. The publicly supported (state) liberal arts college college was founded in 1886. It grants baccalaureate and master's degrees. Enrollment: 4,428.

Library Administration. Shirley M. Tarlton, Dean of Library Services.

Library General Holdings. 320,000 books and bound periodicals; 606,500 microfiche; 84,000 microcards; 26,600 reels of microfilm; 187,000 government documents; 1,840 audiovisual materials; 3,360 periodical and serial titles.

Special Collections

The special collections of the library include the **Eliza Ragsdale Wylie Manuscript Collection,** the **Knox-Wise Family Papers,** and the **Mary Elizabeth Massey Papers.**

1509
Wofford College
Sandor Teszler Library
Spartanburg, South Carolina 29301

Telephone. (803) 585-4821

Institutional Description. The privately supported liberal arts college primarily for men was founded in 1854. It is affiliated with the United Methodist Church. Enrollment: 1,070.

Library Administration. Oakley Herman Coburn, Librarian.

Library General Holdings. 210,000 volumes; 640 current periodical subscriptions.

Special Collections

The special collections contain over 10,000 volumes, including important scholarly books of the sixteenth and seventeenth centuries. Also housed in the library are the **Wofford College Archives** and the records and historical material of the South Carolina Conference of the United Methodist Church.

South Dakota

1510
Augustana College
Mikkelsen Library
29th and Summit Avenue
Sioux Falls, South Dakota 57197

Telephone. (605) 336-5516

Institutional Description. The privately supported Christian liberal arts college is affiliated with the American Lutheran Church. It grants associate, baccalaureate, and master's degrees. Enrollment: 1,560.

Library Administration. Ronelle Thompson, Director.

Library General Holdings. 201,000 volumes; 1,010 current periodical subscriptions; 110,000 government documents; 19,000 microforms.

Special Collections

The library maintains the **College Archives** which include the records of The American Lutheran Church (South Dakota District), the Episcopal Diocese of South Dakota, the South Dakota Ornithologists Union, Minnehaha County, John Morrell and Co., Sioux Falls Bicentennial, and others; the **Dakota Collection,** and the **Norwegian Collection.**

The Center for Western Studies is also housed in the library. The Center houses an extensive library of Western Americana, including the Krause, Manfred, Parker, and other significant private collections, as well as a variety of Western Art and Indian artifact and immigrant collections. Although primarily concerned with the culture and history of South Dakota and its surrounding states, the Center deals with many related aspects of the Great Plains and the Trans-Mississippi West.

1511
Black Hills State College
Leland D. Case Library for Western Historical Studies
College Station, Box 9511
1200 University
Spearfish, South Dakota 57783

Telephone. (605) 642-6361

Institutional Description. The publicly supported state college was founded in 1883. Enrollment: 1,846.

Library Administration. W. Edwin Erickson, Librarian; Dora Ann Jones, Special Collections Librarian.

Library General Holdings. 220,000 volumes; 36,000 microforms; 50,000 pamphlets.

Special Collections

Case Library for Western Historical Studies. Includes over 10,000 monograph and serial volumes, plus local newspapers from 1881, as well as several thousand maps, photographs, and other materials. The library is a depository for several local organizations.

E.Y. Berry Congressional Collection. Consists of the correspondence, files, photographs, and other material (approximately 240 linear feet) covering the period 1950-1970.

Black Hills State College Archives. Includes administrative and historical records of the College.

1512
Dakota State College
Karl E. Mundt Library
Madison, South Dakota 57042

Telephone. (605) 256-5203

Institutional Description. The publicly supported liberal arts and teachers college was founded in 1881. It grants baccalaureate degrees. Enrollment: 710.

Library Administration. Ethelle S. Bean, Director.

Library General Holdings. 77,000 volumes; 575 current periodical subscriptions; 12,000 microforms.

Special Collections

The library maintains the **Karl E. Mundt Archives** which house over 1,200,000 documents covering the 31-year career of Karl Mundt as United States Congressman and Senator. It also maintains a microfilm collection and an oral history collection of South Dakota history.

1513
Dakota Wesleyan University
University Library
1200 West University Avenue
Mitchell, South Dakota 57301

Telephone. (605) 996-6511

Institutional Description. The privately supported liberal arts university is affiliated with the United Methodist Church. Enrollment: 578.

Library Administration. Michael L. Wright, Head Librarian.

Library General Holdings. 76,000 volumes; 326 current periodicals.

Special Collections

Jennewein Collection. Consists of 4,000 monographs, 200 maps, several thousand photographs, and rare and old materials relating to the history and culture of the Dakota region.

Senator Francis Case Collection. Contains the personal and political papers, books, and memorabilia of Senator Case's more than 30 years in the U.S. Congress.

Senator George McGovern Collection. Includes 2,000 volumes and a partial collection of personal and political papers.

1514
Huron College
Ella McIntire Library
Huron, South Dakota 57350

Telephone. (605) 352-8721

Institutional Description. The privately supported liberal arts college was founded in 1883. It is affiliated with the Presbyterian Church (U.S.A.), and grants baccalaureate degrees. Enrollment: 408.

Library Administration. Ethelle Bean, Library Director.

Library General Holdings. 63,000 volumes; 300 periodical subscriptions.

Special Collections

Special collections include the **Blackburn Collection** containing first and early editions; a collection of Lincolniana; the **Crawford Art Collection;** the **Judge A.K. Gardner Collection;** the **A.M. Urquhart Curio Collection;** and the **Dr. Hubert Ketelle Collection.** The Heritage Room houses the **Huron College Archives.** The artifacts of and the books on the Sioux Nation are important holdings of the library.

1515
Mount Marty College
College Library
1105 West 8th Street
Yankton, South Dakota 57078

Telephone. (605) 668-1514

Institutional Description. The privately supported liberal arts college was founded in 1936. It is affiliated with the Roman Catholic Church, and grants baccalaureate degrees. Enrollment: 589.

Library Administration. Sister Marie Kranz, Director.

Library General Holdings. 75,000 volumes; 600 periodical titles.

Special Collections

The curriculum library of more than 5,000 textbooks and other instructional aids is of primary importance to the department of teacher education. Other special collections include works on Catholicism, theology, and Southeast Asia.

1516
National College
Learning Resource Center
321 Kansas City Street
Rapid City, South Dakota 57701

Telephone. (605) 3394-4800

Institutional Description. The privately supported college was founded in 1941 as the National School of Business. Continuing to feature business programs under its new name, the college has 10 branch campuses in South Dakota, California, Colorado, Kansas, Minnesota, and New Mexico. Enrollment: 2,877.

Library Administration. Linda Watson, Librarian.

Library General Holdings. 26,000 books; 400 periodical subscriptions.

Special Collections

The emphases in the library collection are on management, travel hospitality, and data processing.

1517
North American Baptist Seminary
Seminary Library
1321 West 22nd Street
Sioux Falls, South Dakota 57105

Telephone. (605) 336-6588

Institutional Description. The privately supported professional theological seminary was founded in 1858. Affiliated with the North American Baptist Conference, the seminary offers programs at the graduate level only.

Enrollment: 151.

Library Administration. George W. Lang, Library Administrator.

Library General Holdings. 55,000 volumes; 355 current periodical subscriptions.

Special Collections

The library's specialized collections are on Biblical studies, theology, and counseling.

1518
Northern State College
Williams Library
South Jay Street and 12th Avenue
Aberdeen, South Dakota 57401

Telephone. (605) 622-2645

Institutional Description. The publicly supported state liberal arts and teachers college was founded in 1901 as the Northern Normal and Industrial School. Enrollment: 2,321.

Library Administration. Wade Woodward, Librarian; Keith Warne, Archivist.

Library General Holdings. 210,000 books; 910 current periodicals; 23,000 government documents; 51,000 microforms.

Special Collections

The special collections of the Williams Library, all of which contain some rare books, include materials on the history of Aberdeen County and Brown County; a 1,000-volume colleciton on the history of South Dakota; and a 2,000-volume collection on the Great Plains Indians.

1519
Oglala Lakota College
Oglala Lakota College Learning Resources Center
Box 310
Kyle, South Dakota 57752

Telephone. (605) 455-2321

Institutional Description. The tribally supported two-year college is controlled by the Oglala Sioux Tribe and is located on the Pine Ridge Indian Reservation in the southwestern part of the state. There are nine centers throughout the 5,000 square miles of the reservation. Enrollment: 585.

Library Administration. Dicksy June Howe, College Librarian; Theodore L. Hamilton, Archivist.

Library General Holdings. 20,000 volumes; 213 journal subscriptions; 300 video and 16mm films.

Special Collections

The Indian of North America Collection. Consists of over 2,000 volumes dealing with all tribes north of Mexico. The College is attempting to collect comprehensively in the area of Lakota studies. In addition to the published materials, a file of reports and other unpublished materials is available for research. In many cases, these reports contain statistical information concerning the Pine Ridge Indian Reservation.

Oglala Lakota College Archives and Historical Research Center. The Archives is the official repository for the Oglala Sioux Tribe and Oglala Lakota College. It also collects the administrative documents of the American Indian Higher Education Consortium. The Archives has a number of unique oral history collections, tradition Lakota music collections, and an extensive photograph collection. The mission of the archival program is document the history of the people of the Pine Ridge Reservation both historically and currently.

1520
Sioux Falls College
Norman B. Mears Library
1501 South Prairie
Sioux Falls, South Dakota 57101

Telephone. (605) 331-5000

Institutional Description. The privately supported liberal arts college was founded in 1883. It is affiliated with the American Baptist Churches in the U.S.A. Enrollment: 616.

Library Administration. Jane Kolbe, Head Librarian.

Library General Holdings. 75,000 volumes; 400 journal titles.

Special Collections

The curriculum laboratory, several art collections, and the **College Archives** are housed in the library.

1521
South Dakota State University
Hilton M. Briggs Library
Brookings, South Dakota 57007

Telephone. (605) 688-4111

Institutional Description. The publicly supported state university was founded in 1881 as a land-grant college. It awards associate, baccalaureate, master's, and doctorate degrees. Enrollment: 6,268.

Library Administration. Leon Raney, Dean of Libraries.

Library General Holdings. 383,000 volumes; 3,800 current periodical titles; 342,000 government documents; 328,000 microforms.

Special Collections

Special collections include materials on science and technology, nursing, and pharmacy. The library also has a special collection on South Dakota.

1522
University of South Dakota
I.D. Weeks Library
414 East Clark Street
Vermillion, South Dakota 57069

Telephone. (605) 677-5371

Institutional Description. The publicly supported university was founded in 1862. Enrollment: 5,246.

Library Administration. John Van Balen, Acting Director; Karen Zimmerman, Learning Resources Librarian and Archivist.

Library General Holdings. 394,869 volumes; 3,031 current periodical subscriptions; 215 newspaper subscriptions; 282,975 microforms; 10,896 audiovisual items; 232,178 U.S. government documents; 48,638 South Dakota government documents.

Special Collections

Learning Resources Laboratory. Contains 2,850 textbooks, 7,500 children's books, and 4,070 other curriculum materials.

Herman P. Chilson Collection of Western Americana. Includes 10,500 books and pamphlets relating to South Dakota and the immediate region. Subjects include South Dakota history, including local histories; Indians, especially the Sioux; and publications by South Dakota authors.

Map Collection. Contains Geological Survey topographical maps and historical maps of South Dakota and adjacent regions.

Archives. The University of South Dakota Archives contain the official records from several administrative offices of the University as well as a growing collection of faculty papers, departmental papers, and other related University materials.

Rare Book Collections

Richardson Manuscripts Collections. Contains letters, diaries, account ledgers, scrapbooks, pamphlets, and printed items relating to South Dakota and the immediate region. Major collections include papers of several South Dakota governors and U.S. Congressmen. Topically, the collections are a source for research in history, Indian studies, political science, and anthropology.

Tennessee

1523
American Baptist College
T.L. Holcomb Library
1800 Whites Creek Pike
Nashville, Tennessee 37207

Telephone. (615) 228-7877

Institutional Description. The privately supported college and theological seminary is an interracial endeavor by the National Baptist Convention and the Southern Baptist Convention to train pastors, denominational workers, Christian education directors, and other Christian workers. Enrollment: 144.

Library Administration. Dorothy B. Lucas, College Librarian.

Library General Holdings. 30,500 volumes; 220 current periodical and newspaper subscriptions; 165 music scores.

Special Collections

The library's collection is mainly in the areas Bible/Theology and Black Studies.

1524
Austin Peay State University
Felix G. Woodward Library
P.O. Box 4595
Clarksville, Tennessee 37044

Telephone. (615) 648-7618

Institutional Description. The publicly supported university began as a normal school in 1927. Enrollment: 4,741.

Library Administration. Donald Joyce, University Librarian; Susan S. Sparkman, Special Collections Librarian.

Library General Holdings. 242,342 volumes; 1,080 periodical subscriptions; 12,758 microfilm reels; 3,820 recordings; 950 audiotapes; 262,451 microfiche; 191 videotapes; 370 films; 1,271 filmstrips; 1,488 maps; 421 vertical files.

Special Collections

The library contains books on Clarksville-Montgomery County; books by Austin Peay faculty and staff; Austin Peay University yearbooks and newspapers; research projects; theses; the **Center of Excellence for Land Between the Lakes Collection** and the **Center for the Creative Arts Collection.**

Rare Book Collections

Tennessee Room. Contains papers of Elizabeth Meriwether Gilmer (pseudonym Dorothy Dix), noted advice columnist. Miss Meriwether was born on a farm on the Kentucky-Tennessee border (1861) and died in New Orleans (1951). In addition to her columns dating from the 1890s, the library has many personal letters (1910-1949), tear sheets of articles and travel diaries (1917-1933) covering her trips to the Far East, Europe, South America, and Africa. The collection also contains her scrapbooks, articles, clippings, photographs, and her school days autograph album (1877-1879).

1525
Belmont College
Williams Library
1900 Belmont Boulevard
Nashville, Tennessee 37212

Telephone. (615) 385-6782

Institutional Description. The privately supported liberal arts college is affiliated with the Southern Baptist Convention. Enrollment: 2,257.

Library Administration. Ernest W. Heard, Director of Library Services; Jane R. Thomas, Special Collections Librarian.

Library General Holdings. 105,775 volumes; 16,345 non-print items; 710 current periodical subscriptions.

Special Collections

The Curriculum Laboratory has 3,005 items used in the teacher preparation program. The Juvenile Literature section has 2,555 items.

1526
Bethel College
College Library
Cherry Street
McKenzie, Tennessee 38201

Telephone. (901) 352-5321

Institutional Description. The privately supported liberal arts college was founded in 1842 as Bethel Seminary. It now offers a wide variety of programs in addition to theology. It is affiliated with the Cumberland Presbyterian Church. Enrollment: 412.

Library Administration. Bobbye McCarter, Head Librarian.

Library General Holdings. 68,000 volumes; 285 current periodical subscriptions.

Special Collections

The library's special collections include the **Cumberland Presbyterian Church Collection** and the **War of the Rebellion Collection.**

1527
Bryan College
Ironside Memorial Library
Box 7000
Dayton, Tennessee 37321

Telephone. (615) 775-2041

Institutional Description. Officially known as William Jennings Bryan College, the privately supported, independent liberal arts institution was founded in 1930. It grants baccalaureate degrees. Enrollment: 483.

Library Administration. David A. Wright, Director of Library Services.

Library General Holdings. 69,000 volumes; 425 periodical titles.

Special Collections

Included in the religion section of the library are 1,000 volumes from the private library of Dr. Ironside and his son, the late Rev. John S. Ironside of Manhattan, Kansas, and a sizable part of the library of the later Dr. Harris Gregg of Chattanooga, professor of Bible at Bryan College for many years. Other special collections include the **Rader Bible and Rare Book Collection,** the **William Jennings Bryan Mementos Collection,** and the **Birch Arnold Memorial Library of Freedom Collection.** The **Anna Trentham Tennessee History Collection,** named for the late Miss Anna Trentham, first graduate of Spring City (Tennessee High School) and the **College Archives** are also housed in the library.

1528
Christian Brothers College
Plough Memorial Library
650 East Parkway, S.
Memphis, Tennessee 38104

Telephone. (901) 278-0100

Institutional Description. The privately supported business, engineering, and liberal arts college was founded in 1871. It is affiliated with the Roman Catholic Church. Enrollment: 1,377.

Library Administration. A. Wayne Denton, Head Librarian.

Library General Holdings. 91,000 volumes; 585 periodical subscriptions; 5,000 microforms.

Special Collections

Important specialized collections are in the fields of engineering and business. The library maintains a special collection of Napoleonana.

1529
Cleveland State Community College
Library
Box 3570
Cleveland, Tennessee 37320

Telephone. (615) 478-6209

Institutional Description. The publicly supported two-year college features transfer, technology, paraprofessional, and vocational programs. Enrollment: 2,016.

Library Administration. Adeline T. Baskett, Head Librarian.

Library General Holdings. 55,580 volumes; 351 periodical subscriptions; 12 newspaper subscriptions; 24,107 microforms.

Special Collections

The library contains special collections on the history of Polk and Bradley Counties, Tennessee. Included in the collections are the *History of Rebellion in Bradley County* (1866) and the U.S. Bureau of American Ethnology *Annual Report* for 1887 and 1900.

1530
Columbia State Community College
Finney Memorial Learning Resources Center
Columbia, Tennessee 38401

Telephone. (615) 388-0120

Institutional Description. The publicly supported two year college was opened in 1967. Enrollment: 1,597.

Library Administration. Marvin J. Light, Library Director; Richard H. Harrison II, Assistant Librarian/Reference Services.

Library General Holdings. 52,000 volumes; 5,000 non-print titles.

Special Collections

A special collection of Tennesseana materials is maintained, encompassing state history and local genealogy. Collections include 706 volumes, six linear feet of manuscripts (relating to the history of the College), and six linear feet of photographs.

1531
David Lipscomb College
College Library
Granny White Pike
Nashville, Tennessee 37203

Telephone. (615) 385-3855

Institutional Description. The privately supported liberal arts college was founded in 1891 as the Nashville Bible School. Now offering a wide variety of programs, the college grants baccalaureate and master's degrees. It is affiliated with the Churches of Christ. Enrollment: 2,262.

Library Administration. James E. Ward, Director of Library Services.

Library General Holdings. 160,000 volumes; 910 current periodical titles; 30,000 microforms.

Special Collections

The library houses the **Herald of Truth** videotapes, the **Batsell Barrett Baxter Archives,** and the C.E.W. Dorris Collection.

1532
East Tennessee State University
Sherrod Library
Box 22, 450A
Johnson City, Tennessee 37614

Telephone. (615) 929-4337

Institutional Description. The publicly supported state university is organized into eight schools and colleges. It was founded in 1911. Enrollment: 8,276.

Library Administration. Fred P. Borchuck, Director of Libraries.

Library General Holdings. 511,878 volumes; 230,194 government documents; 23,483 maps; 2,434 linear feet of archives, manuscripts, and photographs.

Special Collections

The Sherrod Library has a specialized collection of materials related to genealogy of the upper east Tennessee area. It is non-circulating and consists of more than 1,700 volumes housed in the Genealogy Room. Newspapers and census materials related to area genealogy are also available in microfilm format in the Microforms Department of the library.

Archives of Appalachia. Contains manuscripts, books, photographs, pamphlets, maps, audio and video recordings documenting the political, economic, and cultural development of south central Appalachia. The administrative records of East Tennessee State University are also included. Among the holdings of the Archives are the papers of individuals; records of social, civic, business, cultural, and religious organizations; records of labor unions and citizen groups; and collections of folklore, folk culture, and folk music in south central Appalachia. The most notable collections are Thomas Burton-Ambrose Manning Folklore Collection; Broadside Television Records; Carolina, Clinchfield and Ohio Railroad Company Records; East Tennessee Light and Power Company Records; B. Carroll Reece Papers; Kenneth Murray Photographs; Elizabethton *Star* Negatives.

Instructional Media Center. The Center houses a collection of 16mm films and videotapes about Appalachian life and culture produced by the faculty and filmakers Thomas Burton, Jack Schrader, and Tom Headley. A special focus of this collection is the practice of religious snake handling. Other topics include folk music, mountain crafts, folklore, and violent crime.

Rare Book Collections

Rare Books Collection. Sherrod Library contains a selection of 1,350 volumes derived from gifts provided by the library since 1912. The oldest title, dated 1628, is Sir Walter Raleigh's *The Historie of the World.* The Jones donation comprises a major portion of the collection and contains unique editions of European and American history and literature. The collection also includes numerous significant facsimile editions of early English literature, geography, art, and natural science titles. A special oversize edition room is maintained for pictorial works. Another group of histories and descriptions of the War Between the States continues to be developed.

1533
Fisk University
University Library
1000 Todd Boulevard
Nashville, Tennessee 37203

Telephone. (615) 329-8500

Institutional Description. The privately supported liberal arts college was founded in 1866. It grants baccalaureate and master's degrees. Enrollment: 506.

Library General Holdings. 199,000 volumes; 592 periodical subscriptions; 37 newspaper subscriptions.

Special Collections

Among the special collections of the University Library are the **Julius Rosenwald Fund Archives** (1917-

1918); **George Gershwin Memorial Collection of Music and Musical Literature,** the **Negro Collection** consisting of more than 40,000 titles on the Negro in Africa, America, and the Caribbean plus 2,00 records, 300 pieces of sheet music, and 3,400 Black newspapers, magazines, and dissertations on microfilm.

The archives collection houses 75 manuscript collections of primary source manuscripts, letters, documents, and related materials by and about the Negro in all countries and periods. The manuscripts and literary efforts of Charles Waddel Chesnutt are preserved in this collection, as are the libraries and personal papers of Charles S. Johnson, W.E.B. DuBois, John Mercer Langston, Jean Toomer, Langston Hughes, Aaron Douglas, and John W. Work, III. The most recent collections acquired are those of William L. Dawson, Marcus Garvey, and W.C. Handy.

The new **Black Oral History Collection** contains over 600 taped interviews with persons who have been eyewitnesses, participants, or contributors to the Black experience in America.

1534
Free Will Baptist Bible College
Welch Memorial Library
3606 West End Avenue
Nashville, Tennessee 37205

Telephone. (615) 383-1340

Institutional Description. The privately supported liberal arts and professional Bible college was founded in 1942. It is affiliated with the Free Will Baptist Church. Enrollment: 358.

Library Administration. Lorene Francen, Librarian.

Library General Holdings. 48,000 volumes; 165 current periodical titles.

Special Collections

The library has a substantial collection of Bible study aids.

1535
Freed-Hardeman College
Loden-Daniel Library
158 East Main Street
Henderson, Tennessee 38340

Telephone. (901) 989-4611

Institutional Description. The privately supported liberal arts college was founded in 1869 as the Henderson Male and Female Institute. Now offering a wide variety of programs, it grants associate and baccalaureate degrees. The college is affiliated with the Churches of Christ. Enrollment: 1,016.

Library Administration. Jane W. Miller, Head Librarian.

Library General Holdings. 117,000 volumes; 730 periodical subscriptions; 5,000 microforms; 32,000 audiovisual materials.

Special Collections

In the library's collection are religious books from the personal collections of M.C. Jurfees, F.I. Rowe, T.Q. Martin, Ben F. Taylor, and J.W. Howell. The **Goodpasture Room** houses books provided by the late B.C. Goodpasture, long-time editor of the *Gospel Advocate.* The collections contain much material on the Protestant Restoration Movement in the United States. The library also houses a collection of U.S. War Department Civil War records.

1536
Harding Graduate School of Religion
L.M. Graves Memorial Library
1000 Cherry Road
Memphis, Tennessee 38117

Telephone. (901) 761-1352

Institutional Description. The privately supported graduate school is a branch of Harding College, Searcy, Arkansas. Affiliated with the Churches of Christ, it is an outgrowth of graduate studies in religion which began on the Searcy campus in 1952. Enrollment: 132.

Library Administration. Don Meredith, Librarian.

Library General Holdings. 82,000 volumes; 600 current periodical subscriptions.

Special Collections

Special collections include Greek manuscripts on film; Restoration literature, missions, dissertations produced by members of the Churches of Christ, and the curriculum library of religious education materials.

1537
Johnson Bible College
Glass Memorial Library
7900 Johnson Drive
Knoxville, Tennessee 37998

Telephone. (615) 573-4517

Institutional Description. The privately supported Bible college, founded in 1893, is affiliated with the Christian Church. Enrollment: 368.

Library Administration. Helen Lemmon, Librarian.

Library General Holdings. 59,732 bound books; 4,434 bound periodicals; 2,277 children's books; 1,606 music phonorecords and cassettes; 4,147 cassettes of a general nature.

Special Collections

Special collections holdings consist primarily of books, pamphlets, and archival materials relating to the history of Johnson Bible College. The collection also includes books and pamphlets concerning the history of the Christian Church and also of the Churches of Christ and the Disciples of Christ.

1538
Knoxville College
Alumni Library
901 College Street
Knoxville, Tennessee 37921

Telephone. (615) 524-6511

Institutional Description. The privately supported liberal arts college was founded in 1863. It is affiliated with the Presbyterian Church (U.S.A.), and grants associate and baccalaureate degrees. Enrollment: 335.

Library Administration. D. Elaine Stephens, Director of Library Services.

Library General Holdings. 42,000 volumes.

Special Collections

The Schomburg Microfilm Collection of the Negro in America is available in the Alumni Library.

1539
Lambuth College
Luther L. Gobbel Library
Lambuth Boulevard
Jackson, Tennessee 38301

Telephone. (901) 425-2500

Institutional Description. The privately supported liberal arts college was founded in 1843. It is affiliated with the United Methodist Church. Enrollment: 596.

Library Administration. Judith Hazlewood, Director.

Library General Holdings. 156,000 volumes; 410 current periodical subscriptions; 11,000 microforms.

Special Collections

The library maintains the archives of the United Methodist Church-Memphis Conference.

1540
Lane College
J.K. Daniels Library
545 Lane Avenue
Jackson, Tennessee 38301

Telephone. (901) 424-4600

Institutional Description. The privately supported liberal arts college was founded by the Colored Methodist Episcopal Church in America in 1882. It is affiliated with the Christian Methodist Episcopal Church. Enrollment: 689.

Library Administration. Anna L. Cooke, Library Director.

Library General Holdings. 87,000 volumes including 4,000 bound periodicals; 290 periodical subscriptions; 18 newspaper subscriptions; 7,800 microfilms; 611 filmstrips; 72 films; 355 recordings; 236 cassette tapes; 477 transparencies; 50 slides.

Special Collections

The J.K. Daniels Library has a special collection of over 7,000 volumes dealing with books by and about Blacks. There are also audiovisual materials, cassette tapes, and an Oral History Collection of taped interviews relating to the History of the College. The microfilmed Schomburg Collection with titles dating through 1969 is also housed with this collection.

Rare Book Collections

The library has a small uncatalogued rare books collection of books and materials dealing with the founding and early disciplines of the Colored, now Christian Methodist Episcopal Church.

1541
LeMoyne-Owen College
Hollis F. Price Library
807 Walker Avenue
Memphis, Tennessee 38126

Telephone. (901) 774-9090

Institutional Description. The privately supported liberal arts college was founded in 1871. It is affiliated with the United Church of Christ and the Baptist Church. Enrollment: 951.

Library Administration. Annette C. Berhe, Chief Librarian.

Library General Holdings. 90,000 volumes; 275 current periodical subscriptions.

Special Collections

The major special collection of the library is the **Sweeney Collection** which includes over 4,000 books by Black authors about Black history and culture.

1542
Lincoln Memorial University
Carnegie-Bert Vincent Library
Harrogate, Tennessee 37752

Telephone. (615) 869-3611

Institutional Description. The privately supported university of arts and sciences was chartered in 1897. It offers teacher preparation for certification in Tennessee, Virginia, and Kentucky. Enrollment: 1,101.

Library Administration. William C. Buchanan, Director of the Library.

Library General Holdings. 126,000 volumes; 600 periodical subscriptions; 50,000 microforms.

Special Collections

The library has an extensive collection of books on Abraham Lincoln and the Civil War containing manuscripts, documents, books, pamphlets, and artifacts. There are also special collections of books and manuscripts by and about Jesse Stuart.

1543
Maryville College
Lamar Memorial Library
Maryville, Tennessee 37801

Telephone. (615) 982-6412

Institutional Description. The privately supported liberal arts college was founded in 1819 as a theological seminary. Now offering a wide variety of programs, it is affiliated with the Presbyterian Church (U.S.A.). Enrollment: 554.

Library Administration. Joan H. Worley, Director.

Library General Holdings. 150,000 volumes; 530 current periodical subscriptions.

Special Collections

Special collections include over 2,200 musical scores, nineteenth-century hymnals and songsters, and early travel books.

1544
Memphis State University
J.W. Brister Library
Memphis, Tennessee 38152

Telephone. (901) 454-2201

Institutional Description. The publicly supported state university was founded in 1912 as a normal school. A graduate school was added in 1951. Enrollment: 16,148.

Library Administration. Lester J. Pourciau, University Librarian; Ed Frank, Acting Curator of Special Collections.

Library General Holdings. 920,000 volumes; 9,130 current periodical subscriptions; 2,225,000 microforms.

Special Collections

Mississippi Valley Collection. The collection contains books and maps concerning history, culture, literature, and life in the area from Cairo, Illinois to New Orleans on both sides of the Mississippi River. The collection is particularly strong in Civil War materials, documents concerning the 1968 Memphis Sanitation Strike, the assassination of Martin Luther King, Jr., and materials on the now-defunct *Memphis Press-Scimitar* newspaper.

American Popular Song Sheet Music Collection. Covers the period 1900-1950 and includes 6,270 pieces of sheet music.

Rare Book Collections

Some incunabula and rare books are housed in the library. The bulk of these items are local and regional history materials in manuscript form, including some Andrew Jackson letters, Jefferson Davis letters (post-war), papers of some Memphis mayors, congressmen, editors, and just plain folk.

1545
Memphis Theological Seminary
Seminary Library
168 East Parkway, South
Memphis, Tennessee 38104

Telephone. (901) 458-8232

Institutional Description. The privately supported theological seminary was founded in 1852 and held classes on the Bethel College campus in McKenzie. The present site was opened in 1964. Affiliated with the Cumberland Presbyterian Church, the seminary offers graduate programs only. Enrollment: 164.

Library Administration. Bobbie E. Oliver, Administrative Librarian.

Library General Holdings. 70,000 volumes; 552 periodicals.

Special Collections

The library supports the theological mission of the Seminary and also maintains a special collection in Black Studies.

1546
Mid-America Baptist Theological Seminary
Ora Byram Allison Memorial Library
1255 Poplar Avenue
Memphis, Tennessee 38104

Telephone. (901) 726-9171

Institutional Description. The privately supported theological seminary, affiliated with the Baptist Church, grants associate, professional, master's and doctorate degrees. Enrollment: 349.

Library Administration. William B. Hair, III, Director of Library Services.

Library General Holdings. 96,000 volumes; 820 current periodical subscriptions; 27,000 microforms.

Special Collections

The library supports the theological mission of the Seminary with resource materials for all aspects of the curriculum.

1547
Middle Tennessee State University
Andrew L. Todd Library
Murfreesboro, Tennessee 37132

Telephone. (615) 898-2772

Institutional Description. The publicly supported state university was founded in 1911 as the Middle Tennessee Normal School. Enrollment: 10,432.

Library Administration. J. Donald Craig, Director; Margaret Scott, Special Collections Librarian.

Library General Holdings. 800,000 volumes; 3,000 current periodical subscriptions.

Special Collections

The library receives many United States government publications due to its designation as a partial depository of such materials as well as state government publications many of which are maintained in the **Tennessee Collection.**

1548
Milligan College
P.H. Welshimer Library
Milligan, Tennessee 37682

Telephone. (615) 929-0116

Institutional Description. The privately supported Christian liberal arts college was founded in 1886. It is affiliated with the Christian Church (Independent). Enrollment: 621.

Library Administration. Steven L. Preston, Director of Learning Resources.

Library General Holdings. 115,000 volumes; 400 current periodicals.

Special Collections

The Welshimer Library supports the curriculum of Milligan College which places emphasis on integrating scholarship with a positive, Christian faith.

1549
Rhodes College
Burrow Library
2000 North Parkway
Memphis, Tennessee 38112

Telephone. (901) 726-3000

Institutional Description. The privately supported liberal arts college was formed when the Clarksville Academy and the Masonic University of Tennessee merged in 1848. It is affiliated with the Presbyterian Church, U.S.A. Enrollment: 1,053.

Library Administration. Lynne M. Blair, Director.

Library General Holdings. 195,000 volumes; 955 periodical subscriptions; 4,415 microforms.

Special Collections

Rhodes Collection. This collection consists of publications about Rhodes of an historical nature as well as the books written by faculty and alumni.

The library also maintains the papers of Robinson Topp.

Rare Book Collections

Walter Armstrong Rare Book Collection. Includes first editions of English and American authors, many of them autographed; donated by Mrs. Walter Armstrong.

1550
Shelby State Community College
Midtown Library
P.O. Box 40568
Memphis, Tennessee 38147

Telephone. (901) 528-6743

Institutional Description. The publicly supported two-year college was founded in 1970. Enrollment: 3,384.

Library Administration. Joseph F. Lindenfeld, Head Librarian.

Library General Holdings. 50,000 books; 376 current periodical subscriptions; 4,500 back periodical volumes for 150 titles; 8,000 audiovisual items; 23,00 pamphlets, career file material, college catalogs.

Special Collections

The Shelby State Midtown Library owns over 3,000 items pertaining to Black studies. *A Guide to Black American Materials* was published in 1980 and will be revised in 1988. The library also has an extensive collection of books and audiovisuals relating to Allied Health and Nursing. Another concentration is in the area of career material and contains 2,500 items in pamphlet files. There is also a strong collection in early childhood education and consumer and family studies.

1551
Southern College of Optometry
Library
1245 Madison Avenue
Memphis, Tennessee 38104

Telephone. (901) 725-0180

Institutional Description. The privately supported professional college was founded in 1932. It grants associate, baccalaureate, and professional degrees. Enrollment: 398.

Library Administration. Nancy Gatlin, Director.

Library General Holdings. 18,000 volumes; 205 current periodical subscriptions.

Special Collections

The library has a collection of British theses covering the topic of vision science. There is also an oral history series by pioneers in optometry.

1552
Southern College of Seventh-day Adventists
McKee Library
P.O. Box 629
Collegedale, Tennessee 37315

Telephone. (615) 238-2788

Institutional Description. The privately supported Christian college was founded in 1892 as Graysville Academy. Now a four-year liberal arts college, it is affiliated with the Seventh-day Adventist Church. Enrollment: 1,275.

Library Administration. Peg Bennett, Director of Libraries; Patricia Morrison, Public Services and Special Collections/Rare Books Librarian.

Library General Holdings. 93,199 books; 1,000 periodical subscriptions; 113 microforms; 2,550 audiovisual materials.

Special Collections

Seventh-day Adventists Collection. Consists of material by and about Seventh-day Adventists; includes 9,804 volumes 837 bound journals, 569 audiocassettes, 2,105 microcards, 3,625 microfiche, 77 microfilms, and 253 slides.

Rare Book Collections

Vernon Thomas Memorial Collection. A collection on Abraham Lincoln and the Civil War consisting of books, letters, manuscripts, periodicals, newspapers, pamphlets, pictures, maps, paintings, and artifacts; includes 3,180 volumes and 340 bound periodicals.

1553
State Technical Institute at Memphis
George E. Freeman Library
5983 Macon Cove
Memphis, Tennessee 38134

Telephone. (901) 377-4106

Institutional Description. The privately supported junior college was founded in 1963. Enrollment: 4,328.

Library Administration. Rosa S. Burnett, Director of Library.

Library General Holdings. 40,000 volumes; 400 current periodical and newspaper subscriptions; 15,000 microforms; 4,000 other learning materials.

Special Collections

Morris Collection. This collection contains books and audiovisual materials on oral and written communications.

Tennessee Collection. Begun in early 1987, this collection consists of materials on and about Tennessee and Tennesseans.

Computers and Computer Language. This collection has been developed at the request and suggestion of faculty and students.

1554
Tennessee State University
Martha M. Brown-Lois H. Daniel Library
3500 John Merritt Boulevard
Nashville, Tennessee 37203

Telephone. (615) 320-3131

Institutional Description. The publicly supported state university grew from the A & I State Normal School founded in 1912. Enrollment: 7,006.

Library Administration. Evelyn Fencher, Director.

Library General Holdings. 430,000 volumes; 1,255 periodical subscriptions; 132,000 microforms; 33,250 government documents. The Downtown Library, established in the early 1960s as the University of Tennessee Library, became a branch of the Main campus library concurrently with the merger of the two Universities.

Special Collections

Among the special collections of the library are the **McKissack Architectural Designs Collection,** the **Thomas E. Poag Papers,** and the **Tennessee State University Historical Documents Collection.**

1555
Tennessee Technological University
Jere Whitson Memorial Library
North Dixie Avenue
Cookeville, Tennessee 38505

Telephone. (615) 528-3101

Institutional Description. The publicly supported university was founded in 1915. Begun as a technological college, it has grown into a multi-purpose university. Enrollment: 7,188.

Library Administration. Winston A. Walden, Director, Library Services.

Library General Holdings. 900,000 items including 425,000 microforms; 3,000 serial publications; 52 newspapers.

Special Collections

In addition to supporting the diversified curriculum of this technological university, the library maintains the

Joe L. Evins Collection.

1556
Tennessee Temple University
Cierpke Memorial Library
1815 Union Avenue
Chattanooga, Tennessee 37404

Telephone. (615) 698-6021

Institutional Description. The privately supported Christian university is divided into three divisions: The Bible and Christian Ministries Division; The Arts and Sciences Division; and The Theological Seminary. It is affiliated with the Independent Baptist Church. Enrollment: 1,888.

Library Administration. Sarah Patterson, Director of Library Services.

Library General Holdings. 138,500 volumes; 1,040 periodicals.

Special Collections

Children's Visual Collection. Provides material for child evangelism.

Education Center. Contains materials and textbooks especially for students in elementary and secondary education.

1557
Tennessee Wesleyan College
Merner-Pfeiffer Library
P.O. Box 40
Athens, Tennessee 37303

Telephone. (615) 745-7504

Institutional Description. The privately supported liberal arts college was founded in 1857 by Methodists and is now affiliated with the United Methodist Church. It grants baccalaureate degrees. Enrollment: 376.

Library Administration. Louise I. Harms, Director.

Library General Holdings. 72,000 volumes; 278 current periodical subscriptions; 3,700 microforms; 10,100 audiovisual aids.

Special Collections

Methodist Historical Collection. Contains 1,765 volumes from mid-eighteenth century to the present on regional and national history of Methodism dealing primarily with the Holston Conference.

Mattox Papers. Includes correspondence and other personal papers of a prominent East Tennessee family dating around 1650.

Bolton Papers. A collection of memoirs and personal papers of the historian and college alumnus, David A. Bolton.

1558
Trevecca Nazarene College
Mackey Library
333 Murfreesboro Road
Nashville, Tennessee 37203

Telephone. (615) 248-1200

Institutional Description. The privately supported liberal arts and teachers college was founded in 1901. It is affiliated with the Church of the Nazarene. Enrollment: 1,058.

Library Administration. E. Ray Kohser Thrasher, Director of Library Services.

Library General Holdings. 182,115 accessions.

Special Collections

The library houses a curriculum library, the **College Archives,** and a collection of materials relating to the Church of the Nazarene.

1559
Tusculum College
Carnegie Library
Box 5087
Greenville, Tennessee 37743

Telephone. (615) 638-1111

Institutional Description. The privately supported four-year liberal arts college was founded in 1794. It is affiliated with the United Presbyterian Church. Enrollment: 649.

Library Administration. Cleo Treadway, Director of Library Services.

Library General Holdings. 155,000 volumes (includes microforms); 900 periodical titles.

Special Collections

The Marion C. Edens Special Collection Library house three special collections—The Charles Coffin Collection, the Andrew Johnson Collection, and the College Archives.

Charles Coffin Collection. Of this collection, 2,000 volumes are from the original college library of 1794-1827. As a sizeable collection from a post-Revolutionary frontier college, this collection is a unique resource for scholars of eighteenth-century history. The Coffin collection includes sixteenth-, seventeenth-, and eighteenth-century imprints from renowned European publishing houses and from the early American colonial presses.

Andrew Johnson Collection. Includes books, papers, and memorabilia of the seventeenth President of the United States. This collection was presented to the College by Mrs. Margaret Johnson Patterson Bartlett, great-granddaughter of President Andrew Johnson.

College Archives. The Archives contain documents relating to the history of Tusculum College since its founding in 1794. Most treasured among these items are the original handwritten charter of Tusculum and Greeneville Colleges and the catalogue published in 1846.

1560
Union University
Emma Waters Summar Library
Highway 45 By-Pass
Jackson, Tennessee 38305

Telephone. (901) 668-1818

Institutional Description. The privately supported liberal arts university was founded in 1825. It is affiliated with the Southern Baptist Church. Enrollment: 1,325.

Library Administration. Harold L. Bass, Librarian.

Library General Holdings. 93,500 volumes; 755 current periodical subscriptions; 11,000 microforms.

Special Collections

Special collections of the library include the **Baptist History Collection** which includes rare books; the **Bateman Collection,** and the **Robert G. Lee Library.**

1561
University of Tennessee at Chattanooga
Library
615 McCallie Avenue
Chattanooga, Tennessee 37402

Telephone. (615) 755-4141

Institutional Description. The publicly supported branch of the University of Tennessee was founded in 1886. It grants baccalaureate and master's degrees. Enrollment: 6,485.

Library Administration. Joseph A. Jackson, Dean of Libraries.

Library General Holdings. 359,000 volumes; 3,020 current periodical subscriptions; 777,000 microforms.

Special Collections

The library's special collections include the **Civil War History Collection** and a local manuscripts collection.

1562
University of Tennessee at Knoxville
John C. Hodges Library
1015 Volunteer Boulevard
Knoxville, Tennessee 37996

Telephone. (615) 974-4127

Institutional Description. The publicly supported university was founded in 1794, and is one of four campuses of the University of Tennessee System. Enrollment: 22,-231.

Library Administration. Donald R. Hunt, Dean of Libraries; James Lloyd, Special Collections and Rare Books Librarian. Special collections are housed in the James D. Hoskins Library.

Library General Holdings. 1,585,250 volumes; numerous pamphlets, periodicals, microforms, and sound recordings.

Special Collections

Special Collections, located in the Hoskins Library, is the repository for rare books, manuscripts, the University Archives, and other unusual items of non-standard format (rare maps, prints, historical emphemera).

University Archives. The Archives house published materials issued by the University, its faculty, and student body. Among the publications are catalogs, student newspapers, yearbooks, alumni publications, miscellaneous publications, programs, and various reports of colleges, departments, and other official agencies. Manuscript files, also a part of the Archives, are the records generated by the many units, offices, and bureaus of the University.

Manuscripts. The manuscript collections, which provide resources for original research, number more than 3,000,000 pieces. They include private papers, literary manuscripts, business records, political files, and historical records mostly relating to Tennessee and the Southeast. The World War II Collection is the fastest-growing manuscript group and is expected to become a source of national research interest. There is also a strong group of international papers in the field of radiation research. The largest manuscript set is the Estes Kefauver Collection which amounts to over 59,000 pounds of papers, published items, and memorabilia. There is a permanent exhibit connected with the Kefauver Collection featuring the late Tennessee Senator's office from the Senate Office Building in Washington reassembled with his furnishings and mementoes.

Other manuscript groups are important parts of the library's holdings in primary materials. Documents in the hand of Presidents who hailed from Tennessee (Andrew Jackson, James K. Polk, and Andrew Johnson) may be found here, as may original papers written by founding fathers John Sevier, William Blount, William Cocke, and James Robertson. All stages in the development of the state and region are represented in the manuscript division. The files of historian J.G.M. Ramsey, of educators P.P. Claxton and John Eaton, of politicians Howard Baker and Herbert Walters, of community leader O.P. Temple, of diplomat Horace Maynard, of jurist Sue K. Hicks, of journalist Don Whitehead, of film director Clarence Brown, and of Tennesseans from a diversity of other professions lend support to scholarly study and historical investigation.

Preservation Collection. This collection is a closed stack facility that contains brittle and fragile books, periodicals (mostly nineteenth-century) that are at risk and for which other formats either do not exist or are unacceptable, and volumes that are not rare but require more secure storage to ensure their preservation.

Rare Book Collections

The rare book collection, amounting to some 30,000 volumes, includes books dating from 1481 to the present. Outstanding collection strengths are in the fields of Tennesseana (historical, biographical, literary, political, and descriptive works), North American Indians, nineteenth-century American literature (with many important first editions), early voyages and travels, and early imprints (examples from notable presses). There are also definitive collections of the works of William Congreve and Jane Austen, as well a growing collection of eighteenth- and nineteenth-century shape note song books.

Early Imprints Collections. In addition to examples from Tennessee's early presses, this collection includes a 1481 edition of Cicero's *De Officiis* and another incunabulum, *Biblia Integra,* printed in 1495. The incunabula are accompanied by an array of sixteenth- and seventeenth-century imprints from the presses of continental Europe and Great Britain. The library possesses one of the best collections of Tennessee imprints to be found. Aside from the Roulstone imprints mentioned below, there are many rare pieces which are unique or are now known to exist in only one or two other locations.

Early Voyages and Travels. This collection includes the 1814 edition of *History of the Expedition Under the Command of Captains Lewis and Clark;* a facsimile of *The Log of H.M.S. Bounty;* the 1712 edition of Captain Cooke's *A Voyage to the South Sea; Travels to the Westward of the Allegany Mountains* (1805) by André Michaux; John Bradbury's *Travels in the Interior of America* (1819); and *Early Travels in the Tennessee Country* by Samuel Cole Williams.

Nineteenth-Century American Literature. Prominent in this collection are first editions of works of America's most illustrious authors. Among these are representative titles of Harriet Beecher Stowe, Nathaniel Hawthorne, James Fenimore Cooper, Walt Whitman, Washington Irving, Mark Twain, Henry James, Herman Melville, and many others.

North American Indian Collection. Noteworthy in this collection are a file of *The Cherokee Phoenix,* an Indian newspaper printed in both Cherokee characters and English; a complete run of *The Cherokee Almanac;* first editions of James Adair's *History of the American Indians* and the *Memoirs of Lieut. Henry Timberlake;* compilations of early laws of the Cherokees; books of the Bible, songsters, and other works printed in the Cherokee language; and original color prints of a number of Cherokee chieftains.

Tennessee Collection. Includes the Roulstone imprints, rare and unique examples from the press of Tennessee's first printer, George Roulstone; first printings of the historical treatises of John Haywood and J.G.M. Ramsey; the earliest issues of the Davy Crockett Almanacs; early maps of the Southwest Territory and the infant state of Tennessee; the first compilations of the Acts and Journals of the Tennessee legislature; and the original editions of works produced by the state's leading literary figures.

1563
University of Tennessee at Martin
Paul Meek Library
Martin, Tennessee 38238

Telephone. (901) 587-7000

Institutional Description. The publicly supported branch of the University of Tennessee was founded in 1927 as a junior college. Now offering a wide variety and level of programs, it grants associate, baccalaureate, and master's degrees. Enrollment: 5,191.

Library Administration. Joel E. Stowers, Director.

Library General Holdings. 260,000 volumes; 1,700 periodical subscriptions; 86,000 government documents; 285,000 microforms.

Special Collections

The library houses the **Holland McCombs Papers** and a special collection of books primarily on Tennessee and works by and about Tennesseans.

1564
University of Tennessee at Memphis
Health Sciences Library
800 Madison Avenue
Memphis, Tennessee 38163

Telephone. (902) 528-5500

Institutional Description. The publicly supported branch of the University of Tennessee was founded in 1851. It offers programs in medicine, dentistry, basic medical sciences, nursing, pharmacy, and allied health. Enrollment: 1,999.

Library Administration. Jess A. Martin, Director.

Library General Holdings. 152,000 volumes; 2,000 periodical subscriptions.

Special Collections

The collection of the Health Sciences Library is specialized in that it reflects the curriculum of the University. The **Wallace Collection** contains works by university faculty.

1565
University of the South
Jessie Ball duPont Library
Sewanee, Tennessee 37375

Telephone. (615) 598-5931

Institutional Description. The privately supported liberal arts and theology university was founded in 1857 as a Christian college for men. Coeducational programs began in 1969. It is affiliated with the Episcopal Church. Enrollment: 1,162.

Library Administration. David Arthur Kearley, University Librarian; Melinda Anne Armour, Head of Archives and Special Collections.

Library General Holdings. 370,000 volumes; 2,000 journal subscriptions; 103,000 microforms; 113,100 government documents; 5,550 audiovisual materials.

Special Collections

The Special Collections Department includes a large collection of **Sewaneeana** and materials written by Sewanee authors, along with 8,000 rare books from almost all periods in the history of printing. The rare book collection is particularly strong in Southern literature, fine editions of early theological works, and modern first editions. The **University Archives** provides a collection of over one-half million documents relating to the history of the University, the history of the South, and the development of the Episcopal Church in the South.

1566
Vanderbilt University
Jean and Alexander Heard Library
21st Avenue and West End Avenue
Nashville, Tennessee 37240

Telephone. (615) 322-7100

Institutional Description. The privately supported university was founded in 1873 under the auspices of the Methodist Episcopal Church, South. Now independent, it includes the George Peabody College for Teachers, 8 other colleges and schools, and branch campuses in 7 foreign countries. Enrollment: 8,438.

Library Administration. Malcolm Getz, Director.

Library General Holdings. 1,600,000 volumes; 17,800 periodicals; 1,422,000 microforms; 122,100 audiovisual materials. The Library consists of seven divisions and two special units.

Special Collections

Special Collections include the **Wills Collection of Fugitive and Agrarian Writers;** collections in Southern politics and Tennessee history; the **W.T. Bandy Center for Baudelaire Studies;** and the Vanderbilt University Archives.

A significant collection in astronomy is housed off-campus in the A.J. Dyer Observatory. The Divinity Library houses a collection of 132,000 volumes in Biblical studies, church history, theology, ethics, worship, preaching, pastoral care, and world religions.

Texas

1567
Abilene Christian University
Herman and Margaret Brown Library
ACU Station, Box 8177
Abilene, Texas 79699

Telephone. (915) 674-2344

Institutional Description. The privately supported university is affiliated with the Church of Christ. It was founded in 1906. Enrollment: 4,505.

Library Administration. Marsha Harper, Acting Library Director; Erma Jean Loveland, Special Services Librarian.

Library General Holdings. 315,524 volumes; 1,668 periodical subscriptions; 12 newspaper subscriptions; 378,742 microforms; 21,335 audiovisual materials; 57,164 documents.

Special Collections

Honorable Omar Burleson Congressional Library. Contains congressional correspondence, papers, speeches, scrapbooks, and memorabilia; Congressman Burleson represented the Texas 17th District in the U.S. House of Representatives, 1947-1979.

Books of Yesteryear. A collection of ornate bindings, fiction, turn-of-the century books; representative titles include Horatio Alger and Little Colonel series.

Early Day School Books. Includes selected textbooks from the late 1800s to early 1900s.

Marshall Jackson Collection. A collection of southwestern and genealogical materials.

Orlando Clayton Lambert Collection. Includes books by Lambert and other books and bibliographic imprints which formed the bases for his writings on Catholicism.

Burnya Mae Moore Cookbook Collection. Includes rare, ephemeral, specialized, and encyclopedia cookbooks collected during Moore's 40 years on Abilene Christian University's Home Economics faculty.

Popular Culture Collection. Includes the complete set of works by Edgar Rice Burroughs, Charlie Chan, Earl Derr Biggers, and Dennis Lynds.

Rare Book Collections

Bible Collection. Contains Bibles in various languages from twentieth century versions to early and rare editions, including original editions of the Vinegar Bible (1717); the Geneva (Breeches) Bible (1586); the Bishop's Bible (1575); the Cypriano De Valera revision of 1602.

Jack and Mable Burford Tape Collection. Records of campus events from the 1950s to 1980s.

Price Billingsley Papers. The papers of the early Texas minister includes nearly 700 journals written over a span of 60 years.

Alexander Campbell Letters. Includes 8 letters from Campbell, an early Restoration minister, to Selina Campbell, 1829-1830.

Robert Donner Collection. Deals with conservative American politics and includes pamphlets, periodicals, and leaflets.

Herald of Truth Archives. Tapes and films of weekly evangelistic radio and television programs from 1952 to present; some have printed copies.

John Allen Gano Papers. The papers of the Kentucky early-day preacher covering the period 1851-1901.

Don H. Mooris Papers. The presidential file of the Abilene Christian University President, 1940-1969.

Walter and Nelda Robbins Railroad Collection. A specialized collection of books, periodicals, timetables, passes, clippings, and memorabilia.

Jess Parker Sewell Collection. Papers, photographs, and books of the Abilene Christian University President, 1912-1924.

G. Dallas Smith and John T. Smith Sermon Notes. The sermon notes of the brothers, both ministers.

Lawrence L. Smith Papers. Abilene Christian University historical materials, oral history interviews, photographs, sermons, and notes.

Austin Taylor Hymnbook Collection. Includes Taylor's compilations, Firm Foundation and Gospel Advocate hymnbooks.

Tillet Sidney Teddlie Manuscripts. Consists of a folio book of 26 original song manuscripts by the song writer.

Thorp Spring Christian College Collection. Consists of interviews, albums, and notebooks for the period 1910-1930.

Walt Whitman Collection. Contains 58 pieces including letter (1914), Fellowship Papers, newspapers (1819-1915), and portraits.

1568
Angelo State University
University Library
2601 West Avenue
San Angelo, Texas 76909

Telephone. (915) 942-2131
Institutional Description. The publicly supported state liberal arts university was founded in 1928. Enrollment: 5,134.
Library Administration. Joe B. Lee, Head Librarian.
Library General Holdings. 220,000 volumes; 2,325 journal subscriptions; 161,000 government documents; 457,000 microforms.

Special Collections

The library has collections to support programs in the arts, sciences, teacher education, nursing education, and business administration as well as those programs designed to meet entrance requirements for professional schools of dentistry, engineering, law, and medicine.

1569
Arlington Baptist College
Earl K. Oldham Library
3001 West Division
Arlington, Texas 76012

Telephone. (817) 461-8741
Institutional Description. The privately supported professional Bible college was founded in 1939. It grants baccalaureate degrees, and is affiliated with the Baptist Church. Enrollment: 210.
Library Administration. Sandra Tanner, Librarian.
Library General Holdings. 22,000 volumes; 185 periodical titles; 13,000 microforms.

Special Collections

The library's special collections include the **J. Frank Norris Collection** and the **Heritage Collection** which includes items of historical importance to the Arlington Baptist College.

1570
Austin College
Abell Library Center
900 North Grand Avenue
Sherman, Texas 75090

Telephone. (214) 892-9101
Institutional Description. The privately supported liberal arts college was founded in 1849. It is affiliated with the Presbyterian Church (U.S.A.). Enrollment: 1,203.
Library Administration. Imogene Wyatt Gibson, College Librarian.
Library General Holdings. 153,000 volumes; 775 current periodical subscriptions; 27,000 government documents; 95,000 microforms.

Special Collections

Special collections of the library include the **Berzunza Collection** of materials relating to Alexander the Great; the **Pate Collection** of Texana; and the **Hoard Collection** of Texana.

1571
Austin Presbyterian Theological Seminary
Stitt Library
100 East 27th Street
Austin, Texas 78705

Telephone. (512) 472-6736
Institutional Description. The privately supported theological seminary offers graduate programs only. It is affiliated with the Presbyterian Church, U.S.A. Enrollment: 190.
Library Administration. Calvin C. Klemt, Librarian.
Library General Holdings. 120,000 volumes; 486 current periodicals; 2,150 microfilm reels.

Special Collections

The library is particularly strong in Biblical studies, Biblical archaeology, patristics, the continental Reformation, Calvin, and Presbyterianism.

1572
Baylor College of Dentistry
Library
3302 Gaston Avenue
Dallas, Texas 75246

Telephone. (214) 828-8100
Institutional Description. The privately supported professional college offers programs on the graduate level only. It was founded in 1905. Enrollment: 568.
Library Administration. G. Melvin Hipps, Executive Director.
Library General Holdings. 75,000 volumes; 700 journal titles.

Special Collections

The **Ruth and Lyle Sellars Medical Collection** is housed in the library as well as a collection of rare books with emphasis in otolaryngology.

1573
Baylor College of Medicine
Houston Academy of Medicine-Texas Medical Center Library
One Baylor Plaza
Houston, Texas 77030

Telephone. (713) 797-1230

Institutional Description. The privately supported professional college was founded in 1900. It offers programs on the graduate level only. Enrollment: 834.

Library Administration. Richard A. Lyders, Executive Director; Elizabeth White, Director of Historical Research Center; Dawn Buck, Collection Development.

Library General Holdings. 215,000 volumes; 3,130 current journals.

Special Collections

The library contains volumes dating back to the sixteenth century and is one of the oldest medical libraries in the state of Texas. Special collections include the **Burbank Collection** on arthritis, rheumatism, and gout; the **Mading Collection** on public health; and the **McGovern Collection** on the history of medicine.

1574
Baylor University
Moody Memorial Library
Waco, Texas 76798

Telephone. (817) 755-1011

Institutional Description. The privately supported Christian university consists of 7 colleges and schools located in Waco and Dallas. It is affiliated with the Southern Baptist Church. Enrollment: 10,983.

Library Administration. Jonathan A. Lindsey, Coordinator of Library Affairs.

Library General Holdings. 1,219,000 volumes; 5,755 current periodical subscriptions; 1,136,000 government documents; 873,000 microforms.

Special Collections

Significant special collections are the **Armstrong Brown Library;** the **Texas Collection** which contains many rare volumes and items pertaining to the legal history of Texas; and the **Poague Legislative Library.** The **Peat, Marwick, Mitchell & Co. Tax Library** in the Hankamer School of Business contains a complete listing of all reference materials needed for effective tax research, including all of the major tax services and case law reference materials.

The library's holdings in religion number over 250,000 volumes.

1575
Bee County College
Grady C. Hogue Learning Resources Center
3800 Charco Road
Beeville, Texas 78102

Telephone. (512) 358-3130

Institutional Description. The publicly supported junior college offers the first two years of college degree programs as well as vocational, technical, and general continuing education courses. Enrollment: 1,758.

Library Administration. Marvin Southworth, Learning Resources Center Director.

Library General Holdings. 42,698 volumes; 374 periodical subscriptions; 3,069 microfilm reels; 1,026 disk recordings; 258 videocassettes; 990 other audiovisual materials.

Rare Book Collections

Texas Collection. Includes approximately 900 titles ranging from publication dates as early as 1833 to the present.

1576
Bishop College
Zale Library
3837 Simpson-Stuart Road
Dallas, Texas 75241

Telephone. (214) 372-8000

Institutional Description. The privately supported liberal arts college was founded in 1881. It is affiliated with the American Baptist Church. Enrollment: 1,136.

Library Administration. Francier E. Austin, Director.

Library General Holdings. 181,000 volumes; 450 current periodical subscriptions.

Special Collections

The library houses the **C.A.W. Clark Collection** and the **E.C. Estell Collection** which contain books, papers, and sermons on preaching and on the Black religious experience. The **M.J. Banks Collection** consists of books on the Black experience in Texas.

1577
Corpus Christi State University
University Library
6300 Ocean Drive
Corpus Christie, Texas 78412

Telephone. (512) 991-6810

Institutional Description. The publicly supported state university offers upper level and graduate programs only. Enrollment: 3,885.

Library Administration. Richard L. O'Keeffe, University Librarian; Paul Medley, Special Collections Librarian and Archivist.

Library General Holdings. 284,000 bound volumes; 1,620 current periodical and newspaper subscriptions; 480,000 microforms; 34,840 audiovisual materials.

Special Collections

Daniel E. Kilgore Collection. A collection of 7,500 books and 3,500 documents with emphasis upon southern Texas and northern Mexico.

Sanders Key Stroud II Collection. Includes 155 books in fine bindings, many bound by Stroud; consists of Texana literature of the seventeenth to nineteenth centuries and world history.

Turcotte Collection. Includes court trial documents, especially depositions, from the trials concerning the deposition of the estate of Sarita Kennedy East during the 1960s and 1970s.

Veracruz Archives. 16mm microfilm documents covering the period 1578 to the mid-nineteenth century; film of the documents in the Archivo Notarial de Jalapa and Archivo Paroquial de Cordoba, collectively known as the Veracruz Archives.

Vernon Smylie Collection. Correspondence, scrapbooks, clippings, photographs, and notebooks of information on historical markers in Texas.

Dee Woods Papers. Includes literary items of the chairperson of the annual Southwest Writers Conference: correspondence, scrapbooks, clippings, and files.

DeWitt Hale Papers. Files from Mr. Hale's office while he was in the Texas legislature.

UCC/CCSU Archives. Business and academic records of the University of Corpus Christi 1946-1971, papers covering the transition period 1971-1973, and records of Texas A&I University at Corpus Christi (later Corpus Christi State University) 1973-present.

Isabel and Houston Harte Collection. Non-fiction Texana, with emphasis upon West Texas; includes a number of limited editions with presentation notes to Harte; special emphasis on Texas newspaper history and political history, including Sam Rayburn, Maury Maverick, and Lyndon B. Johnson.

Blucher Papers. Early Nueces County and South Texas maps and survey field notes by Felix von Blucher while he was county surveyor of Nueces County (late nineteenth and early twentieth century).

Hector P. Garcia Papers. Material relating to Dr. Garcia's membership on the Civil Rights Commission of the United Nations and the American G.I. Forum.

William M. Neyland Collection. Personal papers of William M. Neyland, long-time local real estate man, including his work getting streets and highways built in Corpus Christi and south Texas.

Frantz Collection. Includes 550 volumes plus other material with primary focus on Texas; donated by Joe B. Frantz.

Texas/Southwest Collection. Represents the first collection of Texana material owned by the University Library; new material added as acquired.

James Allen Wood Collection. Includes government and private studies and reports concerning water resources in Texas (with emphasis upon south Texas).

Mrs. Ben Christian Papers. Mostly newspaper clippings of events in Corpus Christi and south Texas dating from the early 1960s to 1985.

1578
Criswell College
Wallace Library
525 North Ervay
Dallas, Texas 75201

Telephone. (214) 954-0012

Institutional Description. The privately supported professional Bible college is affiliated with the Baptist Church. It grants associate, baccalaureate, and master's degrees in theology. Enrollment: 283.

Library Administration. John A. Burns, Librarian.

Library General Holdings. 67,000 volumes.

Special Collections

The emphasis of the library's collection is in Biblical studies within the interests of the First Baptist Church of Dallas and the Baptist General Convention of Texas.

1579
Dallas Baptist University
Vance Memorial Library
7777 West Kiest Boulevard
Dallas, Texas 75211

Telephone. (214) 331-8311

Institutional Description. The privately supported liberal arts university was founded in 1898. It is affiliated with the Southern Baptist Church. Enrollment: 1,393.

Library Administration. Margaret A. Gibbs, Director.

Library General Holdings. 270,000 book; 432 current periodical subscriptions.

Special Collections

Special collections include the **Lewis E. and Barbara Harris Bain Memorial Library** and the **Curriculum Collection.**

1580
Dallas Theological Seminary
Mosher Library
3909 Swiss Avenue
Dallas, Texas 75204

Telephone. (214) 824-3094

Institutional Description. The privately supported nondenominational theological seminary for men was founded in 1924. Its emphasis is Evangelical Protestant. Enrollment: 1,032.

Library Administration. Robert D. Ibach, Director.

Library General Holdings. 109,250 volumes; 1,000 current periodical subscriptions; 19,650 microforms.

Special Collections

The library supports the Seminary's programs with resources in the field of theology and related subjects.

1581
East Texas Baptist University
Mamye Jarrett Learning Center
1209 North Grove Street
Marshall, Texas 75670

Telephone. (214) 935-7963

Institutional Description. The privately supported liberal arts university views, as one of its primary objectives, the preparation of teachers for elementary and secondary schools. It is affiliated with the Southern Baptist church. Enrollment: 594.

Library Administration. E.M. Adams, Jr., Director.

Library General Holdings. 91,000 volumes; 610 periodical subscriptions; 6,500 microforms.

Special Collections

Special collection holdings include the **Cope Texana Collection** which includes first editions and rare books; the county and municipal histories of Texas; the **Lentz Collection** of unpublished materials detailing the local history of Harrison County and Marshall, Texas.

1582
East Texas State University
James G. Gee Library
ETSU Station
Commerce, Texas 75428

Telephone. (214) 886-5000

Institutional Description. The publicly supported state university is composed of the Colleges of Business and Technology, Education, Arts and Sciences, and the Graduate School. Enrollment: 5,336.

Library Administration. Mary E. Cook, Director.

Library General Holdings. 934,000 volumes; 3,000 current periodicals; 68 newspapers; 130,000 government documents.

Special Collections

The library's collections support the curriculum which provides a basic foundation for the general education of all undergraduate students as well as further specialized study in a wide range of academic, artistic, preprofessional, and professional fields. Major areas are in agricultural sciences, art, Bible, biological sciences, chemistry, communication and theatre, computer science, earth sciences, history, journalism and graphic arts, literature and languages, mathematics, music, physics, political science, sociology, and anthropology.

1583
East Texas State University at Texarkana
Palmer Memorial Library
2600 North Robinson Road
Texarkana, Texas 75501

Telephone. (214) 838-6514

Institutional Description. The publicly supported branch of East Texas State University was founded in 1971. It offers upper level and graduate programs only. Enrollment: 757.

Library Administration. Arlene Kyle, Librarian.

Library General Holdings. 153,000 volumes; 1,050 periodicals; 1,380,000 microforms.

Special Collections

Specialized collections have emphases in business, education, and nursing.

1584
The Episcopal Theological Seminary of the Southwest
Seminary Library
P.O. Box 2247
Austin, Texas 78768

Telephone. (512) 472-4134

Institutional Description. The privately supported institution is a graduate-level theological seminary offering preparation of students for the Christian ministry. Enrollment: 66.

Library Administration. Harold H. Booher, Librarian.

Library General Holdings. 90,000 volumes.

Special Collections

The library of the Seminary includes subjects typical of those required to support the work of the student and faculty of a theological seminary.

1585
Hardin-Simmons University
Rupert and Pauline Richardson Library
2200 Hickory
Abilene, Texas 79698

Telephone. (915) 677-7281

Institutional Description. The privately supported university was founded in 1891. It is affiliated with the Southern Baptist Church. Enrollment: 1,745.

Library Administration. Joe F. Dahlstrom, Director.

Library General Holdings. 175,000 volumes; 1,100 current periodical subscriptions; 192,000 government documents; 14,500 microforms.

Special Collections

The **Rupert N. Richardson Research Center for the Southwest** houses the R.C. Crane Collection of 5,000 books, letters, and ephemera bearing chiefly on Texas and the Southwest. The library also maintains a collection of 350 books printed and/or designed by El Paso printer Carl Hertzog and a collection of 2,000 books of rare Texana, a large part of the personal library of the late historian Walter Prescott Webb. The **Hoyt Ford Memorial Collection** houses materials relating to life adjustment, counseling, and psychotherapy.

There is a small collection of other rare materials housed in the Betty Woods Rare and Fine Books Room. The **Simmons Collection** consists of several hundred books presented by the family of James B. Simmons, for whom the institution was named. These books constitute the original school library and represent nineteenth-century classics in religion, literature, and history. The library also has a special collection on Thomas Wolfe.

1586
Hill College
Confederate Research Center
P.O. Box 619
Hillsboro, Texas 76645

Telephone. (817) 582-2555

Institutional Description. The publicly supported junior college was founded in 1962. Enrollment: 984.

Library Administration. Eileen Haigh, College Librarian; Harold B. Simpson, Library Director.

Library General Holdings. 30,000 volumes.

Special Collections

American Civil War Collection. This collection includes 3,000 bound volumes on the Civil War with heavy emphasis on the Confederacy. Topics include Hood's Texas Brigade (CSA), Robert E. Lee, Confederate biographies, Civil War battles, and Abraham Lincoln.

Weaponry Collection. Consists of 300 bound volumes on all phases of weaponry—hand guns, shoulder weapons, edged weapons, artillery, ammunition.

1587
Houston Baptist University
Moody Library
7502 Fondren Road
Houston, Texas 77074

Telephone. (713) 774-7661

Institutional Description. The privately supported liberal arts institution was founded by the Baptist General Convention of Texas in 1960. Enrollment: 2,962.

Library Administration. Jon M. Suter, Director of Libraries.

Library General Holdings. 154,000 volumes; 3,300 microfilm reels; 259,000 microfiche; 2,407 phonodiscs; 1,-085 pieces of other media.

Special Collections

The Moody Library has specialized collections on theology (all religions; special emphasis on Southern Baptists); British History and Literature (heavy emphasis on Victorian period); business and computer science; nursing; and curriculum materials.

Rare Book Collections

Rare Book Collections. The rare book collections include the Hicks Collection of Texas and Southwestern History and Politics (first editions and newspapers); Palmer Bradley Collection of Military History (first editions); Robert Bradley Collection of Victorian Literature (first editions plus secondary works); Albert Sidney Johnston Camp of Sons of the Confederate Veterans Collection on the Civil War and Southern History (first editions); and a special collection of miscellaneous first editions, autographed copies, and university-related items.

1588
Howard Payne University
Walker Library
1000 Fisk Avenue
Brownwood, Texas 76801

Telephone. (915) 646-2502

Institutional Description. The privately supported liberal arts university was founded in 1889. It is affiliated with the Southern Baptist Church. Enrollment: 730.

Library Administration. Kim Ross, Head Librarian.

Library General Holdings. 120,000 volumes; 725 current periodical titles; 18,000 government documents.

Special Collections

The library maintains the **Burress Genealogical Collection.**

1589
Huston-Tillotson College
Downs-Jones Library
1820 East Eighth Street
Austin, Texas 78702

Telephone. (512) 476-7421

Institutional Description. The privately supported liberal arts college was founded in 1875 as Tillotson Collegiate and Normal Institute; in 1952 it merged with Samuel Huston College (founded in 1876). It is affiliated with the United Methodist Church and the United Church of Christ. Enrollment: 498.

Library Administration. Patricia Quarterman, College Librarian.

Library General Holdings. 78,000 volumes; 295 current periodical subscriptions.

Special Collections

A curriculum library for the use of the Teacher Education Department is housed in the library. This collection includes textbooks adopted by the state of Texas.

1590
Incarnate Word College
St. Pius X Library
4301 Broadway
San Antonio, Texas 78209

Telephone. (512) 828-1261

Institutional Description. The privately supported liberal arts college was founded in 1881. It is affiliated with the Roman Catholic Church. Enrollment: 1,050.

Library Administration. Mendell Morgan, Director of Library Services.

Library General Holdings. 165,000 volumes; 600 current periodical subscriptions; 23,000 microforms; 37,000 audiovisual materials.

Special Collections

The **Special Collection Room** houses first or limited editions and rare books, including items from the Brackenridge Estate. The **Children's and Young People's Collection** includes a wide variety of children's books to support reading requirements for courses in children's literature. The **Joan Cahill Steves Collection** in religious studies is also maintained. The **Texana Room** contains a selection of books on or about Texas and books by Texas authors. The **Loch Collection** and the **Rosengren Collection** are housed here.

1591
Jacksonville College
Weatherby Memorial Library
500 Pine Street
Jacksonville, Texas 75766

Telephone. (214) 586-2518

Institutional Description. Jacksonville College is a two-year junior college founded by members of the Baptist Church in 1899. It functioned as a senior college until 1918 when it was reorganized on the junior college level. Enrollment: 221.

Library Administration. Anabelle Anderson, Librarian.

Library General Holdings. 22,000 volumes; 183 periodical subscriptions.

Special Collections

The **Historical Records of the Baptist Missionary Association** contains minutes of local, state, and national associations.

1592
Jarvis Christian College
Olin Library
U.S. Highway 80
P.O. Drawer G
Hawkins, Texas 75765

Telephone. (214) 769-2174

Institutional Description. The privately supported liberal arts college, founded in 1912, is an affiliate of Texas Christian University; it awards associate and baccalaureate degrees. The college is also affiliated with the Christian Church (Disciples of Christ). Enrollment: 467.

Library Administration. Kay Varnado, Librarian.

Library General Holdings. 58,000 volumes; 475 current periodical subscriptions.

Special Collections

The library has a special collection of 1,500 volumes by and about Black people; and a collection of 2,500 volumes in young adult literature and career information.

1593
Kilgore College
Randolph C. Watson Library
1100 Broadway
Kilgore, Texas 75662

Telephone. (214) 984-9531

Institutional Description. Founded in 1935, Kilgore College has departed from its original junior college status to encompass university extension programs and a large police academy. Enrollment: 4,652.

Library Administration. Wade L. Pipkin, Director.

Library General Holdings. 74,000 volumes.

Special Collections

The **Adele Habenicht Book Collection** on Texas history and the **Clydene Foster Spear Collection** on literature are maintained in the library.

1594
Lamar University
Mary and John Gray Library
Lamar Station, Box 10001
Beaumont, Texas 77710

Telephone. (409) 880-7011

Institutional Description. The publicly supported liberal arts and professional state university was founded in 1923 as a junior college. It is now composed of 7 colleges and a graduate school. Enrollment: 9,804.

Library Administration. Maxine Johnston, Director of Library Services.

Library General Holdings. 800,000 volumes; 2,950 current periodical subscriptions.

Special Collections

The library maintains special collections on the subject of seventeenth- to nineteenth-century cookery; Texana; and engineering.

1595
Laredo Junior College
Harold R. Yeary Library
West End Washington Street
Laredo, Texas 78040

Telephone. (512) 722-0521

Institutional Description. Laredo Junior College was officially created in 1946 by the voting citizens of the city of Laredo. Laredo State University shares Laredo Junior College facilities. Enrollment: 4,004.

Library Administration. Mayellen Bresie, Director.

Library General Holdings. 138,000 bound volumes; 1,100 current serial subscriptions (including periodicals); 245,000 non-print titles.

Special Collections

The library maintains collections of State Adopted Textbooks, ERIC Documents, regional publications, the Laredo Archives (microfilm), and the Ft. McIntosh papers (microfilm).

1596
Laredo State University
Harold R. Yeary Library
West End Washington Street
Laredo, Texas 78040

Telephone. (512) 722-8001

Institutional Description. The publicly supported state university was founded in 1969. It offers upper division and graduate studies only. Enrollment: 509.

Library Administration. Mayellen Bresie, Director.

Library General Holdings. 148,000 bound volumes; 1,150 current serial subscriptions; 270,000 microforms; 103,000 state and federal government documents.

Special Collections

The library maintains a collection on the local history of South Texas.

1597
LeTourneau College
Margaret Estes Library
2300 South Mobberly Avenue
Longview, Texas 75607

Telephone. (214) 753-0231

Institutional Description. The privately supported liberal arts and professional college was founded in 1946 as a technical institute. In 1961, it added liberal arts curricula. It is an independent, Christian college. Enrollment: 797.

Library Administration. Paul Gray, Director of Library Services.

Library General Holdings. 96,000 volumes; 480 periodical subscriptions; 73,352 varied forms of micromaterials; 2,198 phonorecrods and tapes.

Special Collections

The special collections include memorabilia of R.G. LeTourneau, industrialist and founder of the the college; the **Abraham Lincoln Collection** of 150 volumes, including rare books about Lincoln; and the **Billy Sunday Collection** which includes a scrapbook and a Bible of the early twentieth-century evangelist.

1598
Lubbock Christian College
Moody Library
5601 West 19th Street
Lubbock, Texas 79407

Telephone. (806) 792-3221

Institutional Description. The privately supported liberal arts college was founded in 1957. It is affiliated with the Churches of Christ. Enrollment: 921.

Library Administration. Paula Gannaway and Rebecca Vickers, Librarians.

Library General Holdings. 86,000 volumes; 540 current periodical subscriptions; 51,000 microforms.

Special Collections

The library's collections support the mission of the College which is to stimulate learning, character, and citizenship in a Christian environment.

Curriculum Library. The collection serves the special

needs of students in the teacher education programs.

1599
McMurry College
Jay-Rollins Library
14th and Sayles
Abilene, Texas 79697

Telephone. (915) 692-4130

Institutional Description. The privately supported liberal arts college was founded in 1922. It is affiliated with the United Methodist Church. Enrollment: 1,116.

Library Administration. Joe W. Specht, Director.

Library General Holdings. 132,000 volumes; 460 current periodicals.

Special Collections

Special collections in the Jay-Rollins Library include the **Hunt Library of Texana and the Southwest;** the **Clement-McMurry Rare Book Collection,** and the **Archives of the Northwest Texas Conference** of the United Methodist Church.

1600
Midwestern State University
Moffett Library
3600 Taft Boulevard
Wichita Falls, Texas 76308

Telephone. (817) 692-6611

Institutional Description. The publicly supported university was founded in 1922 as a junior college, and now offers diverse programs at the Associate, Baccalaureate, and Master levels. Enrollment: 3,730.

Library Administration. Allison Breen, Collection Development.

Library General Holdings. 400,000 bound volumes, periodicals, microforms, and cassettes.

Special Collections

The Moffett Library has a specialized interest in American history and railroad books. There is a collection of approximately 100 works by James Joyce including first editions; a collection of original railroad survey maps (mainly of Texas); and local and regional historical materials.

1601
Oblate School of Theology
Library
285 Oblate Drive
San Antonio, Texas 78216

Telephone. (512) 341-1366

Institutional Description. The privately supported theological seminary prepares students for the Roman Catholic priesthood. Special attention is given to the Spanish language and Hispanic culture of the region. Enrollment: 77.

Library Administration. James W. Maney, Director.

Library General Holdings. 37,000 volumes; 260 current journals. The library is primarily in the fields of theology and religious studies.

Special Collections

The library is developing its collection in areas of the social sciences that have religious or value-related implications in philosophy, in minority and ethnic studies with emphasis on Hispanic and Mexican-American questions, and studies of the developing world.

1602
Our Lady of the Lake University of San Antonio
St. Florence Library
411 S.W. 24th Street
San Antonio, Texas 78285

Telephone. (512) 434-6711

Institutional Description. The privately supported liberal arts university was founded in 1911. It was the first Roman Catholic women's college in the South to receive regional accreditation. Now coeducational, it is affiliated with the Roman Catholic Church. Enrollment: 1,274.

Library Administration. Anna Rose Kanning, Director, Learning Resources.

Library General Holdings. 235,000 volumes.

Special Collections

Special collections include a **Texana Collection** and the **Old Spanish Missions Historical Research Library.**

1603
Pan American University
University Library
1201 West University Drive
Edinburg, Texas 78539

Telephone. (512) 381-2011

Institutional Description. The publicly supported (state) liberal arts university was founded in 1927 as the Edinburg Junior College. It now grants associate, baccalaureate, and master's degrees. Enrollment: 7,865.

Library Administration. Leslie M. Gower, Director.

Library General Holdings. 250,000 volumes; 563,365 microforms.

Special Collections

Special collection holdings include a **Mexican-American Collection** and collections on the **Lower Rio**

Grande Valley. Other holdings in special education are also housed.

1604
Paris Junior College
J.H. Newton Library
2400 Clarkville Street
Paris, Texas 75460

Telephone. (214) 785-7661

Institutional Description. Paris Junior College was established in 1924 as part of the Paris City Schools. It became independent of the school district in 1937. Enrollment: 1,736.

Library Administration. LuLane Caraway, Director.

Library General Holdings. 44,629 volumes; 268 periodical titles; 15,025 microforms; 3,479 audiovisual materials.

Special Collections

The **A.M. and Welma Aikin Regional Archives** house the papers and memorabilia of the long-time Dean of the Texas Senate, including a replica of his Austin office, and of other prominent Northeast Texans. The library also maintains a Career Information Center.

1605
Paul Quinn College
Johnson Memorial Library
1020 Elm Street
Waco, Texas 76704

Telephone. (817) 753-6415

Institutional Description. The privately supported liberal arts college was founded in 1872. It is affiliated with the African Methodist Episcopal Church, and grants baccalaureate degrees. Enrollment: 339.

Library Administration. Frank Moorer, Director.

Library General Holdings. 59,000 volumes; 55 current periodical titles; 35,000 microforms.

Special Collections

The **Ethnic Cultural Center** contains books, periodicals, photographs, sculptures, newspapers, old documents, and other memorabilia which related to the culture, history, and heritage of Black and Brown Americans with emphasis on the Black experience.

1606
Prairie View Agricultural & Mechanical University
W.R. Banks Library
P.O. Drawer 188
Prairie View, Texas 77445

Telephone. (409) 857-2625

Institutional Description. The publicly supported state liberal arts and professional university was founded in 1876. Its three aims are to train teachers, offer liberal arts and science, and provide training in agriculture, home economics, engineering, and related fields. Enrollment: 4,182.

Library Administration. Adele S. Dendy, Director of Library Services.

Library General Holdings. 260,000 volumes; 1,976 periodicals and serials; 2,933 Texas State documents; 168,-298 microforms.

Special Collections

Special collections include the **W.D. Lawless Afro-American Collection,** a **Children's Literature Collection,** a collection of Master's theses, curriculum materials, and a Prairie View A & M **Archival Collection.**

1607
Rice University
Fondren Library
600 Main Street
Houston, Texas 77251

Telephone. (713) 527-8101

Institutional Description. The privately supported university was founded in 1912. Enrollment: 4,061.

Library Administration. Samuel M. Carrington, University Librarian; Ferne B. Hyman, Assistant University Librarian; Nancy L. Boothe, Special Collections/Rare Books Librarian.

Library General Holdings. 1,325,000 volumes; 11,721 periodical subscriptions; 1,392,000 microforms; 15,463 recording; 952 audiotapes; 250 videotapes; 16,731 music scores; 22,155 maps.

Special Collections

Specialized collections of the library include annotated scores and monographs of Richard Lert, conductor (Music Library); H.L. Barlett Beethoven Collection (Music Library); Chappalear Science Fiction Collection; nineteenth-century American history; Germanics; Austro-Hungarian history; and the Defense Mapping Agency Map Collection.

University Archives. Includes the official papers of Rice presidents and other administrative officers; the records of student and other Rice-related organization; campus plans, drawings, and blueprints; photographs; ephemeral material and memorabilia; and published material about Rice by Rice faculty, staff, student, and alumni authors.

Rare Book Collections

Woodson Research Center. The Center is Rice University Library's repository for special collections of manuscripts, university archives, and rare books. The Rare Book Collection numbers about 22,000 volumes. Particular subject strengths are the history of science, Texana, eigthteenth-century British plays, and Confederate imprints. Of particular interest is the recent gift of the **Anderson History of Aeronautics Collection,** approximately 4,000 volumes of books, periodicals, photographa, and other materials on the history of manned flight from the time of Leonardo da Vinci until the 1960s, assembled by a private collector over a period of twenty years.

The Center's approximately 400 manuscript collections—mostly historical, literary, scientific, political, and business in nature—occupy approximately 2,000 linear feet. Areas with strong holdings include Texas history, politics, and entrepreneurship; Civil War history; literary authors with Rice connections; and British naval history. Individual collections of note include the 335 linear foot Johnson Space Center History Archive (on deposit), consisting of documentation on space projects Mercury, Gemini, Apollo-Soyuz Test Project, and Skylab; a 90-foot collection of the papers of Julian Sorell Huxley; the James A. Baker III Political Archive; a diverse collection relating to the Imperial Era in Mexico (Maximilian); the papers of entrepreneurs W.W. Fondren, W.B. Sharp, Judge James L. Autry, Judge Harris Masterson, and General William M. Hamman.

The Center also houses the papers of numerous faculty members and alumni in the humanities, science/engineering, social sciences, and the arts. Examples are Norman Hurd Ricker, Fred Terry Rogers, and William V. Houston (physics); Edgar Odell Lovett and Salomon Bochner (mathematics); William Ward Watkin and James Chillman (architecture); William McVey (sculpture); William Goyen and David Westheimer (literature); and Norman Hackerman (chemistry).

1608
St. Edward's University
Scarborough-Phillips Library
3001 South Congress
Austin, Texas 78704

Telephone. (512) 444-2621

Institutional Description. The privately supported liberal arts and teachers university was founded in 1878. An independent institution, it grants baccalaureate and master's degrees. Enrollment: 1,737.

Library Administration. Eileen Shockett, Librarian.

Library General Holdings. 139,000 volumes; 600 current periodicals.

Special Collections

The library collection contains 200 business periodicals and serials and 19,000 books on business, economics, and the behavioral and social sciences which related directly to graduate programs. Also housed in the library are the **University Archives,** the **Social Work Collection,** and the **Curriculum Library.**

1609
St. Mary's University
Academic Library
One Camino Santa Maria
San Antonio, Texas 78284

Telephone. (512) 436-3011

Institutional Description. The privately supported university was founded in 1852. Affiliated with the Roman Catholic Church, it grants baccalaureate, professional (law), and master's degrees. Enrollment: 2,767.

Library Administration. H. Palmer Hall, Director.

Library General Holdings. 200,000 volumes; 1,300 current periodical titles; 137,000 government documents; 78,000 microforms; 18,500 audiovisual materials.

Special Collections

The Academic Library maintains the **Texana Collection,** the **Spanish Archives of Laredo,** and a **Mathematics Collection** which includes materials dating from the 1700s.

1610
Sam Houston State University
Newton Gresham Library
Huntsville, Texas 77341

Telephone. (409) 294-1613

Institutional Description. The publicly supported state university offers programs in liberal arts, teacher training, and professional training. It was founded in 1879. Enrollment: 10,345.

Library Administration. Paul Culp, Special Collections Librarian.

Library General Holdings. 850,000 books, bound journals, and documents; 600,000 microforms; 8,000 phonograph recordings; 4,500 periodical titles.

Special Collections

Special collections include the **University Archives;** the Eliasburg, Bates, and McCormick collections in criminal justice; the **Porter Civil War Collection;** the **Mark Twain Collection,** the **Gertrude Stein Collection;** the **Clark Texas Collection;** and other collections of book and manuscript materials. Other special groups of materials are the library science collections, the curriculum laboratory collection, and the public school textbook collection.

Rare Book Collections

A large collection of rare books on Texas and the Southwest is assembled in the Thomason Room of the library.

1611
San Antonio College
San Antonio College Library
1001 Howard Street
San Antonio, Texas 78284

Telephone. (512) 733-2483

Institutional Description. The publicly supported junior college was founded in 1925. Enrollment: 8,834.

Library Administration. Oscar F. Metzger, College Librarian.

Library General Holdings. 300,000 catalogued items; 600 periodicals; 5,000 government documents; 150 government periodicals.

Rare Book Collections

Morrison Collection. The books, broadsides, periodicals, and pamphlets of this collection reflect a broad picture of the life of the time through items on cartography, cookery, music, women, witchcraft, natural history, religion, literature, and biography. The size of the collection is approximately 5,000 items. Most of the major classical writers are represented in good eighteenth century editions, often edited by major authors, e.g. Pope and Dryden. There are a few first editions of major works, but every major, and many minor, poet of the eighteenth century is represented. Items of special interest include a Baskerville Press edition of Joseph Addison; Baskett's printing of the Bible; and Phillis Wheatley's *Poems on Various Subjects.* The most significant periodical run is for *The Bee* (1733) in nine volumes.

1612
Schreiner College
W.M. Logan Library
Highway 27
Kerrville, Texas 78028

Telephone. (512) 896-5411

Institutional Description. The privately supported liberal arts college was founded in 1923. It is affiliated with the Presbyterian Church (U.S.A.). Enrollment: 462.

Library Administration. M. Rosemary Thomas, Librarian.

Library General Holdings. 45,000 volumes; 360 current periodical titles; 15,000 microforms.

Special Collections

The library has a special collection of materials relating to the Hill Country of Texas and maintains the **College Archives.**

1613
South Plains College
Libraries
1401 College Avenue
Levelland, Texas 79336

Telephone. (806) 894-9611

Institutional Description. South Plains College is a comprehensive community college with its main campus located in Levelland. The college was established by the citizens of Hockley County in 1957. Enrollment: 2,854.

Library Administration. Jimmy Strickland, Director of Libraries.

Library General Holdings. 50,000 volumes; 350 periodical titles; 15,000 microforms.

Special Collections

The Levelland library has a **Rare Book Room** and maintains the **Sam Blair Collection** which has special emphasis on cattle raising and Southwestern history. The Lubbock library contains a rapidly-growing collection of books and periodicals strong in allied health and other technical and occupational fields.

1614
South Texas College of Law
Library
1303 San Jacinto Street
Houston, Texas 77002

Telephone. (713) 659-8040

Institutional Description. The publicly supported professional law college was founded in 1923. It grants the Juris Doctor (J.D.) degree. Enrollment: 1,164.

Library Administration. Frances H. Thompson, Director.

Library General Holdings. 238,000 volumes.

Special Collections

The law collection of the library is the fourth largest collection among law schools in the state of Texas. The library has an agressive acquisition policy in general American law, international materials, and rare books.

1615
Southern Methodist University
DeGolyer Library
P.O. Box 396, SMU Station
Dallas, Texas 75275

Telephone. (214) 692-3231

Institutional Description. The privately supported university, founded in 1911, is affiliated with The United

Methodist Church. Enrollment: 7,895.

Library Administration. Robert W. Oram, University Librarian; David Farmer, Associate Director for Special Collections, Central University Library, and Head, DeGolyer Library; Michael Vinson, Rare Books Librarian.

Library General Holdings. 3,697,796 volumes; 6,795 current periodicals; 1,346,456 microforms; 14,496 audiovisual materials; 520,000 government documents.

Special Collections

The DeGolyer Library's special collections include over 85,000 titles, 1,500 cubic feet of manuscipts, 300,000 photographs, 2,500 model trains, and extensive microform holdings of printed and manuscript material. The holdings include movie scripts and printed promotional materials for Western films; Western Book Club of England novels; early automobile travel accounts, especially in the Americas; early city directories in the Trans-Mississippi West; railroad engine specifications and drawings from Baldwin Locomotive Works; photographs of railroad activities; printed ephemera relating to railroad and land promotions; eighteenth century English drama printed in Dublin.

Rare Book Collections

The rare book collection includes a comprehensive collection of printed books and pamphlets dealing with the discovery, exploration, and settlement of the Trans-Mississippi West, including the Spanish Borderlands. Also, there is comprehensive collection of books on railroad history. Manuscript collections include papers of E.L. DeGolyer, Sr., Earle Cabell, Robert T. Hill, SMU Press and *Southwest Review,* Baldwin Locomotive Works, and Muskogee Company records.

1616
Southwest Texas Junior College
Will C. Miller Memorial Library
Garnerfield Road
Uvalde, Texas 78801

Telephone. (512) 278-4401

Institutional Description. Southwest Texas Junior College is located on the site of what once was an Army Air Force Flying School. The college was established in 1946. Enrollment: 1,754.

Library Administration. Billie Louise Noguess, Librarian.

Library General Holdings. 25,000 volumes; 300 periodical titles; 250,000 microforms.

Special Collections

The library has a special collection of Texana.

1617
Southwest Texas State University
Learning Resources Center
SWTSU Station, Box 1002
San Marcos, Texas 78666

Telephone. (512) 245-2132

Institutional Description. The publicly supported liberal arts and teachers campus of the Texas State University System was founded in 1889. Enrollment: 17,237.

Library Administration. William F. Mears, Director; Richard A. Holland, Special Collections Librarian.

Library General Holdings. 764,000 volumes; 5,700 periodical titles; 261,000 government documents; 996,000 microforms.

Special Collections

Special collections of the library include the **Lyndon B. Johnson Collection,** the **T.E. Lawrence Collection,** and the **John Wesley Hardin Collection** of letters, photographs, newspaper clippings, and books; a collection of early textbooks; and the **Southwestern Collection** which includes the works of J. Frank Dobie, Larry McMurtry, and John Graves.

1618
Southwestern Adventist College
Findley Memorial Library
P.O. Box 567
Keene, Texas 76059

Telephone. (817) 645-3921

Institutional Description. The privately supported liberal arts and teachers college was founded in 1893. It is affiliated with the Seventh-day Adventist Church. Enrollment: 608.

Library Administration. Robert G. Cooper, Librarian.

Library General Holdings. 125,000 volumes; 500 current periodical subscriptions; 10,000 audio and video recordings.

Special Collections

The Findley Library houses the **Haddock Collection** of religious books, the Library of American Civilization (microform), and Ellen G. White books.

1619
Southwestern Assemblies of God College
P.C. Nelson Memorial Library
1200 Sycamore
Waxahachie, Texas 75165

Telephone. (214) 937-4010

Institutional Description. The privately supported Bible college was formed from three schools in 1943: Southwestern Bible School, Shield of Faith Bible School, and Southern Bible College. Enrollment: 635.

Library Administration. Murl M. Winters, Library Director.

Library General Holdings. 104,000 volumes (including 21,000 microforms); 617 periodical subscriptions; 6,100 bound magazine volumes; 2,284 records and tapes; 13,645 other learning materials.

Special Collections

Pentecostal Materials Collection. Contains over 2,000 items of book and non-book materials dealing with various Pentecostal distinctives and history.

Rare Book Collections

William Burton McCafferty Collection. Consists primarily of Pentecostal periodicals (1920-1945) representing examples of some 250 titles.

Dr. Peter Christopher Nelson Papers. The personal papers of Dr. Nelson plus broadsides and ephemera relating to revival campaigns that he and his evangelistic party held in the midwest from 1902-1940.

1620
Southwestern Baptist Theological Seminary
A. Webb Roberts Library
P.O. Box 22000 - 2E
Fort Worth, Texas 76122

Telephone. (817) 923-1921

Institutional Description. The privately supported institution was an outgrowth of the theological department of Baylor University, established in 1901. The graduate-level theological seminary is coeducational and contains three schools: Theology, Religious Education, and Church Music. Enrollment: 4,490.

Library Administration. Carl Wrotenbery, Librarian; Ben Rogers, Archivist.

Library General Holdings. 273,547 books; 1,726 periodical subscriptions; 28,555 bound periodicals; 8,664 microforms; 50,475 convention annuals and association minutes; 26,066 sound recordings; 2,306 video recordings; 807 motion pictures; 2,199 filmstrips; 83,493 music scores; 82,511 sheet music items.

Special Collections

Texas Baptist Historical Collection. This collection has been the official depository of the Executive Board of the Baptist General Convention of Texas since 1933, serving as a resource center for Baptist historians, researchers, and writers. The collection includes church minutes and histories, Texas Baptist Association minutes, State Convention annuals, Baptist newspapers, microfilm, oral history, manuscripts, mission artifacts, photographs, tape recordings, and history books. There is also a Texas Baptist Historical Museum on the premises.

1621
Southwestern Junior College of the Assemblies of God
Nelson Memorial Library
1200 Sycamore Street
Waxahachie, Texas 75165

Telephone. (214) 937-4010

Institutional Description. The two-year college was founded in 1944 as a division of Southwestern Bible Institute. The division became autonomous in 1968. Enrollment: 635.

Library Administration. Murl M. Winters, Director.

Library General Holdings. 90,500 volumes; 500 periodical titles.

Special Collections

The Southwestern Alumni Association sponsors the **Pentecostal Alcove** which holds a collection of materials pertaining to the modern Pentecostal movement. Pentecostal archival material is also being collected relating to the history of Pentecostals in the Southwest.

1622
Southwestern University
Cody Memorial Library
P.O. Box 770
Georgetown, Texas 78627

Telephone. (512) 863-1200

Institutional Description. The privately supported liberal arts and fine arts university was founded in 1840 as Rutesville College. It is now composed of Brown College of Arts and Sciences, and School of Fine Arts. Enrollment: 1,061.

Library Administration. Jon David Swartz, Associate Dean for Libraries and Learning Resources.

Library General Holdings. 161,00 volumes; 920 periodical subscriptions; 10,500 microforms.

Special Collections

Among the special collections in the Cody Library are **Edward A. Clark Texana Collection;** the **Dobie Collection** which includes the Bertha McKee Dobie papers and the Isabel Gaddis Collection; and the **Jackson-Greenwood Collection** of Americana.

1623
Stephen F. Austin University
Ralph W. Steen Library
Box 13055 SFA Station
Nacogdoches, Texas 57962

Telephone. (409) 568-4100

Institutional Description. The publicly supported multi-purpose institution was founded in 1923. Enrollment: 11,244.

Library Administration. Alvin C. Cage, University Librarian; Linda Cheves Nicklas, Special Collections Librarian.

Library General Holdings. 386,608 volumes; 91,621 bound periodical volumes; 3,607 current periodicals; 40 newspaper subscriptions; 498,934 microforms; 23,163 maps.

Special Collections

Historic East Texas. This "collection of collections" emphasizes the life, culture, economy, and history of East Texas. "East Texas" is that region from the Gulf of Mexico north to the Red River, and from the Trinity River east to the western Louisiana area which was once a part of Texas. The collections include personal papers, manuscripts, documents, maps, photographs, books, and other archival materials about East Texas or by East Texans. Among the items in the collections are copies of Samuel E. Asbury's notes and clippings on Texas history; the Barnett family papers (1842-1971); The Robert Bruce Blake Collection of official and private Spanish documents of the Nacogdoches and Bexar Archives; the government proceedings of Spanish Texas; the Robert Donnell Bone letters (1861-1865); Burk-Bone family letters (1834-1900); the papers of J.M. Cartwright; the George L. Crocket papers covering the period 1838-1935 and including materials relating to feuds, rebellions, churches, schools, and colleges in early San Augustine and Nacogdoches; the Burton Crossland collection (1787-1900) of papers and documents of the Lister family of Tennessee and Shelby County, Texas. The collections also include business records of the Angelina and Neches Railroad Company, the Otis Crim Funeral Home, the Kelly Plow Company, and the Nacogdoches Grocery Company as well as business papers of various family enterprises, notably those of Lyne Taliaferro Barret (1832-1913) who drilled the first producing oil well in Texas in 1866.

Charlotte Baker Collection. Consists of original manuscripts, some pen and ink illustrations, and galley proofs of two of this Nacogdoches author's popular books for children, *Necessary Nellie* and *The Green Poodles.*

Karle Wilson Baker Papers. A Nacogdoches writer (1878-1960) who is best known for her poetry reflecting the local color of Texas, the papers contain manuscripts, correspondence, photographs, illustrated articles, speeches, and contributions to the *Yale Review* and other journals.

Virginia Ruth (Fouts) Pochmann Collection. Consists chiefly of the manuscript and working papers of her book, *Triple Ridge Farm,* and correspondence with publishers from 1934-1969.

Forest History. The library is an official North American Forest History Repository. As a result of its repository status, the library has a large collection of business records from several lumber companies, including Angelina County Lumber Company, Kirby Lumber Corporation, Lutcher and Moore Lumber Company, Temple Industries, San Augustine County Lumber Company, and the Newton Country Lumber Company.

Curriculum Collection. 16,625 volumes of the types of materials found in elementary and high school libraries.

Rare Book Collections

Roberts Collection. Consists primarily of books by East Texans or about East Texas.

Arthur Thomas Collection of Texana. Includes scarce Texas county histories, general Texas histories, novels, and many other books relating to Texas and the Southwest.

1624
Sul Ross State University
Bryan Wildenthal Memorial Library
Alpine, Texas 79832

Telephone. (915) 837-8011

Institutional Description. The publicly supported liberal arts and teachers university was founded as a normal school in 1920. It also offers technical programs. Enrollment: 1,584.

Library Administration. Norman L. Spears, Director of Learning Resources.

Library General Holdings. 212,300 volumes; 1,550 current periodical subscriptions; 325,000 microforms; 429 linear feet of manuscript material.

Special Collections

Special collections include a children's collection; a curriculum collection; the **Archives of the Big Bend and the Museum of the Big Bend** containing over 11,000 books, manuscripts, photographs, and artifacts depicting life and culture in the Big Bend area of Texas from the early 1800s to the present.

1625
Tarleton State University
Library
Tarleton Station, Box T-2003
Tarleton, Texas 76402

Telephone. (817) 968-9000

Institutional Description. The publicly supported liberal arts and professional university is a member of the Texas A&M University System. It was founded in 1891. Enrollment: 4,218.

Library Administration. Kenneth W. Jones, University Librarian.

Library General Holdings. 200,000 volumes; 1,700 current periodicals; 432,000 microforms; 19,000 audiovisual materials; 18,000 government documents.

Special Collections

The library maintains collections in the general academic area as well as a special collection of agricultural reports and materials on Texas and Southwest history.

1626
Texas A & I University
James C. Jernigan Library
Texas A&I Station, Box 101
Kingsville, Texas 78363

Telephone. (512) 595-2111

Institutional Description. The publicly supported state university was founded in 1925 as a teachers college. The addition of technological programs prompted the change of name to Texas Arts and Industries University. Enrollment: 5,115.

Library Administration. Paul Goode, Head Librarian.

Library General Holdings. 645,000 volumes; 2,100 current periodicals; 280,000 government documents; 279,-500 microforms.

Special Collections

The **South Texas Archives** contains many historical photographs and manuscript collections of local and regional primary sources. The library maintains the **McGill Collection** of books on Texas and the West and the **Runyon Collection** of botany books.

1627
Texas A & M University
Sterling C. Evans Library
College Station, Texas 77843

Telephone. (409) 845-1951

Institutional Description. The publicly supported university is the state's oldest public institution of higher education. Founded in 1876, it began as a land-grant college. Enrollment: 33,229.

Library Administration. Donald H. Dyal, Head, Special Collections.

Library General Holdings. 1,600,000 volumes; 16,000 periodicals; 2,200,000 microforms.

Special Collections

Roger L. Brooks Matthew Arnold Collections. This collection comprises over 100 volumes of first and variant editions, secondary materials, as well as Arnold manuscript letters. The collection boast first editions of *The Strayed Reveller; Empedocles on Etna and Other Poems; Cromwell: A Prize Poem, Culture and Anarchy; Poems;* and *New Poems;* in addition to many others. Several of the volumes are signed by Arnold; others have the intriguing provenance of Anthony Trollope or Mary Ward. At the time of its acquisition, many of the Arnold letters were unrecorded and unpublished. Robert H. Super donated missing editions and secondary works in 1984 and thereby increased significantly the scholarly value of the Arnold Collection.

C.S. Forester Collection. This collection contains more than 100 of his books in first English, first American, and first Canadian editions, with a few later editions and anthologies. Present are three proof copies, sixteen signed, inscribed, or presentation copies, limited editions, and privately printed books. Present also is a two-page Forester autograph manuscript. Also included is an important group of original letters and commentary by, or in regard to, other writers working in the frigate novel tradition.

Herbert James Frost W. Somerset Maugham Collection. This collection has over 500 volumes—from first editions to paperbacks and translations. Many of the volumes are signed by the author. Over forty of them have long presentation inscriptions by Maugham. In addition, there are several letters from Maugham in the collection.

Great Western Illustrators Collection. Consists of 5,000 volumes covering published illustrations of some sixty illustrators of the West.

Jeff Dykes Range Livestock Collection. One of the important areas of Special Collections is the range livestock industry. Contained within this collection of over 20,000 volumes are several sub-collections of literary interest. The most complete of these is the J. Frank Dobie Collection which was assembled by Jeff Dykes and donated by his daughter, Martha Dykes Goldsmith. Rich in insightful inscriptions, the Dobie collection traces the published career of one of Texas' foremost authors. Other authors such as Owen Wister, Mari Sandoz, Eugene Manlove Rhodes, as well as many others are represented in the range livestock collection.

Edgar B. Kincaid Collection of World Birdlife. Includes ca. 4,000 titles covering birdlife and its habitat worldwide.

Science Fiction Research Collection. The cornerstone of this immense collection is the essentially complete corpus of science fiction and fantasy serial literature published since the first issue of *Weird Tales* in 1923. In addition to the serial literature, the collection possesses over 20,000 volumes of first, variant, and in many cases, translated editions of virtually all American and British science fiction and fantasy authors of the twentieth century. While almost everyone from Poul Anderson to Roger Zelazny is represented, Texan Robert E. Howard and British author Michael Moorcock are particularly complete. There are extensive holdings of historical, critical, and bibliographic works. Special Collections also has a growing collection of manuscripts (some unpublished), galleys, and some notes from Michael Moorcock, Anthony Burgess, Robert Silverberg, Isaac Asimov, and Avram Davidson.

P.G. Wodehouse Collection. The material in this collection is primarily of first English and American editions including the Psmith series, Jeeves, Mulliner, and all of the inimitable Wodehousian characters. There is a growing collection of secondary material.

Rare Book Collections

Loran L. Laughlin Collection of Rare, Antiquarian Books. Includes ca. 200 titles with emphasis on the history of printing. Laughlin was a printer in his youth and collected books which struck his fancy. Later in his career he decided to concentrate on incunables and examples of early non-western printing. Babylonian clay tablets, the Gutenberg Bible, and Hitler's *Mein Kampf* are in this collection.

1628
Texas A & M University at Galveston
Jack K. Williams Library
P.O. Box 1675
Galveston, Texas 77553

Telephone. (409) 740-4566

Institutional Description. The publicly supported division of the Texas A & M University features marine and maritime subjects. Branch campuses are located on Pelican Island at the base of the Galveston ship channel, and on Galveston Island near the beachfront. Enrollment: 586.

Library Administration. Natalie H. Weist, Library Director.

Library General Holdings. 48,000 volumes; 400,000 titles on microfiche.

Special Collections

In keeping with the special purpose designation of Texas A&M University at Galveston, the library has a strong collection of marine and maritime subjects. Topics include oceanography, ships and shipping, marine biology and fisheries, and other related works.

1629
Texas Chiropractic College
Mae Hilty Memorial Library
5912 Spencer Highway
Pasadena, Texas 77505

Telephone. (713) 487-1170

Institutional Description. The privately supported professional college was founded in 1908. It grants the Doctor of Chiropractic degree. Enrollment: 460.

Library Administration. Mara Umpierre, Director.

Library General Holdings. 10,000 volumes; 230 current periodical titles.

Special Collections

The library maintains a collection of chiropractic resources including a collection of rare material.

1630
Texas Christian University
Mary Couts Bernett Library
South University Drive
P.O. Box 32904
Fort Worth, Texas 76129

Telephone. (817) 921-7106

Institutional Description. The privately supported university is affiliated with the Christian Church (Disciples of Christ). Founded in 1873, the institution began as the AddRan Male and Female college in Thorpe Spring. Enrollment: 5,957.

Library Administration. Fred Heath, University Librarian; Charlotte Olin, Special Collections Librarian.

Library General Holdings. 1,205,825 items including 126,129 bound periodicals; 102,697 micromaterials; 45,265 music materials (all formats, including discs); 3,-500 current periodicals.

Special Collections

George T. Abell Collection. A group of over 100 maps from the sixteenth to twentieth century as well as a number of eighteenth-century books on travel. Another part of the collection contains a group of books on southwestern history and geography as well as the oil industry.

Edith and Edgar Deen Collection. This collection is particularly strong in works on women, especially those connected with religion. Mrs. Deen is the author of several books including *All of the Women in the Bible.*

William Luther Lewis Collection. Contains approximately 1,500 titles from 1473 to the mid-twentieth century, in English and and American literature.

Earl Mayfield Collection. Includes over 1,300 books on western outlaws.

Poetry Collection. The library has built a collection of contemporary poetry, particularly that published by small presses in the U.S.

Texas/Southwest History and Literature Collection. The personal libraries of a team of English teachers, Mabel Major and Rebecca Smith Lee and Marion Mullins whose specialty is in history and genealogy.

University Archives. In its depository function, Special Collections holds the University Archives. This body of materials contains the papers of the various Chancellors, beginning with Dr. Cecil Waite, and coming to the present. The permanent University copy of each thesis and dissertation accepted toward a graduate degree is shelved in the department.

The library received a gift of William Faulkner first editions which led to the purchase of a large group of Faulkner books and critical works. Another strength is found in the works of Anthony Trollope.

1631
Texas College
D.R. Glass Libraay
2404 North Grand
Tyler, Texas 75701

Telephone. (214) 531-2503

Institutional Description. The privately supported liberal arts and teachers college was founded in 1894. It is affiliated with the Christian Methodist Episcopal Church. Enrollment: 515.

Library Administration. Mary L. Cleveland, Director.

Library General Holdings. 82,000 volumes; 130 current periodical titles; 23,000 microforms.

Special Collections

The Texas College Library has a special collection on Black studies as well as rare books and memorabilia on the history of the Methodist Episcopal Church and the College.

1632
Texas College of Osteopathic Medicine
Health Sciences Library
3516 Camp Bowie Boulevard
Fort Worth, Texas 76107

Telephone. (817) 735-2380

Institutional Description. The publicly supported institution was founded in 1966. It offers the Professional Degree. Enrollment: 363.

Library Administration. Bobby R. Carter, Librarian; Ray Stokes, Special Collections Librarian; Craig Elam, Associate Director/Technical Services.

Library General Holdings. 1,643 monograph volumes; 200 bound serial volumes; 500 linear feet of archival material; 50 audiocassettes.

Special Collections

Historical Book Collection. Contains over 1,600 volumes which document the founding, growth, and development of osteopathic medicine and which provide historical continuity to the research and instructional activities of the Texas College of Osteopathic Medicine. The collection is especially strong in the following areas:

Osteopathic Medicine. Central to the interests of the college, all works relating to osteopathic medicine and all works by osteopathic physicians are collected comprehensively. Included are the complete works of Andrew Taylor Still, the founder of osteopathic medicine, as well as the writings of the early pioneers of the profession. Contemporary professional and popular works by D.O.'s are extensively represented. The worldwide spread of osteopathic medicine is reflected in books from the United Kingdom, Australia, France, and Germany.

Orthopedic Manipulation, Massage, Bonesetting. The historical development of manipulation as a therapeutic procedure is illustrated in volumes from these and other related areas. Works from Hippocrates to the present are represented, with emphasis on the nineteenth and twentieth centuries. Included are books by such leading figures as J. Cyriax and J.B. Mennell on orthopedic manipulation, J.C. Tissot and D. Graham on massage, and W. Hood and H. Barker on bonesetting.

The rise and development of osteopathic medicine is placed in historical perspective through the works illustrating the state of medical knowledge and education in later nineteenth- and early twentieth-century America. These works, either in original or reprinted editions, include the landmark classics in medical history, as well as the medical textbooks of the day. Besides osteopathic medicine, the nineteenth century saw the rise of many other medical theories and therapies as alternatives to "regular" or "allopathic" medicine. Chiropractic, Herbalism, Homeopathy, Hydrotherapy, Mental Healing, and Naturapathy are among those represented in the collection.

Archives and Manuscripts. The Archives was established to document the history of the college and the osteopathic profession in Texas through the collection and preservation of institutional records; private and professional papers of college faculty, alumni, and other individuals; photographs; and medical memorabilia. Included are the William G. Sutherland Collection of the private papers, publications, and memorabilia of the founder of Cranial Osteopathy and the official records of the Sutherland Cranial Teaching Foundation.

Medical artifacts associated with significant people and events are displayed in the library.

Oral History Collection. This collection aims to preserve through tape-recorded interviews perishable historical information found only in the memories of individuals who have either witnessed or participated in the development of the college and the osteopathic profession in Texas.

1633
Texas Southern University
Central University Library
3100 Cleburne Avenue
Houston, Texas 77004

Telephone. (713) 527-7011

Institutional Description. The publicly supported university was founded in 1947. It is composed of the College of Arts and Sciences, the Graduate School, and the Schools of Law, of Industries, of Business, and of Pharmacy. Enrollment: 7,708.

Library Administration. Spaesio W. Mothershed, University Librarian.

Library General Holdings. 573,000 volumes; 3,500 periodical subscriptions; 221,000 microforms; 7,400 government documents.

Special Collections

Heartman Collection on Negro Life and Culture. A collection of 25,000 items purchased in 1948 from a German-born bookdealer, Charles F. Heartman of Biloxi, Mississippi. The collection contains books, pamphlets, lithographs, oil paintings, musical scores, diaries, Texas slave narratives, scrapbooks, and other documents specifically pertaining to the growth and development of Black people in Texas, the United States, and the world.

Barbara Jordan Archives. A gift from one of TSU's outstanding alumnae, this collection endows the University with a comprehensive collection of historical documents. The collection of Representative Jordan's papers, manuscripts, and personal memorabilia span the period from 1967 through 1976. The early days of her activities in the Texas Senate and her contributions on Capitol Hill are all reflected in the collection.

Gallery of Traditional African Art. The collection includes 160 works of art from East, Central and West Africa with selected works from the Pacific Islands and Meso-America. Included in the collection are rare textiles, musical instruments, ancestral figures, examples of bronze casting, wood carving, and weaving.

1634
Texas State Technical Institute
Library
Waco, Texas 76705

Telephone. (817) 799-3611

Institutional Description. The two-year college was created in 1965 as James Connally Technical Institute. The Institute was part of the Texas A&M system until 1969 when it was given its own Board of Regents and its current name. Enrollment: 4,400.

Library Administration. Linda S. Koepf, Library Director.

Library General Holdings. 52,000 volumes; 520 technical journals.

Special Collections

The library has a special collection of cookbooks including both foreign and U.S. regional. Other collections include sign language, computer science, and commercial art techniques.

1635
Texas Tech University
University Library
P.O. Box 4349
Lubbock, Texas 79409

Telephone. (806) 742-2661

Institutional Description. The publicly supported technological university was founded in 1923. It is composed of the Schools of Agricultural Sciences, Arts and Sciences, Business Administration, Education, Engineering, Home Economics, Law, and the Graduate School. A medical school is planned. Enrollment: 22,243.

Library Administration. E. Dale Cluff, Director.

Library General Holdings. 1,100,000 volumes; 8,200 periodical subscriptions; 800,000 microforms.

Special Collections

The library's special collections include the private library of the twentieth-century Yiddish poet Selig Heller; Lawrence Thompson's *Bibliography of Spanish Plays* (microcard); extensive holdings related to Joseph Conrad; the First and Second Dalhousie Manuscripts containing writings of the English poet John Donne; the Archive of Turkish Oral Narrative; the Center for the Visually Impaired; and the Institute for Studies in Pragmaticism.

Southwest Collection. This collection is both the University archives and a regional repository of historical information pertaining to West Texas and the near Southwest. Nationally recognized for its ranch-related records, the collection also has materials on such topics as agriculture, land colonization, petroleum, mining, water, urban development, politics, pioneering, and the life of the times. In addition to personal papers and noncurrent business and institutional records, there are books, maps, periodicals, photographs, newspapers, taped interviews, movie films, video tapes, and microfilm.

1636
Texas Wesleyan College
Judge George W. Armstrong Library
1201 Wesleyan
P.O. Box 50010
Fort Worth, Texas 76105

Telephone. (817) 534-0251

Institutional Description. The privately supported liberal arts college was founded in 1891. It is affiliated with the United Methodist Church. Enrollment: 1,148.

Library Administration. Douglas Ferrier, Director.

Library General Holdings. 175,000 volumes; 1,075 periodical subscriptions; 202,500 microforms.

Special Collections

The Armstrong Library has the Library of American Civilization collection (microfiche) and the **William S.**

Gray Research Collection on reading.

1637
Texas Woman's University
University Library
TWU Station, Box 23925
Denton, Texas 76204

Telephone. (817) 383-1466

Institutional Description. The publicly supported (state) university for women was founded in 1901. Now a multipurpose institution, men are admitted to health sciences programs and the graduate school. Enrollment: 5,588.

Library Administration. Elizabeth M. Snapp, Librarian.

Library General Holdings. 739,000 volumes; 4,158 periodical subscriptions; 362,000 microforms; 115,000 government documents.

Special Collections

Women's Collection. The collection is an extensive research collection of works by and about women. The book collection of over 39,000 volumes includes such major microform collections as the Gerritsen Collection of Woman's History, Herstory, History of Women, Women and the Law, the National Women's Party Papers, and the National Archives of the American Association of University Women. Also included are over one million pages of manuscripts by or about woman.

Cookbook and Menu Collection. One of the major collections of the world, this collection includes the Julie Benell Cookbook Collection and the greater portion of the Cookery and Gastronomy Library of Mrs. Thomas M. Scruggs and Margaret Cook.

Other special collections include the **D. Genevieve Dixon Collection of Children's and Young Adult's Books;** the collection of works of women writers listed in I.H. Wright, **American Fiction,** 1851-1900; the **L.H. Hubbard Collection of Contemporary Literature;** the **R.P.T. Coffin Collection;** the **Madeleine Henrey Collection** of autographed and inscribed copies of her works, as well as limited issue copies, manuscripts, galleys, and correspondence; and the **Play Collection** (acting editions). Several noteworthy subject areas of research level acquisition include reading, fashion design, textiles, weaving and tapestry, nursing history and trends, nutrition, and Spanish language and literature.

1638
Trinity University
Elizabeth Coates Maddux Library
715 Stadium Drive
San Antonio, Texas 78284

Telephone. (512) 736-8121

Institutional Description. The privately supported university was founded in 1869. It is related by covenant to the United Presbyterian Church, U.S.A. Enrollment: 3,078.

Library Administration. Richard Hume Werking, Director of Libraries; Katherine D. Pettit, Special Collections/Rare Books Librarian.

Library General Holdings. 596,937 volumes; 2,973 current periodical and newspaper subscriptions; 202,043 microforms; 11,019 audiovisual titles.

Special Collections

Encino Press Collection. Each publication of this Austin-based firm was personally designed by William D. Wittliff. Texana is the subject matter of most titles published by the Encino Press and stand as examples of outstanding region publishing. (Part of the Beretta Texana Collection.)

Nicholson Collection. Includes geographies, fine literature, books on ranching, and general Texas history. (Part of the Beretta Texana Collection.)

J.F. Buenz Collection. Contains 19 volumes on such subjects as the Italian Renaissance, Spanish sculpture, and English and French architecture.

Paul A. Campbell International Library of Man and Space. This collection was donated by Dr. Campbell, a pioneer in space and aviation medicine and former Commander of the School of Aerospace Medicine at Brooks Air Force Base in San Antonio. The collection includes books, pamphlets, photographs, maps, transcripts of conversations between the astronauts and NASA, and other material which documents the history of man and space from the earliest theories of the ancients to the incredible ventures of the space program.

Sir Henry Hardman Pamphlet Collection. Spans the years 1920-1973, with the bulk of the material falling into the period 1928-1945. The pamphlets covers a broad range of subjects in twentieth-century British history. The greatest emphasis is on labor-oriented literature, ranging from political theories, primarily Socialism, to practical worker education movements.

George P. Isbell Collection. Includes works by and about Logan Pearsall Smith. The collection includes 46 volumes, and one cubic foot of notes and correspondence with other writers of his day.

Helen Miller Jones Collection of American Literature. Consists of several hundred titles of first and other important editions of works by such authors as William Faulkner, Ernest Hemingway, Willa Cather, and Eugene O'Neill. Two original typescripts, corrected by the authors, are unique: Willa Cather's *My Mortal Enemy,* and Ernest Hemingway's short story, *The Undefeated,* which was published as Number 2 of *This Quarter* (Milan, 1925-26), and afterwards appeared, with many minor alterations, in *Men Without Women* (Charles Scribner's Sons:

1927).

Pola Negri Collection of World Literature and the Theatre. Donated by one of Hollywood's great silent film stars, contains over 500 volumes of the theatre, costume design, and literary works of American and European authors.

Malcolm Lowry Collection. Contains all books by Lowry in hardcover and paperback editions, and nearly all the contributions he made to books and periodicals. Numerous translations of his works into other languages are also part of this collection, as are books about the author, books in which he is mentioned, and other books relating to him, notably those of Conrad Aiken.

Jim Maloney Aerospace Collection. Includes over 200 monographs and more than 35 linear feet of vertical file material documenting the space effort of the United States. The late Mr. Maloney was a reporter for the *Houston Post.*

Pat Ireland Nixon Collection. This collection was presented to Trinity University in 1964 by Dr. Nixon, a prominent San Antonio physician. Includes general histories of Texas, materials on the pre-Revolutionary period, the Revolutionary and Republican periods, the Mexican War, statehood, cowboys, cattlemen, Indians, and gunmen.

Something Else Press/Avant-Garde Poetry Collection. Includes editions of one of the past decade's most prominent avant-garde publishers, Dick Higgins. The press emerged from the non-gallery-oriented, mixed-media, "happening" activities of the Fluxus Group of artists in the early 1960s.

Albert Steves, III Collection. Includes works by and about Sir Winston Churchill; contains 117 volumes, many of them fine editions pertaining to the life and writings of the British author-statesman.

Decherd Turner Collection of William Morris' Kelmscott Press Editions. Contains many fine examples of printing from this press, the most remarkable being the famous edition of *The Works of Geoffrey Chaucer Now Newly Printed* (1896), commonly referred to as the Kelmscott Chaucer.

University Archives. The Archives are the repository for campus records documenting the history of the University and consisting of administrative and academic papers, copies of theses and research projects, press releases, newspaper clippings, photographs, slides, student publications, and other material of significance to the University.

Rare Book Collections

Mr. and Mrs. Walter F. Brown Collection. Among other interesting and rare items, the collection includes the first trade edition of Henry Adams' *History of the United States, from the First Administration of Thomas Jefferson to the Second Administration of James Madison* (New York: 1889); the *Magna Carta...* (London: 1618); and Jonathan Swift's *The History of the Four Last Years of the Queen* (London: 1758).

Gilbert M. Denman, Jr., Collection. Initiated in 1985, this collection holds the *Corpus Vasorum Antiquorum* and other important books on ancient Greek, Roman, and Etruscan art.

Hilton Latin American Collection. The majority of the Hilton books were sent to the general collection when acquired in 1982, but the rare items are housed in the Department of Special Collections. They include materials on Latin America, the Caribbean, Florida, the American Southwest, California, and the Philippines during the Spanish period. In addition, there are 33 autographed letters from famous Latin Americans and others concerning the region—one especially noteworthy from the Argentinian leader, Juan Peron.

C.W. Miller Collection. Contains 20 very sacred volumes with examples of incunabula, early printed books, and manuscripts.

1639
University of Dallas
William A. Blakely Library
1845 East Northgate Drive
Irving, Texas 75062

Telephone. (214) 721-5328

Institutional Description. The privately supported Roman Catholic university was founded in 1956. Enrollment: 1,725.

Library Administration. Nettie L. Baker, University Librarian; Harry A. Butler, Collection Development Librarian.

Library General Holdings. 164,960 books; 812 periodical subscriptions; 16,618 bound periodical volumes; 43,321 microfiche; 27,639 ultrafiche; 3,266 microfilms; 667 audio recordings.

Special Collections

Boyle-Lowther Collection. Donated by William and Javan Kienzle, this collection portrays the history, literature, and culture of Ireland through clippings, phonograph records, and books.

Kendall Memorial Library. This library represents a core collection of 1,000 volumes related to political philosophy. The books are from the private library of Willmoore Kendall, former chairman of the University of Dallas politics and economics departments.

Polish Collection. Contains more than 500 volumes written in English and Polish documenting the history and literature of Poland from past to present. This collection was given to honor Pope John Paul II by Father Francis J. Gabryl.

Limited Editions. One of the most comprehensive sets of Limited Edition Series in Texas was donated to the library in 1968 by Karl Hoblitzelle. This 281-volume gift became the impetus for establishing a library area devoted to rare books and special collections and materials. The original gift has doubled in size and continues to grow.

Rare Book Collections

Rare Books Collection. The library has acquired 865 rare books through individual gifts. This significant collection is the most eclectic of its holdings. The works range from a sixteenth-century cantorella with handwritten, polychrome illuminations to a twentieth-century set of engravings by Pablo Picasso.

1640
University of Houston
M.D. Anderson Library
4800 Calhoun Boulevard
Houston, Texas 77004

Telephone. (713) 749-1011

Institutional Description. The publicly supported (state) university was founded in 1934. It is now a multipurpose institution. Enrollment: 24,077.

Library Administration. Robin N. Downes, Director of Libraries.

Library General Holdings. 1,409,000 volumes; 21,000 journal and serial subscriptions; 2,586,000 microforms.

Special Collections

The Special Collections department of the library houses the **Creative Writing Collection** which includes the Larry McMurtry Papers; the **W.B. Bates Collection of Texana and Western Americana;** the **W.J. Jones Collection** of Latin American plays.

Rare Book Collections

The **Franzheim Memorial Collection** includes rare and historical works on fine arts and architecture.

1641
University of Houston - Clear Lake
Alfred R. Neumann Library
2700 Bay Area Boulevard
Houston, Texas 77058

Telephone. (713) 488-9240

Institutional Description. This publicly supported coeducational university opened for instruction in the fall of 1974. The university is an upper-level institution accepting transfer students at the junior, senior, and graduate levels only. Enrollment: 3,620.

Library Administration. W. Walter Wicker, Director of Learning Resources.

Library General Holdings. 282,000 volumes; 1,760 periodical titles; 1,078,000 microforms; 23,000 government documents.

Special Collections

The library houses the following microform collections: Early English Books 1475-1700; the **Radcliffe/Smith Core Collection** on the History of Women, and the Congressional Information Service.

1642
University of Houston - Downtown
W.I. Dykes Library
One Main Street
Houston, Texas 77002

Telephone. (713) 221-8000

Institutional Description. This branch of the University of Houston is located in the downtown area of the city of Houston. It offers a programs leading to the associate and baccalureate degrees. Enrollment: 5,206.

Library Administration. Robert Chang, Director.

Library General Holdings. 117,000 volumes; 975 current periodical titles; 22,000 microforms.

Special Collections

A special **Energy Collection** is comprised of books, magazines, pamphlets, and newspaper clipping files with information on 1,892 energy-related topics. This collection is especially useful to those in engineering technology, oil and gas accounting, petroleum land management, geology, and related fields.

1643
University of Houston - Victoria
University Library
2602 N. Ben Jordan
Victoria, Texas 77901

Telephone. (512) 576-3157

Institutional Description. The Victoria campus offers upper-division programs only, leading to the baccalaureate and master degrees. Enrollment: 534.

Library Administration. S. Joe McCord, Director; Virginia Allen, Archivist.

Library General Holdings. 185,000 volumes; 1,920 current periodical titles; 38,000 microforms; 95,000 government documents.

Special Collections

The library's special collections include materials on Texas and local history. The library is a regional historical resources depository.

1644
University of Mary Hardin-Baylor
Townsend Memorial Library
MHB Station
Belton, Texas 76513

Telephone. (817) 939-5811

Institutional Description. The privately supported liberal arts university is primarily for women. Founded in 1845, it is operated under the auspices of the Baptist General Convention of Texas. Enrollment: 1,055.

Library Administration. Robert A. Strong, Head Librarian.

Library General Holdings. 113,000 volumes; 650 current periodical subscriptions.

Special Collections

The University emphasizes a strong liberal arts program which is offered in a Christian environment. The library's collections support the curriculum of the University which includes art, biology, business, chemistry, computer and information science, education, home economics, nursing, and physics.

1645
University of North Texas
University of North Texas Libraries
Box 5188 NT Station
Denton, Texas 76203

Telephone. (817) 565-2411

Institutional Description. The publicly supported university was until recently known as North Texas State University. Founded in 1890 as a private normal school, it became a state institution in 1899. Enrollment: 17,057.

Library Administration. Margaret E. Galloway, University Librarian; Richard L. Himmel, University Archivist; Kenneth E. Lavender, Rare Books Librarian.

Library General Holdings. 1,956,150 items including 4,855 current periodicals; 31 newspaper subscriptions; 1,-700,000 microforms (339,693 volume equivalent); 45,973 music scores; and over 46,000 slides, filmstrips, phonodiscs, and phonotapes.

Special Collections

Curriculum Materials Center. The Center houses current, state-adopted textbooks and selected curriculum guides for grades K-12.

Media Library. Maintains a collection of 300 titles in the Gerontological Film Collection concerned with different aspects of aging.

Music Library. The Music Library houses the following specialized collections: The Stan Kenton Collection containing his original jazz charts and scores; the Edward Kennedy "Duke" Ellington Collection containing recordings of discs and tapes, discographies, and biographical sources; the WFAA Collection containing 60,-000 sheet music items and 80,000 stock and original orchestrations of a Dallas radio station; the Leon Breeden Collection of jazz scrapbooks pertaining to the UNT music program; the Whit Ozier Collection of over 60,000 recordings; and the *Source* magazine archives.

Rare Book Collections

Rare Book Collection. This collection has particular strengths in eighteenth-century English literature, miniature books, William Blake, Willa Cather, and Mary Webb.

Texana Collection. Includes travel narratives, Texas fine printing, Anson Jones, Larry McMurtry (manuscripts and first editions), and Warren Norwood (manuscripts and first editions).

University Archives. The Archives contain materials related to the political and business history of north central Texas and the southwest including manuscripts, maps, country records, and the archives of the University. Included in the manuscript collections are the papers of U.S. diplomat Alvin M. Owsley, federal judge Sarah T. Hughes, Texas politician Fred H. Minor, Mary (Mrs. Anson) Jones, and businesswoman Enid Justin.

Music Rare Books Collection. This collection has particular strengths in eighteenth-century printed materials, seventeenth-century French music, and opera of all periods.

1646
University of St. Thomas
Doherty Library
3812 Montrose Boulevard
Houston, Texas 77006

Telephone. (713) 522-7911

Institutional Description. The privately supported Roman Catholic institution admitted its first undergraduate students in 1947. Enrollment: 1,265.

Library Administration. Peter A. Kupersmith, Director.

Library General Holdings. 145,000 volumes; 700 current periodical subscriptions; 301,500 microforms.

Special Collections

The **Hugh Roy Marshall Graduate Philosophy Library** contains more than 7,500 volumes and has especially strong holdings in the area of Thomism. The School of Education maintains its own curriculum collection of 4,-500 volumes in the **Frank E. and Marilyn Tritico Library.** The **Cardinal Beran Library,** located at St. Mary's Seminary, is part of the School of Theology. Currently, it receives 300 periodicals and its holdings of more than 40,000 volumes (25,000 theological titles) are included in the Doherty Library card catalog.

1647
University of Texas at Arlington
UTA Libraries
Box 19125
Arlington, Texas 76019

Telephone. (817) 273-2011

Institutional Description. The campus of UTA is located in the heart of the Dallas-Fort Worth area. The institution was founded in 1895 and during early years had a number of names and missions. It became part of the University of Texas system in 1965. Enrollment: 18,-958.

Library Administration. Charles B. Lowry, Director of Libraries.

Library General Holdings. 970,000 books, journals, documents, and technical reports; 4,000 periodical and newspaper subscriptions.

Special Collections

The Division of Special Collections houses an extensive body of rare books, graphics, manuscripts, newspapers, and microfilm in the **Jenkins Garrett Library.** Specializing in the Spanish, Mexican, and American colonization of Texas, the Civil War, ranching, community histories, politics, biography, and literature, the Garrett Library also contains the nation's most comprehensive collection of books and documents on the Mexican War of 1846-48.

A second major division of the Special Collections is the **Cartographic History Library,** a center for the study of the history of five centuries of exploration and mapping in the New World, with emphasis on Texas and the Gulf of Mexico. The library contains thousands of rare maps and atlases featuring the original works of the world's greatest cartographers and a wide variety of journals and reference works. A wealth of historical documents pertaining to early Texas history is also found in the **Robertson Colony Collection.**

Two other collections relate to historical events of the twentieth century. The **Texas Political History Collection** consists of the papers of elected officials and private citizens, past and present, who have influenced the course of Texas politics and government. The **Texas Labor Archives** serve as the official depository of the Texas AFL-CIO and its affiliates and contains extensive primary records and publications relating to the history of organized labor in Texas and the Southwest.

The Division of Special Collections also contains the **University Archives** which document the history of the campus in publications, photographs, correspondence, and oral history. Also included are extensive collections of microfilm of the state, national, and ecclesiastical archives of Yucatan and Honduras.

The **Minority Cultures Collection,** housed in the Main Library, is a circulating and reference collection covering the political, social, cultural, economic, and intellectual history of American Indians, Blacks, and Mexican Americans in the southwestern United States from U.S. independence to the present with emphasis on twentieth-century problems and progress. The Main Library's collection of American fiction of the late nineteenth century is one of the finest collections of its type in the United States.

1648
University of Texas at Austin
Harry Ransom Humanities Research Center
21st and Guadalupe
Austin, Texas 78713

Telephone. (513) 471-9111

Institutional Description. The publicly supported university, founded in 1881, opened the main campus at Austin and the Medical Branch in Galveston in 1873. Enrollment: 43,137.

Library Administration. Decherd Turner, Director of the Humanities Research Center.

Library General Holdings. 800,000 rare books; 9 million manuscripts; 5 million photographs; 50,000 pieces of literary iconography.

Special Collections

The Humanities Research Center was founded in 1957 and represents one of the greatest collections of manuscript material in the world. The Center serves the advanced intellectual demands of the students and faculty of the University of Texas and serves scholars from all over the world. Begun by the late Harry Huntt Ransom, the Center's collecting pattern changed the basic belief that collecting and criticism were based on the first printed edition of a work to the basic assumption that the first printed edition was not the beginning of a particular text's history, but the end. Thus, the Center began collecting the prepublication materials which charted an author's creative process: notes, the many drafts, the finished draft, the galley proofs, the corrected galley proofs, page proofs, corrected pages proofs. The Center has also aquired a number of writers' libraries, ranging from complete libraries of Evelyn Waugh, Erle Stanley Gardner, J. Frank Dobie, etc., to portions of the libraries of Ezra Pound and the Trieste Library of James Joyce.

The Humanities Research Center's collections are vast and the holdings too numerous to list here, although major collection areas are indexed in the back of this volume. It has been said that the Center has more materials for the study of nineteenth- and twentieth-century French literature than any other institution outside of the Bibliothèque Nationale. This collection also has hundreds of individual British and American writers and literary figures.

The Center also has a major collections of photography and theater arts. These collections have many unique characterisitcs peculiar to their own media, yet the chief reason for being is that they are an integral part of the literary scene as viewed by the Center. A strong collection of materials reflecting the many facets of the book arts has also been developed. Of particular interest to the Center is the field of bookbinding (reliure).

While the holdings of the Humanities Research Center are massive and diverse, it is the central collection of nineteenth- and twentieth-century American, British, and French writers which constitutes the chief basis of its operations. (These comments contributed through the courtesy of Decherd Turner, Director, Humanities Research Center of the University of Texas at Austin).

1649
University of Texas at Dallas
Eugene McDermott Library
P.O. Box 830688
Richardson, Texas 75083

Telephone. (214) 690-2111

Institutional Description. The publicly supported (state) branch campus of the University of Texas System grants baccalaureate, master's, and doctorate degrees. Enrollment: 4,304.

Library Administration. Edward M. Walters, Director of University Libraries.

Library General Holdings. 495,000 volumes; 2,950 current periodical subscriptions; 1,216,000 microforms; 240,000 government documents; 59,000 audiovisual materials.

Special Collections

Special collections include the **Cecil and Ida Green Collection** of Latin American materials; the **Wineburgh Philatelic Research Library;** and the **History of Aviation Collection.** Other notable collections include more than 15,000 art museum catalogs from throughout the world and the **Art Photography Collection.**

Callier Center for Communication Disorders. Maintains material on speech and hearing and their disorders.

Geological Information Library of Dallas. This library houses the world's largest collection of petroleum-well logs and associated geological data.

Rare Book Collections

Rare book collections include the **Lundell Rare Book Library** and the **Louise B. Belsterling Library** of rare botanical books.

1650
University of Texas at El Paso
Central Library
University Avenue at Hawthorne
El Paso, Texas 79968

Telephone. (915) 747-5000

Institutional Description. The publicly supported (state) campus of the University of Texas System was founded in 1913 as the Texas School of Mines and Metallurgy. It now features liberal arts and professional programs. Enrollment: 11,626.

Library Administration. Robert A. Seal, Director of Libraries; Cesar Caballero, Head, Special Collections; Juan A. Sandoval II, Chicano Services Librarian.

Library General Holdings. 710,336 volumes; 5,373 periodicals; 256,576 microforms.

Special Collections

The library has several outstanding special collections of books and other materials which support important academic emphases of the University. The **Southwestern Collection** and the **J. Carl Hertzog Collection** of materials on print, books, and book design are housed in the Hertzog Room. Other special collections include the **Judaica Collection** and the **S.L.A. Marshall Military History Collection.** Rare books, archival, and other manuscript materials are also maintained.

Latin American and Chicano Studies. The library's Chicano Services Section is one of the pioneering efforts in this area of library service.

1651
University of Texas at San Antonio
John Peace Library
6900 FM 1604
San Antonio, Texas 78285

Telephone. (512) 691-4011

Institutional Description. This publicly supported university opened in the summer of 1973 to graduate students. Upper-division undergraduates were admitted for the first time in the fall of 1975 and all four years of the undergraduate program were implemented in the fall of 1976. Enrollment: 6,954.

Library Administration. Michael F. Kelly, Director of Libraries.

Library General Holdings. 629,000 volumes; 2,340 current periodical subscriptions.

Special Collections

The special collections and rare books of the John Peace Library focus on Western Americana and on Texana. Most notable among the special collections are the **John Peace Collection** of books and documents in the period of the Texas Republic and the **Kathryn Stoner**

O'Connor Collection of early Texas and Mexican materials owned by the Sons of the Texas Republic.

1652
University of Texas at Tyler
Robert R. Muntz Library
3900 University Boulevard
Tyler, Texas 75701

Telephone. (214) 566-1471

Institutional Description. The upper-level state supported school was founded in 1971. It grants the baccalaureate and master degrees. Enrollment: 2,247.

Library Administration. C. Olene Harned, University Librarian.

Library General Holdings. 177,500 volumes; 1,250 periodical subscriptions; 111,000 microform volumes.

Special Collections

The library maintains a collection of Texas materials.

1653
University of Texas Health Science Center at San Antonio
Dolph Briscoe Jr. Library
7703 Floyd Curl Drive
San Antonio, Texas 78284

Telephone. (512) 567-2400

Institutional Description. The publicy supported institution is a medical school established in 1959. Enrollment: 2,201.

Library Administration. Virginia M. Bowden, Librarian; Daniel H. Jones, Head, Collection Management.

Library General Holdings. 95,000 volumes; 3,100 current journal subscriptions; 83,000 journals.

Special Collections

The Briscoe Library is an academic health sciences library collecting in the areas of medicine, nursing, dentistry, the allied health professions, and the basic medical sciences.

University Archives. Provides a repository for preservation of historically valuable University records.

Rare Book Collections

Patrick Ireland Nixon Medical Historical Library. Contains more than 3,500 rare and historical medical texts. The collection contains many classics in the history of medicine including works by Albinus, Avicenna, Celsus, Galen, Mascagni, Vesalius, Withering, and John and William Hunter. It is particularly strong in the areas of anatomy, surgery, and ophthalmology.

The Local Medical History Collection. Contains manuscripts, journals, and account books of local physicians, photographs of area hospitals and other medical scenes, and records of other local medical organizations.

1654
University of Texas of the Permian Basin Library
4901 East University Boulevard
Odessa, Texas 79762

Telephone. (915) 367-2114

Institutional Description. The publicly supported institution, founded in 1973, is an upper-level and graduate division of the University of Texas System. Enrollment: 1,281.

Library Administration. Loran Lindsay, Librarian; Bobbie Jean Klepper, Special Services Librarian.

Library General Holdings. 500,000 volumes of books, microforms, and periodicals; 1,200 periodical subscriptions.

Special Collections

The library has a special collections room which contains items relating to the history of the Permian Basin, a sizeable collection of materials by and about J. Frank Dobie, manuscripts of major Texas writers, a Texana collection which supports in-depth research in Texas history and culture, a Spanish language collection, and the University archives. There is also a Curriculum Library containing over 6,000 items including textbooks, children's literature, and curricular materials.

1655
University of Texas - Health Science Center at Houston
Houston Academy of Medicine - Texas Medical Center Library
P.O. Box 20036
Houston, Texas 77225

Telephone. (713) 792-8531

Institutional Description. The Health Science Center at Houston is part of the Texas Medical Center, offering upper-division, graduate, and first-professional study only. Enrollment: 3,778.

Library Administration. Richard A. Lyders, Executive Director.

Library General Holdings. The Houston Academy of Medicine - Texas Medical Center Library is a consortium library for nineteen supporting institutions. The library began in the Texas Medical Center in 1949, when two existing medical libraries, the Houston Academy of Medicine Library and the Baylor College of Medicine Library, combined their respective collections. It is now one of the largest medical libraries in the United States. *See* **Baylor College of Medicine.**

1656
Weatherford College Library
308 East Park Avenue
Weatherford, Texas 76086

Telephone. (817) 594-5471

Institutional Description. Weatherford College was established in 1869 as a Masonic Institute. Private ownership ended in 1949 when Weatherford College of the Parker County Junior College District was mandated by the county voters. Enrollment: 1,178.

Library Administration. Ruth Huse, Librarian.

Library General Holdings. 54,970 volumes; 475 magazine and newspaper subscriptions; 75,644 microforms.

Special Collections

Special collections include the **Weatherford College History Collection,** the **Texas Counties Histories Collection,** and the Southwest Cattle Industry Collection.

1657
West Texas State University
Cornette Library
Canyon, Texas 79016

Telephone. (806) 656-0111

Institutional Description. The publicly supported liberal arts, teachers, and professional university was founded in 1910. Enrollment: 5,083.

Library Administration. John Veenstra, Librarian.

Library General Holdings. 204,000 volumes; 2,315 periodical subscriptions; 625,000 government documents; 530,000 microforms.

Special Collections

The library maintains the **Sheffy Southwestern Americana Collection,** a collection of Texas materials, and a rare book collection.

1658
Wharton County Junior College
J.M. Hodges Learning Center
911 Boling Highway
Wharton, Texas 77488

Telephone. (409) 532-4560

Institutional Description. Wharton County Junior College was established by county voters in 1946. The college moved to its present location in 1949. Enrollment: 1,723.

Library Administration. Patsy I. Norton, Director.

Library General Holdings. 53,333 volumes; 469 periodical titles; 5,000 pamphlets.

Special Collections

The library maintains a special collection of Texana.

1659
Wiley College
Thomas Winston Cole, Sr. Library
711 Rosborough Road
Marshall, Texas 75670

Telephone. (214) 938-8341

Institutional Description. The privately supported liberal arts and teachers college is affiliated with the United Methodist Church. Enrollment: 480.

Library Administration. Patricia Denson, Director of Library Services.

Library General Holdings. 77,407 volumes.

Special Collections

The library has a special collection in Black Studies and a collection of curriculum materials.

Utah

1660
Brigham Young University
University Libraries
Provo, Utah 84602

Telephone. (801) 378-2507

Institutional Description. This private university began as an academy of the Church of Christ of Latter-day Saints in 1875 and became a university in 1903. Enrollment: 36,877.

Library Administration. Sterling J. Albrecht, Director.

Library General Holdings. 1,933,500 volumes; 16,720 current periodical subscriptions; 1,311,500 microforms; 44,000 audiovisual materials.

Special Collections

The library maintains special collections on Mormon Americana, the American West, and the history of printing. The library also has an excellent collection of incunabula and a library of the first editions and other original material of Louisa May Alcott.

1661
College of Eastern Utah
Learning Resource Center
Price, Utah 84501

Telephone. (801) 637-2120

Institutional Description. The publicly supported junior college is a branch of the University of Utah. Founded in 1938, it was originally known as Carbon College. Enrollment: 1,771.

Library Administration. Louis Reinwand, Library Director.

Library General Holdings. 25,000 volumes; 220 periodical subscriptions; 1,000 music scores; 100 microforms.

Special Collections

Musical Scores. This special collection of musical scores was donated by William H. Toy and represents theatre music from the 1880s to the 1920s. Popular band music from that same time period is also included. William Toy owned a theater in Chicago; after moving to Utah, he organized a series of bands to play in small rural mining towns in southeastern Utah.

The library has a collection of secondary Mormon materials and a representative collection of books dealing with coal mining in the United States but particularly in Utah.

Rare Book Collections

Mormonism

1662
Snow College
Lucy A. Phillips Library
150 East College Avenue
Ephraim, Utah 84627

Telephone. (801) 283-4021

Institutional Description. Snow College was founded in 1888 by the Church of Jesus Christ of Latter-day Saints. In 1932, it became part of the Utah System of Higher Education and today the college is an independent institution. Enrollment: 1,408.

Library Administration. Dorothy Floyd, Head Librarian.

Library General Holdings. 30,000 volumes; 240 current periodical subscriptions; 4,000 microforms.

Special Collections

The **Ruth C. Olsen Special Collections Room** preserves materials relevant to local and Utah history.

1663
Southern Utah State College
Library
531 West Center Street
Cedar City, Utah 84720

Telephone. (801) 586-4411

Institutional Description. The publicly supported liberal arts and teachers college was founded in 1897, by an act of the First Utah State Legislature. Enrollment: 2,821.

Library Administration. Diana Graff, Library Director.

Library General Holdings. 129,500 volumes; 700 magazine and newspaper titles; 413,000 microforms; 25,000 government documents; 15,000 audiovisual materials.

Special Collections

The Special Collections area has an abundance of Utah and southern Utah historical materials, Shakespeareana, and recorded music. A separate feature is the Seymour Room with its authentic Victorian furniture and valuable collections in opera, drama, literature, language, and the humanities. Material on southern Utah and the Paiute Indians is housed in the Palmer Room.

1664
University of Utah
J. Willard Marriott Library
Salt Lake City, Utah 84112

Telephone. (801) 581-7200

Institutional Description. The publicly supported university was founded in 1850. Today it offers a varied, comprehensive program of studies. Enrollment: 25,162.

Library Administration. Roger K. Hanson, Director of Libraries.

Library General Holdings. 2,529,643 volumes; 14,000 periodical subscriptions; 2,400,000 microforms.

Special Collections

The **Western Americana** and rare books departments maintain extensive collections of local materials including microfilms of most Utah newspapers, original diaries, and manuscripts.

1665
Utah State University
Merrill Library
University Hill
Logan, Utah 84322

Telephone. (801) 750-1000

Institutional Description. The publicly supported state university was founded in 1888 as a land-grant university. It now includes 8 colleges and a graduate school. Enrollment: 13,029.

Library Administration. Kenneth E. Marks, University Librarian; A.J. Simmonds, Director. Special Collections and Archives.

Library General Holdings. 950,000 volumes; 7,345 current periodical subscriptions; 1,251,000 microforms; 170,000 government documents.

Special Collections

Special collections include material on Utah Mormons and Southern Idaho; the **Jack London Collection;** the Fife Folklore Collection, and the **Gunn McKay Congressional Records.**

1666
Weber State College
Stewart Library
3750 Harrison Boulevard
Ogden, Utah 84408

Telephone. (801) 399-5941

Institutional Description. The state college was founded as the Weber State Academy in 1889 by the Board of Education of the Church of Jesus Christ of Latter-day Saints. In 1933, the Utah Legislature established Weber as a state junior college. It became a four-year degree-granting institution in 1963. Enrollment: 11,366.

Library Administration. Craig S. Hall, Director of Libraries.

Library General Holdings. 304,000 volumes; 2,100 literary, scientific and educational periodicals; 198,000 government documents; 465,000 microforms.

Special Collections

The library houses several special collections, the largest of which is the **Howell Collection** of 10,500 volumes. This collection, willed to the College by the late Judge James A. Howell in 1954, consists mostly of eighteenth- and nineteenth-century American and English literature. Other collections include the **Lawrence J. Burton Congressional Collection,** the **Jeanette McKay Morrell Porcelain Collection,** the **Frank William Becraft Oriental Artifacts Collection,** the **Paul Branson Art Collection,** the **Hyrum and Ruby Wheelright Mormon Literature Collection,** and the **Roland Parry Music Collection.**

1667
Westminster College of Salt Lake City
W.T. Nightingale Memorial Library
1840 South 13th, E.
Salt Lake City, Utah 84105

Telephone. (801) 484-7651

Institutional Description. The privately supported liberal arts and professional college was founded in 1875. It is affiliated with the United Methodist Church, the United Presbyterian Church, and the United Church of Christ. Enrollment: 1,336.

Library Administration. Richard Wunder, Director of Libraries.

Library General Holdings. 63,000 volumes.

Special Collections

As an institution rooted in Judeo-Christian tradition, Westminster seeks to provide an environment that encourages and facilitates the intellectual, spiritual, cultural, and social growth of its students. The collections of the library reflect these goals with strengths in the liberal arts, nursing, and management.

Vermont

1668
Bennington College
Edward Clark Crossett Library
Route 67A
Bennington, Vermont 05201

Telephone. (802) 442-5401

Institutional Description. The privately supported institution was founded in 1932 as a college for women. It became coeducational in 1963. Enrollment: 584.

Library Administration. John C. Swan, Head Librarian.

Library General Holdings. 100,000 volumes; 650 periodical subscriptions; 5,000 microfilm reels; 500 microfiche; 20,000 art slides; 600 spoken-word recordings.

Special Collections

The Edward Clark Crossett Library has a strong book collection in art and in theater as well as particular strengths in areas of literature associated with authors with Bennington connections, such as Bernard Malamud, Ben Belitt, Kenneth Burke, Stanley Edgar Hyman, Howard Nemerov, Erich Fromm, Francis Fergusson, Wallace Fowlie, Nicholas Delbanco, Alan Cheuse, and Stephen Sandy. In the visual arts, former Bennington faculty David Smith, Jules Olitski, and Kenneth Noland are well represented, as is alumna Helen Frankenthaler. The Jennings Music Library is strong in the scores of Bennington faculty Lionel Nowak, Vivian Fine, Lou Calabro, and former faculty Henry Brant and Otto Luening. The Music Library also has a collection of 5,000 music recordings and 10,000 scores.

Rare Book Collections

Friedenberg Collection. Consists of over 400 nineteenth- and twentieth-century first editions of American authors, a small collection of photographic portfolios (Weston, Stand, Adams, Winogrand, Friedlander, Boubat, Doisneau, Bravo, and others), and the collection of student theses, a number of which are the first versions of published novels and other works. There are other archival collections within the college (such as Martha Hill's collection of documents related to the Bennington School for the Dance) currently being reorganized under the auspices of the library, including extensive holdings related to the founding of the college.

1669
Castleton State College
College Library
Castleton, Vermont 05735

Telephone. (802) 468-5611

Institutional Description. Castleton College is a public liberal arts college offering teacher prepartion and other professional programs. Enrollment: 2,043.

Library Administration. William Hannaford, College Librarian.

Library General Holdings. 100,000 volumes; 230 current periodical titles; 55,000 government documents; 33,000 microforms.

Special Collections

The library's collection of Vermontiana is housed in the Vermont Room and includes an extensive collection of town reports, gazetteers, histories, and census data. The **College Archives** contain materials relating directly directly to the College. The library also maintains the **Calvin Coolidge Papers** microfilm collection.

1670
College of St. Joseph
Library
Clement Road
Rutland, Vermont 05701

Telephone. (802) 773-5900

Institutional Description. The privately-supported Catholic college offers two- and four-year programs that combine career preparation with a liberal arts core. Enrollment: 387.

Library Administration. Doreen J. McCullough, Director.

Library General Holdings. 26,000 volumes; 115 current periodical titles.

Special Collections

The library maintains a special collection which includes books, journals, and clippings about Vermont.

1671
Goddard College
William Shipman Library
Plainfield, Vermont 05667

Telephone. (802) 454-8311

Institutional Description. The privately supported liberal arts college operates on two separate but adjoining campuses, each with its own student body, faculty, and community life. Enrollment: 1,416.

Library Administration. Emily Tanner, Director of Educational Resources.

Library General Holdings. 70,000 volumes; 226 current periodical and newspaper subscriptions.

Special Collections

Collected Works of Goddard Graduates. Housed in a separate room, these Senior Studies and master's Theses (numbering 6,000 hard copy volumes and another 1,000 on microform) represent the culminating studies of both undergraduate and graduate students at Goddard College.

1672
Green Mountain College
Library
College Street
Poultney, Vermont 05764

Telephone. (802) 287-9313

Institutional Description. The privately supported liberal arts college is affiliated with the United Methodist Church. Enrollment: 385.

Library Administration. Douglas W. Durkee, Head Librarian.

Library General Holdings. 71,000 volumes; 210 current periodicals; 10,100 audiovisual materials; 3,000 microforms.

Special Collections

The library maintains a unique collection of **Early American Decoration;** and a collection on the Welsh people who settled in Poultney and the surrounding area. The **College Archives** preserves official records and memorabilia of the College.

1673
Johnson State College
John Dewey Library
Johnson, Vermont 05656

Telephone. (802) 635-2356

Institutional Description. The publicly supported liberal arts and teachers college was founded in 1828. Enrollment: 1,128.

Library Administration. Lois Beaty, Library Coordinator.

Library General Holdings. 77,000 volumes; 450 current periodical subscriptions.

Special Collections

The library's collections of art books and children's literature are well known for their depth and range.

1674
Lyndon State College
Samuel Read Hall Library
Lyndonville, Vermont 05851

Telephone. (802) 626-9371

Institutional Description. The four-year liberal arts college is part of the Vermont State College. It prepares teachers for the elementary and junior high grades and offers general education in the liberal arts. Enrollment: 1,014.

Library Administration. Suzanne Gallagher, Head Librarian.

Library General Holdings. 70,000 volumes; 500 current periodical subscriptions.

Special Collections

The **Northeast Kingdom Room** of the library houses historical materials on Vermont.

1675
Marlboro College
Howard and Amy Rice Library
Marlboro, Vermont 05344

Telephone. (802) 257-4333

Institutional Description. Marlboro College is an independent liberal arts college founded in 1947. Enrollment: 190.

Library Administration. Sally W. Andrews, Director.

Library General Holdings. 44,000 volumes; 245 current periodical subscriptions.

Special Collections

The library maintains the **Guernsey Rudyard Kipling Collection** which includes some first editions of Kipling's works.

1676
Middlebury College
Egbert Starr Library
Middlebury, Vermont 05753

Telephone. (802) 388-3711

Institutional Description. The privately supported liberal arts college was founded in 1800. Its summer language schools of English, French, German, Italian, Russian, Spanish, Chinese, Japanese, and Arabic have achieved international reputation. Enrollment: 2,012.

Library Administration. Ronald Rucker, Librarian.

Library General Holdings. 545,500 volumes; 1,800 current periodical subscriptions; 40,000 microforms.

Special Collections

Special library collections include early Vermont imprints, materials relating to Vermont and Middlebury, the College Archives, incunabula, and rare books and manuscripts in various fields. A collection unique in its field is the **Helen Hartness Flanders Ballad Collection** of over 5,000 recorded items, including ballads and folk songs of British and American origin, religious songs, fiddle tunes, and call-sets collected in New England by Mrs. Flanders and her assistants between 1930 and 1959.

Abernethy Library. This library is a special collection of American literature, built around the nucleus of books and manuscripts bequeathed in 1923 by Dr. Julian W. Abernethy. It now contains 15,000 volumes, chiefly in first edition, many of them rare, and manuscripts of 1,200 authors. Especially strong are the materials relating to Thoreau, Emerson, and William Carlos Williams. A part of the Abernethy Library, the Robert Frost Room, has 300 volumes by and about Frost, most of them autographed. In addition, chiefly through the efforts of Mrs. Corinne Tennyson Davids, the collection includes about 2,800 items of such Frostiana as pamphlets and periodicals containing the poet's work, book reviews, news items, photographs, college bulletins, sheet music of his poetry, tape and disc recordings and manuscripts.

1677
Norwich University
Henry Prescott Chaplin Memorial Library
South Main Street
Northfield, Vermont 05663

Telephone. (802) 485-2170

Institutional Description. The publicly supported institution is the Military College of Vermont. Founded in 1819, it combines a wide variety of educational programs with modern military training. Enrollment: 2,528.

Library Administration. Ann B. Turner, Librarian; Jacqueline S. Painter, Documents Librarian and University Archivist.

Library General Holdings. 174,627 volumes; 1,033 current periodicals; 9,011 microfilms; 9,620 microfiche; 55,326 government documents; 1,763 slides; 883 audiocassettes; 62 videocassettes; 817 films; 224 filmstrips.

Special Collections

Archives and Manuscripts. These collections include the papers of Alden Patridge, founder of the University, which reflects his interests in education, mathematics, surveying, engineering, politics, and military affairs, dated from 1800 to 1854. Other important manuscript collections include the papers of Professor Alonzo Jackman (1900-), Major General Ernest N. Harmon (1894-1979), General I.D. White (1900-), and Lt. General Edward H. Brooks (1893-1978). The latter three collections relate mainly to service in World War II and the Korean War.

Caraganis Collection. A collection of 7,000 volumes primarily on military and diplomatic history.

Russian Library. 6,500 volumes in Russian, used primarily by the summer Russian School of Norwich University.

Rare Book Collections

Joel E. Fisher Mountaineering Collection. Includes 74 volumes of late nineteenth- and early twentieth-century books on Alpine and Himalayan mountaineering.

Southard Military History Collection. Approximately 100,000 volumes on military history; the largest portion are British regimental histories. Also includes a number of classic works dating from the sixteenth century.

Other small collections relate to former presidents of Norwich University, published works by Norwich University alumni and faculty, and books that were in the library from its founding (1819) to 1866.

1678
Saint Michael's College
Jeremiah Durick Library
Winooski, Vermont 05404

Telephone. (802) 655-2000

Institutional Description. The four-year liberal arts college was founded in 1903 by the Society of St. Edmund. Enrollment: 1,774.

Library Administration. Joseph T. Popecki, Director.

Library General Holdings. 140,000 volumes of bound books and periodicals; 1,200 current periodical subscriptions; 48,000 microfilm volumes; 38,000 items of nonconventional materials (slides, tapes, pamphlets, musical scores).

Special Collections

Special collections include the **Vermont Collection,** the **Richard Stoehr Collection** of music manuscripts and personal papers, and the **Arcadian Collection.**

1679
School for International Training
Donald B. Watt Library
Kipling Road
Brattleboro, Vermont 05301

Telephone. (802) 257-7751

Institutional Description. The nonprofit, upper-level undergraduate and graduate school was founded in 1964 and is dedicated to cultural exchange and international understanding. Enrollment: 439.

Library Administration. Shirley Capron, Librarian; Michael Green, Librarian.

Library General Holdings. 25,000 volumes; 230 current periodical titles.

Special Collections

The library's special collections include the **Peace Studies Collection** which includes materials dealing with disarmament and the Middle East conflict; the **Languages and Linguistics Collection** consisting primarily of methodology materials for language instruction; and the **International Development Collection** of materials relating to the social and economic development of Third World countries.

1680
Trinity College
Thomas A. Farrell Family Library
Colchester Avenue
Burlington, Vermont 05401

Telephone. (802) 658-0337

Institutional Description. The college is conducted by the Sisters of Mercy and is a four-year liberal arts college for women. Enrollment: 945.

Library Administration. Mark Yerburgh, Library Director.

Library General Holdings. 54,000 volumes; 360 current periodical subscriptions; 41,000 microforms.

Special Collections

A special collection on Vermont consists of 135 volumes about the state. The library also maintains a rare books collection of 400 volumes which includes out-of-print books and limited editions.

1681
University of Vermont
Bailey/Howe Memorial Library
Burlington, Vermont 05405

Telephone. (802) 656-2020

Institutional Description. The publicly supported university, chartered in 1791, is one of the oldest institutions of higher education in the United States. Enrollment: 10,-908.

Library Administration. Nancy L. Eaton, University Librarian; John Buechler, Assistant Director of Libraries for Special Collections.

Library General Holdings. 864,661 volumes; 8,612 current serial subscriptions; 847,814 microforms; 176,306 maps; 244,252 government document titles.

Special Collections

James B. Wilbur Collection of Vermontiana. This is perhaps the largest collection of Vermont materials in the world, from early Vermont imprints to present state documents and dissertations on Vermont. It includes 75,000 volumes; 7,500 printed and manuscript maps; 200,000 photographs; 7,000 linear feet of manuscripts, the latter including personal, family, business, political, literary, and government papers, e.g., Ethan and Ira Allen, Lake Champlain Transportation Company, Henry Stevens Family, and congressmaen, senators, and governors.

The library also has collections on: printing history including books on printing from the sixteenth to nineteenth centuries with a collection of British type specimens prior to 1831; first editions and manuscripts of John Masefield, Diane Wakoski, Hayden Carruth, John Engles, and Willa Cather; Vietnam War ephemera (1967-1972) and fiction; a representative collection of 180 private presses (strong in The Janus Press and Stinehour Press imprints); a small collection of decorated cloth bindings of late nineteenth and early twentieth centuries. Other emphases of special collections are Canadian literature, especially Franco-Canadian literature; Canadian history, especially eastern Canada; Greek and Latin classics; and English history and literature of the Tudor period.

Rare Book Collections

Charles Whittingham Collection. The library of the eminent English printer; includes Chiswick Press imprints.

Publius Ovidius Naso. A collection of illustrated editions of Ovid's works, the majority of them of the *Metamorphoses.* Although the Ovid collection has the works of several editors, commentators, and translators, the emphasis is on the artists who have visually interpreted the works of Ovid.

1682
Vermont Technical College
Hartness Library
Randolph Center, Vermont 05061

Telephone. (802) 728-3391

Institutional Description. Vermont Technical College has a history as a public educational institution that began in 1801. The present name was adopted in 1962. Enrollment: 761.

Library Administration. Dewey Patterson, Director.

Library General Holdings. 50,000 volumes; 400 magazine and journal subscriptions; 8 newspaper subscriptions.

Special Collections

A special collection on **Engineering and Agriculture** is maintained. The agricultural materials have an emphasis on dairying. The library also maintains the **College History Archives.**

Virginia

1683
Bridgewater College
Alexander Mack Memorial Library
East College Street
Bridgewater, Virginia 22812

Telephone. (703) 828-2501

Institutional Description. The privately supported liberal arts college is affiliated with the Church of the Brethren. It was founded in 1880 as Spring Creek Normal and Collegiate Institution. Enrollment: 737.

Library Administration. Ruth Greenawalt, Library Director.

Library General Holdings. 140,000 volumes; 512 periodical subscriptions; 34,000 microform units; 5,600 sound recordings; 450 filmstrips; 400 music scores; 100 videotapes; 16,000 government documents.

Special Collections

Genealogy. The library has a collection of about 600 genealogical sources with an emphasis on German names in Virginia, Pennsylvania, and Maryland.

Rare Book Collections

Church of the Brethren Collection. A collection of 1,500 volumes includes many rare Bibles and hymn books. The papers of Reuel B. Pritchett and M.R. Zigler are also in the collection, as well as the archives of the Southeastern Region of the Church of the Brethren.

Bridgewater College Archives. Includes about 1,300 volumes on Virginia history, including some Confederate imprints and early local imprints. Also included are papers of the late John Wayland, well-known Virginia historian.

1684
CBN University
University Library
CBN Center
Virginia Beach, Virginia 23463

Telephone. (804) 424-7000

Institutional Description. The privately supported university is a professional, graduate-level institution. Enrollment: 534.

Library Administration. Lois J. Lehman, Librarian; Jack L. Ralston, Special Collections Librarian.

Library General Holdings. 200,000 volumes; 2,100 current periodicals; 878,000 microforms; 5,800 audiovisual materials.

Special Collections

Clark Hymnology Collection. Acquired in 1982 from Keith C. Clark, a retired professional Army musician. Mr. Clark had a great love for hymnody and Psalmody and collected over 9,000 volumes in the field from various dealers and individuals. This was the largest private collection of books about hymnody and church music in the United States. Well-known books on the subject from the seventeenth century to the present are to be found here.

C.O. Baptista Film Mission. Formerly located in Wheaton, Illinois, the Mission utilized the medium of the moving picture (live and animation) to spread the Gospel throughout the world. There are some 125 reels of film, several projectors, and archival papers relating to the Mission dating from the 1940s and 1950s.

Archives of CBN and CBN University. Includes copies of all materials published by the CBN Ministries as well as materials published about the Ministry and its constituent groups.

1685
Clinch Valley College
John Cooke Wyllie Library
Wise, Virginia 24293

Telephone. (703) 328-2431

Institutional Description. The four-year college of the University of Virginia offers liberal arts and teacher education programs. Enrollment: 844.

Library Administration. Robin P. Benke, Acting Director of Library Services.

Library General Holdings. 118,000 volumes; 475 current periodical subscriptions; 16,000 microforms.

Special Collections

The library is a depository for United States and Virginia state government documents, with special emphasis on documents relating to education and coal. Many documents and manuscripts relating to Southwest Virginia, including the **James Taylor Adams Papers,** the **Elihu Jasper Sutherland Papers,** and the **Historical Society of Southwest Virginia Collection,** are housed in the Archival Room.

1686
College of William and Mary
Earl Gregg Swem Library
Williamsburg, Virginia 23185

Telephone. (804) 253-4550

Institutional Description. The publicly supported liberal arts college was founded in 1693. Enrollment: 6,290.

Library Administration. Nancy H. Marshall, University Librarian; Margaret Cook, Curator of Manuscripts and Rare Books.

Library General Holdings. 825,000 bound volumes; 6,100 current periodical subscriptions; 98 newspaper subscriptions; 694,000 microforms.

Rare Book Collections

The Swem Library contains a million manuscripts and 25,000 rare books chiefly relating to American history and Virginia history. The manuscript collection is strong in papers of such distinguished alumni as Thomas Jefferson, John Marshall, James Monroe, and John Tyler; papers of eighteenth- and nineteenth-century Virginia families such as those of the Tuckers, Blows, Carters, and Taliaferros; and papers of twentieth-century Virginia political leaders such as former Governor Mills E. Godwin, Jr., William M. Tuck, John Garland Pollard, and former Senator A. Willis Robertson. The rare book collection's strength lies in eighteenth- and early nineteenth-century travel accounts in the United States, American Revolutionary War pamphlets, and collections relating to printing, papermaking, and military history.

1687
Eastern Mennonite College/Seminary
Sadie A. Hartzler Library
Harrisonburg, Virginia 22801

Telephone. (703) 433-2771

Institutional Description. The privately supported college and seminary was founded in 1917 as an academy. It operates under the auspices of the Mennonite Church. Enrollment: 805.

Library Administration. James O. Lehman, Director of Libraries; Lois B. Bowman, Assistant Librarian.

Library General Holdings. 118,454 volumes; 800 periodical subscriptions; 20,000 microform units; 9,000 audiovisual materials.

Special Collections

The library has significant professional collections in the field of education (including a curriculum library), nursing, and sociology/social work. The J.B. Smith Collection (formerly the private library of the college's first president) contains numerous classics in Biblical studies from the early twentieth century.

Rare Book Collections

Menno Simons Historical Library/Archives. A collection relative to Anabaptist and Mennonite history, doctrine, sociology, genealogy, and the arts, including imprints from the sixteenth century to the present. An additional focus is on regional history, especially the German element in the Shenandoah Valley, its history, music, genealogy, and publishing. Also included are the archives of the College and of the Virginia Mennonite Conference.

1688
Emory and Henry College
Kelly Library
Emory, Virginia 24327

Telephone. (703) 944-3121

Institutional Description. The four-year liberal arts college is affiliated with the Holston Conference of the United Methodist Church. The college was founded in 1836. Enrollment: 778

Library Administration. Elaine Zaremba Jennerich, Librarian.

Library General Holdings. 128,000 volumes; 870 current periodical titles; 69,000 government documents; 5,-000 microforms.

Special Collections

The special collections of the library include the **Goodrich Wilson Southwest Virginia Collection,** an **Appalachian Oral History Project,** and the **Holston Conference [United Methodist Church] Archives.**

1689
Ferrum College
Stanley Library
Ferrum, Virginia 24088

Telephone. (703) 365-2121

Institutional Description. The church-related college operates under the auspices of the Virginia Methodist Church. Enrollment: 1,230.

Library Administration. Joe B. Mitchell, Head Librarian.

Library General Holdings. 75,000 volumes; 732 periodical and newspaper subscriptions.

Special Collections

The archives of the **Blue Ridge Institute** are housed in the Stanley Library. The archives serve as a depository for collected data on the history and folk culture of Southwest Virginia and the Blue Ridge Mountains and as a research facility for the use of students and faculty. Holdings include field tapes, written collection, student papers, videotapes, photographs, records, books, and historic manuscripts covering all areas of traditional life and culture.

1690
George Mason University
Charles Rogers Fenwick Library
4400 University Drive
Fairfax, Virginia 22030

Telephone. (703) 323-2000

Institutional Description. The publicly supported (state) university was founded as an extension center of the University of Virginia in 1948. It now offers a wide variety of programs and grants baccalaureate, master's, and doctorate degrees. Enrollment: 12,498.

Library Administration. Charlene S. Hurt, Director.

Library General Holdings. 281,000 volumes; 3,400 periodicals; 451,200 microforms; 134,000 government documents.

Special Collections

Federal Theatre Project Collection. Placed on permanent loan from the Library of Congress, this collection contains the major playscripts, radioscripts, sets, costume designs, and other creative materials produced by the Federal Theatre of the 1930s.

Northern Virginiana. Contains the papers of Congressman William Scott and historical collections from C. Harrison Mann including rare historical maps, atlases, geographies, and law books relating to Virginia; other papers of public officials are also housed.

Performing Arts Archives. Papers from the American Symphony Orchestra League and the Wolf Trap Foundation for the Performing Arts.

Photographic Collections. Prints and negatives, including those of Ollie Atkins, correspondent and photographer for the *Saturday Evening Post* and official White House Photographer from 1965 to 1974.

George Mason University Archives. Contains historical and administrative records of the University.

Rare Book Collections

A Rare Books Collection includes first editions and rare historical materials.

1691
Hampden-Sydney College
Eggleston Library
Hampden-Sydney, Virginia 23943

Telephone. (804) 223-4381

Institutional Description. The privately supported liberal arts college for men was founded in 1776. It is affiliated with the Presbyterian Church in the United States. Enrollment: 828.

Library Administration. David J. Norden, Head Librarian.

Library General Holdings. 154,000 volumes; 890 periodical subscriptions.

Special Collections

John Peter Mettauer Collection. Includes the personal papers of one of the college's first students who later became a teacher and physician; also includes medical journals dealing with his surgical techniques.

Other special collections include an **International Video Collection** and the **Hampden-Sydney Collection.**

1692
Hampton University
Collis P. Huntington Memorial Library
East Queen Street
Hampton, Virginia 23668

Telephone. (804) 727-5000

Institutional Description. The four-year university was founded in 1868 and offers four-year programs leading to the baccalaureate degree. The Division of Graduate Studies offers the M.A. and M.S. degree in 7 areas. Enrollment: 3,786

Library Administration. Jason C. Grant, III, Director.

Library General Holdings. 301,653 volumes; 1,306 periodicals and 52 newspapers; 31,615 microforms; 30,285 pamphlets; 4,373 microfilm reels; 3,000,000 archival items.

Special Collections

The most distinctive group of materials in the library is the **George Foster Peabody Collection,** composed of 28,939 items by and about Blacks. The **Hampton University Archives** includes approximately 7,000,000 items.

1693
Hollins College
Fishburn Library
P.O. Box 9000
Roanoke, Virginia 24020

Telephone. (703) 362-6591

Institutional Description. The privately supported liberal arts college for women was founded in 1842. Men are admitted to graduate programs. Enrollment: 953.

Library Administration. Richard E. Kirkwood, Librarian; Anthony B. Thompson, Archivist.

Library General Holdings. 225,000 volumes; 1,250 serial, continuation, and periodical subscriptions; 160,000 microforms; 1,200 videotapes; 500 audiotapes; 5,000 audio discs; 4,500 music scores.

Special Collections

The Fishburn Library possesses the following special subject collections: the **Enid Starkie Collection** of French symbolist literature (about 4,000 volumes); children's literature; cinema; history of women and women's studies; Benjamin Franklin.

Rare Book Collections

Lucy Winton McVitty Rare Book Room. This room houses rare books, manuscripts, and the archival records of Hollins College. The Archives contain manuscript sources for the history of the college and for the study of women's education. In addition to institutional records, there are the Cocke family papers (Charles Lewis Cocke and his daughter Matty, principally) and letters and diaries of students (mostly nineteenth century). Incunabula (about 60 volumes), fine press books, modern first editions, modern illustrated books, and a small selection of medieval manuscripts constitute the bulk of the rare books collection. Robert Frost, Benjamin Franklin, Margaret Wise Brown, and Enid Starkie are all well represented in collections of first editions and manuscripts. The collection is very broad with examples of written communication from Babylonian cuneiform tablets to Chinese wood block printed books (eleventh century) to a Shakespeare second folio to twentieth century fore-edge paintings.

1694
James Madison University
Carrier Library
Harrisonburg, Virginia 22807

Telephone. (703) 568-6578

Institutional Description. The publicly supported liberal arts and teachers institution was founded in 1908. Enrollment: 9,331.

Library Administration. Dennis Robison, Librarian; Chris Bolgiano, Special Collections Librarian.

Library General Holdings. 350,934 volumes; 2,814 current periodicals; 591,609 microforms; 125,413 government documents.

Special Collections

Educational Material Laboratories. Includes 8,035 pieces of curriculum materials in all media.

Rare Book Collections

Regional Historical Materials. Includes materials for central Shenandoah Valley history (i.e., Shenandoah, Page, and Augusta Counties). There is also a collection of Henkel Press books and manuscript collections of John T. Harris, Charles T. O'Ferrall, and others less prominent from the area.

1695
Liberty University
Liberty Library
Lynchburg, Virginia 24506

Telephone. (804) 582-2220

Institutional Description. The privately supported institution was established in 1971 as the Liberty Baptist College. It operates under the auspices of the Thomas Road Baptist Church. Enrollment: 4,239.

Library Administration. Ernest V. Liddle, Dean of Library Services; Russell File, Special Collections/Rare Books Librarian.

Library General Holdings. 170,000 volumes; 1,352 periodicals; 10 newspaper subscriptions; 450,000 microforms sheets (105,000 volumes); 1,447 music scores; 4,287 other learning materials.

Special Collections

The library houses 4,595 curriculum materials in the Curriculum Library; Sunday School books and other materials dating back to the nineteenth century (250 volumes); books, periodicals, memorabilia, pamphlets, newspaper clippings, gift offers from the Old Time Gospel Hour, and other materials and additional items relating to the ministry of Dr. Jerry Falwell and Thomas Road Baptist Church and its local and and national ministries (1,302 volumes); Church League of America collection of 200 pamphlet files on a large variety of topics concerning fundamentalism and conservative political themes.

1696
Lynchburg College
Knight-Capron Library
Lynchburg, Virginia 24501

Telephone. (804) 522-8399

Institutional Description. The privately supported liberal arts college was founded in 1903. It is affiliated with the Christian Church (Disciples of Christ). Enrollment: 1,764.

Library Administration. Mary C. Scudder, Library Director.

Library General Holdings. 150,654 volumes; 67,002 micro-reproductions (volume equivalent); 782 current periodical and newspaper subscriptions; 21,138 non-print materials including films, recordings, tapes, video.

Rare Book Collections

Rare Books and Manuscripts. Includes the history of the early iron industry in Europe and America; rare and out-of-print Americana; books, pamphlets, and promotional material on travel and accomodations in nineteenth-century America, particularly during the period of the "spas"; eighteenth- and nineteenth-century religious history; eighteenth-century books on "original science"; fifteenth- and sixteenth-century illuminated religious works; seventeenth-, eighteenth-, and nineteenth-century maps of North America, particularly of Virginia.

1697
Mary Baldwin College
Martha Stackhouse Grafton Library
Frederick Street
Staunton, Virginia 24401

Telephone. (703) 887-7000

Institutional Description. The privately supported liberal arts college for women was founded in 1842. It is affiliated with the Presbyterian Church in the United States. Enrollment: 761.

Library Administration. William C. Pollard, College Librarian.

Library General Holdings. 170,000 volumes; 650 periodical subscriptions.

Special Collections

The Charles G. Reigner Room of the main library contains the **Mary Julia Baldwin Collection;** the **Stuart Papers;** and books associated with the early history of the College.

1698
Mary Washington College
E. Lee Trinkle Library
1301 College Avenue
Fredericksburg, Virginia 22401

Telephone. (703) 899-4681

Institutional Description. The state-supported college of liberal arts and sciences was once part of the University of Virginia but became autonomous in 1972. Enrollment: 2,776.

Library Administration. Ruby Y. Weinbrecht, Librarian.

Library General Holdings. 311,000 volumes; 1,300 current magazine and newspaper subscriptions; 171,000 microforms; 98,500 government documents.

Rare Book Collections

The **Daniel H. Woodward Rare Book Room** houses a collection of more than 2,500 unique, rare, or very valuable works. Among the holdings is an incunabulum, a 1496 printing of Pliny's *Naturalis Historia.* A special collection of first and scarce editions of James Joyce's writings and another of the works of Claude Bernard, the nineteenth-century physiologist, are numbered among the items in the Woodward Collection. The library also maintains special collections of the works of Eudora Welty and William Butler Yeats.

1699
Marymount University
Ireton Library
2807 North Glebe Road
Arlington, Virginia 22207

Telephone. (703) 522-5600

Institutional Description. The privately supported college for women was founded in 1950. It is affiliated with the Roman Catholic Church. Enrollment: 1,575.

Library Administration. Deborah Leather, Dean for Library and Learning Services.

Library General Holdings. 68,000 volumes; 580 current periodicals; 76,500 microforms.

Special Collections

Special collections include books on management and English and American literature. The **Gertrude Hoyt Collection** contains books and other materials in the field of economics.

1700
New River Community College
Library
P.O. Box 1127
Dublin, Virginia 24084

Telephone. (703) 674-4121

Institutional Description. In 1966, the Virginia General Assembly formed the Virginia Community College System. The New River Community College was created from the Radford Area Vocation/Technical School. Enrollment: 1,651.

Library Administration. Roberta S. White, Coordinator of Library Services.

Library General Holdings. 25,000 volumes; 238 periodical titles; 25,300 microforms.

Special Collections

The library has a special collection of materials for the hearing impaired.

1701
Norfolk State University
Lyman Beecher Brooks Library
2401 Corprew Street
Norfolk, Virginia 23504

Telephone. (804) 623-8600

Institutional Description. The publicly supported state liberal arts and teachers university grants associate, baccalaureate, and master's degrees. Enrollment: 7,496.

Library Administration. Patricia Gardner Jordan, Director.

Library General Holdings. 200,000 volumes; 2,300 current magazine and journal subscriptions.

Special Collections

The library's collections support the liberal arts and teacher education programs of the University.

H.H. Bozeman Resources Centers. These Centers supply the supplementary materials and instructional media for the School of Education and for other schools and departments for which the collections are relevant. Two centers comprise this component: The Instructional Resource Center and the Multicultural Resource Center. The combined collections include resources and equipment appropriate for use at pre-school through adult education levels, with emphasis on the training and professional development of the teacher. Approximately 20,000 items are housed in the two Centers.

1702
Northern Virginia Community College
Annandale Campus Library
8333 Little River Turnpike
Annandale, Virginia 22003

Telephone. (703) 323-3004

Institutional Description. The publicly supported two-year college consists of five campuses serving the cities of Annandale, Alexandria, Manassas, Sterling, and Woodbridge. Enrollment: 18,521.

Library Administration. Frances Bernhardt, Coordinator of Library Services.

Library General Holdings. 85,000 volumes; 500 current periodical and newspaper titles.

Special Collections

Judy Mann DiStefano Women's History Collection. Includes over 500 books related to the history of women that were donated to the library after the death of Judy Mann DiStefano, a faculty member of the History Department.

1703
Old Dominion University
University Library
5215 Hampton Boulevard
Norfolk, Virginia 23508

Telephone. (804) 440-4141

Institutional Description. The publicly supported (state) liberal arts and professional university was founded in 1930 as a branch of the College of William and Mary. It separated in 1962, and now offers a wide variety of programs. Enrollment: 12,575.

Library Administration. Cynthia Duncan, University Librarian.

Library General Holdings. 535,000 volumes; 4,510 current periodicals; 791,000 microforms; 40,000 audiovisual items; 152,000 government documents.

Special Collections

The Alice Burke Endowment is used to obtain materials in the area of government and political science. The endowment was established by a former faculty member. The Elise Hofheimer Art Library Materials Endowment was established by Linda Hofheimer Kaufman and her husband George in honor of Mrs. Kaufman's mother to purchase materials for the Art Library. Other special collections include the **Moses Myers Collection** and the **George Gay Recording Collection.**

Career Planning and Placement Center. The Center maintains a career-resources library which contains information on occupations.

Women's Center. The Center has a library and reading room and provides information and referral to a variety of services and programs of particular interest to women.

1704
Paul D. Camp Community College
Library
P.O. Box 737
Franklin, Virginia 23851

Telephone. (804) 357-3298

Institutional Description. Paul D. Camp Community College is a two-year institution of higher education which operates under the statewide system of community colleges. Enrollment: 772.

Library Administration. L.M. Weaver, Director.

Library General Holdings. 25,000 volumes; 200 magazine and newspaper subscriptions.

Special Collections

The library has a small collection of children's books and a selection of murder mysteries and current fiction.

1705
Presbyterian School of Christian Education
Library
Route 6, Box 1A
Charlottesville, Virginia 22901

Telephone. (806) 977-3900

Institutional Description. The privately-supported

church-related graduate school was founded in 1914 for the purpose of preparing men and women for service in church vocations with emphasis upon the educational work of the church. Enrollment: 151.

Library General Holdings. The library is located on the campus of Union Theological Seminary, immediately adjacent to the Presbyterian School of Christian Education Campus. *See* **Union Theological Seminary.**

1706
Protestant Episcopal Seminary in Virginia
Bishop Payne Library
Alexandria, Virginia 22304

Telephone. (703) 370-6600

Institutional Description. The privately supported theological seminary, affiliated with the Protestant Episcopal Church, was founded in 1823. It offers programs on the graduate level only. Enrollment: 213.

Library Administration. Jack H. Goodwin, Librarian.

Library General Holdings. 110,000 volumes; 560 periodicals.

Special Collections

The growing reference collection is a rich resource of major works of religious scholarship. The collection dates back to the early years of the nineteenth century.

1707
Radford University
John Preston McConnell Library
Radford, Virginia 24142

Telephone. (703) 831-5471

Institutional Description. The publicly supported university was founded in 1910. Enrollment: 6,260.

Library Administration. John Gaboury, Librarian; Robert Turner, Assistant Director of Public Service.

Library General Holdings. 275,597 volumes; 2,178 current periodical subscriptions; 41,364 bound periodicals; 39,801 periodicals in microform; 10,345 non-print materials.

Special Collections

The McConnell Library houses the papers of John Preston McConnell, the first president of the University. It also has a **Virginia Collection,** a business collection, and an educational books collection.

1708
Randolph-Macon College
McGraw-Page Library
Ashland, Virginia 23005

Telephone. (804) 798-8372

Institutional Description. The privately supported college is affiliated with The United Methodist Church. It was founded in 1830. Enrollment: 958.

Library Administration. Dan T. Bedsole, Librarian; Nancy B. Newins, Reference Librarian.

Library General Holdings. 127,000 volumes; 700 current periodical and newspaper subscriptions (60 in microformat); audiovisual materials including recordings, motion pictures, videotapes, and slides.

Special Collections

William E. Dodd Collection. A book collection with emphasis on nineteenth- and early twentieth-century North Carolina history.

Richard Beale Davis Collection. This collection focuses on the intellectual development of the Colonial South.

Methodist Historical Collections. Emphasis on the Virginia/Baltimore Conferences; primarily print materials; some manuscripts, ephemera.

Rare Book Collections

J. Rives Childs Collections. Includes works by and about Giacomo Casanova and Ange and Sara Goudar, focusing on eighteenth-century Europe; works by and about Henry Miller; biographical materials (print and manuscript) relating to J. Rives Childs.

1709
Randolph-Macon Woman's College
Lipscomb Library
2500 Rivermont Avenue
Lynchburg, Virginia 24503

Telephone. (804) 846-7392

Institutional Description. The privately supported liberal arts college for women was founded in 1891. Although affiliated with the United Methodist Church, the college remains nonsectarian and ecumenical. Enrollment: 785.

Library Administration. Ruth Ann Edwards, Librarian.

Library General Holdings. 153,000 volumes; 780 current periodicals.

Special Collections

Special collections of the Lipscomb Library include a collection of writings by Virginia women; the **Herbert C. Lipscomb Rare Book Collection,** and the Randolph-Macon Women's College Archives which includes the **Pearl S. Buck Collection.**

1710
Saint Paul's College
James Solomon Russell Memorial Library
Lawrenceville, Virginia 23868

Telephone. (703) 848-3111

Institutional Description. Founded in 1882, this private institution is related to the Episcopal Church. Enrollment: 699.

Library Administration. Annie W. Harrison, Librarian.

Library General Holdings. 54,000 volumes; 245 current periodical titles; 26,000 microforms; 15,000 audiovisual materials.

Special Collections

The special collection room houses the **Shelton H. Short, III West Indian Collection** and the **Schomburg Collection on Black History** (microform).

1711
Shenandoah College and Conservatory
Howe Library
Winchester, Virginia 22601

Telephone. (703) 665-4632

Institutional Description. The privately supported institution offers programs in the liberal arts and specializes in music. It was founded in 1875 and is affiliated with The United Methodist Church. Enrollment: 902.

Library Administration. William A. Henderson, Administrative Librarian; Rosemary Green, Assistant Librarian (Reference).

Library General Holdings. 90,000 books; 5,400 bound periodicals; 4,600 microfilms; 9,000 microfiche; 9,700 recordings; 1,800 slides; 500 filmstrips; 500 periodical subscriptions.

Special Collections

EUB Historical Collection. This collection holds materials dealing with the formation, organization, and operation of the United Brethren and Evangelical United Brethren churches of the Virginia Annual conference to the time of merger with the Methodist Church in 1970. The Virginia Conference of the United Methodist Church has designated the Howe Library as the official depository of archival materials of the UB and EUB Virginia Conferences. These materials are housed with the EUB Collection and include histories, diaries, biographies, autobiographies, theological studies, personal papers, and autographs of significant ministerial and lay members of the UB and EUB churches, and General Conference minutes.

1712
Sweet Briar College
Mary Helen Cochran Library
Sweet Briar, Virginia 24595

Telephone. (804) 381-6138

Institutional Description. The privately supported liberal arts college for women was founded in 1901. Enrollment: 709.

Library Administration. John G. Jaffe, Director of Libraries.

Library General Holdings. 200,000 volumes; 975 periodical subscriptions.

Special Collections

Alumnae Collection. A growing body of publications by Sweet Briar College alumnae.

W.H. Auden Collection. Works in part or solely by author, critic, and translator, Wystan Hugh Auden.

Elizabeth G. Caldwell Theatre Collection. Comprised of audiotapes and sound recordings of Broadway musicals and of scripts and play anthologies.

Faculty Collection. Books and articles by Sweet Briar faculty members.

Fanny B. Fletcher Archives. Contains documents, publications by and about the College, student honor theses, photographs, tape recordings, memorabilia, and other materials relating to Sweet Briar's history.

Fletcher Collection. Surviving volumes from the private library of Indiana Fletcher Williams, whose bequest made possible the founding of Sweet Briar College. The Fletcher Collection, together with the Williams Collection, is a fine example of a typical nineteenth-century southern planter's personal library.

Kellogg Library. Originally known as the "Educational Laboratory Library" because it served the Education Department as a major resource, the Kellogg Library is a collection of juvenile literature, both fiction and nonfiction, and of curricular materials, such as teacher's texts and manuals. There is also a growing collection of children's sound recordings.

George Meredith Collection. Works by British novelist, poet, and essayist George Meredith. The most significant items in this collection are the number of first editions: all sixteen of his novels, the three collections of shorter tales, *The Essay of Comedy,* and ten volumes of poetry.

Onegin Collection. Annotated musical scores and books from the personal collection of opera singer Sigrid Onegin.

Evelyn Day Mullen—T.E. Lawrence Collection. This collection was begun by Miss Mullen and focuses on Lawrence the writer rather than Lawrence the legend. Miss Mullen was listed in the directory of American Book Collectors as a major T.E. Lawrence collector.

Rare Book Collections

Fergus Reid Rare Book Room. Contains books designated as rare because of their age, or as examples of fine printing or fine binding, or rare due to being first or limited or signed editions.

Williams Collection. Volumes from the private library of the Williams families, the founding family of Sweet Briar College. As with the Fletcher Collection, the Williams Collection is representative of the typical nineteenth century planter's personal library.

Virginia Woolf Collection. Comprised of many signed, first editions of works by novelist and essayist Virginia Woolf.

1713
Tidewater Community College Library
State Route 135
Portsmouth, Virginia 13703

Telephone. (804) 484-2121

Institutional Description. The former Frederick College was established as the site of the first Tidewater Community College Campus in 1968. There are now three campuses in the system. Enrollment: 7,976.

Library Administration. Henry W. Rejent, Director.

Library General Holdings. 117,462 volumes; 30,923 microfiche; 27,757 microfilms.

Special Collections

The library maintains a special **Virginia Collection** and a collection of career planning items.

1714
Union Theological Seminary in Virginia
Seminary Library
3401 Brook Road
Richmond, Virginia 23227

Telephone. (804) 355-0671

Institutional Description. The privately supported theological seminary was founded in 1812. It is affiliated with the Presbyterian Church (U.S.A.), and offers programs at the graduate level only. Enrollment: 229.

Library Administration. John B. Trotti, Librarian.

Library General Holdings. 254,000 volumes; 1,200 periodicals. The library is a major research library with particular strengths in Biblical studies, Presbyterian history and theology.

Special Collections

In recent years the Seminary purchased the library of Dr. George Gunn (a collection strong in Scots history, literature, and theology) and the library of Dr. H.H. Rowley (an Old Testament collection). In 1976, the library of Dr. Gotthold Muller, a collection of nineteenth- and twentieth-century German technology and philosophy. The Muller library encompasses the formative theological trends of the nineteenth century and adds significant continental reformed writings as well as rich materials from the Lutheran tradition. In 1983, a collection of patristic, Calvin, and other Reformed material was purchased from Dr. Thomas F. Torrance of Edinburgh, significantly strengthening the research collection in Reformed theology.

Reigner Recording Library. This library includes more than 24,000 reels and cassettes of magnetic tape of sermons, worship services, theological lectures, and religious radio programs by leading church persons throughout the world. The library has the only recording of the entire proceedings and assemblies of the World Council of Churches. In 1978, the library became the depository and authorized distributor of the **Reinhold Niebuhr Audio Tape Collection.** The library also serves as the official repository and circulating agent of the radio programs of the Broadcasting and Film Commission of the National Council of Churches. Also included are 1,800 kinescopes of the Council's television programs and numerous productions of the Protestant Radio and Television Center.

1715
University of Richmond
Boatwright Memorial Library
Richmond, Virginia 23173

Telephone. (804) 289-8458

Institutional Description. The privately supported university is affiliated with the Baptist General Association of Virginia. It was founded in 1830. Enrollment: 3,-806.

Library Administration. John Tyson, University Librarian; James E. Gwin, Director of Technical Services.

Library General Holdings. 350,000 books and bound volumes; 3,300 periodical subscriptions; 170,000 microforms; 200,000 government documents; 9,600 sound recordings; 25,000 media items; 9,000 music scores.

Special Collections

Learning Resources Center. Includes the Curriculum Library and some 24,000 items of media (films, audiocassettes, videocassettes, slides, and kits).

Music Library. Includes 18,000 items of music scores, compact discs, LPs, audiocassettes dealing with jazz, the classical period, early childhood education, and the manuscripts of Virginia composer Hilton Rufty. Also includes the complete published works of the noted twentieth-century American composer, F. Flaxington Harker.

Science Library. Includes a special collection of early nineteenth- and twentieth-century books on chemistry from the collection of Dr. E. Emmet Reid.

Virginia Baptist Historical Society and University of

Richmond Archives. Consists of 25,000 volumes of church records, books, serials, manuscripts, and journals dating from the seventeenth century to the present on Southern Baptists and the Baptist Church in Virginia. Included in the collections are the complete archives of the University of Richmond and the congressional papers of David Satterfield and Watkins Abitt.

Rare Book Collections

Rare Books Collection. Contains materials related to Virginia and Richmond, rare editions, Confederate imprints (500 items), pamphlets, incunabula, and special art bindings from the nineteenth century. Included among the collections are first editions of Charles Dickens, Carl Van Vechten, Gertrude Stein, Ernest Hemingway, James Branch Cabell, Clifford Dowdey, and Ellen Glasgow. There is also a collection of 200 volumes of early editions of the Mother Goose series.

1716
University of Virginia
University Libraries
Charlottesville, Virginia 22903

Telephone. (804) 924-3026

Institutional Description. The publicly supported state university, primarily for men, was founded in 1819 under the sponsorship of Thomas Jefferson. The graduate and professional schools are coeducational. Enrollment: 18,485.

Library Administration. W. Frantz, Jr., Director; Edmund Berkeley, Special Collections Librarian.

Library General Holdings. 3,000,000 volumes; 14,000,000 periodicals; 9,000,000 microforms; 4,400 sound recordings; over 10,000,000 manuscripts, maps, photographs, and pictures.

Rare Book Collections

Alderman Library. The Alderman Library collections of American literature and history are internationally known. Foremost among the library's rare books and manuscripts are the collections of Edgar Allan Poe, Nathaniel Hawthorne, Stephen Crane, Mark Twain, William Faulkner, Robert Frost, John Dos Passos, and Ernest Hemingway as well as the original manuscripts of Walt Whitman's *Leaves of Grass,* Thomas Wolfe's *You Can't Go Home Again,* and John Steinbeck's *Grapes of Wrath.* The library's collection of 400 titles by Argentine writer Jorge Luis Borges is the most comprehensive in the United States. In American history, the McGregor Collection focuses on the Southeastern United States. Historical figures represented include Thomas Jefferson, James Madison, James Monroe, Edward R. Stettinius, Hugh Scott, Harry F. Byrd, Sr., Harry F. Byrd, Jr., and Francis Pickens Miller.

1717
Virginia Commonwealth University
James Branch Cabell Library
910 West Franklin Street
Richmond, Virginia 23284

Telephone. (804) 257-1116

Institutional Description. The publicly supported state university was formed in 1968 by the combining of the Richmond Professional Institute and the Medical College of Virginia. Enrollment: 15,474.

Library Administration. William J. Judd, Director; John H. Whaley, Special Collections Librarian and Archivist.

Library General Holdings. 900,000 volumes in all formats; 8,600 periodical subscriptions.

Special Collections

Special collections of the library include the **Book Art Collection;** the **James Branch Cabell Collection;** the **Judaica Collection,** and a collection of medical artifacts.

1718
Virginia Military Institute
Preston Library
Lexington, Virginia 24450

Telephone. (703) 463-6213

Institutional Description. The publicly supported liberal arts and engineering college for men combines academic and military education. A state institution, the school was founded in 1839. Enrollment: 1,273.

Library Administration. Colonel James Edwin Gaines, Jr., Head Librarian.

Library General Holdings. 273,000 volumes; 905 current periodicals; 126,000 government documents.

Special Collections

The library is especially strong in the areas of Confederate history, Civil War history, military science, mathematics, and German literature. The Special Collections Division contains the **United Daughters of the Confederacy Collection;** the **Camillus Christian Collection in Confederate History;** the **Donald E. Rheutan '17 Collection** in typography and history of printing; the **Col. William Couper Collection** in local history.

George C. Marshall Research Library. Dedicated to the General of the Army George Catlett Marshall, the library includes the World War II Chief of Staff's personal papers as well as a collection of material relating to United States military and diplomatic history covering much of the twentieth century.

Rare Book Collections

The library maintains a collection of rare works in military history associated with Robert E. Lee, Joseph Johnston, and "Stonewall" Jackson.

1719
Virginia Polytechnic Institute and State University
University Libraries
Blacksburg, Virginia 24061

Telephone. (703) 961-5593

Institutional Description. The publicly supported institution is the largest in the state. A land-grant university, it was founded in 1872. Enrollment: 22,554.

Library Administration. Paul M. Gherman, University Librarian; Glenn L. McMullen, Head, Special Collections Department.

Library General Holdings. 1,600,000 bound volumes; 19,000 current periodical subscriptions; 3,900,000 microform units; 125,000 maps.

Special Collections

The main strengths of the University Libraries are in the physical and biological sciences and in engineering. The Libraries also collect comprehensively in the area of the history of Southwest Virginia.

Rare Book Collections

Rare Books Collections. The scope of the collections covers the history of technology in the United States and Western Europe in the eighteenth and nineteenth centuries; Southwest Virginia history; the history of the trans-Mississippi American West in the nineteenth century, with an emphasis on the contribution of native Virginians to the area; British and American literature, ca. 1880-1945; and the works of Sherwood Anderson.

Manuscript Collections. These collections cover: the railroad history of the South and Midwest in the nineteenth century (archives of the Norfolk and Western Railway and Southern Railway systems); aeronautical and space history in the United States before 1970 (Archives of American Aerospace Exploration), including the papers of Christopher C. Kraft, Jr., Samuel Herrick, Melvin N. Gough, John T. Parsons, and others; women's involvement in the profession of architecture, especially the pioneer generation of women architects of the early twentieth century (International Archive of Women in Architecture); the history of Southwest Virginia, including the papers of J. Hoge Tyler and the papers of notable Southwest Virginia families, including the Prestons, the Blacks, the Kents, and the Appersons.

1720
Virginia State University
Johnston Memorial Library
Petersburg, Virginia 23803

Telephone. (804) 520-5000

Institutional Description. The publicly supported liberal arts and professional university was founded in 1882. It is composed of the Liberal Arts College, the Teachers College, the Land-Grant College, and the Divisions of General Education, Field Services, and Graduate Studies and Research. Enrollment: 3,748.

Library Administration. Catherine V. Bland, Director.

Library General Holdings. 212,000 volumes; 1,677 periodical and newspaper subscriptions; 333,000 microforms; 82,000 government documents; 300,000 items of archival materials.

Special Collections

The University seeks to promote and sustain academic programs that integrate instruction, research, and extension-public service in a design most responsive to the needs and endeavors of the individuals and groups within its scope of influence. The library's collections reflect these goals with strengths in the liberal arts, research areas, community service, and teacher education fields.

1721
Virginia Union University
University Library
1500 North Lombardy Street
Richmond, Virginia 23220

Telephone. (804) 257-5600

Institutional Description. The private university is affiliated with the American Baptist Convention. It offers a liberal arts program and graduate study in theology. Enrollment: 1,282.

Library Administration. Verdelle V. Bradley, Librarian.

Library General Holdings. 140,000 volumes; 385 current periodical subscriptions; 11,000 microforms.

Special Collections

The library maintains a special collection of materials in Black studies as well as the Schomburg Collection (microform).

1722
Washington and Lee University
University Library
Lexington, Virginia 24450

Telephone. (703) 463-8400

Institutional Description. The privately supported university, primarily for men, was founded by Scotch-Irish pioneers in 1749. It is composed of the College of Arts and Sciences, the School of Commerce, Economics and Politics, and the School of Law. Enrollment: 1,731.

Library Administration. Barbara J. Brown, University Librarian.

Library General Holdings. 334,766 volumes; 1,464 periodical titles; 112,023 microforms; 84,173 government documents; 281,339 manuscript items.

Special Collections

There is a steady growth in the special collections of rare books and manuscripts through gifts of alumni and friends. These collections include valuable resources in the history of the University and Rockbridge County, of the Confederacy, and of the Westward Movement. The special collections include the **Lee Collection** of manuscripts, letters, and other personal papers dating mostly from 1865-1870 while Lee was president of the institution; books from nineteenth-century debating societies such as the Franklin Society, Graham Society, and Washington Society; and collections relating to area pioneer colonial families.

1723
Wytheville Community College
College Library
1000 East Main Street
Wytheville, Virginia 24382

Telephone. (703) 228-5541

Institutional Description. The publicly supported two-year college, a division of the Virginia Community College System, opened in 1963. Enrollment: 1,019.

Library Administration. Anna Ray Roberts, Coordinator, Library Services.

Library General Holdings. 29,000 volumes; 250 serial subscriptions; 1,700 microforms; 2,500 audiovisual titles.

Special Collections

F.B. Kegley Library. Contains materials related to the local history and genealogy of Southwest Virginia. Included in the collection are newspapers, census records and court records on microfilm, historical maps, oral history interviews, local cemetery inventories, and pamphlets.

Washington

1724
Central Washington University
University Library
Ellensburg, Washington 98926

Telephone. (509) 963-1401

Institutional Description. The publicly supported liberal arts and teachers university was founded in 1890. Enrollment: 7,163.

Library Administration. Frank A. Schneider, Director of Library Services.

Library General Holdings. 415,000 volumes; 2,000 journal subscriptions; 516,000 government documents; 811,000 microforms; 26,000 audiovisual materials; 67,000 maps.

Special Collections

The University's primary purpose is academically discovering and creating new knowledge, preserving and transmitting it, and applying it to life's experience. The library's collections support the various programs of the University in the fields of liberal arts and sciences, professional and technical fields, education, business, applied sciences, and engineering technology.

Archival Services. The Archives Collection is designed to preserve all public records, manuscripts, and photographs on local and regional topics.

1725
Centralia College
Learning Resource Center
600 West Locust
Centralia, Washington 98531

Telephone. (206) 736-9391

Institutional Description. The two-year community college was founded in 1926. Enrollment: 2,929.

Library Administration. Deborah York, Coordinator.

Library General Holdings. 30,000 books; 350 periodical titles; 4,000 microforms; 600 audiovisual materials.

Special Collections

The learning resources center maintains a collection of materials on the **Centralia Massacre.**

1726
Eastern Washington University
John F. Kennedy Memorial Library
Mail Stop No. 84, E.W.U.
Cheney, Washington 99004

Telephone. (509) 359-2475

Institutional Description. The publicly supported liberal arts and teachers institution was founded in 1882. Enrollment: 8,200.

Library Administration. Charles H. Baumann, University Librarian; Jay Weston Rea, University Archivist; Charles V. Mutschler, Assistant Archivist.

Library General Holdings. 1,537,659 items including 303,779 classified volumes; 77,759 periodical volumes; 183,797 government documents (full size); 304,290 government documents (microform); and other materials.

Special Collections

A.T. Perry Science Fiction and Fantasy Collection. Contains 2,683 titles including double novels, anthologies, and periodicals from 1942 to 1970 (49 titles).

Ceylon S. Kingston Pacific Northwest Collection. In excess of 21,800 volumes and over 18,000 titles including a retrospective collection of Washington State documents. The collection focuses upon the Inland Empire with supporting materials concerning the Pacific Northwest, including Alberta, British Columbia, Yukon Territory, and Alaska. The Kingston Collection also includes 2,600 maps and 6,800 photographs. Maps are primarily from U.S. government documents and include older topographic maps. Photographs are primarily of Cheney and the University, but do include some other views from the immediate area.

Ye Galleon Press Collection. Contains a nearly complete collection of titles by Ye Galleon Press, a Fairfield, Washington firm specializing in western and local history.

Rare Book Collections

Archives and Special Collections. Includes the following: The Beverly Clarke Mosby Papers, including correspondence with Col. J.S. Mosby; the Byron Opendack Papers which include Mr. Opendack's literary manuscripts; and research notes by faculty members, maps, photographs, and ephemera, most of which relate to the history of the University; the Eastern Regional Branch of the Washington State Archives consisting of over 6,000 cubic feet of public records from municipal, county, state, and other public agencies in the twelve eastern-most counties of the state (includes assessment and tax rolls, voter registration records, court case files, and municipal government records).

1727
Edmonds Community College Library
20000 68th Avenue West
Lynnwood, Washington 98036

Telephone. (206) 771-5000

Institutional Description. The college was founded in 1967 as a state two-year community college. Enrollment: 6,609.

Library Administration. Lena M. Danko, Librarian.

Library General Holdings. 30,022 volumes; 475 periodical titles; 5,000 pamphlets.

Special Collections

The library has a Career Center and maintains specialized collections in horticulture and paralegal studies.

1728
Evergreen State College
Daniel J. Evans Library
Olympia, Washington 98505

Telephone. (206) 866-6000

Institutional Description. The publicly supported liberal arts college was founded in 1947. Enrollment: 2,965.

Library Administration. Sarah Pederson, Acting Director.

Library General Holdings. 177,000 books; 27,000 reference volumes; 1,500 periodical subscriptions.

Special Collections

An Evergreen education is interdisciplinary and helps the student understand the relationships among the arts, humanities, natural sciences, and social sciences. The collections of the Evans Library support this innovative approach by offering students varied and rich holdings in all disciplines.

1729
Gonzaga University
Crosby Library
East 502 Boone Avenue
Spokane, Washington 99258

Telephone. (509) 328-4220

Institutional Description. The privately supported Roman Catholic university was founded in 1887 by the Jesuits. Enrollment: 3,103.

Library Administration. Robert L. Burr, Director; Mary M. Carr, Head of Technical Services.

Library General Holdings. 290,000 volumes (175,000 book titles); 1,615 periodical subscriptions; 65,750 bound periodical volumes; 17,754 microcards; 180,000 microfiche; 6,200 microfilm.

Special Collections

The Crosby Library (named in honor of Bing Crosby, an alumnus of Gonzaga University) has special strengths in philosophy, theology (particularly Roman Catholic), Jesuitica, and Pacific Northwest history.

Rare Book Collections

The rare books and manuscripts collections include the **Hopkins Collection** including works of Gerard Manley Hopkins; **Bing Crosby Collection** of books, records, memorabilia, and papers; **Fox Collection** consisting of radical turn-of-the-century materials, many pertaining to Jay Fox, anarchist and labor radical); and playbills.

1730
Grays Harbor College
John Spellman Library
Aberdeen, Washington 98520

Telephone. (206) 532-902

Institutional Description. The publicly supported junior college was founded in 1930. Enrollment: 2,405.

Library Administration. Susan Moore, Librarian; Don Cates, Librarian.

Library General Holdings. 43,086 volumes; 331 periodical subscriptions; 10 newspaper subscriptions; 1,293 audiovisual materials; 37 microform titles; 170 orchestral scores.

Special Collections

Pacific Northwest Room. Contains books and periodicals related to Washington and its surrounding states and provinces. Some are historical but many represent varied aspects of life and civilization in the Pacific Northwest.

Special Collections Room. Contains books, periodicals, and uncatalogued works on fisheries, oceanography, and water resources relating to Grays Harbor and Washington State, plus more general materials. A second area houses books printed before 1900.

1731
Northwest College of the Assemblies of God
D.V. Hurst Library
P.O. Box 579
Kirkland, Washington 98083

Telephone. (206) 822-8266

Institutional Description. The publicly supported Christian liberal arts college was founded in 1934. It is operated under the Assemblies of God Church, and offers undergraduate programs in general education as well as training for Christian service. Enrollment: 580.

Library Administration. Ann D. Rosett, Head Librarian.

Library General Holdings. 74,800 cataloged items; 468 current periodical subscriptions.

Special Collections

The D.V. Hurst Library houses collections of both Christian education and elementary education curriculum materials. Special collections on the history of the Pentecostal Movement in America and Assemblies of God materials (catalogued and vertical file collections) reflect the history and orientation of Northwest College. **The Henry Ness Collection** consists of different translations of the Bible.

1732
Olympic College
Learning Resources Center
16th and Chester
Bremerton, Washington 98310

Telephone. (206) 478-4551

Institutional Description. The two-year college has several extension centers and a cooperative program through Puget Sound Naval Shipyard for apprenticeship training. The college was founded in 1946. Enrollment: 5,449.

Library Administration. Emmet E. Hoynes, Director.

Library General Holdings. 50,000 books; 475 periodicals; 3,000 microfilm reels.

Special Collections

The **George W. Martin Collection on Mountaineering and Outdoor Literature** is maintained in the library of the learning resources center.

1733
Pacific Lutheran University
Robert A. L. Mortvedt Library
Tacoma, Washington 98447

Telephone. (206) 535-7500

Institutional Description. The privately supported university is affiliated with the American Lutheran Church. It was founded in 1890. Enrollment: 3,855.

Library Administration. John W. Heussman, Library Director; Kerstin Ringdahl, Special Collections Librarian.

Library General Holdings. 325,000 items include a basic core of materials of all types to support an undergraduate curriculum and master's level professional programs in a number of fields; included are 2,000 periodical subscriptions, 500,000 microforms, 6,500 audiovisual and computer software items.

Rare Book Collections

The rare books collections include historical records of people, families, and organizations associated with the Scandinavian (Denmark, Finland, Norway, Sweden, Iceland) immigration to the Pacific Northwest; consists of letters, diaries, biographies, directories, catalogs, rosters, and brochures.

The oral history collection includes 250 cassettes from interviews made with Scandinavian immigrants to the Pacific Northwest; also includes written records of family histories, photographs, and other material collected during the interview.

The library maintains a collection of Scandinavian Bibles and hymnals from the nineteenth and twentieth centuries published in the U.S. for the immigrants. A collection of Scandinavian printing is also maintained showing the art and craft of fine bookmaking and printing in the Scandinavian countries.

1734
Pierce College
Learning Resource Center
9401 Farwest Drive S.W.
Tacoma, Washington 98498

Telephone. (206) 964-6500

Institutional Description. Formerly known as Fort Steilacoom Community College, Pierce College was founded in 1967. Enrollment: 7,109.

Library Administration. Patricia Williams, Librarian.

Library General Holdings. 44,000 volumes; 334 current periodical subscriptions.

Special Collections

Special collections are maintained on early childhood education, criminal justice, and mid-management.

1735
Saint Martin's College
College Library
Lacey, Washington 98503

Telephone. (206) 491-4700

Institutional Description. The four-year coeducational college was founded by Benedictine educators in 1895. Enrollment: 1,006.

Library Administration. Joan McIntyre, Librarian.

Library General Holdings. 85,000 volumes; 350 current periodical subscriptions; 18,000 microforms.

Special Collections

The library has special collections on Northwest history, children's literature, and theology.

1736
Seattle Pacific University
Weter Memorial Library
3307 Third Avenue W.
Seattle, Washington 98119

Telephone. (206) 281-2111

Institutional Description. The privately supported Christian liberal arts university is affiliated with the Free Methodist Church of North America. Enrollment: 2,988.

Library Administration. George E. McDonough, Director of Learning Resources.

Library General Holdings. 137,000 volumes; 1,100 periodical subscriptions; 275,000 microforms.

Special Collections

Special holdings of the library are in the fields of business, education, health sciences, and religion.

1737
Seattle University
Learning Resource Center
Seattle, Washington 98122

Telephone. (206) 626-6868

Institutional Description. The privately supported Roman Catholic university is under the sponsorship and direction of the Jesuit Society. Enrollment: 4,348.

Library Administration. Lawrence E. Thomas, University Librarian.

Library General Holdings. 206,000 volumes; 1,440 current periodical subscriptions; 185,000 microforms.

Special Collections

The collections of the library include special subject holdings in business administration, computer software engineering, and theology.

1738
Shoreline Community College
Ray W. Howard Library/Media Center
16101 Greenwood Avenue North
Seattle, Washington 98133

Telephone. (206) 546-4551

Institutional Description. The two-year college had its beginning in 1964. At that time the college offered college transfer courses in the evening at Shoreline High School. In 1965, the college opened the doors of a new college campus at the present site. Enrollment: 6,660.

Library Administration. Patricia G. Kelley, Librarian.

Library General Holdings. 70,000 books, periodicals, and microfilms.

Special Collections

A special collection of materials on ethnic studies is maintained in the Howard Library.

1739
South Seattle Community College
Library
6000 16th Avenue, S.W.
Seattle, Washington 98103

Telephone. (206) 764-5300

Institutional Description. The two-year college was established in 1969 as one of three colleges comprising the Seattle Community College District. In 1970, the college moved to its current location in south Seattle. Enrollment: 5,775.

Library Administration. Mary E. Petty, Librarian.

Library General Holdings. 20,498 volumes; 360 current periodical titles; 2,535 microforms; 3,028 audiovisual materials.

Special Collections

The **Seattle Folklore Society Archives** are housed in the library. There are also specialized collections on landscaping and horticulture.

1740
Spokane Community College
Library
North 1810 Greene Street
Spokane, Washington 99207

Telephone. (509) 536-7042

Institutional Description. The two-year college was established in 1963 when a transfer program was added to the 47-year-old Spokane Technical and Vocational School. In 1970, the college became a separate unit of the new multi-college concept and was named Spokane Community College. Enrollment: 4,790.

Library Administration. Norma J. Rosenberger, Head Librarian.

Library General Holdings. 32,706 volumes; 536 current periodical subscriptions.

Special Collections

The library maintains specialized collections in automotive technology, electronics, and health occupations.

1741
Tacoma Community College
Library
5900 South 12th Street
Tacoma, Washington 98465

Telephone. (206) 756-5050

Institutional Description. The two-year community college opened in the fall of 1965. Enrollment: 4,489.

Library Administration. Richard Spangler, Director of Learning Resources.

Library General Holdings. 70,000 books; 400 periodical titles.

Special Collections

A special collection on **Ethnic and Northwest History** is maintained in the library.

1742
University of Puget Sound
Collins Memorial Library
1500 North Warner Street
Tacoma, Washington 98416

Telephone. (206) 756-3244

Institutional Description. The privately supported liberal arts institution is affiliated with The United Methodist Church. Enrollment: 4,118.

Library Administration. Desmond Taylor, Library Director.

Library General Holdings. 305,053 bound volumes; 1,376 current periodicals; 122,415 microforms; 14,693 music scores; 122 videotapes; 26,871 recorded compositions; 6,300 cassette tapes.

Special Collections

The liberal arts undergraduate library collections are dedicated to the support of the University curriculum and include a Learning Resource Library in the Education Department. The library also maintains a collection of Holocaust literature.

Homer T. Bone Papers. Correspondence, manuscripts, and personal papers of the mid-twentieth-century U.S. Senator and circuit judge.

Rare Book Collections

Lionel Pries Rare Book Collection. Includes 25 volumes of sixteenth- and seventeenth-century atlases, a 1577 first edition of Holinshed's *Chronicles of England, Scotland, and Ireland.*

1743
University of Washington
Suzzallo Library
1400 N.E. Campus Parkway
Seattle, Washington 98195

Telephone. (206) 543-6616

Institutional Description. The publicly supported state university was founded in 1861. It now offers a wide variety of programs. Enrollment: 33,811.

Library Administration. Merle N. Boylan, Director; Gary L. Menges, Special Collections Librarian.

Library General Holdings. 4,550,000 volumes; 39,000 current serial subscriptions; 4,559,000 microforms.

Special Collections

In addition to the major humanities and social sciences collections, Suzzallo Library contains many specialized collection areas, including Manuscripts and University Archives, the Microforms-Newspapers Section, and Government Publications. The **Pacific Northwest Collection** contains 47,000 book and periodical volumes, 370,600 historical photographs, and 27,000 architectural drawings. The library also maintains the congressional papers of Senators Henry M. Jackson and Warren G. Magnuson.

East Asia Library. This library is the major resource center of its kind north of Berkeley and west of Chicago. The collections are especially strong in anthropology, art, business, communications, languages, literature, law, music, and political science with respect to the cultures of China, Japan, Korea, Inner Asia, and Southeast Asia. The library contains 304,000 volumes.

Health Sciences Library. The library serves as the collection and operations base for the Pacific Northwest Regional Health Sciences Library Services and houses the King County Medical Society Library Services and the Drug Information Services.

1744
Washington State University
Holland Library
Pullman, Washington 99163

Telephone. (509) 335-5586

Institutional Description. Since its founding in 1890, the state-supported university has been a multi-purpose institution. It consists of seven colleges and a graduate school and offers more than 125 undergraduate major fields of study. Enrollment: 14,832.

Library Administration. Donald Bushaw, Director of Libraries.

Library General Holdings. 1,456,181 volumes; 20,200 current periodicals; 2,234,700 microforms.

Special Collections

Holland Library provides strong collections in the social sciences and the humanities, as well as sophisticated service components designed to assist students, faculty and researchers in utilizing these resources. Manuscripts, Archives, and Special Collections contain rich collections of primary resource materials—books, manuscripts, photographs—to support study and research in a number of fields, including Pacific Northwest history, modern British literature, regional publishing, veterinary history, agricultural history, wildlife and outdoor recreation, WSU history, and other subjects.

1745
Western Washington University
Mabel Zoe Wilson Library
Bellingham, Washington 98225

Telephone. (206) 676-3193

Institutional Description. Western Washington University is a state institution founded in 1893. Enrollment: 10,460.

Library Administration. Diane Parker, Director of Libraries; Susan Edmonds, Special Collections and Rare Books Manager.

Library General Holdings. 541,000 volumes of books and bound periodicals; 3,700 periodical subscriptions.

Special Collections

Mongols and Greater Mongolia. This collection include works in many languages with a large number of works in Mongolian languages from all areas of Greater Mongolia. Many rare or unusual items are included and several formats are represented, including microform, serials, monographs, textbooks, and children's literature.

China. This collection deals with minorities in China. Primarily in Chinese, it also includes works in minority languages, especially Mongolian, but also Uighur, Kazakh, and Tibetan.

Small Press Publications. The library recently acquired a group of small press publications that were collected by a local small publisher.

Rare Book Collections

Rare Book Collection. This is a small collection with major emphasis on voyages and exploratory expeditions of the Northwest.

1746
Whitworth College
Harriet Cheney Cowles Memorial Library
Hawthorne Street
Spokane, Washington 99251

Telephone. (509) 466-3260

Institutional Description. The liberal arts college was founded in 1890. Upon the invitation of the Presbyterian Church (U.S.A.), the college moved to its present location in 1914. Enrollment: 1,764.

Library Administration. Hans E. Bynagle, Chief Librarian.

Library General Holdings. 116,000 volumes; 875 current periodical subscriptions; 32,500 microforms.

Special Collections

The library's special collections include the **Presbyterian Church, Synod of Alaska-Northwest Collection,** the microcard collection of Early American Imprints through 1800; and the **Moldenhauer Collection** of twentieth-century music.

West Virginia

1747
Alderson Broaddus College
Pickett Library Media Center
Philippi, West Virginia 26416

Telephone. (404) 457-1700

Institutional Description. Alderson Broaddus College is a private institution affiliated with the American Baptist Churches, U.S.A. Enrollment: 755.

Library Administration. William B. Wartman III, Director, Library Media Services.

Library General Holdings. 92,000 volumes; 400 periodical subscriptions.

Special Collections

The library has special collections of books and periodicals on allied health and houses the **Baptist Historical Collection.**

David Johnson Historical Room. This addition to the library houses the Civil War historical collection of the West Virginia historian, Dr. C. Shirley Donnelly.

1748
Beckley College
Library and Resource Center
609 South Kanawha Street
Beckley, West Virginia 25801

Telephone. (304) 253-7351

Institutional Description. The two-year college was established in 1933 and is a private junior college. Enrollment: 1,216.

Library Administration. Evelyn Paice, Librarian.

Library General Holdings. 15,000 volumes; 140 periodical titles.

Special Collections

The library has special collections on West Virginia and children's literature.

1749
Bethany College
T.W. Phillips Memorial Library
Bethany, West Virginia 26032

Telephone. (304) 829-7000

Institutional Description. Bethany College is a private college affiliated with the Christian Church (Disciples of Christ). Enrollment: 786.

Library Administration. Jonas Barciauskas, Head Librarian.

Library General Holdings. 155,000 volumes; 580 current periodical subscriptions.

Special Collections

Campbell Room. Contains books, nineteenth-century periodicals published by individuals affiliated with the Disciples of Christ, letters, paintings, photographs, and museum pieces related to Bethany's founder and first president, Alexander Campbell.

1750
Concord College
J. Frank Marsh Library
Athens, West Virginia 24712

Telephone. (304) 384-3115

Institutional Description. Founded in 1872, Concord College is a publicaly supported four-year liberal arts college and teacher education institution. Enrollment: 2,032.

Library Administration. Thomas M. Brown, Director of Library and Media Services.

Library General Holdings. 130,000 volumes; 645 current periodical subscriptions; 34,500 microforms.

Special Collections

The library maintains the **West Virginia Collection** of 1,500 items on West Virginia culture and history. The **Wells Goodykoontz Collection** of autographed portraits and photographs of presidents and well-known personalities is housed in the library.

1751
Davis and Elkins College
College Learning Materials Center
Sycamore Street
Elkins, West Virginia 26241

Telephone. (304) 636-1900

Institutional Description. Davis and Elkins College is a private, independent, nonprofit college affiliated with the Presbyterian Church. Enrollment: 828.

Library Administration. Bob L. Mowery, Librarian.

Library General Holdings. 117,000 volumes; 725 current periodicals; 25,000 government documents; 21,000 microforms.

Special Collections

The library maintains the **Applalachian Region Collection** of 2,300 items; the **Don Marion Wolfe Collection** of 150 books by and about John Milton; and collections in the areas of photography and environmental sciences.

1752
Glenville State College
Robert F. Kidd Library
Glenville, West Virginia 26351

Telephone. (304) 462-7361

Institutional Description. Glenville State College was founded in 1873. It became a state normal school in 1898 and a state college in 1943. Enrollment: 1,557.

Library Administration. Ronnie W. Faulkner, Director.

Library General Holdings. 116,000 volumes; 635 current periodical subscriptions; 308,000 microforms; 62,000 government documents.

Special Collections

The **Alma Arbuckle Children's Center** contains more than 2,500 juvenile books supplemented by pamphlets and pictures. The library also maintains the **W.W. Baron Collection** of the papers of the former state governor (1960-64); the **Almira Sexton Letters** of correspondence detailing life in nineteenth-century West Virginia; and the **Bender Collection** of 3,411 art gallery catalogs, mainly from Parke-Benet covering the period 1950 to 1972.

1753
Marshall University
James E. Morrow Library
Huntington, West Virginia 25701

Telephone. (304) 696-2344

Institutional Description. The publicly supported institution was founded as Marshall Academy in 1837. It became a private college in 1858, a normal school under state sponsorship in 1867, and a teachers college in 1920. Enrollment: 8,306.

Library Administration. Kenneth Slack, Acting Director of Libraries; Lisle Brown, Curator of Special Collections; Cora Teel, Archivist/Rare Book Librarian.

Library General Holdings. 375,000 volumes; 2,300 periodical titles; 230,000 microforms; 19,600 audiovisual materials; 550,000 U.S. government documents.

Special Collections

Dr. Charles A. "Carl" Hoffman Library of the History of the Medical Sciences. This collection contains approximately 2,000 volumes dealing with medical history. Rare and scarce medical materials are added to the collection each year from a special endowment fund. While the collection covers the general field of medicine, it focuses on urology, venereal diseases, leprosy, and medical biography.

Dr. Rosanna Blake Library of Confederate History. This collection includes 5,000 volumes on the history of the Confederate States of America. It includes significant volumes on Robert E. Lee, Confederate military unit histories, as well as prints and broadsides. It has a significant number of Confederate imprints (over 700) as well as numerous pamphlets.

Jesse Stuart Collection. This is a collection of all of his first editions. It also has over 800 copies of his publications in magazines, journals, newspapers, and anthologies.

Regional Collection. A collection of materials including manuscripts, photographs, and film recording the history of the Tri-State Region (West Virginia, Ohio, and Kentucky) as well as Virginia. Of significance are the papers of Fred Lambert, Ken Hechler, Chuck Yeager, the WSAZ-TV News Film Archives, court depositions of the Buffalo Creek Flood of 1972, and other notable persons of the region.

University Archives. Contains records of the University, both printed and archival (administrative and department files).

1754
Salem College
Library and Learning Resources
Pennsylvania Avenue
Salem, West Virginia 26426

Telephone. (304) 782-5011

Institutional Description. Salem College is a private, independent, nonprofit college and was established in 1888. Enrollment: 627.

Library Administration. Myron J. Smith, Jr., Director of Libraries.

Library General Holdings. 79,000 volumes; 600 current periodical subscriptions; 163,200 microforms.

Special Collections

The library, housed in the Benedum Learning Resources Building, maintains special collections in the areas of aviation, equestrian education, criminal justice, and political science.

1755
Shepherd College
Ruth Scarborough Library
Shepherdstown, West Virginia 25443

Telephone. (304) 876-2511

Institutional Description. Shepherd College was founded in 1871 and is a publicly supported liberal arts and teacher education institution. Enrollment: 2,577.

Library Administration. George R. Gaumond, College Librarian.

Library General Holdings. 148,000 volumes; 815 current periodical subscriptions; 68,000 microforms.

Special Collections

The **West Virginia Room** houses a special collection of printed materials relating to West Virginia. The library also maintains the **Folk Collection** of materials on regional history.

1756
Southern West Virginia Community College Library
Logan, West Virginia 25601

Telephone. (304) 752-5900

Institutional Description. The two-year college was established from two existing branches of Marshall University in 1971. Enrollment: 1,685.

Library Administration. Barbara Aquirre, Librarian.

Library General Holdings. 36,345 volumes; 496 periodical titles; 7,428 microforms.

Special Collections

The **West Virginia Collection** consists of over 2,000 volumes.

1757
University of Charleston
Andrew S. Thomas Memorial Library
2300 MacCorkie Avenue, Southeast
Charleston, West Virginia 25304

Telephone. (304) 357-4713

Institutional Description. The University of Charleston is a private, independent, nonprofit institution. Enrollment: 1,365.

Library Administration. Frank W. Badger, University Librarian.

Library General Holdings. 102,000 volumes; 700 serial and periodical titles.

Special Collections

Sources for the serious study of American history are provided by the **John Allen Kinnaman Collection** and the **Rocco Gorman Civil War Collection.** The **Thomas Art Collection** includes reproductions of art masterpieces in books format and the **J.W. Herscher Collection** provides exceptional reference materials.

1758
West Liberty State College
Paul N. Elbin Library
West Liberty, West Virginia 26074

Telephone. (304) 336-8000

Institutional Description. The publicly supported state liberal arts and professional college was founded in 1838 as an academy. It grants associate and baccalaureate degrees. Enrollment: 2,481.

Library Administration. Donald R. Strong, Librarian.

Library General Holdings. 193,000 volumes; 1,200 current periodical subscriptions; 40,000 pamphlets.

Rare Book Collections

Nelle M. Krise Rare Book Room. Contains a collection of rare books which illustrate the art of bookmaking.

1759
West Virginia College of Graduate Study Library Services
Institute, West Virginia 25112

Telephone. (304) 768-9711

Institutional Description. West Virginia College of Graduate Studies is a state college and was established in 1972. Enrollment: 2,840.

Library Administration. Sue Forrest, Director of Library Services.

Library General Holdings. The Graduate College provides library services in each region where classes are held. Cooperating libraries include those of neighboring colleges. Students and faculty also make use of the Drain-Jordan Library on the campus of West Virginia State College. *See* **West Virginia State College.**

1760
West Virginia Institute of Technology
Vining Library
Montgomery, West Virginia 25136

Telephone. (304) 442-3146

Institutional Description. West Virginia Institute of

Technology was established in 1895 and is a state institution. Enrollment: 2,890.

Library Administration. Victor C. Young, Director.

Library General Holdings. 137,000 volumes; 1,000 periodicals; 273,000 microforms.

Special Collections

The **West Virginia Collection** includes over 2,000 volumes about West Virginia or by West Virginia authors.

1761
West Virginia School of Osteopathic Medicine
Library
400 North Lee Street
Lewisburg, West Virginia 24901

Telephone. (304) 647-6261

Institutional Description. This is a publicly supported institution. Enrollment: 232.

Library Administration. Donna M. Hudson, Librarian.

Library General Holdings. 11,000 books; 5,000 bound journal volumes; 400 current periodicals; 4 newspaper subscriptions; 4,000 audiovisual items; 50 computer programs.

Special Collections

The library's main subject holdings are in current and older books covering the field of osteopathic medicine.

1762
West Virginia State College
Drain-Jordan Library
Institute, West Virginia 25112

Telephone. (304) 766-3116

Institutional Description. The publicly supported liberal arts and professional state college was founded in 1891. Enrollment: 3,005.

Library Administration. John E. Scott, Librarian; Elizabeth H. Scobell, Special Collections Librarian.

Library General Holdings. 182,702 volumes; 870 periodical subscriptions; 11,242 microfilms; 8,974 other microforms; 15,846 government documents; 3,662 audiovisual titles.

Special Collections

The Drain-Jordan Library maintains an Instructional Materials Center for the Department of Education and the College Archives.

1763
West Virginia University
University Libraries
Morgantown, West Virginia 26506

Telephone. (304) 293-5040

Institutional Description. The publicly supported university was founded in 1867 as the Agricultural College of West Virginia. Enrollment: 15,637.

Library General Holdings. 2,500,000 items including 1,113,455 physical volumes; 1,446,066 microforms; 9,600 periodical titles.

Special Collections

West Virginia and Regional History Collection. This collection serves all researchers investigating topics related to West Virginia, the central Appalachian region, and the University itself. Included in the collection are 28,000 books, 22,000 microforms, 100,000 photographs, oral histories, folk music recordings, films, 15,000 pamphlets, 5,000 maps, 1,200 newspapers, and over 4,500,000 manuscript items. The collection contains a variety of primary and secondary source materials for the study of central Appalachia, the Upper Ohio region, and West Virginia. Among the 3,000 distinct collections are the papers of individuals, families, counties, labor unions, businesses, civic and cultural organizations, and the West Virginia archives. It preserves the papers of over one-half of the governors of West Virginia as well as many of its senators and congressmen, like those of Robert C. Byrd. Some other significant collections are the folklore archives of John Harrington Cox, Louis W. Chappell, and Patrick Gainer; the papers and drawings of David Hunter Strother; manuscripts of John W. and Julia Davis; and the archives of the UMWA Health and Retirement Funds.

Coal Collection. The strong collection on the subject of coal history, economics, and technology includes 8,000 related volumes of books and periodicals.

Rare Book Collections

Rare Book Collections. These collections are housed at the Wise Library, the Medical Center Library, and the Law Library. The Rare Book Room of the Wise Library contains some first editions of Dickens, Scott, and Clemens, as well as a set of Shakespeare's first folios. The Medical Center Library's rare volumes are housed in the McBee Collection which contains historical texts and treatises related to health care. The Colborn Rare Book Room of the Law Library includes volumes of legal scholarship and College of Law related memorabilia and gifts.

1764
West Virginia Wesleyan College
A.M. Pfeiffer Library
College Avenue
Buckhannon, West Virginia 26201

Telephone. (304) 473-7011

Institutional Description. The privately supported liberal arts college was founded in 1890 as the West Virginia Conference Seminary. The college is affiliated with the United Methodist Church. Enrollment: 1,239.

Library Administration. Benjamin Crutchfield, Jr., Director.

Library General Holdings. 150,000 volumes; 690 current periodical and newspaper subscriptions.

Special Collections

The Pfeiffer Library has a collection of **Pearl S. Buck Manuscripts,** a collection on Methodism, and the **Jones Lincoln Collection.**

1765
Wheeling College
Bishop Hodges Learning Center
316 Washington Avenue
Wheeling, West Virginia 26003

Telephone. (304) 243-2000

Institutional Description. Wheeling College is a private, nonprofit college owned by the Society of Jesus, Roman Catholic Church. Enrollment: 1,030.

Library Administration. Eileen Carpino, Director.

Library General Holdings. 123,000 volumes; 635 current periodicals; 48,000 microforms.

Special Collections

The Bishop Hodges Learning Center includes special holdings in theology and religious books and maintains the **Wheeling Archives,** a collection which contains materials on West Virginia history.

Wisconsin

1766
Alverno College
Library Media Center
3401 South 39th Street
Milwaukee, Wisconsin 53215

Telephone. (414) 382-6054

Institutional Description. The privately supported Roman Catholic college was founded in 1936 by the School Sisters of St. Francis. It is now a liberal arts college for women. Enrollment: 1,362.

Library Administration. Jean E. De Lauche, Library Director; Lola Stuller, Librarian, Research Center on Women/Fine Arts; Mary Georgia Matlock, Librarian, Teaching Materials Center; Sara Shulkin, Records Manager (Archives).

Library General Holdings. 89,349 volumes; 158,109 microforms; 13,295 audiovisual items; 10,912 bound periodicals; 404 computer software; 1,039 periodical titles.

Special Collections

Fine Arts Collection. Contains over 2,100 music scores, 7,300 sound recordings (phonographs records and compact discs), and over 7,000 art slides.

Research Center on Women. Includes over 2,800 books and audiovisuals and 106 periodical titles covering women's issues and related topics. Women' biographies are shelved with the general collection of the library.

Teaching Materials Center. Houses materials for education students including over 3,500 books and audiovisuals and 11 periodical titles.

Other collection specialties include peace and higher education.

1767
Beloit College
Col. Robert H. Morse Library
731 College Street
Beloit, Wisconsin 53511

Telephone. (608) 365-3391

Institutional Description. The privately supported liberal arts college, although nonsectarian, retains historic ties to the Congregational Church. It was founded in 1846. Enrollment: 1,018.

Library Administration. Dennis W. Dickinson, Librarian; Holly Lovejoy-Nesvold, Technical Services Librarian.

Library General Holdings. 212,622 books; 31,536 bound periodicals; 672 current periodical subscriptions; 123,074 microforms; 250,000 government documents.

Special Collections

Cullister International Center. Consists of 2,500 books on world affairs, international organizations, and the future world order.

College Archives and Beloitana. Resources include local history of city and college, manuscripts of prominent Beloiters, and college publications.

Beloit Poetry Journal Collection. A collection of contemporary American poetry and small press chapbooks and literary journals that include poetry, fiction, and criticism; numbers around 5,000 volumes.

Martin Luther King, Jr. Collection. Contains 250 items; books on non-violence and pacifism presented at the time of the assassination of Dr. Martin Luther King, Jr. by H. Vail Deale, Director of Libraries from 1953-1980; includes a thirty-year run of *Fellowship Magazine,* and out-of-print items on Mohandas Gandhi.

Joseph C. Rheingold Collection. Contains 300 books by and about Franklin Delano Roosevelt and the New Deal Era, including volumes written by members of his cabinets and magazine articles. These items were acquired from the personal library of Dr. Joseph C. Rheingold of Rockford, Illinois in 1958.

1768
Cardinal Stritch College
Library
6801 North Yates Road
Milwaukee, Wisconsin 53217

Telephone. (414) 352-5400

Institutional Description. Cardinal Stritch College is an independent college sponsored by the Sisters of St. Francis of Assisi, Roman Catholic Church. Enrollment: 2,314.

Library Administration. Meredith Gillette, Director.

Library General Holdings. 101,000 volumes; 600 current periodical subscriptions; 30,000 microforms.

Special Collections

The library's collections include materials on dietetics, management, nursing, reading, and special education.

1769
Carroll College
Carrier Memorial Library
100 N. East Avenue
Waukesha, Wisconsin 53186

Telephone. (414) 547-1211

Institutional Description. The privately-supported liberal arts college was established in 1846. It is the oldest college in the Wisconsin and is referred to as the Pioneer College. Enrollment: 1,500.

Library Administration. Paul D. Starr, Director of Library Services.

Library General Holdings. 172,000 volumes; 600 periodicals titles.

Special Collections

The library maintains a collection of materials on the U.S. Civil War and a children's literature collection.

1770
Carthage College
Ruthrauff Library
2001 Alford Drive
Kenosha, Wisconsin 53141

Telephone. (414) 551-8500

Institutional Description. The privately-supported liberal arts college is affiliated with the Wisconsin-Upper Michigan Synod and Michigan Synod of the Lutheran Church in America. Enrollment: 1,052.

Library Administration. James P. Bishop, Director of Library Services.

Library General Holdings. 171,000 volumes; 680 current periodical titles; 88,500 microforms.

Special Collections

Special collections of the library include a **Civil War Collection,** the **Dawe Collection** of modern English and American literature covering the period 1890-1955; and the **Wilde Collection** on history and historiography.

1771
Concordia College Wisconsin
Rincker Memorial
12800 North Lake Shore Drive
Mequon, Wisconsin 53092

Telephone. (414) 243-5700

Institutional Description. The privately supported college, founded in 1881, is owned and maintained by the Lutheran Church-Missouri Synod. Enrollment: 851.

Library Administration. David O. Berger, Librarian.

Library General Holdings. 70,000 volumes; 600 current periodical and newspaper subscriptions; 17,000 microforms; 2,000 audiovisual materials.

Special Collections

The library maintains a collection of nineteenth- and twentieth-century Protestant hymnals, primarily in German and English.

Rare Book Collections

The rare books collection includes approximately 600 volumes of sixteenth- to nineteenth-century Protestant theology works, including several editions of Martin Luther.

1772
District One Technical Institute
Educational Resources Center
620 West Clairemont Avenue
Eau Claire, Wisconsin 54701

Telephone. (715) 833-6200

Institutional Description. Vocational, technical, and adult education in Eau Claire began in 1912. In 1968, District One was formed when Chippewa, Dunn, Eau Claire, and Pepin counties voted to organize as a district. Enrollment: 1,310.

Library Administration. Lorraine E. Kearney, Librarian.

Library General Holdings. 42,000 volumes; 105 periodical titles.

Special Collections

The library has a special collection on law and technical literature and a collection of corporate annual reports.

1773
Edgewood College
College Library
825 Woodrow Street
Madison, Wisconsin 53711

Telephone. (608) 257-4861

Institutional Description. Edgewood College ia a Roman Catholic liberal arts institution. It was founded in 1927 and developed by the Dominican Sisters of Sinsinawa, Wisconsin. Enrollment: 592.

Library Administration. Sister Janice Costello, College Librarian.

Library General Holdings. 68,000 volumes; 370 cur-

rent periodical subscriptions; 26,500 microforms.

Special Collections

Special collections maintained by the library include the Library of American Civilization (microform), the **Rabbi Swarsensky Hebrew Collection,** and the **Fox Humanities Collection.**

1774
Gateway Technical Institute
Learning Resources Center
3250 30th Avenue
Kenosha, Wisconisn 53142

Telephone. (414) 656-6916

Institutional Description. The two-year college was founded in 1911 as the Racine Vocational School which eventually became the Racine Technical Institute. In 1912, the Kenosha Vocational School was founded and later became the Kenosha Technical Institute. The institutes merged in 1971 to form Gateway Technical Institute. Enrollment: 2,326.

Library Administration. Gerald F. Perona, Librarian; Araxie Kalvonjian, Librarian.

Library General Holdings. 45,000 volumes; 375 periodical titles.

Special Collections

The library maintains specialized collections of materials in aeronautics, career education, hearing impaired, horticulture, hospitality industry, and marketing.

1775
Institute of Paper Chemistry
Library
1043 East South River Street
P.O. Box 1039
Appleton, Wisconsin 54911

Telephone. (414) 738-3384

Institutional Description. The privately supported institute is a graduate-level school affiliated with Lawrence University. Founded in 1929, it provides a broad academic program in the pulp and paper sciences and engineering. Enrollment: 92.

Library Administration. Craig Booher, Librarian; Debra Timmers, Assistant Librarian; George Boeck, Special Collections Librarian.

Library General Holdings. 25,000 books; 18,500 bound periodical volumes; 175,000 patents; 1,770 student reports; 6,800 technical translations; 500,000 technical abstracts; 88 vertical file drawers; 1,800 government reports on microfiche; 25 journal titles on 1,723 microfilm reels; 825 current journal subscriptions.

Special Collections

The library of the Institute of Paper Chemistry is comprised mainly of materials relating to the pulp and paper industry and technology.

David Hunter Collection. Includes 1,300 books and 3,000 documents dealing with the history of papermaking.

1776
Lawrence University
Seely G. Mudd Library
P.O. Box 599
Appleton, Wisconsin 54912

Telephone. (414) 739-3681

Institutional Description. Lawrence University is an independent, private, nonprofit institution. Enrollment: 1,074.

Library Administration. Dennis Ribbens, University Librarian.

Library General Holdings. 271,00 volumes; 1,200 current periodical subscriptions; 100,000 microforms; 244,000 government documents.

Special Collections

The library is the central processing unit for the Associated Colleges of the Midwest (ACM)-Denison Federation of the Inter-University Consortium for Political and Social Research. Special collections include nineteenth-century novels in serial form; Evans Early American Imprints; and a Human Relations Area File.

1777
Marian College of Fond du Lac
Cardinal Meyer Library
45 South National Avenue
Fond du Lac, Wisconsin 54935

Telephone. (414) 923-7600

Institutional Description. Marian College, founded in 1936, is a privately supported Catholic liberal arts college. Enrollment: 397.

Library Administration. Sister Virginia Murphy, C.S.A., Director.

Library General Holdings. 85,000 volumes; 500 current periodical titles.

Special Collections

The library maintains the **Gromme Collection** of materials on birds and special holdings on education and nursing.

1778
Marquette University
Memorial Library
1415 West Wisconsin Avenue
Milwaukee, Wisconsin 53233

Telephone. (414) 224-7214

Institutional Description. The privately supported Roman Catholic university, founded in 1881, is conducted by the Society of Jesus. Enrollment: 9,738.

Library Administration. William Gardner, Librarian; Charles Elston, Special Collections/Rare Books Librarian.

Library General Holdings. 692,317 volumes; 5,941 current periodicals; 247,352 microforms.

Special Collections

Memorial Library Foundation Collection. This collection is part of the national network of regional collections of the Foundation Center in New York. The collection contains complete data on all Wisconsin grantmaking foundations as well as books, periodicals, and pamphlets on the subjects of fund raising, proposal writing, and philanthropy. A biennial, *Foundations in Wisconsin,* is published.

Rare Book Collections

The Department of Special Collections and University Archives contains 7,000 cubic feet of archival and manuscript collections and rare book holdings of over 6,000 volumes. Books holdings are strongest in the subject areas of theology, philosophy, Jesuitica, Catholic Church history, and typography. In addition to the archives of Marquette University and the papers of faculty, students, staff, and alumni, the Department holds major collections relating to Catholic Social Action in the twentieth century. These include the archives of the **Catholic Worker Movement,** including the **Papers of Dorothy Day,** the National Catholic Conference for Interracial Justice, the National Catholic Rural Life Conference, the National Coalition of American Nuns, and the **Papers of Monsignor Luigi Ligutti and Sister Margaret Ellen Traxler.**

Other notable holdings document the history of **Jesuits in Milwaukee, Wisconsin, and the Midwest;** relations between Catholic missionaries and Native Americans from the 1850s largely within a fifteen-state midwest and western area, included in the **Bureau of Catholic Indian Missions Collection;** contributions of Marquette alumni to entertainment and politics as in the **Don McNeill Collection** and the **Clement J. Zablocki Papers;** and a significant movement for the renewal of religious orders in the **Sister Formation Conference/Religious Formation Conference Archives.** In a class by itself is the **John Ronald Reuel Tolkien Collection** containing holograph and typescript drafts of *The Hobbit* and *The Lord of the Rings,* and an extensive collection of publications by and about the author.

1779
Medical College of Wisconsin
Todd Wehr Library
8701 Watertown Plank Road
Milwaukee, Wisconsin 53226

Telephone. (414) 257-8296

Institutional Description. The Medical College of Wisconsin is an independent, private, nonprofit, state-assisted institution. Enrollment: 201.

Library Administration. Patrick W. Brennen, Director of Libraries.

Library General Holdings. 181,000 volumes; 2,415 current periodical subscriptions.

Special Collections

The library's collection covers clinical medicine, basic medical sciences, nursing, public health, and related fields.

Rare Book Collections

A collection of rare volumes, some dating back 400 years, is housed in the Milwaukee Academy of Medicine History of Medicine Room in the library.

1780
Mount Mary College
Patrick and Beatrice Haggerty Library
2900 N. Menomonee River Parkway
Milwaukee, Wisconsin 53222

Telephone. (414) 259-9230

Institutional Description. Mount Mary is Wisconsin's oldest liberal arts college for women. Enrollment: 891.

Library Administration. Sister M. Anne Lucy Hoffman, Director.

Library General Holdings. 108,000 volumes; 805 current periodical titles; 14,500 government documents.

Special Collections

The library maintains the **Age Collection** which represents the complete contents of a Milwaukee gerontology library (donated in 1986) and the **Alfred Lunt Cookbook Collection.**

1781
Mount Senario College
Library
College Avenue West
Ladysmith, Wisconsin 54848

Telephone. (715) 532-5511

Institutional Description. Mount Senario College is an

independent, four-year, nonsectarian, liberal arts college. Enrollment: 611.

Library Administration. James A. Gollata, Director of Library Services; Delores E. Gokee, Director of American Indian Program.

Library General Holdings. 47,000 volumes; 300 periodical and journal subscriptions.

Special Collections

The library maintains a special collection of 1,500 books by and about North American Indians.

1782
Northland College
Dexter Library
1411 Ellis Avenue
Ashland, Wisconsin 54806

Telephone. (715) 682-4531

Institutional Description. The privately supported liberal arts environmental college was founded in 1892 and is affiliated with the United Church of Christ. Enrollment: 541.

Library Administration. Mary D. Fennessey, Head Librarian.

Library General Holdings. 69,000 volumes; 383 current periodical titles.

Special Collections

The library maintains an ethnic heritage collection of oral histories of northern Wisconsin and the upper peninsula of Michigan. The **Sigurd Olson Environmental Institute,** located on the campus, maintains a library of slide/tape programs and films produced by the Institute.

1783
Ripon College
Ripon College Library
Box 248
300 Seward Street
Ripon, Wisconsin 54971

Telephone. (414) 748-8330

Institutional Description. The privately supported liberal arts college, although affiliated with the United Church of Christ, is nondenominational in nature. It was founded in 1851. Enrollment: 818.

Library Administration. Sarah McGowan, Director.

Library General Holdings. 150,000 volumes; 680 periodical titles; 16,500 microforms; 60,000 government publications.

Special Collections

The major special holdings of the library include the Samuel Pedrick Papers (local history), Lincolniana, and a China Collection.

1784
Sacred Heart School of Theology
Leo Dehon Library
P.O. Box 429
Hales Corners, Wisconsin 53130

Telephone. (414) 425-8300

Institutional Description. The privately supported Roman Catholic graduate-level seminary, founded in 1929, now serves over 59 dioceses and religious communities. Enrollment: 106.

Library Administration. Sr. Agnese Jasko, PHJC, Director; Kathy Jastrab, Assistant Librarian.

Library General Holdings. 65,637 books; 5,499 bound periodicals; 363 current periodical subscriptions; 716 microforms; 10,784 LP recordings; 1,120 cassette tapes.

Special Collections

Sacred Heart Collection. Consists of 650 titles in English, French, and German relating to the Sacred Heart of Jesus. They are generally divided into theological works on the subject and devotional materials.

Canon Law Collection. This collection of 1,100 books covers the history and codification of canon law, case studies, dissertations, and textual commentaries, of both the Roman Canon Law (1917 and 1983) and Oriental Canon Law.

Catechetical Curriculum Collection. Includes Catholic religious textbooks, divided into grade level and interest.

1785
St. Francis Seminary
Salzmann Library
3257 South Lake Drive
Milwaukee, Wisconsin 53207

Telephone. (414) 747-6477

Institutional Description. The privately supported Roman Catholic theological seminary provides for the training of priests and lay and religious for ministry. Enrollment: 51.

Library Administration. Rev. Lawrence K. Miech, Library Director; Sr. Colette Zirbes, Associate Librarian.

Library General Holdings. 100,000 volumes (including bound periodicals); 315 current periodical subscriptions.

Special Collections

Catholic Americana. Consists of books written by American Catholic authors printed in the late seventeenth, eighteenth, and nineteenth centuries. Among them are a few books written by Milwaukee's first archbishop,

John Martin Henni, and second archbishop, Michael Heiss. The collection includes works by St. Francis Seminary's first teaching staff.

Bible Collection. Over the years, Salzmann Library has collected Bibles in different languages, a few published before 1500, and various Bibles from the seventeenth and eighteenth centuries. Similarly, a collection of various Missale Romanums dating from the late sixteenth century and upward.

Indian Collection. Includes catechisms, prayer books, hymn books, scripture selections edited by Bishop Frederic Baraga and translated into the Menominee, Chippewa, and Ottawa languages; two books are autographed by Bishop Baraga to Archbishop Henni.

Rare Book Collections

Rare Books Collection. The Salzmann Library has a few incunabula, mainly Bibles and a few commentaries. Books of the early seventeenth century are mostly in the area of scripture, dogmatic and moral theology, and canon law. There are critical editions of the works of Augustine, Bonaventure, and Thomas Aquinas. There is also a sizeable collection of miniature books.

1786
Saint Norbert College
Todd Wehr Library
De Pere, Wisconsin 54115

Telephone. (414) 337-3005

Institutional Description. The privately supported liberal arts college was established in 1898 under the auspices of the Roman Catholic Church. Enrollment: 1,703.

Library Administration. Eugene G. Bunker, Director.

Library General Holdings. 130,000 volumes; 700 current periodical subscriptions; 10,500 bound periodicals; 17,000 microforms.

Special Collections

The **Menomenee Indian Archives** includes the personal papers of the tribal chief from the 1940s. The library also maintains a collection of limited edition classics.

1787
Silver Lake College
Library
2406 South Alvero Road
Manitowoc, Wisconsin 54220

Telephone. (414) 684-6691

Institutional Description. The privately supported Catholic commuter college was founded in 1935 as Holy Family College, an academy and normal school conducted by and for the Franciscan Sisters of Christian Charity until 1957. In 1972 the present name was adopted. The school is now nondenominational. Enrollment: 333.

Library Administration. Sister Mary John Wood, Head Librarian.

Library General Holdings. 85,000 volumes; 170 current periodical subscriptions.

Special Collections

The library subscribes to the Kodaly Music Theory publications. There are also special collections of religious studies journals and related publications and a collection of rare Colonial American and European books.

1788
University of Wisconsin - Eau Claire
McIntyre Library
Eau Claire, Wisconsin 54702

Telephone. (715) 836-2739

Institutional Description. The publicly supported campus of the University of Wisconsin System was founded in 1916 as a normal school. Enrollment: 10,170.

Library Administration. Steve Marquardt, Librarian; Richard L. Pifer, Archivist.

Library General Holdings. 500,000 bound volumes; 5,000 periodical titles; 215,000 government publications; 900,000 microform units.

Special Collections

The Special Collections Department houses a collection of over 1,500 local histories, maps, and atlases documenting the history and development of Wisconsin and of the Chippewa River Valley in particular. The Department has three major subunits: The Area Research Center, the University Archives, and the Rare Book Collection.

Area Research Center. The Center holds approximately 1,300 cubic feet of historical manuscript collections and county/municipal government records documenting the history of Wisconsin's Chippewa River Valley. The Center has a particularly strong genealogical collection. In addition, its holdings reflect the history of the logging industry and of settlement in the Chippewa Valley.

University Archives. Holds approximately 1,000 cubic feet of records documenting the history of the University.

Rare Book Collections

Rare Books Collections. Consists of approximately 1,500 rare and fine print volumes.

1789
University of Wisconsin - Green Bay
Library Learning Center
2420 Nicolet Drive
Green Bay, Wisconsin 54301

Telephone. (414) 465-2000

Institutional Description. University of Wisconsin - Green Bay was established in 1965. A graduate program was added in 1974. Enrollment: 5,062.

Library Administration. Kurt B. Rothe, Executive Director of Learning Resources.

Library General Holdings. 285,000 volumes; 3,815 periodical and serial titles; 332,000 government documents; 44,000 maps; 455,000 items in microformat; 30,500 slides, sound recordings, films, tapes.

Special Collections

The important special collections of the Library Learning Center include the **Leon Kramer Collection of Socialist Materials;** the personal papers of Eleazer Williams; and the **Brown County Historical Records** which are on deposit through the the Wisconsin State Historical Society.

1790
University of Wisconsin - La Crosse
Murphy Library
1631 Pine Street
La Crosse, Wisconsin 54601

Telephone. (608) 785-8505

Institutional Description. The publicly supported campus of the University of Wisconsin System is a multipurpose liberal arts university. Enrollment: 9,111.

Library Administration. Dale Montgomery, Director of Instructional Services; Edwin L. Hill, Special Collections Librarian.

Library General Holdings. 305,900 bound volumes; 1,959 periodical subscriptions; 300,000 microforms.

Special Collections

The general collection of the Murphy Library is strong in the literature and scholarship of physical education.

Area Research Center. These manuscript and public records materials are held here as part of the network of Centers established by the State Historical Society of Wisconsin. Manuscripts include the papers of various families and businesses for a five-county area in western Wisconsin. Public records such as tax rolls, naturalization records, court records, and school records for these same five counties. These records are of special importance for social, political, and genealogical research.

Steamboat Project. This collection includes about 30,000 photographs of inland river steamboats, and a data file for about 20,000 boats. It also includes printed books, pilots' logs, periodicals, government documents on the river and riverboat themes, and portrait and vertical files. The collection of riverboat photographs is generally considered to be the largest in the United States.

Wisconsiana. Contains about 4,000 volumes dealing with Wisconsin, including villages and towns, counties, and the state. This collection is especially strong in materials relating to western Wisconsin and the La Crosse area. There are over 400 maps and about 35,000 historical photographs supporting this collection.

Rare Book Collections

Rare Book Collections. The collections include about 11,000 volumes with special strength in early fantasy, gothic, and science fiction as in the **Skeeters Collection;** in contemporary midwestern little magazines, private presses, and poetry; in inland river steamboating and river life; and in regional history.

1791
University of Wisconsin - Madison
Memorial Library
500 Lincoln Drive
Madison, Wisconsin 53706

Telephone. (608) 262-1234

Institutional Description. The University of Wisconsin was chartered in 1848. Enrollment: 44,584.

Library Administration. D. Kaye Gapen, Director.

Library General Holdings. 4,495,000 volumes; 48,600 periodical subscriptions; 250,000 government documents. UW-Madison has one of the largest research library systems in the United States. It include Memorial Library, 21 other major campus libraries and numerous special campus libraries.

Special Collections

Important special collections include materials on German and Scandinavian studies; the **Burgess Collection** of children's literature; the **C.S. Lewis Letters;** the **Tank Collection** of Calvinist theology and Dutch historical materials; the **Peter G. Toepfer Collection** on chess; the **George B. Wild Collection** of classical and nineteenth-century German literature; the **Deryck Collection** of Belgian Congo archival materials; the **Duveen Collection** on alchemy; the **Robert Boyle Collection,** and the **Cossack Collection.**

Other collections include early American women authors; Buddhism; seventeenth- and eighteenth-century European theology; European socialism; eighteenth-century French literature, French political pamphlets; French Protestantism; French Revolutionary pamphlets; German eighteenth-century theatre; German Expressionism; the history of chemistry; the history of science; natural history; Icelandic history and literature; Irish history and literature; fifteenth- and sixteenth-century Judaica; Lithuanian history and literature; Lutheran theology; Mazarinades; medieval history; National Socialism; Polish history and literature; Russian culture; the Russian Revolutionary Movement; Scandinavian literature; Tibetan materials; Welsh theology; and twentiety-century American and English literature.

Author collections include Dalton Trumbo, Mark Twain, Edna Ferber, and Eugene O'Neill, among others. The library also maintains a collection of little magazines, materials on the American theatre, bookplate literature, private presses, sixteenth-century Italian imprints, Renaissance epics, and English grammars.

The **State Historical Society Library** covers all topics in North American history and holds official publications of U.S. and Canadian governments. It has the second largest newspaper collection in the nation. Memorial Library is the principal research facility on campus for most of the humanities and social sciences. The College Library includes a college catalog collection, ethnic and women's materials, and art slides. The numerous special campus libraries include the Primate Center Library, School of Education Materials Center, and the Map Library.

1792
University of Wisconsin - Milwaukee
Golda Meir Library
P.O. Box 604
Milwaukee, Wisconsin 53201

Telephone. (414) 229-4345

Institutional Description. The publicly supported campus of the University of Wisconsin System was founded in 1956. Enrollment: 18,621.

Library Administration. William C. Roselle, Librarian; Ellen M. Murphy, Special Collections/Rare Books Librarian.

Library General Holdings. 3,500,000 items including 11,000 serial subscription; 500,000 maps and atlases; 143,000 photographs; 500,000 microforms; 40,000 musical scores; 60,000 recordings. The Golda Meir Library is among the 100 largest academic libraries in the United States and is the second largest in Wisconsin.

Special Collections

American Geographical Society Collection. Includes holdings dating from 1452 to the present and supports all facets of geography and related disciplines.

Camus Bibliography Research Collection. This collection is of value to scholars interested in Albert Camus.

Fromkin Memorial Collection. Includes items related to idealistic and reform movements in America from the Civil War to the New Deal.

Shakespeare Research Collection. This collection serves the requirements of the general editorship of the *New Variorum Shakespeare.*

Other collections are related to Hebraica and Judaica, Slovenian music, Franklin Delano Roosevelt, and classical music. Most of the manuscripts are housed in the University Archives/Fromkin Collection area, including *Arena Magazine* office files, the papers of E. Eleanor Fitzgerald, Andrew R. Scher, the **Heinz Roemhold Music Collection,** and the **Kingston Trio Collection.**

Rare Book Collections

Rare Books Department. Contains twentieth-century British and American small press publications; facsimile medieval manuscripts; William Blake engravings and paintings in facsimile; Frank Lloyd Wright and his work; church architecture in Rome; Native American newspapers. The collections include the **Seventeenth-Century Research Collection,** with emphasis on Reformation theology and English literature; the **Layton School of Art Library;** the **Hohlweck and Slichter Civil War Collections;** and the **George Hardie Aerospace Collection** that focuses on aviation history and education.

Manuscripts consist of the **Little Review** papers, including editorial files, correspondence, and manuscripts submitted for publication in this avant-garde literary periodical during its existence from 1914-1929.

1793
University of Wisconsin - Oshkosh
Forrest R. Polk Library
800 Algoma Boulevard
Oshkosh, Wisconsin 54901

Telephone. (414) 424-0202

Institutional Description. The institution was established as Oshkosh Normal School in 1871. Enrollment: 11,655.

Library Administration. John V. Nichols, Director.

Library General Holdings. 355,000 volumes; 1,500 current periodicals; 650,000 microforms; 360,000 government documents; 14,000 audiovisual titles.

Special Collections

Among the special collections of books and films are those of Jay T. Putney, Albert Neumann, Pare Lorentz, and Ruth Rowland. The **Wisconsin Area Research Center,** a collection within the University Archives, includes records of surrounding counties and documents of the Wisconsin State Historical Society that are related to the Fox Valley region. The **Educational Media Collection** contains most of the audiovisual collection as well as teaching materials for all levels from nursery school through the undergraduate university years.

1794
University of Wisconsin - Parkside
Library/Learning Center
Box Number 2000
Kenosha, Wisconsin 53141

Telephone. (414) 553-2273

Institutional Description. The publicly supported campus of the University of Wisconsin System opened in 1969. It features liberal arts and teacher education. Enrollment: 3,486.

Library Administration. Linda Piele, Acting Director; Rebecca Mitchell, Archivist.

Library General Holdings. 341,310 bound volumes; 1,477 current periodical and newspaper subscriptions; 705,749 microfiche; 29,375 microfilm reels; 10,411 audiovisual titles; 400 computer software titles.

Special Collections

Area Research Center. The center is part of a statewide network which operates in conjunction with the State Historical Society of Wisconsin. It contains local government records and manuscripts from Racine and Kenosha counties.

Special Collections. This department of the Library/Learning Center has a collection of literary works published by Perishable Press, a privately owned small press in Mt. Horeb, Wisconsin and the Black Sparrow Press in San Francisco. An additional extensive collection of the work of Irving Wallace consists of correspondence, signed original transcripts, galley and page proofs, research notes, and his novels in various foreign languages. Other notable collections include works by David Kherdian and a collection of eighteenth- and nineteenth-century British and American plays collected by the late H.O. Teisburg.

University Archives. Houses all non-current University of Wisconsin-Parkside records of administrative, legal, financial, or historical importance.

1795
University of Wisconsin - Platteville
Elton S. Karrmann Library
1 University Plaza
Platteville, Wisconsin 53818

Telephone. (608) 342-1101

Institutional Description. The University of Wisconsin - Platteville was established and chartered as Platteville Normal School in 1886. Enrollment: 5,380.

Library Administration. Jerome P. Daniels, Director.

Library General Holdings. 254,000 books, bound periodicals, and instructional materials laboratory printed items; 6,000 audiovisual materials; 2,800 periodical, newspaper, and serial titles; 35,000 maps; 173,000 government publications; 673,000 microforms.

Special Collections

The library maintains a **Southwest Wisconsin Collection** and a **Wisconsin Area Research Center** which collects and preserves historical materials on the region.

1796
University of Wisconsin - Stevens Point
James H. Albertson Center for Learning Resources
2100 Main Street
Stevens Point, Wisconsin 54481

Telephone. (715) 346-4242

Institutional Description. The institution was established in 1893 as Stevens Point Normal School. Enrollment: 9,554.

Library Administration. Mary K, Croft, Dean.

Library General Holdings. 304,000 volumes; 2,100 current periodicals; 450,000 government documents; 329,000 microforms.

Special Collections

Special holdings include collections on education, home economics, and natural resources. The library is an official federal and state documents depository containing a rich selection from 1950, including an extensive congressional series from the year 1825 and a complete microprint edition of United Nations publications. Another strong area of collection is the large and diversified files of national and state newspapers.

Wisconsin Area Research Center. In cooperation with the State Historical Society, the library maintains a Center for the collection of historical material on 12 counties in north central Wisconsin.

University Archives. The function of the Archives is the collecting and preserving of the records of the University's life and activities in all their relationships.

1797
University of Wisconsin - Stout
Library Learning Center
Menonomie, Wisconsin 54751

Telephone. (715) 232-1215

Institutional Description. The publicly supported campus of the University of Wisconsin System was founded in 1893. It features liberal arts and teacher education. Enrollment: 7,336.

Library Administration. John J. Jax, Director of Library; Phillip Q. Sawin, Special Collections Librarian.

Library General Holdings. 201,000 volumes; 1,500 periodical subscriptions; 700,000 microfiche; 1,000 films (16mm); 3,250 audio and video tapes, cassettes, discs.

Special Collections

The specialized collections include materials on tourism and hospitality; commercial lodging operations; trade publications of the American Hotel and Motel Association members; fast and quality food operations; an extensive collection of pamphlets and maps associated with worldwide tourism and travel.

1798
University of Wisconsin - Superior
Jim Dan Hill Library
1800 Grand Avenue
Superior, Wisconsin 54880

Telephone. (715) 394-8101

Institutional Description. The University of Wisconsin - Superior was established in 1893 as the Superior Normal School. Enrollment: 2,205.

Library Administration. Bob Carmack, Director.

Library General Holdings. 285,000 volumes; 955 current periodicals; 299,00 government documents; 883,500 microforms.

Special Collections

The library supports the liberal arts curriculum with a diversity of collections in various academic subjects. The University offers more than 30 academic majors plus a variety of interdisciplinary programs.

1799
University of Wisconsin - Whitewater
Harold Andersen Library
800 West Main Street
Whitewater, Wisconsin 53190

Telephone. (414) 472-1000

Institutional Description. The publicly supported campus of the University of Wisconsin System was established in 1868 as a normal school. It now features liberal arts and teacher education. Enrollment: 9,551.

Library Administration. Hsi-Ping Shao, Librarian; Jerome W. Johnson, Curator, Area Research Center.

Library General Holdings. 324,467 volumes; 3,600 periodical titles; 30 newspaper subscriptions; 821,802 microforms; 247,293 government documents; 60,259 audiovisual materials.

Special Collections

Learning Materials Center. The Center has a 30,893-item curriculum-oriented collection of children's literature, guides, textbooks, tests, pamphlets, and audiovisual materials.

Area Research Center. The Center is a cooperative project of the University and the State Historical Society of Wisconsin and covers Jefferson, Rock, and Walworth counties of Wisconsin. It holds more than 130 series of local government, court, and school district records, the naturalization papers for Walworth and Jefferson counties, and manuscript collections which include memoirs and diaries of early settlers, records of business enterprises, labor unions, social and service organizations, and religious groups as well as the personal papers of regional legislators, educators, lawyers, and veterans.

Wyoming

1800
Casper College
Goodstein Foundation Library
125 College Drive
Casper, Wyoming 82601

Telephone. (307) 268-2269

Institutional Description. The publicly supported two-year college was founded in 1945. Enrollment: 2,534.

Library Administration. Lynette Anderson, Librarian; Jamie C. Ring, Wyoming History Specialist.

Library General Holdings. 71,000 monographs; 612 periodical titles; 29 newspaper subscriptions; 14,000 microform units (136 titles); 4,000 maps.

Special Collections

The Special Collections of the Goodstein Foundation Library contains materials relating to the history of Wyoming and neighboring states. Included in the collection are monographs and maps of the Oregon Trail; monographs relating to Indians who roamed Wyoming, i.e., Arapaho, Cheyenne, Crow, Dakota, Siksika, Shoshoni; monographs by Wyoming authors and about western exploration and travel. There are scattered first editions in the Special Collections.

Notable manuscript collections are the **Robert David Historical Collection** containing maps, diaries, and journals in addition to manuscripts relating to Wyoming history; and the **Frances Seely Webb Historical Collection** containing photographs and some manuscript materials dealing primarily with Casper and Natrona County history.

The collection contains manuscripts for Bill Bragg's books: *Drumm's War, War Horses, Wyoming: Wild and Wooly* and *Wyomings' Wealth;* and for Norman Weis's books: *Ghost Towns of the Northwest; Helldorados, Ghost Towns and Camps of the Southwest;* and *Starduster.*

1801
Central Wyoming College
Learning Resources Center
2660 Peck Avenue
Riverton, Wyoming 82501

Telephone. (307) 856-9291

Institutional Description. Founded in 1966, the two-year college offers the College Transfer Program, Technical Education Program, and Career Education Program. Enrollment: 881.

Library Administration. Jon P. Cobes, Director.

Library General Holdings. 35,000 volumes; 325 current periodical subscriptions.

Special Collections

Special collections include the **Wyoming Collection,** the **American Indian Collection,** and an extensive collection of pamphlets and reports on the Arapahoe and Shoshone tribes and Indian education.

1802
Eastern Wyoming College
Learning Resource Center
3200 West C Street
Torrington, Wyoming 82240

Telephone. (307) 532-7111

Institutional Description. The two-year college was established in 1948 as the Southeast University Center, a part of the University of Wyoming and the local school district. By popular vote in 1956, the Goshen County Community College District was created and the present name of the college was adopted. Enrollment: 859.

Library Administration. James Robert Garcia, Director of Learning Resource Center.

Library General Holdings. 20,000 books; 164 current periodical and newspaper subscriptions.

Special Collections

The **History of the Old West Collection** is maintained in the library.

1803
Laramie County Community College
Library
1400 East College Drive
Cheyenne, Wyoming 82007

Telephone. (307) 634-5853

Institutional Description. The publicly supported (state) junior college, founded in 1968, offers transfer, vocational-technical, and adult continuing education programs. Enrollment: 2,210.

Library Administration. Sandra J. Donovan, Director.

Library General Holdings. 30,000 volumes; 315 periodical subscriptions; 3,000 pamphlets.

Special Collections

A special collection on nursing is available in the library. The **Foundation Collection** was contributed by the Laramie County Community College Foundation, a non-profit corporate body formed to promote, assist, and extend financial support to the college.

1804
University of Wyoming
William Robertson Coe Library
University Station
Laramie, Wyoming 82071

Telephone. (307) 766-1121

Institutional Description. The University of Wyoming is a land-grant college and was founded in 1886. Enrollment: 9,980.

Library Administration. Keith M. Cottam, Director of Libraries.

Library General Holdings. 840,000 volumes; over 12,000 periodical and serial titles; 860,000 government documents; 1,790,000 microforms.

Special Collections

The University's **American Heritage Center** includes collections in Western history, the William M. Fitzhugh, Jr., rare book room, and growing archival and research collections in business history, petroleum history, transportation history, and the performing arts. The **Knapp Collection** includes seventeenth-century English theology and literature and the **Beuf/Gallatin Collection** includes materials on Leonardo da Vinci.

U.S. Trust Territories

1805
American Samoa Community College
College Library
P.O. Box 2609
Pago Pago, American Samoa 96799

Telephone. (684) 699-9155

Institutional Description. American Samoa Community College was established in 1970. Enrollment: 900.

Library Administration. Paula Seethaler, Librarian.

Library General Holdings. 14,915 volumes; 85 serial subscriptions; separate Nursing School library.

Special Collections

1,955 volumes are specialized books on information pertaining to the cultural, biological, and scientific study of the Pacific area.

GENERAL INDEX

Numbers following the headings are Entry Numbers.
Entry Numbers are also used as running heads at the top of each page.

Aandahl, Fred G. 1237
Abbey, Edward 238
Abbey Theater 487
Abbot, Capt. Joel, U.S.N. 694
Abbott, Edith 494
Abbott, Grace 494
Abbott, Jacob 755
Abell, A.S. 695
Aberdeen County (South Dakota) 1518
Abernethy, Frank D. 1676
Abilene Christian University (Texas) 1567
Abitt, Watkins 1715
abolition 106, 358, 596, 681, 764, 1267, 1276, 1444
Abolition Society of Pennsylvania 1445
Abraham Baldwin Agricultural College (Georgia) 349
Abraham Lincoln Brigade 718
abstract expressionism 191
Abzug, Bella 1049
academic freedom 1445
Academy of Art College (California) 76
Academy of Television Arts and Sciences 215
Academy of the New Church (Pennsylvania) 1350
Acadian history 648
accounting 79, 326, 402, 655, 695, 710, 818, 969, 1049, 1123, 1445
acoustics 215
Acta Sanctorum 1124
actuarial science 1046
Adams, Ansel 80, 697
Adams, C.C. 821
Adams, Crosby 1201
Adams, Henry 1638
Adams, James Taylor 1685
Adams, James Truslow 1049
Adams, Léonie 284
Adams, Roger 497
Adams State College (Colorado) 235
Addams, Jane 496, 1444
Addison, Joseph 497, 1611
Ade, George 519
Adelphi University (New York) 1022
Adelsfried, Edmund Woerndle von 1059
Adirondack Community College (New York) 1023
Adirondacks 1023, 1042, 1072, 1107, 1125, 1141
Adler, Felix 1049
Adler, Guido 394
Adler, Herman 1415
Admire, James L. 1301
Adrian College (Michigan) 774
Advent Christian Church 417
Adventist Church 777
Adventist Movement 712, 777
The Adventures of Tom Sawyer 296
advertising art 80
"A.E." 519
aerial photography 564, 721, 841
aeronautics 59, 89, 196, 217, 251, 309, 742, 963, 966, 1045, 1296, 1607, 1774
aerospace 5, 315, 1792
Afghanistan 956
AFL-CIO (Arizona) 55
Africa 31, 608, 1086, 1358, 1439
Africa south of the Sahara 821
African linguistics 1376
African Methodist Episcopal Church 1293
African Methodist Episcopal Zion Church 1196
African music 475
African studies 475, 708, 1032, 1331
Afro-Americans 1, 2, 16, 17, 28, 31, 153, 285, 297, 308, 317, 358, 389, 431, 472, 474, 591, 608, 627, 649, 685, 761, 781, 866, 876, 917, 1171, 1185, 1196, 1203, 1214, 1246, 1254, 1367, 1404, 1414, 1445, 1485, 1507, 1541, 1592, 1605, 1606, 1647, 1692, 1710, 1721
Agee, James 394, 1648
Agee, Rucker 32
aging 1645
Agnes Scott College (Georgia) 350
agrarian writers 1566
agricultural economics 1235

Agricultural Improvement Association of New York State 1158
agricultural machinery 490
agricultural treatises 1000
agriculture 1, 311, 639, 664, 802, 856, 910, 938, 1204, 1372, 1582, 1625, 1626, 1682, 1744
agriculture, history of 212
agriculture, Oklahoma 1301
agriculture, subtropical 216
Aickman, Robert 1243
AIDS (acquired immune deficiency syndrome) 495
Aiken, Conrad 354, 394, 928, 1320
Aikin, A.M. (Texas State Senator) 1604
air pollution 820
air power 251
airborne warfare 1487
Aitken, Hugh 1008
Akeley, Carl Ethan 1158
Akenside, Mark 705
Akin, William S. 500
Alabama 3, 5, 6, 7, 10, 13, 14, 17, 18, 21, 23, 25, 32, 36, 37
Alabama A & M University 1
Alabama Baptist State Convention 25
Alabama Conference of the United Methodist Church 7
Alabama State University 2
Alabama-West Florida Conference of the United Methodist Church 13
Alaska 38, 39, 42, 43, 44, 45, 46, 181, 1726
Alaska Constitutional Convention 45
Alaska Gold Rush 45
Alaska Pacific University 38
Alaskan languages, Native 38
Albany College of Pharmacy (New York) 1024
Albany Junior College (Georgia) 351
Albany Medical Annals 1025
Albany Medical College (New York) 1025
Albany State College (Georgia) 352
Alberta (Canada) 1726
Albertus Magnus College (Connecticut) 259
Albion College (Michigan) 775
Albright College (Pennsylvania) 1351
Albright, Ivan Lorraine 415
Alcenar, Jose Martiniano de 1450
alchemy 266, 284, 1449, 1791
alcohol research 1000
alcoholism 585, 906, 1000, 1089
Alcorn State University (Mississippi) 858
Alcott, Bronson 737
Alcott, Louisa May 737, 755, 1660
Alden Hydraulic Laboratory 772
Alden, Timothy 1352
Alderson Broaddus College (West Virginia) 1747
Aldington, Richard 487, 1445
Aldrich, Thomas Bailey 1123
Alemany, Archbishop Joseph Sadoc 188
Alexander City State Junior College (Alabama) 3
Alexander, George 1158
Alexander, Margaret Walker 866
Alexander the Great 1570
Alfred University (New York) 1026
Alger, Horatio 718, 719, 755, 1567
Alice in Wonderland 1049
Alice Lloyd College (Kentucky) 597
Alighieri, Dante 530, 536, 604, 744, 1081
Allan Hancock College (California) 77
Allegany Community College (Maryland) 669
Allegheny College (Pennsylvania) 1352
Allen, Ethan 1681
Allen, Hervey 394
Allen, Ira 1681
Allen, John W. 487
Allen Press 225
Allen, Reginald Clifford 1504
Allen, W.E.D. 519
Allendale (Michigan) 788
Allentown College of St. Francis de Sales (Pennsylvania) 1353
Allied Occupation of Japan 696
Alma College (Michigan) 776
almanacs 344, 1000
almanacs, eighteenth-century 519
Alpha Boule Society 1445
Alspach, Russell K. 764
alternative movements 279
alternative press publications 1450
Alvernia College (Pennsylvania) 1354
Alverno College (Wisconsin) 1766
Amache Relocation Camp 253
Amber, Dean 1158
America magazine 296
American Academy of Religion 243
American Archives of the Factual Film 549
American Association of Editorial Cartoonists 1278
American Association of Petroleum Geologists 940
American Association of University Women 1637
American Association of University Women (Lowell, Massachusetts) 763
American Bandmasters Association 696
American Baptist Churches, USA 1044, 1520
American Baptist College (Tennessee) 1523
American Baptist Historical Society 1044
American Board of Commissioners for Foreign Missions 737
American Catholic Tribune 1435
American Civil Liberties Union 695, 997
American colonization (Texas) 1647
American Committee on United Europe 296
American Conservatory of Music (Illinois) 414
American Enterprise Institute 232, 351
American Express Company 1164
American Friends Service Committee 1390
American Geographical Society 1792

American Graduate School of International Management (Arizona) 47
American Hall of Aviation History 165
American Heritage School Dictionary 296
American Hotel and Motel Association 1797
American Indian Higher Education Consortium 1519
American Indians 25, 30, 51, 54, 56, 70, 167, 174, 212, 216, 242, 284, 398, 409, 411, 413, 416, 451, 505, 555, 581, 596, 629, 661, 796, 825, 833, 917, 935, 938, 939, 958, 961, 981, 988, 997, 1013, 1063, 1122, 1134, 1158, 1197, 1206, 1214, 1225, 1232, 1254, 1267, 1299, 1302, 1305, 1315, 1318, 1319, 1320, 1332, 1341, 1514, 1518, 1519, 1522, 1562, 1647, 1663, 1778, 1781, 1785, 1786, 1800, 1801
American Insitute of Graphic Arts 1049
American Institute of Architects (Kansas City Chapters) 925
American International College (Massachusetts) 704
American Jewish Archives (West Coast Branch) 146
American Jewish Periodical Center (West Coast Branch) 146
American Lung Association of Maryland 695
American Lutheran Church (South Dakota District) 1510
American Music Resource Center 135
American Playwrights' Theatre 1278
American Political Science Association 296
American Protestant Evangelicalism 1276
American River College (California) 78
American Samoa Community College 1805
American Scientific Affiliation 500
American Society for Microbiology 697
American Society for Testing and Materials 646
American Society of Mechanical Engineers 786
American Society of Pension Actuaries 695
American Symphony Orchestra League 1690
American Tract Society publications 419, 473
American University (District of Columbia) 290
American University of Puerto Rico 1467
American Welding Society 314, 990
Americana 60, 275, 396, 447, 450, 453, 564, 590, 604, 681, 723, 781, 816, 892, 925, 997, 1022, 1055, 1059, 1155, 1217, 1252, 1267, 1269, 1298, 1301, 1352, 1435, 1440, 1449, 1450, 1622, 1696
Americanization Movement 596
Amherst College (Massachusetts) 705
Amherst (Massachusetts) 705
Amis, Kingsley 296
Amish 1242, 1414
"An Evening with Fred Astaire" 215
Anabaptists 137, 157, 575, 920, 931, 1687
anatomical models 1309
anatomy 218, 1471, 1653
Anatomy of Melancholy 118
ancient languages 473
Anderson, Alexander 341
Anderson, Bette 373
Anderson, Clinton P. (U.S. Senator) 1020
Anderson College (Indiana) 501
Anderson, Marian 1449
Anderson, Maxwell 1648
Anderson, Paul B. 497
Anderson, Poul 1627
Anderson, Ritchie and Simon (publishers) 166
Anderson, Sherwood 1719
Andover Newton Theological School (Massachusetts) 706
Andrew College (Georgia) 353
Andrews, Clarence L. 43
Andrews, George 5
Andrews, Harold E. 1240
Andrews, James C. 497
Andrews University (Michigan) 777
Angelina and Neches Railroad Company (Texas) 1623
Angelina County Lumber Company (Texas) 1623
Angell, Sir Norman 503
Angelo State University (Texas) 1568
Anglican Episcopal Church 1060
angling 104, 975, 997, 1399
Anglo-American relations 930
Anglo-American relations, pre-Revolutionary War 519
animal diseases 1372
animal magnetism 742
animal science 980
Ankenbrand, Frank 988
Annenberg Research Institute for Judaic and Near Eastern Studies (Pennsylvania) 1355
Annual Review of Jazz Studies 1000
Anouilh, Jean 1648
Antarctica 810, 829
antebellum South 25, 561, 1181
Antheil, George 1371
Anthony, Susan B. 1158
anthropology 57, 88, 190, 220, 965, 1067, 1158
anti-cult religious groups 142
anti-masonic literature 1158
Antioch College (Ohio) 1239
Anti-Saloon League 1286
antisemitism 1026
anti-slavery 596, 601, 681, 764, 1276, 1390, 1444
APCO Bulletin 423
aphorisms 1217
apiculture 802
Apollo moon landing 519
Apollo-Soyuz Test Project 1607
Apostolic Christian Church 1242
apothecary pottery 1123
Appalachia 597, 601, 613, 622, 669, 1168, 1193, 1197, 1199, 1224, 1532, 1688, 1751, 1763
Appalachian State University (North Carolina) 1168
Appeal to Reason (publishers) 589
Appianus of Alexandria 1026
Appleton-Century (publishers) 519
Aquinas College (Michigan) 778

Aquinas Institute (Missouri) 881
Aquinas, Thomas 209, 293, 881, 1161
Arabian horses 99
Arabian Nights 266
Arabic manuscripts 266
Arapaho Indians 1800, 1801
Arbitron (marketing surveys) 394
Arbuckle, Alma 1752
Arcadia 1678
Arcana Coelestia 1350
archaeology 241, 997
archaeology, Biblical 364, 1571
archaeology, classical 928, 1358
archaeology (Israel) 172
archaeology, Near Eastern 1358
archaeology, southern Illinois 479
archaeology, West Indian 1469
Archibald, Raymond Clare 1475
architects, women 1719
architectural design 1554
architectural drawings 282
architectural history 681
architectural history slides 1051
architecture 5, 31, 215, 391, 415, 436, 440, 444, 488, 496, 536, 593, 646, 688, 713, 742, 798, 925, 938, 993, 997, 1049, 1080, 1101, 1104, 1113, 1115, 1127, 1137, 1158, 1204, 1218, 1363, 1640
architecture, English 1638
architecture, French 1638
architecture, history of 928
architecture, Italian 648
architecture, Roman church 1792
architecture, Southwest 1020
Archives of American Aerospace Exploration 1719
Archives of American Agriculture 549
Archives of American Veterinary Medicine 549
Archivo General de la nacion 1020
Archivo General de las Indias 341, 1020
Archivo Notarial de Jalapa 1577
Archivo paroquial de Cordoba 1577
Arctic 41, 44, 829
Arctic exploration 38, 45, 964
area handbooks 584
Area Research Center (Wisconsin) 1788, 1790, 1794, 1799
Arena Magazine 1792
Arendt, Hannah 1028
Aristotle 1449
arithmetic 1049, 1445
Arizona 49, 51, 54, 55, 56, 57
Arizona Historical Society 55
Arizona Lumber and Timber Co. 55
Arizona State University 48
Arizona Woolgrowers 55
Arkansas 58, 59, 63, 64, 68, 69, 70, 71, 74
Arkansas City (Kansas) 596
Arkansas College 58
Arkansas Medical Societies 73
Arkansas Regional Medical Program 73
Arkansas State Board of Nursing 73
Arkansas State Nurses' Association 73
Arkansas State University 59
Arkansas Tech University 60
Arlington Baptist College (Texas) 1569
Armed Services, Editions of the 32
Arment, Horace 1341
Arment, Roa 1341
Arminian theology 1316
Arminius, James 179, 476
Armour, Richard 106
Armstrong College (California) 79
Armstrong, Edwin H. 1049
Armstrong, Louis 955
Armstrong State College (Georgia) 354
Armstrong, Walter 1549
Arnold, Birch 1527
Arnold, Matthew 1587, 1627
Aroostook County (Maine) 665
Arouet, François Marie 519
art 76, 223, 298, 330, 356, 1098, 1104, 1110, 1113, 1127, 1158, 1223, 1363, 1411, 1429, 1668, 1673, 1703, 1757
art, African 1633
art, American 1000
art, American Indian 1013
art, Baroque 1000
Art Center College of Design (California) 80
art, Chicago Imagist 434
art, Chinese 588
art, Christian 124
art, contemporary 169, 754, 1061
art education 740, 1013
art history 109, 135, 184, 217, 220, 292, 301, 415, 629, 657, 683, 743, 900, 927, 982, 989, 997, 1055, 1150, 1358
Art Institute of Chicago (Illinois) 415
art, Italian Renaissance 1000
art, modern 453, 1000
art, nautical 656
Art of Cookery 583
art, Oriental 50
art photography 1649
art therapy 739, 1292
arthritis 1573
Arthur, Timothy Shay 1049
artists' books 169
Asbury College (Kentucky) 598
Asbury, Francis 248
Asbury, Samuel E. 1623
Asbury Theological Seminary (Kentucky) 599
Ascoli, Max 716
Ashbery, John 1158
Ashendene Press 93
Ashland College (Ohio) 1240

Ashwell, Lena 1158
Asia 1086, 1358, 1439
Asia, southern 821, 856
Asian materials 290
Asian studies 190, 1001
Asimov, Isaac 716, 1627
Aspinwall, Wayne 255
assassination (John F. Kennedy) 642, 894
assassination (Martin Luther King, Jr.) 1544
assassination (Robert F. Kennedy) 758
Assemblies of God 82, 844, 882, 1454, 1731
Assemblies of God Theological Seminary (Missouri) 882
Associated Mennonite Biblical Seminaries (Indiana) 502
Associated Public-Safety Communication Officers 423
Association of Average Adjusters 1046
Association of Commissions on Women 750
Association of Southern Women for the Prevention of Lynching 358
Assumption College (Massachusetts) 707
Assyriana 108, 111
Astaire, Fred 215
astronauts 1638
astronomy 116, 180, 190, 215, 279, 994, 1049, 1382, 1566
astronomy, history of 220
astrophysics 89
Athens State College (Alabama) 4
Atkins, Ollie 1690
Atlanta Christian College (Georgia) 355
Atlanta College of Art (Georgia) 356
Atlanta (Georgia) 369
Atlanta University Center (Georgia) 358
Atlanta University (Georgia) 357
Atlantic and St. Lawrence Railroad 652
Atlantic Christian College (North Carolina) 1169
Atlantic Records 583
Atlantic Union College (Massachusetts) 708
atlases 667, 982, 1159, 1647
atlases, celestial 497
atmospheric sciences 961
atomic energy 217
Atomic Scientists' Movement 494
Atwood, Rufus 608
Auburn University (Alabama) 5
Auburn University at Montgomery (Alabama) 6
auction and booksellers' catalogs 1217
Auden, W.H. 296, 1049, 1320, 1444, 1712
Audubon, John James 737, 1154, 1159, 1403, 1504
Audubon Society (Kansas) 596
Augsburg College (Minnesota) 824
Augusta College (Georgia) 359
Augusta County (Virginia) 1694
Augusta (Georgia) 359
Augustana College (Illinois) 416
Augustana College (South Dakota) 1510
Augustinian Brotherhood at Gemunde 1059
Augustinian Historical Institute 1456
Aull, Dr. George 1489
Aurelius, Marcus 1379
Aurora University (Illinois) 417
Austen, Jane 679
Austin College (Texas) 1570
Austin, Mary 106, 1020
Austin Peay State University (Tennessee) 1524
Austin Presbyterian Theological Seminary (Texas) 1571
Austin, Samuel 1270
Australia 399, 1278, 1421
Austria 912
Austrian revolutionary ephemera 737
Austro-Hungarian Empire 1607
authors, Alabama 7
authors, American Indian 1320
authors, American women 1029, 1791
authors, Black 24, 649
authors, British Catholic 714
authors, California 197
authors, Catholic 296
authors, Celtic 1047
authors, Colorado 252
authors, converted Roman Catholic 1398
authors, English 1217
authors, Florida 325
authors, Georgia 366, 394
authors, Illinois 499
authors, Indiana 517
authors, Iowa 564, 571
authors, Kansas 589
authors, Kentucky 602, 605
authors, Louisiana 645
authors, Maine 653
authors, Maine women 668
authors, Minnesota 825, 847
authors, Mississippi 871
authors, Montana 942
authors, Nebraska 950
authors, New England 341
authors, New Mexico 1009
authors, North Carolina 1184, 1200, 1226
authors, South Dakota 1522
authors, Southern 7, 386, 1565
authors, Tennessee 1563
authors, Texas 1590
authors, Victorian 997
authors, Virginia women 1709
authors, women 1637
authors, Wyoming 1800
autism 947
auto mechanics technology 67
autographs 1180, 1267, 1459
autographs, German literary 737
autographs, papal 1123

autographs, presidential 1059
automobiles 1208
automotive technology 659, 1740
Autry, Judge James L. 1607
avant-garde movements 1067
Avery, Rachel Foster 1158
aviation 59, 296, 309, 694, 966, 1045, 1754
aviation education 1194
aviation, history of 145, 165, 1649, 1792
aviation industry (southern California) 166
aviation technology 525
Azusa Pacific College (California) 81
Babcock, Charles H. 1221
Babson College (Massachusetts) 709
Babson, Roger 734
Babylonian cylinders 997
Babylonian manuscripts 734
Bach, Johann Sebastian 1241
Bacheller, Irving 1125
Bacon, Francis 209
Bacon, Henry 282
Bacon, Leonard 284, 1479, 1482
Bacon, Nathaniel T. 1479
Bacon, Robert Low (U.S. Congressman) 296
Bacote, Clarence A. 358
Bade, Florence 477
Badè Institute of Biblical Archaeology 172
Badillo, Herman 1031
Baer, Carlyle 465
Bafford, Edward L. 697
Bagnold, Enid 1320
bagpipe music 411
Bain, Barbara Harris 1579
Bain, Lewis E. 1579
Bainbridge Junior College (Georgia) 360
Baja California 190, 217, 477
Baker, Charlotte 1623
Baker, Howard 1562
Baker III, James 1607
Baker, Karle Wilson 1623
Baker University (Kansas) 573
Balalaika and Domra Society 497
Baldwin Locomotive Works (Texas) 1615
Baldwin, Mary Julia 1697
Baldwin-Wallace College (Ohio) 1241
Balkan church history 1126
Ball, Elisabeth W. 519
Ball State University (Indiana) 503
ballads 601, 1676
Ballantine, Edward 746
ballet 159, 1259, 1450
balloon flights 251
ballooning 742
Ballou, Hosea 762
Baltic studies 118, 196, 1262
Baltimore Hebrew College (Maryland) 670
Baltimore (Maryland) 695
Balzac, Honoré de 1150
Bancroft, Frederic 1049
Bancroft, Hubert Howe 181
band music scores 715
Bangor Theological Seminary (Maine) 650
bank newsletters 402
Bank Street College of Education (New York) 1027
banking 714, 1049
baptism 996
Baptist Bible Institute (Florida) 304
Baptist Church in Virginia 1715
Baptist College at Charleston (South Carolina) 1483
Baptist Courier 1497
Baptist General Conference (Swedish) 1044
Baptist General Convention of Texas 1620
Baptist Missionary Association 1591
Baptist Missionary Society of Arkansas 61
Baptist publications, early 651
Baptist World Alliance 1044
Baptista Film Mission 1684
Baptists 25, 61, 65, 86, 115, 140, 241, 338, 381, 390, 419, 450, 473, 510, 524, 588, 603, 617, 636, 792, 826, 869, 908, 920, 931, 1172, 1175, 1186, 1197, 1214, 1215, 1221, 1306, 1328, 1346, 1378, 1483, 1497, 1517, 1546, 1556, 1560, 1569, 1574, 1579, 1581, 1587, 1591, 1620, 1644, 1695, 1747
Baptists in colonial America 1044
Baptists, New England 706
Barabas, Stephen 500
Barat College (Illinois) 418
Barbee, David Rankin 296
Barber, Samuel 1371
Barbour, Roger 613
Bard College (New York) 1028
Baring, Maurice 714, 1097
Barker, Shirley 975
Barksdale, Jelks 5
Barlow, Joel 284, 737
Barnard College (New York) 1029
Barnes, Carman 1158
Barnes Company 296
Baron, W.W. 1752
Barret, Lyne Taliaferro 1623
Barrett, William 255
Barrie, Sir James Matthew 284, 519
Barry, Philip 284, 296
Barry, Rev. Michael 722
Barry University (Florida) 305
Barse, Gertrude Massey 1111
Barth, John 1158, 1421
Barthelme, Donald 1158
Bartlett, Elisha 1158
Bartlett, Robert A. 652
Bartok, Bela 1049
Baruch, Bernard 997
Bashkirtseff, Maria 1465
Basic Science and Healing Arts Board (Arkansas) 73

Baskerville Bible 101
Baskerville, John 284
Basque culture 413
Basque studies 961
Basques (Nevada) 958
Basset, Gene 296, 838
Bassist College (Oregon) 1321
Bates College (Maine) 651
Bateson, Gregory 220
Battle, Samuel 1444
Baudelaire, Charles Pierre 1566
Bauhaus Movement 765
Baum, L. Frank 1150
Bax, Clifford 1158
Baxter, Batsell Barrett 1531
Baxter, John E. 1123
Bayh, Birch (U.S. Senator) 519
Baylor College of Dentistry (Texas) 1572
Baylor College of Medicine (Texas) 1573
Baylor University (Texas) 1574
Bays, Bertie Cole 589
BBC radio scripts 519
Beach, Amy 746, 975
Beach, Sylvia 997
Beall, J. Glenn, Jr. (U.S. Congressman and Senator) 678
Bean, Joel 1444
Beaufort Technical College (South Carolina) 1484
Beaumont, Francis 1158, 1339
Beaumont, William 821
Beckett, Samuel 519, 928
Beckford, William 284
Beckley College (West Virginia) 1748
Becquerel, Antoine Henri 737
Becraft, Frank William 1666
Bedou, A.P. 649
The Bee 1611
Bee County College (Texas) 1575
Beecher, John 1648
Beerbohm, Max 225, 296, 737
Beethoven, Ludwig van 196
Behrend, Bernard 1489
Behrend, Ernst 1423
Beigelman, M.N. 166
Beigelman, Paul M. 166
Beinecke, Jr., Walter 1062
Belaval, Emilio S. 1470
Belgian Congo 1791
Belgian culture 421
Belgian Revolution 279
Belgium 369
Belitt, Ben 1668
Bell, Dr. L. Nelson 1201
Bellamarine College (Kentucky) 600
Bellamy, Edward 722, 737
belles lettres, Russian 737
Bellevue College (Nebraska) 943
Bellmont, Henry 1311
Belloc, Hilaire 296, 714, 1097
Bellows, George 705
Belmont Abbey College (North Carolina) 1170
Belmont College (Tennessee) 1525
Beloit College (Wisconsin) 1767
Belt, Dr. Elmer 166
Belvedere Hotel Corporation 695
Bemidji State University (Minnesota) 825
Bemis, Samuel F. 259
Bender, Albert M. 159
Bender, Lauretta 1032
Benedict College (South Carolina) 1485
Benedict, Ruth 1159
Benedictine monastic materials 1170
Benedictine Order 888, 1438
Benell, Julie 1637
Benet, Laura 1032
Benét, Stephen Vincent 284, 394
Benét, William Rose 284
Benezet, Anthony 1444
Benford, Gregory 216
Benitez, Jaime 1470
Benjamin, Mrs. Walter R. 296
Bennett, Arnold 216, 519, 1158, 1280, 1421
Bennett, Charles Alpheus 423
Bennett College (North Carolina) 1171
Bennett, E.H. 415
Bennett Publishing Company 423
Bennington College (Vermont) 1668
Benny, Jack 215
Benson, Louis F. 996
Bentham, Jeremy 497, 1049
Bentley College (Massachusetts) 710
Benton County (Oregon) 1329
Berea College (Kentucky) 601
Berean Institute (Pennsylvania) 1356
Berent, David 651
Berg, Carl 284
Berg, M.D., Sam 1005
Bergdorf-Goodman 1058
Bergen County (New Jersey) 998
Berger, Klaus 629
Berger, Thomas 1158
Berklee College of Music (Massachusetts) 711
Berks County (Pennsylvania) 1351
Berkshire area, northern (Massachusetts) 748
Berkshire Christian College (Massachusetts) 712
Berkson, Bill 279
Berle, Adolf A. 756
Berley Studio 1058
Berlioz, Hector 687, 1049
Bernard Baruch College of the City University of New York 1030
Bernard, Claude 1698
Bernstein, David 1130
Berry, E.Y. 1511

Berryman, John 1049
Besse, Ralph M. 1292
Bessey, Charles E. 955
best sellers 102, 924
Best Sellers book review 1452
Beston, Elizabeth Coatsworth 652
Bestor, Arthur 497
Bethany Bible College (California) 82
Bethany College (Kansas) 574
Bethany College (West Virginia) 1749
Bethany Theological Seminary (Illinois) 419
Bethel College (Kansas) 575
Bethel College (Minnesota) 826
Bethel College (Tennessee) 1526
Bethel Theological Seminary (Minnesota) 827
Bethune, Mary McLeod 306
Bethune-Cookman College (Florida) 306
Betts, Jackson 1256
Bevis, Mildren B. 415
Bewley, Marius 1028
Beyle, Marie Henri 646
B.H. Wragee Inc. 1058
Bibles 5, 83, 101, 172, 221, 319, 419, 437, 473, 494, 497, 502, 506, 519, 552, 568, 571, 573, 601, 636, 670, 706, 734, 766, 776, 777, 838, 854, 902, 920, 951, 993, 1044, 1047, 1060, 1123, 1124, 1155, 1200, 1248, 1265, 1270, 1297, 1316, 1332, 1355, 1418, 1440, 1445, 1461, 1527, 1567, 1597, 1683, 1733, 1785
Biblia Integra 1562
Biblia Latina 101
Biblical studies 26, 82, 115, 146, 176, 195, 204, 229, 322, 364, 367, 466, 471, 544, 563, 599, 700, 789, 801, 823, 884, 888, 948, 1105, 1236, 1248, 1324, 1345, 1378, 1448, 1492, 1517, 1523, 1531, 1534, 1571, 1578, 1714
bibliographic reference 296
bibliography 1217
Bidwell, Louise C. 596
Big Bend area (Texas) 1624
Big Blue Books 589
Biggers, Earl Derr 1567
Bilbo, Theodore G. (U.S. Senator) 877
Billings (Montana) 935
Billingsley, Price 1567
bimetallism 596
bindings, decorated cloth 1681
Binet, Dr. Maurice Emmanuel Hippolyte 764
biochemistry 190, 525, 1144
Biola University (California) 83
biological sciences 380, 666, 856, 1719
biology 190, 1080, 1338
biology, fresh water 477
biomedical engineering technology 239
biomedical sciences 1118
biomedicine 37, 217, 1095, 1389
Bird, Francis William 737
birdlife 1627
Birds of America 1154, 1245, 1403, 1504
Birmingham-Southern College (Alabama) 7
Bishop, Arthur Giles 817
Bishop College (Texas) 1576
Bishop, Elizabeth 1159
Bits Press 921
Bixby, Fred H. 106
Bizzell, W.B. 1306
Black Hawk College - East Campus (Illinois) 420
Black Hawk College - Quad Cities Campus (Illinois) 421
Black Hills State College (South Dakota) 1511
Black Mountain College 1205
Black music 429
Black Muslims 358
Black Power Movement 1445
Black Sparrow Press 1067, 1794
Black studies 1, 16, 22, 29, 130, 153, 158, 219, 280, 284, 297, 302, 306, 317, 352, 389, 429, 438, 491, 526, 551, 585, 627, 643, 644, 645, 649, 692, 698, 756, 764, 821, 858, 859, 875, 904, 927, 977, 1014, 1091, 1185, 1192, 1196, 1202, 1203, 1214, 1246, 1253, 1276, 1278, 1293, 1356, 1362, 1404, 1479, 1485, 1488, 1503, 1507, 1523, 1533, 1538, 1540, 1541, 1545, 1550, 1576, 1592, 1605, 1631, 1633, 1647, 1659, 1692, 1710, 1721
Black Tom Island (New Jersey) 1046
Black World 358
Blackburn College (Illinois) 422
Blackburn, George A. 873
Blackwell, Elizabeth 1049
Blair, Sam 1613
Blake, Robert Bruce 1623
Blake, William 103, 216, 1022, 1154, 1475, 1645, 1792
Blakeslee Lane, Inc. 695
Blanchard, Charles Albert 500
Blanchard, Jonathan 500
Blatty, William Peter 296
Bleeding Kansas 583
Bligh, Captain William 173
blind, studies for the 310
Bliss, Susan Dwight 652
Blockson, Charles L. 1445
Blondheim, David S. 629
Bloomfield College (New Jersey) 977
Bloomsburg University of Pennsylvania 1357
Bloomsbury Group 1026
Blount, William 1562
Blow, Susan 913
Blucher, Felix von 1577
Blue Mountain Community College (Oregon) 1322
Blue Ridge Institute 1689
Blue Ridge Mountains 1689
Bluecher, Heinrich 1028
Bluffton College (Ohio) 1242
Blumenthal, Walter Hart 260

Blunden, Edmund 564
B'nai B'rith International Four Freedoms Library 670
Board of Education of the City of New York 1151
Board of Global Ministries 1268
Bobbs-Merrill (publishing firm) 519
Bodoni, Giambattista 1342
Bogan, Louise 705
Boise State University (Idaho) 407
Boisen, Anton 426
Bole, Dr. Robert 988
Bollingen Foundation 1450
Bolton, David A. 1557
Bomberger, J.H.A. 1453
Bonaparte, Napoleon 296, 319, 431, 1016, 1188, 1217, 1382, 1528
Bone, Home T. 1742
Bone, Robert Donnell 1623
Bonet, Paul 1648
Bonhoeffer, Dietrich 1155
Bonner, James C. 371
book arts 252, 356, 508, 716, 766, 802, 1049, 1067, 1158, 1217, 1219, 1338, 1445, 1475, 1648, 1650, 1717, 1758
Book Club of California 196, 225, 1320
book conservation 1648
book exhibitions 166
book, history of the 252, 255, 716, 755, 792, 1150, 1217, 1245, 1276, 1504, 1650
book illustration 341
Book of Hours 552, 1036
bookbinding 1648
bookbindings, Victorian 997, 1158, 1217
Bookbuilders of Boston 714
bookkeeping 999, 1123
bookplates 279, 465, 1158, 1258, 1278, 1379, 1475, 1791
books for the blind 1096
booksellers 1445
Bookstore Press 279
Boone, Blind 922
Boonslick Historical Society (Missouri) 885
Booth, Edwin 1158
Booth, John Wilkes 296
borderlands, Spanish 1020
Borges, Jorge Luis 802, 1716
Boricua College (New York) 1031
Borlaug, Norman 549
Bornschein, Franz 687
Boston and Maine Railroad 975
Boston and Maine Railroad Historical Association 763
Boston Architectural Center (Massachusetts) 713
Boston Children's Aid Society 755
Boston College (Massachusetts) 714
Boston Conservatory of Music (Massachusetts) 715
Boston (Massachusetts) 765
Boston University (Massachusetts) 716
Boswell, James 284, 497, 1217
Boswell, Roy V. 104
botanical prints 504
botany 180, 422, 549, 593, 802, 1000, 1144, 1363, 1382, 1427, 1459, 1482, 1626, 1649
botany, economic 342
Bothamley, Merrill 423
Botkin, Benjamin 955
Botsford, Edmund 1497
Boudinet, Elias 1318
Bourjaily, Vance 652
Bourke-White, Margaret 1150
Bova, Ben 1445
Bowditch, Nathaniel 1156
Bowdoin College (Maine) 652
Bowdoin, James II 652
Bowdoin, James III 652
Bowen, Elizabeth 1648
Bowen, Henry Lee 688
Bowen, Russell J. 296
Bower, Robert 138
Bowers, Lamont Montgomery 1130
Bowers, Lloyd W. (U.S. Solicitor General) 296
Bowers, Lola 1305
Bowie State College (Maryland) 671
Bowling Green (Kentucky) 624
Bowling Green State University (Ohio) 1243
Bowron, James 32
Boxer, Dr. Charles 519
Boyle, George 687
Boyle, Kay 487
Boyle, Robert 1791
Boynton, Captain Paul 1436
Bozeman Trail 413
Bradbury, Ray 1243
Braddock Military Road 678
Bradford College (Massachusetts) 717
Bradford, Gamaliel 737
Bradley County (Tennessee) 1529
Bradley, Omar 1157
Bradley, Palmer 1587
Bradley, Robert 1587
Bradley University (Illinois) 423
Bradstreet, Anne 519, 766
Brady, Charles A. 1036
Brady, Mrs. Nicholas 296
Bragdon, Claude 1158
Bragg, Bill 1800
Brahe, Tycho 1504
braille 1117
Brainerd Community College (Minnesota) 828
Brandeis, Alice 718
Brandeis, Louis D. 623, 718
Brandeis University (Massachusetts) 718
Brandt, E.H. 497
Brandt, William 497
Branham, William 1313
Branscomb, Dr. Louise 7

Brantley, Jr., William H. 25
Brantner, Chet 52
Bray, Bannister R. 378
Bray, Monsignor James 1038
Bray, Reverend Thomas 688
Brazil 291, 593
Braziller, George 1049
Breathitt, Edward T. 614
Brenau College (Georgia) 361
Brentano, Franz 737
Brenz, Johannes 889
Brescia College (Kentucky) 602
Brethren in Christ Church 1242, 1413
Brett, John Hall 296
Brewer, G.C. 62
Bridges, Robert 1158, 1504
Bridges, Styles 968
Bridgewater College (Virginia) 1683
Bridgewater State College (Massachusetts) 719
Bridson, D.G. 519
Briefs, Goetz A. 296
Brigham Young University - Hawaii 399
Brigham Young University (Utah) 1660
Bright, John 1444
Brin, David 216
Brinkley, Jack T. (U.S. Congressman) 365
Bristow, Gwen 15
British Americana 1444
British Columbia 181, 1726
British seizure of American ships 596
Britton, Henry 497
Broadcast Designers Association 1262
broadcast music 1071
broadcasting 129
Broadside News 764
Broadside Press 764
broadsides 997, 1475
broadsides, American 737
Brodsky, Louis Daniel 919
Bromfield, Louis 1240, 1274, 1279
Bronk, William 975
Bronx (New York) 1079
Brookdale Community College (New Jersey) 978
Brooke, Rupert 1648
Brooklyn Bridge 1115
Brooklyn College of the City University of New York 1032
Brooklyn Law School (New York) 1033
Brooklyn (New York) 1032, 1121
Brooks, Cleanth 877
Brooks Institute of Photography (California) 84
Brooks, Lt. General Edward H. 1677
Brooks, Phillips 737
Broome Community College (New York) 1034
Broome County (New York) 1130
Brown, Alice 975
Brown, Charles Brockden 652
Brown, Clarence 1562
Brown County (South Dakota) 1518
Brown County (Wisconsin) 1789
Brown, Edgar 1489
Brown, Hallie Q. 1246
Brown, Jerry 226
Brown, John 358, 1049, 1445
Brown, John Mason 737
Brown, Margaret Wise 1693
Brown, Marion Marsh 953
Brown, Ollie L. 2
Brown, Theo 772
Brown University (Rhode Island) 1475
Brown, William Wells 1445
Browne, George H. 972
Browning, Elizabeth Barrett 200, 766, 1281
Browning, Robert 766, 1281
Bruce, Sir Frederick William Adolphus 1158
Bruckner, Clayton 1296
Brundage, Avery 497
Brunswick Junior College (Georgia) 362
Bryan College (Tennessee) 1527
Bryan, William Jennings 166, 1527
Bryant, Alys McKey 596
Bryant and Stratton Business Institute (Syracuse, New York) 1035
Bryant College (Rhode Island) 1476
Bryant, William Cullen 341
Brydegaard, Marguerite 119
Bryn Mawr College (Pennsylvania) 1358
Buchan, John 1475
Buchanan, James 1373, 1382
Buchanan, Scott 737
Buck, Pearl S. 1709, 1764
Buckley, Daniel 1343
Buckley, James 1123
Bucknell University (Pennsylvania) 1359
Buckner, Dr. Claudia 102
Buddhism 1083, 1791
Buddhist religious groups 142
Buddhist studies 247
Buena Vista College (Iowa) 541
Buffalo Courier Express 1131, 1134
Buffalo Creek Flood of 1972 (West Virginia) 1753
Buffalo (New York) 1036
building construction 391
Bukowski, Charles 106
Bullard, F. Lauriston 764
Bulloch County (Georgia) 373
Bunche, Ralph J. 215
Bunting, Bainbridge 1020
Bunyan, John 500, 826, 891
Bureau of Catholic Indian Missions 1778
Bureau of Mines 926
Burford, Jack 1567
Burford, Mable 1567
Burgess, Anthony 1627

Burgess, John William 1049
Burguieres, Jules M. 629
Burke, Kenneth 1421, 1668
Burma 1380
Burnet, Gilbert 1445
Burnham, Daniel H. 415
Burnham, Walter E. 596
Burning Deck Press 975
Burns, James A. 355
Burns, Robert 381, 587, 1180
Burr, Aaron 997
Burritt, Elihu 260
Burritt, Elijah 260
Burroughs, Edgar Rice 1567
Burroughs, John 1159
Burroughs, William Seward 48, 1049
Burton, Lawrence J. 1666
Burton, Robert 118
Busch, Fritz 519
Bush, Vannevar 742
business 35, 141, 163, 190, 210, 215, 230, 234, 265, 281, 283, 286, 288, 299, 300, 326, 339, 408, 423, 444, 488, 560, 644, 660, 818, 1030, 1129, 1222, 1375, 1433, 1445, 1449, 1476, 1583, 1587, 1707, 1736, 1804
business administration 324, 459, 626, 662, 816, 1568, 1737
business history 1150
business management 1090
business management, international 1431
business procedures 1123
busing controversy, Providence (Rhode Island) 1479
Butler, John Lloyd 166
Butler, Nicholas Murray 1049
Butler University (Indiana) 504
Butler, Vera 52
Butor, Michel 921
Bynner, Witter 688, 737, 975, 1018
Bynum, Cary 394
Byrd, Harry F., Jr. 1716
Byrd, Harry F., Sr. 1716
Byrd, Richard E. 1278
Byrd, Robert C. 1763
Byrne, Donn 1158
Byrnes, James F. 1489
Byzantine church history 1126
Byzantine manuscripts 494
Byzantine studies 1452
Cabell, Earle 1615
Cabell, James Branch 1717
Cabot, John Moors 762
Cabrillo College (California) 85
Cabrini College (Pennsylvania) 1360
Cade, John Brother 643
Caesar, Doris 596
Cage, John 475
Cajun history 648
Caldecott, Randolph 519
Calder and Boyars (publishers) 519
Caldwell College (New Jersey) 979
Caldwell, Erskine 394, 1320
Calhoun, John C. 1489
California 78, 93, 101, 104, 118, 134, 162, 166, 174, 190, 197, 198, 211, 214, 216, 220, 223
California Baptist College 86
California College of Arts and Crafts 87
California Gold Rush 128
California Institute of Integral Studies 88
California Institute of Technology 89
California Institute of the Arts 90
California Lutheran University 91
California Maritime Academy 92
California Odyssey Project 100
California Polytechnic State University, San Luis Obispo 93
California School of Design (San Francisco) 191
California School of Fine Arts (San Francisco) 191
California School of Professional Psychology 94
California School of Professional Psychology - Berkeley 95
California School of Professional Psychology - Fresno 96
California School of Professional Psychology - Los Angeles 97
California School of Professional Psychology - San Diego 98
California State Polytechnic University, Pomona 99
California State University, Bakersfield 100
California State University, Chico 101
California State University, Dominguez Hills 102
California State University, Fresno 103
California State University, Fullerton 104
California State University, Hayward 105
California State University, Long Beach 106
California State University, Los Angeles 107
California State University, Northridge 108
California State University, Sacramento 109
California State University, San Bernardino 110
California State University, Stanislaus 111
California University of Pennsylvania 1361
California Western School of Law (San Diego) 112
calligraphic manuscripts 737
calligraphy 1255, 1338
Calumet College (Indiana) 505
Calvary Bible College (Missouri) 883
Calvin College (Michigan) 779
Calvin, John 779, 891, 1571
Calvin Theological Seminary (Michigan) 780
Calvinism 779, 1571, 1714, 1791
Cambodia 1380
Camden County College (New Jersey) 980
camellias 1504
Cameron University (Oklahoma) 1299
Camien, Laiten 596

Campbell, Alexander 1567, 1749
Campbell, Carroll 1489
Campbell, James Archibald 1172
Campbell, Leslie H. 1172
Campbell, Roy 1648
Campbell, Thomas 1280
Campbell University (North Carolina) 1172
Campbell, Will D. 876
Campbell, William J. 1445
Campbellsville College (Kentucky) 603
Camus, Albert 1792
Canada 737, 1343
Canada, French 1038
Canadian Northwest Territory 802
canals 455, 519, 763, 1066
Canisius College (New York) 1036
canon law 1449, 1784
Canon Missae 1049
Cantors Institute 1073
Cantrell, Clyde 5
Cape Cod Community College (Massachusetts) 720
Capital University (Ohio) 1244
Capitol Institute of Technology (Maryland) 672
Capote, Truman 394
Capra Press 519
Carberry, Cardinal John Joseph 902
Cardinal Fashion Studios 1058
Cardinal Stritch College (Wisconsin) 1768
cardiology 594
Cardozo, Benjamin Nathan 1049
career planning 23, 56, 149, 152, 163, 323, 427, 662, 710, 759, 795, 797, 812, 835, 859, 976, 1048, 1109, 1165, 1330, 1362, 1604, 1703, 1713, 1727, 1774, 1791
Carey, Hugh L. 1123
Carey, James C. 583
Caribbean 316, 340, 341, 342, 736, 1445, 1473, 1638
Carleton College (Minnesota) 829
Carlow College (Pennsylvania) 1362
Carlson, Lage 1648
Carlucci Commission 296
Carlyle, Thomas 220, 652, 737
Carnap, Rudolf 1450
Carnegie Endowment for International Peace 295, 1049
Carnegie Mellon University (Pennsylvania) 1363
Carney, John 1383
Carofano, Mrs. Edward 1123
Carolina, Clinchfield and Ohio Railroad Company 1532
Carolina Israelite 1218
Carothers, Milton Washington 319
Carrel, Alexis 296
Carriere, Oliver P. 629
Carroll, Archbishop Coleman F. 332
Carroll College (Montana) 933
Carroll College (Wisconsin) 1769
Carroll, John A. 253
Carroll, Lewis 465, 500, 737, 997, 1106
Carson, Rachel 284
Carson, Velma L. 583
Carter, Hodding 870
Carter, Robert 737
Carthage College (Wisconsin) 1770
cartography 104, 118, 475, 638, 721, 1611, 1647, 1791
cartoons 1117
cartoons, editorial 13, 70, 296, 534, 1278
cartoons, political 295, 296, 737, 838
Cartwright, J.M. 1623
Caruso, Enrico 687
Carver, George Washington 31
Casaday, James Lewis 518
Casals, Pablo 48
Casanova, Giacomo 1708
Case, Francis (U.S. Senator) 1513
Case, Nelson 573
Case Western Reserve University (Ohio) 1245
Casement, Dan D. 583
Casper College (Wyoming) 1800
Casper (Wyoming) 1800
Castle, William R. 737
Castleman, Harry 718
Castleton College (Vermont) 1669
Catawba College (North Carolina) 1173
Catawba County (North Carolina) 1195
catechisms 1435
catechisms, New England 737
Cathedral College of the Immaculate Conception (New York) 1048
Cather, Willa 238, 913, 955, 1638, 1645, 1681
Catholic Americana 536, 686, 1785
Catholic Church in America 296
Catholic Conference for Interracial Justice 1778
Catholic Diocese of Youngstown (Ohio) 1262
Catholic Emancipation Act (1829) 187
Catholic Extension Society 459
Catholic history, New Jersey 1001
Catholic News 1087
Catholic Theological Union (Illinois) 424
Catholic University of America (District of Columbia) 291
Catholic University of Puerto Rico 1468
Catholic Worker Movement 1778
Catholicism 81, 186, 197, 293, 305, 334, 424, 459, 484, 521, 528, 531, 536, 585, 590, 600, 618, 619, 634, 690, 800, 811, 813, 888, 902, 906, 982, 1036, 1044, 1124, 1170, 1277, 1289, 1297, 1331, 1376, 1392, 1435, 1478, 1515, 1567, 1729, 1778, 1785
Catledge, Turner 870
Catron, Thomas 1020
cats 284
Cattaraugus County (New York) 1136
cattle industry 519, 579, 583, 938, 1613, 1627, 1656
cattlemen 1638

Catts, Sidney F. 346
Caxton Printers, Ltd. (Caldwell, Idaho) 413
Caxton, William 519
Cayuga County Community College (New York) 1037
CBN University (Virginia) 1684
Cedar Crest College (Pennsylvania) 1364
cello music 48, 1219
Centenary College (New Jersey) 981
Centenary College of Louisiana 625
Center for International Higher Education Documentation 749
Center for the Public Financing of Elections 296
Center for Western Studies 1510
Central America 181
Central Arizona College 49
Central Baptist College (Arkansas) 61
Central Baptist Theological Seminary (Kansas) 576
Central Christian College of the Bible (Missouri) 884
Central Committee for France Overseas 1130
Central Connecticut State University 260
Central Lumber Company (Hanford, California) 103
Central Methodist College (Missouri) 885
Central Michigan University 781
Central Missouri State University 886
Central Oregon Community College 1323
Central Piedmont Community College (North Carolina) 1174
Central Relief Committee 1166
Central State University (Ohio) 1246
Central State University (Oklahoma) 1300
Central University of Iowa 542
Central Washington University 1724
Central Wesleyan College (South Carolina) 1486
Central Wyoming College 1801
Centralia College (Washington) 1725
Centre College of Kentucky 604
Centre County (Pennsylvania) 1421
Centro de Estudios Avanzados (Puerto Rico) 1469
Century Magazine 169, 912
ceramics, Chinese 588
Cerf, Bennett A. 1049
Cerro Maravilla trial 1469
Cervantes 593
Chadron State College (Nebraska) 944
Chadwick, George 746
Chaikin, Joseph 1262
chamber music 497, 756, 915
Chamberlain, Joshua L. 652
Chambers, Martha C. 1139
Chaminade University of Honolulu (Hawaii) 400
Champlain, Hotel 1042
Chan, Charlie 1567
Chandrasekhar, S. 494
Channing, William Ellery 464
chaplaincy materials, World War II 1286
Chapman, Chauncey Brewster 296
Chapman College (California) 113
Chapman, Inoe 613
Chappell, Absalom H. 365
Chappell, Louis W. 1763
Chardin, Teilhard du 296
Charles County Community College (Maryland) 673
Charles, Edward 1320
Charles XV (King of Sweden and Norway, 1859-1872) 416
Charlot, Jean 406
Charlotte (North Carolina) 1218
Charlottesville (Virginia) 1718
Charriere, Gerard 1648
Charters, William F. 504
Charvat, William 1278
Chase, Mary Ellen 653
Chase, Philander 423, 1263
Chatham College (Pennsylvania) 1365
Chattahoochee Valley (Georgia) 365
Chaucer, Geoffrey 519, 1310
Chautauqua County (New York) 1136
Chavez, Cesar 103
checkers 55
Cheeslock, Louis 687
Cheever, John 718
chemical dependency 1089
chemical ecology 1144
chemistry 190, 287, 380, 525, 536, 792, 982, 1202, 1280, 1338, 1445
chemistry, history of 1288, 1449, 1791
Cheney Reservoir (Kansas) 596
Cherokee Advocate 1305
The Cherokee Almanac 1562
Cherokee education 1305
Cherokee Indians 1197, 1224, 1302, 1305, 1318, 1320, 1562
Cherokee medicine formulas 1320
The Cherokee Phoenix 1305, 1562
Cherokee tribal publications 1305
Chesapeake Bay (Maryland) 672
Chesapeake College (Maryland) 674
Chesler, Harry 985
Chesnutt, Charles 1245, 1445, 1533
chess 236, 1791
Chester County Cabinet of Natural Sciences (Pennsylvania) 1459
Chester County (Pennsylvania) 1459
Chesterton, G.K. 296, 714, 1097, 1261, 1383
Chestnut Hill College (Pennsylvania) 1366
Cheuse, Alan 1668
Cheyenne Indians 1800
Cheyney University (Pennsylvania) 1367
Chicago and Pacific Railroad 596
Chicago Architectural Exhibition League 415
Chicago Board of Trade 496
Chicago (Illinois) 472, 474, 496
Chicago State University (Illinois) 425
Chicago Theological Seminary (Illinois) 426

Chicano studies 184, 190, 196, 207, 219, 585, 1650
chickens 583
child care 1222
child development 469, 828
Child, Francis James 737
child labor 755
child psychology 97, 123
child rearing 171
children's book illustration 80
children's literature 10, 20, 22, 52, 62, 66, 93, 119, 123, 152, 171, 177, 252, 256, 257, 261, 274, 279, 329, 335, 384, 385, 410, 421, 427, 433, 467, 469, 475, 494, 519, 544, 545, 564, 565, 569, 578, 579, 593, 618, 628, 640, 677, 684, 698, 699, 700, 719, 731, 755, 770, 773, 781, 795, 815, 820, 833, 837, 838, 847, 856, 864, 868, 877, 890, 899, 912, 944, 946, 950, 976, 988, 990, 1027, 1037, 1049, 1079, 1080, 1109, 1113, 1123, 1129, 1134, 1135, 1137, 1151, 1158, 1159, 1160, 1179, 1218, 1227, 1232, 1240, 1251, 1262, 1269, 1289, 1296, 1300, 1310, 1369, 1388, 1436, 1479, 1483, 1590, 1606, 1624, 1637, 1673, 1693, 1704, 1735, 1748, 1769, 1791, 1799
children's religious literature 1493
Childs, J. Rives 1708
Childs, John 487
Chile 279
Chilson, Herman P. 1522
Chilton, William B. 296
China 1051, 1086, 1743, 1783
China, minorities in 1745
Chinese coins (dynastic era) 573
Ch'ing Dynasty 1475
Chippewa River Valley (Wisconsin) 1788
chiropractic 151, 468, 559, 846, 887, 905, 1099, 1349, 1629
Chiswick Press 1681
chivalric orders 296
chivalry 766
Choctaw Indians 1318
cholera 482
choral books 430
choral music 1007
choreography 715
Chowan College (North Carolina) 1175
Christ College Irvine (California) 114
Christ Evangelical Church (Baltimore, Maryland) 695
Christ the King Seminary (New York) 1038
Christian and Missionary Alliance 201, 851
Christian Brothers College (Tennessee) 1528
Christian, Camillus 1718
Christian Century magazine 487
Christian Church 1239, 1260, 1418, 1537
Christian Church Restoration Movement 170
Christian Churches and Churches of Christ 170, 355
Christian Cynosure 500
Christian education 9, 194, 466, 823, 1400, 1705, 1731
Christian Evangelical Church 176
Christian Heritage College (California) 115
Christian Holiness Association 599
Christian, Marcus 647
Christian Methodist Episcopal Church 19, 1540
Christian Reformed Church 779
Christian Science 477
Christian Theological Seminary (Indiana) 506
Christian values 232
Christianity 532, 768, 1452
Christianity, English 730
Christie, George C. 1181
Christitch, Annie 714
Christmas cards 1475
Chronicles of England, Scotland, and Ireland 1742
church architecture 337, 1124
Church, Clarence M. 1384
Church, Frank (U.S. Senator) 407
church history, American 1401
church history, English 1401
church history, Rhode Island 1475
church leadership 908
Church League of America 1695
church music 879
Church of Christ 456, 1307
Church of God 229, 348, 501, 1303, 1344
Church of the Brethren 222, 520, 586, 1381, 1394, 1683
Church of the Nazarene 248, 726, 911, 1271, 1316, 1558
Church of the United Brethren in Christ 1286
Churches of Christ 9, 62, 1418, 1531, 1536, 1537, 1598
Churchill, Sir Winston 593, 930, 1049, 1638
Ciardi, John 820
cigar industry advertising art 344
Cincinnati Bible College and Seminary (Ohio) 1247
cinema 226, 1143, 1262, 1693
Circleville Bible College (Ohio) 1248
circuit riders 1268
circus, history of the 445, 1320
Cistercian studies 821
The Citadel (South Carolina) 1487
Citizens League Against the Sonic Boom 742
citri-culture 216
citrus 81
Citrus College (California) 116
City College of San Francisco (California) 117
City College of the City University of New York 1039
City University of New York 1040
civil engineering 742
civil liberties 497
civil rights 2, 1218
Civil War, English 494
Civil War novels 1217
Civil War, Spanish 217, 718, 1022
Civil War, U.S. 4, 13, 166, 190, 219, 255, 296, 328,

369, 373, 431, 442, 452, 465, 497, 564, 577, 596, 615, 621, 629, 680, 716, 729, 737, 793, 820, 877, 886, 912, 913, 984, 997, 1001, 1122, 1133, 1181, 1187, 1189, 1267, 1289, 1306, 1331, 1380, 1382, 1385, 1504, 1526, 1532, 1535, 1542, 1544, 1552, 1561, 1586, 1587, 1607, 1610, 1647, 1718, 1747, 1757, 1769, 1770, 1792
Claflin College (South Carolina) 1488
Clandel, Paul 849
Clapp, W.W. 737
Clare County (Michigan) 804
Claremont Colleges (California) 118
Claremont Graduate School (California) 119
Claremont McKenna College (California) 120
Clarion University (Pennsylvania) 1368
Clark, Barrett H. 284
Clark, C.A.W. 1576
Clark College (Georgia) 363
Clark County (Arkansas) 65
Clark County (Nevada) 960
Clark, Edward A. 1622
Clark, General Mark W. 1487
Clark, Jamie 1223
Clark, John Bates 1049
Clark, J.S. 643
Clark, Thomas A. 497
Clark, Tom 279
Clark University (Massachusetts) 721
Clarke, Dr. Norman E. 781
Clarke, Lucile 781
Clarkson University (New York) 1041
Clarksville (Tennessee) 1524
classics, Greek 792, 993, 1161, 1270
classics, Latin 792, 993, 1161, 1270
Claxton, P.P. 1562
Clayton, Henry DeLamar 32
Cleaveland, Parker 652
Clemens, Samuel 284, 497, 519, 679, 1056, 1159, 1221, 1610, 1716, 1763
Clemson, Thomas Green 1489
Clemson University (South Carolina) 1489
Clendening, Dr. Logan 594
Clendening History of Medicine Library 594
Cleveland Chiropractic College (Missouri) 887
Cleveland City Club (Ohio) 1250
Cleveland, Grover 979, 997
Cleveland Institute of Music (Ohio) 1249
Cleveland State Community College (Tennessee) 1529
Cleveland State University (Ohio) 1250
Cleveland Technical College (North Carolina) 1176
Cleverdon, Douglas 519
Clewell, Clarence E. 1213
Clifford, James L. 534
Clinch Valley College (Virginia) 1685
clinical psychology 95
Clinton Community College (New York) 1042
Clinton County (Pennsylvania) 1405
Clinton, DeWitt 1049
Clinton Railroad Company 695
clocks 279
Clune, Henry W. 1158
Coach House Press 1450
Coahoma Junior College (Mississippi) 859
coal mining 678, 1393, 1661, 1685, 1763
Coan, Carl (U.S. Senator) 296
Cobbett, William 1000, 1022, 1059
Coburn, Charles 394
Cochise College (Arizona) 50
Cochran, Warren Baldwin 573
Cocke, Charles Lewis 1693
Cocke, William 1562
Cocteau, Jean 1648
codex manuscripts 552
codices, medieval 997, 1059
Coe College (Iowa) 543
Coe, William Robertson 284
Coffeyville Community College (Kansas) 577
Coffin, Robert P.T. 652, 975, 1637
Cogswell College (California) 121
coinage 722, 997
Coker College (South Carolina) 1490
Coker, Elizabeth Boatwright 1494
Coker, Major James Lide 1490
Colby College (Maine) 653
Colby-Sawyer College (New Hampshire) 962
Coleman College (California) 122
Coleridge, Samuel Taylor 529
Colette 1648
Colgate Rochester Divinity School (New York) 1044
Colgate University (New York) 1043
College for Developmental Studies (California) 123
College Misericordia (Pennsylvania) 1369
College of Aeronautics (New York) 1045
College of Charleston (South Carolina) 1491
College of DuPage (Illinois) 427
College of Eastern Utah 1661
College of Great Falls (Montana) 934
College of Idaho 408
The College of Insurance (New York) 1046
College of Lake County (Illinois) 428
College of Mount St. Joseph (Ohio) 1251
College of Mount Saint Vincent (New York) 1047
College of Notre Dame (California) 124
College of Notre Dame of Maryland 675
College of Osteopathic Medicine of the Pacific (California) 125
College of Our Lady of the Elms (Massachusetts) 722
College of Saint Benedict (Minnesota) 830
College of St. Catherine - St. Mary's Campus (Minnesota) 832
College of St. Catherine (Minnesota) 831
College of St. Elizabeth (New Jersey) 982
College of St. Joseph (Vermont) 1670
College of St. Mary (Nebraska) 945

College of St. Scholastica (Minnesota) 833
College of St. Thomas (Minnesota) 834
College of San Mateo (California) 126
College of Santa Fe (New Mexico) 1009
College of the Albemarle (North Carolina) 1177
College of the Atlantic (Maine) 654
College of the Holy Cross (Massachusetts) 723
College of the Sequoias (California) 127
College of the Southwest (New Mexico) 1010
College of William and Mary (Virginia) 1686
College of Wooster (Ohio) 1252
Collins Overland Telegraph Expedition 45
Colman, Anson 1158
Colmer, William M. 877
Colonial Period, U.S. 296, 319
Colophon 1123
Colorado 235, 236, 249, 252, 255, 257, 258
Colorado College 236
Colorado Plateau 55
Colorado River water rights 960
Colorado School of Mines 237
Colorado State University 238
Colorado Technical College 239
Colum, Mary 1130
Colum, Padraic 1130
Columbia Bible College (South Carolina) 1492
Columbia Christian College (Oregon) 1324
Columbia College (Columbia, California) 128
Columbia College (Illinois) 429
Columbia College (Los Angeles, California) 129
Columbia College (South Carolina) 1493
Columbia State Community College (Tennessee) 1530
Columbia Studios 215
Columbia Theological Seminary (Georgia) 364
Columbia Union College (Maryland) 676
Columbia University (New York) 1049
Columbus, Christopher 519
Columbus College (Georgia) 365
Columbus (Georgia) 365
Combe, William 1280
Comenius, John Amos 1415
comic art 985
comic books 802, 1450
comics, underground 549
Comly, John 1444
commercial art 80
Commission on Government Efficiency and Economy (Maryland) 695
Commission on Interracial Cooperation 358
Common Cause 997
communal societies 537
communism 55
Communism, international 1182
Communist Party (U.S.) 1218, 1276
Community College of Beaver County (Pennsylvania) 1370
community colleges 1034
community psychology 97
community service 765, 1720
Community Service Society 1049
Compleat Angler 1450
composers 340
composers, American 192
composers, Pennsylvania 1414
Compton Community College (California) 130
Compton, Karl T. 742
compulsory military service 1444
computer languages 1553
computer science 215, 217, 239, 265, 286, 324, 339, 532, 792, 963, 1363, 1587, 1634
computer software engineering 1737
computer-integrated manufacturing 980
computers 1553
Conception Seminary College (Missouri) 888
concert programs 497
Concord College (West Virginia) 1750
Concordia College - Moorhead (Minnesota) 835
Concordia College - St. Paul (Minnesota) 836
Concordia College (Illinois) 430
Concordia College (Michigan) 782
Concordia College (Wisconsin) 1771
Concordia Seminary (Missouri) 889
Concordia Teachers College (Nebraska) 946
Concordia Theological Seminary (Indiana) 507
Confederate Army, Official Records of the 13
Confederate history 1718
Confederate States of America 386, 394, 877, 1586, 1587, 1718, 1722, 1753
Congregationalism 284, 426
Conkle, Ellsworth P. 953
Conn, Jack T. 1301
Connecticut 259, 262, 271, 274
Connecticut College 261
Connett, Eugene V. 997
Connolly, Cyril 1320
Conolly, Admiral Richard Lansing 1080
Conrad, Joseph 216, 284, 296, 519, 1043, 1445, 1635
conscientious objection 1444
conscription 1444
conservation of natural resources 1489
Conservative Baptist Association of America 241, 1346
Constable & Co. (London) 1445
Constitution, U.S. 30, 519
consumer education 784
consumer information 168
consumer studies 525, 1550
contemplative thought 1330
controversial literature, Catholic 1124
Converse College (South Carolina) 1494
Converse, Frederick 746
Conway, Moncure D. 1049
Conwell, Russell H. 1445
Cook County (Illinois) 472, 474
Cook, Dr. Robert A. 1076

Cook, Margaret 1637
Cook, Thomas M. 1144
cookbooks 219, 346, 750, 766, 1159, 1328, 1567, 1634, 1637, 1780
Cooke, Alistair 716
cookery 255, 583, 802, 1594, 1637
Coole, Thomas Henry 573
Coolidge, Calvin 1669
Cooper, James Fenimore 284, 296, 519, 1562
Cooper, Peter 1050
Cooper, Thomas 1504
The Cooper Union (New York) 1050
Cooperative Movement 1450
Coover, Robert 1158
Copeland, Jo 1058
Copernicus, Nicolaus 519
Copiah-Lincoln Junior College (Mississippi) 860
Coppard, A.E. 1648
Coppin State College (Maryland) 677
Corbin, Edythe Patten 296
Corcoran School of Art (District of Columbia) 292
Cordell, Suzanne 517
Cordell, Warren N. 517
Coriolanus 590
Cork County (Ireland) 25
Corliss, George 1475
Corman, Cid 1648
Cormier, Robert 731
Cornell College (Iowa) 544
Cornell University (New York) 1051
corporate planning 402
corporate reports 434
Corpus Christi State University (Texas) 1577
Corpus Vasorum Antiquorum 1638
Corso, Gregory 1049, 1320, 1648
Corthell, Elmer 1475
Corvo, Baron 552, 564
Costain, Thomas 1648
costume 109, 129, 136, 214, 341, 394, 497, 583, 982, 1039, 1058, 1217, 1321, 1638
Cosumnes River College (California) 131
Cottey College (Missouri) 890
cotton mills 975
Cotton, Norris (U.S. Congressman, U.S. Senator) 975
Cottrell, Alvin J. 296
counseling 88
counter-culture 279
Counts, George 487
county fairs (California) 93
county histories, Pennsylvania 1394
Couper, Col. William 1718
court reporting 326, 699
Cousins, Norman 1032
Covenant Theological Seminary (Missouri) 891
covert activities 296
Covey, Arthur 591
cowboys 579, 1638
Cowdrey, Mary Bartlett 1000
Cowper, William 1280
Cox, John Harrington 1763
Crabb, A.L. 624
Crabb, Richard 500
Crabbe, George 1280
Craddock, Charles 1289
craft unions 696
crafts 657
Craig, Edward Gordon 1648
Craigie, Mrs. Pearl Mary Teresa 1158
Cramer, William C. 345
Cranbrook Academy of Art (Michigan) 783
Cranbrook Press 783
Crane, Hart 296, 1049, 1245
Crane, Julia 1142
Crane, R.C. 1585
Crane, Richard T. 296
Crane School of Music 1142
Crane, Stephen 279, 519, 1049, 1150, 1320, 1399, 1716
Crane, Walter 284, 519
Crapsey, Adelaide 1158
Crary, Dorcas 654
Craven, Avery O. 561
Craven Community College (North Carolina) 1178
Craven, Rear Admiral Thomas Tingey 296
crawfish 629
Crawford, George A. 596
Crawford, Johnson Tal 1301
Creamer, David 984
creation science 59, 70
creation/evolution controversy 313
creative arts 1524
creative studies 1134
creative writing 1640
creativity in children 119
Credit Foncier 103
Creek Indians 30, 1320
Creeley, Robert 279, 928
Creighton University (Nebraska) 947
creole languages 406
The Creole Testament 1445
cricket (sport) 1390
crime 1217
criminal court transcripts, New York 1074
criminal justice 2, 213, 276, 595, 659, 910, 989, 1074, 1222, 1408, 1610, 1734, 1754
criminology 802
Crissey, Orlo 817
Criswell College (Texas) 1578
criticism, history of 214
Crittenden, Ethel Taylor 1221
Crocchiola, Father Stanley 1011
Crocket, George L. 1623
Crone, Dr. Ruth 953
Crosby, Bing 215, 1729
Cross, Milton 1071

cross-cultural research 965
Crow Indians 1800
Crowe, Philip Kingsland 762
Cruikshank, George 997, 1217
cryptography 1262
Cuala Press 652, 653, 1022
Cuba Cane Sugar Corporation 341
Cuban refugee exodus 1268
Cuba-U.S. commercial relations 341
Cuesta College (California) 132
cuisine 219, 451, 750, 969, 1594, 1637
Cuite, Thomas 1121
culinary arts 255, 451, 564, 583, 659, 750, 969, 1052, 1477, 1594
Culinary Institute of America (New York) 1052
cults 878
culture, contemporary 1445
Culver-Stockton College (Missouri) 892
Cumberland County College (New Jersey) 983
Cumberland Presbyterian Church 1526
Cumming, William P. 1180
cummings, e.e. 737
Cummington Press 705, 956
Cunard, Nancy 1648
cuneiform script 1258
cuneiform tablets 238, 902, 997, 1049
Cuney, Norris Wright 1171
Curie, Marie Sklodowska 1391
Curley, James M. 723
Curll, Edmund 593
currency 997
Current-Garcia, Eugene 5
curriculum materials 30, 74, 108, 109, 135, 216, 260, 274, 278, 280, 343, 397, 410, 423, 467, 469, 475, 477, 515, 541, 603, 621, 642, 663, 674, 691, 692, 708, 732, 751, 762, 773, 791, 815, 843, 897, 912, 913, 967, 990, 1001, 1008, 1078, 1094, 1142, 1183, 1203, 1220, 1228, 1275, 1289, 1291, 1315, 1325, 1347, 1348, 1361, 1377, 1380, 1394, 1397, 1398, 1400, 1434, 1455, 1483, 1525, 1575, 1587, 1610, 1623, 1624, 1645, 1654, 1687, 1694, 1695, 1712, 1715, 1731, 1742, 1762, 1766, 1793, 1799
Curry College (Massachusetts) 724
Curtis Brown Ltd. 1049
Curtis, Dr. Ford E. 1450
Curtis, Edward S. 737
Curtis, Harriet R. 1450
Curtis Institute of Music (Pennsylvania) 1371
Custer, Elizabeth B. 935
Custer, General George Armstrong 781, 935, 1318
Cutler, Ephraim 1267
Cutler, William P. 1267
Cuyahoga Community College (Ohio) 1253
Cylke, Frank Kurt 296
Czarnikow-Rionda Company 341
Czech-Americans 441, 955
Czechoslovakia 296, 737
Dada Movement 564, 1067
Dade County (Florida) 323
daguerreotypes 1278
Dahlberg, Edward 1320, 1648
Daily Oklahoman 1307
dairy industry 1682
Dakota Indians 1800
Dakota State College (South Dakota) 1512
Dakota Territory 1513
Dakota Wesleyan University (South Dakota) 1513
Dale, George 1301
Dale, Samuel S. 1049
Dallas Baptist College (Texas) 1579
Dallas Theological Seminary (Texas) 1580
Dalton College (Georgia) 366
Daly, Augustin 705, 1049
Dana, Jr., Richard Henry 341, 1156
dance 159, 214, 715, 820, 1127, 1219, 1450
Danenbarger, William F. 583
Daniel Webster College (New Hampshire) 963
Danish Immigrant Archival Listing Project 547
Danish-Norwegian Baptist Conference 1044
Dann, Jack 1445
Dante 530, 536, 604, 744, 1081
Dante Society 737
Darlington, Philip 654
Darlington, William 1459
Dartmouth College (New Hampshire) 964
Darton, Harvey 1151
Darwin, Charles 1393, 1403
data processing 122
date culture 216
Davenport, Eugene 497
David Lipscomb College (Tennessee) 1531
Davids, Corinne Tennyson 1676
Davidson, A. Wolfe 1489
Davidson, Avram 1627
Davidson College (North Carolina) 1180
Davidson County Community College (North Carolina) 1179
Davidson, George 45
Davies, A. Powell 464
Davis and Elkins College (West Virginia) 1751
Davis, Bette 716
Davis, Beulah 685
Davis, Dorothy Salisbury 1032
Davis, Hallie Flanagan 1159
Davis, Jefferson 1544
Davis, John W. 296, 678, 1763
Davis, Julia 1763
Davis, Mrs. Verina (Jefferson) 1200
Davis, Richard Harding 319, 737
Davison, George 282
Davy Crockett Almanacs 1562
Dawson, Fielding 279
Dawson, William L. 1533

Day, Dorothy 1778
Day, Jerome J. 413
Day, Mrs. Lucy 413
Daytona Beach Community College (Florida) 307
De Anza College (California) 133
De Copia Verborum 891
De Fabrica 1245
De Officiis 1562
deaf education 310
deafness 108, 294, 310, 1117
Dean Junior College (Massachusetts) 725
debating societies 1722
DeBellis, Anthony 924
Debs, Eugene V. 517
December Magazine 1475
DeCiantis, Michael 1479
Decker, George 1122
Declaration of Independence, signers of 1390
decoration, early American 1672
Defiance College (Ohio) 1254
Defoe, Daniel 284, 497, 519, 1000
DeGolyer, Sr., E.L. 1615
Deland, Margaret 1460
Delano, Frederic A. 296
Delaware 285
Delaware County (Pennsylvania) 1463
Delaware State College 285
Delaware Valley College of Science and Agriculture (Pennsylvania) 1372
Delbanco, Nicholas 1668
DeLillo, Don 1158
Delta State University (Mississippi) 861
Democrats for Willkie 1158
Dempster, Charlotte Louisa Hawkins 714
Denning, John 596
dental assisting 1408
dental hygiene 612, 980, 1284, 1408
dentistry 150, 218, 254, 950, 955, 1005, 1106, 1449, 1572, 1653
dentistry, history of 1333
Denton, Jeremiah 5
Denver (Colorado) 253
Denver Conservative Baptist Seminary (Colorado) 241
Department of Defense films 296
DePaul, St. Vincent 431
DePaul University (Illinois) 431
DePauw University (Indiana) 508
Depression Era 639, 820
Depression Era Relief Collection 596
Der Deutsche Markur 1245
dermatology 432, 594
Derrydale Press 997
desert research 961
design 169, 1110, 1375
desk-top publishing 1467
detection 1217
detective fiction 519, 1320
Detroit (Michigan) 815
devotional works 1435
DeVry Institute of Tèchnology (Missouri) 893
Dewey, Chester 1158
Dewey, John 487, 1049
Dewey, Melvil 1049
Dewey, Thomas E. 1158
Diablo Valley College (California) 134
Dial 284
Dibrell Family 73
Dichter, Ernst 1092
Dickens, Charles 216, 284, 296, 431, 552, 590, 694, 719, 997, 1217, 1280, 1320, 1715, 1763
The Dickensian 431
Dickerson, Russell 1489
Dickey, James 394, 928
Dickinson College (Pennsylvania) 1373
Dickinson, Emily 341, 705, 737, 1127
Dickinson, John 1373
Dickinson, Jr., Fairleigh S. (New Jersey State Senator) 985
Dickinson School of Law (Pennsylvania) 1374
Dickinson State University (North Dakota) 1229
dictation 326
dictionaries 517, 1000
Dies, Laura Woodworth (Stedman) Gould 284
dietetics 1411, 1768
digital systems 1112
Dillard University (Louisiana) 626
Dillingham, Louise Bulkley 1358
dime novels 251, 564, 718, 1158, 1276
Dine, Jim 169
diplomacy 287, 295, 664, 716, 762, 997
diplomatic history, U.S. 296, 1718
Direction magazine 296
disarmament 1444
Disciples of Christ 113, 435, 506, 610, 620, 892, 932, 1169, 1260, 1332, 1418, 1537, 1548, 1592, 1749
discovery and exploration 593, 681
discovery and exploration (Great Lakes) 820
discovery and exploration (North America) 802
displaced persons 738
Disraeli, Benjamin 1158
dissent and social change 109
District of Columbia 295
District One Technical Institute (Wisconsin) 1772
Divina Providentia 578
divine healing 1313
Dix, Dorothea Lynde 737
Dix, Dorothy 1524
Dixon, D. Genevieve 1637
Dixon, Thomas R. 1186
DNA, recombinant 742
Dobie, Bertha McKee 1622
Dobie, J. Frank 1617, 1627, 1648, 1654
Doheny Collection 185
Doheny, E.L. 166

Dolci, Danilo 716
Dombey and Son 590
domestic arts 802
Dominican College of San Rafael (California) 135
Dominican Friars of the Province of St. Albert the Great 881
Dominican House of Studies (District of Columbia) 293
Dominican Order 293
Dominick, Peter 255
Donaldson, Stephen R. 1262
Donalson, Colonel John E. 360
Donne, John 519, 1635
Donnelley, Elliott 453
Donner, Robert 1567
Doolittle, Hilda 284
Dorman, Caroline 639
Dorn, Ed 279
Dorn, Frances E. 1032
Dorr Rebellion of 1842 1475
Dorris, C.E.W. 1531
Dos Passos, John 1320, 1716
Douglas, Aaron 1533
Douglas, Norman 284, 1320
Douglass, Frederick 1293
Dowdey, Clifford 1715
Dowling College (New York) 1053
Dowling, Enos E. 456
Dowling, Father Edward J. 906
Downes, Olin 394, 1028
Downs, Kendall 1587
Doyle, Arthur Conan 1217, 1648
Dozenal Society 1096
Dozois, Gardner 1445
Dr. Martin Luther College (Minnesota) 837
Dr. William M. Scholl College of Podiatric Medicine (Illinois) 432
Drabble, Margaret 1158, 1320
Drake, Daniel 33
Drake, Sir Francis 587
Drake University (Iowa) 545
drama 1343, 1450, 1663
drama, American 494, 1049, 1158, 1449, 1791, 1794
drama, English 497, 1049, 1158, 1607, 1794
drama, English neoclassical 494
drama, French 1390
drama, French neoclassical 494
drama, Spanish 1276
dramatic arts 190
dramatists, Irish 714
Draper, Muriel Gurdon (Sanders) 284
Dreier, Katherine S. 284
Dreiser, Theodore 296, 519, 1449
Dresel, Ellis Loring 737
Drew, John T. Jr. 1305
Drew University (New Jersey) 984
Drexel, A.J. 1375
Drexel University (Pennsylvania) 1375
Dreyfus Affair 737
drill team materials 1393
Drinan, S.J., Rev. Robert F. 714
Drinker, Henry 1444
drug abuse 585, 741
drug enforcement 1421
Drury, Clifford M. 81
Drury College (Missouri) 894
Dryden, John 118, 215, 1158
D.S. Morgan Company 1133
Dubinsky, David 1058
Dubois, Fred T. (U.S. Senator) 409
DuBois, W.E.B. 756, 1293, 1445, 1533
Dubuque (Iowa) 552
Duffer, Casper 1301
Duff-Gordon, Lady (Lucille) 1058
Duke University (North Carolina) 1181
Dulles, Allen W. 997
Dulles, John Foster 997
Dunbar, Paul Laurence 1289
Duncan, John 975
Duncan, Robert 279
Dunning, John Wert 776
Dunsany, Lord 1359
Duquesne University (Pennsylvania) 1376
Durant, Henry Fowle 766
Durham (New Hampshire) 975
Durrell, Lawrence 487
Dust Bowl 100
Dutch heritage materials 492, 558
Dutch settlement (Michigan) 791
Dutch settlement (New York) 1049
Dutchess Community College (New York) 1054
Dutchess County (New York) 1085
DuVal, Jr. Miles P. 296
Dwyer, Florence (U.S. Congresswoman) 990
Dyer, John 705
Dyers, D.B. 596
Dyke College (Ohio) 1255
Dyke, Henry Van 1123
Dykes, Jeff 1627
E. Haldeman-Julius Publications 589
Earlham College (Indiana) 509
early childhood 123, 263
early childhood education 30, 1550, 1734
Early, Eleanor 714
earth science 536
earthquake engineering 89
East Asia 696, 1049, 1276, 1475, 1743
East Carolina University (North Carolina) 1182
East Central College (Missouri) 895
East Central University (Oklahoma) 1301
East Mississippi Junior College (Mississippi) 862
East Stroudsburg University of Pennsylvania 1377
East Tennessee Light and Power Company 1532
East Tennessee State University 1532

East Texas Baptist University 1581
East Texas State University 1582
East Texas State University at Texarkana 1583
Eastern Arizona College 51
Eastern Baptist Theological Seminary (Pennsylvania) 1378
Eastern College (Pennsylvania) 1379
Eastern Connecticut State University 262
Eastern Europe 1049
Eastern Illinois University 433
Eastern Kentucky University 605
Eastern Mennonite College/Seminary (Virginia) 1687
Eastern Michigan University 784
Eastern Montana College 935
Eastern Nazarene College (Massachusetts) 726
Eastern New Mexico University 1011
Eastern Oregon State College 1325
Eastern Shore (Maryland) 672, 674
Eastern Washington University 1726
Eastern Wyoming College 1802
Eastman, George 1158
Eastman, Max 519
East-West comparative studies 88
Eaton, John 1562
ecclesiastical history 1449
ecclesiology 722
Eckman, Thomas F. 1243
ecology 190, 821
economic history 593, 681, 997
economic movement 1129
economic thought 525
economics 120, 381, 444, 497, 525, 560, 629, 790, 808, 943, 971, 1030, 1049, 1144, 1699, 1796
Ecumenical Movement 1155
Eden Theological Seminary (Missouri) 896
Edgewood College (Wisconsin) 1773
Edinboro University of Pennsylvania 1380
Edison rolls 1320
Editions of the Armed Services 32
Edman, Dr. V. Raymond 500
Edmonds Community College (Washington) 1727
Edson, James S. 5
education 26, 35, 75, 119, 210, 324, 331, 374, 408, 459, 469, 472, 474, 480, 500, 505, 517, 525, 605, 626, 633, 639, 681, 704, 857, 899, 924, 973, 987, 989, 1146, 1151, 1277, 1348, 1409, 1422, 1429, 1441, 1455, 1525, 1583, 1595, 1687, 1707, 1736, 1762, 1766, 1791, 1796
education, computer science 792
education, higher 977
education, Jewish 738
education philosophies 1001
educational technology 1467
educational theory 1139
Edward Waters College (Florida) 308
Edwardian fiction 1320
Effingham County (Georgia) 373
Egbert, Laurence D. 296
Eggleston, Edward 514
Eggleston, George Cary 514
Egyptology 647
Eikon Basilike 1158
Einstein, Albert 519
Eire Society of Boston 714
Eisenhower, Dwight D. 1254
Elbert, Ella Smith 766
Eleazer, James 1489
electrical engineering 239
electricity 694, 742
electronic components, manufacturers of 893
electronic engineering 239
electronics 67, 121, 217, 659, 1484, 1740
elementary education 322, 533, 739, 1731
Elinore Sisters vaudeville act 1158
Eliot, Daniel 792
Eliot, George 284, 1320
Eliot, Thomas Lamb 1338
Eliot, T.S. 705, 737, 1290, 1320, 1648
Elizabeth City State University (North Carolina) 1183
Elizabeth Seton College (New York) 1055
Elizabethan Club 284
Elizabethton Star (Tennessee) 1532
Elizabethtown College (Pennsylvania) 1381
Ellerbrock, Lee 113
Ellington, Duke 1645
Elliott, Carl 32
Elliott, Lang 1111
Ellis, Michael 1450
Ellis, Richard 1445
Elmhurst College (Illinois) 434
Elmira College (New York) 1056
Elon College (North Carolina) 1184
Ely, Richard T. 629
Elzevier imprints 1129, 1449
emancipation 766, 1185
emblem books 1049
Embry-Riddle Aeronautical University (Florida) 309
Emerson College (Massachusetts) 727
Emerson, Edwin 296
Emerson, Ralph Waldo 341, 519, 737, 1158, 1676
émigré literature 226
Emmanuel College and School of Christian Ministry (Georgia) 367
Emmanuel College (Massachusetts) 728
Emmanuel County Community College (Georgia) 368
Emmanuel County (Georgia) 368
Emory and Henry College (Virginia) 1688
Emory University (Georgia) 369
Empire State Forest Products Association 1144
Emporia State University (Kansas) 578
Encino Press 1638
Endicott College (Massachusetts) 729
endocrinology 33
energy 372, 924, 1041, 1101, 1422, 1642

energy advocates 1445
energy, alternative 959
energy conservation 490
Engel, Julia 1049
Engel, Solton 1049
Engels, John 1681
engineering 89, 121, 145, 230, 237, 265, 277, 311, 372, 444, 488, 516, 525, 527, 536, 633, 742, 803, 926, 970, 1101, 1112, 1204, 1363, 1555, 1594, 1719
engineering technology 391, 856
Engle, Paul 543
English Tudor literature 1681
engraving 107
Enid (Oklahoma) 1314
enology 103
Enterprise State Junior College (Alabama) 8
entertainers, Black 297, 1445
entertainment, popular 737
entomology 190, 549, 802, 955, 1144, 1204
environmental design 1144
environmental engineering 148
environmental hazards 721
environmental issues 1144
environmental science 1144, 1751
environmental studies 661, 736, 959, 1144, 1422, 1782
The Envoy magazine 487
Ephraim (Utah) 1662
Epigrammatum Libri Quattuor 988
epigraphy specimens 1049
Episcopal Church 1060
Episcopal Diocese of South Dakota 1510
Episcopal Divinity School (Massachusetts) 730
The Episcopal Theological Seminary of the Southwest (Texas) 1584
Episcopalianism 730, 1044, 1565, 1706
Epping Brick Company 975
Epstean, Edward 1049
equestrian arts 932, 1092, 1477, 1754
equine studies 583, 1198
Erasmus, Desiderius 891, 1044
Erie Canal 1066
Erie Community College - South Campus (New York) 1057
Erie (Pennsylvania) 1383
erotica 1218
Erskine College and Seminary (South Carolina) 1495
Escambia County (Alabama) 14
Eskimo art 807
Eskimos 825
Esmeralda County (Nevada) 960
Esperanto 1342
Esquire 1058
Estell, E.C. 1576
Estonia 196
Etherington, Don 1648
ethnic studies 77, 436, 579, 585, 1367, 1408, 1738, 1741
ethnography 268, 302, 943, 965, 1061, 1067, 1167, 1776
ethnomusicology 192, 215, 475
etiquette 1159, 1290
Eton College 1217
Etting, Ruth 955
etymology 1000
eugenics 912
Eureka College (Illinois) 435
European expansion before 1800 856
Evangelical and Reformed Church 853, 1173
Evangelical Association 573
Evangelical Association of North America 1286
Evangelical Church 1286, 1347
Evangelical Covenant Church 471
Evangelical Free Church of America 493
Evangelical Friends Church 1266
Evangelical Synod of North America 896
Evangelical United Brethren Church 1286, 1711
evangelicalism 83, 86, 229, 232, 419, 473, 617, 826, 1401, 1425, 1567, 1580, 1619
evangelism, child 1556
Evans, Billy 373
Evans, Richard X. 296
Evans, Sr., Dr. Louis 500
Everett, Robert 614
Evergreen State College (Washington) 1728
Everson, William 296
evolution 654
Evolution/Creation Archive 549
Ewert, William B. 975
Ewing, Charles 296, 1303
Ewing, Juliana Horatia 755
"Excelsior" 1314
exhibition catalogs 76, 169, 356, 783, 1000, 1223, 1429, 1469, 1649
Exley, Frederick 1158
exonumia 997
expatriate authors 802
expatriate writers 487, 1022
exploration and settlement, sixteenth-century 1358
expositions and fairs 103, 260, 1318
Expressionist Movement 1067
extremist literature 55
fables 997
faculty development 458
Fair Campaign Practices Committee 296
Fair Play Township (Kansas) 596
Fairbanks, Charles 519
Fairchild, Herman LeRoy 1158
Fairfield (Washington) 1726
Fairleigh Dickinson University (New Jersey) 985
Fairlie, John 497
fairy tales 766
falconry 251
Fales, De Coursey 1081
Falk, Karl 103

Fall, Albert 1020
Falwell, Jerry 1695
family life 525
family relations 18, 577
family studies 1550
family therapy 97
fanzines 1445, 1450
Far East 223, 275
farm cooperatives 583
Farm Security Administration 694
Farmers' Library of Wheatland (New York) 1158
farming systems research 583
Farnam, Lynnwood 1371
Farrell, James T. 1449
Fascism 1067
fashion design 136, 1058, 1637
fashion illustration 1321
Fashion Institute of Design and Merchandising (California) 136
Fashion Institute of Technology (New York) 1058
fashion merchandising 1077, 1411
fast food operations 1797
Fatherless Children of France Memorial Volume Records 714
Fatzer, Harold R. 583
Faubus, Orval 69
Faucette, J.P. 74
Faucette, W.C. 74
Faulkner University (Alabama) 9
Faulkner, Virginia 955
Faulkner, William 552, 647, 876, 919, 1290, 1320, 1630, 1648, 1716
Faur, Faber du 284
Faust, Ehrhardt 284
Fayetteville State University (North Carolina) 1185
Federal Land Bank/Farm Credit Banks system 764
Federal Theatre Project 1690
Federal Writers' Project (Kansas) 596
Federalist Period 279
Feibleman, James K. 487
Fein, Irving Jay 1479
Felician College (Illinois) 436
Felician College (New Jersey) 986
Fellowship Magazine 1767
feminism 917, 1444
feminists 1342
fencing 802
Fenwick, Millicent 1049
Ferber, Edna 1791
Fergusson, Erna 1020
Fergusson, Francis 1668
Fermi, Enrico 494
Ferraro, Geraldine A. 1088
Ferrero, Guglielmo 1049
Ferris State College (Michigan) 785
Ferrum College (Virginia) 1689
Fessenden, William Pitt 652
Feurbron, Harvey 477
Ficke, Arthur Davison 284
fiction, nineteenth-century 215, 1320, 1466
fiddle tunes 1676
Field, Bernard T. 742
field sports 431
Fielding, Henry 497, 1320
Fields, J.T. 737
Fike, Dr. Rupert 1489
Fillmore, Millard 1140
film industry 1143, 1262
film-making, independent 1130
films 1130
finance 79
Finch, Robert 166
Findlay College (Ohio) 1256
fine arts 35, 76, 80, 148, 224, 269, 292, 330, 356, 429, 435, 488, 496, 500, 557, 683, 703, 740, 754, 762, 765, 783, 842, 993, 1049, 1051, 1080, 1092, 1363, 1429, 1439, 1480, 1640
fine arts presses 956
fine bindings 413, 475, 535, 564, 1150, 1217, 1342
fine printing 57, 93, 104, 131, 166, 196, 200, 203, 214, 219, 224, 225, 236, 252, 295, 296, 423, 475, 496, 519, 622, 667, 737, 813, 924, 1159, 1221, 1342, 1359, 1445, 1504, 1693, 1788
fine printing, California 106, 108, 1320
Finkler, M.D., Rita 1005
Finlay, Ian Hamilton 519, 1119
Finley, Martha 755
Finn, S.J., Fr. Francis 1297
Finnish-Americans 806
Fiore, Dr. Jordan 719
fire protection 189, 1312
fire science 182, 1112, 1408
Firestone Tire and Rubber Company 746
First Amendment freedoms 487
First Casualty Press 279
First Church of Christ (Salem, Massachusetts) 714
First Interstate Bank of Arizona 55
First Ladies, U.S. 457
First World 358
Fischer, Margarita 596
Fish, E.J. 792
Fisher, Vardis 284
fisheries 5, 1628, 1730
fishing 975
Fisk University (Tennessee) 1533
Fitch, Clyde 705
Fitchburg State College (Massachusetts) 731
Fitzgerald, E. Eleanor 1792
Fitzgerald, F. Scott 296, 519, 997, 1320
Five Civilized Tribes (Oklahoma) 1305
Flaccus, Quintus Horatius 552
Flagler College (Florida) 310
Flaherty, Robert J. 1049
Flaming Rainbow University (Oklahoma) 1302

Flathead Valley Community College (Montana) 936
Flaubert, Gustav 1648
Fleming, Alexander 519
Fletcher, John Gould 59, 69, 70, 284, 1158, 1339
flight, history of 1296
Fling, Fred Morrow 955
Flint (Michigan) 817
Flood, Daniel J. (U.S. Congressman) 296, 1396
Florida 307, 319, 320, 321, 322, 325, 328, 331, 333, 335, 340, 341, 342, 344, 345
Florida Agricultural and Mechanical University 311
Florida Atlantic University 312
Florida Baptists 338
Florida College 313
Florida Community College 314
Florida Institute of Technology 315
Florida International University 316
Florida Memorial College 317
Florida Southern College 318
Florida State University 319
Fluxus Group 1638
Fogarty, John E. (U.S. Congressman) 1478
Folio Society 1139
folk music 147, 252, 1197, 1217, 1475
folk songs 1241, 1676
folklore 497, 809, 955, 1532, 1665, 1739
folklore, Black 17
folklore, Colorado 252
folklore, North Dakota 1230
folklore, northeastern Pennsylvania 1396
folklore, Ozark 589
folklore, Pennsylvania 1394
folklore, Southern 1217
folklore, Southwestern 57
folklore, West Virginia 1755
Folsom, Marion Bayard 1158
Fondren, W.W. 1607
Fontbonne College (Missouri) 897
food marketing 1437, 1467
food services management 669
Foote, Arthur 746
Foote, Samuel 1280
Forbes, John Murray 737
Forbes Military Road 678
Forbes. W. Cameron 737
Force, Manning Ferguson 737
Ford, Daniel 975
Ford, Ford Maddox 928
Ford, Gerald R. 816
Ford, John 519
Ford, Paul Leicester 284
Fordham University (New York) 1059
fore-edge paintings 166, 238, 319, 477, 529, 629, 635, 675, 1117, 1693
foreign affairs, Japanese 776
forensic medicine 218
forensic science 1074
forest chemistry 1144
Forester, C.S. 1627
forestry 23, 71, 669, 1144, 1204, 1235, 1343
forests 1627
Forrest, Richard A. 393
Forrestal, James V. 997
Forster, E.M. 596, 1320
Fort Fletcher (Kansas) 579
Fort Hays (Kansas) 579
Fort Hays State University (Kansas) 579
Fort Hill plantation (South Carolina) 1489
Fort Leavenworth (Kansas) 590
Fort Lewis College (Colorado) 242
Fort Necessity (Pennsylvania) 678
Fort Schuyler (New York) 1149
Fort Union (New Mexico) 1014
Fort Valley State College (Georgia) 370
Fort Zarah (Kansas) 579
fortifications 1157
Forward, Robert L. 216
Fossum, M. Truman 1235
Foster, Stephen Collins 1393, 1450
Fowler, Henry True 1423
Fowlers and Wells (publishers) 705
Fowles, John 394, 1320
Fowlie, Wallace 1668
Fox, George 1390
fox hunting 431
Fox, Jay 1729
Fox Valley (Wisconsin) 1793
Framingham State College (Massachusetts) 732
France, Anatole 519
France, pre-revolutionary 876
Francis Marion College (South Carolina) 1496
Francis, Robert 764
Franciscan Order 752, 1120
Francisco Sugar Company 341
Franck, James 494
Franco-American Alliance 296
Franco-Canadian literature 1681
Franges, Nikola 1049
Frank, Glenn 912
Frank, Waldo 1449
Franklin and Marshall College (Pennsylvania) 1382
Franklin, Benjamin 1693
Franklin College 1382
Franklin College of Indiana 510
Franklin County (Maine) 663
Franklin Pierce College (New Hampshire) 965
Franklin Society (debating) 1722
Franklin University (Ohio) 1257
Frantz, Harry W. 296
Fraser, James Earle 1150
Fréchette, Dr. Van Derck 1026
Free Methodist Church 1116, 1347
Free Will Baptist College (Tennessee) 1534
Free Will Baptists 1534

Freed-Hardeman College (Tennessee) 1535
Freedom Center of Political and Social Ephemera, Periodicals, and Books 104
freedom of expression 497
freedom of information 206
freedom of the press 487
Freemasonry 500, 1421
Freewill Baptist General Conference 1044
Freikorps 764
French and Indian War 1450
French Canada 1038
French monarchy 802
French Revolution 494, 519, 564, 764, 802, 955, 1059
French, Samuel 705
French symbolist literature 1693
Fresno (California) 103
Fresno Pacific College (California) 137
Fresno Republican 103
Friendly Moralist Society 1491
Friends Historical Library 1444
Friends University (Kansas) 580
frigate novels 1627
Froben, Johann 101
Fromm, Erich 1668
frontier life, Kansas 579
frontier religion 350
Frost, Robert 296, 341, 350, 564, 705, 964, 972, 975, 1106, 1217, 1320, 1475, 1504, 1676, 1693, 1716
Frostburg State University (Maryland) 678
Fry, Elizabeth 1444
Fugitive Poets 1320
fugitive writers 1566
Fuld, Helene 677
Fulkner, William 646
Fullbright, J. William (U.S. Senator) 69
Fuller, Dr. Charles E. 138
Fuller, General J.F.C. 1000
Fuller, Hoyt W. 358
Fuller, Margaret 737
Fuller Theological Seminary (California) 138
Fullerton, George E. 81
Fulton County (Illinois) 490
fund raising 1778
fur industry 519
fur trade 935
Furman, Richard 1497
Furman University (South Carolina) 1497
furniture design 794
G. Wilson Knight Interdisciplinary Society 1096
Gaddis, Isabel 1622
Gade, Niels 216
Gadsden State Junior College (Alabama) 10
Gaelic language 1059
Gagliardo, Ruth Garver 578
Gainer, Patrick 1763
Gaines, Pierce Welch 279
Galileo, Galilei 519
Gallatin Valley (Montana) 938
Gallaudet University (District of Columbia) 294
Gallery, Rear Admiral Daniel Vincent, U.S.N. 694
Gallicanism 187
Gallico, Paul W. 1049
Galsworthy, John 216, 296, 519, 1158, 1280
gambling 960
Gandhi, Mahatma 1444, 1767
Ganey, Hertha 1134
Gann, Ernest 1043
Gannett, Lewis Stiles 737
Gannon, Archbishop John Mark 1383
Gannon University (Pennsylvania) 1383
Gano, John Allen 1567
Garcia, Hector P. 1577
garden plants 639
Gardner, Erle Stanley 1648
Gardner, Fay Webb 1186
Gardner, John 1158
Gardner, Judge A.K. 1514
Gardner, O. Max 1186
Gardner-Webb College (North Carolina) 1186
Garfield County (Oklahoma) 1314
Garfield, James A. 1260
Garland, Hamlin 226
Garland, Judy 215
Garner, Alexander 697
Garrett, John B. 1390
Garrett, John Work 681
Garrett-Evangelical Theological Seminary (Illinois) 437
Garrison, William Lloyd 596
Garst, Roswell 549
Garvey, Marcus 1533
Gascoyne, David 1320
Gaston College (North Carolina) 1187
gastronomy 219, 255, 451, 564, 750, 969, 1052, 1594, 1637
Gatch, Philip 1268
Gateway Technical Institute (Wisconsin) 1774
Gathings, E.C. 59
Gauss, C.F. 639
Gavilan College (California) 139
Gay, Sydney Howard 1049
Gazette du Bon Ton 1058
Geer, Peter Zack 373
Gehrnan, Richard 1414
genealogy, Alabama 5, 8, 11
genealogy, Celtic 1047
genealogy, Georgia 353, 394
genealogy, Italian 497
genealogy, Kentucky 614
genealogy, Louisiana 630
genealogy, Maryland 1683
genealogy, Michigan 819
genealogy, Mississippi 877
genealogy, New Hampshire 975

genealogy, New Jersey 988, 993
genealogy, New Mexico 1014
genealogy, New York 1042
genealogy, North Carolina 1176, 1179, 1194, 1199, 1210
genealogy, North Dakota 1237
genealogy, Ohio 1272
genealogy, Oregon 1325, 1336
genealogy, Pennsylvania 1683
genealogy, Scottish 453, 1384
genealogy, South Carolina 1486
genealogy, Tennessee 1530, 1532
genealogy, Texas 1567, 1588, 1630
genealogy, Virginia 1683, 1687, 1723
genealogy, Wisconsin 1788, 1790
General Church of the New Jerusalem 1350
The General Theological Seminary (New York) 1060
Genesee County (Michigan) 817
Genesee County (New York) 1122, 1133
Genesee Valley (New York) 1137
genetics 519
Geneva College (Pennsylvania) 1384
Geneva Medical College Library (New York) 1147
Geneva (New York) 1066
genocide studies 998
Gentleman's Magazine 578
Gentleman's Quarterly (eighteenth century) 346
geography 667, 1792
Geological Society of America 940
geological subsidence 106
geology 57, 190, 237, 245, 926, 937, 1015, 1172, 1504, 1649
George C. Wallace State Community College - Dothan (Alabama) 11
George Corley Wallace State Community College (Alabama) 12
George Fox College (Oregon) 1326
George III 1245, 1314
George Mason University (Virginia) 1690
George Washington University (District of Columbia) 295
Georgetown College (Kentucky) 606
Georgetown University (District of Columbia) 296
Georgetown (Washington, D.C.) 296
Georgia 349, 354, 362, 368, 369, 381, 385, 394, 395, 396
Georgia Baptist Convention 381
Georgia College 371
Georgia Institute of Technology 372
Georgia, Republic of (U.S.S.R.) 737
Georgia Southern College 373
Georgia Southwestern College 374
Georgia State University 375
Georgia, west 397
Georgian Court College (New Jersey) 987
geoscience 215, 525
Gerald R. Ford Presidential Library 816
Gerardiionnis Vossii de Historicus Latinus 55
German Americana 1288, 1382
German culture 190
German expressionism 1791
German intellectual émigrés 1129
German Reformed Church (North Carolina) 1173
German Revolution of 1918 764
German studies 1791
German-Americans 550, 1453
Germans from Russia 238
Germany 207, 583, 816, 1421, 1607
Gernsback, Hugo 1150
gerontology 149, 982, 1645, 1780
Gershwin, George 1533
Gertz, Elmer 487
Gettysburg College (Pennsylvania) 1385
Gilbert and Sullivan 519
Gilbert, Christine B. 1080
Gilbert, O.P. 381
Gilchrist, James Grant 596
Giles, Janice Holt 624
Giligia Press 279
Gill, Eric 225, 296, 341, 714, 1648
Gilman, Henry 549
Gilmer, Elizabeth Meriwether 1524
Gimbel, Sophie 1058
Ginn, Ronald "Bo" 373
Girardeau, John L. 873
Giraudoux, Jean 1421
Gissing, George 284
Gitlow, Benjamin 1218
Givernaud, Joseph 1059
Gladding, John W. 596
Glasgow, Ellen 1715
glass 742
Glassboro State College (New Jersey) 988
Glasse, Hannah 583
glassmaking 742
Glaze, Bud 52
Glennon, Cardinal John 902
Glenville State College (West Virginia) 1752
GMI Engineering and Management Institute (Michigan) 786
Goddard College (Vermont) 1671
Goddard, Robert H. 721
Godkin, E.L. 737
Godwin, Jr., Mills E. 1686
Goethe, Charles Mathias 109
Gogarty, St. John 1359
Golden Cockerel Press 1067
Golden Gate Baptist Theological Seminary (California) 140
Golden Gate University (California) 141
Golden, Harry 1218
Goldey Beacom College (Delaware) 286
Goldsmith, Oliver 155, 497
Goldstein, David 714

Goll, Colonel Miriam E. Perry 755
Gonzaga, Alessandro Andrea 296
Gonzaga University (Washington) 1729
Good, James I. 896
Goodrich, Samuel G. 705
Goodspeed, Charles Eliot 766
Gordon College (Massachusetts) 733
Gordon, Harold J. 764
Gordon-Conwell Theological Seminary (Massachusetts) 734
Gorey, Edward 646
Gorman, Herbert 487
Goshen Biblical Seminary (Indiana) 511
Goshen College (Indiana) 512
Gospel of Mark 552
Gosse, Edmund 1158
gothic novels 1790
Gott, Charles 762
Goucher College (Maryland) 679
Goudar, Ange 1708
Goudar, Sara 1708
Goudy, Frederic 260
Gough, Melvin N. 1719
Gould, John 792
gout 1573
Gove, Robert W. 1149
government 1703
Governors State University (Illinois) 438
Gowen, John Curtis 1134
Graaff, Robert J. Van de 742
Grabhorn Press 93, 196, 225, 1020
Grace Brethren Church 513
Grace College (Indiana) 513
Grace College of the Bible (Nebraska) 948
Graceland College (Iowa) 546
Graduate School and University Center of the City University of New York 1061
Graduate Union Theological Union (California) 142
Graf, Oscar Maria 820
Graham, Billy 617
Graham, Sheilah 997
Graham Society (debating) 1722
Grambling State University (Louisiana) 627
grammars 1000, 1791
Grand Army of the Republic 1122
Grand Canyon 55
Grand Canyon College (Arizona) 52
Grand Rapids Junior College (Michigan) 787
Grand Valley State College (Michigan) 788
Grand View College (Iowa) 547
Grandi, Dino 296
Grange, Harold "Red" 500
Graniteville County (South Carolina) 1505
Grant, Ulysses S. 13, 487
grant-making foundations 1778
grants 495
Grants Branch Community College (New Mexico) 1012
graphic arts 80, 93, 269, 330, 550, 662, 997, 1358, 1582
graphic design 76, 292, 794, 1262
Gratz College (Pennsylvania) 1386
Graves, John 1617
Graves, Robert 225, 487, 583, 1320
Gray, Glen 749
Gray, William S. 1014, 1636
Grays Harbor College (Washington) 1730
Great Basin Indians 961
Great Lakes 781, 796
Great Lakes Bible College (Michigan) 789
Great Lakes-St. Lawrence Winter Navigation Season Extension Project 1144
Great Plains 579, 1237, 1510
Great Plains Indians 1518
Great Smoky Mountains National Park 1224
Greater Hartford Community College (Connecticut) 263
Greater New Haven State Technical College (Connecticut) 264
Greece, ancient 494
Greek manuscripts 1181
Green, Julian 394
Green, Julien 1398
Green Mountain College (Vermont) 1672
Green, Roger Sherman 737
Greenaway, Kate 519
Greenberg, Noah 1143
Greene County (Ohio) 1246
Greene, Graham 296, 714, 1320, 1398, 1648
Greene, Zula Bennington 589
Greenfield Community College (Massachusetts) 735
Greensboro College (North Carolina) 1188
Greenville College (Illinois) 439
greeting cards 344
Gregg, Dr. Harris 1527
Gregg, Rev. Wilbur R. 1488
Gregorian chants 332
Gregory, Voris (U.S. Congressman) 614
Grey, Dr. J.D. 636
Grey, Zane 55
Griffin, Alva H. 156
Griffin, Marion Mahony 415
Griffin, Martin I.J. 296
Griffin, S. Marvin 360
Griffis, William Elliot 1000
Grinnell College (Iowa) 548
Grogan, Florence 378
Grolier Club First Editions 1217
Gropius, Walter 737
Gross, Alfred Otto 652
Gross, Dr. Charles Russell 1479
Grosshut, Friedrich 975
Grossmont Community College (California) 143
Grove City College (Pennsylvania) 1387

Grunwald, Fred 215
Guatemala 593, 646
Guild, Edward Chipman 652
Guilford College (North Carolina) 1189
Guiney, Louise Imogen 723
guitar music 192
Gulf Coast 346
Gumby, L.S. Alexander 1049
gunmen 1638
Gunn, Dr. George 1714
Gurney, Joseph John 1444
Gustavus Adolphus College (Minnesota) 838
Guyer, Tennyson 1256
Guyman, Jr., E.T. 166
Gwynedd Mercy College (Pennsylvania) 1388
gynecology 218, 1447
Hackensack Meadowlands Development Commission 985
Haenschen, Gustav 1071
Hagan, Helen 1220
Hagedorn, Hermann 284
Haggard, H. Rider 1049
Haggerty, Louis C. 296
Haggerty, William J. 1130
Hahnemann University (Pennsylvania) 1389
Hailperin, Rabbi Herman 1376
Haire, Hazel 1058
Haire, William 1058
Haiti 341
Haitian art 340
Haitian Presidential Papers 1445
Hale, DeWitt 1577
Hale, Edward Everett 596, 1158
Hale, George E. 89
Haley, James A. (U.S. Congressman) 318
Hall, Dr. Jabez 506
Hall, Elise Coolidge 746
Hall, G. Stanley 721
Hall, James Norman 548
Hall, Kendrick C. 999
Hall, Radclyffe 1648
Halleck, Charles 519
Hallmark Company 215
Halpern, Seymour 1123
Halsman, Phillipe 697
Hamerik, Asger 687
Hamilton, Alexander 1049
Hamilton College (New York) 1062
Hamline University (Minnesota) 839
Hamman, General William M. 1607
Hammarskjöld, Dag 296
Hammer, Preston C. 792
Hammer, Victor 225
Hammond, Ben F. 596
Hampden-Sydney College (Virginia) 1691
Hampshire College (Massachusetts) 736
Hampton, Milton Edward Earle 596
Hampton University (Virginia) 1692
Handel, George Frederick 519
Handel's anthems 1000
Handlin, Oscar 1032
Handy, W.C. 1533
Handy Writers' Colony 485
Hanford Hardware Company (California) 103
Hanna, Richard (U.S. Congressman) 106
Hannaford, Mark (U.S. Congressman) 106
Hannah, Barry 876
Hannibal-LaGrange College (Missouri) 898
Hanover College (Indiana) 514
Hapgood, Hutchins 284
Hapgood, Neith (Boyce) 284
Harbor Press 705
Hardin, John Wesley 1617
Harding, Earl 296
Harding University (Arkansas) 62
Harding University Graduate School of Religion (Tennessee) 1536
Hardin-Simmons University (Texas) 1585
Hardy, Thomas 216, 260, 284, 319, 653
Harker, F. Flaxington 1715
Harlan, John M. 623
Harlan, John Marshall 997
Harlem Renaissance 1290, 1445
Harmon, Major General Ernest N. 1677
harp music 397, 1084
Harper and Row (publishers) 1049
Harper, Francis 1445
Harper, William Rainey 494
Harper's Bazaar 1058
Harper's Weekly 169
Harrington Institute of Interior Design (Illinois) 440
Harrington, Michael 753
Harris, Edward Melvin 1393
Harris, Frank 583
Harris, General Hugh P. 1487
Harris, John T. 1694
Harris, Roy 107
Harris, Thomas 1162
Harris, Townsend 1039
Harrison, Charles I. 919
Harrison County (Texas) 1581
Harrison, Everett 138
Harrison, Jim 1158
Harris-Stowe State College (Missouri) 899
Hart, George 596
Hart, Oliver 1497
Harte, Bret 508
Harte, Houston 1577
Harte, Isabel 1577
Hartford Graduate Center (Connecticut) 265
Hartford Seminary (Connecticut) 266
Hartley, L.P. 1320
Hartley, Marsden 651
Hartmann, Sadakichi 216

Hartnell College (California) 144
Hartog, Jan de 233
Hartwick College (New York) 1063
Hartwick, Johann Christopher 1063
Hartzog, George 1489
Harvard University (Massachusetts) 737
Harvey, Dorothy Dudley 1158
Harvey Mudd College (California) 145
Harvey, Thomas 1264
Harvey, William 519
Harwell, Richard B. 652
Haskell Indian Junior College (Kansas) 581
Hassidism 738
Hastings, W.W. 1305
Hauan, Martin 1301
Haughawout, Margaret E. 589
Hauptmann, Gerhart 1022
Haven, George W. 975
Haverford College (Pennsylvania) 1390
Havre (Montana) 939
Hawaii 399, 400, 402, 403, 404, 405, 406
Hawaii Loa College 401
Hawaii Pacific College 402
Hawkes, John 737
Hawkins, Robert 613
Hawthorne College (New Hampshire) 966
Hawthorne, Julian 296, 1158
Hawthorne, Nathaniel 287, 341, 519, 652, 1125, 1320, 1562, 1716
Hay, John 1475
Hayden, Floyd S. 116
Haydon, Benjamin Robert 737
Haynes, F. Jay 938
Hays, Brooks 69
Hays, William S. 624
Hayslip, Rev. Ross 1316
Hayward, Max and Virginia 166
Haywood, John 1562
Hazen, David Wheeler 1343
hazzanic music 1073
"H.D." 284, 1415
Heady, Earl 549
Healey, Dorothy Ray 106
health 669
health care 666, 1275, 1763
health care, alternative 559
health care, Oklahoma 1319
health planning 714
health psychology 97
health sciences 150, 218, 254, 278, 311, 314, 323, 482, 495, 496, 525, 623, 741, 867, 970, 1025, 1049, 1147, 1148, 1222, 1319, 1333, 1389, 1459, 1550, 1564, 1613, 1653, 1736, 1740, 1743, 1747
Healy, Catherine 653
Healy, John 653
Heaney, Seamus 1217, 1444
hearing disorders 1649
hearing impaired 175, 1209, 1700
Hearn, Lafcadio 25, 32, 635, 646, 1280
Hearney, Seamus 714
Hearst Metrotone News 215
heavier-than-air flying machines 251
Hebraica 146, 341, 489, 670, 1073, 1166, 1217, 1258, 1355, 1376, 1386, 1792
Hebrew College (Massachusetts) 738
Hebrew language 146
Hebrew manuscripts 738
Hebrew studies 738, 1773
Hebrew Union College - Jewish Institute of Religion (California) 146
Hebrew Union College - Jewish Institute of Religion (New York) 1064
Hebrew Union College - Jewish Institute of Religion (Ohio) 1258
Hechler, Ken 1753
Hecht, Anthony 1158
Heckewelder, John 1026
Heidelberg College (Ohio) 1259
Heinrich, Karl 1450
Heiss, Archbishop Michael 1785
Heller, Joseph 718, 1158, 1421
Heller, Saul 1123
Heller, Selig 1635
Hellman, Lillian 1648
Hellriegel, Monsignor Martin B. 902
hematology 762
Hemberger, Theodore 687
Hemingway, Ernest 452, 519, 1320, 1638, 1715, 1716
Hemphill, Paul 5
Henderson State University (Arkansas) 63
Hendrick, Bishop Thomas Augustine 1097
Hendrix College (Arkansas) 64
Henley, Beth 876
Henni, Archbishop John Martin 1785
Henrey, Madeleine 1637
Henry, Bill 166
Henry, Dr. Carl F.H. 493
Henty, George Alfred 344
heraldry 296
herbals 218, 279, 319, 1000, 1363, 1427, 1459, 1482, 1489, 1649
Herberg, Will 984
Herbut, Peter A. 1447
Hering, Leonora 583
Heritage Press 1067
Herkimer County Community College (New York) 1065
hero fiction 997
Herrán, Thomás 296
Herrick, Samuel 1719
Herschel, J.F.W. 737
Hersey, John 284
Hershberger, Arthur W. 583
Herter, Christian 737

Hertzog, J. Carl 1585, 1650
Herz, Martin F. 296
Hesse, Herman 820
Heston, Charlton 215
Heusler, Andreas 820
Heuven, Alexander Van 1103
Hewitt, Abram 1050
Hewlett, Maurice 1280
Heyen, William 1158
Heyen, William H. 1133
Hiawatha legend 796
Hibbard, Howard 1000
Hicks, Edward 1444
Hicks, Elias 1444
Hicks, Sue K. 1562
Hidy, Lance 975
Higginson, Fred H. 583
Higginson, Jeanette 583
higher education 977
highway administration 475
highway building, Texas 1577
Hilberseimer, Ludwig Karl 415
Hildreth, Samuel P. 1267
Hill College (Texas) 1586
Hill Country (Texas) 1612
Hill, Dr. Charles L. 1293
Hill, Lister 32
Hill Monastic Manuscript Library 848
Hillsdale College (Michigan) 790
Hillyer, Judge George 381
Hilquit, Morris 1167
Himes, Chester 1445
Hinds Junior College (Mississippi) 863
Hindu religious groups 142
Hinduism 1083
Hine, Lewis 697
Hinkson, Katharine Tynan 487
Hinsdale, Burke A. 1260
Hiram College (Ohio) 1260
Hirsch, Felix 1004
Hispanic culture 139
Hispanic studies 1031
Histoire de la Notation Musicale 1245
historical markers, Texas 1577
The Historie of the World 1532
history, American 109, 307, 540, 544, 551, 716, 979, 997, 1080, 1150, 1154, 1240, 1287, 1317, 1343, 1450, 1482, 1504, 1600, 1716, 1757
history, ancient Middle Eastern 241
History and Annals of Hebrew Printing 1258
history, California 133
history, Canadian 109
history, Catholic Church (U.S.) 1083
history, Cuban 1069
history, Eastern European 296
history, English 207, 369, 450, 519, 540, 856, 928, 997, 1273, 1403, 1587
history, European 296
history, French 369, 431, 1217
history, French colonial 1130
history, French pre-Revolutionary 834
history, Icelandic 1791
history, Irish 1001, 1036, 1055, 1322, 1435, 1456, 1791
history, Latin American 166, 519
history, Lithuanian 1791
history, Near Eastern 670
history, New York 1150
history, nineteenth-century American 717
history, North American 1791
History of the American Indian 1320
History of the Indian Tribes of North America 1320
history, Pennsylvania-German 1402
history, Polish 436, 1791
history, Portuguese 737
history, Russian 955
history, Spanish 332
history, United States 519, 924
Hitchcock, Edward 705
Hite, Kathleen 596
Hitler, Adolf 340, 1376
Hjortsberg, William 1158
Hoag, Enoch 1390
Hobart and William Smith Colleges (New York) 1066
Hockney, David 169
Hoffman, Charles Fenno 1049
Hoffman, Malvina 1245
Hofmann, Josef 1371
Hofstader, Richard 1049
Hofstra University (New York) 1067
Hogan, Dr. John C. 234
Hogan, John A. 975
Hogan, William Ransom 646
Hogarth Press 1067
Hogarth, William 58, 680
Hogrogian, Nonny 975
Hohenberger, Frank 519
Holden, Miriam Y. 997
Holiness Movement 599, 911
holistic health 149
Holland Society 1049
Holley, Dr. Joseph Winthrop 352
Holley, Marietta 1125
Hollins College (Virginia) 1693
Hollywood 537
Holmes, Alester 1489
Holmes Book Company 131
Holmes, Ezekial 664
Holmes Junior College (Mississippi) 864
Holmes, Mary Jane 1133
Holmes, Oliver Wendell 341, 681, 737, 1379
Holmes, Sherlock 1217
Holocaust 723, 998, 1130, 1386, 1742
holograph music 1371
Holt, Hamilton 331

Holy Family College (Pennsylvania) 1391
Holy Land 1258
Holy Names College (California) 147
home economics 314, 755
home remedies 1275
homeopathic medicine 151, 1389
Homer 1049
homesteading 935
Honduras 1647
Honeyman, Robert B. 1403
Honolulu Community College (Hawaii) 403
Hood College (Maryland) 680
Hood, Thomas 1280
Hood's Texas Brigade 1586
Hooker, Samuel Cox 820
Hooper, Edward William 737
Hoover, Calvin 1192
Hoover Dam 960
Hoover, Herbert 1326
Hope College (Michigan) 791
Hope, John 358
Hope, Lugenia Burns 358
Hope, Welborn 1301
Hopkins, Gerard Manley 675, 1729
Hopkins, Harry L. 296
Hopkins, Joseph 1059
Hopkins, Kenneth 1320
Hopkinsville Community College (Kentucky) 607
Hoppin, William Jones 737
Horace 997, 1475
Horgan, Paul 284, 1016, 1020
The Horn Book 755
Horn, Robert D. 593
horn-books 519, 1049
Horne, Bernard S. 1450
horse racing 431
horses 583
Horsford, Eben N. 1115
Horsford, Eben Norton 766
horticulture 214, 331, 648, 654, 659, 802, 1235, 1312, 1445, 1504, 1727, 1739, 1774
Horton, Frank (U.S. Congressman) 1158
Horton, George Van Ruis 296
Horton, Omah Scott 596
Hosmer, Helen 1142
hospitality industry 117, 281, 336, 1408, 1467, 1516, 1797
hospitals, French 1151
hotel management 117, 281, 1100, 1111, 1408
Houdini, Harry 737
Hough, Cass S. 59
Houghton College (New York) 1068
Houghton Mifflin Company 737
Hound and Horn 284
House Committee on Un-American Activities 1276
household manuals 1159
Houser, Martin L. 423
Housman, A.E. 225
Housman, Laurence 225
Houston Baptist University (Texas) 1587
Houston, David Franklin 737
Howard, Bronson 1049
Howard, Dr. Minnie 409
Howard, Frank 820
Howard, Oliver Otis 652
Howard Payne University (Texas) 1588
Howard, Robert E. 1627
Howard Shipyards (Indiana) 519
Howard University (District of Columbia) 297
Howe, Stewart 497
Howell, Edwin Eugene 1158
Howell, Judge James A. 1666
Howell, Roger 652
Howells, William Cooper 1026
Howells, William Dean 519, 653, 737, 1000, 1123, 1158, 1243, 1269, 1290
Howland, Emily 1164, 1444
Howse, A.E. 596
Hoyt, Gertrude 1699
Hubbard, Dr. David Allan 138
Hubbard, Elbert 55, 1158
Hubbard, Kin 504
Hubbard, Margaret C. 975
Hubbell, Walter Sage 1158
Hudson Valley (New York) 1153
Hudson, W.H. 1026
Huff, Robert 975
Hughes, Langston 346, 1245, 1445, 1533
Hughes, Richard 519
Hughes, Sarah T. 1645
Hughes, Ted 519
Huguenots 652
Hull, General William 737
Hulter, Archer Butler 236
human development 171
human rights 670, 1102
human services 969, 1090
humanism 1158
humanities 79, 147, 159, 207, 212, 224, 281, 289, 324, 425, 453, 480, 525, 626, 742, 1743, 1773, 1791
Humboldt State University (California) 148
humor 497
Humphrey, Dr. Clarence J. 99
Humphrey, Inez Faith 613
Hungary 1355
Hunkins, Eusebia 1280
Hunleth Music Store (St. Louis, Missouri) 497
Hunt, Arthur Billings 1049
Hunt, Henry G. 296
Hunt, Leigh 564, 1280, 1290
Hunt, Morton M. 1445
Hunter College of the City University of New York 1069
Hunter, Dard 1144

Hunter, David 1775
Hunter, John 1653
Hunter, William 1653
Huntingdon College (Alabama) 13
Huntington, Anna Hyatt 1150
Huntington College (Indiana) 515
Hurley, Patrick 1318
Huron College (South Dakota) 1514
Hurston, Zora Neale 341
Husa, Karel 1071
Husson College (Maine) 655
Husted, Margaret 255
Huston-Tillotson College (Texas) 1589
Hutchins, Robert Maynard 494
Hutterian Brethren 1242
Hutton, Laurence 997
Hutzler, Abram G. 681
Huxley, Aldous 1137
Huxley, Julian 1607
hydraulics 564
hydrology 215
Hyman, Stanley Edgar 1668
hymnals 118, 243, 282, 430, 434, 456, 464, 497, 636, 836, 840, 931, 984, 996, 1155, 1286, 1316, 1332, 1425, 1430, 1475, 1543, 1567, 1683, 1684, 1771
hymnody 1684
hymnody, Scandinavian 826
hypnotism 596
Icarian studies 499
ice skating 279
Iceland 174, 1051
iconography 1475
Idaho 413
Idaho, southern 1665
Idaho State University 409
idealistic movements 1792
Iliff School of Theology (Colorado) 243
Illinois 485, 488
Illinois and Michigan Canal 455
Illinois Benedictine College (Illinois) 441
Illinois College 442
Illinois College of Optometry 443
Illinois Institute of Technology 444
Illinois Regional Archives Depository 485
Illinois, southern 479, 486
Illinois State University 445
Illinois Valley Community College 446
Illinois Wesleyan University 447
illuminated manuscripts 224, 279, 737, 766, 802, 1258, 1696
illustrated books 737, 924, 1049, 1129, 1150, 1450
illustrated books, French 284
illustrators of the West 1627
imaginary voyages 1445
imaginary wars 238
imaging sciences 1112
Imagists 1445
Immaculata College (Pennsylvania) 1392
immigrants, Danish 547
immigrants, Scandinavian 1733
immigration 1445
imprints, Aldine 215
imprints, Auburn (New York) 1097
imprints, Charlotte (North Carolina) 1207
imprints, Confederate 5, 32, 394, 497, 615, 629, 1181, 1217, 1220, 1607, 1683, 1753
imprints, Dutch 993
imprints, early American 1133, 1150, 1213, 1276, 1559, 1776
imprints, early American medical 1147
imprints, early English 1276
imprints, early European 1129, 1276
imprints, early New Hampshire 975
imprints, early Pennsylvania-German 1394
imprints, eighteenth-century American 5
imprints, Elzevier 1129, 1449
imprints, European 70
imprints, German-American 1382
imprints, Hebrew 146
imprints, Irish 1124
imprints, Louisiana 629
imprints, New Jersey 997
imprints, Pacific Northwest 1744
imprints, sixteenth-century Italian 1791
imprints, Swedish 574
imprints, Tennessee 1562
imprints, Vermont 1676
Incarnate Word College (Texas) 1590
incunabula 33, 200, 211, 224, 238, 284, 293, 301, 431, 442, 497, 519, 552, 681, 723, 766, 771, 821, 889, 997, 1049, 1059, 1083, 1120, 1123, 1124, 1155, 1158, 1159, 1170, 1180, 1217, 1245, 1258, 1267, 1283, 1297, 1342, 1358, 1435, 1445, 1456, 1461, 1475, 1660, 1676, 1693, 1696, 1698, 1785
Independence Community College (Kansas) 582
The Independent magazine 331
India 274, 591
Indian Missionary 1305
Indian Territory Reports 1305
Indiana 510, 519, 521, 537, 538
Indiana Cotton Mills 519
Indiana Friends Meetings 509
Indiana Institute of Technology 516
Indiana, northwest 526
Indiana State University 517
Indiana Territory 539
Indiana University 519
Indiana University at South Bend 518
Indiana University of Pennsylvania 1393
individual rights 141
Indonesia 1380
industrial arts 1361
industrial design 80, 87
industrial education 423

industrial efficiency 1421
industrial firms, Pennsylvania 1421
industrial management 525
industrial psychology 97
industrial relations 1101, 1431
industrial society 1450
Industrial Union of Marine and Shipbuilding Workers of America 696
infectious diseases 218
inflation money, German 103
Inge, William 582, 589
Ingersoll, Robert G. 487
Ingraham, Martha Wheatland 770
Innes, William T. 1445
Inquisition sermons 1258
Institute for Research on Poverty 1167
Institute of American Indian Arts (New Mexico) 1013
Institute of American Values 747
Institute of Cistercian Studies 821
Institute of Paper Chemistry (Wisconsin) 1775
instrumental methods 498
insurance 1046
integral studies 88
Inter American University of Puerto Rico 1470
intercultural resources 1223
The Interdenominational Theological Center (Georgia) 376
interdisciplinary studies 1728
interfaith projects 467
interior design 76, 149, 269, 298, 330, 440, 1058, 1104, 1411
international arbitration 1444
International Archive of Women in Architecture 1719
International Brotherhood of Pottery and Allied Workers 1262
International Cyclopedia of Aviation Biography Records 1296
international development 1679
international events, 1948- 1221
International Institute of Flint (Michigan) 817
international law 324
international management 47
international monetary fund 947
international organizations 331, 1767
International Pentecostal Holiness Church 367
International Piano Archives at Maryland 696
International Publishers 1276
international relations 47, 295
international studies 1, 160, 207, 316, 444, 696, 704, 762, 790, 1278
International Union of Mine, Mill and Smelter Workers 252
interpersonal communications 30
investment 1476
Iona College (New York) 1070
Iowa 174, 545, 550
Iowa Public Employment Relations Board 562
Iowa State University of Science and Technology 549
Iowa United Methodist Conference 550
Iowa Wesleyan College 550
Ireland 25, 639, 1639
Ireland, Joseph N. 284
Ireland, Tom 922
Irish culture 1388
Irish Literary Renaissance 341, 369, 487, 653, 802
iron industry 1696
Ironside, Dr. H.A. 1527
Ironside, Rev. John S. 1527
Iroquois Indians 1122, 1134, 1158
irrigation 103
irrigation, trickle 216
Irving, Edward 1313
Irving, Henry 1158
Irving, Washington 284, 1049, 1158, 1393, 1449, 1562
Isabella I, Queen 431
Isherwood, Christopher 1320
Ishill, Joseph 341
Islam 730, 768
Islamic manuscripts 997
Islamic materials 266
Islands Community College (Alaska) 39
Isles of Shoals 975
Isothermal Community College (North Carolina) 1190
Israel 738
Israel (archaeology) 172
Israeli popular music 146
Israeli publications 489
Italian cities and towns 497
Italian Renaissance 118, 215, 1449, 1638
Italian Risorgimento Period 802
Itallie, Jean-Claude van 1262
Itawamba Junior College (Mississippi) 865
Ithaca College (New York) 1071
Ivask, George 705
Ives, Burl 499
Ives, Frederick Eugene 1445
J. and W. Seligman and Company 1318
Jackman, Alonzo 1677
Jackson, Andrew 1544, 1562
Jackson, Helen Hunt 236
Jackson, Henry M. (U.S. Senator) 1743
Jackson, Mrs. Thomas Jonathan "Stonewall" 1200
Jackson, Peter Huntington 688
Jackson, Rodney 196
Jackson State University (Mississippi) 866
Jackson, Thomas Jonathan ("Stonewall") 1718
Jackson, William Henry 697
Jackson, William S. 236
Jacksonville College (Texas) 1591
Jacksonville Historical Society (Florida) 320
Jacksonville University (Florida) 320
Jacobi, Lotte 697
Jacobs, William Plumer 1502
Jaeger, Werner 737

Jager, Dr. Thor 594
Jamaica 714
Jamaica Alamanack 1445
James, Alice 737
James, Fob 5
James, Henry 296, 519, 653, 675, 681, 737, 1020, 1026, 1158, 1320, 1562
James Madison University (Virginia) 1694
James, Ollie (U.S. Congressman) 614
James, William 737
Jamestown College (North Dakota) 1230
Jamestown (North Dakota) 1230
Jamieson, Helen T. 1425
Jamieson, Janet P. 1425
Jansenism 187
Janus Press 1681
Japan 284, 290, 385, 1086, 1441, 1743
Japanese art books 330
Japanese internment (World War II) 70, 78, 253
Jarrell, Randall 1219
Jarvis, Charles H. 1371
Jarvis Christian College (Texas) 1592
Javits, Jacob K. (U.S. Senator) 1132
Jay, John 1049
jazz 428, 470, 488, 593, 605, 646, 662, 711, 955, 1000, 1123, 1475, 1645, 1715
Jeffers, Robinson 32, 106, 166, 225, 284, 296, 1648
Jefferson Community College (New York) 1072
Jefferson County (New York) 1072
Jefferson Davis State Junior College (Alabama) 14
Jefferson, Thomas 1686, 1716
Jemison, Robert 32
Jenks, William H. 1390
Jennings, M.D., Roscoe G. 73
Jersey City State College (New Jersey) 989
Jessye, Eva 589
Jestrab, Elvira 1237
Jestrab, Frank 1237
Jesuit history, U.S. 296
Jesuit missionaries 296, 1122
Jesuitica 634, 723, 916, 1036, 1059, 1078, 1297, 1729, 1778
jewelry 331
Jewett, Sarah Orne 341, 653, 737
Jewish Archives of Greater Buffalo (New York) 1131
Jewish communal studies 146
Jewish culture 1026
Jewish education 1355
Jewish evangelism 995
Jewish Federation of Metropolitan Chicago 489
Jewish law 1374
Jewish life 221, 670
Jewish music 146, 1073
Jewish political figures 738
Jewish studies 738, 839, 1152, 1216, 1386
Jewish Theological Seminary of America (New York) 1073
Jillson, Willard R. 624
Jimenez, Juan Ramon 1473
Jimenez, Zenobia 1473
Joan of Arc 1049
John A. Logan College (Illinois) 448
John Carroll University (Ohio) 1261
John Crerar Library 494
John F. Kennedy University (California) 149
The John Hopkins University (Maryland) 681
John Jay College of Criminal Justice of the City University of New York 1074
John Marshall Law School (Illinois) 449
John Morrell and Company (South Dakota) 1510
John Wesley College (North Carolina) 1191
Johnson and Wales College (Rhode Island) 1477
Johnson, Andrew 1559, 1562
Johnson, Barbara 1493
Johnson Bible College (Tennessee) 1537
Johnson C. Smith University (North Carolina) 1192
Johnson, Charles S. 1533
Johnson, Earl A. 1192
Johnson, Harold E. 504
Johnson, James Weldon 284
Johnson, Lyndon B. 1577, 1617
Johnson, Paul 877
Johnson, Samuel 497, 500, 1049, 1158, 1217
Johnson Space Center History Archive 1607
Johnson State College (Vermont) 1673
Johnson, Thomas Moore 924
Johnson, William Samuel 1049
Johnston, Joseph 1718
Johnston, Wayne 497
Jones, Anson 1645
Jones, Ernest Larue 296
Jones, Herbert 596
Jones, James 485, 649
Jones, Jenkin Lloyd 464
Jones, Madison 5
Jones, Mary (Mrs. Anson) 1645
Jones, Robert E. 975
Jones, Robert (U.S. Congressman) 34
Jones, Rufus M. 1390
Jones. T.Z.R. 792
Jones, Warren L. 629
Jones, William J. 921
Jonson, Ben 1339
Joplin, Scott 922
Jordan, Barbara (U.S. Congresswoman) 1633
Jordan, Len B. (U.S. Senator) 407
Joseffy, Rafael 497
Joseph Love Inc. 1058
Josephson, Ben 1106
The Journal of Negro History 431
journalism 331, 394, 564, 1431
journalists 716
journals, eighteenth-century 292
journals, nineteenth-century medical 379

Jova, Joseph John 296
Joyce, James 284, 487, 552, 583, 593, 849, 1320, 1600, 1648
Judaic studies 995, 1032, 1355
Judaica 146, 221, 255, 280, 284, 341, 400, 489, 494, 651, 670, 767, 820, 1073, 1129, 1166, 1192, 1217, 1258, 1386, 1650, 1791, 1792
Judeo-Christian relations (Middle Ages) 1376
Judson College (Alabama) 15
Judson College (Illinois) 450
Juilliard School (New York) 1075
Juliano, Rev. Anthony J. 1343
jump rope rhymes 579
Juniata College (Pennsylvania) 1394
junior colleges 1034
jurisprudence, European 816
juvenile literature 344, 430, 663, 718, 766, 1236, 1525, 1712
Kabbalah 738
Kahn, Albert 798
Kaifeng (China) 1258
KAKE-TV (Wichita, Kansas) 596
Kalamazoo College (Michigan) 792
Kalamazoo (Michigan) 821
Kaminsky, Marc 1262
Kane, Grenville 997
Kanner, Leo J. 670
Kansas 573, 579, 593
Kansas City Art Institute (Missouri) 900
Kansas State University 583
Kansas Territory 596
Kansas Water Resources Board 596
Kansas Wesleyan University 584
Kansas West Conference of the United Methodist Church 591
Kaplan, Louis I. 670
Kapp Putsch 764
Karman, Theodore von 89
Kasura, Walter J. 497
Kaufman, George 1703
Kaufman, Linda Hofheimer 1703
Kavan, Anna 1320
Kazakh language 1745
Kazel, Sr. Dorothy 1292
Kean, Charles John 1158
Kean College of New Jersey 990
Kearney State College (Nebraska) 949
Keating, Kenneth B. (U.S. Senator) 1158
Keats, John 166
Keen, William Williams 1475
Keene, Paul Edwin 437
Keene State College (New Hampshire) 967
Kefauver, Estes 1562
Kelley, Robert F. 296
Kellogg Community College (Michigan) 793
Kellogg, Elijah 652
Kellogg, W.K. 99
Kelly, Alexander 1218
Kelly, James A. 1121
Kelly Plow Company (Texas) 1623
Kelmscott Press 93, 319, 653, 1067, 1638
Kempter Military School and College (Missouri) 901
Kendall College (Illinois) 451
Kendall College of Art and Design (Michigan) 794
Kendall, Paul, M. 1280
Kendall, Willmoore 1639
Kennan, George F. 997
Kennedy, John F. 296, 642, 894
Kennedy, Robert F. 758
Kennesaw College (Georgia) 377
Kenrick, Archbishop Francis Patric 902
Kenrick, Archbishop Peter Richard 902
Kenrick Seminary (Missouri) 902
Kent, Rockwell 1049, 1141
Kent State papers 975
Kent State University (Ohio) 1262
Kenton, Stan 1645
Kentucky 494, 602, 603, 604, 605, 608, 609, 613, 614, 615, 619, 620, 622, 623, 624, 1753
Kentucky High School Athletic League 608
Kentucky Methodist Heritage Center 609
Kentucky State University 608
Kentucky Wesleyan College 609
Kentucky, western 616
Kenyon College (Ohio) 1263
Kenyon, John S. 1260
Keogh, Eugene (U.S. Congressman) 1121
Kephart, Horace 1224
Kepler, Johannes 519
Kern County (California) 100
Kerouac, Jack 975, 1049
Kerry County (Ireland) 25
Kesey, Ken 1158, 1342
Kester, Howard 1201
Keswick Holiness Movement 500
Ketchikan Community College (Alaska) 40
Ketelle, Dr. Hubert 1514
Ketler, Dr. Isaac C. 1387
Key, Francis Scott 296
Keystone Junior College (Pennsylvania) 1395
Kherdian, David 975, 1794
Kienbusch, Otto von 997
Kierkegaard, Soren 850
Kilgore College (Texas) 1593
Killian, Jr., James R. 742
Kilmer, Joyce 296
Kilpatrick, James H. 381
Kilroe, Edwin P. 1049
Kimball, George 975
Kimball, Stanley 345
Kincaid, William 1371
kindergarten 913, 1151
kinesiology 215, 1099
King, Hamilton 296

King, Jr., Martin Luther 387, 716, 1767
King Library Press 622
King, Muriel 1058
King, Stephen 664
The King's College (New York) 1076
King's College (Pennsylvania) 1396
Kingston, Ceylon S. 1726
Kingston Trio 1792
Kinnaman, John Allen 1757
Kinnell, Galway 519
Kinston (North Carolina) 1194
Kipling, Rudyard 1049, 1150, 1280, 1675
Kirby Lumber Company (Texas) 1623
Kircher, Ann 821
Kirksville College of Osteopathic Medicine (Missouri) 903
Kirkwood Community College (Iowa) 551
Kirtland Community College (Michigan) 795
Kistler, Lynton 406
kites 251
Kline, Peter B. 1296
Klingberg, Haddon 826
Klingberg, J.E. 826
Knapp, Dorothy Elizabeth 755
Knickerbocker literature 1049
Knight, Damon 1342
Knight, Etheridge 1290
Knipp, Buddie 613
Knoblock, Edward 737
Knoop, Faith Yingling 59
Knox College (Illinois) 452
Knox, Ronald 296
Knoxville College (Tennessee) 1538
Kodaly music theory 1787
Kolb, Emery 55
Kolbe, Saint Maximilian 752
Koo, Vi-Kyuin Wellington 1049
Koob, Kathryn 569
Korea 1380, 1743
Korean Conflict 1487, 1677
Korson, George 1396
Koschmann, Renata 946
KPIX (San Francisco) 193
KQED (San Francisco) 193
Kraft, Jr., Christopher C. 1719
Krainis, Bernard 756
Kramer, Leon 1789
Krannert Center for the Performing Arts 497
Krauskopf, Joseph 1372
Krauss, E.A. 889
Krohn, Ernst 928
Krupsak, Mary Ann 1158
Kulturkampf 187
Kuskokwim Community College (Alaska) 41
Kutztown University (Pennsylvania) 1397
La Crosse (Wisconsin) 1790
La Salle, Saint John Baptist de 187
La Salle University (Pennsylvania) 1398
La Verne (California) 222
labor 291, 1030, 1101
labor history 1280, 1288
labor history, New Jersey 1008
labor issues 70
labor law 141
labor movement 517, 1243, 1421
labor movement, Jewish 1355
labor movement, New York City 1106
labor organizations (Arkansas) 70
labor unions 252, 375, 1763
Laboratory Institute of Merchandising (New York) 1077
Lackey, Richard S. 877
Ladd, George Eldon 138
Lady, Wendell 583
LaFarge, Oliver 1648
Lafayette College (Pennsylvania) 1399
Lafayette, Marquis de 378, 519, 1200, 1399
Lagerlog, Selma 838
LaGrange College (Georgia) 378
Laguna Verde Imprenta 166
Lake Champlain Transportation Company (Vermont) 1681
Lake Charles (Louisiana) 637
Lake Erie College (Ohio) 1264
Lake Forest College (Illinois) 453
Lake Superior State College (Michigan) 796
Lake Tahoe (Nevada) 959
Lake-Sumter Community College (Florida) 321
Lakota Indians 1519
Lamar University (Texas) 1594
Lambert, Fred 1753
Lambert, Orlando Clayton 1567
Lambuth College (Tennessee) 1539
Lampner, Dr. Carl 1386
Lancaster Bible College (Pennsylvania) 1400
Lancaster Theological Seminary (Pennsylvania) 1401
Lancey, William Lewis 981
land colonization, Texas 1635
land reclamation 612
Land Run of 1893 (Oklahoma) 1314
Lander College (South Carolina) 1498
Landram, Russell 594
Landrum, Phil 388
landscape architecture 287, 1144, 1480
landscape gardening 802
landscaping 1445, 1739
Lane College (Tennessee) 1540
Lane, James H. 5
Langston, John Mercer 1533
language books, American Indian 1305
language, Russian 1677
languages, African 1445
languages, American Indian 296, 766
languages, ancient 419

languages, Baltic 1262
languages, Celtic 296
languages, Germanic 928
languages, Ibero-American 1106
languages, Jewish 670
languages, Near Eastern 419, 1106
languages, Romance 928, 1278
Lanier, Sidney 385, 681
Lanman, Charles 32
Lansford, Bascom Lamar 1197
Lansing Community College (Michigan) 797
lantern projection photography 90
Lantz, Walter 215
Laos 1380
Lapwai Indians 413
Laramie County Community College (Wyoming) 1803
Larcom, Lucy 769
Laredo Junior College (Texas) 1595
Laredo State University (Texas) 1596
Las Vegas (Nevada) 960
laser technology 980
Lasseter, Dillard R. 386
Latah County (Idaho) Historical Society Oral History Program 413
Latin America 190, 207, 279, 316, 342, 646, 1086, 1268, 1358, 1439, 1638, 1649, 1650
Latin American politics 1000
Latin American studies 1473
Latin Americana 928
Latin Christian literature 1331
Latin manuscripts 1181
Latvia 196, 955
Laughlin, Clarence J. 629
Laughlin, Harry 912
Laughton, Charles 215
Laver, James 296
law 149, 163, 213, 228, 234, 444, 449, 606, 607, 1012, 1127, 1158, 1370, 1614, 1772
law, California 127, 130, 143, 167, 184, 231
law, comparative 112, 1374
law enforcement 23, 454, 605
law, European 1181
law, foreign 816
law, intellectual property 1374
law, international 112, 997, 1033, 1049, 1102, 1181, 1374
Law, Jan 106
law, Jewish 1374
law, labor 1102
law, media 1102
law (Pacific Rim countries) 112
law, People's Republic of China 206
law, space 112
Lawes, Lewis E. 1074
Lawrence, Abbot 737
Lawrence, D.H. 217, 284, 487, 519, 593, 1020, 1049, 1217, 1288, 1320, 1359, 1648
Lawrence Institute of Technology (Michigan) 798
Lawrence, T.E. 737, 1617, 1648, 1712
Lawrence University (Wisconsin) 1776
Lawson, John Howard 487
Lawson State Community College (Alabama) 16
Lazarsfeld, Paul F. 1049
Le Gallienne, Richard 225
Le Guin, Ursula 1342
Le Ideés Nouvelles de la Mode 1058
Le Moyne College (New York) 1078
League of Women Voters of the City of New York 1049
League of Women Voters (Ohio) 1280
Lear, Edward 737
learning disabled 175
Leary & Co. (Philadelphia) 1445
Leaue of Nations documents 696
Leavenworth (Kansas) 590
Lebanan Valley College (Pennsylvania) 1402
Lee, Arthur 737
Lee, Dr. Robert G. 636
Lee, George Washington 1200
Lee, Lawrence 1450
Lee, Robert E. 1586, 1718, 1722, 1753
Lees-McCrae College (North Carolina) 1193
legal history 1449
legal history, English 231
legal history, European 802
legal research 449
legal scholarship 1763
LeGallienne, Eva 284
Leggat, Alexander 938
Legrain, Pierre 1648
Lehigh University (Pennsylvania) 1403
Lehman College (New York) 1079
Lehman, Edith Altschul 1049
Lehman, Harvey 1280
Lehman, Herbert H. 1049
Lehman, John 1648
Leigh, John Highfield 1158
Lemhi Indian Agency 409
LeMoyne-Owen College (Tennessee) 1541
Lenoir Community College (North Carolina) 1194
Lenoir-Rhyne College (North Carolina) 1195
Lenski, Lois 59, 319, 578, 1131, 1134, 1219, 1244, 1393
Leo Hart Printing Company (Rochester, New York) 1158
lepidoptera 279, 1295
leprosy 1753
Lert, Richard 1607
Lesley College (Massachusetts) 739
Leslie, Sir Shane 296
Lesser Antilles 1062
Lessing, Doris 1320
LeTourneau College (Texas) 1597
LeTourneau, R.G. 1597

letters (American), published 1259
letters (British), published 1259
Leuba, Martha 1450
Leuba, Walter 1450
Levenson, Sam 1032
Lever, A. Frank 1489
Leverton, Garrett 453
Levi, Peter 714
Lewes, George Henry 284
Lewis and Clark College (Oregon) 1327
Lewis and Clark Community College (Illinois) 454
Lewis and Clark expeditions 1240, 1327
Lewis, Arthur H. 1445
Lewis, C.S. 500, 592, 1217, 1791
Lewis, Eleanor C. 1239
Lewis, Graceanna 1444
Lewis, John L. 1167
Lewis, Sinclair 1648
Lewis University (Illinois) 455
Lewis-Clark State College (Idaho) 410
Lewisohn, Ludwig 718, 1648
Lexington Theological Seminary (Kentucky) 610
Ley, Willy 34
Libbey-Owens-Ford Corporation 1290
Libby, Orin G. 1237
liberation movements 1445
Liberty Association of General Baptists 524
Liberty County (Georgia) 373
Liberty University (Virginia) 1695
Library of Living Philosophers 487
library science 57, 196, 369, 481, 816, 1049, 1113, 1203, 1375, 1441, 1610
libretti 341, 715, 1475
Liddle, E.A. 770
Lieb, John 1002
Lieberman, Stanley 997
life sciences 525, 536
life-styles, alternative 1445
Lifshin, Lyn 1445
Ligutti, Monsignor Luigi 1778
Lilienthal, David E. 997
Lily, William 519
Limited Editions Club 629, 652, 1351, 1639
Lincoln, Abraham 81, 166, 236, 296, 306, 358, 423, 441, 442, 457, 461, 470, 471, 494, 504, 518, 519, 564, 573, 590, 601, 605, 615, 621, 629, 716, 729, 774, 787, 809, 820, 912, 938, 977, 981, 1006, 1252, 1289, 1318, 1343, 1352, 1399, 1423, 1466, 1475, 1514, 1542, 1552, 1586, 1597, 1764, 1783
Lincoln, Charles Eric 358
Lincoln Christian College (Illinois) 456
Lincoln College (Illinois) 457
Lincoln County (Nevada) 960
Lincoln Land Community College (Illinois) 458
Lincoln Lore Newsletter 981
Lincoln Memorial University (Tennessee) 1542
Lincoln Park Conservation Association 431
Lincoln University (Missouri) 904
Lincoln University (Pennsylvania) 1404
Lind, Jenny 471
Lindquist, Jennie 976
Lindsay, Vachel 1260, 1648
Linfield College (Oregon) 1328
linguistics 734, 742, 1278, 1679
Link, Edwin A. 1130
Linn County (Oregon) 1329
Linnaeus, Carolus 583
Linn-Benton Community College (Oregon) 1329
Lion, Leon M. 1158
Lipsky, Joan 556
"Listening to Indians" 1305
literary criticism 708
literary translation, art of 764
literature, African 1404
literature, Afro-American 1290
literature, Afro-French 644
literature, American 57, 59, 159, 166, 207, 215, 252, 276, 287, 394, 422, 445, 450, 453, 475, 536, 558, 565, 587, 601, 606, 622, 629, 725, 744, 782, 792, 856, 878, 892, 923, 925, 928, 964, 997, 1078, 1080, 1081, 1106, 1150, 1159, 1181, 1217, 1218, 1240, 1243, 1262, 1278, 1320, 1403, 1409, 1435, 1439, 1475, 1504, 1532, 1549, 1562, 1593, 1630, 1637, 1638, 1647, 1648, 1663, 1666, 1668, 1676, 1699, 1716, 1719, 1770
literature, Black 341, 429, 438, 526, 761
literature, Brazilian 1450
literature, Caribbean 736
literature, Celtic 834
literature, classical 540
literature, English 57, 59, 63, 135, 159, 166, 207, 212, 215, 252, 284, 287, 341, 369, 381, 394, 418, 423, 431, 435, 445, 450, 478, 481, 497, 519, 528, 532, 534, 536, 544, 558, 587, 593, 601, 609, 622, 681, 692, 737, 744, 792, 820, 856, 878, 892, 925, 928, 965, 997, 1055, 1069, 1078, 1080, 1081, 1106, 1132, 1159, 1181, 1218, 1240, 1243, 1261, 1262, 1280, 1288, 1320, 1342, 1403, 1439, 1449, 1450, 1458, 1463, 1464, 1475, 1504, 1532, 1549, 1611, 1630, 1637, 1641, 1645, 1648, 1663, 1666, 1681, 1699, 1719, 1744, 1770, 1791, 1792, 1804
literature, European 166, 737
literature, Franco-Canadian 1681
literature, French 177, 214, 352, 519, 589, 648, 764, 820, 973, 1049, 1161, 1451, 1648, 1693, 1791
literature, French pre-Revolutionary 834
literature, Gaelic 1059
literature, German 284, 519, 681, 764, 928, 1718, 1791
literature, Greek 284, 1288
literature, Hebrew 1064, 1167, 1355, 1386
literature, Icelandic 1791
literature, illustrated Victorian 1245
literature, Irish 589, 593, 623, 653, 658, 714, 1001, 1036, 1047, 1055, 1070, 1078, 1243, 1359, 1366,

1456, 1791
literature, Italian 530, 766
literature, Italian Renaissance 924
literature, Jewish 670, 738, 1064
literature, Latin 284, 1132
literature, Latin American 57, 764
literature, Lithuanian 1791
literature, Louisiana French 629
literature, Norwegian 568
literature, Polish 436, 752, 986, 1065, 1160, 1354, 1391, 1791
literature, Russian 737, 1677
literature, Scandinavian 838, 850, 1791
literature, Scottish 453, 1211, 1504
literature, seventeenth-century English 1413
literature, Spanish 57, 483, 792, 820, 1343, 1450, 1637
literature, Spanish-American 478, 1358
literature, Victorian 622
literature, Welsh 1498
literature, Yiddish 1167
literature, Yiddish-American 1475
lithography 1445
Lithuania 196
Little Blue Books 549
Little Blue Books 589
Little Colonel series 1567
Little Dorritt 413, 590
little magazines 279, 1278, 1450, 1791
Little Review 1792
Little Rock School Crisis 70
Littlejohn, J.C. 1489
liturgical works, Roman Catholic 1438
liturgy 714, 888, 1124
livestock 1372
Livingston University (Alabama) 17
Livingstone College (North Carolina) 1196
Lloyd, Alan C. 999
Lloyd-Butler, John 166
Lock Haven University (Pennsylvania) 1405
Locke, Leslie Leland 1387
Locklin, Gerald 106
Lodge, Gonzalez 1049
Loesser, Jean Bassett 1249
Logan College of Chiropractic (Missouri) 905
Logan, John A. 448
Logan, Joshua 1049
logging industry, Wisconsin 1788
Loma Linda University (California) 150
London Blitz 1450
London (England) 519
London, Jack 1665
Long Beach (California) 106
Long, Chester I. 596
Long, Huey P. 646
Long Island (New York) 1053
Long Island Studies Institute (New York) 1067
Long Island University, C.W. Post Campus (New York) 1080
Long, Perry 107
Longfellow, Henry Wadsworth 341, 652, 737, 792, 1475
Loras College (Iowa) 552
Lord, Sr., Franklin B. 1080
Lorentz, Pare 1793
Loretto Heights College (Colorado) 244
Loring, Charles Greely 737
Los Angeles 102
Los Angeles College of Chiropractic (California) 151
Los Angeles historical photography 106
Los Angeles Mission College (California) 152
Los Angeles Southwest College (California) 153
Los Angeles Valley College (California) 154
lost mines 55
Louisiana 32, 629, 630, 631, 635, 637, 640, 645, 646, 648
Louisiana College 628
Louisiana Purchase 1318
Louisiana State University 629
Louisiana State University at Eunice 630
Louisiana State University Medical Center 632
Louisiana Tech University 633
Louisville Conference of the United Methodist Church 609
Louisville (Kentucky) 623
Louisville Presbyterian Theological Seminary (Kentucky) 611
Lourdes College (Ohio) 1265
Love, John 255
Love, Tom 59
Lovecraft, H.P. 1475
Low Countries 369
Low, Seth 1049
Lowande, Joseph A. 103
Lowell, Amy 737
Lowell, James Russell 737
Lowell, Robert 216, 737
Lowes, John Livingston 737
Lowrie, Donald 497
Lowrie, Helen 497
Lowry, Malcolm 1320, 1638
Loyola College (Maryland) 682
Loyola Marymount University (California) 155
Loyola University (Louisiana) 634
Loyola University of Chicago (Illinois) 459
Lubbock Christian College (Texas) 1598
Lubell, Samuel 296
Ludenorff political group (Germany) 816
Luhan, Mabel Dodge 284
Lum and Abner 70
Lumbee Indians 1206
lumber industry 1623
Lummis, Charles 238, 1020
lunar flight 251
Lunt, Alfred 1780

Lurie, George S. 429
Lurleen B. Wallace State Junior College (Alabama) 18
Lush, Jay 549
Lutcher and Moore Lumber Company (Texas) 1623
Luther College (Iowa) 553
Luther, Martin 430, 519, 777, 837, 840, 889, 1155, 1195, 1295, 1771
Luther Northwestern Theological Seminary (Minnesota) 840
Lutheran Brotherhood Insurance Company 840
Lutheran Church in America 951
Lutheran Historical Society 1406
Lutheran Theological Seminary at Gettysburg (Pennsylvania) 1406
Lutheran Theological Seminary at Philadelphia (Pennsylvania) 1407
Lutheran Theological Southern Seminary (South Carolina) 1499
Lutheranism 91, 114, 416, 507, 538, 553, 570, 782, 835, 836, 850, 889, 951, 1006, 1285, 1295, 1385, 1406, 1407, 1499, 1501, 1714, 1771, 1791
Luzerne County Community College (Pennsylvania) 1408
Lynchburg College (Virginia) 1696
lynching 358
Lyndon State College (Vermont) 1674
Lynds, Dennis 1567
Lynn, Charles J. 514
Lyric Theatre (Baltimore, Maryland) 695
MacCord, Charles 1002
MacCormac Junior College (Illinois) 460
MacDiarmid, Hugh 1217
Macdonald, Duncan Black 266
MacDonald, George 284
MacDonald, John D. 252, 341
MacDonald, Ramsay 1504
MacDowell, Edward A. 975, 1049
Machen, Arthur 820, 1280
Macias, Salvador 1343
MacInnes, Colin 1158
Mackenzie, Compton 1320, 1648
MacLees, William A. 1059
MacLeish, Archibald 735
MacLeod, Norman 284
MacMillan, Donald B. 652
MacMillan, E.A. 1301
Macmillan, Frances 1267
MacMurray College (Illinois) 461
MacNeil, Neil 296
Macready, William Charles 1067
Macy, William K. 1080
Madison, James 997, 1716
Madisonville Community College (Kentucky) 612
Madonna College (Michigan) 799
madonnas 982
Madrid (Spain) 279
magic 266
magic lantern 90
Magna Carta 1638
Magnetic Core Memory Project 742
magnetic resonance imaging 495
magnetism 694
Magnuson, Warren G. (U.S. Senator) 1743
Mahan, Asa 598
Maharishi International University (Iowa) 554
Mahwah Township (New Jersey) 998
Mailer, Norman 1393
Mainbocher 1058
Maine 652, 658, 664, 665
Maine Maritime Academy 656
majolica jars 1123
Malamud, Bernard 1668
Malarme, Stephane 921
Malaysia 1380
Malone College (Ohio) 1266
Malone, Henry 596
Maloney, Jim 1638
Malthus, Thomas Robert 497
management 79, 149, 156, 215, 265, 300, 314, 326, 372, 560, 742, 808, 1433, 1516, 1667, 1699, 1768
Manati Sugar Company 341
Manchester College (Indiana) 520
Mancini, Henry 215
Mangione, Jerre 1158
Manhart, George B. 508
Manhattan College (New York) 1081
Manhattan School of Music (New York) 1082
Manhattanville College (New York) 1083
Manheim, Ralph 764
Mankato State University (Minnesota) 841
Manley, Edward B. 1267
Manly, Basil 32
Manly, Jr., Basil 1497
Mann, Horace 749, 1239
Mann, Merle B. 398
Mann, Thomas 1320
Mannes College of Music (New York) 1084
Mannes, Leopold Damrosch 1084
Manning, Cardinal Henry E. 751
Manning, Francis M. 1198
manorial records, English 494
Mansfield, Katherine 1320
Mansfield, Mike (U.S. Senator) 941
Mansfield University of Pennsylvania 1409
Manton, Jr., Robert 975
Manual Arts Press 423
manual education 423
manufacturers' catalogs 264
Manutius, Aldus 1245
Maori 406
maps 32, 48, 57, 207, 215, 219, 223, 237, 296, 372, 409, 413, 433, 475, 497, 564, 667, 721, 821, 841, 1015, 1180, 1258, 1397, 1504, 1607, 1696, 1791

March, M.D., Alden 1025
marching band music 30, 1393
Marckwardt, Albert 296
Marcus, William Elder 331
Mare, Walter de la 1382, 1445
Marian College (Indiana) 521
Marian College of Fond du Lac (Wisconsin) 1777
Marianist literature 1289
Marietta College (Ohio) 1267
marine biology 217, 1628
marine engineering 1163
marine insurance 1046
marine sciences 277, 342, 656, 1149, 1156, 1163, 1472, 1491, 1506, 1628
Marine Society of New York 1149
marine technology 659
Marion College (Indiana) 522
Marion, General Francis 1496
Marion, Ira 1039
Marist Brothers 1085
Marist College (New York) 1085
maritime history 656, 664, 694, 1149, 1156, 1163
Mark Hopkins Institute of Art (San Francisco) 191
marketing 79, 326, 1433
Markham, Edwin 596, 708, 1162
Marlboro College (Vermont) 1675
Marlborough, 1st Duke of 593
Marquand, John Phillips 284
Marquette University (Wisconsin) 1778
Marquis, Don 394
marriage 18, 577
marriage manuals 1290
Mars Hill College (North Carolina) 1197
Marshall, Arthur 922
Marshall, Bruce 296
Marshall, Catherine 350
Marshall College 1382
Marshall, General George C. 1718
Marshall, John 1686
Marshall, Murray 296
Marshall, S.L.A. 1650
Marshall (Texas) 1581
Marshall University (West Virginia) 1753
Martin Community College (North Carolina) 1198
Martin County (North Carolina) 1198
Martin, Jr., Joseph W. (U.S. Congressman) 760
Martin, Thomas E. (U.S. Senator) 296
Martinon, Jean 475
Martland, M.D., Harrison 1005
Mary Baldwin College (Virginia) 1697
Mary Immaculate Seminary (Pennsylvania) 1410
Mary Queen of Scots 1049
Mary Washington College (Virginia) 1698
Marygrove College (Michigan) 800
Maryknoll School of Theology (New York) 1086
Maryland 296, 423, 671, 677, 686, 689, 691, 698, 701
Maryland Institute, College of Art 683
Maryland, southern 673
Maryland, western 678
Marylhurst College (Oregon) 1330
Marymount College (Kansas) 585
Marymount College (New York) 1087
Marymount Manhattan College (New York) 1088
Marymount University (Virginia) 1699
Maryville College (Missouri) 906
Maryville College (Tennessee) 1543
Marywood College (Pennsylvania) 1411
Masaryk, Thomas G. 1450
Masefield, John 25, 284, 1049, 1158, 1445, 1648, 1681
Maser, Fred 984
Mason, Alexandra 593
Mason, James 215
Mason, John M. 1430
Mason, William Smith 118
mass communications 1150
mass media 802
Massachusetts College of Art 740
Massachusetts College of Pharmacy and Allied Health Sciences 741
Massachusetts Institute of Technology 742
massacres 1725
Massee, May 578
Massey, Mary Elizabeth 1508
Mast, Gerald 1262
Masters, Edgar Lee 296, 1475, 1648
Masterson, Judge Harris 1607
Mater Dei College (New York) 1089
mathematics 5, 90, 145, 180, 190, 215, 290, 496, 519, 525, 536, 718, 792, 994, 1049, 1338, 1387, 1609, 1718
mathematics, history of 623
Mather, Cotton 737
Mathews, John E. 343
Mattatuck Community College (Connecticut) 267
Matthews, Brander 1049
Matthews, Jack 1240
Matthews, John Joseph 1320
Matthiessen, F.O. 284, 737
Maugham, W. Somerset 233, 519, 1627, 1648
Maui Community College (Hawaii) 404
Maverick, Maury 1577
May Fourth Collection (Kent State) 1262
Mayan civilization 1365
Maybank, Burnett Rhett 1491
Mayer, Doris 982
Mayer, Yisrael 982
Mayfield, Earle B. (U.S. Senator) 296
Mayland Technical College (North Carolina) 1199
Maynard, Horace 1562
Maynard, Theodore 296
Maytag, Robert E. 342
Mayville State College (North Dakota) 1231
Mazarinades 737, 1217, 1791
McAlister, Heber 74

McBrayer, Pearl L. 613
McCann, William R. 296
McCardell, Claire 1058, 1110
McCarthy, Eugene J. (U.S. Senator) 296
McCarthy, Joseph 714
McCarthy, Mary 1159
McCartney, Clarence E. 1384
McClain, Alva J. 513
McClellan, John L. (U.S. Senator) 65
McClelland, General George B. 1387
McClintock, John 984
McClure, Russell E. 596
McCollum, Matthew 1488
McCombs, Holland 1563
McConnell, John Preston 1707
McCormack, John W. 716
McCormick, Daniel 596
McCormick Theological Seminary (Illinois) 462
McCullers, Carson 394, 1648
McCutcheon, George 1289
McDavid, Jr., Raven I. 1497
McDonald, Gerald D. 1143
McFee, William 284
McGhee, George C. 296
McGovern, George (U.S. Senator) 1513
McGrath, Joseph 1078
McGraw, James P. 911
McGuane, Thomas 1158
McGuffey readers 1123, 1269
McGuiness, Peter 1121
McIlhenny, Edward Avery 629
McIlvaine, Charles Pettit 1263
McIntyre, Thomas J. (U.S. Senator) 975
McKay, Gunn 1665
McKendree College (Illinois) 463
McKenzie, Kenneth 997
McKevitt, Michael 255
McKinney, Jean Webster 1159
McKnight, J. Hudson 596
McLintock, Walter 284
McMaster Homer E. 1252
McMurry College (Texas) 1599
McMurtrie, Douglas C. 802
McMurtry, Larry 1617, 1640, 1645
McNeese State University (Louisiana) 635
McNeice, Louis 1648
McNeill, Don 1778
McNutt, Paul 519
McPherson College (Kansas) 586
McVey, William 1245
McWilliams, Carey 215
Mead, George Herbert 494
Mead Johnson and Company 537
Mead, Margaret 296
Meadville/Lombard Theological School (Illinois) 464
Mears, Louise 953
mechanical engineering 121
Mecklenburg County (North Carolina) 1207, 1218
Mecklenburg Declaration of Independence 1180
medals 722, 997
Medaris, Major General John 315
Medger Evers College - CUNY (New York) 1091
Medialle College (New York) 1090
medical artifacts 218, 1717
medical botany 279, 319
medical caricatures 1500
Medical College of Georgia 379
Medical College of Wisconsin 1779
medical education 218
medical ephemera 1500
medical ethics (Jewish) 738
medical history, Louisiana 632
medical instruments 1275
medical jurisprudence 1374
medical laboratory science 662
medical sciences 379, 1564
medical technology 339
Medical University of South Carolina 1500
medicine 379, 380, 495, 594, 620, 1025, 1095, 1147, 1158, 1275, 1421, 1424, 1426, 1500, 1564, 1572, 1653, 1655
medicine, clinical 1779
medicine, history of 150, 254, 352, 482, 564, 762, 856, 1005, 1103, 1131, 1147, 1148, 1181, 1319, 1333, 1573, 1691, 1753, 1779
medicine, military 693
medicine, nineteenth-century American 1632
medicine, Spanish colonial 218
medieval codices 997, 1059
medieval manuscripts 238, 296, 593, 1245, 1342, 1504
medieval studies 536, 821, 1059
Meem, John Gaw 1020
Meeter, H. Henry 779
Meiklejohn, Alexander 705
Mein Kampf 1627
Meir, Golda 1792
Meissner, George N. 928
Melancthon, Philip 891
Melanesia 399, 406
Melson, Irene W. 378
Melville, Herman 341, 737, 1320, 1504, 1562
Melvin, Frank E. 593
Memphis Press-Scimitar 1544
Memphis State University (Tennessee) 1544
Memphis Theological Seminary (Tennessee) 1545
Mencken, H.L. 190, 284, 296, 346, 593, 679, 1057, 1385
Mendel, Dr. Bernardo 519
Mendelsohn, Jack 464
Menke, Eric F. 296
Menlo College (California) 156
Mennonite Biblical Seminary (Indiana) 523
Mennonite Brethren 137, 157, 592
Mennonite Brethren Biblical Seminary (California)

157
Mennonite Church 512
Mennonites 575, 1242, 1414, 1687
Menomenee Indians 1786
mental health 1444
mental illness 906
mental retardation 1209
menus 117, 1052, 1100
Mercer, Johnny 375
Mercer University, Atlanta (Georgia) 380
Mercer University, Macon (Georgia) 381
Mercersburg Reform 1382
merchandising 136, 1321
merchant marine 1149
Mercy College (New York) 1092
Mercyhurst College (Pennsylvania) 1412
Meredith, George 284, 1712
Meridian Junior College (Mississippi) 867
Merrill, Elbridge Warren 43
Merrill, James 705
Merrimack River (Massachsuetts) 763
Merritt College (California) 158
Mertins, Dr. Louis 931
Merton, Thomas 600, 714, 902, 1049, 1097
Merwin, W.S. 497
Mesa College (Colorado) 245
Meserole, Harriet 1058
Mesopotamia 111
Messersmith, George 287
Messiah College (Pennsylvania) 1413
Messner, Elmer 1117
metallurgy 145, 252, 926, 937, 1015
Metamorphoses 1681
meteorology 215
Methodism 4, 7, 64, 179, 199, 227, 243, 248, 303, 318, 353, 369, 386, 396, 437, 476, 508, 535, 550, 584, 598, 599, 609, 839, 868, 878, 885, 911, 984, 1068, 1150, 1188, 1268, 1270, 1281, 1488, 1557, 1599, 1708, 1711, 1736, 1764
Methodist College (North Carolina) 1200
Methodist Episcopal Church 66, 387, 1631
Methodist Theological School (Ohio) 1268
Metro-Goldwyn-Mayer 226
Metrolina region (North Carolina) 1218
Metropolitan Technical Community College (Nebraska) 950
Mettauer, John Peter 1691
Metzdorf, Robert 997
Mexican Americans 1647
Mexican colonization (Texas) 1647
Mexican political, economic, and social life (pre-1917) 166
Mexican War of 1846-48 1647
Mexican-American studies 1603
Mexico 181, 211, 519, 622, 646
Mexico, Imperial Era of 1607
Mexico, northern 1577
Meynell, Alice 714
Miami Christian College (Florida) 322
Miami Radio Monitoring Service 1450
Miami University (Ohio) 1269
Miami Valley (Ohio) 1296
Miami-Dade Community College (Florida) 323
Michalson, Carl 984
Michelson, Albert Abraham 694
Michener, James 592
Michigan 776, 785, 805, 816, 1782
Michigan Baptist Convention 792
Michigan Christian College 801
Michigan, southwest 821
Michigan State University 802
Michigan Technological University 803
Micronesia 399, 406
microscopy 594
Mid Michigan Community College 804
Mid-America Baptist Theological Seminary (Tennessee) 1546
Mid-America Bible College (Oklahoma) 1303
Mid-America Nazarene College (Kansas) 587
Mid-Arkansas Valley Development Association, Inc. 596
Middle Ages 190, 1059, 1358, 1449
Middle East 156, 207, 544, 730, 738, 1337, 1679
Middle Eastern history, ancient 241
Middle Eastern manuscripts 1049
Middle Tennessee State University 1547
Middlebury College (Vermont) 1676
Middlebury (Vermont) 1676
Middlesex Canal Association (Massachusetts) 763
Middletown Studies 503
Midland Lutheran College (Nebraska) 951
Midwestern State University (Texas) 1600
Mierow, Charles C. 236
Miles College (Alabama) 19
Miles, Dr. Wyndham Davies 62
Milhaud, Darius 159
military affairs 1182
military handbooks 1157
military history 242, 384, 579, 716, 901, 1157, 1475, 1487, 1587, 1650, 1677, 1686, 1718
military history, Alabama 5
military medicine 693
military science 345, 1157, 1487, 1718
Mill, John Stuart 497
Millar, Ethel K. 64
Millay, Edna St. Vincent 1128, 1482
Miller, Arthur 1158, 1648
Miller, Dawn Logan 1458
Miller, Francis Pickens 1716
Miller, Henry 215, 487, 1648, 1708
Miller, Jr., Winlock 284
Millerites 712
Miller-Lux lands 103
Millersville University of Pennsylvania 1414

Milligan College (Tennessee) 1548
Millikan, Robert A. 89
Milliken University (Illinois) 465
Mills College (California) 159
Mills Music Company 161
Millsaps College (Mississippi) 868
Milne, A.A. 1648
Milton, Frederick 1058
Milton, John 416, 497, 519, 622, 792, 1000, 1751
Mineral Area College (Missouri) 907
Mineral King (California) 103
mineral science 937
miniature books 203, 1117, 1645, 1785
miniature soldiers 1475
mining 145, 237, 242, 612, 678, 909, 926, 937, 938, 960, 1015, 1338, 1635
Minneapolis College of Art and Design (Minnesota) 842
Minnehaha County (South Dakota) 1510
Minnesota 843, 847, 852, 854, 855
Minnesota Jewish Historical Society 839
Minnesota, northeast 854
Minnestota 841
Minor, Fred H. 1645
minorities 32, 982
minorities in China 1745
Minot State College (North Dakota) 1232
minstrel music 1475
Miriam, R.S.M., Sister 296
Mises, Ludwig von 1387
Mishima, Yukio 1211
Miskimon, T.B. 596
missiology 138, 266, 734, 1456
missionaries 81, 248, 450, 544, 884, 1086, 1122, 1276, 1425
missionary service 1182
missions, Spanish 1602
Mississippi 860, 861, 865, 866, 870, 871, 872, 874, 876, 877
Mississippi College 869
Mississippi Methodist Archives 868
Mississippi River 452, 1544
Mississippi State University 870
Mississippi University for Women 871
Mississippi Valley 70, 416, 629
Mississippi Valley State University 872
Missouri 898, 912, 913, 922, 927, 931
Missouri Baptist College 908
Missouri Baptist Historical Society 931
Missouri Southern State College 909
Missouri Western State College 910
Mistral, Gabriela 1029
Mitchell, Everett 500
Mitchell, Margaret 373, 394, 876
Mitchell, Maria 1159
Mitford, Jessica 1648
Mitford, Nancy 1320
Mobile (Alabama) 27
Mobile College (Alabama) 20
Moffett, Admiral William Adger, U.S.N. 694
Mohave Community College (Arizona) 53
Mohave County (Arizona) 53
Mohawk Valley Community College (New York) 1093
Mojave Desert 110, 216
Molière 1049
Molina, Edward C. 994
Momaday, N. Scott 1320
monastic history 821
monastic manuscripts 848
Moncrieff, William Thomas 1158
Mongolia 1745
Monmouth College (New Jersey) 991
monographs, historical 806
Monroe County (New York) 1133
Monroe, James 1686, 1716
Monroe, Vaughn 746
Mont Saint Michel and Chartres 1245
Montaigne, Michel de 1451
Montana 934, 935, 936, 937, 938, 939, 941, 942
Montana College of Mineral Science and Technology 937
Montana State University 938
Montcalm Community College (Michigan) 805
Montclair State College (New Jersey) 992
Monterey Institute of International Studies (California) 160
Montgomery, C.B. 1402
Montgomery College - Germantown (Maryland) 684
Montgomery County (Tennessee) 1524
Montgomery, Robert H. 1049
Montreat-Anderson College (North Carolina) 1201
Montserrat College of Art (Massachusetts) 743
Moody Bible Institute (Illinois) 466
Moody, Dwight L. 1044
Mooney, James D. 296
Moorcock, Michael 1627
Moore, Burnya Mae 1567
Moore, Clement C. 319, 1060
Moore, George 894, 1280
Moore, Henry Ludwell 1049
Moore, Marianne 296, 1358
Moorhead State University (Minnesota) 843
Mooris, Don H. 1567
Mora, Jo 55
Moravian Church 1213, 1415
Moravian College and Theological Seminary (Pennsylvania) 1415
More, Thomas 155, 225, 619, 1048, 1081, 1087
Morehead State University (Kentucky) 613
Morehouse, Albert P. 913
Morehouse College (Georgia) 382
Morgan, Arthur E. 1239
Morgan, Julia 93, 109
Morgan, Junius Spencer 997

Morgan, Lewis Henry 1158
Morgan State University (Maryland) 685
Morley, Christopher 216, 1022, 1158, 1390, 1648
Mormonism 255, 399, 500, 546, 997, 1660, 1665, 1666
Morningside College (Iowa) 555
Morrell, Jeanette McKay 1666
Morris Brown College (Georgia) 383
Morris, Gouverneur 1049
Morris, William 341, 792
Morrison, James (U.S. Congressman) 642
Morrow County (Oregon) 1322
Morrow Cove (California) 92
Morton, David 624
Morton, Sterling 955
Mosby, Beverly Clarke 1726
Mosby, Colonel J.S. 1726
Moseley, Franklin S. 13
Mosely, Philip, E. 497
Mosher Press 344, 652, 653, 1067, 1139
Moss, John E. (U.S. Congressman) 109
Mother Goose 778, 1715
Mother Lode Region (California) 128
motion picture technology 90
motor vehicles 820
Mount Aloysius Junior College (Pennsylvania) 1416
Mount Angel Seminary (Oregon) 1331
Mount Holyoke College (Massachusetts) 744
Mount Marty College (South Dakota) 1515
Mount Mary College (Wisconsin) 1780
Mount Mercy College (Iowa) 556
Mount Saint Clare College (Iowa) 557
Mount Saint Mary College (New York) 1094
Mount St. Mary's College (California) 161
Mount St. Mary's College (Maryland) 686
Mount Senario College (Wisconsin) 1781
Mount Sinai School of Medicine - CUNY (New York) 1095
Mount Union College (Ohio) 1270
Mount Vernon College (District of Columbia) 298
Mount Vernon Nazarene College (Ohio) 1271
mountain crafts 1532
mountaineering 252, 1677, 1732
movie stars 537
movie stills 975
Mt. San Antonio Community College (California) 162
Muehlstein, Herman 1287
Muggeridge, Malcolm 500
Muhlenberg College (Pennsylvania) 1417
Muir, John 227
Mullan, John 296
Muller, Herman J. 519
Mumford, Lewis 1449
Mundelein College (Illinois) 467
Mundt, Karl E. (U.S. Congressman and Senator) 1512
Munn, Charles Allen 1059
Munn, Edwin George 1158
Murdoch, Iris 564
Murdock, Kermit 892
Murdock, Marcellus 596
Murga, Monsignor Vicente 1468
Murphy, Father Francis X. 1049
Murray State College (Oklahoma) 1304
Murray State University (Kentucky) 614
Murrow, Edward R. 215, 762
Muse, Bishop Daniel T. 1313
museum studies 149
music 60, 234, 290, 394, 450, 497, 498, 583, 605, 711, 1084, 1429
music, Afro-American 358
music, American Indian 1013
music, chamber 497
music, church 617
music criticism 1443
music, Dutch 497
music education 1082, 1249
Music Educators National Conference 696
music, ensemble 497
music, folk 1532
music, French 497, 1645
music genres, American 1320
music, holograph 1371
music, Jewish 1258
music, liturgical 224
music manuscripts 284, 1371
music, medieval 1143
music, popular 375, 583, 711, 714
music publishers' catalogs 497
music, ragtime 922
music, religious 636
music, Renaissance 1143
music, rock 711, 1475
music, sacred 1078, 1124
music scores 57, 219, 256, 257, 280, 340, 341, 414, 455, 480, 488, 497, 519, 678, 715, 762, 915, 932, 1008, 1022, 1049, 1075, 1241, 1347, 1376, 1661, 1715
music scores, motion picture 497
music, Slovenian 1792
music therapy 1411
Musica Transalpina 1245
musical instruments 1022, 1075, 1143
musicology 215, 252, 622
Muskingham College (Ohio) 1273
Muskingum Area Technical College (Ohio) 1272
Muskogee Company (Texas) 1615
Muskogee Phoenix 1305
Musmanno, Justice Michael A. 1376
Mussolini, Benito 1087
Mutiny on the Bounty 173
mycology 99
Myer, Joseph C. 1123
Myers, Isabel Briggs 341
Myers, Moses 1703
Mylai Incident 596

mystery fiction 166, 447, 1139, 1315, 1704
mysticism 1390
mythology 688
Nabokov, Vladimir 1320
Nacogdoches Grocery Company (Texas) 1623
Nadel, Norman 583
Nampa (Idaho) 412
The Naropa Institute (Colorado) 247
Nash, John Henry 93, 225, 1020
Nash, Ogden 1648
Nassau Community College (New York) 1096
Nassau County (New York) 1067
Natchez Episcopal Library 641
Nathan, Robert 284
National Aeronautics and Space Administration 926
National Association for the Advancement of Colored People 1293
National Association of College Wind and Percussion Instructors 696
National Association of Lesbian and Gay Alcoholism Professionals 1000
National Book Award winners 1421
National Catholic Rural Life Conference 1778
National Christian Association 500
National Civic League 253
National Coalition of American Nuns 1778
National College of Chiropractic (Illinois) 468
National College of Education (Illinois) 469
National College (South Dakota) 1516
National Council for Social Studies 1151
National Council of Churches 1268, 1714
National Immigration Archives 1445
National Indian Education Association 825
National Kindergarten Association 1151
National Normal University (Ohio) 1294
National Organization for Women 750
National Park Service 1489
National Resources Council of Onondaga County (New York) 1144
National Socialism 764, 1791
National Stereoscopic Association 1379
National Track and Field Hall of Fame Historical Research Library 504
National University (California) 163
National Women's Party 1637
Native American Resource Center 1206
Natrona County (Wyoming) 1800
natural history 144, 252, 279, 341, 629, 651, 654, 681, 1504, 1791
natural resources 148, 245, 1796
natural science 623, 626, 1101, 1158, 1444, 1459
Naturalis Historia 1698
nautical art 656
nautical education 1149
nautical science 656
Navajo Community College (Arizona) 54
naval architecture 1149, 1163
naval history 164, 1080, 1156, 1163
naval history, English 214
Naval Postgraduate School (California) 164
naval science 694
navigation 284, 742
Nayler, James 1390
Nazarene Bible College (Colorado) 248
Nazarene Theological Seminary (Missouri) 911
Nazareth College of Rochester (New York) 1097
Nazi Germany 547, 737, 816
Nazi propaganda 1026
Nazi War Crimes Trials 1301, 1376
Nazism 538, 1067
Near East 501
Near East (archaeology) 172
Near Eastern languages 473
Near Eastern manuscripts 284, 1049
Near Eastern studies 1355
Nearing, Scott 1290
Nebraska 944, 949, 956
Nebraska, southeastern 953
Nebraska Synod of the Lutheran Church in America 951
Nebraska Wesleyan University 952
Needham, James J. 1123
Negri, Pola 1638
Negro Digest 358
Nehrling, Henry 331
Neighborhood Union (Atlanta, Georgia) 358
Neighbors, Darrell 106
Nellis Air Force Base 960
Nelson & Sons, Thomas 1445
Nelson, Father Thomas J. 902
Nelson, Knox 72
Nemerov, Howard 1668
Neo-Pagan religious groups 142
Neoplatonists 924
Neslon, Dr. Peter Christopher 1619
Ness, Henry 1731
Nestorians 111
Netherland Reformed Church 542
Netherlands 369
Neumann, Albert 1793
Nevada 958, 961
Nevada, southern 960
Nevada Test Site 960
Nevins, Allan 1049
New Age religious groups 142
New American Practical Navigator 1156
New Brunswick Theological Seminary (New Jersey) 993
New Century Publishers 1276
New Colophon 1123
New Deal Era 1767
New England 974
New England College (New Hamphsire) 968
New England College of Optometry (Massachusetts)

745
New England Conservatory (Massachusetts) 746
New England Drug Information Service 741
New France 737
New Hampshire 967, 968, 972, 975
New Hampshire Academy of Science 975
New Hampshire College 969
New Hampshire Technical Institute 970
New Jersey 423, 978, 983, 985, 987, 988, 990, 991, 1000, 1004, 1008
New Jersey Institute of Technology 994
New Jersey Pine Barrens 1003
New London County (Connecticut) 261
New Mexico 1010, 1011, 1014, 1017, 1020
New Mexico Highlands University 1014
New Mexico Institute of Mining and Technology 1015
New Mexico Military Institute 1016
New Mexico State University 1017
New Orleans Academy of Science 646
New Orleans Baptist Theological Seminary (Louisiana) 636
New Orleans (Louisiana) 32, 629, 646, 647, 649
New Realism Movement 1067
New River Community College (Virginia) 1700
New School for Social Research (New York) 1098
New Testament 730
New Testament Abstracts 768
New York American Canadian Geneological Society 1042
New York Chiropractic College 1099
New York City Technical College - CUNY 1100
New York Forest Owners Association, Inc. 1144
New York Institute of Technology 1101
New York Law School 1102
New York Medical College 1103
New York, northern 1142
New York Pro Musica Antiqua 1143
New York School of Interior Design 1104
New York (State) 1056, 1139
New York State Forestry and Park Association 1144
New York Theological Seminary 1105
New York University 1106
New York, western 1038
New Zealand 399
Newberry College (South Carolina) 1501
Newburgh (New York) 1094
Newman, Cardinal John Henry 161, 187, 296, 723, 751
newspapers 1791, 1796
newspapers, Alabama 32
newspapers, alternative 253
newspapers, American colonial 1114
newspapers, American Indian 1792
newspapers, Catholic 296
newspapers, early American 737
newspapers, early California 215
newspapers, early Colorado 252
newspapers, Florida 341
newspapers, Geneva (New York) 1066
newspapers, Jewish 489
newspapers, New Hampshire 975
newspapers, nineteenth-century 1021, 1181
newspapers, U.S. 924
newspapers, Utah 1664
Newton County Lumber Company (Texas) 1623
Newton, Sir Isaac 709, 1489
Ney, Peter Stuart 1180
Neyland, William M. 1577
Niagara frontier, history of the (New York) 1038
Niagara Movement 1293
Nicaragua and Isthmian Canal Commission 596
Nicholls State University (Louisiana) 637
Nichols, Alice C. 583
Nichols, William F. 5
Nicholson, Roy S. 1486
Nickell, Otto L. 613
Nicklès, François Joseph Jérôme 1445
Nicols College (Massachusetts) 747
Nicolson, Harold 519
Nields, John W. 1127
Nietz, Dr. John A. 1450
"The Night Before Christmas" 319, 1060, 1217
Nightingale, Charles Lowell 737
Nightingale, Florence 33, 681, 1151
Niles, John Jacob 605
Nin, Anais 215, 1320
Nixon, E.D. 2
Nixon, Richard 233
Nodel, Julius J. 400
Nolan, J. Bennett 1351
Nolan, T.C. 381
Nonesuch Press 714, 1067
No-Popery literature 187
Nordic epics 820
Norell, Alney 614
Norfolk and Western Railway 1719
Norfolk State University (Virginia) 1701
Norris, Frank 319
North Adams State College (Massachusetts) 748
North, Alex 215
North American Baptist Conference (German) 1044
North American Baptist Fellowship 1044
North American Baptist Seminary (South Dakota) 1517
North American Indians 174, 505, 629, 981, 1063, 1214, 1562, 1781
North Carolina 1170, 1177, 1178, 1179, 1182, 1188, 1189, 1190, 1200, 1208, 1210, 1217, 1220, 1224, 1708
North Carolina Agricultural and Technical State University 1202
North Carolina Central University 1203
North Carolina, northwest 1226
North Carolina State University 1204

North Carolina Wesleyan College 1205
North Central Bible College (Minnesota) 844
North Central College (Illinois) 470
North Central Technical College (Ohio) 1274
North Country Community College (New York) 1107
North Country (New York) 1042, 1072, 1125, 1141
North Dakota 1230, 1231, 1232, 1234, 1237
North Dakota State College of Science 1233
North Dakota State University 1234
North Dakota State University - Bottineau Branch and Institute of Forestry 1235
North Georgia College 384
North Idaho College 411
North Park College and Theological Seminary 471
North Shore (Long Island, New York) 1080
Northcote, James Spencer 714
Northeast Louisiana University 638
Northeast Missouri State University 912
Northeastern Bible College (New Jersey) 995
Northeastern Christian Junior College (Pennsylvania) 1418
Northeastern Illinois University 472
Northeastern Junior College (Colorado) 249
Northeastern Ohio Universities College of Medicine 1275
Northeastern State University (Oklahoma) 1305
Northeastern University (Massachusetts) 749
Northern Arizona University 55
Northern Baptist Theological Seminary (Illinois) 473
Northern Illinois University 474
Northern Kentucky University 615
Northern Michigan University 806
Northern Montana College 939
Northern Nevada Community College 958
Northern State College (South Dakota) 1518
Northern Virginia Community College 1702
Northland College (Wisconsin) 1782
Northrop, John K. 166
Northrop University (California) 165
Northwest Alabama State Junior College 21
Northwest Christian College (Oregon) 1332
Northwest College of the Assemblies of God (Washington) 1731
Northwest Community College (Alaska) 42
Northwest Minnesota Historical Center 843
Northwest Missouri State University 913
Northwest Nazarene College (Idaho) 412
Northwest Territory 452, 539, 781, 1267
Northwestern Americana 1326
Northwestern College (Iowa) 558
Northwestern College (Minnesota) 845
Northwestern College of Chiropractic (Minnesota) 846
Northwestern Michigan College 807
Northwestern State University of Louisiana 639
Northwestern University (Illinois) 475
Northwood Institute (Michigan) 808
Norton, C.E. 737
Norwalk Community College (Connecticut) 268
Norwegian-Americana 1351
Norwegian-Americans 553, 850, 1510
Norwich University (Vermont) 1677
Norwood, Warren 1645
Notre Dame College (New Hampshire) 971
Nouy, Pierre Lecomte du 57
Nova University (Florida) 324
Novak, Michael 760
Noyes, Alfred 1158
nuclear energy 217
nuclear reactor accidents 1373
Nuclear Regulatory Commission 446, 863
Nueces County (Texas) 1577
nullification controversy 1489
numismatics 296, 928, 997
nursing 50, 132, 218, 254, 263, 267, 278, 323, 361, 380, 434, 458, 522, 525, 618, 626, 643, 655, 662, 677, 714, 832, 857, 910, 974, 1329, 1353, 1369, 1370, 1408, 1411, 1432, 1455, 1462, 1484, 1550, 1564, 1568, 1583, 1644, 1653, 1667, 1687, 1768, 1777, 1779, 1803
nursing history 1151, 1637
nursing novels 970
nursing, practical 828
nursing, public health 755
nutrition 151, 1375
Nutting, Adelaide 1151
Nutting, John Danforth 500
Nye Country (Nevada) 960
Oakland City College (Indiana) 524
Oakland University (Michigan) 809
Oakwood College (Alabama) 22
Oates, Joyce Carol 1158
Obenchain, Lida Calvert 624
Oberlin College (Ohio) 1276
Oblate School of Theology (Texas) 1601
O'Brien, Justin 1049
obstetrics 218, 1447
Occidental College (California) 166
occult 284, 1421, 1475
Occult religious groups 142
occult sciences 497
Oceania (Pacific) 1805
oceanography 217, 324, 1628, 1730
O'Connell, J. Harlin 997
O'Connor, Flannery 371, 394, 1320
O'Connor, Jeremiah J. 296
O'Connor, Kathryn Stoner 1651
Oddfellows, Independent Order of 695
O'Dwyer, Paul 1123
O'Ferrall, Charles T. 1694
Office of Indian Affairs 1305
Office of Military Government for Germany, U.S. Zone 296
Official Record of the Union and Confederate Navies 1862-1865 897, 913

Oglala Lakota College (South Dakota) 1519
Oglala Sioux Indians 1519
Oglethorpe, James Edward 385
Oglethorpe University (Georgia) 385
O'Hara, Frank 279
O'Hara, John 1421
O'Hegarty, P.S. 593
Ohio 1273, 1280, 1290, 1753
Ohio Company of Associates 1267
Ohio Dominican College 1277
Ohio River Valley 494
Ohio State University 1278
Ohio State University - Mansfield Campus 1279
Ohio University 1280
Ohio Valley 1450, 1457
Ohio Wesleyan University 1281
Ohlone College (California) 167
Ohlone Indians 167
Oil, Chemical and Atomic Workers (Ohio) 1280
Ojibwa Indians 825
Okaloosa-Walton Junior College (Florida) 325
Oklahoma 1300, 1301, 1304, 1308, 1315
Oklahoma Baptist University 1306
Oklahoma Christian College 1307
Oklahoma City (Oklahoma) 1308
Oklahoma City University (Oklahoma) 1308
Oklahoma College of Osteopathic Medicine and Surgery 1309
Oklahoma Land Runs 1318
Oklahoma, northeastern 1305
Oklahoma Panhandle State University 1310
Oklahoma State Federation of Labor 1318
Oklahoma State University 1311
Oklahoma State University Technical Institute 1312
Old Catholic Movement 187
Old Dominion University (Virginia) 1703
"Old Fashioned Revival Hour" 138
"Old Time Gospel Hour" 1695
Oliphant, Patrick 1444
Oliphant Press 705
olives 103
Olivet College (Michigan) 810
Olivet Nazarene College (Illinois) 476
Olsen, Ruth C. 1662
Olson, Charles 279
Olson, Sigurd 1782
Olympic College (Washington) 1732
Olympic Games 166, 504
Omaha Federal Writers Project 956
O'Malley, Cormac 1123
Ondreyco, Michael A. 1276
Onegin, Sigrid 1712
Oneida Community 1067, 1150
O'Neill, Carlotta 1080
O'Neill, Eugene 261, 284, 705, 1080, 1269, 1475, 1638, 1791
O'Neill, Jr., Thomas P. (U.S. Congressman, Speaker of the House) 714
O'Neill, Lottie Holman 500
Open Church Foundation 734
Open Court Press 487
Open Theater 1262
Opendack, Byron 1726
opera 593, 915, 1130, 1645, 1663
Opera Omnia 209, 891
opera productions 1371
opera scores 497, 715
operations research 1112
operettas 1414
ophthalmology 443, 1653
Oporto (Portugal) 1320
Oppenheimer, Joel 279
Optic, Oliver 718
Opticks 1245
optics 90, 1158
optometry 205, 443, 745, 1145, 1335, 1419, 1551
oral history, Afro-American 1445
oral history, American Indian 1318
oral history, Arkansas 62
oral history, California 78, 100, 133, 167, 211, 215
oral history, Colorado 236
oral history, Florida 325
oral history, Georgia 375
oral history, Idaho 413
oral history, Kentucky 597, 605
oral history, Mennonite 575
oral history, Michigan 1782
oral history, Mississippi 872
oral history, New York 1140
oral history, Oklahoma 1314
oral history, Pennsylvania 1421, 1450
oral history, Puerto Rico 1469, 1472, 1473
oral history, South Dakota 1512
oral history, Tennessee 1540
oral history, Texas 1632
oral history, U.S. 1049
oral history, Wisconsin 1782
Oral Roberts University (Oklahoma) 1313
Orange Coast College (California) 168
Orange County (California) 104
Orange County Community College (New York) 1108
Orange County (New York) 1108
oratory 583
orchestra music 455, 715, 1075
orchestral methods 498
orchidology 190, 829
Order of St. Augustine 1456
Order of St. Vincent de Paul 1410
Oregon 1325, 1328, 1339, 1342
Oregon, central 1323
Oregon Health Sciences University 1333
Oregon Shakespearian Festival Association 1339
Oregon State University 1334
Oregon Trail 1800

organ building and design 497, 955
Orient, Westerners in the 1000
Oriental art 103, 583, 595, 1342, 1666
Oriental languages 260
Oriental studies 57, 183
origami 279
Origin of the Species 1403
Oriole Press 341, 1278
Orlando College (Florida) 326
Orleans County (New York) 1133
Orlovsky, Peter 1049
Ormond, Dr. Alexander 1387
ornamental horticulture 287
ornithology 144, 275, 279, 284, 331, 342, 544, 549, 593, 629, 792, 802, 1217, 1777
O'Rourke, Martha L. 28
Orozco, José Clemente 964
Orthodox Christianity 1126
orthopedic surgery 594
orthopedics 432, 468, 887
Orwell, George 1269
Osler, William 33
osseous material 905
osteopathic medicine 125, 566, 666, 903, 1280, 1309, 1426, 1632, 1761
O'Sullivan, Timothy 697
Oswego County (New York) 1140
Otero, Miguel 1020
Otis Art Institute of Parsons School of Design (California) 169
Otis Crim Funeral Home (Texas) 1623
Otis, Elizabeth 503
otolaryngology 1572
Ottawa University (Kansas) 588
Otterbein College (Ohio) 1282
Ottoman Empire 296
Ouachita Baptist University (Arkansas) 65
Our Lady of Holy Cross College (Louisiana) 640
Our Lady of the Lake University (Texas) 1602
Our Mutual Friend 590
Oursler, Fulton 296
Outdoor Advertising Association of America 985
outdoor recreation 1732, 1744
outlaws, western 1630
Overbrook Press 1067
Ovid 1681
Owen, Robert 1159
Owen, Robert Dale 59
Owen, Sir Richard 1445
Owsley, Alvin M. 1645
Oxford College of Emory University (Georgia) 386
Oxford (England) 118
Oxford Movement 161, 187, 1124
Oxford University (England) 118
oxygen 792, 1373
Oyez Press 279
Ozark Mountains 58

Paccioli, Lucca 695
Pace University (New York) 1109
Pacific Christian College (California) 170
Pacific coast, U.S. 181
Pacific linguistics 406
Pacific Lutheran University (Washington) 1733
Pacific Northwest 148, 284, 410, 411, 413, 1326, 1328, 1332, 1342, 1343, 1726, 1729, 1730, 1733, 1735, 1741, 1743, 1744, 1745
Pacific Northwest Railroad 1298
Pacific Oaks College and Children's School (California) 171
Pacific Ocean 190
Pacific Ocean, islands of the 399, 401, 402, 403, 1805
Pacific Ocean, northern 118
Pacific Relations Institute 1049
Pacific School of Religion (California) 172
Pacific Union College (California) 173
Pacific University (Oregon) 1335
Pacific voyages 217
pacifism 1444
Paddleford, Clementine 583
Paddock, Munson 453
Paducah Community College (Kentucky) 616
Paducah (Kentucky) 616
Page County (Virginia) 1694
Paier College of Art, Inc. (Connecticut) 269
Paine, Albert Bigelow 589
Paine College (Georgia) 387
Paiute Indians 1663
Palace of Fine Arts (San Francisco) 191
paleography 284
paleontology 190, 1504
paleontology, invertebrate 215
Palisades Nuclear Power Plant (Michigan) 791
Palm Beach Atlantic College (Florida) 327
Palm Beach Junior College (Florida) 328
Palmer, Betsy 500
Palmer, B.J. 1099
Palmer College of Chriropractic (Iowa) 559
Palomar College (California) 174
pamphlets, Catholic Apostolic Church 1313
pamphlets, Communist Party 279, 1276
pamphlets, early U.S. 955
pamphlets, eighteenth-century English 593
pamphlets, English Civil War 1039
pamphlets, French political 279, 1791
pamphlets, French revolutionary 593, 1449
pamphlets, German 596
pamphlets, poetical eighteenth-century British 1288
pamphlets, political 214
pamphlets, Populist Period 596
pamphlets, Prohibition Period 596
pamphlets, Quaker 1390
pamphlets, religious 1059
pamphlets, Socialist 279

pamphlets, Southern U.S. 1217
pamphlets, World War I 955
pamphlets, World War I propaganda 1260
Pan American University (Texas) 1603
Panama Canal 296, 519, 596
Pantheon Books 1049
Panton, Leslie & Company 346
papal bulls 1124
paper industry 1775
papermaking 1144, 1423, 1686, 1775
papyri 172, 284, 816, 997, 1049
Paracelsus, Theophrastus 1389
parachutes 251
Paraguay 216
paralegal studies 857, 1174, 1727
Paramount Pictures 215
parapsychology 149, 1262
Paris Junior College (Texas) 1604
Parish, James Robert 1262
Parish, Maxfield 1243
Parish, Peggy 1493
Park, Benjamin 1049
Park Hill (Oklahoma) 1305
Parke-Benet art catalogs 1752
Parker Society 891
parks administration 60
Parks, Gordon 583
Parley, Peter 705
Parrish, Morris L. 997
Parry, Roland 1666
Parsifal epic 1059
Parsons, John T. 1719
Parsons School of Design (New York) 1110
Parsons, William Barclay 1049
Partch, Harry 497
Partridge, Alden 1677
Partridge, Eric 975
Pasadena City College (California) 175
Pasadena Playhouse 106
Pascal, Blaise 1067
Paskow, David G. 1445
Passaic (New Jersey) 1008
Passman, Otto E. 638
Pasteur, Louis 33
pastoral counseling 364, 1378
pastoral psychology 734
pastoral theology 1400
Pastore, John O. (U.S. Senator) 1478
pataphysics 1320
Patchen, Kenneth 220
patents 372
Paterson (New Jersey) 1008
Paterson, William 1008
pathology 594
Patrick Henry State Junior College (Alabama) 23
Patrick, Walton 5
patristics 364
Pattee, Fred Lewis 1421
Patten College (California) 176
Patterson, Captain Joseph Medill 453
Patterson, George Washington 1158
Patterson, Robert 997
Paul, Arthur 956
Paul D. Camp Community College (Virginia) 1704
Paul Quinn College (Texas) 1605
Paul, Robert L. 687
Paul Smith's College (New York) 1111
Pauling, Linus 1334
Pavlova, Anna 1450
Peabody, George Foster 687, 1692
Peabody Institute Awards 394
Peabody Institute of The Johns Hopkins University (Maryland) 687
Peabody Sisters 1239
Peabody, Stuyvesant 431
Peace, John 1651
peace studies 207, 295, 331, 520, 555, 569, 580, 704, 791, 1065, 1189, 1292, 1326, 1362, 1444, 1679, 1766
Pearlman, Myer 844
Pease, Arthur Stanley 737
pedagogy 1414
pedagogy, Jewish 738
Pedrick, Samuel 1783
Pee Dee region (South Carolina) 1496
Pell, John H.G. 1080
Pella (Iowa) 542
Pelton, Jeanette Siron 504
Pembroke State University (North Carolina) 1206
Pendleton Farmer's Society 1489
Penn, William 1059, 1390
Pennington, Isaac 1390
Pennington, Walter 589
Pennsylvania 423, 1382, 1393, 1397, 1414, 1434, 1438
Pennsylvania, central 1440
Pennsylvania Coal and Iron Police 1376
Pennsylvania College of Optometry 1419
Pennsylvania College of Podiatric Medicine 1420
Pennsylvania Dutch 1402
Pennsylvania Folklife Center 1382
Pennsylvania, northeastern 1396, 1399
Pennsylvania, northwestern 1412
Pennsylvania, southwestern 1458
Pennsylvania State University 1421
Pennsylvania State University - Capitol Campus 1422
Pennsylvania State University, Erie 1423
Pennsylvania State University, M.S. Hershey Medical Center 1424
Pennsylvania, western 1450, 1457
Pennsylvania-Dutch 1453
Pennsylvania-German materials 1417
Peno, Raul de la 937
Penrose, Spencer 236
Pentecostal Movement 844, 882, 1454, 1619, 1621,

1731
Pentecostal-Charismatic Movement 1313
Peoria Historical Society Library 423
Peoria (Illinois) 423
Pepper, Claude (U.S. Senator) 319
Pepperdine University (California) 177
Pepys, Samuel 461
Pequot Library 284
Percival, James Gates 284
percussion instruments 48
Percy, Thomas 319
Percy, Walker 649, 1398
performance, history of 737
performing arts 210, 212, 297, 831, 1320, 1429, 1431, 1690, 1804
periodicals, early American 692
periodicals, French nineteenth-century satirical 279
periodicals, nineteenth-century 4
periodicals, nineteenth-century women's rights 418
periodontal materials 762
Perishable Press 1794
Perkins, Frances 1049
Perkins, George Walbridge 1049
Permian Basin 1654
Peron, Juan 1638
Perry, A.T. 1726
Perry, George Sessions 1648
personal counseling 906
Peru 519
Peru State College (Nebraska) 953
Peter Pauper Press 1143
Peterich, Gerda 975
Peterkin, Julia 1489
Peters, Eugene H. 1260
Peters, Paul O. 1252
Peters, Roberta 1071
Peterson, Donald G. 450
petroleum industry 1318, 1623, 1630, 1635, 1649, 1804
Pettit, James M. 1032
pharmaceutical literature 218, 741, 914, 1427
pharmacology 1123
pharmacopoeias 218
pharmacy 380, 525, 545, 741
pharmacy, history of 1024, 1427
phenomenology 1376
Phi Delta Kappa 420
Philadelphia 1435
Philadelphia College of Osteopathic Medicine 1426
Philadelphia College of Pharmacy and Science 1427
Philadelphia College of Textiles and Science (Pennsylvania) 1428
Philadelphia College of the Bible (Pennsylvania) 1425
Philadelphia Colleges of the Arts (Pennsylvania) 1429
Philadelphia (Pennsylvania) 1391, 1445
Philander Smith College (Arkansas) 66
philanthropy 755, 1778
philately 1649
Philippines 1086
Philips, George Morris 1459
Philips, William Pyle 1390
Phillips County Community College (Arkansas) 67
Phillips, David Graham 514
Phillips, Helen C. 982
Phillips, H.H. 1314
Phillips, T.W. 1314
Phillips University (Oklahoma) 1314
Phillips, Wendell 737
Phillpotts, Eden 216, 1405
philology 629
philosophy 88, 138, 155, 186, 190, 273, 293, 332, 418, 484, 487, 531, 664, 690, 737, 881, 1161, 1277, 1283, 1331, 1435, 1482, 1584, 1646, 1706, 1729, 1778, 1785
philosophy, medieval 494
philosophy, Renaissance 494
Phoenix Theatre 284
photogrammetry 1144
photographers 697
photographic archives 697
photography 57, 80, 84, 269, 292, 629, 657, 662, 950, 1049, 1117, 1342, 1421
photojournalism 1445
photomechanical processes 1049
physical education 1219, 1441, 1459
physical sciences 211, 1719
physical therapy 1198
physics 190, 207, 525, 536, 1338
physiology 218
piano music 497
piano rolls 497
Picasso, Pablo 1639
Pickering, Timothy 596
Pickett, Bishop J. Waskom 598
Pickford, Grace E. 1260
pidgin English 406
Piedmont College (Georgia) 388
Pierce College (Washington) 1734
Pierce, C.S. 737
Pierce, Franklin 652, 965
Pierson, John Shaw 997
pietistic studies 471
Pilgrim Holiness Church 1448
Pilgrim's Progress 500, 826, 891
Pine Barrens of New Jersey 1003
Pine Ridge Indian Reservation 1519
Pinero, Sir Arthur Wing 1158
Pinter, Harold 519
pioneer life 835, 935, 1722
Pioneer Valley (Massachusetts) 735
Pissarro, Lucien 792
Pitcairn Island 173
Pitlik, Dr. Samuel 1386
Pittsburgh Comix Club 1450
Pittsburgh (Pennsylvania) 1450

Pittsburgh Playhouse 1450
Pittsburgh State University (Kansas) 589
Pittsburgh Theological Seminary (Pennsylvania) 1430
Pitzer College (California) 178
planetary science 215
plant pathology 99, 1144
plant rusts 579
plantations 639
plantations, Georgia rice 984
plantations, Louisiana 637
Plante, David 1320
Plantin, Christopher 578
Plath, Sylvia 519, 757, 766
Plato 924
playbills 341, 394, 497, 583, 714, 997, 1049, 1067, 1114, 1158, 1211, 1320, 1450, 1729
playing cards 284
plays (acting editions) 344, 705, 924, 1049, 1450, 1637
plays, American 453, 978, 1475
plays, eighteenth-century 1039
plays, eighteenth-century French 1449
plays, English 519
plays, Latin American 1640
plays, nineteenth-century French 1449
plays, Regency Period 1039
plays, Restoration Period 1039
plays, Spanish 820
plays, twentieth-century 438
Plimpton, Frances Taylor Pearsons 766
Plimpton, George Arthur 766, 1049
Plumpp, Sterling 876
Plutzik, Hyam 1158
Plymouth (New Hampshire) 972
Plymouth State College (New Hampshire) 972
Poag, Thomas E. 1554
Pochmann, Virginia Ruth Fouts 1623
podiatry 432, 566, 1420
Poe, Edgar Allan 519, 564, 688, 1018, 1049, 1475, 1716
Poe Society 695
poetics 247
poetry 106, 217, 247, 284, 296, 319, 331, 931, 997, 1288, 1450
poetry, American 341, 386, 503, 732, 766, 964, 992, 1039, 1225, 1243, 1475, 1767
poetry, Asian-American 1475
poetry, avant-garde 212, 1119, 1638
poetry, Black 1293
poetry, contemporary 214, 475, 494, 1364
poetry, contemporary American 593, 1630
poetry, English 564, 593, 732, 766, 1053, 1243, 1320
poetry, Irish 714
Poetry magazine 494
poetry, modern British 341
poetry, San Francisco Bay Area 105
poetry, Yiddish 1635
poets, American women 1417
poets, San Francisco Bay Area 193
poets, women 1119
Pogo comics 1489
Point Loma Nazarene College (California) 179
Point Park College (Pennsylvania) 1431
poker 629
Poland 260, 296, 1355, 1639
polar exploration 45, 964
polar regions 41, 44, 45
police administration 475
Polish studies 1354
Polish-Americans 260, 799, 814, 1065, 1160, 1354
political campaigns 1301
political cartoons, nineteenth-century 737
political development, U.S. 573
political exiles 226
political exiles, German 1129
political history, American 1158
political history, Texas 1647
political issues 802
political movements, radical 816
political parties 764
political philosophy 55, 1639
political research 1776
political science 2, 120, 402, 643, 906, 923, 1080, 1278, 1703, 1754
political studies 178
political studies, Georgia 394
political theory 1158
political tracts, English 924
politicians 716
politics 927, 1252, 1567
politics, Alabama 5
politics, Southern U.S. 1566
politics, Texas 1607, 1635
Poliziano, Angelo 118
Polk Community College (Florida) 329
Polk County (North Carolina) 1190
Polk County (Tennessee) 1529
Polk, James K. 1562
Pollard, Harry 596
Pollard, John Garland 1686
Polledo, Manuel Rionda y 341
Pollock, Anna Marble 284
polymer chemistry 1144
polymer research 1112
Polynesia 399, 406
Polytechnic University (New York) 1112
Pomona College (California) 180
Ponce Medical School (Puerto Rico) 1471
Pontifical College Josephinum (Ohio) 1283
Pony Express 931
Pope, Alexander 497
Popper, Karl 1450
pop-up books 80
porcelain 1666
Porcupine, Peter 1059

Porgy and Bess 589
Portales (New Mexico) 1011
Porter, Bern 653
Porter, Cole 284
Porter, Katherine Anne 394, 696, 1398
Porter, Linda 284
Porterville College (California) 181
Portland Community College (Oregon) 1336
Portland School of Art (Maine) 657
Portland State University (Oregon) 1337
portraits, eighteenth-century 330
Portsmouth Naval Shipyard 975
Posey, Walter 350
Post College (Connecticut) 270
postage stamps, U.S. 103
postcards 1475
postcards, Russian 103
posters, American 296, 1117
posters, European 1117
Post-Revolutionary Period, U.S. 319
Potsdam Normal School 1142
Poultney (Vermont) 1672
poultry 583, 1372
Pound, Ezra 216, 284, 413, 519, 705, 1062, 1290, 1320, 1475, 1482, 1648
poverty studies 1167
Powell, Anthony 1320
Powell, Dick 215
Powell, Lawrence Clark 196
Powys, John Cowper 279, 1043, 1648
Powys, Llewelyn 279, 1043, 1648
Powys, Theodore Francis 279, 1043, 1648
Pradeau, Alberto 48
pragmatism 1635
Prairie View A & M University (Texas) 1606
Prang, Louis 1445
Prange, Gordon W. 696
Pratt Institute (New York) 1113
Pratt, Theodore 312
prayer books 1155
preaching 734, 1566
preclinical sciences 1424
Pregel, Sophie 497
Presbyterian College (South Carolina) 1502
Presbyterian School of Christian Education (Virginia) 1705
Presbyterianism 75, 194, 364, 462, 514, 611, 873, 918, 996, 1207, 1387, 1430, 1458, 1461, 1502, 1545, 1549, 1571, 1746
presidential campaign artifacts 1280
presidential campaigns 166, 781
presidential papers, U.S. 1061
Presidents, books owned by U.S. 737
Presidents, U.S. 457, 997
Presley, Elvis 191
Press, Frank 742
Preston, Harry B. 967
Preston, John A. 746
Price, Bolton C. 866
Priestley, J.B. 1648
Priestley, Joseph 652, 1373
primate studies 1791
primers 93
primers, New England 737
Princeton Borough Agricultural Association (New Jersey) 997
Princeton Theological Seminary (New Jersey) 996
Princeton University Library Chronicle 997
Princeton University (New Jersey) 997
Principia College (Illinois) 477
printing 80, 107, 1686
printing, California 104
printing, history of 255, 519, 583, 596, 622, 681, 757, 792, 802, 928, 964, 975, 1113, 1217, 1245, 1262, 1338, 1475, 1565, 1627, 1660, 1718
printmaking 1429
prisons, Arkansas 70
Pritchett, Reuel B. 1683
private presses 105, 149, 169, 225, 394, 445, 487, 564, 583, 769, 975, 1067, 1139, 1158, 1217, 1219, 1245, 1269, 1444, 1450, 1745, 1792
profit sharing 402
Progressive Party 737
proletarian literature 1320
promptbooks 737, 1363
propaganda warfare 296
propaganda, World War II 477
Prophet, Nancy Elizabeth 1479
proposal writing 1778
Prose magazine 1262
Protestant Episcopal Theological Seminary in Virginia 1706
Protestant Radio and Television Center 1714
Protestant Restoration Movement 9, 177, 313, 789, 1247, 1324, 1418, 1535, 1536
Protestantism 558, 1276
protests against war 1444
Proust, Marcel 497
proverbs 1217
Providence College (Rhode Island) 1478
psalmody 397, 746, 1684
psalters 636
psychological tests 95
psychology 88, 95, 96, 97, 98, 138, 163, 210, 247, 324, 444, 525, 925, 1067, 1287
psychology, clinical 1335
psychotherapy 95, 1585
public administration 190, 324, 797
public affairs 215, 1129
public communications 324
public health 1573, 1779
public policy 997
public service 765
publishing 1061

publishing, magazine 593
Puerto Rican studies 1031, 1069
Puerto Rico 279, 1470, 1471, 1472, 1473, 1474
Pulaski County (Arkansas) Medical Society 73
Pulaski County (Arkansas) Women's Auxiliary 73
Pulitzer, Joseph 1049
Pulitzer Prize winners 1421
Pulliam, Eugene Collins 573
Punch 423
Punch and Judy 93
Pupin, M.I. 1049
puppetry 93
Purdue University Calumet (Indiana) 526
Purdue University (Indiana) 525
Purdy, James 284, 1648
Puritan theology 996
Puritanism 891, 1000, 1445
Putney, Jay T. 1793
Pyle, Howard 1444
Pynchon, Thomas 1158
pyrotechnics 251
Quaker literature 1444
Quakerism 233, 509, 572, 580, 988, 1067, 1080, 1189, 1242, 1266, 1294, 1326, 1390, 1444
Quattlebaum, Paul 1489
Quayle, William Alfred 573
Queens College (North Carolina) 1207
Queens College of the City University of New York 1114
Queens County (New York) 1114
Quetzalcoatl 1195
Quietism 187
Quigley, Carroll 296
Quigley Publications 296
Quillian, Hubert T. 378
Quillian, James 361
Quincy College (Illinois) 478
Quinnipiac College (Connecticut) 271
Quitman, John Anthony 737
Qumran 576
Qur'anic interpretations 266
Rabassa, Gregory 764
rabbinics 670, 738, 1258
Rackham, Arthur 1049, 1296
Radcliffe College (Massachusetts) 750
Rader, Lloyd 1300
Radford University (Virginia) 1707
radiation technology 536
radical movements 1445
radical politics 106
radicalism 1729
radicalism, American 802
radicalism, French eighteenth-century 416
Radin, Paul 1067
radiology 594, 846, 887
radium 594, 1391
ragtime music 922
railroads 5, 110, 166, 242, 453, 485, 519, 564, 1049, 1208, 1298, 1301, 1567, 1600, 1615, 1719
Railsback, Tom 499
Rains, Albert 32
raisins 103
Ralston, Samuel 519
Ramapo College of New Jersey 998
Ramsey, Frank Plumpton 1450
Ramsey, J.G.M. 1562
ranch records, Texas 1635
ranching 1638
Rancho San Pedro (California) 102
Rancho Santiago College (California) 182
RAND Graduate School (California) 183
Rand, Reverend Silas 766
Randall, David 519
Randolph, Vance 69
Randolph-Macon College (Virgina) 1708
Randolph-Macon Woman's College (Virginia) 1709
Random House (publishers) 1049
range livestock industry 1627
rangelands 1627
Rank, Otto 1049
Ranke, Leopold Von 1150
Ransom, Bishop Reverdy E. 1293
Ransome, Arthur 296
rationing 103
Ravenel, Henry 1489
Rawdon, Herb 596
Rawlings, Marjorie Kinnan 341
Raworth, Tom 279
Rayburn, Sam 1577
Raymond Walters General and Technical College (Ohio) 1284
reading 1014, 1067, 1090, 1636, 1768
Reading Area Community College (Pennsylvania) 1432
Reading (Pennsylvania) 1351
Reagan, Ronald 435
real estate 314
Realey, Charles B. 593
Reconstruction Period 25, 639, 766
recorded sound 207
recreation and sports 1441
recreation management 966
recreational resources 1489
Red River Settlement 802
Red River Valley (Minnesota) 835
Reece, B. Carroll 1532
Reece, Byron Herbert 398
Reed College (Oregon) 1338
Reed, John 737
Reed, Simeon Garnet 1338
Reed, Thomas Brackett 652
Reese, William 352
reference for rare books 1217
reform movements 1792
Reformation Movement 364, 369, 492, 519, 836, 837,

840, 889, 984, 1155, 1158, 1278, 1295, 1430, 1571, 1792
Reformed Church in America 791, 822, 993
Reformed Church in the United States 896
Reformed Presbyterian Church of North America 1384
Reformed Theological Seminary (Mississippi) 873
Regency Period 1039
regimental histories, British 296, 1677
regimental histories, U.S. Civil War 255
regional planning 215
Regis College (Colorado) 250
Regis College (Massachusetts) 751
Register of 1794 1445
Reichenbach, Hans 1450
Reichswehr 764
Reiff, Henry 1125
Reigner, Charles G. 1458
Reiner, Fritz 475
Reinhardt, Max 1130
Reinhold Niebuhr Audio Tape Collection 1714
religion 88, 114, 138, 176, 273, 519, 625, 726, 778, 782, 830, 906, 1574, 1580, 1765
religion, Afro-American 358
religion, American frontier 350
religion, history of 353, 1413, 1696
religions, Asian 1132
religions, world 1132, 1566
religious controversies 341, 1444
religious education 467, 1105, 1155, 1191, 1209, 1536, 1548
religious fundamentalism 1695
religious life, seventeenth-century 497
religious movements 142
religious studies 250, 272, 422, 436, 560, 583, 707, 879, 917, 987, 1064, 1324, 1330, 1344, 1346, 1601, 1618, 1646, 1705, 1736, 1787
religious thought, French (16th-18th century) 187
religious tracts 140
religious tracts, English 924
religious tracts, Quaker 1390
reliure, art of 1648
Remington, Frederic 1125
Renaissance epics 1791
Renaissance literature 1339, 1358, 1390, 1403
Renaissance manuscripts 593, 766, 1342
Rend Lake College (Illinois) 479
Renewed Moravian Church 1415
Rensselaer Polytechnic Institute (New York) 1115
Rensselaer, Stephen Van 1115
Reorganized Church of Jesus Christ of Latter Day Saints 546
respiratory therapy 950
Responsiones Scriptae 891
restaurant management 117, 1100, 1111, 1408
Restoration drama 341
Restoration Period 1039
retailing 820, 1077, 1321
Reuel, John Ronald 1778
Revard, Carter 1320
revolution 207
revolution, roots and results of 737
Revolutionary War, American 319, 519, 681, 816, 993, 1059, 1450
Reynolds, Lloyd 1338
Reynolds, Mary Ross 802
Reynolds, Paul Revere 1049
Rheingold, Dr. Joseph C. 1767
rhetoric 253, 583
rheumatism 1573
Rheutan, Donald E. 1718
Rhoades, Rendell 629
Rhode Island 1475, 1479, 1481, 1482
Rhode Island College 1479
Rhode Island School of Design 1480
Rhodes College (Tennessee) 1549
Rhodes, Eugene Manlove 1627
Rhys, Jean 1320
Ricardo, David 497
Rice, Alice Hegan 624
Rice, Cale Young 624
Rice, Merton Stacher 573
rice plantations, Georgia 984
Rice University (Texas) 1607
Richard, Father Gabriel 813
Richards, Grant 296
Richards, Janet 296
Richards, Jonathan 1390
Richards, Ralph 596
Richards, Stanley 1445
Richardson, Dorothy 1320
Richardson, Dr. Rupert N. 1585
Richardson, H.H. 737
Richardson, Louise 319
Richardson, Roy D. 1032
Richardson, Samuel 1320
Richmond County (Georgia) 359
Richmond, Mary E. 1049
Richmond, Mary L. 956
Richmond Technical College (North Carolina) 1208
Richmond (Virginia) 1715
Riddick, Frank S. 1181
Rider College (New Jersey) 999
Ridge, John Rollin 1320
Riding, Laura 1320
Riel, Louis 802
Riemenschneider Bach Institute 1241
Rigdon, Commander William M. 373
Riggs, Lynn 1320
Riley, James Whitcomb 519
Riley, W.B. 845
Riley, William L. 596
Rilke, Rainer Maria 497, 593
Rimbaud, Jean Arthur 921

Rinehart, Mary Roberts 1450
Ringling School of Art and Design (Florida) 330
Rinhart, Floyd 1278
Rinhart, Marion 1278
Rio Grande Valley (Texas), lower 1603
Rio Hondo College (California) 184
Ripon College (Wisconsin) 1783
Ripon (England) 1450
The Rise and Fall of the Third Reich 543
Ritchie, Ward 166
Rittenhouse, Jesse B. 331
River Rouge (Michigan) 820
Rivera, Diego 191
Rivera, Tomas 216
riverboats 639, 1790
rivers 1292
Riverside (California) 216
Rivier College (New Hampshire) 973
Roanoke Bible College (North Carolina) 1209
Robbins, Nelda 1567
Robbins, Walter 1567
Robert Morris College (Pennsylvania) 1433
Roberts, Benjamin Titus 1116
Roberts, Charles 1390
Roberts, Clete 215
Roberts, Kenneth 653, 975
Roberts, M.M. 877
Roberts, Oral 1313
Roberts Wesleyan College (New York) 1116
Robertson, A. Willis 1686
Robertson, Alice M. 1320
Robertson, Ben 1489
Robertson, James 1562
Robertson, Merle Greene 646
Robeson County (North Carolina) 1206
Robeson, Paul 297, 596, 1445
Robins, Margaret Dreier 341
Robinson, Edwin Arlington 296, 341, 653, 737, 975, 1020, 1125, 1276, 1482
Robinson, Joe T. 69
Robinson, Lennox 487
robotics 1363
Rochester Academy of Science 1158
Rochester and Pittsburgh Coal Company 1393
Rochester Friendly Home (New York) 1158
Rochester Institute of Technology (New York) 1117
Rochester (Michigan) 809
Rockbridge County (Virginia) 1722
Rockefeller University (New York) 1118
Rockefeller, Winthrop 70
rocketry 34, 694, 721
Rockhill, William Woodville 737
Rockingham Community College (North Carolina) 1210
Rocky Mountain College (Montana) 940
Rocky Mountain Conference of the United Methodist Church 243
Rocky Mountain states 997
Rocky Mountains 181, 257, 258
Rodda, Albert (State Senator, California) 109
Roebling, John A. 1115
Roemhold, Heinz 1792
Roerich, Elena 705
Roethke, Theodore 1421
Roger Williams College (Rhode Island) 1481
Rogers, Bruce 260, 284, 714, 1180, 1379
Rogers, Byron 255
Rogers, Samuel 1280
Rohe, Mies van der 415
Rolfe, Frederick 552, 564
Rollins College (Florida) 331
Rollins, Philip Ashton 997
Romanarum Historiarum de Bellis Punicis Liber Basileae 1026
Romance languages 207
romantic literature 166
Rome, ancient 494
Ronsard, Pierre 279
Rookmaaker, Hans 500
Rooney, John (U.S. Congressman) 1121
Roosevelt County (New Mexico) 1011
Roosevelt, Franklin Delano 1243, 1360, 1767, 1792
Roosevelt, Theodore 236, 719, 737, 1080, 1229
Roosevelt University (Illinois) 480
Roosevelt Wildlife Forest Station 1144
Roper, Sam 589
Rosary College (Illinois) 481
Rose-Hulman Institute of Technology (Indiana) 527
Roselle, Anne 340
Rosemont College (Pennsylvania) 1434
Rosenfeld, Azriel 697
Rosenwald, Julius 1533
Ross, John M. 72
Rosser, George 381
Rouault, Georges 415
Roudneff, Vadim 497
Roulstone, George 1562
Rounce and Coffin Club 166
Routh, E.C. 1306
"Rowan Oak" Papers 876
Rowell, Chester Harvey 103
Rowland, Ruth 1793
Rowley, Dr. H.H. 1714
Rowse, A.L. 394
Roxburghe Club 564
Royce, William Hobart 1150
Roycroft Press 55, 93, 1139, 1158
Ruark, Robert 1220
Rudolf, Max 1371
Rufty, Hilton 1715
Rumaker, Michael 279
Rumely, Edward Aloysius 519
rural life 212
Ruscha, Ed 169

Rush, Benjamin 482, 1373
Rush University (Illinois) 482
Ruskin, Gertrude M. 1197
Ruskin, John 25, 284, 766, 1049, 1158, 1280
Russell, Bertrand 1450
Russell, George 519, 1359
Russell, Henry Norris 997
Russell, John B. 500
Russell, Lillian 1158
Russell, Rosalind 215
Russell Sage College (New York) 1119
Russia 207, 284, 639, 1049, 1397
Russia, pre-revolutionary 1269
Russian America 45
Russian folk art 415
Russian history 55
Russian Revolution 928
Russian Revolutionary Movement 1791
Russian sheet music 497
Russian theological literature 1126
Russo-Turkish relations, nineteenth-century 519
Rust, Colonel Gordon A. 1111
Rutgers, The State University of New Jersey 1000
Rutherford Country (North Carolina) 1190
Rutledge, Dr. John J. 678
Ryan, Cornelius 1280
Saalfield Publishing Company 1262
Sabbath, history of the 173
Sacco-Vanzetti 764, 1376
Sackville-West, Vita 519
Sacramento Peace Center 109
Sacramento, Port of 109
sacred harp music 397
Sacred Heart of Jesus 1784
Sacred Heart School of Theology (Wisconsin) 1784
Sacred Heart Seminary College (Michigan) 811
Sacred Heart University (Connecticut) 272
sacred music 879, 1083
sacro-occipital technique 1099
Sadtler Standard Spectra 955
safety 886
Sage, Russell 1039
Sager, Charles 678
Saginaw Valley State College (Michigan) 812
Sahlin, Nils 838
Saia, Joe 589
sailing 709, 1156
Sailor's Snug Harbor Archives 1149
St. Alphonsus College (Connecticut) 273
St. Ambrose College (Iowa) 560
St. Andrews College (North Carolina) 1211
St. Anne's Hermitage 1085
St. Anselm College (New Hampshire) 974
St. Augustine College (Illinois) 483
St. Bonaventure University (New York) 1120
St. Charles Borromeo Seminary (Pennsylvania) 1435
St. Cloud State University (Minnesota) 847
St. David, Lord 196
St. Edward's University (Texas) 1608
St. Francis College (New York) 1121
St. Francis College (Pennsylvania) 1436
St. Francis Seminary (Wisconsin) 1785
St. George, Elizabeth 982
St. Hyacinth College and Seminary (Massachusetts) 752
St. John Fisher College (New York) 1122
St. John Vianney College Seminary (Florida) 332
Saint John's College and Seminary (California) 185
St. John's College (Maryland) 688
St. John's College (New Mexico) 1018
St. John's Provincial Seminary (Michigan) 813
St. Johns River Community College (Florida) 333
Saint John's University (Minnesota) 848
St. John's University (New York) 1123
Saint Joseph Seminary College (Louisiana) 641
St. Joseph's College (California) 186
Saint Joseph's College (Indiana) 528
St. Joseph's College (Maine) 658
St. Joseph's Seminary (New York) 1124
Saint Joseph's University (Pennsylvania) 1437
St. Lawrence University (New York) 1125
St. Lawrence Valley (New York) 1142
St. Leo College (Florida) 334
St. Louis Catholic Historical Society 902
St. Louis College of Pharmacy (Missouri) 914
St. Louis Conservatory of Music (Missouri) 915
St. Louis (Missouri) 927
St. Louis (Missouri) public schools 899
Saint Louis University (Missouri) 916
Saint Martin's College (Washington) 1735
Saint Mary College (Kansas) 590
St. Mary of the Lake Seminary (Illinois) 484
Saint Mary-of-the-Woods College (Indiana) 529
Saint Mary's College (Indiana) 530
St. Mary's College (Michigan) 814
St. Mary's College (Minnesota) 849
St. Mary's College (North Carolina) 1212
St. Mary's College of California 187
St. Mary's College of Maryland 689
St. Mary's Seminary and University (Maryland) 690
St. Mary's University (Texas) 1609
St. Meinrad College and School of Theology (Indiana) 531
Saint Michael's College (Vermont) 1678
Saint Nicholas 755
Saint Norbert College (Wisconsin) 1786
St. Olaf College (Minnesota) 850
St. Patrick's Seminary (California) 188
St. Paul Bible College (Minnesota) 851
St. Paul School of Theology (Missouri) 917
St. Paul's College (Virginia) 1710
St. Petersburg Junior College (Florida) 335
St. Thomas University (Florida) 336
St. Vincent's College (Pennsylvania) 1438

St. Vladimir's Orthodox Theological Seminary (New York) 1126
Saintsbury, George 1450
Salem College (North Carolina) 1213
Salem College (West Virginia) 1754
Salem State College (Massachusetts) 753
Salesian philosophy 1353
Salisbury, Leah 1049
Salisbury State University (Maryland) 691
Salmon, Lucy Maynard 1159
Salzedo, Carlos 1084, 1371
Sam Houston State University (Texas) 1610
Samford University (Alabama) 25
Samuels, Jack Harris 1049
San Antonio College (Texas) 1611
San Augustine County Lumber Company (Texas) 1623
San Diego County (California) 190
San Diego Miramar College (California) 189
San Diego State University (California) 190
San Fernando Valley (California) 108, 154
San Francisco Art Association 191
San Francisco Art Institute (California) 191
San Francisco Conservatory of Music (California) 192
San Francisco Museum of Art 191
San Francisco State University (California) 193
San Francisco Theological Seminary (California) 194
San Joaquin Valley (California) 100
San Joaquin Valley farm workers 103
San Jose Bible College (California) 195
San Jose State University (California) 196
San Juan College (New Mexico) 1019
San Luis Valley (Colorado) 235
Sandburg, Carl 497, 574, 1158, 1218
Sanders, Ed 279
Sandoz, Mari 238, 944, 955, 1627
Sandy Hook Pilot Association (New York) 1149
Sandy, Stephen 1668
Sanford (C.E.) and Son General Store (Texas) 1623
Sangamon State University (Illinois) 485
Sanger, Margaret 757
Sanskrit texts 247
Santa Anna, Antonia Lopez de 296
Santa Clara University (California) 197
Santa Clara Valley (California) 133
Santa Cruz County (California) 85
Santa Rosa Junior College (California) 198
Santayana, George 1049
Santo Domingo (Dominican Republic) 341
Santos, Bienvenido 596
Sarah Lawrence College (New York) 1127
Sargent, Pamela 1445
Saroyan, William 103
Sarton, George 737
Sartre, Jean Paul 1648
Sasso, Pamfilo 988
Sassoon, Siegfried 596, 1320, 1648
satellite imagery 219
Satterfield, David 1715
Satterthwaite, Elizabeth 988
Sault Ste. Marie (Michigan) 796
Savannah (Georgia) 354
Savannah State College (Georgia) 389
Savitz, Beatrice C. 738
Savitz, Harry A. 738
saxophone 746
Saylor, John P. (U.S. Congressman) 1393
Scandinavia 118, 471
Scandinavian printing 1733
Scandinavian studies 856, 1791
Scandinavians (western U.S.) 91
Scarborough, William S. 1293
Sceptre Press 975
Schaffner, John 1049
Schatken, Florence 1058
Schenker, Heinrich 216
Scher, Andrew R. 1792
Schilder, Paul F. 1032
Schlesinger, Dr. Frank 116
Schlumberger, M.D., Hans G. 73
Schmidt, Carl F 1137
Schmidt, Emanuel 826
Schmitter, Charles 802
Schmitter, Ruth 802
Schofield, Stephen 500
Scholte, Dominie Hendrik Pieter 542
School for International Training (Vermont) 1679
School of the Museum of Fine Arts (Massachusetts) 754
School of the Ozarks (Missouri) 918
School of Theology at Claremont (California) 199
Schreiner College (Texas) 1612
Schroeder, Theodore 487
Schulte, Archbishop Paul 521
Schuster, Max Lincoln 1049
Schutt, Harold G. 103
Schuylkill Seminary (Pennsylvania) 1351
Schweitzer, Albert 113, 1150
Schwenckfelders 1242
Schwengel, Ethel 912
Schwengel, Fred D. 912
science 148, 211, 444, 496, 718, 742, 1115, 1363, 1375, 1384
science fiction 57, 190, 216, 519, 593, 684, 697, 1011, 1150, 1189, 1278, 1320, 1421, 1445, 1450, 1607, 1627, 1726, 1790
Science Fiction Society of New Hampshire 975
science, history of 57, 166, 190, 287, 409, 494, 497, 742, 1000, 1051, 1318, 1403, 1450, 1464, 1475, 1489, 1791
Science of Creative Intelligence 554
scientific expeditions, early 549
Scotland 319, 453
Scott, Clement William 1158

Scott, Hugh 1716
Scott, James Brown 296
Scott, Paul 1320
Scott, Paul M. 743
Scott, Sir Walter 32, 413, 552, 1320, 1763
Scott, William (U.S. Congressman) 1690
Scottsdale Community College (Arizona) 56
screenplays 129
Scribner, Charles 997
Scripps College (California) 200
scripts, motion picture 564
Scruggs, Mrs. Thomas M. 1637
sculpture 1429
sculpture art prints 143
sculpture, Spanish 1638
S.D. Bishop State Junior College (Alabama) 24
sea, history of the 40
Seabury, Samuel 1060
Seasongood, Murray 253
Seattle Folklore Society Archives 1739
Seattle Pacific University 1736
Seattle University (Washington) 1737
Sebald, William J. 694
secession controversy 1489
Secker, Martin 1320
secretarial sciences 1467
Seitz, Frederick 497
Selden, Armistead 32
Selig, Richard Jay 737
Seligman, Edwin R.A. 1049
Seneca Indians 1134
Sequoia National Forest 103
serial novels, nineteenth-century 1776
serials, early scientific 549
sermons, Elizabethan 1415
Serna, Ramon Gomez de la 1450
set designs 394, 497
Seton Hall University (New Jersey) 1001
Seton Hill College (Pennsylvania) 1439
Seventh Day Baptists 1026
Seventh-day Adventist Church 173, 676, 954
Seventh-day Adventists 22, 150, 708, 777, 1552
Sevier, John 1562
Sévigné, Mme. de 1245
Sewanee (Tennessee) 1565
Seward, William Henry 1158
Sewell, Jess Parker 1567
sex roles 97
Sexton, Almira 1752
Sexton, Anne 1648
sexuality 97
Shakers 1067
Shakespeare, William 417, 519, 590, 968, 1212, 1217, 1310, 1339, 1340, 1449, 1663, 1763
Shakespearean criticism 717
Shakespearian studies 497, 1792
Shannon, Monsignor William H. 1097
shape note singing 397
shape note song books 1562
Sharp, W.B. 1607
Sharpe, R. Bowdler 792
Sharples, James 1444
Shaw, George Bernard 287, 296, 1217, 1359, 1421, 1648
Shaw, Irwin 716
Shaw, John Mackay 319
Shaw, Joseph Coolidge 714
Shaw, Robert Gould 737
Shaw University (North Carolina) 1214
Shea, John Gilmary 296
Shedd, John A. 601
Sheen, Archbishop Fulton J. 1044
sheet music 57, 161, 234, 252, 344, 358, 394, 497, 519, 681, 687, 876, 922, 1049, 1276, 1291, 1414, 1475, 1544
sheet music, Confederate 319
sheet music, World War I 1260
Shelby State Community College (Tennessee) 1550
Sheldon Jackson College (Alaska) 43
Shelley, Percy Bysshe 381, 792
Shenandoah College and Conservatory (Virginia) 1711
Shenandoah Valley (Virginia) 1687, 1694
Shenk, Hiram Herr 1402
Shepard, Ernest 519
Shephard, Dr. Esther 196
Shepherd College (West Virginia) 1755
Sheppard, Moses 1444
Sheraton-Belvedere Corporation 695
Sherman, William T. (General) 296
Sherwood, Robert 737
shipbuilding 92, 742, 1163
Shippensburg University of Pennsylvania 1440
shipping 1628
ships 92, 694, 1156, 1628
Shirer, William L. 543
Shirk, George 1308
Shoemaker, Henry W. 1394
Shore, Melvin 109
Shoreline Community College (Washington) 1738
Shorter College (Georgia) 390
shorthand 999, 1123
Shoshone Indians 1800, 1801
Shotwell, James T. 1049
Shugerman, Albert 7
Shute, Henry 975
Sibelius, Jean 504
Sibley, U. Erwin 371
Siddons, Anne Rivers 5
Siegel, Robert 500
Sierra Nevada College (Nevada) 959
Sieveking, Lancelot 519
Sigma Delta Chi 508
Sigma Pi Phi (Philadelphia) 1445
sign language 1634

Sigurd Olson Environmental Institute 1782
Sikh religious groups 142
Siksika Indians 1800
Sillers, Walter 861
Sills, Kenneth C.M. 652
Silva, Luigi 1219
Silver, Ernest L. 972
Silver, Hyman 670
Silver Lake College (Wisconsin) 1787
Silverberg, Robert 1627
Silverman, Simon 1376
silviculture 1144
Simmons College (Massachusetts) 755
Simmons, James B. 1585
Simon, Charlie May 59, 70
Simon, William E. 1399
Simon's Rock of Bard College (Massachusetts) 756
Simpson, Adele 1058
Simpson College (California) 201
Simpson College (Iowa) 561
Sinclair, John 1020
Sinclair, Upton 106, 166, 519
Sinel, Jo 87
Sing Sing prison 1074
singing 746
singing instruction 461
Sinnott, Francis 1121
Sino-Soviet relations 295, 519
Sioux Falls College (South Dakota) 1520
Sioux Indians 825, 1514, 1522
Sissman, L.E. 737
Sister Formation Conference 1778
Sisters of Charity of Leavenworth 590
Sisters of Mercy 1412
Sisters of Providence 529
Sitwell, Edith 714, 1648
Sitwell, Osbert 1648
Sitwell, Sacheverell 1648
Skarstedt, C.W. 826
skepticism 1451
Skidmore College (New York) 1128
Skinner, Cornelia Otis 1158
Skinner, Frank 497
Skubitz, Joe (U.S. Congressman) 589
Skyline College (California) 202
Slaughter, Henry P. 358
slave narratives 1445
slavery 1, 755, 766, 984, 1185, 1267
Slavic studies 183
slip ballads 997
Slippery Rock University of Pennsylvania 1441
Slovenian music 1792
slum life 755
Smart, Charles Allen 1280
Smith, Adam 497
Smith, Al 296
Smith, Alva C. 365
Smith, Charles H. 1479
Smith College (Massachusetts) 757
Smith, David Eugene 1049
Smith, Dr. Wilber 493
Smith, Dr. Wilbur 138
Smith, E.F. 1449
Smith, G. Dallas 1567
Smith, H. Alexander 997
Smith, Holland M. 5
Smith, Hugh McCormick 296
Smith, John T. 1567
Smith, Lawrence L. 1567
Smith, Lillian 341, 394
Smith, Logan Pearsall 1320, 1638
Smith, Nila Banton 1067
Smith Printing Company (Rochester, New York) 1158
Smith, Stevie 1320
Smith, William S. 519
Smollett, Tobias 497
Snail's Pace Press 705
snake handling, religious 1532
Snell, Bertand 1142
Snelling, Lois 59
Snow College (Utah) 1662
Snow, C.P. 1648
Snow, Martin 975
Sobeloff, Simon F. 670
social action, Catholic 1778
social activism 253
social change 1456
social change, non-violent 1444
Social Credit Movement 1290
social ethics, Christian 734
social issues 802
social movements 816, 1129
social protest 211, 1445
social reform 564, 1444, 1445
social research 1776
social science 2, 79, 159, 207, 525, 626, 1088, 1098, 1743, 1791
social welfare 755, 1000, 1039
social work 755, 976, 1411, 1608, 1687
socialism 1789
Society for Historians of Foreign Relations 296
Society of American Foresters-New York Section 1144
Society of Automotive Engineers 786
Society of Biblical Literature 243
Society of Friends 509, 580, 1189, 1294, 1326, 1390
Society of Jesus 296, 462
Society of Manufacturing Engineers 786
Society of Professional Journalists 508
sociology 494, 1277, 1299, 1687
soil conservation 1311
soil science 99, 1144
solar energy 48
Soleri, Paolo 48
Solidarity (Poland) 737

Sollee, Arthur 343
Solzhenitsyn, Aleksandr Isayevich 592
Something Else Press 1119, 1638
Sommer, William 1245
Sondheim, Herbert 1058
song books 497, 1543
song sheets 1475
songsters 344, 1475
Sonneborn, Tracy M. 519
Sonoma County (California) 198, 203
Sonoma State University (California) 203
Sons of the Texas Republic 1651
Soper, Joanne 555
Source magazine 1645
South Carolina 1170, 1483, 1489, 1491, 1494, 1501, 1502
South Carolina State College 1503
South Dakota 1510, 1511, 1512, 1513, 1518, 1521, 1522
South Dakota Ornithologists Union 1510
South Dakota State University 1521
South Plains College (Texas) 1613
South Seas 504
South Seattle Community College (Washington) 1739
South Texas College of Law 1614
South (U.S.), history of the 1495, 1505
Southeast Asia 297, 591, 839, 1051, 1380, 1515, 1743
Southeast Missouri State University 919
Southeastern Americana 345
Southeastern Architectural Archive 646
Southeastern Baptist Theological Seminary (North Carolina) 1215
Southeastern Bible College (Alabama) 26
Southeastern College (Florida) 337
Southeastern Community College (Iowa) 562
Southeastern Illinois College 486
Southeastern Louisiana University 642
Southeastern Massachusetts University 758
Southeastern Oklahoma State University 1315
Southeastern University (District of Columbia) 299
Southern Americana 1181
Southern Arkansas University 68
Southern Baptist Convention 140, 908
Southern Baptist Theological Seminary 617
Southern Baptists 65, 86, 304, 338, 1172, 1197
Southern California 102
Southern California College 204
Southern California College of Optometry 205
Southern California Western Theological Library Association 199
Southern College of Seventh-day Adventists (Tennessee) 1552
Southern College of Technology (Georgia) 391
Southern Conference for Human Welfare 358
Southern Connecticut State University 274
Southern Education Foundation 358
Southern fiction 876
Southern Highlands 1216
Southern Illinois University - Carbondale 487
Southern Illinois University - Edwardsville 488
Southern Maine Vocational-Technical Institute 659
Southern Methodist University (Texas) 1615
Southern Methodists 369
Southern Nazarene University (Oklahoma) 1316
Southern Oregon State College 1339
Southern Railway 1719
Southern Regional Council 358
Southern School of Optometry (Tennessee) 1551
Southern Tenant Farmer's Union 1201
Southern University at Baton Rouge (Louisiana) 643
Southern University in New Orleans (Louisiana) 644
Southern University at Shreveport (Louisiana) 645
Southern Utah State College 1663
Southern West Virginia Community College 1756
Southey, Robert 646, 1158
Southwest Baptist University (Missouri) 920
Southwest Minnesota Historical Center 852
Southwest Mississippi Junior College 874
Southwest Missouri State University 921
Southwest Review 1615
Southwest State University (Minnesota) 852
Southwest Territory 1562
Southwest Texas Junior College 1616
Southwest Texas State University 1617
Southwest Writers Conference 1577
Southwestern Adventist College (Texas) 1618
Southwestern Americana 54, 55, 56, 57, 223, 242, 1009, 1017, 1019, 1308, 1585, 1599, 1613, 1625, 1626, 1630, 1635, 1638, 1645, 1650, 1657
Southwestern Assemblies of God College (Texas) 1619
Southwestern Baptist Theological Seminary (Texas) 1620
Southwestern College (Kansas) 591
Southwestern Junior College of the Assemblies of God (Texas) 1621
Southwestern Oregon Community College 1340
Southwestern University School of Law (California) 206
Southwestern University (Texas) 1622
Southworth-Anthonensen Press 652
Soviet Union 207, 1049
Soviet-American relations 55
space exploration 34, 251, 315, 340, 567, 1607, 1638, 1719
space sciences 215, 217
Spalatin, George 840
Spalding University (Kentucky) 618
Spanish Archives of Laredo (Texas) 1609
Spanish colonies in Latin America 519
Spanish colonization (Texas) 1647
Spanish culture 155
Spanish Golden Age 820
Spanish Inquisition 1449
Spanish language popular reading 323

Spanish missions 1602
Spanish Refugee Relief Organization 1049
Spanish-Pueblo architecture 1020
Sparkman, John 32
Spaulding, Albert T. 381
Spaulding, E. Wilder 912
special education 30, 123, 310, 469, 739, 1386, 1467, 1603, 1768
Speck, William A. 284
spectroscopy 215
speech disorders 1649
Spelman College (Georgia) 392
Spencer, Stanley 596
Spender, Stephen 519, 1320, 1648
Spenser, Edmund 416, 519
Sperisen, Albert 225
Spertus College of Judaica (Illinois) 489
Spinoza 1049
spirituality 186
Spock, Benjamin 1150
Spokane Community College (Washington) 1740
Spoon River College (Illinois) 490
sporting books 284, 431, 997
sports 1080
sports administration 336
sports medicine 151, 468
sports rule-books 431
Spring Garden College (Pennsylvania) 1442
Spring Hill College (Alabama) 27
Springer, William 809
Springfield Technical Community College (Massachusetts) 759
Spurgeon, Charles H. 931
spying 296
Squires, J. Duane 975
Stafford, William 1342
stage, history of American 341
stagecoach lines 1164
Stagg, Amos Alonzo 494
stained glass 762
Stanbrook Abbey Press 714
Stanford University (California) 207
Stapleton, Jean 1465
Starkie, Enid 1693
Starr King School for the Ministry (California) 208
"The Star-Spangled Banner" 296
State Community College of East Saint Louis (Illinois) 491
State Fair Community College (Missouri) 922
state fairs (California) 93
State Technical Institute at Memphis (Tennessee) 1553
State University of New York at Albany 1129
State University of New York at Binghamton 1130
State University of New York at Buffalo 1131
State University of New York at Oneonta 1139
State University of New York at Stony Brook 1132
State University of New York College at Brockport 1133
State University of New York College at Buffalo 1134
State University of New York College at Cortland 1135
State University of New York College at Fredonia 1136
State University of New York College at Geneseo 1137
State University of New York College at New Paltz 1138
State University of New York College at Oswego 1140
State University of New York College at Plattsburgh 1141
State University of New York College at Potsdam 1142
State University of New York College at Purchase 1143
State University of New York College of Environmental Science and Forestry 1144
State University of New York College of Optometry 1145
State University of New York College of Technology 1146
State University of New York Health Science Center at Syracuse 1147
State University of New York Health Science Center at Brooklyn 1148
State University of New York Maritime College 1149
statecraft 997
statistical reference materials 183
Statistics Archive 549
STC books 737
steamboats 629, 639, 1790
steamships 695, 1156
Steele, Fletcher 1144
Stefansson, Vilhjalmur 964
Steffens, Lincoln 1049
Steichen, Edward J. 694
Steiglitz, Alfred 697
Stein, Gertrude 253, 284, 1221, 1320, 1610, 1648, 1715
Stein, Leo 284
Steinbeck, John 196, 238, 287, 296, 503, 1049, 1245, 1320, 1648, 1716
Steinbeck Research Center 196
Steinberg, William 1450
Steloff, Frances 1128
Stendhal 646
Stennis, John C. 870
stenography 1123
Stephen F. Austin State University (Texas) 1623
Stephens, Charles Asbury 652
Stephens College (Missouri) 923
Stephens, James 1320
stereoscopic slides 394, 975, 1379

Stern, Dr. Alfred 1472
Stern, Louis E. 1000
Sterne, Laurence 341, 519
Stetson, Eugene W. 381
Stetson University 338
Stettinius, Edward R. 1716
Stevens, Edwin Augustus 1002
Stevens, Henry 1681
Stevens Institute of Technology (New Jersey) 1002
Stevens, Wallace 1320
Stevenson, Adlai E. 997
Stevenson, Robert Louis 284, 394, 997, 1049, 1445
Steves, Joan Cahill 1590
Stewart, Alexander 234, 1122
Stewart, Charles 737
Stewart, Frank H. 988
Stewart, Joseph L. 5
Stieglitz, Alfred 284
Stiles, Ezra 284
Still, Andrew Taylor 566, 1632
Still, James 613
Still, William 1445
Stillman College (Alabama) 28
Stinehour Press 1681
Stockbridge, Nellie 413
Stockton State College (New Jersey) 1003
Stoeckhardt, Georg 889
Stoehr, Richard 1678
Stoelzer, Richard 1022
Stokes, James G. Phelps 1049
Stokowski, Leopold 1371
Stone Country 1475
Stone, Edward Durrell 69
Stone, Harlan Fiske 1049
Stone, Norman 500
Stonehill College (Massachusetts) 760
Storm, Alfred 101
Stouffer, Jean 579
Stout, Rex 714
Stove, Julia 319
Stowe, Harriet Beecher 564, 1562
Straker, Robert L 1239
Strasberg, Lee 1049
Stratton, Charles W. 583
Strayer College (District of Columbia) 300
street cries, London 519
Street, Oliver Day 32
Streeter, Floyd B. 596
Streeter, Thomas W. 284
Strode, Hudson 32
Strom Thurmond Institute of Government and Public Affairs 1489
Strother, David Hunter 1763
Stroud II, Sanders Key East, Sarita Kennedy 1577
Strouse, Charlotte 220
Strouse, Norman 220
Strube, Gustav 687
Stuart, E.S. 1445
Stuart, Jesse 613, 614, 624, 1542, 1753
Stubblefield, Frank Albert (U.S. Congressman) 614
Stuckenberg, John H.W. 1385
Student Army Training Corps (World War I) 1382
student protests 193
studio art 657
Styron, William 394, 1180
Suez Canal 519
Suffolk University (Massachusetts) 761
Sufi religious groups 142, 424
sugar beet industry, Colorado 238
sugar industry 629
sugar industry, Cuban 341
Sul Ross State University (Texas) 1624
Sullivan, Leonor K. (U.S. Congressman) 296
Sullivan, Louis 415, 488
Sullivan, Richard H. 596
Sully, George Washington 346
Sulzer, William 596
Summit meetings 988
Sumner, Charles 737
Sumter County (Alabama) 17
Sunday, Billy 513, 1597
Sunday, history of 173
Sunday school materials 337
sundials 279
Supreme Court of Louisiana 647
surgery 1653
surgical instruments 1275
surgical techniques 1691
surrealism 415, 1320
Surrealist Movement 1067
survey field books 203
Susquehanna University (Pennsylvania) 1443
Sutherin, Charles 1270
Sutherland Cranial Teaching Foundation 1632
Sutherland, Donald (literary critic) 253
Sutherland, Elihu Jasper 1685
Sutphin, John 1133
Sutton Movement Shorthand 715
Sutton, Valerie 715
Swann vs. Charlotte/Mecklenburg Board of Education 1218
Swanson, Robert D. 776
Swarthmore College (Pennsylvania) 1444
Swasey, Samuel 975
Swedenborg, Emanuel 1350
Swedenborgian Church 1291
Swedish immigrants (U.S.) 574
Swedish-American books 838
Swedish-American Historical Society and Archives 471
Swedish-Americans 416
Sweet Briar College (Virginia) 1712
Sweet, Emma Biddlecom 1158
Swenson, Carl A. 574
Swift, Jonathan 497, 1449, 1638

Swinburne, Algernon 1000, 1217
Sydenstricker, Dorothy P. 58
Sykes, Christopher 296
symbolism 688
Symonds, John Addington 820
Synge, J.M. 519
Syracuse University (New York) 1150
Syriac manuscripts 1155
System on Automotive Safety Information 820
Szigeti, Joseph 497
Tabb, Rev. John Bannister 296
Tabor College (Kansas) 592
Tacoma Community College (Washington) 1741
Taft, Lorado 497
Taggard, Genevieve 1127
Tahlequah (Oklahoma) 1305
Tait, Dr. Ian M. 891
Talbott, Katherine Houk 1007
The Tales of the Heike 55
Talladega College (Alabama) 29
Tallapoosa County (Alabama) 3
Talmudic commentaries 670
Tamiment Institute 1106
Tammany Hall 1049
Tampa Bay region 344
Tampa College (Florida) 339
tap dancers, Black 1445
tapestry 1637
Tarbell, Ida M. 1352
Tarkington, Booth 519, 666, 1289
Tarleton State University (Texas) 1625
Tate, James 589, 1648
Tauber, Maurice Falcolm 1049
Tauchnitz editions 1158
taxation 141, 156, 206, 270, 767, 818, 1257, 1433, 1574
taxonomy 593
Taylor, Alice Bemis 236
Taylor, Frederick Winslow 1002
Taylor, Gene (U.S. Congressman) 909
Taylor, Kenneth P. 500
Taylor, Robert H. 997
Taylor, Thomas 319
Taylor University (Indiana) 532
Tchelitchew, Pavel 284
teacher education 374, 438, 439, 478, 488, 541, 569, 595, 676, 698, 704, 724, 739, 748, 788, 851, 852, 886, 957, 986, 1069, 1094, 1135, 1138, 1202, 1238, 1310, 1357, 1436, 1515, 1525, 1556, 1568, 1589, 1598, 1659, 1701, 1720, 1724, 1793, 1798
Teachers College of Columbia University (New York) 1151
teaching methodology 517
Teale, Edwin Way 279
Teapot Dome 764
technology 516, 1375, 1555
technology, history of 212, 494, 742, 1000, 1054, 1442, 1444, 1450, 1719
Teddlie, Tillet Sidney 1567
Tedlock, Anne 589
Teisberg, H.O. 1794
telecommunications 742, 1112
teleplays 129
television commercials 500
television news archives, San Francisco Bay Area 193
television production 129
Telford, Alexander 596
Tell en-Nasbeh (Israel) 172
temperance 733, 1276
Temple Industries (Texas) 1623
Temple, O.P. 1562
Temple University (Pennsylvania) 1445
Tennessee 1530, 1547, 1553, 1557, 1559, 1562, 1563, 1566
Tennessee State University 1554
Tennessee Technological University 1555
Tennessee Temple University 1556
Tennessee Wesleyan College 1557
tennis 1123
Tennyson, Alfred 25, 593, 1158, 1217, 1280
The Tenth Muse Lately Sprung up in America 519
Terris, Benjamin 1444
Tesla, Nicola 1049
Texas 1570, 1574, 1575, 1577, 1581, 1585, 1587, 1590, 1593, 1594, 1596, 1599, 1600, 1602, 1603, 1607, 1609, 1610, 1616, 1622, 1623, 1624, 1626, 1627, 1630, 1638, 1640, 1643, 1645, 1651, 1652, 1654, 1656, 1657, 1658
Texas A & I University 1626
Texas A&M University 1627
Texas A&M University at Galveston 1628
Texas AFL-CIO 1647
Texas Baptist Association 1620
Texas Chiropractic College 1629
Texas Christian University 1630
Texas College 1631
Texas College of Osteopathic Medicine 1632
Texas Historical Commission 1577
Texas, northeast 1604
Texas Republic 1651
Texas Southern University 1633
Texas State Technical Institute 1634
Texas Tech University 1635
Texas Wesleyan College 1636
Texas, west 1635
Texas Woman's University 1637
textbook adoption list, New Mexico 1010
textbooks, early American 274, 344, 517, 719, 753, 836, 972, 988, 1004, 1027, 1049, 1083, 1134, 1139, 1151, 1269, 1450, 1617
textbooks, scientific 1318
textile design 1058
textile industry, Philadelphia 1428
textiles 78, 136, 149, 1204, 1428, 1637

Thackeray, William Makepeace 997, 1217, 1320, 1489
Thailand 1380
Thatcher, Howard 687
Thaxter, Celia 653
Thayer, Anna Chittenden 358
theater 207, 215, 297, 327, 394, 453, 497, 518, 537, 716, 727, 737, 762, 997, 1067, 1158, 1217, 1252, 1278, 1320, 1343, 1353, 1450, 1668, 1712
Theater Group 20 1158
theater (Los Angeles) 106
theater models 1049
Theatre Guild Archive 284
theatrical biographies 1049, 1067
theatrical touring companies 1011
Theodore Roosevelt Association 1080
theologians, New England 266
theology 26, 83, 113, 114, 115, 138, 176, 179, 185, 186, 188, 194, 199, 243, 273, 293, 303, 305, 327, 332, 369, 381, 418, 419, 424, 434, 462, 471, 473, 476, 484, 492, 493, 494, 501, 505, 507, 531, 557, 563, 583, 590, 610, 611, 617, 650, 686, 690, 702, 706, 708, 734, 768, 813, 823, 827, 848, 850, 853, 883, 888, 902, 911, 916, 917, 933, 947, 952, 974, 984, 993, 996, 1026, 1036, 1038, 1060, 1063, 1068, 1086, 1105, 1126, 1155, 1158, 1215, 1236, 1247, 1268, 1277, 1283, 1285, 1289, 1316, 1345, 1346, 1347, 1400, 1406, 1415, 1430, 1435, 1446, 1452, 1456, 1461, 1468, 1483, 1492, 1495, 1499, 1515, 1517, 1523, 1536, 1545, 1546, 1565, 1566, 1571, 1580, 1584, 1587, 1601, 1646, 1706, 1711, 1714, 1729, 1735, 1737, 1765, 1771, 1778, 1784, 1785, 1804
theology, eighteenth-century European 1791
Thiel College (Pennsylvania) 1446
Third World 369, 1292
Thomas Aquinas College (California) 209
Thomas College (Maine) 660
Thomas, Dylan 296, 519, 1648
Thomas, Edward 1158
Thomas Jefferson University (Pennsylvania) 1447
Thomas, John Charles 687
Thomas More College (Kentucky) 619
Thomas Road Baptist Church (Virginia) 1695
Thomas, Vernon 1552
Thomas, Vincent (State Assemblyman, California) 106
Thomas, William Holland 1224
Thomas, William M. 1158
Thomism 1646
Thomistic philosophy 293
Thompson, Amy 1479
Thompson, Clark W. (U.S. Congressman) 296
Thompson, Dorothy 1150
Thompson, Francis 714
Thompson, Lawrence 1635
Thompson, T.P. 32
Thomson, James 705
Thomson, Virgil 1049
Thonssen, Lester 253
Thoreau, Henry David 296, 341, 792, 849, 1245, 1475, 1676
Thorndike, R. Amory 654
Thorp Spring Christian College (Texas) 1567
Three Mile Island 1373
Thurber, James 1278, 1320
Thurman, Howard 387
Thurmond, Strom 1489
Tibet 1791
Tibetan language 1745
Tibetan texts 247
Ticknor and Fields 737
Tidewater Community College (Virginia) 1713
Tillman, Benjamin R. 1489
Timberlake, C.L. 614
time-pieces 1301
Tinterow, Maurice M. and Jean H. 596
tissue specimens 1309
Tittle, Walter 1295
Tlingit culture (Alaska) 43
tobacco 1182, 1490
Toccoa Falls College (Georgia) 393
Toch, Ernst 215
Tofias, Arnold 760
tokens 997
Toledo (Ohio) 1290
Tolkien, J.R.R. 1778
Tollope, Anthony 1630
Tolly, Michael Andreas Barclay de 737
Toole, John Lawrence 1158
Toomer, Jean 1533
Toomey, Ursula 722
Topp, Robinson 1549
Torch Press 552
Torello, Anton 1371
Torontoy Estate 103
Torrens, Robert 497
Totem Pole Theater (Pennsylvania) 1465
Tougaloo College (Mississippi) 875
Toulouse-Lautrec 1648
tourism 281, 336, 960, 1797
Tournquist, Nels A. 583
Touro College (New York) 1152
Towns, George Alexander 358
Towson State University (Maryland) 692
toy theater 394
Toy, William H. 1661
track and field events 504
tracts, political 1000
tracts, Quaker 1390
tracts, Reformation 1155
trade bindings 104
trade catalogs 1129
trade manuals 1233
traffic engineering 820
trains 110

Trans-Mississippi West 212, 284, 1510, 1615, 1719
transportation 133, 475, 1112, 1338, 1804
Transylvania University (Kentucky) 620
Traubel, Gertrude 1445
travel accounts, nineteenth-century American 1686
Traven, B. 216
Traxler, Sister Margaret Ellen 1778
Treasure Valley Community College (Oregon) 1341
treaties, Iroquois Indian Nation 1134
treaties, Seneca Indian Nation 1134
Trebra, Louis Von 583
Trenholm, George Francis 714
Trentham, Anna 1527
Trenton State College (New Jersey) 1004
Trevecca Nazarene College (Tennessee) 1558
Trianon Press 220
Trinity Bible College (North Dakota) 1236
Trinity Christian College (Illinois) 492
Trinity College (Connecticut) 275
Trinity College (District of Columbia) 301
Trinity College (Vermont) 1680
Trinity Evangelical Divinity School (Illinois) 493
Trinity Lutheran Seminary (Ohio) 1285
Trinity University (Texas) 1638
Tri-State University (Indiana) 533
Trollope, Anthony 997
tropical studies 342
Trotsky, Leon 737
Troy State University (Alabama) 30
The True Christian Religion 1350
Trumbo, Dalton 1791
Trumbull, John 1059
Trust Territory Archives 406
Truth, Sojourner 1138
Tuban, Frank H. 156
Tuck, William M. 1686
Tufts University (Massachusetts) 762
Tulane University (Louisiana) 646
Tulare County history (California) 103
Tulsa Junior College (Oklahoma) 1317
Tunxis Community College (Connecticut) 276
Tureck, Rosalyn 716
Turkey 296
Turkey, early printing in 519
Turkish books 279
Turkish Oral Narrative, Archives of 1635
Turnbull, Agnes Sligh 1460
Tusculum College (Tennessee) 1559
Tusiani, Joseph 1047
Tuskegee University (Alabama) 31
Twain, Mark 211, 497, 519, 564, 679, 912, 1056, 1221, 1269, 1449, 1562, 1610, 1716, 1763, 1791
Twentieth Century Fox Film Corporation 215, 226, 564
Twomey, S.J., Louis 634
Tykociner, Joseph 497
Tyler, George 1445
Tyler, Glenn 409
Tyler, J. Hoge 1719
Tyler, John 1686
Tyler, Moses Coit 806
type specimen books 737
typeface design 1263
typefaces, Anglo-Saxon 593
typewriters, antique 460
typewriting 999
typography 76, 80, 211, 564, 583, 596, 714, 1217, 1718, 1778
UCLA Film Archives 215
UCLA Radio Archives 215
UCLA Television Archives 215
Uighur language 1745
Ulster County Community College (New York) 1153
Ulster County (New York) 1153
Umatilla County (Oregon) 1322
underground presses 475
Underground Railroad 737, 1445
Underhill, Dudley Field 1080
Unger-Bassler Collection 1382
Unicorn Press 1475
Uniformed Services University of the Health Sciences (Maryland) 693
Union Army, Official Records of the 13
Union College (Kentucky) 621
Union College (Nebraska) 954
Union College (New York) 1154
Union of Concerned Scientists 742
Union Pacific Railroad 564
Union Theological Seminary in Virginia 1714
Union Theological Seminary (New York) 1155
Union University (Tennessee) 1560
Unitarian Universalist Association, Central Midwest 464
Unitarianism 208, 464, 1338
Unitas Fratrum 1415
United Brethren Church 535, 1711
United Brethren in Christ 515, 573
United Church of Christ 426, 434, 626, 650, 853, 894, 1173, 1184, 1401
United Daughters of the Confederacy 614, 1718
United Evangelical Church 1286
United Methodist Church 64, 199, 243, 437, 463, 535, 573, 591, 621, 625, 626, 775, 839, 880, 885, 1241, 1282, 1513, 1599, 1688, 1711
United Methodist Church (Memphis Conference) 1539
United Methodist Church (South Carolina Conference) 1509
United Methodist Commission on Archives and History 984
United Mine Workers 589
United Mine Workers (District Two, Pennsylvania)) 1393
United Mine Workers (Ohio) 1280
United Negro College Fund 1167

United Presbyterian Church 1430
United States Air Force Academy (Colorado) 251
United States Blind Athletes Association 504
United States International University (California) 210
United States Merchant Marine Academy (New York) 1156
United States Military Academy (New York) 1157
United States Mint 988
United Steel Workers (Local 1397, Homestead, Pennsylvania) 1393
United Steelworkers of America 1421
United Theological Seminary of the Twin Cities (Minnesota) 853
United Theological Seminary (Ohio) 1286
United Verde Mine (Arizona) 55
United Wesleyan College (Pennsylvania) 1448
Unity College (Maine) 661
Universal Studios 226
Universalism 464
University and College Design Association 1262
University of Akron (Ohio) 1287
University of Alabama 32
University of Alabama at Birmingham 33
University of Alabama in Huntsville 34
University of Alaska - Anchorage 44
University of Alaska - Fairbanks 45
University of Alaska - Juneau 46
University of Arizona 57
University of Arkansas at Fayetteville 69
University of Arkansas at Little Rock 70
University of Arkansas at Monticello 71
University of Arkansas at Pinebluff 72
University of Arkansas for Medical Sciences 73
University of Baltimore (Maryland) 695
University of Bridgeport (Connecticut) 278
University of California, Berkeley 211
University of California, Davis 212
University of California, Hastings College of Law 213
University of California, Irvine 214
University of California, Los Angeles 215
University of California, Riverside 216
University of California, San Diego 217
University of California, San Francisco 218
University of California, Santa Barbara 219
University of California, Santa Cruz 220
University of Central Arkansas 74
University of Central Florida 340
University of Charleston (West Virginia) 1757
University of Chicago (Illinois) 494
University of Cincinnati (Ohio) 1288
University of Colorado at Boulder 252
University of Colorado at Denver 253
University of Colorado Health Sciences Center 254
University of Connecticut 279
University of Dallas (Texas) 1639
University of Dayton (Ohio) 1289
University of Delaware 287
University of Denver (Colorado) 255
University of Detroit (Michigan) 815
University of Dubuque (Iowa) 563
University of Evansville (Indiana) 534
University of Florida 341
University of Georgia 394
University of Hartford (Connecticut) 280
University of Hawaii at Hilo 405
University of Hawaii at Manoa 406
University of Health Sciences - The Chicago Medical School (Illinois) 495
University of Houston - Clear Lake (Texas) 1641
University of Houston - Downtown (Texas) 1642
University of Houston - Victoria 1643
University of Houston (Texas) 1640
University of Idaho 413
University of Illinois - Urbana-Champaign 497
University of Illinois at Chicago 496
University of Indianapolis (Indiana) 535
University of Iowa 564
University of Judaism (California) 221
University of Kansas 593
University of Kansas Medical Center 594
University of Kentucky 622
University of La Verne (California) 222
University of Louisiana in Shreveport 631
University of Louisville (Kentucky) 623
University of Lowell (Massachusetts) 763
University of Maine at Augusta 662
University of Maine at Farmington 663
University of Maine at Orono 664
University of Maine at Presque Isle 665
University of Mary Hardin-Baylor (Texas) 1644
University of Maryland at College Park 696
University of Maryland, Baltimore County 697
University of Maryland, Eastern Shore 698
University of Massachusetts at Amherst 764
University of Massachusetts at Boston 765
University of Medicine and Dentistry of New Jersey 1005
University of Miami (Florida) 342
University of Michigan 816
University of Michigan - Flint 817
University of Minnesota - Duluth 854
University of Minnesota - Morris 855
University of Minnesota - Twin Cities 856
University of Mississippi 876
University of Missouri - Columbia 924
University of Missouri - Kansas City 925
University of Missouri - Rolla 926
University of Missouri - St. Louis 927
University of Montana 941
University of Montevallo (Alabama) 35
University of Nebraska - Lincoln 955
University of Nebraska - Omaha 956
University of Nevada, Las Vegas 960

University of Nevada, Reno 961
University of New England (Maine) 666
University of New Hampshire 975
University of New Haven (Connecticut) 281
University of New Mexico 1020
University of New Orleans (Louisiana) 647
University of North Alabama 36
University of North Carolina at Asheville 1216
University of North Carolina at Chapel Hill 1217
University of North Carolina at Charlotte 1218
University of North Carolina at Greensboro 1219
University of North Carolina at Wilmington 1220
University of North Dakota 1237
University of North Florida 343
University of North Texas 1645
University of Northern Colorado 256
University of Northern Iowa 565
University of Notre Dame (Indiana) 536
University of Oklahoma 1318
University of Oklahoma Health Sciences Center 1319
University of Oregon 1342
University of Osteopathic Medicine and Health Sciences (Iowa) 566
University of Pennsylvania 1449
University of Pittsburgh at Bradford (Pennsylvania) 1451
University of Pittsburgh (Pennsylvania) 1450
University of Portland (Oregon) 1343
University of Puerto Rico, Mayaguez Campus 1472
University of Puerto Rico, Rio Piedras Campus 1473
University of Puget Sound (Washington) 1742
University of Redlands (California) 223
University of Rhode Island 1482
University of Richmond (Virginia) 1715
University of Rochester (New York) 1158
University of St. Thomas (Texas) 1646
University of San Diego (California) 224
University of San Francisco (California) 225
University of Scranton (Pennsylvania) 1452
University of South Alabama 37
University of South Carolina 1504
University of South Carolina - Coastal Carolina College 1506
University of South Carolina at Aiken 1505
University of South Dakota 1522
University of South Florida 344
University of Southern California 226
University of Southern Colorado 257
University of Southern Indiana 537
University of Southern Maine 667
University of Southern Mississippi 877
University of Southwestern Louisiana 648
University of Tampa (Florida) 345
University of Tennessee at Chattanooga 1561
University of Tennessee at Knoxville 1562
University of Tennessee at Martin 1563
University of Tennessee at Memphis 1564
University of Texas - Health Science Center at Houston 1655
University of Texas at Arlington 1647
University of Texas at Austin 1648
University of Texas at Dallas 1649
University of Texas at El Paso 1650
University of Texas at San Antonio 1651
University of Texas at Tyler 1652
University of Texas Health Science Center at San Antonio 1653
University of Texas of the Permian Basin 1654
University of the District of Columbia 302
University of the Ozarks (Arkansas) 75
University of the Pacific (California) 227
University of the Sacred Heart (Puerto Rico) 1474
University of the South (Tennessee) 1565
University of Toledo (Ohio) 1290
University of Tulsa (Oklahoma) 1320
University of Utah 1664
University of Vermont 1681
University of Virginia 1716
University of Washington 1743
University of West Florida 346
University of West Los Angeles (California) 228
University of Wisconsin - Eau Claire 1788
University of Wisconsin - Green Bay 1789
University of Wisconsin - La Crosse 1790
University of Wisconsin - Madison 1791
University of Wisconsin - Milwaukee 1792
University of Wisconsin - Oshkosh 1793
University of Wisconsin - Parkside 1794
University of Wisconsin - Platteville 1795
University of Wisconsin - Stevens Point 1796
University of Wisconsin - Stout 1797
University of Wisconsin - Superior 1798
University of Wisconsin - Whitewater 1799
University of Wyoming 1804
Updike, John 705, 737, 1320
Upham, Thomas C. 652
Upland (Indiana) 532
Upper Iowa University 567
Upper Peninsula (Michigan) 796, 803, 806, 1782
Upsala College (New Jersey) 1006
urban education 899
Urban, Joseph 1049
Urban League of Flint (Michigan) 817
urban studies 647, 928, 977
Urbana University (Ohio) 1291
urology 1753
Ursinus College (Pennsylvania) 1453
Ursuline College (Ohio) 1292
Ursuline materials 1048
U.S. Bureau of the Census 791
U.S. Coast Guard Academy (Connecticut) 277
U.S. Geological Survey 926, 940, 1015
U.S. Naval Academy (Maryland) 694
U.S.S. Monitor 1002

Utah 1662, 1663, 1664, 1665
Utah State University 1665
utopian communities 103, 927, 1061
utopian literature 1421
Vaad Hatzalah 1166
Valdosta State College (Georgia) 395
Valencia Community College (Florida) 347
valentines 1475
Vallance, William Roy 1158
Valley City State College (North Dakota) 1238
Valley Forge Christian College (Pennsylvania) 1454
Valparaiso University (Indiana) 538
Van Vechten, Carl 284
Vanbrugh, Irene 1158
Vanderbilt University (Tennessee) 1566
VanderCook College of Music (Illinois) 498
Vanderlip, Frank Arthur 1049
Vandeventer, Harry B. 997
Vassar College (New York) 1159
Vatican Council I 187
Vatican Council II 1376
Vatican manuscripts 916
vaudeville 564, 737
Vaughan, Dr. John A. 652
Vechten, Carl Van 551, 1715
Vega, Lope de 279
Vendettuoli, Maurice and Vera 1479
venereal diseases 1753
Venetian *laudi* 687
Vergil 593, 997
Vermont 1669, 1670, 1674, 1678, 1680, 1681
Vermont Technical College 1682
Verne, Jules 519, 1445
Versailles Treaty 764
Very, Jones 737
veterinary history 1744
veterinary medicine 5, 31, 525, 856
Victoria (Texas) 1643
Victorian literature 1587
Victorian novelists 997
Vidor, King 215
Vietnam 1380
Vietnam War 238, 279, 297, 407, 765, 913, 1398, 1681
Viking exploration of America 1351
Villa Julie College (Maryland) 699
Villa Maria College of Buffalo (New York) 1160
Villa Maria College (Pennsylvania) 1455
Villanova University (Pennsylvania) 1456
Villar, Henry 737
Villard, Oswald 1049
Vincennes University (Indiana) 539
Vincentian Community 1410
Vinci, Leonardo da 215, 718, 1002, 1158, 1804
Vining, Edward Payson 734
Violin Society of America 1276
Virchow, Rudolf 594
Virgin Mary 1289
Virginia 1686, 1690, 1694, 1707, 1713, 1715, 1753
Virginia Baptist Historical Society 1715
Virginia Commonwealth University 1717
Virginia Mennonite Conference 1687
Virginia Military Academy 1718
Virginia Polytechnic Institute and State University 1719
Virginia, southwest 1685, 1688, 1689, 1719
Virginia State University 1720
Virginia Union University 1721
visual arts 87, 169, 210, 280, 743, 842, 900, 1668
visual communications 490
visual resources 330
visual science 1145
visually impaired 175, 1473, 1635
vocal arts 1130
vocational education 1222
Vogue 1058
voice instruction 461
"Voice of Firestone" 746
Volkhovskii, Feliks Vadimovich 737
Volpe, John A. 749
Voltaire 519, 1245
Volterra, Vito 718
Voorhees College (South Carolina) 1507
Voorhees, Donald 1071
voyages and travels 997
V-12 program (World War II) 1382
V-5 program (World War II) 1382
Wabash College (Indiana) 540
Waccamaw region (South Carolina) 1506
WACO Aircraft Company 1296
Wadhams Hall Seminary-College (New York) 1161
Wagner College (New York) 1162
Wagner, Henry Raup 284
Wagner, Robert F. 296, 1106
Wahlberg, Edgar 253
Wahlstrom, Carl E. 729
Waid, H. Warner 1026
Wain, John 1648
Wake Forest University (North Carolina) 1221
Wake Technical College (North Carolina) 1222
Wakefield, Edmund B. 1260
Wald, Lillian D. 1049
Walden 1245
Waldorf College (Iowa) 568
Waley, Arthur 1000
Walker, Admiral John G. 596
Walker Army Air Field (Kansas) 579
Walker, Emery 1648
Walker, Henry P. 1457
Walker, Ludwig 591
Walker, Major T.P. 894
Walker, Ronald 1489
The Walker-Talker 579
Wall, Florence E. 982
Wallace, George C. 33

Wallace, Henry A. 564
Wallace, Irving 118, 718, 1648, 1794
Wallace, James B. 975
Wallace, Lew 519
Wallace, Robert 921
Wallcut, Thomas 652
Walpole, Hugh 1320, 1648
Walpole, Sir Robert 593
Walser, Richard 1179
Walsh College of Accountancy and Business Administration (Michigan) 818
Walsh, David I. (U.S. Senator) 723
Walsh, S.J., Reverend Edmund A. 296
Walsh, William 296
Walters, Herbert 1562
Walther, C.F.W. 889
Walton, Izaak 1450
war 207, 664
War of the Rebellion 613
War of 1812 1276, 1450, 1475
war posters 1445, 1475
Ward, Henry Augustus 1158
Ward, May Williams 596
Ward Ritchie Press 166
Ward, Roswell 1158
Waring, Joseph I., M.D. 1500
Warner Brothers 215, 226
Warner, Emily Smith 296
Warner Pacific College (Oregon) 1344
Warner Southern College (Florida) 348
Warren Edward Royal 236
Warren, Robert Penn 284, 394
Warren Wilson College 1223
Warrington, James 1430
Warshawsky, Abraham 1245
Wartburg College (Iowa) 569
Wartburg Theological Seminary (Iowa) 570
Washburn, Philip 236
Washburn University of Topeka (Kansas) 595
Washington and Jefferson College (Pennsylvania) 1457
Washington and Lee University (Virginia) 1722
Washington Bible College (Maryland) 700
Washington, Booker T. 31, 1293, 1445
Washington College (Maryland) 701
Washington County (New York) 1023
Washington (D.C.) 295, 296
Washington, George 1059
Washington Society (debating) 1722
Washington State Archives 1726
Washington State University 1744
Washington Theological Union (Maryland) 702
Washington University (Missouri) 928
Washtenaw Community College (Michigan) 819
watches 1301
water resource management 1262
water resources 302, 961, 1144, 1311, 1635, 1730
Water Resources Council 1144
water resources, southern California 118
water resources, Texas 1577
Waterfield, Harry Lee 614
Watergate investigation 300
Waters, Frank 1020
waterways 455, 519, 763, 1066
Watie, Stand 1318
Watson, Charles E. 501
Watson, J.B. 72
Watson, Robert 1450
Watson, Tom 361
Watson, William 1158
Watts, Ted 589
Waugh, Alec 1648
Waugh, Evelyn 296, 714, 1320, 1648
Waugh, Frederick J. 596
Wayland, John 1683
Wayne, Anthony 596
Wayne State College (Nebraska) 957
Wayne State University (Michigan) 820
Waynesburg College (Pennsylvania) 1458
weaponry 1586
Weatherford College (Texas) 1656
Weaver, Harriet Shaw 1320
Weaver, Rufus W. 381
weaving 78, 1637
Webb, Frances Seely 1800
Webb Institute of Naval Architecture (New York) 1163
Webb, Walter Prescott 1585
Weber, Orlando F. 997
Weber State College (Utah) 1666
Webster, Daniel 260, 718
Webster University (Missouri) 929
Weed, Thurlow 1158
Weeks, Gerald R. 500
Weidman, Jerome 1648
weights and measures 1049
Weimar Republic 737, 764
Weingrow, Howard L. 1067
Weingrow, Muriel 1067
Weintraub, Stanley 1421
Weird Tales 1627
Weis, Norman 1800
Weiss, Paul 487
Welch, Denton 1648
welding 314
Weller, Earle V. 166
Welles, Orson 519
Wellesley College (Massachusetts) 766
Wells College (New York) 1164
Wells Fargo 1164
Wells, Henry 1164
Wells, H.G. 216, 497, 1280, 1445
Welsh language 1498
Welsh settlers, Vermont 1672
Welsh theology 1791

Welter, C. Bernice 596
Welty, Eudora 346, 394, 649, 868, 876, 1698
Wenger, M.D., Oliver Clarence 73
Wesenberg, Alice Bidwell 504
Wesley, Charles 248, 303, 984
Wesley College (Delaware) 288
Wesley College (Mississippi) 878
Wesley, John 36, 179, 199, 248, 303, 369, 396, 476, 522, 911, 984, 1068, 1191, 1448, 1486
Wesley Theological Seminary (District of Columbia) 303
Wesleyan Church 1448, 1486
Wesleyan College (Georgia) 396
Wesleyan Methodist Church 1448
Wesleyan University (Connecticut) 282
Wesleyan/Holiness Movement 1347
West, Benjamin 1444
West Chester University (Pennsylvania) 1459
West Coast Christian College (California) 229
West Coast Poetry Review 1475
West Coast University (California) 230
West Florida 346
West Georgia College 397
West Indies 340, 341, 1469, 1710
West, Jessamyn 233
West Liberty State College (West Virginia) 1758
West, Paul 1421
West Point (New York) 1157
West, Rebecca 284
West Texas State University 1657
West Virginia 1747, 1748, 1750, 1752, 1753, 1755, 1756, 1760
West Virginia College of Graduate Studies 1759
West Virginia Institute of Technology 1760
West Virginia School of Osteopathic Medicine 1761
West Virginia State College 1762
West Virginia University 1763
West Virginia Wesleyan College 1764
Westbrook College (Maine) 668
Westchester Academy of Medicine 1103
Westchester Community College (New York) 1165
Western Americana 40, 81, 91, 118, 131, 166, 211, 219, 227, 238, 252, 255, 284, 413, 447, 564, 584, 829, 916, 925, 931, 935, 938, 939, 997, 1010, 1011, 1014, 1020, 1299, 1318, 1342, 1510, 1522, 1626, 1640, 1651, 1660, 1664, 1800, 1802, 1804
Western Baptist College (Oregon) 1345
Western Book Club of England 1615
Western Carolina University (North Carolina) 1224
Western Connecticut State University 283
Western Conservative Baptist Seminary (Oregon) 1346
Western European studies 792
Western Evangelical Seminary (Oregon) 1347
Western Federation of Miners 252
Western films, movie scripts for 1615
Western Illinois University 499
Western Kentucky University 624
Western Maryland College 703
Western Michigan University 821
Western Montana College 942
Western New England College (Massachusetts) 767
Western New Mexico University 1021
western novels 1139, 1320
Western Oregon State College 1348
Western Piedmont Community College (North Carolina) 1225
Western Reserve area (Ohio) 1275
Western State College (Colorado) 258
Western State University College of Law - Orange County (California) 231
Western States Black Research Center 627
Western States Chiropractic College (Oregon) 1349
Western Theological Seminary (Michigan) 822
Western Washington University 1745
Westmar College (Iowa) 571
Westminster Choir College (New Jersey) 1007
Westminster College (Missouri) 930
Westminster College of Salt Lake City (Utah) 1667
Westminster College (Pennsylvania) 1460
Westminster Theological Seminary (Pennsylvania) 1461
Westmont College (California) 232
Westmoreland County Community College (Pennsylvania) 1462
Weston, Dr. Edward 994
Weston School of Theology (Massachusetts) 768
westward expansion, U.S. 519
Wetmore, Henry S. 596
Wexler, Jerry 583
Weyl, Walter 1000
WGN radio station (Chicago) 497
whaling 1475
whaling ships 737
Wharton County Junior College (Texas) 1658
Wharton, Edith 284, 519, 681, 1123, 1648
Wheatley, Phillis 1445, 1611
Wheaton College (Illinois) 500
Wheaton College (Massachusetts) 769
Wheeling College (West Virginia) 1765
Wheelock College (Massachusetts) 770
Wheelright, Hyrum 1666
Wheelright, Ruby 1666
Whipple, William 737
Whistler, James McNeill 415
Whitcomb, James C. 508
White, Amelia 1018
White, Dora 935
White, Eartha M.M. 343
White, Ellen G. 173, 708, 777, 1618
White, General I.D. 1677
White, Gilbert 737
White, Mary 578
White Mountains (New Hampshire) 975
White Pines College (New Hampshire) 976

White, T.H. 1398
White, William Allen 578
Whitehead, Donald 1562
Whitehead, George 1390
Whitehead, Joseph 1058
Whiteman, Paul 771
Whitman, Walt 196, 296, 331, 385, 485, 564, 705, 1000, 1022, 1049, 1281, 1449, 1475, 1482, 1504, 1562, 1567, 1716
Whitney, Stephen Phoenix 1049
Whittier College (California) 233
Whittier, John Greenleaf 233, 341, 737, 1393, 1444
Whittingham, Charles 1681
Whittington, "Dick" 106
Whitworth College (Washington) 1746
Wichita State University (Kansas) 596
Widener University (Pennsylvania) 1463
Wieman, Henry Nelson 487
Wiener, Norbert 742
Wieners, John 279
Wiesner, Jerome B. 742
Wiggin, Kate Douglas 652
Wilberforce University (Ohio) 1293
Wilbur, Richard 705
Wilcox, Frank 1245
Wilcox, Molly Warren 596
Wilde, Oscar 225, 681, 1245
Wilder, Thornton 284
wildlife 1744
wildlife biology 1144
Wiley College (Texas) 1659
Wilhelm, Kate 1342
Wilkes College (Pennsylvania) 1464
Wilkes County (North Carolina) 1226
Wilkes County Technical Institute (North Carolina) 1226
William Carey College (Mississippi) 879
William Jewell College (Missouri) 931
William Paterson College of New Jersey 1008
William Penn College (Iowa) 572
William Tyndale College (Michigan) 823
William Woods College (Missouri) 932
Williams, Annie Laurie 1049
Williams, Ben Ames 653
Williams College (Massachusetts) 771
Williams, Gaar 504
Williams, George Washington 1445
Williams, Indiana Fletcher 1712
Williams, John A. 1158
Williams, Maynard Owen 792
Williams, Nicholas M. 714
Williams, Sr., R.T. 1316
Williams, T. Harry 629
Williams, Talcott 705
Williams, Tennessee 394, 876, 1049, 1648
Williams, William Carlos 284, 519, 992, 1676
Williamson, Charles C. 1049
Williamson, Jack 1011
Willingham, Calder 394
Willis, Nathaniel Parker 1049
Willis, William 652
Willkie, Wendell L. 519, 1158
Wilmington College (Delaware) 289
Wilmington College (Ohio) 1294
Wilson, Angus 564
Wilson, Carroll 519, 742
Wilson College (Pennsylvania) 1465
Wilson, Dr. Walter 883
Wilson, Edmund 284, 1320
Wilson, Goodrich 1688
Wilson III, Robert E. Lee 59
Wilson, Joseph 1445
Wilson, M.L. 938
Wilson, Robert 1049
Wilson, Woodrow 997, 1180
Windell, Paul 1032
Windham, Donald 394
Windsor Castle 13
Wingate College (North Carolina) 1227
Winkler, Dr. Norman 1450
Winkler, Flora 1450
Winkler, Karl Gottfried Theodor 284
Winona State University (Minnesota) 857
Winston-Salem State University (North Carolina) 1228
Winthrop College (South Carolina) 1508
Winton, Alma 1440
Wisconsin 1793, 1795, 1796
Wisconsin, northern 1782
Wister, Owen 238, 1627
witchcraft 1449, 1475, 1611
Witherspoon, John 997
Witt, Joyce Bell 1320
Wittenberg University (Ohio) 1295
Wittgenstein, Ludwig 1450
Wittliff, William E. 1638
Wodehouse, P.G. 1627
Wofford College (South Carolina) 1509
Wohlberg, Dr. Gerald 738
Wolcot, John 1218
Wolf Creek Generating Station 596
Wolf, J. Quincy 58
Wolf Trap Foundation for the Performing Arts 1690
Wolfe, Ann Fox 982
Wolfe, Don Marion 1751
Wolfe, Gregg D. 1252
Wolfe, Henry C. 982
Wolfe, James 737
Wolfe, Thomas 596, 737, 1200, 1212, 1220, 1585
Wolff, Kurt 284
Wolfing, John M. 928
Wolverton, Charles A. (U.S. Congressman) 988
women and religion 853
women architects 1719

women artists 203
women authors, American 1029, 1791
women, history of 32, 622, 750, 757, 927, 982, 997, 1056, 1159, 1290, 1641, 1702
women in business 1035
women in literature 809
women in religion 1105
women, Third World 583
women's antebellum literature 1489
women's education 1693
Women's Equity Action League 750
Women's International League for Peace and Freedom 485
women's movement 475, 1444
women's rights 418, 1062
women's studies 7, 21, 109, 200, 202, 244, 298, 369, 577, 593, 692, 708, 728, 750, 830, 831, 890, 917, 923, 945, 962, 982, 1000, 1029, 1032, 1088, 1093, 1119, 1171, 1212, 1219, 1276, 1278, 1329, 1364, 1417, 1439, 1475, 1630, 1637, 1703, 1766, 1791
women's suffrage 1062, 1158, 1159, 1276
women's trade union movement 341
The Wonderful Wizard of Oz 1049
Wood, Grant 543
Wood Junior College (Mississippi) 880
Wood, Lulu L. 1240
wood products engineering 1144
woodblock books 415
Woodbury University (California) 234
Woodford, Alfred O. 180
Woodruff, Douglas 296
Woods, Dee 1577
Woodward, Daniel H. 1698
Woolf, Virginia 552, 757, 1245, 1712
Woolsey, C.L. 922
Wooster, Lyman Dwight 579
Worcester Polytechnic Institute (Massachusetts) 772
Worcester State College (Massachusetts) 773
Wordsworth, William 519, 705
Work, John W., III 1533
Workers Library Publishers 1276
Works Progress Administration 938
world affairs 1767
World Baptist Fellowship 1569
World Council of Churches 1268, 1714
World Evangelism Fellowship 1620
World War I 174, 196, 596, 1217, 1301, 1320
World War II 508, 596, 639, 678, 790, 1217, 1306, 1450, 1487, 1562, 1677
World War II combat photographs 694
world's fairs 260, 1318
Wouk, Herman 1049
W.R. Grace and Company 1049
Wright Brothers 1296
Wright, Dr. Milton S.J. 1293
Wright, Frank Lloyd 415, 593, 1792
Wright, Harold Bell 589
Wright, James 1263
Wright, Richard 876, 1445
Wright, Roy V. (New Jersey State Senator) 994
Wright State University (Ohio) 1296
WSB (Channel 2, Atlanta) 394
Wulsin, F.R. 737
W.W. Norton (publishers) 1049
Wyckoff, George 981
Wyler, William 215
Wylie, Eliza Ragsdale 1508
Wyoming 1800, 1801, 1802
Wytheville Community College (Virginia) 1723
Xavier University of Louisiana 649
Xavier University (Ohio) 1297
x-ray powder diffraction 109
Yager, Willard E. 1063
Yale Review 284
Yale University (Connecticut) 284
Yale, William 975
Yarkovsky, Rev. J.J. 737
Yasui, Minoru 253
Yates, Elizabeth 578, 967
Ye Galleon Press 1726
Yeager, Chuck 1753
Yeats, William Butler 217, 287, 296, 319, 487, 519, 593, 764, 1039, 1132, 1263, 1359, 1648, 1698
yellow fever 632
Yellowstone National Park 938
Yerby, Frank 387
Yeshiva University (New York) 1166
Yogi, Maharishi Mahesh 554
Yolla Bolly Press 93, 196
York College of Pennsylvania 1466
York College of the City University of New York 1167
York County (Pennsylvania) 1466
Young, Allie 613
Young, Barnard 497
Young, Edward 1489
Young, Fred E. 576
Young, George 613
Young Harris College (Georgia) 398
Young, Jr., Whitney M. 1049
Young, Mary 1230
Young, Morris 497
Young, Owen D. 1125
Young, Philip 1421
Young, Sr., Whitney M. 608
Young, Stark 394
Young, Victor 718
Youngstown State University (Ohio) 1298
Yourcenar, Marguerite 652
Youth's Companion 755
Yucatan 1647
Yugoslavia 257
Yuker, Harold E. 1067
Yukon Territory 1726

Zablocki, Clement J. 1778
Zebrowski, George 1445
Zelazny, Roger 1627
Zigler, M.R. 1683
Zimbalist, Efrem 1371
Zimmerman, Jeremiah 1406
Zitterbart, Fidelis 1450
Zola, Emile 1475
zoology 1144, 1482
zoology, economic 342
Zukofsky, Louis 681, 1648
Zuppke, Robert 497
Zweig, Stefan 1136

INSTITUTION INDEX

Numbers following the names of schools are Entry Numbers.
Entry Numbers are also used as running heads at the top of each page.

Abilene Christian University 1567
Abraham Baldwin Agricultural College 349
Academy of Art College 76
Academy of the New Church 1350
Adams State College 235
Adelphi University 1022
Adirondack Community College 1023
Adrian College 774
Agnes Scott College 350
Alabama Agricultural and Mechanical University 1
Alabama State University 2
Alaska Pacific University 38
Albany College of Pharmacy 1024
Albany Junior College 351
Albany Medical College 1025
Albany State College 352
Albertus Magnus College 259
Albion College 775
Albright College 1351
Alcorn State University 858
Alderson Broaddus College 1747
Alexander City State Junior College 3
Alfred University 1026
Alice Lloyd College 597
Allan Hancock College 77
Allegany Community College 669
Allegheny College 1352
Allentown College of St. Francis de Sales 1353
Alma College 776
Alvernia College 1354
Alverno College 1766
American Baptist College 1523
American Conservatory of Music 414
American Graduate School of International Management 47
American International College 704
American River College 78
American Samoa Community College 1805
American University 290
American University of Puerto Rico 1467
Amherst College 705
Anderson College 501
Andover Newton Theological School 706
Andrew College 353
Andrews University 777
Angelo State University 1568
Annenberg Research Institute for Judaic and Near Eastern Studies 1355
Antioch College 1239
Appalachian State University 1168
Aquinas College 778
Aquinas Institute 881
Arizona State University 48
Arkansas College 58
Arkansas State University 59
Arkansas Tech University 60
Arlington Baptist College 1569
Armstrong State College 354
Armstrong University 79
Art Center College of Design 80
The Art Institute of Chicago 415
Asbury College 598
Asbury Theological Seminary 599
Ashland College 1240
Assemblies of God Theological Seminary 882
The Associated Mennonite Biblical Seminaries 502
Assumption College 707
Athens State College 4
Atlanta Christian College 355
Atlanta College of Art 356
Atlanta University 357
Atlanta University Center 358
Atlantic Christian College 1169
Atlantic Union College 708
Auburn University 5
Auburn University at Montgomery 6
Augsburg College 824
Augusta College 359
Augustana College (IL) 416
Augustana College (SD) 1510
Aurora University 417
Austin College 1570

Austin Peay State University 1524
Austin Presbyterian Theological Seminary 1571
Azusa Pacific University 81
Babson College 709
Bainbridge Junior College 360
Baker University 573
Baldwin-Wallace College 1241
Ball State University 503
Baltimore Hebrew College 670
Bangor Theological Seminary 650
Bank Street College of Education 1027
Baptist Bible Institute 304
Baptist College at Charleston 1483
Barat College 418
Bard College 1028
Barnard College 1029
Barry University 305
Bassist College 1321
Bates College 651
Baylor College of Dentistry 1572
Baylor College of Medicine 1573
Baylor University 1574
Beaufort Technical College 1484
Beckley College 1748
Bee County College 1575
Bellamarine College 600
Bellevue College 943
Belmont Abbey College 1170
Belmont College 1525
Beloit College 1767
Bemidji State University 825
Benedict College 1485
Bennett College 1171
Bennington College 1668
Bentley College 710
Berea College 601
Berean Institute 1356
Berklee College of Music 711
Berkshire Christian College 712
Bernard Baruch College of the City University of New York 1030
Bethany Bible College 82
Bethany College (KS) 574
Bethany College (WV) 1749
Bethany Theological Seminary 419
Bethel College (KS) 575
Bethel College (MN) 826
Bethel College (TN) 1526
Bethel Theological Seminary 827
Bethune-Cookman College, Inc. 306
Biola University 83
Birmingham-Southern College 7
Bishop College 1576
Black Hawk College - East Campus 420
Black Hawk College - Quad Cities Campus 421
Black Hills State College 1511
Blackburn College 422
Bloomfield College 977
Bloomsburg University of Pennsylvania 1357
Blue Mountain Community College 1322
Bluffton College 1242
Boise State University 407
Boricua College 1031
Boston Architectural Center 713
Boston College 714
Boston Conservatory 715
Boston University 716
Bowdoin College 652
Bowie State College 671
Bowling Green State University 1243
Bradford College 717
Bradley University 423
Brainerd Community College 828
Brandeis University 718
Brenau College 361
Brescia College 602
Bridgewater College 1683
Bridgewater State College 719
Brigham Young University 1660
Brigham Young University - Hawaii 399
Brookdale Community College 978
Brooklyn College of the City University of New York 1032
Brooklyn Law School 1033
Brooks Institute of Photography 84
Broome Community College 1034
Brown University 1475
Brunswick Junior College 362
Bryan College 1527
Bryant and Stratton Business Institute - Syracuse 1035
Bryant College 1476
Bryn Mawr College 1358
Bucknell University 1359
Buena Vista College 541
Butler University 504
Cabrillo College 85
Cabrini College 1360
Caldwell College 979
California Baptist College 86
California College of Arts and Crafts 87
California Institute of Integral Studies 88
California Institute of Technology 89
California Institute of the Arts 90
California Lutheran University 91
California Maritime Academy 92
California Polytechnic State University, San Luis Obispo 93
California School of Professional Psychology 94
California School of Professional Psychology - Berkeley 95
California School of Professional Psychology - Fresno 96

California School of Professional Psychology - Los Angeles 97
California School of Professional Psychology - San Diego 98
California State Polytechnic University, Pomona 99
California State University, Bakersfield 100
California State University, Chico 101
California State University, Dominguez Hills 102
California State University, Fresno 103
California State University, Fullerton 104
California State University, Hayward 105
California State University, Long Beach 106
California State University, Los Angeles 107
California State University, Northridge 108
California State University, Sacramento 109
California State University, San Bernardino 110
California State University, Stanislaus 111
California University of Pennsylvania 1361
California Western School of Law 112
Calumet College 505
Calvary Bible College 883
Calvin College 779
Calvin Theological Seminary 780
Camden County College 980
Cameron University 1299
Campbell University 1172
Campbellsville College 603
Canisius College 1036
Cape Cod Community College 720
Capital University 1244
Capitol Institute of Technology 672
Cardinal Stritch College 1768
Carleton College 829
Carlow College 1362
Carnegie-Mellon University 1363
Carroll College (MT) 933
Carroll College (WI) 1769
Carthage College 1770
Case Western Reserve University 1245
Casper College 1800
Castleton State College 1669
Catawba College 1173
Catholic Theological Union 424
Catholic University of America 291
Catholic University of Puerto Rico 1468
Cayuga County Community College 1037
CBN University 1684
Cedar Crest College 1364
Centenary College 981
Centenary College of Louisiana 625
Central Arizona College 49
Central Baptist College 61
Central Baptist Theological Seminary 576
Central Christian College of the Bible 884
Central Connecticut State University 260
Central Methodist College 885
Central Michigan University 781
Central Missouri State University 886
Central Oregon Community College 1323
Central Piedmont Community College 1174
Central State University (OH) 1246
Central State University (OK) 1300
Central University of Iowa 542
Central Washington University 1724
Central Wesleyan College 1486
Central Wyoming College 1801
Centralia College 1725
Centre College of Kentucky 604
Centro de Estudios Avanzados de Puerto Rico y el Caribe 1469
Chadron State College 944
Chaminade University of Honolulu 400
Chapman College 113
Charles County Community College 673
Chatham College 1365
Chesapeake College 674
Chestnut Hill College 1366
Cheyney University 1367
Chicago State University 425
Chicago Theological Seminary 426
Chowan College 1175
Christ College Irvine 114
Christ the King Seminary 1038
Christian Brothers College 1528
Christian Heritage College 115
Christian Theological Seminary 506
Cincinnati Bible College and Seminary 1247
Circleville Bible College 1248
The Citadel, The Military College of South Carolina 1487
Citrus College 116
City College of San Francisco 117
City College of the City University of New York 1039
City University of New York 1040
Claflin College 1488
Claremont Colleges 118
Claremont Graduate School 119
Claremont McKenna College 120
Clarion University 1368
Clark College 363
Clark University 721
Clarkson University 1041
Clemson University 1489
Cleveland Chiropractic College 887
Cleveland Institute of Music 1249
Cleveland State Community College 1529
Cleveland State University 1250
Cleveland Technical College 1176
Clinch Valley College 1685
Clinton Community College 1042
Coahoma Junior College 859
Cochise College 50

Coe College 543
Coffeyville Community College 577
Cogswell College 121
Coker College 1490
Colby College 653
Colby-Sawyer College 962
Coleman College 122
Colgate University 1043
Colgate-Rochester Divinity School 1044
College for Developmental Studies 123
College Misericordia 1369
College of Aeronautics 1045
College of Charleston 1491
College of DuPage 427
College of Eastern Utah 1661
College of Great Falls 934
College of Idaho 408
The College of Insurance 1046
College of Lake County 428
College of Mount St. Joseph 1251
College of Mount St. Vincent 1047
College of New Rochelle 1048
College of Notre Dame 124
College of Notre Dame of Maryland 675
College of Osteopathic Medicine of the Pacific 125
College of Our Lady of the Elms 722
College of Saint Benedict 830
College of St. Catherine 831
College of St. Catherine - St. Mary's Campus 832
College of Saint Elizabeth 982
College of St. Joseph 1670
College of St. Mary 945
College of St. Scholastica 833
College of St. Thomas 834
College of San Mateo 126
College of Santa Fe 1009
College of the Albemarle 1177
College of the Atlantic 654
College of the Holy Cross 723
College of the Sequoias 127
College of the Southwest 1010
College of William and Mary 1686
College of Wooster 1252
Colorado College 236
Colorado School of Mines 237
Colorado State University 238
Colorado Technical College 239
Columbia Bible College 1492
Columbia Christian College 1324
Columbia College (Columbia, CA) 128
Columbia College (Hollywood, CA) 129
Columbia College (IL) 429
Columbia College (SC) 1493
Columbia State Community College 1530
Columbia Theological Seminary 364
Columbia Union College 676
Columbia University 1049
Columbus College 365
Community College of Beaver County 1370
Community College of Denver 240
Compton Community College 130
Conception Seminary College 888
Concord College 1750
Concordia College Wisconsin 1771
Concordia College (IL) 430
Concordia College (MI) 782
Concordia College - Moorehead 835
Concordia College - St. Paul 836
Concordia Seminary 889
Concordia Teachers College 946
Concordia Theological Seminary 507
Connecticut College 261
Converse College 1494
The Cooper Union 1050
Copiah-Lincoln Junior College 860
Coppin State College 677
Corcoran School of Art 292
Cornell College 544
Cornell University 1051
Corpus Christi State University 1577
Cosumnes River College 131
Cottey College 890
Covenant Theological Seminary 891
Cranbrook Academy of Art 783
Craven Community College 1178
Creighton University 947
Criswell College 1578
Cuesta College 132
The Culinary Institute of America 1052
Culver-Stockton College 892
Cumberland County College 983
Curry College 724
The Curtis Institute of Music 1371
Cuyahoga Community College 1253
Dakota State College 1512
Dakota Wesleyan University 1513
Dallas Baptist University 1579
Dallas Theological Seminary 1580
Dalton College 366
Daniel Webster College 963
Dartmouth College 964
Davidson County Community College 1179
David Lipscomb College 1531
Davidson College 1180
Davis and Elkins College 1751
Daytona Beach Community College 307
De Anza College 133
Dean Junior College 725
Defiance College 1254
Delaware State College 285
Delaware Valley College of Science and Agriculture 1372

Delta State University 861
Denver Conservative Baptist Seminary 241
DePaul University 431
DePauw University 508
DeVry Institute of Technology 893
Diablo Valley College 134
Dickinson College 1373
Dickinson School of Law 1374
Dickinson State University 1229
Dillard University 626
District One Technical Institute 1772
Dominican College of San Rafael 135
Dominican House of Studies 293
Dowling College 1053
Dr. Martin Luther College 837
Dr. William M. Scholl College of Podiatric Medicine 432
Drake University 545
Drew University 984
Drexel University 1375
Drury College 894
Duke University 1181
Duquesne University 1376
Dutchess Community College 1054
Dyke College 1255
Earlham College 509
East Carolina University 1182
East Central College 895
East Central University 1301
East Mississippi Junior College 862
East Stroudsburg University of Pennsylvania 1377
East Tennessee State University 1532
East Texas Baptist University 1581
East Texas State University 1582
East Texas State University at Texarkana 1583
Eastern Arizona College 51
Eastern Baptist Theological Seminary 1378
Eastern College 1379
Eastern Connecticut State University 262
Eastern Illinois University 433
Eastern Kentucky University 605
Eastern Mennonite College/Seminary 1687
Eastern Michigan University 784
Eastern Montana College 935
Eastern Nazarene College 726
Eastern New Mexico University 1011
Eastern Oregon State College 1325
Eastern Washington University 1726
Eastern Wyoming College 1802
Eden Theological Seminary 896
Edgewood College 1773
Edinboro University of Pennsylvania 1380
Edmonds Community College 1727
Edward Waters College 308
Elizabeth City State University 1183
Elizabeth Seton College 1055
Elizabethtown College 1381
Elmhurst College 434
Elmira College 1056
Elon College 1184
Embry-Riddle Aeronautical University 309
Emerson College 727
Emmanuel College 728
Emmanuel College and School of Christian Ministry 367
Emmanuel County Junior College 368
Emory and Henry College 1688
Emory University 369
Emporia State University 578
Endicott College 729
Enterprise State Junior College 8
Episcopal Divinity School 730
The Episcopal Theological Seminary of the Southwest 1584
Erie Community College - South Campus 1057
Erskine College and Seminary 1495
Eureka College 435
Evergreen State College 1728
Fairleigh Dickinson University 985
Fashion Institute of Design and Merchandising 136
Fashion Institute of Technology 1058
Faulkner University 9
Fayetteville State University 1185
Felician College (IL) 436
Felician College (NJ) 986
Ferris State College 785
Ferrum College 1689
Findlay College 1256
Fisk University 1533
Fitchburg State College 731
Flagler College 310
Flaming Rainbow University 1302
Flathead Valley Community College 936
Florida Agricultural and Mechanical University 311
Florida Atlantic University 312
Florida College 313
Florida Community College at Jacksonville 314
Florida Institute of Technology 315
Florida International University 316
Florida Memorial College 317
Florida Southern College 318
Florida State University 319
Fontbonne College 897
Fordham University 1059
Fort Hays State University 579
Fort Lewis College 242
Fort Valley State College 370
Framingham State College 732
Francis Marion College 1496
Franklin and Marshall College 1382
Franklin College of Indiana 510
Franklin Pierce College 965

Franklin University 1257
Free Will Baptist Bible College 1534
Freed-Hardeman College 1535
Fresno Pacific College 137
Friends University 580
Frostburg State University 678
Fuller Theological Seminary 138
Furman University 1497
Gadsden State Junior College 10
Gallaudet University 294
Gannon University 1383
Gardner-Webb College 1186
Garrett-Evangelical Theological Seminary 437
Gaston College 1187
Gateway Technical Institute 1774
Gavilan College 139
The General Theological Seminary 1060
Geneva College 1384
George C. Wallace State Community College - Dothan 11
George Corley Wallace State Community College 12
George Fox College 1326
George Mason University 1690
George Washington University 295
Georgetown College 606
Georgetown University 296
Georgia College 371
Georgia Institute of Technology 372
Georgia Southern College 373
Georgia Southwestern College 374
Georgia State University 375
Georgian Court College 987
Gettysburg College 1385
Glassboro State College 988
Glenville State College 1752
GMI Engineering and Management Institute 786
Goddard College 1671
Golden Gate Baptist Theological Seminary 140
Golden Gate University 141
Goldey Beacom College 286
Gonzaga University 1729
Gordon College 733
Gordon-Conwell Theological Seminary 734
Goshen Biblical Seminary 511
Goshen College 512
Goucher College 679
Governors State University 438
Grace College 513
Grace College of the Bible 948
Graceland College 546
Graduate School and University Center of the City University of New York 1061
Graduate Theological Union 142
Grambling State University 627
Grand Canyon College 52
Grand Rapids Junior College 787
Grand Valley State College 788
Grand View College 547
Grants Branch Community College 1012
Gratz College 1386
Grays Harbor College 1730
Great Lakes Bible College 789
Greater Hartford Community College 263
Greater New Haven State Technical College 264
Green Mountain College 1672
Greenfield Community College 735
Greensboro College 1188
Greenville College 439
Grinnell College 548
Grossmont Community College 143
Grove City College 1387
Guilford College 1189
Gustavus Adolphus College 838
Gwynedd Mercy College 1388
Hahnemann University 1389
Hamilton College 1062
Hamline University 839
Hampden-Sydney College 1691
Hampshire College 736
Hampton University 1692
Hannibal-LaGrange College 898
Hanover College 514
Hardin-Simmons University 1585
Harding Graduate School of Religion 1536
Harding University 62
Harrington Institute of Interior Design 440
Harris-Stowe State College 899
Hartford Graduate Center 265
Hartford Seminary 266
Hartnell College 144
Hartwick College 1063
Harvard University 737
Harvey Mudd College 145
Haskell Indian Junior College 581
Haverford College 1390
Hawaii Loa College 401
Hawaii Pacific College 402
Hawthorne College 966
Hebrew College 738
Hebrew Union College - Jewish Institute of Religion (CA) 146
Hebrew Union College - Jewish Institute of Religion (NY) 1064
Hebrew Union College - Jewish Institute of Religion (OH) 1258
Heidelberg College 1259
Henderson State University 63
Hendrix College 64
Herkimer County Community College 1065
Hill College 1586
Hillsdale College 790
Hinds Junior College 863

Hiram College 1260
Hobart and William Smith Colleges 1066
Hofstra University 1067
Hollins College 1693
Holmes Junior College 864
Holy Family College 1391
Holy Names College 147
Honolulu Community College 403
Hood College 680
Hope College 791
Hopkinsville Community College 607
Houghton College 1068
Houston Baptist University 1587
Howard Payne University 1588
Howard University 297
Humboldt State University 148
Hunter College of the City University of New York 1069
Huntingdon College 13
Huntington College 515
Huron College 1514
Husson College 655
Huston-Tillotson College 1589
Idaho State University 409
Iliff School of Theology 243
Illinois Benedictine College 441
Illinois College 442
Illinois College of Optometry 443
Illinois Institute of Technology 444
Illinois State University 445
Illinois Valley Community College 446
Illinois Wesleyan University 447
Immaculata College 1392
Incarnate Word College 1590
Independence Community College 582
Indiana Institute of Technology 516
Indiana State University 517
Indiana University at South Bend 518
Indiana University of Pennsylvania 1393
Indiana University - Bloomington 519
Institute of American Indian Arts 1013
Institute of Paper Chemistry 1775
Inter American University of Puerto Rico 1470
The Interdenominational Theological Center 376
Iona College 1070
Iowa State University of Science and Technology 549
Iowa Wesleyan College 550
Islands Community College 39
Isothermal Community College 1190
Itawamba Junior College 865
Ithaca College 1071
Jackson State University 866
Jacksonville College 1591
Jacksonville University 320
James Madison University 1694
Jamestown College 1230
Jarvis Christian College 1592
Jefferson Community College 1072
Jefferson Davis State Junior College 14
Jersey City State College 989
The Jewish Theological Seminary of America 1073
John A. Logan College 448
John Carroll University 1261
John F. Kennedy University 149
John Jay College of Criminal Justice of the City University of New York 1074
John Marshall Law School 449
John Wesley College 1191
The Johns Hopkins University 681
Johnson and Wales College 1477
Johnson Bible College 1537
Johnson C. Smith University 1192
Johnson State College 1673
Judson College (AL) 15
Judson College (IL) 450
The Juilliard School 1075
Juniata College 1394
Kalamazoo College 792
Kansas City Art Institute 900
Kansas State University 583
Kansas Wesleyan University 584
Kean College of New Jersey 990
Kearney State College 949
Keene State College 967
Kellogg Community College 793
Kemper Military School and College 901
Kendall College 451
Kendall College of Art and Design 794
Kennesaw College 377
Kenrick Seminary 902
Kent State University 1262
Kentucky State University 608
Kentucky Wesleyan College 609
Kenyon College 1263
Ketchikan Community College 40
Keystone Junior College 1395
Kilgore College 1593
The King's College 1076
King's College 1396
Kirksville College of Osteopathic Medicine 903
Kirkwood Community College 551
Kirtland Community College 795
Knox College 452
Knoxville College 1538
Kuskokwim Community College 41
Kutztown University 1397
La Salle University 1398
Laboratory Institute of Merchandising 1077
Lafayette College 1399
LaGrange College 378
Lake Erie College 1264
Lake Forest College 453

Lake Superior State College 796
Lake-Sumter Community College 321
Lamar University 1594
Lambuth College 1539
Lancaster Bible College 1400
Lancaster Theological Seminary 1401
Lander College 1498
Lane College 1540
Lansing Community College 797
Laramie County Community College 1803
Laredo Junior College 1595
Laredo State University 1596
Lawrence Institute of Technology 798
Lawrence University 1776
Lawson State Community College 16
Le Moyne College 1078
Lebanon Valley College 1402
Lees-McCrae College 1193
Lehigh University 1403
Lehman College 1079
LeMoyne-Owen College 1541
Lenoir Community College 1194
Lenoir-Rhyne College 1195
Lesley College 739
LeTourneau College 1597
Lewis and Clark College 1327
Lewis and Clark Community College 454
Lewis University 455
Lewis-Clark State College 410
Lexington Theological Seminary 610
Liberty University 1695
Lincoln Christian College 456
Lincoln College 457
Lincoln Land Community College 458
Lincoln Memorial University 1542
Lincoln University (MO) 904
Lincoln University (PA) 1404
Linfield College 1328
Linn-Benton Community College 1329
Livingston University 17
Livingstone College 1196
Lock Haven University 1405
Logan College of Chiropractic 905
Loma Linda University 150
Long Island University, C. W. Post Campus 1080
Loras College 552
Loretto Heights College 244
Los Angeles College of Chiropractic 151
Los Angeles Mission College 152
Los Angeles Southwest College 153
Los Angeles Valley College 154
Louisiana College 628
Louisiana State University 629
Louisiana State University at Eunice 630
Louisiana State University in Shreveport 631
Louisiana State University Medical Center at New Orleans 632
Louisiana Tech University 633
Louisville Presbyterian Theological Seminary 611
Lourdes College 1265
Loyola College 682
Loyola Marymount University 155
Loyola University 634
Loyola University of Chicago 459
Lubbock Christian College 1598
Lurleen B. Wallace State Junior College 18
Luther College 553
Luther Northwestern Theological Seminary 840
Lutheran Theological Seminary at Gettysburg 1406
Lutheran Theological Seminary at Philadelphia 1407
Lutheran Theological Southern Seminary 1499
Luzerne County Community College 1408
Lynchburg College 1696
Lyndon State College 1674
MacCormac Junior College 460
MacMurray College 461
Madisonville Community College 612
Madonna College 799
Maharishi International University 554
Maine Maritime Academy 656
Malone College 1266
Manchester College 520
Manhattan College 1081
Manhattan School of Music 1082
Manhattanville College 1083
Mankato State University 841
Mannes College of Music 1084
Mansfield University of Pennsylvania 1409
Marian College 521
Marian College of Fond du Lac 1777
Marietta College 1267
Marion College 522
Marist College 1085
Marlboro College 1675
Marquette University 1778
Mars Hill College 1197
Marshall University 1753
Martin Community College 1198
Mary Baldwin College 1697
Mary Immaculate Seminary 1410
Mary Washington College 1698
Marygrove College 800
Maryknoll School of Theology 1086
Maryland Institute, College of Art 683
Marylhurst College for Lifelong Learning 1330
Marymount College (KS) 585
Marymount College (NY) 1087
Marymount Manhattan College 1088
Marymount University 1699
Maryville College (MO) 906
Maryville College (TN) 1543
Marywood College 1411
Massachusetts College of Art 740

Massachusetts College of Pharmacy and Allied Health Sciences 741
Massachusetts Institute of Technology 742
Mater Dei College 1089
Mattatuck Community College 267
Maui Community College 404
Mayland Technical College 1199
Mayville State College 1231
McCormick Theological Seminary 462
McKendree College 463
McMurry College 1599
McNeese State University 635
McPherson College 586
Meadville/Lombard Theological School 464
Medaille College 1090
Medgar Evers College - CUNY 1091
Medical College of Georgia 379
Medical College of Wisconsin 1779
Medical University of South Carolina 1500
Memphis State University 1544
Memphis Theological Seminary 1545
Menlo College 156
Mennonite Biblical Seminary 523
Mennonite Brethren Biblical Seminary 157
Mercer University, Atlanta 380
Mercer University, Macon 381
Mercy College 1092
Mercyhurst College 1412
Meridian Junior College 867
Merritt College 158
Mesa College 245
Messiah College 1413
Methodist College 1200
Methodist Theological School in Ohio 1268
Metropolitan State College 246
Metropolitan Technical Community College 950
Miami Christian College 322
Miami University 1269
Miami-Dade Community College 323
Michigan Christian College 801
Michigan State University 802
Michigan Technological University 803
Mid Michigan Community College 804
Mid-America Baptist Theological Seminary 1546
Mid-America Bible College 1303
Mid-America Nazarene College 587
Middle Tennessee State University 1547
Middlebury College 1676
Midland Lutheran College 951
Midwestern State University 1600
Miles College 19
Millersville University of Pennsylvania 1414
Milligan College 1548
Millikin University 465
Mills College 159
Millsaps College 868
Mineral Area College 907
Minneapolis College of Art and Design 842
Minot State University 1232
Mississippi College 869
Mississippi State University 870
Mississippi University for Women 871
Mississippi Valley State University 872
Missouri Baptist College 908
Missouri Southern State College 909
Missouri Western State College 910
Mobile College 20
Mohave Community College 53
Mohawk Valley Community College 1093
Monmouth College 991
Montana College of Mineral Science and Technology 937
Montana State University 938
Montcalm Community College 805
Montclair State College 992
Monterey Institute of International Studies 160
Montgomery College - Germantown 684
Montreat-Anderson College 1201
Montserrat College of Art 743
Moody Bible Institute 466
Moorehead State University 843
Moravian College and Theological Seminary 1415
Morehead State University 613
Morehouse College 382
Morgan State University 685
Morningside College 555
Morris Brown College 383
Mount Aloysius Junior College 1416
Mount Angel Seminary 1331
Mount Holyoke College 744
Mount Marty College 1515
Mount Mary College 1780
Mount Mercy College 556
Mount Saint Clare College 557
Mount Saint Mary College 1094
Mount St. Mary's College 161
Mount St. Mary's College and Seminary 686
Mount Senario College 1781
Mount Sinai School of Medicine - CUNY 1095
Mount Union College 1270
Mount Vernon College 298
Mount Vernon Nazarene College 1271
Mt. San Antonio Community College 162
Muhlenberg College 1417
Mundelein College 467
Murray State College 1304
Murray State University 614
Muskingum Area Technical College 1272
Muskingum College 1273
The Naropa Institute 247
Nassau Community College 1096
National College 1516

National College of Chiropractic 468
National College of Education 469
National University 163
Navajo Community College 54
Naval Postgraduate School 164
Nazarene Bible College 248
Nazarene Theological Seminary 911
Nazareth College of Rochester 1097
Nebraska Wesleyan University 952
New Brunswick Theological Seminary 993
New England College 968
New England College of Optometry 745
New England Conservatory 746
New Hampshire College 969
New Hampshire Technical Institute 970
New Jersey Institute of Technology 994
New Mexico Highlands University 1014
New Mexico Institute of Mining and Technology 1015
New Mexico Military Institute 1016
New Mexico State University 1017
New Orleans Baptist Theological Seminary 636
New River Community College 1700
New School for Social Research 1098
New York Chiropractic College 1099
New York City Technical College - CUNY 1100
New York Institute of Technology 1101
New York Law School 1102
New York Medical College 1103
New York School of Interior Design 1104
New York Theological Seminary 1105
New York University 1106
Newberry College 1501
Nicholls State University 637
Nichols College 747
Norfolk State University 1701
North Adams State College 748
North American Baptist Seminary 1517
North Carolina Agricultural and Technical State University 1202
North Carolina Central University 1203
North Carolina State University at Raleigh 1204
North Carolina Wesleyan College 1205
North Central Bible College 844
North Central College 470
North Central Technical College 1274
North Country Community College 1107
North Dakota State College of Science 1233
North Dakota State University 1234
North Dakota State University - Bottineau Branch and Institute 1235
North Georgia College 384
North Idaho College 411
North Park College and Theological Seminary 471
Northeast Louisiana University 638
Northeast Missouri State University 912
Northeastern Bible College 995
Northeastern Christian Junior College 1418
Northeastern Illinois University 472
Northeastern Junior College 249
Northeastern Ohio Universities College of Medicine 1275
Northeastern State University 1305
Northeastern University 749
Northern Arizona University 55
Northern Baptist Theological Seminary 473
Northern Illinois University 474
Northern Kentucky University 615
Northern Michigan University 806
Northern Montana College 939
Northern Nevada Community College 958
Northern State College 1518
Northern Virginia Community College 1702
Northland College 1782
Northrop University 165
Northwest Alabama State Junior College 21
Northwest Christian College 1332
Northwest College of the Assemblies of God 1731
Northwest Community College 42
Northwest Missouri State University 913
Northwest Nazarene College 412
Northwestern College 558, 845
Northwestern College of Chiropractic 846
Northwestern Michigan College 807
Northwestern State University of Louisiana 639
Northwestern University 475
Northwood Institute 808
Norwalk Community College 268
Norwich University 1677
Notre Dame College 971
Nova University 324
Oakland City College 524
Oakland University 809
Oakwood College 22
Oberlin College 1276
Oblate School of Theology 1601
Occidental College 166
Oglala Lakota College 1519
Oglethorpe University 385
Ohio Dominican College 1277
Ohio State University 1278
Ohio State University - Mansfield Campus 1279
Ohio University 1280
Ohio Wesleyan University 1281
Ohlone College 167
Okaloosa-Walton Junior College 325
Oklahoma Baptist University 1306
Oklahoma Christian College 1307
Oklahoma City University 1308
The Oklahoma College of Osteopathic Medicine and Surgery 1309
Oklahoma Panhandle State University 1310
Oklahoma State University 1311

Oklahoma State University Technical Institute 1312
Old Dominion University 1703
Olivet College 810
Olivet Nazarene University 476
Olympic College 1732
Oral Roberts University 1313
Orange Coast College 168
Orange County Community College 1108
Oregon Health Sciences University 1333
Oregon State University 1334
Orlando College 326
Otis Art Institute of the Parsons School of Design 169
Ottawa University 588
Otterbein College 1282
Ouachita Baptist University 65
Our Lady of Holy Cross College 640
Our Lady of the Lake University of San Antonio 1602
Oxford College of Emory University 386
Pace University 1109
Pacific Christian College 170
Pacific Lutheran University 1733
Pacific Oaks College and Children's School 171
Pacific School of Religion 172
Pacific Union College 173
Pacific University 1335
Paducah Community College 616
Paier College of Art, Inc. 269
Paine College 387
Palm Beach Atlantic College 327
Palm Beach Junior College 328
Palmer College of Chiropractic 559
Palomar College 174
Pan American University 1603
Paris Junior College 1604
Parsons School of Design 1110
Pasadena City College 175
Patrick Henry State Junior College 23
Patten College 176
Paul D. Camp Community College 1704
Paul Quinn College 1605
Paul Smith's College 1111
Peabody Institute of The Johns Hopkins University 687
Pembroke State University 1206
Pennsylvania College of Optometry 1419
Pennsylvania College of Podiatric Medicine 1420
Pennsylvania State University 1421
Pennsylvania State University - Capitol Campus 1422
Pennsylvania State University, Erie, The Behrend College 1423
Pennsylvania State University, M.S. Hershey Medical Center 1424
Pepperdine University 177
Peru State College 953
Philadelphia College of Bible 1425
Philadelphia College of Osteopathic Medicine 1426
Philadelphia College of Pharmacy and Science 1427
Philadelphia College of Textiles and Science 1428
Philadelphia Colleges of the Arts 1429
Philander Smith College 66
Phillips County Community College 67
Phillips University 1314
Piedmont College 388
Pierce College 1734
Pittsburg State University 589
Pittsburgh Theological Seminary 1430
Pitzer College 178
Plymouth State College 972
Point Loma Nazarene College 179
Point Park College 1431
Polk Community College 329
Polytechnic University 1112
Pomona College 180
Ponce School of Medicine 1471
Pontifical College Josephinum 1283
Porterville College 181
Portland Community College 1336
Portland School of Art 657
Portland State University 1337
Post College 270
Prairie View Agricultural & Mechanical University 1606
Pratt Institute 1113
Presbyterian College 1502
Presbyterian School of Christian Education 1705
Princeton Theological Seminary 996
Princeton University 997
Principia College 477
Protestant Episcopal Seminary in Virginia 1706
Providence College 1478
Purdue University 525
Purdue University - Calumet 526
Queens College 1207
Queens College of the City University of New York 1114
Quincy College 478
Quinnipiac College 271
Radcliffe College 750
Radford University 1707
Ramapo College of New Jersey 998
Rancho Santiago College 182
The RAND Graduate School 183
Randolph-Macon College 1708
Randolph-Macon Woman's College 1709
Raymond Walters General and Technical College 1284
Reading Area Community College 1432
Reed College 1338
Reformed Theological Seminary 873
Regis College (CO) 250
Regis College (MA) 751
Rend Lake College 479

Rensselaer Polytechnic Institute 1115
Rhode Island College 1479
Rhode Island School of Design 1480
Rhodes College 1549
Rice University 1607
Richmond Technical College 1208
Rider College 999
Ringling School of Art and Design 330
Rio Hondo College 184
Ripon College 1783
Rivier College 973
Roanoke Bible College 1209
Robert Morris College 1433
Roberts Wesleyan College 1116
Rochester Institute of Technology 1117
Rockefeller University 1118
Rockingham Community College 1210
Rocky Mountain College 940
Roger Williams College 1481
Rollins College 331
Roosevelt University 480
Rosary College 481
Rose-Hulman Institute of Technology 527
Rosemont College 1434
Rush University 482
Russell Sage College 1119
Rutgers, The State University of New Jersey 1000
S.D. Bishop State Junior College 24
Sacred Heart School of Theology 1784
Sacred Heart Seminary College 811
Sacred Heart University 272
Saginaw Valley State College 812
St. Alphonsus College 273
St. Ambrose University 560
St. Andrews Presbyterian College 1211
St. Anselm College 974
St. Augustine College 483
St. Bonaventure University 1120
St. Charles Borromeo Seminary 1435
St. Cloud State University 847
St. Edward's University 1608
St. Francis College (NY) 1121
St. Francis College (PA) 1436
St. Francis Seminary 1785
St. Hyacinth College and Seminary 752
Saint John Fisher College 1122
St. John Vianney College Seminary 332
Saint John's College and Seminary 185
St. John's College (MD) 688
St. John's College (NM) 1018
St. John's Provincial Seminary 813
Saint John's University (MN) 848
St. John's University (NY) 1123
St. Johns River Community College 333
Saint Joseph Seminary College 641
St. Joseph's College 186
Saint Joseph's College 528
St. Joseph's College 658
St. Joseph's Seminary 1124
Saint Joseph's University 1437
St. Lawrence University 1125
St. Leo College 334
St. Louis College of Pharmacy 914
St. Louis Conservatory of Music 915
St. Louis University 916
Saint Martin's College 1735
Saint Mary College 590
St. Mary of the Lake Seminary 484
Saint Mary-of-the Woods College 529
Saint Mary's College 530
St. Mary's College of California 187
St. Mary's College of Maryland 689
St. Mary's College (MI) 814
St. Mary's College (MN) 849
Saint Mary's College (NC) 1212
St. Mary's Seminary and University 690
St. Mary's University 1609
St. Meinrad College and School of Theology 531
Saint Michael's College 1678
Saint Norbert College 1786
St. Olaf College 850
St. Patrick's Seminary 188
St. Paul Bible College 851
St. Paul School of Theology 917
Saint Paul's College 1710
St. Petersburg Junior College 335
St. Thomas University 336
St. Vincent College and Seminary 1438
St. Vladimir's Orthodox Theological Seminary 1126
Salem College (NC) 1213
Salem College (WV) 1754
Salem State College 753
Salisbury State University 691
Sam Houston State University 1610
Samford University 25
San Antonio College 1611
San Diego Miramar College 189
San Diego State University 190
San Francisco Art Institute 191
San Francisco Conservatory of Music 192
San Francisco State University 193
San Francisco Theological Seminary 194
San Jose Bible College 195
San Jose State University 196
San Juan College 1019
Sangamon State University 485
Santa Clara University 197
Santa Rosa Junior College 198
Sarah Lawrence College 1127
Savannah State College 389
School for International Training 1679
School of the Museum of Fine Arts 754

School of the Ozarks 918
School of Theology at Claremont 199
Schreiner College 1612
Scottsdale Community College 56
Scripps College 200
Seattle Pacific University 1736
Seattle University 1737
Seton Hall University 1001
Seton Hill College 1439
Shaw University 1214
Shelby State Community College 1550
Sheldon Jackson College 43
Shenandoah College and Conservatory 1711
Shepherd College 1755
Shippensburg University of Pennsylvania 1440
Shoreline Community College 1738
Shorter College 390
Sierra Nevada College 959
Silver Lake College 1787
Simmons College 755
Simon's Rock of Bard College 756
Simpson College (CA) 201
Simpson College (IA) 561
Sioux Falls College 1520
Skidmore College 1128
Skyline College 202
Slippery Rock University of Pennsylvania 1441
Smith College 757
Snow College 1662
Sonoma State University 203
South Carolina State College 1503
South Dakota State University 1521
South Plains College 1613
South Seattle Community College 1739
South Texas College of Law 1614
Southeast Missouri State University 919
Southeastern Baptist Theological Seminary 1215
Southeastern Bible College 26
Southeastern College of the Assemblies of God 337
Southeastern Community College 562
Southeastern Illinois College 486
Southeastern Louisiana University 642
Southeastern Massachusetts University 758
Southeastern Oklahoma State University 1315
Southeastern University 299
Southern Arkansas University 68
Southern Baptist Theological Seminary 617
Southern California College 204
Southern California College of Optometry 205
Southern College of Optometry 1551
Southern College of Seventh-day Adventists 1552
Southern College of Technology 391
Southern Connecticut State University 274
Southern Illinois University at Carbondale 487
Southern Illinois University - Edwardsville 488
Southern Maine Vocational-Technical Institute 659
Southern Methodist University 1615
Southern Nazarene University 1316
Southern Oregon State College 1339
Southern University at Baton Rouge 643
Southern University in New Orleans 644
Southern University - Shreveport 645
Southern Utah State College 1663
Southern West Virginia Community College 1756
Southwest Baptist University 920
Southwest Mississippi Junior College 874
Southwest Missouri State University 921
Southwest State University 852
Southwest Texas Junior College 1616
Southwest Texas State University 1617
Southwestern Adventist College 1618
Southwestern Assemblies of God College 1619
Southwestern Baptist Theological Seminary 1620
Southwestern College 591
Southwestern Junior College of the Assemblies of God 1621
Southwestern Oregon Community College 1340
Southwestern University 1622
Southwestern University School of Law 206
Spalding University 618
Spelman College 392
Spertus College of Judaica 489
Spokane Community College 1740
Spoon River College 490
Spring Garden College 1442
Spring Hill College 27
Springfield Technical Community College 759
Stanford University 207
Starr King School for the Ministry 208
State Community College of East St. Louis 491
State Fair Community College 922
State Technical Institute at Memphis 1553
State University of New York at Albany 1129
State University of New York at Binghamton 1130
State University of New York at Buffalo 1131
State University of New York at Stony Brook 1132
State University of New York College at Brockport 1133
State University of New York College at Buffalo 1134
State University of New York College at Cortland 1135
State University of New York College at Fredonia 1136
State University of New York College at Geneseo 1137
State University of New York College at New Paltz 1138
State University of New York College at Oneonta 1139
State University of New York College at Oswego 1140
State University of New York College at Plattsburgh 1141

State University of New York College at Potsdam 1142
State University of New York College at Purchase 1143
State University of New York College of Environmental Science and 1144
State University of New York College of Optometry 1145
State University of New York College of Technology 1146
State University of New York Health Science Center at Syracuse 1147
State University of New York Health Sciences Center at Brooklyn 1148
State University of New York Maritime College 1149
Stephen F. Austin University 1623
Stephens College 923
Stetson University 338
Stevens Institute of Technology 1002
Stillman College 28
Stockton State College 1003
Stonehill College 760
Strayer College 300
Suffolk University 761
Sul Ross State University 1624
Susquehanna University 1443
Swarthmore College 1444
Sweet Briar College 1712
Syracuse University 1150
Tabor College 592
Tacoma Community College 1741
Talladega College 29
Tampa College 339
Tarleton State University 1625
Taylor University 532
Teachers College of Columbia University 1151
Temple University 1445
Tennessee State University 1554
Tennessee Technological University 1555
Tennessee Temple University 1556
Tennessee Wesleyan College 1557
Texas A & I University 1626
Texas A & M University 1627
Texas A & M University at Galveston 1628
Texas Chiropractic College 1629
Texas Christian University 1630
Texas College 1631
Texas College of Osteopathic Medicine 1632
Texas Southern University 1633
Texas State Technical Institute 1634
Texas Tech University 1635
Texas Wesleyan College 1636
Texas Woman's University 1637
Thiel College 1446
Thomas Aquinas College 209
Thomas College 660
Thomas Jefferson University 1447
Thomas More College 619
Tidewater Community College 1713
Toccoa Falls College 393
Tougaloo College 875
Touro College 1152
Towson State University 692
Transylvania University 620
Treasure Valley Community College 1341
Trenton State College 1004
Trevecca Nazarene College 1558
Tri-State University 533
Trinity Bible College 1236
Trinity Christian College 492
Trinity College (CT) 275
Trinity College (DC) 301
Trinity College (VT) 1680
Trinity Evangelical Divinity School 493
Trinity Lutheran Seminary 1285
Trinity University 1638
Troy State University 30
Tufts University 762
Tulane University 646
Tulsa Junior College 1317
Tunxis Community College 276
Tusculum College 1559
Tuskegee University 31
Ulster County Community College 1153
Uniformed Services University of the Health Sciences 693
Union College (KY) 621
Union College (NE) 954
Union College (NY) 1154
Union Theological Seminary 1155
Union Theological Seminary in Virginia 1714
Union University 1560
United States Air Force Academy 251
United States Coast Guard Academy 277
United States International University 210
United States Merchant Marine Academy 1156
United States Military Academy 1157
United States Naval Academy 694
United Theological Seminary 1286
United Theological Seminary of the Twin Cities 853
United Wesleyan College 1448
Unity College 661
University of Akron 1287
University of Alabama 32
University of Alabama at Birmingham 33
University of Alabama in Huntsville 34
University of Alaska - Anchorage 44
University of Alaska - Fairbanks 45
University of Alaska - Juneau 46
University of Arizona 57
University of Arkansas at Fayetteville 69
University of Arkansas at Little Rock 70

University of Arkansas at Monticello 71
University of Arkansas at Pine Bluff 72
University of Arkansas for Medical Sciences 73
University of Baltimore 695
University of Bridgeport 278
University of California, Berkeley 211
University of California, Davis 212
University of California, Hastings College of Law 213
University of California, Irvine 214
University of California, Los Angeles 215
University of California, Riverside 216
University of California, San Diego 217
University of California, San Francisco 218
University of California, Santa Barbara 219
University of California, Santa Cruz 220
University of Central Arkansas 74
University of Central Florida 340
University of Charleston 1757
University of Chicago 494
University of Cincinnati 1288
University of Colorado at Boulder 252
University of Colorado at Denver 253
University of Colorado Health Sciences Center 254
University of Connecticut 279
University of Dallas 1639
University of Dayton 1289
University of Delaware 287
University of Denver 255
University of Detroit 815
University of Dubuque 563
University of Evansville 534
University of Florida 341
University of Georgia 394
University of Hartford 280
University of Hawaii at Hilo 405
University of Hawaii at Manoa 406
University of Health Sciences - The Chicago Medical School 495
University of Houston 1640
University of Houston - Clear Lake 1641
University of Houston - Downtown 1642
University of Houston - Victoria 1643
University of Idaho 413
University of Illinois at Chicago 496
University of Illinois at Urbana-Champaign 497
University of Indianapolis 535
University of Iowa 564
University of Judaism 221
University of Kansas 593
University of Kansas Medical Center 594
University of Kentucky 622
University of La Verne 222
University of Louisville 623
University of Lowell 763
University of Maine at Augusta 662
University of Maine at Farmington 663
University of Maine at Orono 664
University of Maine at Presque Isle 665
University of Mary Hardin-Baylor 1644
University of Maryland at College Park 696
University of Maryland, Baltimore County 697
University of Maryland, Eastern Shore 698
University of Massachusetts at Amherst 764
University of Massachusetts at Boston 765
University of Medicine and Dentistry of New Jersey 1005
University of Miami 342
University of Michigan 816
University of Michigan - Flint 817
University of Minnesota - Duluth 854
University of Minnesota - Morris 855
University of Minnesota - Twin Cities 856
University of Mississippi 876
University of Missouri - Columbia 924
University of Missouri - Kansas City 925
University of Missouri - Rolla 926
University of Missouri - St. Louis 927
University of Montana 941
University of Montevallo 35
University of Nebraska - Lincoln 955
University of Nebraska - Omaha 956
University of Nevada, Las Vegas 960
University of Nevada, Reno 961
University of New England 666
University of New Hampshire 975
University of New Haven 281
University of New Mexico 1020
University of New Orleans 647
University of North Alabama 36
University of North Carolina at Asheville 1216
University of North Carolina at Chapel Hill 1217
University of North Carolina at Charlotte 1218
University of North Carolina at Greensboro 1219
University of North Carolina at Wilmington 1220
University of North Dakota 1237
University of North Florida 343
University of North Texas 1645
University of Northern Colorado 256
University of Northern Iowa 565
University of Notre Dame 536
University of Oklahoma 1318
University of Oklahoma Health Sciences Center 1319
University of Oregon 1342
University of Osteopathic Medicine and Health Sciences 566
University of Pennsylvania 1449
University of Pittsburgh 1450
University of Pittsburgh at Bradford 1451
University of Portland 1343
University of Puerto Rico, Mayaguez Campus 1472
University of Puerto Rico, Rio Piedras Campus 1473
University of Puget Sound 1742

University of Redlands 223
University of Rhode Island 1482
University of Richmond 1715
University of Rochester 1158
University of St. Thomas 1646
University of San Diego 224
University of San Francisco 225
University of Scranton 1452
University of South Alabama 37
University of South Carolina 1504
University of South Carolina at Aiken 1505
University of South Carolina at Coastal Carolina College 1506
University of South Dakota 1522
University of South Florida 344
University of Southern California 226
University of Southern Colorado 257
University of Southern Indiana 537
University of Southern Maine 667
University of Southern Mississippi 877
University of Southwestern Louisiana 648
University of Tampa 345
University of Tennessee at Chattanooga 1561
University of Tennessee at Knoxville 1562
University of Tennessee at Martin 1563
University of Tennessee at Memphis 1564
University of Texas at Arlington 1647
University of Texas at Austin 1648
University of Texas at Dallas 1649
University of Texas at El Paso 1650
University of Texas at San Antonio 1651
University of Texas at Tyler 1652
University of Texas Health Science Center at San Antonio 1653
University of Texas of the Permian Basin 1654
University of Texas - Health Science Center at Houston 1655
University of the District of Columbia 302
University of the Ozarks 75
University of the Pacific 227
University of the Sacred Heart 1474
University of the South 1565
University of Toledo 1290
University of Tulsa 1320
University of Utah 1664
University of Vermont 1681
University of Virginia 1716
University of Washington 1743
University of West Florida 346
University of West Los Angeles 228
University of Wisconsin - Eau Claire 1788
University of Wisconsin - Green Bay 1789
University of Wisconsin - La Crosse 1790
University of Wisconsin - Madison 1791
University of Wisconsin - Milwaukee 1792
University of Wisconsin - Oshkosh 1793
University of Wisconsin - Parkside 1794
University of Wisconsin - Platteville 1795
University of Wisconsin - Stevens Point 1796
University of Wisconsin - Stout 1797
University of Wisconsin - Superior 1798
University of Wisconsin - Whitewater 1799
University of Wyoming 1804
Upper Iowa University 567
Upsala College 1006
Urbana University 1291
Ursinus College 1453
Ursuline College 1292
Utah State University 1665
Valdosta State College 395
Valencia Community College 347
Valley City State College 1238
Valley Forge Christian College 1454
Valparaiso University 538
Vanderbilt University 1566
VanderCook College of Music 498
Vassar College 1159
Vermont Technical College 1682
Villa Julie College 699
Villa Maria College 1455
Villa Maria College of Buffalo 1160
Villanova University 1456
Vincennes University 539
Virginia Commonwealth University 1717
Virginia Military Institute 1718
Virginia Polytechnic Institute and State University 1719
Virginia State University 1720
Virginia Union University 1721
Voorhees College 1507
Wabash College 540
Wadhams Hall Seminary-College 1161
Wagner College 1162
Wake Forest University 1221
Wake Technical College 1222
Waldorf College 568
Walsh College of Accountancy and Business Administration 818
Warner Pacific College 1344
Warner Southern College 348
Warren Wilson College 1223
Wartburg College 569
Wartburg Theological Seminary 570
Washburn University of Topeka 595
Washington and Jefferson College 1457
Washington and Lee University 1722
Washington Bible College 700
Washington College 701
Washington State University 1744
Washington Theological Union 702
Washington University 928
Washtenaw Community College 819

Wayne State College 957
Wayne State University 820
Waynesburg College 1458
Weatherford College 1656
Webb Institute of Naval Architecture 1163
Weber State College 1666
Webster University 929
Wellesley College 766
Wells College 1164
Wesley College (DE) 288
Wesley College (MS) 878
Wesley Theological Seminary 303
Wesleyan College 396
Wesleyan University 282
West Chester University 1459
West Coast Christian College 229
West Coast University 230
West Georgia College 397
West Liberty State College 1758
West Texas State University 1657
West Virginia College of Graduate Study 1759
West Virginia Institute of Technology 1760
West Virginia School of Osteopathic Medicine 1761
West Virginia State College 1762
West Virginia University 1763
West Virginia Wesleyan College 1764
Westbrook College 668
Westchester Community College 1165
Western Baptist College 1345
Western Carolina University 1224
Western Connecticut State University 283
Western Conservative Baptist Seminary 1346
Western Evangelical Seminary 1347
Western Illinois University 499
Western Kentucky University 624
Western Maryland College 703
Western Michigan University 821
Western Montana College 942
Western New England College 767
Western New Mexico University 1021
Western Oregon State College 1348
Western Piedmont Community College 1225
Western State College 258
Western State University College of Law (Orange County) 231
Western States Chiropractic College 1349
Western Theological Seminary 822
Western Washington University 1745
Westmar College 571
Westminster Choir College 1007
Westminster College of Salt Lake City 1667
Westminster College (MO) 930
Westminster College (PA) 1460
Westminster Theological Seminary 1461
Westmont College 232
Westmoreland County Community College 1462
Weston School of Theology 768
Wharton County Junior College 1658
Wheaton College (IL) 500
Wheaton College (MA) 769
Wheeling College 1765
Wheelock College 770
White Pines College 976
Whittier College 233
Whitworth College 1746
Wichita State University 596
Widener University 1463
Wilberforce University 1293
Wiley College 1659
Wilkes College 1464
Wilkes Community College 1226
William Carey College 879
William Jewell College 931
William Paterson College of New Jersey 1008
William Penn College 572
William Tyndale College 823
William Woods College 932
Williams College 771
Wilmington College (DE) 289
Wilmington College (OH) 1294
Wilson College 1465
Wingate College 1227
Winona State University 857
Winston-Salem State University 1228
Winthrop College 1508
Wittenberg University 1295
Wofford College 1509
Wood Junior College 880
Woodbury University 234
Worcester Polytechnic Institute 772
Worcester State College 773
Wright State University 1296
Wytheville Community College 1723
Xavier University 1297
Xavier University of Louisiana 649
Yale University 284
Yeshiva University 1166
York College of Pennsylvania 1466
York College of the City University of New York 1167
Young Harris College 398
Youngstown State University 1298